D1195813

PATROLOGY

VOL. III

THE GOLDEN AGE OF GREEK PATRISTIC LITERATURE FROM THE COUNCIL OF NICAEA TO THE COUNCIL OF CHALCEDON

PATROLOGY

by

JOHANNES QUASTEN

PROFESSOR OF ANCIENT CHURCH HISTORY
AND CHRISTIAN ARCHAEOLOGY
THE CATHOLIC UNIVERSITY OF AMERICA
WASHINGTON D.C.

VOLUME III

*The Golden Age of Greek Patristic Literature
From the Council of Nicaea
to the Council of Chalcedon*

CHRISTIAN CLASSICS, INC.
WESTMINSTER, MARYLAND
1983

First Published, 1960
Reprinted by Christian Classics, Inc., 1983

ISBN: 0-87061-086-4
Library of Congress Catalog Card Number: 83-72018
All Rights Reserved
Printed in the United States of America

PREFACE

In presenting this volume comprising the Greek Patristic Literature from the Council of Nicaea (325) to the Council of Chalcedon (451), I wish to take the opportunity of thanking scholars of many lands for their fraternal cooperation. I cannot name each one here, but I am grateful to all of them for their generous assistance. The copies of articles and books they sent me have greatly facilitated the difficult task of incorporating their findings and furnishing an adequate bibliography of critical texts, translations and studies.

I have followed in this volume the system adopted for the previous ones of indicating the exact place where the editions and translations of each work can be found. Thus the reader will be brought into contact with the sources as speedily as possible.

The first two volumes have been translated into French by J. Laporte and were published by *Les Éditions du Cerf* at Paris under the title *Initiation aux Pères de l'Église*, vol. I (1955), II (1957). In this French edition I have made a number of additions to the text and brought the bibliographies up to date.

I cannot fail to mention the help I received from my colleague in this University, Rt. Rev. Dr. M. J. Higgins, and from Rev. Dr. C. A. Bouman at the University of Nijmegen in the preparation of the manuscript and the indexes and in the reading of the proofs.

The Catholic University of America
Washington D.C.

JOHANNES QUASTEN

TABLE OF CONTENTS

CHAPTER I

CHAPTER II

CHAPTER III

LIST OF ABBREVIATIONS

AAB	Abhandlungen, Berlin Academy. Phil.-hist. Klasse, 1815ff.
AAM	Abhandlungen, Munich Academy. Phil.-hist. Klasse, 1835ff.
AAWW	Anzeiger der Österreichischen Akademie der Wissenschaften. Vienna, 1864ff.
AB	Analecta Bollandiana. Brussels, 1882ff.
AC	Antike und Christentum, ed. by F. J. Dölger. Münster i.W., 1929-1950.
ACL	Antiquité Classique. Louvain.
ACO	Acta Conciliorum Œcumenicorum, ed. by E. Schwartz. Berlin, 1914ff.
ACW	Ancient Christian Writers, ed. by J. Quasten and J. C. Plumpe. Westminster (Md.) and London, 1946ff.
AER	American Ecclesiastical Review. Washington (D. C.), 1889ff.
AGP	Archiv für Geschichte der Philosophie. Berlin, 1889-1932.
AGWG	Abhandlungen der Gesellschaft der Wissenschaften zu Göttingen.
AHD	Archives d'histoire doctrinale et littéraire. Paris, 1926ff.
AIPh	Annuaire de l'Institut de philologie et d'histoire orientales et slaves. Paris and Brussels, 1932ff.
AJA	American Journal of Archaeology. Princeton, 1885ff.
AJPh	American Journal of Philology. Baltimore, 1880ff.
AKK	Archiv für katholisches Kirchenrecht. Mainz, 1857ff.
AL	Acta Linguistica. Copenhagen.
ALMA	Archivum Latinitatis Medii Aevi (Bulletin Du Cange). Brussels and Paris, 1924ff.
ALW	Archiv für Liturgiewissenschaft. Regensburg, 1950ff.
ANF	Ante-Nicene Fathers. Buffalo and New York.
Ang	Angelicum. Rome, 1924ff.
ANL	Ante-Nicene Christian Library. Edinburgh, 1864ff.
Ant	Antonianum. Rome, 1926ff.
AnTh	L'Année Théologique. Paris, 1940ff.
AnThA	L'Année Théologique Augustinienne. Paris, 1951ff.
APF	Archiv für Papyrusforschung. Leipzig, 1901ff.
APh	Archives de Philosophie. Paris.
AR	Archivum Romanicum. Florence.
ARW	Archiv für Religionswissenschaft. Berlin and Leipzig, 1898ff.
ASS	Acta Sanctorum, ed. by the Bollandists. Antwerp and Brussels, 1643ff.
AST	Analecta Sacra Tarraconensia. Barcelona, 1925ff.
ATG	Archivo Teológico Granadino. Granada, 1938ff.
AThR	Anglican Theological Review. New York, 1918ff.
Aug	Augustiniana. Louvain, 1951ff.
AugMag	Augustinus Magister. Congrès international augustinien. Paris, 21-24 septembre 1954. Vols. 1 and 2: Communications, vol. 3: Actes. Paris, 1954-1955.
BAB	Bulletin de la Classe des Lettres de l'Académie Royale de Belgique. Brussels.
BAC	Biblioteca de Autores Cristianos. Madrid, 1945ff.
BAGB	Bulletin de l'Association G. Budé. Paris.
BAPC	Bulletin of the Polish Academy. Cracow.
Bazmavep	(Polyhistor) Journal of the Mechitarists. Venice, 1843ff.
BBI	Bulletin of the Byzantine Institute. Boston.
BBR	Bulletin de l'Institut historique belge de Rome.
BEHE	Bibliothèque de l'École des hautes études. Paris.
Bess	Bessarione. Rome, 1896ff.

BFC	Bolletino di Filologia Classica. Turin.
BFTh	Beiträge zur Förderung der Theologie. Gütersloh.
BGDS	Beiträge zur Geschichte der deutschen Sprache.
BHM	Bulletin of the History of Medicine. Baltimore.
BHTh	Beiträge zur historischen Theologie. Tübingen, 1929ff.
Bibl	Biblica. Rome, 1920ff.
BICS	Bulletin of the Institute of Classical Studies of the University of London.
BiNJ	Bijdragen van de Philosophische en Theologische Faculteiten der Nederlandsche Jezuïeten. Roermond and Maastricht, 1938ff.
BiZ	Biblische Zeitschrift. Paderborn and Freiburg 1903-1939; 1957ff.
BJ	Bursians Jahresbericht über die Fortschritte der klassischen Altertumswissenschaft. Leipzig.
BJR	Bulletin of John Rylands Library. Manchester, 1903ff.
BKV	Bibliothek der Kirchenväter, ed. by F. X. Reithmayr and V. Thalhofer. Kempten, 1860-1888.
BKV²	Bibliothek der Kirchenväter, ed. by O. Bardenhewer, T. Schermann, C. Weyman. Kempten and Munich, 1911ff.
BKV³	Bibliothek der Kirchenväter. Zweite Reihe, ed. by O. Bardenhewer, J. Zellinger, J. Martin. Munich, 1932ff.
BLE	Bulletin de Littérature Ecclésiastique. Toulouse, 1899ff.
BM	Benediktinische Monatsschrift. Beuron, 1919ff.
BNJ	Byzantinisch-neugriechische Jahrbücher. Athens, 1920ff.
BOR	Biserica Ortodox Română. Bucarest, 1874ff.
BoS	Bogoslovska Smotra. Zagreb, 1912ff.
BoZ	Bonner Zeitschrift für Theologie und Seelsorge. Düsseldorf, 1925ff.
BPEC	Bolletino del Comitato per la preparazione dell'Edizione nazionale dei Classici greci e latini. Rome.
BTAM	Bulletin de Théologie Ancienne et Médiévale. Louvain, 1929ff.
BV	Bogoslovni Vestnik. Ljubljana, 1921ff.
BVM	Bogoslovskij Vestnik. Moscow, 1892ff.
Byz	Byzantion. Brussels, 1924ff.
BZ	Byzantinische Zeitschrift. Leipzig, 1892-1943. Munich, 1950ff.
CBQ	The Catholic Biblical Quarterly. Washington (D. C.), 1939ff.
CC	Civiltà Cattolica. Rome, 1850ff.
CCL	Corpus Christianorum. Series Latina. Turnhout and Paris, 1953ff.
CD	La Ciudad de Dios. Madrid, 1891ff.
CE	The Catholic Encyclopedia. New York, 1907-1914; Suppl. 1922.
CGG	Das Konzil von Chalkedon. Geschichte und Gegenwart. Ed.: A. Grillmeier and H. Bacht. Würzburg, I (1951), II (1953), III (1954).
CH	Church History. Chicago, 1931ff.
ChQ	The Church Quarterly Review. London, 1875ff.
CHR	The Catholic Historical Review. Washington (D. C.), 1915ff.
CJ	Classical Journal. Chicago.
CPh	Classical Philology. Chicago.
CPT	Cambridge Patristic Texts.
CQ	Classical Quarterly. London and Oxford.
CR	The Classical Review. London and Oxford.
CRI	Comptes-rendus de l'Académie des Inscriptions et Belles-Lettres. Paris.
CSCO	Corpus Scriptorum Christianorum Orientalium. Louvain, 1903ff.
CSEL	Corpus Scriptorum Ecclesiasticorum Latinorum. Vienna, 1866ff.
CSHB	Corpus Scriptorum Historiae Byzantinae. Bonn, 1828-1897.
CTh	Collectanea Theologica. Lwow, 1920ff.

DA   Dissertation Abstracts. Ann Arbor, Michigan.

DAC   Dictionary of the Apostolic Church, ed. J. Hastings. Edinburgh, 1915-1918.

DAL   Dictionnaire d'Archéologie Chrétienne et de Liturgie, ed. F. Cabrol and H. Leclercq. Paris, 1907-1953.

DAp   Dictionnaire Apologétique, ed. A. d'Alès. Paris, 1925ff., 4th ed.

DB   Dictionnaire de la Bible, ed. F. Vigouroux. Paris, 1895-1912; Suppl. 1926ff.

DCA   Dictionary of Christian Antiquities, ed. W. Smith and S. Cheetham. London, 1875/1880. 2 vols.

DCB   Dictionary of Christian Biography, Literature, Sects and Doctrines, ed. W. Smith and H. Wace. London, 1877-1887. 4 vols.

DDC   Dictionnaire de droit catholique, ed. V. Villien, E. Magnin, R. Naz. Paris, 1924ff.

DHC   Documents Illustrative of the History of the Church, ed. B. J. Kidd. London, 1938. 2 vols.

DHG   Dictionnaire d'Histoire et de Géographie Ecclésiastique, ed. A. Baudrillart. Paris, 1912ff.

DLZ   Deutsche Literaturzeitung für Kritik der internationalen Wissenschaft. Berlin, 1880ff.

DOP   Dumbarton Oaks Papers. Cambridge (Mass.), 1941ff.

DOS   Dumbarton Oaks Studies. Cambridge (Mass.), 1950ff.

DR   Downside Review. Stratton on the Fosse n. Bath, 1880ff.

DSp   Dictionnaire de la Spiritualité, ed. M. Viller. Paris, 1932ff.

DSt   Dominican Studies. Oxford, 1948ff.

DT   Divus Thomas. Fribourg (Switzerland), 1914ff.

DTC   Dictionnaire de Théologie Catholique, ed. A. Vacant, E. Mangenot, and E. Amann. Paris, 1903-1950.

DTP   Divus Thomas. Piacenza, 1880ff.

EA   Enchiridion Asceticum, ed. M. J. Rouet de Journel and J. Dutilleul. 4th ed. Barcelona, 1947.

EB   Estudios Biblicos. Madrid.

EBrit   Encyclopaedia Britannica. 14th ed. Chicago, London, Toronto, 1929ff.

EC   Enciclopedia Cattolica, ed. P. Paschini and others. Rome, 1949-1954.

ECQ   Eastern Churches Quarterly. Ramsgate, 1936ff.

EE   Estudios Ecclesiasticos. Madrid, 1922ff.

EEBS   Ἐπετηρὶς τῆς Ἑταιρείας Βυζαντινῶν Σπουδῶν. Athens, 1931ff.

EH   Enchiridion Fontium Historiae Ecclesiasticae Antiquae, ed. C. Kirch. 6th ed. by L. Ueding. Barcelona, 1947.

EHPR   Études d'Histoire et de Philosophie Religieuse.

EHR   English Historical Review. London, 1886ff.

EL   Ephemerides Liturgicae. Rome, 1887ff.

EO   Échos d'Orient. Paris, 1897-1942.

Eos   Eos. Commentarii Societatis Philologicae Polonorum. Lwow, 1894ff.

EP   Enchiridion Patristicum, ed. M. J. Rouet de Journel, 18th ed. Freiburg i. B., 1953.

EPh   Ἐκκλησιαστικὸς Φάρος. Alexandria.

Eranos   Eranos. Göteburg.

ES   Enchiridion Symbolorum, ed. H. Denzinger and C. Rahner. 30th ed. Freiburg i.B., 1955.

Et   Études. Paris, 1856ff. (until 1896: Études religieuses).

EtByz   Études Byzantines. Paris, 1943-1945.

ETL   Ephemerides Theologicae Lovanienses. Louvain, 1924ff.

ExpT   The Expository Times. Edinburgh, 1898ff.

FC	The Fathers of the Church, ed. R. J. Deferrari. New York, 1947ff.
FF	Forschungen und Fortschritte. Berlin, 1925ff.
FKDG	Forschungen zur Kirchen- und Dogmengeschichte. Göttingen, 1953ff.
FLDG	Forschungen zur christlichen Literatur- und Dogmengeschichte. Mainz, 1900ff.; Paderborn, 1906ff.
Folia	Folia. Studies in the Christian Perpetuation of the Classics. New York, 1947ff.
FP	Florilegium Patristicum. Bonn, 1904ff.
FRL	Forschungen zur Religion und Literatur des Alten und Neuen Testamentes. Göttingen.
FS	Franciscan Studies. St. Bonaventure (N. Y.), N.S. 1941ff.
FThSt	Freiburger theologische Studien. Freiburg i.B., 1910ff.
GAb	Abhandlungen der Gesellschaft der Wissenschaften zu Göttingen.
GCS	Die griechischen christlichen Schriftsteller. Leipzig, 1897ff.
GGA	Göttingische Gelehrte Anzeigen. Berlin, 1738ff.
Gno	Gnomon. Kritische Zeitschrift für die gesamte Altertumswissenschaft. Munich, 1925ff.
Greg	Gregorianum. Rome, 1920ff.
GTT	Gereformeerd Theologisch Tijdschrift. Aalten.
HA	Handes Ansorya. Monatsschrift für armenische Philologie. Vienna, 1887ff.
HAPhG	Heidelberger Abhandlungen zur Philosophie und ihrer Geschichte. Heidelberg.
Hermathena	Hermathena. A Series of Papers on Literature, Science and Philosophy. Dublin and London, 1874ff.
Hermes	Hermes. Zeitschrift für klassische Philologie. Berlin, 1866ff.
HJ	The Hibbert Journal. London, 1902ff.
HJG	Historisches Jahrbuch der Görresgesellschaft. Cologne, 1880ff.; Munich, 1950ff.
HS	Harvard Studies and Notes in Philology and Literature. Cambridge (Mass.).
HSCP	Harvard Studies in Classical Philology. Cambridge (Mass.).
HThR	Harvard Theological Review. Cambridge (Mass.), 1908ff.
HTS	Harvard Theological Studies. Cambridge (Mass.), 1916ff.
HVS	Historische Vierteljahrsschrift. Leipzig, 1898-1937.
HZ	Historische Zeitschrift. Munich, 1859ff.
IER	The Irish Ecclesiastical Record. Dublin, 1864ff.
IKZ	Internationale kirchliche Zeitschrift. Bern, 1911ff.
Isis	Isis. Quarterly Organ of the History of Science Society. Bruges and Cambridge (Mass.), 1913ff.
ITQ	The Irish Theological Quarterly. Dublin, 1864ff.
JA	Journal Asiatique. Paris, 1822ff.
JAC	Jahrbuch für Antike und Christentum. Münster i.W., 1958ff.
James	M. R. James, The Apocryphal New Testament. Oxford, 1924.
JBL	Journal of Biblical Literature. New Haven and Boston, 1881ff.
JDAI	Jahrbuch des Deutschen Archäologischen Instituts. Berlin, 1886ff.
JEH	The Journal of Ecclesiastical History. London, 1950ff.
JHS	Journal of Hellenic Studies. London, 1880ff.
JL	Jahrbuch für Liturgiewissenschaft. Münster, 1921-1941.
JLH	Jahrbuch für Liturgik und Hymnologie. Kassel, 1955ff.
JNES	Journal of Near Eastern Studies. Chicago, 1942ff.
JOBG	Jahrbuch der Österreichischen Byzantinischen Gesellschaft. Vienna, 1951ff.

JQR	Jewish Quarterly Review. Philadelphia, 1888ff.
JR	The Journal of Religion. Chicago, 1921ff.
JRS	Journal of Roman Studies. London, 1911ff.
JS	Journal des Savants. Paris.
JSOR	Journal of the Society of Oriental Research. Chicago, 1917-1932.
JThSt	Journal of Theological Studies. London, 1900-1905; Oxford, 1906-1949; N.S.: Oxford, 1950ff.
KA	Kyrkohistorisk Årskrift. Stockholm.
KGA	Kirchengeschichtliche Abhandlungen, ed. M. Sdralek. Breslau, 1902-1912.
KT	Kleine Texte für Vorlesungen und Übungen, ed. H. Lietzmann. Berlin, 1903ff.
Latomus	Latomus. Revue des études latines. Brussels.
LCC	Library of Christian Classics, ed. J. Baillie, J. T. McNeill, H. P. van Dusen. Philadelphia and London, 1953ff.
LCL	Loeb Classical Library. London and Cambridge (Mass.), 1912ff.
LF	Liturgiegeschichtliche Forschungen. Münster, 1918ff.
LFC	Library of the Fathers of the Holy Catholic Church, ed. E. B. Pusey, J. Keble and J. H. Newman. Oxford, 1838-1888.
LJ	Liturgisches Jahrbuch. Münster, 1951ff.
LNPF	A Select Library of Nicene and Post-Nicene Fathers of the Christian Church, ed. by Ph. Schaff and H. Wace. Buffalo and New York, 1886-1900; reprinted: Grand Rapids, 1952ff.
LQ	Liturgiegeschichtliche Quellen. Münster, 1918ff.
LQF	Liturgiegeschichtliche Quellen und Forschungen. Münster, 1929-1940; 1957ff.
LThK	Lexikon für Theologie und Kirche. Freiburg i.B., 1930-1938.
LThK²	Lexikon für Theologie und Kirche. 2nd ed. Freiburg i.B., 1957ff.
LThPh	Laval Théologique et Philosophique. Québec.
LZB	Literarisches Zentralblatt. Leipzig, 1850ff.
MAH	Mélanges d'Archéologie et d'Histoire. Paris and Rome, 1881ff.
Mansi	J. D. Mansi, Sacrorum Conciliorum Nova et Amplissima Collectio. Florence, 1759-1798. Reprint and continuation: Paris and Leipzig, 1901-1927.
MBTh	Münsterische Beiträge zur Theologie. Münster, 1923ff.
MC	Monumenta Christiana. Bibliotheek van Christelijke Klassieken. Utrecht, 1948ff.
MDAI	Mitteilungen des Deutschen Archäologischen Instituts. Römische Abteilung. Heidelberg.
MG	Migne, Patrologia Graeca.
MGH	Monumenta Germaniae Historica. Hannover and Berlin, 1826ff.
MGWJ	Monatsschrift für Geschichte und Wissenschaft des Judentums. Breslau, 1851ff.
ML	Migne, Patrologia Latina.
Mnem	Mnemosyne. Bibliotheca philologica Batavorum. Leiden.
MS	Mediaeval Studies. Toronto, 1939ff.
MSCA	Miscellanea Agostiniana. Rome, 1931.
MSCI	Miscellanea Isidoriana. Rome, 1935.
MSLC	Miscellanea di Studi di Letteratura Cristiana Antica. Catania.
MSR	Mélanges de Science Religieuse. Lille, 1944ff.
MStHTh	Münchener Studien zur historischen Theologie. Munich, 1921-1937.

MTS   Münchener theologische Studien. Munich, 1950ff.
MTZ   Münchener theologische Zeitschrift. Munich, 1950ff.
Mus   Le Muséon. Revue d'études orientales. Louvain, 1881ff.

NA   Neues Archiv der Gesellschaft für ältere deutsche Geschichtskunde.
            Hannover, 1876-1936.
NAKG   Nederlandsch Archief voor Kerkgeschiedenis. The Hague.
NC   La Nouvelle Clio. Brussels, 1947ff.
ND   Nuovo Didaskaleion. Catania, 1947ff.
N.F.   Neue Folge.
NGWG   Nachrichten der Gesellschaft der Wissenschaften zu Göttingen. Phil.-
            hist. Klasse. Göttingen, 1865ff.
NJKA   Neue Jahrbücher für das klassische Altertum. Leipzig.
NKZ   Neue kirchliche Zeitschrift. Leipzig, 1890ff.
NRTh   Nouvelle Revue Théologique. Tournai, 1879ff.
NS   Νέα Σίων. Jerusalem, 1901ff.
N.S.   New Series.
NSch   New Scholasticism. Washington, 1927ff.
NTA   Neutestamentliche Abhandlungen. Münster, 1909ff.
NTT   Nieuw Theologisch Tijdschrift. Haarlem.

OC   Oriens Christianus. Leipzig, 1901-1941. Wiesbaden, 1953ff.
OCh   Orientalia Christiana. Rome, 1923-1934.
OCP   Orientalia Christiana Periodica. Rome, 1935ff.
ODC   The Oxford Dictionary of the Christian Church, ed. by F. L. Cross.
            London, 1957.
OLZ   Orientalistische Literaturzeitung. Leipzig, 1898ff.
Or   Orientalia. Commentarii periodici Pont. Instituti Bibl. Rome, 1920ff.
Orph   Orpheus. Rivista di umanità classica e cristiana. Catania.
OrSyr   L'Orient Syrien. Paris, 1956ff.
OstkSt   Ostkirchliche Studien. Würzburg, 1952ff.

PB   Pastor Bonus. Trier, 1889ff. Since 1947: TThZ.
PC   Paraula Cristiana. Barcelona.
Phil   Philologus. Zeitschrift für das klassische Altertum. Leipzig. Wiesbaden,
            1946ff.
PhJ   Philosophisches Jahrbuch der Görresgesellschaft. Fulda, 1888ff.
PhW   Philologische Wochenschrift. Leipzig.
PO   Patrologia Orientalis, ed. by R. Graffin and F. Nau. Paris, 1903ff.
PP   La Parola del Passato. Rivista di studi classici. Naples, 1946ff.
PrOChr   Le Proche-Orient Chrétien. Jerusalem, 1951ff.
PS   Patrologia Syriaca, ed. by R. Graffin. Paris, 1894-1926. 3 vols.
PSt   Patristic Studies, ed. by R. J. Deferrari. Washington, 1922ff.
PThR   Princeton Theological Review. Princeton.
PWK   Pauly-Wissowa-Kroll, Realencyklopädie der klassischen Altertums-
            wissenschaft. Stuttgart, 1893ff.

QLP   Questions Liturgiques et Paroissiales. Louvain, 1918ff.

RAC   Rivista di Archeologia Cristiana. Rome, 1924ff.
RACh   Reallexikon für Antike und Christentum, ed. by T. Klauser. Leipzig,
            1941ff. Stuttgart, 1950ff.
RAL   Rendiconti della Reale Accademia Nazionale dei Lincei. Classe di scienze
            morali, storiche e filologiche. Rome.

RAM	Revue d'Ascétique et de Mystique. Toulouse, 1920ff.
RAp	Revue Apologétique. Paris, 1905-1940.
RB	Revue Bénédictine. Maredsous, 1884ff.
RBibl	Revue Biblique. Paris, 1891ff. N.S.: 1904ff.
RBPh	Revue Belge de Philologie et d'Histoire. Brussels.
RC	Revue Critique d'Histoire et de Littérature. Paris.
RCC	Revue des Cours et Conférences. Paris.
RDC	Revue de Droit Canonique. Strasbourg, 1951ff.
RE	Realencyklopädie für protestantische Theologie und Kirche, founded by J. J. Herzog, 3rd ed. by A. Hauck. Leipzig, 1896-1913.
REA	Revue des Études Arméniennes. Paris.
REAN	Revue des Études Anciennes. Bordeaux, 1899ff.
REAug	Revue des Études Augustiniennes. Paris, 1955ff.
REB	Revue des Études Byzantines. Paris, 1946ff.
REG	Revue des Études Grecques. Paris, 1888ff.
RELA	Revue des Études Latines. Paris, 1923ff.
RelC	Religión y Cultura. Madrid.
Religio	Religio, ed. by E. Buonaiuti. Rome, 1925-1939.
RES	Revista Española de Teologia. Madrid, 1941ff.
RevR	Review of Religion. New York.
RF	Razón y Fé. Madrid, 1901ff.
RFE	Revista de Filologia Española. Madrid.
RFIC	Rivista di Filologia e Istruzione Classica. Turin.
RFN	Rivista di Filosofia Neoscolastica. Milan, 1909ff.
RGG²	Religion in Geschichte und Gegenwart. 2nd ed. by H. Gunkel and L. Zscharnack. Tübingen, 1927-1932.
RGG³	Religion in Geschichte und Gegenwart. 3rd ed. by K. Galling. Tübingen, 1957ff.
RH	Revue Historique. Paris, 1876ff.
RHE	Revue d'Histoire Ecclésiastique. Louvain, 1900.
RHEF	Revue d'Histoire de l'Église de France. Paris, 1910ff.
RHL	Revue d'Histoire et de Littérature Religieuses. Paris, 1896-1907.
RhM	Rheinisches Museum für Philologie. Bonn, 1833ff.
RHPR	Revue d'Histoire et de Philosophie Religieuses. Strasbourg, 1921ff.
RHR	Revue de l'Histoire des Religions. Paris, 1880ff.
RIL	Rendiconti del R. Istituto Lombardo di Scienze e Lettere. Milan.
RLM	Revue Liturgique et Monastique. Maredsous.
RML	Revue du Moyen-âge Latin. Lyons and Strasbourg, 1945ff.
ROC	Revue de l'Orient Chrétien. Paris, 1896ff.
ROL	Revue de l'Orient Latin. Paris, 1893ff.
RPh	Revue de Philologie, de Littérature et d'Histoire Anciennes. Paris, 1914ff.
RQ	Römische Quartalschrift. Freiburg i.B., 1891ff.
RQH	Revue des Questions Historiques. Paris, 1866ff.
RR	Ricerche Religiose. Rome, 1925ff.
RSCI	Rivista di Storia della Chiesa in Italia. Rome, 1947ff.
RSFR	Rivista di Studi Filosofici e Religiosi. Rome.
RSH	Revue de Synthèse Historique. Paris.
RSO	Rivista degli Studi Orientali. Rome, 1908ff.
RSPT	Revue des Sciences Philosophiques et Théologiques. Paris, 1907ff.
RSR	Recherches de Science Religieuse. Paris, 1910ff.
RSRUS	Revue des Sciences Religieuses. Strasbourg and Paris, 1921ff.
RStR	Ricerche di Storia Religiosa. Rome, 1954ff.
RT	Revue Thomiste. Paris, 1893ff.
RTAM	Recherches de Théologie Ancienne et Médiévale. Louvain, 1929ff.

RTP	Revue de Théologie et Philosophie. Lausanne, 1868ff.
RTr	Rivista Trimestrale di Studi Filosofici e Religiosi. Perugia.
RUO	Revue de l'Université d'Ottawa.
SA	Studia Anselmiana. Rome, 1933ff.
SAB	Sitzungsberichte der Preussischen Akademie der Wissenschaften. Phil.-hist. Klasse. Berlin, 1882ff.
SAH	Sitzungsberichte der Heidelberger Akademie der Wissenschaften. Phil.-hist. Klasse. Heidelberg, 1910ff.
SAM	Sitzungsberichte der Bayerischen Akademie der Wissenschaften. Phil.-hist. Klasse. Munich, 1871ff.
SAW	Sitzungsberichte der Wiener Akademie der Wissenschaften. Phil.-hist. Klasse. Vienna, 1847ff.
SC	Scuola Cattolica. Milan, 1873ff.
SCA	Studies in Christian Antiquity, ed. by J. Quasten. Washington, 1941ff.
SCH	Sources Chrétiennes, ed. by H. de Lubac and J. Daniélou. Paris, 1941ff.
Schol	Scholastik. Freiburg i.B., 1926ff.
SD	Studies and Documents, ed. by K. Lake and S. Lake. London and Philadelphia, 1934ff.
SE	Sacris Erudiri. Jaarboek voor godsdienstwetenschappen. Bruges, 1948ff.
SIF	Studi Italiani di Filologia Classica. Florence.
SJMS	Speculum. Journal of Medieval Studies. Cambridge (Mass.), 1926ff.
SKGG	Schriften der Königsberger Gelehrtengesellschaft. Berlin, 1924ff.
SM	Studien und Mitteilungen zur Geschichte des Benediktinerordens und seiner Zweige. Munich, 1880ff.
SO	Symbolae Osloenses. Oslo, 1920ff.
So	Sophia. Milan and Padua.
SP	Studia Patristica. Papers Presented to the Second International Conference on Patristic Studies held at Christ Church Oxford 1955 (TU 63/64). Berlin, 1957. 2 vols.
SPCK	Society for Promoting Christian Knowledge. London.
SPM	Stromata Patristica et Mediaevalia, ed. by C. Mohrmann and J. Quasten. Utrecht, 1950ff.
SQ	Sammlung ausgewählter Quellenschriften zur Kirchen- und Dogmengeschichte. Tübingen, 1893ff.
SSL	Spicilegium Sacrum Lovaniense. Louvain, 1922ff.
ST	Studi e Testi. Pubblicazioni della Biblioteca Vaticana. Rome, 1900ff.
StBN	Studi Bizantini e Neoellenici. Rome, 1947ff.
StC	Studia Catholica. Roermond and Nijmegen 1924ff.
StGKA	Studien zur Geschichte und Kultur des Altertums. Paderborn.
STh	Studia Theologica. Lund, 1948ff.
StP	Studia Patavina. Padua, 1954ff.
ThBl	Theologische Blätter. Leipzig, 1922ff.
ThGl	Theologie und Glaube. Paderborn, 1909ff.
ThJ	Theologische Jahrbücher. Leipzig, 1842ff.
ThLB	Theologisches Literaturblatt. Leipzig, 1880ff.
ThLZ	Theologische Literaturzeitung. Leipzig, 1878ff.
ThQ	Theologische Quartalschrift. Tübingen, 1819ff.; Stuttgart, 1946ff.
ThR	Theologische Revue. Münster, 1902ff.
ThStKr	Theologische Studien und Kritiken. Gotha, 1828ff.
TJHC	Theology. Journal of Historic Christianity. London.
TP	Transactions and Proceedings of the American Philological Association. Boston (Mass.).

INTRODUCTION

The victory of Constantine at the Milvian Bridge constitutes the turning-point in the history of the early Church. It marks the end of pagan Rome and inaugurates the Christian Empire. From an outlawed religion, Christianity became a tolerated, and finally the preferred religion. After the short-lived attempt of the Emperor Julian (361-363) to restore paganism failed, the Christian religion becomes under Theodosius I a few years later the religion of the state.

Thus the Church enters a new era as does her science, her liturgy and her art. The period of the great Church Fathers begins, the golden age of ecclesiastical literature. The Christian writers of the fourth and fifth centuries are at liberty to devote their talents to causes other than the defense of the Church against the pagans. The development of ecclesiastical science is the distinctive feature of this epoch. Free from external oppression, the Church dedicates herself to the preservation of her doctrine from heresy and to the definition of her main dogmas. It is the age of the great ecumenical councils and its salient characteristic, the effect of the Christological disputes, is intense activity in theology. Most writers, engrossed in the contemporary burning issues, devote themselves to polemic and dogma. It is especially in the East, where the famed councils of Nicaea (325), Constantinople (381), Ephesus (431) and Chalcedon (451) took place, that a large number of outstanding authors deal with the heresies of Arianism, Macedonianism, Sabellianism, Nestorianism, Apollinarianism and Monophysitism. Thus this period produces such great theologians as Athanasius, the Cappadocian Fathers, John Chrysostom, Cyril of Alexandria and others, whose works echo the intellectual conflicts of their times.

There is, in addition to the interior growth of theological science, a second element that contributed to the achievements of Christian literature in the post-Constantinian period. The victory of the Christian religion is accompanied by wholesale assimilation of secular learning and education and unrestricted appropriation of traditional literary forms. Thus the classical authors of the Greek Church like Basil the Great, Gregory of Nyssa and Gregory of Nazianzus combine excellent theological training with Hellenistic culture, with brilliant eloquence and a mastery of style learnt in the ancient schools and academies. A Christian humanism was born in which ecclesiastical literature reached its perfection.

The freedom of worship granted by Constantine resulted very soon in mass conversion. The Church thus becomes a dominant factor in the world. The great danger was that there might be a lowering of Christian morals and spirituality and an insufficient change of heart and mind. To offset this, the world Church produced monasticism, which renounces the world and advocates a life of asceticism and mysticism. In the beginning, the new movement reacted strongly against all attempts at Christian humanism and against any intermarriage between classical culture and Christian religion. Manual labor and prayer were recommended rather than sacred science and literary activity in the earliest communities of cenobites. As time went on, this attitude towards literature and learning changed completely. On the contrary, many monasteries became cradles of theology and Christian philosophy and not a few of their inhabitants took an active part in the dogmatic controversies of their times. Furthermore, the rise of monasticism created an entirely new type of Christian literature. Lives of famous monks and anecdotes about the sayings and doings of the most renowned solitaries and abbots were composed, ascetical manuals were written in order to promote spiritual perfection and explain the special duties of the monk. The founders of monasticism drew up disciplinary rules and regulations. Once again the East was the place of origin of this genre: it was Egypt that instituted the monastic life.

Meanwhile the ancient centers of ecclesiastical learning, the Schools of Alexandria and Antioch, did not interrupt their efforts to interpret the Book of Books, Holy Scripture. Their different points of view have been sufficiently described in a previous volume (II, p. 2-4, 121-123). In the fourth and fifth centuries they were closely involved in the great dogmatic controversies that preceded and followed the ecumenical councils. As a result, their opposition to each other increased to such a degree that several of their members fell into heresies.

The School of Alexandria, which reached its peak under Origen, saw a second spring in the fourth century. Following in the main the impulse and ideas of its great master, it nevertheless freed itself from some of his errors, using allegorical exegesis for edification only. Thus there is a difference between the elder and younger members of this school. Since Arius and other heretics made every effort to prove their erroneous opinions from Scripture, the Neo-Alexandrine School in order to refute them, adopted in all polemical and theological discussions and controversies the historico-gramma-tical interpretation of Scripture which had always been advocated by the School of Antioch. The allegorical method had proved itself insufficient for such purposes. The leader of this new school was St. Athanasius, the defender of the faith against Arius. Its most brilliant disciples were Eusebius of Caesarea, the three Cappadocians, Didymus the Blind, Hesychius of Jerusalem and

Cyril of Alexandria, the protagonist of orthodoxy against Nestorius. It was, however, the adherence to the older principle of interpretation that contributed to such vague speculations as Monophysitism and Monotheletism.

During this period the School of Antioch reached the height of its fame, while Diodorus of Tarsus was its head. He and his great disciples St. John Chrysostom, Meletius of Antioch, Theodore of Mopsuestia, upheld the principles of its founder Lucian (cf. vol. II, p. 142-144), who laid great stress on a literal rendering of the biblical text and a historical and grammatical study of its sense. However, the rationalistic tendencies of this school, which tried to eliminate the element of mystery from Christian doctrine, brought a number of its representatives into conflict with the traditional teaching of the Church. Arius, a disciple of its founder, Lucian, was not the only heretic who received his theological training at Antioch. Nestorius and Apollinaris of Laodicea belonged to this exegetical school, as well as Theodore of Mopsuestia. The latter, however, deserves a more positive evaluation than has been hitherto accorded him; his biblical commentaries, together with those of the other writers of the Antiochene School like Theodoret of Cyrus, exhibit both in form and content the greatest exegetical skill.

The progress made in the elucidation and interpretation of Holy Scripture as well as the skill developed by the Hellenistic schools of rhetoric contributed to the great success of another form of Christian literature in the post-Constantinian period, which surpasses all others in importance, the homily. Sermons of the fourth and fifth centuries have reached us in countless numbers, thanks in many instances to the tireless efforts of Christian stenographers. The most famous example is St. John Chrysostom.

The glorious termination of three centuries of conflict with the State occasioned the first attempt at a comprehensive history of the Church. The Father of this new science is Eusebius of Caesarea. His work was continued, but never surpassed, by a great number of other ecclesiastical historians, Socrates, Sozomen, Theodoret, Philip of Side and Hesychius of Jerusalem. Their works, although of no great literary value, have immense importance as the sources of our knowledge of the early Church.

Excellent information is also supplied by the numerous letters left by many of the most outstanding Christian writers of this period. The freedom given the Church occasioned a great increase in Christian correspondence, which continued in form and style the tradition of the highly developed epistolary literature of the Hellenistic world. Since most of it was composed with a view to ultimate publication, even private missives follow the rules laid down by the Greek stylists. Although the epistle is the oldest Christian literary form, the post-Constantinian period witnesses the beginnings of the great collections. They reveal not only the many interests of their authors but provide interspersed with doctrinal discussions, first class evidence on every phase of life, economic and professional, social, political and religious; the whole society of the time passes before us and lives before our eyes. They have so far not been adequately evaluated in their theological, philological and historical aspect, and they are a mine of information far from being exhausted. Thus the festal, encyclical and personal letters of Athanasius present a surprisingly rich source for the history of the Egyptian Church, the Trinitarian controversies, the Arian heresy and the beginnings of monasticism. The letters of Basil the Great are pearls of Christian epistolary art, unsurpassed in language and style, in depth and warmth of sentiment, or in breadth of interest and variety of personal acquaintances. There are the sparkling, Atticistic epistles of Gregory of Nazianzus, the practical and wise missives of Gregory of Nyssa and the touching and courageous communications of St. John Chrysostom as well as the elegant correspondence of Synesius of Cyrene. All types of ancient epistolography find their perfection in these great collections.

It was in the East, as we have seen (vol. I, p. 158-171) that Christian poetry began and the first Christian hymns were sung. They do not follow ancient prosody because they were formed after the prose translation of the psalms. However, in post-Constantinian times the Church enters upon a rivalry with dying heathenism as well as with heretics who attempted to render their doctrines popular by means of popular songs. Arius, the elder and the younger Apollinaris of Laodicea, the Empress Eudocia composed such hymns for their purposes and the ancient philosophical schools made use of similar compositions in order to spread their metaphysics. Following in the footsteps of Neoplatonism, Gregory of Nazianzus wrote verse which praises the incomprehensible and unknown God. He is the author of more than 400 Christian poems. Synesius of Cyrene, even more brilliant, has hymns in honor of the Holy Trinity. Both of them were faithful to the laws of antique metre, though in Gregory we meet already here and there a new form of rhythm dependent on word stress. Here we see the first influence of Syriac poetry, which produced the greatest Christian poet of this period, Ephraem Syrus.

The difference between the times of persecutions and the new era is no less evident in the development of the liturgy. The Eucharist, at the beginning a simple Lord's Supper in the private homes of the Christians, takes the form more and more of a court ceremonial for the reception of a king. Especially the Eastern liturgies see a rapid growth in this direction. The leading centres are, as in theological thought, Alexandria and Antioch. The sudden increase of communities in size and number, to which the many ecclesiastical buildings, the basilicas of Constantine, testify, leads to a codification of public prayer. Thus in the East the first sacramentaries appear in the fourth century. There are especially three collections of texts, the Euchologion of Bishop Serapion of Thmuis for Alexandria and Egypt, the Liturgy of the eighth book of the *Apostolic Constitutions*, the so-called Clementine Liturgy, for Antioch and Syria (cf. vol. II, p. 184f), and the so-called Liturgy of St. Basil for Asia Minor.

CHAPTER I

THE WRITERS OF ALEXANDRIA AND EGYPT

In the preceding volume attention has been drawn to the important position which Alexandria in Egypt occupies in the history of Christian thought. This city of learning, famous for its monumental library and its schools of religion, philosophy, and sciences, was the place where Christianity came in greater contact with Hellenism than in any other metropolis of the East or West. Thus in this setting the fundamental problem of theology arose, the problem of faith and science and the connected problem of the philosophical foundation and defense of the faith. The intellectual power of the Greek genius helped to make Christianity a spiritual force and aided it in developing a lofty theory of knowledge capable of going far toward satisfying even exalted minds. The quest, however, for higher wisdom and the incipient theological research were not without danger to the purity of the faith. Alexandria becomes the sphere of doctrinal speculation as well as of dogmatic controversies, of the elaboration and formulation of dogma, as well as of novel theories and personal interpretations often at variance with the traditional teaching of the Church. The city of the most famous theological school is the birthplace of the greatest heresy of Christian antiquity which attempted to substitute philosophical principles and methods for revealed truth. The cradle of sacred science is the cradle of Arianism.

Almost all of the writers in the present chapter and most of the others are more or less involved in the great controversy created by the revolt of the Alexandrian priest. Despite the numerous studies made in recent years, the origin of Arianism and its pre-Nicaean history still present several unsolved problems. Thus it is still debated whether the ideological forerunner of Arius' doctrine must be sought in the theories of Origen, or of Paul of Samosata, or of Lucian of Antioch. Similarly, historians still disagree on the dates of several events in the pre-Nicaean stage of the Arian dispute. Gwatkin, Seeck, Snellman, Opitz and Schneemelcher assign the outbreak of the dispute to the year 318 or 320, before the Licinian persecution. Schwartz, on the contrary, Batiffol, Bardy and Telfer, believe that the first open conflict of Arius with his bishop, Alexander, and his condemnation of the same, date from as late as the spring or fall of 323, and that the following events developed rather swiftly, within 18 or 22 months.

Sources: H. G. Opitz, Urkunden zur Geschichte des arianischen Streites 318-328 (Athanasius' Werke, Band III, 1). Berlin and Leipzig, 1934-1935, to be continued by E. Schneemelcher and M. Tetz.

Studies: On Egypt and its Church in this period: H. I. Bell, Jews and Christians in Egypt. The Jewish Troubles in Alexandria and the Athanasian Controversy. London, 1924. — J. G. Milne, A History of Egypt under Roman Rule, 3rd ed. London, 1924. — G. Bardy, Les premiers temps du christianisme de langue copte en Égypte: Mémorial M. J. Lagrange. Paris, 1940, 203-216. — E. R. Hardy, Christian Egypt: Church and People. New York, 1952. Cf. vol. II, 2-3.

On Arianism: H. Gwatkin, Studies of Arianism, 2nd ed. Cambridge, 1890. — C. Hefele and H. Leclercq, Histoire des conciles I 1, 349-385. — O. Seeck, Untersuchungen zur Geschichte des nicänischen Konzils: ZKG 17 (1896) 1-71 and 319-362. — P. Batiffol, Sozomène et Sabinos: BZ 7 (1898) 265-284. — P. Snellman, Der Anfang des arianischen Streites. Helsingfors, 1904. — E. Schwartz, Zur Geschichte des Athanasius: NGWG 5 (1904) 338-401 and 518-547; 6 (1905) 164-187 and 257-299; 9 (1908) 305-374; 12 (1911) 367-426. — S. Rogala, Die Anfänge des arianischen Streites (FLDG 7, 1). Paderborn, 1907. — G. Schoo, Die Quellen des Kirchenhistorikers Sozomenos. Berlin, 1911, 97-110. — G. Bardy, Le symbole de Lucien d'Antioche et les formules du synode In Encaeniis (341): RSR 3 (1912) 139-155; *idem*, La politique religieuse de Constantin après le concile de Nicée: RSRUS 8 (1928) 516-551; *idem*, Saint Lucien d'Antioche et son école: les collucianistes: RSR 22 (1932) 437-462. — J. Zeiller, Arianisme et religions orientales dans l'Empire romain: RSR 18 (1928) 73-86. — H. G. Opitz, Die Zeitfolge des arianischen Streites von den Anfängen bis 328: ZNW 33 (1934) 131-159. — E. Schwartz, Zur Kirchengeschichte des 4. Jahrhunderts: ZNW 34 (1935) 129-213. — G. Bardy, Recherches sur saint Lucien d'Antioche et son école. Paris, 1936; *idem*, L'Occident en face de la crise arienne: Irénikon 16 (1939) 385-424; *idem*, L'Occident et les documents de la controverse arienne: RSRUS 20 (1940) 28-64. — R. V. Sellers, Two Ancient Christologies. A Study in the Christological Thought of the Schools of Alexandria and Antioch (SPCK). London, 1940. — G. Gentz, Arianer: RACh 1 (1943) 647-652. — W. Telfer, When did the Arian Controversy begin?: JThSt 47 (1946) 129-142. — N. H. Baynes, Sozomen, Ecclesiastica Historia I 15: JThSt 49 (1948) 165-168. — W. Telfer, Sozomen I 15. A Reply: JThSt 50 (1949) 187-191 (against Baynes). — E. Ivanka, Hellenisches und Christliches im frühbyzantinischen Geistesleben. Vienna, 1948, 17-24. — G. Gigli, L'ortodossia, l'arianesimo e la politica di Costanzo II (337-361). Rome, 1950. — G. H. Williams, Christology and Church-State Relations in the Fourth Century: Church History 20 (1951) n. 3, 3-33; n. 4, 3-26. — V. De Clercq, Ossius of Cordova (SCA 13). Washington, 1954, 189-195. — W. Schneemelcher, Zur Chronologie des arianischen Streites: ThLZ 79 (1954) 393-400. — T. E. Pollard, The Origins of Arianism: JThSt 9 (1958) 103-111.

ARIUS

Arius (256-336), a native of Libya, received his theological training at Antioch in the School of Lucian, whom bishop Alexander of Alexandria called one of the fathers of Arianism. From Antioch he went to Alexandria where, ordained deacon and later priest, he was appointed to the Church of St. Baucalis. About the year 318 he began to excite much discussion by a theological doctrine of his own, which he presented in his sermons as the faith of the Church. Since he wrote very little and only a few fragments remain, satisfactory insight into his original teaching is difficult to obtain.

However, his basic ideas can be ascertained and summarized in a few words.

At the foundation of his system is an axiom which blocked from the beginning his understanding of the true relation between God the Father and God the Son. This principle proclaimed it necessary that the Godhead should be not only uncreated but unbegotten (ἀγέννητος). The logical sequence is that the Son of God, the Logos, cannot be truly God. He is the first of God's creatures and like the others was brought out of nothingness (ἐξ οὐκ ὄντων), not from the divine substance. He differs essentially from the Father. He is a secondary God. There was a time when the Son of God was not (ἦν ὅτε οὐκ ἦν). He is the Son of God not in the metaphysical, but in the moral sense of the word. The title of God is improperly given to Him, because the only true God adopted Him as Son in prevision of his merits. From this sonship by adoption results no real participation in the divinity, no true likeness to it. God can have no like. The Logos holds a middle place between God and the world. God created Him to be the instrument of creation. The Holy Spirit is the first of the creatures of the Logos. He is still less God than the Word. The Logos was made flesh in the sense that He fulfilled in Jesus Christ the function of a soul.

This doctrine is a typical product of theological rationalism. It satisfied superficial minds to a high degree because it gave a simple and easy answer to the very difficult question of the relation existing between God the Father and God the Son. It saved Arius and his followers the trouble of investigating God's inner life because it denied all internal divine relations. This rationalistic character is what attracted many to the heresy. Moreover, the false views are closely connected with Neoplatonic theories, still current at the time, of intermediaries between God and the world, among which many were thus already prepared to class the God of the Christians. Finally, it must be remembered, in order to understand the force behind the movement, that the theology of Arius was not entirely new. It was nothing but the theory of subordinationism, that in a more moderate form had been taught before Arius and had many adherents, developed to an extreme.

The doctrine was soon to be denounced as contrary to tradition. It attacked in fact the very nature of Christianity, because it attributed redemption to a God who was not a true God at all and for this reason incapable of redeeming mankind. Thus it deprived the faith of its essential character.

The situation became grave when Arius and his followers, first entreated and then commanded to abandon the innovation, obstinately refused. Alexander, then bishop of Alexandria, thought it his duty to summon the whole Egyptian hierarchy. Nearly one hundred rallied for a synod in the year 318 at Alexandria. Arius was condemned and he and his adherents deposed. Far from accepting his excommunication, he objected to the sentence and tried to gain associates among his former fellow-students at Antioch. Some of them were already bishops, among whom the most influential, Eusebius of Nicomedia, extended a warm welcome to the heresiarch and gave him his full support; himself a disciple of Lucian of Antioch, Arius' teacher, he shared all his ideas. Thus dissension invaded the Greek Church and the danger increased. To settle the issue, Constantine called the first ecumenical council at Nicaea and more than 300 bishops participated. The sentence of Alexander against Arius was not only sustained but confirmed. In order to prevent a revival of the controversy, the council drew up the celebrated Nicaean Creed.

The Emperor exiled Arius to Illyria but recalled him in 328. The bishops assembled at the Synod of Tyre and Jerusalem in 335 decided to readmit him into the Church and to reinstate him into the ranks of the clergy. Constantine ordered a solemn reconciliation by the Bishop of Constantinople. But on the eve of the appointed day Arius died suddenly (336).

Studies: See above p. 7. — The chief sources for his life and his doctrine are the writings of Athanasius and the Church Historians of the fourth and fifth centuries, supplemented by the letters of St. Basil and by Epiphanius (*Haer.* 69). — J. GUMMERUS, Die homöusianische Partei bis zum Tode des Konstantius. Leipzig, 1900. — X. LE BACHELET, Arianisme: DTC 1 (1901) 1779-1848. — N. H. BAYNES, Athanasiana: Journal of Egyptian Archaeology 11 (1925) 58-69 (the recall of Arius from exile). — G. BARDY, Le souvenir d'Arius dans le Praedestinatus: RB 40 (1928) 256-261. — F. J. KELLY, Athanasius and the Arian Controversy: AER 79 (1928) 173-183. — G. BARDY, Fragments attribués à Arius: RHE 26 (1930) 253-268. W. ELLIGER, Bemerkungen zur Theologie des Arius: ThStKr 103 (1931) 224-251. — W. E. BARNES, Arius and Arianism: ExpT 46 (1934) 18-24. — W. TELFER, Arius takes refuge at Nicomedia: JThSt 37 (1936) 59-63. — M. J. LUBATSCHIWSKYJ, Des hl. Basilius liturgischer Kampf gegen den Arianismus: ZkTh 66 (1942) 20-38. — M. RICHARD, Saint Athanase et la psychologie du Christ selon les Ariens: MSR 4 (1947) 5-54. — W. TELFER, St. Peter of Alexandria and Arius: AB 67 (1949) 117-130. — G. MÖNNICH, De achtergrond van de Ariaanse Christologie: NTT 4 (1950) 378-412. — J. N. D. KELLY, Early Christian Creeds. London, 1950, 231-262. — A. GRILLMEIER, Die theologische und sprachliche Vorbereitung der christologischen Formel von Chalkedon: CGG I (1951) 68-77. — H. DÖRRIES, Das Selbstzeugnis Kaiser Konstantins. Göttingen, 1954. — P. GALTIER, Saint Athanase et l'âme humaine du Christ: Greg 36 (1955) 553-589. — P. WORRALL, St. Thomas and Arianism: RTAM 23 (1956) 208-259; *idem*, Was St. Athanasius a Source for Aquinas on Arianism?: SP I (1957) 168-176. — H. A. WOLFSON, The Philosophy of the Church Fathers. Cambridge (Mass.), 1956, 217-219, 306-307, 585-587, 593-594. — G. L. PRESTIGE, God in Patristic Thought. London, 1956, 146-156, 209-213. — T. E. POLLARD, Logos and Son in Origen, Arius and Athanasius: SP II (1957) 282-287; *idem*, The Exegesis of John X 30 in the Early Trinitarian Controversies: New Testament Studies 3 (1957) 334-349. — L. UEDING and J. LIÉBAERT, Arianismus: LThK² 1 (1957) 842-848. — W. SCHNEEMELCHER, Arianischer Streit: RGG³ 1 (1957) 593-595. — J. N. KELLY, Early Christian Doctrines. London, 1958, 226-233, 236-240, 244-251.

THE WRITINGS OF ARIUS

We know of three writings composed by Arius in the ante-Nicene period of the controversy.

1. *Letter to Eusebius of Nicomedia*

The first is a communication which he sent (ca. 318) to Eusebius of Nicomedia (cf. below, p. 190) after he had been excommunicated by Alexander. Its Greek text is preserved by Epiphanius, *Haer.* 69,6 and Theodoret, *Hist. eccl.* 1,5, 1-4. In addition two Latin versions are extant. It begins: 'Arius, unjustly persecuted by bishop Alexander on account of that all-conquering truth which you also uphold, sends greetings in the Lord to his very dear lord, the man of God, the faithful and orthodox Eusebius'. It complains 'that the bishop oppresses and persecutes us most severely and causes us much suffering: he has driven us out of the city as atheists, because we do not concur in what he publicly preaches, namely, that the Father has always been, and that the Son has always been; that as the Father so is the Son; that the Son is unbegotten as the Father; that He is always being begotten, without having been begotten; that neither by thought nor by any interval does God precede the Son, God and the Son having always been; and that the Son proceeds from God'. Most characteristic is the conclusion:

> We are persecuted because we say that the Son had a beginning, but that God was without beginning. This is really the cause of our persecution; and likewise, because we say that He is from nothing. And this we say because He is neither part of God, nor of any subjacent matter. For this we are persecuted; the rest you know. Farewell. As a fellow-disciple of Lucian *(συλλουκιανιστά)* and as a truly pious man, according to the import of your name, remember our afflictions.

Editions: H. G. OPITZ, Athanasius' Werke III, 1, 1-3 (Urkunde 1). — Theodoret, *Hist. eccl.* 1, 5, 1-4 (GCS 19, 25-27 ed. Parmentier). — Epiphanius, *Haer.* 69, 6 (GCS 37, 156-157 ed. Holl). The most convenient collection of the surviving fragments of Arius' own writings is to be found in G. BARDY, Recherches sur Lucien d'Antioche. Paris, 1936, 216-278 (L'héritage littéraire d'Arius).

Old Latin Versions: One is found in Marius Victor, *Adv. Arium*, prol. (ML 8, 1035f), the other was published by D. DE BRUYNE, RB 26 (1909) 93f from Codex 54 (f. 158ᵛ) of the Cologne Cathedral.

Translations: English: B. JACKSON, LNPF ser. 2, vol. 3, 41. — E. R. HARDY, Christology of the Later Fathers (LCC 3). London and Philadelphia, 1954, 329-331. — *German:*

A. Seider, BKV² 51 (1926). — *French:* A. d'Alès, Le dogme de Nicée. Paris, 1926, 57-58.

Studies: P. Snellman, Der Anfang des arianischen Streites. Helsingfors, 1904, 79f. — E. Schwartz, Zur Geschichte des Athanasius: NGWG 6 (1905) 260-270. — G. Bardy, l.c. 185f. — P. Nautin, Deux interpolations dans une lettre d'Arius: AB 67 (1949) 131-141.

2. *Letter to Alexander of Alexandria*

Invited by Eusebius, Arius and a number of his followers went to Nicomedia. There he composed (ca. 320) an Exposition of his faith (ἔκθεσις πίστεως) in the form of a public but polite letter addressed to bishop Alexander of Alexandria. Athanasius, *De synodis* 16, and Epiphanius, *Haer.* 69,7-8, have preserved its Greek text. Hilary, *De Trinitate* 4,12-13; 6,5-6, offers a Latin translation. Epiphanius is the only one to record the signature of Arius and the members of the Alexandrian clergy who accompanied him to Nicomedia.

Editions: H. G. Opitz, Athanasius' Werke III, 1, 12-13 (Urkunde 6). — Athanasius, *De synodis* 16 (MG 26, 709). — Epiphanius, *Haer.* 69, 7-8 (GCS 37, 157-159 ed. Holl).

Latin Version: Hilary, *De Trinitate* 4, 12-13; 6, 5-6 (ML 10, 104-107; 39-40; 160-161).

Translations: English: J. H. Newman, LNPF ser. 2, vol. 4, 458. — E. R. Hardy, LCC 3, 332-334. — *French:* A. d'Alès, Le dogme de Nicée. Paris, 1926, 58-59.

Studies: R. Arnou, Arius et la doctrine des relations trinitaires: Greg 14 (1933) 269-272. — J. De Ghellinck, Qui sont les ὥς τινες λέγουσι de la lettre d'Arius: Miscellanea G. Mercati I (ST 121). Rome, 1946, 127-144. — N. H. Baynes, Sozomen, Ecclesiastica Historia I 15: JThSt 49 (1948) 165-168. — W. Telfer, Sozomen I 15. A Reply: JThSt 50 (1949) 187-191.

3. *The Banquet (θάλεια)*

It was in the same place, at Nicomedia, that Arius composed the *Thalia*, of which we have only fragments consisting mainly of sentences quoted by Athanasius, *Oratio contra Arianos* 1,2-10, *De decretis syn. Nic.* 16, *De sent. Dionys.* 6, *De synodis* 15, and elsewhere. It seems that this long rhapsody in which he drew up his heresy and extolled the beauties of metaphysics, was written, at least partly, in metric form, because Athanasius calls it an imitation of the banquet songs of the Egyptian Sotades and speaks of 'the dissolute tone of the metre' (*De syn.* 15) and its 'effeminate tune and nature' (*Or. Ar.* 1,5). Moreover, the Arian Philostorgius reports (*Hist. eccl.* 2,2) that Arius in order to popularize his doctrine 'wrote songs for the sea and for the mill and for the road and then set them to suitable music'. We have reason to believe that the *Thalia* contained some of them and was most probably a mixture of verse and prose. According to Athanasius it began:

According to the faith of God's elect, God's prudent ones, Holy children, rightly dividing, God's Holy Spirit receiving, have I learned this from the partakers of wisdom. Accomplished, divinely taught, and wise in all things. Along their track, have I been walking, with like opinions, I the very famous, the much suffering for God's glory; and taught of God, I have acquired wisdom and knowledge (*Or. Ar.* 1,5 LNPF).

The same Athanasius quotes the following passage from the *Thalia*:

God Himself then, in His own nature, is ineffable to all men. Equal or like Himself He alone has none, or none in glory. And ingenerate we call Him, because of Him who is generate by nature. We praise Him as without beginning and adore Him as everlasting, because of Him who in time has come to be. The Unbegun made the Son a beginning of things originated; and advanced Him as a Son to Himself by adoption. He has nothing proper to God in proper subsistence. For He is not equal, nor one in essence with Him. There is full proof that God is invisible to all beings; both to things which are through the Son, and to the Son He is invisible. I will say it expressly, how by the Son is seen the Invisible; by that power by which God sees, and in His own measure, the Son endures to see the Father, as is lawful. Thus there is Triad, not in equal glories. Not intermingling with each other are their subsistencies. Foreign from the Son in essence is the Father, for He is without beginning. Understand that the Monad was; but the Dyad was not, before it was in existence. It follows at once that, though the Son was not, the Father was God. Hence the Son, not being — for He existed at the will of the Father —, is God Only-begotten, and He is alien from either. Wisdom existed as Wisdom by the will of the wise God. Hence He is conceived in numberless conceptions: Spirit, Power, Wisdom, God's glory, Truth, Image, and Word. Understand that He is conceived to be Radiance and Light. One equal to the Son, the Superior is able to beget; but one more excellent, or superior or greater, He is not able. At God's will the Son is what and whatsoever He is. And when and since He was, from that time He has subsisted from God. He, being a strong God, praises in His degree the Superior. To speak in brief, God is ineffable to His Son. For He is to Himself, what He is, that is, unspeakable. So that nothing which is called comprehensible does the Son know how to speak about; for it is impossible for Him to investigate the Father, who is by Himself. For the Son does not know His own essence. For, being the Son, He really existed, at the will of the Father. What argument then allows, that He who is from the Father should not know His own parent by comprehension? For it is plain, that for that which had a beginning to conceive how the Unbegun is, or to grasp the idea, is not possible (*De syn.* 15 LNPF).

Edition: G. BARDY, La Thalie d'Arius: RPh 53 (1927) 211-233.

Translations: See below (p. 28 and 63) the translations of Athanasius, *Orat. contra Arianos* and *De synodis.*

Studies: P. MAAS, Die Metrik der Thaleia des Areios: BZ 18 (1909) 511-515. — W. WEYH, Eine unbemerkte altchristliche Akrostichis (Thaleia): BZ 20 (1911) 139. — G. BARDY, Saint Alexandre d'Alexandrie a-t-il connu la Thalie d'Arius?: RSRUS 16 (1926) 527-532; *idem,* La Thalie d'Arius: RPh 53 (1927) 211-233.

4. Letter to the Emperor Constantine

Of the post-Nicene period we have a letter which Arius and Euzoius addressed to the Emperor Constantine at the end of 327. Preserved by Socrates (*Hist. eccl.* 1, 26, 2) and Sozomen (*Hist. eccl.* 2, 27, 6) it contains a Creed by which Arius and Euzoius intend to prove their orthodoxy.

Editions: H. G. OPITZ, Athanasius' Werke III, 1, 64 (Urkunde 30). — Socrates, *Hist. eccl.* 1, 26, 2 (MG 67, 149). — Sozomen, *Hist. eccl.* 2, 27, 6 (MG 67, 1012).

Translations: See the translations of Socrates and Sozomen below p. 533 and 535.

Studies: G. BARDY, Recherches sur saint Lucien d'Antioche et son école. Paris, 1936, 274f. — J. N. D. KELLY, Early Christian Creeds. London, 1950, 189-190 with Greek text and English translation of the Creed.

The number of Arian writings which have perished must be considerable, see J. DE GHELLINCK, En marge des controverses ariennes. Quelques allusions à des écrits disparus. Réminiscences d'écrits d'adversaires: Miscellanea Historica Alberti De Meyer. Louvain, 1946, 159-180. For an Arian homily on the devil ascribed to Athanasius, see below. For two other sermons of an unknown Arian author in Cod. n. 212 of the Bibl. Nat. at Athens, see M. RICHARD, Bull. d'inform. de l'Inst. de Recherches et d'Hist. des Textes 1 (1952) 76. — Draguet showed that a commentary on Job ascribed to Origen (LOMMATZSCH 16, 3-24), preserved in a Latin version and consisting of three books, cannot be a work of Julian of Halicarnassus, as Usener thought to have proved, but was written by an Arian, most probably in the fourth century: R. DRAGUET, Un commentaire grec arien sur Job: RHE 25 (1924) 38-65. Cf. E. AMAND DE MENDIETA, Fatalisme et liberté dans l'antiquité grecque. Louvain, 1945, 533-548. — E. AMAND and M. CH. MOONS, Une curieuse homélie grecque inédite sur la virginité, adressée aux pères de famille: RB 63 (1953) 18-69 and 211-238, published an interesting homily *On Virginity* which the manuscripts attribute to St. Basil the Great. The author is most probably an Arian ascetic of the pre-Nicene period who has a leaning to the ascetic views of the Encratites. Amand and Moons furnish an annotated edition and French translation of the sermon, a study of the manuscript tradition, the principal theological and moral ideas, the style and rhetorical devices of the author.

ALEXANDER OF ALEXANDRIA

One of the key figures at the Council of Nicaea (325) was Alexander who succeeded Achillas as bishop of Alexandria about A.D. 312. During his pontificate the Arian controversy arose and the Meletian schism continued. Alexander defended the faith against both dangers. With Arius he first tried kindness and fatherly admonition and attempted to win him back by showing that his views were contrary to tradition. When, however, the heresiarch and his followers refused to submit, nearly one hundred bishops rallied round Alexander in a synod (318), censured the false teaching and excommunicated both its author and his adherents. This step proving ineffectual, the Council of Nicaea was convened (325), and Arius, with Meletius as well, was finally condemned. Only three years later (328) Alexander died after enduring many trials in combating Arianism.

I. HIS WRITINGS

1. *Epistles*

According to Epiphanius (*Haer.* 69,4) there existed a collection of seventy letters by Alexander. All of them have been lost except for two very important encyclicals concerned with the Arian controversy.

a. Theodoret of Cyrus preserved in his *Hist. eccl.* 1,4 an Epistle addressed to 'Alexander, bishop of the city of Byzantium' which had been sent to all the bishops outside Egypt, to warn of Arius and his followers in case any of them presumed to set foot in their dioceses. It must have been written ca. 324 after the first condemnation of Arius at the Synod of Alexandria:

Arius, therefore, and Achilles, having lately entered into a conspiracy, emulating the ambition of Colluthus, have turned out far worse than he. For Colluthus, indeed, who reprehends these very men, found some pretext for his evil purpose; but these, beholding his bartering of Christ, endured no longer to be subject to the Church; but building for themselves dens of thieves, they hold their assemblies in them unceasingly, night and day directing their calumnies against Christ and against us. For since they call in question all pious and apostolic doctrine, after the manner of the Jews, they have constructed a workshop for contending against Christ, denying the Godhead of our Saviour, and preaching that He is only the equal of all others. And having collected all the passages which speak of His plan of salvation and His humiliation for our sakes, they endeavour from these to collect the preaching of their impiety, ignoring altogether the passages in which His eternal Godhead and unutterable glory with the Father is set forth. Since, therefore, they back up the impious opinion concerning Christ which is held by the Jews and Greeks, in every possible way they strive to gain their approval; busying themselves about all those things which they are wont to deride in us, and daily stirring up against us seditions and persecutions... And we, indeed, though we discovered rather late, on account of their concealment, their manner of life and their unholy attempts, by the common suffrage of all have cast them forth from the congregation of the Church which adores the Godhead of Christ (1-2 ANF 6).

Alexander does not hesitate to trace the Arian heresy back to Lucian of Antioch and Paul of Samosata:

> For you yourselves are taught of God, nor are you ignorant that this doctrine, which has lately raised its head against the piety of the Church, is that of Ebion and Artemas; nor is it aught else but an imitation of Paul of Samosata, bishop of Antioch, who, by the judgment and the counsel of all the bishops, and in every place, was separated from the Church. To whom Lucian succeeding, remained for many years separate from the communion under three bishops. And now lately having drained the dregs of their impiety, there have risen amongst us those who teach this doctrine of a creation from things which are not, their hidden sprouts, Arius and Achilles, and the gathering of those who join in their wickedness (9 ANF 6).

Alexander admits that three bishops in Syria have given Arius their support. On the other hand, Alexander has received many letters of approval from his fellow bishops and he asks the bishop for a similar statement. Though Theodoret mentions Alexander of Byzantium as the recipient, it is more likely that Alexander of Thessalonica is meant, as Opitz suggests.

Editions: H. G. OPITZ, Athanasius' Werke III, 1, 19-29 (Urkunde 14).—MG 18, 547-572.

Translations: English: J. B. H. HAWKINS, ANL 6, 291-296. — *German:* A. SEIDER, BKV² 51 (1926) 6-25 (Theodoret).

Studies: V. HUGGER, Wie sind die Briefe Alexanders von Alexandrien chronologisch zu ordnen? ThQ 91 (1909) 66-86. — G. LOESCHKE, Zur Chronologie der beiden grossen antiarianischen Schreiben des Alexander von Alexandrien: ZKG 31 (1910) 584-586. — O. SEECK, Die Chronologie der beiden Schreiben des Alexander: ZKG 32 (1911) 277-281 (against Loeschke). — H. OPITZ, Die Zeitfolge des arianischen Streites von den Anfängen bis zum Jahre 328: ZNW 33 (1934) 131-159.

b. Socrates (*Hist. eccl.* 1,6) and Gelasius Cyzicus (*Hist. concil. Nic.* 2,3) quote another encyclical, addressed 'To our beloved and most reverend fellow-ministers of the Catholic Church in every place'. It seems to have been written ca. 319 before the above Epistle and shows the beginning of the Arian heresy. Eusebius, bishop of Nicomedia, the imperial residence, 'imagining that with him rest all ecclesiastical matters' (1), has joined the apostates and undertaken to write everywhere for the propagation of the new heresy. In such circumstances Alexander feels obliged 'no longer to remain silent, but to announce to you all, that you may know both those who have become apostates, and also the wretched words of their heresy; and if Eusebius (of Nicomedia) writes, not to give heed to him' (1). On this occasion Alexander gives a very important summary of the Arian doctrine:

God was not always the Father; but there was a time when God was not the Father. The Word of God was not always, but was made from things that are not; for He who is God fashioned the non-existing from the non-existing; wherefore there was a time when He was not. For the Son is a thing created, and a thing made; nor is He like to the Father in substance; nor is He the true and natural Word of the Father; nor is He His true Wisdom; but He is one of the things fashioned and made. And He is called the Word and Wisdom by a misapplication of the terms, since He is Himself made by the proper Word of God and by that Wisdom which is in God, in which, as God made all other things, so also did He make Him. Wherefore, He is by His very nature changeable and mutable, equally with other rational beings. The Word, too, is alien and separate from the substance of God. The Father also is ineffable to the Son; for neither does the Word perfectly and accurately know the Father, neither can He perfectly see Him. For neither does the Son indeed know His own substance as it is. Since He for our sakes was made, that by Him as by an instrument God might create us; nor would He have existed had not God wished to make us. Some one asked of them whether the Son of God could change even as the devil changed; and they feared not to answer that He can; for since He was made and created, He is of mutable nature.

Since those about Arius speak these things and shamelessly maintain them, we, coming together with the bishops of Egypt and the Libyas, nearly a hundred in number, have anathematized them together with their followers (2-3 ANF 6).

Editions: H. G. OPITZ, Athanasius' Werke III, 1, 6-11 (Urkunde 4b). — MG 18, 571-578.

Translations: English: J. H. NEWMAN, Select Treatises of St. Athanasius in controversy with the Arians, Vol. I. 4th ed. 11th impr. London, 1920, 3-7. — M. ATKINSON, Historical Tracts of St. Athanasius (LFC). Oxford, 1873, 299-304. — J. B. H. HAWKINS, ANL 14 (1869) 333-363. Reprinted: ANF 6 (1886) 296-299.

Studies: G. BARDY, Saint Alexandre d'Alexandrie a-t-il connu la Thalie d'Arius?: RSR 6 (1926) 527-532. — T. E. POLLARD, Logos and Son in Origen, Arius and Athanasius: SP II (TU 64). Berlin, 1957, 282-287.

c. This second encyclical, which Socrates and Gelasius preserved in the Greek original, is also found in some manuscripts of Athanasius' works under the heading *Deposition of Arius and his Followers (Καθαίρεσις Ἀρείου καὶ τῶν σὺν αὐτῷ).* Here the text is preceded by a letter which Alexander addressed to the clergy of Alexandria and the Mareotis, asking all its members to sign the above encyclical.

Editions: H. G. OPITZ, Athanasius' Werke III, 1, 6 (Urkunde 4a). — MG 18, 581-582.

Translations: English: M. ATKINSON, l.c. 297-298. — J. B. HAWKINS, ANF 6 (1886) 299.

2. *Sermons*

Of his sermons one is preserved in a Syriac and a Coptic translation: *De anima et corpore deque passione Domini.* The introduction deals with the relation between soul and body, the main part with the necessity and the fruit of the Lord's Passion. Strongly rhetorical in character, the sermon is influenced both in thought and in language by Melito's newly discovered *Homily on the Passion* (cf. vol. I, p. 243f).

Editions: Syriac text: A. MAI first published the Syriac version from Vatican Cod. Syr. 368 in: Nova Patrum Bibliotheca 2, Rome, 1844, 529-539 with a Latin translation (reprinted MG 18, 585-604). — E. A. W. BUDGE edited the Syriac version from Cod. Brit. Mus. Syr. add. 17192 in: Coptic Homilies in the Dialect of Upper Egypt. London, 1910, 407-415. *Coptic text:* BUDGE, 115-132. The Coptic version is complete, the Syriac represents an abbreviated form.

Modern Translations: English: From the Syriac: BUDGE, 417-424. — J. B. H. HAWKINS, ANF 6 (1886) 299-302. From th· Coptic: BUDGE, 258-274.

Studies: G. KRÜGER, Melito von Sardes oder Alexander von Alexandrien?: Zeitschr. f. wiss. Theologie 31 (1888) 434-448. — C. THOMAS, Melito von Sardes. Osnabrück, 1893, 40-51. — C. BONNER, The Homily on the Passion by Melito of Sardis (SD 14), London, 1940, 46-47, 62-65 shows that Alexander's sermon is based in part upon a sermon of Melito *On the Soul and Body* and that Melito's *Homily on the Passion* was used in the latter part. — W. SCHNEEMELCHER, Der Sermo 'de anima et corpore', ein Werk Alexanders von Alexandrien?: Festschrift für G. Dehn, Neukirchen, 1957, 119-143, too, suggests that Alexander worked up a homily by Melito.

Of other genuine discourses we have only small fragments in Syriac and Coptic translation. A Coptic panegyric edited by H. Hyvernat (cf. vol. II, p. 117), though attributed to Alexander, is a late falsification. The eulogy praises his predecessor Peter and is supposed to have been delivered on the anniversary of that Alexandrian martyr and in the oratory dedicated to him.

Editions: H. HYVERNAT, Les actes des martyrs de l'Égypte. Paris, 1886, 247-262. — L. TH. LEFORT, Athanase: Sur la virginité: Mus 42 (1929) 256-259 Coptic text and French translation of a sermon on virginity attributed to Alexander.

2. THEOLOGICAL ASPECTS

Alexander's description of the Arian heresy corresponds to the information provided by the other sources at our disposal. He is correct in his view that the error was derived from the subordinationism of Paul of Samosata and Lucian of Antioch, because in a letter addressed to Eusebius of Antioch Arius calls himself a disciple of Lucian (cf. vol. II, p. 143). Alexander designates his own teaching 'the apostolic dogma for which we die'. He declares

that the Son of God was not made 'from things which are not' and
that there was no 'time when He was not' (1,4), but that He was
begotten of the Father (1,11). He is equally with the Father unchangeable and immutable, wanting in nothing. He is the very
exact image of the Father, in no way differing from Him (1,12).
The Lord says: 'I and My Father are one' (John 10,30), not as
proclaiming Himself to be the Father, nor to demonstrate that two
persons are only one person, but to show that the Son of the Father
most exactly preserves the expressed likeness of the Father, who has
by nature impressed upon Him His similitude in every respect, is
the image of the Father in no way discrepant, and the expressed
figure of the primitive exemplar (1,9):

> Therefore to the unbegotten Father, indeed, we ought to preserve
> His proper dignity, in confessing that no one is the cause of His being;
> but to the Son must be allotted His fitting honor, in assigning to Him,
> as we have said, a generation from the Father without beginning, and
> allotting adoration to Him, so as only piously and properly to use
> the words, 'He was', and 'always', and 'before all worlds', with respect
> to Him; by no means rejecting His Godhead, but ascribing to Him
> a similitude which exactly answers in every respect to the Image and
> Exemplar of the Father. But we must say to the Father alone belongs
> the property of being unbegotten, for the Saviour Himself said, 'My
> Father is greater than I' (John 14,28) (1,12 ANF 6).

Since the Epistles of Alexander were the only written protests
against the Arian heresy before the Council of Nicaea, it is interesting to note that the *homoousios* does not appear as yet, although
it is stated that the Son 'was begotten of the Father Himself',
ἐξ αὐτοῦ ὄντος πατρός (1,11) — a formula which is almost identical
with the ἐκ τῆς οὐσίας. Moreover, Alexander asks: 'How is He
unlike to the substance of the Father *(πῶς ἀνόμοιος τῇ οὐσίᾳ τοῦ
πατρός)* who is the perfect image and brightness of the Father, and
who says, "He that hath seen Me hath seen the Father" (John 14,9)?
And how, if the Son is the Word or Wisdom and Reason of God, was
there a time that He was not? It is the same as if they said that
there was a time when God was without reason and wisdom'
(ἄλογος καὶ ἄσοφος) (2,4 ANF 6):

> How, then, is it not impious to say, that the wisdom of God once
> was not, which speaks thus concerning itself: 'I was with Him forming
> all things; I was His delight' (Prov. 8,30); or that the power of God
> once did not exist; or that His Word was at any time mutilated; or
> that other things were ever wanting from which the Son is known and
> the Father expressed? For he who denies that the brightness of the
> glory existed, takes away also the primitive light of which it is the
> brightness. And if the image of God was not always, it is clear also

that He was not always, whose image it is. Moreover, in saying that the character of the subsistence of God was not, He also is done away with who is perfectly expressed by it (1,7 ANF 6).

The Word is the Son of God not by adoption *(θέσει)* but by nature *(φύσει):*

Hence one may say that the Sonship of our Saviour has nothing at all in common with the sonship of the rest. For just as it has been shown that His inexplicable subsistence excels by an incomparable excellence all other things to which He has given existence, so also His Sonship, which is according to the nature of the Godhead of the Father, transcends, by an ineffable excellence, the sonship of those who have been adopted by Him *(ibid.)*.

Moreover, in the Psalms the Saviour says: 'The Lord hath said unto Me, *Thou art My Son*' (Ps. 12,7). Where, showing that He is the true and genuine Son, He signifies that there are no other genuine sons besides Himself. And what, too, is the meaning of this: 'From the womb before the morning I begat thee' (Ps. 110,3)? Does He not plainly indicate the natural sonship of paternal bringing forth, which He obtained not by the careful framing of His manners, not by the exercise of and increase in virtue, but by property of nature? Wherefore, the only-begotten Son of the Father, indeed, possesses an indefectible Sonship; but the adoption of rational sons belongs not to them by nature, but is prepared for them by the probity of their life, and by the free gift of God (1,8 ANF 6).

For this reason Mary is really the Mother of God and Alexander calls her therefore *theotokos*:

After this we know of the resurrection of the dead, the first fruit of which was our Lord Jesus Christ who in very deed, and not in appearance merely, carried a body of Mary, Mother of God *(ἐκ τῆς θεοτόκου Μαρίας)*.

The Son is the only-begotten mediator by whom God the Father brings the universe from nothing into existence:

Those ignorant men do not know how great is the difference between the unbegotten Father and the things which were by Him created from the things which are not, as well the rational as the irrational. Between which two, as holding the middle place, the only-begotten nature *(ὡς μεσιτεύουσα φύσις μονογενής)* of God, the Word by which the Father formed all things out of nothing, was begotten of the true Father Himself (1,11 ANF 6).

Studies: A. v. HARNACK, Lehrbuch der Dogmengeschichte. 5th ed. vol. 2. Tübingen, 1931, 204-207. — H. M. GWATKIN, Studies of Arianism. 2nd ed. Cambridge, 1900, 17f. — C. E. RAVEN, Apollinarianism. An Essay on the Christology of the Early Church. Cambridge, 1926, 72-78. — G. BARDY, Recherches sur saint Lucien d'Antioche et son école. Paris, 1936. — A. GRILLMEIER, CGG I (1951) 79f., 125f. — V. C. DE CLERCQ, Ossius of Cordova (SCA 13). Washington, 1954, 224-226, 267f.

ATHANASIUS

Alexander was succeeded in 328 by one of the most imposing figures in all ecclesiastical history, and the most outstanding of all Alexandrian bishops, St. Athanasius. Of undaunted courage, unflinching in the face of danger or adversity and cowed by no man, he was the steadfast champion and great defender of the faith of Nicaea, 'the pillar of the Church', as St. Gregory of Nazianzus calls him (*Or.* 21,26). The Arians regarded him as their chief enemy and did everything to destroy him. To silence him, they enlisted the aid of secular power and corrupt ecclesiastical authority. Five times was he banished from his episcopal see and spent more than seventeen years in exile. But all this suffering could not break his resistance. He was convinced that he fought for the truth and employed every means at his disposal to combat his powerful adversaries. Despite his uncompromising hostility towards error and the fierceness with which he opposed it, he had the quality, rare in such a character, of being capable, even in the heat of battle, of tolerance and moderation towards those who had in good faith been led astray. Many of the eastern bishops had rejected the *homoousios* through misunderstanding, and Athanasius evinces great sympathy and patience in winning them back to the truth. The Greek Church called him later 'the Father of Orthodoxy', whereas the Roman Church counts him among the four great Fathers of the East.

The most important sources for the history of his life are his own writings and the Syriac introduction to his Festal Letters. There is in addition an *Historia Athanasii* preserved in Latin, usually called *Historia acephala* on account of its mutilated condition, Gregory Nazianzen's, *Oration* 21, and some fragments of a Coptic eulogy.

Athanasius was born about 295 at Alexandria where he received his classical and theological education. From the Introduction to his *Life of St. Antony* it appears that he had dealings with the monks of the Thebais at an early time. In 319 he was ordained deacon by his bishop Alexander and served shortly afterwards as his secretary. As such he accompanied his bishop to the Council of Nicaea (325), where his debates with the Arians attracted attention (Athanasius, *Ap. c. Arian.* 6; Socr., *Hist. eccl.* 1,8). Three years later he succeeded Alexander.

His new task was not an easy one. The Arian doctrine, though condemned at Nicaea, could still muster considerable support at Alexandria. To add to the difficulties, the Meletians personally disliked the new bishop. Soon all sorts of false accusations were launched against him by these circles, and calumnies only increased when Athanasius was ordered by Constantine to readmit Arius to communion and refused. His enemies gathered at a synod at Tyre in 335 and deposed him. Soon afterwards the emperor exiled him to Treves. His contact with the West was to exercise vast and lasting influence. Constantine died in 337 and Athanasius was able to return to his diocese by November 23rd of that year.

But his opponents did not rest. At the instigation of Eusebius, bishop of Nicomedia, they again deposed Athanasius in a synod at Antioch (339) and elected Pistus, an excommunicated priest, as bishop of Alexandria. When he proved to be impossible, they installed the Cappadocian Gregory by force. Athanasius took refuge at Rome. A synod held there in 341 at the invitation of Pope Julius I completely exonerated him and at the great synod of Serdica in 343 he was reaffirmed las the only legal bishop of Alexandria. Nevertheless he was not able to return to Egypt before Gregory of Cappadocia died (345). He reached the city October 21st, 346. Soon the intrigues began anew. Athanasius' protector, Constans, died in 350. Constantius, now sole emperor of the East and West, ready to take action against Athanasius, had a synod summoned at Arles in 353 and at Milan in 355 to condemn Athanasius and introduced another usurper, a certain George of Cappadocia, into the see of Alexandria. Athanasius was forced a third time to leave his diocese. This time he fled to the monks of the Egyptian desert. He remained there for six years devoting himself to the composition of the *Apology to Constantius*, *Apology for his Flight*, the *Letter to the Monks* and the *History of the Arians*. The situation changed rapidly after Constantius died in 361. The usurper George of Cappadocia was murdered on December 23rd of the same year. Julian, the new emperor, recalled the exiled bishops. Thus on February 22nd, 362 Athanasius re-entered the Egyptian capital.

Without delay he began his work for the reconciliation of the Semi-Arians and the orthodox party. He held a synod at Alexandria in 362 to clear up the misunderstandings. But none of this was to Julian's taste who did not want peace but discord and dissension among the Christians. Thus Athanasius was expelled by imperial order as a 'disturber of the peace and enemy of the gods'. But Julian died the following year (363) and Athanasius was able to return. He was exiled a fifth time in 365 after Valens became ruler of the East (364-378). He took up his abode in a country house outside the city for four months. When the people of Alexandria threatened to revolt against this order, Valens, afraid of the possible consequences, recalled the primate. He was restored to his office February 1st, 366. He spent his remaining days in peace and died May 2nd, 373.

Sources for the history of his life: Syriac introduction to his Festal Letters: W. CURETON, The Festal Letters of Athanasius. London, 1848. Latin translation: MG 26, 1351f. — English translation by A. ROBERTSON, LNPF ser. 2, vol. 4, 503-506. The *Historia acephala* covers the period from 346 until his death in 373. Contained in the famous *Collectio Theodosii Diaconi* of Cod. Veron. LX (cf. E. SCHWARTZ, Über die Sammlung des Cod. Veron. LX: ZNW 35 (1936) 1-23), it represents the partial translation of an Alexandrian chronicle composed in the fourth century. It was first published by S. MAFFEI, Osservazioni letterarie 3. Verona, 1783, reprinted MG 26, 1443f. The best edition is that of C. H. TURNER, Ecclesiae occidentalis monumenta iuris antiquissima (Oxford, 1899-1939) 1, 2, 663-671; English translation by A. ROBERTSON, LNPF ser. 2, vol. 4, 496-499. Cf. H. FROMEN, Athanasii historia acephala. Jena Diss. Münster, 1914. — Gregory of Naz., Oration 21 '*On the Great Athanasius*', delivered at Constantinople in 379 or 380 (see below p. 243). — For the fragments of the Coptic eulogy, see: O. v. LEMM, Koptische Fragmente zur Patriarchengeschichte Alexandriens (Mémoires de i'Académie imp. de St. Pétersbourg. Sér. 7, t. 36, no. 11) 1888; *idem*, Kleine koptische Studien Nr. 57 (Mémoires. Sér. 8, t. 11, no. 4) 1912. — For the legendary *Vitae*, see: B. BECK, Die griechischen Lebensbeschreibungen des Athanasius auf ihr gegenseitiges Verhältnis und ihre Quellen untersucht. Jena Diss. Weida, 1912.

Monographs: J. A. MÖHLER, Athanasius der Grosse. 2nd ed. Mainz, 1844. — F. LAUCHERT, Leben des hl. Athanasius des Grossen. Cologne, 1911. — LE BACHELET, Athanase: DTC 1 (1901) 2143-2178. — G. BARDY, Saint Athanase (Les Saints) 3rd ed. Paris, 1925; *idem*, Athanase: DHG 4 (1930) 1313-1340. — M. CONSTANTINIDES, Ὁ Μέγας Ἀθανάσιος καὶ ἡ ἐποχὴ αὐτοῦ. Athens, 1937. — G. GENTZ, RACh 1 (1943) 860-866. — H. F. VON CAMPENHAUSEN, Griechische Kirchenväter. Stuttgart, 1955, 72-85. — P. T. CAMELOT, Athanasios der Grosse: LThK² 1 (1957) 976-981.

Special Studies: H. LIETZMANN, Chronologie der ersten und zweiten Verbannung des Athanasius: Zeitschr. f. wiss. Theologie 44 (1901) 380-390. — E. SCHWARTZ, Zur Geschichte des Athanasius: NGWG 5 (1904) 338-401 and 518-547; 6 (1905) 164-187 and 257-299; 9 (1908) 305-374; 12 (1911) 367-426. — N. W. SHARPE, Athanasius the Copt and his Times: Bibl. sacra 72 (1915) 618. — N. H. BAYNES, Athanasiana: Journal of Egyptian Archaeology II (1925) 58-69 (return of Athanasius from his first exile). — K. F. HAGEL, Kirche und Kaisertum in Lehre und Leben des Athanasius. Diss. Giessen, 1933. — For the date of his death, see S. EUSTRATIADES, Ἀθανάσιος ὁ μέγας, πατριάρχης Ἀλεξανδρείας : Ῥωμανός 1 (1932/33) 55-58. — O. SEEL, Die Verbannung des Athanasius durch Julian: Klio 32 (1939) 175-188. — K. M. SETTON, Christian Attitude towards the Emperor in the Fourth Century. New York, 1941, 67-83, 198-199. — W. SCHNEEMELCHER, Athanasius von Alexandrien als Theologe und als Kirchenpolitiker: ZNW 43 (1950/51) 242-256. — P. PEETERS, Comment St. Athanase s'enfuit de Tyr en 335 (Recherches d'histoire et de philologie orientales: Subsidia hagiographica 27). Brussels, 1951. — V. C. DE CLERCQ, Ossius of Cordova (SCA 13). Washington, 1954, 232-303, 315-358, 401-438, 460-480, 506-527.

I. HIS WRITINGS

It is astonishing that despite such privations and amidst all his activities, Athanasius found time for a great number of literary productions. Most of his writings, it is true, are intimately connected with his fight for the defense of the faith of Nicaea. Again and again he submits the dialectical and exegetical argumentation of his opponents to a critical examination and refutes the accusations which unscrupulous enemies flung against him. He does not show himself a professional scholar and he willingly left to others the task of exploring the secrets of learning. But his knowledge of Scripture, his skill in debate and the depth of his conviction have gained the admiration of succeeding generations. Photius remarks that 'in all his works his style is clear, free from redundancies and simple, but earnest and deep, and the arguments, of which he has an abundant store, are extremely forceful' (*Bibl. cod.* 140). Nevertheless, there is a certain negligence in form and a lack of order in the arrangement of his material that cause prolixity and frequent repetition. In his *Apologies* and especially in his *Life of St. Antony* he created new forms of literature.

Editions: MG 25-28. New critical edition in three volumes for Berlin Academy in progress since 1934. So far published: Athanasius' Werke herausgegeben im Auftrage der Kirchenväter-Kommission der Preussischen Akademie der Wissenschaften von H. G. OPITZ, II, 1, 1-280: Die Apologien. Berlin and Leipzig, 1935; III, 1, 1-76: Urkunden zur Geschichte des arianischen Streites 318-328. Berlin and Leipzig, 1934; to be continued by W. SCHNEEMELCHER and M. TETZ. Cf. E. SCHWARTZ, DLZ 6 (1935) 715-720; F. SCHEIDWEILER, Zur neuen Ausgabe des Athanasios: BZ 47 (1954) 73-94 with very valuable textual criticism; M. TETZ, Studien zur Überlieferung der dogmatischen Schriften des Athanasius, Diss. Bonn, 1955; *idem*, Zur Edition der dogmatischen Schriften des Athanasius von Alexandrien: ZKG 67 (1955/56) 1-28. — W. LORIMER, Critical notes on Athanasius: JThSt 40 (1939) 37-46. For the tradition of the text indispensable: H. G. OPITZ, Untersuchungen zur Überlieferung der Schriften des Athanasius (Arbeiten zur Kirchengeschichte 23). Berlin and Leipzig, 1935. — For Greek manuscripts, see: F. WALLIS, On Some MSS of the Writings of S. Athanasius: JThSt 3 (1902) 97-110, 245-258; K. LAKE, Some Further Notes on the MSS of the Writings of S. Athanasius: JThSt 5 (1904) 108-114; R. P. CASEY, Greek Manuscripts of Athanasian Corpora: ZNW 30 (1931) 49-70.

Greek Dictionary: Lexicon Athanasianum, digessit et illustravit G. MÜLLER. Berlin, 1944/52. Cf. H. EMONDS, Eine neue Lexicon Athanasianum und seine Beziehung zur Liturgiewissenschaft: ALw 2 (1952) 110-114.

Versions: Old Latin: B. ALTANER, Altlateinische Übersetzungen von Schriften des Athanasios von Alexandreia: BZ 41 (1941) 45-59. — G. BARDY, Sur les anciennes traductions latines de saint Athanase: RSR 41 (1947) 239-242. — A. SIEGMUND, Die Überlieferung der griechischen christlichen Literatur in der lateinischen Kirche. München-Pasing, 1949, 49-50. — *Syriac:* J. LEBON, Athanasiana Syriaca: Mus 40 (1927) 205-248; 41 (1928) 169-216. — R. P. CASEY, A Syriac Corpus of Athanasian Writings: JThSt 35 (1934) 66-67. — H. G. OPITZ, Das syrische Corpus Athanasianum: ZNW 33 (1934) 18-31. — *Armenian:* F. C. CONYBEARE, On the Sources of the Text of S. Athanasius: The Journal of Philology 24 (1896) 285-300. — R. P. CASEY, Armenian Manuscripts of St. Athanasius of Alexandria: HThR 24 (1931) 43-60. — *Coptic:* L. T. LEFORT, S. Athanase, écrivain copte: Mus 46 (1933) 1-33. — *Arabic:* G. GRAF, Geschichte der arabischen Literatur. I Die Übersetzungen (ST 118). Vatican City, 1944, 310-316.

Modern Translations: English: J. H. NEWMAN, Select Treatises of St. Athanasius in Controversy with the Arians. 4th ed. 11th impression. London and New York, 1920. — LFC, vols. 8 (1842) and 19 (1844) Select Treatises in Controversy with the Arians by J. H. NEWMAN; vol. 13 (1843) Historical Tracts by M. ATKINSON; vol. 38 (1854) The Festal Epistles by H. BURGESS; vol. 45 (1881) Later Treatises by W. BRIGHT. — A. ROBERTSON,

LNPF series 2, vol. 4 contains the most complete collection of Athanasian works in English. — *German:* Sämtliche Werke der Kirchenväter, vols. 13-18. Kempten, 1835-1837. — J. Fisch, BKV Ausgewählte Schriften des hl. Athanasius. 2 vols. Kempten, 1872-1875. — J. Lippl and A. Stegmann, BKV² 13 (1913); A. Stegmann and H. Mertel, BKV² 31 (1917). — *French:* J. Lebon, SCH 15 (1947); T. Camelot, SCH 18 (1947); J. M. Szymusiak, SCH 56 (1958). — *Russian:* A. P. Sostin, 4 vols. 1st ed. Moscow, 1851-1854, 2nd ed. 1902-1903.

Studies: K. Hoss, Studien über das Schrifttum und die Theologie des Athanasius. Freiburg i.B., 1899. — A. Stülcken, Athanasiana. Literar- und dogmengeschichtliche Untersuchungen (TU 19, 4). Leipzig, 1899. — J. Lebon, Pour une édition critique des œuvres de saint Athanase: RHE 21 (1925) 524-530. — M. J. Bastgen, Athanasius. Wirtschaftsgeschichtliches aus seinen Schriften. Giessen Diss. Darmstadt, 1928. — F. L. Cross, The Study of St. Athanasius. Oxford, 1945 (lecture). — F. Chatillon, La 'région de la dissemblance' signalée dans saint Athanase: Revue du Moyen Age Latin 3 (1947) 376 (une citation de Platon). — B. Altaner, Augustinus und Athanasius. Eine quellenkritische Studie (De Trinitate): RB (1949) 82-90. — G. Rochefort, Une anthologie grecque du XIe siècle, le Parisinus Suppl. Gr. 690 (texte de S. Athanase): Scriptorium 4 (1950) 3-17.

1. *Apologetical and Dogmatic Writings*

1. *Against the Heathen* and *The Incarnation of the Word*

The treatises *Oratio contra gentes (Λόγος κατὰ 'Ελλήνων)* and *Oratio de incarnatione Verbi (Λόγος περὶ τῆς ἐνανθρωπήσεως)* are in reality two parts of a single work to which St. Jerome (*De vir. ill.* 87) refers as *Adversum gentes duo libri.* The first is a refutation of pagan mythologies, worship and beliefs. After a study of the nature of evil, its origin and its history, the author describes the immorality and folly of idolatry in all its varieties. The refutation of popular polytheism is followed by a rejection of the higher form of nature-worship or philosophical pantheism. Since nature and God are distinct, monotheism is the only reasonable religion. The knowledge of God is possible because the soul of man is by its immortality akin to God. As a mirror of the Logos it can know God at least through creation. Arrangement and content of this tract follow the pattern of the apologies of the second century.

The *Incarnation of the Word* in continuing the preceding work, shows that there was no remedy for the corruption of mankind and no restoration to the original creation and constitution of man except through the Incarnation. The reasons for the Incarnation, Death and Resurrection of Christ are given and the Christian faith in this great mystery is defended against the objections of Jews and pagans. The tract might be called the classical exposition of the doctrine of redemption and the patristic counterpart to St. Anselm's *Cur Deus homo.*

A shorter second recension of the *De incarnatione* remained unknown until a few decades ago. J. Lebon drew attention to it and R. P. Casey studied the tradition of its text, extant in four manuscripts. H. G. Opitz gives good reasons to believe that it originated in the fourth century at Antioch, because an anti-Apollinaristic tendency appears in it. Casey, however, concludes his investigation with the following summary (xi): 'The Long Recension still appears to have been the original, the Short Recension a secondary, literary revision, revealing no clearly defined dogmatic motive. In view of the absence of important dogmatic changes in the true texts of both recensions and of the similarity in matter and style between the additions and substitutions of the Short Recension and the Long Recension, the former may plausibly be attributed to Athanasius himself or to one of his immediate circle'. M. Tetz in a recent article signalizes the very fluid state of this problem.

E. Schwartz thinks that Athanasius wrote both, *Against the Heathen* and *Incarnation of the Word* about 336 when he was in exile at Treves. But the fact that there is no trace of the Arian controversy nor of the Nicene theology in these tracts favors an earlier date. They were most probably composed about 318 before Arius' doctrine became widely known.

Editions: MG 25, 3-96 *Contra gentes*, 95-198 *De incarnatione*. Separate: A. ROBERTSON, St. Athanasius on the Incarnation. London, 1882. 2nd ed., 1893. In his first edition Robertson merely reprinted the text of Montfaucon and Migne; the second is based on Codex Seguerianus (Coisl. gr. 45) of the Bibliothèque Nationale at Paris. The same manuscript has been used in the new edition by F. L. CROSS, Athanasius De incarnatione, an Edition of the Greek Text (SPCK Texts for Students 39). London, 1939. — J. LEBON discovered the Short Recension in a fourteenth century paper manuscript of Mt. Athos (Codex Dochariou 78). He found the same text translated in a Syrian manuscript of the sixth century (Cod. Vat. Syr. 104). — G. J. RYAN and R. P. CASEY, The De incarnatione of Athanasius (SD 14): Part I, G. J. Ryan, the Long Recension Manuscripts; Part II, R. P. Casey, The Short Recension. London and Philadelphia, 1945/1946. Casey gives a full collation of the text of Cod. Dochariou 78 and reprints the text of Robertson's second edition as an appendix of Part II (1-86). Cf. F. L. CROSS, JThSt 49 (1948) 88-95. M. RICHARD, MSR 6 (1949) 128-130. E. R. SMOTHERS, HThR 41 (1948) 39-50.

Translations: English: A. ROBERTSON, LNPF series 2, vol. 4, 1-30 *Contra gentes*, 31-67 *De incarnatione*. The latter reprinted in LCC 3 (1954) 55-110. — T. H. BINDLEY, Athanasius On the Incarnation (Christian Classics Series 3) 2nd ed. London, 1903. — Anon., The Incarnation of the Word of God, Being the Treatise of St. Athanasius De incarnatione Verbi Dei, newly translated into English by a Religious of C.S.M.V., with an Introduction by S. C. Lewis. London and New York, 1944 (modern version with occasional paraphrase and abridgment). — *German:* J. FISCH, BKV Ausgewählte Schriften des hl. Athanasius vol. I (1872) 27-116 *Contra gentes*, 117-195 *De incarnatione*. — A. STEGMANN, BKV² 31 (1917) 11-81 *Contra gentes*, 82-156 *De incarnatione*. — L. A. WINTERSWYL, Athanasius, Die Menschwerdung Gottes (selections). Leipzig, 1937. — *French:* P. TH. CAMELOT, Athanase, Contre les païens et Sur l'incarnation du Verbe (SCH 18). Paris,

1947 (with a very valuable introduction 7-106). — *Dutch:* H. BERKHOF, Athanasius, Oratio de incarnatione. Amsterdam, 1949.

Studies: S. WOLDENDORP, De incarnatione, een geschrift van Athanasius. Groningen Diss. The Hague, 1919. — E. SCHWARTZ, Der sogenannte Sermo maior de fide des Athanasius (SAM Phil.-hist. Klasse Jahrg. 1924, 6). Munich, 1925, 44-46. — J. LEBON, Pour une édition critique des œuvres de saint Athanase: RHE 21 (1925) 525-530, deals with Codex Dochiariou 78 and Codex Vat. Syr. 104. — J. LEBON, Une ancienne opinion sur la condition du corps du Christ dans la mort: RHE 23 (1927) 5-43, 209-241, investigates a point of historical theology involved: the death of Christ as a separation of the body from the Logos. — K. LAKE and R. P. CASEY, The Text of the De incarnatione of Athanasius: HThR 19 (1926) 259-270, give an account of another Greek copy of the text of the Short Recension in a tenth century parchment at Athens. — R. P. CASEY, The Athens Text of Athanasius' Contra Gentes and De Incarnation: HThR 23 (1930) 51-89 publishes a full collation of this text. — H. G. OPITZ, Untersuchungen zur Überlieferung der Schriften des Athanasius. Berlin and Leipzig, 1935, 190-203. — J. LEBON, Altération doctrinale de la 'Lettre à Epictète' de saint Athanase: RHE 31 (1935) 713-761. — A. D. NOCK, Neotera, queen or goddess?: Aegyptus 33 (1953) 283-296. — J. R. LAURIN, Orientations maîtresses des apologistes chrétiens de 270 à 361. Rome, 1954, 402-416. — M. TETZ, Athanasiana: I. Athanasius' De incarnatione in der Überlieferung des Codex Dochiariou 78; II. Ein De incarnatione-Fragment bei Justinian als Testimonium für die 'lange' Rezension: VC 9 (1955) 159-175, provides a list of variants of Codex Dochiariou 78 and reports of a discovery of the earliest known quotation from the Long Recension text of *De Incarnatione* in Justinian's *Contra Monophysitas* from the middle of the sixth century; *idem,* Zur Edition der dogmatischen Schriften des Athanasius von Alexandrien: ZKG 67 (1955/56) 1-28.

2. *The Discourses against the Arians*

The three *Orationes contra Arianos* represent the chief dogmatic work. The first summarizes the Arian doctrine as contained in Arius' *Thalia*, and defends the definition of the Council of Nicaea that the Son is eternal, increated *(ἀγέννητος)* and unchangeable and that there is a unity of Divine Essence between the Father and the Son. The second and third books give a careful explanation of Scriptural texts bearing on the generation of the Son (Hebr. 3, 2; Acts 2, 36; Prov. 8, 22), on the relation of the Son to the Father from the Fourth Gospel, and on the Incarnation (Matth. 28, 18; John 3, 35; Matth. 26, 39; John 12, 27; Mark 13, 32; Luke 2, 52). The Arian exegesis is refuted and the true sense established.

A considerable discussion has arisen regarding the date of these three discourses. It has been customary to assign them to the third exile, 356-362, when Athanasius took refuge with the monks in the desert of Egypt. But the author speaks in the introduction (1,1) of the Arian heresy as that 'which has now risen' and is afraid that 'her smooth sophistry may deceive men into wrong thoughts of Christ', considering that 'she has already seduced certain of the foolish'. It does not seem probable that such a statement would be made of a heresy which had existed for a whole generation. Thus

F. Loofs and A. Stülcken suggested an earlier date, namely 338/9, shortly before the second exile. However in his *First Letter to the Monks* Athanasius remarks:

> I thought it needful to represent to your Piety what pains the writing of these things has cost me, in order that you may understand hereby how truly the blessed Apostle has said, 'O the depth of the riches both of the wisdom and knowledge of God' (Rom. 11, 33), and may kindly bear with a weak man such as I am by nature. For the more I desired to write, and endeavoured to force myself to understand the Divinity of the Word, so much the more did the knowledge thereof withdraw itself from me; and in proportion as I thought that I apprehended it, in so much I perceived myself to fail of doing so. Moreover also I was unable to express in writing even what I seemed to myself to understand; and that which I wrote was unequal to the imperfect shadow of the truth which existed in my conception. Considering therefore... what is said in the Psalms, 'The knowledge of Thee is too wonderful for me, it is high, I cannot attain unto it' (Ps. 139, 6)... I frequently designed to stop and to cease writing; believe me, I did. But lest I should be found to disappoint you, or by my silence to lead into impiety those who have made enquiry of you, and are given to disputation, I constrained myself to write briefly, what I have sent to your piety (*Ep.* 52, 1 LNPF).

It appears that the *Discourses against the Arians* had not been in existence for twenty years when he wrote these words in 358. An author who had dealt so extensively and aptly with the Arian doctrine would not have found it so difficult to compose a brief summary of what he had treated before. It is quite evident that he refers to his first attempt. The *Discourses* were composed at the same time as the *Historia Arianorum ad Monachos*, which dates from about 358. Serapion had asked Athanasius for three things: a history of recent events, an exposition of the Arian heresy and an exact account of the death of Arius. In his letter to Serapion Athanasius furnishes the latter and sends for the two former what he had 'addressed to the monks against the heresy' (*Ep.* 54, 2), when he took refuge with them (358-362). We shall not err if we see here a reference to the *History of the Arians* and the *Discourses against the Arians*.

A number of manuscripts add a fourth *Discourse* and thus the Benedictine edition speaks of *Four Orations against the Arians*. But whereas the first three form a homogeneous work, the fourth differs in address, content and style. In fact, it is not written against the Arians at all but against the Marcellians. The introductory chapters 1-8 deal predominantly with the Arians, it is true, and they are mentioned again in chapters 11. 14 f. 17 and 25. Chapters 2. 3. 9.

25, however, are a refutation of the Sabellian, and the end, of the Samosatene heresy. But the main body of the work, chapters 3-4 and 8-29, is written against Marcellus and his followers. Thus the so-called fourth discourse does not continue the three and has no connecting link with them, but enters abruptly into its subject. Moreover, style and phraseology contrast so strikingly that Athanasius cannot be considered its author. It is not an Oration, although J. H. Newman goes too far when he calls it only 'a collection of fragments or memoranda of unequal lengths and on several subjects'. The compiler remains unknown and it must have been added to the three *Discourses* at a later time. That explains why some of the manuscripts do not have it.

Editions: MG 26, 12-468. The 'fourth Oration': MG 26, 469-526. Separate edition: W. BRIGHT, The Orations of St. Athanasius against the Arians according to the Benedictine Text. Oxford, 1873. A Slavonic version of the first book was edited by A. VAILLANT, Discours contre les Ariens de St. Athanase. Version slave et traduction en français. Sofia, 1954.

Translations: English: J. H. NEWMAN published a translation of the four Orations in the Library of the Fathers, vol. 19, Oxford, 1844; reprinted but revised by A. ROBERTSON, LNPF series 2, vol. 4, 303-447. Of a totally different kind, amounting to a condensed paraphrase is the translation of the three Orations which he published in 1881 in his work: Select Treatises of St. Athanasius in controversy with the Arians. Vol. I. 4th ed. 11th impression. London and New York, 1920, 155-428. — *German:* J. FISCH, BKV Athanasius vol. I (1872) 197-585 Vier Bücher gegen die Arianer. — A. STEGMANN, BKV² 13 (1913) 17-387 Vier Reden gegen die Arianer. — *Dutch:* C. J. DE VOGEL, Athanasius, Redevoeringen tegen de Arianen (Monumenta Christiana I, 2). Utrecht, 1949 (Three Orations). — *Italian:* E. SALA, S. Atanasio, Cristo Dio (Contra Arianos) (I classici cristiani 64). Siena, 1937.

Studies: F. LOOFS, Athanasius: Realencyklopädie f. prot. Theol. u. Kirche, 3d ed. vol. 2 (1897) 200f. — A. STÜLCKEN, Athanasiana (TU 4, 4). Leipzig, 1899, 44-58. — A. STEGMANN, Zur Datierung der 'drei Reden des h. Athanasius gegen die Arianer': ThQ 96 (1914) 423-450, 98 (1916) 227-231 favors ca. 357 as date. — A. STEGMANN, Die pseudoathanasianische 'IVte Rede gegen die Arianer' als κατὰ 'Αρειανῶν λόγος, ein Apollinarisgut, Rottenburg, 1917 with a new edition of the fourth Oration. — A. GAUDEL, La date des trois discours contre les Ariens: RSR 19 (1929) 524-539 suggests 339 as presumable date. Cf. J. LEBON, St. Athanase a-t-il employé l'expression 'Ο κυριακὸς ἄνθρωπος?: RHE 31 (1935) 324-329. — H. G. OPITZ, Untersuchungen 139-141, 171-172.

3. *Concerning the Incarnation and against the Arians*

A shorter treatise *De incarnatione et contra Arianos* has come down to us, whose authenticity has been questioned. Nevertheless, no convincing reasons have been advanced against the Athanasian authorship. The objection that Athanasius could not have referred to the Trinity as 'One God in three Hypostases' (εἰς θεὸς ἐν τρισὶν ὑποστάσεσιν), since he always uses the word *hypostasis* as a synonym for *essence*, is no proof. First of all, at the Alexandrian synod of 362

Athanasius admitted that the term *hypostasis* could be used also in the meaning of *person* and therefore one could speak of 'three hypostases' (*Tom. ad Antioch.* 5-6, ML 26, 801). Secondly, even if this was not the case at such an early date, the possibility of a later interpolation still remains. In addition, the tract is quoted as genuine by Theodoret (*Dial.* 2, 3) who calls it an *Oration against the Arians*, and by Gelasius (*De duabus naturis*). The content is concerned with the divinity of Christ, which is proved from Scripture, and that of the Holy Spirit (13-19).

Edition: MG 26, 983-1028.

Studies: T. SCHERMANN, Die griechischen Quellen des hl. Ambrosius in libris 3 de Spiritu Sancto. Munich, 1902, 36f. — J. LEBON, Pour une édition critique des œuvres de S. Athanase: RHE 26 (1925) 528-530. — J. RUCKER, Das Dogma von der Persönlichkeit Christi und das Problem der Häresie des Nestorius. Oxenbronn, 1934, 108-110. — H. G. OPITZ, Untersuchungen 177-178. — M. SIMONETTI, Sulla paternità del De incarnatione Dei Verbi et contra Arianos: Nuovo Didaskaleion 5 (1952) 5-19, denies the authenticity.

2. *Spurious Dogmatic Writings*

The reputation which Athanasius gained as a theologian explains why a number of other dogmatic treatises have been attributed to him.

a. The two books *De incarnatione contra Apollinarem* were most probably written about 380 after Athanasius had died. They differ in language and style from his works. The name of Apollinaris of Laodicea, against whom they are directed, does not appear in the text. The two books seem to be independent tracts and not parts of a single work.

Editions: MG 26, 1093-1166. Separate: T. H. BENTLEY, St. Athanasii De incarnatione contra Apollinarium. London, 1887. Extract: EP 796-800. Of the first book two independent versions exist in Syriac. Cf. C. MOSS, A Syriac Version of Pseudo-Athanasius contra Apollinarium I: OCP 4 (1938) 65-84. No Syriac Version of the second book has yet been discovered. See: J. LEBON, Une ancienne opinion sur la condition du corps du Christ dans la mort: RHE 23 (1927) 33-44.

Studies: H. STRÄTER, Die Erlösungslehre des hl. Athanasius, Freiburg i. Br., 1894, 75-90 advocated its authenticity. He was refuted by A. STÜLCKEN, Athanasiana. Literar- und dogmengeschichtliche Untersuchungen (TU 19, 4). Leipzig, 1899, 70-75. J. DRÄSEKE, Gesammelte patristische Untersuchungen, Altona, 1889, 169-207, thought that Didymus of Alexandria composed the first, and his disciple Ambrose of Alexandria the second book. However, J. LEIPOLDT, Didymus der Blinde von Alexandrien, Leipzig, 1905, 24-26 and G. BARDY, Didyme l'Aveugle, Paris, 1910, 39-42 disproved this opinion. P. CH. DEMETROPULOS, Τὸ πρόβλημα τῆς γνησιότητος τοῦ "Περὶ σαρκώσεως τοῦ Κυρίου ἡμῶν Ἰησοῦ Χριστοῦ, κατὰ Ἀπολλιναρίου Λόγοι δύο" τοῦ μεγάλου Ἀθανασίου: Θεολογία 24 (1953) 442-461, is in favor of Athanasian authorship.

b. Sermo maior de fide (Περὶ πίστεως λόγος ὁ μείζων)

This document has points of contact with the earliest works of Athanasius but it is hardly more than an artless compilation from the *Oratio de incarnatione Verbi*, and other works of his. It cannot be attributed to him despite Theodoret's remarkable testimony (*Dial.* 1, 2, 3) to the contrary. Its Greek text is incomplete but an Armenian version has preserved the entire work. E. Schwartz and R. P. Casey think that it was originally a letter addressed to the Church of Antioch. In fact, the Florilegium of *Cod. Vatic. gr.* 1431, Facundus of Hermiane and the Armenian version call it *Epistle to the Antiochenes*. While its character is definitely anti-Arian, the treatise makes a peculiar use of the word *anthropos*, which is constantly reiterated to designate sometimes the human nature of our Lord, sometimes the seat of personality. E. Schwartz suggested Eustathius of Antioch as the author. F. Scheidweiler recently came after a careful examination of the different Greek and Armenian texts, to the conclusion that it was composed about 358 by Marcellus of Ancyra (see below p. 200).

Editions: Greek fragments: MG 26, 1263-1294. The best edition of these by E. SCHWARTZ, Der sogenannte Sermo maior de fide des Athanasius (SAM Phil.-hist. Kl. 1924, 6). Munich, 1925. Cf. J. LEBON, Le sermo maior de fide pseudo-Athanasien: Mus 38 (1925) 243-260; G. KRÜGER, Gno 4 (1928) 36-40. — *Armenian version:* R. P. CASEY, The Armenian Version of the Pseudo-Athanasian Letter to the Antiochenes and of the Expositio fidei. Part I (SD 15). London and Philadelphia, 1947. Cf. M. RICHARD, MSR 6 (1949) 130-133. CASEY adds a new edition of the Greek fragments p. 48-62.

Translation: English, R. P. CASEY, l.c. 13-42.

Studies: R. P. CASEY, The pseudo-Athanasian Sermo maior de fide: JThSt 35 (1934) 394-395. — F. SCHEIDWEILER, Wer ist der Verfasser des sogenannten Sermo maior de fide?: BZ 47 (1954) 333-357; *idem, Καίπερ,* nebst einem Exkurs zum Hebräerbrief: Hermes 83 (1955) 220-230.

c. Expositio fidei ("Εκθεσις πίστεως)

Among the sources of the *Sermo maior de fide* is a highly interesting document, entitled *Statement of Faith*. E. Schwartz regards Eustathius of Antioch as the author (cf. below p. 304), whereas Scheidweiler thinks of Marcellus of Ancyra. The content consists of a trinitarian creed (1), which is followed by a comment emphasizing the distinct existence of the Son, and his essential uncreatedness (2-4). There is no express reference to the Arian controversy, although most of it might be directed against this heresy. The Sabellians are mentioned by name: 'For neither do we hold a Son-Father, as do the Sabellians, calling Him of one but not of the same essence (μονοούσιον καὶ οὐχ ὁμοούσιον), and thus destroying the existence of the Son. Neither do we ascribe the passible body, which He bore for the salvation of the whole world, to the Father. Neither can we imagine three Subsistencies separated from each other, as results from their bodily nature in the case of men, lest we hold a plurality of gods like the heathen' (2 LNPF).

Edition: The text is extant in the Greek original (MG 25, 199-208) and an Armenian version. For the latter, see: R. P. CASEY, The Armenian Version of the Pseudo-Athanasian Letter to the Antiochenes and of the Expositio fidei. Part I (SD 15). London and Philadelphia, 1947, 7-10.

Translation: English: A. ROBERTSON, LNPF 4, 83-85.

Studies: E. SCHWARTZ, l.c. — F. SCHEIDWEILER, BZ 47 (1954) 333-357.

d. Interpretatio in symbolum

C. P. Caspari thinks that this *Interpretation of the Creed* was written at Alexandria, not by Athanasius but by one of his first successors, Peter or Timotheus. F. Kattenbusch finds the proof for its Egyptian origin insufficient.

Editions: MG 26, 1231-1232. — A. HAHN, Bibliothek der Symbole und Glaubensregeln der alten Kirche. 3rd ed. Breslau, 1897, 137-139.

Studies: C. P. CASPARI, Ungedruckte Quellen zur Geschichte des Taufsymbols und der Glaubensregel 1. Christiania, 1866, 1-72. — F. KATTENBUSCH, Das apostolische Symbol 1. Leipzig, 1894, 300f, 317f.

e. Dialogi de sancta Trinitate quinque; Dialogi contra Macedonianos duo

These dialogues contain disputations of an orthodox with an Anomoean, a Macedonian and an Apollinarist. According to A. Günthör, it seems that their author is Didymus the Blind (cf. below, p. 89), since they show a close affinity to his style and theology. In fact, they appear to be preparatory studies to his three books *De Trinitate*, composed between 381 and 392.

Editions: Dialogi de sancta Trinitate quinque: MG 28, 1115-1286. *Dialogi contra Macedonianos duo:* MG 28, 1291-1338.

Studies: F. LOOFS, Zwei Makedonische Dialoge: Sitzungsberichte der Preuss. Akademie der Wiss. (1914) 526-551. — A. SEGOVIE, Contribución al estudio de la tradición manuscrita del Pseudo-atanasiano 'Dialogo I contra un Macedoniano o Pneumatomaco': Archivo Teológico Granadino 1 (1938) 87-107. — A. GÜNTHÖR, Die sieben pseudo-athanasianischen Dialoge, ein Werk Didymus' des Blinden von Alexandrien. Rome, 1941. — B. DIETSCHE, L'héritage littéraire de Didyme l'Aveugle: RSPT 2 (1941/42) 380-414. Cf. K. RAHNER, ZkTh 65 (1941) 111f. — P. SMULDERS, Greg 24 (1943) 254-256. — P. MEINHOLD, Pneumatomachen: PWK 21 (1951) 1066-1101.

f. Symbolum Athanasianum

The Athanasian Creed, also called *Symbolum Quicunque* from its opening word, was thought to be the composition of the great bishop of Alexandria whose name it bears until the seventeenth century, when it became evident that its language and structure point to a later and to a Western origin. It was not ascribed to Athanasius before the seventh century. The Latin text is the original, the Greek a translation. In content it is a clear exposition of the Trinity and the two natures in the one Divine Person of Christ. At various points the author calls attention to the penalties which will follow the rejection of the articles of faith therein set down. Thus it opens with the pronouncement, 'Whosoever will be saved, before all things it is necessary that he hold the Catholic Faith', and closes with the verse, 'This is the Catholic Faith, which except a man believe faithfully and firmly, he cannot be saved'. Consisting of forty rhythmical sentences, it gained a world-wide reputation, and has since the ninth century been used in the ordinary Sunday office, on the Feast of the Trinity and in the *exorcismus obsessorum*. Until recently the Church enjoined its recitation at Prime on certain Sundays of the year. Today it is said at Prime on Trinity Sunday only. In the Carolingian period it was recited by the people after the Sunday sermon. Western writers quoted it again and again as a proof for the correctness of the *Filioque*. The Greeks rejected it in their controversy with the Latins, whereas the authors of the Reformation valued it highly. It is also used in the liturgical service of the Anglican Church.

The time of its composition and the identity of its author are still matters of dispute. St. Hilary, St. Vincent of Lerins, Eusebius of Vercelli, Vigilius, Fulgentius of Ruspe and Martin of Bracara have been suggested. Brewer was of the opinion that Ambrose was the author and he has found many adherents. G. Morin maintained for a while that Caesarius of Arles was the only one to be considered if it was written by an individual at all. There is no doubt that Caesarius knew this symbol and it seems that it was inserted into the Caesarean collections by his own wish, but there is not enough evidence to justify the conclusion that he was the composer. Others have suggested that it grew out of several provincial synods. Most probably it is of Gallican origin and dates from the second half of the fifth century.

Editions: MG 28, 1582-1583. — ML 88, 585A f. — Mansi 2, 1354B f. — ES 39-40. — C. H. TURNER, A Critical Text of the Quicumquevult: JThSt 11 (1910) 401-411 with variants of all the manuscripts. — Greek and Syriac text: H. LIETZMANN, Apollinaris von Laodicea und seine Schule 1. Tübingen, 1904, 250-253; J. FLEMMING and H. LIETZ-

MANN, Apollinaristische Schriften syrisch. Berlin, 1904, 33-34. *Ethiopic*: H. GUERRIER, Un texte éthiopien du symbole de saint Athanase: ROC 20 (1915/1917) 68-76, 133-141.

Studies: A. E. BURN, The Athanasian Creed and its Early Commentaries (TSt 4, 1). Cambridge, 1896 (four Latin commentaries). — G. D. W. OMMANEY, A Critical Dissertation on the Athanasian Creed. Its original language, date, authorship, titles, text, reception and use. Oxford, 1897. — H. BRADSHAW, The Use of the Quicumquevult in the Book of Common Prayer: JThSt 5 (1904) 458f. — K. KÜNSTLE, Antipriscilliana, Freiburg i.B., 1905, 204ff., advocated Spanish origin; *idem*, ThR 5 (1906) 201-205. — R. H. MALDEN, Quicumque vult salvus esse: JThSt 8 (1907) 301-303. — E. VACANDARD, Notes sur les Symboles des Apôtres de Constantinople et de saint Athanase: RQH 2 (1909) 559-566. — H. BREWER, Das sogenannte Athanasianische Glaubensbekenntnis, ein Werk des hl. Ambrosius (FLDG 9). Paderborn, 1909. — M. JUGIE, Sévérien de Gabala et le Symbole athanasien: EO (1911) 193-204. — G. MORIN, À propos du Quicumque. Extraits d'homélies de saint Césaire d'Arles sous le nom de saint Athanase: RB 28 (1911) 417-424; *idem*, L'origine du symbole d'Athanase: JThSt 12 (1911) 161-190, 337-361. — A. E. BURN, The Athanasian Creed. Oxford, 1912. — J. STIGLMAYR, Das 'Quicumque' und Fulgentius von Ruspe: ZkTh 49 (1925) 341-357; *idem*, Athanase (Le prétendu symbole d'): DHG 4, 1345. — A. E. BURN, The Authorship of the 'Quicumque vult': JThSt 27 (1925/26) 19-28. — C. R. PASTÉ, Del simbolo Quicumque: SC 3 (1932) 142-147 regards Eusebius of Vercelli as the author. — G. MORIN, L'origine du symbole d'Athanase: témoignage inédit de S. Césaire d'Arles: RB 44 (1932) 207-219. — J. R. PALANQUE, Saint Ambroise et l'empire romain. Paris, 1933, 508; *idem*, RHE 32 (1936) 941. N. 2. — M. J. RYAN, The Date of the Athanasian Creed: AER 88 (1933) 625-627 dates its composition before 451. — H. LINDROTH, Triniteten och inkarnationen enligt Athanasianum: Svensk Theologisk Kvartalskrift 9 (1933) 134-146. — F. H. DUDDEN, The Life and Times of St. Ambrose. Oxford, 1935, 676f. — V. LAURENT, Le symbole Quicumque et l'Église byzantine. Notes et documents: EO 39 (1936) 385-404. — P. SCHEPENS, Pour l'histoire du symbole Quicumque: RHE 32 (1936) 548-569 against Ambrose; cf. E. CATTANEO, Ambrosius 19 (1943) 2-6. — F. J. BADCOCK, The History of the Creeds. 2nd ed. London, 1938. — J. MADOZ, Le symbole du IVᵉ concile de Tolède: RHE 34 (1938) 5-20, thought of Isidore of Seville as author, but decided later for Vincent of Lerins: J. MADOZ, Un Tratado disconocido de San Vincente de Lérins: Greg 21 (1940) 88; *idem*, Excerpta Vincentii Lerinensis (Estudios Onienses I, 1). Madrid, 1940, 65-90: Lenta elaboración del Quicumque. — L. HUGHES, The Quicumque vult: ExpT 57 (1945/46) 184-185 originated in France or Spain in the fifth century. — E. SCHILTZ, La comparaison du Symbole Quicumque vult: ETL 24 (1948) 440-454. — M. CAPPUYNS, L'auteur de la Regula Magistrie: Cassiodore: RTAM 15 (1948) 209-268, thinks that Nicetas of Remesiana composed the Athanasianum. — J. A. DE ALDAMA, Una nueva tentativa sobre el autor del 'Quicumque': EE 24 (1950) 237-239, refutes Cappuyns. — J. F. BETHUNE-BAKER, An Introduction to the Early History of Christian Doctrine. 9th ed. London, 1951, 252-254. — J. MADOZ, Quicumque vult: Enciclopedia Cattolica 10 (1953) 411f.

g. *Pseudo-Athanasii De Trinitate Libri XII*

The twelve books *De Trinitate* attributed to St. Athanasius, which Migne (ML 62, 237-334) has printed among the works of the African bishop Vigilius of Thapsus, who lived in the second half of the fifth century, are not by Athanasius nor by Vigilius. They represent a collection of treatises by several unknown authors of the West, who composed them approximately in the second half of the fourth and in the fifth century. They are very valuable as documents of the struggle of the Western Church against Arianism. Their dependence upon the Greek Fathers and their influence on the later writers of the West, as for instance St. Ambrose, St. Augustine and others, has still to be investigated. A new edition is being prepared by M. Simonetti. So far the last three books have been published comprising the *Expositio fidei catholicae* (p. 19-39), the *Professio Ariana et confessio catholica* (p. 41-68) and the *De Trinitate et De Spiritu Sancto* (p. 69-145). They are three independent works by three different authors. Since St. Augustine makes use of the first two treatises in his *Ep.* 148 n. 10, they must have been composed before A. D. 413/414. The last tract is important for the doctrine of the Holy Spirit and seems to be of an earlier date. Simonetti proved that it must have been written before 381, because St. Ambrose shows acquaintance with it in his own *De Spiritu Sancto*. Bulhart's new edition provides the complete text.

Editions: ML 62, 237-334. — New crit. ed.: M. SIMONETTI, Pseudo-Athanasii De Trinitate libri X-XII. Bologna, 1956. — V. BULHART, CCL 9 (1957) 1-205 (libri I-XII).

Studies: M. SIMONETTI, Studi sul De Trinitate pseudo-atanasiano: Nuovo Didaskaleion 3 (1949) 57-72; *idem,* Sul De Spiritus Sancti potentia di Niceta di Remesiana e sulle fonti del De Spiritu Sancto di S. Ambrogio: Maia 4 (1951) 239-248, proves that Nicetas depends on books X and XII and Ambrose on book XII.

3. *Historico-Polemical Writings*

Athanasius was often forced to appeal to history and tradition in his defense against calumnies. But more than once these historico-polemical writings go beyond the justification of his own and the condemnation of his enemies' conduct. They attack and expose.

1. *Apology against the Arians*

The *Apologia contra Arianos* (*'Απολογητικὸς κατὰ 'Αρειανῶν*) was written about 357 after the return from his second exile. When the Eusebian party renewed the old charges against him, he prepared a collection of documents for his own defense. Since it contains the proceedings and decisions of previous synods and important letters of high ranking persons dealing with Athanasius, it represents an historical source of primary value for the history of the Arian controversy. For his own vindication Athanasius gives first a series of documents from the eve of his departure to Rome down to his return to Alexandria (339-347). Thus chapters 3-19 offer the Encyclical Letter of the Council of Egypt held at the end of 338, in which the Egyptian prelates relate the election of Athanasius, the calumnies against him, the testimony available for his defense and call upon all bishops to be the avengers of such injustice. In chapters 20-35 follows the letter which Pope Julius wrote at the request of a Roman synod (341) to the bishops of the Eusebian party at Antioch, defending Athanasius and reproaching them for their disrespect to the Council of Nicaea and to the See of Rome. Concerning the latter the Bishop of Rome asks:

> Are you ignorant that the custom has been for word to be written first to us, and then for a just decision to be passed from this place? If then any such suspicion rested upon the Bishop there [at Alexandria], notice thereof ought to have been sent to the Church of this place; whereas, after neglecting to inform us, and proceeding on their own authority as they pleased, now they desire to obtain our concurrence in their decisions, though we never condemned him [Athanasius]. Not so have the constitutions of Paul, not so have the traditions of the Fathers directed; this is another form of procedure, a novel practice. I beseech you, readily bear with me: what I write is for the common good. For what we have received from the blessed Apostle Peter, that I signify to you (35 LNPF).

Chapters 36-50 contain three letters of the Council of Serdica (343/4), one encouraging the Church of Alexandria to patience and confirming Pope Julius' decision, another, almost identical with the first, to the bishops of Egypt and Libya, and a third, an Encyclical Letter of the Council announcing its decisions, the rehabilitation of Athanasius, Marcellus and Asclepas, and the deposition and excommunication of the Arian leaders. Chapters 51-58 produce letters of the Emperor Constantius, Pope Julius, of the bishops of Palestine, of Valens and Ursacius, all of which form a sequel to the Council of Serdica.

In the second part of the Apology, Athanasius deals with documents earlier than those of the first, because he wants to show the evidence upon which his acquittal was based. Thus he goes back to the year 331 and quotes the letters of Constantine previous to the Synod of Tyre (335) (ch. 59-63), the proceedings of this synod (ch. 71-83) and documents subsequent to it (ch. 84-88). In the two concluding chapters (89-90), Athanasius points to the sufferings of the bishops of Italy, Gaul and Spain — he singles out for mention especially Pope Liberius and the great bishop Ossius — as proof that they believed in his innocence, since they endured exile rather than desert his cause.

Editions: MG 25, 247-410. — New critical edition by H. G. Opitz, Athanasius' Werke II, 1, 87-168 *Apologia secunda.*

Translations: English: M. Atkinson, LFC 13 (1843) 13-124, reprinted LNPF series 2, vol. 4, 97-147. — *German:* J. Fisch, BKV Athanasius II (1875) 45-169.

Studies: R. Seiler, Athanasius' Apologia contra Arianos. Ihre Entstehung und Datierung (Tübingen Phil. Diss.). Düsseldorf, 1932. Seiler's analysis and date is rejected by H. G. Opitz, Untersuchungen 158-159, note 3; see Opitz' own evaluation of the Apology: Untersuchungen 104-109. I. Gelzer, Das Rundschreiben der Synode von Serdika: ZNW 40 (1941) 1-24 (*Apologia contra Arianos* 3, 44-50). — A. H. M. Jones, The Date of the Apologia contra Arianos of Athanasius: JThSt N.S. 5 (1954) 224-227 suggests that Athanasius revised the Apology after 367 against the opinion of Opitz that it did not pass through two stages or editions. — V. De Clercq, Ossius of Cordova (SCA 13). Washington, 1954, 478-479, 510-512.

2. *Apology to the Emperor Constantius*

Soon new and serious charges were made against Athanasius. He was supposed to have poisoned the mind of Emperor Constans against his brother, Emperor Constantius. He defended himself in his *Apologia ad Constantium imperatorem (Πρὸς τὸν βασιλέα Κονστάντιον ἀπολογία)*, his most careful work, written in forceful and dignified language and with artistic skill and finish. Its present form dates from the year 357.

Editions: MG 25, 595-642. Of the new Berlin edition by H. G. Opitz, only two pages were published: Athanasius' Werke II, 1, 279-280. — A new critical text was edited by J. M. Szymusiak, Athanase d'Alexandrie: Apologie à l'Empereur Constance. Apologie pour sa fuite (SCH 56). Paris, 1958, 89-132 (with valuable introduction).

Translations: English: M. Atkinson, LFC 13 (1843) 154-187, reprinted: LNPF series 2, vol. 4, 236-253. — *German:* J. Fisch, BKV Athanasius II (1875) 171-213. — *French:* J. M. Szymusiak, SCH 56 (1958) 89-132.

Studies: K. F. Hagel, Kirche und Kaisertum in Lehre und Leben des Athanasius (Tübingen Diss.). Leipzig, 1933, 11-12, 44f. — K. M. Setton, Christian Attitude towards the Emperor in the Fourth Century. New York, 1941, 73-80.

3. *Apology for his Flight*

Of the same year is his *Apologia pro fuga sua*, which refutes the charge of cowardice circulated against him by giving the reasons for his flight and citing as justification the example of Our Lord and the Saints of Scripture. Addressed to the entire Church, it is one of the most famous Athanasian writings.

Editions: MG 25, 643-680. New critical edition by H. G. Opitz, Athanasius' Werke II, 1, 68-86. — Newest edition: J. M. Szymusiak, SCH 56 (1958) 133-167.

Translations: English: M. Atkinson, LFC 13 (1843) 189-209, reprinted: LNPF series 2, vol. 4, 254-265. — *French:* J. M. Szymusiak, SCH 56 (1958) 133-167.

Studies: H. G. Opitz, Untersuchungen 153-154. — V. C. De Clercq, Ossius of Cordova (SCA 13). Washington 1954, 228-238.

4. *History of the Arians*

Mention has been made of the *Historia Arianorum ad monachos* which Athanasius compiled in 358 at the invitation of the monks with whom he had taken refuge. Whereas in the *Apology to the Emperor Constantius* Athanasius tried to gain his favor, he now attacks him as an enemy of Christ, a patron of heresy and a precursor of Antichrist. The fragment of this Arian History, that has been preserved, begins with the admission of Arius to communion at the synod of Jerusalem and deals with the events of the years 335-357. In manuscripts and printed editions it is preceded by a dedicatory *Letter to the Monks* and followed by a *Letter to Bishop Serapion* on the death of Arius.

Editions: MG 25, 691-796. — New crit. edition: H. G. OPITZ, Athanasius' Werke II, 1, 183-230 fragment of the *Historia Arianorum*, 181-182 *Epistula ad monachos*, 178-180 letter to Bishop Serapion.

Translations: English: M. ATKINSON, LFC 13 (1843) 210-214 Epistle to Serapion, 215-218 Epistle to the Monks, 219-296 History of the Arians, reprinted LNPF ser. 2, vol. 4, 266-302 Arian History, 563-564 Epistle to the Monks, 564-566 Epistle to Serapion.

4. *Exegetical Writings*

Of his exegetical writings only fragments have reached us in *Catenae*. For this reason it is difficult to determine their date of composition.

1. *To Marcellinus on the Interpretation of the Psalms*

The *Epistula ad Marcellinum de interpretatione Psalmorum* deals with the content, the Messianic character and the devotional use of the Psalms. Inspired by the discourse of a venerable old man, the author praises the beauty of the Psalter, especially its universality, its fitness for every soul, every condition and every spiritual need. He refers to the singing of the Psalms and remarks that this liturgical custom was introduced not for its musical effect but in order to give the worshippers more time to meditate upon the meaning.

Editions: MG 27, 11-46. Several fragments of a Syriac version are extant, see: A. BAUM-STARK, Geschichte der syrischen Literatur. Bonn, 1922, 164, n. 7.

Translation: German: J. FISCH, BKV Athanasius II (1875) 331-366.

Studies: J. QUASTEN, Musik und Gesang in den Kulten der heidnischen Antike und christlichen Frühzeit (LQF 25). Münster, 1930, 120, 144-146. — H. G. OPITZ, Untersuchungen 206.

2. Commentary on the Psalms

Of a commentary on the Psalms, fragments survive, most of which have come down to us through the *Catenae* of the Psalms by Nicetas of Heraclea, the learned metropolitan of the eleventh century. The Benedictine editors published a collection of such fragments under the title *Expositiones psalmorum*, to which additions were made by Cardinal Pitra. Although some of the items are doubtful, most of them can be regarded as genuine. St. Jerome mentions (*De vir. ill.* 87) an Athanasian work *De psalmorum titulis*. But the treatise *De titulis Psalmorum*, consisting of brief notes on the Psalter verse by verse and first published by Antonelli in 1746, is not by Athanasius but by Hesychius of Jerusalem, as the investigations of M. Faulhaber and G. Mercati have shown. Other fragments of a genuine commentary on the psalms were found by R. Devreesse, and J. David edited Coptic fragments of an Athanasian explanation of the psalms. From all that remains it is evident that Athanasius had a predilection for the allegorical and typological interpretation of the Psalter in contradistinction to the more jejune exegesis predominant in his dogmatico-polemical writings, especially in his *Discourses against the Arians.*

Editions: Expositiones psalmorum: MG 27, 55-590; cf. J. B. PITRA, Analecta sacra et classica. Paris, 1888, pars 1, 3-20. *De titulis psalmorum:* MG 27, 649-1344. — R. DEVREESSE, Dictionnaire de la Bible, Suppl. 1, 1109, 1125, 1187. — J. DAVID, Les éclaircissements de saint Athanase sur les psaumes. Fragments d'une traduction en copte sahidique: ROC 24 (1924) 3-57.

Translation: German: J. FISCH, BKV Athanasius II (1875) 371-835 (*Expositiones psalmorum*).

Studies: H. STRÄTER, Die Erlösungslehre des hl. Athanasius. Freiburg i.B., 1894, 29-35 (*De titulis psalmorum* not authentic). — M. FAULHABER, Isaiasglossen des Hesychius. Freiburg i.B., 1900, XVI-XX; *idem,* Eine wertvolle Oxforder Handschrift: ThQ 83 (1901) 227-232. — G. MERCATI, Note di letteratura biblica e cristiana antica (ST 5). Rome, 1901, 145-179; *idem,* ThR 4 (1905) 368-372; *idem,* Sull' autore del De titulis psalmorum stampato fra le opere di S. Atanasio: OCP 10 (1944) 7-22.

3. Commentary on Ecclesiastes and Song of Songs

According to Photius (*Bibl. cod.* 139) Athanasius composed a commentary on Ecclesiastes and Canticle of Canticles. He states, that 'the style is clear, like that of all his writings. But neither this nor any other of his works with which I am acquainted approaches the grace and beauty of the letters containing an apology for his flight and an account of his exile'. Except for a few fragments found in *Catenae* and printed in the Benedictine edition, the commentary is lost.

Edition: Fragments of Canticum: MG 27, 1347-1350.

4. Commentary on Genesis

Codex Barb. 569 preserves seven fragments of a commentary on Genesis by Athanasius and the Catena of Nicephorus adds another. They deal with Genesis 1,1; 1,6; 2,17; 3,10; 3,21; 3,23; 5,31ff; 48, 18-20. Through the same Nicephorus a fragment of a commentary on Exodus 28,4 has come down to us.

Studies: For Genesis and Exodus: R. Devreesse, Anciens commentateurs grecs de l'Octateuque: RBibl 44 (1935) 180. — A. Recheis, Sancti Athanasii Magni doctrina de primordiis seu quomodo explicaverit Genesim 1-3: Ant 28 (1953) 219-260.

There are also fragments on Job in some catenae, as well as on Matthew, Luke and 1 Corinthians, but it seems that they are not from lost commentaries on these books but from other works of St. Athanasius, perhaps some sermons no longer extant. No ancient author ever mentions that Athanasius wrote commentaries on any part of the New Testament.

Finally, the Synopsis Scripturae Sacrae (MG 28, 283-438), a compilation that gives a kind of introduction to Holy Scripture by describing the contents and origin of all the biblical books, is not of Athanasian authorship.

5. Ascetical Writings

1. The Life of St. Antony

Athanasius is the author of the most important document of early monasticism, the biography of St. Antony, the father of Christian monachism, born about the year 250. He composed it about 357, shortly after the death of the great hermit (356), and addressed it to monks who, according to the prologue, had asked him for an account of 'how Antony came to practice asceticism, what he was previous to this, what his death was like, and whether everything said about him was true'. Athanasius complied readily and in his answer indicates at the same time the purpose of his Vita:

> I am very happy to accede to your request, for I, too, derive real profit and help from the mere recollection of Antony; and I feel that you also, once you have heard the story, will not merely admire the man but will wish to emulate his resolution as well. Really, for monks the life of Antony is an ideal pattern of the ascetical life (ACW).

Thus Athanasius wrote it in order to present a model of a life consecrated to the service of God. He wants to induce his readers to imitate the holiness of his hero, not his miracles and visions.

Gregory of Nazianzus rightly calls it 'a rule of monastic life in the form of a narrative' (*Orat.* 21,5). The author reports from personal acquaintance with Antony: 'I make haste to write to Your Reverence what I myself know — for I have seen him often — and whatever I was able to learn from him who was his companion over a long period and poured water on his hands. Throughout I have been scrupulously considerate of the truth' (Prol. ACW). The Greek original in its present form does not give further information about the addressees. However, only a few years after its appearance, almost certainly not later than 375, the *Life of Antony* was translated into Latin by Evagrius of Antioch and this version preserves probably the original heading 'Athanasius the bishop to the brethren in foreign parts' *(ad peregrinos fratres)*. This seems to refer to monks in the West. But even if this were not the case, it remains a fact, that the *Vita* played an important part in diffusing the ideals of monastic life in general and in introducing monasticism into the West. St. Augustine testifies in the *Confessions* (8, 6, 14) to the decisive influence the book had on his own conversion and on the vocations of others to monastic life.

St. Jerome mentions (*De vir. ill.* 87, 88, 125) both, the original and the Latin version, and specifies Athanasius as the author and Evagrius, his own friend, as the translator. Migne's edition is only a reprint of the Benedictine. The latter was based on six manuscripts, all of which seem to derive from Metaphrastes' well-known collection of lives compiled in the tenth century. A new edition is being prepared by G. Garitte, which for the first time will make use of a number of non-Metaphrastic Greek manuscripts.

The Latin translation of Evagrius is often more a paraphrase than a literal translation. For this reason it is very important that a second Latin version has been found in a single manuscript in the Chapter Library of St. Peter's at Rome. Discovered by A. Wilmart and first published by G. Garitte in 1939, it cannot compare with that of Evagrius in elegancy and style, but appears to be even older and represent the best check upon the Metaphrastic text. Due to its extreme literalness, its Latin is awkward and ungraceful, a shortcoming, which makes it unlikely to believe that it was made after Evagrius' cultivated version had found universal recognition. There is in addition a Syriac and a Coptic translation, published by Garitte in 1949.

CONTENTS

The *Vita* narrates the birth and youth of Antony, his call and first steps in asceticism, his life in the tombs and in the desert, his solitude and his becoming the father and teacher of monks (1-15).

There follows Antony's address to the monks, which takes up a substantial part of the biography (16-43). Athanasius then tells of his longing for martyrdom when the persecution of Maximin Daja befell the Church, of his visit to the brethren along the Nile, of his miracles in the desert and his visions. His loyalty to the faith and his preaching against the Arians are recorded:

> Answering the appeal of both the bishops and all the brethren, he came down from the mountain, and entering Alexandria, he denounced the Arians. He said that their heresy was the worst of all and a fore-runner of the Antichrist. He taught the people that the Son of God is not a creature nor has He come into being 'from non-existence' but He is the eternal Word and Wisdom of the substance of the Father. Hence, too, it is impious to say, 'there was a time when He was not', for the Word was always coexistent with the Father. Wherefore, do not have the least thing to do with the most godless Arians: there simply is no fellowship of light and darkness. You must remember that you are God-fearing Christians, but they, by saying that the Son and Word of God the Father is a creature, are in no respect different from the pagans, who worship the created in place of God the Creator. And you may be sure that all creation is incensed against them because they count among created things the Creator and Lord of all, to whom all things owe their existence (69 ACW).

The rest of the book deals with his practical wisdom and his discussion with two Greek philosophers on idolatry, reason and faith (72-80), Constantine's letter to him (81), his prophecies, his miracles and his death (82-93). An epilogue (94) admonishes the addressees to 'read this to the brethren, that they may learn what the life of the monks should be like', and, if the occasion presents itself, to 'read it also to the pagans, that at least in this way they may learn that our Lord Jesus Christ is not only God and the Son of God, but that the Christians by their faithful service to Him and their orthodox faith in Him prove that the demons whom the Greeks consider gods are no gods; that moreover, they trample them under foot and drive them out for what they are — deceivers and corrupters of men'.

The demons take up considerable space in this biography, and especially the long address given to his fellow monks strikes the modern reader almost like a discourse on demonology. The *Vita* is full of strange encounters with Satan and his helpers, which kindled the inspiration of artists again and again. There is no doubt that Antony was not entirely free from popular ideas regarding evil spirits and that he lays perhaps too great stress on the tempta-tions caused by them. However, we have to keep in mind that he regards monastic life as a martyrdom and the monk as the successor to the martyr. Just as the martyr was thought to fight with Satan in his suffering, so the monk was supposed to wage a continuous battle against the demons. Athanasius explains that Antony, having failed to obtain the grace of dying for the faith in the persecution of Maximin Daja, returned to his monastery and imposed upon himself a daily martyrdom:

> When the persecution finally ceased and bishop Peter of blessed memory had suffered martyrdom, he left and went back to his solitary cell; and there he was a daily martyr to his conscience, ever fighting the battles of the faith. For he practised a zealous and more intense ascetic life (47 ACW).

He looked upon monastic life as a warfare in which the chief enemy was the devil and the demons. Thus, giving instructions to his monks, he told them:

> Living this life, let us be carefully on our guard and, as is written, 'with all watchfulness keep our heart' (Prov. 4, 23). For we have enemies, powerful and crafty — the wicked demons; and it is against these that our wrestling is (21).

To Antony perfection is acquired by the return to our original state, the state in which we were created:

> Virtue has need only of our will, since it is within us and springs from us. Virtue exists when the soul keeps in its natural state. It is kept in its natural state when it remains as it came into being. Now it came into being fair and perfectly straight... For the soul is said to be straight when its mind is in its natural state as it was created. But when it swerves and is perverted from its natural condition, that is called vice of the soul.
> So the task is not difficult: If we remain as we were made, we are in the state of virtue; but if we give our minds to base things, we are accounted evil. If the task had to be accomplished from without, it would indeed be difficult; but since this is within us, let us guard ourselves from foul thoughts. And having received the soul as something entrusted to us, let us guard it for the Lord, that He may recognize His work as being the same as He made it (20).

To reach this state of soul we must gain control of our passions and victory over Satan and sin. Such stability cannot be achieved without daily examination of conscience, which, according to Antony, should be written down: 'Let every man daily take an accounting with himself of the day's and the night's doings, and if he has sinned, let him stop sinning; and if he has not, let him not boast of it... Let this observation be a safeguard against sinning: let us note and write down our actions and impulses of the soul as though we were to report them to each other' (55 ACW). Cardinal Newman's final appraisal of Antony's stature, as it appears in this biography, may be quoted: 'His doctrine surely is pure and unimpeachable; and his temper is high and heavenly, — without cowardice, without gloom, without formality, and without self-complacency. Superstition is abject and crouching, it is full of thoughts of guilt; it distrusts God, and dreads the powers of evil. Antony at least has nothing of this, being full of holy confidence, divine peace, cheerfulness, and valorousness' (*Hist. Sketches* 2, 11).

LITERARY FORM

If we compare the *Vita* with ancient biographies we may call it an encomium. Thus Cavallin thinks that Athanasius imitates Xenophon's *Bios* of the heroic Agesilaus and sees in Antony the ideal monk as Xenophon in Agesilaus the ideal king. According to Reitzenstein, he used a *Vita* of Pythagoras no longer extant, and transferred the portrait of the ideal sage with all his virtues into the Christian world. Holl points to Philostratus' account of Apollonius of Tyana and to the treatise *Quis dives salvetur* (cf. vol. II, p. 15/16) of Clement of Alexandria as sources for the *Vita*. There are a number of striking parallels between the *Life of Plotinus* by his disciple Porphyry and the *Life of St. Antony*, so that, in the opinion of List, Athanasius had this in mind. It would be difficult to trace the literary influence in detail, although there cannot be any doubt that the ancient classical model of the hero's as well as the newer type of *Vita* of the sage served as inspiration for Athanasius. But it remains his great achievement that he recasted these inherited expressions of popular ideals in the Christian mold and disclosed the same heroism in the imitator of Christ aided by the power of grace. Thus he created a new type of biography that was to serve as a model for all subsequent Greek and Latin hagiography.

Editions: Greek text: MG 26, 835-976, reprint of the Benedictine edition (Paris, 1698). Published separately by A. F. MAUNOURY, Paris, 1887, 1890. Cf. G. GARITTE, Histoire du texte imprimé de la Vie grecque de S. Antoine: Bulletin de l'Institut historique belge de Rome 22 (1942/43) 5-29; *idem*, Le texte grec et les versions anciennes de la Vie de S. Antoine: SA 38 (1956) 1-12.

Ancient Versions: Latin text of Evagrius: MG 26, 835-976, ML 73, 125-170. Text of the earliest Latin version: G. GARITTE, Un témoin important du texte de la Vie de S. Antoine par S. Athanase. La version latine inédite des Archives du Chapitre de Saint-Pierre à Rome (Études de philol., d'archéol. et d'hist. anc. publ. par l'Inst. hist. belge de Rome 3). Brussels, 1939. Cf. A. WILMART, Une version latine inédite de la Vie de saint-Antoine: RB 31 (1914) 163-173. — C. MOHRMANN, Note sur la version latine la plus ancienne de la Vie de S. Antoine par S. Athanase: SA 38 (1956) 35-44.

Syriac version: P. BEDJAN, Acta martyrum et sanctorum. Paris, 1895, 1-121. Cf. also the recension made by the seventh-century monk Anan-Isho: The Book of Paradise, ed. by E. A. BUDGE. London, 1904, 1, 1-108 English translation; 2, 1-93 Syriac text. *Coptic version:* G. GARITTE, S. Antonii Vitae versio Sahidica (CSCO 117, 118). Louvain, 1949.

Modern Translations: English: H. ELLERSHAW, LNPF second series 4 (1892) 195-221. — E. A. BUDGE, l.c. — J. B. MCLAUGHLIN, St. Anthony the Hermit by St. Athanasius. London and New York, 1924. — R. T. MEYER, ACW 10 (1950). — M. E. KEENAN, FC 15 (1952) 127-216. — *French:* B. LAVAUD, Antoine le Grand, père des moines. Sa vie par S. Athanase et autres textes. Lyon, 1943. — R. DRAGUET, Les Pères du désert. Paris, 1949, 1-74 reprints the translation of Robert ARNAULD D'ANDILLY (1653). — *German:* L. CLARUS, Das Leben des heiligen Antonius von Athanasius dem Grossen. Münster i. W., 1857. — P. A. RICHARD, BKV (1875) Ausgewählte Schriften des hl. Athanasius 2, 217-330. — H. MERTEL, BKV² (1917) 11-101. — N. HOVORKA, Leben und Versuchung des hl. Antonius nach der im 4. Jahrhundert von Bischof Athanasius verfassten Biographie. Vienna, 1925. — *Danish:* H. F. JOHANNSEN, Den hellige Antonius' Liv og andre skrifter om munke og helgener i Aegypten, Palaestina og Syrien. Copenhagen, 1955.

Studies: For form of composition: H. MERTEL, Die biographische Form der griechischen Heiligenlegenden. Diss. Munich, 1909, 11-19. — R. REITZENSTEIN, Hellenistische Wundererzählungen. Leipzig, 1906, 55-59; *idem*, Des Athanasius Werk über das Leben des Antonius. Ein philologischer Beitrag zur Geschichte des Mönchtums (SAH). Heidelberg, 1914. — A. PRIESSNIG, Die biographischen Formen der griechischen Heiligenlegende in ihrer geschichtlichen Entwicklung. Münnerstadt, 1924, 18-35. — K. HOLL, Die schriftstellerische Form des griechischen Heiligenlebens: Gesammelte Aufsätze zur Kirchengeschichte II. Der Osten. Tübingen, 1928, 249-269. — J. LIST, Das Antoniusleben des hl. Athanasius des Grossen. Eine literarhistorische Studie zu den Anfängen der byzantinischen Hagiographie (Texte und Forschungen zur byzantinisch-neugriechischen Philologie 11). Athens, 1931. — S. CAVALLIN, Literarhistorische und textkritische Studien zur Vita Caesarii Arelatensis. Lund, 1934. — A. J. FESTUGIÈRE, Sur une nouvelle édition du 'De vita Pythagorica' de Jamblique: REG 50 (1937) 470-494. — M. SCHUETT, Vom hl. Antonius zum hl. Guthlac. Ein Beitrag zur Geschichte der Biographie: Antike und Abendland 5 (1956) 75-91.

For content and historical value etc.: J. STOFFELS, Die Angriffe der Dämonen auf den Einsiedler Antonius: ThGl 2 (1910) 721-732, 809-830. — A. VON HERTLING, Antonius der Einsiedler. Innsbruck, 1929, 6-12. — K. HEUSSI, Der Ursprung des Mönchtums. Tübingen, 1936, 78-108. Cf. L. LEFORT, RHE 33 (1937) 343f. — M. VILLER - K. RAHNER, Aszese und Mystik in der Väterzeit. Freiburg i.B., 1939, 84-89. — J. VERGOTE, L'Égypte, berceau du monachisme chrétien (et l'influence de la Vita Antonii d'Athanase): Chronique d'Égypte 17 (Brussels, 1942) 329-345. — H. DÖRRIES, Die Vita Antonii als Geschichtsquelle: NGWG Philol.-hist. Kl. 14 (1949) 359-410. — P. L. BOUYER, La Vie de S. Antoine. Essai sur la spiritualité du monachisme primitif. St-Wandrille, 1950. — E. E. MALONE, The Monk and the Martyr (SCA 12). Washington, 1950, 44-46, 101-103, 107-109, 127, 141; *idem*, SA 38 (1956) 201-228. — A. C. BAYNES, St. Antony and the Demons: Journal of Egyptian Archaeology 40 (1954) 7-10. — J. DANIÉLOU, Les démons de l'air dans la 'Vie d'Antoine': SA 38 (1956) 136-145. — M. J. MARX, Incessant Prayer in the Vita Antonii: SA 38 (1956) 108-135. — E. T. BETTENCOURT, L'idéal religieux de S. Antoine et son actualité: SA 38 (1956) 45-65. — L. TH. A. LORIÉ, Spiritual Terminology in the Latin Translations of the Vita Antonii with reference to the fourth and fifth century monastic literature (Latinitas Christianorum Primaeva 19). Nymegen, 1955. — B. STEIDLE, Homo Dei Antonius. Zum Bild des 'Mannes Gottes' im alten Mönchtum: SA 38 (1956) 148-200. — L. VON HERTLING, Studi storici Antoniani negli ultimi trent' anni: SA 38 (1956) 13-24. — G. GARITTE,

Réminiscences de la Vie d'Antoine dans Cyrille de Scythopolis: Silloge bizantina in onore di Silvio G. Mercati. Rome, 1957, 117-122.

2. On Virginity

a. St. Jerome testifies (*De vir. ill.* 87) that Athanasius dealt with this subject on several occasions. There exists a treatise *On Virginity* (περὶ παρθενίας) among his works that has been the object of a long and lively controversy. The Benedictine editors and P. Batiffol pronounced it dubious because of several passages that appeared incompatible with Athanasius' way of speaking. E. von der Goltz strongly defended its authenticity. However, M. Aubineau who has recently given a thorough evaluation of all the Athanasian writings on virginity, proved that it cannot be considered as genuine on account of its tendencies, its style and its vocabulary. He found 121 words which Athanasius never used.

Nevertheless, this small book had considerable importance for the history of asceticism. It forms a kind of manual for the Christian virgin, giving her detailed instruction about the conduct and religious duties of a bride of Christ, and supplying her with beautiful prayers. There are no indications whatsoever of the date of its composition. The new edition by E. von der Goltz gives a full discussion of the variant readings. Some further improvements have been made in the text by K. Lake and R. P. Casey, who had a better knowledge of the Patmos (P) manuscript and made use of two additional codexes, the Vatopedi manuscripts A and K.

Editions: MG 28, 251-282. — New critical edition by E. v. d. Goltz, Λόγος σωτηρίας πρὸς τὴν παρθένον. Eine echte Schrift des Athanasius (TU 29, 2a). Leipzig, 1905, 25-50. Improvements of this text by K. Lake and R. P. Casey, The Text of the De virginitate of Athanasius: HThR 19 (1926) 173-190.

Translation: Spanish: B. Vizmanos, Las virgenes cristianas de la Iglesia Primitiva (BAC 45). Madrid, 1949, 1089-1109.

Studies: P. Batiffol, Le περὶ παρθενίας du pseudo-Athanase: RQ 7 (1893) 275-286. — E. v. d. Goltz, l.c. 1-144. Cf. P. Batiffol, RBibl (1906) 295-299. V. Burch, The American Journal of Theology 10 (1906) 295-299. A. Souter, JThSt 9 (1906) 140-141. P. Delehaye, AB (1906) 180-181. J. Leipoldt, ZKG 27 (1906) 225-226. G. Krüger, ThLZ (1906) 352-355. — R. H. Connolly, The So-called Egyptian Church Order and Derived Documents (TSt 8). Cambridge, 1916, 156-157 (*Canones Hippolyti* influenced by *De virginitate*). — E. Buonaiuti, Saggi sul cristianesimo primitivo. Castello, 1923, 242-254: Evagrio Pontico e il De Virginitate di Ps. Atanasio. — F. Zucchetti, Il Sinodo di Gangra e un scritto di pseudo-Atanasio: RR 1 (1925) 548-551. — G. Bardy, Athanase: Dictionnaire de Spiritualité I (1935) 1048-1052. — M. Aubineau, Les écrits de S. Athanase sur la virginité: RAM 31 (1935) 144-151.

b. Lefort has edited Coptic fragments of an *Epistle to the Virgins* amounting to 65 pages. It seems to be related to the above-mentioned work and was used by St. Ambrose and Shenoute of Atripe (cf.

below p. 185). The former makes ample use of it in *De virginibus* without mentioning his source. The latter quotes a long passage from it and states explicitly that he takes it from 'the letters' of archbishop Athanasius. Unfortunately, Lefort's Coptic text is mutilated at the beginning and the author's name and the title of the work are lacking. Ephraem of Antioch (d. ca. 544), however, mentions an *Epistle to the Virgins* by St. Athanasius (Photius: MG 103, 993). Thus Lefort is of the opinion that Athanasius is the real author. The Epistle contains an excellent exposition of the christological doctrine of the hypostatic union.

Editions: Editio princeps: L. Th. Lefort, S. Athanase sur la virginité: Mus 42 (1929) 197-275. This Coptic text is based on Cod. Neapol. Zoega 245, Cod. Paris. B.N. 131 and Paris. B.N. 78. Newest edition: L. Th. Lefort, S. Athanase. Lettres Festales et Pastorales en copte (CSCO 150). Louvain, 1955, 73-99. — For Shenoute's quotation, see: J. Leipoldt, Sinuthii archimandritae vita et opera omnia (CSCO 42). Louvain, 1908, p. 108, 1. 19-21.

Translation: French: L. Th. Lefort, Mus 42 (1929) 240-264; *idem*, CSCO 151 (1955) 55-80.

Studies: L. Th. Lefort, S. Athanase sur la virginité: Mus 42 (1929) 197-275; *idem*, Athanase, Ambroise et Chenoute 'sur la virginité': Mus 48 (1935) 55-73. — O. von Lemm, Zu einer nicht identifizierten Rede 'de virginitate', in: Koptische Miszellen: Bulletin de l'Académie impériale des sciences de Saint-Pétersbourg, VIe série, t. 3 (1909) 393-403; *idem*, Koptische Miszellen I. Leipzig, 1914, 163-173. — A. Janssens, Een Marialeven vermeld bij S. Athanasius en S. Ambrosius, in: De heilige Maagd en Moeder Gods Maria I. Het Dogma en de Apocryphen. Antwerpen-Nijmegen, 1930, 332-336. — L. Dossi, S. Ambrogio e S. Atanasio de virginibus: Acme. Annali della Facoltà di Filosofia e Lettre dell' università statale di Milano 4 (1951) 241-262. — M. Aubineau, l.c. 19-30. — L. Th. Lefort, CSCO 150 (1955) XVIII-XXII.

c. There is another treatise *On Virginity (Λόγος περὶ παρθενίας)* that has a good chance of being recognized as genuine. A large Syriac fragment of it has been edited by Lebon and the complete text is extant in an Armenian version published by Casey. Both Lebon and Casey agree that the original was Greek. The title *Discourse on Virginity* corresponds to its content. The author addresses not one particular virgin but all who are willing to live in the state of virginity. He does not deal with the monastic life but with virgins who live at home with their relatives. He regards them as brides of Christ who have signed a contract with Christ which will last to their death. He calls their life 'angelic' and admonishes them to abstain from baths and secular amusements, to practice silence, to read the Scriptures and sing the psalms, to work in order to support themselves, but to remain poor. The author gives a long list of examples of virginity from the Old Testament which he quotes from the Greek text of the Septuagint and cites a long passage from the *Acta Pauli et Theclae* (cf. vol. I p. 131f.). The Syriac manuscript (*addit.* 14.607 of the British Museum) of the 6th or 7th century attributes the work to St. Athanasius and the Armenian version, made from the Greek in the sixth century, was found in a collection of Athanasian writings. The content furnishes no reason to deny his authorship.

Editions: Syriac fragment: J. LEBON, Athanasiana Syriaca I. Un λόγος περὶ παρθενίας attribué à saint Athanase d'Alexandrie: Mus 40 (1927) 209-218. *Armenian version:* R. P. CASEY, Der dem Athanasius zugeschriebene Traktat περὶ παρθενίας : SAB 33 (1935) 1026-1034 based on the two manuscripts Cod. 648 of the 14th (?) and Cod. 629 of the 19th century, both of the Library of the Mechitarists at Vienna.

Translations: French: J. LEBON, l.c. 219-226. — *German:* R. P. CASEY, l.c. 1035-1045.

Study: M. AUBINEAU, l.c. 14-18 gives a good summary of Lebon's and Casey's investigations.

d. The same Syriac manuscript *addit.* 14.607 of the British Museum contains a *Letter to the Virgins who went to Jerusalem to pray and returned, by St. Athanasius, Archbishop of the Alexandrians.* The author recalls in the first part the pilgrimage to Bethlehem and Jerusalem from which a group of virgins returned. He feels sorry for them that they had to leave these holy places but assures them that they can remain with Christ for ever by a holy life. The second part is a treatise on virginity with detailed rules for this state. The author recommends first of all, vigilance against the devil, discusses the conduct of the virgin in church, noble bearing and dignity, charity in speaking. He warns against sensuality and condemns the communal life of ascetics of both sexes living together under one roof. The text is most probably the copy of a much older Syriac version. The original must have been in Greek. The style has all the characteristics of that of St. Athanasius: clarity, precision and simplicity.

Edition: Syriac text by J. LEBON, Athanasiana Syriaca II. Une lettre attribuée à saint Athanase d'Alexandrie: Mus 41 (1928) 170-188.

Translation: French: J. LEBON, l.c. 189-203.

Studies: J. LEBON, l.c. 204-213. — M. AUBINEAU, l.c. 12-14.

e. A. van Lantschoot published a hitherto unknown Coptic letter of ostensibly Athanasian origin dealing with *Love and Self-control.* He found it in manuscript *Or.* 8802 of the British Museum dating from the 11th or 12th century. It carries the title: '*Letter* of our holy Father, venerable in every regard, apa Athanasius, archbishop of Alexandria, *on* the subject of *love (ἀγάπη) and self-control (ἐγκράτεια)*'. Lefort has clearly shown that this letter is related to a long Coptic exhortation, entitled '*Catechesis* delivered by our very venerable holy Father apa Pachomius, the holy archimandrite, *on the occasion when one brother monk had a resentment against another'*. The identity of words and phrases is so great that one must have copied the other, unless both made use of the same source. Lefort who arranges the texts of both in parallel columns, proved that Pachomius copied Athanasius and that the latter is most probably the real author. It seems that he composed it in Coptic.

Editions: Editio princeps: A. van Lantschoot, Lettre de saint Athanase au sujet de l'amour et de la tempérance: Mus 40 (1927) 267-279. — New edition: L. Th. Lefort, S. Athanase. Lettres Festales et Pastorales en copte (CSCO 150). Louvain, 1955, 110-120.

Translations: French: A. van Lantschoot, l.c. 280-292. — L. Th. Lefort, CSCO 151 (1955) 88-98. — *English:* An English translation of the Catechesis of Pachomius is given with the Coptic text by E. A. W. Budge, Coptic Apocrypha in the Dialect of Upper Egypt. London, 1913, 35-98.

Studies: L. Th. Lefort, St. Athanase écrivain copte: Mus 46 (1933) 1-33; *idem*, CSCO 150 (1955) XXVIII-XXXI. — M. Aubineau, l.c. 18-19.

f. Of even greater importance is a discovery which Lefort made in a manuscript from the White Monastery (now *Cod. Paris.* B.N. 131). He found almost two thirds of the so-called First Pseudo-Clementine Epistle addressed to the virgins (see vol. I, p. 58f.) in a Coptic version which attributes this letter to Athanasius. Lefort is inclined to think of Athanasius as its real author, whereas Wagenmann rejects this possibility. At any rate the Coptic version is by far older and more reliable than the Syriac text. Since the manuscript of the White Monastery is from the fourth or fifth century, it proves that the monastic circles of Egypt knew this letter. In fact, Shenoute and his successor Besa quote this Coptic text.

Editions: Editio princeps: L. Th. Lefort, Le De Virginitate de saint Clément ou de saint Athanase?: Mus 40 (1927) 254-264 and Mus 42 (1929) 265-269, gives the Coptic text based on Cod. Paris. B.N. 131 and 130 and a Latin translation. New edition: L. Th. Lefort, Les Pères Apostoliques en copte (CSCO 135). Louvain, 1952, 32-43.

Translation: French: L. Th. Lefort, CSCO 136 (1952) 29-37. For other translations, see vol. I, p. 59.

Studies: L. Th. Lefort, Mus 40 (1927) 265-269. Cf. J. Wagenmann, ThLZ 54 (1929) 589f. — L. Th. Lefort, Saint Athanase sur la virginité: Mus 42 (1929) 265-269; *idem*, Une citation copte de la pseudo-Clémentine De Virginitate: Bulletin de l'Institut français d'archéol. orient. 30 (1930) 509-511; *idem*, CSCO 135 (1952) XV-XIX. — H. Duensing, Die dem Klemens von Rom zugeschriebenen Briefe über die Jungfräulichkeit: ZKG 63 (1950/51) 166-188 (against Athanasian authorship).

g. In 1949 Lefort published Coptic fragments of another treatise on virginity hitherto unknown, from *Cod.* 130² of the Bibliothèque Nationale at Paris originating from Shenoute's monastery. The title of the entire work is given on f. 85 verso:' Here are the instructions and precepts concerning the virgins given by apa Athanasius archbishop'. The fragment calls virginity 'a divine virtue', 'the wealth of the Church' and 'a sacrificial gift reserved for God'. The virgin is a woman by nature but by her free choice and firm resolution she surpasses nature and lives an immortal life in a mortal body. There follow rules for the dress of virgins. Their hands and feet must be covered and their dress modest. These general ideas on virginity and precise instructions are in perfect agreement with those of St. Athanasius. We find the same expressions and precepts in his other treatises.

In 1951 Lefort edited another fragment of an Athanasian treatise on virginity from *Cod. Paris.* B.N. 131⁵ of the eleventh century. There is a possibility that the above-mentioned *Instructions and Precepts concerning Virgins* and this fragment belong to the same work. The new piece has no title; beginning and end are mutilated. The author gives a long list of persons of the Old Testament who have been blessed by God, like Enoch, Noe, Abraham, Jacob, Joseph, Moyses, Aaron, etc. He praises virginity in a similar way as the author of the *Instructions and Precepts.*

Editions: Editio princeps of the fragments from the *Instructions and Precepts concerning Virgins:* L. Th. Lefort, Un nouveau 'De Virginitate' attribué à saint Athanase: AB 67 (1949) = Mélanges Peeters, 145-146. New edition: L. Th. Lefort, CSCO 150 (1955) 99-100. Editio princeps of the fragment from Cod. Paris. B.N. 131⁵: L. Th. Lefort, Encore un 'De Virginitate' de saint Athanase?: Mélanges De Ghellinck (Museum Lessianum Sect. Hist. 13). Gembloux, 1951, 216-218. New edition: L. Th. Lefort, CSCO 150 (1955) 101-106.

Translations: French: L. Th. Lefort, AB 67 (1949) 147-148; *idem*, CSCO 151 (1955) 80-82. — L. Th. Lefort, Mélanges De Ghellinck, 219-221; *idem*, CSCO 151 (1955) 82-84.

Studies: M. Aubineau, l.c. 30-31. — L. Th. Lefort, CSCO 150 (1955) XXII-XXVII.

3. *Other Ascetical Treatises*

Codex Vaticanus 2200 written between 750 and 850 A.D. contains two fragments of a hitherto unknown ascetical treatise 'By St. Athanasius, Patriarch of Alexandria, *On Sickness and Health*'. Style and content do not offer anything which would contradict this attribution. On the contrary, both are worthy of this Church Father. The great age and reliability of the manuscript are additional factors in favor of Athanasian authorship.

The author refutes heretics who demand a continuous and uninterrupted divine service of praise and for this reason do not tolerate any sleep. They base their ideas on a wrong interpretation of biblical texts, like Proverbs 6, 4. Perhaps the Messalians (cf.

below p. 163) are meant who emphasized Scripture passages like
I Thess. 5, 17: 'Pray without ceasing' (Euchites).

Edition: F. DIEKAMP, Analecta Patristica (Orientalia Christiana Analecta 117). Rome,
1938, 5-8.

Fragments of a long ascetical treatise have been published by
L. Th. Lefort from two manuscripts, one of John Rylands Library
at Manchester and the other of the British Museum (*Or.* 6007).
The text is acephalous but Besa, Shenoute's disciple and successor,
quotes a passage from it and attributes it explicitly to St. Athanasius. The content deals with marriage and procreation of children,
the use of wine and the 'conveniences of the flesh'. The author
admonishes 'his brothers' to avoid the excesses of the taverns but
does not demand total abstention from wine. He regards matrimony
as a means of escaping prostitution. He recommends the singing
of psalms as a medicine for the soul.

Edition: L. TH. LEFORT, CSCO 150 (1955) 121-138.

Translation: French: L. TH. LEFORT, CSCO 151 (1955) 99-109.

Studies: For the manuscripts, see W. E. CRUM, Catalogue of the Coptic Manuscripts
in the John Rylands Library, Manchester, 62 and 63 with the citation of Besa. For
the latter, see K. H. KUHN, Mus 66 (1953) 228. For British Museum, Or. 6007, see
CRUM, Catalogue of the Coptic Manuscripts in the British Museum, London, 1905,
n. 990. — L. TH. LEFORT, CSCO 150 (1955) XXXI-XXXIII.

4. *Sermons*

The Benedictine editors declared dubious or spurious all of the
sermons attributed to Athanasius. A careful examination of the
great number listed by A. Ehrhard which so far has not been made,
will most probably modify this judgment and prove some of them
genuine. Hoss thought that the homilies *De sabbatis et circumcisione
ex libro Exodi* and *De passione et cruce Domini* are of Athanasian
authorship and not to be regarded as doubtful. In fact, the latter
closely resembles the authentic works in many passages.

The sermons *De patientia* and *In ramos palmarum* (MG 26,1297-1315)
and the homily *In canticum canticorum* (MG 27,1349-1362) do not
belong to Athanasius. Budge edited three sermons which have
come down in a Coptic version, *On Charity and Discord, On Matthew
20,1-16,* and *On Soul and Body.*

The Syriac version of several extracts from the last mentioned
homily *On Soul and Body,* in Syriac manuscript *add.* 7.192 of the
British Museum, attributes it to Alexander, Athanasius' predecessor
in the see of Alexandria (cf. above p. 17).

Casey has published a *Homily on the Devil,* ascribed to Athanasius, which he found in a single manuscript of the fifteenth century in the Ambrosiana (*Cod. Gr.* 235, D 51 sup.) at Milan. The people addressed in this homily have retained their pagan associations though their devotion to the Christian religion is assumed. Sacrifices to the old gods is still a common practice. Casey pointed out that on the grounds of style and literary composition Athanasian authorship is improbable. Recent investigations by Tetz and Scheidweiler have definitely shown that this sermon must have been composed at or near Alexandria by an Arian.

Burmester discovered three Coptic homilies attributed to Athanasius in a Holy Week Lectionary. Bernardin edited 'A Sermon of St. Athanasius, Archbishop of Alexandria: *On the Suffering of Christ-Jesus and on Fear of the Judgment-Place*' from a Coptic manuscript (M 595) belonging to the Pierpont Morgan Library at New York (100v-108r). It seems to be meant for Good Friday or Holy Saturday. The references to the equality of the Son with the Father presuppose the Arian controversy and the mention of the Manichaeans suggests the fourth century. The same manuscript contains 'A Discourse *Concerning Lazarus whom Christ raised from the Dead*' attributed to Athanasius, which J. B. Bernardin published in 1940. The homily is one of the ten found in a synaxary formerly in use during Eastertide and Whitsuntide at the Monastery of the Archangel Michael at Hamouli on the southern border of the province of Fayum. Another sermon ascribed to Athanasius in the same manuscript, *Catechesis in festum Pentecostes*, has not as yet been published. The genuineness of these and other Coptic Athanasian homilies remains to be investigated.

Lantschoot published from a Coptic manuscript of the National Library at Naples an allocution addressed to monks who came to see Athanasius and pay their respects. There is no good reason to doubt its authenticity. The content deals with the vocation to monastic life.

Three other sermons attributed to Athanasius seem to belong to a certain Timothy of Jerusalem whose identification remains difficult. He must have lived between the sixth and eighth century. The first (MG 28, 905-914) deals with the annunciation of the births of John the Baptist and of Christ; the second (MG 28, 943-958) with Mary and Joseph's journey to Bethlehem and the Nativity; the third (MG 28, 1001-1024) with the healing of the blind man (John 9, 1f). Jugie proved that the *Homily on the Annunciation* (MG 28, 917-943) is not by Athanasius but by an author of the end of the seventh or the beginning of the eighth century. L. Th. Lefort has recently drawn our attention to Coptic fragments of a manuscript of ca. 600 A.D. in the Egyptian Museum of Turin

containing 'Discourses pronounced by holy apa Athanasius, archbishop of Alexandria, when he returned from his second exile:
*On the Virgin and Theotokos Mary who gave Birth to God, On Elisabeth,
the Mother of John,* in which he refutes Arius, and *On the Nativity of
our Lord Jesus Christ*'.

Editions, Translations and Studies: MG 28, 133-250; 501-1114. — K. Hoss, Studien über
das Schrifttum und die Theologie des Athanasius. Freiburg i.B., 1899, 96-103. —
A. EHRHARD, Überlieferung und Bestand der hagiographischen und homiletischen
Literatur der griechischen Kirche (TU 50-52). Berlin and Leipzig, 1938-1952, passim.
— E. A. W. BUDGE, Coptic Homilies in the Dialect of Upper Egypt. London, 1910,
Coptic texts: 58-65, 80-89, 115-132; English translation: 204-211, 226-234, 258-274;
Syriac version of the homily *On Soul and Body:* 407-415; English translation: 417-424. —
R. P. CASEY, An Early Homily on the Devil ascribed to Athanasius of Alexandria:
JThSt 36 (1935) 1-10; Greek text: 4-10. Cf. M. TETZ, Eine arianische Homilie unter
dem Namen des Athanasius von Alexandrien: ZKG 64 (1952/53) 299-307. New edition
by F. SCHEIDWEILER, Eine arianische Predigt über den Teufel: ZKG 67 (1955/56)
132-140. — O. H. E. BURMESTER, The Homilies or Exhortations of the Holy Week
Lectionary: Mus 45 (1932) 44-48 Coptic texts and English translation. — J. B. BERNARDIN,
A Coptic Sermon attributed to St. Athanasius: JThSt 38 (1937) 113-129 Coptic text
with English translation. — J. B. BERNARDIN, The Resurrection of Lazarus: American
Journal of Semitic Languages and Literatures 57 (1940) 262-290 (Coptic text: 277-290,
English translation: 262-273). — A. VAN LANTSCHOOT, Une allocution à des moines en
visite chez S. Athanase: Ang 20 (1943) 249-253 (Coptic text: 250-252, French translation:
252-253). — B. CAPELLE, Les homélies liturgiques du prétendu Timothée de Jérusalem:
EL 63 (1949) 5-26. — M. JUGIE, Deux homélies patristiques pseudépigraphes: EO 39
(1941/42) 283-289. — L. TH. LEFORT, Athanasiana Coptica: Mus 69 (1956) 233-241;
idem, L'homélie de S. Athanase des papyrus de Turin: Mus 71 (1958) 5-50 (à suivre).

6. *Letters*

Of Athanasius' large correspondence only a portion has survived.
Most of his letters are not personal and private, but represent
official decrees and sometimes entire treatises. For this reason they
are highly important for the history of the Arian controversy and
the development of Christian doctrine in the fourth century.

1. *Festal Letters* (Ἐπιστολαὶ ἑορταστικαί)

During the third century it had become a custom with the bishops
of Alexandria to announce the beginning of Lent and the correct
date of Easter each year to the suffragan sees by a letter issued
usually shortly after Epiphany. Such a pastoral contained in
addition a discussion of current ecclesiastical affairs or problems
of Christian life and exhortations to observe the fast, to almsgiving
and the reception of the sacraments. Dionysius of Alexandria is
the first known to have sent such Easter Letters (cf. vol. II, p. 108).
Athanasius remained loyal to this tradition, even when he was

in exile. Shortly after his death these letters were brought together by one of his friends and the collection was given wide distribution. Of the Greek original only fragments are extant but in Syriac thirteen, written in the years 329-348, are completely preserved. Lefort recently published the Coptic text of seventeen letters of which we so far had only small Greek quotations. This new discovery proves Schwartz's chronology impossible.

We notice in them the same simplicity of style, vigor and warmth, that pervades his other writings. Naturally the coming Easter season occupies a prominent place and a tone of joy predominates. The instructions for Lent indicate that even in Egypt the forty-day fast before Easter had become customary. The first Festal Letter for the year 329 speaks only of a six-day fast (10) but from the year 330 onwards Athanasius emphasizes again and again that the observance had to begin on Monday of the sixth week before Easter. Thus he says in his Festal Letter for the year 332:

> The beginning of the fast of forty days is on the fifth of Phamenoth [March 1]; and when, as I have said, we have first been purified and prepared by those days, we begin the holy week of the great Easter on the tenth of Pharmuthi [April 1], in which, my beloved brethren, we should use more prolonged prayers, and fastings, and watchings, that we may be enabled to anoint our lintels with precious blood, and to escape the destroyer. Let us rest then, on the fifteenth of the month of Pharmuthi [April 10], for on the evening of that Saturday we hear the angels' message, 'Why seek ye the living among the dead? He is risen'. Immediately afterwards that great Sunday receives us, I mean on the sixteenth of the same month Pharmuthi [April 11], on which our Lord having risen, gave us peace towards our neighbours (3, 6 LNPF).

Editions: Greek fragments: MG 26, 1431-1444. More fragments have been found since but never been assembled in a new critical edition.
Syriac version: W. CURETON, The Festal Letters of Athanasius. London, 1848. This Syriac text was reprinted by Mai, Nova Patrum Bibl. 6, Rome, 1853, pars I, with a rather unreliable Latin translation made from an Italian version. The Latin text was reprinted by MG 26, 1351-1432. An additional fragment was published by G. BICKELL, Conspectus rei Syrorum literariae. Münster i. W., 1871, 52. For the fragments of the three Festal Letters 27, 29 and 44 found in Severus of Antioch, see: J. LEBON, Severi Antiocheni liber contra impium Grammaticum CSCO 101 (1933) 293-295 Syriac text, CSCO 102 (1933) 216-217 Latin translation. Eight additional quotations from the Festal Letters have been found in a treatise of Timotheus Aelurus (d. 477) preserved in Armenian and edited by K. TER-MEKERTTSCHIAN and E. TER-MINASSIANTZ, Timotheos Ailuros' des Patriarchen von Alexandrien Widerlegung der auf der Synode zu Chalkedon festgesetzten Lehre. Leipzig, 1908.
Coptic version: L. TH. LEFORT, Lettres Festales et Pastorales de S. Athanase en copte (CSCO 150). Louvain, 1955, 1-72. — M. PIEPER, Zwei Blätter aus dem Osterbrief des Athanasius vom Jahre 364 (Pap. Berol. 11948): ZNW 37 (1938) 73-76 mit Coptic text, German translation and commentary.

Modern Translations: English: H. BURGESS, Library of Fathers 38. Oxford, 1854, reprinted LNPF 4, 506-553. — *German:* F. LARSOW, Die Festbriefe des hl. Athanasius aus dem Syrischen übersetzt und durch Anmerkungen erläutert. Berlin, 1852. — *French:* L. TH. LEFORT, CSCO 151 (1955) 1-54.

Studies: For the chronology, see: E. SCHWARTZ, Zur Geschichte des Athanasius: NGWG Philol.-hist. Klasse (1904) 333-356. — F. LOOFS, Die chronologischen Angaben des sogenannten 'Vorberichts' zu den Festbriefen des Athanasius: SAB (1908) 1013-1022. — E. SCHWARTZ, Zur Kirchengeschichte des vierten Jahrhunderts: ZNW 34 (1935) 129-137. — L. TH. LEFORT, Les lettres Festales de S. Athanase: Bulletin de la Classe des Lettres de l'Académie Royale de Belgique 39 (1953) 643-656, 41 (1955) 183-185; *idem,* À propos des Festales de saint Athanase: Mus 67 (1954) 43-50.

Other Studies: P. PEETERS, L'épilogue du synode de Tyr en 335 (dans les Lettres Festales d'Athanase): AB (1945) 131-144. — L. TH. LEFORT, La chasse aux reliques des martyrs en Égypte au IVe siècle: La Nouvelle Clio 6 (1954) 225-230, deals with Festal Letters of the years 369 and 370.

None of these Festal Letters has attracted more attention in ancient and modern times than the 39th for the year 367. This condemns the attempt of the heretics to introduce apocryphal works as divinely inspired Scripture and enumerates the books of the Old and New Testament included in the Canon, and handed down and accepted by the Church. Its text has been almost completely restored from Greek, Syriac and Coptic fragments. The twenty-seven books of our present New Testament are here for the first time declared to be alone canonical. According to Athanasius the deutero-canonical books of the Old Testament do not belong to the Canon: 'There are other books besides these not indeed included in the Canon, but appointed by the Fathers to be read by those who newly join us, and who wish for instruction in the word of godliness: the Wisdom of Solomon, and the Wisdom of Sirach, and Esther, and Judith, and Tobias, and that which is called the Teaching of the Twelve Apostles, and the Shepherd' (7 LNPF). Thus they are classed together with the Didache and the Shepherd of Hermas as of a secondary rank serving only for the edification of neophytes. This Athanasian list is in content and sequence of the biblical books identical with the Canon of the most valuable of all the manuscripts of the Greek Bible, the *Codex Vaticanus* of the beginning of the fourth century. In both the books of the Maccabees are omitted. This explains to a certain extent why they are also absent from the Ethiopic version of the Bible. It is possible that *Codex Vaticanus* represents the copy which was prepared for the Emperor Constans by Alexandrian scribes in 340 at Rome while Athanasius lived there.

Editions: Greek fragment: MG 26, 1435-1440 with a Latin translation from the Syriac. — TH. ZAHN, Geschichte des neutestamentlichen Kanons 2. Erlangen, 1892, 203-212; *idem,* Grundriss der Geschichte des neutestamentlichen Kanons, 2nd ed. Leipzig, 1904,

Beilage 6. — E. Preuschen, Analecta. Kürzere Texte zur Geschichte der alten Kirche und des Kanons. II Zur Kanongeschichte. 2nd ed. Tübingen, 1910, 42-45. Preuschen gives in addition on p. 45-52 a German translation of the Coptic fragments of this letter edited by C. Schmidt, Der Osterfestbrief des Athanasius vom Jahre 367: NGWG Philol.-hist. Klasse (1898) 167-203; *idem*, Ein neues Fragment des Osterfestbriefes des Athanasius vom Jahre 367: NGWG Philol.-hist. Klasse (1901) 326-349. See the new edition of the Coptic text by L. Th. Lefort, S. Athanase. Lettres Festales et Pastorales en copte (CSCO 150). Louvain, 1955, 58-62. Lefort gives the text of the Greek fragment CSCO 151 (1955) 34-35.

Modern Translations: English from the Syriac: H. Burgess, LNPF second series, n. 4 (1891) 551-552. — *German from the Syriac:* F. Larsow, l.c. — *French from the Coptic:* L. Th. Lefort, CSCO 151 (1955) 31-40. — *German from the Coptic:* Preuschen, l.c.

Studies: Th. Zahn, Athanasius und der Bibelkanon: Festschrift der Universität Erlangen. Erlangen, 1901, 1-36. — G. Mercati, Il canone biblico athanasiano con sticometrie interpolate: ST 95 (1941) 78-80. — J. Ruwet, Le canon alexandrin des Écritures. S. Athanase: Bibl 33 (1952) 1-29.

2. Three Synodal Letters

a. Tome to the People of Antioch

The *Tomus ad Antiochenos* was written in the name of the Alexandrian synod of 362. It deals with the state of the Church at Antioch and recommends the best course to be taken in order to reestablish peace and concord. The terms on which communion should be granted to those Arians willing to reunite are laid down. Except for an express anathema against the doctrine of Arius, they were to be asked for nothing beyond the Nicene Creed. The integrity of Christ's human nature and its perfect union with the Word are defended against the Arian Christology. Since this involved an important question of theological terminology, the use of the word *hypostasis* is discussed and the two different meanings *Subsistence* or *Person* are recognized. The two parties were admonished not to press the question of one or three *hypostases*, since disputes merely about words must not be suffered to divide those who think alike.

Edition: MG 26, 795-810.

Translations: English: W. Bright, Later Treatises of St. Athanasius (LFC 46). Oxford, 1881. — A. Robertson, LNPF, second series 4, 483-486.

Studies: H. Lietzmann, Apollinaris von Laodicea und seine Schule. Tübingen, 1904, 6-7. — A. Grillmeier, CGG I (1951) 91-99: Die Stellung des Tomus von Alexandrien 362 in der Christologie des hl. Athanasios.

b. Letter to the Emperor Jovian concerning the Faith

The *Epistula ad Jovianum imperatorem* gives an exposition of the true faith for which the emperor had asked. Athanasius composed it by order of the great Alexandrian synod of 363.

Edition: MG 26, 813-820. Best edition: Theodoret, *Hist. eccl.* 4, 3 (L. PARMENTIER, GCS 19 (1911) 212-216).

Translation: English: A. ROBERTSON, LNPF, second series 4, 567-568.

c. Letter to the African Bishops

The *Epistula ad Afros episcopos*, written in the name of ninety bishops of Egypt and Libya assembled at an Alexandrian synod in 369, warns the hierarchy of Western Africa against the Arian efforts to represent the synod of Ariminum as a final settlement of the faith at the expense of the definitions of the Council of Nicaea. For this purpose the latter is contrasted with the local synods held since. The Nicene formula is proved to be in accordance with Scripture and the reasons for the adoption of the word *homoousios* are given. The Arian position that the Son is a creature is shown to be inconsistent and untenable and the Son's relation to the Father to be essential, not merely moral. The letter insists that the Nicene Creed implies the Godhead of the Holy Spirit. The conclusion issues a warning against Auxentius, the Arian bishop of Milan.

Editions: MG 26, 1029-1048. Theodoret, *Hist. eccl.* 1, 8, 7-16 quotes *Epist. ad Afros* 5-6 (J. PARMENTIER, GCS 19, 35, 8-37, 14) and *Hist. eccl.* 2, 23, 1-9 cites *Ep. ad Afros* 3-4 (GCS 19, 150, 11-152, 17). A Syriac version found in Cod. Mus. Brit. Or. 8606f. 43a-50a has not been published yet.

Translations: English: W. BRIGHT, LFC 46. Oxford, 1881. — A. ROBERTSON, LNPF, second series 4, 488-494.

Studies: H. G. OPITZ, Untersuchungen 154, 174. — For the old Latin translation of the *Ep. ad Afros* in Cod. Berol. Phill. Lat. 1671 s. IX, see: B. ALTANER, Altlateinische Übersetzungen von Schriften des Athanasios von Alexandrien: BZ 41 (1941) 50f. — A. SIEGMUND, Die Überlieferung der griechischen christlichen Literatur in der lateinischen Kirche. Munich, 1949, 49-50.

3. Two Encyclical Letters

a. Encyclical Epistle to the Bishops throughout the World

The *Epistula ad episcopos encyclica*, written about the middle of 339 is an urgent appeal to all the bishops of the Catholic Church to regard Athanasius' cause as their own and to unite against Gregory, the Arian bishop who has intruded on the Church of Alexandria. The outrages which took place at the time of Gregory's arrival on April 15, 339 and the acts of violence of the governor, who seized the churches and gave them to the Arians, are given in detail. The letter represents the oldest polemical treatise of Athanasius.

Editions: MG 25, 221-240. Best ed.: OPITZ, Athanasius' Werke II, 1, 169-177.

Translations: English: Oxford translation by M. ATKINSON, LFC 13 (1843) 1-121, with notes of J. H. Newman, reprinted and revised by A. ROBERTSON, LNPF, second series 4, 91-96.

Studies: H. G. OPITZ, Untersuchungen 132-135.

b. Circular to the Bishops of Egypt

The *Epistula encyclica ad episcopos Aegypti et Libyae* was written after Athanasius' expulsion from Alexandria on February 9, 356 and before the arrival of George, the new Arian bishop, on February 24, 357. Its primary purpose is to warn the hierarchy against the attempt of the heretics to substitute another Creed for the Nicene. For this reason the second part confronts the false teaching with passages from Scripture. At the end a description of the death of Arius is given and the strange coalition 'of sordid Meletians with insane Arians' denounced.

Edition: MG 25, 537-594.

Translations: English: M. ATKINSON, LFC 13. Oxford, 1843, 125-153, revised by A. ROBERTSON, LNPF, second series 4, 222-235. — *German:* J. FISCH, BKV Athanasius II (1875) 1-43.

Studies: H. G. OPITZ, Untersuchungen 109-132. — J. LEBON, S. Athanase a-t-il employé l'expression ὁ κυριακὸς ἄνθρωπος?: RHE 31 (1935) 303-329, proves that St. Jerome borrowed the term 'dominicus homo' from this letter.

4. Dogmatic-Polemical Letters

a. The Letters concerning the Holy Spirit

The *Epistulae IV ad Serapionem episcopum Thmuitanum* were written in 359 or early in 360 when Athanasius had taken refuge with the monks in the desert of Egypt. They form a homogeneous work not only because they are addressed to the same person but because all of them deal with the same subject, the doctrine of the Holy Spirit. The question of his divinity was intimately connected with the question of the divinity of the Son and the Arian controversy, although the issue was not debated in the earlier stages. Serapion had written to Athanasius regarding 'certain persons, having forsaken the Arians on account of their blasphemy against the Son of God, yet oppose the Holy Spirit, saying that He is not only a creature, but actually one of the ministering spirits, and differs from the angels only in degree' (1,1). The first of Athanasius' letters refutes these new heretics. He calls them tropicists (τροπικοί), because they explained in a tropical, i.e. metaphorical sense, the passages from Scripture opposed to their doctrine. The letter reveals his profound and vigorous grasp of his subject by his insistence that our knowledge of the Spirit must be derived from our knowledge of the Son. It is the theology of the New Testament when he stresses that the Holy Spirit is the Spirit of the Son, not only inasmuch as the Son gives and sends Him, but because He is the principle of Christ's life within us. The second and the third letters are written in answer to a further request from Serapion for an abridgement of the elaborate contents of the first. Since Athanasius promises such a summary at the beginning of the second but gives first an account of the Son and fulfils his promise only at the beginning of the third, it is evident that originally the letters II and III were one. The very abrupt ending of II and the lack of a doxology lead to the same conclusion. The last letter deals with an argument of the tropicists which Athanasius had outlined and answered in the first (I,15-21) but omitted in the third: 'If the Spirit is not a creature, so they objected, nor one of the angels, but proceeds from the Father, then He is Himself also a son, and He and the Word are two brothers; and if He is a brother, how is the Word only-begotten? How is it then that They are not equal, but the one is named after the Father, and the other after the Son? How, if He is from the Father, is He not also said to be begotten or called son, but just Holy Spirit? But if the Spirit is of the Son, then the Father is the Spirit's grandfather' (I,15 Shapland 95-98).

Athanasius refutes this idea in letter IV, 1-7 in a way which makes this more than a summary of the corresponding passage in the first letter. It is a new and independent treatise, ending in the doxology of IV 7, and having no connection with what immediately follows, IV 8-23, an explanation of Matthew 12,32. It is, consequently, a separate work or perhaps the rest of another letter addressed to Serapion. The content suggests that it belongs to an earlier period of Athanasius' life.

Edition: MG 26, 529-676.

Translations: English: C. R. B. SHAPLAND, The Letters of Saint Athanasius concerning the Holy Spirit. London - New York, 1951. — *French:* J. LEBON, Lettres à Sérapion sur la divinité du Saint Esprit (SCH 15). Paris, 1947. — *German:* J. LIPPL, Vier Briefe an Serapion. BKV² 13 (1913) 400-497.

Studies: G. CRONE, Athanasius, Briefe an Serapion, erläutert. Steyl, 1939. — C. R. B. SHAPLAND, l.c. 11-49. — J. LEBON, l.c. 7-77. — H. R. SMYTHE, The Interpretation of Amos 4, 13 in St. Athanasius and Didymus: JThSt 1 (1950) 158-168 concerning *Ep.* I, 3.

In addition to the Letters concerning the Holy Spirit two other extant communications are addressed to Serapion. One, rather brief, from the year 339, was united with the collection of Festal Letters; the other, written between the years 356-358, gives an account of the death of Arius.

Editions: The first letter: MG 26, 1412-1414. The second concerning the death of Arius: MG 25, 685-690. New critical ed.: H. G. Opitz, Athanasius' Werke II, 1, 178-180.

Translations: English: M. Atkinson, LFC 13. Oxford, 1843, 210-214: concerning the death of Arius; reprinted and revised by A. Robertson, LNPF, second series 4, 564-566.

b. Letter to Epictetus

The *Epistula ad Epictetum episcopum Corinthi* deals with the relation of the historical Christ to the eternal Son. The bishop of Corinth had submitted a memorandum to Athanasius regarding certain questions raised in his diocese. Their nature can be deduced from Athanasius' answer:

What lower region has vomited the statement that the Body born of Mary is coessential with the Godhead of the Word? or that the Word has been changed into flesh, bones, hair, and the whole body, and altered from its own nature? Or who ever heard in a Church, or even from Christians, that the Lord wore a body putatively, not in nature; or who ever went so far in impiety as to say and hold, that this Godhead, which is coessential with the Father, was circumcised and became imperfect instead of perfect; and that what hung upon the tree was not the body, but the very creative Essence and Wisdom? Or who that hears that the Word transformed for Himself a passible body, not of Mary, but of His own Essence, could call him who said this a Christian? Or who devised this abominable impiety, for it to enter even his imagination, and for him to say that to pronounce the Lord's Body to be of Mary is to hold a Tetrad instead of a Triad in the Godhead? — those who think thus, saying that the Body of the Saviour which He put on from Mary, is of the Essence of the Triad. Or whence again have certain vomited an impiety as great as those already mentioned, saying namely, that the body is not newer than the Godhead of the Word, but was coeternal with it always, since it was compounded of the Essence of Wisdom? Or how did men called Christians venture even to doubt whether the Lord, Who proceeded from Mary, while Son of God by Essence and Nature, is of the seed of David according to the flesh, and of the flesh of Saint Mary? (9 LNPF)

All these questions suggest that the difficulties came from Arian and Apollinaristic groups that shared Docetic views. The *Letter to Epictetus* gained almost canonical reputation and was much quoted in the Christological controversies. Epiphanius (*Haer.* 77,3-13) made use of it in his refutation of the heresy of Apollinaris of Laodicea. The Council of Chalcedon adopted it as the best expression of its own conviction (Mansi, *Conc.* 7,464). When the Nestorians tried to falsify the text for their own purpose, Cyril of Alexandria (*Ep.* 40) unmasked the corruptions.

Two different Armenian versions of this letter exist. The one was published by Tajezi (*S. Athanasii Sermones*, Venice 1899, 324-

343) and is quoted in full in *The Seal of the Faith*, a seventh century dogmatic *catena*, edited by Karapet Ter-Mekerttschian, Etchmiadzin, 1914 (cf. J. Lebon, *Les citations patristiques grecques du 'Sceau de la Foi'*: RHE 25 (1929) 8). The other, published by R. P. Casey, is found in two manuscripts of the Mechitarists at Vienna and belongs to an Armenian corpus of Athanasian writings compiled early in the eighth century. We have besides a Syriac translation which already shows the corruptions of the Apollinarists, as J. Lebon has proved in his edition.

Editions: MG 26, 1049-1070. Separate ed. by G. LUDWIG, Ep. ad Epictetum. Jena, 1911. Two Latin versions are extant, one of them in the Acts of the Council of Ephesus. E. SCHWARTZ, Acta Conciliorum Oecumenicorum I 5, 2, 321ff., gives the text of both. — Syriac version based on the only manuscript Cod. Mus. Brit. add. 14557 s. VII by P. BEDJAN, Nestorius, Le livre d'Héraclide de Damas, Paris, 1910, 577ff.; J. LEBON, Severi Antiocheni liber contra impium Grammaticum (CSCO 102) 300, 10ff. text, (CSCO 101) 211, 2ff. version. — Armenian version: R. P. CASEY, An Armenian Version of Athanasius's Letter to Epictetus: HThR 26 (1933) 127-150.

Translations: English: A. ROBERTSON, LNPF second series 4, 570-574. — *German:* J. LIPPL, BKV² 13 (1913) 504-517.

Studies: H. G. OPITZ, Untersuchungen 173f. — A. SIEGMUND, Die Überlieferung der griechischen christlichen Literatur in der lateinischen Kirche. Munich, 1949, 49f. — J. LEBON, Altération doctrinale de la Lettre à Épictète de saint Athanase: RHE 31 (1935) 713-761.

c. Letter to Adelphius

The *Epistula ad Adelphium episcopum et confessorem* was written in 370 or 371 in answer to a report which Adelphius had sent to Athanasius about the Arian charge of creature-worship brought against the Christology of Nicaea. Athanasius traces their error back to the Valentinians, Marcionists and Manichaeans, and points out that Catholics do not worship the human nature of Christ as such, but the Word Incarnate:

> We do not worship a creature. Far be the thought. For such an error belongs to heathens and Arians. But we worship the Lord of creation, Incarnate, the Word of God. For if the flesh also is in itself a part of the created world, yet it has become God's body. And we neither divide the body, being such, from the Word, and worship it by itself, nor when we wish to worship the Word do we set Him far apart from the flesh, but knowing, as we said above, that 'the Word was made flesh', we recognize Him as God also, after having come in the flesh (3 LNPF).

Edition: MG 26, 1071-1084.

Translation: English: A. ROBERTSON, LNPF second series 4, 575-578.

Studies: H. G. OPITZ, Untersuchungen 136-139. For the Syriac version, see: H. G. OPITZ,

Das syrische Corpus Athanasianum: ZNW 33 (1934) 18-31. R. P. Casey, A Syriac Corpus of Athanasian Writings: JThSt 35 (1934) 66-67. This Syriac text is preserved in two manuscripts: Cod. Mus. Brit. add. 14531 (Wright n. 769 p. 739) s. VII/VIII f. 102b-108b and in Cod. Mus. Brit. Or. 8606a. 723 f. 6b-10b. — For the Armenian version, cf. R. P. Casey, Armenian Manuscripts of St. Athanasius of Alexandria: HThR 24 (1931) 45 n. 6.

d. Letter to the Philosopher Maximus

The *Epistula ad Maximum philosophum* congratulates the addressee on his successful refutation of heretics who shared the Arian views that Christ was only the adopted Son of God while others advocated the doctrine of Paul of Samosata that Christ's humanity was distinct in person from God the Word. Athanasius is convinced that what was confessed by the Fathers at Nicaea will finally prevail: 'For it is correct, and enough to overthrow every heresy however impious, and especially that of the Arians, which speaks against the Word of God, and as a logical consequence profanes His Holy Spirit' (5 LNPF).

Edition: MG 26, 1085-1090.

Translation: English: A. Robertson, LNPF second series 4, 578-579.

e. Letter concerning the Decrees of the Council of Nicaea

The *Epistula de decretis Nicaenae synodi* is a defense of the Nicene definition, especially the non-scriptural terms ἐκ τῆς οὐσίας and ὁμοούσιος, to which the Arians objected. Addressed to a friend to whom the Arian claim had caused confusion, it was written about 350/351. Athanasius shows that these expressions do not differ in sense from what is to be found in Scripture and that they had already been in ecclesiastical use as far back as Origen, Dionysius of Rome, Dionysius of Alexandria and Theognostus. Passages from all these writers are quoted. The letter is of special interest for its description of the proceedings at Nicaea. In order to show that the Eusebians then signed what they now complain of, Athanasius appends the letter of Eusebius of Caesarea to his flock, the only surviving account that dates from the actual year of the Council. It is of special importance because it contains the rule of faith presented to the Council by Eusebius himself and the revised form of it which was finally adopted (cf. below, p. 344). There are reasons to believe that originally a number of other Nicene documents followed. On the other hand, the *Epistula de sententia Dionysii episcopi Alexandrini* seems to be a later addition. Athanasius' quotation from Dionysius in support of the Nicene term *homoousios* had challenged the Arians, who claimed Dionysius for their side. The present letter refutes the heretical party's interpretation of certain passages in Dionysius as favorable to themselves. Athanasius proves all these citations orthodox although they are only an incomplete presentation of his belief.

Editions: MG 25, 415-476. New crit. ed.: H. G. OPITZ, Athanasius' Werke II, 1, 1-45. Separate ed.: H. G. OPITZ, Athanasius, Über die Entscheidungen des Konzils von Nicäa (*De decretis Nicaenae synodi*). Sonderdruck für Seminarübungen. Berlin and Leipzig, 1935.

Translations: English: J. H. NEWMAN, Select Treatises of St. Athanasius in Controversy with the Arians, vol. I. 4th ed. London, 1887. 11th impression, London and New York, 1920, 11-59. Reprinted, slightly revised by A. ROBERTSON, LNPF ser. 2, vol. 4, 150-172, 73-76.

Studies: H. G. OPITZ, Untersuchungen 102-104. — A. D'ALÈS, Pour le texte de Saint Athanase (*De decretis* 27): RSR (1924) 61. — P. BATIFFOL, Les sources de l'histoire du Concile de Nicée: EO 28 (1925) 385-402; 30 (1927) 5-17. — H. CHADWICK, Athanasius, De decretis 40, 3: JThSt 49 (1948) 168-169. — J. N. D. KELLY, Early Christian Creeds. London, 1950, 211-230.

Editions of the Epistula de sententia Dionysii: MG 25, 479-522. — New crit. ed.: H. G. OPITZ, Athanasius' Werke II, 1, 46-47.

Translation: English: A. ROBERTSON, LNPF ser. 2, vol. 4, 173-187.

Study: H. G. OPITZ, Dionys von Alexandrien und die Libyer: Studies presented to K. Lake, ed. by R. P. Casey. London, 1937, 41-53.

f. Letter concerning the Synods of Ariminum and Seleucia

The *Epistula de synodis Arimini in Italia et Seleuciae in Isauria celebratis* was written in the autumn of 359, the year of the twin synods of Ariminum and Seleucia. It is an extensive report going far beyond the ordinary size of a letter. The first part (1-14) deals with the history of the two synods. Athanasius shows that there was no reason for any new council, since the decisions of Nicaea made it unnecessary. The heretics are still the same. There follow the proceedings at Ariminum, the letter of the synod to the Emperor Constantius, and its decree, the proceedings of Seleucia, the deposition of Acacius, the report to the emperor and reflections on the conduct of the Arians. The second part (15-32) gives a history of Arian creeds beginning with the belief of Arius as expressed in his *Thalia* (cf. above, p. 11) and his letter to Alexander of Alexandria. The third part (33-40) contains a refutation of the Homoeans and an appeal to the Semi-Arians, showing that the terms objected to are misunderstood. To clear the way for a reunion with the Homoeousians like Basil of Ancyra (cf. below, p. 201) and others, he exhorts them to look at the sense, not at the wording. Although there are weighty reasons why the term *coessential* (ὁμοούσιος) is better than *like in essence*, (ὁμοιούσιος), he admits that the latter is capable of a correct interpretation. After Athanasius had written his account of the two synods he received information that the Emperor Constantius had sent a letter to the synod of Ariminum. He added a copy of it together with the reply of the bishops in a postscript, which forms the last chapter (55). It appears that chapters 30-31 in the second part are also a later insertion.

Editions: MG 26, 681-794. New crit. ed.: H. G. OPITZ, Athanasius' Werke II, 1, 231-278. Opitz rejects the idea of later insertions and thinks that *De synodis* was composed after the death of Constantius and perhaps before the return of Athanasius (February 21, 362).

Translations: English: J. H. NEWMAN, Select Treatises of St. Athanasius. 4th ed., 11th impression. London and New York, 1920, 63-152. — J. H. NEWMAN, LNPF ser. 2, vol. 4, 448-480, revised by A. Robertson.

Studies: J. GUMMERUS, Die homöusianische Partei bis zum Tode des Konstantius. Leipzig, 1900. — H. G. OPITZ, Untersuchungen 98-101. — J. N. D. KELLY, Early Christian Creeds. London, 1950, 288-291.

g. Letter to Rufianus

The *Epistula ad Rufianum episcopum*, written after 362, deals with the reception of Arians who return to the Church. Rufianus had asked for advice in this difficult question. Athanasius refers to the decisions of the councils in this matter: 'The same decision was come to here and everywhere, namely, in the case of those who had fallen and been leaders of impiety, to pardon them upon their repentance, but not to give them the position of clergy; but in the case of men not deliberate in impiety, but drawn away by necessity and violence, that they should not only receive pardon, but should occupy the position of clergy' (LNPF). The letter gained such reputation that it was incorporated in the canonical collection of the Greek Church.

Editions: MG 26, 1179-1182. — J. B. F. PITRA, Juris ecclesiae Graecorum historia et monumenta I. Rome, 1864, 572-575.

Translation: English: A. ROBERTSON, LNPF ser. 2, vol. 4, 566-567.

h. Letter to the Monks

In his *Epistula ad monachos* Athanasius sees himself compelled to write to the solitaries 'because there are certain persons who hold with Arius and go about the monasteries with no other object save that under color of visiting you and returning from us they may deceive the simple'. He asks his readers not to give occasion of scandal to the brethren and to shun those who entertain Arian views as well as those who, while they pretend not to hold with Arius, yet worship with the heretics. A Latin version of this letter is preserved in *Codex Vatic. lat. 133* saec. IX/X. However, this translation, slavish in other respects, contains interpolations that show the influence of Lucifer of Calaris' *De non conveniendo cum haereticis*.

Editions: MG 26, 1185-1188. — Old Latin version: G. HARTEL, CSEL 14 (1886) 332-333. Best ed.: L. SALTET, Fraudes littéraires des schismatiques Lucifériens aux IVe et Ve siècles: Bulletin de littérature ecclés. (1906) 306-307.

Translation: English: A. ROBERTSON, LNPF ser. 2, vol. 4, 564.

Studies: L. SALTET, l.c. 300-326. — G. DE JERPHANION, La vraie teneur d'un texte de S. Athanase rétablie par l'épigraphie: RSR 20 (1930) 529-544; *idem,* La voix des monuments. Paris, 1938, 95-110, proves with the use of fragments of an inscription found by American excavators in Upper Egypt and published in 'The Monastery of Epiphanius' (New York, The Metropolitan Museum of Art, 1927) that the Old Latin version seems to be more reliable than has been thought. The inscription has preserved a part of the *Epistula ad monachos* in its Greek original.

5. Ascetical Letters

a. Letter to Amun

The *Epistula ad Amunem monachum* was written before 356 in order to calm the overscrupulous conscience of certain monks, who were worried about involuntary thoughts and nocturnal pollutions. 'If we believe man to be, as the divine Scriptures say, a work of God's hands, how could any defiled work proceed from a pure Power, and if, according to the divine Acts of the Apostles (17, 28), "we are God's offspring", we have nothing unclean in ourselves. For then only do we incur defilement, when we commit sin, that foulest of things. But when any bodily excretion takes place independently of will, then we experience this, like other things, by a necessity of nature'. The letter treats then of the 'two ways of life', the one, the moderate and ordinary, marriage; the other, angelic and unsurpassed, namely virginity.

Edition: MG 26, 1169-1176.

Translation: English: A. ROBERTSON, LNPF ser. 2, vol. 4, 556-557.

b. Letter to Dracontius

The *Epistula ad Dracontium* was written in 354 or 355 to urge an abbot not to refuse the episcopate. Athanasius refers to the surprising unanimity of his election and to the danger that unfit persons will grasp at the office if Dracontius did not accept. 'If the organizing of the churches is distasteful to you, and you do not think the ministry of the episcopate has its reward—why!—then you have brought yourself to despise the Saviour that ordered these things... For if all were of the same mind as your present advisers, how would you have become a Christian, since there would be no bishops?' (3-4 LNPF). In order to show that Dracontius is not the only one who has been elected from among the monks, he mentions a number of monastic superiors who became bishops. It seems that the letter was successful because Dracontius participated in the synod of Alexandria in 362 as bishop of Hermupolis Parva.

Edition: MG 25, 523-534.

Translation: English: A. ROBERTSON, LNPF ser. 2, vol. 4, 557-560.

6. *Dubious Letters*

Scipio Maffei published in 1738 from a Latin manuscript in the Chapter Library of Verona two letters which Hefele regards as of doubtful genuineness, whereas Schwartz and others think Athanasius their real author. Both were written by him while he attended the synod of Serdica in 343. The one is addressed 'to the presbyters and deacons and the people of the Catholic Church in the Mareotis', the other 'to all the presbyters and deacons of the holy Catholic Church at Alexandria and the Parembola'. The first contains a long list of signatures. Both of them inform the Churches of the praise bestowed by the council on their courageous stand against the Arians and of the excommunication of the leaders of the heresy, Theodore, Valens, Ursacius and others. The Latin is poor and seems to be a translation from Greek.

Editions: ML 56, 850-854. Best ed.: C. H. TURNER, Ecclesiae occidentalis monumenta iuris antiquissima. Oxford, 1899-1939, 1, 2, 654-662.

Studies: C. J. HEFELE - H. LECLERCQ, Histoire des conciles I, 2. Paris, 1907, 811-812. — E. SCHWARTZ, Zur Geschichte des Athanasius: NGWG Phil.-hist. Kl. 5 (1904) 381. — J. ZEILLER, Les origines chrétiennes dans les provinces danubiennes de l'Empire romain, Paris, 1918, 242-243, defends their authenticity.

Two other letters attributed to Athanasius are preserved in Latin only. They are addressed to bishop Lucifer of Calaris (Cagliari) in Sardinia. The first asks him for a copy of his letters to the Emperor Constantius and the second thanks him for sending these. Both are highly complimentary on the firmness of his faith and the courage of his defense of the Church against the Arians. Saltet, however, has proved both of these communications to be forgeries by a Luciferian.

Editions: MG 26, 1181-1186, ML 13, 1037-1042. — G. HARTEL, CSEL 14 (1886) 322-327. — Best ed.: L. SALTET, Fraudes littéraires des schismatiques Lucifériens aux IVe et Ve siècles: Bulletin de littérature ecclés., sér. 3, 8 (1906) 303-306.

Studies: L. SALTET, l.c. 300-326. — G. BARDY, Faux et fraudes littéraires dans l'antiquité chrétienne: RHE 32 (1936) 15-16.

H. I. Bell published from the Coptic a letter pretending to be from Athanasius to Paphnutius, but it does not seem genuine.

Edition: H. I. BELL, Jews and Christians in Egypt. Oxford, 1924, 118.

Translations: English: H. I. BELL, op-cit. 119. — A. DEISSMANN, Athanasiana: ExpT 36 (1924/25) 8-11.

II. THE THEOLOGY OF ATHANASIUS

Athanasius was not a scientific theologian. He contributed almost nothing speculative, nor did he develop any system nor invent new terminology. Yet the history of dogma in the fourth century is identical with the history of his life. His greatest merit remains his defense of traditional Christianity against the danger of Hellenization hidden in the heresy of Arius and his followers. A true disciple of Origen, he uses forms and concepts of Greek thought but fills them with a content taken from revelation. All his efforts purpose to substantiate 'the very tradition, teaching, and faith of the Catholic Church from the beginning, which the Lord gave, the Apostles preached, and the Fathers kept' (*Ep. ad Serap.* 1, 28). Against the rationalistic tendencies of his opponents he establishes the priority of faith over reason. The latter cannot be the judge in metaphysical matters. By reason man is unable to investigate his own nature and things on earth, not to speak of the divine and ineffable nature (*In illud* 6).

If Athanasius makes use of philosophy, he does it in order to unfold and clarify the doctrine of the Church, not to penetrate the divine essence with the human mind. He is by nature and talent a controversialist, less concerned about formulas than about ideas. As such he possesses a mind more accurate than broad; but, armed with an inflexible logic, he knows how to separate Greek thought and Christian revelation whenever there is danger that the truth of the Gospel might be darkened or falsified.

Thus he defended not only the consubstantiality of the Son with the Father but he explained the nature and generation of the Logos more successfully than any of the earlier theologians. He laid in fact the foundations of theological development for centuries to come. His teaching furnished the basic ideas for the trinitarian and christological doctrine of the Church.

1. *Trinity*

In his *first Letter to Serapion* Athanasius states:

There is then a Triad, holy and complete, confessed to be God in Father, Son and Holy Spirit, having nothing foreign or external mixed with it, not composed of one that creates and one that is originated, but all creative; and it is consistent and in nature indivisible, and its activity is one. The Father does all things through the Word in the Holy Spirit. Thus the unity of the holy Triad is preserved. Thus one God is preached in the Church, 'who is over all (Ephes. 4, 6), and through all, and in all' — 'over all' as Father, as beginning, as fountain; 'through all', through the Word; 'in all', in the Holy Spirit. It is a Triad not only in name and form of speech, but in truth and actuality. For as the Father is He that is, so also His Word is one that is and God over all. And the Holy Spirit is not without actual existence, but exists and has true being. Less than these [Persons] the Catholic Church does not hold, lest she sink to the level of the modern Jews, imitators of Caiphas, and to the level of Sabellius. Nor does she add to them by speculation, lest she be carried into the polytheism of the heathen (Shapland p. 134-136).

The words 'not composed of one that creates and one that is originated, but all creative' make it quite clear that Athanasius does not share the belief that God needed the Logos as a medium for the creation of the world, as Arius thought following the ideas of Philo and Origen. He refutes the Arian doctrine that God, willing to create nature, saw that it could not endure the untempered hand of the Father, but made and created first the Son and Word, that through Him as a medium, all things might thereupon be brought to be:

If they shall assign the toil of making all things as the reason why God made the Son only, the whole creation will cry out against them as saying unworthy things of God; and Isaias too who said in Scripture, 'The Everlasting God, the Lord, the Creator of the ends of the earth, fainteth not, neither is weary: there is no searching of his understanding' (Is. 40, 28). And if God made the Son alone, as not deigning to make the rest, but committed them to the Son as an assistant, this on the other hand is unworthy of God, for in Him there is no pride. Nay the Lord reproves the thought, when He says: 'Are not two sparrows sold for a farthing?' and 'one of them shall not fall on the ground without your Father that is in heaven' (Matth. 10, 29)... If then it be not unworthy of God to exercise His Providence, even down to things so small, a hair of the head, and a sparrow, and the grass of the field, also it was not unworthy of Him to make them. For what things are the subjects of His Providence, of those He is Maker through His proper Word. Nay a worse absurdity lies before the men who thus speak; for they distinguish between the creatures and the framing; and consider the latter the work of the Father, the creatures the work of the Son; whereas either all things must be brought to be by the Father with the Son, or if all that is originate comes to be brought through the Son, we must not call Him one of the originated things (*Or. Arian.* 2, 25 LNPF).

Thus Arius placed the Logos on the side of the creatures, Athanasius placed him on the side of God. The Word is not created, He is begotten. Arius asserted that the Son is a creature of the Father, a work of the will of the Father. Athanasius refuted this claim pointing to the fact that the very name 'Son' presupposes His being generated; but to be begotten means to be an offspring of the Father's essence, not of His will. Generation belongs to nature, not to will. For this reason the Son cannot be called a creature of the Father. He has in common with the Father the fulness of the Father's Godhead and the Son is entirely God (*ibid.* 1, 16; 3, 6). Athanasius recalls repeatedly the comparison of the light issuing from the sun, so familiar to the School of Alexandria, in order to demonstrate that begetting in God differs from human begetting because God is indivisible:

> Since He is God's Word and own Wisdom, and, being His Radiance, is ever with the Father, therefore it is impossible, if the Father bestows grace, that He should not give it in the Son, for the Son is in the Father as the radiance in the light. For, not as if in need, but as a Father in His own Wisdom hath God founded the earth, and made all things in the Word which is from Him, and in the Son confirms the Holy Laver. For where the Father is, there is the Son, and where the light, there the radiance; and as what the Father worketh, He worketh through the Son and the Lord Himself says, 'What I see the Father do, that do I also'; so also when baptism is given, whom the Father baptizes, him the Son baptizes, and whom the Son baptizes, he is consecrated in the Holy Spirit. And again as when the sun shines, one might say that the radiance illuminates, for the light is one and indivisible, nor can it be detached, so where the Father is or is named, there plainly is the Son; and is the Father named in baptism, then must be the Son named with Him (*ibid.* 2, 41 LNPF).
>
> For the Son is in the Father, as it is allowed us to know, because the whole Being of the Son is proper to the Father's essence, as radiance from light, and stream from fountain; so that whoso sees the Son, sees what is proper to the Father, and knows that the Son's Being, because from the Father, is therefore in the Father. For the Father is in the Son, since the Son is what is from the Father and proper to Him, as in the radiance the sun, and in the word the thought, and in the stream the fountain: for whoso thus contemplates the Son, contemplates what is proper to the Father's essence, and knows that the Father is in the Son (*ibid.* 3, 3).

For this reason the Son is eternal like the Father. Father and Son are two, but the same (*ταὐτόν*), because they have the same nature (*φύσις*):

> For they are one, not as one thing divided into two parts, and these nothing but one, nor as one thing twice named, so that the Same becomes at one time Father, at another His own Son, for this Sabellius holding was judged an heretic. But they are two, because the Father

is Father and is not also Son, and the Son is Son and not also Father; but the nature (physis) is one; (for the offspring is not unlike its parent, for it is his image), and all that is the Father's is the Son's. Wherefore neither is the Son another God, for He was not procured from without, else were there many, if a godhead be procured foreign from the Father's; for if the Son be other as an Offspring, still He is the Same as God; and He and the Father are one in propriety and peculiarity of nature, and in the identity of the one Godhead, as has been said. For the radiance also is light, not second to the sun, nor a different light, nor from participation of it, but a whole and proper offspring of it. And such an offspring is necessarily one light; and no one would say that they are two lights, but sun and radiance two, yet one, the light from the sun enlightening in its radiance all things. So also the Godhead of the Son is the Father's; whence also it is indivisible; and thus there is one God and none other but He. And so, since they are one and the Godhead itself one, the same things are said of the Son, which are said of the Father, except His being said to be the Father (*ibid.* 3, 4 LNPF).

Moreover, there can be only one Son, since, taken by Himself, He suffices to exhaust the Father's fecundity:

The offspring of men are portions of their fathers, since the very nature of bodies is not uncompounded, but in a state of flux, and composed of parts; and men lose their substance in begetting, and again they gain substance from the accession of food. And on this account men in their time become fathers of many children; but God, being without parts, is Father of the Son without partition or passion; for there is neither effluence of the Immaterial, nor influx from without, as among men; and being uncompounded in nature, He is Father of One Only Son. This is why He is Only-begotten, and alone in the Father's bosom, and alone is acknowledged by the Father to be from Him, saying, 'This is My beloved Son, in Whom I am well pleased' (Matth. 3, 17). And He too is the Father's Word, from which may be understood the impassible and impartitive nature of the Father, in that not even a human word is begotten with passion or partition, much less the Word of God (*De decr.* 11 LNPF).

There remains no room for subordinationism in such a doctrine of the Logos. If the Son says: 'The Father is greater than I', this means: The Father is the origin, the Son the derivation (*Or. Arian.* 3, 3; 4 EF 760/776). Eternally begotten, the Son is of the Father's substance, ἐκ τῆς οὐσίας τοῦ πατρός, He is consubstantial to the Father, He is ὁμοούσιος. Both terms were used by the Council of Nicaea and Athanasius deems them absolutely essential, whereas he discards the expression ὅμοιος as unsatisfactory:

For only to say 'like according to essence' (ὅμοιος κατ' οὐσίαν), is very far from signifying 'of the essence' (ἐκ τῆς οὐσίας), by which rather, as they say themselves, the genuineness of the Son to the Father is signified. Thus tin is only like to silver, a wolf to a dog, and gilt brass to the true metal; but tin is not from silver, nor could a wolf be accounted the offspring of a dog. But since they say that He is 'of the essence' and 'Like-in-essence', what do they signify by these but 'Consubstantial'? For, while to say only 'Like-in-essence', does not necessarily convey 'of the essence', on the contrary, to say 'Consubstantial', is to signify the meaning of both terms, 'Like-in-essence' and 'of the essence'. And accordingly they, the Semi-Arians themselves, in controversy with those who say that the Word is a creature, instead of allowing Him to be genuine Son, have taken their proofs against them from human illustrations of son and father, with this exception that God is not as man, nor the generation of the Son as issue of man, but such as may be ascribed to God, and is fit for us to think. Thus they have called the Father the Fount of Wisdom and Life, and the Son the Radiance of the Eternal Light, and the Offspring from the Fountain, as He says, 'I am the Life', and, 'I Wisdom dwell with Prudence' (John 14, 6; Prov. 8, 12). But the Radiance from the Light, and Offspring from Fountain, and Son from Father, how can these be so fitly expressed as by 'Consubstantial'? (*De syn.* 41 LNPF).

Thus he defends the *homoousios* not only against the Arians, but also against the Semi-Arians, to whom he makes overtures in order to gain them back to the Nicene formula.

Studies: L. Atzberger, Die Logoslehre des hl. Athanasius. Munich, 1880. — F. Lauchert, Die Lehre des hl. Athanasius des Grossen. Leipzig, 1895. — K. Hoss, Studien über das Schrifttum und die Theologie des Athanasius. Freiburg i.B., 1899. — L. Coulange, Métamorphose du consubstantiel: Athanase et Hilaire: RHL (1922) 168-214. — A. Gaudel, La théorie du Logos chez saint Athanase: RSR 19 (1929) 524-539; 21 (1931) 1-26. — G. Prestige, 'Αγέν[ν]ητος and cognate words in Athanasius: JThSt 34 (1933) 258-265. — J. Lebon, S. Athanase a-t-il employé l'expression ὁ κυριακὸς ἄνθρωπος?: RHE 31 (1935) 307-329. — C. Hauret, Comment le 'Défenseur de Nicée' a-t-il compris le dogme de Nicée? Bruges, 1936. — J. B. Berchem, Le rôle du Verbe dans l'œuvre de la création et de la sanctification d'après saint Athanase: Ang 15 (1938) 201-232. — F. L. Cross, The Study of St. Athanasius. Oxford, 1945. — G. L. Prestige, Fathers and Heretics. London, 1948. — J. N. D. Kelly, Early Christian Creeds. London, 1950, 231-262. — J. Lebon, Le sort du consubstantiel nicéen: RHE 47 (1952) 485-529. — G. L. Prestige, God in Patristic Thought. London, 1956, 197-218. — H. A. Wolfson, The Philosophy of the Church Fathers. Cambridge (Mass.), 1956, 227-230. — T. E. Pollard, Logos and Son in Origen, Arius and Athanasius: SP 2 (TU 64). Berlin, 1957, 282-287; *idem,* The Exegesis of John X 30 in the Early Trinitarian Controversies: New Testament Studies 3 (1957) 334-349. — J. N. D. Kelly, Early Christian Doctrines. London, 1958, 240-247.

2. *Logos and Redemption*

The root of the Athanasian doctrine of the Logos is the idea of redemption. Nothing is so typical of his theology as sentences like the following:

He was made man that we might be made God *(θεοποιηθῶμεν)* and He manifested Himself by a body that we might receive the idea of the unseen Father; and He endured the insolence of men that we might inherit immortality (*De incarn.* 54 LNPF).

The Word, perceiving that no otherwise could the corruption of men be undone save by death as a necessary condition, while it was impossible for the Word to suffer death, being immortal, and Son of the Father; to this end He takes to Himself a body capable of death, that it, by partaking of the Word Who is above all, might be worthy to die instead of all, and might, because of the Word which was come to dwell in it, remain incorruptible, and that henceforth corruption might be stayed from all by the grace of the resurrection. Whence, by offering unto death the body He Himself had taken, as an offering and sacrifice free from any stain, straightway He put away death from all His peers by the offering of an equivalent. For being over all, the Word of God naturally by offering His own temple and corporeal instrument for the life of all satisfied the debt by His death. And thus He, the incorruptible Son of God, being conjoined with all by a like nature, naturally clothed all with incorruption by the promise of the resurrection. For the actual corruption in death has no longer holding-ground against men, by reason of the Word, which by His one body has come to dwell among them (*ibid.* 9).

Thus Athanasius infers the necessity of the incarnation and of the death of Christ from God's redeeming will. We would not have been redeemed, if God Himself had not become man and if Christ were not God. The Logos assuming human nature, deified mankind. He overcame death not only for Himself but for all of us:

And thus taking from our bodies one of like nature, because all were under penalty of the corruption of death, He gave it over to death in the stead of all, and offered it to the Father — doing this, moreover, of His loving-kindness, to the end that, firstly, all being held to have died in Him, the law involving the ruin of men might be undone inasmuch as its power was fully spent in the Lord's body, and had no longer holding-ground against men, his peers, and that, secondly, whereas men had turned toward corruption, He might turn them again toward incorruption, and quicken them from death by the appropriation of His body and by the grace of the resurrection, banishing death from them like straw from the fire (*ibid.* 8).

If Christ was God not by nature, but by participation, he could never have formed the likeness of God in anyone. For he who possesses nothing but that which he has borrowed from another cannot hand down anything to others:

By partaking of Him, we partake of the Father; because that the Word is the Father's own. Whence, if He was Himself too from participation, and not from the Father His essential Godhead and Image, He would not deify being deified Himself. For it is not possible that He, who merely possesses from participation, should impart of that partaking to others, since what He has is not His own, but the Giver's; and what He has received, is barely the grace sufficient for Himself (*De syn.* 51 LNPF, EP 787).

Studies: H. STRÄTER, Die Erlösungslehre des hl. Athanasius. Freiburg i.B., 1894. — K. BORNHÄUSER, Die Vergottungslehre des Athanasius und Joh. Damascenus (BFTh 7, 2). Gütersloh, 1903. — V. CREMER, De Verlossingsidee bij Athanasius den Groote. Turnhout, 1921. — G. BARDY, La vie spirituelle d'après saint Athanase: VS 18 (1928) 97-113. — J. B. BERCHEM, L'incarnation dans le plan divin d'après saint Athanase: EO 33 (1934) 316-330; *idem*, Le Christ sanctificateur d'après saint Athanase: Ang 15 (1938) 515-558. — J. GROSS, La divinisation du chrétien d'après les Pères grecs. Paris, 1938, 201-218. — K. PRÜMM, 'Mysterion' und Verwandtes bei Athanasius: ZkTh 63 (1939) 350-359. — J. B. SCHOEMANN, Eikon in den Schriften des hl. Athanasius: Schol 16 (1941) 335-350. — D. UNGER, A Special Aspect of Athanasian Soteriology: FS 6 (1946) 30-53, 171-194. — R. BERNARD, L'image de Dieu d'après saint Athanase. Paris, 1952. — P. C. DEMETROPULOS, 'Η ἀνθρωπολογία τοῦ μεγάλου 'Αθανασίου. Athens, 1954.

3. *Christology*

The thorough discussion of the relation of the Son to the Father did not prevent Athanasius from answering strictly christological questions. Upholding the real distinction between the divinity and humanity after the Incarnation, he nevertheless emphasizes the personal unity of Christ:

> For just as He is Word of God, so afterwards 'the Word was made flesh'; and while 'in the beginning was the Word', the Virgin at the consummation of the ages conceived, and the Lord has become man. And He who is indicated by both statements is one Person, for 'the Word was made flesh'. But the expressions used about His Godhead, and His becoming man, are to be interpreted with discrimination and suitably to the particular context. And he that writes of the human attributes of the Word knows also what concerns His Godhead: and he who expounds concerning His Godhead is not ignorant of what belongs to His coming in the flesh: but discerning each as a skilled and 'approved money-changer', he will walk in the straight way of piety; when therefore he speaks of His weeping, he knows that the Lord, having become man, while He exhibits His human character in weeping, as God raised up Lazarus; and he knows that He used to hunger and thirst physically, while divinely He fed thousands of persons from five loaves; and knows that while a human body lay in the tomb, it was raised as God's body by the Word Himself (*De sent. Dion.* 9 LNPF).

Thus whatever the Lord did as God and as man belongs to the same person:

Being Son of God in truth, He became also Son of Man, and being God's Only-begotten Son, He became also at the same time 'firstborn among many brethren'. Wherefore neither was there one Son of God before Abraham, another after Abraham: nor was there one that raised up Lazarus, another that asked concerning him; but the same it was that said as man, 'Where does Lazarus lie?' (John 11,34), and as God raised him up: the same that as man and in the body spat, but divinely as Son of God opened the eyes of the man blind from his birth; and while, as Peter says (1 Pet. 4,1), in the flesh He suffered, as God He opened the tomb and raised the dead (*Tom. ad Ant.* 7 LNPF).

However, recent investigations have shown that in Athanasius' Christology there is no prominent place for the human soul of Christ. A. Stülcken deserves credit for having recognized that Athanasius as a theologian does not assign any important role to the human soul of Christ. Though G. Voisin attempted to refute this view, M. Richard and A. Grillmeier have come to the same conclusion. Richard's careful analysis of *Contra Arianos* III 35-37 reveals the weakness of Athanasius' argumentation against the Arians. The latter based their objections to the divinity of Christ on Scriptural passages which mention the inner suffering, fear and affliction of the Logos. One would expect Athanasius to show that all this has nothing to do with his divinity but is caused by his human soul. But he never avails himself of this opportunity and never attacks the Arians for having made this mistake. The reason is that the characteristic form of Christology in early times was a Logos-Sarx Christology. Arius and Apollinaris, though at extremes in other respects, are its typical exponents. Neither of them admits the presence of a human soul in Christ because they are convinced that the Logos has taken its place. Even Athanasius might be called a moderate but orthodox representative of this form of Christology, though he differs from both, Arius and Apollinaris, in so far as he never explicitly denies the existence of a human soul in Christ. From his predominantly soteriological point of view he contents himself with giving prominence to the Logos and Sarx in Christ, but abstains from answering questions regarding the connecting link between the Logos and his Flesh. This is even more surprising, if we remember that a century before Origen had introduced the concept of the soul of Christ as being intermediate between God and the Flesh (cf. vol. II, p. 80).

There is one passage in Athanasius, *Tom. ad Antioch.* 7 which has been adduced to prove that Athanasius did believe in a human soul of Christ. Its usual translation runs as follows:

> The Saviour had not a body without a soul *(οὐ σῶμα ἄψυχον)*, not without sense or intelligence; for it was not possible, when the Lord

had become man for us, that His body should be without intelligence: nor was the salvation effected in the Word Himself of the body only, but of the soul also (LNPF).

However, Grillmeier is of the opinion that the words οὐ σῶμα ἄψυχον must be rendered 'not a lifeless body', rather than 'not a soulless body' or 'a body without a soul', if justice be done to the context.

Though Athanasius knows very well of the concept of death as the separation of the soul from the body, in speaking of Christ's death he does not mention the soul at all but following the Logos-Sarx Christology, he replaces the soul with the Logos. Thus Christ's death is to him a separation of Logos and body. This idea appears in his early as well as in his later writings. In his early *De incarnatione* (22) he remarks:

> If, then, once more, His body had fallen sick, and the Word had been sundered from it in the sight of all, it would have been unbecoming that He who healed the diseases of others should suffer His own instrument to waste in sickness. For how could His driving out the diseases of others have been believed in if His own temple fell sick in Him (LNPF).

In his chief dogmatic work *Orationes contra Arianos* he explains the death of Christ in the same terms of Logos-Soma. Discussing John 12, 27 and 10, 18, he states:

> He said humanly, *Now is My soul troubled;* and He said divinely, *I have power to lay down My life, and power to take it again.* For to be troubled was proper to the flesh, but to have power to lay down his life and take it again, when He would, was no property of men but of the Word's power. For man dies, not at his own arbitrement, but by necessity of nature and against his will; but the Lord being Himself immortal, but having a mortal flesh, had at His own free will, as God, to become separate from the body and to take it again, when He would (3,57).

Thus there is no place in his explanation of Christ's death for the human soul. Finally, in his *Epistle to Epictetus*, dealing with some who claim that the Logos was changed into flesh, he points to Christ's *descensus ad inferos* without even mentioning the soul:

> But in the Body which was circumcised, and carried, and ate and drank, and was weary, and was nailed on the tree and suffered, there was the impassible and incorporeal Word of God. This Body it was that was laid in a grave, when the Word had left it... And this above all shows the foolishness of those who say that the Word was changed into bones and flesh. For if this had been so there would be no need of a tomb. For the Body would have gone by itself to preach to the

spirits in Hades. But as it was, He Himself [the Word] went to preach, while the Body Joseph wrapped in a linen cloth, and laid it away at Golgotha. And so it was shown to all that the Body was not the Word, but Body of the Word (5/6 LNPF).

Thus he does not speak of the soul leaving the body at all, which proves that Christ's soul does not really figure in his concept of the Saviour's death and descent.

The personal unity existing between the divine and the human nature is the reason that Mary is really and in truth 'bearer of God' (θεοτόκος): 'Scripture contains a double account of the Saviour; that He was ever God, and is the Son, being the Father's Word and Radiance and Wisdom; and that afterwards for us He took flesh of a Virgin, Mary, Bearer of God (θεοτόκου), and was made man' (Or. Arian. 3,29; 3,14).

A second consequence of the personal unity of Christ is the *communicatio idiomatum*. Thus Christ deserves adoration even in his human nature:

We do not worship a creature. Far be the thought. For such an error belongs to heathens and Arians. But we worship the Lord of creation, Incarnate, the Word of God. For if the flesh also is in itself a part of the created world, yet it has become God's body. And we neither divide the body, being such, from the Word, and worship it by itself, nor when we wish to worship the Word do we set Him far apart from the flesh, but knowing, as we said above, that 'the Word was made flesh', we recognize Him as God also, after having come in the flesh. Who is so senseless as to say to the Lord: 'Leave the Body that I may worship Thee' (*Epist. ad Adelph.* 3 LNPF).

On the contrary, the incarnation and the death of Christ was not to the shame of God but the glory of God and have given us even more reason to adore the Lord:

The Word was not impaired in receiving a body, that He should seek to receive a grace, but rather He deified that which He put on, and more than that, gave it graciously to the race of man. For as He was ever worshipped as being the Word and existing in the form of God, so being what He ever was, though become man and called Jesus, He none the less has the whole creation under foot, and bending their knees to Him in this Name, and confessing that the Word's becoming flesh, and undergoing death in flesh, has not happened against the glory of His Godhead, but to the glory of God the Father. For it is the Father's glory that man, made and then lost, should be found again; and when dead, that he should be made alive, and should become God's temple. For whereas the powers in heaven, both Angels and Archangels, were ever worshipping the Lord, as they are now worshipping Him in the Name of Jesus, this is our grace and high

exaltation, that even when He became man, the Son of God is worshipped, and the heavenly powers will not be astonished at seeing all
of us, who are of one body with Him, introduced into their realms
(*Or. Arian.* 1, 42 LNPF).

Studies: A. STÜLCKEN, Athanasiana. Literatur- und dogmengeschichtliche Untersuchungen (TU NF 4, 4). Leipzig, 1899. — G. VOISIN, La doctrine christologique de
saint Athanase: RHE 1 (1900) 226-248. — E. WEIGL, Untersuchungen zur Christologie
des hl. Athanasius (FLD 12, 4). Paderborn, 1914. Cf. J. LIÉBAERT, Saint Cyrille
d'Alexandrie et l'arianisme. Lille, 1948, 130-136. — J. LEBON, Une ancienne opinion
sur la condition du corps du Christ dans la mort: RHE 23 (1927) 5-43; 209-241. —
E. MERSCH, Le Corps Mystique du Christ. 2nd ed. Brussels and Paris, 1936, 374-409.
English translation: E. MERSCH, The Whole Christ. Translated by J. R. Kelly.
Milwaukee, 1938, 263-287. — R. V. SELLERS, Two Ancient Christologies. London, 1940.
— T. TSCHIPKE, Die Menschheit Christi als Heilsorgan. Freiburg, 1940, 28-30. —
L. BOUYER, L'incarnation et l'Église corps du Christ dans la théologie de saint Athanase.
Paris, 1943. — M. RICHARD, Saint Athanase et la psychologie du Christ selon les Ariens:
MSR 4 (1947) 5-54. — A. GRILLMEIER, Die theologische und sprachliche Vorbereitung
der christologischen Formel von Chalkedon: CGG I (1951) 77-102. — I. ORTIZ DE
URBINA, L'anima umana di Cristo secondo S. Atanasio: OCP 20 (1954) 27-43. —
P. GALTIER, Saint Athanase et l'âme humaine du Christ: Greg 36 (1955) 553-589. —
T. E. POLLARD, The Impassibility of God: Scottish Journal of Theology 8 (1955) 353-364.
— J. N. D. KELLY, Early Christian Doctrines. London, 1958, 284-289.

4. *Holy Spirit*

The Athanasian teaching on the divinity of the Holy Spirit and
his being of the same essence as the Father follows the line of
christological thinking of the Alexandrians. The Holy Spirit must
be God because if he were a creature, we should have no participation of God in Him: This thought occurs again and again in his
Letters to Serapion:

> He, therefore, who is not sanctified by another, nor a partaker of
> sanctification, but Who is Himself partaken, and in Whom all the
> creatures are sanctified, how can He be one from among all things or
> pertain to those who partake of Him?
> If by participation in the Spirit, we are made 'sharers in the divine
> nature' (2 Pet. 1, 4), we should be mad to say, that the Spirit has a
> created nature and not the nature of God. For it is on this account
> that those in whom He is are made divine. If He makes men divine,
> it is not to be doubted that His nature is of God (1, 23/24 Shapland
> 123/26).

Secondly, the Holy Spirit is of the Trinity, and since the Trinity
is homogeneous the Spirit is not created but He is God:

> It is madness to call Him a creature. If He were a creature, He
> could not be ranked with the Triad. For the whole Triad is one God.
> It is enough to know that the Spirit is not a creature, nor is He num-
> bered with the things that are made. For nothing foreign is mixed
> with the Triad; it is indivisible and consistent (1,17 Shapland 103).

He is as the Son consubstantial *(ὁμοούσιος)* with the Father:

> If the Holy Spirit is one, and the creatures many and angels many — what likeness can there be between the Spirit and things originate? It is obvious that the Spirit does not belong to the many nor is He an angel. But because He is one, and still more, because He is proper to the Word Who is one, He is proper to God Who is one, and one in essence with Him *(ὁμοούσιος)*.
>
> These sayings [of Scripture] concerning the Holy Spirit by themselves alone, show that in nature and essence He has nothing in common with or proper to creatures, but is distinct from things originate, proper to, and not alien from, the Godhead and essence of the Son; in virtue of which essence and nature He is of the Holy Triad (1,27 Shapland 133).

It was Origen's idea that the Holy Spirit owes His existence to the Son. There is a similar train of thought in the writings of Athanasius. He states e.g.: 'For the Son does not merely partake the Spirit, that therefore He too may be in the Father; nor does He receive the Spirit, but rather He supplies It Himself to all; and the Spirit does not unite the Word to the Father, but rather the Spirit receives from the Word... He, as has been said, gives to the Spirit, and whatever the Spirit has, He has from the Word' (*Or. Arian.* 3,24).

Athanasius definitely states that the Holy Spirit 'proceeds from the Father' (*Ep. Ser.* 1,2). The question is whether he teaches a doctrine of double procession, from the Son as well as from the Father. He nowhere states explicitly that the Holy Spirit proceeds from the Son, but the procession of the Spirit from the Son or from the Father through the Son is a necessary corollary of his whole argument. In fact, all that he says about the procession of the Holy Spirit would make no sense if he was not convinced that the Holy Spirit proceeds from the Son also. His very procession from the Father is itself perceived by us from our knowledge of his mission from the Word, as is evident from Athanasius' remark: 'As the Son, the living Word, is one, so must the vital activity and gift whereby he sanctifies and enlightens, be one, perfect and complete; which is said to proceed *(ἐκπορεύεσθαι)* from the Father, because it is from the Word, who is confessed to be from the Father, that it shines forth and is sent and is given' (*Ep. Ser.* 1, 20).

Studies: T. Schermann, Die Gottheit des Heiligen Geistes nach den griechischen Vätern des 4. Jahrhunderts. Freiburg i.B., 1901, 47-89. — P. Galtier, Le Saint Esprit en nous d'après les Pères grecs. Rome, 1946, 117-134. — C. R. B. Shapland, The Letters of S. Athanasius Concerning the Holy Spirit. New York, 1951, 34-43: Athanasius' doctrine of the Holy Spirit.

5. *Baptism*

Athanasius regards baptism conferred by the Arians as invalid. In his *first Letter to Serapion* (30) he says: 'The faith in the Triad, which has been delivered to us, joins us to God; he who takes anything away from the Triad, and is baptized in the name of the Father alone, or in the name of the Son alone, or in the Father and the Son without the Holy Spirit, receives nothing... for the rite of initiation is in the Triad. He who divides the Son from the Father, or reduces the Spirit to the level of the creatures, has neither the Son nor the Father, but is without God, worse than an unbeliever, and anything rather than a Christian' (Shapland 139f).

From these words it could be suggested that Athanasius found fault with the baptism of the Arians because they failed to use the requisite Trinitarian formula. However, this is not the case. Athanasius' chief objection is the same as that of Cyril of Jerusalem, Basil the Great, the *Apostolic Canons* (46; 47) and the *Apostolic Constitutions* (19). It rests on the fact that the faith in which it is given is defective, as is evident from his second *Discourse against the Arians* (42):

> And these [the Arians] hazard, too, the fullness of the sacrament, I mean baptism; for if the initiation is given to us in the name of Father and Son, and they do not confess a true Father, because they deny also the true Son, and name another of their own framing as created out of nothing, is not the rite administered by them altogether empty and unprofitable, making a show, but in reality being no help towards religion? For the Arians do not baptize into Father and Son, but into Creator and creature, and into Maker and work. And as a creature is other than the Son, so the baptism, which is supposed to be given by them, is other than the truth, though they pretend to name the name of the Father and the Son, because of the words of Scripture. For not he who simply says, 'O Lord', gives baptism; but he who with the name has also the right faith. On this account therefore our Saviour also did not simply command to baptize, but first says, 'Teach'; then thus: 'Baptize in the name of the Father, the Son and the Holy Ghost'; that the right faith might follow upon learning, and together with faith might come the consecration of baptism.
>
> There are many other heresies too, which use the words only, but not in a right sense, as I have said, nor with sound faith, and in consequence the water which they administer is unprofitable, as deficient in piety, so that he who is sprinkled by them is rather polluted by irreligion than redeemed... So Manicheans and Phrygians, and the disciples of the Samosatene, though using the names, nevertheless are heretics, and the Arians follow in the same course though they read the words of Scripture and use the names, yet they mock those who receive the rite from them.

It is interesting to note that Athanasius here mentions the followers of Paul of Samosata among the heretics who used the prescribed formula of baptism. Even the Council of Nicaea (*canon* 19) regards their baptism, as Athanasius, to be invalid, because it commands: 'Regarding the Paulianists who wish to return to the Catholic Church, the rule is to be observed that they must be rebaptized'.

Studies: J. ERNST, Der Ketzertaufstreit in der altchristlichen Kirche nach Cyprian. Mit besonderer Berücksichtigung der Konzilien von Arles und Nicaea. Mainz, 1901; *idem*, Die Ketzertaufangelegenheit auf den Konzilien von Arles und Nicaea: ZkTh 27 (1903) 759-767. — W. SATTLER, Die Stellung der griechischen Kirche zur Ketzertaufe bis ca. 500. 1911.

6. *Eucharist*

In a fragment of his sermon *To the Newly Baptized*, preserved by Eutychius of Constantinople (MG 26, 1325), Athanasius says clearly:

> You shall see the levites bring loaves and a chalice of wine, and place them on the table. As long as the invocation and prayers have not begun, there is only bread and wine. But after the great and wonderful prayers have been pronounced, then the bread becomes the body of Our Lord Jesus Christ, and the wine becomes His blood. Let us come to the celebration of the mysteries. As long as the prayers and invocations have not taken place, this bread and this wine are simply [bread and wine]. But after the great prayers and holy invocations have been pronounced, the Word descends into the bread and wine, and the body of the Word is.

Another passage dealing with the Eucharist is to be found in his *Letters to Serapion* 4,19. Some scholars have quoted it in order to prove that Athanasius regarded the Eucharist as a symbol of the body and blood of the Lord, not as His real body and blood. But the passage taken as a whole in its context does not justify such an interpretation. Athanasius introduces Jesus promising the Apostles to give them His body and blood as a spiritual food (πνευματικῶς). Using this expression Athanasius intends to refute the misunderstanding of the inhabitants of Capharnaum who thought of the flesh of Christ in its natural state. The body and the blood of the Lord will be given to the Apostles in a spiritual way (πνευματικῶς δοθήσεται τροφή), as a token of the resurrection to eternal life. Thus there is no idea of a symbolical interpretation in the sense of Zwingli.

SERAPION OF THMUIS

Serapion had been superior of a colony of monks before he became bishop of Thmuis, a town in Lower Egypt. Sozomen (*Hist. eccl.* 4,9) calls him 'a prelate distinguished by the wonderful sanctity of his life and the power of his eloquence'. St. Jerome (*De vir. ill.* 99) states that he was given the title *Scholasticus* on account of his great learning. He was an intimate friend of St. Antony the hermit who made him the confident of his visions (Athanasius, *Vita Ant.* 82) and bequeathed him one of his two sheepskins (*ibid.* 91); Athanasius received the other. He was the recipient of a number of important epistles from the latter. As early as 339 Athanasius sent one of his Festal Letters 'to the beloved brother and our fellow minister' (MG 26, 1412-1414), which indicates that Serapion must have been consecrated before this date. In another missive Athanasius, by describing the death of Arius, refutes the notion that the heretic had been reconciled to the Church. The details were furnished him by his presbyter Macarius, who was at Constantinople when Arius passed away while Athanasius was himself in exile at Treves. It was written evidently in 358. But, most important of all, Athanasius addressed to him four letters concerning the Holy Spirit (cf. above, p. 57), which present the first formal treatise ever written upon this subject and bear witness to their mutual regard and frequent intercourse. Moreover, in 356 Athanasius sent Serapion with four other Egyptian bishops and three presbyters to the court of Constantius in order to refute the calumnies of the Arian party and conciliate the ruler. It was under the same emperor that he was ousted from his see and suffered as 'confessor'. The exact date of his death is unknown. According to Epiphanius (*Haer.* 73,26) one Ptolemaeus attended the synod of Seleucia in 359 as bishop of Thmuis. It would be rash to assume from this that Serapion was by this time dead. It is more probable that Ptolemaeus was an Arian usurper and that Serapion had been exiled. Moreover, a fragment of a letter from Apollinaris to Serapion in Pseudo-Leontius, *Adv. fraudes Apollinaristarum* alludes to a communication sent by Athanasius to Corinth on the christological question. The latter seems to be nothing but the Athanasian letter to Epictetus (cf. above, p. 59), the date of which makes it impossible that Serapion had departed this life by the autumn of 359. Even if Lietzmann (*Apollinaris*, p. 279) was wrong in assigning its composition to 370, there is enough evidence to show that Serapion must have died after 362.

Studies: G. BARDY, DTC 14 (1941) 1908. — H. DÖRRIES, PWK Suppl. 8 (1956) 1260-1267.

St. Jerome (*De vir. ill.* 99) tells us that Serapion wrote an excellent treatise against the Manichæans (cf. below, p. 356), another on the titles of the Psalms and useful Epistles to various persons. The work on the Psalms is lost, but that against the Manichæans has only recently been recovered entire.

1. *Against the Manichæans*

Its text had a complicated history. It first appeared in Canisius' *Antiquae Lectiones*, vol. V (Ingolstadt, 1608), in a Latin translation made by the Spanish Jesuit Francisco de Torres. The earliest Greek edition was prepared by J. Basnage from a single manuscript of the seventeenth century in the *Stadtbibliothek* at Hamburg, containing also the treatise of Titus of Bostra against the Manichæans. This remained the basis of all printed Greek texts until Cardinal Pitra drew attention to a codex of the eleventh century in the *Biblioteca di San Carlo* at Genoa, which, like the Hamburg manuscript, contained a fragmentary copy of Serapion's treatise, followed by books 1-3 of Titus' *Contra Manichaeos*. The new find proved to be the archetype of the manuscript at Hamburg as well as of two other manuscripts at Rome of the seventeenth and eighteenth centuries, respectively. Moreover, the same codex led A. Brinkmann to an important discovery. No exemplar of Serapion's study was complete, but he proved by a clever analysis of the Genoa volume that it had been thrown into disorder at an early period. The disarray was the blunder of some binder, who displaced folios amounting to three quarters of the whole. One leaf was lost, but the rest were scattered in Titus of Bostra's tract. Brinkmann thus succeeded in restoring practically all of Serapion's treatise, and also made it obvious that Migne (MG 40, 900-924) contains but a fourth of the original. So matters stood until 1924, when the catalogue of the library of the Monastery of Vatopedi on Mount Athos was published by Eustratiades and Arkadios. It gave notice of a manuscript of the twelfth century hitherto unknown, which contains among a variety of patristic treatises Serapion's *Against the Manichæans* complete. A year later R. P. Casey obtained a facsimile and Brinkmann's deductions were proved remarkably exact. The text agrees with his conclusions and in addition supplies the lacuna caused by the loss of one sheet. Finally, in 1931 Casey published a new edition based on the Athos codex and that of Genoa. It was the first time that Serapion's tract had been made available in its entirety to modern scholars.

Now it became clear why St. Jerome calls it an *egregius liber* and why its author was surnamed *Scholasticus*. There is ample evidence of his rhetorical, philosophical and theological erudition. Serapion, it is true, did not intend to refute the entire Manichæan system as Alexander of Lycopolis and later on St. Augustine. He limits himself to a criticism of the main points, especially of the dualistic theory of a good and a bad first principle, of the objections to the Old Testament and certain parts of the New. But he reveals great skill and acumen in showing these basic tenets of Manichæism to be illogical and inconsistent.

As for Serapion's christological doctrine, it is to be noticed that despite his friendly relations with Athanasius he does not use the Nicene *homoousios* for the Son of God but the simple *homoios* (48, 20f.). The term *homoousios* occurs 27, 6, where the author states that the creatures are not of the same substance as the Creator *(homoousia)*. From 25, 13-18 and 37, 11-13 it appears that the Gospel of St. Mark occupied the first place in Serapion's canon and that of St. Matthew the second. In 11,1f. we have one of the earliest references to the Christian cult of the relics. Chapters 29 and 30 deal with the relation existing between the demons and the abyss (see Luke 8, 31). Although Serapion regards the *abyss* of the Gospel as a place of punishment and torture, its principal purpose is to serve as a remedy for the sinner (30, 1-5); it exists only to sober and enlighten him (30, 9). This concept of hell seems to be influenced by Origen.

Edition: R. P. CASEY, Serapion of Thmuis against the Manichees (HTS 15). Cambridge (Mass.), 1931.

Studies: A. BRINKMANN, Die Streitschrift des Serapion von Thmuis gegen die Manichäer: SAB (1894) 479-491. — R. P. CASEY, The Text of the Anti-Manichaean Writings of Titus of Bostra and Serapion of Thmuis 21 (1928) 97-111. — A. PETERS, Het tractaat van Serapion van Thmuis tegen de Manichaeën: SE 2 (1949) 55-94.

2. *The Euchologion*

A unique eleventh century manuscript (no. 149) of the Laura Monastery of Mount Athos contains an *euchologion* or sacramentary, which is ascribed to Serapion, the bishop of Thmuis. Consisting of thirty prayers, the collection is certainly Egyptian and dates in its present form from the fourth century, most probably before rather than after A.D. 350. The name Serapion is found in the entries to the first and fifteenth prayers, but the others were composed by the same author as can be proved from their terminology and contents. Eighteen are connected with the eucharistic liturgy, seven with baptism and confirmation, three with ordination, two with the blessing of the oils and funerals. The thirty prayers are followed in the manuscript by a dogmatic *Letter concerning Father and Son*.

The prayer of the oblation is an anaphora consisting of the Preface ending in the *Sanctus*, the oblation and recital of the Institution, invocation of the Logos, the intercession for the living, the intercession for the departed, the recitation of the Diptychs and the prayer for those who have offered.

There are several most striking points to be observed in this anaphora. We have here the earliest certain evidence of the use of the *Sanctus* in the eucharistic liturgy. The transition from the *Sanctus* to the words of the Institution is typical also of the later Egyptian liturgy. But most astonishing is the fact that between the words of the Institution for the bread and the cup is inserted a prayer for the union of the Church, drawn from the Didache (9,4). It is true that certain sentences in the Preface agree word for word with the Liturgy known as that of St. Mark. On the other hand, close examination makes it evident that the anaphora has many peculiarities. Several passages show a predominantly speculative and theological, to be more specific, 'gnostic' colouring, which is not based on ancient tradition but constitutes Serapion's own contribution. The author shows a bold independence leading to the creation of entirely new prayers and the insertion of revisions of early Christian forms. Thus his eucharistic Canon, although precious for the history of the liturgy, represents only a second class witness to tradition. Even the epiklesis of the Logos seems to be Serapion's own contribution. Peter and Theophilus, the patriarchs of Alexandria, testify that Athanasius and the Liturgies of Alexandria never knew of any invocation asking for the coming of the Logos upon the bread and cup; but it is traceable, and has in fact certain analogies to Gnostic eucharistic prayers.

The *Letter concerning Father and Son*, which in the manuscript follows immediately after the thirty prayers of the *Euchologion*, does not bear any name. G. Wobbermin holds that it must be attributed to Serapion, but the style differs from his treatise *Against the Manichæans* and his *Euchologion*. The doxology at the end of the letter 'To the unseen wise God honor and might, greatness, magnificence both now and ever, yea was and is and shall be to generations of generations and to the ageless incorruptible ages of the ages. Amen' is very much unlike the strictly trinitarian doxology directed to God through Christ in the Holy Spirit, which appears in almost identical phrasing at the end of all the prayers of Serapion's sacramentary. The author of the Letter has a confused idea of the Third Person. Following 'the holy teachers of the Catholic and apostolic Church', he wants to prove that the Son is coeternal with the Father. Most probably he belongs to an older generation of opponents of the Arian heresy.

The manuscript in which Serapion's *Euchologion* is contained was found by A. Dimitrijewsky, who also published the first edition in 1894. It was published anew four years later by G. Wobbermin, who did not know of the previous one. Other editions were prepared by F. E. Brightman, who restored the correct sequence of the prayers, and by F. X. Funk.

Editions: A. DIMITRIJEWSKY, Ein Euchologium aus dem 4. Jahrhundert, verfasst von Sarapion, Bischof von Thmuis. Kiev, 1894. — G. WOBBERMIN, Altchristliche liturgische Stücke aus der Kirche Aegyptens nebst einem dogmatischen Brief des Bischofs Serapion von Thmuis (TU 18, 3b). Leipzig, 1898. — F. E. BRIGHTMAN, The Sacramentary of Serapion of Thmuis: JThSt 1 (1900) 88-113, 247-277. — F. X. FUNK, Didascalia et Constitutiones Apostolorum II. Paderborn, 1905, 158-195 (with Latin translation). — *Eucharistic Prayers:* J. QUASTEN, Monumenta eucharistica et liturgica vetustissima (FP 7). Bonn, 1935, 48-67.

Translations: English: J. WORDSWORTH, Bishop Serapion's Prayer-book. An Egyptian Sacramentary dated probably about A.D. 350-356, translated from the edition of G. Wobbermin (SPCK). London, 1899. 2nd ed., revised, 1923. — *German:* R. STORF, BKV² 5 (1912) 135-157.

Studies: P. DREWS, Über Wobbermins 'Altchristliche liturgische Stücke aus der Kirche Aegyptens': ZKG 20 (1900) 291-328, 415-441. — A. BAUMSTARK, Die Anaphora von Thmuis und ihre Überarbeitung durch den hl. Serapion: RQ 18 (1904) 123-142. — T. SCHERMANN, Aegyptische Abendmahlsliturgien in ihrer Überlieferung dargestellt (StGKA 6, 1-2). Paderborn, 1912, 100-114. — L. DUCHESNE, Origines du culte chrétien. 5th ed. Paris, 1925, 76-81. — H. LIETZMANN, Messe und Herrenmahl. Bonn, 1926, 186-197. — P. BATIFFOL, L'Eucharistie. La présence réelle et la transsubstantiation (Études d'hist. et de théologie positive, sér. 2) 9th ed. Paris, 1930, 311-317. — H. LECLERCQ, DAL 11 (1933) 606-612. — B. CAPELLE, L'anaphore de Sérapion. Essai d'exégèse: Mus 49 (1946) 425-443. — G. DIX, The Shape of the Liturgy. 4th impr. Westminster, 1949, 162-172.

3. *Letters*

Of the 'useful epistles to various persons', which Serapion wrote according to St. Jerome (*De vir. ill.* 99), only few are extant. Two were discovered by Cardinal Mai. The one is a brief word of consolation addressed to a bishop Eudoxius suffering from illness, the other a longer letter of encouragement to monks at Alexandria, in which he uses the expression 'consubstantial Trinity' (ὁμοούσιος τριάς). However, a Greek fragment published by Cardinal Pitra (*Analecta sacra* 2, Paris, 1884, Proleg. XL; *Analecta sacra et classica* 1, Paris, 1888, 47) shows that there existed at one time a collection of as many as twenty-three letters. There is hope that some of these might still be found. Thus Draguet recently published a letter that Serapion addressed to some disciples of St. Antony the hermit on the occasion of his death (356). An Armenian version published in 1885 comprises only half of the text. The Syriac version discovered by Draguet provides the complete epistle, which seems to be authentic. Both translations have been made from the Greek original no longer extant.

Editions: MG 40, 923-942 reprints the two letters which Mai published, Classici auctores 5, Rome, 1883, 364-365 and Spicilegium Romanum 4, Rome, 1840, Praef. 45-67. — R. DRAGUET, Une lettre de Sérapion de Thmuis aux disciples d'Antoine (A.D. 356) en version syriaque et arménienne: Mus 64 (1951) 1-25, gives the text of both versions, a French translation and a commentary.

The Syriac extracts from a *Homily on Virginity*, a *Letter to Confessors*, and a short dogmatic fragment published by Pitra (*Analecta sacra* 4, Paris, 1883, 214-215; 443-444) are of doubtful authenticity. Fragments of a commentary on Genesis have been published by Devreesse. The *Life of John the Baptist* preserved in an Arabic version and attributed to an Egyptian bishop Serapion cannot be genuine.

Editions: R. DEVREESSE, Anciens commentateurs grecs de l'Octateuque: RBibl (1935) 181. — The *Life of John the Baptist* was edited and translated into English by A. MINGANA, Bulletin of the John Rylands Library 11 (1927) 342-349, 438-491, reprinted in Woodbrooke Studies 1. Cambridge, 1927, 234-287, cf. 138-145. German translation: R. BOOS, Goetheanum 6 (1927) 318-320.

DIDYMUS THE BLIND

Didymus, surnamed 'the Blind', stands out among the heads of the catechetical school of Alexandria in the fourth century. Born about the year 313, he had lost his sight at the age of four, as Palladius (*Hist. Lausiac.* 4) tells us. The high esteem that he won during his lifetime sprang partly from spontaneous admiration for a man who, despite the tremendous handicap of lifelong blindness, amassed an amazing treasure of erudition, and that, too, without ever going to school or even learning to read. He was a veritable prodigy of encyclopaedic knowledge, but not by any standard a brilliant or original intellect. He kept out of the religious controversies of his time, yet had a genuinely powerful effect on contemporary theological thought. Athanasius did not hesitate to place him in the highly responsible position as head of the catechetical school of Alexandria (Rufinus, *Hist. eccl.* 2, 7). He was the last of its famous teachers, since that celebrated institution closed down soon after his death. His best known pupils are St. Jerome and Rufinus. The first mentions Didymus repeatedly as his *magister* (*Epist.* 50,1; 84,3; *comm. in Osee proph.*, prol.; *comm. in epist. ad Ephes.*, prol.), praises his learning, and testifies to his influence on the divines of his time in the West as well as in the

East (*Liber de Spir. Sancto*, Praef. ad Paulin.). The second calls him a 'prophet' and 'apostolic man' (Rufinus, *Apol. in Hier.* 2,25). But it was not only by his learning that Didymus attracted his contemporaries. His asceticism had won him no less renown. He lived almost a hermit's life. St. Antony, the father of monasticism, saw him several times in his cell and Palladius paid him four visits there over a period of ten years (*Hist. Lausiac.* 4). He was 85 years old when he died about the year 398.

Monographs: J. LEIPOLDT, Didymus der Blinde von Alexandria (TU 29, 3). Leipzig, 1905. — G. BARDY, Didyme l'Aveugle. Paris, 1910. — W. J. GAUCHE, Didymus the Blind, an Educator of the Fourth Century. Diss. Washington, 1934.

I. HIS WORKS

The extensive erudition which astonished his contemporaries found expression in a great number of writings. According to Palladius 'he interpreted the Old and the New Testament word by word, and such attention did he pay to the doctrine, setting out his exposition of it subtly yet surely, that he surpassed all the ancients in knowledge' *(l.c.)*. This fits exactly St. Jerome's report; he calls his works *plura et nobilia*, mentions in addition to commentaries on a great number of biblical books, treatises such as *De Spiritu Sancto*, *De dogmatibus* and two books *Contra Arianos*, but adds at the end of his enumeration 'and many other things, to give an account of which would be a work of itself' (*De vir. ill.* 109).

Unfortunately, very little remains of this great literary output due to the cloud of suspicion which hung over Didymus' name and reputation during the Origenistic controversies. After all, he had dared to defend the great Alexandrian and his work *De principiis* as entirely orthodox. No wonder then that in the sixth and following centuries he was condemned as a believer in the pre-existence of the soul and in the Apokatastasis. The bishops who gathered at Constantinople for the Fifth General Council in 553 anathematized Origen, Didymus and the deacon Evagrius Ponticus for those doctrines. As a consequence, almost all of Didymus' works have perished.

Editions: MG 39, 131-1818. Though this is the only collected edition of his works, it remains very incomplete. A careful investigation of the catenae would furnish additional texts. K. STAAB, Pauluskommentare aus der griechischen Kirche, Münster, 1933, 1-45, presents a critical edition of many exegetical fragments.

1. *On the Trinity*

Fortunately, among those which have come down to us, is his main work, the three books *On the Trinity (Tὰ περὶ τριάδος* τρία βιβλία), composed between 381 and 392. Perhaps we owe its preservation to the fact that it was not marred by Origenism. Even Jerome admits: 'Certe in Trinitate catholicus est' (*Lib. II adv. Rufin.*, 16). In fact, he is in full agreement with Athanasius in his defense of the consubstantiality of the three divine persons. He rejects any subordinationism and at the end answers the objections raised by the Arians and Macedonians. The first book deals with the Son, the second with the Holy Spirit, the third summarizes the two and discusses the most important biblical passages on which the opponents based their conclusions. Although the treatise testifies to the enormous biblical erudition of its author, it remains a vast collection of Scriptural texts, studied sometimes with real depth but occasionally, too, distorted.

Editions: MG 39, 269-992. Selections: EP 1068-1076.

Studies: T. SCHERMANN, Lateinische Parallelen zu Didymus (*De Trinitate* 2, 14): RQ 16 (1902) 232-242 (in Tertullian and Ambrose). — A. JAHN and J. DRÄSEKE, Zur Schrift über die Trinität: Zeitschrift f. wissenschaftl. Theologie 45 (1902) 410-415, deal with quotations from Greek poets. — H. R. SMYTHE, The interpretation of Amos IV, 13 in St. Athanasius and Didymus: JThSt N.S. 1 (1950) 158-168 (*De Trinitate* 3, 31). — L. DOUTRELEAU, Le De Trinitate est-il l'œuvre de Didyme l'Aveugle?: RSR 45 (1957) 514-557.

2. On the Holy Spirit

In his *De Trinitate* Didymus refers twice (3, 16, 21) to his treatise *On the Holy Spirit* (Περὶ τοῦ ἁγίου πνεύματος λόγος). Although the Greek original has been lost, a Latin version is extant, which St. Jerome, following a suggestion of Pope Damasus, prepared between 384 and 392 (ML 39, 1031-1086). St. Ambrose used the Greek text in 381 as a source for his *De Spiritu Sancto*, so that Jerome accuses him in the introduction to his Latin translation of plagarism; Didymus' work was thus composed at least before 381. It is one of the best monographs on the subject written during the fourth century. The first part (ch. 4-29) adduces proof that the Holy Spirit is not a creature but consubstantial with the Father and the Son, the second (ch. 30-59) deals with Scriptural texts which confirm the Catholic doctrine and refute the objections of the Pneumatomachi. Except for the unreliable rendering of trinitarian terms and expressions, St. Jerome's translation is so faithful that it even repeats misquotations.

Editions: Latin version: MG 39, 1031-1086. ML 23, 101-154. — A new critical ed. will be published soon: G. BARDY, Didyme, Traité du Saint-Esprit. Texte, introduction, traduction et notes (SCH). — Selections: EP 1066-1067.

Translations: French: G. BARDY, l.c. — *German:* G. CRONE, Didymus, Der Heilige Geist, erläutert. Steyl, 1939.

Studies: T. Schermann, Die griechischen Quellen des hl. Ambrosius in ll. III de Spir. S. Munich, 1902, 87-92. — E. Stolz, Didymus, Ambrosius, Hieronymus: ThQ 87 (1905) 371-401 with a valuable study of the reliability of Jerome's translation. — B. Altaner, Augustinus und Didymus der Blinde, Eine quellenkritische Untersuchung: VC 5 (1951) 116-120, proves that Augustine knew *De Spiritu Sancto.* A. Quattrone, La pneumatologia nel trattato De Spiritu Sancto di Didimo Allessandrino: Regnum Dei 8 (1952) 82-88, 140-152; 9 (1953) 81-88.

3. *Against the Manichæans*

This treatise is extant in Greek and consists of 18 short chapters. In its present form the introduction is mutilated and the impression prevails that the text represents only an excerpt from a larger work. Nevertheless it seems to be authentic; for Didymus engages in polemics against the Manichæans in *On the Trinity* and *On the Holy Spirit* as well as in his commentaries to the Bible. There is hardly any indication that the author was influenced by Serapion's book of the same name (cf. above, p. 81), although he seems to know it.

Editions: MG 39, 1085-1110. Selection: EP 1077.

Translation: Spanish: M. Parpal, Obras escogidas de Patrologia griega. Barcelona, 1916.

4. *Lost Dogmatical Works*

a. *De dogmatibus et contra Arianos*

In his *De trinitate* Didymus refers not less than fourteen times to another work from his pen which he calls πρῶτος λόγος, the *First Word*, and which for a long time was thought to be lost. Yet this treatise, probably the same as the two books *De dogmatibus et contra Arianos* mentioned by St. Jerome (*De vir. ill.* 109), seems identical with the fourth and fifth books appended to St. Basil's *Contra Eunomium* by many manuscripts and most printed editions (cf. below, p. 210). The added material, though attributed to St. Basil as early as the fifth century, definitely does not belong to him. On the other hand, it has a number of features in common with our blind author's *De Trinitate* and *De Spiritu Sancto*, and what is more important, though it appears to be only a compendium or excerpt, its text fits the fourteen allusions in *De Trinitate*. The unabridged original must have been composed before 392, the year in which St. Jerome's *De viris illustribus* was published. There are reasons to assume that Didymus in *De Spiritu Sancto* 32 has this same work in mind, when he speaks of a *Dogmatum volumen* as one of his previous writings.

Editions: MG 29, 671-774. — J. Drāseke, Apollinarios von Laodicea (TU 7, 3-4). Leipzig, 1892, 205-251.

Studies: F. X. Funk, Die zwei letzten Bücher der Schrift Basilius' des Gr. gegen Eunomius:
Kirchengeschichtliche Abhandlungen und Untersuchungen 2, Paderborn, 1899, 291-329,
attributed the two books to Didymus. When J. Leipoldt, l.c. 26-31, raised objections,
Funk answered: Kirchengeschichtl. Abh. und Unters. 3. Paderborn, 311-323. Bardy,
l.c. 23-27 agreed with Funk. Finally J. Lebon, Le Pseudo-Basile (*Adv. Eunom.* IV-V)
est bien Didyme d'Alexandrie, Mus 50 (1937) 61-83, proved that Didymus must be
the author.

b. Sectarum volumen

Nothing remains of his treatise *Sectarum volumen* mentioned in
De Spir. Sancto 5 and 21, in which Didymus explained among other
things that the Holy Spirit does not receive wisdom but is wisdom.

c. Defense of Origen

According to Socrates (*Hist. eccl.* 4, 25) Didymus devoted a work
to the defense and exposition of Origen's *On First Principles* of
which nothing is extant. He endeavored to show that Origen had
been misunderstood by simple people who could not grasp his
ideas. St. Jerome reports that Didymus gave an orthodox interpretation of Origen's trinitarian doctrine but accepted without
hesitation his other errors regarding the sin of the angels, the
pre-existence of souls, the Apokatastasis, etc. (*Adv. Rufin.* 1, 6; 2, 16).
The same informant tells us of another treatise with Origenistic
leanings. Written at the suggestion of Rufinus, who spent the years
371 to 377 in Egypt, it answered the question: 'Quare moriantur
infantes, cum propter peccata corpora acceperint?' Didymus'
explanation was: 'non eos multa peccasse et ideo corporum carceres
tantum eis tetigisse sufficere' (Jerome, *Adv. Rufin.* 3, 28).

d. St. John of Damascus mentions two other works of Didymus,
Ad philosophum and *De incorporeo*, from which his *Sacra Parallela*
takes a few brief quotations (MG 96, 248. 524). Nothing else is
known about them.

e. According to K. Holl, Didymus also composed the little book
Adversus Arium et Sabellium found among the works of Gregory of
Nyssa (MG 45, 1281-1302). This opinion won the support of
J. Leipoldt, but not of G. Bardy. The latter showed that while
Holl proved that the work was not Gregory's, he did not establish
that it was Didymus'.

Studies: K. Holl, Über die Gregor von Nyssa zugeschriebene Schrift Adv. Arium et
Sabellium: ZKG 25 (1904) 380-398. Reprinted: K. Holl, Gesammelte Aufsätze II.
Tübingen, 1928, 298-309. — J. Leipoldt, l.c. 9. — G. Bardy, l.c. 17f.

f. A. Günthör regards Didymus as the author of the seven
Pseudo-Athanasian Dialogues (cf. above, p. 31). He is not the first

to advocate that view. E. Stolz held the same opinion. Others have thought of Maximus Confessor, Theodoret of Cyrus, Apollinaris of Laodicea or Diodorus of Tarsus. Günthör examines the exegesis, the theology, especially the trinitarian terminology, and the style of these dialogues. As a result he is convinced that only Didymus could have written them. His theory has met with both approval and opposition. W. Dietsche agrees, whereas H. Rahner has serious doubts.

Studies: E. Stolz, Didymus, Ambrosius, Hieronymus: ThQ 87 (1905) 371-401. — F. Loofs, Zwei Makedonische Dialoge: SAB (1914) 526-551. — A. Segovie, Contribución al estudio de la tradición manuscrita del Pseudo-atanasiano 'Dialogo I contra un Macedoniano o Pneumatomaco': Archivo Teológico Granadino 1 (1938) 87-107. — A. Günthör, Die sieben pseudo-athanasianischen Dialoge, ein Werk Didymus' des Blinden von Alexandrien. Rome, 1941. Cf. H. Rahner, ZkTh 65 (1941) 111f. — W. Dietsche, L'héritage littéraire de Didyme l'Aveugle: RSPT 2 (1941/42) 380-414.

g. W. Dietsche also attributed to Didymus the treatise *On the Vision of the Seraphim* which G. Morin edited in Anecdota Maredsolana III, 3, 103-122. B. Altaner does not subscribe to this hypothesis and suggests Theophilus of Alexandria as its author (cf. below p. 106).

Editions: Editio princeps: A. M. Amelli, S. Hieronymi Stridonensis presb. tractatus contra Origenem de visione Isaiae. Monte Cassino, 1901. — New edit. G. Morin, Anecdota Maredsolana III, 3 (1903) 103-122. Amelli and Morin regarded St. Jerome as the author.

Studies: F. Diekamp, Literarische Rundschau für das katholische Deutschland 27 (1901) 293f, was the first to suggest Theophilus of Alexandria as the real author. — B. Dietsche, Didymus von Alexandrien als Verfasser der Schrift über die Seraphenvision. Untersuchungen zur Urheberschaft des sogenannten Anecdoton von Amelli. Freiburg i.B., 1942. — B. Altaner, Wer ist der Verfasser des Tractatus in Isaiam VI, 1-7?: ThR 42 (1943) 147-151.

5. *Exegetical Works*

a. *Old Testament*

According to Jerome, Didymus composed commentaries to the following books of the Old Testament: the Psalms, Job, Isaias, Osee and Zacharias. There existed also one on Proverbs, mentioned by Cassiodorus, *Inst. div. litt.* 5. None of these has been preserved entire but many fragments are found in *catenae*. Moreover, some of the papyri discovered at Toura in Egypt in 1941 contain excerpts of considerable length from Didymus' explanations of Genesis, Job and Zacharias. These texts are being edited by O. Guérand and J. Scherer.

Studies: G. Bardy, Du nouveau sur Didyme l'Aveugle: Science religieuse. Travaux et recherches. 1944, 247-250. — H. C. Puech, Les nouveaux écrits d'Origène et de Didyme découverts à Toura: RHPR 31 (1951) 293-329. — L. DOUTRELEAU and J. AUCAGNE, Que savons-nous aujourd'hui des papyrus de Toura?: RSR 43 (1955) 161-193 furnish an edition and a French translation of the excerpts of the third book of the commentary on Zacharias. The papyrus contains so many fragments of this work that the text will be almost complete.

The Commentary to the Psalms of which St. Jerome speaks (*De vir. ill.* 109; *Epist.* 112, 20) must have been a monumental work. The large number of quotations extant enables us to gain an impression of Didymus' allegorico-mystical method of exegesis, which proves him a true follower of Origen. Like the Alexandrian master, he shows an interest in textual criticism and compares the different manuscripts of the Septuagint as well as the Hexapla. But his endeavor to determine the exact reading does not prevent a freely figurative interpretation. Thus he is convinced that the Old Testament contains everywhere an important Christian message and that every Psalm points to Christ.

Of the Commentary on Proverbs only a few fragments are extant. It was translated, at the suggestion of Cassiodorus *(l.c.)* by Epiphanius the Scholastic, but this version has been entirely lost.

The Commentary on Isaias counted no less than eighteen volumes although it dealt only with Isaias 40-66, a section that Didymus regarded as a book of its own (Jerome, *De vir. ill.* 109; *Prol. comm. in Is. proph.*).

Texts: Fragmenta *in Genesin et Exodum:* MG 39, 1111-1115; *in Regum* 1.2.: MG 39, 1115-1120; *in Job:* MG 39, 1119-1154; *in Psalmos:* MG 39, 1155-1616, 1617-1622; *in Proverbia:* MG 39, 1621-1646. Migne's collection of fragments is by no means complete. For further fragments, see: M. FAULHABER, Hohelied-, Proverbien- und Predigerkatenen. Vienna, 1902, 168. — J. LEIPOLDT, l.c. 17-21 and 148. — G. BARDY, Didyme l'Aveugle. Paris, 1910, 44-48. — R. DEVREESSE, Chaînes exégétiques grecques: DB Suppl. I (1928) 1125f. etc.; *idem,* Anciens commentateurs grecs de l'Octateuque: RBibl (1935) 181-186 Fragmenta *in Genesin et Exodum.* — H. C. PUECH, l.c.

Study: L. MARIÈS, Un commentaire de Didyme publié sous le nom de Diodore: RSR 5 (1914) 73-78, 246-251, deals with scholia on the Psalms which Cardinal Mai attributed to Diodor of Tarsus, but evidently belong to Didymus.

b. New Testament

Our blind author composed commentaries on the following writings of the New Testament: The Gospel of Matthew, that of John, the Acts of the Apostles, I and II Corinthians, Galatians and Ephesians. St. Jerome made use of the work on St. Matthew for his own interpretation of the same evangelist (*De vir. ill.* 109; *Comm. in evang. Matth.* prol.). Nothing else is known about it. Of the explanation to the Fourth Gospel a few fragments survive (MG 39, 1645-54).

Citations from Didymus on the Acts can be found in many

Catenae and in Theophylactus' exegesis of the same book. Migne's edition is far from being complete (MG 39, 1653-78). Thirty additional excerpts are given by J. A. Cramer, *Catenae Graecorum patrum in Novum Testamentum*, Oxford, 1844, t. III, 21. 90. 187-413. To judge from the number of quotations, the original must have been of considerable size.

Very little was left of his commentary on I Corinthians (a quotation in Jerome's *Ep.* 119, 5), until K. Staab published 38 fragments of this work from *Codex Athous Pantokrat.* 28 which restore the greater part of Didymus' notes on chapters 15 and 16 of I Corinthians. The same manuscript and *Cod. Vat.* 762 contain a number of fragments of his commentary on II Corinthians.

Edition: K. STAAB, Pauluskommentare aus der griechischen Kirche aus Katenen-handschriften gesammelt. Münster, 1933, 6-14 Fragments on I Corinthians, 14-44 Fragments on II Corinthians. MG 39, 1677-1732 is incomplete and based on Cod. Vat. 762 only. Staab publishes p. 1-6 a long fragment on the seventh chapter of Romans, which does not belong to a commentary, but most probably to his treatise *Against the Manichaeans*.

His exposition of Galatians, written before 387, served as a source for Jerome's (*Ep.* 112, 4; *Comm. in Epist. ad Gal.*, prol.). The latter's interpretation of Ephesians also made good use of Didymus' brief commentary on that Epistle (Jerome, *Adv. Rufin.* 1, 16. 21; *Comm. in Epist. ad Ephes.*, prol.). Of these works nothing remains.

Cassiodorus mentions an *Expositio septem canonicarum* (i.e. *catholicarum*) *epistolarum* of Didymus as having been turned into Latin by Epiphanius the Scholastic (*Inst. div. litt.* 8). The version has reached us (MG 39, 1749-1818), whereas the original survives in only a few excerpts (MG *l.c.*; Cramer, *l.c.*, VIII, 2. 30. 52. 63. 22. 65). The authorship of this commentary has been much disputed. E. Klostermann had shown that several passages of the Latin translation appear in Cramer's edition of the Greek fragments under the names of Origen, John Chrysostom and Severus of Antioch. It seemed therefore that the work which Cassiodorus and Epiphanius the Scholastic regarded as that of Didymus was in reality a *catena*, compiled not earlier than the sixth century from Greek exegetical treatises by different authors. However, K. Staab's careful investigation has left little doubt that Didymus is the author.

Editions: MG 39, 1749-1818. New crit. ed. by F. ZOEPFL, Didymi Alex. in epistolas canonicas brevis enarratio (Neutest. Abhandl. 4, 1). Münster, 1913.

Studies: E. KLOSTERMANN, Über des Didymus von Alexandrien In epistolas canonicas enarratio (TU 28, 2). Leipzig, 1905. — K. STAAB, Die griechischen Katenenkommentare zu den katholischen Briefen: Bibl (1924) 314-318.

II. THE THEOLOGY OF DIDYMUS

For the historian of theology the writings of Didymus are of considerable value. They do not, it is true, give one the impression of an original or monumental achievement, but rather of a rich mosaic, in which we admire the variety of colorful stones. Nevertheless, they are important for the development of the trinitarian and christological doctrines. Since he stands between Athanasius and the great Cappadocian Fathers, he bears witness to one of the most interesting transitions in the history of thought. Moreover, his treatises are the fruit of his lectures at the catechetical school of Alexandria. They show the influence of his predecessors, of Origen as well as Athanasius, but at the same time, by improving on the traditional Alexandrian teaching, they lay the foundations for the christology of Cyril of Alexandria.

Studies: See monographs above p. .... — W. BRIGHT, DCB 1, 827-829. — M. PELLEGRINO, EC 4, 1567f. — G. BARDY, DSp fasc. 20-21, 668-671; *idem*, Post apostolos ecclesiarum magister: RML 6 (1950) 313-316 (title given to Origen by Didymus). — T. BAROSSE, The Unity of the Two Charities in Greek Patristic Exegesis: TS 15 (1954) 355-388. — W. C. LINSS, The Four Gospel Text of Didymus the Blind. Diss. Boston Univ., 1955.

1. *Trinity*

Didymus is above all the theologian of the Trinity. His doctrine on this subject found its best expression in the catch-word μία οὐσία, τρεῖς ὑποστάσεις which he uses again and again in his controversies. This formula, which does not occur in the works of St. Athanasius, appears for the first time in the *Discourse against Arius and Sabellius* dating from before 358 (cf. above, p. 89). From the existence of only one substance in the Trinity, Didymus concludes that there can be only one operation of the three Divine Persons:

> It is proved that in all things there is one same operation of the Father, the Son, and the Holy Ghost. There is but one operation where there is but one substance, because whatever are *homoousia* with the same substance, have likewise the same operations (*De Spir. Sancto* 17).

On other occasions he argues from the unity of operation to the unity of nature:

> Since, therefore, these *homoousia* are worthy of the same honor and have the same operation, they have the same nature, and do not differ from one another either in divinity or in operation: they alone can exist together, be placed together in the same grade of dignity, and be everywhere understood with Him Who is one (*De Trin.* 2, 6, 4).

Speaking of Divine Providence he states that Father, Son and Holy Spirit share in it because of their unity of substance: 'Those who share in the same guiding have the same glory and the same essence' (*ibid.* 2, 8, 4). Of course, this absolute unity of nature, will and operation transcends human understanding: 'It is impossible to grasp even this, how the Trinity has one will, and speaks and grants favors in such a way that this speech and granting of favors is common to all the Persons' (*ibid.* 2, 5, 1). The same conclusions are drawn in his book *De Spiritu Sancto:*

> Whoever communicates with the Holy Ghost communicates immediately with the Father and the Son. And whoever shares in the glory of the Father has this glory from the Son, contributed through the Holy Spirit. So it is proved that in everything there is one same operation for the Father, the Son, and the Holy Ghost (17).
>
> At the end of the second epistle which Paul wrote to the Corinthians he says: 'The grace of our Lord Jesus Christ, and the charity of God, and the communication of the Holy Ghost be with you all' (2 Cor. 13, 13). From these words is shown one assumption of the Trinity: since whoever receives the grace of Christ has it as much through the administration of the Father as through the distribution of the Holy Ghost. For this grace is given by God the Father and by Jesus Christ, according to the words: 'Grace be with you and peace from God the Father and from our Lord Jesus Christ'; the Father does not give one kind of grace, and the Son another. But St. Paul describes this grace as being given by the Father and by our Lord Jesus Christ and completed by the communication of the Holy Ghost (6).
>
> For when anyone has received the grace of the Holy Ghost he will have it as a gift from the Father and our Lord Jesus Christ. By one same grace, however, which is from the Father and the Son, completed by the operation of the Holy Spirit, is proved the Trinity of one substance (16).

2. *Christology*

The Christology of Didymus has exceptional value for the history preceding the christological controversies. It is far from following the soteriological trend that characterizes Athanasius. On the other hand, it is much clearer on the question of the human soul of Christ. In *De Trinitate* he openly refutes the Arian doctrine that Jesus had no human soul at all. Perhaps we can detect here the influence of Origen, who had already taught that the Logos had united himself to the body through the medium of the soul (cf. vol. II, p. 80). Didymus declares without hesitation that no human body without a soul can eat and sleep, nor can the divinity of the Logos do this. Since we know that Jesus did both, a human soul is needed (*De Trin.* 3, 2, 27; 3, 21). He stresses the union between the Logos and the human soul stating that this union is eternal and indissoluble (*In psalm.* 1284 C; 1465 C). From the fact that Jesus is a perfect man (ἄνθρωπος τέλειος) follows that he is subject — saving sin — to all our infirmities, weaknesses and needs. He has kept all the consequences of the Incarnation (*De trin.* 3, 21). While his humanity has been sanctified through its union with the Logos, still it has preserved its passibility.

Whereas Athanasius regards the resurrection as the reunion of the Logos with his body, Didymus declares more correctly that while his body was in the grave, his human soul was for three days and three nights in Hades, to be reunited with the body in the resurrection (*In psalm.* 1233 ABC). As a consequence, Didymus emphasizes (*De Trin.* 3, 6; 3, 21; 3, 13) that there was no fusion of the divinity and the humanity in Christ to constitute a third nature but that the two elements were joined without change (ἀτρέπτως) and without fusion (ἀσυγχύτως). Thus he recognizes in Christ two natures or two wills, the divine and the human (*ibid.* 3, 12). Although he does not as yet use the formula δύο φύσεις, his approach constitutes a definite step forward in christological doctrine. His distinguishing of two natures in Christ does not prevent him from expressing the personal unity: 'We do not believe that the Son who is from the Father is one being (ἄλλον), and He who became flesh and was crucified is another being (καὶ ἄλλον)' (*De Trin.* 3, 6; *De Spir. S.* 52).

3. *The Holy Spirit*

For Didymus as for St. Athanasius, the doctrine of the Spirit stands in the closest possible relation to that of the Son. In the Arian controversy, the heresy about the former arose out of the heresy about the latter. Thus Didymus not only devotes the second book of his *De Trinitate* to the Holy Ghost, he wrote a special treatise *De Spiritu Sancto*, so that he has been called 'the theologian of the Holy Spirit' and the Council of Florence praised him for his manifold and explicit testimony to the procession of the Holy Ghost from both the Father and the Son.

Against the Arian doctrine that the Holy Spirit is a creature, he repeatedly asserts that he is uncreated like the Son. Comparing the Baptism of Christ with the baptism of the catechumens, he remarks:

> The creature is anointed with a created and sanctified oil in baptism. The Saviour, as God, was anointed with His all-holy and, like Himself, uncreated Spirit, above His fellows, which is to say, us. But if the Holy Spirit were creature, He Who is uncreated would not be anointed by Him (*De Trin.* 2, 23).

The third person of the Trinity is not a creature but God and equal to the Father:

> It has been proved that the Holy Ghost is not only God, but also equal and similar to the Father, because in an equal and similar way man is a temple of the three persons; and likewise whoever is the dwelling-place of the Father has the Son also dwelling within him, as well as the Spirit of God: just as in turn, whoever has the dignity of having the Holy Spirit or the Son, has the Father also (*De Trin.* 2, 10).

Regarding the procession of the Holy Ghost from the Father and the Son, Didymus in his treatise *De Trinitate* does not go farther than to state that the Holy Spirit 'proceeds from the Father and remains divinely in the Son' (1, 31). He mentions, however, that the Holy Spirit is the image of the Son, as the Son is the image of the Father (2, 5) and that He is the Spirit of the Son, of the Logos, of the Saviour (1, 18; 2, 6; 3, 1). As the Son is *homoousios* to the Father, so the Holy Spirit is consubstantial with the Father and the Son (1,27; 1,19). If the Latin translation of St. Jerome does justice to the original, Didymus progresses in *De Spiritu Sancto* and formulates plainly the doctrine of the procession of the Holy Spirit from the Father and the Son:

> Non loquetur [Spiritus Sanctus] a semetipso: hoc est non sine me, et sine meo et Patris arbitrio, quia inseparabilis a mea et Patris est voluntate, quia non ex se est sed ex Patre et me est, hoc enim ipsum quod subsistit et loquitur a Patre et me illi est (34).
>
> Spiritus quoque Sanctus qui est Spiritus veritatis, Spiritusque sapientiae, non potest, Filio loquente, audire quae nescit, cum hoc ipsum sit quod profertur a Filio, id est procedens a veritate, consolator manans de consolatore, Deus de Deo, Spiritus veritatis procedens (36).
>
> Neque enim quid aliud est Filius exceptis his quae ei dantur a Patre, neque alia substantia est Spiritus Sancti praeter id quod datur ei a Filio (37).

Following the traditional lines of Greek theology, Didymus considers the work of the sanctification of the soul as belonging in some particular way to the Holy Spirit. He is convinced that the Holy Ghost renovates us in baptism. He is the plenitude, the culminating point of all God's gifts to man. He is in the Trinity as the common Gift of the Father and the Son. He is the first Gift, because He is Love, and love is the reason for all other gifts. Hence all gifts are recapitulated in Him. 'In the substance of the Holy Ghost is understood the plenitude of all gifts' (*De Spir. S.* 28):

> It is impossible for anyone to acquire the grace of God if he have not the Holy Ghost: in Whom we prove that all the gifts of God consist (*ibid.* 9).

Whence it is evident that the Holy Ghost is the plenitude of all gifts, and that nothing is given in the Divinity without Him, because all the advantages which are received from the favor of God's gifts flow from this Fountain-Head (*ibid.* 4).

Studies: T. Schermann, Die Gottheit des Heiligen Geistes nach den griechischen Vätern des vierten Jahrhunderts. Freiburg i.B., 1901, 189-223. — E. L. Heston, The Spiritual Life and the Role of the Holy Ghost in the Sanctification of the Soul as Described in the Works of Didymus of Alexandria. Notre Dame (Indiana), 1938. — P. Galtier, Le Saint Esprit en nous d'après les Pères grecs. Rome, 1946, 206-216. — A. Quattrone, La pneumatologia nel trattato De Spiritu Sancto di Didimo Alessandrino: Regnum Dei 8 (1952) 82-88, 140-152; 9 (1953) 81-88.

4. *The Church*

It is the same Holy Spirit who distributes the different graces in the Church founded by Christ:

He founded His Church upon the rivers, making it, through His divine legislation, capable of receiving the Holy Ghost, from Whom, as from their fountain-head, the different graces flow as fountains of living water (*In Ps.* 23, 4).

It is the same Spirit through Whom the Church becomes the Mother of all, who from her virginal womb gives birth in the baptismal font to her children:

The baptismal pool of the Trinity is a workshop for the salvation of all those who believe. It frees from the serpent sting all those who are washed therein, and, remaining a virgin, becomes the mother of all through the Holy Ghost (*De Trin.* 2, 13).

So it is in Alexandria with Didymus the Blind that we find the font itself described, apparently for the first time, as the ever-virgin mother of the baptized, fruitful through the Holy Spirit. It is only logical that on another occasion he should call the Church not only the bride of Christ (*De Trin.* 2,6,23; *In Ps.* 1369 AB, 1372 A, 1465 C) but our Mother (*In Prov.* 1624 C), most probably following an idea of his master Origen. More pronounced, however, is his doctrine of the Church as the Mystical Body of Christ (*In Ps.* 1281 C), on which he is much clearer than St. Athanasius.

5. *Original Sin and Baptism*

To Didymus the fall of the first parents is the sin of old (παλαιὰ ἁμαρτία), from which Jesus cleansed us in His Baptism in the Jordan (*De Trin.* 2,12). All the children of Adam have inherited it by transmission (κατὰ διαδοχήν) through the intercourse of their parents. This is why Jesus, born of a Virgin, has not been stained with it (*Contra Man.* 8).

Speaking of the effects of baptism, he mentions both the negative and the positive aspect, the cleansing from original sin and all its consequences as also from personal guilt, and the adoption as children of God:

> The Holy Spirit as God renovates us in baptism, and in union with the Father and the Son, brings us back from a state of deformity to our pristine beauty and so fills us with His grace that we can no longer make room for anything that is unworthy of our love; He frees us from sin and death and from the things of the earth; makes us spiritual men, sharers in the divine glory, sons and heirs of God and of the Father. He conforms us to the image of the Son of God, makes us co-heirs and His brothers, we who are to be glorified and to reign with Him; He gives us heaven in exchange for earth, and bestows paradise with a bounteous hand, and makes us more honorable than the angels; and in the divine waters of the baptismal pool extinguishes the inextinguishable fire of hell (*De Trin.* 2, 12).

> For when we are immersed in the baptismal pool, we are by the goodness of God and the Father and through the grace of His Holy Spirit stripped of our sins as we lay aside the old man, are regenerated and sealed by His own kingly power. But when we come up out of the pool, we put on Christ our Saviour as an incorruptible garment, worthy of the same honor as the Holy Spirit who regenerated us and marked us with His seal. For as many of you, says Holy Scripture, as have been baptized in Christ have put on Christ (Gal. 3, 27). Through the divine insufflation we had received the image and likeness of God, which the Scripture speaks of, and through sin we had lost it, but now we are found once more such as we were when we were first made: sinless and masters of ourselves (*De Trin.* 2, 12).

Baptism is absolutely necessary for salvation. Not even the perfection of a faultless life can make up for it: 'No one not regenerated by the Holy Spirit of God and marked with the seal of His sanctification has attained heavenly gifts, even through the perfection of a faultless life in all the rest' (*De Trin.* 2, 12). The only exception to the indispensability of the baptism of water is the baptism of blood, which is also the work of the Holy Spirit: 'Those who suffered martyrdom before baptism, having been washed in their own blood, were vivified by the Holy Spirit of God' (*ibid.*). He sums up the effects of baptism on the soul as follows: 'Thus, renovated in baptism, we enjoy the familiarity of God, in so far as the powers of our nature permit, as someone has said: In so far as mortal man can be likened to God' (*ibid.*).

Didymus mentions once (*De Trin.* 2,15) that the Catholic Church does not recognize baptism conferred by the Montanists or the Eunomians, because the former held a trinitarian doctrine of modalistic-monarchian character and did not baptize in the three divine Persons, while the latter made use of a peculiar formula, baptizing 'in the death of the Lord' (εἰς τὸν θάνατον τοῦ κυρίου).

6. The Mother of God

Didymus calls Mary by preference 'the Mother of God' (θεοτόκος), a title which originated at Alexandria (cf. vol. II, p. 81). He proclaims her virginity *in partu* and *post partum* and addresses her as 'the perpetual virgin' (ἀειπαρθένος), an expression which Athanasius had used (*Contra Arianos* 2,70).

7. Anthropology

The influence of Origen can be seen in the doctrine of the human soul. Although quite a few passages seem to imply that man consists of only body and soul (*De Spir. S.* 54; *In Ps.* 1520 BC), others show that Didymus, following Origen and Plato, believed in three principles and made a real distinction between the rational soul (νοῦς), the animal soul (ψυχή) and the body (φύσις) (*De Spir. S.* 54, 55, 59; *De Trin.* 1,9; 1,15; 3,31).

He follows Origen also in his ideas of the origin of the soul. He is convinced that the soul has been created but shares his predecessor's error that it existed before the body in which it was enclosed in punishment for sins committed (*Enarr. in Epist. Petr. I*, 1; *De Trin.* 3,1). The same belief in its pre-existence is at the basis of the treatise which he addressed to Rufinus (cf. above, p. 89) on the early death of children.

8. Apokatastasis

According to Jerome (*Adv. Ruf.* 1,6), Didymus defended even Origen's doctrine of the universal restoration of all things in their original, purely spiritual state (ἀποκατάστασις). At first glance his writings seem to contradict this statement. He speaks many times of the inextinguishable fire of hell, of eternal punishment etc. (*De Trin.* 2,12; 2,26; *In Ps.* 1244 D, 1316 A, 1585 B). He affirms (*In Ps.* 1372 C) that there is time for penance only in this world. All these passages seem to exclude the idea of the Apokatastasis. However, upon closer examination there is evidence enough to support St. Jerome's assertion. Didymus remarks that the fallen angels are anxious to be saved (*In Petr. I* 1759 B) and were redeemed by Christ (*ibid.* 1770 BC). He is of the opinion that there will be no sinners in the life to come because their state of sin has ceased (*In Ps.* 1340 C). He never tires of refuting the Manichæans by showing that evil is not an essence (οὐσία) but an accidental condition, and that God will totally destroy it (*Contra Man.* 2,1088). He is convinced that if God punishes he does so only to educate, to train and to improve. Retribution as such or to avenge justice is absolutely foreign to his mind.

Thus Didymus has inherited from Origen the idea of purgatory. He states that God's 'spiritual fire' (νοητόν πῦρ) completes the purification of man that had begun in the waters of baptism (*De Trin.* 2,12). If he calls the fire or chastisement 'eternal', he seems to use the word not in the strict sense, but in the meaning of 'long lasting'. He declares explicitly that *aionios* can be applied literally only to God but, when said of punishment, it must be understood merely as 'timeless' (*De Trin.* 2, 6, 4).

THEOPHILUS OF ALEXANDRIA

Theophilus, patriarch of Alexandria, was the third successor to St. Athanasius and the predecessor of St. Cyril, his nephew. He ruled the Church of Egypt for 28 years (385-412), fully conscious of the important role that his see had played in the history of both Church and Empire. E. Gibbon (*Decline and Fall* 1,103f.) calls him 'the perpetual enemy of peace and virtue, a bold, bad man, whose hands were alternately polluted with gold and with blood'. This may be an exaggeration, but the sources at our disposal make him out a sorry figure of a bishop, violent and extremely unscrupulous. Undoubtedly a man of great intellectual ability, he too often devoted his gifts to the consolidation and increase of his power by very dubious means. He made his tremendous influence felt in all the political questions that in his day affected either Church or State.

Three important events are especially connected with his name—the decay of paganism in Egypt, the controversy over Origen, and the deposition and exile of St. John Chrysostom. In a concentrated attack on the last survivals of heathen cults in Egypt he destroyed in 391 with the consent of the Emperor Theodosius a number of shrines, especially the famous Sarapeum, the Mithraeum and the temple of Dionysos. He welcomed the opportunity thus offered to decorate the patriarchal city with a great number of new churches. For reasons that were not at all metaphysical, Theophilus changed sides in the quarrel about Origen. An ardent admirer of his until 399 and a friend of his adherents like John of Jerusalem, he later condemned him. It seems that Theophilus in one of his Paschal Letters had expressed himself in favor of God's incorporeity. Thereupon some monks conceived grave doubts regarding his orthodoxy and sent a commission to examine him. To forestall a riot by these anthropomorphists and, at the same time, anxious for political reasons to come to terms with them, he condemned Origenism at a Synod of Alexandria in 401 (Socrates, *Hist. eccl.* 6,75; Sozomen, *Hist. eccl.* 8,11). Moreover, he now took advantage of the decision to initiate a reckless persecution in the Nitrian desert of the supporters of the great Alexandrian, prominent among them the 'Four Long Brothers' Dioscurus, Ammon, Eusebius and Euthymus. But, he is most notorious for the evil part that he took in the banishment of St. John Chrysostom; forming a coalition of the different factions, both episcopal and imperial, opposed to the intrepid preacher, he called in 403 in the neighborhood of Chalcedon the Synod of the Oak that deposed St. John and sent him into exile.

In all justice, however, we must remember that most of our information comes from the enemies of Theophilus, especially Palladius, *Dialogus de vita Joh. Chrysostomi.* Arnobius (*Conflictus* 2,18), Theodoret (*Ep.* 170), Pope Leo the Great (*Ep.* 53.63.74), Vigilius Taps. (*C. Eut.* 1,15) and others regard Theophilus as a Father of the Church. The *Apophthegmata Patrum* prove the reputation he enjoyed in monastic circles. He was on excellent terms with the two famous abbots Horsiesi and Ammon, whom he always venerated as his spiritual fathers. The Coptic Church celebrates his feast on October 15, the Syriac, October 17.

Studies: G. LAZZATI, Teofilo d'Alessandria. Milan, 1936. — S. VISMARA, Un patriarca alessandrino del V secolo: SC (1935) 513-517. — W. BRIGHT, DCB 4, 999-1008. — J. FAIVRE, DHG 2 (1914) 319-323. — B. EVETTS, History of the Patriarchs of the Coptic Church of Alexandria: PO 1, 425-430. — E. WEIGL, Christologie vom Tode des Athanasius bis zum Ausbruch des nestorianischen Streites. Munich, 1925, 113-120. — R. DELOBEL et M. RICHARD, Théophile d'Alexandrie: DTC 15 (1946) 523-530. — A. FAVALE, Teofilo d'Alessandria: Salesianum 18 (1950) 215-246, 498-535; 19 (1951) 34-82.

HIS WRITINGS

Theophilus must have been a prominent ecclesiastical author; his literary bequest was of considerable volume (cf. Theodoret, *Ep.* 83; Leo M., *Ep.* 75; Gelasius, *Ep.* 42, 3, 3; Gennadius, *De vir. ill.* 34). Unfortunately, very little remains. An extensive list of his works is given by H. G. Opitz, but the most complete by M. Richard. Only a few can be mentioned here.

Edition: MG 65, 29-68, 401-404 (incomplete).

Studies: H. G. OPITZ, Theophilus von Alexandrien: PWK II, 5 (1934) 2149-2165. — M. RICHARD, Les écrits de Théophile d'Alexandrie: Mus 52 (1939) 33-50. — C. ASTRUC, Théophile d'Alexandrie et les manuscrits de la correspondance de Mélétios Pigas: Scriptorium 1 (1946/47) 162.

1. *Paschal Canon*

Theophilus composed a Table showing the Easter cycle for the years 380 to 479, which he sent to the victorious Emperor Theodosius about 388 or a little later. He wanted to make himself independent of Rome and induce the Emperor to adopt by imperial law the Alexandrian Paschal date as universal. The attempt failed and the Emperor refused to do so. Of this work the prologue is all that remains, complete only in a Latin translation.

Editions: MG 65, 47-52. Best ed.: B. KRUSCH, Studien zur christlich-mittelalterlichen Chronologie. Leipzig, 1880, 220-226.

Study: E. SCHWARTZ, Christliche und jüdische Ostertafeln: AGWG Phil.-hist. Kl., N.F. 8, 6 (1905) 3ff.

2. *Epistles*

Of his voluminous correspondence several letters were translated into Latin by St. Jerome and are preserved among his collected epistles. *Ep.* 92 (CSEL 55,147ff), received through Epiphanius, is a synodical of Sept. 400 to the bishops of Palestine and Egypt and reports on a gathering in Alexandria about 399 against the adherents of Origen. Two others were addressed in the summer of 400 to Jerome himself, *Ep.* 97 (CSEL 55,140) asking his aid in hunting out the Origenists, and *Ep.* 89 (CSEL 55,142) introducing the monk Theodore, who was on his way to Rome. The last (CSEL 55,143), sent to Epiphanius in 401, admonishes that prelate to call a synod to condemn the Origenists and suggests that the hierarchy of Asia Minor should follow suit.

A communication to the archimandrite Horsiesi and another to the Pachomian monks in Pbau both survive in a Coptic version and have been edited by W. E. Crum with a German translation.

Edition: W. CRUM, Der Papyruscodex saec. VI-VII der Philippsbibliothek in Cheltenham. Koptisch-theologische Schriften. Herausgegeben und übersetzt. Mit einem Beitrag von A. Ehrhard. Strasbourg, 1915, 65f, 70f.

Studies: A. EHRHARD, *ibidem:* 132-145. — W. HENGSTENBERG, Pachomiana mit einem Anhang über die Liturgie von Alexandrien: Festgabe Albert Ehrhard, herausg. v. A. M. Koeniger. Bonn and Leipzig, 1922, 238-252.

We know of many more of his letters. Of some fragments remain, of others nothing. Thus, according to Socrates (*Hist. eccl.* 6, 2, 6), he sent two epistles through the presbyter Isidore to Theodosius or Maximus around 388. Several were composed in 394 in reference to the dispute between Rufinus and Jerome, in which Theophilus places himself on the side of Rufinus (Jerome, *Contra Ruf.* 3,18). In another of the year 395 he approves of the apology of John of

Jerusalem against the accusations of Jerome (Jerome, *Contra Joh.* 5). A little later he wrote twice to Jerome regarding the ordination of his brother Paulinus, to which Jerome answered in *Ep.* 63 and 82. In 402 he corresponded with John Chrysostom regarding 'the Long Brothers'. Besides, we find mention of letters written about 399/400 to Pope Anastasius of Rome (Jerome, *Ep.* 88), to Flavian of Antioch in 401, to Pope Innocent I of Rome in July 404, to Porphyrius of Antioch after 404.

3. *Paschal Letters*

Following the custom of the Alexandrian patriarchs, Theophilus composed a great number of Easter Letters, twenty-six at least, that we know of. Three, preserved in translation of Jerome's, were issued in 401, 402 and 404 and have an anti-Origenistic tendency, although they also polemize against Apollinaris of Laodicea. Those of 401 and 402 are especially rich in theological content. The Latin version is found in Jerome's *Ep.* 96 (CSEL 55,159), 98 (CSEL 55,185) and 100 (CSEL 55,213). Of the first we have in addition a number of fragments of the original Greek and a remnant of a Coptic rendering.

Of his earliest Paschal Letter written in 386 nothing survives but the quotation in Cosmas Indicopleustes (*Top. Christ.* 10). That of 388, the third, is mentioned by Timotheus Aelurus in his refutation of the doctrine of Chalcedon. Some portions also remain of the fifth (390), of the sixth (391), of the tenth (395), several fragments of the twenty-first (406), of the twenty-second (407) and an undated excerpt from some other. The twenty-sixth (411) is alluded to by Synesius, *Ep.* 9. Cassian (*Coll.* 10,2: *longa disputatio, liber enormis*) and Gennadius *(De vir. ill.* 33: *disputatio longissima)* describe a further Easter circular to refute the anthropomorphists, i.e., those who attributed to God a human body.

Studies: See: Timotheos Ailuros, Widerlegung der auf der Synode von Chalkedon festgesetzten Lehre, herausgegeben von K. TER-MEKERTTSCHIAN und E. TER-MINASSIANTZ. Leipzig, 1908, 105, 160, 161, 195. Cf. E. SCHWARTZ, Codex Vaticanus Gr. 1431 eine antichalkedonische Sammlung aus der Zeit Kaiser Zenons: AAM 32, 6 (1927) 107 n. 191. 192; 112 n. 289. 290. 291; 114 n. 337. — For the Greek fragments of the Paschal Letter for 401, see: F. DIEKAMP, Doctrina Patrum de incarnatione Verbi. Münster, 1907, 180-183. — For the letter mentioned by Cassian and Gennadius, see: E. DRIOTON, La discussion d'un moine anthropomorphite audien avec le patriarche Théophile d'Alexandrie en année 399: ROC 20 (1915/17) 92-100, 113-132.

4. Facundus of Hermiane (*Pro defens. trium capit.* 6,5) testifies that Theophilus composed a violent pamphlet against St. John Chrysostom for giving shelter to some of the Origenist monks driven out of Egypt by the Alexandrian. Facundus gives a detailed account

together with a number of citations of this work, which he calls 'enormem librum, non solum contumeliis, sed ipsa quoque saepe repetita maledictorum recapitulatione nimis horribilem'. Jerome did not hesitate to render it into Latin and a fragment of his translation is preserved in his *Ep.* 113, as we know from *Ep.* 114, which implies that Theophilus denounced St. John Chrysostom for having desecrated the liturgy and the altar. That this was one of the charges brought by the Synod of the Oak, we learn from Facundus, who quotes it verbatim (*l.c.* 6,5; Photius, *Bibl. cod.* 59). It is possible that Theophilus concocted the libel in rage at the return of St. John Chrysostom in October 403.

Studies: C. BAUR, S. Jérôme et S. Chrysostome: RB 23 (1906) 430-436; *idem*, Der hl. Johannes Chrysostomus und seine Zeit, vol. 2. Munich, 1930, 280-283.

5. *Against Origen*

Gennadius (*De vir. ill.* 33) does not mention the diatribe against Chrysostom but is acquainted with 'one large volume against Origen'. Most probably this was merely a collection of the anti-Origenistic synodical and Paschal Letters. Thus Theodoret (*Dial.* 2) quotes from Theophilus' *Against Origen* two passages which occur in the Paschal Letter of 401 (Jerome, *Ep.* 96,4) and 402 (*ibid.* 98,16).

6. *Homilies*

A *Homily on the Judgement* is preserved in its Greek text in the *Apophthegmata Patrum* (MG 65,200,4). A Syriac version was published by M. Brière, ROC 18(1913)79f.

A *Homily on Contrition and Abstinence* is extant in a Coptic translation, edited by E. A. W. Budge, *Coptic Homilies in the Dialect of Upper Egypt ed. from the Papyrus Codex or. 5001 in the British Museum*, London 1910, 66f., 212f.

A *Homily on the Cross and the Thief* survives also in Coptic and was edited by F. de Rossi, *Papiri coptici di Torino* I,1,64.

A *Homily on the Institution of the Eucharist* was discovered by M. Richard, by proving that the sermon *In mysticam cenam* attributed to S. Cyril of Alexandria (MG 77,1016-1029) is really a discourse of Theophilus directed against the Origenist monks and can be dated to March 400. M. Richard, *Une homélie de Théophile d'Alexandrie sur l'institution de l'Eucharistie:* RHE 33 (1937) 46-56.

A *Homily on Penance* is known from a fragment preserved in the *Doctrina Patrum de incarnatione* 18, IX, ed. F. Diekamp, p. 120,10f.

Several homilies extant in Coptic and Ethiopic have not been edited as yet. Of others only fragments remain.

Other Texts: H. De Vis, Homélies coptes de la Vaticane, Texte copte publié et traduit, vol. 2, Copenhagen, 1929, 124-157, published the Coptic text and a French translation of a sermon for the dedication of the 'Church of the Three Children' at Alexandria. Cf. H. J. Polotsky, OLZ 33 (1930) 873. — An Arabic homily of Monophysite tendency was published and translated into French by H. Fleisch, Une homélie de Théophile d'Alexandrie en l'honneur de St. Pierre et de St. Paul. Texte arabe publié pour la première fois et traduit: ROC 10 (1936) 371-419.

SPURIOUS WRITINGS

A number of writings are of doubtful authenticity. Thus A. Mingana edited the *Vision of Theophilus*, dealing with the flight of the Holy Family into Egypt and the life that they led there. Although the story is preserved only in Syriac, it is thoroughly Coptic in origin. The actual writer is given at the end of the narrative as Cyril, who avers that he had heard it from the mouth of his father, the patriarch Theophilus. This Cyril is evidently the great Cyril of Alexandria, who succeeded Theophilus in 412. However, it seems for several reasons that both Theophilus and Cyril are fictitious names. The document appears to be a speech or homily delivered on the feast of the Virgin by a Coptic bishop, who wrote the original in Arabic. The Syriac translation was most probably made by a West Syrian Monophysite living near or in Egypt. In the introduction it is stated that the Emperor Theodosius gave Theophilus 'the keys to the temples of the idols throughout Egypt from Alexandria to Assuan, in order that he might take the wealth contained in them and spend it in erecting buildings for the Church of our Lord Jesus Christ'.

Editions: A. Mingana, Vision of Theophilus or the Book of the Flight of the Holy Family into Egypt: BJR 13 (1929) 383-474. Reprinted: Woodbrooke Studies 3, 1. Cambridge, 1931, 44-92 Syriac Text, 8-43 English Translation. — Arabic version from Cod. Vat. Ar. 698 (J. 1371): M. Guidi, RAL Serie V, Classe di scienze storiche 26 (1917) 441-469. Ethiopic version: C. Conti Rossini, RAL 21 (1912) 395-471.

Studies: F. Nau, La version syriaque de la vision de Théophile sur le séjour de la Vierge en Égypte: ROC 15 (1910) 125-132. Cf. AB 29 (1910) 457. — M. Guidi, La omelia di Teofilo di Alessandria sul monte Coscam nelle letterature orientali: RAL Serie V, Classe di scienze storiche 26 (1917) 381-391. — F. J. Dölger, Drei Theta als Schatzsicherung und ihre Deutung durch den Bischof Theophil von Alexandrien. Eine Szene aus dem Kampf gegen die Heidentempel: AC 3 (1932) 189-191. — G. Lazzati, l.c. 87-89. — G. Graf, Geschichte der christlichen arabischen Literatur I. Die Übersetzungen (ST 118). Vatican City, 1944, 229-232.

The *Lady Meux manuscript* no. 2 and British Museum manuscript *Orient.* no. 604 contain an Ethiopic discourse which Theophilus is said to have preached on the Virgin Mary on the sixth day of the month of Hadar, and in which he describes at great length the life of Mary. E. A. W. Budge has turned into English an extract from this discourse comprising the words that the Virgin herself is said to have spoken to Theophilus in a vision. It was a well-known rhetorical device of Coptic preachers to address Mary by name and then to recite to the audience what purports to be her answer. Theophilus, as a great historical personage, has been introduced by the orator here simply to lend authority to his words.

Translation: English: History of the Virgin Mary as told by her to Theophilus, Patriarch of Alexandria: E. A. W. BUDGE, Legends of Our Lady Mary the Perpetual Virgin. Oxford, 1933, 61-80. — A Coptic sermon attributed to Theophilus was published by W. H. WORRELL, A Homily On the Virgin by Theophilus, Patriarch of Alexandria, in: The Coptic Manuscripts in the Freer Collection (University of Michigan Humanistic Series 10, Part 2). New York, 1923, 249-322, 359-380.

It was F. Diekamp who for the first time raised the question whether the anti-Origenistic treatise *On the Vision of Isaias VI,1-7*, which A. M. Amelli edited under the name of St. Jerome, should not rather be attributed to Theophilus. B. Dietsche advocated Didymus the Blind, but B. Altaner favors Theophilus as the most probable author (cf. above p. 90).

Lefort reports about a Coptic treatise hitherto unedited whose writer seems to be Theophilus. Its content is exegetical and dogmatic. The number of fragments preserved in *Catenae* indicate that Theophilus had a name as an exegete as well.

Studies: L. TH. LEFORT, S. Athanase écrivain copte: Mus 16 (1933) 31. This treatise is found in Codex Zoega 246 of the sixth century. — A. MINGANA, The Work of Dionysius Barsalibi Against the Armenians (Woodbrooke Studies 4), Cambridge, 1931, 14 contains a passage: 'And Theophilus of Alexandria says: "Christ who saved us was not defiled and polluted when he strengthened His flesh by a virginal blood, in His anthropophile union with us" '. This quotation must be of another unknown work of Theophilus because it is not found in any of his extant writings. — For his exegetical works, see: M. RICHARD, Les fragments exégétiques de Théophile d'Alexandrie et de Théophile d'Antioche: RBibl 47 (1938) 387-397. The fragment on Matthew 4, 23 has been published by J. REUSS, Matthäus-Kommentare aus der griechischen Kirche, aus Katenenhandschriften gesammelt und herausgegeben (TU 61). Berlin, 1957, 151f.

SYNESIUS OF CYRENE

Synesius belongs to those historical figures between dying Hellenism and rising Christianity which attract our attention at once. He has been called 'the Platonist in the mitre', and not without reason. Born at Cyrene in Libya between 370 and 375 of a noble pagan family, he received his early schooling in his native town. For his higher studies he betook himself to Alexandria, where the famous Hypatia initiated him into the mysteries of Neo-Platonist philosophy. He kept a lifelong, unbounded enthusiasm for her whom he calls his 'master', 'mother', and 'the philosopher'. He visited Athens and was deeply disappointed because 'philosophy had departed from the city'. In 399 the citizens of the Pentapolis sent him as their ambassador to the imperial court at Constantinople. He returned in 402 after he had obtained a remittal of the excessive taxes levied on his country. Soon afterwards he went to Alexandria to be married. His words 'God and the law and the sacred hand of Theophilus gave me my wife' (*Ep.* 105) indicate that it was a Christian wedding ceremony, performed by the patriarch of Alexandria.

Nevertheless it remains doubtful whether he was baptized when in 410 the grateful clergy and people of the Ptolemais, remembering his courageous defense of his native town against the marauding hordes of the Macheti in 405 and 406, elected him as bishop and metropolitan of the Pentapolis. Synesius was very reluctant to accept. He finally agreed on two conditions, namely, that he should be permitted to continue his marriage, and should not be forced to abandon his philosophical opinions regarding the pre-existence of the soul, the eternity of creation and the allegorical concept of the resurrection of the flesh:

> You know that philosophy is opposed to the opinions of the vulgar. I shall certainly not admit that the soul is posterior in existence to the body. I cannot assert that the world and all its parts will perish together. The resurrection which is so much talked about, I consider something sacred and ineffable and I am far from sharing the ideas of the multitude on the subject... For what has the multitude to do with philosophy? The truth of divine mysteries is not a thing to be talked about. But if I am called to the episcopate, I do not think it right to pretend to hold opinions which I do not hold. I call God and man as witnesses to this. Truth is the property of God, before whom I wish to be entirely blameless. Though I am fond of amusements — for from my childhood I have been accused of being mad after arms and horses — still, I will consent to give them up — though I shall regret to see my darling dogs no longer allowed to hunt, and my bows moth-eaten! Still, I will submit to this if it is God's will. And though I hate all cares and troubles, I will endure these petty matters of business, as rendering my appointed service to God, grievous as it will be. But I will have no deceit about dogmas, nor shall there be variance between my thoughts and my tongue... It shall never be said of me that I got myself consecrated without my opinions being known. But let Father Theophilus, dearly beloved by God, decide for me with full knowledge of the circumstances of the case, and let him tell me his opinion clearly. Then he will either leave me in private life to philosophize quietly by myself, or else he will have no opening left for afterwards judging me, and removing me from the episcopal body (*Ep.* 105, DCB 4, 774f.).

The patriarch of Alexandria did not hesitate to consecrate him.

As a bishop Synesius governed his diocese very successfully with strong sentiment for justice and peace. Nevertheless in his heart he remained more of a Platonist than a Christian, as his writings betray. He must have died shortly afterwards because none of his letters exhibit a date later than 413.

Studies: A. GARDNER, Synesius of Cyrene, Philosopher and Bishop. London, 1886. — T. R. HALCOMB, Synesius: DCB 4 (1887) 756-780. — W. S. CRAWFORD, Synesius the Hellene. London, 1901. — A. J. KLEFFNER, Synesius von Kyrene, der Philosoph und Dichter, und sein angeblicher Vorbehalt bei seiner Wahl und Weihe zum Bischof von Ptolemais. Paderborn, 1901. — H. KOCH, Synesius von Kyrene bei seiner Wahl und Weihe zum Bischof: HJG 23 (1902) 751-774. — G. GRÜTZMACHER, Synesios von Kyrene, ein Charakterbild aus dem Untergang des Hellenentums. Leipzig, 1913. — J. STIGLMAYR, Synesius von Kyrene, Metropolit der Pentapolis: ZkTh 38 (1914) 509-563. — P. MAAS, Verschiedenes II: Hesychios, Vater des Synesios von Kyrene: Phil (1913) 449-456. — N. TERZAGHI, Sinesio di Cirene: Atene e Roma (1917) 1-37. — H. v. CAMPENHAUSEN, Synesios: PWK II 4 (1932) 1362-1365. — G. BETTINI, L'attività publica di Sinesio. Udine, 1938. — J. C. PANDO, The Life and Times of Synesius of Cyrene as Revealed in his Works (PSt 63). Washington, 1940. — C. H. COSTER, Synesius, a Curialis of the Time of Arcadius: Byz 15 (1940/41) 10-38. — C. BIZZOCHI, La tradizione storica della consecrazione episcopale di Sinesio di Cirene: Greg 25 (1944) 130-170; *idem*, La irregolarità della consecrazione di Sinesio come congettura?: Greg 27 (1946) 261-299. — P. C. VAN DEN HORST, Augustinus en Synesius: Hermeneus 20 (1949) 73-77. — H. I. MARROU, La 'conversion' de Synésius: REG 65 (1952) 474-484. — C. LACOMBRADE, Synésius de Cyrène, hellène et chrétien. Paris, 1951. — A. J. VISSER, Synesios van Cyrene, literator, mysticus, bisschop: Ned. Arch. Kerkgeschiedenis 39 (1952) 67-80. — H. VON CAMPENHAUSEN, Griechische Kirchenväter. Stuttgart, 1955, 125-136.

HIS WRITINGS

His literary pursuits testify to his classical erudition and philosophical talent. Admired in Byzantine times for their excellent Attic style, they are sources of considerable importance for the history of his age and his country, especially for the study of the relations between Christianity and Platonism.

Editions: MG 66, 1021-1756. This only complete ed. is a reprint of the text of the complete works edited by D. PETAVIUS, Paris, 1612, except that the text of the *Calvitii Encomium* is a reprint from the edition of that work by J. KRABINGER, Stuttgart, 1834. Krabinger prepared a complete edition of which only the first vol. was published, Landshut, 1850. It contains all writings but the letters and hymns. Other crit. editions will be listed below with the individual works.

Translations: English: A. FITZGERALD, The Letters of Synesius of Cyrene. London, 1926; *idem*, The Essays and Hymns of Synesius of Cyrene, Including the Address to the Emperor Arcadius and the Political Speeches. 2 vols. London, 1930. — *French:* H. DRUON, Œuvres de Synésius, traduites entièrement pour la première fois en français et précédées d'une étude biographique et littéraire. Paris, 1878.

Studies: R. SOLLERT, Die Sprichwörter bei Synesios von Kyrene. Teil I. Augsburg, 1909; *idem*, Sprichwörter und sprichwörtliche Redensarten bei Synesios von Kyrene. Teil II. Augsburg, 1910. — A. HAUCK, Welche griechischen Autoren der klassischen Zeit kennt und benützt Synesius von Kyrene? Ein Beitrag zur παιδεία des 4. Jahrhunderts n. Chr. (Progr.). Friedland in Mecklenburg, 1911. — N. TERZAGHI, Per la prossima edizione critica degli Opuscoli di Sinesio: Didaskaleion 1 (1912) 11-29 (manuscript tradition); *idem*, Le clausole ritmiche negli Opuscoli di Sinesio: Didaskaleion 1 (1912) 205-225, 319-360. — A. SOUTER, Lexical Notes on the Writings of Synesius of Cyrene: JThSt 36 (1935) 176-178. — P. HENRY, Études plotiniennes I. Les états du texte de Plotin. Paris and Brussels, 1938, 202-205. — G. LAZZATI, L'Aristotele perduto e gli scrittori cristiani. Milan, 1938, 55-58, 74. — E. A. PEZOPULOS, Συνεσίου τοῦ Κυρηναίου περὶ Ὁμήρου καὶ τῶν ἐν ταῖς ῥητορείαις σχημάτων : EEBS 15 (1939) 288-351 (claims that the work on Homer attributed to Plutarch was composed by Synesius). — R. PACK, Folklore and Superstitions in the Writings of Synesius: Classical Weekly 43 (1949) 51-56. — C. LACOMBRADE, En marge de Synésius: Mélanges V. Magnien. Toulouse, 1949, 47-55. — H. HUNGER, Zwei unbekannte Libanioshandschriften der Österreichischen National-bibliothek: Scriptorium 6 (1952) 26-32 (with fragments of Synesius). — K. LATTE, Textkritische Beiträge zu Synesios: Classica et Mediaevalia 17 (1956) 91-97 (critical notes on De regno, Dion, De insomniis, Ad Paeonium, Encomium calvit.). — A. WIFSTRAND, Brief an Bertil Axelson über Synesios: Classica et Mediaevalia 18 (1957) 130-132 (*Ad Paeonium* 308D, *De regno* 26a, *Encom. calv.* 84b).

1. *The Discourse on Royalty (Περὶ βασιλείας)* is a courageous speech made in 400 at Constantinople in the presence of the Emperor Arcadius, in which he describes the duty of a young ruler to be an image of God. His criticism of the existing conditions at the imperial court is of astonishing frankness:

> Nothing has done more harm to the Roman State than the habit of surrounding the person of the king with a theatrical pomp and a sort of divine mystery. Do not be vexed at what I say. The fault is not yours. It is the fault of those who began this evil custom, and have handed it down to posterity as a thing to be proud of. The fear that if you are often seen you will be reduced to the level of mere men makes you state prisoners. You see nothing, you hear nothing which can give you any practical wisdom. Your only pleasures are the most sensual pleasures of the body. Your life, is the life of a sea-anemone. The result of this studied seclusion is that you repel the wise and the noble, while you admit to your familiarity creatures who are the counterfeits of humanity; creatures with small heads and scanty brains, who with idiotic grins and gestures of buffoons, help you kill the time, and lessen the burden of that cloud which the unnatural character of your life brings upon you (*Oratio de regno* 10, DCB 4, 758).

Editions: MG 66, 1053-1108. Separate: J. G. KRABINGER, Synesius, Rede über das Königtum. Munich, 1825.

Translations: English: A. FITZGERALD, l.c. — *French:* C. LACOMBRADE, Le Discours sur la royauté de Synésius de Cyrène, trad. nouv. avec introd., notes et commt. Paris, 1951. — *German:* J. G. KRABINGER, l.c.

Studies: G. GRÜTZMACHER, l.c. 111-120. — K. M. SETTON, Christian Attitude towards the Emperor in the Fourth Century. New York, 1941, 152-162. — E. DEMOUGEOT, La théorie du pouvoir impérial au Ve siècle: Mélanges de la Société toulousaine d'études classiques I. Toulouse, 1946, 191-206. — C. LACOMBRADE, Notes sur deux panégyriques: Pallas 4 (1956) 15-26.

2. *The Egyptian Discourses or on Providence* is the title of a strange treatise the content of which is mostly supplied by conditions and events at the imperial capital, disguised as the native myth of Osiris and Typhos, the one the image of virtue, the other of crime. Begun at Constantinople and finished in Egypt, the book reveals its author as a true disciple of Plato, who believes in the return of all things and the unlimited succession of worlds.

Editions: MG 66, 1209-1282. Separate: J. G. KRABINGER, Synesius, Aegyptische Erzählungen. Sulzbach, 1835.

Translations: See above p. 108. — *German:* J. G. KRABINGER, l.c.

Studies: E. GAISER, Des Synesius von Kyrene Aegyptische Erzählungen oder über die Vorsehung. Darstellung des Gedankeninhalts dieser Schrift und ihrer Bedeutung für die Philosophie des Synesius unter Berücksichtigung ihres geschichtlichen Hintergrundes. Erlangen Diss. Wolfenbüttel, 1886. — O. SEECK, Studien zu Synesius I. Der historische Gehalt des Osirismythos: Phil 52 (1893) 442-458. — C. LACOMBRADE, Synésios et l'énigme du loup: REAN (1946) 260-266 (wolves mean Huns MG 66, 1209A).

3. *Dion or His Mode of Life* was written in his own defense about 405. It consists of three parts. The first deals with Dion of Prusa and his writings; the second justifies his preoccupation with philosophy and rhetoric, an ideal found in Dion; in the third Synesius gives his own philosophy of life as Dion's follower. He is highly critical of the monks, those 'barbarians' who despise literary work, and makes it quite clear that he prefers the Greek way of life to 'the other', the Christian (*Dion* 9,13). He attacks the sophists for their ambition, because they look only for honor and reputation, not for truth. He is proud of his own independence, that he is his own master.

Edition: MG 66, 1111-1164.

Translations: See above p. 108.

Studies: J. R. ASMUS, Synesius und Dio Chrysostomus: BZ 9 (1900) 85-119. — G. MISCH, Geschichte der Autobiographie I. Leipzig, 1907, 380-383. — K. TREU, Synesios von Kyrene. Ein Kommentar zu seinem 'Dion' (TU 71). Berlin, 1958.

4. *The Praise of Baldness (Φαλάκρας ἐγκώμιον)* is a humorous sophistic on the advantages of being bald. The author proves with many arguments from nature, history and mythology that baldness is a decoration of man, a sign of wisdom and a stamp of similarity with God. Being bald, he wrote it to refute a treatise of Dio Chrysostom, entitled *The Praise of Hair*.

Editions: MG 66, 1167-1206. Separate: J. G. KRABINGER, Synesius, Lob der Kahlköpfigkeit. Stuttgart, 1834.

Translations: English: A. FITZGERALD, l.c. *French:* H. DRUON, l.c. (cf. above p. 108). *German:* J. G. KRABINGER, l.c.

Studies: J. R. Asmus, Synesius und Dio Chrysostomus: BZ 9 (1900) 119-151. — J. Geffcken, Kynika und Verwandtes. Heidelberg, 1909, 149-151. — G. Pasquali, Synesius, Encomium calv. 186, 2: Didaskaleion (1912) 519-521 (critical note). — L. Kotynski, Meander 12 (1957) 157-168; 185-197.

5. *On Dreams (Περὶ ἐνυπνίων)* composed in 403 or 404 in a single night, is a tractate on the causing and meaning of dreams, which the author regards as divine revelations. He sent it to Hypatia (*Ep.* 154) asking for her own opinion.

Edition: MG 66, 1281-1320.

Translations: English: A. Fitzgerald, l.c. — I. Myer, Synesius, On Dreams. Philadelphia, 1888. *French:* H. Druon, l.c. *German:* W. Lang, Das Traumbuch des Synesius von Cyrene. Übersetzung und Analyse der philosophischen Grundlagen (HAPhG 10). Tübingen, 1926.

Studies: N. Terzaghi, Sul commento di Nicephorus Gregoras al περὶ ἐνυπνίων : SIF (1904) 181-217; *idem*, Nota sul Cod. Monac. gr. 29: SIF (1905) 437-442. — M. Gelzer, Zwei Einteilungsprinzipien der antiken Traumdeutung: Juvenes dum sumus. Aufsätze zur klassischen Altertumswissenschaft der 49. Versammlung deutscher Philologen. Basel, 1907, 40-51 (threefold division by Synesius). — A. Ludwig, Die Schrift περὶ ἐνυπνίων des Synesios von Kyrene: ThGl 7 (1915) 547-558. — R. C. Kipling, The Ὄχημα-Πνεῦμα of the Neo-Platonists and the De insomniis of Synesius of Cyrene: AJPh 43 (1922) 318-330. — W. Lang, l.c. — C. Lacombrade, Retouche à la biographie de Libanius: AIPH 10 (1950) 361-366 (regarding MG 66, 1317-1320). — R. Weiss, New Light on Humanism in England during the 15th century: Journal of the Warburg and Courtauld Institute 14 (1951) 21-33 (on the Latin translation of *De insomniis* by John Free). — W. L. Dulière, Synésius de Cyrène, analyste du rêve et inventeur du densi-mètre: Le Flambeau 35 (1952) 233-250, 383-405.

6. *The Gift (Περὶ τοῦ δώρου)* is a little work dedicated to a certain Paeonius at Constantinople, to whom he sent it with a fine astronom-ical instrument, an astrolabe.

Edition: MG 66, 1577-1588.

Translations: English: A. Fitzgerald, l.c. *French:* H. Druon, l.c. *German:* B. Kolbe, Der Bischof Synesius von Cyrene als Physiker und Astronom. Berlin, 1850 (with improved Greek text).

Studies: B. Kolbe, l.c. — W. L. Dulière, l.c. — O. Neugebauer, The Early History of the Astrolabe: Isis 40 (1949) 240-256.

7. *Letters*

The collection of his correspondence consists of 156 items, written between 399 and 413. The circle of correspondents is not particularly wide and comprises about forty persons, among them Hypatia, his teacher, to whom several letters are addressed. A hundred or so are personal notes to relatives or friends, thirty-five introduce some person or request assistance for people involved in difficulties. Several have to do with civil or military business and some twenty with events and conditions resulting from the invasions of the barbarian raiders into the Pentapolis. About a dozen letters have to do with ecclesiastical matters. Among them is the encyclical *Ep.* 58 (MG 66, 1401-1404) which informs the bishops of the excommunication of Andronicus, a high government official. The letters 72 and 90 deal with the same person. The latter addressed to Theophilus, the patriarch of Alexandria, intercedes for Andronicus, because 'formerly he acted unjustly, now he suffers unjustly'. Letters 66 and 67 are reports to Theophilus about the conditions of the diocese, which testify to the conscientious care that Synesius extended to his faithful. In letter 5 he warns his priests against the 'godless sect of Eunomius', whereas in letter 11 he introduces himself to the clergy as the new bishop. Obviously there is no discernible plan underlying the order of the Epistles as they have come down to us, and the arrangement is not due to Synesius himself. Most probably it is but a selection made from a much larger collection that he composed.

Nevertheless, the letters have the highest value for their information about the personality of the author, his fine education and noble qualities of heart, his syncretistic belief and philosophical and theological opinions. Moreover, they are an outstanding source for the history and geography of the Late Empire in general and the Pentapolis in particular. Evagrius, Photius and Suidas admired them for their grace and charm. They were regarded as models of the art. More than one hundred manuscripts testify to their popularity in later ages. In fact, Synesius was the last pagan epistolographer of recognized importance.

Editions: MG 66, 1321-1560. New ed.: R. HERCHER, Epistolographi Graeci. Paris, 1873, 638-739. Migne has 156, Hercher 159 letters, but the last three letters of Hercher's edition are not genuine.

Translations: English: A. FITZGERALD, The Letters of Synesius of Cyrene, translated into English with introduction and notes. London, 1926. — *French:* H. DRUON, l.c. — F. LAPATZ, Lettres de Synésius, traduites pour la première fois et suivies d'Études sur les derniers moments de l'hellénisme. Paris, 1870.

Studies: R. HERCHER, l.c. LXXII-LXXIX. — O. SEECK, Studien zu Synesios II. Die Briefsammlung: Phil 52 (1893) 458-483. — W. FRITZ, Die Briefe des Bischofs Synesius von Kyrene, ein Beitrag zur Geschichte des Attizismus im 4. und 5. Jahrhundert. Leipzig, 1898; *idem*, Die handschriftliche Überlieferung der Briefe des Bischofs Synesius: AAM Philos.-philol. Klasse 23 (1905) 319-398; *idem*, Unechte Synesiosbriefe: BZ 14 (1905) 75-86 (*Epp.* 157, 158, 159 Hercher). — N. TERZAGHI, L'epistola 159 di Sinesio: RAL (1917) 624-633 (for authenticity). — H. LECLERCQ, DAL 8 (1929) 2851-2855. — X. H. SIMEON, Untersuchungen zu den Briefen des Bischofs Synesios von Kyrene. Paderborn, 1933. — J. HERMELIN, Zu den Briefen des Bischofs Synesius von Kyrene. Upsala, 1934. — G. J. DE VRIES, Maiorem infante mamillam: Mnem 12 (1944) 160 (*Ep.* 4). — G. W. H. LAMPE, Βαρύλλιον (*Ep.* 15): CR (1948) 114-115. — G. KARLSSON, Une lettre byzantine attribuée à Synésius: Eranos 50 (1952) 144-145 (*Ep.* 158 Hercher not authentic, belongs to Nicetas Magister). — L. CASSON, Bishop Synesius' Voyage to Cyrene: The American

Neptune 12 (1952) 291-296 (*Ep.* 4). — G. BUEHRING, Zum Topos Hom., Ilias VI, 429f: Gymnasium 61 (1954) 418 (*Ep.* 16). — C. LACOMBRADE, Sur les traces des Axomites: Annales publ. par la Faculté des Lettres de Toulouse. Pallas 3 (1955) 5-14 (*Ep.* 122).

8. *Hymns*

There are about ten hymns preserved in the editions but it remains doubtful whether the last can be attributed to Synesius since the best manuscripts do not have it. Although they exhibit a strange mixture of pagan and Christian ideas they are lyrical outpourings of a profoundly religious soul. Composed according to the laws of ancient prosody and in the Doric dialect, they show the influence of classical models as well as liturgical chants of his times. The first of them reminds one of the Neo-Platonic mysticism of a Jamblichus and his concept of the Trinity. The second, a beautiful morning song, combines Neo-Platonic and Christian doctrines in a surprising confession of Father, Son and Holy Spirit. The third and fourth hymns praise the identity of the divine Monas and Trias. Those that follow indicate a greater familiarity with the Christian faith. Thus the fifth, perhaps the best of the entire collection, and the sixth, extol the divine Son of the Virgin. The seventh deals with the adoration of the magi and interprets their gifts. Synesius remarks in this hymn, not without pride, that he is the first to compose a lyrical song on Christ to the accompaniment of the cithara (7,1). The eighth is a prayer to 'the illustrious Son of the Virgin' for natural and supernatural gifts. The ninth is a hymn on Christ's descent into Hades, a powerful poem full of mythological imagery.

Editions: MG 66, 1587-1616. — W. CHRIST et M. PARANIKAS, Anthologia Graeca carminum Christianorum. Leipzig, 1871, 3-23. — J. FLACH, Synesii episcopi hymni metrici. Tübingen, 1875. — New crit. ed.: N. TERZAGHI, Synesius, Hymni et opuscula. I. Hymni. Rome, 1939; II. Rome, 1944. Separate: M. M. HAWKINS, Der 1. Hymnus des Synesios. Text u. Kommentar. Diss. Munich, 1939.

Translations: English: A. FITZGERALD, The Essays and Hymns of Synesius. 2 vols. London, 1930. — *French:* M. MEUNIER, Synésius, Hymnes, trad. et notes. Paris, 1947. — *German:* G. M. DREVES, Der Sänger der Kyrenaika: Stimmen aus Maria-Laach 52 (1897) 545-562 (selections). — T. MICHELS, Mysterien Christi. Frühchristliche Hymnen aus dem Griechischen übertragen. Münster, 1952 (two hymns).

Studies: C. VELLAY, Études sur les hymnes de Synésius de Cyrène. Paris, 1904. — U. v. WILAMOWITZ-MOELLENDORFF, Die Hymnen des Proklos und Synesios: SAB (1907) 272-295 (with textual crit. and translat. of *Hymn* 9). — C. WEYMAN, Analecta sacra et profana: Festgabe H. Grauert. Freiburg i.B., 1910, 2-4 (*hymn.* 7). — N. TERZAGHI, La tradizione manoscritta degli Inni di Sinesio: SIF 20 (1913) 450-497; *idem*, Synesii Cyrenensis hymni metrici: Atti della r. Accademia di archeologia, lettere e belle arti di Napoli 4 (1915) 63-123; *idem*, Studi sugli inni di Sinesio: Rivista indo-greco-italica di filologia (1921) 11-25, 192f; (1922) 1-18; *idem*, Il Cod. Barocc. gr. 56 e l'autore del X inno di Sinesio: BZ 38 (1938) 287-298. — E. A. PEZOPULOS, Ποιήματα Συνεσίου:

EEBS 13 (1937) 305-352; 14 (1938) 342-392 (metrical composition). — A. FERRUA, Gli inni di Sinesio: CC 91 (1940) 126-133. — W. THEILER, Die chaldäischen Orakel und die Hymnen des Synesios. Halle, 1942. — A. KURFESS, Synesios, Hymn. 9 (1), 32: PhW (1943) 288. — C. BIZZOCHI, L'ordine degli inni di Sinesio: Greg 23 (1942) 91-115, 202-237. — A. FESTUGIÈRE, Sur les hymnes de Synésius: REG 58 (1945) 208-277. — S. MARIOTTI, De Synesii hymnorum memoria: SIF 22 (1947) 215-230 (manuscripts and crit. notes). — M. COCCO, Neoplatonismo e cristianesimo nel primo inno di Sinesio di Cirene: Sophia 16 (1948) 199-202, 351-356. — C. BIZZOCHI, Gli inni di Sinesio interpretati come mistiche celebrazioni: Greg 32 (1951) 347-387. — A. BONADIES-NANI, Gli inni di Proclo: Aevum 26 (1952) 385-409. — S. MARIOTTI, Probabili varianti d'autore in Ennio, Cicerone, Sinesio: La Parola del Passato 38 (1954) 368-375 (*hymn.* 1); *idem,* Adversaria philologa II. Studi in onore di U. E. Paoli. Florence, 1955, 507-511 (*hymn.* 9). — C. LACOMBRADE, Sur deux vers controversés de Synésius, *Ὑμνος ἑβδομος*: REG 69 (1956) 67-72. — R. KEYDELL, Zu den Hymnen des Synesios: Hermes 84 (1956) 151-162 (*hymn.* 6, 9, 1, 2).

9. *Two Orations (καταστάσεις)*

They belong to the last period of his life, when he was bishop and metropolitan of the Pentapolis, although they are political in character. Both of them are masterpieces of rhetoric. The first expresses the thanks of the country to the military commander Anysios after his victory over the barbarians (406/407). The second, delivered in 412, when they invaded the Pentapolis a second time, laments the unfortunate situation and admonishes the inhabitants to resist the enemy to the last drop of blood.

Editions: MG 66, 1561-1578. — J. G. KRABINGER, Synesii Cyrenaei orationes et homiliarum fragmenta. Landshut, 1850, 376-379 (*or.* I), 380-390 (*or.* II).

Translations: English: A. FITZGERALD, l.c. *French:* H. DRUON, l.c.

10. *Homilies*

Only two fragments remain to leave us an impression of Synesius as a preacher. The first is of a sermon he gave at the beginning of Easter and consists of an allegorical interpretation of Psalm 74,9. The second is of a homily to the newly baptized at the Easter Vigil, in which he praises 'the holy night' brighter than any day.

Editions: MG 66, 1561-1578. — J. G. KRABINGER, l.c. 371-372 (*hom.* I), 373 (*hom.* II).

Translations: English: A. FITZGERALD, l.c. *French:* H. DRUON, l.c. *German:* B. KOLBE, l.c. (with improved Greek text).

NONNUS OF PANOPOLIS

Another pagan poet of Egypt who seems to have embraced the Christian faith after he had won great fame is Nonnus. Hardly any biographical details are available, except that he was born at

Panopolis in Upper Egypt, most probably about the year 400. He is the author of the longest extant Greek epic, the *Dionysiaca*, which describes in 48 books the legendary journey of the pagan god Dionysus to India. Composed at Alexandria, it gives no indication that the author was a Christian at that time, despite some allusions that have been interpreted as references to Christian doctrine. Baroque in language and style, this creation is at any rate totally pagan in its contents.

Editions: A. LUDWICH, Dionysiaca. 2 vols. (Bibl. Teubneriana). Leipzig, 1909, 1911. — Dionysiaca, with an English translation by W. H. D. ROUSE, mythological introduction by H. J. ROSE and notes on text criticism by L. R. LIND (LCL) 3 vols. London and Cambridge (Mass.), 1940. New ed.: R. KEYDELL, Nonni Pan. Dionysiaca. 2 vols., 1959.

Translations: English: W. H. D. ROUSE, l.c. — *French:* C. DE MARCELLUS, Les Diony-siaques. Paris, 1856. — M. MEUNIER, Les Dionysiaques. Paris, 1919. — *German:* T. VON SCHEFFER, Die Dionysiaka des Nonnos von Panopolis, deutsch. 2 vols. Munich, 1929, 1933 with notes by H. BOGNER; 2nd ed. Wiesbaden, 1955. Cf. J. HOLTERMANN, Gymnasium 62 (1955) 266-268.

Studies: General: R. KEYDELL, PWK 17 (1937) 904-921. — *Special:* J. LA ROCHE, Zur Verstechnik des Nonnos: WSt (1900) 194-221. — J. NEGRISOLI, Studio critico interno alle Dionisiache di Nonno. Rome, 1903. — F. SCHILLER, De iteratione Nonniana. Trebnitz, 1908. — P. FRIEDLÄNDER, Die Chronologie des Nonnos von Panopolis: Hermes 47 (1912) 43-59. — A. LUDWICH, Epimetrum Nonnianum. Königsberg, 1913. — F. BRAUN, Hymnen bei Nonnos von Panopolis. Diss. Königsberg, 1915. — T. TIEDKE, Zur Textkritik der Dionysiaka des Nonnos: Hermes 49 (1914) 214-228, 50 (1915) 444-455, 58 (1923) 305-321. — T. SINKO, Zu Nonnos: Berliner Philologische Wochenschrift (1918) 861-864 (metrical compos.). — A. LUDWICH, Nachlese zu Nonnos: *ibid.* 373-384. — T. SINKO, De expositione Pseudo-Nonniana historiarum quae in orationibus Gregorii Nazianzeni commemorantur: Charisteria C. de Morawski oblata. Cracow, 1922, 124-148. R. KEYDELL, Zu Nonnos: BNJ 4 (1923) 14-17, 6 (1928) 19-24; *idem,* Zur Komposition der Bücher 13-40 der Dionysiaka des Nonnos: Hermes 62 (1927) 393-434. — P. MAAS, Zur Verskunst des Nonnos: BZ 27 (1927) 17-18. — P. COLLART, Nonnus de Panopolis. Études sur la composition et le texte des Dionysiaques (Rech. d'arch. de philol. et d'hist. I). Cairo, 1930. — V. STEGMANN, Astrologie und Universalgeschichte. Studien und Interpretationen zu den Dionysiaka des Nonnos von Panopolis. Leipzig, 1930. — L. CASTIGLIONI, Epica Nonniana: Rendiconti del R. Istituto Lomb. 65 (1932) 6-10. — J. BRAUNE, Nonnos und Ovid. Greifswald, 1935. — L. R. LIND, A Note on Nonnus, Dionysiaca I 69-71: CPh 30 (1935) 78; *idem,* Un-hellenic Elements in the 'Dionysiaca': ACL 7 (1938) 57-65. — S. BEZDECHI, Vulgarismes dans l'épopée de Nonnus: Anuarul Inst. de Studii Clasice 3 (1936/40) 34-74 (syntax). — H. GERSTINGER, Zur Frage der Komposition, literarischen Form und Tendenz der Dionysiaka des Nonnos von Panopolis: WSt 61/62 (1943/47) 71-87. — R. KEYDELL, Textkritisches zu Nonnos: Hermes, 79 (1944) 13-24. — H. HAIDACHER, Quellen und Vorbilder der Dionysiaka des Nonnos von Panopolis. Diss. Graz, 1949 (typewritten). — P. BERNARDINI MARZOLLA, Il testo dei Dionysiaca di Nonno: SIF 26 (1952) 191-209. — A. DILLER, A Lost Manuscript of Nonnus' Dionysiaca: CPh 48 (1953) 177. — R. KEYDELL, Wortwiederholungen bei Nonnos: BZ 46 (1953) 1-17 (textcritical problems). — J. MEHLER, Nonnos' Dionysiaka: Hermeneus 28 (1956) 27-35. — R. DOSTÁLOVÁ-JENIŠTOVÁ, Die Sagen über den Eponymos der Blemmyer bei Nonnos von Panopolis: Listy Filologické N.S. 4 (1956) 174-177 (*Dionys.* 17, 385-397); *idem,* Tyros und Beirut in den Dionysiaka des Nonnos aus Panopolis: Listy Filologické N.S. 5 (1957) 36-54.

The same Nonnus, however, is regarded as the author of the famous metrical *Paraphrase of St. John's Gospel*, composed in hexameters after 431. Its style has many characteristics in common with the *Dionysiaca* and numerous verses have been taken from the pagan work. While the oldest manuscript, *Codex Laurent. s.* XI and the *Vatican Codex* s. XIV do not give any author for the *Paraphrase*, the *Codex Paris. s.* XIII and a number of earlier manuscripts attribute it to 'Nonnus the poet of Panopolis', as do the index of the *Anthol. Pal.* and the interpolation of Suidas. Most probably the *Paraphrase* represents a work, which Nonnus wrote after becoming a Christian. The author refers repeatedly to Mary as the *Theotokos*.

Editions: MG 43, 749-1228 reprint of the ed. by D. HEINSIUS, Leiden, 1627. — F. PASSOW, Leipzig, 1834. — C. DE MARCELLUS, Paris, 1861. Best crit. ed.: A. SCHEINDLER, Bibliotheca Teubneriana. Leipzig, 1881.

Translation: French: C. DE MARCELLUS. Paris, 1861.

Studies: General: .E. AMANN, DTC 11 (1931) 793-795. — R. KEYDELL, PWK 17 (1937) 917-920. — *Special:* G. KINKEL, Die Überlieferung der Paraphrase des Evangeliums Johannis von Nonnos. Zürich, 1870. — A. SCHEINDLER, Zur Kritik der Paraphrase des Nonnos von Panopolis: WSt 3 (1881) 219-252, 4 (1882) 77-95. — H. TIEDKE, Nonniana (Progr.). Berlin, 1883. — R. JANSSEN, Das Johannes-Evangelium nach der Paraphrase des Nonnus Panopolitanus (TU 23, 4). Leipzig, 1903. Cf. W. BOUSSET, ThLZ (1903) 587. — A. KUHN, Literarhistorische Studien zur Paraphrase des Johannes-Evangeliums von Nonnos aus Panopolis (Progr.). Kalksburg, 1908. — W. KUIPER, De Nonno evangelii Joannei interprete: Mnem 46 (1918) 225-270. — J. GOLEGA, Studien über die Evangeliendichtung des Nonnos von Panopolis. Ein Beitrag zur Geschichte der Bibeldichtung im Altertum. Breslau, 1930. — G. COSTA, Problemi di storia e religione I. Il Nonno di Panopoli e la Madre di Dio: Bilychnis (1931) 143-150. (Finds it difficult to attribute the *Dionysiaca* and the *Paraphrase* to the same author. The latter was composed, he thinks, not by a neophyte but by a disciple of Cyril of Alex. about A.D. 431.) — R. KEYDELL, Über die Echtheit der Bibeldichtungen des Apollinaris und des Nonnos: BZ 33 (1933) 243-254. — H. BOGNER, Die Religion des Nonnos von Panopolis: Phil 89 (1934) 320-333. (There must have been a conversion of the author since the *Dionysiaca* is positively pagan and the *Paraphrase* Christian.) — Q. CATAUDELLA, Cronologia di Nonno di Panopoli: SIF N.S. 11 (1934) 15-32 (tries to prove that Gregory of Naz. depends on Nonnus). — R. DOSTÁLOVÁ-JENIŚTOVÁ, Der Name Nonnos: Nonnosforschungen I: Studia antiqua A. Salač sept. oblata. Prague, 1955, 102-109.

CYRIL OF ALEXANDRIA

When the Alexandrian patriarch Theophilus died on October 15, 412, the government wanted a certain archdeacon Timothy to succeed, but two days afterwards Cyril, a nephew of the late patriarch, was elected and elevated to the famous see of the Egyptian metropolis. His name is for ever connected with the second great Christological controversy, which led to the Council of Ephesus (431) and the condemnation of Nestorius. Born at Alexandria, he evidently received his classical and theological training at this great centre of learning. Three letters (*Ep.* 1, 25, 310, 370) of St. Isidore of Pelusium (cf. below, p. 184) give the impression that Cyril lived for a time in the desert with the monks, but Severus of Antioch (CSCO 101,252f.) is doubtful of their authenticity. Moreover, Cyril never refers to such a sojourn, not even in his later correspondence with the monks. The first certain date in his life is 403, when he accompanied his uncle to Constantinople and took part in the deposition of St. John Chrysostom at the 'Synod of the Oak' near Chalcedon. As patriarch of Alexandria he remains a controversial figure. It seems that he had inherited from his uncle certain prejudices. Thus his grudge against St. John Chrysostom lasted for a long time and it was not before the year 417 that he had the name of this great saint restored to the diptychs of the Alexandrian Church. He shared with his uncle a certain ruthlessness of action against his opponents. His harsh treatment of the Jews and the Novatians did not shrink from expulsion and confiscation and created great dissensions between him and the imperial city-prefect Orestes. His relentless fight against the last remnants of paganism was most probably the reason why he has been accused, as Socrates (*Hist. eccl.* 7,15) insinuates, of being responsible for the murder of the famous philosopher Hypatia, cruelly torn to pieces on the steps of a Church by a mob of Christians in March 415. However, there seems to be no proof that he was guilty of this hideous crime.

We are better informed for the period which follows 428, when Nestorius became bishop of Constantinople. It is in the defense of orthodoxy against Nestorianism that Cyril appears as a prominent factor in ecclesiastical and dogmatic history. A student of the theological school of Antioch, Nestorius in his episcopal sermons asserted that there are two persons in Christ, a divine person, the Logos, dwelling in a human person, the man Jesus, and that the Blessed Virgin could not be called *Theotokos*, Mother of God. His arguments were refuted as early as the spring of 429 by Cyril in his Paschal Letter. Soon after the Alexandrian defended the orthodox doctrine in a long encyclical to the monks of Egypt. Thus the latent antagonism which existed for two generations in the Christological question between the two great theological centres of the East, became a public conflict not only between the representatives of the two schools but between Alexandria and Constantinople. It was the long history of mutual enmity between these two sees that added a political factor to the theological controversy and gave it the appearance of a bitter personal quarrel. After a fruitless exchange of letters between Nestorius and Cyril both appealed to Pope Celestine. A synod held at Rome in August 430 condemned Nestorius and approved of Cyril's theology. The Pope entrusted Cyril with communicating this decision to Nestorius. Cyril drew up twelve Anathemas against the new heresy which he added to the Pope's letter and threatened Nestorius with deposition and excommunication unless within ten days he retracted his errors.

There remained only one possibility of avoiding an open break in the Eastern Church, a general council. Thus the Emperor Theodosius II, urged especially by Nestorius, summoned all metropolitans and bishops of the empire to Ephesus for the Pentecost of 431, to the synod which became famous throughout the world as the Third Ecumenical Council. In the first session (June 22, 431), in which Cyril as the Papal delegate presided, Nestorius was deposed and excommunicated. Cyril's twelve anathemas were confirmed, the Christological doctrine of Nestorius condemned, and the title *Theotokos* solemnly recognized.

Four days later John of Antioch arrived at Ephesus with his bishops. He did not hesitate to hold a synod of his own with his bishops and the friends of Nestorius, in which he deposed and excommunicated Cyril. When Theodosius heard of the proceedings, he thought of a master-stroke, declared both Cyril and Nestorius deposed and sent them to jail. After further examinations, Cyril was permitted to return to Alexandria. He arrived on October 30 to be received in his see as a second Athanasius, whereas Nestorius retired to a monastery in Antioch.

It was not until 433 that the bad feeling between Alexandria and Antioch ended in a reconciliation. John of Antioch accepted the condemnation of Nestorius, whereas Cyril of Alexandria signed a profession of faith very probably drawn up by Theodoret of Cyrus, in which the divine maternity of the Blessed Virgin was clearly acknowledged. Although Cyril wrote to Pope Sixtus III that peace was restored, he was forced to defend his Christology again and again. Since Theodore of Mopsuestia had been Nestorius' master, there was agitation to have him condemned too, and Cyril came close to doing so between the years 438 and 440. However, on his deathbed he declared himself against such a move, in order to avoid a revival of the controversy. He died on June 27, 444.

Studies: General: J. KOPALLIK, Cyrillus von Alexandrien, eine Biographie nach den Quellen gearbeitet. Mayence, 1881. — J. MAHÉ, DTC 3 (1908) 2476-2527. — C. PAPADOPOULOS, Ὁ ἅγιος Κύριλλος Ἀλεξανδρείας. Alexandria, 1933. — M. JUGIE, Cirillo d'Alessandria: EC 3 (1950) 1715-1724. — H. DU MANOIR, DSp 2 (1953) 2672-2683. — G. JOUASSARD, RACh 3 (1956) 499-516. — G. BARDY, DHG 13 (1956) 1169-1177.

Special: C. HEFELE-H. LECLERCQ, Histoire des conciles II, 1. Paris, 1908, 248-422. — F. NAU, St. Cyril and Nestorius: ROC 15 (1910) 365-391; 16 (1911) 1-54. — J. MASPÉRO,

Horapollon et la fin du paganisme égyptien: Bull. Inst. fr. Archéol. orient. 11 (1914) 163-195. — K. PRAECHTER, Hypatia: PWK 9 (1916) 242-249. — J. RUCKER, Cyrillus von Alexandrien und Timotheus Aelurus in der alten armenischen Christenheit: HA (1927) 699-714. — E. SCHWARTZ, Cyrill und der Mönch Viktor (SAW Phil.-hist. Klasse 208, 4). Vienna, 1928. — D. FRANSES, Cyrille au Concile d'Éphèse: StC 7 (1931) 369-398. — P. BAPHIDES, St. Cyril and his Struggle against Nestorius (in Greek). Thessalonike, 1932. — C. PAPADOPOULOS, Ὁ ἅγιος Κύριλλος ὁ ᾽Αλεξανδρείας καὶ ἡ Δ᾽ Οἰκουμενικὴ Σύνοδος: Θεολογία 15 (1937) 337f. — H. I. BELL, Anti-Semitism in Alexandria: JRS 31 (1941) 1-18. — F. M. ABEL, Cyrille d'Alexandrie dans ses rapports avec la Palestine: Kyrilliana, Spicilegia edita Sancti Cyrilli Alexandrini XV recurrente saeculo (444-1944). Cairo, 1947, 203-230. — E. DRIOTON, Cyrille d'Alexandrie et l'ancienne religion égyptienne: ibidem 231-246. — H. MUNIER, Le lieu de la naissance de Saint Cyrille d'Alexandrie: ibidem 197-202. — G. NEYRON, Saint Cyrille et le Concile d'Éphèse: ibidem 37-57. — R. RÉMONDON, L'Égypte et la suprême résistance au christianisme: Didaskaleion 51 (1952) 116-128. — F. PERICOLI-RIDOLFINI, La controversia tra Cirillo d'Alessandria e Giovanni d'Antiochia nell'epistolario di Andrea da Samosata: Rivista degli Studi Orientali 29 (1954) 187-217. — J. LIÉBAERT, Saint Cyrille d'Alexandrie et la culture antique: MSR 12 (1955) 5-26. — H. VON CAMPENHAUSEN, Griechische Kirchenväter. Stuttgart, 1955, 153-164.

I. HIS WRITINGS

Cyril is one of the greatest figures of early Christian literature. His works fill ten volumes of Migne's edition (MG 68-77) even today after many of them have been lost. He was still living when the first translations appeared: Marius Mercator is the author of a Latin and Rabbulas of Edessa of a Syriac version of some of his writings. Armenian, Ethiopian and Arabic renditions followed. Thanks to these translations some of his writings no longer preserved in the original Greek have been rediscovered.

His style and language are far from attractive; he is diffuse and sometimes overelaborate and ornate. The content, however, reveals a depth of thought and richness of ideas, a precision and clarity of argument that prove the speculative and dialectic talent of the author, and make his writings first class sources for the history of dogma and Christian doctrine.

The Nestorian controversy divides his literary activity into two periods: the first extending to 428, is devoted to exegesis and polemics against the Arians, the second ending with his death is almost completely taken up by his refutation of the Nestorian heresy.

His exegetical works form the greater but not the better part of his literary output. His interpretation of the Old Testament is strongly influenced by Alexandrian tradition and therefore highly allegorical though he differs from Origen because of the emphasis with which he insists that not all the details of the Old Testament yield a spiritual signification. His New Testament exegesis is more literal but, nevertheless, betrays a disinclination to the historico-philological approach.

Collections: J. AUBERT, Sancti Cyrilli Alexandrini opera omnia Graece et Latine. Paris, 1638, 6 vols. Additional texts were published by A. MAI, Nova Patrum Bibliotheca 2-3. Rome, 1844-1845. MG 68-77 is a reprint of Aubert's edition together with the additions by Mai. A new critical edit. of certain treatises by P. E. PUSEY. 7 vols. Oxford, 1868-1877: Sancti patris nostri Cyrilli archiepiscopi Alexandrini in XII prophetas. 2 vols. Oxford, 1868. — Sancti patris nostri Cyrilli archiepiscopi Al. in d. Joannis evangelium. Accedunt fragmenta varia necnon tractatus ad Tiberium diaconum duo. 3 vols. Oxford, 1872. — Sancti patris nostri Cyrilli arch. Al. Epistolae tres oecumenicae, Libri V contra Nestorium, XII capitum explanatio, XII capitum defensio utraque, Scholia de incarnatione Unigeniti. Oxford, 1875. — Sancti patr. nostri Cyrilli arch. Al. De recta fide ad imperatorem, De incarnatione Unigeniti dialogus, De recta fide ad principissas, De recta fide ad augustas, Quod unus Christus dialogus, Apologeticus ad imperatorem. Oxford, 1877. — A new critical text of many Anti-Nestorian writings is found in E. SCHWARTZ, Acta conciliorum oecumenicorum. Concilium universale Ephesinum. I. vols 1-5. Berlin and Leipzig, 1927-1930. — The Syriac version of the Commentary on Luke was published in CSCO 70 by J. B. CHABOT, Paris and Leipzig, 1912, and CSCO 140 by R. M. TONNEAU (Latin transl.), Louvain, 1953. Other edit. will be listed with the individual works. Many additional fragments are found in the new edition of Severus of Antioch by J. LEBON, CSCO 93-94, 101-102, 111-112, 119-120.

Translations: English: P. E. PUSEY, LFC 43 (1874), 47 (1881); T. RANDELL, LFC 48 (1885). — *German:* H. HAYD, BKV (1879); O. BARDENHEWER, BKV³ 12 (1935).

Studies: For a list of manuscripts (40, without those of Vatican Library) and of printed editions (51), see: P. RENAUDIN, La théologie de saint Cyrille. Tongerloo, 1937, 67f. — For the Old Latin versions, cf. A. SIEGMUND, Die Überlieferung der griechischen christlichen Literatur in der lateinischen Kirche. Munich-Pasing, 1949, 61-64. — For Syriac versions, cf. A. BAUMSTARK, Geschichte der syrischen Literatur. Bonn, 1922, 71f, 160f. — For Armenian versions, cf. F. C. CONYBEARE, The Armenian Version of Revelation and of Cyril of Alexandria's Scholia on the Incarnation. London, 1907, 165f. — For Arabic versions, cf. G. GRAF, Geschichte der christlichen arabischen Literatur I (ST 118). Vatican City, 1944, 358-365. — For the chronology of Cyril's works, see: G. JOUASSARD, L'activité littéraire de saint Cyrille d'Alexandrie jusqu'à 428. Essai de chronologie et de synthèse: Mélanges E. Podechard. Lyons, 1945, 159-174. — For language and style: A. VACCARI, La grecità di S. Cirillo d'Alessandria: Studi dedicati alla memoria di P. Ubaldi. Milan, 1937, 27-40. Cf. F. L. CROSS, Actes VIᵉ Congr. int. Étud. byz. I. Paris, 1950, 392. — For his exegesis, cf. F. M. ABEL, Parallélisme exégétique entre saint Jérôme et saint Cyrille d'Alexandrie: Vivre et Penser 1 (1941) 94-119, 212-230. — A. KERRIGAN, St. Cyril of Alexandria, Interpreter of the Old Testament. Rome, 1952; *idem*, The Objects of the Literal and Spiritual Senses of the New Testament according to St. Cyril of Alexandria: SP I (TU 63). Berlin, 1957, 354-374.

1. *Commentaries on the Old Testament*

a. *De adoratione et cultu in spiritu et veritate*

The 17 books *The Adoration and Worship of God in Spirit and in Truth (Περὶ τῆς ἐν πνεύματι καὶ ἀληθείᾳ προσκυνήσεως καὶ λατρείας)* present in the form of a dialogue between Cyril and Palladius an allegorico-typological exegesis of specifically chosen passages of the Pentateuch which do not follow the order of the Old Testament text but are assembled without any reference to their sequence in order to prove that the Law was abrogated only in the letter and not in the spirit. The institutions of the Old Dispensation must be understood as typical prefigurations of the adoration in the spirit.

Taking as a starting point the sin of Adam and Eve, the first book deals with the deliverance of man from the slavery of sin and Satan, the second and third with justification through Christ as the means of obtaining that deliverance, the fourth and fifth with the resolution of the human will to persevere and preserve it. The basis of our salvation is the love of God (book 6) and of our neighbour (books 7 and 8). Books 9-13 show the Church and the priesthood, books 14-16, the spiritual worship of the Christians, forshadowed in the institutions of the Old Testament. The last book is devoted to the feasts of the Jews, especially the Pasch. The time of composition for this treatise, which occupies an entire volume of Migne's edition, is long before 429 but after 412.

Edition: MG 68, 133-1125.

Studies: J. H. BERNARD, On Some Fragments of an Uncial MS. of S. Cyril of Alexandria Written on Papyrus (Transactions of the Royal Irish Academy 29, 18). Dublin, 1892, 653-672 (manuscript of the sixth century containing the end of book 7 and the entire text of book 8). — D. SERRUYS, Un 'Codex' sur papyrus de St. Cyrille d'Alexandrie: RPh 34 (1910) 101-117 (on the same manuscript Pap. Louvre E 10295=R 1). — For a Syriac version of the sixth century, cf. R. DUVAL, La littérature syriaque. 3rd ed. Paris, 1907, 365. — W. J. BURGHARDT, Cyril of Alexandria on 'wool and linen': Traditio 2 (1944) 484-486 (*De ador. et cultu* 9, 390). — P. SANZ, Griechische liturgische Papyri. Vienna, 1946, 11-124 (book 9).

b. Glaphyra (Γλαφυρά)

The thirteen books of *Elegant Comments* belong to the same period and are complementary to *De adoratione in spiritu*. Actually, the latter work refers to the former and vice versa. The content is also an exposition of select Pentateuch passages, which follows, however, the order of the Old Testament books and is not presented in the form of a dialogue. Seven books are devoted to Genesis, three to Exodus, and one book each to Leviticus, Numbers and Deuteronomy.

Edition: MG 69, 9-678.

Studies: Fragments of a Syriac version by Moses of Agel (6th cent.) are extant: J. GUIDI, Atti della R. Accademia dei Lincei. Serie 4 Rendiconti, vol. 2. Rome, 1886, 397-416, 545-547. Cf. R. DUVAL, op. cit. 364f. — For the relations existing between Origen's homilies and the spiritual explanations of *Glaphyra*, see: A. KERRIGAN, op. cit. 419-423.

c. The Commentary on Isaias

Consists of five *biblia*, some of which are divided into *logoi*, and others into *tomoi*. The introduction outlines the task of the interpreter

to expound first the literal and then the spiritual sense. The five
biblia offer a continuous commentary on Isaias 1-10, 10-24, 25-42,
42-51, 52-66. This extensive work, which fills almost the entire
volume 70 of Migne's edition, was most probably composed after
the two works on the Pentateuch but before 429.

Edition: MG 70, 9-1450.

d. The Commentary on the Minor Prophets

Has twelve main sections corresponding to their number, subdivided into *tomoi*. A prologue precedes each prophecy and an
introduction the entire commentary.

Editions: MG 71 and 72, 9-364. Best ed.: P. E. Pusey, Sancti patris nostri Cyrilli archiepiscopi Alexandrini in XII prophetas. 2 vols. Oxford, 1868.

Studies: For the general historical introduction, see: A. Kerrigan, op. cit. 295-297, for
peculiarities of style, *ibid.* 333-334, for changes of persons speaking and of addressees,
ibid. 334-338. For Cyril's interpretation of Joel, see: A. Merx, Die Prophetie des Joel
und ihre Ausleger. Halle, 1879, 152-156.

Numerous fragments of other commentaries on the Old Testament
are extant in the *Catenae*, some of them very extensive; they are
from Kings, Psalms, some Canticles, Proverbs, the Canticle of
Canticles, Jeremias, Ezechiel and Daniel. That Cyril wrote an
exegesis of the Psalms is implied by Ephrem of Antioch (according
to Photius, *Bibl. cod.* 229) and the florilegium *Doctrina Patrum de
incarnatione Verbi* (F. Diekamp, Münster i.W. 1907, 186). The
fragments in the Chains do not go beyond Psalm 119 but there
cannot be any doubt that Cyril's work dealt with the whole Psalter
as G. Mercati has sufficiently shown. An Armenian manuscript
of the Bodleian Library contains extracts from a commentary on
Ezechiel attributed to Cyril. Some of them seem to correspond to
fragments of the same work published by Migne, MG 70, 1457f.
See S. Baronian and F. C. Conybeare, in *Catalogus mss. bibliothecae
Bodleianae*, pars XIV, Oxford 1918, 164.

Fragments: Explanatio in Psalmos: MG 69, 717-1273. However, a careful scrutiny of these
fragments will be necessary before they can be used with confidence; cf. R. Devreesse,
Chaînes exégétiques grecques: DB Suppl. I. Paris, 1928, 1134. Cf. G. Mercati, Osservazioni a proemi del Salterio di Origine, Ippolito, Eusebio, Cirillo Alessandrino e altri
con frammenti inediti (ST 142). Vatican City, 1948, 127-144. — MG 69, 679-698
fragments on Kings; 69, 1277 a fragment on Proverbs; 69, 1277-1294 on the Canticle
of Canticles; 70, 1451-1458 on Jeremias and Baruch; 70, 1457-1462 on Ezechiel and
Daniel. For an Armenian manuscript of a commentary on Ezechiel, see: L. Mariès,
Hippolyte de Rome: PO 27 (1954) 33. — A number of quotations of the commentary
on Canticle of Canticles is found in the *Catena* of Procopius of Gaza MG 87, 1545-1754.
Cf. W. Riedel, Die Auslegung des Hohen Liedes in der jüdischen Gemeinde und in
der griechischen Kirche. Leipzig, 1898, 101-102; L. Welsersheimb, Das Kirchenbild
der griechischen Väterkommentare zum Hohen Liede: ZkTh 70 (1948) 433-435.

2. Commentaries on the New Testament

a. The Commentary on the Gospel of St. John

This commentary has more of a dogmatico-polemical tendency. The introduction states that special attention will be given to the dogmatic sense of the text and the refutation of heretical doctrines. The author is anxious to prove from the fourth Gospel that the Son is of the same divine substance as the Father and that both have their own personal subsistence. He inveighs against the Arians, Eunomians and the Christology of the School of Antioch. The name of Nestorius is not mentioned nor does the term *Theotokos* and the terminology of Cyril's later writings occur. For this reason it is quite certain that the book was composed before the outbreak of the Nestorian controversy, i.e. before 429. The *terminus a quo* is still a matter of dispute. J. Lebon and N. Charlier hold that this explanation of the Gospel of St. John is the oldest of Cyril's exegetical works. G. Jouassard thinks that it was begun in 425 but not completed until 428. The enormous commentary consists of twelve books subdivided into chapters. Books seven and eight containing the exposition of St. John 10, 18-12, 48 are not preserved except for a few fragments in the Chains, the authenticity of which, however, remains doubtful.

Editions: MG 73 and 74, 9-756. Best ed.: P. E. Pusey, Sancti patris nostri Cyrilli arch. Alexandrini in d. Joannis evangelium. 3 vols. Oxford, 1872. MG 74, 9-104 and Pusey, vol. 2, 243-334 (fragments from the *Catenae*) should be subjected to rigorous scrutiny. A critical edition of these pieces is in preparation. Cf. J. Reuss, Matthäus-, Markus-, und Johannes-Katenen nach den handschriftlichen Quellen untersucht. Münster, 1941, 253f.

Translation: English: LFC 43 (Oxford, 1832), 48 (London, 1885). Commentary on the Gospel according to John, the first vol. translated by P. E. Pusey, the second by T. Randell.

Studies: J. Mahé, La date du Commentaire de saint Cyrille d'Alexandrie sur l'Évangile selon saint Jean: BLE 8 (1907) 41-45. — J. Lebon, RHE 22 (1926) 90. — Maric, Cyrille sur Jean VI, 54: Bogoslovska Smotra (1934) 296-306. — L. Turrado, *Δόξα* en el Ev. de S. Juan seg. San Cirilo de Al. Rome, 1939. — J. Reuss, Cyrill von Alexandrien und sein Kommentar zum Johannes-Evangelium: Bibl 25 (1944) 207-209. — G. Jouassard, L'activité littéraire de saint Cyrille d'Alexandrie jusqu'à 428: Mélanges E. Podechard. Lyons, 1945, 169-170. — J. Liébaert, Saint Cyrille d'Alexandrie et l'arianisme. Lille, 1948, 9-11. — N. Charlier, Le 'Thesaurus de Trinitate' de Saint Cyrille d'Alexandrie: RHE 45 (1950) 60-62. — G. Langevin, Le thème de l'incorruptibilité dans le commentaire de S. Cyrille d'Alexandrie sur l'évangile selon Jean: Sciences Ecclésiastiques 8 (1956) 295-316. — A. Kerrigan, The Objects of the Literal and Spiritual Senses of the New Testament according to St. Cyril of Al.: PS 1 (1957) 365-366.

b. The Commentary on the Gospel of St. Luke

Is of a different type, being in reality a series of *Homilies on St. Luke* with practical rather than dogmatic purpose. Of the Greek original only three complete sermons and some fragments in the Chains remain. However, a Syriac version of the sixth or seventh century preserves not less than 156 homilies. Their content provides us with valuable clues as to their date. The polemic against Nestorius and his adherents predominates and A. Rücker has found at least one allusion to Cyril's Anathemas in homily 63, which indicates that the Homilies on St. Luke date from the end of the year 430.

Editions: Greek text of the three sermons: MG 77, 1009 *In transfigurationem Domini*, 77, 1039-1050 *In occursum Domini*. The latter combines two original homilies. Catenae fragments: MG 72, 475-950. A. RÜCKER, Die Lukashomilien des hl. Cyrill von Alexandrien, Breslau, 1911, 33f, has carefully examined these fragments. The one on Luke 2, 52 (MG 72, 508) does not belong to Cyril but to Theodoret of Cyrus. Additional fragments on Luke 9-10 and 24, 51 have been published by J. SICKENBERGER, Fragmente der Homilien des Cyrill von Alexandrien zum Lukasevangelium (TU 34, 1), Leipzig, 1909, 63-108, from the *Catena* of Nicetas of Heraclea.

Syriac version: R. PAYNE SMITH, S. Cyrilli Alexandriae archiepiscopi Commentarii in Lucae evangelium quae supersunt syriace e manuscriptis apud Museum Britannicum. Oxford, 1858. Additions to the text of homilies 112-116 were published by W. WRIGHT, Fragments of the Homilies of Cyril of Alexandria on the Gospel of S. Luke, edited from a Nitrian ms. London, 1874. New fragments of several homilies were edited by A. RÜCKER, op. cit. 87-101. Of a new critical edition of the Syriac version the first part was published comprising homilies 1-80: J. B. CHABOT, S. Cyrilli Alexandrini commentarii in Lucam I: CSCO 70, Scriptores Syri 27. Paris and Leipzig, 1912.

Translations: Latin: R. M. TONNEAU, S. Cyrilli Alexandrini commentarii in Lucam I: CSCO 140, Scriptores Syri 70. Louvain, 1953. — *English:* R. PAYNE SMITH, A Commentary upon the Gospel according to St. Luke by St. Cyril, Patriarch of Alexandria. 2 vols. Oxford, 1859. — *German:* A. RÜCKER, op. cit., translated the Syriac fragments 87-101.

Studies: J. SICKENBERGER, op. cit. — A. RÜCKER, op. cit. Cf. F. NAU, ROC 16 (1911) 443-444.

c. Commentary on the Gospel of St. Matthew

Leontius of Byzantium, Ephrem of Antioch and others know of a commentary on the Gospel of St. Matthew composed by Cyril. Only a number of small fragments remain in the Chains. They cover all 28 chapters and make it quite clear that this work was a biblical commentary in the proper sense of the word, similar to the one on the Gospel of St. John. The date of composition seems to be after 428.

Editions: MG 72, 365-374. A new critical ed. of these fragments was recently published by J. REUSS, Matthäus-Kommentare aus der griechischen Kirche (TU 61). Berlin, 1957, 103-269.

Study: J. REUSS, Matthäus-, Markus- und Johannes-Katenen nach den handschriftlichen Quellen untersucht. Münster, 1941, 49f.

d. The Chains contain in addition a number of fragments of Cyril's lost commentaries on the Epistle to the Romans, on First and Second Corinthians and on the Epistle to the Hebrews.

Fragments: Epist. ad Romanos: MG 74, 773-856. Pusey, In Joannem, vol. 3 (cf. above p. 123) 173-248. — *Ep. I ad Corinthios:* MG 74, 856-916. Pusey, op. cit. 3, 249-319. — *Ep. II ad Cor.:* MG 74, 916-952. Pusey, op. cit. 3, 320-361. *Ep. ad Hebraeos:* MG 74, 953-1006. Pusey, op. cit. 3, 362-440. Armenian fragments of the commentary on Hebrews were published by J. Lebon, Fragments arméniens du commentaire sur l'Épître aux Hébreux de saint Cyrille d'Alexandrie: Mus 44 (1931) 69-114, 46 (1933) 237-246. A Syriac fragment of the same commentary is found in Barsalibi's treatise *Against the Armenians,* published by A. Mingana, Woodbrooke Studies 4. Cambridge, 1931, 47.

Studies: S. Lyonnet, S. Cyrille d'Alexandrie et 2 Cor. 3, 17: Bibl 32 (1951) 25-33. — G. Giudici, La dottrina della grazia nel Commento ai Rom. di S. Cirillo d'Alessandria. Diss. Greg. Rome, 1951.

3. *Dogmatic-Polemical Writings against the Arians*

The earliest of Cyril's dogmatic-polemic works are directed against the Arians. The most important of the two treatises against this heresy is

a. Thesaurus de sancta et consubstantiali Trinitate

A trinitarian summa comprising the Arian objections, their refutation and the lasting results of the controversies of the fourth century. Here Cyril follows entirely his master Athanasius; almost a third of the extensive work is a reproduction of Athanasius, *Contra Arianos* III, as J. Liébaert has sufficiently shown. It seems that Cyril used in addition a work of Didymus the Blind, *Contra Eunomium,* no longer extant. The preface gives a table of contents of the 35 chapters. Photius *(Bibl. cod.* 136) does not hesitate to state that 'this work is the clearest of all Cyril's works, especially to those who are able to grasp the significance of his logical methods'. While there cannot be any doubt that the *Thesaurus* was composed before the outbreak of the Nestorian controversy, opinions differ as to the exact date. G. Jouassard thinks that Cyril wrote it between 423 and 425. J. Liébaert and N. Charlier hold it to be the first of Cyril's greater works and therefore to have been written at the beginning of his episcopal career which began in 412.

Edition: MG 75, 9-656.

Studies: G. Jouassard, L'activité littéraire 169. — J. Liébaert, Saint Cyrille d'Alexandrie et l'arianisme. Les sources et la doctrine christologique du 'Thesaurus' et des 'Dialogues sur la Trinité'. Lille, 1948. — N. Charlier, Le 'Thesaurus de Trinitate' de saint Cyrille d'Alexandrie: RHE 45 (1950) 25-81.

b. De sancta et consubstantiali Trinitate

The second of the anti-Arian writings was composed shortly after the *Thesaurus* and dedicated to the same 'brother' Nemesius. It consists of seven dialogues of the author with his friend Hermias and refers clearly to his first work. Cyril states in the preface that the subtlety of the questions that he intends to answer demands the adoption of this form. Moreover, compared with the *Thesaurus*, the seven dialogues are more personal in character and form more of a unity than the 35 chapters of the first treatise. Dialogues 1-6 deal with the consubstantiality of the Son, the seventh with that of the Holy Spirit.

Edition: MG 75, 657-1124. The treatise *De sancta et vivifica Trinitate* (MG 75, 1147-1190) is not by Cyril, but by Theodoret of Cyrus; cf. below p. 546.

Translation: German: H. HAYD, BKV (1879) 43-469.

4. Dogmatic-Polemical Writings against the Nestorians

a. Adversus Nestorii blasphemias

The first of the anti-Nestorian treatises is the *Five Tomes against Nestorius* composed in the spring of 430. They represent a critical examination of a collection of sermons published by Nestorius in the previous year. His name does not appear in Cyril's work but many quotations from his homilies. Thus the first book refutes selected passages attacking the Marian title *theotokos*, the four others, those defending a duality of persons in Christ.

Editions: MG 76, 9-248. New ed. by P. E. PUSEY, Epistolae tres oecumenicae etc. Oxford, 1875, 54-239. Best ed.: E. SCHWARTZ, ACO I, 1, 6, 13-106.

Translation: English: P. E. PUSEY, LFC 47 (1881).

b. De recta fide

It was shortly after the beginning of the Nestorian controversy in 430 that Cyril submitted to the imperial court three memorials *On the True Faith* in order to counteract any Nestorian influence. The first of them was addressed to the Emperor Theodosius II, the two others *ad reginas* (ταῖς βασιλίσσαις) without mentioning any specific names. However, John of Caesarea at the beginning of the sixth century seems to be correct, when he states that the first of the two was addressed to the emperor's two younger sisters Arcadia and Marina, and the second to his elder sister Pulcheria and his wife Eudocia.

Editions: De recta in dominum nostrum Jesum Christum fide ad imperatorem Theodosium: MG 76, 1133-1200. — P. E. PUSEY, S. Cyrilli Alex. De recta fide ad imperatorem etc., Oxford,

1877, 1-153, provides a new edition of the Greek text and the Syriac version by Rabbula of Edessa. The latter is also found in P. BEDJAN, Acta Martyrum et Sanctorum 5. Paris, 1895, 628-696. The best edition of the Greek text: E. SCHWARTZ, ACO 1, 1, 1, 42-72. *De recta fide ad dominas:* MG 76, 1201-1336; *De recta fide ad augustas:* MG 76, 1335-1420. New ed. by PUSEY, op. cit. 154-333. Best ed.: E. SCHWARTZ, ACO 1, 1, 5, 62-118 and 1, 1, 5, 26-61.

Translation: German: O. BARDENHEWER, BKV³ (1935) 21-78.

Study: F. DIEKAMP, Das Glaubensbekenntnis des apollinaristischen Bischofs Vitalis von Antiochien: ThQ 86 (1904) 497-511 (*De recta fide ad reginas* 1, 10).

c. The Twelve Anathemas against Nestorius

Were written in the same year 430 (cf. below, p. 134). Cyril found it necessary to defend them in three apologies. In the first two he refutes two attacks which accused him of Apollinarianism and Monophysitism, one by Andrew of Samosata, the other by Theodoret of Cyrus. Thus Cyril's first apology *Against the Oriental Bishops* answers the charges of Andrew, who represented the Syrian bishops, and the second, the *Letter to Euoptius*, those of Theodoret. Both of these treatises must have been composed in the earlier half of 431 since there is no reference whatsoever to the Council of Ephesus. The third defense of the Anathemas is found in the brief commentary *Explicatio duodecim capitum Ephesi pronuntiata*, written while Cyril was in prison at Ephesus in August or September 431. The author is anxious to prove each one of the Anathemas by quotations from Scripture.

Editions: Explicatio pro duodecim capitibus adversus orientales episcopos: MG 76, 315-385. — *Epistola ad Euoptium adversus impugnationem duodecim capitum a Theodoreto editam:* MG 76, 385-452. A new edition of both treatises by PUSEY, S. Cyrilli Alex. epistolae tres oecumenicae etc. Oxford, 1875, 259-497. — *Explicatio duodecim capitum Ephesi pronuntiata:* MG 76, 293-312. New edit. by PUSEY, op. cit. 240-258. The first two treatises are preserved in a Latin translation by Marius Mercator: ML 48, 933-1002. Pusey reprints this Latin text with the Greek original and consults in addition a Syriac version. The best edition of the three writings is found in E. SCHWARTZ, ACO I, 1, 7, 33-65 *Adversus orientales episcopos;* I, 1, 6, 107-146 *Contra Theodoretum;* I, 1, 5, 15-25 *Explicatio duodecim capitum;* Latin version: ACO I, 5, 116-142; 142-165; 15-25.

d. Apologeticus ad imperatorem

Is an apology addressed to the Emperor Theodosius II immediately after Cyril's release and his return to Alexandria. Cyril justifies therein his actions, both before and during the Council of Ephesus.

Editions: MG 76, 453-488. PUSEY, De recta fide ad imperatorem. Oxford, 1877, 425-456. Best ed.: E. SCHWARTZ, ACO 1, 1, 3, 75-90.

e. Scholia de incarnatione Unigeniti

Composed after 431, gives first an explanation of the names of Christ, Emmanuel and Jesus, and then defines the hypostatic union as opposed to a mixture or external association only. The author refers to the combination of body and soul in man as the closest comparison in the created world. The entire text is extant in an old Latin, Syriac and Armenian translation, while of the original Greek only a small portion remains (EP 2124).

Editions: Greek fragments: MG 75, 1369-1412. The Old Latin version: ML 48, 1005-1040. Both in new ed. by P. E. PUSEY, S. Cyrilli Alex. epistolae tres oecumenicae etc. Oxford, 1875, 498-579. Best edition: E. SCHWARTZ, ACO I, 5, 219-231 Greek fragments; I, 5, 184-215 Latin version. The Armenian translation was published by F. C. CONYBEARE, The Armenian Version of Revelation and of Cyril of Alexandria's Scholia on the Incarnation and Epistle on Easter, ed. from the oldest MSS. and Englished. London, 1907. 95-143: Armenian text.

Translations: English: From the Old Latin version: P. E. PUSEY, LFC 47 (1881). — From the Armenian: F. C. CONYBEARE, op. cit. 168-214.

Studies: M. RICHARD, Le pape Léon le Grand et les Scholia de incarnatione Unigeniti de saint Cyrille d'Alexandrie: RSR 40 (1952) 116-128, proves that the Latin version used by Leo the Great goes back to Cyril himself. — G. JOUASSARD, Impassibilité du Logos et impassibilité de l'âme humaine chez Cyrille d'Alexandrie: RSR 45 (1957) 209-224.

f. Adversus nolentes confiteri sanctam Virginem esse Deiparam

The Emperor Justinian I testifies in his *Tractatus contra Monophysitas* 13-14 (MG 86,1,1132) about the year 542 that the treatise *Against Those That Do Not Acknowledge Mary to be the Mother of God* is a genuine work of Cyril. The first to publish it was Cardinal Mai.

Editions: MG 76, 255-292. Best ed. E. SCHWARTZ, ACO I, I, 7, 19-32.

Translations: German: H. HAYD, BKV (1879) 531-560. — O. BARDENHEWER, BKV³ (1935) 205-236.

g. Contra Diodorum et Theodorum

This tractate was written against Diodore of Tarsus and Theodore of Mopsuestia, the teachers of Nestorius. Consisting of three books, it was most probably composed about 438. Considerable fragments are extant in Greek and Syriac.

Editions: Greek and Syriac fragments (in Latin translation): MG 76, 1437-1452. Additional fragments: PUSEY, S. Cyrilli Al. in S. Joannis evangelium. Oxford, 1872, vol. 3, 492-537. Cf. M. RICHARD, Les traités de Cyrille d'Alexandrie contre Diodore et Théodore et les fragments dogmatiques de Diodore de Tarse: Mélanges F. Grat. Paris, 1946, 99-116.

Translation: English: PUSEY, LFC 47 (1881).

Studies: M. RICHARD, l.c. — R. DEVREESSE, Essai sur Théodore de Mopsueste (ST 141). Vatican City, 1948, 156-159. — F. A. SULLIVAN, The Christology of Theodore of

Mopsueste. Rome, 1956, 46-54, 173-179. — L. ABRAMOWSKI, Der Streit um Diodor und Theodor zwischen den beiden ephesinischen Konzilien: ZKG 67 (1955/56) 252-287.

h. Quod unus sit Christus

This dialogue on the unity of person in Christ, represents a thorough refutation of the false doctrine that the Word of God was not made flesh but was united only to a man, with the result that there is the true and natural Son of God and 'another one', an adopted son of God, who does not share the dignity and honor of the first. The author refers to his earlier polemic against the Nestorian heresy and exhibits such a maturity of thought and expression that the dialogue, highly prized in antiquity, seems to be one of Cyril's last anti-Nestorian writings.

Editions: MG 75, 1253-1361. New ed. by P. E. PUSEY, De recta fide ad imperatorem etc. Oxford, 1877, 334-424.

Translations: P. E. PUSEY, LFC 46 (1881). — *German:* O. BARDENHEWER, BKV³ 12 (1935) 109-204.

5. The Apology against Julian

After more than twenty-five years of his episcopal career, Cyril found it necessary to write a large apologetic work *For the Holy Religion of the Christians Against the Books of the Impious Julian.* Dedicated to Theodosius II, it refutes Julian the Apostate's three books *Against the Galilaeans* of the year 363. The introduction indicates that paganism was far from being dead in Egypt and that Julian's accusations against the Christian religion had remained very popular and were regarded as unanswered. Not more than the first ten books of Cyril's work are extant in entirety in the original Greek. Dealing with the relations between Christianity, Judaism and heathenism, they reply only to Julian's first book, in which the emperor intended to prove that Christianity was but a debased Judaism with an admixture of pagan elements. Cyril seems to employ a method similar to Origen's in his *Contra Celsum,* following his adversary step by step and always quoting the text of his opponent's argument. The result is an analytic criticism without any attempt at synthesis. Since Julian's polemic is lost, Cyril's work remains the principal source for a partial reconstruction of it. The Greek and Syriac fragments of books 11-20 of Cyril's treatise seem to indicate that they were devoted to the refutation of Julian's second book. For this reason C. J. Neumann suggested that Cyril's apology consisted altogether of thirty books and that the last ten contained the reply to book 3 of Julian's *Against the Galilaeans.* However, this remains doubtful, since nothing of these last ten books is extant. There is no hint that Cyril wrote more than twenty books against Julian, nor that he attempted a refutation of the entire work of the Apostate. We know from a letter of Theodoret of Cyrus (*Ep.* 83) that Cyril sent his work to the patriarch John of Antioch. Thus the date of composition must be before 441, the year in which John died. It cannot be earlier than 433, the year of reconciliation between John and Cyril.

Editions: Books 1-10: MG 76, 509-1058. Greek fragments of books 11-19: MG 76, 1057-1064. Additional fragments of books 11-20 are found in: C. J. NEUMANN, Iuliani Imperatoris librorum contra Christianos quae supersunt (Scriptorum Graecorum qui Christianam impugnaverunt religionem quae supersunt, fasc. 3), Leipzig, 1880: 42-63 Cyrilli Alexandrini librorum contra Iulianum fragmenta Syriaca edidit E. Nestle, and 64-87: Cyrilli Alexandrini librorum contra Julianum 11-20 fragmenta Graeca et Syriaca Latine reddita disposuit C. J. Neumann. Cod. Venet. Marc. 165 contains some Greek fragments of books 12-14 which so far have not been edited. Cf. F. DIEKAMP, SAB (1901) 1051 note 1; *idem*, Doctrina Patrum de incarnatione Verbi. Münster, 1907, Introd. L. For the unreliable quotations from Plotinus in books 2 and 8, see: P. HENRY, Études plotiniennes I. Les états du texte de Plotin. Paris, 1938, 71-74, 125-140. For further fragments, see: PO 14, 1, 245-246 and R. DRAGUET, Pour l'édition du Philalèthe de Sévère d'Antioche: BZ 30 (1929/30) 278-279. L. FRUECHTEL, Neue Zeugnisse zu Clemens Alexandrinus: ZNW 36 (1937) 88-90.

Studies: J. GEFFCKEN, Kaiser Julianus und die Streitschriften seiner Gegner: Neue Jahrbücher für das klassische Altertum 21 (1908) 188f. — H. LECLERCQ, DAL 8 (1928) 380-387. — P. REGAZZONI, Il Contra Galilaeos dell'Imperatore Giuliano e il Contra Julianum di S. Cirillo Alessandrino: Didaskaleion 6 (1928) 1-114. — H. DU MANOIR, Dogme et spiritualité chez saint Cyrille d'Alexandrie, Paris, 1944: 448-453 citations d'auteurs profanes dans le 'Contra Julianum'.

6. *Paschal Letters*

Cyril continued the custom of the bishops of Alexandria of sending every year to all the Churches of Egypt an announcement in the form of a pastoral epistle on the date of Easter and the preceding fast. The editions of Cyril's works list 29 of such Paschal Letters under the somewhat misleading heading *Homiliae Paschales*. Written between 414 and 442, they exhort to fast and abstinence, to vigilance and prayer, almsgiving and works of mercy. Despite their predominantly moral and practical character, they contain several dogmatic expositions, which reecho the christological controversies of the times. Thus *Hom.* 5, 8, 17, 27 defend the doctrine of the Incarnation against the heretics who deny the eternity of the Son, while *Hom.* 12 discusses the dogma of the Trinity. The author's zeal against pagan and Jews betrays itself all too often in intemperate polemic. The Christians are warned against *dipsychia*, an attitude, in which the soul is divided between Christianity and paganism, practicing rites of both (*Hom.* 12 and 14), against false gods and their adherents (*Hom.* 6 and 9), against the Jews and their infidelity (*Hom.* 1, 4, 10, 20, 21, 29).

Editions: MG 77, 401-982. Paschal Letter 17 for the year 429 in which Cyril objects to Nestorius for the first time, is also extant in an Old Latin translation falsely attributed to Arnobius iunior: MG 77, 789-800. A new edition of this version was published by J. SCHARNAGL, S. Cyrilli XVII. homiliae sive epistulae paschalis interpretatio quae vulgo Arnobii iunioris dicitur Latina. Vienna, 1909. Arnobius used this translation but is not the author of it. Cf. G. MORIN, Études, textes, découvertes I. Maredsous, 1913, 344f. For the tendency of this Latin translation, see: H. KAYSER, Die Schriften des sogenannten Arnobius iunior dogmengeschichtlich und literarisch untersucht. Gütersloh, 1912, 125f.

Translation: Dutch: M. COSTANZA, Cyrillus van Alexandrië, Preeken. Bussum, 1946, 21-44 Paschal Letter 8; 45-66 Paschal Letter 17.

Studies: C. PAPADOPOULOS, Οἱ ἑορταστικοὶ λόγοι τοῦ ἁγίου Κυρίλλου ᾽Αλεξανδρείας : EPh 31 (1932) 25-45. — P. MELONI, Il digiuno quaresimale e S. Cirillo Alessandrino: Kyrilliana. Cairo, 1947, 247-272.

The *Paschal Table* for the years 403-512 which Cyril prepared for the Emperor Theodosius II. is no longer extant, but Cyril's covering letter to the ruler survives in an old Armenian translation, published for the first time by Conybeare in 1907.

Edition: Armenian text of the letter to Theodosius II: F. C. CONYBEARE, The Armenian Version of Revelation and Cyril of Alexandria's Scholia on the Incarnation and Epistle on Easter. London, 1907, 143-149. The letter clearly indicates that it was accompanied by the Paschal Table. Dionysius Exiguus, *Ep. ad Petronium* (ML 67, 19f), reports about Cyril's Paschal Table and quotes the last part of it covering the years 437-531. However, this cannot be the original table but must be a later revision or continuation. The Latin *Prologus de ratione paschae* and the Latin *Epistola ad Leonem papam* on Easter (Cyril, *Ep.* 86-87: MG 77, 377-390) are falsifications.

Translation: English: F. C. CONYBEARE, op. cit. 215-221: The letter to the Emperor Theodosius II.

Studies: B. KRUSCH, Studien zur christlich-mittelalterlichen Chronologie. Leipzig, 1880, 88-98, 101-109, 337-349. — E. SCHWARTZ, Christliche und jüdische Ostertafeln (Abh. Kgl. Gesellsch. der Wissenschaften zu Göttingen, Phil.-histor. Kl. N.F. 8, 6). Berlin, 1905, 22-24. — G. MERCATI, Über die Ostertafel des hl. Cyrill von Alexandrien: ThR 6 (1907) 126-127. — A. CORDOLIANI, Les computistes insulaires et les écrits pseudo-alexandrins: Bibliothèque de l'École des Chartes 106 (1945) 5-34, proves the forgery of the Easter Table by Irish authors.

7. *Sermons*

Not more than 22 sermons remain of all the homilies which Cyril delivered during his long pontificate, and even they are sometimes in only fragmentary condition. The editors have gathered them under the heading *Homiliae diversae* to distinguish them from the *Homiliae Paschales*. The first eight of the collection were supposedly given in the summer of 431 during the Council at Ephesus. Of six we have the complete text. Homily n. 4 (MG 77, 991-996) is the most famous Marian sermon of antiquity. Cyril delivered it in the Church of St. Mary at Ephesus between June 23rd and 27th, 431.

The eleventh homily, entitled *Encomium in S. Mariam Deiparam*
(MG 77, 1029-1040) is nothing more than the fourth, retouched and
enlarged between the seventh and the ninth century, as A. Ehrhard
has sufficiently shown. Homilies 3, 15, 16 and 20 deal with the
Incarnation. The homily *In mysticam cenam* (MG 77, 1016-1029)
is not by Cyril but by his uncle Theophilus, as M. Richard has
shown (cf. above, p. 104). The homily *In exitu animi* is of doubtful
authenticity. Homily 8 *In transfigurationem Domini* and 12 *In occursum
Domini* belong to Cyril's series of homilies on the Gospel of St. Luke
mentioned above, p. 123.

Editions: MG 77, 981-1116 *(Homiliae diversae)* gives the text of 17 complete sermons
and the fragments of five others. Of the seventeen ns. 10, 11 and 13 are spurious; 3, 12
and 20 probably authentic. The rest must be subjected to a careful scrutiny, even those
supposed to have been given at Ephesus. Pusey, St. Cyrilli in d. Joannis evangelium.
Accedunt fragmenta varia, vol. 3. Oxford, 1872: 452-476, 538-545 seem to be genuine
fragments. For those delivered at Ephesus, E. Schwartz has published a new edition,
ACO I, 1, 2, 92f; 4, 14f; 7, 173. He denies the authenticity of the Marian sermon *(hom. 4)*:
ACO I, 1, 2, 102; 4, xxv.

Translations: German: O. Bardenhewer, Marienpredigten aus der Väterzeit, übersetzt.
Munich, 1934 (translation of homily 4). — *Dutch:* M. Costanza, Cyrillus van
Alexandrië, Preeken, ingeleid en vertaald, Bussum, 1946, furnishes a translation of
homilies ns. 1-7, 9-13, 15-17 and 20.

Studies: A. Ehrhard, Eine unechte Marienhomilie des hl. Cyrill von Alexandrien:
RQ 3 (1889) 97-113. — A. d'Alès, S. Cyrille d'Alexandrie et les Sept à Sainte-Marie
d'Éphèse: RSR 22 (1932) 62-70. — H. du Manoir, Dogme et spiritualité chez Cyrille
d'Alexandrie. Paris, 1944, 58-60. — C. Papadopoulos, Λόγος εἰς τὴν ἀνάληψιν τοῦ
κυρίου ἀνέκδοτος ἐπ' ὀνόματι Κυρίλλου 'Αλεξανδρείας: Εἰς μνήμην Σπ. Λάμπρου
Athens, 1935, 35-41, published a sermon on the Ascension which four manuscripts
of Mount Athos attribute to Cyril of Alexandria. Ch. Martin, Un discours prétendument
inédit de S. Cyrille d'Alexandrie sur l'ascension: RHE 32 (1936) 345-350, proved that
this homily, far from being unedited, is found among the spurious of St. John Chrysostom
(MG 64, 45-48) and does not belong to Cyril nor to Chrysostom. — A. Dillmann,
Chrestomathia Aethiopica, Leipzig, 1866, 88-98, published the Ethiopic version of two
homilies on Melchisedech purporting to be Cyril's. A German translation of these
sermons was given by S. Euringer, Übersetzung der Homilien des Cyrillus von
Alexandrien, des Severus von Synnada und des Theodotus von Ancyra in Dillmanns
'Chrestomathia Aethiopica': Orientalia 12 (1943) 114-127. — For the two sermons
on the 'Anargyroi' (MG 77, 1100-1105), see: P. Sinthern, Zum Kult der Anargyroi:
ZkTh 69 (1947) 354-360. — B. Koetting, Peregrinatio religiosa. Münster, 1950, 203-205.

8. *Letters*

Cyril's large correspondence is extremely important for the
history of State and Church, ecclesiastical doctrine and law, the
relations between East and West and the rivalry between theological
schools and episcopal sees. Fortunately, quite a number of his
letters are extant. Migne's edition counts 88, though some of them
are spurious and 17 addressed to Cyril by others. E. Schwartz

published in addition the Greek text of five others, four of them hitherto entirely unknown, and one in a Latin version only. Some survive in old Syriac, Coptic and Armenian translations.

Editions: MG 77, 401-981. — E. SCHWARTZ, Konzilsstudien II. Strasbourg, 1914, 67-70; *idem,* Neue Aktenstücke zum Ephesinischen Konzil 431 (AAM 30, 8). Munich, 1920, 52f: *Ep. ad Juvenalem,* 57f: *Ep. ad Acacium,* 67f: *Epp. ad Johannem Antioch.,* 75f: *Ep. ad Maximianum Constant.; idem,* ACO 1 passim.

Studies: For the letter 84 *ad Euoptium,* see above p. 127. — For *Ep.* 81 *ad monachos in Phua constitutos,* cf. E. HONIGMANN, Patristic Studies (ST 173). Vatican City, 1953, 52f. — *Ep.* 74 *ad Rabbulam episcopum Edessae* is not preserved in the Greek original but in a Syriac version: OVERBECK, S. Ephraemi Syri, Rabbulae episc. Edesseni, Balaei aliorumque opera selecta. Oxford, 1865: 226-229 Syriac text. BICKELL, Ausgewählte Schriften der syrischen Kirchenväter (BKV). Kempten, 1874: 246-249 German translation. — For *Ep.* 82 *ad Amphilochium ep. Sidae,* cf. G. FICKER, Amphilochiana, vol. 1. Leipzig, 1906, 259f. — For *Ep.* 86 *ad Leonem papam,* and *Ep.* 87 *seu Prologus de ratione paschae,* see above p. 131. — For the Armenian version of the letter addressed to the Emperor Theodosius II, see above p. oo. — A. VAN ROEY, Deux fragments inédits des lettres de Successus, évêque de Diocésarée à saint Cyrille d'Alexandrie: Mus 55 (1942) 87-92 (Syriac text and Latin translation of two excerpts from the letters of Successus, to whom Cyril addressed *Epp.* 45 and 46). — *Ep.* 55 contains a brief explanation of the Nicene Creed *In sanctum symbolum,* composed about 438 (MG 77, 289-320. Best ed.: E. SCHWARTZ, ACO 1, 1, 4, 49-61), and addressed to the deacon and archimandrite Maximus of Antioch who had asked for it. German translation: O. BARDENHEWER, BKV³ 12 (1935) 240-263.

First class sources for the history of dogma are those addressed to Nestorius, among them especially *Ep.* 4, the so-called *epistola dogmatica,* which represents the second of those he wrote to this heretic. The first meeting of the Council of Ephesus on June 22, 431, approved it solemnly by a unanimous vote of all the bishops present. Each of the 125 ecclesiastical rulers recommended the acceptance of this letter as in full agreement with the Nicene Creed and a true expression of the Catholic doctrine; the very wording of their endorsement is still preserved. Leo the Great in 450 (*Ep. Contra Eutych. haer.* 1) subscribes to their judgment of the epistle, 'evidentius fidem Nichaenae definitionis exponens'. The Councils of Chalcedon in 451 and of Constantinople in 553 also approved it for the same reason.

Editions: MG 77, 43-50. New ed. by P. E. PUSEY, S. Cyrilli epistolae tres oecumenicae etc. Oxford, 1875, 2-11: Greek text with Latin version by Marius Mercator. — Best ed.: E. SCHWARTZ, ACO I, 1, 1, 25-28.

Translations: English: P. E. PUSEY, The Three Epistles of St. Cyril. Oxford, 1872. — C. A. HEURTLEY, On the Faith and the Creed. Dogmatic Teaching of the Church of the Fourth and Fifth Centuries. Oxford, 1886, 156-161. — T. H. BINDLEY, The Oecumenical Documents of the Faith. London, 1899. Reprinted, 1906. — J. KIDD, Documents Illustrative of the History of the Church (SPCK) vol. 2, London, 1938, 251-255 (reprint of Heurtley's translation). — *German:* O. BARDENHEWER, BKV³ 12 (1935) 81-86.

Studies: I. ORTIZ DE URBINA, Das Glaubenssymbol von Chalkedon: CGG I (1951) 398-401. — G. JOUASSARD, Un problème d'anthropologie et de christologie chez saint Cyrille d'Alexandrie: RSR 43 (1955) 361-378.

The third letter to Nestorius (*Ep.* 17), which Cyril sent in the name of the Alexandrian synod at the end of 430, created great difficulties on account of the twelve anathemas attached to it and the peculiar terminology used by the author. Although it was added to the *Acta* of the Council of Ephesus, it did not receive formal ratification by vote. Nevertheless, the opinion prevailed later on that this letter and the anathemas had been adopted by the Councils of Ephesus and Chalcedon.

Editions: MG 77, 105-122. PUSEY, op. cit. 12-39: Greek text with Latin translation by Marius Mercator. Best ed.: E. SCHWARTZ, ACO I, 1, 1, 33-42.

Translations: English: PUSEY, The Three Epistles (cf. above p. 133). — C. A. HEURTLEY, op. cit. 162-176. — T. H. BINDLEY, op. cit. — J. KIDD, op. cit. 255-265. — *German:* O. BARDENHEWER, BKV³ 12 (1935) 86-100. — *French:* F. NAU, ROC 16 (1911) 189f. — H. DU MANOIR, Dogme et spiritualité chez Cyrille d'Al. Paris, 1944, 492-493.

Studies: J. MAHÉ, Les Anathématismes de Saint Cyrille d'Alexandrie et les évêques orientaux du patriarchat d'Antioche: RHE 7 (1906) 505-543. — C. L. SOUVAY, The Twelve Anathematizations of S. Cyril: CHR 5 (1926) 627-635. — J. PUIG DE LA BELLACASA, Los doce anatematismos de S. Cirilo. Fueron aprobados por el Concilio de Efeso?: EE 11 (1932) 5-25. — A. DENEFFE, Der dogmatische Wert der Anathematismen Cyrills: Schol 8 (1933) 64-88, 203-216. — P. GALTIER, Les Anathématismes de S. Cyrille et le Concile de Chalcédoine: RSR 23 (1933) 45-57. — H. DU MANOIR, op. cit. 491-510 Les Anathématismes de Cyrille et son monophysitisme. —A. GRILLMEIER, Die theologische und sprachliche Vorbereitung der christologischen Formel von Chalkedon: CGG I (1951) 176-184, 189-193. — P. GALTIER, Saint Cyrille d'Alexandrie et saint Léon le Grand à Chalcédoine: CGG I (1951) 372-377. — C. MOELLER, Le chalcédonisme et le néo-chalcédonisme en Orient de 451 à la fin du VIe siècle: CGG I (1951) 652-662. — H. BACHT, Die Rolle des orientalischen Mönchtums in den kirchenpolitischen Auseinandersetzungen um Chalkedon: CGG II (1953) 203-206. — H. DIEPEN, Les douze Anathématismes au Concile d'Éphèse et jusqu'en 519: Revue Thomiste 55 (1955) 300-338.

The third of the so-called ecumenical letters is *Ep.* 39, which Cyril addressed to John of Antioch in the spring of 433 and which has become known as the *Symbolum Ephesinum.* Here the patriarch of Alexandria expresses his joy and satisfaction that peace has been restored between himself and the bishops of Antioch: 'Let the heavens rejoice and the earth be glad, for the mid-wall of partition is broken down, and the cause of sorrow removed, and all manner of dissension taken away, Christ, our common Saviour, awarding peace to His own Churches' (1). At the end he sums up the faith of both parties in the symbol which had been submitted by the bishops of Antioch and gives the exact text of the formula of union to which both groups had subscribed. The Council of Chalcedon in 451 recommended this letter without restriction.

Editions: MG 77, 173-182. — Pusey, S. Cyrilli epistolae tres oecumenicae. Oxford, 1875, 40-53: Greek text with Old Latin version, and use of Syriac version. Best ed.: E. Schwartz, ACO I, 1, 4, 15-20. — An Ethiopic version was published by A. Dillmann, Chrestomathia Aethiopica. Leipzig, 1866, 72-76.

Translations: English: Pusey, The Three Epistles of Cyril. Oxford, 1872. — C. A. Heurtley, op. cit. 177-184, reprinted by J. Kidd, op. cit. 26-270. — T. H. Bindley, op. cit. — German: O. Bardenhewer, BKV³ 12 (1935) 100-107.

Studies: A. d'Alès, Le Symbole d'union de 433: RSR 3 (1931) 257-268. — P. Galtier, L'unité du Christ. Paris, 1939, 13-88. — I. Ortiz de Urbina, Das Glaubenssymbol von Chalkedon. Sein Text, sein Werden und seine dogmatische Bedeutung: CGG I (1951) 398-401, 414-417.

II. THE THEOLOGY OF CYRIL

Cyril's contemporary, Pope Celestine I, did not hesitate to honor him with titles like 'bonus fidei catholicae defensor', 'vir apostolicus' and 'probatissimus sacerdos'. After his death his reputation increased to such an extent that in the Greek Church he was regarded as the ultimate authority in all christological questions. Indeed, he was called the 'Seal of the Fathers' by Anastasius Sinaita in the seventh century. The S. Congregation of Rites on July 28, 1882 gave him the title 'Doctor ecclesiae'.

1. *Theological Method*

It is not only through his ideas that Cyril influenced the sacred sciences but also through his method. He is in fact the main representative of the scholastic procedure among the Greek Fathers. It seems that he consciously and purposely extended the long established practice of adducing 'proofs from Scripture' to include also 'proofs from the Fathers'. He did not invent this method. It had been used before. But nobody so far had employed it with such technical skill and perfection. It is certainly his merit that from now on Patristic testimony stands with Scriptural as authority in theological argumentation. In his trinitarian works he intends to sum up in a systematic presentation the teaching of the Church Fathers. The beginning of his controversy with Nestorius convinces him that there is no other way to win the battle than by making agreement with the Fathers the decisive element in all questions regarding orthodoxy. He follows this line as early as 429 in his letter to the monks (*Ep.* 1). In his second letter to Nestorius in the spring of 430 he states:

> We shall succeed [in rightly expounding the doctrine of faith to those who are seeking the truth] if, betaking ourselves to the statements of the Fathers, we are careful to esteem them highly and putting our own selves to test as to whether we are in the faith, as it is written

(2 Cor. 13,5), thoroughly conform our own beliefs to their sound and unexceptionable doctrines (*Ep.* 4).

Moreover, in his third letter to Nestorius, he calls himself 'a lover of sound doctrine, treading in the religious footsteps of the Fathers' and establishes the doctrine of the Incarnation by 'following in every particular the confessions of the holy Fathers, which they have drawn up under the guidance of the Holy Spirit speaking in them, and keeping close to the meaning which they had in view, and journeying, so to speak, along the king's highway' (*Ep.* 17). The Council of Ephesus in its meetings of June 22 (*Acta Conc. Oec.* 1, 1, 2, 39-45) and July 22 (*ibid.* 1, 1, 7, 89-95) adopts the proof from the Fathers and since then it has become the classical procedure in all theological argumentation in the Orient.

However, this is not the only methodological contribution that Cyril made to the scholasticism of a later period. He is largely responsible for introducing the proof from reason into ecclesiastical science. Again, he is not the first to do so. The Arians and Apollinarists had set the precedent. Perhaps this is why Cyril employs this method particularly in his anti-Arian writings. In his *Thesaurus* especially, Cyril regularly adds a number of proofs from reason to each thesis. He becomes so accustomed to this system that we find it again and again in all his other anti-Arian writings up to his *Commentary on the Gospel of St. John*.

Studies: J. N. HEBENSBERGER, Die Denkwelt des hl. Cyrill von Alexandrien. Eine Analyse ihres philosophischen Ertrags. Augsburg, 1927. — H. DU MANOIR, L'argumentation patristique dans la controverse nestorienne: RSR 25 (1935) 441-461, 531-560. — P. RENAUDIN, La théologie de saint Cyrille d'Alexandrie d'après saint Thomas d'Aquin. Tongerloo, 1937. — H. DU MANOIR, Dogme et spiritualité chez saint Cyrille d'Alexandrie. Paris, 1944. — J. SALAVERRI, El argumento de tradición patristica en la antigua Iglesia: RES 5 (1945) 107-119. — A. RIDOLFI, S. Cirillo nella luce del Pontificato Romano: Kyrilliana. Cairo, 1947, 17-36. — N. M. HARING, The Character and Range of Influence of St. Cyril of Alexandria on Latin Theology (430-1260): Mediaeval Studies 12 (1950) 1-19. — M. RICHARD, Les florilèges diphysites du Ve et du VIe siècle: CGG I (1951) 721-748 (proofs from the Fathers).

2. *Christology*

Cyril's writings enable us to follow the development of his Christology very closely. There is a great difference between the earlier and the later works. The Christology of the former, e.g. the *Thesaurus* and the *Dialogues*, merely repeats that of St. Athanasius. We find the same form of Logos-Sarx Christology without the slightest indication of the theological importance of the soul of Christ. It did not occur to Cyril, any more than to Athanasius, to refute the Arian difficulties about the immutability of the Logos by pointing to the existence of a human soul in Christ. Both of them attribute Christ's suffering to his flesh, without adverting to the soul's participation therein. The flesh is likewise the subject of his sanctity and his glory. Moreover, Cyril repeats the main formula of the Athanasian Christology, which provides the foundation for the entire Logos-Sarx Christology: 'The Word was made man, but did not descend upon a man' (Athanasius, *Contra Arian.* 3, 30; Cyril, *Dialog.* 1). In this period he does not hesitate to refer to inhabitation as a designation of the relation between God and man in Christ. Thus we encounter the concepts of 'temple' and 'house' quite frequently in his older works, when he speaks of the indwelling of the Logos in the flesh (*Thesaurus* 23, 24, 28; *Dialog.* 5).

It is in the year 429/430 that Cyril devotes himself to a deeper investigation of the christological doctrine in order to prepare himself for a refutation of Nestorius. His terminology becomes more pointed and his ideas more acute. Whereas in the earlier period he had not shrunk from employing 'assume' with reference to the Incarnation, he now teaches that the Word became man but did not assume a man (*Ep.* 45 *ad Succ.*). In his second letter to Nestorius he explains the Incarnation as follows:

> For we do not affirm that the nature of the Word underwent a change and became flesh, or that it was transformed into a whole or perfect man consisting of soul and body; but we say that the Word, having in an ineffable and inconceivable manner personally united to Himself flesh instinct with a living soul, became man and was called the Son of Man, yet not of mere will or favor, nor again by the simple taking to Himself of a person (i.e. of a human person to His divine person), and that while the natures which were brought together into this true unity, were diverse, there was of both one Christ and one Son: not as though the diverseness of the natures were done away by this union, but rather the Godhead and Manhood completed for us the one Lord and Christ and Son by their inutterable and unspeakable concurrence and unity. And thus, although He subsisted and was begotten of the Father before the worlds, He is spoken of as having been born also after the flesh of a woman: not that His divine nature had its beginning of existence in the holy Virgin, or needed of necessity on its own account a second generation after its generation from the Father, for it is foolish and absurd to say that He who subsisted before all worlds, and was co-eternal with the Father, stood in need of a second beginning of existence, but forasmuch as the Word having 'for us and for our salvation' personally united to Himself human nature, came forth of a woman, for this reason He is said to have been born after the flesh. For He was not first born an ordinary man of the holy Virgin, and then the Word descended upon Him, but having been made one with the flesh from the very womb itself, He is said to have submitted to a birth according to the flesh, as appropriating and making His own the birth of His own flesh. (*Ep.* 4)

From these words it is quite evident that Cyril teaches the hypostatic union, ἕνωσις καθ᾽ ὑπόστασιν, between the Logos and the flesh which He united to Himself. He states very clearly: 'If we reject this hypostatic union either as impossible or unmeet, we fall into error of making two sons' (*Ep.* 4). He maintains this union was an ἀσύγχυτος ἕνωσις, i.e. a union without a mixture of the two natures, preserving both without any change or alteration:

> He vouchsafed to be born as we, and proceeded forth, a man from a woman, not ceasing to be what He was, but even when He became man by taking upon Him flesh and blood, still continuing what He was, — God in nature and truth. Neither do we say that the flesh was converted into the divine nature, nor surely that the ineffable nature of God the Word was debased and changed into the nature of flesh, for it is unchangeable and unalterable, ever continuing altogether the same according to the Scriptures: but we say that the Son of God, while visible to the eyes, and a babe in swaddling clothes, and still at the breast of His Virgin Mother, filled all creation as God, and was seated with His Father. For the divine nature is without quantity and without magnitude and without limit (*Ep.* 17, 3).
>
> But let Thy Holiness vouchsafe to stop the mouths of those who say that there was a mixture of confusion or blending of God the Word with the flesh, for it is likely that some are spreading the report, that I hold or say this also. But so far am I from holding anything of the sort that I look upon those as mad who at all imagine that 'shadow of turning' can befall the divine nature of the Word, and that He is susceptible of change: for He remains what He is always and has undergone no alteration. Nor could He ever undergo alteration (*Ep.* 39).

Since the hypostatic union does not change the two natures, there is a rational soul, ψυχὴ λογική, in the human nature, even when united to the divine: 'His holy Body, embued with a rational Soul, was born of her, to which Body also the Word was personally united' (*Ep.* 4).

Cyril finds the best comparison for this union of the two natures in Christ in the relation of body and soul in every human being: 'For the one and sole Christ is not twofold, although we conceive of Him as consisting of two distinct substances inseparably united, even as a man is conceived of as consisting of soul and body, and yet is not twofold but one of both' (*Ep.* 17,8). For this reason there is no possibility of separating the two subsistences after the union:

> If any one in the one Christ divides the subsistences (ὑποστάσεις) after the union, connecting them only by a conjunction of dignity or authority or rule, and not rather by a union of natures (ἕνωσις φυσική), be he anathema (*Ep.* 17, anath. 3).

For the same reason it is not permissible to separate the sayings, ἰδιώματα, which the Scriptures contain about Christ, some of which seem to apply to Him as man, some as the Logos:

> If any one distributes to two Persons or Subsistences (προσώποις ἤγουν ὑποστάσεσι) the expressions used both in the Gospels and in the Epistles, or used of Christ by the Saints, or by Him of Himself, attributing some to a man, conceived of separately, apart from the Word which is of God, and attributing others, as befitting God, exclusively to the Word which is of God the Father, be he anathema (Ep. 17, anath. 4).

> To one Person, therefore, must be attributed all the expressions used in the Gospels, the one incarnate hypostasis of the Word (μία ὑπόστασις τοῦ θεοῦ λόγου σεσαρκωμένη, Ep. 17, 8).

Cyril rejects the terminology of the Nestorians who called the union of the two natures an 'indwelling' (ἐνοίκησις), or a 'connection' (συνάφεια) or 'close participation' (ἕνωσις σχετική):

> But neither again do we say that the Word which is of God dwelt in Him Who was born of the Holy Virgin as in an ordinary man, lest Christ should be understood to be a man who carries God (within him), for though the Word 'dwelt in us' (John 1, 14), and 'all the fullness of the Godhead' as it is said (Col. 2, 9) 'dwelt in Christ bodily', yet we understand, that when He became flesh the indwelling was not such as when He is said to dwell in the saints, but that having been united by a union of natures (ἕνωσις κατὰ φύσιν) and not converted into flesh, He brought to pass such an indwelling as the soul of man may be said to have with its own body.

> There is then one Christ and Son and Lord, not as though He were a man connected with God simply by a unity of dignity or authority, for equality of honor does not unite natures. Peter and John are equal in honor in that they are apostles and holy disciples, but the two are not one. Nor certainly do we understand the mode of connection to be that of juxtaposition, for this does not suffice to express a union of natures (ἕνωσις φυσική). Nor do we understand the union to be in the way of close participation (ἕνωσις σχετική), as we, 'being joined to the Lord', as it is written (1 Cor. 6, 17), 'are one spirit with Him'; but rather we reject the term 'connection' (συνάφεια) altogether, as insufficient to signify the union (τὴν ἕνωσιν, Ep. 17, 4-5).

To sum up, it is evident that Cyril in reality sees the union in Christ resulting from the person, the duality from the natures. In this he has anticipated the decision of the Council of Chalcedon and prepared the theological foundation for it. However, his terminology is by no means satisfactory and was no doubt a source of great misunderstanding. He used the terms φύσις and ὑπόστασις without any distinction to signify 'nature' as well as 'person'. He

speaks of the 'one incarnate nature of the Word', μία φύσις τοῦ
λόγου σεσαρκωμένη (*Ep.* 46, 2; EP 2061), when he intends to denote
the unity of the person, thinking that St. Athanasius was responsible
for this dangerous expression (*Rect. Fid. ad Reg.* 1, 9). As a matter
of fact, the formula had been invented by Apollinaris of Laodicea
who identified nature with person and taught that there was only
one nature in Christ. Cyril, however, by his *mia-physis* phrase,
intends only to admit for an ideal moment the conceptual distinction
of two individual entities; in other words, he teaches the union of
the Logos with a perfect human nature, composed of a body and
a rational soul; this nature, however, does not subsist independently
in itself but in the Logos. For this reason, he does not hesitate to
speak repeatedly of two natures *(δύο φύσεις)* before the union,
and one nature *(μία φύσις)* after the union of the Logos with the
flesh. Thus he declares: 'We say that two natures *(δύο φύσεις)*
are united, but that after the union there is no longer a division
into two (natures); we believe, therefore, in one nature of the Son
(μίαν εἶναι πιστεύομεν τὴν τοῦ υἱοῦ φύσιν), because He is one,
though become man and flesh' (*Ep.* 40 *ad Acac.*). From such and
similar statements it can be easily understood why Cyril was accused
of Apollinarism and Monophysitism. In reality, he endeavored to defend the traditional doctrine against both extremes, Apollinarianism
and Nestorianism. There is no doubt that the terminology of the
Antiochenes was clearer, but Cyril's was the deeper theological
thought. It took the Council of Chalcedon (451) to combine both
in the definition that there is in Christ a union of both natures into
one person: δύο φύσεις εἰς ἓν πρόσωπον καὶ μίαν ὑπόστασιν (ES 148).

Studies: SCHÄFER, Die Christologie des hl. Cyrillus von Alexandrien in der römischen
Kirche 432-534: ThQ 77 (1895) 421-447. — A. REHRMANN, Die Christologie des hl.
Cyrillus von Alexandrien. Hildesheim, 1902. — M. JUGIE, La terminologie christologique
de saint Cyrille d'Alexandrie: EO 15 (1912) 12-27. — E. WEIGL, Christologie vom
Tode des Athanasius bis zum Ausbruch des nestorianischen Streites. Munich, 1925,
123-203. — I. MARIĆ, Celebris Cyrilli Alexandrini formula christologica de una activitate
Christi in interpretatione Maximi Confessoris et recentiorum theologorum: Bogoslovska
Smotra 14 (1926) 56-102. — I. BACKES, Die Christologie des hl. Thomas von Aquin
und die griechischen Kirchenväter (FLDG 17, 3-4). Paderborn, 1931, 14-25. —
I. RUCKER, Das Dogma von der Persönlichkeit Christi und das Problem der Häresie
(Studien zum Concilium Ephesinum IV). Oxenbronn, 1934; *idem,* Cyrill und Nestorius
im Lichte der Ephesus-Enzyklika. Oxenbronn, 1934. — E. MERSCH, Le Corps Mystique
du Christ. 2nd ed. Brussels and Paris, 1936, 487-536. English translation: E. MERSCH,
The Whole Christ, transl. by J. R. Kelly, Milwaukee, 1938, 337-364. — A. GAUDEL,
La théologie de l' 'Assumptus Homo': RSRUS 17 (1937) 64-90, 214-234. — H. DU
MANOIR, Le problème de Dieu chez Cyrille d'Alexandrie: RSR 27 (1937) 385-407,
549-596. — J. VAN DEN DRIES, The Formula of S. Cyril of Alexandria μία φύσις τοῦ
Θεοῦ Λόγου σεσαρκωμένη. Rome, 1939. — A. M. DUBARLE, L'ignorance du Christ
dans saint Cyrille d'Alexandrie: ETL (1939) 111-120. — R. V. SELLERS, Two Ancient
Christologies. London, 1940, 80-106. — M. RICHARD, L'introduction du mot 'hypostase'

dans la théologie de l'incarnation: MSR 2 (1945) 243-252. — H. DU MANOIR, Dogme et spiritualité 99-162. — G. BASETTI-SANI, Il primato di Cristo in San Cirillo: Kyrilliana. Cairo, 1947, 137-196. — B. DE M. V. MONSEGÚ, Unidad y Trinidad, propiedad y apropiación en las manifestaciones trinitarias, según la dotrina de San Cirilo Alejandrino: RES 8 (1948) 1-57. — A. HULSBOSCH, De hypostatische vereniging volgens den H. Cyrillus van Alexandrië: StC 24 (1949) 65-94. — G. L. PRESTIGE, Fathers and Heretics. London, 1948. — J. LIÉBAERT, La doctrine christologique de saint Cyrille d'Alexandrie avant la querelle nestorienne. Lille, 1951. — A. GRILLMEIER, Die theologische und sprachliche Vorbereitung der christologischen Formel von Chalkedon: CGG I (1951) 160-193. — P. GALTIER, Saint Cyrille d'Alexandrie et saint Léon le Grand à Chalcédoine: CGG I (1951) 345-387. — J. LEBON, La christologie du monophysisme syrien: CGG I (1951) 516-522, 528-531, 557-562, 578-580. — P. GALTIER, L' 'unio secundum hypostasim' chez saint Cyrille: Greg 33 (1952) 351-398. — G. JOUASSARD, Une intuition fondamentale de saint Cyrille d'Alexandrie en christologie dans les premières années de son épiscopat: REB 11 (1953) 175-186; idem, Une problème d'anthropologie et de christologie chez saint Cyrille d'Alexandrie: RSR 43 (1955) 361-378; idem, Saint Cyrille d'Alexandrie et le schéma de l'incarnation Verbe-chair: RSR 44 (1956) 234-242; idem, Impassibilité du Logos et impassibilité de l'âme humaine chez Cyrille d'Alexandrie: RSR 45 (1957) 209-244. — P. GALTIER, saint Cyrille et Apollinaire: Greg 37 (1956) 584-609. — H. M. DIEPEN, La christologie de S. Cyrille d'Alexandrie et l'anthropologie néoplatonicienne: Euntes Docete 9 (1956) 20-63; idem, Aux origines de l'anthropologie de saint Cyrille d'Alexandrie. Bruges, 1957 (against Liébaert and Jouassard); idem, Stratagèmes contre la théologie de l'Emmanuel: Divinitas 1 (1957) 444-478. — J. N. D. KELLY, Early Christian Doctrines. London, 1958, 317-329. For Cyril's soteriology, see: E. WEIGL, Die Heilslehre des hl. Cyrill von Alexandrien. Mayence, 1905. — J. MAHÉ, La sanctification d'après saint Cyrille d'Alexandrie: RHE 10 (1909) 30-40, 469-492. — J. F. DE GROOT, De leer van den hl. Cyrillus van Alexandrië over de heiligmakende genade: Theolog. Studiën 31 (1913) 343-358, 501-515. — L. JANSSENS, Notre filiation divine d'après saint Cyrille d'Alexandrie: ETL 15 (1938) 233-278. — A. M. DUBARLE, Les conditions du salut avant la venue du Sauveur chez saint Cyrille d'Alexandrie: RSPT 32 (1948) 359-362. — G. GIUDICI, La dottrina della grazia nel Commento ai Romani di S. Cirillo d'Alessandria. Diss. Greg. Rome, 1951. — B. FRAIGNEAU-JULIEN, L'inhabitation de la sainte Trinité dans l'âme selon Cyrille d'Alexandrie: RSR 30 (1956) 135-156. — W. J. BURGHARDT, The Image of God in Man according to Cyril of Alexandria (SCA 14). Washington, 1957. — H. J. M. DIEPEN, Stratagèmes contre la théologie de l'Emmanuel. À propos d'une nouvelle comparaison entre saint Cyrille et Apollinaire: Divinitas 1 (1957) 444-478. — J. N. D. KELLY, Early Christian Doctrines. London, 1958, 396-399.

For Cyril's ecclesiology, see: L. MALEVEZ, L'Église dans le Christ. Étude de théologie historique et théorique: RSR 25 (1935) 257-291, 418-440. — H. DU MANOIR, L'Église, Corps du Christ chez saint Cyrille d'Alexandrie: Greg 19 (1939) 537-603, 83-100, 161-188. — P. POLAKES, Orthodoxia. Constantinople, 1948. — J. CAPMANY, La comunicación del Espíritu Santo en la Iglesia-Cuerpo Mistico como principio de su unidad según San Cirilo de Alejandría: RES 17 (1957) 173-204. — H. DU MANOIR, Dogme et spiritualité 287-366.

For Cyril's eucharistic doctrine, see: E. MICHAUD, Saint Cyrille d'Alexandrie et l'Eucharistie: Revue internat. de théologie 10 (1902) 599-614, 675-692. — J. MAHÉ, L'Eucharistie d'après saint Cyrille d'Alexandrie: RHE 8 (1907) 677-696. — A. STRUCKMANN, Die Eucharistielehre des hl. Cyrill von Alexandrien. Paderborn, 1910. — H. DU MANOIR, Dogme et spiritualité 184-218.

For Cyril's teaching on the Holy Spirit: J. B. WOLF, Commentationes in S. Cyrilli Alexandrini de Spiritu Sancto doctrinam. Würzburg, 1934. — P. GALTIER, Le Saint-

Esprit en nous d'après les Pères grecs. Rome, 1946, 217-272. — B. DE M. V. MONSEGÚ, La teología del Espíritu Santo según San Cirilo de Alejandría: RES 7 (1947) 161-220. — J. SAGÜÉS, El Espíritu Santo en la santificación del hombre según la dotrina de San Cirilo de Alejandría: EE 21 (1947) 35-83. — S. TROOSTER, De H. Geest en de Mens-wording bij Cyrillus van Alexandrië: BiNJ 18 (1957) 375-397. — N. CHARLIER, La doctrine sur le Saint-Esprit dans le 'Thesaurus' de saint Cyrille d'Alexandrie: SP II (TU 64). Berlin, 1957, 187-193.

3. *Mariology*

It is only a conclusion drawn from the *communicatio idiomatum* that Cyril calls Mary the Mother of God, and found the formula for the true doctrine in the word θεοτόκος, as opposed to the Χριστοτόκος or ἀνθρωποτόκος of the Nestorians. If it was God Who was born and crucified, then Mary is truly the Mother of God:

> But forasmuch as the Holy Virgin brought forth after the flesh God personally united to flesh, for this reason we say of her that she is 'the Mother of God' (θεοτόκος), not as though the nature of the Word had its beginning of being from the flesh, for He was 'in the beginning', and 'the Word was God and the Word was with God', and He is the maker of the world, co-eternal with the Father, and the Creator of the universe, but, as we said before, because having personally united man's nature to Himself, He vouchsafed also to be born in the flesh, of her womb (*Ep.* 17, 11).

This is by no means a new doctrine. The title *theotokos* had been employed in the School of Alexandria for a long period to express Mary's divine motherhood. The historian Sozomen reports (*Hist. eccl.* 7, 32; EH 866) that Origen used the title (cf. vol. II, p. 81). Cyril is well aware of this long tradition:

> This is the doctrine which strict orthodoxy everywhere prescribes. Thus shall we find the Holy Fathers to have held. So did they make bold to call the Holy Virgin 'the Mother of God' (θεοτόκος). Not as though the nature of the Word or His Godhead had its beginning from the Holy Virgin, but forasmuch as His holy Body, embued with a rational soul, was born of her, to which Body also the Word was personally united, on this account He is said to have been born after the flesh (*Ep.* 4).

Moreover, Cyril regarded this word *theotokos* as a kind of compendium of Christology since it presupposes the unity of the person and the duality of natures in Christ: 'A correct, sufficient and irreproachable profession of faith is found in the assertion of the divine maternity of the Blessed Virgin': ἀρκεῖ τὸ θεοτόκον λέγειν καὶ ὁμολογεῖν τὴν ἁγίαν παρθένον (*Hom.* 15 *de incarnatione Verbi;* EP 2058).

Studies: A. EBERLE, Die Mariologie des hl. Cyrillus von Alexandrien (FThSt 27). Freiburg, 1921. — NILUS A S. B., De maternitate div. B.M.V. Nestorii et Cyrilli sententiae. Rome, 1944. — H. DU MANOIR, Dogme et spiritualité 257-286.

TWO LITURGICAL PAPYRI OF EGYPT

Among the great number of Christian Papyri, two have special importance for the history of the Egyptian liturgy.

1. The Dêr-Balizeh Papyrus

In 1907 Flinders Petrie and W. E. Crum discovered in the ruins of the monastery Dêr-Balizeh in Upper Egypt a papyrus of three incomplete leaves and thirty to forty fragments, a few considerable, but most very small. It is now housed in the Bodleian Library at Oxford. Dom P. de Puniet was the first to publish its text from a transcript given him by W. E. Crum, but he limited himself to the three incomplete leaves only. All subsequent editions were based on this, until C. H. Roberts and Dom B. Capelle recently in a new edition included the hitherto unpublished fragments mentioned above.

The document was written in the sixth or seventh century. In content, however, it seemed to represent the practice of the fourth as F. E. Brightman thought, or even the third century, as Th. Schermann suggested. B. Capelle, admitting that it has conserved very ancient elements, holds that nothing warrants a date prior to the end of the sixth, whereas J. N. D. Kelly is inclined to accept Brightman's view.

The find amounts to part of an early Egyptian *Euchologium*. Its Eucharistic rite contains three prayers belonging to the first part of Mass, an anaphora and a communion prayer. Between the *Sanctus* and the narrative of the Institution, there is an invocation (epiclesis) of the Holy Spirit that the consecration may take place for the advantage of the faithful: 'Deign to send down Thy Holy Spirit upon these creatures and change the bread into the Body of the Lord and Saviour Jesus Christ, but the cup into the Blood of the New Testament'. Immediately preceding the words of the Institution there is a petition for unity in the Church, borrowed from *Didache* 9, 4 and describing the grain from which the eucharistic bread has been made as originally scattered on the tops of the mountains but brought together into a single whole (cf. vol. I, p. 32). We find a similar quotation from the *Didache* in the *Euchologium* of Serapion (cf. above, p. 83), but there it is placed between the words of the Institution for the bread and for the chalice which completely destroys the symmetry and seems to be Serapion's own arrangement.

The Communion Prayer is as follows: 'Grant that, as partakers of Thy grace, we may receive the power of the Holy Spirit, may be strengthened and fortified in faith and may have the hope of a future eternal life through our Lord Jesus Christ'.

Important and unique is the inclusion towards the end, of a simple creed, which reads as follows:

> I believe in God the Father almighty
> and in His only-begotten Son
> our Lord Jesus Christ,
> and in the Holy Spirit, and in the
> resurrection of the flesh in the
> holy Catholic Church.

Nowhere else do we find anything similar. Although it has several Egyptian parallels and may well be much more ancient than the liturgy, yet at the close of no other Eucharistic service do we encounter such a declaration of belief. It cannot have belonged in the Mass, both because of the place it now occupies and because it is a baptismal formula. Unfortunately the rubric preceding it has been mutilated and there remains only: '...confesses the faith, saying'. The words which have fallen out, if supplied, perhaps read: 'The candidate of baptism confesses the faith, saying'. Thus the writer seems to have copied part of the baptismal rite. The extremely archaic form of the creed has occasionally led scholars to date the liturgy of the papyrus very early. But it must be remembered that collections of this kind compile materials of different age and place.

Editions: P. DE PUNIET, Le nouveau papyrus liturgique d'Oxford: RB 26 (1909) 34-51. — T. SCHERMANN, Der liturgische Papyrus von Dêr-Balyzeh. Eine Abendmahlsliturgie des Ostermorgens (TU 36, 1 b). Leipzig, 1910. Cf. F. E. BRIGHTMAN, JThSt 12 (1911) 310f. — F. CABROL and H. LECLERCQ Reliquiae liturgicae vetustissimae (Monumenta ecclesiae liturgica I, 1, 1913) CLXIV-CLXXV. — C. WESSELY, Les plus anciens monuments du christianisme écrits sur papyrus II: PO 18 (1924) 425-429. — C. DEL GRANDE, Liturgiae, preces, hymni Christianorum e papyris collecti. 2nd ed. Naples, 1934, 1-5. — J. QUASTEN, Monumenta eucharistica et liturgica vetustissima (FP 7). Bonn, 1935, 37-44. — New crit. edition: C. H. ROBERTS and B. CAPELLE, An Early Euchologium. The Dêr-Balyzeh Papyrus enlarged and reedited. Louvain, 1949.

Translations: Latin: J. QUASTEN, op. cit. — A. BUGNINI, L'Eucologio di Dêr-Balizeh: EL 65 (1951) 157-170. — *English:* P. F. PALMER, Sources of Christian Theology, vol. 1: Sacraments and Worship. Westminster (Md), 1955, 46-47. — *German:* L. A. WINTERSWYL, Gebete der Urkirche. Freiburg i.B., 1940, 13-15.

Studies: P. DE PUNIET, À propos de la nouvelle anaphore égyptienne: EO 13 (1910) 72-76. — S. SALAVILLE, Le nouveau fragment d'anaphore égyptienne de Dêr-Balyzeh: EO 12 (1909) 329-335; idem, La double épiclèse des anaphores égyptiennes: EO 13 (1910) 133-134. — T. SCHERMANN, op. cit. — J. A. JUNGMANN, Zwei Textergänzungen im liturgischen Papyrus von Dêr-Balyzeh: ZkTh 48 (1924) 465-471. — F. CABROL,

Canon: DAL 2 (1925) 1881-1895. — H. LIETZMANN, Messe und Herrenmahl. Bonn, 1926, 37-39, 74-80, 154. — P. BATIFFOL, L'Eucharistie. La présence réelle et la trans-substantiation (Études d'histoire et de théologie positive 2), 9th ed. Paris, 1930, 327-334. — P. NAUTIN, Je crois à l'Esprit-Saint dans la Sainte Église pour la résurrection de la chair. Étude sur l'histoire et la théologie du symbole. Brussels and Paris, 1947. — J. N. D. KELLY, Early Christian Creeds. London, 1950, 88-89, 121-122. — B. CAPELLE, op. cit. 39-61. — K. GAMBER. Das Eucharistiegebet im Papyrus von Dêr-Balizeh und die Samstagabend-Agapen in Ägypten: OstkSt 7 (1958) 48-65.

2. *Papyrus Fragment of the Anaphora of St. Mark*

M. Andrieu and P. Collomp published in 1928 a papyrus of the University Library of Strasbourg, which contains fragments of an anaphora. A thorough examination proved that we have here a part of the so-called prayer of intercession, which in the Liturgy of St. Mark was recited by the celebrant and deacon between the beginning of the Canon and the Trishagion for the whole Catholic Church, for all orders and ranks of the Christian people, for all emergencies, for the living and for the dead. It is a fourth-century papyrus and the service described here was probably used already at the time of St. Athanasius (295-373). In other words, our fragment represents the original type of the Liturgy of St. Mark and is not less than 800 years older than the earliest manuscripts we possess thereof. Since the Liturgy of St. Mark was later on strongly influenced by the Byzantine type, it is of special importance to have recovered a text of a period preceding this change.

Editions: M. ANDRIEU and P. COLLOMP, Fragments sur papyrus de l'anaphore de saint Marc: RSRUS 8 (1928) 489-515. — J. QUASTEN, Monumenta eucharistica et liturgica vetustissima (FP 7). Bonn, 1935, 44-48.

Translations: Latin: J. QUASTEN, op. cit. 45-49. — *English:* P. F. PALMER, Sources of Christian Theology, vol. 1: Sacraments and Worship. Westminster (Md), 1955, 44-46.

CHAPTER II

THE FOUNDERS OF EGYPTIAN MONASTICISM

Monasticism is a creation of Christian Egypt. Its founders were not the phiiosophers of the Hellenistic world but the fellahin of the country of the Nile, who were untouched by Greek ideas. Its beginnings are intimately connected with the history of asceticism, which was inherent in Christian teaching from the first. Whereas in the earliest times individual asceticism was practised without involving separation from home and family or absence from the ecclesiastical community and city life, the representatives of the new movement retired from the world and sought silence and solitude away from human habitation. The climate was ideal for such a development. Tradition connects the origin of monasticism with the Decian persecution (c. 250), when many Christians fled from the populous parts of Egypt to the surrounding deserts and remained there for some time (Eusebius, *Hist. eccl.* 6, 42). Some of them settled there permanently to lead a holy life and thus became the forerunners of the hermits.

However, it is not without reason that the ʿourth century witnessed the great development of monasticism. It was a natural reaction against the danger of secularisation after the Church had been given freedom and Christianity had been adopted as the State religion. Thus the spread of worldliness was counteracted by a flight from the world. As a result, monasticism in its early stage was opposed to learning and literature and rejected any attempt at a reconciliation between faith and philosophy, Christian religion and Hellenistic culture. Some of these ascetics were bitter enemies of the famous teachers of the School of Alexandria, especially of Origen. However, this hostility did not last. As time went on, their attitude toward education and knowledge became gradually more sympathetic. There was a slow but steady growth in appreciation of the treasures of ancient culture. It is still within the fourth century that hermits and monks appear among Christian authors. They created a literary type, monastic rules and ascetical treatises, collections of spiritual Sayings of the Fathers of the desert, hagiographic and edifying writings, sermons and letters. Soon, too, they ceased to limit themselves to works mirroring the ideals of the spiritual life. They composed very learned essays of high theological and historical value. Moreover, many of the monasteries developed into outstanding centres of sacred science.

We owe our information regarding the origin and spread of the movement in part to the biographies of its founders written by their disciples, to a greater extent, however, to two special documents dealing with the history of Egyptian monasticism. The one is the *Lausiac History* of Palladius, bishop of Helenopolis (cf. below, p. 177), the other, an anonymous *History of the Monks of Egypt*, preserved in Greek and in a Latin translation by Rufinus. We have in addition the reports in the *Ecclesiastical Histories* of Socrates and Sozomen and the oldest parts of the *Apophthegmata Patrum*.

Two different forms of the new asceticism developed in Egypt. The older one is anchoritism or hermitism, i.e. life in isolation, the younger, cenobitism or monasticism proper, i.e. life in common.

Selected Texts: H. Koch, Quellen zur Geschichte der Askese und des Mönchtums in der alten Kirche. Tübingen, 1933.

Translations: English: H. Waddell, The Desert Fathers. New York, 1936. — *French:* J. Brémond, Les Pères du désert. 2 vols. 2nd ed. Paris, 1927. — H. Draguet, Les Pères du désert. Textes choisis et présentés. Paris, 1949. — *German:* S. Feldhohn, Blühende Wüste. Aus dem Leben palästinensischer und ägyptischer Mönche im 5. und 6. Jahrhundert. Aus dem Griechischen übersetzt. Düsseldorf, 1957.

Studies: H. Weingarten, Der Ursprung des Mönchtums im nachkonstantinischen Zeitalter: ZKG 1 (1877) 1-35. — O. Zöckler, Askese und Mönchtum. 2nd ed. Frankfurt a.M., 1897. — D. Völter, Der Ursprung des Mönchtums. Freiburg i.B., 1900. — J. M. Besse, Les moines d'Orient antérieurs au Concile de Chalcédoine. Paris, 1900. — E. Lucius, Das mönchische Leben des 4. und 5. Jahrhunderts in der Beleuchtung seiner Vertreter und Gönner: Festgabe für H. J. Holtzmann. Tübingen, 1902, 123-156. — J. O. Hannay, The Spirit and Origin of Christian Monasticism. London, 1903. — E. Lucius, Die Anfänge des Heiligenkults in der christlichen Kirche, herg. v. G. Anrich. Tübingen, 1904, 337-409. — S. Schiwietz, Das morgenländische Mönchtum I. Das Aszetentum der ersten drei Jahrhunderte und das ägyptische Mönchtum im 4. Jahrhundert. Mayence, 1904. — H. Leclercq, Cénobitisme: DAL 2 (1910) 3047-3248. — P. van Cauwenbergh, Étude sur les moines d'Égypte depuis le Concile de Chalcédoine (451) jusqu'à l'invasion arabe (640). Paris and Louvain, 1914. — W. H. Macklean, Christian Monasticism in Egypt to the Close of the Fourth Century. London, 1920. — P. Gobillot, Les origines du monachisme chrétien et l'ancienne religion de l'Égypte: RSR 10 (1920) 303-354; 11 (1921) 29-86, 168-213, 328-361; 12 (1922) 46-68. — A. v. Harnack, Das Mönchtum, seine Ideale und seine Geschichte. 10th ed. Giessen, 1921. — W. Bousset, Das Mönchtum in der sketischen Wüste: ZKG 42 (1923) 1-41. — A. Saudreau, La prière chez les moines de l'antiquité: VS 8 (1923) 288-293. — J. Lebreton, Les origines du monachisme et de la mystique chrétienne: RSR 14 (1924) 357-364. — H. G. White and W. Hauser, The Monasteries of the Wâdi n'Natrûn. 3 vols. New York, 1926, 1932, 1933. Cf. Ch. Martin, Les monastères du Wâdi n'Natroun: NRTh 62 (1935) 113-134, 238-252. — F. Bauer, Die Heilige Schrift bei den Mönchen des christlichen Altertums: ThGl 17 (1925) 512-532. — D. Gorce, La 'lectio divina' des origines du cénobitisme à St. Benoît et Cassiodore I. Paris, 1925; idem, Sur la tonsure chrétienne et ses prétendues origines païennes: RHE 20 (1925) 399-454. — A. Brémond, Le moine et le stoïcien: RAM 8 (1927) 26-40. — J. Zellinger, Bad und Bäder in der altchristlichen Kirche. Munich, 1928, 47-67. — E. Buonaiuti, Le origini dell'ascetismo cristiano. Pinerolo, 1928. — A. L. Schmitz, Die Welt der ägyptischen Einsiedler und Mönche: RQ 37 (1929) 189-243. — H. F. v. Campenhausen, Die asketische Heimatlosigkeit im altkirchlichen und frühmittelalterlichen Mönchtum. Tübingen, 1930. — C. Baur, Der weltflüchtige und der welttätige Gedanke in der Entwicklung des

Mönchtums: BoZ 7 (1930) 113-126. — J. QUASTEN, Musik und Gesang in den Kulten der heidnischen Antike und christlichen Frühzeit (LQF 25). Münster, 1930, 147-157 (katanyxis and liturgical singing in Egyptian monasteries). — P. RESCH, La doctrine ascétique des premiers maîtres égyptiens du quatrième siècle. Paris, 1931. — H. DÖRRIES, Mönchtum und Arbeit. Leipzig, 1931. — P. OPPENHEIM, Das Mönchskleid im christlichen Altertum. Eine kultur- und religionsgeschichtliche Studie (RQ Suppl. 28). Freiburg i.B., 1931; idem, Symbolik und religiöse Wertung des Mönchskleides im christlichen Altertum. Münster, 1932. — P. DE MEESTER, Autour de quelques publications récentes sur les habits des moines d'Orient: EL 47 (1933) 446-458. — H. LECLERCQ, Monachisme: DAL 11 (1934) 1774-1947. — J. BIDEZ, Le texte du prologue de Sozomène et de ses chapitres (VI 28-34) sur les moines d'Égypte et de Palestine (SAB). Berlin, 1935. — G. BARDY, La vie spirituelle d'après les Pères des trois premiers siècles. Paris, 1935. — F. KOZMAN, Textes législatifs touchant le cénobitisme égyptien. Rome, 1935. —K. HEUSSI, Der Ursprung des Mönchtums. Tübingen, 1936. — M. VILLER and M. OLPHE-GALLIARD, Ascèse, ascétisme: DSp 1 (1936) 916-981. — P. DE LABRIOLLE, Les débuts du monachisme: A. FLICHE and V. MARTIN, Histoire de l'Église III. Paris, 1936, 299-369; English translation by E. C. MESSENGER: The Church in the Christian Roman Empire, vol. 2. New York, 1953, 421-477.—J. HAUSHERR, Ignorance infinie: OCP (1936) 351-361. -— G. BARDY, Apatheia: DSp 1 (1937) 727-746. — H. B. DE WARREN, Le travail manuel chez les moines à travers les âges: VS 52 (1937) 80-123. — B. STEIDLE, Das Lachen im alten Mönchtum: BM 20 (1938) 271-280; idem, Die Tränen, ein mystisches Problem im alten Mönchtum: BM 20 (1938) 181-187. — M. LOT-BORODINE, Le mystère du 'don des larmes' dans l'Orient chrétien: VS 48 (1936) 65-110. — M. VILLER and K. RAHNER, Aszese und Mystik in der Väterzeit. Freiburg i.B., 1939, 80-121. — H. DÖRRIES, Die Bibel im ältesten Mönchtum: ThLZ 72 (1947) 215-222. — H. STRATHMANN and P. KESELING, Askese: RACh 1 (1943) 763-795. — P. WILPERT, Ataraxie: RACh 1 (1943)· 844-854. — J. HAUSHERR, Penthos. La doctrine de la componction dans l'Orient chrétien. Rome, 1944. — A. T. GEOGHEGAN, The Attitude towards Labor in Early Christianity and Ancient Culture (SCA 6). Washington, 1945, 162-174. — M. MARX, Incessant Prayer in Ancient Monastic Literature. Vatican City, 1947. — A. J. PHYTRAKIS, Ὁ κλαυθμὸς τῶν μοναχῶν. Athens, 1946; idem, Μαρτύριον καὶ μοναχικὸς βίος. Athens, 1948. — E. E. MALONE, The Monk and the Martyr (SCA 12). Washington, 1950; idem, Martyrdom and Monastic Profession as a Second Baptism: A. MAYER, J. QUASTEN, B. NEUNHEUSER, Vom christlichen Mysterium. Düsseldorf, 1951, 115-134. — E. DEKKERS, Les anciens moines cultivaient-ils la liturgie?: ibid. 87-114. — G. BARDY, Les origines des écoles monastiques en Orient: Mélanges J. De Ghellinck. Gembloux, 1951, 293-309. — J. E. STEWART, The Influence of the Idea of Martyrdom in the Early Church. Diss. St. Andrews, 1951. — P. T. CAMELOT, Mystique et continence. Bruges, 1952, 273-292. — J. LECLERCQ, Pour l'histoire de l'expression 'Philosophie chrétienne': MSR (1952) 221-226. — M. CRAMER, Thebanische Mönche, ihr asketisches und kultisches Leben: ALW 2 (1952) 103-109. — H. MUSURILLO, The Problem of Ascetical Fasting in the Greek Patristic Writers: Traditio 12 (1956) 1-64. — I. HAUSHERR, Comment priaient les Pères?: RAM 32 (1956) 33-58. — K. D. MOURATIDIS, Ἡ μοναχικὴ ὑπακοὴ ἐν τῇ ἀρχαίᾳ ἐκκλησίᾳ. Athens, 1956. — A. DIHLE, Demut: RACh 3 (1956) 765-771. — O. ROUSSEAU, Monachisme et vie religieuse d'après l'ancienne tradition de l'Église. Chevetogne, 1957. — A. VAN DER MENSBRUGGHE, Prayer-time in Egyptian Monasticism (320-450): SP II (TU 64). Berlin, 1957, 435-454.

ST. ANTONY

The one who initiated the older type is St. Antony, well known from the classical biography by St. Athanasius (cf. above, p. 39). Born of Christian parents about 250 at Coma in Middle Egypt, he sold all his belongings after their death, gave the money to the poor and began to practise the ascetic life not far from his old home. After fifteen years, at the age of thirty-five, he moved to the right side of the Nile, to the 'Outer Mountain' at Pispir; here, for the next twenty years he occupied an abandoned fort. Many gathered around him to follow his example. Thus great colonies of monks arose, the most famous of which were at Nitria and Scete. Although St. Antony became their leader, he remained ever true to his eremitic vocation. He as well as all of his disciples lived alone. He died in 356 at the age of one hundred and five years on Mount Colzim near the Red Sea, the recognized founder of the anchoritic type of monachism.

According to Athanasius (*Vita* 72f.) Antony was a man of 'divine wisdom', 'of grace and urbanity' although he never learnt to read or write. If people teased him about this shortcoming, he used to answer: 'Well, what do you say, which is first, the mind or the letters? And which is the cause of which—the mind of letters, or letters of the mind?' When they admitted that the mind is first and the inventor of letters, Antony answered: 'Therefore, one who has a sound mind has no need of letters'. About his attitude towards literature, Socrates (*Hist. eccl.* 4,23) relates:

To the good Antony there came a philosopher of the day and said: 'Father, how do you hold up deprived as you are of the solace of books?' Antony said: 'My book, philosopher, is nature, and thus I can read God's language at will'.

His biographer remarks: 'Antony gained renown not for his writings, nor for worldly wisdom, nor for any art, but solely for his service to God' (*Vita* 93).

Studies: For the *Vita Antonii*, see above p. 43-45 (editions, translations and studies). — S. SCHIWIETZ, Das morgenländische Mönchtum I. Mayence, 1904, 68-79. — E. AMÉLINEAU, Saint Antoine et les commencements du monachisme chrétien en Égypte: RHR 65 (1912) 16-78. — J. DAVID, Antoine: DHG 3 (1924) 726-734. — E. BUONAIUTI, Le origini dell' ascetismo cristiano. Pinerolo, 1928, 177-182. — P. MONCEAUX, Saint Augustin et saint Antoine. Contribution à l'histoire du monachisme: Miscellanea Agostiniana, vol. II. Rome, 1931, 61-89. — K. HEUSSI, Der Ursprung des Mönchtums. Tübingen, 1936, 78-108. — G. BARDY, Antoine: DSp 1 (1936) 702-708. — D. BROOKE, Pilgrims were they all. London, 1937 (ch. I). — G. BARDY, Les premiers temps du christianisme de langue copte en Égypte: Memorial Lagrange. Paris, 1940, 203-216. — P. NOORDELOOS and F. HALKIN, Une histoire latine de saint Antoine, la 'Légende de Patras': AB (1943) 211-250. — G. GARITTE, Panégyrique de saint Antoine par Jean, évêque d'Hermopolis: OCP 9 (1943) 100-131, 330-365 (Coptic text and French translation of this Coptic homily). — H. QUEFFÉBE, Saint Antoine du désert. Paris, 1950. English translation by J. WHITALL: H. Queffébe, Saint Anthony of the Desert. New York, 1954. — W. NIGG, Vom Geheimnis der Mönche. Zurich and Stuttgart, 1953, 29-63. — B. STEIDLE, Antonius Magnus Eremita 356-1956 (SA 38). Rome, 1956 (a collection of

articles by 14 different authors). A survey of all studies of the last 30 years, *ibid.* 13-24
L. v. HERTLING, Studi storici Antoniani negli ultimi trent' anni. — G. GIAMBERARDINI.
S. Antonio Abate. Astro del deserto. Cairo, 1957.

Letters

Nevertheless, he carried on a correspondence with monks as well
as with emperors and high officials. Athanasius reports about his
letter to the emperors:

> The fame of Antony reached even the emperors; for when
> Constantine Augustus and his sons Constantius Augustus and Constans
> Augustus heard about these things, they wrote to him as to a father
> and begged him to write back. He, however, did not make much of
> the documents nor did he rejoice over the letters; but he was the same
> as he was before the emperors wrote to him. When the documents
> were brought to him, he called the monks and said: 'You must not
> be surprised if an emperor writes to us, for he is a man; but you should
> rather be surprised that God has written the law for mankind and has
> spoken to us through His own Son'. Indeed, he did not like to accept
> the letters, saying that he did not know what to answer to such things.
> But being persuaded by the monks, who urged that the emperors were
> Christians and that they might take offense at being ignored, he had
> them read. And he wrote back, commending them for worshipping
> Christ, and giving them salutary advice not to think highly of the
> things of this world, but rather to bear in mind the judgment to come;
> and to know that Christ alone is the true and eternal King. He begged
> them to show themselves humane and to have a regard for justice
> and for the poor. And they were glad to receive his answer (*Vita* 81
> ACW).

Athanasius knows also of a letter addressed to the imperial official
Balacius, 'who in his partisanship for the execrable Arians bitterly
persecuted us Christians. And since he was so barbaric as to beat
virgins and strip and flog monks, Antony sent him a letter with the
following contents: "I see God's judgment approaching you;
stop, therefore, persecuting Christians, that the judgment may
not seize you; even now it is on the point of overtaking you"' (*ibid.*
86).

None of these letters is extant. Seven others addressed to various
monasteries in Egypt survive in versions. They are first mentioned
by St. Jerome (*De vir. ill.* 88), who had read them, however, not
in Coptic—the language in which they were probably dictated
by St. Antony—but in Greek. As F. Klejna proved, the collection
has come down to us complete in late Latin translations of translations: one, very poor, done out of the Greek by Valerius de Sarasio
and edited by Symphorianus Champerius at Paris in 1515 (MG

40,977-1000); and a second, made from an Arabic manuscript by the Maronite Abraham Ecchellensis. The latter, published also in Paris in 1641 (MG 40,999-1066), comprises *Ep.* 1-7 of a group of twenty, the rest of which were written not by St. Antony but partly by his disciple and successor Ammonas and partly by unknown correspondents. Of the seven authentic, the first exists also in Syriac, and we have besides in Coptic the seventh, the beginning of the fifth and end of the sixth. G. Garitte has recently found a Georgian version of all seven.

These letters contain exhortations to perseverance and warnings against a return to the world. The addressees are called repeatedly *filii Israelitae, viri Israelitae sancti* because they follow the words of the Lord: *Exi de terra et de cognatione tua*—an indication that they are monks. The first of the letters is an introduction to the monastic life for novices. Another addressed to the monks at Arsinoë receives special praise from St. Jerome. The seventh mentions the terrible end of Arius. It is quite evident that Antony wrote to the different monastic colonies in order to immunize them against all Arian propaganda.

These communications glow with religious enthusiasm but indulge in no polemics. Though there is a total absence of mysticism, they preach a solid and healthy asceticism. The first obligation of the monk is to know himself because only those who know themselves will be able to know God. This self-knowledge is understood as an evergrowing perception of divine grace given to us. The first letter explains the operation of the Holy Spirit in the making of a monk. It mentions three roads leading to the monastic profession. The direct road is taken by those who follow the call of God from a virtuous and holy life in the world. The reading of Holy Scripture marks the beginning of the second. Here the soul, after becoming conscious of the terrible end of those who die in sin and the great and heavenly promises given to the saints, decides on the persuit of perfection. The third is the road of atonement after evildoing and impenitence, from which the soul is called by many afflictions and tribulations. The letters present monastic life as a continuous battle for which the beginner must arm himself by exterior and interior mortification. Fortunately, he has the support of the Holy Spirit in this fight, who guides him and opens the eyes of his soul to the great task, the sanctification of soul and body, the final goal of his vocation. The last cannot be reached without the exstirpation of all passions. There are three kinds of 'emotions' in man. Some are purely natural and under the guidance of the soul. Other result from overindulgence in food and drink and excite the body against the soul. The third kind is caused by the evil spirits, who attack the soul directly or through the body. There is an extensive passage (MG 40,983-984) dealing with the manifold wiles of the devil but there is no hint at a 'discerning of the spirits' in the modern sense. There follow recommendations for the purification of the different senses, which will lead to a preparation of the whole man for the resurrection. Finally, the passions like pride, hate, jealousy, anger and impatience are treated. These will be overcome by the instruction of the Holy Ghost; he who yields to His guidance will be saved.

The small but interesting letter by Antony which the Egyptian bishop Ammon, a contemporary of Athanasius, reproduces in its entirety, has all the earmarks of genuineness (MG 40,1065). It is addressed to the archimandrite Theodore and his monks and reports a private revelation regarding the forgiveness of sins committed after baptism. It informs the monks that God has taken away the offenses of those whose contrition and penance are sincere. Ammon gives it in a Greek version, while the original was in Coptic.

Editions: MG 40, 977-1000; 999-1019; 1065. — The Georgian version and the Coptic fragments: G. GARITTE, Lettres de saint Antoine. Version géorgienne et fragments coptes: CSCO 148 text, 149 Latin translation. Louvain, 1955. — The Coptic fragments were first published by O. WINSTEDT, The Original Text of One of St. Antony's Letters: JThSt 7 (1906) 540-545. — For the Syriac version of the first letter, see: F. NAU, La version syriaque de la première lettre de saint Antoine: ROC 14 (1909) 282-297. — For the letter to Theodore: F. HALKIN, Sancti Pachomii vitae Graecae (Subsidia hagiographica 19). Brussels, 1932, 116, 19-33. — For the Arabian Corpus of Letters, Rules and Sayings, a later compilation, see: G. GRAF, Geschichte der christlichen arabischen Literatur. I (ST 118). Vatican City, 1944, 456-459.

Studies: L. v. HERTLING, Antonius der Einsiedler. Innsbruck, 1929, 56-70 (for the authenticity of the two collections of letters). — F. KLEJNA, Antonius und Ammonas. Eine Untersuchung über die Herkunft und Eigenart der ältesten Mönchsbriefe: ZkTh 62 (1938) 309-348. — G. GARITTE, A propos des lettres de saint Antoine l'Ermite: Mus 52 (1939) 11-32 (for the authenticity of both collections). — KRAUS, Der Hl. Geist in den Briefen des hl. Antonius des Einsiedlers: Festschrift zum 50-jährigen Bestandsjubiläum des Missionshauses St. Gabriel. Kaldenkirchen, 1939, 117-134. — G. GARITTE, Une lettre grecque attribuée à S. Antoine: Mus 55 (1942) 97-129 (although very old, this letter, found in the manuscript app. 46 of the Municipal Library of Nuremberg, is not by S. Antony); *idem,* Les lettres de saint Antoine en géorgien: Mus 64 (1951) 267-278 (importance of the Georgian version for the tradition of the text).

Rule

The so-called *Rule of St. Antony* is spurious. St. Athanasius does not mention it in his biography. A careful analysis of the document, extant in two Latin versions, reveals its composite character. At least two compilers contributed to its present form. One of the Latin translations was made from an Arabic text and published by A. Ecchellensis in 1646, the other was edited for the first time by L. Holstenius in 1661.

Edition: MG 40, 1065-1074 reprints both editions side by side.

Study: B. CONTZEN, Die Regel des hl. Antonius (Progr.). Metten, 1896 (thinks that some parts of the Rule are genuine).

Sermons

Athanasius remarks that Antony 'by ceaseless conferences fired the zeal of those who were already monks, and incited most of the others to a love of the ascetic life; and soon, as his message drew men after him, the number of monasteries multiplied, and to all he was a father and guide' (*Vita* 15 ACW). Perhaps this passage is responsible for the fact that a number of sermons have been falsely attributed to the founder of monasticism. There is a collection of twenty *Sermones ad filios suos monachos* and one *Sermo de vanitate mundi et resurrectione mortuorum* extant in Latin (MG 40,961-1102). None of them seems to be genuine. The only discourse of Antony's we possess is found in his biography. Athanasius who gives a Greek translation (*Vita* 16-43) does not fail to state that it was delivered in Coptic. It is an address to the monks on the virtues and difficulties of their life. There is reason to assume that it is several conferences condensed into one by St. Athanasius.

Editions: For the address to the monks, see the editions and translations of the *Vita* (above p. 43). Codex Vatic. Graec. 1579 contains a fragment attributed to an hitherto unknown treatise of St. Antony *Admonitions addressed to Monks.* Cf. G. GARITTE, Un fragment grec attribué à saint Antoine l'Ermite: BBR 20 (1939) 165-170. — I. HAUSHERR, Un écrit stoïcien sous le nom de saint Antoine l'Ermite: OCh 30 (1933) 212-216 (a pagan treatise used by the monks as a work of St. Antony). — F. v. IVANKA, Kephalaia. Eine byzantinische Literaturform und ihre antiken Wurzeln: BZ 47 (1954) 285-291 (a collection of meditations attributed to St. A.).

AMMONAS

After Antony's death the colony of hermits at Pispir was under the guidance of Ammonas, one of his oldest disciples, whom the *Apophthegmata Patrum* (65,119-123) praises for his unending kindness of heart. Seven of his letters have come down in a Greek version and fifteen in Syriac, the latter offering a more reliable text. Some occur in the larger collection of St. Antony's epistles in the Latin translation of Abraham Ecchellensis (cf. above, p. 151).

If we compare the correspondence of Ammonas with St. Antony's, the former is by far the more interesting. Except for the *Apophthegmata*, it appears to be the most instructive and precious source for the history of the earliest monachism in the desert of Scete. These documents reveal an original and genuine mysticism, free of all system and theory. There is not the slightest sign of Origen's terminology or of the later school culminating in Evagrius Ponticus. The ancient idea of the long and arduous journey of the soul to heaven is very prominent. After the soul has conquered every temptation, it ascends from the nether world, from light to light, from one heaven to another. However, in its passage to the beyond it will be opposed by all kinds of enemies and powers of the air. To overcome these numerous foes God will appoint as a custodian and guide a divine power *(δύναμις θεϊκή)*. Although the idea of the passage of the soul was usually understood of its time after death, Ammonas applies it to the mystical ascent on earth, reminding one of the *Ascensio Isaiae* (cf. vol. I, p. 110). Ammonas in fact quotes this work. Thus the letters remain important for the history of the earliest Christian mysticism and show that it was totally different from the later Evagrian type destined to have a lasting influence on all mysticism of the Christian Orient.

Editions: Greek text: F. Nau, PO 11 (1916) 432-454. — Syriac version: M. Kmosko, Les lettres d'Ammon: PO 10 (1915) 555-639. — Latin version: MG 40, 1019-1066.

Translations: Latin: From the Syriac version: M. Kmosko, op. cit. — *French:* From the Greek: F. Nau, op. cit.

Studies: E. Peterson, Irrige Zuweisungen asketischer Texte: ZkTh 57 (1933) 273f. — F. Klejna, Antonius und Ammonas. Eine Untersuchung über die Herkunft und Eigenart der ältesten Mönchsbriefe: ZkTh 62 (1938) 309-348 (regards the *Ep.* 15 of the Syriac version as spurious).

PACHOMIUS

During the time when anchoritism was in process of development in the northern provinces of Egypt, in the south Pachomius the Copt gave shape to its second form, cenobitism or the monastic life properly so-called. Born of pagan parents, he became a convert to the faith at the age of twenty and was educated in the ascetical school of the hermit Palemon. About A. D. 320 he started the first great *coenobium* or monastery of the common life at Tabennisi near Dendera in the Thebaid on the right bank of the Nile. He followed elsewhere with eight additional foundations for men and two for women, over all of which he presided as abbot general. His important contribution was not only that he housed the monks together—such grouping existed before his time—but that he created a genuine fellowship; he drew up the first rule providing for a government in the spirit of community, uniformity, poverty, obedience and discretion. Thus he became the founder of cenobitism, the form of monastic life which was destined to spread through the whole world and survive to our times. He died in 346. Numerous biographies testify to the esteem and admiration in which he was held.

Studies: O. Grützmacher, Pachomius und das älteste Klosterleben. Freiburg i.B., 1896. — P. Ladeuze, Étude sur le cénobitisme Pakhomien pendant le IVe siècle et la première moitié du Ve. Louvain and Paris, 1898. — S. Schiwietz, Das morgenländische Mönchtum I. Mayence, 1904, 119-148. — W. Bousset, Apophthegmata. Studien zur Geschichte des ältesten Mönchtums. Tübingen, 1923, 209-280. — L. T. Lefort, St. Pacôme et Amen-em-ope: Mus 40 (1927) 65-74. — H. Heussi, Der Ursprung des Mönchtums. Tübingen, 1936, 115-131. — H. Leclercq, Pakhome: DAL 13 (1937) 499-510. — H. Bacht, Pakhome — der Grosse 'Adler': Geist und Leben 22 (1949) 367-382; *idem*, L'importance de l'idéal monastique de S. Pacôme pour l'histoire du monachisme chrétien: RAM 26 (1950) 308-326; *idem*, Vom gemeinsamen Leben. Die Bedeutung des pachomischen Mönchideals für die Geschichte des christlichen Mönchtums: Mönchtum in der Entscheidung (Liturgie und Mönchtum, 3. Folge, Heft 11). Maria Laach, 1952, 91-110. — V. Monachino, EC 9 (1952) 511-514. — W. Nigg, Vom Geheimnis der Mönche. Zurich and Stuttgart, 1953, 64-85. — H. Bacht, Antonius und Pachomius. Von der Anachorese zum Cönobitentum: SA 38 (1956) 66-107. — E. Amand de Mendieta, Le système cénobitique basilien comparé au système cénobitique pacômien: RHR 152 (1957) 31-80. — D. J. Chitty, A Note on the Chronology of the Pachomian Foundations: PS II (TU 64). Berlin, 1957, 379-385.

THE RULE OF PACHOMIUS

Thanks to the efforts of Dom A. Boon, the unsatisfactory texts of the Pachomian Rule have been replaced by the critical edition that this highly important document deserves. It was originally drawn up in Coptic. About a fourth of this is extant in large fragments, first brought out by L. Th. Lefort and contained also in Boon in an appendix. The early Greek translation has disappeared completely, and the so-called *Excerpta Graeca* represent remains of an abbreviated text adapted to a different milieu, most probably outside Egypt. The second half of the fourth century saw so many Latins joining the Pachomians, especially at Canopus to the northeast of Alexandria, that St. Jerome who lived at Bethlehem was asked by the priest Silvanus to provide a Latin version. Prepared about 404 from the Greek, it paved the way for the lasting influence which the work of Pachomius had in the West. This has survived and is the only form in which we possess the entire text today. A *recensio longior* and a *recensio brevior* exist and for a long time the latter was regarded as the authentic work of St. Jerome. Thus even in 1923 P. Albers edited it as such (FP 16). However, the discovery of the Coptic fragments in 1919 made it clear that the *recensio brevior*, though widespread, was only an adaptation of the Rule for Italian monasteries. The original is, therefore, the *recensio longior*. This is preserved in eighteen manuscripts, six derived from one and the same archetype, but together with the rest constituting a sound basis for the text. A ninth-century copy in the National Library at Munich, *Clm* 28118, possesses special importance, since it contains some unique readings. The short recension has come down in twelve manuscripts, the oldest of the eleventh century.

This first Rule had an extraordinary influence on all subsequent monastic legislation. St. Basil made use of it for his own Rule (cf. below, p. 212). The *Regula Orientalis* or *Regula Vigilii* (so called because attributed to the deacon Vigilius) shows such a strong literary dependence that it helps us to reconstruct Pachomius' work. Written in Gaul about 420, it borrows a quarter of its text from the Latin translation of Jerome. Reminiscences can also be found in the two Rules of St. Caesarius of Arles and in that of his successor, Aurelius of Arles. The so-called *Regula Tarnatensis* of the seventh century shows an even greater indebtedness. The famous Rule of St. Benedict, the Father of Western monasticism, reminds one of the Egyptian in a great number of passages. Dom C. Butler in his critical edition has noticed twenty-six such, but this figure seems too low and a thorough study would disclose more. In several instances the parallelism is so close as to suggest direct borrowing. Finally, St. Benedict of Aniane († 821) made use of Pachomius in his great reform. His *Liber ex regulis diversorum patrum collectus* (ML 103,423-702) gives the text of the Pachomian Rule in Jerome's version and his *Concordia regularum* (ML 103,717-1380) refers to it again and again.

According to Palladius (*Hist.Laus.* 32,1) the Rule was dictated by an angel who instructed the saint to exchange the life of a hermit for that of a Father of monks, to live with him under one roof:

> To him as he sat in his cave an angel appeared and said: 'You have successfully ordered your own life. So it is superfluous to remain sitting in your cave. Up! go out and collect all the young monks and dwell with them, and according to the model which I now give you, so legislate for them; and he gave him a brass tablet on which this was inscribed (SPCK).

Then follow the different paragraphs of the Rule. St. Jerome repeats the legend in the Preface to his Latin version. The fact, however, is that the code was composed only gradually, as it is evident from the haphazard way in which the different regulations follow one another. Far from being dictated by an angel, they were accumulated in the course of the abbot's practical experience. Many sections appear to be addenda to the original corpus and frequent repetitions occur. Thus it is possible that the Rule of Pachomius may be a sort of compilation of instructions to monks drawn up by several superiors.

Jerome's text consists of four parts entitled: precepts, precepts and institutions, precepts and penal statutes, precepts and laws of Pachomius. Altogether this comprises 192 sections, generally short, dealing in detail with the conditions of monastic life. Many concern physical labor. The majority of the monks were employed in agricultural tasks, while others plied a trade, but all manual work was regarded as divine service. Among the group of artisans were to be found tailors, smiths, carpenters, dyers, tanners, shoemakers, gardeners, copyists, cameldrivers, especially weavers, who prepared mats and baskets from the rushes of the Nile and palm-leaves. One of the regulations directed that all the monks were to be assigned work in proportion to their strength. No particulars are given about liturgical worship. Only two prayers are mentioned as being said in common, the morning and the evening prayer. The novice before being accepted had to learn how to read and write. It is worth noticing that no one at all is to be admitted to the monastery who cannot read. But the Rule did not gain its importance from such items. Its lasting value consists in its having provided an economic, and especially a spiritual basis for the *koinos bios*, the *vita communis*. This rests on the monastic virtues of obedience, chastity and poverty which, however, were practised without any vows.

Editions: A. Boon and L. T. Lefort, Pachomiana Latina. Règles et épîtres de S. Pacôme. Épître de S. Théodore et Liber de S. Orsiesius. Texte latin de S. Jérôme, ed. A. Boon (11-74). Appendice: La Règle de S. Pacôme, fragments coptes (155-168) et Excerpta grecs (169-182), ed. L. T. Lefort (Bibl. de RHE 7). Louvain, 1932. Lefort has added a Latin translation of the Coptic fragments. New Coptic fragments were published by Lefort, La Règle de S. Pacôme: Mus 48 (1935) 75-80; 54 (1941) 111-138; *idem*, Œuvres de S. Pacôme et de ses disciples (CSCO 159). Louvain, 1956, 30-36. — Antiquated editions: MG 40, 947-956, ML 23, 61-86. — P. B. Albers, Sancti Pachomii abbatis Tabennensis Regulae monasticae (FP 16). Bonn, 1923, 9-59, 74-90. — Three Ethiopic versions were edited by A. Dillmann, Chrestomathia Aethiopica. Leipzig, 1866, 57-69. — E. A. W. Budge, Coptic Apocrypha in the Dialect of Upper Egypt, London, 1913, 146-176 published the Coptic text of *The Instructions of Apa Pachomius, the Archimandrite*.

Translations: English: G. H. Schodde, The Rules of Pachomius, translated from the Ethiopic: Presbyterian Review 6 (1885) 678-689. — E. A. W Budge, op. cit. 352-382. — W. K. L. Clarke, The Lausiac History of Palladius (SPCK). London, 1918, 112-115. — *French:* R. Basset, Les apocryphes éthiopiens traduits en français. Fasc. 8. Paris, 1896. — L. T. Lefort, CSCO 160 (1956) 30-37. — *German:* E. König, ThStKr 51 (1878) 323-337. — *Swedish:* O. Löfgren, Pakomius' etiopiska klosterregler. I svensk tolkning: KA 48 (1948) 163-184.

Studies: See studies on Pachomius, above p. 155. — L. T. Lefort, La Règle de S. Pacôme (en grec): Mus 37 (1924) 1-28. — R. Draguet, Le chapitre de l'Histoire Lausiaque sur les Tabennésiotes dérive-t-il d'une source copte?: Mus 58 (1945) 15-95. — B. Steidle, 'Der Zweite' im Pachomiuskloster: BM 24 (1948) 174-179. — P. Gnolfo, Pedagogia Pacomiana: Salesianum 10 (1948) 569-596. — H. Bacht, Ein Wort zur Ehrenrettung der ältesten Mönchsregel: ZkTh 72 (1950) 350-359, examines the Rule and compares it with Sozomen, *Hist. eccl.* 3, 14 for relations between monachism and the ancient Egyptian religion. — K. Lehmann, Die Entstehung der Freiheitsstrafe in den Klöstern des heiligen Pachomius: ZSK 37 (1951) 1-94. — C. DE CLERCQ, L'influence de la Règle de saint Pacôme en Occident: Mélanges L. Halphen. Paris, 1951, 169-176. — H. BACHT, 'Meditatio' in den ältesten Mönchsquellen: Geist und Leben 28 (1955) 360-373. — L. T. LEFORT, CSCO 159 (1956) IX-XII. — A. BAUMSTARK, Nocturna Laus. Typen frühchristlicher Vigilienfeier und ihr Fortleben vor allem im römischen und monastischen Ritus (LQF 32). Münster, 1957, 105-123 (vigil in Pachomian monasteries).

Letters

In St. Jerome's version the Rule of Pachomius is followed by some exhortations to the monks and eleven letters addressed to abbots and brothers of his monasteries. Two of the latter, sent to the abbots Cornelius and Syrus, are written in a still undeciphered code which uses the different letters of the Greek alphabet.

Editions: ML 23, 85-99. Best ed.: A. BOON, op. cit. 75-101. — L. T. LEFORT, CSCO 159 (1956), 1-24 has published the Coptic text of a Pachomian catechesis for a rancorous monk, and 25-26 of a catechesis on the six Easter days. French translation: CSCO 160 (1956) 1-26, 26-27.

The Lives of St. Pachomius

At least six biographies of the famous abbot have come down to us. Preserved in Sahidic and Bohairic Coptic, in Arabic, Syriac, Greek and Latin, they are of unequal value. Some of them may have been composed no more than fifteen or twenty years after his death. Apparently, several accounts of his life were current in Coptic monastic circles before they were set down in written form. The most exact data are provided by *Vita I* and *II*, but even Greek *Vita I* is not simply identical with the original. The interrelation of the biographies is not sufficiently cleared up as yet. All are now available in critical texts except the Arabic. This will be published soon by the Bollandists. Thus the edition of the *Corpus Pachomium* will have been completed and the question of priority may be re-examined. So far the best Greek redaction seemed superior to the Coptic, Arabic and Syriac sources. Lefort, however, is firmly convinced that the Coptic Lives are the most important.

Editions: Greek Lives: F. HALKIN, S. Pachomii Vitae Graecae (Subsidia hagiographica 19). Brussels, 1932. Cf. L. T. LEFORT, RHE 29 (1933) 424-428. — F. HALKIN, Les Vies grecques de S. Pacôme: AB 47 (1929) 376-388; *idem*, L'Histoire Lausiaque et les Vies grecques de S. Pacôme: AB 48 (1930) 257-301. — R. DRAGUET, Un morceau grec inédit des Vies de Pacôme apparié à un texte d'Évagre en partie inconnu: Mus 70 (1957) 267-306 (le plus ancient fragment grec).

Coptic Lives: L. T. LEFORT, Sancti Pachomii Vita bohairice scripta, (CSCO 89), Louvain, 1925, reprinted 1953 (Text); CSCO 107, Louvain, 1925, reprinted 1953 (Versio). Cf. L. T. LEFORT, Littérature bohairique: Mus 44 (1931) 115-135. — L. T. LEFORT, S. Pachomii Vitae sahidice scriptae (CSCO 99/100). Louvain, 1933/34, reprinted 1952

(Text). Cf. P. Peeters, A propos de la Vie sahidique de S. Pacôme: AB 52 (1934) 286-320. — L. T. Lefort, Vies de S. Pacôme (Nouveaux fragments): Mus 49 (1936) 219-230. — P. Peeters, L'édition critique des Vies coptes de S. Pacôme par le Prof. Lefort: Mus 59 (1936) 17-34; *idem*, L'œuvre de L. T. Lefort: Mus 59 (1946) 41-62; *idem*, Le dossier copte de S. Pacôme et ses rapports avec la tradition grecque: AB 64 (1946) 258-277.

Arabic Lives: E. Amélineau, Histoire de S. Pakhome et de ses communautés (Annales du Musée Guimet 17). Paris, 1889, 337-711. — W. E. Crum, Theological Texts from Coptic Papyri edited with an Appendix upon the Arabic and Coptic Versions of the Life of Pachomius (Anecdota Oxoniensia. Semitic series 12). Oxford, 1913: Appendix II, 86-94 and 94-170. Cf. P. Ladeuze, Étude sur le cénobitisme Pakhomien pendant le IVe siècle et la première moitié du Ve. Louvain and Paris, 1898, 45-69, 78, 108. — G. Graf, Geschichte der christlichen arabischen Literatur I (ST 118). Vatican City, 1944, 459-461. — A new fragment of an Arabic Life was published by P. Peeters, Un feuillet d'une Vie arabe de saint Pacôme: AB 59 (1946) 412.

Syriac Lives: P. Bedjan, Acta Martyrum et Sanctorum 5. Paris, 1895, 122-176.

Translations: French: L. T. Lefort, Les Vies coptes de S. Pacôme et de ses premiers successeurs. Louvain, 1943. — E. Amélineau, op. cit. — R. Draguet, Les Pères du désert. Paris, 1949, 87-126. — *German:* H. Mertel, BKV² 31 (1917) 20-122 (from Codex Vat. 819 representing Halkin's *Vita altera*).

Studies: L. T. Lefort, S. Athanase écrivain copte: Mus 46 (1933) 1-33, proves that S. Pachomius used several Coptic ascetical treatises of S. Athanasius for his sermons and catecheses. — L. T. Lefort, Les premiers monastères Pacômiens. Exploration topographique: Mus 52 (1939) 379-408. — W. Hengstenberg, Pachomiana. Festschrift A. Ehrhard. Bonn, 1922, 228-252. — W. Bousset, Apophthegmata. Studien zur Geschichte des ältesten Mönchtums. Tübingen, 1923, 209-280 Untersuchungen zur Vita Pachomii. — K. Heussi, Der Ursprung des Mönchtums. Tübingen, 1936, 115-131. — H. Bacht, Die Rolle des orientalischen Mönchtums in den kirchenpolitischen Auseinandersetzungen um Chalkedon: CGG II (1953) 300-308. — L. Ueding, Die Kanones von Chalkedon in ihrer Bedeutung für Mönchtum und Klerus: CGG II (1953) 580-590. — D. J. Chitty, Pachomian Sources Reconsidered: JEH 5 (1954) 38-77, stresses the great significance of the Greek *Vita prima* and its reliability assigning to it the first place in all studies on the Lives. — L. T. Lefort, Les sources coptes Pacômiennes: Mus 67 (1954) 217-229 refuting Chitty, regards the Coptic Lives as the most important.

HORSIESI

Before Pachomius died he appointed Petronius to be his successor. The latter lived only two months. Under Horsiesi († ca. 380) who then assumed the leadership, the monastic corporation greatly increased. In 350, when difficulties arose within the organization, he appointed a coadjutor, named Theodore, to reestablish peace and order. St. Jerome's version of the Rule of Pachomius contains as an appendix a treatise by Horsiesi entitled *Doctrina de institutione monachorum*, which testifies to his high religious and monastic ideals. In 56 chapters he instructs his monks on their duties so thoroughly that this document gives more insight into the spirit of the Pachomian creation than the Rule of the founder. The final section indicates that Horsiesi composed it shortly before his death.

For this reason Gennadius (*De vir. ill.* 9) refers to it as his testament. W. E. Crum and A. Ehrhard published a letter of Theophilus of Alexandria to Horsiesi (cf. above, p. 102) with very interesting details about the liturgy of Holy Week at Alexandria and a report about Horsiesi's participation in the celebration of Easter at the Egyptian metropolis. W. Hengstenberg does not agree with A. Ehrhard in thinking the letter to Horsiesi genuine. Gennadius does not mention it nor does he know of a *Libellus de sex cogitationibus sanctorum* attributed to Horsiesi and preserved in Latin (MG 40,895-896).

Editions: Doctrina de institutione monachorum: MG 40, 869-894; ML 103, 453-476 in Benedict of Aniane's *Codex Regularum.* — P. B. ALBERS, S. Pachomii abbatis Tab. Regulae monasticae. Accedit S. Orsiesii eiusdem Pachomii discipuli Doctrina de institutione monachorum (FP 16). Bonn, 1923, 91-125. Best ed.: A. BOON, op. cit. 109-147. — L. T. LEFORT, Œuvres de S. Pacôme et de ses disciples (CSCO 159). Louvain, 1956, published Coptic fragments of Horsiesi's Letters 63-66, Catecheses 66-80, and Rules 82-99; French translation: CSCO 160 (1956) 63-66, 67-80, 81-99.

Studies: L. T. LEFORT, Un document Pacômien méconnu: Mus 60 (1947) 269-283 (Sahidic fragment of Horsiesi's 'monita'); *idem,* CSCO 159 (1956) XVII-XXX. — H. BACHT, Studien zum 'Liber Orsiesii': HJG 77 (1958) 98-124.

THEODORE

Horsiesi's coadjutor and assistant, Theodore, was a person of outstanding achievements that won him the admiration of his contemporaries. As mentioned above (p. 159) he succeeded in settling the revolt which threatened to wreck the Pachomian organization. Several new monasteries were founded by him. He died on the 27th of April 368 after having ruled for eighteen years. On that occasion St. Athanasius addressed a letter to Horsiesi begging him to reassume full leadership. It testifies to the high esteem which Theodore enjoyed:

I have heard about the decease of the blessed Theodore and the tidings caused me great anxiety, knowing as I did his value for you. Now if it had not been Theodore, I should have used many more words to you with tears, considering what follows after death. But since it is Theodore whom you and I have known, what need I say in my letter save 'Blessed is' Theodore, 'who hath not walked in the council of the ungodly' (Ps. 1, 1). But if 'he is blessed that feareth the Lord' (Ps. 111, 1), we may now confidently call him blessed, having the firm assurance that he has reached as it were a haven, and has a life without care... Wherefore, brethren beloved and most longed-for, weep not for Theodore, for he 'is not dead, but sleepeth' (Matth. 9, 24). Let none weep when he remembers him, but imitate his life. For one must not grieve over one that is gone to the place where grief is not. This I write to you all in common: but especially to you, beloved and most longed-for Horsiesi, in order that, now that he is fallen asleep, you may take up the whole charge, and take his place among the brethren. For while he survived, you two were as one, discoursing to the beloved ones what made for their good. Thus act, then, and so doing write and tell me of the safety of yourself and of the brotherhood (LNPF).

It is not known for how long Horsiesi presided after Theodore's death. The biographies of Pachomius end at this instant, indicating clearly that Theodore's efforts completed Pachomius' work.

Letters

Gennadius (*De vir. ill.* 8-9) mentions three letters from Theodore's pen, intended at least in part to restore peace after the disorders in the Pachomian monasteries. Only one of them survives in the translation of Jerome appended to the Rule of Pachomius. Headed *Ad omnia monasteria de pascha*, it exhorts all to celebrate the approaching Easter in unanimity and harmony. The novices are admonished to prepare themselves by honest contrition for the reception of the body and blood of the Lord.

Another brief note of Theodore's is preserved in a communication of the Egyptian bishop Ammon to Theophilus of Alexandria. Addressed to the monks of the Nitrian mountains, it encourages them to perseverance and steadfastness in the faith against all attempts of the Arian party.

Editions: ML 23, 99-100. Best ed.: A. Boon, op. cit. 105-106. The Letter of the Egyptian bishop Ammon is not found in Migne, but in: Acta SS. Maii 3. Antwerp, 1680, 63-71, ch. 22. Latin translation *ibid.* 347-357. Cf. P. Ladeuze, Étude sur le cénobitisme Pakhomien. Louvain, 1898, 108-111. — Coptic fragments of three of Theodore's catecheses have been published by L. T. Lefort, CSCO 159, Louvain, 1956, 37-60. French translation: CSCO 160, Louvain, 1956, 38-66. Cf. L. T. Lefort, Un document Paclômien méconnu: Mus 60 (1947) 269-283 (Sahidic fragment of a catechesis).

MACARIUS THE EGYPTIAN

Although Ammon, a contemporary of St. Antony, was regarded as the founder of the famous monastic colony of Scetis, its spiritual hero was Macarius the Egyptian, also surnamed the Elder or the Great. Palladius (*Hist. Laus.* 17), Rufinus (*Hist. monach.* 28) and the *Apophthegmata* testify to his important position in the history of Egyptian monachism. Born about the year 300 in a village of Upper Egypt, he retired at the age of thirty to the desert of Scetis to live there for sixty years as a hermit, very soon surrounded by disciples. Because of his unusual judgment and discernment, his brethren called him 'the aged youth' (παιδαριογέρων), as Palladius (ibid.) informs us. His rapid progress in virtue and his good example won him the confidence of many souls. When he was forty, he received the grace of healing and forecasting the future. Palladius and the other sources write with great admiration of his miracles. He was then accounted worthy of the priesthood and became famous for his sermons and instructions. His fiery eloquence won him repeated invitations to address the anchorites in the Nitrian mountains. He paid several visits to St. Antony, the Father of the monks. At an advanced age he was exiled to an island of the Nile by the Arian bishop Lucius of Alexandria, who felt authorized to do so by an edict of the Emperor Valens. He returned soon to his desert and died shortly before 390.

WRITINGS ATTRIBUTED TO MACARIUS

Neither Palladius nor Rufinus know of any literary works of Macarius the Egyptian but later manuscripts attribute quite a number of writings to him, sayings, letters, prayers, homilies and treatises.

Edition: MG 34, 235-262, 405-822.

Studies: S. Schiwietz, Das morgenländische Mönchtum, vol. 1. Mayence, 1904, 97-101. — C. Flemming, De Macarii Aegyptii scriptis quaestiones. Göttingen, 1911. — E. Amann, Macaire: DTC 9 (1926) 1452-1455. — H. G. E. White, New Coptic Texts from the Monastery of St. Macarius (The Monasteries of the Wâdi n'Natrûn I). New York, 1926. — G. Graf, Geschichte der christlichen arabischen Literatur I (ST 118). Vatican City, 1944, 389-395. — E. Peterson, Macario il Grande: EC 7 (1951) 1740f.

1. The Spiritual Homilies ('Ομιλίαι πνευματικαί)

Our Egyptian won his fame through a collection of fifty *Spiritual Homilies* attributed to him a few generations after his death and preserved in a number of manuscripts. The first to publish them under Macarius' name was Johannes Picus in 1559, who added a Latin translation. Based on manuscripts of Paris (*Paris. gr.* 587 s. XVI and 1157 s. XIII), his edition was improved by H. J. Floss from a Berlin Codex (*Cod. Berol. gr.* 16 s. XII/XIII), and reprinted by Migne (MG 34, 449-822). Seven additional homilies found in an Oxford manuscript were brought out by G. L. Marriott in 1918.

These homilies entitle their author to a pre-eminent position in the history of early Christian mysticism and have proved a source of inspiration to modern mystics. Thus the author of *De vero Christianismo* (1708), John Arndt, knew all of them by heart and Gottfried

Arnold translated them into German as early as 1696. Finally John Wesley, the founder of the Methodists, whose hymns show the influence of these sermons, published an English version of twenty-two of them.

The problem of authorship has occasioned extensive research. Macarius of Egypt, to whom O. Bardenhewer (vol. II, p. 89) was still inclined to attribute the homilies, is out of the question. Dom L. Villecourt was the first to discover in them traces of Messalianism. The Messalians, whose name is derived from the Syriac *mesallein*, εὐχῖται, 'praying men', arose in the second half of the fourth century at Edessa and in the neighboring parts of Mesopotamia and were condemned in 431 by the Council of Ephesus; a number of propositions taken from their representative work, the *Ascetic Book* or the *Asketikon*, were stigmatized as 'blasphemous and heretical'. The list of these propositions has been transmitted to us by both Timothy, presbyter of Constantinople (*De receptione haereticorum*, MG 86,1,45-52), and John of Damascus (*De haeresibus liber* 80; MG 94,1,728-737). The latter states expressly that he took his version, which consists of eighteen sentences, from the *Asketikon* itself. Traces of all, except the fourteenth and fifteenth excerpts, can be found in the homilies. In some cases the wording is identical, as for instance, in Proposition 18 compared with Homily 8,3. Thus it appeared, especially after the investigations of H. Dörries, that the anathema of the Council of Ephesus proved unable to destroy the *Ascetic Book* of the Messalians. Its peculiarities were normalized, its errors corrected and, under the protection of a great name, the work was preserved as the homilies of Macarius the Egyptian, an attribution made as early as A. D. 534, the date of the Syriac *Ms. add.* 12175 in the British Museum. Thanks to his reputation and to the refined character of mysticism in these sermons, they were regarded as unobjectionable and gained universal acclaim. Villecourt's discovery, which seemed to throw an entirely new light on the authorship, was acknowledged by A. Wilmart, A. Jülicher and G. L. Marriott.

However, the problem remained, who was the real author of these writings. No answer could be made to this vexed question without careful study of the manuscripts, especially after Villecourt had drawn attention to the fact that manuscripts of an Arabic version of the corpus existed in the Vatican and Marriott had pointed out that Syriac codexes in the British Museum offered, besides the known homilies, many other pieces attributed to Macarius. The Arabic tradition was thoroughly investigated by W. Strothmann. Further progress was made in the excellent studies of H. Dörries, who discovered in a Moscow manuscript (*Cod.*

Mosqu. 177 $\frac{320}{\text{CCCVII}}$) the same fifty-seven homilies as at Oxford but in a text considerably older. Another Moscow Codex (*Cod. Mosqu.* 178 $\frac{319}{\text{CCCVI}}$ = *Codex simul* 61 of the Berlin Staatsbibliothek) contains 24 almost entirely different sermons. A Vatican Greek manuscript (*Cod. Vat. gr.* 710) has 27 and an Arabic 26. The most extensive is the Greek manuscript *Cod. Vat. gr.* 694 with 64 *logoi*. Not even half of them are to be found in the printed editions. In several cases brief prayers and questions are added to the homilies. The different collections show a strange mixture and disarray in the material. H. Dörries, however, succeeded in bringing it all into some order and was thus able to reconstruct the most probable original form, both of the *Asketikon* itself, i.e. the Ascetic Book of the Messalians condemned at Ephesus, and of two additions to it. Theodoret (*Hist. eccl.* 4,11,2) says of these sectarians:

> About the same time the heresy of the Messalians sprang up. Those who have rendered their name into Greek call them Euchites. Besides the above, they bear other appellations. They are sometimes called Enthusiasts, because they regard the agitating influences of a demon by whom they are possessed as indications of the presence of the Holy Ghost. Those who have thoroughly imbibed this heresy shun all manual labor as a vice; they abandon themselves to sleep, and declare their dreams to be prophecies. The following were the leaders of this sect: Dadoes, Sabbas, Adelphius, Hermes, Symeon, and many others.

Dörries believes that the last named Symeon, was the author of the Macarian writings. He was a native of Mesopotamia, as we know from other sources, and it is evident from various statements in the work that its author lived in Upper Mesopotamia. He repeatedly alludes to war between the Romans and Persians, which indicates that he dwelt on the frontier of the two Empires. Moreover, the only river mentioned is the Euphrates. For the dating of the *Asketikon*, it is important that the Messalians were first condemned at the close of the fourth century at the Council of Side (390), presided over by Amphilochius the metropolitan of Iconium (cf. below, p. 297) and that there was no mention in the synod of any books by them. In fact, our reports of this earlier ecclesiastical action seem to imply that they were then totally illiterate, whereas it was on a written work that the Council of Ephesus (431) passed judgment. Thus the *Ascetic Book* must have been composed between 390 and 431.

However, the entire hypothesis of the Messalian origin of the homilies has recently been challenged by an important discovery of W. Jaeger (cf. below, p. 274). If the author of the homilies and of the 'Great Letter' of Macarius is one, then Messalian origin seems unlikely. Nevertheless, a final judgment is impossible as long as we lack a critical edition of the writings of Macarius. W. Jaeger (p. 227) admits that 'their origin remains a mystery', but is of the opinion that as *terminus ante quem* we can establish the date 534.

Editions: MG 34, 449-822. — G. L. Marriott, Macarii anecdota. Seven unpublished Homilies of Macarius (HTS 5). Cambridge (Mass.), 1918.

Translations: English: J. Wesley, A Christian Library I. Bristol, 1749; 2nd ed. London, 1819. — A. J. Mason, Fifty Spiritual Homilies of St. Macarius the Egyptian (SPCK). London, 1921 (based on a revision of Migne's text). — *German:* G. Arnold, Leipzig, 1696; 2nd ed. Goslar, 1702; 3rd ed. 1716. — N. Casseder, 2 vols. Bamberg, 1819, 1820. — M. Jocham, Sämtliche Schriften des hl. Makarius des Grossen, BKV. Kempten, 1878, 63-424. — D. Stiefenhofer, BKV² 10 (1913).

Studies: J. Stoffels, Die mystische Theologie Makarius' des Ägypters und die ältesten Ansätze christlicher Mystik. Bonn, 1908. Cf. J. Stiglmayr, Altchristliche Mystik: ThR 8 (1909) 234-240. — J. Stoffels, Makarius der Ägypter auf den Pfaden der Stoa: ThQ 92 (1910) 88-105, 243-265. — J. Stiglmayr, Makarius der Grosse und das christliche Kultleben: ThGl 1 (1909) 734-736; *idem*, Makarius der Grosse und Gregor von Nyssa: ThGl 2 (1910) 571; *idem*, Der Mystiker Makarius und die 'Weltweisen', insbesondere Sokrates: Katholik 90, 2 (1910) 55-59; *idem*, Bilder und Vergleiche aus dem byzantinischen Hofleben in den Homilien des Makarius: Stimmen der Zeit 80 (1911) 414-427; *idem*, Makarius der Grosse im Lichte der kirchlichen Tradition: ThGl 3 (1911) 274-288; *idem*, Sachliches und Sprachliches bei Makarius von Ägypten (Programm Feldkirch). Innsbruck, 1912; *idem*, Die Agrapha bei Makarius von Ägypten: ThGl 5 (1913) 634-641. — G. L. Marriott, The Lausiac History of Palladius and a Homily ascribed to Macarius of Egypt: JThSt 18 (1917) 68-69; *idem*, The Seven Homilies of Macarius in Florilegia: JThSt 18 (1917) 70-71; *idem*, Symeon Metaphrastes and the Seven Homilies of Macarius of Egypt: JThSt 18 (1917) 71-72; *idem*, The Tractate of Symeon Metaphrastes 'De perfectione in spiritu': JThSt 19 (1918) 331-333; *idem*, Isaac of Nineveh and the Writings of Macarius of Egypt: JThSt 20 (1919) 345-347; *idem*, The Authorship of a Homily attributed to St. Macarius of Egypt: JThSt 21 (1920) 177-178. — J. Pacheu, L'expérience mystique de Macaire l'Égyptien: Revue de philosophie 20 (1920) 109-136. — L. Villecourt, Homélies spirituelles de Macaire en arabe sous le nom de Siméon Stylite: ROC 21 (1918/19) 337-344; *idem*, La date et l'origine des 'homélies spirituelles' attribuées à Macaire: Comptes rendus de l'Académie d'Inscriptions et de Belles-Lettres (1920) 250-258. — A. Wilmart, Origine véritable des homélies pneumatiques: RAM 1 (1920) 361-377. — A. Jülicher, Geheiligte Ketzer: Prot. Monatshefte 25 (1921) 67f. — G. L. Marriott, The Homilies of Macarius: JThSt 22 (1921) 259-262. — J. Stiglmayr, Pseudo-Makarius und die Aftermystik der Messalianer, ZkTh 49 (1925) 244-260. — M. Viller, La question du Pseudo-Macaire: RAM 6 (1925) 421-422. — G. L. Marriott, The Messalians and the Discovery of their Ascetic Book: HThR 19 (1926) 191-198. — E. Amann, Messaliens: DTC 10, 792-795. — E. Peterson, Die Häretiker der Philippusakten: ZNW 31 (1932) 97-111; *idem*, Die Schrift des Eremiten Markus über die Taufe und die Messalianer: ZNW 31 (1932) 273-288; *idem*, Zum Messalianismus der Philippus-Akten: OC 29 (1932) 172-179; *idem*, Irrige Zuweisung asketischer Texte: ZkTh 57 (1933) 271-273 (25th homily). — W. Strothmann, Die arabische Makariustradition. Diss. Göttingen. Schönhütte, 1934. — J. Hausherr, L'erreur fondamentale et la logique du messalianisme: OCP 1 (1935) 328-360; *idem*, Quanam aetate prodierit 'Liber graduum': OCP 1 (1935) 495-502. — K. Rahner, Ein messalianisches Fragment über die Taufe: ZkTh 61 (1937) 258-271 (concerning MG 40, 847). — J. Ziegler, Dulcedo Dei. Münster, 1937, 85-88 (Macarius on the sweetness of mystical experience). —

A. Kemmer, Charisma Maximum. Louvain, 1938 (relation of Cassian's doctrine to the Messalian heresy). — H. Dörries, Symeon von Mesopotamien. Die Überlieferung der messalianischen Makarios-Schriften (TU 55, 1). Leipzig, 1941. — E. Klostermann, Symeon und Makarius. Bemerkungen zur Textgestalt zweier divergierender Überlieferungen (AAB 11, 1943), Berlin, 1944; idem, ThLZ 73 (1948) 687-690. — W. Völker, Neue Urkunden des Messalianismus?: ThLZ 68 (1943) 129-136 (against the Messalian character of Pseudo-Macarius' writings, related to Gregory of Nyssa). — R. A. Klostermann, Die slavische Überlieferung der Makariusschriften. Göteborg, 1950. — W. Jaeger, Two rediscovered Works of Ancient Christian Literature: Gregory of Nyssa and Macarius. Leiden, 1954, 208-230. Cf. H. Dörries, Christlicher Humanismus und mönchische Geist-Ethik: ThLZ 79 (1954) 643-656. — E. Klostermann, Vor einer neuen Ausgabe der Homilien des Makarius-Symeon: FF 28 (1954) 361-363. — J. Darrouzès, Notes sur les homélies du Pseudo-Macaire: Mus 67 (1954) 297-309 (manuscript tradition). — A. Wenger, Grégoire de Nysse et le pseudo-Macaire: REB 13 (1955) 145-150. — A. Kemmer, Gregor von Nyssa und Pseudo-Makarius. Der Messalianismus im Lichte östlicher Herzensmystik: SA 38 (1956) 268-282. — D. Staniloae, Autour des 'Homélies Spirituelles' de S. Macaire d'Égypte: Mitropolia Oltenei (Craïova) 9 (1957) 15-38. — The main sources for the history of the Messalians are conveniently collected by M. Kmosko in the preface of his ed. of the Liber Graduum: Patrologia Syriaca 3. Paris, 1926. For additional studies on the Messalians, cf. below p. 275.

2. Letters

Of the letters attributed to Macarius, four are to be found in Migne (MG 34,405-446). The first is given not in the original Greek but only in a Latin version. However, there exists in addition a collection of eight epistles in Syriac. The first is identical with Migne's first. Entitled *Ad filios Dei*, it could perhaps be that which Gennadius (*De vir. ill.* 10) mentions as the only writing from Macarius' pen:

> Macarius, the Egyptian monk, distinguished for his miracles and virtues, wrote one letter which was addressed to the younger men of his profession. In this he taught them that he could serve God perfectly who, knowing the condition of his creation, should devote himself to all labors, and by wrestling against everything which is agreeable in this life, and at the same time imploring the aid of God would attain also to natural purity and obtain continence, as a well-merited gift of nature (LNPF).

A. Wilmart prepared a critical edition of this first letter but its authenticity is by no means certain. The rest of the collection is absolutely spurious. The epistle *Signorum copia* (MG 34,441-444) is a later patchwork of Nilus and Ephraem Syrus.

Editions: Epistola Sancti Macarii monachi ad filios Dei: MG 34, 406-410 (Latin). — New crit ed. by A. Wilmart, La lettre spirituelle de l'abbé Macaire: RAM 1 (1920) 58-83. For the Syriac version of this letter, see: A. Baumstark, Eine syrische Übersetzung des Makariosbriefes 'ad filios Dei': OC 9 (1919) 130-132. — G. L. Marriott, Macarius of Egypt: his Epistle ad Filios Dei in Syriac: JThSt 20 (1919) 42-44. — Coptic fragments of this letter: E. Amélineau, Monuments pour servir à l'histoire de l'Égypte chrétienne.

Histoire des monastères de la Basse-Égypte (Annales du Musée Guimet 25). Paris, 1894, 122-125.

Translation: German: M. JOCHAM, BKV (1878) 23-28.

Studies: G. L. MARRIOTT, Gennadius of Marseilles on Macarius of Egypt: JThSt 20 (1919) 347-349. — A. BAUMSTARK, Geschichte der syrischen Literatur. Bonn, 1922, 85. — For a spurious letter, cf. A. WILMART, La fausse lettre latine de Macaire: RAM 3 (1922) 411-419. — P. RESCH, La doctrine ascétique des premiers maîtres égyptiens. Paris, 1931, 39-41.

3. *The Great Letter*

None of these letters has attracted more attention than the so-called 'Great Letter' of Macarius, Ep. 2 in Migne's edition. J. Stiglmayr discovered that the second half of it corresponds to the second part of Gregory of Nyssa's treatise *De instituto Christiano* (cf. below, p. 274), and H. Dörries, that its first part is copied from the 40th of the *Spiritual Homilies* ascribed to Macarius. Stiglmayr was of the opinion that Pseudo-Macarius had borrowed the second part of his letter from Gregory of Nyssa. Villecourt on the contrary held that the treatise *De instituto Christiano* was not by Gregory of Nyssa but by a later author and that this later author had used Ps.-Macarius as a source. W. Jaeger has now definitely established the authenticity of *De instituto Christiano* and it follows that the 'Great Letter' depends on that treatise, not vice versa. Furthermore, if we accept Jaeger's date for Gregory's work, after 390, then all efforts hitherto made to show Messalianism in our document are proven abortive. Since the 'Great Letter' is the most extensive theological tract extant under Macarius' name and since on the basis of content and style, its author has so far been identified by scholars with that of the homilies, the question of Messalian origin of the latter needs an entire revaluation. The difficulty remains, however, that the writer of the letter has yet to be found. It cannot be overlooked that the Arabic versions of the homilies and the 'Great Letter' give his name as Symeon, which occurs also in the Slavic translations of some other works of Macarius. If this Symeon is not the leader of the Messalians, then who he is still needs to be determined. Secondly, the fact will have to be explained that Gregory's treatise in its original form remained relatively unknown, compared with the great reputation which the letter of Macarius gained.

In the new edition of the letter by W. Jaeger, the text is based chiefly on three Greek manuscripts (*Codex Vaticanus Gr.* 710 saec. XII-XIII, *Codex Vaticanus Gr.* 694 saec. XII-XIII, *Codex Hierosolymitanus Gr. S. Saba* 157 saec. XI), an Arabic version (found in *Codex Vaticanus Arab.* 70 and *Codex Vaticanus Arab.* 80), and a Syriac epitome.

Editions: MG 34, 409-441. — New critical ed. by W. JAEGER, Two rediscovered Works of Ancient Christian Literature: Gregory of Nyssa and Macarius. Leiden, 1954, 233-301 (Greek text).

Translation: German: M. JOCHAM, BKV (1878) 29-55.

Studies: J. STIGLMAYR, Makarius der Grosse und Gregor von Nyssa: ThGl 2 (1910) 571. — L. VILLECOURT, La grande lettre de Macaire, ses formes textuelles et son milieu littéraire: ROC 22 (1921) 29-56. — W. JAEGER, op. cit. 145-230.

4. *Treatises*

There are in addition to the homilies and letters, seven *opuscula* on the ascetic life, which the manuscripts attribute to Macarius. Among them are the two treatises *On Perfection* (MG 34, 841-852) and *On Prayer* (MG 34, 853-865). They are only excerpts from the 'Great Letter' and represent, as W. Jaeger has shown, a further stage in the process of paraphrasing Gregory of Nyssa's *De instituto Christiano*. Taken together, they reproduce the entirety of this treatise, the tract *On Perfection*, the first part, and that *On Prayer*, the second. But the author of this further development cannot be the same as the writer of the 'Great Letter'.

Edition: MG 34, 821-968.

Studies: J. STIGLMAYR, Sachliches und Sprachliches bei Makarius von Ägypten. Innsbruck, 1912, 7, 2. — L. VILLECOURT, St. Macaire, les opuscules ascétiques et leur relation avec les homélies spirituelles: Mus 35 (1922) 203-212. — W. JAEGER, op. cit. 156-162.

MACARIUS THE ALEXANDRIAN

A contemporary of the Egyptian Macarius was Macarius the Alexandrian, also called 'the town's man', from the place of his birth, and to distinguish him from the former, who was born in Upper Egypt. Although he seems to have possessed the gifts of prophecy and healing and power over the demons in a still higher degree, posterity has paid less attention to him than to his namesake, as is evident from the few *Apophthegmata* or 'Sentences of the Fathers' dealing with him. Born a little earlier, he died about 394, almost a hundred years old. About the year 335 he established himself in the desert of Cellia *(τὰ κέλλια)*. It was here that Palladius, the author of the *Lausiac History*, who admits that he never saw Macarius the Egyptian, met the Alexandrian three years before his death. He tells (ch. 18) of his heroic asceticism and informs us that he was a priest. For a time he must have been in charge of a monastic colony in the Nitrian desert.

Palladius does not mention any of his works, and it seems that he wrote nothing. At any rate, the three sayings (MG 34, 261-263), the *Sermo S. Macarii Alexandrini de exitu statuque animarum post hanc vitam* (MG 34, 385-392) and the two monastic rules *S. Macarii Alexandrini abbatis Nitriensis regula ad monachos* (MG 34, 967-970) and *S. Serapionis, Macarii, Paphnutii et alterius Macarii regula ad monachos* (MG 34, 971-978) are not authentic.

EVAGRIUS OF PONTUS

A disciple of the two Macarii was Evagrius (Socrates, *Hist. eccl.* 4, 23), surnamed Ponticus, because he was born at Ibora in Pontus. He was ordained reader by Basil the Great and deacon by Gregory of Nazianzus. He accompanied the latter at the Council of Constantinople (381) and 'since he was skilled in argument against all heresies' (*Hist. Laus.* 38, 2) he remained with Nectarius, the patriarch of that city, in which he soon 'flourished, speaking with youthful zeal against every heresy' *(ibid.)*. When dangers threatened his soul and temptations his virtue, he left the capital and went to Jerusalem where he was received by Melania, the Roman lady, and shortly afterwards about 382, to Egypt. He exiled himself for two years in the mountains of Nitria and then entered the desert to live for fourteen years in Cellia. It was here that he became acquainted with the Macarii so that 'he emulated their course of conduct, and miracles were done by his hands as numerous and as important as those of his preceptors', as the historian Socrates (*Hist. eccl.* 4, 23) tells us. He earned his livelihood by writing, 'since he wrote the Oxyrhynchus characters excellently', according to Palladius (*Hist. Laus.* 38, 10), who was one of his disciples. When Theophilus of Alexandria wished to make him a bishop, he refused. He died in 399 at the age of 54.

HIS WRITINGS

Evagrius is the first monk to have written numerous and comprehensive works that were of great influence in the history of Christian piety. He is in fact the founder of monastic mysticism and the most fertile and interesting spiritual author of the Egyptian desert. The monks of East and West alike studied his writings as classical documents and invaluable text-books. Recent investigations have shown that his ideas live on not only in Palladius but also in the Byzantine writers John Climacus, Hesychius, Maximus Confessor, Nicetas Stethatos down to the Hesychasts, in the Syrian authors Philoxenus of Mabbug, Isaac of Ninive, John Bar Caldun up to Barhebraeus, and in the West in John Cassian. In fact, the great Oriental School of Evagrian mysticism reaches from the fourth to the fifteenth, nay to the twentieth century.

Unfortunately, except for small fragments the original Greek text of his treatises has been lost, owing to the fact that the fifth (553) and the following ecumenical councils condemned him as an Origenist. However, some of his works are extant in Latin translations prepared by Rufinus (Jerome, *Ep.* 133, 3) and Gennadius (*De vir. ill.* 11), others in Syriac and Armenian, Arabic and Ethiopian versions. Some, too, have been found among the publications of others, like St. Basil the Great and Nilus of Ancyra. There is hope that the progress of patristic research, the study of oriental manuscripts and the *Catenae* will bring to light more of his treatises. Only then will it be possible to find out exactly to what extent Evagrius shared the errors of Origen.

His spirituality is definitely based on the mysticism of the great Alexandrian. He is the first ecclesiastical writer to put his teaching in aphorisms, imitating thereby the gnomic literature of philosophy. He is the creator of the so-called spiritual 'centuries', a literary form which became famous in Byzantine times.

Editions: MG 40, 1213-1286 (incomplete). — Syriac version: W. FRANKENBERG, Evagrius Pontikus (AGWG N.F. 13, 2). Berlin, 1912 (Syriac text with retranslation into Greek). — J. MUYLDERMANS, Evagriana Syriaca. Textes inédits. Louvain, 1952. — Armenian version: P. B. SARGHISEAN, The Life and Works of the Holy Father Evagrius Ponticus in an Armenian Version of the Fifth Century with Introduction and Notes (in Armenian). Venice, 1907, 217-323.

Studies: Greek text: J. MUYLDERMANS, A travers la tradition manuscrite d'Évagre le Pontique. Essai sur les manuscrits grecs conservés à la Bibliothèque Nationale de Paris (Bibl. du Mus. 3), Louvain, 1932; *idem,* Evagriana: Mus 44 (1931) 36-68, 369-383; *idem,* Evagriana. Paris, 1931; *idem,* Nouveaux fragments inédits: Mus 45 (1932) 49-59; *idem,* Evagriana. Le Vatic. Barb. Graecus 115: Mus 51 (1938) 191-226; *idem,* Evagriana de la Vaticane: Mus 54 (1941) 1-15. — E. PETERSON, Zu griechischen Asketikern I. Zu Euagrios Pontikos: BNJ 4 (1923) 5-8; *idem,* Noch einmal Euagrios Pontikos: BNJ 5 (1926/27) 412-418; *idem,* Miszellen zur altkirchlichen und byzantinischen Literatur: ThLZ 55 (1930) 256-257; *idem,* Zur Textkritik des Clemens Alexandrinus und Euagrios: ThLZ 56 (1931) 69-70; *idem,* Irrige Zuweisungen asketischer Texte: ZkTh 57 (1933) 271-273; *idem,* Zu griechischen Asketikern III: BNJ 9 (1932/33) 51-54; *idem,* Miszellen zur altkirchlichen und byzantinischen Literatur: ThR 32 (1933) 242-243.

For Syriac and Armenian versions: A. BAUMSTARK, Geschichte der syrischen Literatur. Bonn, 1922, 86-88. — I. HAUSHERR, Les versions syriaque et arménienne d'Évagre le Pontique. Leur valeur, leur relation, leur utilisation: OCh 22 (n. 69) (1931) 69-118; 24 (n. 73) (1931) 38-40. — J. MUYLDERMANS, Le discours de Xystus dans la version arménienne d'Évagre le Pontique: REA 9 (1929) 183-201; *idem,* Miscellanea Armeniaca: Mus 47 (1934) 293-296; *idem,* Sur les séraphins et sur les chérubins d'Évagre le Pontique dans les versions syriaque et arménienne: Mus 59 (1946) 367-379.

For Arabic versions: G. GRAF, Geschichte der christlichen arabischen Literatur I (ST 118). Vatican City, 1944, 397-399.

For a survey of recent publications: A. WENGER, Le texte véritable d'Évagre le Pontique: REB 13 (1955) 150-152.

Studies on thought and influence: O. Zöckler, Evagrius Pontikus (Biblische und kirchen-historische Studien 4). Munich, 1893. — S. Schiwietz, Das morgenländische Mönchtum I. Mayence, 1904, 265-274. — R. Reitzenstein, Historia monachorum und Historia Lausiaca. Göttingen, 1916, 124-142 (Evagrius and Diadochus of Photice). — E. Buonaiuti, Evagrio Pontico e il De Virginitate Atanasiano: RTr 1 (1920) 208-220. — W. Bousset, Apophthegmata. Tübingen, 1923, 281-341. — M. Viller, Aux sources de la spiritualité de saint Maxime. Les œuvres d'Évagre le Pontique: RAM 11 (1930) 156-184, 239-268, 331-336. — K. Rahner, Le début d'une doctrine des cinq sens spirituels: RAM 13 (1932) 136-141; *idem*, Die geistliche Lehre des Evagrius Pontikus: ZAM 8 (1933) 21-38. — I. Hausherr, Contemplation et sainteté, une remarquable mise au point par Philoxène de Mabboug: RAM 14 (1933) 171-195. — M. Lot-Borodine, Le mystère du 'don des larmes': VS 48 (1936) 65-110. — A. Saudreau, La spiritualité d'Évagre le Pontique: VS 46 (1936) 180-190. — I. Hausherr, 'Ignorance infinie': OCP 2 (1936) 351-362. — S. Marsili, Giovanni Cassiano ed Evagrio Pontico. Dottrina sulla carità e contemplazione (SA 5). Rome, 1936. — J. Maréchal, Études sur la psychologie des mystiques II. Paris, 1937, 120-128. — M. Olphe-Galliard, La science spirituelle d'après Cassien: RAM 18 (1937) 141-160. — M. Viller and K. Rahner, Aszese und Mystik in der Väterzeit. Freiburg i.B., 1939, 97-109. — J. Gouillard, Un auteur spirituel byzantin du XIIᵉ siècle, Pierre Damascène (influenced by Evagrius): EO 38 (1939) 257-278. — N. Crainic, Das Jesusgebet: ZKG 60 (1941) 341-353. — R. Draguet, L'Histoire Lausiaque, une œuvre écrite dans l'esprit d'Évagre: RHE (1946) 321-364, (1947) 5-49. — B. Blumenkranz, Die jüdischen Beweisgründe im Religionsgespräch mit den Christen in den christlich-lateinischen Sonderschriften des 5. bis 11. Jahrhunderts: ThZ 4 (1948) 119-147. — J. De Ghellinck, Patristique et Moyen Age 3. Gembloux, 1948, 216f. (bibliography). — C. Guillaumont-Boussac, Une théorie du rêve chez Évagre le Pontique: REG 65 (1952) 1-16.

1. *Antirrhetikos*

Socrates (*Hist. eccl.* 4, 23) mentions that Evagrius composed a book which 'contained selections from Holy Scripture against tempting spirits, distributed into eight parts according to the number of arguments, designated *Antirrhetikos ('Ἀντιρρητικός)*'. Gennadius (*De vir. ill.* 11) has evidently the same work in mind when he informs us that Evagrius wrote a work 'Suggestions against the eight principal sins', adding that he 'was the first to mention or among the first at least to teach these, setting against them eight books taken from the testimony of the Holy Scriptures only, after the example of our Lord, who always met his tempter with quotations from Scripture, so that every suggestion, whether of the devil or depraved nature had a testimony against it. This work I have, under instructions, translated into Latin, translating with the same simplicity which I found in the Greek'. Gennadius' translation has met the same fate as the original: both are lost. The Greek excerpt published by Migne (MG 40, 1272-1276) *De octo vitiosis cogitationibus ad Anatolium* does not belong to the *Antirrhetikos* but to the one hundred sentences of the *Praktikos* (below). Fortunately, the entire *Antirrhetikos* is preserved in Syriac and Armenian versions.

It deals in eight books with the eight evil spirits which keep the monk under constant attack: the demons of gluttony, adultery, avarice, despondency, irritability, weariness of being a monk, sloth, arrogance. For each of these eight vices the author investigates the causes and diabolical influences at work, concluding with a quotation from the Bible that would enable the monk to defeat the attack. Thus Evagrius intends to give a useful *vademecum* for what he calls the 'active' monk, i.e. one who is still struggling. He is not the author of, but the first literary witness to the doctrine of the eight vices, which preceded that of the seven capital sins. Cassian, Nilus, Gregory the Great, John Climacus, John of Damascus and others attached great importance to it.

Editions: W. FRANKENBERG, Evagrius Pontikus. Berlin, 1912, 472-545 Syriac text with retranslation into Greek-Armenian text: P. B. SARGHISEAN, The Life and Works of the Holy Father Evagrius Ponticus in an Armenian Version of the Fifth Century with Introduction and Notes (in Armenian). Venice, 1907, 217-323. An Ethiopic version of *De octo vitiosis cogitationibus* was published by J. BACHMANN, Äthiopische Lesestücke. Inedita Aethiopica. Leipzig, 1893, 26-103. O. SPIES, Die äthiopische Überlieferung der Abhandlung des Evagrius περὶ τῶν ὀκτὼ λογισμῶν: OC 7 (1932) 203-228, furnishes a collation of five manuscripts against Bachmann's printed text and an English translation.

Studies: S. SCHIWIETZ, Die Achtlasterlehre des Evagrius Pontikus und die griechische Philosophie: Katholik 83, 2 (1903) 311-322; *idem*, Das morgenländische Mönchtum I. Mayence, 1904, 266-274; *idem*, Stammt das christliche Hauptsündenschema aus der astronomischen Planetenlehre?: ThGl 4 (1912) 374-383. — F. HÖRHAMMER, Die sieben Hauptsür.den. 1. Teil: Das Achtlasterschema und dessen Umbildung durch Gregor d. Grossen. Diss. Munich, 1924. — L. WRZOL, Die Hauptsündenlehre des Johannes Cassianus und ihre historischen Quellen: DT 2, 9 (1923) 385-404. — P. RESCH, La doctrine ascétique des premiers maîtres égyptiens du IVe siècle. Paris, 1931, 125-134. — I. HAUSHERR, L'origine de la théorie orientale des huit péchés capitaux: OCh 30, 3 (n. 86) 164-175. — J. STELZENBERGER, Die Beziehungen der frühchristlichen Sittenlehre zur Ethik der Stoa. Munich, 1933, 379-402. — A. VÖGTLE, Achtlasterlehre, RACh 1 (1941) 74-79.

2. *Monachikos*

Evagrius compiled in addition a work of two parts called *The Monk*, the first of which consists of one hundred sentences devoted to the *Praktikos*, the second, of fifty for the *Gnostikos*. Gennadius shows himself very familiar with this treatise: 'Evagrius composed also a book of one hundred sayings for those living simply as anchorites, arranged by chapters, and fifty sayings for the erudite and studious'. He adds that he first translated the second part into Latin because the first part had been previously translated. However he remarks that he himself 'restored this translation partly by translating and partly by emendation, so as to represent the true meaning of the author, because I saw that the translation was vitiated and confused by time'. He does not give the name of the translator but it must have been Rufinus of Aquileia, whom he mentions on another occasion (*De vir. ill.* 17) as a translator of the Sentences of Evagrius (cf. Jerome, *Ep.* 133, 3). All of these Latin versions have been lost. However, the first part, the *Praktikos*, is extant in two Greek editions (one of 70, the other of 100 sentences), and the second, the *Gnostikos*, in a Syriac version. The content consists of Sayings of the Fathers and masters of the ascetical life, e.g. Antony, Macarius the Egyptian, Athanasius, Serapion, Didymus, Basil the Great and others.

Editions: a. Praktikos: MG 40, 1220-1236, 1244-1252, 1272-1276. For the order in which these texts have to be arranged, see: W. FRANKENBERG, op. cit. 4. — J. MUYLDERMANS, La teneur du Practicos d'Évagre le Pontique: Mus 42 (1929) 74-89 (survey of translations and editions); *idem*, A travers la tradition manuscrite d'Évagre le Pontique (Bibliothèque du Mus. 3). Louvain, 1932, 39.

b. Gnostikos: W. FRANKENBERG, op. cit. 546-553 Syriac text and retranslation into Greek. — Greek fragments furnished by Cod. Mosq. 425, fol. 216v-219 (16th cent.): I. HAUSHERR, Nouveaux fragments grecs d'Évagre le Pontique: OCP 5 (1939) 229-233.

3. Mirror for Monks and Nuns

Under this title a collection of fifty sentences is extant in the Greek original. They were translated into Latin by Rufinus (MG 40, 1277-1286). The introduction to the *Mirror for Nuns* is preserved in *Ep.* 19 and 20 of Evagrius, as I. Hausherr has proved.

Editions: Greek text: H. GRESSMANN, Nonnenspiegel und Mönchsspiegel des Euagrios Pontikos zum ersten Male in der Urschrift herausgegeben (TU 39, 4b). Leipzig, 1913, 146-165. For a collation of the Armenian version, see: H. GRESSMANN and W. LÜDTKE, ZKG 35 (1914) 87-96. In addition to Rufinus' translation of both, the Mirror for Monks and Nuns (MG 40, 1277-1286), A. Wilmart edited an old Latin version of the Mirror for Nuns: A. WILMART, Les versions latines des sentences d'Évagrius pour les vierges: RB 28 (1911) 143-153, (from Cod. Paris. nov. acquis. Lat. 239 (s. X), and J. Leclercq published only recently an old Latin version of the Mirror for Monks which has proved more literal than that in MG: J. LECLERCQ, L'ancienne version latine des sentences d'Évagre pour les moines: Scriptorium 5 (1951) 195-213. Leclercq shows in his philological commentary that Migne's text is most probably a later revision of this newly discovered version. M. MUEHMELT, Zu der neuen lateinischen Übersetzung des Mönchsspiegels des Evagrius: VC 8 (1954) 101-103, shares this opinion and proves it by a comparison of texts concerning sentence 55. For *Ep.* 19 and 20 forming the preface, see: I. HAUSHERR, Le traité de l'oraison d'Évagre le Pontique: RAM 15 (1934) 44. For aphorism n. 9 of Gressmann's text, see: L. T. LEFORT, À propos d'un aphorisme d'Évagre Ponticus: BAB 36 (1950) 70-79, who shows that Evagrius depends on Pachomius. For Armenian fragments of the Mirror for Monks, see J. MUYLDERMANS, À propos d'un feuillet de manuscrit arménien (Brit. Mus. Cod. Arm. 118): Mus 65 (1952) 11-16; of the Mirror for Nuns: J. MUYLDERMANS, Fragment arménien du 'Ad virgines' d'Évagre: Mus 53 (1940) 77-87.

4. Gnostic Problems

Problemata Gnostica is a collection of six hundred sentences divided into six books of one hundred maxims, customarily referred to as the *Centuries*. The Greek text is lost but the work has survived in a Syriac and an Armenian version. The content concerns questions of a dogmatic and ascetical nature. The Trinity, the angels, the restoration of all things, are among the topics discussed. In this as in his other works Evagrius consciously adopted the sententious form avoiding long discussions and dispensing altogether with continuous and unbroken discourse. He aimed at concision, facilitating the work of memory, that the reader might have a store\of pithy sayings to ruminate on and develop at leisure. Gennadius does not mention this work but Socrates (*Hist. eccl.* 4, 23) refers to it as *The Six Hundred Prognostic Problems*. Most probably 'prognostic' is to be read 'gnostic', as the Syriac manuscripts suggest.

Editions: W. FRANKENBERG, op. cit. 49-471 Syriac text. Frankenberg based his text on Cod. Vaticanus Syr. 178. A new edition of the Syriac text has been published by A. GUILLAUMONT, Les six centuries des 'Kephalaia Gnostica' d'Évagre le Pontique: PO 28, 1 (1958); cf. A. and C. GUILLAUMONT, Le texte véritable des Gnostica d'Évagre le Pontique: RHR 142 (1952) 156-205. Using a manuscript of the British Museum (add. 17167), this new edition furnishes a more reliable text than that by Frankenberg. For both, the Syriac and the Armenian versions, cf. J. MUYLDERMANS, Évagre le Pontique: les Capita cognoscitiva dans les versions syriaque et arménienne: Mus 47 (1934) 73-106. For Greek fragments in Codex Mosq. 425, fol. 216v-219, see: I. HAUSHERR, Nouveaux fragments d'Évagre le Pontique: OCP 5 (1939) 229-233. — For the concept of '*apatheia*', cf. I. HAUSHERR, Une énigme d'Évagre le Pontique, Centurie II, 50: RSR 23 (1933) 21-38. — For the literary form of the 'centuries', cf. I. HAUSHERR, DSp 2 (1938) 416-418. An Ethiopic version of a collection of sentences was published by S. GRÉBAUT, Sentences d'Évagre. Texte et traduction: ROC 20 (1915/17) 211-214, 435-439; 22 (1920/21) 206-211.

5. *On Prayer*

Evagrius seems to be the author of the treatise *De oratione (Περὶ προσευχῆς)* found among the writings of Nilus of Ancyra, although eight sentences of this work are quoted in the *Apophthegmata Patrum* as Sayings of Nilus (MG 65, 305 A-C) and Photius (*Bibl. Cod.* 201) attributes it to Nilus. The content is completely in the thought and style of Evagrius. Moreover, the Syriac version of this work goes under the name of Evagrius, and the Syrians, whenever they quote it, know of no other author than Evagrius. The entire work consists of 153 chapters preceded by a short introduction.

Editions: MG 79, 1165-1200 (among the works of Nilus). An Arabic and a Syriac version were published by I. HAUSHERR, Le De oratione d'Évagre le Pontique en syriaque et en arabe: OCP 5 (1939) 7-71.

Translation: French: I. HAUSHERR, Le traité de l'oraison d'Évagre le Pontique (pseudo-Nil): RAM 15 (1934) 34-93, 113-170 (with textual criticism and commentary).

Studies: I. HAUSHERR, Par delà l'oraison pure grâce à une coquille. À propos d'un texte d'Évagre: RAM 13 (1932) 184-188. — I. HAUSHERR, Le De oratione de Nil et Évagre: RAM 14 (1933) 196-199; *idem*, Evagrii Pontici tria capita de oratione: OCh 30, 3 (n. 86)

(1933) 149-152 (deals with a text not belonging to the treatise); *idem*, Le traité de l'oraison d'Évagre le Pontique: RAM 15 (1934) 34-93, 113-170; *idem*, Comment priaient les Pères?: RAM 32 (1956) 33-58, 284-296.

6. *De malignis cogitationibus*

This treatise is also found among the writings of Nilus. Nevertheless, it is by Evagrius, as Hausherr has amply demonstrated.

Editions: MG 79, 1199-1228 (among the works of Nilus). Migne's text is incomplete and must be supplemented by the texts which were added by J. MUYLDERMANS, A travers la tradition manuscrite d'Évagre le Pontique. Louvain, 1932, 47-55, 16. — E. PETERSON, Irrige Zuweisungen asketischer Texte: ZkTh 57 (1933) 271, proved that the text attributed to Evagrius by Muyldermans l.c. 15, 17-60 does not belong to him.

Studies: K. HEUSSI, Untersuchungen zu Nilus dem Asketen (TU 42, 2). Leipzig, 1917, 163-166. — I. HAUSHERR, Le traité de l'oraison d'Évagre le Pontique: RAM 15 (1934) 34-38.

7. *Ad Eulogium monachum*

Nicephorus Callistus in the 14th century was the first to attribute this exhortation to Nilus. In reality it seems to have been written by Evagrius. There are quite a number of manuscripts in which it appears under his name and the Syriac and Armenian versions assign it to him. It deals with perfection and the constant vigilance necessary for the monk against the temptations of the demons.

Edition: MG 79, 1093-1140.

Studies: J. MUYLDERMANS, A travers la tradition manuscrite d'Évagre le Pontique. Louvain, 1932, 62-65. Cf. M. VILLER, RAM 14 (1933) 102. — K. HEUSSI, op. cit. 156 n. 7.

8. *Biblical Commentaries*

Evagrius learned from his master Origen not only his mystical theology but also his biblical exegesis. Urs von Balthasar has shown that the *Selecta in Psalmos* contain a great number of fragments of his *Commentary on the Psalms*. This commentary differed from all previous ones in that it was composed in the form of sentences like his other works. Its syllogisms and 'blessed's', its ideas on God and on Gnosis, on the world and asceticism make its authorship by Evagrius quite evident.

He must have composed in addition a *Commentary on Proverbs*. A great portion of it can be found in Origen's commentary; fragments occur in *Catenae* and among the remains of Hippolytus, Eusebius, Apollinaris, Basil, Chrysostom and Didymus. The *Book of Proverbs* had greater influence in forming the sententious style of Evagrius than any other in the Bible. His *Mirror for Monks and Nuns* is a direct imitation of *Proverbs*.

Evagrius wrote also a *Commentary on Job*. M. Faulhaber found twenty-five *scholia* of this lost work in *Vallic*. C 41. Vestiges exist, too, of a *Commentary on Luke*. The seven *scholia* from the latter preserved in the *Catena* of Nicetas indicate that Evagrius did, at times, abandon his pithiness for a more discursive style. Most probably he was the author of commentaries no longer extant on Numbers, Kings and the Canticle of Canticles.

Studies: M. FAULHABER, Proverbien- und Predigerkatenen. Vienna, 1902. — G. MERCATI, Intorno ad un scolio creduto di Evagrio: RBibl 14 (1914) 534-542; reprinted: G. MERCATI, Opere minori, vol. 3 (ST 78). Vatican City, 1937, 393-401 (schol. on Proverbs). — R. DEVREESSE, Chaînes exégétiques grecques: DB Suppl. I (1928) 1084-1233 *passim.* — H. URS VON BALTHASAR, Die Hiera des Evagrius: ZkTh 63 (1939) 86-106, 181-206.

9. *Letters*

About 67 of his *letters* have come down to us in a Syriac version. Frankenberg made an edition of them, retranslating them into Greek. Most are short and without any indication of the addressees. Among the longer epistles is one to Melania, whom he met at Jerusalem. Another, sent to some monks near Caesarea is preserved in the original Greek; it is, as R. Melcher has proved, *Epistle* 8 among the letters of St. Basil the Great (cf. below, p. 224). It warns against the Arians, gives an exposition of the trinitarian dogma and demonstrates from Scripture the consubstantiality of the Father with the Son. It also contains a critical examination of Arian exegesis and biblical proof of the divinity of the Holy Spirit.

Editions: W. FRANKENBERG, op. cit. 554-635. Letter to Melania: 613-619. — MG 32, 245-268: Greek text of *Ep.* 8 of St. Basil, corresponds to Frankenberg 621-635 Syriac text.

Translations: English: R. J. DEFERRARI, Saint Basil, The Letters (LCL) vol. 1. Cambridge (Mass.), 1926, 47-93. — *German:* A. STEGMANN, BKV² 46 (1925) 25-42.

Studies: R. MELCHER, Der achte Brief des Basilius, ein Werk des Evagrius Ponticus (MBTh 1). Münster, 1923. — W. BOUSSET, Apophthegmata. Tübingen, 1923, 335-336.

PALLADIUS

The most outstanding historian of Egyptian monasticism was Palladius, a pupil of Evagrius Ponticus. Born in Galatia in 363 or 364, he received a thorough education in the classics. In 388 he went to Egypt to get acquainted with the hermits. After a year at Alexandria the priest Isidore who gave him the first introduction to the ascetic life, handed him over to the Theban hermit Dorotheus in the so-called Solitudes five miles away from the city in order to complete there a kind of novitiate. Being unable to finish the three years owing to a breakdown in health, he went on in 390 to Nitria and then to Cellia, where he spent nine years, first with Macarius and then with Evagrius. The latter had a lasting influence on him. When he fell ill again, the doctors advised him to betake himself to Palestine in search of a better climate. About 400 he was consecrated bishop of Helenopolis in Bithynia and soon became involved in the Origenistic controversies. In 405 he travelled to Rome to plead the cause of St. John Chrysostom. The following year the Emperor Arcadius exiled him to Upper Egypt. When in 412-413 he was permitted to return, he became bishop of Aspuna in Galatia. He died shortly before the Council of Ephesus (431).

Studies: E. Amann, Palladius: DTC 11 (1932) 1823-1830. — E. Schwartz, Palladiana: ZNW 36 (1937) 161-204. — H. Leclercq, Palladius: DAL 13 (1937) 912-930. — K. Heussi and A. Kurfess, Palladios: PWK 18, 3 (1943) 203-207.

HIS WRITINGS

1. *Historia Lausiaca*

His greatest work is entitled the *Lausiac History (Λαυσιακόν)* after Lausus, chamberlain at the court of Theodosius II, to whom he dedicated it. Composed in 419/420, it gives a description of the monastic movement in Egypt, Palestine, Syria and Asia Minor in the fourth century and therefore represents an extremely important source for the history of early monasticism. Palladius combines his personal reminiscences with information he had received from others into a series of biographies, intended to edify the reader. The strongly legendary character of many of the narratives gives no reason to doubt the author's good faith or mistrust his statements when he describes what he saw for himself. He never tries to write a defense of monasticism and does not hesitate to tell of the apostasies and weaknesses of the monks. He condemns pride and arrogance and states in his introduction: 'To drink wine with reason is better than to drink water with pride' (Prol. 10). There is no sign of any ascetic theory in his work, but only facts and stories. It is written in the spirit of Evagrius Ponticus.

Though it remains a question whether he made use of written sources for the content, he certainly did so for the form. The nearest literary model is the *Vita Antonii* of St. Athanasius (cf. above, p. 39) but we also find striking parallels in the biographical works of Hellenistic literature which portray the ideal sage in all his virtues and give graphic accounts of the extraordinary deeds performed by the philosophers.

The *Lausiac History* was soon translated into Latin. A great number of Oriental versions followed. The history of its Greek text was for a long time a puzzle until Abbot Butler brought order out of confusion. He proved that it was at an early time fused with the anonymous *History of the Monks in Egypt*, composed about the year 400 and similar in content to the work of Palladius. It describes a visit paid by a party of seven to the Egyptian ascetics in 394-395. C. Butler was of the opinion that the archdeacon Timotheus of Alexandria was perhaps its author, whereas F. Diekamp thought of Rufinus. The latter, at any rate translated it into Latin (ML 21, 387-462).

Editions: MG 34, 995-1260 (interpolated). — Best ed.: C. BUTLER, The Lausiac History of Palladius. 2 vols. (TSt 6, 1-2). Cambridge, 1904. Butler's edition of the Greek text (found in vol. 2) leaves much to be desired, as Draguet has recently proved (cf. his articles below). Old Latin versions: ML 74, 249-342 (*Paradisus Heraclidis*) and ML 74, 343-382. For the oriental versions, cf. BUTLER, vol. 1, 77-171. — The Latin text of the *Historia monachorum in Aegypto* is found in ML 21, 387-462. The Greek text was published by E. PREUSCHEN, Palladius und Rufinus. Giessen, 1897, 1-131. Cf. BUTLER, vol. 1, 268-276 for the various recensions. — F. DIEKAMP, Analecta Patristica (Orientalia Christiana Analecta 117). Rome, 1938, 23-27. — F. X. MURPHY, Rufinus of Aquileia. His Life and Works. Washington, 1945, 175-179.

Translations: English: W. K. L. CLARKE, The Lausiac History of Palladius (SPCK). London and New York, 1918. — *French:* A. LUCOT, Palladius. Histoire Lausiaque. Texte grec, introduction et trad. Paris, 1912 (with improvements of Butler's text). — *German:* S. KROTTENTHALER, Des Palladius von Helenopolis Leben der heiligen Väter (BKV² 5). Kempten and Munich, 1912. — Translation of the *Historia monachorum:* T. Rufinus, Mönchsgeschichte. 2 vols. Vienna, 1927, 1930. — *Danish:* H. F. JOHANNSEN, Skrifter om munke og helgener i Aegypten og Palaestina og Syrien, oversat. Copenhagen, 1955.

Studies: E. PREUSCHEN, Palladius und Rufinus. Ein Beitrag zur Quellenkunde des ältesten Mönchtums. Giessen, 1897. — C. H. TURNER, The Lausiac History of Palladius: JThSt 9 (1905) 321-355. — S. SCHIWIETZ, Das morgenländische Mönchtum I. Mayence, 1904, 80-90. — E. W. WATSON, Palladius and Egyptian Monasticism: ChQ 64 (1907) 105-128. — R. REITZENSTEIN, Historia monachorum und Historia Lausiaca. Eine Studie zur Geschichte des Mönchtums und der frühchristlichen Begriffe Gnostiker und Pneumatiker. Göttingen, 1916. — W. BOUSSET, Komposition und Charakter der Historia Lausiaca: NGWG (1917) 173-217. — C. BUTLER, Palladiana: JThSt 22 (1921) 21-35, 138-155, 222-238. — W. BOUSSET, Zur Komposition der Historia Lausiaca: ZNW 21 (1922) 81-98. — M. CHAINE, La double recension de l'Histoire Lausiaque dans la version copte: ROC 25 (1926) 232-275 (Coptic fragments in Codd. Vat. Borgia 59 and 64). — D. TABACHOVITZ, Ein paar lexikalische Bemerkungen zur Historia Lausiaca des Palladius: BZ 30 (1930) 228-231. — F. HALKIN, L'Histoire Lausiaque et les Vies grecques de St. Pacôme: AB 48 (1930) 257-301. — H. HERGT, Die Traumoperation in der christlichen Asketik: Bayerische Blätter f. das Gymnasial-Schulwesen 71 (1935) 64-71 (ch. 29 on castration). — P. PEETERS, Une vie copte de St. Jean de Lycopolis: AB 54 (1936) 359-383 (severe critique of Palladius' accuracy and of Butler's defense thereof). — W. TELFER, The Trustworthiness of Palladius: JThSt 38 (1937) 379-383 (echoes Peeters's article). — E. C. TAPPERT, A Greek Hagiological Manuscript in Philadelphia: TP 68 (1937) 264-276 (*Hist. Laus.* and *Apophthegmata*). — I. HAUSHERR, Aux origines de la mystique syrienne: Grégoire de Chypre ou Jean de Lycopolis?: OCP 4 (1938) 497-520 (*Hist. Laus.* ch. 35). — G. B. CALVI, La Storia Lausiaca di Palladio: Salesianum 1

(1939) 269-279; 2 (1940) 204-223; 3 (1941) 129-156. — S. Morenz, Ein koptischer Diogenes. Griechischer Novellenstoff in ägyptischer Mönchserzählung: Zeitschrift f. ägyptische Sprache und Altertumskunde 77 (1941) 52-54 (*Hist. Laus.* ch. 35). — S. Linnér, Syntaktische und lexikalische Studien zur Historia Lausiaca des Palladios. Diss. Upsala, 1943. — R. Draguet, Le chapitre de l'Histoire Lausiaque sur les Taben- nésiotes dérive-t-il d'une source copte?: Mus 57 (1944) 53-146 and 58 (1945) 15-96 (against trustworthiness of ch. 32); *idem*, L'inauthenticité du proémium de l'Histoire Lausiaque: Mus 59 (1946) 529-534; *idem*, L'Histoire Lausiaque, une œuvre écrite dans l'esprit d'Évagre: RHE (1946) 321-364, (1947) 5-49; *idem*, Une nouvelle source copte de Pallade: le ch. VIII (de l'Histoire Lausiaque): Mus 60 (1947) 227-255 (the new source is Amoun). — F. X. Murphy, Melania the Elder: A Biographical Note: Traditio 5 (1947) 59-77. — R. Draguet, Réminiscences de Pallade chez Cyrille de Scythopolis: RAM 25 (1949) 123-128, 213-218; *idem*, Un nouveau témoin du texte G de l'Histoire Lausiaque: AB 67 (1949) 300-308 (Cod. Athen. 281); *idem*, Butler et sa Lausiac History face à un ms. de l'édition 1ᵉ Wake 67: Mus 63 (1950) 205-230 (Butler did not pay enough attention to a manuscript of Christ Church at Oxford); *idem*, Un texte G de l'Histoire Lausiaque dans le Laura 333 T 93: RSR 40 (1952) 107-115 (important manuscript of Mount Athos furnishing a non-metaphrastic text). — E. Honigmann, Patristic Studies (ST 173). Vatican City, 1953, 104-122 (*Hist. Laus.* and Heraclidas of Nyssa). — J. Muyldermans, A propos d'un text grec attribué à Jean de Lycopolis: RSR 43 (1955) 395-401 (*Hist. Laus.* ch. 35, edit. of Cod. Athen. B.N. 1050). — A. J. Festugière, Le problème littéraire de l'Historia Monachorum: Hermes 83 (1955) 257-284 (three Greek recensions). — D. J. Chitty, Dom Cuthbert Butler and the Lausiac History: JThSt N.S. 6 (1955) 102-110 (defense of Butler's edition against Draguet). — R. Draguet, Butleriana: Une mauvaise cause et son malchanceux avocat: Mus 68 (1955) 238-258 (refutation of Chitty). — R. T. Meyer, Lexical Problems in Palladius' Historia Lausiaca: PS I (TU 63). Berlin, 1957, 44-52.

2. Dialogus de vita S. Joannis

About the year 408, while in exile at Syene, Palladius composed the famous *Dialogue on the Life of St. John Chrysostom*, which is the most important biographical source for the later years of the Saint. Plato's *Phaedo* served as a model. The fictitious dialogue is supposed to have taken place at Rome shortly after Chrysostom's death in 407 or 408 between an oriental bishop and the Roman deacon Theodore. It consists mainly of a defense of the great patriarch of Constantinople against the libellous pamphlet of Theophilus, the patriarch of Alexandria, his worst enemy (cf. above, p. 103). The invective of the latter is no longer extant but its accusations can be reconstructed from the present *Dialogue*.

Editions: MG 47, 5-82. — Best ed.: P. R. Coleman-Norton, Palladii Dialogus de vita sancti Johannis Chrysostomi. Edited with revised text. Cambridge (Mass.), 1928.

Translation: English: H. Moore, The Dialogue of Palladius concerning the Life of Chrysostom (SPCK). New York and London, 1921.

Studies: P. Ubaldi, Appunti sul Dialogo storico di Palladio: Memorie della R. Accademia delle Scienze di Torino. Ser. II, tom. 56 (1906) 217-296 (Plato's Phaedo and the *Dialogue*). — E. C. Butler, Authorship of the Dialogus de vita Chrysostomi: Χρυσοστομικά, Studi e ricerche intorno a S. Giovanni Crisostomo I. Rome, 1908, 35-46. — F. Aengen-

VOORT, Der Dialog des Palladius über das Leben des hl. Johannes Chrysostomus: Progr. des Collegium Augustinianum zu Gaesdonck, 1913. — E. C. BUTLER, The Dialogus de vita Chrysostomi and the Historia Lausiaca: JThSt 22 (1921) 138-155. — L. FRUECHTEL, Zur Johannes Chrysostomus-Vita des Palladios von Helenopolis: PhW (1942) 621-623. — C. BAUR, Wo wurde der dem Palladius von Helenopolis zugeschriebene Dialog über das Leben des hl. Johannes Chrysostomus verfasst?: ZkTh 71 (1949) 466-468. — E. HONIGMANN, The Lost End of Menander's Epitrepontes: BAB 46, 2. Brussels, 1950, 3-43 (quotation from Menander in *Dialogue*). — J. DUMORTIER, La valeur historique du Dialogue de Palladius et la chronologie de S. Jean Chrysostome: MSR 7 (1951) 51-56.

3. On the People of India and the Brahmins

The small treatise Περὶ τῶν τῆς Ἰνδίας ἐθνῶν καὶ τῶν Βραχμάνων, preserved under the name of Palladius, consists of four parts, of which only the first seems to be from his pen. It gives an account of the experiences of an Egyptian scholar on his journey to India. The second and third part are perhaps by the historian Arrian; the fourth by an unknown Christian author. The second and fourth contain an address delivered by Dadamis, the third a report of a meeting between Alexander the Great and the Brahmins. The entire text is extant in manuscript A of the *Alexander Novel, Codex Paris. Gr. 1711* and in a Latin translation attributed to St. Ambrose.

Editions: · C. MÜLLER, Pseudo-Callisthenes III 7-16, in: F. DÜBNER, Opera Arriani. Paris, 1846, 102-120. — Latin version: F. PFISTER, Kleine Texte zum Alexanderroman. Heidelberg, 1910, 1-5.

Studies: W. KROLL, PWK 10 (1919) 1720-1721. — L. FRUECHTEL, Παλλαδίου περὶ τῶν τῆς Ἰνδίας ἐθνῶν καὶ τῶν Βραχμάνων. Diss. Erlangen, 1920. — P. R. COLEMAN-NORTON, The Authorship of the Epistola de Indicis Gentibus et de Bragmantibus: CPh 21 (1926) 154-160. — A. WILMART, Les textes latins de la lettre de Palladius sur les mœurs des Brahmanes: RB 45 (1933) 29-42. — F. PFISTER, Das Nachleben der Überlieferung von Alexander und den Brahmanen: Hermes 76 (1941) 143-169. — R. DESMED, Pseudo-Palladius, Les peuples de l'Inde et les brahmanes. Thèse de lic. Brussels University, 1949. — F. PFISTER, Alexander der Grosse in den Offenbarungen der Griechen, Juden, Mohammedanern und Christen. Berlin, 1956. — G. CARY, The Medieval Alexander. Cambridge (Mass.), 1956, 12-13.

ISIDORE OF PELUSIUM

Isidore who was born at Alexandria and died about the year 435 is commonly believed to have been abbot of a mountain monastery near Pelusium in Egypt. However, recent investigations have shown that there is no reason to suppose that he was head of a cenobitic community. The oldest source of information is Severus of Antioch and he never refers to him in such a capacity. He calls him 'a priest, correct in faith, full of divine wisdom and biblical knowledge'. He remarks that he saw a letter of an ascetic, in which Isidore is saluted as 'the venerable priest Isidore, the altar of Christ, the vessel for the service of the churches, the treasury of Holy Scripture'. Thus the oldest document, dating practically from Isidore's lifetime, says nothing of Isidore being an abbot. Moreover, his 2000 letters still extant fail to provide any justification for the title. The first time we hear of it is in the *Apophthegmata Patrum*, which introduce six of his sentences with 'the *abbas* Isidore of Pelusium said'. However, here the title by no means connotes presiding over a community, but simply means 'Father of the desert' or 'Father of the monks', i.e., a hermit who instructed others in the spiritual life. It is noteworthy, too, that the official lists of the Saints in the Greek Church, the *Menologium* of Basilius II and the *Synaxarium ecclesiae Constant.*, do not call Isidore an abbot. He was so designated for the first time in the sixth century by the Roman deacon Rusticus, who prepared a selection of 49 letters of Isidore, translated them into Latin and added them to the *Acts* of the Council of Ephesus. Here in the pompous heading of the first letter he is called a *doctor ecclesiae* and *abbas monasterii circa Pelusium*. But this witness remains doubtful.

To sum up: Isidore was a priest of Pelusium, famous for his piety and his knowledge of Holy Scripture, as Severus testifies. His letters prove that he led a monastic life and enjoyed a great reputation among the ascetics so that he might be called a Father of the monks, but hardly 'head of a monastery' or abbot of a coenobium. Ephraem, the patriarch of Antioch, informs us, that Alexandria was the place of his birth. The date is unknown, most probably about 360 A. D. Nicephorus Callistus (*Hist. eccl.* 14, 53) remarks that Isidore was a pupil of St. John Chrysostom but there is no reason to take this statement literally. His letters do not imply so close a personal relationship between the two, despite the enthusiastic praise which Isidore lavishes on the great bishop and preacher on several occasions (*Ep.* 1, 152, 156). Photius (*Ep.* 2, 44) lists him with Basil the Great and Gregory of Nazianzus among the ancient Christian masters of epistolography and calls Isidore specifically a model not only of the priestly and ascetical life but also of style and phraseology.

HIS LETTERS

Isidore's correspondence reveals indeed an outstanding personality with a classical education and excellent theological training. His main source is Holy Writ, but he knows the early Christian writers too. Some of his letters are taken almost word for word from Clement of Alexandria, as Fruechtel has shown. Isidore holds that even the secular sciences have high value if they are glorified by divine truth (3, 65). The Christian should like a bee extract nourishment even from the writings of pagan philosophers (2, 3). Demosthenes, Plato, Aristotle and Homer are his favorites. His quotations from some of them, e.g. Demosthenes, are so numerous as to be the basis of textual studies. With this great learning he combined a lively interest in all questions pertaining to world and Church, hierarchy and laity, secular and ecclesiastical government, morals and dogma. Unafraid and unbending, he dares to pass judgment on emperors and bishops, to warn and to advise high and low.

His collected letters cover a period of about four decades, from 393 to 433, and a great variety of persons and subjects. It is unfortunate that the standard edition is very unsatisfactory. Published at Paris in 1638 and reprinted by Migne (MG 78), it comprises 2012 letters in five books. Such a division into five sections is justified neither by the contents nor by the manuscripts. C. H. Turner and K. Lake have drawn our attention to Codex Bα1 of Grottaferrata, the oldest and most important manuscript of Isidore's letters, which so far has never been collated. The existing editions are all based on the collection of two thousand letters which was formed in the century from 450 to 550 A.D. in the Akoimete monastery at Constantinople. This *Corpus Isidorianum* was mentioned by Facundus, bishop of Hermiana, in his *Pro defensione trium capitulorum* (ML 67, 573), composed between 546 and 548, and eighteen years later the Roman deacon Rusticus had independent access to it (*Acta Concil. oecum.* ed. Schwartz 1,4,1,25). The latter remarks that the collection consisted of four codexes, each containing five hundred epistles. The 2012 letters of Migne include at least 19 doublets. It would be unreasonable to doubt that the figure 2000 resulted from a selection by the Akoimetes deliberately designed to attain a round number. As a matter of fact, Severus of Antioch speaks of 'almost three thousand' (CSCO Scriptores Syri, ser. 4, tom. 6, ed. Lebon, 182-183), and the Lexicon of Suidas (2, 668) confirms this. A new critical edition based on the Grottaferrata manuscript would not only provide a vastly improved text but restore the original order of the letters.

However, the two thousand epistles which have been preserved are enough to make Isidore's correspondence unique in the patristic period. Their form is an illustration of the author's own principle of unaffected elegance (*Ep.* 5, 133) while their content concerns theological as well as secular subjects. Among the latter are those addressed to the state authorities, in order to intercede for the city of Pelusium (2, 25; cf. 1, 175), to Quirinius, the prefect of Egypt (1, 174-175) reprimanding him for his use of force, to the Emperor Theodosius II, exhorting him to be gentle and generous, since these are the noble virtues of a ruler (1, 35).

Most treat of exegetical questions. The writer follows the historical and grammatical method of the School of Antioch (cf. vol. II, p. 121f.) and rejects allegorism (4, 117). He condemns the attempt to see figures of Christ everywhere in the Old Testament, since this will encourage pagans and heretics to be suspicious of the true Messianic passages (2, 195; cf. 2, 63; 3, 339). The Old Testament is a mixture of history and prophecy and these two should not be confused (2, 63; 4, 203). Nevertheless he welcomes allegorical interpretations if they serve only for edification. Among the exegetical letters more than sixty are devoted to the Pauline Epistles.

Not a few of his missives deal with ascetical and moral subjects. Containing the simplest rules of ethics as well as the highest principles of perfection, they testify to Isidore's depth of wisdom and honesty of soul. The kingdom of God is based on voluntary poverty and abstinence (1, 129) but only if all commandments are obeyed and all virtues are practised (1, 287). Asceticism is not enough (1, 129), the spirit is the essential. Thus he says: 'You are not a perfect ascetic, if you have the food, drink and bed of St. John the Baptist. In order to reach perfection, you must have his spirit' (1, 162). Virginity is as much above married life as heaven above earth or the soul above the body (4, 192), but virginity without love of our neighbour or virginity without humility has no value (1, 286). Such are the principles which he never tires of recalling to the minds of monks, priests and bishops who do not live up to their vocation.

THEOLOGICAL ASPECTS

Most interesting are those of his letters which reveal Isidore as a dogmatic theologian. He defends the ecclesiastical Christology against the different heresies on many occasions. Thus he maintains first of all the divinity of Christ against the Arians and refutes them by a careful, literal interpretation of Holy Scripture. Since he regards the Arians as the most dangerous enemies of all, he sees his main task as a theologian in their defeat (1, 389). His exact analysis of biblical texts (3, 335; 1, 353; 3, 334; 3, 31; 1, 67; 3, 166; 4, 142; 1, 139; 4, 166), his philological approach to their meaning and his scientific method of exegesis show again the influence of the School of Antioch. He uses the Nicene expression *homoousios* or *homoousiotes* repeatedly (1, 67, 422; 3, 18, 31, 112, 334, 335; 4, 99, 142). Moreover, he explicitly refers to this Council in his letter 4, 99: 'One must follow the holy synod which met at Nicaea without adding or detracting anything, because filled by the Spirit of God, it has taught the truth'.

On the other hand, he defends the true humanity of Christ against the Manicheans (1, 102; 2, 133). 'The Lord selected his mother from the posterity of Abraham and assumed flesh from her. Thus he was in truth made man, in all like us, except sin' (1, 264).

At least eight of Isidore's letters are addressed to Cyril of Alexandria: 1, 310, 323, 324, 370; 2, 127; 3, 306; 5, 79, 268. In one of them (1, 310) he does not hesitate to reproach the patriarch for his behavior at Ephesus:

> Sympathy does not see distinctly; but antipathy does not see at all. If then you would be clear of both sorts of bleariness of vision, do not indulge in violent negations, but submit any charges made against you to a just judgment. God Himself, Who knows all things before they come to pass, vouchsafed to come down and see the cry of Sodom; thereby teaching us the lesson to look closely into things and weigh them well. Many of those who were assembled at Ephesus speak satirically of you as a man bent on pursuing his private animosities, not as one who has at heart the cause of Jesus Christ (DHC).

This warning, however, does not prevent him from admonishing Cyril in another letter (1, 324) not to sacrifice one jot of his doctrine. He petitions the Emperor Theodosius to stop those court-officials who tried at Ephesus to assume judicial authority in matters of faith (1, 311).

Regarding the hypostatic union Isidore rejects a mixture as well as a separation of the two natures in Christ. He warns the lector Timotheus against the Manicheans who taught only one nature in Christ (1, 102). He speaks clearly of δύο φύσεις and ἕν πρόσωπον καὶ μία ὑπόστασις (1, 23, 303, 323, 405), thus anticipating in a certain way the definition of Chalcedon.

LOST WRITINGS

Isidore mentions occasionally in his letters two treatises he composed. Twice (2, 137 and 228) he refers to a tract *Against the Greeks (Λόγος πρὸς "Ελληνας)* and once (3, 253) to a work *On the Non-existence of Fate (Λογίδιον περὶ τοῦ μὴ εἶναι εἱμαρμένην)*. It seems that the former corresponded to an epistle no longer extant, and the latter is identical with the lengthy missive to the sophist Harpocras (3, 154).

Editions: MG 78. For the 19 doublets, see: C. BAUR, Duplikate in Mignes Patrologia Graeca: ThQ 100 (1919) 252-254. An Old Latin version of 49 letters, preserved in the *Synodicon adversus tragoediam Irenaei*, was edited from a Vatican and Monte Cassino manuscript by R. AIGRAIN, Quarante-neuf lettres de S. Isidore de Péluse, édition critique de l'ancienne version latine contenue dans deux manuscrits du Concile d'Éphèse. Paris, 1911, and again by E. SCHWARTZ, ACO I, 4 (1922/23) 9-25.

Studies: General: D. S. BALANOS, 'Ισίδωρος ὁ Πηλουσιώτης. Athens, 1922. — G. BAREILLE, Isidore de Péluse: DTC 8 (1924) 94-97.

Special: P. B. Glueck, Isidori Pelusiotae summa doctrinae moralis. Würzburg, 1848. — L. Bober, De arte hermeneutica S. Isidori Pelusiotae. Cracow, 1878. — E. Bouvy, De S. Isidoro Pelusiota libri tres. Nîmes, 1884. — E. Bouvy, S. Jean Chrysostome et S. Isidore de Péluse: EO 1 (1897/98) 190-201. — V. Lundström, De Isidori Pelusiotae epistolis recensendis praelusiones: Eranos 2 (1897) 67-80 (furnishes a new text of three letters based on new manuscripts: *Ep.* 2, 212; 1, 1.2). — G. Mercati, Due supposte lettere di Dionigio Alessandrino: Note di letteratura biblica e cristiana antica (ST 5). Rome, 1901, 82-86 (*Ep.* 1, 39 and 3, 219). — N. Capo, De Isidori Pelusiotae Epist. locis ad antiquitatem pertinentibus: Bess 6 (1901/02) 342-363; *idem*, De S. Isidori Pelusiotae epistolarum recensione ac numero quaestio: SIF 9 (1901) 449-466; cf. C. Baur, ThQ 100 (1919) 254. — C. H. Turner, The Letters of Isidore of Pelusium: JThSt 6 (1905) 70-86 (important for the text tradition). — K. Lake, Further Notes on the MSS of Isidore of Pelusium: JThSt 6 (1905) 270-282. — J. L. Sicking, Isidorus van Pelusium: De Katholiek 130 (1906) 109-129 (regards many letters as spurious). — E. Lyon, Le droit chez Isidore de Péluse: Études d'histoire juridique offertes à P. F. Girard. Paris, 1913, vol. 2, 209-222. — L. Bayer, Isidors von Pelusium klassische Bildung (FLDG 13, 2). Paderborn, 1915. — Joasaph, St. Isidore of Pelusium as a Commentator of Holy Scripture (in Russian): Bogoslovski Vrem. 1 (1915) 535-561, 727-834. — E. Fehrle, Satzschluss und Rhythmus bei Isidor von Pelusion: BZ 24 (1924) 315-319. — A. N. Diamantopulos, Ἰσίδωρος ὁ Πηλουσιώτης: NS 18 (1925/26) 99-115, 288-303. — G. Redl, Isidor von Pelusion als Sophist: ZKG 47 (1928) 325-332. — H. Grégoire, Les sauterelles de saint Jean-Baptiste: Byz 5 (1929/30) 109-128 (*Ep.* 1, 132: MG 78, 269). — A. J. Phytrakes, Οἱ πολιτικοὶ καὶ ἐκκλησιαστικοὶ ἄρχοντες κατὰ Ἰσίδωρον τὸν Πηλουσιώτην. Mytilene, 1936. — L. Fruechtel, Isidoros von Pelusion als Benützer des Clemens Alexandrinus und anderer Quellen: Berliner PhW 58 (1938) 61-64; *idem*, Neue Quellennachweise zu Isidoros von Pelusion: Berliner PhW 58 (1938) 764-768. — F. La Cava, Una lettera di sant' Isidoro Pelusiota. Nuove considerazioni sullo scopo delle parabole: DTP 39 (1936) 529-533 (*Ep.* 2, 270). — B. Altaner, Hat Isidoros von Pelusion einen Λόγος πρὸς Ἕλληνας und einen Λόγος περὶ τοῦ μὴ εἶναι εἱμαρμένην verfasst?: BZ 42 (1942) 91-100. — R. Gröhl, Gedanken des hl. Isidor von Pelusium über das Priestertum: Haec loquere et exhortare 38 (1944) 187-189. — A. Schmid, Die Christologie Isidors von Pelusium (Paradosis 2). Fribourg, 1948. — E. Demougeot, Quelques témoignages de sympathie d'Orientaux envers saint Jean Chrysostome exilé: Atti dello VIII° Congresso intern. di Studi bizantini I. Palermo, 1951, 44-54. — S. Y. Rudberg, Codex Upsaliensis Graecus 5: Eranos 50 (1952) 60-70 (containing fragments hitherto unpublished). — M. Smith, The Manuscript Tradition of Isidore of Pelusium: HThR 47 (1954) 205-210. — C. Astruc, Miscellanea Graeca dans un recueil provenant de Charles de Montchal: Scriptorium 8 (1954) 293-296 (Cod. Paris. B.N. Lat. 3282 containing Greek excerpts partly inedited).—J. Darrouzès, Un recueil épistolaire byzantin, le manuscrit de Patmos 706: REB 14 (1956) 87-121 (containing some letters of Isidore). — G. J. Bartelink, Θεοκάπηλος et les synonymes chez Isidore de Péluse: VC 12 (1958) 227-231.

SHENOUTE OF ATRIPE

Shenoute is, next to Pachomius, the most important representative of Egyptian cenobitism. As abbot of the famous White Monastery of Atripe in the desert of Thebes for 83 years (383-466), he ruled over 2200 monks and 1800 nuns, as Besa, his pupil and successor, informs us. Although of an irascible and passionate temperament, he was an outstanding organizer, who brought his communities to a flourishing state. In his Rule he did not hesitate to depart from the prescriptions of Pachomius. It mentions explicitly a written monastic profession to be signed by the monks and the permission to withdraw to the desert after a few years of cenobitic life, without completely severing connections with the monastery. In 431 Shenoute accompanied Cyril of Alexandria to the Council of Ephesus. He died at the age of 118. Biographies in Coptic, Arabic and Syriac praise his personality and his achievements. The oldest of them is that of his disciple, Besa, which served as a source for all the others.

Shenoute is the most outstanding Christian writer in Coptic. According to Besa he left a great number of letters and sermons. Most of the former, addressed to monks and nuns, deal with monastic questions, others combat pagans and heretics. His sermons are spirited and predominantly eschatological in character. In addition, several apocalypses and visions are attributed to him. Some of his works survive in Ethiopic, Arabic and Syriac versions. So far it has been very difficult to sift the authentic writings from the spurious.

Editions: J. Leipoldt and W. E. Crum, Sinuthii archimandritae vita et opera omnia: CSCO 41 (Copt. 1), Louvain, 1906; CSCO 42 (Copt. 2) 1908; CSCO 73 (Copt. 5) 1913. — E. Amélineau, Œuvres de Chenoudi. Texte copte et traduction française. 2 vols. Paris, 1907, 1911 (This ed. is far less reliable than that by Leipoldt; cf. the crit. review by F. Nau, ROC 12 (1907) 313-328). — Separate: P. Du Bourget, Entretien de Chenoute sur les problèmes de discipline ecclésiastique et de cosmologie: Bull. Inst. français d'archéol. orient. 57 (1958) 99-104 (crit. ed. of a discussion in the 4th book of the *Discussions and Letters* of Shenoute).

Translations: Latin: H. Wiesmann, Sinuthii archimandritae vita et opera omnia: CSCO 96 (Copt. 8, translation of CSCO 42), Louvain, 1931; CSCO 108 (Copt. 12, translat. of CSCO 73), 1936, reprint. 1952; CSCO 129 (translat. of CSCO 41), 1951. — *French:* E. Amélineau, op. cit.

Studies: J. Leipoldt, Schenute von Atripe und die Entstehung des national-ägyptischen Mönchtums (TU 25, 1). Leipzig, 1903; *idem*, Geschichte der christlichen Literaturen des Orients (Die Literaturen des Ostens in Einzeldarstellungen 7, 2). Leipzig, 1907, 146-153. — W. E. Crum, Inscriptions from Shenoute's Monastery: JThSt 5 (1904) 552-569. — J. F. Bethune-Baker, The Date of the Death of Nestorius: JThSt 9 (1908) 601-605 (date of Shenoute's death: 466). — E. Tisserant, Étude sur une traduction arabe d'un sermon de Chenoudi: ROC 13 (1908) 81-89 (sermon on penance). — A. Grohmann, Die im Äthiopischen, Arabischen und Koptischen erhaltenen Visionen Apa Schenutes von Atripe: ZDMG 67 (1913) 187-267; 68 (1914) 1-16 (edition and German translation). — O. H. E. Burmester, The Homilies or Exhortations of the Holy Week Lectionary: Mus 45 (1932) 21-70 (ten Bohairic homilies, edition and English translation). — L. T. Lefort, Un passage obscur des hymnes à Chenoute: Orientalia 4 (1935) 411-415; *idem*, Athanase, Ambroise et Chenoute: 'Sur la virginité': Mus 48 (1935) 55-74 (shows that Shenoute used Athanasius as a source, cf. above p. 45). — D. P. Buckle, A Noteworthy Sahidic Variant in a Shenoute Homily in the John Rylands Library: BJR 20 (1936) 383-384. — G. Graf, Geschichte der christlichen arabischen Literatur I (ST 118). Vatican City, 1944, 461-464. — A. van Lantschoot, A propos du Physiologus: Coptic Studies in honor of W. E. Crum. Boston, 1950, 339-363 (doubts that Shenoute borrowed from the *Physiologus*). — D. G. Müller, Die alte koptische Predigt. Versuch eines Überblicks. Diss. Heidelberg, 1953. Published: 1954. Cf. ThLZ 79 (1954) 122-123; *idem*, Einige Bemerkungen zur 'ars praedicandi' der alten koptischen Kirche: Mus 67 (1954) 231-270. — S. Morenz, Mitteilungen des Instituts für Orient-forschung 1 (1953) 250-255. — L. T. Lefort, La chasse aux reliques des martyrs en Égypte au IVe siècle: NC 6 (1954) 225-230 (French translation of Shenoute's Catechesis against superstition). — K. H. Kuhn, The Observance of the 'Two Weeks' in Shenoute's Writings: SP II (TU 64). Berlin, 1957, 427-434. — U. Treu, Aristophanes bei Schenute: Phil 101 (1957) 325-328.

Besa's *Life of Shenoute* is found in Leipoldt's edition CSCO 41 (Copt. 1), Latin translation by H. Wiesmann, CSCO 129. For Besa's other writings, see the edition by K. H. Kuhn, Letters and Sermons of Besa: CSCO 157 (1956) Coptic text, CSCO 158 (1956) English translation. German translation of one of his letters, reminding his monks of the vow of poverty: W. Erichsen, Ein Sendbrief eines ägyptischen Klostervorstehers: Jahrbuch für das Bistum Mainz 5 (1950) 310-313. Cf. K. H. Kuhn, Besa's Letters and Sermons: Mus 66 (1953) 225-243; *idem*, A Fifth-Century Egyptian Abbot: JIhSt 5 (1954) 36-48 (Besa and his background), 174-187 (Monastic life in Besa's day); 6 (1955) 35-48 (Besa's Christianity).

THE APOPHTHEGMATA PATRUM

There is hardly any work which gives a better idea of the spirit of Egyptian monachism than the anonymous collection of spiritual maxims called *Apophthegmata Patrum* or *Sayings of the Fathers*. Compiled perhaps about the end of the fifth century, it contains pronouncements (λόγοι) of the most famous abbots and solitaries of the Egyptian desert and anecdotes about their miracles and virtues (ἔργα). Before it was written down in Greek, there must have been an oral tradition in Coptic. Probably in the sixth century the anthology was arranged in the alphabetical order of the personalities whose words and works were reported. The first is abbot Antony, the last abbot Or. This series is extant in a number of later redactions and translations. Giving as they do a vivid picture of monastic life in the Natron Valley, these *Sayings of the Fathers* represent an invaluable source of information for the history of religion and civilization.

The *Verba seniorum* which the Jesuit Rosweyde published in 1615 as books III, V, VI and VII of his great *Vitae Patrum* (ML 73/74) represents a Latin version of four different *Apophthegmata* collections, all of them originally in Greek and related to the above-mentioned. The translation was most probably made by the Roman deacon and later Pope Pelagius I (556-561), the subdeacon and later Pope John III (561-574), the deacon Paschasius and the abbot Martin of Dumio. A Coptic version was published by Zoëga, an Armenian by the Mechitarists of S. Lazzaro at Venice. Various Syriac versions also exist.

Editions: Greek text of the alphabetic anthology from Codex Regius 2466: Editio princeps: J. B. COTELIER, Ecclesiae Graecae monumenta I (1677) 338-712, reprinted MG 65, 71-440. This collection was supplemented by the 400 anonymous Apophthegmata from Codex Coislinianus 126 published by F. NAU, Histoires des solitaires égyptiens: ROC 12 (1907) 43-47 comprising Ap. 1-37; ROC 12 (1907) 171-189 comprising Ap. 38-62; ROC 12 (1907) 393-413 comprising Ap. 63-132; ROC 13 (1908) 47-66 comprising Ap. 133-174; ROC 13 (1908) 266-297 comprising Ap. 175-215; ROC 14 (1909) 357-379 comprising Ap. 216-297; ROC 17 (1912) 204-211 comprising Ap. 298-334; ROC 17 (1912) 294-301 comprising Ap. 335-358; ROC 18 (1913) 137-146 comprising Ap. 359-400. After Ap. 132 the chapter should be inserted which F. NAU published in his article: Le chapitre Περὶ ἀναχωρητῶν ἁγίων et les sources de la Vie de St. Paul de Thèbes: ROC 10 (1905) 387-417 (text 409-414). — Additional and related texts are found: PO 8, 164-183. New Apophthegmata were discovered by E. C. TAPPERT, A Greek Hagiological Manuscript in Philadelphia: TP 68 (1937) 264-276.

Verba seniorum: The Latin text of the four different Apophthegmata collections in ML 73, 855-1022 (translated by Pelagius and John); 73, 1025-1062 (translated by Paschasius); 74, 381-394 (translated by Martin of Dumio); 73, 739-810 (Pseudo-Rufinus). Addition to Rosweyde's collection: A. WILMART, Le recueil latin des Apophthegmes: RB 34 (1922) 185-198.
Syriac collection: P. BEDJAN, Acta Martyrum et Sanctorum VII. Paris, 1897. — E. A. W. BUDGE, The Book of Paradise II. London, 1904.
Coptic collection: G. ZOËGA, Catalog. cod. Copt. Rome, 1910.
Armenian collection: The Writings of the Holy Fathers and their Lives (in Armenian), Venice, 1855, vol. I, 413-722; vol. II, 1-504: Sayings and Stories of the Holy Fathers.

Translations: English: Verba seniorum: H. WADDELL, The Desert Fathers. Translated from the Latin with an introduction. London, 1936 (selections from Rosweyde's second edition of the Latin text printed in 1628). — Syriac collection: E. A. W. BUDGE, The Book of Paradise II. London, 1904 (with Syriac text). Translation separately: E. A. W. BUDGE, The Paradise of the Fathers II. London, 1907; *idem*, The Wit and Wisdom of the Christian Fathers of Egypt of the Apophthegmata Patrum by 'Anân îshô of Bêth 'Abhê. Oxford, 1934 (Apophthegmata only). — *French: Verba seniorum:* M. ARNAULD D'ANDILLY, Les Vies des saints Pères des déserts et de quelques saintes écrites par les Pères de l'Église et autres anciens auteurs ecclésiastiques. Brussels, 1694. Selection: R. DRAGUET, Les Pères du désert. Paris, 1949, 203-228. — F. NAU, ROC 12 (1907) 43-47, 171-189, 393-413; 13 (1908) 47-66, 266-297. — *Dutch:* H. ROSWEYDE, 't Vadersboeck. 't Leven en de spreucken der Vaderen. Bruges, 1699.

Studies: General: The basic and indispensable work is: W. BOUSSET, Apophthegmata. Tübingen, 1923, 1-208 (Untersuchungen über Textüberlieferung und Charakter der *Apophthegmata*). — F. CAVALLERA, Apophthegmes: DSp 1, (1937) 765-770. — P. DE LABRIOLLE, Apophthegmata: RACh 1 (1942) 545-550.

Special: C. BUTLER, The Lausiac History of Palladius. Cambridge, 1898, 208-214. — M. CHAINE, Le texte original des Apophthegmes des Pères: Université Saint-Joseph, Beyrouth (Syrie). Mélanges de la Faculté Orientale, t. 5, 2 (1912) 541-569. — F. NAU, Notes sur le texte original des Apophthegmes des Pères: ROC 18 (1913) 208f. — G. GRAF, Arabische Apophthegmen-Sammlung: OC N.S. 5 (1915) 314-318. — T. HOPFNER, Über die koptisch-sahidischen Apophthegmata Patrum Aegyptiorum und verwandte griechische, lateinische, koptisch-bohairische und syrische Sammlungen (AAWW Phil.-hist. Klasse 61, 2). Vienna, 1918.—A. H. SALONIUS, Vitae Patrum. Lund, 1920 (textual crit., vocabulary etc.). — W. BOUSSET, Die Textüberlieferung der Apophthegmata Patrum: Festgabe A. v. Harnack. Tübingen, 1921, 102-116. — A. WILMART, Le recueil latin des Apophthegmes: RB 34 (1922) 185-198. — A. BAUMSTARK, Geschichte der syrischen Literatur. Bonn, 1922, 92-93, 201-203. — L. VILLECOURT, Une même parabole commune aux Apophthegmes des Pères et à Calila et Dimna: Mus 36 (1923) 243-248. — T. Hermann, Einige bemerkenswerte Fragmente zu den griechischen Apophthegmata Patium: ZNW 23 (1924) 102-109. — J. Lebreton, Chronique d'histoire des origines chrétiennes IV. Les origines du monachisme: RSR 14 (1924) 357-364. — W. Gemoll, Das Apophthegma. Literarhistorische Studien. Vienna, 1926 – D. Gorce, La part des 'Vitae patrum' dans l'élaboration de la Règle bénédictine: RLM 14 (1929) 338-399. — K. Heussi, Der Ursprung des Mönchtums. Tübingen, 1936, 104-108, 132-280. — G. Morin, Un ms. bavarois des Vitae patrum à la Bibliotheque Royale de Bruxelles: SM 55 (1937) 15-18. — E. C. Tappert, A Greek Hagiological Manuscript in Philadelphia: TP 68 (1937) 264-276. — I. Herwegen, Väterspruch und Mönchsregel. Münster, 1937. — A. Wilmart, Les rédactions latines de la Vie d'Abraham Ermite: RB 50 (1938) 222-245 (ML 73, 651-690). — M. Viller and K. Rahner, Aszese und Mystik in der Väterzeit. Freiburg i.B., 1939, 115-121. — N. Schedl, Jesus Christus. Sein Bild bei den Mönchen der Sketis. Diss. Vienna, 1942. — S. Morenz, Ein koptischer Diogenes. Griechischer Novellenstoff in ägyptischer Mönchserzählung: Zeitschrift für ägyptische Sprache 77 (1941) 52-54. — J. Doresse, A propos d'un apophtegme copte. Diogène et les moines égyptiens: RHR 128 (1944) 84-93. — H. Duensing, Neue christlich-palästinensisch-aramäische Fragmente (NGWG 1944) 215-227 (fragments of an Aramaic version). — G. Garitte, Deux manuscrits italo-grecs (Vat. Gr. 1238 et Barber. Gr. 475): Miscellanea Mercati III (ST 123). Vatican City, 1946, 16-40 (containing Greek apophthegmata). — H. Dörries, Die Bibel im ältesten Mönchtum Th Z 72 (1947) 215-222. — M. Jugie, Un apophthegme des Pères inédit sur le purgatoire: Mémorial L. Petit. Bucarest, 1948, 245-253 (apophthegma of Paul the Simple). — E. Mioni, Le Vitae Patrum nella tradizione di Ambrogio Traversari: Aevum 24 (1950) 319-331. — R. Draguet, Le Paternikon de l'Add. 22508 du British Museum: Mus 63 (1950) 25-46 (important for the Greek tradition of the *Ap.*); *idem*, Une nouvelle attestation de ἕλκειν τὰς ἐξ: Mélanges J. De Ghellinck I. Gembloux, 1951, 287-291 (expression attributed to abbot Poemen). — J. C. Guy, Remarques sur le texte des Apophthegmata Patrum: RSR 43 (1955) 252-258. — E. C. Tappert, Desert Wisdom: The Sayings of the Anchorites: Lutheran Quarterly 9 (1957) 157-172.

CHAPTER III

THE WRITERS OF ASIA MINOR

It was in Asia Minor at Nicomedia that Arius took refuge after he had been condemned by the synod of Alexandria in 318. Here he found strong support from many influential bishops and from the emperors. It was in the same Asia Minor that the First Ecumenical Council of Nicaea convened in 325 to settle the burning issue. However, despite the decisions of the great assembly, the conflict continued. The problem involved in the quarrel was solved, but the quarrel itself was far from being ended. On the contrary, in the years which followed Arianism became predominant in the two political dioceses of Pontica and Asiana. It is typical that the leaders of the four Arian · parties, the bishops Eusebius of Nicomedia, Eustathius of Sebaste, Eunomius of Cyzicus, Basil of Ancyra and the sophist Asterius, the first Arian writer, lived in Asia Minor. It was the same Asia Minor that saw the first Christian Emperor baptized by an Arian bishop in Achyron near Nicomedia. He permitted Arius to return from exile and banished Athanasius as a disturber of the peace. He and his successor Constantius were completely under the influence of Eusebius of Nicomedia. Thus Asia Minor became the center of Arian power. Yet it is the same Asia Minor that produced the three great doctors of the Eastern Church, the staunch defenders of the Nicene faith against Arianism and its imperial supporters, the 'Cappadocian Fathers', who gave the final shape to the doctrine of the Trinity.

EUSEBIUS OF NICOMEDIA

Eusebius, to whom Arius went after he had been excommunicated at Alexandria, was by far his most powerful friend. A disciple of Lucian of Antioch, he was first made bishop of Berytus and later, shortly before 318, appointed to the more important see of Nicomedia. There in close proximity to the court, in high favor with the Empress Constantia, the sister of Constantine and the wife of Licinius, he occupied a position the influence of which was soon to be felt in the controversy. He set himself at once upon Arius' arrival to work for his ideas and to support him against his own ordinary. He addressed a great number of letters to the hierarchy of Asia Minor and the Orient in order to convince them that the heresiarch had been treated unjustly and that a reversal of his deposition should be demanded of the bishop of Alexandria. He participated in the Council of Nicaea and submitted a Creed, which was rejected as blasphemous. He signed the Nicene formula of Faith only to become afterwards the protagonist of the most extreme Arian party, the Eusebians, who defended the crudest form of the false doctrine and constituted the strongest reaction against the Nicaenum. For this reason, as well as on account of his former relations with Licinius, Constantine exiled him to Gaul three months after the Council. Recalled in 328 at the intercession of Constantia, he won the Emperor's favor. He succeeded in having Eustathius of Antioch in 330, Athanasius at a synod of Tyre in 335 and Marcellus of Ancyra in 336 deposed. In 337 he baptized the first Christian Emperor, Constantine. At the end of 338 he was elevated to the episcopal see of Constantinople, the new national capital. He died at the end of 341 or the beginning of 342. His adherents have called him 'the great'. He transformed what might have remained an Egyptian dispute into an ecumenical controversy. He was more an ecclesiastical politician than a theologian, experienced in worldly affairs and ambitious, ready for any intrigue.

Studies: H. R. REYNOLDS, Eusebius of Nicomedia: DCB 2 (1880) 360-367. — A. LICHTEN-STEIN, Eusebius von Nikomedien. Versuch einer Darstellung seiner Persönlichkeit und seines Lebens unter besonderer Berücksichtigung seiner Führerschaft im arianischen Streite. Halle, 1903. — S. ROGALA, Die Anfänge des arianischen Streites. Paderborn, 1907, 77-85. — C. HEFELE and H. LECLERCQ, Histoire des conciles I. Paris, 1907, 639-647. — F. J. DÖLGER, Die Taufe Konstantins und ihre Probleme: Konstantin der Grosse und seine Zeit. Festgabe zum Konstantins-Jubilaeum (RQ Suppl. 19). Freiburg i.B., 1913, 377-447. — G. BARDY, Recherches sur St. Lucien d'Antioche et son école. Paris, 1936. — G. BAREILLE, Eusèbe de Nicomédie: DTC 5 (1939) 1539-1552. — V. C. DE CLERCQ, Ossius of Cordova. A Contribution to the History of the Constantinian Period (SCA 13). Washington, 1954, 193-198, 284-286, 293-298.

HIS LETTERS

1. *Letter to Paulinus of Tyre*

The historian Theodoret of Cyrus has preserved (*Hist. eccl.* 1, 5) a letter that Eusebius addressed to bishop Paulinus of Tyre. It belongs to the kind of letters with which he inundated the East after Arius left Alexandria and found shelter at his house in Nicomedia, and is as such an interesting document. A Latin translation of it is found in Marius Victorinus, *Adv. Arium* (prol). Eusebius informs the addressee that he is disappointed by his silence and reserve in the controversy which has arisen. Paulinus is urgently requested to speak out and show his true color. The Arian doctrine is outlined and it is suggested that Paulinus should write to bishop Alexander, Arius' ordinary, to get him to change his mind.

Edition: H. G. OPITZ, Athanasius' Werke III, 1. Berlin and Leipzig, 1934, 15-17 (Urkunde 8): Greek and Latin text.

Translations: See the translations of Theodoret's *Historia ecclesiastica* below p. 551.

2. *Letter to Arius*

Athanasius mentions a letter addressed by Eusebius to Arius before the Council of Nicaea took place. He quotes the following sentence: 'Since your sentiments are good, pray that all adopt them; for it is plain to any one, that what has been made was not before its origination; but what came to be has a beginning of being' (*De syn.* 17).

Edition: H. G. OPITZ, op. cit. 3 (Urkunde 2).

Translations: See translations of Athanasius' *De synodis*, above p. 63.

3. *Letter to Athanasius*

According to Socrates (*Hist. eccl.* 1, 23) Eusebius wrote to Athanasius asking him to re-admit Arius and his adherents into the Church. 'The tone of his letter indeed was that of entreaty, but openly he menaced him'. This document has not been preserved.

4. *Letter to the Bishops of the Nicene Council*

Socrates (*Hist. eccl.* 1, 14) and Sozomen (*Hist. eccl.* 2, 16) preserved a letter which Eusebius and Theognis of Nicaea sent to the principal bishops who participated in the Council. Socrates calls it 'a penitential confession' and Sozomen 'a retractation'. Although the genuineness of this document has been doubted occasionally (for instance by Bardenhewer, vol. 3, p. 43) it seems to be authentic. The two bishops composed it while they were in exile and Sozomen mentions that they owed their restoration to this document because shortly afterwards they were recalled by an imperial edict. According to its text, the two had subscribed to the articles of faith at Nicaea but not to the condemnation of Arius:

> We, having been sometime since condemned by your piety without a formal trial, ought to bear in silence the decisions of your sacred abjudication. But since it is unreasonable that we by silence should countenance calumniators against ourselves, we on this account declare that we entirely concur with you in the faith; and also, after having closely considered the import of the term *homoousios*, we have been wholly studious of peace, having never followed the heresy. After suggesting whatever entered our thought for the security of the churches and fully assuring those under our influence, we subscribed to the declaration of faith; we did not subscribe to the anathematizing; not as objecting to the creed, but as disbelieving the party accused to be

such as was represented, having been satisfied on this point, both from his own letters to us, and from personal conversations. But if your holy council was convinced, we, not opposing but concurring in your decisions, by this statement give them full assent and confirmation: and this we do, not as wearied with our exile, but to shake off the suspicion of heresy. If therefore you should now think fit to restore us to your presence, you will have us on all points conformable and acquiescent in your decrees: especially since it has seemed good to your piety to deal tenderly with and recall even him who was primarily accused. It would be absurd for us to be silent and thus give presumptive evidence against ourselves, when the one who seemed responsible has been permitted to clear himself from the charges brought against him; vouchsafe then, as is consistent with that Christ-loving piety of yours, to remind our most religious emperor, to present our petitions, and to determine speedily concerning us in a way becoming yourselves (Socrates, *Hist. eccl.* 1, 14 LNPF).

From this letter it appears that Arius had succeeded in defending himself against the charges brought against him and had been recalled. Bardenhewer thinks that the document is nothing but a forgery, designed to propagate the falsehood that Arius had been pardoned by the Fathers of the Nicene Council.

Edition: H. G. OPITZ, op. cit. 65-66 (Urkunde 31).

Translations: See translations of Socrates and Sozomen, below p. 534 and 536.

Studies: O. SEECK, Untersuchungen zur Geschichte des nicänischen Konzils: ZKG 17 (1896) 361-363. — E. SCHWARTZ, Zur Geschichte des Athanasius VIII: NGWG (1911) 380-386. — K. MÜLLER, Kleine Beiträge zur alten Kirchengeschichte. Zu der Eingabe der Bischöfe Euseb von Nikomedien und Theognis von Nicaea an die (zweite) Synode von Nicaea (327): ZNW 24 (1925) 290-292. — N. H. BAYNES, Athanasiana: Journal of Egyptian Archaeology 11 (1925) 58-61. — G. BARDY, Sur la réitération du concile de Nicée: RSR 23 (1933) 430-450 (against authenticity).

THEOGNIS OF NICAEA

Theognis, bishop of Nicaea, was according to Philostorgius (*Hist. eccl.* 2, 14) a disciple of Lucian of Antioch. At the Council of 325 he opposed its decisions at first but finally gave his signature to the Creed. He was deposed together with Eusebius of Nicomedia three months after the Council for communicating with the Arians. Constantine banished them to Gaul. Recalled from exile, supposedly after they had written the above letter of recantation, Theognis became one of the most outspoken enemies of Athanasius. This contributed to the story that he had bribed the notary to whom the Emperor had entrusted the custody of the documents of the Nicene Council and the latter had effaced his signature. He participated in the synod of Eusebius of Nicomedia at Antioch which condemned Eustathius. He was one of the chief conspirators against Athanasius at the court of Constantine (Socrates, *Hist. eccl.* 1, 27, 7), accusing him before the Emperor 'of being the author of all the seditions and troubles that agitated the Church, and of excluding those who were desirous of joining the Church; and alleged that unanimity would be restored were he alone to be removed' (Sozomen, *Hist. eccl.* 2, 22, 1). The Emperor thereupon called a synod at Caesarea in 334, which Athanasius refused to attend (Theodoret, *Hist. eccl.* 1, 28, 2). A year later Theognis appeared at the synod of Tyre and was a member of the committee sent into the Mareotis to investigate certain ecclesiastical affairs, especially the charge of the broken cup brought against Athanasius (Athan., *Apol. c. Arian.* 77). After carrying out his commission, he brought new accusations against Athanasius at the court of Constantinople. He continued these efforts when Constantius II took possession of the government. He signed the communication addressed to Pope Julius against Athanasius. At the synod of Serdica (343) his letters against Athanasius, Marcellus of Ancyra and Asclepas of Gaza were publicly read (Mansi 3, 60 D; 71 A; Theodoret, *Hist. eccl.* 2, 8, 4). However, it seems that he had died before, because his name does not appear among those of the Arian leaders excommunicated at this synod. The teaching of Theognis was condemned at the Council of Constantinople in 381.

Studies: D. DE BRUYNE, Deux lettres inconnues de Théognis l'évêque arien de Nicée: ZNW 27 (1928) 106-110. — W. ENSSLIN, Theognis: PWK II 5 (1934) 1984-1985.

ASTERIUS THE SOPHIST

Asterius the Sophist owes his name to the profession which he had practised before he became a Christian. He had been a rhetorician or philosopher. He was a disciple of Lucian of Antioch but apostatized in the persecution of Maximinus, the same in which his teacher died as a martyr. He was perhaps the first Arian writer and Arius himself made use of his works in his rejection of the doctrine of Nicaea, as Athanasius testifies, calling him 'the sacrificer' on account of his apostasy and 'the advocate' of the Arian heresy. Thus Athanasius writes:

> But let us suppose that the other creatures could not endure to be wrought by the absolute Hand of the Unoriginate, and therefore the Son alone was brought into being by the Father alone, and other things by the Son as an underworker and assistant, for this is what Asterius the sacrificer has written, and Arius has transcribed and bequeathed to his own friends, and from that time they use this form

of words, broken reed as it is, being ignorant, the bewildered men, how brittle it is. For if it was impossible for things originate to bear the hand of God, and you hold the Son to be one of their number, how was he too equal to this formation by God alone? And if a mediator became necessary that things originate might come to be, and you hold the Son to be originated, then must there have been some medium before Him, for His creation; and that mediator himself again being a creature, it follows that he too needed another mediator for his own constitution. And though we were to devise another, we must first devise his mediator, so that we shall never come to an end (*De decret.* 8 LNPF).

More information about Asterius, his origin, his associations, his ambitions and his doings is supplied in Athanasius, *De synodis* 18:

And one Asterius from Cappadocia, a many-headed Sophist, one of the fellows of Eusebius, whom they could not advance into the clergy, as having done sacrifice in the former persecution in the time of Constantius' grandfather, writes, with the countenance of Eusebius and his fellows, a small treatise, which was on a par with the crime of his sacrifice, yet answered their wishes; for in it, after comparing, or rather preferring, the locust and the caterpillar to Christ, and saying that Wisdom in God was other than Christ, and was the Framer as well of Christ as of the world, he went round the Churches in Syria and elsewhere, with introductions from Eusebius and his fellows, that as he once made trial of denying, so now he might boldly oppose the truth. The bold man intruded himself into forbidden places, and seating himself in the place of the clergy, he used to read publicly this treatise of his, in spite of the general indignation (LNPF).

HIS WRITINGS

1. *The Syntagmation*

The small treatise mentioned by Athanasius in which Asterius defended the principle that there could not be two ἀγένητα is the *Syntagmation* written after the Council of Nicaea. Except for the fragments which Athanasius (*Or. c. Arian.* 1, 30-34; 2, 37; 3, 2, 60; *De decr.* 8, 28-31; *De syn.* 18 - 20,47) and Marcellus of Ancyra (Eusebius, *C. Marcellum* 1, 4) have preserved, the entire work is lost. Regarding its sources, Marcellus informs us that Asterius made use of a great number of passages taken from episcopal encyclicals dealing with the Arian case. He mentions especially the letter of Eusebius of Nicomedia to Paulinus of Tyre (cf. above, p. 191) as one of them. Among the Athanasian excerpts the following are typical:

Although His eternal Power and Wisdom, which truth argues to be Unbegun and Ingenerate, would appear certainly to be one and the same, yet many are those powers which are one by one created by Him, of which Christ is the First-born and Only-begotten. All however equally depend upon their Possessor, and all his powers are rightly called His, Who created and uses them; for instance, the Prophet says that the locust, which became a divine punishment of human sin, was called by God Himself, not only a power of God, but a great power (Joel 2, 25). And the blessed David too in several of the Psalms invites, not Angels alone, but Powers also to praise God. And he invites them all to the hymn, he presents before us their multitude, and is not unwilling to call them ministers of God, and teaches them to do His will (*De syn.* 18 LNPF).

The Son is one among others; for He is first of things originate, and one among intellectual natures; and as in things visible the sun is one among phenomena, and it shines upon the whole world according to the command of its Maker, so the Son, being one of the intellectual natures, also enlightens and shines upon all that are in the intellectual world (*De syn.* 19).

Although Athanasius links him with Eusebius of Nicomedia, it is interesting to note Marcellus' remark that he toned down the bolder phrases of his letter to Paulinus. This agrees with Epiphanius (*Haer.* 76, 3), who declares Asterius to be the leader of those Arians who observed a more cautious attitude. It may also explain why Philostorgius the Arian (*Hist. eccl.* 2, 14, 15) accuses Asterius of having falsified the true Arian doctrine of Lucian of Antioch.

2. *Refutation of Marcellus*

Socrates (*Hist. eccl.* 1, 36) reports that Marcellus of Ancyra, wishing to counteract Asterius' influence, 'in his overanxiety to confute him, fell into the diametrically opposite error; for he dared to say, as the Samosatene had done, that Christ was a mere man'. St. Jerome (*De vir. ill.* 86) mentions that Asterius answered Marcellus and charged him with Sabellianism. This work seems to be lost.

3. *Commentaries and Homilies on the Psalms*

The *Syntagmation* and the *Refutation of Marcellus* were not the only writings of Asterius. St. Jerome (*De vir. ill.* 94) thought him important enough to be listed in his catalogue of famous men with the following information: 'He wrote during the reign of Constantius commentaries on the Epistle to the Romans, on the Gospels and on the Psalms and also many other works which are diligently read by those of his party'. All of these works were thought to be lost until M. Richard and E. Skard discovered a number of his expositions of the Psalms. The new edition by Richard contains 31 homilies,

29 of them on the Psalms (though the authenticity of some remains doubtful) and 27 fragments of the Commentary on the Psalms, some of them of considerable size. There are nine panegyrics for Easter week. These new texts add an entirely new chapter to the history of the Arian heresy in so far as they shed fresh light not only on the exegesis of the School of Antioch but also on the personality of Asterius and his training as a jurist. They provide more information on his doctrine of the Logos and on other dogmatic questions. He was evidently an excellent orator and preacher.

It seems that he died about 341 because at the synod of Antioch held that year he appears for the last time, as a companion to bishop Dianius of Caesarea in Cappadocia. The Asterius Scythopolita or Scythopolitanus mentioned by Jerome in *Ep.* 112, 20 is nobody else than Asterius the Sophist, especially since he calls him the author of a lengthy commentary on the Psalms. The surname must be supposed an error because Asterius was a Cappadocian.

Editions: M. RICHARD, Commentariorum in Psalmos quae supersunt, accedunt aliquot homiliae anonymae (SO Suppl. 16). Oslo, 1956. Some sermons among those of Asterius of Amasaea and St. John Chrysostom: MG 40, 389-478; 55, 35-39, 539-544, 549-558. Ns. 1, 10, 14, 24, 26 and 27 of Richard's edition are of doubtful authenticity. The most convenient collection of fragments is to be found in: G. BARDY, Recherches sur St. Lucien d'Antioche et son école. Paris, 1936, 316-357. — For the fragments in the letters of Severus of Antioch, see: E. W. BROOKS, The Sixth Book of the Select Letters of Severus of Antioch I, 2. London, 1902, 321-322.

Studies: G. BARDY, Astérius le Sophiste: RHE 22 (1922) 221-272. — M. RICHARD, Les homélies d'Astérius sur les Psaumes IV-VII: RBibl 44 (1935) 548-558; *idem,* Une ancienne collection d'homélies grecques sur les Psaumes I-XV: SO 25 (1947) 54-73; *idem,* Le recueil d'homélies d'Astérius le Sophiste: SO 29 (1951) 24-33 (revision of the preceding article; new manuscripts, especially Athos Laura θ 210); *idem,* Deux homélies inédites du Sophiste Astérius: SO 29 (1952) 93-98 (preliminary edition from Cod. Athos Laura θ 210). — J. C. DIDIER, Le pédobaptisme au IVe siècle. Documents nouveaux: MSR 6 (1949) 233-246. — E. SKARD, Asterios von Amaseia und Asterios der Sophist: SO 20 (1940) 86-132 (*Homilies on the Psalms*); *idem,* Eine Bemerkung über spätrömisches Strafrecht in einer Homilie des 'Sophisten' Asterios: SO 25 (1947) 80-82. Cf. L. WENGER, Strafweise Verbrennung des Mantels statt des Mannes: AAWW 84 (1947) 293-299. — E. SKARD, Bemerkungen zu den Asterios-Texten: SO 27 (1949) 54-69; *idem,* Nochmals strafweise Verbrennung des Mantels: SO 31 (1955) 138-140.

MARCELLUS OF ANCYRA

Marcellus, bishop of Ancyra in Galatia, was at Nicaea (325) with St. Athanasius one of the staunch defenders of the orthodox faith against the Arians. He continued his relentless war on them even after the Council and published in 335, when he was already advanced in years, a comprehensive treatise against the heretical Sophist Asterius of Cappadocia (cf. above, p. 194). Therein he not only refuted the latter's errors but also attacked the two Eusebii. The reaction of the Eusebian party was instantaneous and virulent. Eusebius of Caesarea wrote his *Contra Marcellum* and *De ecclesiastica theologia*, wherein he not only defends himself but goes on to accuse Marcellus of Sabellianism (cf. below, p. 341). Marcellus' treatise was referred to Constantine with an accusatory letter. As a result a synod was convened at Constantinople in 336 where the book was condemned and Marcellus himself was deposed and exiled. He attended with Athanasius the synod convoked by Pope Julius in Rome in the fall of 340. Those of its members who were present at the Council of Nicaea testified how strongly the bishop of Ancyra had there opposed the Arians. Since he had been accused of heresy, Pope Julius requested of him an account of his faith in writing. This written *professio fidei* was judged to be orthodox and the synod refused to sanction his deposition. The Council of Serdica (343/344) also cleared him of the same charge, although he had been accused of 'blending the falsehood of Sabellius, the malice of Paul of Samosata and the blasphemies of Montanus into a confused system' (*Epist. synod. Sardic. Orient.* 2, CSEL 65, 50). The encyclical of the assembly states:

> The book of our fellow-minister Marcellus was also read, by which the fraud of Eusebius and his fellows was plainly discovered. For what Marcellus had advanced by way of enquiry, they falsely represented as his professed opinion; but when the subsequent parts of the book were read and the parts preceding the queries themselves, his faith was found to be correct. He had never pretended, as they positively affirmed, that the Word of God had His beginnings from Holy Mary, nor that His kingdom had an end; on the contrary he had written that His kingdom was both without beginning and without end (*op. cit.* 6, CSEL 65, 117-118).

Thereupon Marcellus was restored to his see. The historians Socrates (*Hist. eccl.* 2, 24) and Sozomen (*Hist. eccl.* 3, 23-24) relate that his reinstatement caused considerable disturbance at Ancyra. A few years later, in 347, he was again deposed and exiled, this time by the Emperor Constantius. He died about 374. Canon I of the Second Ecumenical Council at Constantinople in 381 condemned him as a heretic.

WRITINGS AND DOCTRINE

1. The book which made him famous but caused all his troubles was his treatise against Asterius, the first and undoubtedly the most important of his works. Unfortunately, we do not even know its

title. Hilarius refers to it as the 'liber, quem de subiectione Domini Christi ediderat' (*Ex. op. hist. fragm.* 2, 22), scarcely an indication of its name but rather a casual reference to one of its objectionable doctrines. Nor do we know anything of its outline and divisions. Under the circumstances it is important that not less than 127 passages are quoted by Eusebius of Caesarea in his *Contra Marcellum* and *De ecclesiastica theologia*. Another excerpt is found in Epiphanius as part of the refutation which Acacius of Caesarea, Eusebius' successor, composed against Marcellus. The first collection of the fragments of Marcellus by Rettberg was completed by Klostermann in his edition of the works of Eusebius.

These citations enable the reader to grasp the gist of Marcellus' treatise. Despite the fact that Eusebius was undoubtedly a biased witness, it can hardly be denied that the bishop of Ancyra laid himself open to the accusation of Sabellianism. The Council of Serdica was correct in its statement that Marcellus never had asserted that the Word of God had a beginning. Nevertheless, he seemed to have held that the Word became Son only with the Incarnation. Generally speaking he is more reactionary than revolutionary. In his attempt to prove the Arian heresy no more than a poorly veiled polytheism, he himself teaches a monotheism which knows only an economical trinity, not identical with, but closely related to the concept of the rationalist or dynamic Monarchians of former times. It is this tendency which leads him to the heretical doctrine that before the creation of the world the Logos was only in God and that at the end he will be only in God. The Logos therefore is absolutely consubstantial with the Father *(ὁμοούσιος τῷ πατρί)* but He is not generated and not a person. Only the God-man Christ is a person, He alone is called and is in reality Son of God. There was no Son of God before the Incarnation. God was simply *Monas*.

Editions: C. H. G. RETTBERG, Marcelliana. Göttingen, 1794. New crit. ed.: E. KLOSTERMANN, GCS Eusebius' Werke, vol. 4. Berlin, 1906, 183-214.

Translation: German: W. GERICKE, Marcell v. Ancyra. Halle, 1940, 192-244.

Studies: T. ZAHN, Marcellus von Ancyra. Ein Beitrag zur Geschichte der Theologie. Gotha, 1867. — F. LOOFS, Die Trinitätslehre Marcells von Ancyra und ihr Verhältnis zur älteren Tradition: SAB (1902) 764-781. — D. CHENU, Marcel d'Ancyre: DTC 9 (1927) 1993-1998. — W. GERICKE, Marcell von Ancyra, der Logos-Christologe und Biblizist: sein Verhältnis zur antiochenischen Theologie und zum Neuen Testament. Halle, 1940. — G. W. H. LAMPE, Exegesis of some Biblical Texts by Marcellus of Ancyra and Pseudo-Chrysostom's Homily on Ps. 96: JThSt 49 (1948) 169-175. — J. M. FONDEVILLA, Ideas trinitarias y cristologicas de Marcelo de Ancyra. Diss. Pont. Univ. Greg. Madrid, 1953 (extract); *idem*, Ideas cristologicas de Marcelo de Ancyra: EE 27 (1953) 20-64. — F. SCHEIDWEILER, Marcell von Ancyra: ZNW 46 (1955) 202-214 (textual crit. and interpretation, corrections of Gericke's translat.).

2. The *profession of faith* which Marcellus wrote down at the request of Pope Julius is extant. Epiphanius preserves the entire text as an introduction to his chapter on the Marcellians, *Haer.* 72, 2-3. There is no doubt that it could be interpreted as in agreement with the orthodox doctrine.

Edition: E. KLOSTERMANN, op. cit. 214-215.

Studies: C. P. CASPARI, Ungedruckte Quellen zur Geschichte des Taufsymbols und der Glaubensregel, vol. 3. Christiania, 1875, 28-161: Über den griechischen Text des altrömischen Symbols in dem Briefe des Marcellus von Ancyra an den römischen Bischof Julius. — J. N. D. KELLY, Early Christian Creeds. London, 1950, 102-104, 108-111, 273-277.

3. Marcellus is the author of a small tract *De sancta ecclesia* as M. Richard has sufficiently proved. It is extant in two manuscripts of the 13th and 14th century, which attribute it to Anthimus, bishop of Nicomedia in Bithynia, who died as a martyr about 302. G. Mercati who discovered its text in *Cod. Ambros.* H 257 *inf.* saec. XIII and *Cod. Scorial.* Y II, 7 saec. XIV, made an edition of it in 1901. The content shows that Anthimus cannot be its author. The treatise deals with the marks by which the true Church can be recognized: oneness, catholicity and apostolicity. The heretical sects are in comparison of later origin and of limited expansion, and all are derived from pagan philosophy, from the doctrines of Hermes Trismegistos, Plato and Aristotle. A great number of heretical groups are named, among them the Arians, represented by Asterius the Sophist and Eusebius of Caesarea. This excludes the possibility of Anthimus' authorship for chronological reasons. Many similarities existing between Marcellus' first work against Asterius and this treatise lead to the conclusion that he must be its author.

Edition: G. MERCATI, Note di letteratura biblica e cristiana antica (ST 5). Rome, 1901, 87-98: Anthimi Nicomediensis episcopi et martyris de sancta ecclesia.

Studies: G. MERCATI, Alcune note di letteratura patristica: RIL ser. 2, 31 (1898) 1033-1036. — A. HARNACK, Geschichte der altchristlichen Literatur bis Eusebius 2, 2. Leipzig, 1904, 158-160. — M. RICHARD, Un opuscule méconnu de Marcel évêque d'Ancyre: MSR 6 (1949) 5-28.

4. The above mentioned writings are not the only ones Marcellus composed. St. Jerome remarks (*De vir. ill.* 86) that he wrote many volumes, especially against the Arians, in which he defended himself against their accusations and referred to his friendship with the bishops of Rome and Alexandria as a proof of his orthodoxy. None of these later works has survived. F. Scheidweiler thinks that Marcellus is the author of the *Sermo maior de fide* and the *Expositio fidei* wrongly attributed to St. Athanasius (cf. above, p. 30).

Studies: F. SCHEIDWEILER, Wer ist der Verfasser des sogenannten Sermo maior de fide?: BZ 47 (1954) 333-357; *idem, Καίπερ,* nebst einem Exkurs zum Hebräerbrief: Hermes 83 (1955) 220-230.

BASIL OF ANCYRA

The same synod at Constantinople, that deposed and exiled Marcellus in 336, appointed as his successor a certain Basil, who had been a physician, 'a man of great eloquence and learning' (Sozomen, *Hist. eccl.* 2, 33). His position in the dogmatic controversies of his times is evident from what St. Athanasius says about him in *De synodis* 41:

> Those who deny the Council [of Nicaea] altogether, are sufficiently exposed by these brief remarks. Those, however, who accept everything else that was defined at Nicaea, and doubt only about the 'consubstantial' (ὁμοούσιος), must not be treated as enemies; nor do we here attack them as Ariomaniacs, nor as opponents of the Fathers, but we discuss the matter with them as brothers with brothers, who mean what we mean and dispute only about the word. For, confessing that the Son is from the essence of the Father, and not from other subsistence, and that He is not a creature nor work, but His genuine and natural offspring, and that He is eternally with the Father as being His Word and Wisdom, they are not far from accepting even the phrase 'consubstantial'. Now such is Basil who wrote from Ancyra concerning the faith.

The last sentence refers to a letter by Basil, sent to all the bishops after a synod at Ancyra in 358, over which he presided and which rejected the *homoousios*, anathematizing every one who did not faithfully confess the essential likeness of the Son to the Father and in particular all those who so misinterpreted the sayings of Jesus in the Gospel as to conceive him to be 'unlike' (ἀνόμοιος) the Father. As the now established leader of the Semi-Arians or Homoiousians, he, together with Eustathius of Sebaste and Eleusius of Cyzicus, went to the imperial court at Sirmium in the summer of the same year and interceded successfully for the acceptance of the so-called third Sirmian formula, the Creed of the Homoiousians. The emperor entrusted Basil with the preparations for a general council which was supposed to make peace among the different Arian parties. While Basil was discussing the place to be chosen for this assembly with the bishops of the Orient, the strict Arians or Anomoeans gained the support of the emperor for their plan to summon two synods — one for the Westerns at Ariminum and another for the Easterns at Seleucia. A second conference was held at Sirmium under the presidency of Constantius to draw up a

Creed to be accepted by these two synods. The result was that on May 22, 359, the third Sirmian formula was superseded by the fourth, which rejected the word *ousia* as not contained in the Scriptures and not understood by the people and launched the watchword 'like in all respects' *(ὅμοιος κατὰ πάντα)* as the rallying-point of all moderates. Even Basil signed this Creed by which it was hoped to restore harmony to the Church. However, he felt it necessary to draw up a statement that the formula 'like in all respects' really embraces not only the will, but everything, the hypostasis as well as the essence. He proves at length that though the term *ousia* is not contained in either the Old or the New Testament, yet its sense can be found everywhere. It is an important manifesto of Homoiousian theology which reproduces essentially the teaching of St. Athanasius and has been preserved by Epiphanius, *Haer.* 73,12-22 (MG 42,425-444).

The Western synod met at Ariminum but did not accept the dated Creed and the watchword 'like in all things'. The κατὰ πάντα was dropped and a bare ὅμοιος retained. The Eastern synod at Seleucia ended in a split. Basil of Ancyra, Eustathius of Sebaste and Eleusius of Cyzicus were sent to the emperor at Constantinople who succeeded in securing their signature for the definition of Ariminum on December 31, 359. Thus the victory of Arianism in the Homoian form was complete. It was of the proceedings of this year that Jerome said (*Dial. adv. Lucif.* 19): 'The whole world groaned and wondered to find itself Arian'.

Thus the leader of the Homoiousians had fallen and Acacius of Caesarea, the Homoian, was now the dominating spirit. A synod held at Constantinople in 360 under his presidency deposed and exiled his enemies, among them Basil of Ancyra, Eustathius and Eleusius. Basil was forced to go to Illyria, where he evidently died in exile about 364, not without having revoked his consent to the definition of Ariminum (Philost., *Hist. eccl.* 5, 1).

Studies: J. Schladebach, Basilius von Ancyra. Eine historisch-philosophische Studie. Diss. Leipzig, 1898. — J. Gummerus, Die homöusianische Partei bis zum Tode des Konstantius. Leipzig, 1900, 121f. — R. Janin, Basile d'Ancyre: DHG 6 (1932) 1104-1107. — E. Schwartz, Zur Kirchengeschichte des vierten Jahrhunderts: ZNW 34 (1935) 149-158. — O. Perler, Basileios von Ankyra: LThK² 2 (1958) 31-32.

HIS WRITINGS

The above-mentioned treatise on the trinitarian doctrine preserved by Epiphanius, which Basil composed together with George of Laodicea, was not the only work from his pen. St. Jerome (*De vir. ill.* 89) testifies that he published in addition *Against Marcellus,* in which he refuted his predecessor, besides a book *On Virginity* and a number of other tracts.

For a long time all of these writings were believed to have been lost, until F. Cavallera in 1905 identified Basil's treatise *On Virginity* with a tract always previously listed among the spurious works of Basil the Great *On the True Purity of Virgins (Περὶ τῆς ἐν παρθενίᾳ ἀληθοῦς ἀφθορίας)*. The title indicates the author's purpose in this long treatise: he intends to show the virtues which a virgin must have, if her life is to lead her to sanctity and heavenly bliss. In ch. 65 he finds it necessary to justify himself for going too much into physiological details. Such an apology would very well fit the bishop of Ancyra, who had been a physician before entering the priesthood. His investigation of the relation between food and chastity (7-12, MG 30, 681-693) is very interesting. His discussion of trinitarian questions reveals Homoiousian influence and has much in common with the synodical letter which Basil composed after the Synod of Ancyra in 358. Thus Cavallera's identification is highly probable.

Editions: MG 30, 669-809. — A. VAILLANT, De virginitate de saint Basile. Texte vieux slave. Paris, 1943.

Studies: X. LE BACHELET, Basile d'Ancyre: DTC 2 (1905) 461-463. — F. CAVALLERA, Le 'De virginitate' de Basile d'Ancyre: RHE 6 (1905) 5-14. — J. JANINI CUESTA, Dieta y virginidad: Misc. Comillas 14 (1950) 187-197 (relation between Basil of Ancyra and Gregory of Nyssa). — F. CAVALLERA, Basile d'Ancyre: DSp 1 (1937) 1283.

THE CAPPADOCIAN FATHERS

The life and times of Marcellus and Basil of Ancyra show to what extent the Church in Asia Minor suffered from the Arian controversies in the first half of the fourth century. It was not before the middle of that century that the province of Cappadocia produced three great theologians, Basil of Caesarea, his friend Gregory of Nazianzus and his brother Gregory of Nyssa whom we call 'the three great Cappadocians'. In this splendid triad the theological work of Athanasius found its continuation and reached its climax. When they died, the overthrow of Arianism and the glorious victory of the faith of Nicaea was in sight. Their contribution to the progress of theology, to the solution of the problem 'Hellenism and Christianity', to the restoration of peace and to the expansion of monasticism is such, that it has had a lasting influence on the Church universal. Though united by common interests of mind and spirit as well as by the bonds of a close and life-long friendship, each one of them represents a different type of personality. Thus Basil is known as the man of action, Gregory of Nazianzus as the master of oratory and Gregory of Nyssa as the thinker.

Studies: H. WEISS, Die grossen Kappadozier Basilius, Gregor von Nazianz und Gregor von Nyssa als Exegeten. Braunsberg, 1872; *idem*, Die Erziehungslehre der drei Kappadozier. Freiburg i.B., 1903. — K. UNTERSTEIN, Die natürliche Gotteserkenntnis nach der Lehre der kappadozischen Kirchenväter Basilius, Gregor von Nazianz und Gregor von Nyssa. Straubing, 1902/1903 (2 Progr.). — K. HOLL, Amphilochius von Ikonium in seinem Verhältnis zu den grossen Kappadoziern. Tübingen, 1904. — C. GRONAU, De Basilio, Gregorio Naz., Nyssenoque Platonis imitatoribus. Diss. Göttingen, 1908. — J. MAIER, Die Eucharistielehre der drei grossen Kappadozier. Diss. Breslau, 1915. — E. IVANKA, Hellenisches und Christliches im frühbyzantinischen Geistesleben. Vienna, 1948, 28-67. — G. SOELL, Die Mariologie der Kappadozier im Lichte der Dogmengeschichte: ThQ 131 (1951) 163-188, 288-319, 426-457. — J. F. CALLAHAN, Greek Philosophy and the Cappadocian Cosmology: DOP 12 (1958) 29-57. — B. OTIS, Cappadocian Thought as a Coherent System: DOP 12 (1958) 95-124.

BASIL THE GREAT

There is only one among the three Cappadocian Fathers to whom the cognomen *Great* has been attributed: Basil. His outstanding qualifications as an ecclesiastical statesman and organizer, as a great exponent of Christian doctrine and as a second Athanasius in the defense of orthodoxy, as the Father of oriental monasticism and reformer of the liturgy, warrant the conferring of such a title. Born at Caesarea in Cappadocia about 330 in a family no less renowned for its Christian spirit than for its nobility and wealth, he received his elementary training from his father Basil, a famous rhetorician at Neocaesarea in Pontus, who was a son of St. Macrina the Elder, a pupil of St. Gregory the Wonderworker. His mother Emmelia, the daughter of a martyr, gave birth to ten children, three of whom became bishops: St. Basil, St. Gregory of Nyssa and St. Peter of Sebaste, while her oldest daughter is well known as St. Macrina the Younger, a model of the ascetic life. The talented youth attended for his higher education the schools of rhetoric at his native Caesarea, at Constantinople, and finally, after 351, at Athens. In this last city he met Gregory of Nazianzus with whom he entered upon a life-long friendship. He returned to his native city about 356 and began his career as a rhetorician, which he renounced soon, to embrace a life entirely devoted to God. He describes this spiritual awakening in his *Ep.* 223, 2:

I had wasted much time on follies and spent nearly all my youth in vain labors, and devotion to the teachings of a wisdom that God had made foolish (1 Cor. 1, 20). Suddenly I awoke as out of a deep sleep. I beheld the wonderful light of the Gospel truth, and I recognized the nothingness of the wisdom of the princes of this world that was come to naught (1 Cor. 2, 6). I shed a flood of tears over my wretched life, and I prayed for a guide who might form in me the principles of piety.

His first step was to receive the sacrament of baptism, the next to journey through Egypt, Palestine, Syria and Mesopotamia, in order to meet the most famous ascetics. Their lives inspired him:

> I admired their continence in living, and their endurance in toil. I was amazed at their persistency in prayer, and at their triumphing over sleep. Subdued by no natural necessity, ever keeping their soul's purpose high and free in hunger and thirst, in cold and nakedness, they never yielded to the body; they were never willing to waste attention on it. Always, as though living in a flesh that was not theirs, they showed in very deed what it is to sojourn for a while in this life, and what to have one's citizenship and home in heaven. All this moved my admiration. I called these men's lives blessed, in that they did indeed show that 'they bear about in their body the dying of Jesus'. And I prayed that I too, as far as in me lay, might imitate them (LNPF).

On his return he divided his fortune among the poor and went into solitude not far from Neocaesarea on the Iris. He was soon surrounded by companions who shared the cenobitic life with him. When Gregory of Nazianzus paid a visit to him in 358, they prepared together the *Philocalia*, an anthology of Origen's works, and the two *Rules* which had a decisive influence in the expansion of the cloistered life in common and earned Basil the name of Lawgiver of Greek monasticism. Even in this period he proved himself the man of action and in a short time founded a number of monasteries. It is not surprising that Eusebius, the metropolitan of Caesarea, was eager to make use of his great talents for his diocese. About 364 he persuaded Basil to become a priest. Basil accepted and 'was all in all to him, a good counsellor, a skilful helper, an expounder of the Scriptures, an interpreter of his duties, the staff of his old age, the prop of his faith, more trustworthy than all his clerics, more experienced than any layman', as Gregory of Nazianzus (*Orat.* 43, 33) reports. After Eusebius died in 370, he became his successor as bishop of Caesarea, metropolitan of Cappadocia and exarch of the civil diocese of Pontus. As such he soon won the love of his people. He established hospitals for the sick and victims of contagious diseases, homes for the poor and hospices for travellers and strangers, so that Gregory of Nazianzus speaks of an entire 'new city'. In his fight against state-supported Arianism he combined ceaseless activity with wisdom and prudence. He knew no fear or intimidation in his dealings with the Emperor Valens and his prefects. He appeared as a real Prince of the Church in his conversation with the Prefect Modestus, who sent by the emperor, threatened him with confiscation and exile, in order to obtain from him a signed statement of his adherence to the Arian cause. Gregory of Nazianzus has recorded his reply (*Orat.* 43, 49):

> The confiscation of goods does not harm one who has nothing, unless perchance, for these tortures and sufferings you need a cloak and a few books which are my whole life. Exile I do not know, for I am bound to no one place: not only this my own land in which I live, but the whole world into which I may be banished, I hold as my own, for the whole world is of God, whose dweller and sojourner I am. These tortures, what harm could they do me, not having a body, except so to speak, the first blow. Of these things only are you lord. But death would be an act of kindness for it will bring me nearer to God, for Whom I live and for Whom I have been created and to Whom in the greater part I have died and towards Whom I hasten.

Modestus, astonished at such words, responded: 'No one until now has spoken to me in such a manner and with such liberty of words'. To this Basil replied:

> Perhaps you have never met a bishop before... Where God is endangered and exposed, there all other things are considered as nothing. Him alone do we look to. Fire, swords, beasts and the instruments for tearing the flesh are wished for by us as delights more than horrors. Afflict us with such tortures, threaten, do all that you can now devise, enjoy your power. Also, let the Emperor hear this, that at all events you will not persuade us nor win us over to the impious doctrine [Arianism], though you threaten with cruel deeds (43, 50).

This intrepidity and resoluteness made such an impression on the emperor, that he abandoned the attempt to subdue the bishop and rescinded the decree for his banishment.

Basil's main concern was the unity of the Church. The almost total lack of such unity among the Christians in the East and between the bishops of the East and West caused him to enlist the patronage of Athanasius in his attempt to establish better relations between Rome and the Orient. He even addressed a letter to Pope Damasus in which he described the terrible condition of the Churches in the East and begged him to pay them a visit (*Ep.* 70). He was convinced that orthodoxy could succeed only if there were no dissensions and no waste of strength among the believers. Unfortunately, one obstacle stood out prominently in the way of the desired harmony between East and West, namely, the dispute of

Paulinus and Meletius as to which of the two was the lawful bishop of Antioch. Basil's appeal to Athanasius and to Rome for the healing of this schism was rejected, mainly because the hierarchy of the West was opposed to Meletius whom he favored, and recognized Paulinus. Thus the letters which came back from Rome, affirmed the community of faith, but offered no assistance. Nevertheless, he lived to see at least the dawning of better days, when the Emperor Valens died on August 9, 378, and external conditions permitted the restoration of peace. Basil himself passed away on January 1, 379, not more than fifty years of age. Two years later the so-called Second Ecumenical Council met at Constantinople, by which the Emperor Theodosius the Great brought order and unity to the Church, opening the doors to all who adhered to the faith of Nicaea. There is no doubt that Basil had laid the foundations for this great moment in the history of Christianity.

Studies: E. VENABLES, Basil of Caesarea: DCB 1 (1900) 282-297. — P. ALLARD, Saint Basile. 4th ed. Paris, 1903. — P. ALLARD and J. BESSE, Basile de Césarée: DTC 2 (1905) 441-459. — J. SCHÄFER, Basilius' des Grossen Beziehungen zum Abendlande. Münster, 1909. — J. PARGOIRE, Basile de Césarée et Basiliens: DAL 2 (1910) 501-510. — J. WITTIG, Die Friedenspolitik des Papstes Damasus I. und der Ausgang der arianischen Streitig-keiten (KGA 10). Breslau, 1912; *idem*, Leben, Lebensweisheit und Lebenskunde des hl. Metropoliten Basilius des Grossen von Caesarea: Ehrengabe Joh. Georg Herzog v. Sachsen ed. by F. Fessler. Freiburg i.B., 1920, 617-638. — V. GRUMEL, Saint Basile et le siège apostolique: EO 21 (1922) 280-292. — F. SCHEMMEL, Basilius und die Schule von Caesarea: PhW 42 (1922) 620-624. — J. RIVIÈRE, Saint Basile, évêque de Césarée. Paris, 1925. — F. ZUCCHETTI, Eustathius von Sebaste und Basilius von Caesarea: RR 2 (1926) 17-22. — M. CROVINI, I malintesi di un famoso episodio storico del secolo IV. S. Basilio e Papa Damaso: SC 6 (1928) 321-344. — R. JANIN, Saint Basile, archevêque de Césarée et docteur de l'Église. Paris, 1929. — G. PESENTI, Un rifacimento greco-volgare della vita di S. Basilio scritta da Gregorio Asceta: Festgabe Heïsenberg, ed. by F. Dölger. Leipzig, 1929, 316-322. — G. BARDY, Basile de Césarée: DHG 6 (1932) 1111-1126. — K. V. ZETTERSTEEN, Eine Homilie des Amphilochius von Ikonium über Basilius von Caesarea: OC 9 (1934) 67-98. — E. SCHWARTZ, Zur Kirchengeschichte des vierten Jahrhunderts: ZNW 34 (1935) 158-213 (Melet. schism). — J. DE GHELLINCK, Un cas de conscience dans la carrière de S. Basile: Miscellanea Vermeersch I (Analecta Gregor. 9/10). Rome, 1935, 217-237. — H. ENGBERDING, Die Verehrung des hl. Basilius des Grossen in der byzantinischen Liturgie: Der christliche Osten in Vergangenheit und Gegenwart 2 (1937) 16-22. — M. M. FOX, The Life and Times of St. Pasil the Great as Revealed in his Works. Washington, 1939. — S. GIET, Sasimes. Une méprise de saint Basile. Paris, 1941; *idem*, Les idées et l'action sociales de saint Basile le Grand. Paris, 1941. — M. J. LUBATSCHIWSKYJ, Des hl. Basilius' liturgischer Kampf gegen den Arianismus: ZkTh 66 (1942) 20-38. — M. RICHARD, Saint Basile et la mission du diacre Sabinus: AB 67 (1949) 178-202. — G. BARDY, Basilius von Caesarea: RACh 1 (1950) 1261-1265. — L. VISCHER, Basilius der Grosse. Diss. Basel, 1953. — H. v. CAMPEN-HAUSEN, Griechische Kirchenväter. Stuttgart, 1955, 86-100. — S. GIET, Saint Basile et le concile de Constantinople de 360: JThSt N.S. 6 (1955) 94-99. — J. M. RONNAT, Basile le Grand. Paris, 1955. — O. ROUSSEAU, La rencontre de saint Ephrem et de saint Basile: L'Orient Syrien 2 (1957) 261-284. — K. RAHNER, Basileios der Grosse: LThK² 2 (1958) 33-35. — J. GRIBOMONT, Eustathe le Philosophe et les voyages du jeune Basile de Césarée: RHE 54 (1959) 115-124.

I. HIS WRITINGS

It would be incorrect to see in Basil only the ecclesiastical administrator and organizer. Among all his time-consuming tasks he remains the great theologian. In fact, in the liturgical books of the Greek Church he ranks as the first of 'the great ecumenical teachers'. He might with some reservations be called 'a Roman among the Hellenes', since even his writings reveal a man of action and a leaning to the practical and ethical aspects of the Christian message, while the rest of the Greek Church Fathers show a decided preference for the metaphysical side of the gospel.

Nevertheless, Gregory of Nazianzus testifies (*Orat.* 43, 66) that his writings were highly appreciated by his contemporaries for their content as well as for their form. The educated and the unlearned, Christians and pagans read them. He does not hesitate to praise their influence on his own thinking, life and aspirations and calls him 'the master of style' (*Ep.* 51). Photius (*Bibl. cod.* 141) is even more enthusiastic about them:

> He [Basil] is admirable in all his writings. More than any one else he knows how to use a style that is pure, distinct, suitable, and in general, forensic and panegyrical; in arrangement and purity of sentiment he is second to none. He is fond of persuasiveness and sweetness and brilliancy, his words flow like a stream gushing forth spontaneously from a spring. He employs probability to such an extent, that if any one were to take his discourses as a model of forensic language, and practise himself in them, provided he had some acquaintance with the rules connected with it, I do not think he would need to consult any other author, not even Plato nor Demosthenes, whom the ancients recommend those to study who desire to become masters of the forensic and panegyrical style (SPCK).

His writings comprise dogmatic, ascetic, pedagogic and liturgical treatises besides a great number of sermons and letters. Fortunately, his literary remains suffered no great loss during the centuries. His name was a protection against oblivion, and such was his reputation that many tracts, homilies and letters composed by others were attributed to him. A critical edition of his complete works is badly needed. E. Amand de Mendieta's comprehensive history of the hitherto existing editions and J. Gribomont's and Stig Y. Rudberg's recent studies of the manuscript tradition represent very valuable preliminary contributions to such a task.

Editions: J. GARNIER and P. MARAN, 3 vols. Paris, 1721/1730, repr. MG 29-32. Cf. E. AMAND, Essai d'une histoire critique des éditions générales grecques et gréco-latines de S. Basile de Césarée: RB 52 (1940) 141-161, 53 (1941) 119-151, 54 (1942) 124-144, 56 (1944/45) 126-173. — G. MERCATI, Opere minori 4 (ST 79). Vatican City, 1937, 372-76 (Cod. Vaticanus Gr. 428); *idem*, Nota sul Codex Hauniensis 1343: Classica et

Mediaevalia 17 (1956) 109-118 (Cod. Vat. Barb. Gr. 462). — S. Y. Rudberg, Codex Upsaliensis Graecus 5: Eranos 50 (1952) 60-70; *idem*, Études sur la tradition manuscrite de saint Basile. Upsala, 1953; *idem*, Indications stichométriques contenues dans quelques mss. de Basile: Eranos 52 (1954) 191-194. — J. Gribomont, Études suédoises et reclassement de la tradition manuscrite de saint Basile: Mus 67 (1954) 51-69; *idem*, Études sur l'histoire du texte de saint Basile: Scriptorium 8 (1954) 298-304. — E. Amand, La tradition manuscrite des œuvres de saint Basile: RHE 49 (1954) 507-521.

For the Old *Latin versions*, see: B. Altaner, Beiträge zur Geschichte der altlateinischen Übersetzungen von Väterschriften: HJ 61 (1941) 208-212 (translation of Rufinus). — A. Siegmund, Die Überlieferung der griechischen christlichen Literatur in der lateinischen Kirche. Munich-Pasing, 1949, 51-55. For the Armenian manuscripts in the Library of the Mechitarists at San Lazzaro, cf. I. W. Driessen, Les recueils manuscrits arméniens de saint Basile: Mus 66 (1953) 65-95.

Translations: English: B. Jackson, LNPF series 2, vol. 8 (1895). — *German:* Sämtliche Schriften des hl. Basilius des Grossen (Sämtliche Werke der Kirchenväter 19-26). Kempten, 1838-1842. — V. Gröne, BKV 3 vols. Kempten, 1875-1881. — A. Stegmann, BKV² 46. 47. Kempten, 1925. — *French:* B. Pruche, SCH 17 (1945); S. Giet, SCH 26 (1949). Other translations with individual works.

Studies: T. L. Shean, The Influence of Plato on St. Basil the Great. Diss. Baltimore, 1906. — C. Gronau, De Basilio, Gregorio Naz., Nyssenoque Platonis imitatoribus. Diss. Göttingen, 1908, 34-43. — J. Trunk, De Basilio Magno sermonis Attici imitatore. Progr. Ehingen, 1911. — G. Lazzati, L'Aristotele perduto e gli scrittori cristiani. Milan, 1933, 34-43. — P. Henry, Les états du texte de Plotin. Paris, 1938, 159-196. — J. Joosen (P. Calasanctius), De beeldspraak bij den heiligen Basilius den Grote met een inleiding over de opvattingen van de griekse en romeinse rhetoren aangaande beeldspraak. Nijmegen, 1941. — E. Amand, A propos d'un livre récent: 'Bildersprache' et critique d'authenticité des œuvres basiliennes: RB 54 (1942) 145-150. — W. M. Roggisch, Platons Spuren bei Basilius dem Grossen. Diss. Bonn, 1949 (typ.). — B. Altaner, Augustinus und Basilius der Grosse. Eine quellenkritische Untersuchung: RB (1950) 17-24. — L. Vischer, Das Problem der Freundschaft bei den Kirchenvätern: ThZ 9 (1953) 173-200. — L. Busch, Basilius und die Medizin: Therapeutische Berichte 29 (Leverkusen, 1957) 111-121.

1. *Dogmatic Writings*

All his extant dogmatic treatises are devoted to the overthrow of Arianism.

1. *Against Eunomius*

The oldest of his dogmatic writings is his *Adversus Eunomium*, in three books, composed between the years 363-365. Its original title Ἀνατρεπτικὸς τοῦ Ἀπολογητικοῦ τοῦ δυσσεβοῦς Εὐνομίου indicates that it represents a refutation of the small treatise *Apologia* which Eunomius, one of the leaders of the extreme form of Arianism, the Anomoians, published about 361. Book I refutes the argument that the essence of God consists in his innascibility *(ἀγεννησία)* and that for this reason the Word cannot be the true Son of God, since He is generated and not more than a creature.

Book II defends the doctrine of Nicaea that the Word is consubstantial (ὁμοούσιος) with the Father. Book III asserts with the same emphasis the consubstantiality of the Holy Spirit. The printed editions add two other books also devoted to the defense of the consubstantiality of the Son and the Holy Spirit, composed, however, not by Basil but, apparently, by Didymus the Blind (cf. above, p. 88).

Edition: MG 29, 497-669.

Studies: M. ALBERTZ, Untersuchungen über die Schriften des Eunomius. Diss. Wittenberg, 1908. — F. DIEKAMP, Literargeschichtliches zur Eunomianischen Kontroverse: BZ 18 (1909) 1-13, 190-194. — E. VANDENBUSSCHE, La part de la dialectique dans la théologie d'Eunomius 'le technologue': RHE 40 (1944/45) 47-72. — J. LEBON, Le Pseudo-Basile (*Adv. Eunom.* IV-V) est bien Didyme d'Alexandrie: Mus 50 (1938) 61-83.

2. *On the Holy Spirit*

The work *On the Holy Spirit* (Περὶ τοῦ ἁγίου πνεύματος), written about 375, treats also of the consubstantiality of the two divine persons, the Son and the Holy Spirit, with the Father. It begins by explaining that Basil had been criticized because he had used in public worship the doxology: Glory be to the Father with the Son together with the Holy Spirit (μετὰ τοῦ υἱοῦ σὺν τῷ πνεύματι τῷ ἁγίῳ) instead of the usual formula: Glory be to the Father through the Son in the Holy Spirit (διὰ τοῦ υἱοῦ ἐν τῷ ἁγίῳ πνεύματι). The first was regarded as an innovation. Basil justifies the former as no less orthodox than the latter and insists that the Church knows both. Since the Son and the Holy Spirit are of one and the same nature with the Father, equal honor with the Father belongs to both, as Scripture and tradition prove. Therefore the first formula 'with the Son together with the Holy Spirit' is even more appropriate than the second because it establishes the distinction of the divine persons but also bears conspicuous witness to the eternal communion and perpetual conjunction which exists between Them. Thus it refutes Sabellianism as well as Arianism. The treatise, dedicated to Basil's friend Amphilochius, bishop of Iconium, served St. Ambrose as a source for his *De Spiritu Sancto* six years later, so that many of St. Basil's ideas reached the West.

Editions: MG 32, 67-217. Crit. ed.: C. F. H. JOHNSTON, The Book of St. Basil the Great On the Holy Spirit. Oxford, 1892. — New crit. ed.: B. PRUCHE, Basile de Césarée, Traité du Saint-Esprit. Texte, trad. et notes (SCH 17). Paris, 1947.

Translations: English: B. JACKSON, LNPF ser. 2, vol. 8 (1895) 2-50. — *French:* B. PRUCHE, op. cit.

Studies: T. SCHERMANN, Die Gottheit des Heiligen Geistes nach den griechischen Vätern des vierten Jahrhunderts. Freiburg i.B., 1901, 89-145; *idem*, Die griechischen Quellen des hl. Ambrosius in ll. III de Spir. S. Munich, 1902, 59-70. — P. HENRY, Les états du texte de Plotin. Paris, 1938, 162-170 (composed about 360). — P. GALTIER, Le Saint-Esprit en nous d'après les Pères grecs. Rome, 1946, 143-165. — B. PRUCHE, L'originalité du traité de saint Basile sur le Saint-Esprit: RSPT 32 (1948) 207-221. — H. DÖRRIES, De Spiritu Sancto. Der Beitrag des Basilius zum Abschluss des trinitarischen Dogmas (AGWG Philolog.-Hist. Kl. 3 Nr. 39). Göttingen, 1956. — W. JAEGER, Basilius und der Abschluss des trinitarischen Dogmas: ThLZ 83 (1958) 255-258.

2. *Ascetic Treatises*

Ascetica is the title of a group of thirteen writings attributed to Basil, that includes a number of unauthentic works besides some which are beyond doubt from his pen. J. Gribomont's study of the text tradition of these *Ascetica* presents for the first time an exact description and classification of their manuscripts and a critical examination of the old Armenian, Georgian, Arabic and Slavic translations.

Edition: MG 31, 620-1428. Cf. J. GRIBOMONT, Histoire du texte des Ascétiques de saint Basile (Bibl. du Mus. 32). Louvain, 1953.

Translations: English: W. K. L. CLARKE, The Ascetic Works of Saint Basil (SPCK). London, 1925. — M. M. WAGNER, FC 9 (1950) 9-430. — *German:* V. GRÖNE, BKV (1877). — *Italian:* E. LEGGIO, L'Ascetica di S. Basilio il Grande. Turin, 1934. — *Polish:* A. SEPTICKIJ. Lwow, 1929.

Studies: G. BARDY, DSp 1, 1273-1283. — P. HUMBERTCLAUDE, La doctrine ascétique de saint Basile de Césarée. Paris, 1932. — O. RING, Das Basiliusproblem: ZKG 51 (1932) 365-383. — J. HAUSHERR, Les grands courants de la spiritualité orientale: OCP 1 (1935) 129-132 (Basil's ascetical doctrine). — E. AMAND, Les Ascétiques de S. Basile de Césarée. Exposé des problèmes d'authenticité. Louvain, 1935. — M. VILLER and K. RAHNER, Aszese und Mystik in der Väterzeit. Freiburg i.B., 1939, 123-133. — F. M. GUÉTET, La tradition manuscrite des Ascétiques attribuées à S. Basile: Mélanges Bénédictins. St. Wandrille, 1947. — E. AMAND, L'ascèse monastique de saint Basile. Essai historique. Paris, 1949 (with a complete list of the authentic ascetical works p. XXVI). — A. DIRKING, Die Bedeutung des Wortes Apathie beim hl. Basilius dem Grossen: ThQ 134 (1954) 202-212. — J. GRIBOMONT, L'exhortation au renoncement attribuée à saint Basile: OCP 21 (1955) 375-398 (MG 31, 625-648 *De renuntiatione saeculi* is not authentic). — T. PICHLER, Das Fasten bei Basilius dem Grossen und im antiken Heidentum. Innsbruck, 1955.

1. *Moralia (Τὰ ἠθικά)*

The *Moralia* is a collection of eighty rules or moral instructions *(regulae)*, each of them supported by quotations from the New Testament. Although the work is addressed to the Christians as such and treats first of the general duties, it is in effect a single forceful admonition in support of the ascetic life. It is the oldest and most important piece of the *Corpus asceticum*. St. Basil composed it during his sojourn at the Iris in Pontus while Gregory of Nazianzus was with him. It represents his first ascetic work which he published with prologue 7 *De judicio Dei* as a preface. Prologue 8 *De fide* was added by himself later on. According to Gribomont only the *Moralia* deserves the title *Rules* (*"Οροι*).

Edition: MG 31, 700-869 *Moralia*; 31, 653-699 *De iudicio Dei* and *De fide*.

Studies: J. GRIBOMONT, Obéissance et Évangile selon saint Basile le Grand: VS Suppl. 21 (1952) 192-215; *idem*, Les Règles Morales de saint Basile et le Nouveau Testament: SP II (TU 64). Berlin, 1957, 416-426.

2. *The Two Monastic Rules*

Of later origin are the two sets of 'rules' which are the result of questions asked by the monks whom St. Basil visited. In their present form, the first, entitled *Detailed Rules (Regulae fusius tractatae)*, discusses under 55 heads the principles of monastic life, the second, the *Short Rules (Regulae brevius tractatae)*, under 313 heads, their application to the day-to-day life of a cloistered community. Both are arranged in the form of question and answer, and based on notes of pastoral conversations between Basil and members of his monasteries, as they were written down by tachygraphs. The oldest redaction of such a collection of questions and answers is no longer extant in its original Greek, but only in Syriac versions and in a Latin translation by Rufinus. The latter seems to have received it from his Egyptian master Evagrius Ponticus (cf. above, p. 170), who took it along on his flight to Constantinople and Palestine. This first form betrays the influence of Eustathius of Sebaste, the older friend of St. Basil, who had spread the monastic life in Asia Minor, before Basil embarked upon it. That explains why the historian Sozomen (*Hist. eccl.* 3, 14) remarks:

> It is said that Eustathius, who governed the Church of Sebaste in Armenia, founded a society of monks in Armenia, Paphlagonia and Pontus, and became the author of a zealous discipline, both as to what meats were to be partaken of or to be avoided, what garments were to be worn, and what customs and exact course of conduct were to be adopted. Some assert that he was the author of the ascetic treatises commonly attributed to Basil of Cappadocia.

Gribomont notices a Messalian atmosphere in some ·of the questions and an intended restraint in the answers, of this earliest redaction or 'Small Asketikon', which goes back to about 358/59. As time went on, Basil freed himself and his monks from the influence of Eustathius and developed his own idea of the monastic life. Only the first 23 of the *Detailed Rules* are based on the 'Small Asketikon', the numbers 24-55 presuppose a more advanced state of Basilian cenobitism.

A second redaction of this collection of questions and answers seems to go back to St. Basil's monastery at Caesarea. Here we find in addition the *Epitimia*, rules of punishments for monks and nuns who violate the monastic code. This second form was later on resumed by Theodore Studites.

A third redaction improved the literary form. Basil himself combined this form with the *Moralia* and sent it to his pupils in Pontus, whom he was unable to visit personally. He called it humbly an 'outline' or 'draft', ὑποτύπωσις ἀσκήσεως.

But none of these redactions was as wide spread as the so-called *Vulgata* prepared by a compiler in the sixth century. He made use of the third which he found in Pontus manuscripts. It begins with prologue 6 which opens a collection consisting of prologues 7, 8, the *Moralia* and the questions. All of these pieces must be regarded as authentic after Gribomont's investigations. This Vulgate edition inserts prologue 5 and 4 between the *Moralia* and the *Detailed Rules*, and prologue 9 between the *Detailed* and the *Shorter Rules*, which are here divided for the first time. There follows at the end the *Epitimia*, which is preceded by a compilation of two of St. Basil's letters, *Ep.* 173 and 22. Prologue 5 and the *Epitimia* might be by one of his pupils. Prologue 6, 7 *(De judicio)* and 8 *(De fide)* are by St. Basil, but prologue 9 is not from his pen but an excerpt of Homily 25 by Pseudo-Macarius.

This 'Great Asketikon' was enlarged during the Middle Ages. Thus the *Constitutiones asceticae*, comprehensive directions and admonitions to monks, and the treatise *De baptismo* were added at the end. The origin of the former remains uncertain. There is a Messalian influence noticible in the first chapter. The tract *On Baptism* in two books treats of the preparation for baptism and Holy Communion and of a life in accord with the baptismal vows. Although the author in the second book alludes to the *Moralia* and the *Regulae* as his own, its authenticity has been contested and it has been attributed to Severian of Gabala. Gribomont's proof for St. Basil's authorship is very convincing.

In the East St. Basil's legislation has survived to the present time, in the principal monastic Rule of the Greek Church. The Basilians are the one great order of the Orient. Even in the West the influence of these constitutions was far-reaching. Translated even before the end of the fourth century by Rufinus of Aquileia, they were known to the later Western monastic lawgivers, St. Cassian and St. Benedict. They are mentioned by Gregory of Tours *(Hist. Franc.* 10, 29) and in the great *Concordia* of St. Benedict of Aniane in the ninth century they appear again *(Concordia reg.* 3, 3).

Editions: MG 31, 889-1052 *Regulae fusius tractatae;* 31, 1080-1305 *Regulae brevius tractatae;* 31, 620-625 *Praevia institutio ascetica;* 31, 1305-1316 *Epitimia;* 31, 1315-1428 *Constitutiones asceticae;* 31, 1513-1628 *De baptismo.* — Latin version of the Rules by Rufinus: ML 103,

487-554. — MG 31, 648-652 *De ascetica disciplina*. Old Latin version: A. WILMART, Le discours de saint Basile sur l'ascèse en latin: RB 27 (1910) 226-233.

Translations: English: W. K. L. CLARKE, op. cit. — *German:* Sämtliche Werke der Kirchenväter aus dem Urtexte in das Deutsche übersetzt, vol. 21, Kempten, 1839, 226-398; vol. 22, Kempten, 1839, 3-40. — V. GRÖNE, Ausgewählte Schriften des hl. Basilius des Grossen, vol. 2 (BKV, 1877) 53-364. — H. URS VON BALTHASAR, Die grossen Ordensregeln. Einsiedeln, 1948, 29-98 (repr. of Gröne's translation of the Rules). — *Italian:* E. LEGGIO, op. cit.

Studies: G. BARDY, DDC 2, 218-224 (Rules). — E. F. MORISON, St. Basil and his Rule. Oxford, 1912. — W. K. L. CLARKE, St. Basil the Great. A Study in Monasticism. Cambridge, 1913. — M. ROTHENHÄUSLER, Der hl. Basilius und die klösterliche Profess: BM 4 (1922) 280-290. — F. LAUN, Die beiden Regeln des Basilius, ihre Echtheit und hre Entstehung: ZKG 44 (1925) 1-61. — M. G. MURPHY, Saint Basil and Monasticism. Washington, 1930. — H. DÖRRIES, Symeon von Mesopotamien (TU 4, 10, 1). Leipzig, 1941, 451-465 (Rules). — A. T. GEOGHEGAN, The Attitude towards Labor in Early Christianity and Ancient Culture (SCA 6). Washington, 1945, 175-181. — M. LOOTENS, De H. Basilius de Groote en het monnikenwezen. Louvain, 1946. — F. M. GUÉTET, La tradition manuscrite des Ascétiques attribuées à S. Basile: Mélanges Bénédictins. St. Wandrille, 1947 (une recension studite des Règles basil.). — E. AMAND, L'ascèse monastique de saint Basile de Césarée. Maredsous, 1949. — S. GIET, Le rigorisme de saint Basile: RSR (1949) 333-342. — P. DE GUCHTENEERE, Les 'Constitutions ascétiques' attribuées à saint Basile. État des questions. Louvain, 1954 (typ.). — L. T. LEFORT, Les Constitutions ascétiques de saint Basile: Mus 69 (1956) 5-10 (fragments of a Coptic version of the Rules).

3. *Educational Treatises*

1. *Ad adolescentes*

In his *Exhortation to Youths as to How they shall Best Profit by the Writings of Pagan Authors* St. Basil deals with a special problem of education, the Christian attitude towards pagan literature and learning. Although the tract has the unpretentious form of advice given to his nephews, who were attending pagan schools, it is of far greater importance, since it reveals St. Basil's opinion of the value of Greek classical literature. He assigns it a place far below Holy Scripture, but he does not forbid its use for educational purposes. The study of the ancient writers can be valuable if a good selection is made among the works of the poets, historians and rhetoricians, and everything is excluded which could be dangerous for the souls of the students. He seems to be concerned only about the morality of the readers, but has no worries about their faith. In such literature one should look for the honey and avoid the poison. Thus the young Christians of Caesarea would be able to find many examples of virtue in Homer, Hesiod, Theognis, Solon and Euripides, and the philosophers, above all Plato, whom he quotes on several occasions. The exhortation is written with extraordinary feeling for the lasting values of Hellenistic learning and its broadmindedness has had a strong influence on the attitude of the Church toward the classical tradition. Basil is fully aware of the advantage of an erudition which combines the Christian truth with the inherited culture: 'The fruit of the soul is pre-eminently truth, yet to clothe it with external wisdom is not without merit, giving a kind of foliage and covering for the fruit and an aspect by no means ugly' (175).

Editions: MG 31, 563-590. — *Separate:* E. SOMMER. Paris, 1903. — A. DIRKING. Münster, 1934. — F. BOULENGER, Aux jeunes gens, sur la manière de tirer profit des lettres helléniques. Texte établi et trad. 2nd ed. Paris, 1952. — R. J. DEFERRARI, Address to Young Men on Reading Greek Literature: St. Basil, Letters vol. 4 (LCL). London, 1934, 249-348 (Greek text and transl.). — A. NARDI, Discorso ai giovani sulla letteratura di classici. Turin, 1931. — E. NERI and G. BALPONI, S. Basilius Magnus, Le omelie: Ai giovani. Siena, 1938.

Translations: English: F. M. PADELFORD, Address to Young Men on the Right Use of Greek Literature: Essays on the Study and Use of Poetry by Plutarch and Basil the Great. New York, 1902, 97-120. — R. DEFERRARI, op. cit. — *French:* F. BOULENGER, op. cit. — *Italian:* A. NARDI, op. cit. — *German:* A. STEGMANN, BKV² 47 (1925) 445-468.

Studies: H. EICKHOFF, Zwei Schriften des Basilius und Augustinus als geschichtliche Dokumente der Vereinigung von klassischer Bildung und Christentum. Schleswig, 1897. — G. BÜTTNER, Basileios' des Grossen Mahnworte an die Jugend über den nütz-lichen Gebrauch der heidnischen Literatur. Eine Quellenuntersuchung. Munich, 1908. — C. WEYMAN, St. Basilius über die Lektüre der heidnischen Klassiker: HJ 30 (1909) 287-296. — L. V. JACKS, St. Basil and Greek Literature. Washington, 1922. — M. GOEMANS, Het tractaat van Basilius den Groote over de klassieke studie. Nijmegen, 1945. — G. SOURY, Le traité de saint Basile sur les lettres helléniques. Influence de Plutarque: Actes du Congrès de l'Assoc. G. Budé. Grenoble, 1948, 152-154 (résumé). — A. G. AMATUCCI, Qualche osservazioni sul *Πρὸς τοὺς νέους* di Basilio: RFIC (1949) 191-197. — P. KOUKOULES, Basil, Gregory of Naz. and John Chrysostom as Educators (in Greek). Athens, 1951.

2. *Admonitio S. Basilii ad filium spiritualem*

This Latin tract was since the ninth century regarded as a work by St. Basil, but since the sixteenth universally held to be by an unknown author. However, P. Lehmann, its most recent editor, is of the opinion that Basil the Great actually wrote it and that the Latin text represents the translation by Rufinus. He bases his conclusion mainly on a comparison with the Rules of St. Basil. He proves that St. Benedict of Nursia knew the *Admonitio* and esteemed it highly. The ample use of the Bible, especially of Proverbs, is typical for early Egyptian monasticism. There are many similarities between the *Admonitio* and the works of Evagrius Ponticus (cf. above, p. 169), for instance, the sayings on *humilitas*, on fasting to be combined with silence, etc. Everything points to the Egyptian monasticism of the Scetis as the place of origin. This would not disagree with Basil's authorship, since he visited these monks in 360. But there is not more than a mere possibility that he composed the treatise and no positive proof. However, several other features point to about 350/360 as the time of composition. Thus the content reminds one of the *Vita Antonii* (cf. above, p. 39) in many instances, especially in the rather limited use of the title 'monachus'.

Edition: P. LEHMANN, Die Admonitio S. Basilii ad filium spiritualem (SAM Phil.-hist. Kl. 1955, H. 7). Munich, 1955. Cf. A. ADAM, DLZ 78 (1957) 579-582.

Translation: Anglo-Saxon: H. W. NORMAN, The Anglo-Saxon Version of the Hexameron of St. Basil and the Saxon Remains of St. Basil's Admonitio ad filium spiritualem with a Translation. London, 1848.

Study: P. LEHMANN, Ein Ermahnungsschreiben Basilius' des Grossen, die Benediktiner-Regel und der Basilius-Übersetzer: FF 29 (1955) 214-215.

4. *Homilies and Sermons*

St. Basil differs from his great contemporaries in that he did not write any scholarly commentaries to the books of Holy Writ. His exegetical skill appears in his numerous homilies, in which he employed the artifices of ancient rhetoric. He makes generous use of the devices of the Second Sophistic, of metaphor, comparison, ecphrasis, of Gorgianic figures and parallelism, as was the custom of the times, but he is more restrained than the two Gregories and he never regards these refinements as the most important element of his sermons. He is certainly one of the most brilliant ecclesiastical orators of antiquity, who combines rhetorical display with simplicity of thought and clarity of expression. Above all, he appears as the physician of souls, who does not want to please his listeners, but to touch their consciences.

Fortunately, the text tradition of the homilies has received a thorough investigation by Stig Y. Rudberg. He has examined 169 manuscripts which he reduced to 14 or 18 different types.

Studies: See Rudberg's studies above p. 209. — J. M. CAMPBELL, The Influence of the Second Sophistic on the Style of the Sermons of St. Basil the Great (PSt 2). Washington, 1922. — W. HENGSBERG, De ornatu rhetorico, quem Basilius Magnus in diversis homiliarum generibus adhibuit. Diss. Bonn, 1957.

1. *In Hexaemeron*

The place of honor among his homilies belongs to the nine on the Hexaemeron, the narrative of the 'Six Days' of creation in Genesis 1, 1-26, which he delivered before 370 while still a presbyter. He gave them as Lenten sermons within one week, since on some days he preached twice, in the morning and in the evening. Although they show traces of improvisation, they were held in high esteem in East and West. There is no work in late Greek literature which could be compared with these homilies in rhetorical beauty. Ambrose made ample use of them in his own homilies on the same subject. A Latin translation by the African Eustathius appeared as early as 440.

Basil makes it clear that he is not interested in the allegorical interpretation of Genesis:

> I know the laws of allegory, though not from my own works but from the works of others. Some preachers do not concede the ordinary sense of the Scriptures. They will not call water water, but something else. They interpret a plant or fish as their fancy wishes. They change the nature of the reptiles and wild beasts to fit their allegories, like those who explain phenomena that appear in dreams to suit their own ends. When I hear the word grass, I understand that grass is meant. Plant, fish, wild beast, domestic animal, — I take all in a literal sense, 'for I am not ashamed of the Gospel' (*Hex.* 9, 80).

He intends to provide a Christian idea of the world in contrast to ancient pagan notions and Manicheism, and to show the Creator behind creation. He paints a colorful picture of the beauty of nature and unfolds the miracles of the cosmos in an amazing display of natural science and philosophy, which shows him abreast of contemporary research and scholarship. The central position of the earth is to him merely a theory. Many of his explanations are borrowed from Aristotle, Plato and Poseidonios. He is in addition indebted to Plotinos, although he never mentions him. Thus the homilies are important for their sources, too. The last of them announces a lecture on man as the image of God. It seems never to have been delivered because Ambrose knows of only nine homilies and Gregory of Nyssa composed his *De hominis opificio* with the special purpose of completing his brother's work. The two sermons, *De hominis structura* (MG 30, 9-61) and another *De paradiso* (MG 30, 61-72), are not authentic.

Editions: MG 29, 3-208. — New crit. ed.: S. Giet, Basile de Césarée. Homélies sur l'Hexaéméron. Texte grec, introd. et traduction (SCH 26). Paris, 1949. — The Old Latin version of Eustathius: MG 30, 869-968. New crit. ed.: E. Amand de Mendieta and S. Y. Rudberg, Eustathius. Ancienne version latine des neuf homélies sur l'Hexaméron de Basile de Césarée. Ed. crit. avec prol. et tables (TU 66). Berlin, 1958.

Translations: English: B. Jackson, LNPF ser. 2, vol. 8 (1895) 52-107. — *French:* S. Giet, op. cit. — *German:* A. Stegmann, BKV² 47 (1925) 8-153. — *Anglo-Saxon:* H. W. Norman, The Anglo-Saxon Version of the Hexameron of St. Basil. London, 1848.

Studies: C. Gronau, Poseidonios, eine Quelle für Basilius' Hexahemeron. Braunschweig. 1912; *idem,* Poseidonios und die jüdisch-christliche Genesisexegese. Leipzig, 1914, 7-112. — J. Levie, Les sources de la septième et huitième Homélie de St. Basile sur l'Hexaméron: Musée Belge (1920) 113-149. — J. H. van Haeringen, Qui fuerit Basilii Magni de mundi procreatione orationum ordo: Mnem N.S. 63 (1925) 53-56. — M. Cesaro, Natura e cristianesimo negli Exameron di san Basilio e di sant' Ambrogio: Didaskaleion 7

(1929) 53-123. — E. Stéphanu, Le sixième jour de l'Hexaméron de saint Basile: EO 35 (1932) 385-398 (*De hominis structura* authentic). — Y. Courtonne, Saint Basile et l'hellénisme. Étude sur la rencontre de la pensée chrétienne avec la sagesse antique dans l'Hexaméron de Basile le Grand. Paris, 1934. — J. Torossian, The Armenian Version of St. Basil's Homilies In Hexaemeron (in Armenian): Bazmavep. 91 (1934) 327-336, 412-425. — E. v. Ivanka, Die Autorschaft der Homilien Εἰς τὸ Ποιήσωμεν ἄνθρωπον κατ' εἰκόνα ἡμέτεραν καὶ ὁμοίωσιν : BZ 36 (1936) 46-57 (*De hominis structura* not authentic). — J. Bidez, Le traité d'astrologie cité par saint Basile dans son Hexaéméron: ACL 7 (1938) 19-21. — B. Altaner, Eustathius, der lateinische Übersetzer der Hexaemeron-Homilien Basilius' des Grossen: ZNW 39 (1940) 161-170. — A. S. Pease, Caeli enarrant: HThR 34 (1941) 163-200. — S. Giet, Saint Basile a-t-il donné une suite aux homélies de l'Hexaméron?: RSR 33 (1946) 317-358. — E. Amand, Les états de texte des homélies pseudo-basiliennes sur la création de l'homme: RB (1949) 3-54 (deals with the two homilies *De hominis structura* attributed to Basil: MG 30, 10-62, and Gregory of Nyssa: MG 44, 257-297, preserved in two different recensions, a longer and a shorter. The longer cannot be attributed to Basil nor to Gregory). — R. Leys, L'Image de Dieu chez Grégoire de Nysse. Brussels, 1951, 130-138 (regards Gregory of Nyssa as the author of *De structura hominis*). — H. Merki, Ὁμοίωσις Θεῷ. Von der platonischen Angleichung an Gott zur Gottähnlichkeit bei Gregor von Nyssa. Fribourg, 1952, 165-173.

2. Homilies on the Psalms

There are about 18 homilies on the Psalms attributed to St. Basil. Not more than 13 seem to be authentic. They deal with Psalms 1, 7, 14, 28, 29, 32, 33, 44, 45, 48, 59, 61 and 114 (according to the Greek numeration). Their purpose is to edify, and to provide a moral application rather than an exegetical interpretation of the text, as the introduction proves: 'The prophets teach one thing, the historical books another, still another is taught in the Law, and something else in the Sapiential Books. The Book of Psalms brings together what is most serviceable in all the others; it foretells the future, it recalls the past, it lays down the laws of life, it teaches us our duties, — in a word, it is a general treasury of excellent instructions' (*Hom. in Ps.* 1, n. 1). The author makes extensive use of Eusebius of Caesarea's *Commentary on the Psalms* (cf. below, p. 337).

Editions: MG 29, 209-494: the 13 authentic homilies; MG 30, 71-118: the five spurious.

3. Commentary on Isaias

The lengthy Commentary on Isaias 1-16 also borrows heavily from Eusebius' *Commentary on the Psalms* and his *Commentary on Isaias*. Formerly, Garnier's view was universally received, that imperfection in form and content would exclude any possibility of Basil's authorship. Wittig, however, has defended its authenticity and has been seconded by Jülicher and Humbertclaude. Wittig supposes that the commentary consists of sermons or lectures delivered by Basil in Neocaesarea in the winter of 374/75 at an episcopal conference held at Dazimon. This hypothesis fails, because the series is too extensive and too learned for such an occasion. Today the opinion prevails that the work is not authentic.

Editions: MG 30, 118-668. — *Separate:* P. TREVISAN, San Basilio. Commento al profeta Isaia. Testo, introd., versione e note (Corona Patrum Salesiana. Series Graeca 4-5) 2 vols. Turin, 1939 (reprint of Garnier's text).

Translations: Italian: P. TREVISAN, op. cit. — *German:* Sämtliche Werke der Kirchenväter, vol. 23/24. Kempten, 1840.

Studies: J. WITTIG, Des heiligen Basilius des Grossen geistliche Übungen auf der Bischofs-konferenz von Dazimon, 374/375, im Anschluss an Isaias 1-16. Breslau, 1922. Cf. A. JÜLICHER, ThLZ 47 (1922) 361-364. — P. HUMBERTCLAUDE, A propos du commentaire sur Isaïe attribué à saint Basile: RSRUS 10 (1930) 47-68; *idem,* La doctrine ascétique de saint Basile de Césarée. Paris, 1932, 4-27. — R. DEVREESSE, L'édition du commentaire d'Eusèbe de Césarée sur Isaïe. Interpolations et omissions: RB 42 (1933) 540-555 (against Basil's authorship). — E. STÉPHANU, EO 37 (1934) 238-240 (against authenticity). — E. AMAND, L'ascèse monastique de saint Basile. Paris, 1949, 30 n. 1 (against authenticity).

4. *Other Sermons*

There are in addition to these homilies about 23 other sermons which might be regarded as authentic (MG 31, 163-618, 1429-1514). They are miscellaneous in subject matter and reveal even more than the others the pastoral side of his activity. Some of them are on Feasts of the Lord or the Martyrs, as for instance, *In sanctam Christi generationem* (Epiphany), *In martyrem Julittam* (5), *In Barlaam martyrem* (17), *In Gordium martyrem* (18), *In sanctos quadraginta martyres* (19), *In sanctum martyrem Mamantem* (23). Most treat of Christian duties, of fasting, of the right of the use of riches, of neighbourly love: n. 1 and 2 *De ieiunio,* n. 7 *In divites,* n. 8 *Homilia dicta tempore famis et siccitatis,* n. 20 *De humilitate,* n. 21 *Quod rebus mundanis adhaerendum non sit.* Others warn against vices such as anger, avarice drunkenness, jealousy: n. 6 *De avaritia,* n. 10 *Adversus eos qui irascuntur,* n. 11 *De invidia,* n. 14 *In ebriosos.* All of them are a rich source of information for the history of the morals and customs of the times.

Editions: MG 31, 163-618, 1429-1514. — *Separate:* Y. COURTONNE, S. Basile. Homélies sur la richesse. Édition critique et exégétique. Paris, 1935. — Crit. ed. of *Oratio in Barlaam:* STAURONIKITA, Γρηγόριος ὁ Παλαμᾶς. 1933, 281-285. — H. DE VIS, Homélies coptes de la Vaticane. Texte copte et traduit. Vol. 2. Copenhagen, 1929, 203-241 (Homélie sur l'arche de Noé, texte et traduction). — For the Old Latin versions: cf. E. AMAND, Une ancienne version latine inédite de deux homélies de saint Basile: RB 57 (1947) 12-81: gives a description of Cod. Parisinus Lat. 10593, edition of the Latin text of the homilies *On Grace* and *In martyrem Julittam,* and a comparison of the Greek and Latin. — M. HUGLO, Les anciennes versions latines des homélies de saint Basile: RB 64 (1954) 129-132 (dates of the Old Latin versions).

Translations: English: M. M. WAGNER, FC 9 (1950) 431-512 (6 homilies). — *German:* A. STEGMANN, BKV² 47 (1925) 165-444 (20 sermons). — E. NERI and G. BALPONI,

S. Basilius Magnus. Le omelie (Classici cristiani). Siena, 1938. — *Spanish:* L. DEL
PARAMO, A. DE LAICO, P. OLIVER, Homilias escogidas de San Basilio el Grande (Biblioteca
de Autores griegos y latinos). Barcelona, 1915.

Studies: A. DIRKING, S. Basilii M. de divitiis et paupertate sententiae quam habeant
rationem cum veterum philosophorum doctrina. Diss. Münster, 1911. — C. GRONAU,
Poseidonios und die jüdisch-christliche Genesisexegese. Leipzig, 1914, 281-293 (*Or.* 2).
— G. BARDY, L'homélie de saint Basile Adversus eos qui calumniantur nos: RSR 16
(1926) 21-28. — M. R. P. McGUIRE, S. Ambrosii De Nabuthe (PSt 15). Washington,
1927, 4-6 (indebtedness of St. Ambrose to B.). — O. RING, Drei Homilien aus der
Frühzeit Basilius' des Grossen. Paderborn, 1930. — A. M. BUSQUETS, San Basilio
predicador de la limosna: PC 19 (1934) 16-31. — S. GIET, De saint Basile à saint Ambroise.
La condemnation du prêt à intérêt au IVᵉ siècle: RSR (1944) 95-128. — H. DRESSLER,
A Note on the De Nabuthe of St. Ambrose: Traditio 5 (1947) 311-312 (comparison
with St. B.). — S. GIET, La doctrine de l'appropriation des biens chez quelques-uns
des Pères: RSR (1948) 55-91; *idem*, Comment naissent les légendes: RSR (1948) 273-276
(on usury). — E. AMAND, Une homélie grecque inédite antinestorienne du Vᵉ siècle
sur l'Incarnation du Seigneur: RB 58 (1948) 223-263 (text and translation of this homily
falsely attributed to S. Basil; study of dogmatic concepts and style suggests Proclus of
Constantinople as probable author); *idem*, A propos d'une édition princeps: RB 62
(1952) 300-301 (deals with the same homily, the use of *theotokos* and a description of
Cod. Vaticanus Gr. 2056). — S. Y. RUDBERG, Le texte de l'homélie pseudo-basilienne
sur l'Incarnation du Seigneur: RB 62 (1952) 189-200 (studies the same homily and
examines the editio princeps in the light of five new manuscripts. R. shares Amand's
opinion that Proclus might be the author). — E. AMAND and M. C. MOONS, Une curieuse
homélie grecque inédite sur la virginité, adressée aux pères de famille: RB 63 (1953)
18-69, 211-238 (edition and translat. of the homily *On Virginity* attributed to Basil.
The author is an Arian; cf. above p. 13). — S. GIET, A propos des danses liturgiques:
RSR 27 (1953) 131-133 (homily 14, 1). — J. BERNARDI, Le mot τρόπαιον appliqué
aux martyrs: VC 8 (1954) 174-175 (*Or.* 17, *Or.* 19). — M. SIMONETTI, Sulla struttura
dei Panegirici di S. Giovanni Crisostomo: RIL 86 (1953) 159-180 (élément nouveau
du panégyrique avec S. Basile). — E. F. BRUCK, Kirchenväter und Seelgerät: ZSR 72
(1955) 191-210 (*Hom. dicta temp. fam. et sicc.*, *In divit.*). — E. AMAND DE MENDIETA, La
virginité chez Eusèbe d'Émèse et l'ascétisme familial dans la première moitié du IVᵉ
siècle: RHE 50 (1955) 777-820 (Pseudo-Basilian homily *On Virginity*). — A. VÖÖBUS,
Syrische Herkunft der Pseudo-Basilianischen Homilie über die Jungfräulichkeit: OC 40
(1956) 69-77 (Biblical quotations prove Syriac origin of the homily *On Virginity*).
— E. ROUILLARD, Recherches sur la tradition manuscrite des 'Homélies diverses' de
S. Basile: Revue Mabillon 48 (1958) 81-98.

5. *Letters*

The Letters of St. Basil reveal his fine education and literary
taste even more than his homilies. They were very soon regarded as
models. When a certain Nicobulus asked for the rules of epistolography, St. Gregory of Nazianzus (*Ep.* 51) referred in his answer
to Basil as a master of that art and when the same Nicobulus
requested him to send him some of his letters, Gregory made a
collection of them and forwarded it to Nicobulus (*Ep.* 53). The
Benedictines of St. Maur published in their edition not less than
365 epistles, among them a number not composed by St. Basil but

addressed to him. This collection is divided into three classes: I (n. 1-46) letters written before his episcopate in the years 357 to 370; II (n. 47-291) letters assigned to the period of his episcopal career from 370 to 378, two thirds of the entire collection; III (n. 292-365) letters which cannot be dated, since there is no indication whatsoever of their time of composition, and many doubtful and spurious ones. The chronological order of this edition was challenged by Ernst, but defended as substantially correct by Loofs and Schäfer. The manuscript tradition of the correspondence has been investigated by M. Bessières, A. Cavallin and Stig Y. Rudberg. The last-named was able to add three old manuscripts to the most important Family Aa. Thus a new critical text will supplant the Benedictine one. Rudberg gives us an idea of it in his masterly edition of *Ep.* 2 addressed to Gregory of Nazianzus, which is based on 123 manuscripts, of *Ep.* 150 to Amphilochius of Iconium and *Ep.* 173 to Theodora. Courtonne's new edition constructs the text on the basis of the six oldest manuscripts of the Family Aa.

St. Basil's correspondence is a copious and invaluable store of information for the history of the Eastern Church in the fourth century, particularly in Cappadocia. Since he never found a real biographer, his letters represent the best source for his life and times, for his many activities and far-reaching influence, especially for his personality and his character. Although they were not primarily intended as literature, they are literary in the best sense. Their great variety makes it impossible to classify them according to their content. We can mention only a few groups.

Editions: MG 32, 220-1112. — R. DEFERRARI, Saint Basil, The Letters. (LCL) 4 vols. London and Cambridge (Mass.), 1926-1939, reprinted 1950. New crit. ed.: Y. COURTONNE, Saint Basile, Lettres, vol. I (*Epp.* 1-100). Texte établi et traduit. Paris, 1957.

Translations: English: B. JACKSON, LNPF ser. 2, vol. 8 (1895) 109-327. — R. DEFERRARI, op. cit. — A. C. WAY, FC 13 (1951); FC 28 (1955). — *French:* Y. COURTONNE, op. cit. — *German:* A. STEGMANN, BKV² 46 (1925).

Manuscript Tradition: M. BESSIÈRES, La tradition manuscrite de la correspondance de saint Basile. Oxford, 1923. — G. COPPOLA, I codici Laurenziani delle lettere di S. Basilio e il papiro Berol. 6795: Rivista indo-greco-italiana 7 (1923) 19-28 (this fifth-century Berlin papyrus contains an anthology of Basil's letters); *idem,* L'archetipo dell' epistolario di Basilio: Studi italiani di filologia classica 3 (1923) 137-150. — A. CAVALLIN, Studien zu den Briefen des hl. Basilius. Lund, 1944. — S. Y. RUDBERG, Études sur la tradition manuscrite de S. Basile. Upsala, 1953.

Studies: V. ERNST, Basilius' des Grossen Verkehr mit den Okzidentalen: ZKG 16 (1896) 626-664 (chronology). — F. LOOFS, Eustathius von Sebaste und die Chronologie der Basiliusbriefe. Halle, 1898. — J. SCHÄFER, Basilius' des Grossen Beziehungen zum Abendlande. Münster, 1909, 11-34 (chronology). — E. BUONAIUTI, Attraverso l'Epistolario di S. Basilio: Rivista stor.-crit. delle scienze teol. 4 (1908) 122-132. — G. PASQUALI, Gregorii Nysseni Opera. Epistulae. Berlin, 1925, LIX-LXI, 70/71 (*Ep.* 10

not authentic). — A. C. WAY, The Language and Style of the Letters of St. Basil (PSt 13).
Washington, 1927; *eadem*, The Authenticity of Letter 41 in the Julio-Basilian Correspondence: AJPh (1930) 67-69. — H. GRÉGOIRE, Dazmana est bien Dazimon: Byz 10
(1935) 760-763 (*Ep.* 212). — G. DE JERPHANION, Une nouvelle méthode en géographie
historique? Dazmana-Dazimon?: OCP 2 (1936) 260-272; 491-496. — G. LAZZATI,
Aristotele perduto. Milan, 1938, 34-43 (*Ep.* 22). — A. CAVALLIN, Die Legendenbildung
um den Mailänder Bischof Dionysius: Eranos (1945) 136-149 (*Ep.* 197 addressed to
Ambrose, the second part not authentic); *idem*, Zum Verhältnis zwischen regierendem
Verb und Participium coniunctum: Eranos (1946) 280-295 (*Ep.* 109). — M. TADIN,
La lettre 91 de saint Basile a-t-elle été adressée à l'évêque d'Aquilée Valérin?: RSR 37
(1950) 457-468. — W. VÖLKER, Basilius, Ep. 366 und Clemens Alexandrinus: VC 7
(1953) 23-26 (*Ep.* 366 not authentic, contains excerpts of *Stromateis*). — P. VON DER
MUEHLL, Basilius und der letzte Brief Epikurs, Museum Helveticum 12 (1955) 47-49
(Basil's *Ep.* 11 beginning reminiscent of Epicur). — J. GRIBOMONT, Eustathe le Philosophe et les voyages du jeune Basile de Césarée: RHE 54 (1959) 115-124 (*Ep.* 1).

1. *Letters of Friendship*

Basil had a great longing for friendship and loyalty. Thus the
letters addressed to friends for the exchange of ideas, for consolation,
encouragement and advice are especially numerous. He is always
anxious to hear from his friends and often asks them to write. Cf.
Ep. 1, 3, 4, 7, 12-14, 17, 19-21, 27, 56-58, 63, 64, 95, 118, 123, 124,
132-135, 145-149, 152-158, 162-165, 168, 172-176, 181, 184-186,
192-196, 198, 200, 201, 208-210, 232, 241, 252, 254, 255, 259, 267,
268, 271, 278, 282, 284, 285, 320, 332-334.

2. *Letters of Recommendation*

Always ready to help, Basil addressed a great number of letters
to high authorities and wealthy persons in order to recommend the
poor and oppressed, to intercede for cities and towns, for relatives
and friends, as in *Ep.* 3, 15, 31-37, 72-78, 83-88, 96, 104, 108-112,
137, 142-144, 177-180, 271, 273-276, 279-281, 303-319.

To the same class of letters belongs his correspondence with
Libanius of Antioch, which comprises 25 communications: *Ep.*
335-359. Their authenticity has been the subject of much dispute.
Some of them are spurious, or at least very doubtful; others like
Ep. 335-346 and 358 must be authentic because of their position
in the manuscript tradition and because of the historical information
they contain. Basil's missives to Libanius introduce young Cappadocian students to the distinguished Greek sophist and rhetorician;
Libanius' letters to Basil are notes of thanks. Basil here makes more
use of rhetorical devices than elsewhere in his epistles, so that
Libanius in one of his answers (*Ep.* 338) states: 'I have been van-
quished in beauty of epistolary style and it is Basil who has gained
the victory'. The entire correspondence is interesting for the history

of the personalities involved as well as for the fact that such an exchange between a priest and a pronounced pagan was at all possible. Here we have two great representatives of the Christian and the Hellenistic world on the best of terms with each other.

Edition: R. FOERSTER, Libanii Opera XI: Epistulae 840-1544 una cum pseudepigraphis et Basilii cum Libanio commercio epistolico. Leipzig, 1922.

Studies: O. SEECK, Die Briefe des Libanius zeitlich geordnet (TU 30, 1/2). Leipzig, 1906, 30-34, 468-471 (defends the authenticity and dates the letters 356-372). — P. MAAS, Der Briefwechsel zwischen Basileios und Libanios: SAB (1912) 1112-1126 (regards some of the letters as authentic). — H. MARKOWSKI, Zum Briefwechsel zwischen Basileios und Libanios: Berliner PhW (1913) 1150-1152 (against authenticity). — A. LAUBE, De litterarum Libanii et Basilii commercio. Breslau, 1913 (against authenticity). Cf. G. PASQUALI, Berliner PhW 34 (1914) 1508-1519 (for authenticity except *Ep.* 1590 and 1603). — G. PASQUALI, De litterarum Libanii et Basilii commercio: SIF 3 (1923) 129-136. — M. BESSIÈRES, La tradition manuscrite de la correspondance de saint Basile: JThSt 23 (1922) 351.

3. *Letters of Consolation*

Letters n. 5, 6, 28, 29, 62, 101, 107, 139, 140, 206, 227, 238, 247, 256, 257, 269, 300-302 are expressions of sympathy addressed to parents and husbands who suffered a loss of their dear ones, to bishops, priests and monks living in depression, to churches deprived of their pastors, to clergy and faithful attacked by heretics.

4. *Canonical Letters*

Basil wrote many letters for the sole purpose of reestablishing order wherever there had been disturbances or canon law had fallen into neglect. Such are *Ep.* 53 and 54 addressed 'to the Chorepiscopi' at the beginning of his episcopate about 370. Famous are the three so-called *Canonical Letters* 188, 199 and 217, sent to Amphilochius, bishop of Iconium. They contain minute ecclesiastical regulations concerning penitential discipline and are very important for its history. Their authenticity has been wrongly denied. They soon gained universal recognition in the entire East and acquired the authority of law in the Greek Church.

Edition: C. PITRA, Iuris eccles. Graecorum historia et monumenta I. Rome, 1864, 576-618 (*Ep.* 188. 199. 217).

Studies: F. GILLMANN, Das Institut der Chorbischöfe im Orient (Veröffentlichungen aus dem Kirchenhistor. Seminar München 2, 1). Munich, 1903, 99-105. — J. SCHÄFER, Basilius' des Grossen Beziehungen zum Abendlande. Münster, 1909, 5-7 (against authenticity of *Ep.* 53 and 54). — E. SCHWARTZ, Die Kanonessammlungen der alten Reichskirche: ZSK 25 (1936) 1-114. — K. BONES, Αἱ τρεῖς Κανονικαὶ Ἐπιστολαὶ τοῦ Μεγάλου Βασιλείου πρὸς τὸν Ἀμφιλόχιον : BZ 64 (1951) 62-78 (manuscript tradition and character of the *Canonical Letters*).

5. Moral-ascetical Letters

The promotion of morality and asceticism is the goal of many letters to the clergy, to laymen and religious. Basil calls the lapsed back to the fold and to a new life, he exhorts bishops and priests to fulfill their duties conscientiously, he shows ways and means to perfection and praises monastic life with great enthusiasm. To this group belong n. 2, 10-11, 14, 18, 22-26, 49, 65, 83, 85, 97, 106, 112, 115, 116, 161, 173, 174, 182, 183, 197, 219, 220-222, 240, 246, 249, 251, 259, 277, 283, 291-299, 366.

6. Dogmatic Letters

Some of the dogmatic letters are so long that they amount to real treatises. Most of them deal directly with points of Trinitarian doctrine, with the Nicene Creed and with the defense of the consubstantiality of the Son and the Holy Spirit against Arians, Eunomians, Sabellians and Apollinarists. N. 233-236, addressed to bishop Amphilochius of Iconium, form a coherent whole and investigate the relations between faith and reason, nature and revelation, as the sources of our knowledge of God. Other such epistles are n. 9, 52, 105, 113, 114, 125, 129, 131, 159, 175, 210, 214, 226, 251, 258, 261, 262.

However, the long letter 38 addressed to his brother Gregory of Nyssa *On the difference between substance and person* is not authentic according to Cavallin. Furthermore, n. 8, entitled *An Apology to the Caesareans for his Withdrawal and on Faith*, which has formed the core of many discussions regarding St. Basil's theology, must be assigned to Evagrius Ponticus, as Bousset and Melcher have independently demonstrated. *Ep.* 16 *Adversus Eunomium haereticum* is not a letter and not by St. Basil but an excerpt from Gregory of Nyssa's *Contra Eunomium*, ch. 10.

Studies: F. DIEKAMP, Ein angeblicher Brief des hl. Basilius gegen Eunomius: ThQ 77 (1895) 277-285. — W. BOUSSET, Apophthegmata. Tübingen, 1923, 335-336. — R. MELCHER, Der achte Brief des Basilius ein Werk des Evagrius Ponticus. Münster, 1923 (cf. above p. 176).

The epistles of Basil to Apollinaris of Laodicea and the latter's replies, n. 361-364, were generally regarded as spurious until, in 1892, J. Dräseke sought to establish their authenticity. His arguments, however, convinced only a few. Bonwetsch had no greater success. In his posthumous work G. L. Prestige has recently presented a fresh, cogent and persuasive defense of their genuineness. He compares their style and vocabulary with Basil's authentic writings; he further shows that Basil never denied this interchange, but actually admitted that he had written at least one letter. What Basil in 375 did repudiate is the so-called *Eustathian Document*, which is not in this group and seems to have been by Apollinaris. Prestige provides a new English translation of the correspondence. The Document is given in its Greek text and an English version.

Ep. 189 *To Eustathius on the Holy Trinity*, of which G. Mercati (ST 11, 1903, 57 ff.) published a new critical edition, is generally considered today to be a letter of Gregory of Nyssa written against the Pneumatomachi.

Editions: MG 32, 1099-1108 (*Ep.* 361-364). New crit. ed.: H. DE RIEDMATTEN, JThSt N.S. 7 (1956) 202-205.

Translation: English: G. L. PRESTIGE, St. Basil the Great and Apollinaris of Laodicea, edited by H. Chadwick. London, 1956.

Studies: J. DRÄSEKE, Apollinaris von Laodicea. Leipzig, 1892, 100-121. — G. BONWETSCH, Zum Briefwechsel zwischen Basilius und Apollinaris: ThStKr 82 (1909) 625-628. — A. C. WAY, On the Authenticity of the Letters attributed to St. Basil in the so-called Basil-Apollinaris Correspondence: AJPh (1931) 57-65. — G. L. PRESTIGE, op. cit. — H. DE RIEDMATTEN, La Correspondance entre Basile de Césarée et Apollinaire de Laodicée: JThSt N.S. 7 (1956) 199-210; 8 (1957) 53-70 (textual crit.). — R. WEIJEN-BORG, De authenticitate et sensu quarundam epistularum S. Basilio Magno et Apollinario Laodiceno adscriptarum: Ant 33 (1958) 197-240.

7. *Liturgical Letters*

A number of letters are important for the history of the liturgy. Thus *Ep.* 207 addressed to the clergy at Neocaesarea and written in the late summer of 375, gives an excellent description of the vigil service. *Ep.* 93 recommends daily Communion.

8. *Historical Letters*

The range of St. Basil's correspondence was enormous. In his letter 204 he remarks: 'Let Pisidia, Lycaonia, Isauria, both Phrygias, as much of Armenia as is near you, Macedonia, Achaea, Illyria, Gaul, Spain, all Italy, Sicily, Africa, the sound part of Egypt, whatever is left of Syria — let all, whoever send letters to us and receive letters from us in return, be questioned'. With such far-reaching contacts Basil's letters represent a first-class source for the history of the Empire and the conditions of State and Church, for the relations between East and West, for the controversies between orthodoxy and heresy.

The correspondence between the Saint and the Emperor Julian, consisting of n. 39, 40, 41, 60, is spurious and was recognized as such even in Byzantine times.

According to Wittig, letters 50 and 81 addressed 'Innocentio episcopo' were composed by St. John Chrysostom and sent to Pope Innocent I.

Studies: For *Ep.* 169-171, see: W. M. RAMSAY, The Church in the Roman Empire. 2nd ed. London, 1893, 443-464. — For *Ep.* 50 and 81: J. WITTIG, Studien zur Geschichte des Papstes Innozenz I. und der Papstwahlen des 5. Jahrhunderts: ThQ 84 (1902) 388-439. — For *Ep.* 155, 164 and 165: G. PFEILSCHIFTER, Kein neues Werk des Wulfila: Veröffentlichungen aus dem Kirchenhistor. Seminar München 3, 1 (1907) 192-224.

6. *The Liturgy of St. Basil*

Gregory of Nazianzus in the eulogy on his friend mentions among his lasting achievements the reform of the liturgy of Caesarea, which he made while still a presbyter of that city (*Orat.* 43, 34). We know from Basil's own writings that he was accused of innovations on several occasions. In his book *De Spiritu Sancto* (cf. above, p. 210) he has to defend himself for using a new doxology. In his *Ep.* 207 he answers the charge of having inaugurated a different method of singing. He reformed the Divine Office for his monasteries and introduced Prime and Compline, as the *Rules* sufficiently prove.

A universal tradition of the Orient attributes to him the so-called *Liturgy of St. Basil*, which is still employed in the Churches of the Byzantine rite on the Sundays in Lent (except Palm Sunday), on Maundy Thursday, Easter Eve, Christmas Eve, the Eve of Epiphany and January the first, the Feast of St. Basil. On the other days, the shorter Liturgy of St. Chrysostom is followed.

There is no reason whatsoever to doubt that St. Basil's Liturgy actually goes back to him. In a letter addressed about 520 by the monks of Scythia to the African bishops in exile in Sardinia, Petrus Diaconus writes:

> Hinc etiam beatus Basilius Caesariensis episcopus in oratione sacri altaris, quam paene universus frequentat Oriens, inter cetera: 'dona', inquit, 'Domine, virtutem ac tutamentum: malos, quaesumus, bonos facito, bonos in bonitate conserva: omnia enim potes, et non est qui contradicat tibi: cum enim volueris, salvas, et nullus resistit voluntati tuae'.

Shortly afterwards, about 540, Leontius of Byzantium accuses Theodore of Mopsuestia of having shamelessly replaced with his own *Anaphora* that of the Apostles and that which St. Basil composed under the inspiration of the Holy Ghost (MG 86, 1368). He evidently refers here to the two Liturgies of St. John Chrysostom and St. Basil. Canon 32 of the Trullian Synod of 692 condemns the Armenians for using unmixed wine in their Eucharistic service, while James the Brother of the Lord and Basil the Great of Caesarea, who handed down the liturgy in written form, prescribe wine mingled with water. From all these testimonies it can be concluded that the *Liturgy of St. Basil* rightly bears the name of the eminent bishop of Caesarea. Recent investigations have shown, though, that he is not its creator but its theological reviser, who did not shorten the original but enlarged it. As time went on, it underwent many changes, but the pith remained and still gives evidence of being the work of a master of the Greek language. Basil's great reputation and his importance for Greek monasticism explain the far-reaching influence of his Liturgy — an influence illustrated best by its adoption by the patriarchal see of Constantinople, and also evidenced by its rapid spread over the whole East, as well as to Sicily and Italy. It was translated into Slavonic by Sts. Cyril and Methodius in the ninth century, and introduced into Russia in 987 by Grand-Duke Wladimir. The Coptic Liturgy of St. Basil is an abbreviated form of the Greek.

The oldest manuscript is *Codex Barberini* of the year 795, now *Codex Vat. Barb.* III, 55 of which the eleventh-century *Codex Sevastianof C.* is only a copy. *Codex Paris. Gr.* 325 of the 14th century contains the Coptic Anaphora of St. Basil in Greek.

Besides several oriental versions there are two extant Latin translations of the twelfth century. One of them, made by Nicholas of Otranto, is found in a South-Italian manuscript of the thirteenth century containing the Greek original and a Latin translation in parallel columns. This codex is now in the Landesbibliothek of Karlsruhe, Germany.

Editions: MG 31, 1629-1656. — H. A. DANIEL, Codex liturgicus ecclesiae orientalis. Leipzig, 1853, 421-438. — C. A. SWAINSON, The Greek Liturgies chiefly from original authorities. Cambridge, 1884, 76-87, 151-171. — F. E. BRIGHTMAN, Liturgies Eastern and Western, vol. 1. Oxford, 1896, 309-344, 400-411. — R. ENGDAHL, Beiträge zur Kenntnis der byzantinischen Liturgie. Berlin, 1908, 78ff. (the Greek text and Nicholas of Otranto's translation in parallel columns). — H. ENGBERDING, Das Eucharistische Hochgebet der Basileiosliturgie. Textgeschichtliche Untersuchungen und kritische Ausgabe. Münster, 1931. — S. EURINGER, Die äthiopische Anaphora des hl. Basilius. Nach vier Handschriften herausgegeben, übersetzt und mit Bemerkungen versehen (Orientalia Christiana t. 36, fasc. 3). Rome, 1934. — Oldest Latin version: A. STRITT-MATTER, Missa Grecorum. Missa sancti Johannis Chrysostomi. The Oldest Latin Version Known of the Byzantine Liturgies of St. Basil and St. John Chrysostom: Traditio 1 (1943) 79-137.

Translations: English: J. N. W. B. ROBERTSON, The Divine Liturgies of Chrysostom and Basil. London, 1894. — *French:* C. CHARON, Les saintes et divines Liturgies de nos saints Pères Jean Chrysostome, Basile le Grand et Grégoire le Grand. Beyrouth, 1904. French translation of the Coptic text: C. MACAIRE, Liturgie copte alexandrine, dite de St. Basile. Paris, 1899. — *German:* R. STORF, Griechische Liturgien: BKV² 5 (1912) 263-278. — S. EURINGER, op. cit. — *Dutch:* J. MUIJSER, Het heilig Offer in den Koptischen ritus volgens den H. Basilius den Groote, 2nd ed. Nijmegen, 1928.

Studies: P. DE MEESTER, Authenticité des liturgies de saint Basile et de saint Jean Chrysostome: DAL 6 (1925) 1596-1604. — J. MOREAU, Les anaphores des Liturgies de saint Jean Chrysostome et de saint Basile comparées aux canons romain et gallican. Paris, 1927. — D. M. MORATTES, 'Η λειτουργία τοῦ M. Βασιλείου: Θεολογία 7 (1929) 70-75. — S. SALAVILLE, Liturgies orientales. Paris, 1932. — S. ANTONIADES, Place de la liturgie dans la tradition des lettres grecques. Leiden, 1939, 149-152, 346-357. — M. JUGIE, De epiclesi eucharistica secundum Basilium Magnum: Acta Academiae Velehradensis 19 (1948) 202-207. — M. S. H. GELSINGER, The Epiclesis in the Liturgy of Saint Basil: Eastern Church Quarterly 10 (1954) 243-248. — A. RAES, L'authenticité de la liturgie byzantine de saint Basile: Mélanges S. Salaville = REB 16 (1958) 143-157.

II. THE THEOLOGY OF ST. BASIL

The teaching of St. Basil is centred around the defense of the Nicene doctrine against the different Arian parties. His life-long friendship with Athanasius was based on their common cause. He adhered to the patriarch of Alexandria with unswerving devotion, because he recognized him as the champion of orthodoxy. He declares: 'We can add nothing to the Creed of Nicaea, not even the slightest thing, except the glorification of the Holy Spirit, and this only because our fathers mentioned this topic incidentally' (*Ep.* 258, 2 LCL). Despite this assertion, it is Basil's great merit that he went beyond Athanasius and contributed in a high degree to the clarification of Trinitarian and Christological terminology.

1. *Trinitarian Doctrine*

Regarding the doctrine of the Trinity, St. Basil's chief work consisted in bringing back the Semi-Arians to the Church and in fixing once for all, the meaning of the words *ousia* and *hypostasis*.

The framers of the Creed of Nicaea, and among them Athanasius, used *ousia* and *hypostasis* as synonyms. Thus Athanasius even in one of his latest writings *Ad Afros* 4, in refuting the objections brought against these two words as non-scriptural, states: '*Hypostasis* is *ousia* and means nothing else but simply being'. Even the Synod of Alexandria in 362, presided over by Athanasius, gave formal recognition to both expressions, i.e. one *hypostasis* or three *hypostases* in God. This decision led to endless misunderstandings and controversies. St. Basil was the first to insist upon the distinction, one *ousia* and three *hypostases* in God, and to maintain that μία οὐσία, τρεῖς ὑποστάσεις is the only acceptable formula. For him, *ousia* means the existence or essence or substantial entity of God, whereas *hypostasis* signifies the existence in a particular mode, the manner of being of each of the Persons. *Ousia* corresponds to the Latin *substantia* as that essential being which Father, Son and Spirit have in common, while St. Basil defines *hypostasis* as τὸ ἰδίως λεγόμενον, denoting a limitation, a separation of certain circumscribed conceptions from the general idea, corresponding to *persona* in the legal terminology of the Latins. Thus he says (*Ep.* 214): '*Ousia* has the same relation to *hypostasis* as the common has to the particular. Every one of us both shares in existence by the common term *ousia* and is such or such a one by his own properties. In the same manner, in the matter in question, the term *ousia* is common, like goodness or Godhead or any similar attribute, while *hypostasis* is contemplated in the special property of Fatherhood, Sonship, or the power to sanctify'. Thus he regards *hypostasis* as a better term than *prosopon*, since Sabellius had used the latter to express distinctions in the Godhead which were merely temporal and external:

> It is indispensable to have clear understanding that, as he who fails to confess the community of the essence or substance falls into polytheism, so he who refuses to grant the distinction of the *hypostases* is carried away into Judaism. For we must keep our mind stayed, so to say, on a certain underlying subject matter, and, by forming a clear impression of its distinguishing lines, so arrive at the end desired. For suppose we do not bethink us of the Fatherhood, nor bear in mind Him of Whom this distinctive quality is marked off, how can we take in the idea of God the Father? For merely to enumerate the differences of Persons (πρόσωπον) is insufficient; we must confess each Person (πρόσωπον) to have a natural existence in a real *hypostasis*. Now Sabellius did not even object to the word *prosopon* so long as it was not used as synonymous with *hypostasis*. [*Prosopon*, like *persona*, means either a mask, a stage disguise or person, but in the Greek word, unlike the Latin, the notion of 'impersonation' is much more prominent than the notion of 'autonomous personality'.] For, he said, that the same God, being one in matter, was metamorphosed, as the need of the moment required, and spoken of now as Father, now as Son, and now as the Holy Spirit. The inventors of this unnamed heresy are renewing the old long-extinguished error; those, I mean, who are repudiating the *hypostases*, and denying the name of the Son of God. They must give up uttering iniquity against God, or they will have to wail with them that deny Christ (*Ep.* 210, 5 LNPF).

Thus Basil advanced the Trinitarian doctrine and especially its terminology along the way that ultimately led to the definition of the Council of Chalcedon (451). The two other Cappadocians, Gregory of Nazianzus and Gregory of Nyssa, followed in the footsteps of their master, securing his theological position and using it as a base for further progress.

Studies: T. B. STRONG, The History of the Theological Term 'Substance': JThSt 2 (1901) 224-235; 3 (1902) 22-40; 4 (1903) 28-45. — R. ROUGIER, Le sens des termes οὐσία, ὑπόστασις et πρόσωπον dans les controverses trinitaires postnicéennes: RHR 73

(1916) 48-63; 74 (1917) 133-189. — A. GRANDSIRE, Nature et hypostases divines dans saint Basile: RSR 13 (1923) 130-152.

2. *The Homoousios*

Basil's clarification of the two terms, *ousia* and *hypostasis*, contributed in a high degree to the universal adoption of the Nicene *homoousios* and the triumph of the Cappadocian position at the Council of Constantinople (381). However, it is with reference to this point that Zahn, Loofs, and especially Harnack have brought the charge against St. Basil and his fellow-Cappadocians of holding the consubstantiality of the three divine Persons only in the sense of the *homoiousios* and reducing the unity to a mere matter of likeness. Harnack distinguishes between the old and the new Nicenes, — the old being represented by the champions of the *homoousios* at Nicaea, by the West and Alexandria, especially St. Athanasius, the new, by St. Basil and the two Gregories. The Cappadocians would in reality be Semi-Arians, who could speak the language of Nicaea only by twisting the primitive *homoousios* into the sense of *homoiousios*. What they ultimately adopted, according to Harnack, was the theology of Basil of Ancyra (cf. above, p. 201), which amounted to the Homoian view, that there is a community of substance only in the sense of likeness of substance, not in that of unity of substance.

This charge is far from being supported by the evidence cited in its favor. St. Basil most emphatically proclaimed the numerical unity of God. The passage of his *Letter* 210, 5, which we have quoted above (p. 229), proves to anyone who scrutinizes it closely that Basil is very anxious to avoid the pitfalls of polytheism as well as of Sabellianism. He says: 'He who fails to confess the community of the essence or substance falls into polytheism', and his *Homily* 24, 3 provides the parallel: 'Confess only one *ousia* in both [the Father and the Son], so as not to fall into polytheism'. Such statements cannot be reconciled with the Homoian view, that there are three forms of existence of like nature with one another, together making up the Godhead, instead of one Godhead, existing permanently in three distinct forms of existence. Harnack's view is therefore mistaken. The distinction between 'old Nicenes' and 'new Nicenes' is justified only if we keep in mind that there is no real but only a formal difference between the two groups, in so far as with the new Nicenes there is more emphasis on the three divine Persons than on the unity of the divine substance.

Studies: J. F. BETHUNE-BAKER, The Meaning of Homoousios in the Constantinopolitan Creed. Cambridge, 1901. — J. RASNEUR, L'homoiousianisme dans ses rapports avec l'orthodoxie: RHE 4 (1903) 189-206, 411-431. — K. HOLL, Amphilochius von Ikonium in seinem Verhältnis zu den grossen Kappadoziern. Tübingen, 1904, 122-158 (Basil's

Trinitarian and Christological doctrine). — F. NAGER, Die Trinitätslehre des hl. Basilius des Grossen. Paderborn, 1912. — A. v. HARNACK, Lehrbuch der Dogmengeschichte, vol. 2, 5th ed. Tübingen, 1931, 259-284. — R. ARNOU, Unité numérique et unité de nature chez les Pères après le Concile de Nicée: Greg 15 (1934) 242-254. — C. PERA, I teologi e la teologia dal III al IV secolo: Ang 19 (1942) 78-95 (L'azione di Eunomio e la reazione di S. Basilio). — J. LEBON, Le sort du consubstantiel nicéen: RHE 48 (1953) 632-682. — H. A. WOLFSON, The Philosophy of the Church Fathers, vol. I. Faith, Trinity, Incarnation. Cambridge (Mass.), 1956, 337-346. — J. N. D. KELLY, Early Christian Doctrines. London, 1958, 263-269.

3. *Holy Spirit*

One of the reasons which contributed to the suspicion that Basil shared Semi-Arian views was the fact that he never calls the Holy Spirit explicitly 'God' in his treatise *De Spiritu Sancto*. It was because of this reserve that Basil was attacked by the monks. Athanasius (*Ep.* 62 and 63) wrote in his support and urged them to consider his intention and purpose (his *oikonomia*): 'to the weak he becomes weak to gain the weak'. We learn more of this reserve which caused several bishops to reproach Basil severely (cf. Gregory Naz., *Ep.* 58) in Gregory of Nazianzus' panegyric (68/69):

> The enemies were on the watch for the unqualified statement 'the Spirit is God', which, although it is true, they and the wicked patron of their impiety imagined to be impious; so that they might banish him and his power of theological instruction from the city and themselves be able to seize upon the Church, and make it the starting point and citadel, from which they could overrun with their evil doctrine the rest of the world. Accordingly, by the use of other terms, and by statements which unmistakably had the same meaning, and by arguments necessarily leading to this conclusion, he so overpowered his antagonists, that they were left without reply, and involved in their own admissions — the greatest proof possible of dialectical skill. His [Basil's] treatise on this subject makes it further manifest being evidently written by a pen borrowed from the Spirit's store. He postponed for a time the exact term, begging as a favor from the Spirit Himself and His earnest champions, that they would not be annoyed at his *oikonomia* [in refraining from the express assertion 'The Holy Spirit is God'], nor, by clinging to a single expression, ruin the whole cause, from an uncompromising temper, at a crisis when religion was in peril. He assured them that they would suffer no injury from a slight change in their expressions, and from teaching the same truth in other terms. For our salvation is not so much a matter of words as of actions.
>
> That he, no less than any other, acknowledged that the Spirit is God, is plain from his often having publicly preached this truth, whenever opportunity offered, and eagerly confessed it when questioned in private. But he made it more clear in his conversations with me, from whom he concealed nothing during our conferences upon this subject. Not content with simply asserting it, he proceeded, as he had

but very seldom done before, to imprecate upon himself that most terrible fate of separation from the Spirit, if he did not adore the Spirit as consubstantial and coequal with the Father and the Son. And if anyone would accept me as having been his fellow laborer in this cause, I will set forth one point hitherto unknown to most men. Under the pressure of the difficulties of the period, he himself under took the *oikonomia*, while allowing freedom of speech to me, whom no one was likely to drag from obscurity to trial or banishment, in order that by our united efforts our Gospel might be firmly established. I mention this not to defend his reputation, for the man is stronger than his assailants, if there are any such; but to prevent men from thinking that the terms found in writings are the utmost limit of the truth, and so have their faith weakened, and consider that their own error is supported by his theology, which was the joint result of the influences of the time and of the Spirit, instead of considering the sense of his writings, and the object with which they were written, so as to be brought closer to the truth, and enabled to silence the partisans of impiety. At any rate let his theology be mine, and that of all dear to me (LNPF).

Gregory's statement is in full agreement with the fact that Basil taught the divinity and consubstantiality of the Holy Spirit implicitly in his writings, though he never uses the ὁμοούσιος τῷ πατρί of the third Person in the Trinity. He speaks unequivocally in *Adv. Eunomium* 3, 4 and 3, 5 of his divinity *(θεότης αὐτοῦ)* and proves it all through his treatise *De Spiritu Sancto* (41-47, 58-64, 71-75).

In his *Ep.* 189, 5-7, he states clearly and unmistakably:

What ground is there for conceding to the Spirit fellowship with Father and Son in all other terms, and isolating Him from the Godhead alone? There is no escape from the position that we must either allow the fellowship here, or refuse it everywhere. If He is worthy in every other respect, He is certainly not unworthy in this. If, as our opponents argue, He is too insignificant to be allowed fellowship with Father and with Son in Godhead, He is not worthy to share any single one of the divine attributes: for when the terms are carefully considered, and compared with one another, by the help of the special meaning contemplated in each, they will be found to involve nothing less than the title of God.

But they contended that this title sets forth the nature of that to which it is applied; that the nature of the Spirit is not a nature shared in common with that of Father and of Son; and that for this reason the Spirit ought not to be allowed the common use of the name. It is, therefore, for them to show by what means they have perceived this variation in nature... We are of necessity guided in the investigation of the divine nature by its operations. Suppose we observe the operations of the Father, of the Son, of the Holy Ghost, to be different from one another, we shall then conjecture, from the diversity of operations, that the operating natures are also different. For it is impossible that things which are distinct, as regards their nature, should be associated as regards the form of their operations; fire does not freeze; ice does not warm; difference of natures implies difference of the operations proceeding from them. Grant then that we perceive the operation of the Father, Son and Holy Ghost to be one and the same, in no respect showing difference or variation; from this identity of operation we necessarily infer the unity of nature... Identity of operation in the case of the Father and of the Son and of the Holy Ghost clearly proves invariability of nature. It follows that, even if the name of Godhead does not signify nature, the community of essence proves that this title is very properly applied to the Holy Spirit (LNPF).

St. Basil manifestly holds the common view of most of the Greek Fathers that the Holy Spirit proceeds from the Father through the Son. He comes from the Father but not by generation as the Son: He is the breath of his mouth (*De Spiritu Sancto* 46, 38), but also 'the natural goodness and the inherent holiness and the royal dignity extended from the Father through the Only-Begotten to the Spirit' (*ibid.* 47). He is also called the Spirit of Christ, but that does not mean that the Son is the only source of the Spirit, as Eunomius maintained (*Adv. Eunomium* 2, 34). Holy Scripture calls Him the 'Spirit of the Father' as well as 'the Spirit of the Son', since the Son has everything in common with the Father (*de Sp. S.* 18, 45). Basil indicates rather than expresses the conception that the Holy Spirit is in some sense through the Son and proceeds from Him (*Adv. Eunomium* 2, 32).

Studies: L. Lohn, Doctrina sancti Basilii Magni de processionibus divinarum personarum: Greg 10 (1929) 329-364, 461-500. — J. De Ghellinck, Patristique et Moyen Age, vol. III. Gembloux, 1948, 311-338 (Un cas de conscience dans les conflits trinitaires sur le Saint-Esprit). — H. Dörries, De Spiritu Sancto. Der Beitrag des Basilius zum Abschluss des trinitarischen Dogmas. Göttingen, 1956. — J. N. D. Kelly, op. cit. 258-263 (the *homoousion* of the Spirit). Cf. above p. 210.

4. *Eucharist*

One of the most remarkable documents regarding the Eucharist and the history of Holy Communion is Basil's *Ep.* 93, addressed to the patrician lady Caesaria in 372. It testifies to the reservation of the sacrament by private persons in their own houses for their own use, to the custom of daily communion and the belief in the presence of the body and blood of the Lord:

It is good and beneficial to communicate every day, and to partake of the holy body and blood of Christ. For he distinctly says, 'He that eats my flesh and drinks my blood has eternal life' (John 6, 54). And who doubts that to share frequently in life, is the same thing as to have manifold life? I, indeed, communicate four times a week, on the Lord's day, on Wednesday, on Friday, and on the Sabbath, and on the other days if there is a commemoration of any Saint. It is needless to point out that for anyone in times of persecution to be compelled to take the communion in his own hand without the presence of a priest or minister is not at all a serious offence, as long custom sanctions this practice from the facts themselves. All the solitaries in the desert, where there is no priest, take the communion themselves, keeping communion at home. And at Alexandria and in Egypt, each one of the laity, for the most part, keeps the communion at his own house, and participates in it when he likes. For when once the priest has completed the offering, and given it, the recipient, participating in it each time as entire, is bound to believe that he properly takes and receives it from the giver. And even in the church, when the priest gives the portion, the recipient takes it with complete power over it, and so lifts it up to his lips with his own hand. It has the same validity whether one portion or several portions are received from the priest at the same time (LNPF).

5. *Confession*

K. Holl is of the opinion that St. Basil originated auricular confession in the Catholic sense as a regular and obligatory confession of all sins, even the most secret (*Enthusiasmus*, p. 257, 2nd ed. 267). However, he erroneously identifies sacramental confession with the 'cloister confession', which was merely a means of discipline and spiritual direction, and involved no sacramental reconciliation or absolution. In his *Rule* (*Reg. fus. tract.* 25. 26. 46) St. Basil ordains that the monk has to reveal his heart and confess all his offences, even his innermost thoughts, to his superior or to others worthy of trust 'who enjoy the confidence of the brethren'. The place of the superior can in this instance be taken by someone elected as his representative. There is not the slightest indication that either the superior or his substitute must be a priest. Thus Basil might be said to have inaugurated what is known as the 'cloister confession' but not the auricular confession that forms an essential part of the sacrament of Penance.

From his so-called Canonical Letters (cf. above, p. 223) it appears that the discipline which had existed in the Churches of Cappadocia ever since the time of Gregory Thaumaturgos was still maintained. Expiation consisted in the separation of the penitent from the Christian assembly during the liturgical service. Four degrees had been mentioned in Gregory's *Epistula canonica* (cf. vol. II, p. 126): the state of 'weepers', who stayed outside the Church (προίσκλαυσις); the state of 'hearers', who were present for the reading of Holy Writ and the sermon (ἀκρόασις); the state of the 'prostrate' who assisted at the prayer on their knees *(ὑπόστασις)*; lastly, the state of those who stood during the whole office, but did not participate in the Communion *(σύστασις)*. In Basil's third Canonical Letter *(Ep.* 217, EH 593/6), which adds valuable information about the duration of the different periods, we have the same four classes of penitents, as is evident from canon 75:

> The man who has been polluted with his own sister, either on the father's or the mother's side, must not be allowed to enter the house of prayer, until he has given up his iniquitous and unlawful conduct. And, after he has come to a sense of that fearful sin, let him *weep* for three years standing at the door of the house of prayer, and entreating the people as they go in to prayer that each and all will mercifully offer on his behalf their prayers with earnestness to the Lord. After this let him be received for another period of three years to *hearing* alone, and while hearing the Scriptures and the instruction, let him be expelled and not be admitted to prayer. Afterwards, if he has asked it with tears and has fallen before the Lord with contrition of heart and great humiliation, let *kneeling* be accorded to him during other three years. Thus when he shall have worthily shown the fruits of repentance, let him be received in the tenth year to the prayer of the faithful without oblation; and after *standing* with the faithful in prayer for two years, then, and not till then, let him be held worthy of the *communion* of the good thing (LNPF).

Studies: K. HOLL, Enthusiasmus und Bussgewalt. Leipzig, 1898, 257-268. — A. LAGARDE (= J. TURMEL), La confession dans saint Basile: RHL 8 (1922) 534-548. — J. JANINI CUESTA, La penitencia medicinal desde la Didascalia Apostolorum a S. Gregorio de Nisa: RES 7 (1947) 337-362. — J. GROTZ, Die Entwicklung des Bussstufenwesens in der vornicänischen Kirche. Freiburg i.B., 1955, 404f.; 407f.; 415f.
For other studies on Basil's teaching, see: E. SCHOLL, Die Lehre des hl. Basilius von der Gnade. Freiburg i.B., 1881. — G. BÜTTNER, Beiträge zur Ethik Basileios' des Grossen (Progr.). Landshut, 1913. — C. GRONAU, Das Theodizeeproblem in der altchristlichen Auffassung. Tübingen, 1922. — T. PAPAKONSTANTINU, Ὁ Μέγας Βασιλείος, ἡ δογματικὴ αὐτοῦ διδασκαλία, 3rd ed. Athens, 1931. — B. KOSTITS, Τὸ πρόβλημα τῆς σωτηρίας. Athens, 1936 (Basil's soteriology). — B. K. EXARCHOS, Παιδαγωγαὶ γνῶμαι τοῦ Μ. Βασιλείου. Athens, 1938. — B. SCHEVE, Basilius der Grosse als Theologe. Ein Beitrag zur Frage nach der theologischen Arbeitsweise der Väter. Nijmegen, 1943. — G. BLOND, L'hérésie encratite vers la fin du IVᵉ siècle (chez Basile): RSR (1944) 157-210. — G. F. REILLY, Imperium and Sacerdotium according to St. Basil the Great. Washington, 1945. — I. COMAN, Plutarch's, St. Cyprian's and Basil the Great's Opinions on Envy (in Rumanian): Prinos. Studies in honor of Patriarch Nicodin. Bucarest, 1946, 255-272. — J. GRIBOMONT, Obéissance et Évangile selon saint Basile le Grand: VS Suppl. 21 (1952) 192-215 (no influence of Pachomius in the Rules). — W. A. TIECK, Basil of Caesarea and the Bible. Diss. Columbia Univ. New York, 1953. — D. M. NOTHOMB, Charité et Unité. Doctrine de saint Basile le Grand sur la charité envers le prochain: Proche-Orient Chrétien 4 (1954) 310-321. — E. BRUCK, Kirchenväter und soziales Erbrecht. Berlin, 1956, 3-10. — For Basil's ecclesiology, see: P. BATIFFOL, L'ecclésiologie de saint Basile: EO 21 (1922) 9-30. — V. GRUMEL, Saint Basile et le siège apostolique: EO 21 (1922) 280-292. — E. CASPAR, Geschichte des Papsttums I. Tübingen, 1930, 220-232. — A. N. DIAMANTOPOULOS, Basil the Great and Rome (in Greek): Ἐναίσιμα

[Studies in honor of Papadopoulos], ed. by G. Papamichail. Athens, 1931, 38-51 (B. did not admit any primacy of jurisdiction). For Basil's cosmology, see: J. F. CALLAHAN, Greek Philosophy and the Cappadocian Cosmology: DOP 12 (1958) 31-57. — For his influence on Augustine, see: J. F. CALLAHAN, Basil of Caesarea. A New Source for St. Augustine's Theory of Time: HSCP 63 (1958) 437-454.

ST. GREGORY OF NAZIANZUS

Gregory of Nazianzus was, like his friend Basil, the son of a wealthy aristocratic family in Cappadocia. He was almost the same age as Basil and followed the same course of studies. Nevertheless, he is a totally different type. He does not share the vigor of the great prince bishop of Caesarea nor his ability as a leader. He might be called the humanist among the theologians of the fourth century in so far as he preferred quiet contemplation and the union of ascetic piety and literary culture to the splendor of an active life and ecclesiastical position. Yet his weak and highly sensitive nature did not permit him to follow the yearning of his soul and to resist, consequently, all influences from the outside. As a result there appears a certain lack of resoluteness in his entire life. He longs for solitude and yet the prayers of his friends, his accommodating disposition and his sense of duty call him back to the turbulent world and the controversies and conflicts of his time. Thus his entire career is a succession of flights from, and returns to, the world.

Yet he has fascinated scholars for more than a thousand years as the 'Christian Demosthenes', as he was called in Byzantine times. He is beyond doubt one of the greatest orators of Christian antiquity and surpasses his friend Basil in his command of the resources of Hellenistic rhetoric. If he had any success in life, he owes it chiefly to the power of his eloquence.

Gregory was born about 330 at Arianzum in south-western Cappadocia, a country estate in the neighborhood of Nazianzus, of which his father, who bore the same name as himself, was bishop. His holy mother Nonna was the daughter of Christian parents. It was her example that had a decisive influence on the conversion of her husband in 325 and on the earliest training of her son, who tells us in one of his Orations (2, 77) that he was consecrated to God by his mother even before birth. He became first acquainted with Basil when as a youth he was sent to the school of rhetoric at Caesarea in Cappadocia. The latter went soon to Constantinople to continue his education while Gregory attended for a short time the Christian schools of Caesarea in Palestine and Alexandria in Egypt. His former acquaintance with Basil grew into an intimate friendship when he reached Athens in order to complete his studies at this famous seat of learning. In the funeral oration which he delivered over the body of his friend in 381 he has given us a most interesting account of University life at Athens in the middle of the fourth century. He left the city about 357, shortly after Basil, and returned home. It seems that he received baptism between this return to Cappadocia and his extensive visit in 358/59 with Basil, who lived in monastic retirement in the wilds of the Iris in Pontus. We have mentioned above (p. 205), the support he gave on that occasion to his friend Basil in the compilation of the *Philocalia* and the *Monastic Rules*. He became so fascinated by this kind of life that he would perhaps have remained in solitude, but his father wanted him ordained in order to have him as an aid to his own declining years and failing strength. When the people of Nazianzus seconded this desire, he did not have the courage to resist and was raised to the priesthood by his father about 362, actually against his will. In his displeasure at the violence done him, which he even years after describes as an act of tyranny (*Carmen de vita*, l. 345), he fled to his friend in Pontus, but soon returned with a truer view of his duty, and from now on faithfully assisted in the administration of the diocese and the care of souls. He explained and defended his flight and his return in his *Apologeticus de fuga* (cf. below, p. 243) which amounts to a complete treatise on the nature and responsibilities of the priestly office.

About the year 371 the Emperor Valens subdivided the civil province of Cappadocia into two, naming Caesarea, the centre of Basil's metropolitanship, as the capital of Cappadocia Prima, and Tyana as the capital of Cappadocia Secunda. Insisting that ecclesiastical divisions should parallel civil, Anthimus, the bishop of Tyana, thereupon pretended to be the metropolitan of the new province and claimed jurisdiction over some of Basil's suffragan sees. The latter strenuously objected and determined to erect several new bishoprics in the disputed territory in order to assert his rights and strengthen his position. Sasima was one of the towns selected and Basil consecrated his friend Gregory, who was very reluctant, as bishop of this miserable little village. Gregory never got possession of his see, but remained at Nazianzus, where he continued to help his father. When the latter died in 374, he took over the administration of the diocese of Nazianzus, but not for long. A year later he withdrew to Seleucia in Isauria to enter a life of retirement and contemplation.

Again it was only for a short period that he could enjoy his solitude. In 379 the small Nicene minority at Constantinople turned to Gregory with an urgent plea to come to their aid and to reorganize their Church, which, oppressed by a succession of Arian emperors and archbishops, hoped for a better future now that Valens had died. Gregory accepted and thus became for two years a conspicuous figure in the political history of the Church. When he arrived at the capital, he found all ecclesiastical buildings in the hands of the Arians. One of his relatives offered him his house, which he consecrated under the promising title of Anastasia, Church of the Resurrection. He soon won a large audience by his eloquent sermons and it was here that he preached the famous *Five Orations on the Divinity of the Logos* (cf. below, p. 242). When the new ruler of the East, Theodosius, made his triumphal entry into the city, December 24th, 380, the Catholics had all their edifices restored and Gregory was installed in the church of the Apostles, to which the Emperor conducted him personally in solemn procession. The Second Ecumenical Council, which Theodosius convoked and opened at Constantinople in May 381, recognized Gregory as bishop of the capital. However, when the hierarchy of Egypt and Macedonia objected to his nomination for canonical reasons and also because it had been made before their arrival, he was so disgusted that he resigned from the second see of Christendom within a few days. Before his departure he delivered in the Cathedral his farewell sermon (*Orat.* 42) to the episcopal assembly and the people. He returned to Nazianzus and took charge of the diocese until two years later (384) in his friend Eulalius a satisfactory successor to his father was consecrated. Relieved of his burden, Gregory spent the last years of his earthly life on his family's estate at Arianzum, entirely devoted to his literary pursuits and monastic practices, until the last burden, his sickly body, was taken from him. He died in 389 or 390.

Studies: H. LECLERCQ, Grégoire de Nazianze: DAL 6 (1925) 1667-1711; *idem*, Nazianze: DAL 12 (1935) 1054-1065. — W. RUGE, Nazianzos: PWK 16 (1935) 2099-2101. — Q. CATAUDELLA, Gregorio Nazianzeno: EC 6 (1951) 1088-1096. — The most important sources for his life are his letters and his poems. A Greek *Vita S. Gregorii* was composed by a priest Gregorios in the seventh century (Text: MG 35, 243-304). Cf. J. COMPERNASS, Gregorios Presbyter. Bonn, 1907. For six other Lives and the many encomia, see: J. SAJDAK, Historia critica scholiastarum et commentatorum. Gregorii Naz. I (Meletema Patristica I). Cracow, 1914, 255f.; 248f.; 256f. Selections of the encomium by Johannes Kyriotes Geometres of the tenth century were published by P. TACCHI-VENTURI, De Ioanne Geometra eiusque in S. Gregorium Nazianzenum inedita laudatione in cod. Vaticano-Palatino 402 adservata: Studi e documenti di Storia e Diritto 14 (1893) 133-162.

Gregory's last will and testament, written most probably at Constantinople on May 31, 381, is extant: MG 37, 389-396. New edition: Card. PITRA, Iuris ecclesiae Graecorum hist. et monumenta, vol. 2. Rome, 1868, 153-160. Gregory bequeathed all his property to the 'Catholic community of Nazianzus for the benefit of the poor'. Cf. F. MARTROYE, Le testament de saint Grégoire de Nazianze: Mémoires de la Société nationale des Antiquaires de France 76 (1923) 219-263; repr. sep. Paris, 1924.

C. ULLMANN, Gregorius von Nazianz der Theologe. Ein Beitrag zur Kirchen- und

Dogmengeschichte des vierten Jahrhunderts. 2nd ed. Gotha, 1867. — A. Benoît, St. Grégoire de Nazianze. Sa vie, ses œuvres et son époque. 2nd ed. Paris, 1885, 2 vols. — E. Fleury, Hellénisme et christianisme: Saint Grégoire de Nazianze et son temps. Paris, 1930. — I. G. Coman, Geniul Stantului Grigorie din Nazianz. Bucarest, 1937 (the genius of St. Greg.). — S. Giet, Sasimes, une méprise de saint Basile. Paris, 1941 (relations between Basil and Gregory). — P. Gallay, La Vie de saint Grégoire de Nazianze. Lyon, 1943. — J. Lercher, Die Persönlichkeit des hl. Gregorius von Nazianz und seine Stellung zur klassischen Bildung (aus seinen Briefen). Diss. Innsbruck, 1949. — E. Rapisarda, Il pessimismo di Gregorio Nazianzeno: MSLC 3 (1951) 136-161; reprinted: Atti dello VIIIº Congr. internaz. di Studi bizantini (Palermo, 1951) vol. I. Rome, 1953, 189-201. — K. G. Bones, Γρηγόριος ὁ Θεολόγος. Πατρολογικὴ καὶ γενεαλογικὴ μελέτη. Athens, 1953; cf. H. M. Werhahn, BZ 67 (1954) 414-418 and Bones' reply: BZ 68 (1955) 211f. — F. Lefherz, Studien zu Gregor von Nazianz. Mythologie, Überlieferung, Scholiasten. Diss. Bonn, 1958.

I. HIS WRITINGS

Gregory of Nazianzus was by no means a prolific writer. He never composed a biblical commentary nor any learned dogmatic treatise. His literary bequest consists solely of orations, poems and letters. He is the only poet among the great theologians of the fourth century. In his prose as well as in his verse, he always remains the great rhetorician with a perfection in form and style unattained by any of his Christian contemporaries. It is mainly for this reason that his works attracted the interest of the medieval Byzantine commentators as well as the humanists of the Renaissance. A critical text of Gregory is badly needed. The Cracow Academy of Sciences undertook the task before 1914. A number of preparatory studies were published but no new edition has as yet appeared.

Collections: Maurist ed. by C. Clémencet and A. B. Caillau. Paris, vol. 1, 1778; vol. 2, 1840; repr. MG 35-38. Cf. D. Meehan, Editions of Saint Gregory of Nazianzus: ITQ 3 (1951) 203-219.

Translations: English: C. G. Browne and J. E. Swallow, LNPF ser. 2, vol. 7 (1894) 185-498. — *German:* J. Röhm, BKV vol. 1 (1874), vol. 2 (1877). — P. Häuser, BKV² 59 (1928), BKV³ 3 (1939). — *French:* P. Gallay, Grégoire de Nazianze, Textes choisis. Trad. et annot., 2 vols. Paris, 1941.

Studies: I. R. Asmus, Gregor von Nazianz und sein Verhältnis zum Kynismus: ThStKr 67 (1894) 314-338. — R. Gottwald, De Gregorio Nazianzeno Platonico. Diss. Breslau, 1906. — J. Sajdak, De Gregorio Nazianzeno posteriorum rhetorum, grammaticorum, lexicographorum fonte: Eos 16 (1910) 94-99; *idem,* De Gregorio Nazianzeno poetarum Christianorum fonte: Eos 18 (1912) 1-30. — L. Deubner, Kerkidas bei Gregor von Nazianz: Hermes 54 (1919) 438-441. — H. Pinault, Le Platonisme de saint Grégoire de Nazianze (Paris thesis). La Roche-sur-Yon, 1925. ·Cf. G. Bardy, RAp 42 (1926) 681-685. — E. C. E. Owen, St. Gregory at Nazianzus: JThSt 26 (1925) 64-71 (notes on grammar, vocabulary and style). — For the influence of the sophists on his language and style, see: E. Fleury, op. cit. — M. T. Disdier, Nouvelles études sur Grégoire de Nazianze: EO 34 (1931) 485-497 (covers the period 1918-1931). — P. Gallay, Langue et style de saint Grégoire de Nazianze. Paris, 1933. — M. E. Keenan, St. Gregory of

Nazianzus and Early Byzantine Medicine: BHM 9 (1941) 8-30. — R. DE L. HENRY
The Late Greek Optative and its Use in the Writings of Gregory of Nazianzus.
Washington, 1943. Cf. M. J. HIGGINS, Why another Optative Dissertation?: Byz 15
(1940/41) 443-448. — B. ALTANER, Augustinus, Gregor von Nazianz und Gregor von
Nyssa: RB 61 (1951) 54-62 (shows that Augustine knew Gregory's writings). —
AGATHANGELOS VON KYDONIA, 'Ο κωμῳδοποιὸς 'Αριστοφάνης καὶ Γρηγόριος ὁ
Ναζιανζῆνος: Γρηγόριος ὁ Παλαμᾶς 36 (1953) 20-24 (influence of Aristophanes).

1. *The Orations*

The finest of his compositions are the 45 extant *Orations*. Evidently
only a selection made soon after his death, most of them belong to
the years 379-381, the most important period of his life, when, as
bishop of Constantinople, he drew world-wide attention. The
orations gave Gregory greater opportunity to display his rhetorical
skill than all his other writings and we find in them all the devices of
Asianic eloquence-figures, images, antitheses, interjections, staccato
sentences — employed to an extent that appears to the modern
reader excessive. There is no doubt that he was making every effort
to please an audience that appreciated such cleverness. Here he
proves himself an apt pupil of his teachers at Athens, Himerius and
Prohaeresius (Socrates, *Hist. eccl.* 4, 26), and of the sophist Polemon
(Jerome, *De vir. ill.* 117). These speeches were soon read and studied
in the schools of rhetoric. As a result there appeared numerous
scholia within a short time, the oldest of which date from the
beginning of the sixth century. Those of Elias, a tenth-century
archbishop of Crete, are still useful. The poetical rhythm of Gregory's
prose was the reason that passages of his orations were in later times
made the basis of ecclesiastical hymns and poems. Such borrowings
can be found in the verse of Dorotheus of Maiuma, John Damascene,
Cosmas of Maiuma, Arsenius of Corcyra, Nicephorus Blemmydes
and in a number of anonymous compositions.

As early as 399 or 400 Rufinus of Aquileia translated nine of the
orations into Latin. They are n. 2, 6, 16, 17, 26, 27, 38-40. Unfortunately, his work was very hasty and careless. There exist in
addition old versions in Armenian, Syriac, Slavonic, Coptic,
Georgian, Arabic and Ethiopic.

Editions: MG 35-36 (*Or.* 35 is spurious). Latin translation by Rufinus: A. ENGELBRECHT,
Tyrannii Rufini Orationum Gregorii Nazianzeni novem interpretatio: CSEL 46 (1910).

Translations: English: C. G. BROWNE and J. E. SWALLOW, Select Orations: LNPF ser. 2,
vol. 7, 203-434 (24 Orations). — *German:* J. RÖHM, BKV 2 vols. (1874/1877), translated
25 Orat. — P. HÄUSER, BKV² 59 (1928), BKV³ 3 (1939). — T. MICHELS, Gregor von
Nazianz, Macht des Mysteriums. Sechs geistliche Reden an den Hochtagen der Kirche.
Düsseldorf, 1956 (MG 36, 312-333, 336-360, 396-401, 427-452, 607-664). — *Italian:*
Q. CATAUDELLA, Greg. Naz., Orazioni scelte. Turin, 1936. — *Spanish:* L. DEL PARAMO,
Homilias de San Gregorio Nazianceno: Obras escogidas de patrologia griega. Barcelona,
1916.

Manuscript tradition: T. SINKO, I. De traditione orationum Gregorii Nazianzeni (Meletema Patristica II). Cracow, 1917; II. De traditione indirecta (Meletema Patristica III). Cracow, 1923. — F. LEFHERZ, op. cit. — G. ROCHEFORT, Une anthologie grecque du XIe siècle, le Parisinus Suppl. Gr. 690: Scriptorium 4 (1950) 3-17.

Versions: For the Old versions, see: W. LÜDTKE, Zur Überlieferung der Reden Gregors von Nazianz: OC N.S. 3 (1913) 263-276. — For the Arabic versions: G. GRAF, Geschichte der christlichen arabischen Literatur I. Vatican City, 1944, 330-332. — The Coptic homily on Genesis 22 attributed to Gregory and edited and translated by M. CHAÎNE, ROC 17 (1912) 395-409, 18 (1913) 36-38, is nothing but an excerpt from Gregory of Nyssa's *Oratio de deitate Filii et Spiritus Sancti* (MG 46, 553f.). — W. E. CRUM, Theological Texts from Coptic Papyri, Oxford, 1913, 36-53, published the Coptic text and an English translation of a homily on repentance and Rom. 4, 15, ascribed to Gregory of Naz. For an Armenian oration On the Holy Cross, see: Bazmavep (Venice) 91 (1933) 444-449. A Slavonic version of 13 orations was published by A. BUDILOVIC, St. Pétersbourg, 1875.

Scholia: MG 36, 737-1256; MG 127, 1177-1480. — J. SAJDAK, Historia critica scholiastarum et commentatorum Gregorii Nazianzeni I (Meletema Patristica I). Cracow, 1914; *idem*, Die Scholiasten der Reden des Gregor von Nazianz. Ein kurzgefasster Bericht über den jetzigen Stand der Forschung: BZ 30 (1930) 268-274. — P. A. BRUCKMAYR, Untersuchungen über die Randscholien der 28 Reden des hl. Gregorios von Nazianz im Cod. theol. Gr. 74 der Wiener Nationalbibliothek. Diss. Vienna, 1940 (typ. copy available at the Philol. Seminar of the University). — K. A. DE MEYIER, Un manuscrit grec de la Bibliothèque d'Antoine Perrenot de Granvelle à la Bibliothèque Universitaire de Leyde: Scriptorium 2 (1948) 290-291 (Voss. Gr. F 45 containing the scholia of Basil Minimus). — F. LEFHERZ, Studien zu Gregor von Nazianz. Mythologie, Überlieferung, Scholiasten. Bonn, 1958.

Studies: S. PETRIDES, Notes d'hymnographie byzantine: BZ 13 (1904) 421-428 (commentaries of the archimandrite Dorotheus on Gregory of Nazianzus, proof of the early dependence of Byzantine lyric poetry upon the rhetorical prose of Gregory). — E. NORDEN, Antike Kunstprosa, vol. 2. Leipzig, 1909, 562-569. — A. DONDERS, Der hl. Kirchenlehrer Gregor von Nazianz als Homilet. Münster, 1909. — M. GUIGNET, Saint Grégoire de Nazianze et la rhétorique. Thèse. Paris, 1911; *idem*, Saint Grégoire de Nazianze orateur et épistolier. Paris, 1911. — J. SAJDAK, De Gregorio Nazianzeno poetarum Christianorum fonte. Cracow, 1917 (passages of Gregory's homilies in Dorotheus, John Damascene and others). — T. SINKO, De expositione Pseudo-Nonniana historiarum quae in orationibus Gregorii Nazianzeni commemorantur: Charisteria C. de Morawski oblata. Cracow, 1922, 124-148. — H. FUCHS, Augustin und der antike Friedensgedanke. Berlin, 1926, 96-125 (*Orat.* 6). — J. SAJDAK, Anonymi Oxoniensis Lexicon in Orationes Gregorii Nazianzeni: Mélanges Rozwadowski. Cracow, 1927, 153-179. — J. LIST, Zwei Zeugnisse für die Lobrede bei Gregor von Nazianz: BNJ 6 (1928) 24-31 (*Orat.* 21). — S. SKIMINA, De Gregorii Nazianzeni sermonum proprietatibus ad prosam rhythmicam pertinentibus: Acta II. Congressus philol. class. Slav. Prague, 1931, 229-235. — E. BIGNONE, Nuove testimonianze e frammenti del 'Protrettico' di Aristotele: RFIC 64 (1936) 225-237 (*Orat.* 40). — F. J. DÖLGER, Nonna. Ein Kapitel über christliche Volksfrömmigkeit des vierten Jahrhunderts: AC 5 (1936) 44-75 (*Orat.* 18). — B. WYSS, Gregorius Nazianzenus, Orat. 28, 8: Hermes (1938) 360 (text. crit.). — H. FRANK, Das Alter der römischen Laudes- und Vesperantiphonen der Weihnachtsoktav und ihrer griechischen Originale: OC 36 (1939) 14-18 (*Or.* 39 *In sancta lumina*). — L. BROU, Saint Grégoire de Nazianze et l'antienne 'Mirabile Mysterium' des Laudes de la Circoncision: EL 58 (1944) 14-22 (*Orat.* 39). — B. WYSS, Zu Gregor von Nazianz: Phyllobolia P. Von der Mühll. Basel, 1946, 153-183 (*Orat.* 28, 11 text. crit.). — J. VOGT, Berichte über Kreuzeserscheinungen aus dem vierten Jahrhundert: AIPh 9 (1949) 593-606 (*Orat.* 5). — DOUBOUNIOTIS, Niketas of Herakleia. Introduction to the

Orations of Gregory of Naz.: Θεολογία (1950) 354-384. — O. Strunk, St. Gregory of Nazianzus and the Proper Hymns for Easter: Late Classical and Mediaeval Studies in Honor of A. M. Friend, ed. by K. Weitzmann. Princeton, 1955, 82-87 (*Orat.* 1 and 45, *Or.* 33). — D. Ruiz, La homilia como forma de predicación: Helmatica 7 (1956) 79-111 (Gregory's rhetorical talent).

a. The Five Theological Orations (27-31), delivered at Constantinople in the summer or fall of 380, have won Gregory greater admiration than any of his other compositions. It is to them that he owes the distinctive title, 'the Theologian'. They defend the Church's dogma against Eunomians and Macedonians, and, though they were preached with the special purpose of protecting the Nicene faith of his own congregation, they represent the mature result of long and intensive study of the trinitarian doctrine. The first serves as an introduction to the series and treats of the pre-requisits for a discussion of divine truths. The second deals with *theologia* in the strict sense, i.e. the existence, nature and attributes of God, so far as human intellect can comprehend and define them. The third demonstrates the unity of nature in the three divine Persons, particularly the divinity of the Logos and his coequality with the Father. The fourth is a refutation of the Arian objections against the divinity of the Son and of the scriptural passages abused by them. The fifth oration defends the divinity of the Holy Spirit against the Macedonians. Gregory himself calls (*Orat.* 28, 1) the last four orations τῆς θεολογίας λόγοι.

Separate Edition: A. J. Mason, The Five Theological Orations of Gregory of Nazianzus (Cambridge Patristic Texts). Cambridge, 1899 (with valuable commentary).

Translations: English: C. G. Browne and J. E. Swallow, LNPF ser. 2, vol. 7 (1894) 284-328; reprinted: E. R. Hardy, Christology of the Later Fathers (LCC 3). London and Philadelphia, 1954, 128-214. — *German:* P. Häuser, BKV³ 3 (1939). — *French:* P. Gallay, Grégoire de Nazianze. Les discours théologiques. Lyons and Paris, 1942.

b. Oration n. 20 *On the Order and Establishment of Bishops* and n. 32 *On Moderation and Purpose in Controversies* denounce the passion of the Constantinopolitans for dogmatic controversies and arguments. The first gives in addition a detailed definition of the trinitarian teaching.

c. The *apologetic* group of his orations consists of two invectives against Julian the Apostate (n. 4 and 5), whom Gregory had personally known at Athens. They were composed after the Emperor's death (June 26, 363) but probably never delivered in public. Hate and anger so predominate in them that their historical value is almost nil.

Separate Edition: R. Montagu, Eaton, 1610.

Translations: English: C. W. KING, Julian the Emperor, containing Gregory Nazianzen's two invectives and Libanius' Monody, with Julian's extant theosophical works. London, 1888. — *German:* P. HÄUSER, BKV² 59 (1928) 71-191.

Studies: R. ASMUS, Die Invektiven des Gregorius von Nazianz im Lichte der Werke des Kaisers Julian: ZKG 31 (1910) 325-367. — J. COMAN, S. Grigorie din Nazianz despre imperatul Julian. Incercare asupra discursurilor 4 si 5. Vol. I. Bucarest, 1938. — F. DVORNIK, The Emperor Julian's 'Reactionary' Ideas on Kingship: Late Classical and Mediaeval Studies in Honor of A. M. Friend, ed. by K. Weitzmann. Princeton, 1955, 71-80 (*Orat.* 4). — J. BERNARDI, La formule πού εἰσιν : saint Jean Chrysostome a-t-il imité saint Grégoire de Nazianze?: SP I (TU 63). Berlin, 1957, 178-181 (*Contra Jul.* 2, 25; MG 35, 693-696).

d. The *panegyrical* and *hagiographic* group includes far more of his orations than the dogmatic. Some of them are liturgical sermons for Christmas, Epiphany, Easter, Low Sunday, Pentecost; others, encomiums of the Maccabees, St. Cyprian of Carthage, St. Athanasius, Maximus the philosopher; others again, funeral orations over his father, his brother Caesarius, his sister Gorgonia, his friend St. Basil.

Separate Editions: V. QUENTIER, Paris, 1880 (*Orat.* 7: panegyric on his brother Caesarius). — F. BOULENGER, Paris, 1908 (*Or.* 7 and 43 panegyric on Caesarius and on Basil).

Separate Translations: J. COLLIER, A Panegyric upon the Maccabees by St. Gregory Nazianzen. London, 1716. — *French:* F. BOULENGER, op. cit. (*Or.* 7 and 43). — *Italian:* P. GAZZOLA, Asti, 1913 (*Orat.* 7 and 43). — *German:* T. MICHELS, op. cit. (liturgical homilies).

Studies: For the sermons on Christmas and Epiphany, see: H. USENER, Das Weihnachtsfest. 2nd ed. Bonn, 1911, 260f. — For the funeral orations: L. RULAND, Die Geschichte der kirchlichen Leichenfeier. Regensburg, 1901, 154-157. — X. HÜRTH, De Gregorii Naz. orationibus funebribus. Strasbourg, 1907. — A. N. MALIN, Οἱ ἐπιτάφιοι λόγοι Γρηγορίου N. Athens, 1929. — For the panegyric on Cyprian in which Gregory mixes the legend of the pagan magician Cyprian of Antioch with the history of St. Cyprian of Carthage, see: T. SINKO, De Cypriano martyre a Gregorio Naz. laudato. Cracow, 1916. — H. DELEHAYE, Cyprien d'Antioche et Cyprien de Carthage: AB 39 (1921) 314-332. — A. D. NOCK, Cyprian of Antioch: JThSt 28 (1927) 411-415. — L. KRESTAN - A. HERMANN, RACh 2 (1956) 467-477. — For Gregory's brother Caesarius, see: O. SEECK, PWK 3 (1897) 1298-1300. — V. CASOLI, Cesario medico del sec. 4. Modena, 1931. — C. NOPPEN, Lofrede van Caesarius door St. Gregorius Nazianzenus. Brussels, 1934. — The 'Questions and Answers' entitled *Dialogi quattuor* attributed to Caesarius (MG 38, 851-1190) are spurious. K. G. BONES, EEBS (1953) 261-279, thinks that Severus of Antioch might be the author. P. DUPREY, Quand furent composés les 'Dialogues' attribués à Césaire de Nazianze?: Proche-Orient Chrétien 5 (1955) 14-30, 297-315, is of the opinion that they originated in the first half of the sixth century.

e. The largest group is made up of *occasional orations*. In the most important, n. 2, the *Apologeticus de fuga*, he describes at great length the character and responsibilities of the sacerdotal office, in order to justify himself for first fleeing from its burdens and then returning to submit to them. This is virtually a complete treatise on the priesthood and it was used by St. John Chrysostom as the model and source for his *Six Books on the Priesthood*. It also inspired Gregory the Great's *Pastoral Rule*. Gregory of Nazianzus seems to have preached only a part of it in 362 and enlarged it at a later date.

Separate Edition: Apologeticus de fuga: J. ALZOG, Freiburg i.B., 1858, 2nd ed. 1869.

Separate Translation: German: G. WOHLENBERG, Gregorius' von Nazianz Schutzrede und Chrysostomus' sechs Bücher vom Priestertum (Bibliothek theol. Klassiker 29). Gotha, 1890.

Studies: J. VOLK, Die Schutzrede des Gregor von Nazianz und die Schrift über das Priestertum von Johannes Chrysostomus: Zeitschrift für praktische Theologie 17 (1895) 56-63. — MENN, Zur Pastoraltheologie Gregors von Nazianz: Revue internat. de Théologie 12 (1904) 427-440. — M. M. WAGNER, Rufinus the Translator. A Study of his Theory and his Practice as Illustrated in his Version of the 'Apologetica' of St. Gregory Nazianzen (PSt 73). Washington, 1945.

Among his other occasional orations we find one on his elevation to the see of Sasima, another on the consecration of Eulalius as successor to his father, and, the last of this group, his Farewell Address after his resignation, with which he took leave of the Council and the congregation of Constantinople in 381 (*Orat.* 42).

2. Poems

It was at the end of his life, during his retirement at Arianzum, that Gregory composed his poems. Although he could not be called an inspired poet, some of his verses nevertheless show real poetic feeling and rise to genuine beauty. Other compositions are nothing more than prose in meter. In all, about 400 poems are extant. One of them, entitled *In suos versus* explains in detail why he turned to poetry in his old age. He wished first of all to prove that the new Christian culture was no longer inferior in any way to the pagan. Secondly, since certain heresies, especially that of Apollinaris, did not hesitate to spread their teachings in poetical garb, he finds it necessary to make use of the same weapon for a successful refutation of their false doctrines. Thus 38 of his poems are dogmatic and deal with the Trinity, the works of God in creation, Divine Providence, the Fall, the Incarnation, the genealogies, miracles and parables of Our Lord and the canonical books of Holy Scripture. Forty of the poems are moral. The best of the entire collection are found among the 206 historical and autobiographical poems. Here he finds an opportunity to express his innermost thoughts and feelings, his longing for relatives and friends who rest in God, his hopes and desires, his disillusions and errors. The longest work is his autobiography, *De vita sua*, which counts 1949 iambic trimeters. It represents not only the principal source for the life of Gregory from his birth to his departure from Constantinople but also the highest achievement in autobiography of all Greek literature. He wrote also several other autobiographical poems: *Querela de suis calamitatibus* (2, 1, 19), *De animae suae calamitatibus lugubre* (2, 1, 45) and *Carmen lugubre pro sua anima*. All these works together depict for us the inner life of a Christian soul with such power and vividness that they can be compared only with the *Confessions* of St. Augustine.

Among Gregory's other verses are numerous epitaphs, epigrammatic maxims and aphorisms — types in which he excelled. He is master of a great variety of metres. It has been noted that his rhythm is based on stress, not quantity, in his works, *Hymnus vespertinus* and *Exhortatio ad virgines* (1, 1, 32 and 1, 2, 3). But they seem to be unauthentic. R. Keydell has proved that at least the latter cannot be attributed to Gregory. The tragedy, *Christus patiens*, found among his works (MG 38, 133-338), is certainly spurious. It was written most probably in the eleventh or twelfth century and remains the only extant drama of the Byzantine period.

Opinion is still divided as to a just evaluation of Gregory's poetry. Pellegrino and Wyss differ diametrically in their conclusions. Keydell is convinced that his poetry shows in form and content a complete break with classical antiquity, is independent of any tradition and has never had an imitator. Werhahn, however, who offers a new critical edition of *Comparatio vitarum* (MG 37, 649-667), has, on the whole, proved that Gregory used extensively philosophical sources like Plato, Stoa and the diatribe literature and reworked familiar commonplaces, for instance, in his description of the life of the rich. In his verse Gregory appears to have his roots deep in the classical tradition. He takes over its treasures whenever he thinks them useful for a Christian philosophy of life, but his creative mind melts them down and forms something new which has definitely the stamp of his own Christian soul.

A complete critical edition of the poems was prepared by L. Sternbach. Unfortunately the manuscript was lost during the last world war. Migne contains many spurious pieces.

Editions: MG 37-38. 16 are spurious or doubtful. A good edition of some epic and didactic poems is found in W. CHRIST and M. PARANIKAS, Anthologia Graeca carminum Christianorum. Leipzig, 1871, 23-32. Separate ed.: H. M. WERHAHN, Gregorii Nazianzeni Σύγκρισις βίων. Carmen edidit, apparatu critico munivit, quaestiones peculiares adiecit. Wiesbaden, 1953. A Syriac version of Gregory's Iambic poems was published by J. BOLLIG and H. GISMONDI, S. Gregorii Theologi liber carminum iambicorum, versio Syriaca antiquissima. 2 vols. Beyrouth, 1895/96.

Translations: English: H. S. BOYD, Select Poems of Synesius and Gregory Nazianzen. London, 1814. — W. R. PATON, The Epigrams of Saint Gregory the Theologian: The Greek Anthology (LCL). London, 1917, 399-505. — H. Card. NEWMAN translated several poems in: Historical Sketches, vol. 2, 55-72. — *French:* P. GALLAY, Grégoire de Nazianze.

Poèmes et lettres choisies. Lyons and Paris, 1941. — *Italian:* M. PELLEGRINO, Poesie scelte. Turin, 1939. — F. CORSARO, Poesie scelte: MSLC 6 (1955) 1-42.

General Studies: M. SCHUBACH, De b. patris Gregorii Nazianzeni Theologi carminibus commentatio patrologica. Koblenz, 1871. — P. STOPPEL, Quaestiones de Gregorii Nazianzeni poetarum scaenicorum imitatione et arte metrica. Diss. Rostock, 1881. — A. LUDWICH, Nachahmer und Vorbilder des Dichters Gregorios von Nazianz: RhM 42 (1887) 233-238. — E. DUBEDOUT, De D. Gregorii Nazianzeni carminibus. Paris, 1901. — W. ACKERMANN, Die didaktische Poesie des Gregorius von Nazianz. Diss. Leipzig, 1903. — J. GEFFCKEN, Kynika und Verwandtes. Heidelberg, 1909 (influence of the Cynic-Stoic diatribe on Gregory's *poemata moralia*). — Q. CATAUDELLA, Le poesie di Gregorio Nazianzeno: Atene e Roma 8 (1927) 88-96. — M. PELLEGRINO, La poesia di S. Gregorio Nazianzeno (Pubbl. Univ. Sacro Cuore, sc. filol. 13). Milan, 1932. — G. GHEDINI, La poesia di S. Gregorio Nazianzeno: SC (1932) 256-260. — J. COMAN, Tristetea poeziei lirice a St. Grigorie de Nazianz. Bucarest, 1938 (the melancholic character of Gregory's lyric poetry). — H. L. DAVIDS, De gnomologieën van Sint Gregorius van Nazianze. Diss. Amsterdam, 1940. — B. WYSS, Zu Gregor von Nazianz: Phyllobolia für P. Von der Mühll. Basel, 1946, 153-183 (text. crit.); *idem*, Gregor von Nazianz. Ein griechisch-christlicher Dichter des vierten Jahrhunderts: Museum Helveticum 6 (1949) 177-210. — T. SINKO, Chronologia poezji św. Grzegorza z Nazjianzu. Cracow, 1947. — H. M. WER-HAHN, op. cit. — R. KEYDELL, Die literarhistorische Stellung der Gedichte Gregors von Nazianz: Atti del VIII° Congresso internazionale di Studi bizantini I. Rome, 1953, 143-143. — F. CORSARO, Gregorio Nazianzeno poeta: MSLC 6 (1956) 5-21. — F. SCHEIDWEILER, Zu den Gedichten Gregors von Nazianz bei Cantarella und Soyter: BZ 49 (1956) 345-348. — I. G. COMAN, The Poetry of Gregory of Nazianzus (in Rumanian): Studii teologice 10 (1958) 68-92.

Special Studies: For the autobiographical poems, see: L. F. M. DE JONGE, De S. Gregorii Nazianzeni carminibus quae inscribi solent περὶ ἑαυτοῦ. Amsterdam, 1910. — G. MISCH Geschichte der Autobiographie, vol. 1: Das Altertum, 2. Hälfte, 3rd ed. Frankfurt a. M. 1950, 383-402; English translation: G. MISCH, A History of Autobiography in Antiquity, vol. 2. London, 1950, 600-624 (the autobiographical poems of Gregory of Naz.). — A. GANGI, Il De vita sua di Gregorio Nazianzeno. Thesis. Catania Univers. Cf. Nuovo Didaskaleion 1 (1947) 99. — P. COURCELLES, Antécédents autobiographiques des Confessions de saint Augustin: RPh 31 (1957) 23-51. — For the *Carmen ad Vitalianum*, see: Q. CATAUDELLA, Derivazioni da Saffo in Gregorio Nazianzeno: BFC 33 (1926/27) 282-284. — For the spurious *Exhortatio ad virgines*, cf. R. KEYDELL, Die Unechtheit der Gregor von Nazianz zugeschriebenen Exhortatio ad virgines: BZ 43 (1950) 334-337. — For eight of the dogmatic poems in hexameters (MG 38, 397-456) see: R. KEYDELL, Ein dogmatisches Lehrgedicht Gregors von Nazianz: BZ 44 (1951) 315-321. — For the spurious *Christus patiens*, see: E. A. PULLIG, Χριστὸς πάσχων. Der leidende Christus. Christliche Tragödie, als deren Verfasser lange Zeit Gregor von Nazianz gegolten hat. Beilage zum Jahresbericht der Oberrealschule zu Bonn, 1893 (German translation preserving the original metre). — K. KRUMBACHER, Geschichte der byzantinischen Litera-tur. 2nd ed. Munich, 1897, 746-749. — K. HORNA, Der Verfasser des Christus patiens: Hermes 64 (1929) 429-431 (Constantinus Manasses in the first half of the 12th century the author). — A. MOMIGLIANO, Un termino post quem per il Christus patiens: SIF 10 (1933) 47-51 (compares Romanos Melod. with *Christus pat.* 454-460). — F. J. DÖLGER, Die Blutsalbung des Soldaten mit der Lanze im Passionsspiel Christus patiens. Zugleich ein Beitrag zur Longinus-Legende: AC 4 (1934) 81-94. — A. TUILIER, La datation et l'attribution du Χριστὸς πάσχων et l'art du centon: Actes du 6e Congrès internat. d'Études byzantines I. Paris, 1950, 403-409 (time of composition: 4th century). Cf. F. DÖLGER, BZ (1952) 159 (against Tuilier). — R. CANTARELLA, Anonimo bizantino del secolo XII (Pseudo-Gregorio Nazianzeno). La passione di Cristo. Azione drammatica in 5 quadri e 12 scene: Dioniso 16 (1953) 188-207 (Italian translation).

3. Letters

Gregory was the first Greek author to publish a collection of his letters; he did so at the request of Nicobulus (cf. above, p. 220), a grandson of his sister Gorgonia. Incidentally, he also sets forth a theory of epistolography; he demands that a good letter should have four characteristics: shortness, clearness, charm and simplicity (*Ep.* 51 and 54). Although he refuses to present his own epistles as models, they are carefully written, in many cases not without humor, and most of them are brief and pointed. Thus St. Basil declares conciseness to be typical of his friend's correspondence. In writing (*Ep.* 19) to Gregory he remarks: 'The day before yesterday a letter came to me from you. It was indeed strictly yours, not so much in handwriting as in the letter's peculiar quality. For, though the sentences were few they offered much thought'.

There are 244 extant letters in Migne and another, addressed to Basil, was discovered by G. Mercati. Most of them were written during his retirement at Arianzum during the years 383-389. Though pleasant in style and spirit, they have not the importance of St. Basil's correspondence. Their value is predominantly autobiographical, and, in general, they do not go beyond the circle of his friends and relatives. A few have gained repute for their theology, especially two addressed to the priest Cledonius, *Ep.* 101 and 102. Both were probably written in 382, in order to furnish material for a refutation of the Apollinarists. The Council of Ephesus (431) adopted a long passage of *Ep.* 101, that of Chalcedon (451), the entire letter. Another communication dealing with Apollinarianism is *Ep.* 202, in which in 387 Gregory warned his successor bishop Nectarius of Constantinople against the increasing activity of this sect. Sozomen (*Hist. eccl.* 6, 27) quotes most of it.

Editions: MG 37. G. MERCATI, Nuova lettera di Gregorio Nazianzeno e risposta di Basilio Magno: Varia Sacra, fasc. 1 (ST 11). Rome, 1903, 53-56 (from Cod. Vatic. Gr. 435). *Ep.* 42 is not by Gregory but by his father, *Ep.* 241 is by St. Basil, *Ep.* 243 is by Gregory Thaumaturgos.

Translations: English: C. G. BROWNE and J. E. SWALLOW, Select Letters: LNPF ser. 2, vol. 7, 437-482. — The translation of *Ep.* 101 and 102 to Cledonius and *Ep.* 202 to Nectarius has been reprinted in: E. R. HARDY, Christology of the Later Fathers (LCC 3). London and Philadelphia, 1954, 215-232. — *French:* P. GALLAY, Grégoire de Nazianze. Textes choisis. Vol. I. Poèmes et lettres. Paris, 1941. — *Polish:* J. STAHR, Poznań, 1933.

Manuscript Tradition: G. PRZYCHOCKI, The Vatican Manuscripts of the Letters of St. Gregory of Nazianzus (in Polish): Eos 16 (1910) 100-136; *idem*, De Gregorii Naz. epistularum codicibus Laurentianis: WSt (1911) 251-263; *idem*, De Gregorii Naz. epistularum codicibus Britannicis, qui Londini, Oxoniae, Cantabrigiae asservantur: BAPC (1912) 5-6 and Rozprawy Akademji umiejętności w Krakowie III ser. V, 230-246. — P. GALLAY, Notes sur quelques manuscrits parisiens des lettres de saint Grégoire de Nazianze: Mélanges A. M. Desrousseaux. Paris, 1937, 165-170; *idem*, Liste des manuscrits des lettres de saint Grégoire de Nazianze: REG (1944) 106-124; *idem*, Recherches sur les manuscrits des lettres de saint Grégoire de Nazianze conservés à la Bibliothèque Nationale de Paris: Mélanges J. Saunier. Lyon, 1944, 81-93; *idem*, Catalogue des manuscrits parisiens des lettres de saint Grégoire de Nazianze. Mâcon, 1945. — G. Przychocki, Historia listów św. Grzegorza z Nazjianzu. Cracow, 1946. — P. Gallay, Les manuscrits des lettres de saint Grégoire de Nazianze. Paris, 1957. — F. Lefherz, op. cit.

Studies: J. Freeland, St. Gregory Nazianzen from his Letters: Dublin Review 130 (1902) 333-354 (Gregory's character). — M. Guignet, Les procédés épistolaires de saint Grégoire de Nazianze comparés à ceux de ses contemporains. Paris, 1911; *idem*, St. Grégoire de Nazianze orateur et épistolier. Paris, 1911. — G. Przychocki, De Gregorii Naz. epistulis quaestiones selectae. Cracow, 1912. Cf. W. Jaeger, DLZ (1912) 180-183. — H. Gerstinger, Zwei Briefe des Gregorios von Nazianz im Papyrus Gr. Vindob. 29788 A-C (SAW Phil.-hist. Kl. 208, 3). Vienna, 1928 (*Ep.* 80 and 90). — P. Gallay, Langue et style de S. Grégoire de Nazianze dans sa correspondance. Paris, 1933. — B. Wyss, Zu Gregor von Nazianz: Phyllobolia P. Von der Mühll. Basel, 1946, 153-183 (text. crit. *Ep.* 178). — H. L. Davids, De Gregorii Nazianzeni Epistula LXV: VC 1 (1947) 244-246 (text. crit.); *idem*, De Gregorii Nazianzeni Epistula CXCIX: VC 2 (1948) 113-114 (text. crit.). — J. Lercher, Die Persönlichkeit des hl. Gregorius von Nazianz und seine Stellung zur klassischen Bildung (aus seinen Briefen). Diss. Innsbruck, 1949. — M. F. A. Brok, A propos des lettres festales: VC 5 (1951) 101-110 (*Ep.* 115, 120 and 172 represent answers to Paschal Letters).

II. THEOLOGICAL ASPECTS

Gregory opens one of his letters addressed to St. Basil with the sentence: 'From the first I have taken you, and I take you still, for my guide of life and my teacher of dogma'. With these words Gregory himself acknowledges his obligation to the great bishop of Caesarea in theology. An intensive study of his thought will always confirm this dependence. Nevertheless, he shows definite progress beyond St. Basil, not only in his improvement of the terminology and the dogmatic formulas but also in his realization of theology as a science, and in a deeper grasp of its problems. Thus it is not without reason that posterity has bestowed the title 'the Theologian' on him. More than once he gives an explicit treatment of the nature of theology in his works. In fact, in his *Five Theological Orations* (27-31) and in the closely related *Sermons* 20 and 32 he provides a series of 'discourses on method', a methodology in the fullest sense of the term. He discusses the sources of theology, the characteristics of the theologian, the *ecclesia docens* and the *ecclesia discens*, the object of theology, the spirit of theology, faith and reason, and the Church's power to formulate binding dogmatic definitions.

Studies: F. K. Hümmer, Des hl. Gregor von Nazianz, des Theologen, Lehre von der Gnade. Kempten, 1890. — J. Sajdak, The Educational Ideas of Gregory of Nazianzus. Poznań, 1933 (in Polish). — L. Stephan, Die Soteriologie des hl. Gregor von Nazianz. Vienna, 1938. — J. Tyciak, Wege östlicher Theologie. Bonn, 1946, 245-260 (concept of truth). — J. PLAGNIEUX, Saint Grégoire de Nazianze Théologien. Paris, 1951. — F. X. PORTMANN, Die göttliche Paidagogia bei Gregor von Nazianz. Eine dogmengeschichtliche Studie. Sankt Ottilien, 1954. — M. SERRA, La carità pastorale in S. Gregorio Nazianzeno: OCP 21 (1955) 337-374.

1. Trinitarian Doctrine

The defense of the doctrine of the Trinity is one of the themes to which he returns in almost every discourse. In the oration *On Holy Baptism* (*Orat.* 40, 41) he gives an accurate summary of his teaching:

> I give you this profession of faith as a life-long guide and protector: One sole divinity and one power, found in the Three in Unity, and comprising the Three separately, not unequal in substances or natures, neither increased nor diminished by addition or subtraction, in every respect equal, in every respect one and the same; just as the beauty and the greatness of the heavens is one; the infinite conjunction of Three Infinite Ones, each being God as considered apart, as the Father so the Son, as the Son so the Holy Ghost, each being distinct by his personal property *(ἰδιότης, proprietas)*, the Three one God when contemplated together; each God because of the consubstantiality *(ὁμοουσιότης)*, one God because of the monarchia *(μοναρχία)*.

With this confession Gregory intends to avoid the heresy of Arius as well as of Sabellius, as he clearly states:

> Three in individualities or *hypostases*, if any prefer to call them, or persons *(πρόσωπον)*, for we will not quarrel about names so long as the syllables amount to the same meaning; but one in respect of the substance — that is the Godhead. For They are divided without division, if I may say so; and They are united in division. For the Godhead is one in Three, and the Three are one, in Whom the Godhead is, or to speak more accurately, Who are the Godhead. Excesses and defects we will omit, neither making the unity a confusion, nor the division a separation. We would keep equally far from the confusion of Sabellius and from the division of Arius, which are evils diametrically opposed, yet equal in their wickedness. For what need is there heretically to fuse God together, or to cut Him up into inequality (*Or.* 39, 11 LNPF).

If we compare Gregory's teaching with that of St. Basil, we notice a much stronger emphasis on the unity and *monarchia*, the one sovereignty of God, on the one hand, and, on the other, a much clearer definition of the divine relations. In fact, the doctrine of relations, which forms the heart of the later scholastic analysis of the Trinity, and which the Council of Florence (Febr. 4, 1441) summarizes in the sentence: *in Deo omnia sunt unum, ubi non obviat relationis oppositio*, basically goes back to Gregory's sentence: There is complete identity among the three divine Persons except for the relations of origin (*Orat.* 34, MG 36, 352A; *Orat.* 20, MG 35, 1073A; *Orat.* 31, MG 36, 165B; *Orat.* 41, MG 36, 441C). Gregory uses this doctrine of relations to prove the coeternity of the divine Persons and Their identity of substance against the rationalistic distortions of the heretics. The three Persons have each a property of relation. Their properties are relations of origin. Whereas Basil deals with this character of relation as a property of the Son only, Gregory offers in addition a detailed discussion of it as a property of the Holy Spirit.

It is Gregory's great merit to have given for the first time a clear definition of the distinctive characters of the divine Persons, the *notions* which are involved in their origin and in their mutual opposition. Here is another point in which Gregory advances beyond Basil. The latter, though he shows a clear understanding of the properties (ἰδιότητες) of the first two Persons of the Trinity in his *Adv. Eunom.* 2, 28, declared himself unable to express the property of the third, which he expected to grasp only in the beatific vision (*Adv. Eunom.* 3, 6-7). Gregory overcomes this difficulty completely and declares the distinctive characters of the three divine Persons to be ἀγεννησία, γέννησις and ἐκπόρευσις or ἔκπεμψις (cf. *Orat.* 25, 16; 26, 19). Thus the distinctive character of the Holy Spirit is clearly defined as *procession*. He states for instance: 'The proper name of the Unoriginate is Father, and that of the unoriginately Begotten is Son, and that of the unbegottenly Proceeding or Going forth is the Holy Spirit' (*Or.* 30, 19). Gregory is fully aware of the fact that he contributed this term 'procession':

> The Father is Father and is Unoriginate, for He is of no one, the Son is Son, and is not unoriginate, for He is of the Father. But if you take the word 'origin' in a temporal sense, He too is Unoriginate, for He is the Maker of time, and is not subject to time. The Holy Ghost is truly Spirit, coming forth from the Father indeed, but not after the manner of the Son, for it is not by generation but by procession since I must coin a word for the sake of clearness; for neither did the Father cease to be Unbegotten because of His begetting something, nor the Son to be begotten because He is of the Unbegotten, nor is the Spirit changed into Father or Son because He proceeds, or because He is God — though the ungodly do not believe it (*Or.* 39, 12 LNPF).

Studies: J. HERGENRÖTHER, Die Lehre von der göttlichen Dreieinigkeit nach dem hl. Gregor von Nazianz, dem Theologen. Regensburg, 1850. — K. HOLL, Amphilochius von Ikonium in seinem Verhältnis zu den grossen Kappadoziern. Tübingen, 1904, 158-196. — J. DRÄSEKE, Neuplatonisches in des Gregorios von Nazianz Trinitätslehre: BZ 15 (1906) 141-160. — J. N. D. KELLY, Early Christian Doctrines. London, 1958, 264-268.

2. *Holy Spirit*

The last words indicate further progress in the development of the Christian doctrine: Gregory does not hesitate, as St. Basil did (cf. above, p. 231), to give a clear and formal expression of the divinity of the Holy Ghost. As early as 372 he calls the latter 'God' (τὸ πνεῦμα ἅγιον καὶ θεός) in a public sermon and adds the question: 'How long shall we hide the lamp under the bushel, and withhold from others the full knowledge of the divinity [of the Holy Spirit]? The lamp should rather be placed on the candlestick that it may give light to all churches and souls and to the whole fullness of the world, no longer by means of metaphors, or intellectual sketches, but by distinct declaration' (*Or.* 12, 6). While he defended the reserve (οἰκονομία) and the prudence of Basil in setting forth this truth, he claimed for himself the right of full freedom of speech (cf. above, p. 231). In the fifth of his *Theological Orations*, which is entirely devoted to the Holy Spirit, he derives the consubstantiality of the latter from the fact that He is God: 'Is the Spirit God? Most certainly. Well, then, is He consubstantial? Yes, if He is God' (*Or.* 31, 10). He explains on that occasion the uncertainty of former times as in harmony with the appointed order of development in the divine revelation of truth:

> The Old Testament proclaimed the Father clearly, but the Son more darkly; the New Testament plainly revealed the Son, but only indicated the deity of the Spirit. Now the Holy Spirit lives among us and makes the manifestation of Himself more certain to us; for it was not safe, so long as the divinity of the Father was still unrecognized, to proclaim openly that of the Son; and so long as this was still not accepted, to impose the burden of the Spirit, if so bold a phrase may be allowed (*Or.* 31, 26).

Studies: T. SCHERMANN, Die Gottheit des Heiligen Geistes nach den griechischen Vätern des vierten Jahrhunderts. Freiburg i.B., 1901, 145-167. — P. GALTIER, Le Saint-Esprit en nous d'après les Pères grecs. Rome, 1946, 175-180.

3. *Christology*

Even more advanced than his doctrine on the Trinity and the Holy Spirit is his Christology, which won the approval of the Council of Ephesus (431) and of Chalcedon (451). His famous letters to Cledonius provided an excellent guide for the Church in the debates of the following century, because they strongly defend the essential doctrine of the complete manhood of Christ, including a human soul, against the teaching of Apollinaris, which finds in the humanity of Christ a body and an animal soul, but with the indwelling deity replacing the higher human soul. He declares that the humanity of Christ is a *physis* because it consists of body and soul. He explicitly rejects the Logos-Sarx Christology and makes that of the Logos-Man his own (*Ep.* 102, MG 37, 200BC). 'There are two natures [in Christ], God and Man, since there is a soul as well as a body in Him' (*Ep.* 101, MG 37, 180A; cf. *Ep.* 102, MG 37, 201B). Whoever claims that there is no human soul in Christ, takes the 'wall of partition' between God and man away. There had to be a human mind *(νοῦς)* in Christ, because it is the mind which is the image of the divine intellect. Thus the human mind in Christ is the connecting link between God and the flesh: 'Mind is mingled with mind, as nearer and more closely related, and through it with flesh, being a Mediator between God and carnality' (*Ep.* 101, 10).

Gregory is the first among the Greek theologians to apply the trinitarian terminology to the christological formula. He states that in Christ 'both natures are one by combination, the deity being made man, and the manhood deified or however one should express it'. He states:

> And if I am to speak concisely, the Saviour is made of elements *(ἄλλο καὶ ἄλλο)* which are distinct from one another, for the invisible is not the same with the visible, not the timeless with that which is subject to time, yet he is not two persons *(ἄλλος καὶ ἄλλος)*. God forbid! For both natures are one by the combination, the deity being made man, and the manhood deified or however one should express it. And I say different elements because it is the reverse of what is the case in the Trinity; for there we acknowledge different Persons so as not to confound the *hypostases:* but not different elements, for the Three are one and the same in the Godhead (*Ep.* 101, MG 37, 180).

This comparison of the trinitarian dogma with the christological will finally lead in the next century to the adoption of the one-hypostasis formula with reference to Christ — a formula which Gregory and the two other Cappadocians, however, did not as yet have.

Gregory furthermore testifies unmistakably to the unity of person in Christ. Speaking of Christ, he says: 'He deigned to be One made out of two; two natures meeting in One, not two Sons' (*Orat.* 37, 2; EP 1001). This union was not by grace; Gregory coins the expression 'united in essence': κατ' οὐσίαν συνῆφθαί τε καὶ συνάπτεσθαι (*Ep.* 101, 5), which proved to be of great importance for the future development of the christological doctrine.

Studies: J. DRÄSEKE, Gregorios von Nazianz und sein Verhältnis zum Apollinarismus: ThStKr 65 (1892) 473-512. — E. WEIGL, Christologie vom Tode des Athanasius bis zum Ausbruch des nestorianischen Streites. Munich, 1925, 53-79. — E. MERSCH, Le Corps Mystique du Christ. 2nd ed. Brussels and Paris, 1936, 438-450; English translation: E. MERSCH, The Whole Christ. Translated by J. R. Kelly, Milwaukee, 1938, 303-314.

— M. Richard, L'introduction du mot 'hypostase' dans la théologie de l'incarnation: MSR 2 (1945) 29-32, 189-190. — A. Grillmeier, Die theologische und sprachliche Vorbereitung der christologischen Formel von Chalkedon: CGG 1 (1951) 157-158. — J. Lebon, Le sort du consubstantiel nicéen: RHE 48 (1953) 632-682. — H. A. Wolfson, The Philosophy of the Church Fathers, vol. 1. Cambridge, 1956, 370-371, 396-397.

4. Mariology

The term 'Theotokos' became through Gregory of Nazianzus, long before the Council of Ephesus (431), the touchstone of orthodoxy:

> If anyone does not believe that Saint Mary is the Mother of God (θεοτόκος), he is severed from the Godhead. If anyone should assert that He passed through the Virgin as through a channel, and was not at once divinely and humanly formed in her (divinely, because without the intervention of a man; humanly, because in accordance with the laws of gestation), he is in like manner godless. If any assert that the manhood was formed and afterward was clothed with the Godhead, he too is to be condemned. For this would not be a generation of God, but a shirking of generation. If any introduces the notion of two Sons, one of God the Father, the other of the mother, and discredits the unity and identity, may he lose his part in the adoption promised to those who believe aright... If anyone assert that His flesh came down from heaven, that is not from hence, nor of us but above us, let him be anathema... If anyone has put his trust in Him as a man without a human mind, he is really bereft of mind, and quite unworthy of salvation. For that which He has not assumed He has not healed; but that which is united to His Godhead is also saved (*Ep.* 101, 4-6 LNPF).

This passage shows that Gregory regards the dogma of Mary's motherhood as the pivot of the Church's teaching about Christ and salvation. He explains Christ being born of a virgin as follows: 'A great thing is virginity and celibacy, a being ranked with the angels, and with the single nature; for I shrink from calling it Christ's, who, though He willed to be born for our sakes who are born, by being born of a Virgin, enacted the law of virginity, to lead us away from this life, and cut short the power of the world, or rather, to transmit one world to another, the present to the future' (*Orat.* 43, 62).

Study: G. Soell, Die Mariologie der Kappadozier im Lichte der Dogmengeschichte: ThQ 131 (1951) 288-319.

5. Eucharistic Doctrine

Gregory of Nazianzus is firmly convinced of the sacrificial character of the Eucharist. Recovered from illness, he writes to Amphilochius, the bishop of Iconium: 'The tongue of a priest meditating on the Lord raises the sick. Do, then, the greater thing by celebrating the liturgy, and loose the great mass of my sins when you lay hold of the Sacrifice of the Resurrection. Most Reverend friend, cease not both to pray and to plead for me when you draw down the Word by your word, when with a bloodless cutting you sever the Body and the Blood of the Lord, using your voice for the lance' (*Ep.* 171 LNPF). In his *Apologeticus de fuga* he calls the Eucharist 'the external sacrifice, the antitype of the great mysteries' (*Or.* 2, 95 LNPF):

> Since then I knew these things, and that no one is worthy of the mightiness of God, and the sacrifice, and priesthood, who has not first presented himself to God, a living, holy sacrifice, and set forth the reasonable, well-pleasing service, and sacrificed to God the sacrifice of praise and the contrite spirit, which is the only sacrifice required of us by the Giver of all; how could I dare offer to Him the external sacrifice, the antitype of the great mysteries (μεγάλων μυστηρίων ἀντίτυπον)?

Studies: J. MAIER, Die Eucharistielehre der drei grossen Kappadozier. Diss. Breslau, 1915. — O. CASEL, Das Mysteriengedächtnis der Messliturgie im Lichte der Tradition: JLw 6 (1926) 148-151. — J. BETZ, Die Eucharistie in der Zeit der griechischen Väter, vol. I, 1. Freiburg i.B., 1955, 225-226, 284-285.

GREGORY OF NYSSA

Gregory of Nyssa was neither an out-standing administrator and monastic legislator like Basil, nor an attractive preacher and poet like Gregory of Nazianzus. But as a speculative theologian and mystic he is certainly the most gifted of the three great Cappadocians. He was born about the year 335 and was educated chiefly by his elder brother, St. Basil, whom he often calls his teacher. After he had been lector in the Church, he decided for a wordly career, became a teacher of rhetoric and married. It was the influence of his friends, especially Gregory of Nazianzus, which eventually determined him to retire to the monastery in Pontus which St. Basil had founded on the Iris (cf. above, p. 205). In the autumn of 371 he was raised to the see of Nyssa, an insignificant town in his brother's metropolitan district of Caesarea. Although he had received the episcopal consecration against his own free will, he did not disappoint Basil as Gregory of Nazianzus did. He actually went to Nyssa and remained there, but failed to live up to the expectations of his brother and metropolitan, who criticized his lack of firmness in dealing with people and his unfitness for Church politics (Basil, *Ep.* 100, 58, 59, 60), not to mention financial matters. Moreover, he met with violent opposition from the heretics of that place, who did not hesitate to undermine his position with trumped-up charges of misappropriation of Church funds. The result was that a synod of Arian bishops and court prelates met at Nyssa in 376 and deposed him in his absence. He has left us (*Ep.* 6) a vivid account of the triumphal reception which was given to him, when he returned to his diocese after the death of the Arian Emperor Valens in 378. A year later he attended the Synod of Antioch, which sent him as a visitator to the diocese of Pontus. While on this mission, he was elected in 380 archbishop of Sebaste, which he had to administer for a few months much against his will. In 381 he took a prominent part in the Second Ecumenical Council at Constantinople side by side with Gregory of Nazianzus. He returned to the capital on several other occasions, as for instance to preach the funeral orations of the princess Pulcheria in 385 and of her mother, the Empress Flaccilla, soon afterwards. The last time he appeared there was in 394, when he participated in a synod. He died most probably in the same year.

Studies: P. GODET, DTC 6 (1920) 1847-1852. — J. DANIÉLOU, EC 6 (1951) 1096-1111. — J. RUPP, Gregors des Bischofs von Nyssa Leben und Meinungen. Leipzig, 1834. — F. DIEKAMP, Die Wahl Gregors von Nyssa zum Metropoliten von Sebaste im Jahre 380: ThQ 90 (1908) 384-401. — H. F. v. CAMPENHAUSEN, Griechische Kirchenväter. Stuttgart, 1955, 114-124. — J. DANIÉLOU, Le mariage de Grégoire de Nysse et la chronologie de sa vie: REAug 2 (1956) 71-78.

I. HIS WRITINGS

Among the three great Cappadocians Gregory of Nyssa is by far the most versatile and successful author. His writings reveal a depth and breadth of thought which surpass that of Basil and Gregory of Nazianzus. The reader is struck by his openmindedness towards contemporary currents of intellectual life, by his great adaptability and the keenness of his thought.

In his style Gregory shows himself more indebted to the contemporary sophistic and less restrained in the adoption of its devices than the other Cappadocian Fathers. In the selection of words he consciously follows classical authors. There is an accumulation of Atticisms, which however, does not exclude borrowings from the world of the Koine and the Septuagint. His predilection for ecphrasis and metaphor, for the linguistic jugglery of the paradox and oxymoron shows how strongly he let himself be influenced by the eccentric characteristics of contemporary Greek rhetoric. Yet, he never became a master of the art. His style remains very often without charm. His sentences are too heavy and appear to be over-charged. In his panegyrics and funeral orations, and especially in his polemical treatises, his diction is full of fire and energy, but often falls into exaggerated pathos and bombast, making it very difficult for the modern reader to appreciate the depth of his thought and religious conviction.

The complete edition of Gregory's works in Migne is very unsatisfactory. The French Revolution prevented the Maurist Fathers from bringing them out. The *editio princeps* was published by Morellus at Paris in 1615, an enlargement of which appeared in 1638 and was reprinted in Migne. W. Jaeger has been working on a definitive text since 1908, when the plan was first conceived by U. von Wilamowitz-Moellendorff at the University of Berlin. So far six volumes have been published. Moreover, we have a number of good editions of special treatises. Jaeger has for the first time succeeded in cutting a path through the intricacies of the manuscript tradition, a gigantic task, which meant a careful examination of hundreds of manuscripts scattered throughout the world. The question of authenticity will in many cases remain unanswered until his work is completed.

Even the undoubtedly genuine works represent a great problem: their exact chronology. The attempts made so far have produced only presumptions. However, it seems certain that most of the writings belong to the last period of Gregory's life, beginning with the year 379. The fascinating problem of his inner development and of the evolution of his thought cannot be solved until more definite results become available.

Editions: MG 44-46. Attempts to produce emended texts of Gregory's works were made by several scholars. J. G. Krabinger published between 1835 and 1840 separate editions of several treatises for which he used manuscripts of the Munich Library. These excellent editions will be listed with the individual works below. G. H. Forbes and F. Oehler intended to furnish complete critical editions, but they published only a few treatises. Of G. H. Forbes's edition: S.P.N. Gregorii Nysseni Basilii M. fratris quae supersunt omnia, t. I, fasc. 1-2, Burntisland, 1855-1861 (comprising the *Hexaemeron*, *De hominis opificio* and a part of *De vita Moysis*), is all that was published. This edition provides a comprehensive apparatus crit. F. Oehler published only: S. Gregorii episc. Nysseni opera, t. I, continens libros dogmaticos. Halle, 1865. — Of the new critical edition: Gregorii Nysseni Opera auxilio aliorum virorum doctorum edenda curavit W. Jaeger, the following six volumes have been published: vol. I/II: Contra Eunomium, ed. by W. Jaeger, Berlin, 1921; vol. III, 1: Opera dogmatica minora, Pars I, ed. by F. Mueller, Leiden, 1958; vol. VI: In Canticum Commentarius, ed. by H. Langerbeck, Leiden, 1960; vol. VIII, 1: Opera ascetica, ed. by W. Jaeger, J. P. Cavarnos, V. W. Callahan, Leiden, 1952; vol. VIII, 2: Epistulae, ed. by G. Pasquali, Berlin 1925, 2nd ed. Leiden 1959.

Translations: English: W. Moore and H. A. Wilson, LNPF ser. 2, vol. 5 (1893). — C. Richardson, LCC 3 (1954) 235-331. — H. Graef, ACW 18 (1954). — *German:* F. Oehler, Bibliothek der Kirchenväter I. Leipzig, 1858-1859, 4 vols. — H. Hayd and J. Fisch, BKV, 2 vols. 1874, 1880. — K. Weiss and E. Stolz, BKV² 56 (1927) with an introduction by J. Stiglmayr. — *French:* J. Daniélou, SCH 1, 1942, 2nd ed. 1956. — J. Laplace, SCH 6, 1944.

Studies: L. MÉRIDIER, L'influence de la seconde sophistique sur l'œuvre de Grégoire de Nysse. Rennes, 1906. — E. C. E. OWEN, St. Gregory of Nyssa. Grammar, Vocabulary and Style: JThSt 26 (1925) 64-71. — G. W. P. HOEY, The Use of the Optative Mood in the Works of Gregory of Nyssa (PSt 26). Washington, 1930. — A. PUECH, Histoire de la littérature grecque chrétienne, vol. 3. Paris, 1930, 396-436. — M. E. KEENAN, St. Gregory of Nyssa and the Medical Profession: BHM 15 (1944) 150-161. — For Arabic versions, see: G. GRAF, Geschichte der christlichen arabischen Literatur, vol. 1 (ST 118). Vatican City, 1944, 332-335. — E. v. IVANKA, Hellenisches und Christliches im frühbyzantinischen Geistesleben. Vienna, 1948, 28-67. — B. ALTANER, Augustinus, Gregor von Nazianz und Gregor von Nyssa: RB 61 (1951) 54-62. — H. MUSURILLO, History and Symbol. A Study of Form in Early Christian Literature: TS 18 (1957) 357-386. G. DOWNEY, Ekphrasis : RACh 4 (1959) 932-943.

1. *Dogmatic Treatises*

Most of the writings of this group are controversial and directed against the heresies of his times.

1. *Adversus Eunomium*

Gregory wrote not less than four treatises against Eunomius. The first, composed about 380, is a reply to the first book of the Ὑπὲρ τῆς ἀπολογίας ἀπολογία, in which Eunomius after fourteen years has answered St. Basil (cf. above, p. 209). The second, written soon afterwards, is a rebuttal of the second book of the same work of Eunomius. In the third he refuted between 381 and 383 a new attack of the Arian leader on Basil. This last was at an early time divided into ten books. Thus he defended his lately (379) deceased brother in three different treatises against Eunomius. At the Second Ecumenical Council at Constantinople in 381 Gregory, the leading theologian of the assembly, read the first two treatises to Gregory of Nazianzus and Jerome (*De vir. ill.* 128).

When Eunomius in 383 submitted a 'Confession of Faith' (Ἔκθεσις πίστεως) to the Emperor Theodosius, Gregory wrote a very detailed criticism of it. This fourth treatise against Eunomius has nothing to do with the first three tracts or twelve books written in defense of his brother.

Unfortunately as early as the sixth century the order of these twelve books was disturbed. It seems that the second treatise, forming the second book of the twelve, on account of its more speculative character, did not meet with the same appreciation as the rest in the monasteries, and was therefore replaced by Gregory's refutation of Eunomius' 'Confession of Faith'. As a result the second book of the collection was forgotten and Photius in his *Bibl. Cod.* 6/7 speaks only of two treatises by Gregory in support of Basil. Even when the revival of scholarly interest in the ninth century led to its rediscovery, it was simply added at the end of the collection as a second part of the twelfth book (12b), or, in other manuscripts, as book 13. This was the order in all the printed editions of *Against Eunomius (Πρὸς Εὐνόμιον ἀντιρρητικοὶ λόγοι)* until Jaeger restored the original: 1, 12b, 3-12a.

This work represents one of the most important refutations of Arianism.

Editions: MG 45, 237-1122. — New crit. ed.: W. JAEGER, Contra Eunomium libri. Berlin, 1921. Pars Prior: Liber I et II (vulgo I et XIIb). Pars Altera: Liber III (vulgo III-XII) p. 1-295, Refutatio Confessionis Eunomii (vulgo lib. II) p. 296-389.

Translations: English: H. C. OGLE, H. A. WILSON, M. DAY, LNPF ser. 2, vol. 5, 33-248, 250-314. — *German:* F. OEHLER, Bibliothek der Kirchenväter I. Leipzig, 1858.

Studies: M. ALBERTZ, Untersuchungen über die Schriften des Eunomius. Wittenberg, 1908. — F. DIEKAMP, Literargeschichtliches zur Eunomianischen Kontroverse: BZ 18 (1909) 1-13, 190-194. — A. JÜLICHER, Textkritische Studien: Defensio trium capitulorum des Bischofs Facundus von Hermiane in Verbindung mit Gregors Schriften Contra Eunomium: ThLZ 47 (1922) 398-400. — E. VANDENBUSSCHE, La part de la dialectique dans la théologie d'Eunomius 'le technologue': RHE 40 (1944/45) 47-72. — T. A. GOGGIN, The Times of St. Gregory of Nyssa as Reflected in his Letters and the Contra Eunomium (PSt 79). Washington, 1947.

2. *Adversus Apollinaristas ad Theophilum episcopum Alexandrinum*

This small tract addressed to the patriarch of Alexandria (cf. above, p. 100) asked Theophilus for a detailed refutation of Apollinarianism. Gregory rejects the charge of this sect that Catholics believed in two Sons of God. Since Theophilus was consecrated in 385, this pamphlet must have been written in the last few years of Gregory's life.

Editions: MG 45, 1269-1278. New crit. ed. by F. MUELLER, Gregorii Nysseni Opera dogmatica minora. Leiden, 1958, 119-128.

3. *Antirrheticus adversus Apollinarem*

Soon afterwards Gregory published this most important of all extant anti-Apollinarian writings. It contains a vehement reply to Apollinaris' book *Demonstration of the Incarnation of God in the Image of Man.* Gregory deals with the union of the two natures in Christ and refutes the heretical doctrine that the flesh of Christ came down from heaven and the Logos occupies the place of the human rational soul in Christ.

Editions: MG 45, 1123-1270. New crit. ed. by F. MUELLER, op. cit. 131-233.

Studies: H. LIETZMANN, Apollinaris von Laodicea und seine Schule, vol. 1. Tübingen, 1904, 83-87. — C. E. RAVEN, Apollinarianism. Cambridge, 1923, 262-270.

4. *Sermo de Spiritu Sancto adversus Pneumatomachos Macedonianos*

The sermon is directed against the *Pneumatomachi* (contenders against the Spirit). Macedonius, the leader of this sect and the chief representative known to us of the Arian teaching with regard to the Holy Spirit, had been appointed bishop of Constantinople after the deposition of Paul (a Nicene), but was himself in turn deposed by the Synod of Constantinople in 360. First published by Cardinal Mai in 1833, the ideas correspond with Gregory's. We are, therefore, justified in regarding it authentic. Mai edited it with another sermon attributed to Gregory *Sermo adversus Arium et Sabellium*, which is not from Gregory's pen and which K. Holl ascribes to Didymus the Blind (cf. above, p. 89).

Editions: Card. Mai, Script. vet. nova collectio 8. Rome, 1833, pars 2, 1-25. Reprinted: Mai, Nova Patrum Bibl. 4. Rome, 1847, pars 1, 1-39. MG 45, 1301-1334. New crit. ed.: F. Mueller, op. cit. 89-115. This new edition furnishes for the first time the complete text restoring the concluding part not found in previous editions. *Adversus Arium et Sabellium:* MG 45, 1281-1302. New crit. edition: F. Mueller, op. cit. 71-85.

Translation: English: H. A. Wilson, LNPF ser. 2, vol. 5, 315-325 (*On the Holy Spirit against the Macedonians*).

Studies: K. Holl, Über die Gregor von Nyssa zugeschriebene Schrift 'Adversus Arium et Sabellium': ZKG 25 (1904) 380-398; republished in: Gesammelte Aufsätze zur Kirchengeschichte II. Tübingen, 1928, 298-309. — F. Loofs, Macedonianism: Encyclopedia of Religion and Ethics 8 (1915) 225ff. — G. Bardy, Macédonius et les Macédoniens: DTC 9 (1927) 1464ff. — P. Meinhold, Pneumatomachoi: PWK 21 (1951) 1066-1101.

5. *Ad Ablabium quod non sint tres dii*

Several treatises of Gregory's are devoted to the defense and clarification of the Church's teaching on the Trinity. Such is the tract *That there are not three Gods*, addressed to Ablabius, a certain ecclesiastic, who had raised the question on why we should not speak of three Gods when we recognize the divinity of Father, Son and Holy Spirit. It is usually assigned to the year 375. However, a number of considerations suggest a later date, probably 390, because Gregory introduces himself in the beginning as an old man. He points out that 'god' is a term indicative of essence (being), not of persons. Therefore it must always be used in the singular with each of the names of the persons. So we say 'God the Father, God the Son, and God the Holy Spirit'. Father, Son and Spirit are modes of being, are the three relations, but the being remains one and the same, and the term expressing it must therefore always be used in the singular.

Editions: MG 45, 115-136. New crit. ed.: F. Mueller, op. cit. 37-57.

Translations: English: H. A. WILSON, LNPF ser. 2, vol. 5, 331-336. — C. RICHARDSON, LCC 3 (1954) 256-267. — *German:* F. OEHLER, Bibliothek der Kirchenväter. Part I, vol. 1. Leipzig, 1858, 186-217.

6. *Ad Graecos ex communibus notionibus*

The treatise *On Common Notions* deals with all the expressions used in explaining the Trinity, and is a refutation based on the commonly recognized principles of reasoning. The new edition by F. Mueller restores the complete text. So far introduction and conclusion had been lacking.

Editions: MG 45, 175-186. New crit. ed.: F. MUELLER, op. cit. 19-33.

7. *Ad Eustathium de sancta Trinitate*

This treatise addressed to the physician Eustathius is a refutation of the *Pneumatomachi*. Gregory describes their point of view and his own as follows:

> They allow that the power of the Godhead extends from the Father to the Son, but they divide the nature of the Spirit from the divine glory. Against this view, to the best of my ability I must enter a brief defense of my own position. They are charging me with innovations and they base their charge on my confession of three *hypostases*, and blame me for asserting one Goodness, one Power, one Godhead. In this they are not far from the truth, for I do so assert (3/4).

The greater part of this treatise is found among the letters of St. Basil as *Ep.* 189, to whom it has been falsely attributed. This is perhaps the reason that in Migne's edition it does not appear among the works of Gregory.

Editions: F. OEHLER, Bibliothek der Kirchenväter. Part I, vol. 2. Leipzig, 1858, 180ff. — G. MERCATI, ST (1903) 71-82. — New crit. ed.: F. MUELLER, op. cit. 3-16.

Translations: English: H. A. WILSON, LNPF ser. 2, vol. 5, 326-330. — *German:* F. OEHLER, l. c.

Studies: G. MERCATI, La lettera ad Eustazio De sancta Trinitate: Varia sacra, fasc. 1 (ST 11). Rome, 1903, 57-70. Cf. F. DIEKAMP, ThR 2 (1903) 476-478.

8. *Ad Simplicium de fide sancta*

This tract addressed to the tribune Simplicius defends the divinity and consubstantiality of the Son and the Holy Spirit against the Arians and attacks their heretical interpretation of Scriptural passages. Introduction and conclusion are not preserved.

Editions: MG 45, 136-145. — New crit. ed.: F. MUELLER, op. cit. 61-67.

Translation: English: H. A. WILSON, LNPF ser. 2, vol. 5, 337-339.

9. *Dialogus de anima et resurrectione qui inscribitur Macrinia*

This dialogue of Gregory with his sister Macrina on the soul and resurrection is a counterpart to Plato's Phaedo. The conversation took place in 379 shortly after their brother Basil's death, when Gregory returned from a synod at Antioch to visit his sister, at that time superior of a convent on the river Iris in Pontus, and found her dying. Gregory tells us of the origin of the dialogue in his *Vita Macrinae*:

> And that she might cause me no depression of spirit, she somehow subdued the noise and concealed the difficulty of her breathing, and assumed perfect cheerfulness. She not only started pleasant topics herself, but suggested them as well by the questions which she asked. The conversation led naturally to the mention of our great Basil. While my very soul sank and my countenance was saddened and fell, she herself was far from going with me into the depths of mourning, that she made the mention of that saintly name an opportunity for the most sublime philosophy. Examining human nature in a scientific way, disclosing the divine plan that underlies all afflictions, and dealing as if inspired by the Holy Spirit, with all the questions relating to a future life, she maintained such a discourse that my soul seemed to be lifted along with her words almost beyond the compass of humanity and, as I followed her argument, to be placed within the sanctuary of heaven... And if my tract would not thereby be extended to an endless length, I would have reported everything in its order; i.e. how her argument lifted her as she went into the philosophy both of the soul, and of the causes of our life in the flesh, and of the final cause of Man and his mortality, and of death and the return thence into life again. In all of it her reasoning continued clear and consecutive; it flowed on so easily and naturally that it was like the water from some spring falling unimpeded downwards (LNPF).

Macrina died the next day and Gregory must have composed this dialogue soon afterwards. The views concerning the soul, death, resurrection and the final restoration of all things (apocatastasis) which Gregory puts into her mouth, are of course his own. She speaks as 'the Teacher' and the discourse has often been given the title *Macrinia*.

Editions: MG 46, 11-160. — Separate ed.: J. G. KRABINGER, Leipzig, 1837.

Translations: English: W. MOORE, LNPF ser. 2, vol. 5, 428-468. — *German:* H. HAYD, BKV (1874) 321-417. — K. WEISS, BKV² 56 (1927) 243-334.

Studies: A. M. AKULAS, Plato's Idea of the Immortality of the Soul compared with Gregory of Nyssa's (in Greek). Jena Diss. Athens, 1888. — M. PELLEGRINO, Il Platonismo di San Gregorio Nisseno nel Dialogo intorno all' anima e alla risurrezione: RFN 30 (1938) 437-474. — J. DANIÉLOU, La résurrection des corps chez Grégoire de Nysse: VC 7 (1953) 154-170.

10. *Contra Fatum*

The small tract *Against Fate* contains a dispute of the author with a pagan philosopher at Constantinople in 382. Gregory defends the freedom of the will against astrological fatalism. He reduces to absurdity the idea that the position of the stars at a man's birth determines his fate.

Editions: MG 45, 145-174. — Separate ed.: P. C. JORDACHESCU and T. SIMENSCHY, Sancti Gregorii Nysseni Contra Fatum. Chisinau, 1938. — New crit. ed.: J. A. McDONOUGH, The Treatise of Gregory of Nyssa Contra Fatum, a Critical Text with Prolegomena. Diss. Harvard University. Cf. summary in: HSCP 61 (1953) 179-180. This crit. text will be published in W. JAEGER's edition.

Studies: F. BOLL, Studien über Claudius Ptolemaeus: Jahrbücher für klassische Philologie. Supplementband 21 (1904) 181ff. — E. AMAND DE MENDIETA, Fatalisme et liberté dans l'antiquité grecque. Louvain, 1945, 405-439. — J. GAITH, La conception de la liberté chez Grégoire de Nysse (Études de Philosophie Médiévale 43). Paris, 1953.

11. *Oratio catechetica magna*

The most important of all his dogmatic writings is his large *Catechesis*, composed about 385. It is a compendium of Christian doctrine which he dedicated to the teachers who 'have need of system in their instructions' (prolog.). In fact, it represents the first attempt after Origen's *De principiis* to create a systematic theology. Gregory gives a remarkable presentation of the principal dogmas and defends them against pagans, Jews and heretics. He seeks to establish the whole complex of Christian doctrines on a foundation of metaphysics rather than on the authority of Scripture alone. He treats of God, Redemption and Sanctification. The first part, chapters 1-4, considers the one God in three Persons, the con-substantiality of the Son with the Father and the divinity of the Holy Spirit. The second part, chapters 5-32, discusses Christ and his mission. Beginning with the creation of man and original sin, Gregory shows the restoration of the primitive order by the Incarnation and Redemption. The third part, chapters 33-40, studies the application of the grace of Redemption through the two sacraments, Baptism and Eucharist, and the essential condition for regeneration, the belief in the Trinity.

In general, Gregory shows significant dependence on Origen as well as on Methodius. His universalist teaching on the Last Things especially betrays the influence of the great Alexandrian. Nevertheless, Gregory's manual of dogma was a great achievement, as its wide circulation in the Eastern Church proves.

Editions: MG 45, 9-106. — Separate ed.: J. G. KRABINGER, Munich, 1835. — J. H. SRAWLEY, The Catechetical Oration of St. Gregory of Nyssa (CPT). Cambridge,

1903. — Srawley's text, based on sixteen manuscripts, was reprinted by L. Méridier, Grégoire de Nysse, Discours catéchétique. Paris, 1908.

Translations: English: W. Moore, LNPF ser. 2, vol. 5, 473-509. — J. H. Srawley, The Catechetical Oration of St. Gregory of Nyssa (SPCK). London, 1917. — C. Richardson, LCC 3 (1954) 268-325. — *German:* H. Hayd, BKV (1874) 123-205. — K. Weiss, BKV² 56 (1927) 1-85. — *French:* L. Méridier, op. cit. — *Dutch:* W. C. van Unnik, Oratio catechetica, ingel. en vertaald (Klass. der Kerk I, 4). Amsterdam, 1949. — *Rumanian:* D. Cristescu and N. I. Barbu, Λόγος κατηχητικὸς ὁ μέγας. Bucarest, 1947.

Studies: J. H. Srawley, The Manuscripts and Text of the Oratio Catechetica of St. Gregory of Nyssa: JThSt 3 (1902) 421-428. — J. Dräseke, Textverbesserungen zur Oratio catechetica (Review of Méridier's edition): ThLZ 33 (1908) 531-534.

2. *Exegetical Works*

More evident in his exegetical writings is Gregory's admiration of Origen, whose hermeneutical principles he follows, except in the two works on the narrative of Creation, both written at the request of his brother Peter, the bishop of Sebaste.

1. *De opificio hominis*

This first work was meant to complete the homilies of Basil on the *Hexaemeron* (cf. above, p. 217). In the introductory letter Gregory states that, in sending it to his brother Peter as an Easter gift, he intended to add to the treatise of Basil, 'our common father and teacher', the consideration of man's creation lacking in the *Hexaemeron*, 'not so as to interpolate his work by insertion but so that the glory of the teacher may not seem to be failing among his disciples'. Though the *De opificio* consists in the main of an anthropological and physiological explanation of Genesis 1, 26, the theological point of view is by no means neglected, as he indicates right at the beginning: 'The scope of our proposed enquiry is not small: it is second to none of the wonders of the world, — perhaps even greater than any of those known to us, because no other existing thing, save the human creation, has been made like God'. The date of its composition is perhaps shortly after St. Basil's death (January 1, 379), if not in the last period of Gregory's life.

Editions: MG 44, 125-256. — G. H. Forbes, S. P. N. Gregorii Nysseni quae supersunt omnia, t. 1. Burntisland, 1855/61, 96-319 (with excellent apparat. crit.). — Separate ed.: J. Laplace, Grégoire de Nysse, La création de l'homme (SCH 6). Paris, 1943 (with notes by J. Daniélou). Laplace reprints Migne's text with some of Forbes's emendations. — An Old Latin translation by Dionysius Exiguus: ML 67, 345-408. Cf. P. Levine, Two Early Latin Versions of St. Gregory of Nyssa's περὶ κατασκευῆς ἀνθρώπου: HSCP 63 (1958) 473-492. — For the two homilies *Faciamus hominem* which follow the text of *De opificio* in MG 44, 257-298 and Basil's *Hexaemeron*

(MG 30, 61-72), see above p. 218 Ivanka's, Giet's and Amand's studies. They cannot be attributed to Gregory nor to Basil.

Translations: English: H. A. WILSON, LNPF ser. 2, vol. 5, 387-427. — *French:* J. LAPLACE, op. cit. — *German:* H. HAYD, BKV (1874) 209-317.

Studies: E. W. MÖLLER, Gregorii Nysseni doctrinam de natura hominis et illustravit et cum Origeniana comparavit. Diss. Halle, 1854. — A. KRAMPF, Der Urzustand des Menschen nach der Lehre des hl. Gregor von Nyssa. Würzburg, 1889. — F. HILT, Des hl. Gregor von Nyssa Lehre vom Menschen systematisch dargestellt (Diss. Tübingen). Cologne, 1890. — J. DRÄSEKE, Gregorios von Nyssa in den Anführungen des Johannes Erigena: ThStKr 82 (1909) 530-576 (quotations from this treatise in Scotus Erigena). — E. STEPHANU, La coexistence initiale du corps et de l'âme d'après saint Grégoire de Nysse et saint Maxime l'Apologète: EO 31 (1932) 304-315. — E. v. IVANKA, Die Quelle von Ciceros De natura deorum II 45-60: Archivum Philologicum (Budapest) 59 (1935) 10-21 (Posidonius is the source of Cicero and of Gregory of Nyssa's *De hominis opificio:* MG 44, 125-127). — J. B. SCHOEMANN, Gregors von Nyssa theologische Anthropologie als Bildtheologie: Schol 18 (1943) 31-53, 175-200. — L. REBECCHI, L'antropologia naturale di San Gregorio Nisseno: DTP 46 (1943) 176-195, 309-341. — J. JANINI CUESTA, La antropologia y la medicina pastoral de San Gregorio de Nisa. Madrid, 1946 (*De opificio hominis* and Galenus). — W. JAEGER, Greek Uncial Fragments in the Library of Congress in Washington: Traditio 5 (1947) 79-102 (containing two passages of *De opificio hom.:* MG 44, 180B-181B and 44, 196A-197A). — E. V. McCLEAR, The Fall of Man and Original Sin in the Theology of Gregory of Nyssa: TS 9 (1948) 175-212. — A. H. ARMSTRONG, Platonic Elements in St. Gregory of Nyssa's Doctrine of Man: Dominican Studies 1 (1948) 113-126. — E. v. IVANKA, Die stoische Anthropologie in der lateinischen Literatur: AAWW 87 (1950) 178-192 (Posidonius as a source of *De opif. hominis*). — F. FLOERI, Le sens de la division des sexes chez Grégoire de Nysse: RSR 27 (1953) 105-111 (in *De opif. hom.*). — A. N. ZOUBOS, Eine Frage des Anaxagoras in der Anthropologie des Gregor von Nyssa. Athens, 1956. — G. B. LADNER, The Philosophical Anthropology of St. Gregory of Nyssa: DOP 12 (1958) 59-94. — See all studies on the image of God in man, below p. 293.

2. *Explicatio apologetica in Hexaemeron*

The second work on the Creation was written to correct some misunderstandings of the biblical text and of Basil's exegesis, and also to engage in metaphysical speculations. It was evidently composed soon after *De opificio*, to which it refers towards the conclusion. Since Basil, *Hexaem.* 9, 80, explicitly states that he was interested in the literal sense only and not in allegory (cf. above, p. 217), Gregory is anxious to follow in his footsteps throughout the two works that supplement his brother's treatise. Thus towards the end he asserts with a certain satisfaction that he never distorted the literal sense of the Bible into figurative allegory *(εἰς τροπικὴν ἀλληγορίαν)*. This is all the more remarkable since elsewhere in his exegesis he delights in seeking and finding an allegorical meaning beneath every word of Holy Writ.

Editions: MG 44, 61-124. — G. H. FORBES, Greg. Nyss. quae supersunt omnia, t. 1, fasc. 1. Burntisland, 1855, 1-95.

Studies: K. GRONAU, Poseidonios und die jüdisch-christliche Genesisexegese. Leipzig, 1914, 112-141. — E. F. SUTCLIFFE, St. Gregory of Nyssa and Paradise. Was it Terrestrial?: AER 84 (1931) 37-350. — C. M. EDSMANN, Schöpferwille und Geburt. Eine Studie zur altchristlichen Kosmologie: ZNW (1939) 11-44. — E. CORSINI, Nouvelles perspectives sur le problème des sources de l'Hexaéméron de Grégoire de Nysse: PS I (TU 63). Berlin, 1957, 94-103. — J. F. CALLAHAN, Greek Philosophy and the Cappadocian Cosmology: DOP 12 (1958) 31-57.

3. *De vita Moysis*

In this mystical treatise Gregory provides a guide to a life of virtue in the form of an ideal portrait of Moses. It consists of two parts, which exhibit two different types of Scriptural exegesis. The first summarizes the actual life of Moses after Exodus and Numbers. Here he pays special attention to the literal sense. The second and essential part is an allegorical interpretation *(θεωρία)* in which the great lawgiver and spiritual leader of Israel becomes the symbol of the mystic migration and ascension of the soul to God. The entire work shows the influence of Plato and Philo. Several references to his old age and the content in general prove sufficiently that it was written about 390/392.

The new edition of this treatise by J. Daniélou is based on ten manuscripts representing all three families of the text tradition and contains many and important emendations.

Editions: MG 44, 297-430. — New crit. ed.: J. DANIÉLOU, Grégoire de Nysse. La Vie de Moïse ou traité de la perfection en matière de vertu (SCH 1). Paris, 2nd ed. 1955 (the first ed. of 1942 contains only the French transl.).

Translation: French: J. DANIÉLOU, op. cit.

Studies: K. BURDACH, Faust und Moses: SAB (1912) 358-403, 627-659, 736-789. — J. DANIÉLOU, op. cit. I-XXXV. — W. JAEGER, Two Rediscovered Works of Ancient Christian Literature. Leiden, 1954, 132-142 (*Vita Moysis* an important source of *De instituto Christiano*). — J. DANIÉLOU, Moïse exemple et figure chez Grégoire de Nysse: Cahiers Sion (1955) 386-400.

4. *In psalmorum inscriptiones*

In his two essays on the titles of the Psalms Gregory develops the idea that the five books of Psalms form as many steps on the ladder to perfection (ch. 1-9), and that the sole purpose of the Septuagint titles is to lead us to goodness (ch. 10-25). His allegorical interpretation permits him to find a consistent plan of ascetical and mystical precepts in the entire arrangement of the Psalter. A homily on the sixth Psalm is added to this treatise in the editions of his works.

Edition: MG 44, 431-608.

5. Eight Homilies on Ecclesiastes

An Accurate Exposition of Ecclesiastes consists of eight homilies on Eccl. 1,1 - 3,13, which serve the same mystical purpose. The allegorical interpretation intends to prove that this 'truly sublime and divinely inspired' book has for its aim 'the uplifting of the spirit above the senses'. By a complete renunciation of all the things that are apparently great and splendid in this world the spirit will conduct the senses into a world of peace.

Edition: MG 44, 615-754.

6. Fifteen Homilies on the Canticle of Canticles

Gregory's Accurate Exposition of the Canticle of Canticles ('Εξήγησις ἀκριβὴς εἰς τὸ ᾆσμα τῶν ᾀσμάτων) is a commentary consisting of fifteen homilies on Cant. 1,1 - 6,8. In the preface he defends against several ecclesiastical authors the necessity for, and the right to, a spiritual interpretation of Scripture, whether it might be called tropology or allegory. The foreword concludes with high praise of Origen, whose mystical exegesis has beyond any doubt had a powerful influence on Gregory. Nevertheless, Gregory is too deep and independent a thinker to follow slavishly the Alexandrian master. On God, on the relation of all created beings to Him, on the sanctifying action of the Holy Spirit, he has his own ideas, in which he enlists the support of Plotinus' speculations. The Song of Songs represents to him the union of love between God and the soul under the figure of a wedding (Hom. 1; MG 44, 772). It is this aspect of the book that predominates in Gregory's commentary in contrast to Origen, who, particularly in his homilies on the subject (cf. vol. II, p. 50), prefers to regard the bride of the Canticle as the Church — an interpretation that Gregory does not neglect, but relegates to a minor role.

Editions: MG 44, 755-1120. — New crit. ed.: H. LANGERBECK, Gregorii Nysseni In Canticum Commentarius (Greg. N. Op. ed. cur. W. Jaeger, vol. VI). Leiden, 1960. For the Syriac version made between 450 and 550, see the study of C. VAN DEN EYNDE, La version syriaque du Commentaire de Grégoire de Nysse sur le Cantique des cantiques. Ses origines, ses témoins, son influence (Bibl. du Mus. 10). Louvain, 1939. Cf. R. H. CONNOLLY, JThSt 41 (1940) 84-86. This version has not been edited so far.

Translation: German: H. U. v. BALTHASAR, Gregor von Nyssa, Der versiegelte Quell. Auslegung des Hohen Liedes (abbreviated transl.). Salzburg, 1939.

Studies: W. RIEDEL, Die Auslegung des Hohen Liedes in der jüdischen Gemeinde und der griechischen Kirche. Leipzig, 1898, 66-74. — H. U. v. BALTHASAR, op. cit. 7-36. — L. WELSERSHEIMB, Das Kirchenbild der griechischen Väterkommentare zum Hohenlied: ZkTh 70 (1948) 423-433. — H. PÉTRÉ, Ordinata caritas: RSR 42 (1954) 40-57 (influence of Origen).

7. *On the Witch of Endor*

The brief tract *De pythonissa*, addressed to bishop Theodosius, deals with 1 Kings 28, 12f., and sets out to prove that 'the witch of Endor' did not, as Origen thought, see Samuel but a demon who put on the appearance of the prophet.

Editions: MG 45, 107-114. — Separate ed.: E. KLOSTERMANN, Eustathius von Antiochien und Gregor von Nyssa über die Hexe von Endor (KT 83). Bonn, 1913.

8. *De oratione dominica*

The treatise on the Lord's Prayer consists of five homilies. The first stresses the need for prayer and its neglect by most Christians, while the following four explain the various petitions of the Our Father, mostly from the moral point of view. Luxury and gluttony are favorite objects of the author's strictures. From time to time, beginning even in his first sermon, he forsakes the literal meaning for the mystical interpretation, and then the divine image in man's soul becomes his favorite theme. The third sermon has a passage very important for the doctrine of the Trinity:

> Hence the characteristic of the Father's Person cannot be transferred to the Son or the Spirit, nor, on the other hand, can that of the Son be accommodated to one of the others, or the property of the Spirit be attributed to the Father and the Son. But the incommunicable distinction of the properties is considered in the common nature. It is the characteristic of the Father to exist without cause. This does not apply to the Son and the Spirit; for the Son 'went out from the Father' (John 16, 28), as says the Scripture, and 'the Spirit proceedeth' from God and 'from the Father' (John 5, 26). But as the being without cause, which belongs only to the Father, cannot be adapted to the Son and the Spirit, so again the being caused, which is the property of the Son and of the Spirit, cannot by its very nature, be considered in the Father. On the other hand, the being not ungenerated is common to the Son and to the Spirit; hence in order to avoid confusion in the subject, one must again search for the pure difference in the properties, so that what is common be safeguarded, yet what is proper be not mixed. For He is called the Only-Begotten of the Father by the Holy Scripture; and this term establishes His property for Him. But the Holy Spirit is also said to be from the Father, and is testified to be the Son's. For it says: 'If any man have not the Spirit of Christ, he is none of His' (Rom. 8, 9). Hence the Spirit that is from God is also Christ's Spirit; but the Son, Who is from God, neither is nor is said to be from the Spirit; and this relative sequence is permanent and inconvertible. Hence the sentence cannot properly be resolved and reversed in its meaning so that as we say the Spirit to be Christ's, we might also call Christ the Spirit's. Since therefore, this individual property

distinguishes one from the other with absolute clarity, but as, on the other hand, the identity of action bears witness to the community of nature, the right doctrine about the Divinity is confirmed in both; namely that the Trinity is numbered by the Persons, but that it is not divided into parts of different nature (ACW 18).

While Krabinger and Oehler regard the foregoing as authentic, it is missing in a number of manuscripts and in the older editions. The passage was first published by Cardinal Mai in 1833. K. Holl went so far as to declare it a 'Western forgery' made in the interest of the *Filioque*. Yet, all the evidence, its style, its theology and its text tradition points clearly to its genuineness, as F. Diekamp has convincingly shown. Its phrases occur — sometimes verbatim — in other writings of Gregory of Nyssa. It appears in the *Doctrina Patrum de Verbi incarnatione* as early as 700 A.D. and in *Codex Vaticanus Graecus* 2066 of the seventh or eighth century as a part of Gregory's third sermon on the Lord's Prayer.

Editions: MG 44, 1120-1193. — J. G. KRABINGER, S. Gregorii episc. Nysseni De precatione orationes V. Landshut, 1840. — F. OEHLER, Bibliothek der Kirchenväter I, 3. Leipzig, 1859. — For the Trinitarian passage of the third homily, see: Card. MAI, Script. vet. nova coll. 7, Rome, 1883, pars 1, 6-7. — F. DIEKAMP, Doctrina Patrum de Verbi incarnatione. Münster, 1907, 4-5. A Syriac version of the first homily is found in ZINGERLE and MOESINGER, Monumenta Syriaca ex Romanis codicibus collecta. Innsbruck, 1869-1878, 1, 111-116.

Translations: English: H. C. GRAEF, ACW 18 (1954) 21-84. — *German:* J. FISCH, BKV (1880) 10-81. — K. WEISS, BKV² 56 (1927) 89-150.

Studies: K. HOLL, Amphilochius von Ikonium in seinem Verhältnis zu den grossen Kappadoziern. Tübingen, 1904, 215. Cf. F. DIEKAMP, ThR 3 (1904) 332. — J. DRÄSEKE, Zu Gregorios von Nyssa: ZKG 28 (1907) 387-400 (on the Trinitarian passage in Hom. 3). — G. WALTHER, Untersuchungen zur Geschichte der griechischen Vaterunserexegese (TU 40, 3). Leipzig, 1914, 31-49. — H. MERKI, Ὁμοίωσις θεῷ. Von der platonischen Angleichung an Gott zur Gottähnlichkeit bei Gregor von Nyssa. Fribourg, 1952, 124-128 (*Sermo* 2). — R. LEANEY, The Lucan Text of the Lord's Prayer (in Gregory of Nyssa): Novum Testamentum 1 (1956) 103-111.

9. *De beatitudinibus*

The second exegetical treatise dealing with the New Testament is a series of eight homilies on the Beatitudes. They are compared to a ladder by which the Divine Word conducts us gradually up to the heights of perfection. Many of Gregory's conceptions remind one of the Enneads of Plotinus, especially his teaching on purification as leading to deification, but he has thoroughly Christianized his Neo-Platonist borrowings.

Edition: MG 44, 1193-1302.

Translations: English: H. C. GRAEF, ACW 18 (1954) 85-175. — *German:* J. FISCH, BKV (1880) 85-192. — K. WEISS, BKV² 56 (1927) 153-240.

10. *Two Homilies on I Corinthians*

There are in addition two homilies on I Corinthians. The first on I Cor. 6, 18, is listed among Gregory's orations as *Oratio contra fornicarios*. The other on I Cor. 15, 28 proves from the words of St. Paul the true divinity of the Son.

Editions: MG 46, 489-498; 1107-1110: *In illud: Qui fornicatur in proprium corpus peccat* (1 Cor. 6, 18). MG 44, 1303-1326: *In illud: Quando sibi subiecerit omnia, tunc ipse quoque Filius subicietur ei qui sibi subiecit omnia.* — New crit. ed. of the latter: J. K. DOWNING, The Treatise of Gregory of Nyssa: In illud: Tunc et ipse Filius. A Critical Text with Prolegomena. Diss. Harvard Univ., as yet unpublished. Cf. the summary: HSCP 58/59 (1948) 221-223.

3. *Ascetic Works*

The spiritual doctrine of Gregory of Nyssa is found chiefly in his ascetic writings, which in recent times have finally received the attention they deserve. They justify the title 'Father of Mysticism', which has been given to this great Cappadocian. While his brother Basil was the lawgiver for Eastern asceticism, and his sister Macrina played an important role in the development of communities for women, Gregory supplements his brother's and sister's efforts with a teaching on spirituality. Basil gave Eastern monasticism its organization, and Gregory inspired its characteristic religious outlook.

Fortunately, most of Gregory's ascetic works are now available in the excellent critical edition, based on more than one thousand manuscripts, of the Harvard Institute for Classical Studies conducted by W. Jaeger.

Edition: Gregorii Nysseni Opera, vol. VIII, 1: Gregorii Nysseni Opera Ascetica ediderunt W. JAEGER, J. P. CANARVOS, V. W. CALLAHAN. Leiden, 1952.

1. *De virginitate*

Gregory's book *On Virginity* is not only the earliest of his ascetic treatises but of all his works, since it was written shortly after Basil had been elected bishop in 370 and before Gregory himself was consecrated to the see of Nyssa in 371. Gregory refers to Basil in the introduction as 'to that most godly bishop and our father in God' and he alludes to his brother's monastic *Rules*, stating: 'All the particular rules obeyed by the followers of this calling will, to avoid prolixity, be omitted here; the exhortation in the discourse will be introduced only in general terms, and for cases of wide application; but in a way particulars will be included, and so nothing will be overlooked'. He declares that Basil 'alone could be the master of such instructions' and that for this reason he will be presented as the ideal ascetic. 'He will not indeed be mentioned by name, but by certain indications we shall say in cipher that he is meant. Thus future readers will not think our advice unmeaning, when the candidate for this life is told to school himself by recent masters' (LNPF). Gregory fulfills this promise of the introduction in chapter 23, in which Basil appears as the example and tutor of ascetics. There is again at the beginning a reference to his *Rules:* 'Now the details of the life of him who has chosen to live in such a philosophy as this, the things to be avoided, the exercises to be engaged in, the rules of temperance, the whole method of training, and all the daily regimen which contributes towards this great end, has been dealt with in certain written manuals of instruction for the benefit of those who like details. Yet there is a plainer guide to be found than verbal instruction, and that is practice... Any theory divorced from living examples, however admirably it may be dressed out, is like the unbreathing statue, with its show of a blooming complexion impressed in tints and colors; but the man who acts as well as teaches, as the Gospel tells us, he is the man who is truly living, and has the bloom of beauty, and is efficient and stirring. It is to him that we must go' (23 LNPF).

Virginity is for Gregory, as he says in the introduction, 'a necessary door of entrance to a holier life'. Moreover, 'it is the channel which draws down the Deity to share man's estate, it keeps wings for man's desire to rise to heavenly things, and is a bond of union between the Divine and the human, by its mediation bringing into harmony these existences so widely divided' (2). Gregory sees the entire divine economy, the whole chain of salvation in the light of virginity. This chain reaches from the three Persons in the Trinity and the angelic powers of heaven to mankind as its last link. Thus he calls Christ the 'archvirgin' ($\dot{\alpha}\rho\chi\iota\pi\dot{\alpha}\rho\theta\epsilon\nu\sigma$).

The striking example of virginity is the Blessed Virgin. There is a spiritual incarnation of God in every virginal soul: 'What happened in the stainless Mary when the fulness of the Godhead which was in Christ shone out through her, that happens in every soul that leads by rule the virgin life. No longer indeed does the Master come with bodily presence; "we know Christ no longer according to the flesh" (2 Cor. 5, 16); but spiritually He dwells in us and brings us His Father with Him, as the Gospel somewhere tells' (2). Virginity is the foundation of all virtues: 'Let the virtuous life have for its substructure the love of virginity; but upon this let every result of virtue be reared' (17). Virginity is in fact the preparation for the vision of God: 'It has been proved as well that this union of the soul with the incorruptible Deity can be accomplished in no other way but by herself attaining by her virgin state to the utmost purity possible, — a state which, being like God, will enable her to grasp that to which it is like, while she places herself like a mirror beneath the purity of God and moulds her own beauty at the touch and the sight of the Archetype of all beauty' (11). 'The real virginity, the real zeal for chastity, ends in no other goal than this, viz. the power thereby of seeing God' (11).

Of course Gregory knows that virginity cannot be reached by human efforts alone, it must be supported by grace: 'It belongs to those alone whose struggles to gain this object of a noble love are favoured and helped by the grace of God' (1). Gregory who was himself married feels sorry that he is excluded from this state of virginity:

> Would indeed that some profit might come to myself from this effort! I should have undertaken this labor with the greater readiness, if I could have hope of sharing, according to the Scripture, in the fruits of the plough and the threshing-floor; the toil would then have been a pleasure. As it is, this my knowledge of the beauty of virginity is in some sort vain and useless to me, just as the corn is to the muzzled ox that treads the floor, or the water that streams from the precipice to a thirsty man when he cannot reach it. Happy they who have still the power of choosing the better way, and have not debarred themselves from it by the engagements of the secular life, as we have, whom a gulf now divides from glorious virginity (3; MG 46, 325 B, LNPF).

> If only, before experience comes, the results of experience could be learnt, or if, when one has entered on this course, it were possible by some other means of conjecture to survey the reality, then what a crowd of deserters would run from marriage into the virgin life (3; MG 46, 328 C, LNPF).

In ch. 20 he compares the two kinds of marriage, the earthly and the spiritual, which cannot exist simultaneously in the same soul: 'No more do our emotional powers possess a nature which can at once pursue the pleasures of sense and court the spiritual union; nor, besides, can both those ends be gained by the same courses of life; continence, mortification of the passions, scorn of fleshly needs, are the agents of the one union; but all that are the reverse of these are the agents of bodily cohabitation... When two marriages are before us to choose between, and we cannot contract both, it would be the aim of a sound mind not to miss choosing the more profitable one... The soul which cleaves to the undying Bridegroom should have the fruition of her love for the True Wisdom which is God' (20).

In these and similar thoughts Gregory follows in the footsteps of Origen and Methodius. His frequent and conscious use of philosophic terms shows that he sees in the ascetic life the fulfillment of the dreams of the philosophers of ancient Greece concerning the *vita contemplativa*.

The many manuscripts of the treatise prove that it was widely read in the Middle Ages. The first printed edition was brought out by Johannes Livineius at Antwerp in 1574, long before the *editio princeps* of Gregory's works by Morellus at Paris in 1615.

J. P. Cavarnos, author of the new edition, shows that Gregory continued to add to his favoured treatise even after it had been published. As a result there were two slightly different versions. This explains certain variants in the manuscripts. Cavarnos thinks (p. 237) that the introductory letter and the *capitulatio* belong to the later revision. It is possible that the subtitle of the treatise Προτρεπτικὴ ἐπιστολὴ εἰς τὸν κατ'ἀρετὴν βίον refers only to the introductory epistle.

Editions: MG 46, 317-416. — New crit. ed.: J. P. CAVARNOS, op. cit. 215-343.

Translations: English: W. MOORE, LNPF ser. 2, vol. 5, 343-371. — *Spanish:* F. DE B. VIZMANOS, San Gregorio Niseno, Acerca de la virginidad o epistola exhortatoria a la vida virtuosa: Las virgenes cristianas. Madrid, 1949, 1110-1172.

Studies: J. STIGLMAYR, Die Schrift des heiligen Gregor von Nyssa über die Jungfräulichkeit: ZAM 2 (1927) 334-359. — H. O. KNACKSTEDT, Die Theologie der Jungfräulichkeit beim hl. Gregor von Nyssa. Diss. Rome, 1940.

2. *Quid nomen professiove Christianorum sibi velit*

His treatise *What is the Christian name and profession?* is couched as a letter addressed to a certain Harmonius. This is not merely a literary device, since Harmonius had actually written to him several times. As he compares his correspondent to a plectrum which has struck the strings of his old lyre, it is a safe conclusion that Gregory wrote it in the last years of his life. Gregory defines the Christian profession as 'the imitation of the divine nature'. He anticipates Harmonius' objection that this is 'too lofty for the lowliness of our nature', thereby touching upon one of the fundamental teachings of his theology of the spiritual life, namely, the doctrine of man as the image of God:

> Let no one misrepresent the definition as excessive and surpassing the lowliness of our nature, for it has not exceeded our nature. Should anyone consider the first state of man, he will find from the lessons of the Scriptures that the definition does not exceed the limits of our nature, for the first condition of man was according to the imitation of the likeness of God. Moses explains this when he says, 'God made man, according to the image of God He made him' (Gen. 1, 27). The profession of Christianity then is the restoration of man to his

pristine good fortune. If from the beginning man was a likeness of God, perhaps we have not extended the definition beyond the mark in saying that Christianity is the imitation of the divine nature (244 C/D).

Editions: MG 46, 237-249. — New crit. ed.: W. JAEGER, op. cit. 129-142.

Studies: M. E. KEENAN, De Professione Christiana and De Perfectione. A Study of the Ascetical Doctrine of Saint Gregory of Nyssa: DOP 5 (1950) 167-207. — W. JAEGER, op. cit. 93-128.

3. *De perfectione et qualem oporteat esse Christianum*

This tract is addressed to the monk Olympius who had asked for direction in attaining perfection 'by means of the life according to virtue'. It is based entirely on the great christological texts of St. Paul, whom Gregory considers the safest guide for the Christian in his efforts to imitate Christ. Sanctification is viewed not only in terms of free will, but in terms of Christ's operations in the soul. Thus Gregory deals with Christ as the power and wisdom of God, as the peace of the soul, as the true light, as redemption, as our Pasch and our High Priest, as propitiation, as the brightness of His glory and the imprint of His substance, as spiritual food and drink, as the rock, as the foundation of faith and the corner-stone, as the image of the invisible God, as the head of the body of the Church, as the first-born of creation, first-born from the dead and first-born among many brethren, as the mediator of God and man, as the only-begotten Son, as Lord of glory, as the principle of being, as king of justice and peace. All these different names of Christ are discussed. The author distinguishes between First-born and Only-Begotten and touches upon christological questions. The real topic *On Perfection* receives a fuller treatment than in the letter to Harmonius. In concluding Gregory states: 'True perfection never stands still, but is always growing toward the better: perfection is limited by no boundaries' (285 C/D).

It seems that this treatise was written after the letter to Harmonius. The addressee is the same Olympus to whom Gregory dedicated his *Life of Macrina*. The epistolary form is but a literary fiction.

Editions: MG 46, 251-286. — New crit. ed.: W. JAEGER, op. cit. 173-214.

Studies: M. E. KEENAN, op. cit. — W. JAEGER, op. cit. 145-172.

4. *De instituto Christiano*

W. Jaeger has given us the first complete edition of this treatise, known so far only in the form of a highly defective late Byzantine excerpt printed by Migne (MG 46, 287-306) under the title *De proposito secundum Deum et exercitatione iuxta veritatem et ad religiosos qui proposuerant quaestionem de pietatis scopo.* The title *De instituto Christiano* is used by Migne in the headlines of every page. The Greek title is Περὶ τοῦ κατὰ θεὸν σκοποῦ καὶ τῆς κατὰ ἀλήθειαν ἀσκήσεως. Since the second part of the treatise corresponds to the second part of the 'Great Letter' of the so-called Macarius (cf. above, p. 164), *De instituto christiano* was formerly regarded as spurious and its second part as a copy of that letter. The rediscovery of the entire work in its original form establishes the priority of *De instituto Christiano*. Thus new light has been cast upon the 'Macarius problem' and we have been brought considerably closer to a solution.

This essay of Gregory's is of the highest importance. It seems to be his final statement on the nature of asceticism and expresses the quintessence of his thought. Jaeger (p. 119) is convinced that the treatise was composed during the last few years of his life, after 390; it makes ample use of his earlier writings, from *De virginitate* down to *De vita Moysis*, which are separated by a quarter of a century and have contributed the greater part of its contents. Thus it combines all the leading ideas of the great Christian Platonist into a perfect and harmonious whole. Gregory remarks that he wrote it by selecting from 'the fruits previously given him by the Spirit' (p. 42, 17). The work is, therefore, the culmination of Gregory's spiritual thinking.

He himself gives a brief outline (41, 10-24) of its contents in mentioning the occasion of its composition. Some monks had requested (1) a summary of his doctrine on the true object of the contemplative life and the means of attaining it, (2) advice for superiors in the guidance of their communities, and (3) instruction on exercises that would prepare their souls for the reception of the Spirit.

It is in this admirable form that Gregory's teaching penetrated the monastic world and influenced the educational system of the East. The author's purpose is to harmonize the concept of grace with the Hellenistic ethical tradition and the classical ideal of virtue *(ἀρετή)*. The roots of his 'Christian philosophy' go back to Platonism and the Stoa, but he forms something entirely new in this intermarriage of Hellenism and Christianity.

There are only five manuscripts on which to base the new edition. Three of them can be traced to a manuscript of the Abbot Arsenios of the year 911, unfortunately no longer extant. An older archetype of the ninth century is represented by a manuscript from Thessaly now at Milan.

Editions: MG 46, 287-306 (excerpt only). — First crit. ed.: W. JAEGER, op. cit. 40-89.

Studies: J. STIGLMAYR, Makarius der Grosse und Gregor von Nyssa: ThGl 2 (1910) 571.
— G. L. MARRIOTT, The De Instituto Christiano attributed to Gregory of Nyssa: JThSt 19 (1918) 328-330. — A. WILMART, La tradition de l'hypotypose ou traité sur l'ascèse attribué à S. Grégoire de Nysse: ROC 21 (1919) 412-421. — L. VILLECOURT, La grande lettre grecque de Macaire, ses formes textuelles et son milieu littéraire: ROC 22 (1920/21) 29-56. — W. JAEGER, op. cit. 3-39; *idem,* Two Rediscovered Works of Ancient Christian Literature: Gregory of Nyssa and Macarius. Leiden, 1954, 37-142, 174-207. — H. DÖRRIES, Christlicher Humanismus und mönchische Geist-Ethik: ThLZ 79 (1954) 643-656. — A. WENGER, Grégoire de Nysse et le pseudo-Macaire: REB 13 (1955) 145-150. — A. KEMMER, Gregorius Nyssenus estne inter fontes Joannis Cassiani numerandus?: OCP 21 (1955) 451-466. — R. LEYS, La théologie spirituelle de Grégoire de Nysse: SP II (TU 64). Berlin, 1957, 495-511. — For the *Great Letter* of Macarius and his *Spiritual Homilies,* see above p. 162-168.

5. De castigatione

This is the shortest of the ascetic treatises and of somewhat restricted interest because of its theme. The exact title *Adversus eos qui castigationes aegre ferunt* is explained by the fact that it is addressed to those members of Gregory's flock who were 'angered exceedingly at the admonitions of their teacher' and on this account withdrew from the Church.

Edition: MG 46, 307-316.

6. Vita Macrinae

In the introduction to his *De virginitate* Gregory writes: 'Each of us is inclined to embrace some course of life with the greater enthusiasm, when he sees personalities who have already gained distinction in it. We have therefore made the requisite mention of saints who have gained their glory in celibacy'. In keeping with this principle, Gregory, as he himself states, composed the *Life of Macrina,* his beloved sister, in order that the example of her 'who had reached the highest summit of human virtue by true wisdom (διὰ φιλοσοφίας), should not fall into oblivion but be of advantage for others'. Thus her biography, written shortly after her death in Dec. 379 at the request of the monk Olympus, belongs definitely to the ascetic works despite its literary form. Macrina is presented as a model of Christian perfection, to be imitated by others who have the same ambition. The author stresses his intention to give an accurate and reliable account of her life and to exclude for this reason anything not based on his own personal knowledge and information. He describes in simple and touching language Macrina's love for the reading of Scripture, and the help she gave her mother in raising her younger brothers and sisters. He does not forget the influence she had on Basil and on himself. He relates in all candor how she rescued Basil for the ascetic life:

> When the mother had arranged excellent marriages for the other sisters, such as was best in each case, Macrina's brother, the great Basil, returned after his long period of education, already a practised rhetorician. He was puffed up beyond measure with the pride of oratory and looked down on the local dignitaries, excelling in his own estimation all the men of leading and position. Nevertheless, Macrina took him in hand, and with such speed did she draw him also toward the mark of philosophy that he forsook the glories of this world and despised fame gained by speaking, and deserted it for this busy life where one toils with one's hands. His renunciation of property was complete, lest anything should impede the life of virtue (27f. SPCK).

Gregory is at his best when he depicts his sister as the model of the spiritual mother in the convent on the banks of the river Iris. She fosters by precept and example the angelic life that she shares with her daughters in religion. A rare combination of natural and supernatural gifts equipped her for this leadership among women devoted whole-heartedly to God and their neighbour. The bishop of Nyssa gives a moving account of the last conversation between himself and his saintly sister. In his dialogue *De anima et resurrectione* (cf. above, p. 261) he has used this scene as a frame for his doctrine on the resurrection. Death appears in his *Life of Macrina* only as the crowning of the bride of Christ. The *Vita* is a gem of early hagiographic literature and an important historical source as well for the two great Cappadocians, Basil and Gregory of Nyssa. It provides in addition interesting information about ecclesiastical, liturgical and monastic customs of the fourth century.

The great number of manuscripts testifies to the esteem in which it was held. Its latest editor, V. Woods Callahan, has demonstrated that a number of them come from a monastery, where the memory of St. Macrina never faded. The *editio princeps* was issued in 1618 by J. Gretser S. J. It does not appear in the first printing of the complete works by Morellus at Paris in 1615, but was incorporated into the enlarged publication of 1638.

Editions: MG 46, 959-1000. — New crit. ed.: V. W. CALLAHAN, op. cit. 370-414.

Translations: English: W. K. LOWTHER CLARKE, St. Gregory of Nyssa, The Life of St. Macrina (SPCK). London, 1916. — *German:* E. STOLZ, BKV² 56 (1927) 337-368.

Studies: F. J. DÖLGER, Das Anhängekreuzchen der hl. Makrina und ihr Ring mit der Kreuzpartikel. Ein Beitrag zur religiösen Volkskunde des 4. Jahrhunderts nach der Vita Macrinae des Gregor von Nyssa: AC 3 (1932) 81-116. — V. W. CALLAHAN, op. cit. 347-367.

4. Orations and Sermons

Besides the homilies mentioned above (p. 266 f.), there is a collection of sermons and orations, which though not numerous, display great variety in subject matter. They exhibit even more than his other writings his fondness for rhetorical ornament. The chronology of the sermons has received a thorough investigation by J. Daniélou.

Edition: MG 46, 431-1000.

Studies: J. DANIÉLOU, Le mystère du culte dans les sermons de saint Grégoire de Nysse: Vom christlichen Mysterium. Festschrift O. Casel. Düsseldorf, 1951, 76-93; *idem*, La chronologie des sermons de Grégoire de Nysse: RSR 29 (1955) 346-372.

1. Liturgical Sermons

Most of them are devoted to the solemn days of the ecclesiastical year. One of them, *In diem Luminum sive in baptismum Christi* (MG 46, 577-600), was most probably delivered on Epiphany 383. The sermon *In sanctum Pascha et in resurrectionem* (MG 46, 652-681) was delivered on Easter Sunday 379. It is related to his treatise *On the Creation of Man* which he composed during the preceding months (cf. above, p. 263). Only the first, third and fourth of the five Easter sermons *In sanctum Pascha sive in Christi resurrectionem* (MG 46, 599-690) seem to be authentic. The first was preached on Easter 382. Next comes *In ascensionem Christi* (MG 46, 690-694) which was given on May 18th, 388. It represents the first reliable testimony for a feast of the Ascension distinct from Pentecost. Of the same month and year (May 28, 388) is *De Spiritu Sancto sive in Pentecosten* (MG 46, 696-701). The Christmas sermon *In natalem Christi* (MG 46, 1128-1149), highly important for the history of the feast of the Nativity, was delivered on the 25th of December, 386. H. Usener denied its authenticity (*Weihnachtsfest*, p. 247); K. Holl (*Amphilochius v. Ikon.*, p. 231) defended it and has found approval.

Translations: English: H. A. WILSON, LNPF ser. 2, vol. 5, 518-524 (*On the Baptism of Christ*). — *German:* J. FISCH, BKV (1880) 253-395 (*On the Baptism of Christ, five Easter sermons, Ascension sermon*).

Studies: M. A. KUGENER, Une homélie de Sévère d'Antioche attribuée à Grégoire de Nysse et à Hésychius de Jérusalem: ROC 3 (1898) 435-451 (proved that the second of the five Easter sermons belongs to Severus of Antioch). — G. SOELL, Die Mariologie der Kappadozier im Lichte der Dogmengeschichte: ThQ 131 (1951) 178-188, defends the authenticity of the Christmas sermon: MG 46, 1127-1150. — P. NAUTIN, Homélies pascales III (SCH 48), Paris, 1957, 84-105, has shown that the seventh in the collection of Easter sermons of Pseudo-Chrysostom (MG 69, 745-755) has great similarities with Gregory's theological ideas. Nevertheless, it cannot be attributed to him.

2. Panegyrics on Martyrs and Saints

The first of his two *Sermons on St. Stephen* (MG 46, 701-721) defends (1) the divinity of the Holy Spirit against the objection that the martyr at the moment of his death saw only two Persons of the Godhead and (2) the divinity of the Son against an Arian interpretation of the words 'standing at the right hand of the Father'. This sermon was delivered on the 26th of December, 386, the second (MG 46, 721-736) the next day.

The long *Panegyric on Gregory Thaumaturgus* (MG 46, 893-958) describes his great achievements in sacred science, philosophy and rhetoric, and compares him to Moses. In his *Praise of Theodore the Martyr* (MG 46, 735-748) the martyr is called upon to save the Empire from an invasion, which would destroy the sanctuaries and the altars. Gregory delivered it on February 7, 381, at Euchaïta, where the *martyrion* of this saint was. He gives a long description of it (MG 46, 737-740). Of the three *Sermons on the Forty Martyrs* the first two (MG 46, 749-772) were given at Sebaste, the place of their martyrdom, in their chapel on the 9th and 10th of March, 383; the third (46, 775-786) delivered at Caesarea on the 9th of March, 379, tells the story of their sufferings.

Translation: German: J. FISCH, BKV (1880) 399-556 (sermons *On the Forty Martyrs, On Theodore the Martyr, On Gregory Thaumaturgus*).

Studies: J. SIMON, Où et quand furent prononcées les 'Orationes in XL Martyres' de S. Grégoire de Nysse?: HA 41 (1927) 733ff. (at Sebaste on March 7, 380). — W. TELFER, The Latin Life of St. Gregory Thaumaturgus: JThSt 31 (1929/30) 142-155, 354-363. — F. HALKIN, La prétendue Passion inédite de saint Alexandre de Thessalonique: NC 6 (1954) 70-72 (manuscript of Gregory of Nyssa's *Panegyric on Gregory Thaumaturgus*).

3. Funeral Orations

Strictly speaking, there are only three funeral orations by Gregory of Nyssa, all delivered at Constantinople at the month's mind. The fact that he was called upon to give these sermons in the capital over outstanding figures of his time, shows the great reputation he enjoyed as an orator. The discourses take the form of a Christian *Consolatio*, modelled, as J. Bauer has shown, on the παραμυθικὸς λόγος of the ancient rhetoricians. The first was pronounced over Bishop Meletius of Antioch (MG 46, 851-864), who died in May 381 while attending the Second Ecumenical Council at Constantinople; the second was for the princess Pulcheria, the only child of Theodosius the Great; her death occurred in 385, when she was only six years of age (MG 46, 864-877). The last of the three (MG 46, 877-892) delivered on September 15, 385, is the funeral oration on the Empress Flaccilla, the wife of Theodosius, who passed away soon after her daughter.

The discourse on his brother Basil (MG 46, 787-818) is authentic but cannot be regarded as a funeral oration. It was preached on some anniversary of Basil's death, but whether the first, the second or the third, is difficult to determine. J. Daniélou is of the opinion that it was given at Caesarea on the first of January, 381, and this seems to be correct. Devoted entirely to the praise of Basil without any admixture of *threnos* or *paramythia*, it should be classed as an *encomium*. Gregory compares his great brother to St. John the Baptist and St. Paul. His main purpose is to establish a feast day for him in the Martyrology, for he was convinced that Basil was a saint. The genuineness of the oration has been defended by H. Delehaye and K. Holl against H. Usener.

The sermon on St. Ephraem Syrus extols this illustrious saint (MG 46, 819-850) and compares him to St. Basil. It too should be classed as an *encomium*. There is, however, great doubt about its authenticity.

Editions: J. G. KRABINGER added a new crit. text of the oration on Meletius to his ed. of the *Oratio catechetica*, Munich, 1835, 79ff., 165ff. Separate ed.: J. A. STEIN, Encomium of St. Gregory, Bishop of Nyssa, on his Brother St. Basil, Archbishop of Cappadocian Caesarea. A Commentary, with a Revised Text, Introduction and Translation (PSt 17). Washington, 1928. Cf. P. MAAS, BZ 28 (1928) 437ff.

Translations: English: W. MOORE, LNPF ser. 2, vol. 5, 513-517 (on Meletius). — J. A. STEIN, op. cit. (on Basil). — *German:* J. FISCH, BKV (1880) 399-425 (on Basil), 462-490 (on Ephraem), 557-569 (on Meletius), 570-582 (on Pulcheria), 583-596 (on Flaccilla).

Studies: J. BAUER, Die Trostreden des Gregorios von Nyssa in ihrem Verhältnis zur antiken Rhetorik. Marburg, 1892. — K. HOLL, Amphilochius von Ikonium. Tübingen, 1904, 197. — H. USENER, Das Weihnachtsfest. 2nd ed. Bonn, 1911, 255. — H. DELEHAYE, Les passions des martyrs et les genres littéraires. Brussels, 1921, 188. — J. DANIÉLOU, art. cit.

4. *Moral Sermons*

The most unaffected and natural sermons are those that deal with moral questions. Two of them are entitled *De pauperibus amandis et benignitate complectendis*. The first (MG 46, 455-469) was delivered in March, 382, the second (MG 46, 472-489) apparently in March, 384.

The discourse against usurers, *Contra usuarios* (MG 46, 433-453), mentions explicitly St. Basil's utterance on the same topic, and condemns usury because it breaks all the laws of charity. It seems to have been preached in March, 379.

Adversus eos qui differunt baptismum (MG 46, 415-432) represents an earnest effort to dissuade catechumens from postponing their baptism and running the risk of dying in sin. It alludes again and again to the baptism of Christ in the Jordan, the theme of Epiphany, which was after Easter the solemn date of baptism in the East. It was pronounced at Caesarea on January 7, 381.

Translation: German: J. Fisch, BKV (1880) 195-226 (*De pauperibus amandis* 1-2), 227-242 (*Contra usuarios*).

Study: S. Giet, De saint Basil à saint Ambroise: La condamnation du prêt à intérêt au IVe siècle (chez Grégoire de Nysse): RSR (1944) 95-128 (against usurers).

5. *Dogmatic Sermons*

The *Oratio de deitate Filii et Spiritus Sancti* (MG 46, 553-576) is the most important of the dogmatic sermons. Gregory compares the heretics of his time to the Stoics and Epicureans of St. Paul's day, refutes some of their notions regarding the Trinity, defends the divinity of the Son and the Spirit and praises the faith of Abraham. This oration was delivered at the Synod of Constantinople in May 383. It was quoted often and held in high esteem by later writers of the Greek Church.

The divinity of the Holy Spirit is again the subject of a short discourse usually called *In suam ordinationem* (MG 46, 544-553). O. Bardenhewer (vol. 3, p. 205) thinks that it was preached at the Synod of Constantinople in 394. If this is the case, it is his last sermon, so far as we know, because Gregory died soon afterwards. However, it is more probable that it was pronounced at the Council of Constantinople in May, 381. Its theological topics are the same as those of the Council. It alludes especially to the *Pneumatomachoi* and there are in addition historical reasons for this date, as J. Daniélou has shown.

Translation: J. Fisch, BKV (1880) 385-395 (*In suam ordinationem*).

Studies: M. Chaine, Une homélie de saint Grégoire de Nysse attribuée à saint Grégoire de Nazianze: ROC 17 (1912) 395-409, 18 (1913) 36-38, published the Coptic text and a translation of a homily that is but an excerpt of the above mentioned *Oratio de deitate Filii et Spiritus Sancti*. — H. I. Bell, Sermons by the Author of the 'Theognosia', Attributed to Gregory of Nyssa: JThSt 26 (1925) 364-373, deals with sermons on the Gospel of St. John which Bell discovered in Cod. Mus. Brit. add. 39605. They belong in reality to the Iconoclastic era and to a writer of the circle of Theodore, Abbot of Studium. A critical edition of this commentary was published by K. Hansmann, Ein neuentdeckter Kommentar zum Johannesevangelium (FLDG 16, 4-5). Paderborn, 1930. — W. Jaeger, Der neuentdeckte Kommentar zum Johannesevangelium und Dionysios Areopagites (SAB). Berlin, 1930. — For the two homilies *Faciamus hominem ad imaginem et similitudinem nostram* (MG 44, 257-298), see above p. 217 and 263; also W. J. Burghardt, The Image of God in Man according to Cyril of Alexandria (SCA 14). Washington, 1957, 5-6, n. 19.

5. *Letters*

There are thirty letters in the new edition by G. Pasquali. They give an idea of Gregory's diverse interests and contacts. Some of them, like *Ep.* 9, 11, 12, 28 are purely social communications.

Others introduce or intercede for people, e.g. *Ep.* 7 and 8. Several deal with theological questions. Thus *Ep.* 5 contains a brief defense of the doctrine of the Trinity. *Ep.* 24 is devoted to an exposition of the one substance and three Persons in the Godhead. According to Cavallin's recent investigations Basil's *Ep.* 38, identical with that of Gregory of Nyssa to his brother Peter, bishop of Sebaste, belongs rightfully to Gregory of Nyssa, although it was ascribed to Basil at the Council of Chalcedon (451). It discusses in detail the difference between *ousia* and *hypostasis*. Leontius of Byzantium and John of Damascus quote a passage of Gregory's *Epistola ad Philippum monachum*, which is no longer extant in the original Greek. The fragment treats of the two natures in Christ and, after G. Bardy's careful study, must be regarded as authentic. A Latin version of the entire letter was discovered by G. Mercati.

Ep. 4 explains the mystical reason why the feast of Christmas occurs at the winter solstice and not at the vernal equinox.

Two of his letters led to lively controversies between Catholics and Protestants in the 16th and 17th centuries: *Ep.* 2 warns against indiscriminate pilgrimages to the Holy Land by ascetics, both men and women; *Ep.* 3, addressed to three pious women living in the Holy Land, Eustathia, Ambrosia and Basilissa, relates the deep impression made on him by the sight of the sacred places, when he visited Palestine on his journey to Arabia. He speaks with sorrow of the unhappy conditions in the Holy Land and warns them that despite their hallowed environment, they are not immune to the contagion of vice and heresy.

Ep. 2 testifies vividly to the popularity of pilgrimages and protests against undue esteem for them. He addresses himself especially to those that have taken up the 'higher life', the 'life according to philosophy'. He advises them to refrain from making such journeys, first of all because the Lord in his teachings nowhere prescribes them as necessary for salvation: 'When the Lord invites the blest to their inheritance in the kingdom of heaven, He does not include a pilgrimage to Jerusalem amongst their good deeds. When He announces the Beatitudes, He does not name amongst them that sort of devotion'. Secondly, these pilgrimages are fraught with moral dangers, especially for women, and 'those who have entered upon the perfect life'. Thirdly: 'What advantage, moreover, is reaped by him who reaches those celebrated spots themselves? He cannot imagine that our Lord is living in the body there at the present day, but has gone away from us foreigners; or that the Holy Spirit is in abundance at Jerusalem, but unable to travel as far as us. Whereas, if it is really possible to infer God's presence from visible symbols, one might more justly consider that He dwelt in the

Cappadocian nation than in any of the spots outside. For how many altars there are there, on which the name of our Lord is glorified! One could hardly count so many in all the rest of the world'.

Gregory confesses that he himself did not experience an increase in faith as a result of his own pilgrimage:

We confessed that the Christ Who was manifested is very God, much before as after our sojourn at Jerusalem. Our faith in Him was not increased afterwards any more than it was diminished. Before Bethlehem we knew His being made man by means of the Virgin. Before we saw His grave we believed in His Resurrection from the dead. Apart from seeing the Mount of Olives, we confessed that His Ascension into heaven was real. We derived only this much of profit from our travelling thither, namely that we came to know, by being able to compare them, that our own places are far holier than those abroad.

Change of place does not affect any drawing nearer unto God, but wherever you may be, God will come to you, if the chambers of your soul be found of such a sort that He can dwell in you. But if you keep your inner man full of wicked thoughts, even if you were on Golgotha, even if you were on the Mount of Olives, even if you stood on the memorial-rock of the Resurrection, you will be as far away from receiving Christ into yourself, as one who has not even begun to confess Him (LNPF).

Both letters, 2 and 3, seem to have been written about 383. The authenticity of *Ep.* 2 has been called in question by some Catholic authors like Cardinal Bellarmine and the Jesuit Gretser. Today it is generally accepted as genuine.

Ep. 25, addressed to Amphilochius of Iconium, is very valuable for the history of Christian architecture and art. It describes in detail a *martyrion* in the construction of which Gregory was interested and for which he asked Amphilochius to procure some workmen. The shrine is to be cruciform in keeping with the common type of contemporary church building, as Gregory remarks. He prefers a self-sustained vaulting to one that rests on supports. Pillars and capitals are to be carved in the Corinthian style. The various kinds of material, fire-baked brick, marble, stones found in the vicinity, timber, are mentioned. The design and ornamentation of the panels are discussed. All of this makes the letter an excellent source of Christian archaeology.

Editions: MG 44, 999-1108. New crit. ed.: Gregorii Nysseni Opera VIII, 2: Epistulae, edidit G. PASQUALI. Berlin, 1925, 2nd ed. Leiden, 1959. — F. Diekamp published a fragment of a hitherto unknown letter *Ad Xenodorum Grammaticum* which deals with the concept of *energeia:* F. DIEKAMP, Analecta Patristica (Orientalia Christiana Analecta 117).

Rome, 1938, 13-15. — For the *Ep. ad Eustathium de sancta Trinitate,* see above p. 260. — For the Latin version of the *Ep. ad Philippum,* see: G. MERCATI, ST 75 (1938) 191-199. For the Greek fragments of this letter, see: G. BARDY, Saint Grégoire de Nysse, *Ep. ad Philippum:* RSR 11 (1921) 220-222.

Translations: English: W. MOORE, H. C. OGLE, H. A. WILSON, LNPF ser. 2, vol. 5, 382-383 (*On Pilgrimages*), 527-548 (18 letters). — *German:* B. Keil furnished a German translation of *Ep.* 25 with commentary in: J. STRZYGOWSKI, Kleinasien ein Neuland der Kunstgeschichte. Leipzig, 1903, 70ff.

Studies: P. MAAS, Zu den Beziehungen zwischen Kirchenvätern und Sophisten I, Drei neue Stücke aus der Korrespondenz des Gregorios von Nyssa: SAB (1912) 988-999, 1112ff., attributes three letters to Gregory which appear in slightly different form in the correspondence between Libanius and St. Basil, *Ep.* 347, 348, 352; cf. above p. 222. — G. PASQUALI, Le lettere di Gregorio di Nissa: SIF 3 (1923) 75-136. — F. MUELLER, Der zwanzigste Brief des Gregor von Nyssa: Hermes 74 (1939) 66-91. — M. E. KEENAN, The Letters of St. Gregory of Nyssa: Classical Weekly 37 (1943/44) 75-77. — C. CAVALLIN, Studien zu den Briefen des hl. Basilius. Lund, 1944 (*Ep.* 38 belongs to Gregory). — T. A. GOGGIN, The Times of Saint Gregory of Nyssa as Reflected in the Letters and the Contra Eunomium. Washington, 1947. — M. M. WAGNER, A Chapter in Byzantine Epistolography: DOP 4 (1948) 129-140. — B. KÖTTING, Peregrinatio religiosa. Wallfahrt und Pilgerwesen in Antike und alter Kirche. Münster, 1950, 421-424 (*Ep.* 2). — W. JAEGER, Vom Affen und wahren Christen: Varia Variorum. Festgabe für K. Reinhardt. Cologne, 1952, 161-168 (*Ep. ad Harmonium*). — J. DARROUZÈS, Un recueil épistolaire byzantin, le manuscrit de Patmos 706: REB 14 (1956) 87-121 (containing letters of St. Gregory).

II. THEOLOGICAL ASPECTS

If we compare Gregory of Nyssa as a theologian with the two other Cappadocians, Basil and Gregory of Nazianzus, we recognize his superiority immediately. He furnished the first organic and systematic presentation of the Christian faith after Origen. His doctrinal speculations reach far beyond the contemporary controversies and contribute to the progress of theology as such.

1. *Philosophy and Theology*

No other Father of the fourth century made so extensive a use of philosophy as did Gregory of Nyssa in his endeavour to bring the mysteries of faith nearer to human understanding. He likens philosophy to the Bride in the Canticle of Canticles, because it teaches us what attitude to take towards the Divine (*In Cant. cant. hom.* 6, MG 44, 885B). He does not hesitate, it is true, to criticize pagan philosophy and he compares it with the childless and barren daughter of the Egyptian king (Exod. 2,1-10):

Childless, indeed, is pagan philosophy; always in pains of childbirth it never engenders living offspring. What fruit has philosophy brought forth worthy of such labor? Are not all [its fruits] inane and undeveloped and miscarried before they enter the light of the knowledge of God? (*De vita Moysis* 2, 11).

Nevertheless, he considers it an obligation to make discreet use of pagan wisdom. As the treasures of the Egyptians were destined to serve a better purpose in the hands of the children of Israel, so wisdom must be redeemd from the bondage of pagan philosophy, to be employed in the service of the higher life of virtue:

> For there is, indeed, something in pagan learning which is worthy of being united to us for the purpose of engendering virtue. It must not be rejected. For the philosophy of both ethics and nature may well become consort, friend, and life-companion of the higher life, if only that which is born of her bring with itself nothing of the foreign stain (*De vita Moysis* 2, 37/38).

In this as in his whole attitude towards philosophy Gregory proves himself a loyal follower of Origen (cf. vol. II, p. 42). Of course, Gregory knows very well that philosophy cannot be absolute and independent: 'We are not allowed to affirm what we please. We make Holy Scripture the rule and the measure of every tenet. We approve of that alone which may be made to harmonize with the intention of those writings' (*De anima et resurr.*, MG 46, 49B). Holy Writ is for him 'the guide of reason' (*Contra Eunom.* 1, 114, 126), 'the criterion of truth' (*ibid.* 107) and an advantage over the wisdom of the pagans (*De anima et resurr.*, MG 46, 46B). As a result, 'whatever was useful he made his own, what was unprofitable he discarded' (*De vita Ephraem Syr.*, MG 46, 82B). With these words Gregory describes Ephraem's attitude towards pagan philosophy as well as his own.

Gregory's frequent recourse to secular learning has misled some modern scholars into underestimating his achievements in theology, misinterpreting his essentially Christian attitude, and putting a false emphasis on his close relationship to Plato. Thus Cherniss (p. 62) does not hesitate to claim that 'but for some few orthodox dogmas, which he could not circumvent, Gregory had merely applied Christian names to Plato's doctrines and called it Christian theology' — an exaggeration which proves a lack of understanding for this great Christian thinker and for the place he holds in the chain of patristic tradition. Although it was Plato who exercised the profoundest influence upon Gregory, upon his training, his outlook, his terminology and his approach to a problem, he by no means constitutes the sole basis of Gregory's system. Neo-Platonism left definite traces on his teaching, especially Plotinus, and certain Stoic elements appear in his ethical doctrine. In determining the various factors, however, it must be kept in mind that much of what is Platonic or Neo-Platonic in Gregory of Nyssa had by this time become the common property of all the schools of philosophy. It remains the great merit of J. Daniélou's investigation of Gregory's relation to Plato that it shows on the one hand the literary dependence but, on the other, the complete Christian metamorphosis of Plato's thought.

In method, Gregory has paid far more attention to the *ratio theologica* than Basil and Gregory of Nazianzus. He is convinced that he should make use of reason to substantiate as far as possible even the deepest mysteries of revelation. However, in all these attempts to penetrate faith with mind, he lets himself be guided by the tradition of the Fathers: 'If our reasoning be found unequal to the problem, we must keep for ever firm and unmoved the tradition which we received by succession from the Fathers' (*Quod non sint tres dii*, MG 45, 117).

Studies: W. MEYER, Die Gotteslehre des Gregor von Nyssa. Eine philosophische Studie aus der Zeit der Patristik. Leipzig, 1894. — F. DIEKAMP, Die Gotteslehre des hl. Gregor von Nyssa. Ein Beitrag zur Dogmengeschichte der patristischen Zeit. Teil I. Münster, 1896. — F. PREGER, Die Grundlagen der Ethik bei Gregor von Nyssa. Würzburg, 1897. — A. REICHE, Die künstlerischen Elemente in der Welt- und Lebensanschauung des Gregor von Nyssa. Diss. Jena, 1897. — C. GRONAU, De Basilio, Gregorio Nazianzeno Nyssenoque Platonis imitatoribus. Göttingen, 1908. — H. F. CHERNISS, The Platonism of Gregory of Nyssa (University of California Publications in Classical Philology XI, 1). Berkeley, 1930. — E. v. IVANKA, Ein Wort Gregors von Nyssa über den Patriarchen Abraham: StC 11 (1934) 45-47 (concept of God). — J. BAYER, Gregors von Nyssa Gottesbegriff. Diss. Giessen, 1935. — M. PELLEGRINO, Il platonismo di San Gregorio Nisseno: RFN 30 (1938) 437-474. — S. GONZALES, El realismo platonico de S. Gregorio de Nisa: Greg 20 (1939) 189-206. — H. U. v. BALTHASAR, La philosophie religieuse de saint Grégoire de Nysse: RSR (1939) 513-549; *idem*, Présence et pensée. Essai sur la philosophie religieuse de Grégoire de Nysse. Paris, 1942. — J. DANIÉLOU, Platonisme et théologie mystique. Essai sur la doctrine spirituelle de saint Grégoire de Nysse. Paris, 1944, 2nd ed. 1954. — W. VÖLKER, Die Ontologie Gregors von Nyssa in ihren Grundzügen: Festschrift G. Biundo (Veröffentlichungen des Vereins für Pfälz. Kirchengeschichte 4). Grünstadt, 1952, 9-16. — J. DANIÉLOU, Akolouthia chez Grégoire de Nysse: RSR 27 (1953) 219-249 (Aristotelian, Stoic and Christian concept). — S. STOLPE, Platonism och kristendom. Eros och agape hos Gregorius av Nyssa: Credo 34 (1953) 152-157. — J. DANIÉLOU, Grégoire de Nysse et Plotin: Association G. Budé. Actes du Congrès de Tours et de Poitiers (1953) 259-262. — W. VÖLKER, Zur Gotteslehre Gregors von Nyssa: VC 9 (1955) 103-128 (influence of Plato and the School of Alexandria). — J. F. CALLAHAN, Greek Philosophy and the Cappadocian Cosmology: DOP 12 (1958) 31-57. For other studies on cosmology, see above p. 265.

2. Trinitarian Doctrine

Gregory is following in the footsteps of Plato and at the same time anticipating the extreme realism of the Middle Ages in his attempts to reconcile the Trinity and the Unity. In the opening paragraph of his treatise *That there are not three Gods* he says:

We say then to begin with that the practice of calling those who are not divided by nature by the very name of their common nature in the plural and saying they are 'many men' is a customary abuse of language, and that it would be much the same thing to say there are 'many human natures' ...Thus there are many who have shared in the same nature — many disciples, say, or apostles, or martyrs — but the man in them all is one; since, as has been said, the term 'man' does not belong to the nature of the individual as such, but to that which is common... Thus it would be much better to correct our erroneous habit, so as no longer to extend to a plurality the name of the nature. We should then be no longer tempted to project our error of speech into theological doctrine (LNPF).

Here Gregory seems to admit under the influence of the Platonic doctrine of ideas, even in finite things, the numerical unity of essence or nature. He confuses the abstract that excludes plurality with the concrete that exacts plurality, when he states that 'man' designates nature but not the individual, and that Peter, Paul and Barnabas should be called one man not three men. Thus he attributes reality to the universal idea in order to explain the divine Trinity better and to refute the accusation of tritheism:

Since the correction of the habit is impracticable, we are not so far wrong in not going contrary to the prevailing habit in the case of the lower nature, since no harm results from the mistaken use of the name: but in the case of the statement concerning the Divine nature the various use of terms is no longer free from danger: for that which is of small account is in these subjects no longer a small matter. Therefore we must confess one God, according to the testimony of Scripture, 'Hear, o Israel, the Lord thy God is one Lord', even though the name of the Godhead extends through the Holy Trinity *(ibid.).*

According to Gregory, the distinction of the three divine Persons consists exclusively in their immanent mutual relations. For this reason their activity *ad extra* can only be one and the divine Persons have it in common:

Since among men the action of each in the same pursuits is discriminated, they are properly called many, since each of them is separated from the others within his own environment, according to the special character of his operation. But in the case of the Divine nature we do not similarly learn that the Father does anything by Himself in which the Son does not work conjointly, or again that the Son has any special operation apart from the Holy Spirit; but every operation extends from God to the creation, and is named according to our variable conceptions of it, has its origin from the Father, and proceeds through the Son, and is perfected in the Holy Spirit.

Since then the Holy Trinity fulfills every operation in a manner similar to that of which I have spoken, not by separate action according to the number of the Persons, but so that there is one motion and disposition of the good will, which is communicated from the Father through the Son to the Spirit, so neither can be called Those Who exercise this Divine and superintending power and operation towards ourselves and all creation, conjointly and inseparably, by Their mutual action, three Gods (*ibid.* LNPF).

However, there is a difference between their activity *ad extra* and their mutual and immanent relations:

While we confess the invariable character of the nature we do not deny the difference in respect of cause, and that which is caused, by which alone we apprehend that one Person is distinguished from another; namely, by our belief, that one is the Cause, and another is of the Cause. Again in that which is of the Cause we recognize yet another distinction. For one is directly *(προσεχῶς)* from the first Cause, and another only mediately and through that which is directly from the first Cause; so that the character of being Only-Begotten *(μονογενές)* abides without doubt in the Son, and the mediation *(μεσιτεία)* of the Son, while it guards His character of being Only-Begotten, does not exclude the Spirit from His natural relation to the Father (*ibid.* LNPF).

From these words it appears that Gregory with the other Greek Fathers conceives the Holy Spirit as proceeding from the Father through the Son, i.e. immediately from the Son and mediately from the Father. He expresses exactly the same idea in his treatise *De Spiritu Sancto* 3. There he compares the Father, the Son and the Holy Ghost to three torches, the first of which imparts its light to the second, and through the second it imparts its light to the third. However, in the passage of his *De oratione* which we quoted above (p. 267) he goes further stating: 'The Holy Spirit is also said to be from the Father and is testified to be from the Son *(ἐκ τοῦ υἱοῦ)*... Hence the Spirit that is from God is also Christ's Spirit'. Thus Gregory not only teaches the divinity and consubstantiality of the Holy Spirit and his proceeding from the Father, but he also makes a deeper study of his relation to the Son than the two other Cappadocians.

Studies: K. HOLL, Amphilochius von Ikonium in seinem Verhältnis zu den grossen Kappadoziern. Tübingen, 1904, 196-235. — G. ISAYE, L'unité de l'opération divine dans les écrits trinitaires de S. Grégoire de Nysse: RSR 27 (1937) 422-439. — S. GONZALES, El simbolo de S. Gregorio de Nisa y su posición entre los simbolos de Cappadocia: Greg 19 (1938) 130-134; *idem*, La identidad de operación en las obras exteriores y la unidad de la naturaleza divina en la teologia trinitaria de S. Gregorio de Nisa: Greg 19 (1938) 280-301. — M. GOMES DE CASTRO, Die Trinitätslehre des hl. Gregor von Nyssa. Freiburg i.B., 1938. — S. GONZALES, La formula *Μία οὐσία τρεῖς ὑποστάσεις* en San Gregorio de Nisa. Diss. Rome, 1939. — J. LEBON, Le sort du consubstantiel nicéen: RHE 48 (1953) 632-682.

3. Christology

His Christology is characterized by a sharp differentiation of the two natures in Christ: 'Our contemplation of the respective properties of the flesh and of the Godhead remains free from confusion, so long as each of these is contemplated by itself, as for example, "the Word was made before the ages, but the flesh came into being in the last times": but one could not reverse the statement, and say that the latter is pretemporal, or that the Word has come into being in the last times. The Word was in the beginning with God, the man was subject to the trial of death and neither was the Human Nature from everlasting, nor the Divine Nature mortal: and all the rest of the attributes are contemplated in the same way. It is not the Human Nature that raises up Lazarus, nor is it the power that cannot suffer, that weeps when he lies in the grave: the tear proceeds from the Man, the life from the true Life' (*Contra Eunom.* 5, 5 LNPF).

Nevertheless, Gregory recognizes fully the possibility of the *communicatio idiomatum* and justifies it very clearly: 'By reason of contact and the union of Natures the proper attributes of each belong to both, as the Lord receives the stripes of the servant, while the servant is glorified with the honor of the Lord. For this is why the Cross is said to be the Cross of the Lord of glory (Phil. 2, 2), and why every tongue confesses that Jesus Christ is Lord, to the glory of God the Father' (*ibid.*). These sentences prove at the same time Gregory's conviction that the two Natures still remain distinct after the exaltation of Christ. Nevertheless, despite the two Natures in Christ, there are not two Persons in him, but one: 'This is our doctrine, which does not, as Eunomius charges against it, preach a plurality of Christs, but the union of the Man with the Divinity' (*ibid.*). Thus there is one Person, ἐν πρόσωπον.

Studies: J. Rivière, Le dogme de la rédemption. 2nd ed. Paris, 1905, 151-159, 384-387. — J. H. Srawley, St. Gregory of Nyssa on the Sinlessness of Christ: JThSt 7 (1906) 434-441. — J. B. Aufhauser, Die Heilslehre des hl. Gregor von Nyssa. Munich, 1910. — J. Lenz, Jesus Christus nach der Lehre des hl. Gregor von Nyssa. Trier, 1925. — L. Malevez, L'Église dans le Christ: RSR (1935) 257-280. — V. Koperski, Doctrina S. Gregorii Nysseni de processione Filii Dei. Diss. Rome, 1936. — E. Mersch, Le Corps Mystique du Christ. 2nd ed. Brussels, 1936, 450-463; English translation: E. Mersch, The Whole Christ. Translated by J. R. Kelly, Milwaukee, 1938, 314-322. — J. Daniélou, L'état du Christ dans la mort d'après Grégoire de Nysse: HJG 77 (1958) 63-72.

4. Mariology

It is against Apollinaris and his followers that Gregory defends the completeness of the human nature in Christ. In his *Antirrheticus*

(45) he declares that Christ had a real human soul, a human νοῦς and that He possessed a free will. Otherwise His life could neither be a real example and moral pattern for us, nor could it redeem the human race. The Son of God formed for Himself a human nature out of the flesh of the Virgin (*Adv. Apollin.*, MG 45, 1136). Therefore she must be called Mother of God. Gregory employs the term *theotokos* five times and rejects the term *anthropotokos* used by some innovators, the Antiochenes. In his letter to Eustathia, Ambrosia and Basilissa (*Ep.* 17), he asks the question: 'Do we announce another Jesus? Do we produce other Scriptures? Have any of ourselves dared to say "Mother of Man" of the Holy Virgin, the Mother of God, which is what we hear that some of them say without restraint?' He sees in the sister of Moses, Miriam, a type of Mary, the Mother of God. Her virginity broke the power of death: 'In the age of Mary, the Mother of God, he [death] who had reigned from Adam to her time, found, when he came to her and dashed his forces against the fruit of her virginity as against a rock, that he was shattered to pieces upon her' (*De virg.* 13). He testifies to her *virginitas in partu:* 'In the same strain the womb of the Holy Virgin, which ministered to an Immaculate Birth, is pronounced blessed in Gospel (Luke 11, 27). For that birth did not annul the virginity, nor did the virginity impede so great a birth' (*ibid.* 19). In the 13th Homily *on the Canticle of Canticles* he states: 'Death came through one man, and Redemption through another. The first fell by sin, the second raised him again. The woman found her advocate in a woman' (MG 44, 1052). Here Mary appears as the *advocata Evae*, a thought which goes back to Irenaeus (cf. vol. I, p. 298).

Study: G. SOELL, Die Mariologie der Kappadozier: ThQ 131 (1951) 178-188.

5. *Eschatology*

It is especially in his eschatological views that Gregory proves himself a disciple of Origen. He does not share his ideas regarding the pre-existence and migration of souls and explicitly rejects the doctrine that they are enclosed in material bodies as a punishment for sins committed in a preceding world (*De an. et resurr.*, MG 46, 125). But he agrees with the Alexandrian in maintaining that the pains of hell are not eternal but temporary, because they are only medicinal. Although he speaks repeatedly of 'the inextinguishable fire' and the immortality of 'the worm', of an 'eternal sanction' (*Orat. cat.* 40), although he threatens the sinner with eternal suffering and eternal punishment, he could not imagine an eternal estrangement from God of his intellectual creatures and explains elsewhere these expressions as referring only 'to long periods of time' (*ibid.* 26). He believes with Origen in the universal restoration at the end of time (*ἀποκατάστασις*), and in the complete victory of good over evil, but rejects Origen's opinion that the Apokatastasis was not the end of the world but a passing phase, only one of an unlimited succession of worlds in which apostasy from God and return to God follow each other again and again. Gregory sees in the Apokatastasis the magnificent and harmonious conclusion of the entire history of salvation, when every creature shall intone a chant of thanksgiving to the Saviour and even 'the inventor of evil' shall be healed:

> When after long periods of time, the evil of our nature, which is now mixed up with it and has grown with its growth, has been expelled, and when there has been a restoration of those who are now lying in sin to their primal state, a hymn of thanksgiving will arise from all creation,. as well as from those who in the process of the purgation have suffered chastisement, as from those who needed not any purgation at all. These and the like benefits the great mystery of the Divine Incarnation bestows. For in those points in which He was mingled with humanity, passing as He did through all the accidents proper to human nature, such as birth, rearing, growing up, and advancing even to the taste of death, He accomplished all the results before mentioned, freeing both man from evil, and healing even the introducer of evil himself (*Orat. cat.* 26 LNPF).

In order to safeguard Gregory's orthodoxy, well-meaning but ill-advised admirers attempted to prove that his writings had been interpolated by Origenist heretics. The first such effort was made by Germanus, Patriarch of Constantinople (d. 733), in the second part of his *Antapodotikos* or *Anodeutikos*. According to Photius (*Bibl. cod.* 233) Germanus believed that especially the *Oratio catechetica* and *De anima et resurrectione* were interpolated. However, such a hypothesis is without foundation. Moreover, Gregory's views on the universal restoration are found not only in the two treatises mentioned above, but also in his other works. He simply erred in the attempt to conquer heights of speculation where but few mortals dare to tread.

Studies: W. VOLLERT, Die Lehre Gregors von Nyssa vom Guten und Bösen und von der schliesslichen Überwindung des Bösen. Leipzig, 1897. — E. MICHAUD, St. Grégoire de Nysse et l'Apocatastase: Revue internationale de théologie 10 (1902) 37-52. — T. OKSIJUK, The Eschatology of St. Gregory of Nyssa (in Polish). Kiev, 1914. — E. F. SUTCLIFFE, St. Gregory of Nyssa and Paradise. Was it Terrestrial?: AER 84 (1931) 337-350. — W. VOLLERT, Hat Gregor von Nyssa die paulinische Eschatologie verändert? ThBl 14 (1935) 106-112. — J. DANIÉLOU, L'apocatastase chez Grégoire de Nysse: RSR 30 (1940) 328-347; *idem*, Notes sur trois textes eschatologiques de saint Grégoire de Nysse: RSR 30 (1940) 348-356 (translation and commentary: In Psalm. 2, 6, MG 44,

508B-509A; *In Ascens.*, MG 46, 693; *In Nativit.*, MG 46, 1128-1129). — J. JANINI CUESTA, La penitencia medicinal desde la Didascalia Apostolorum a S. Gregorio de Nisa: RES 7 (1947) 337-362. — J. DANIÉLOU, La résurrection des corps chez Grégoire de Nysse: VC 7 (1953) 154-170.

III. THE MYSTICISM OF GREGORY OF NYSSA

Gregory's intellectual achievement reaches its climax and culminates in his mystical theology, to which, however, scholars have only recently devoted much study. F. Diekamp and K. Holl were the first to call attention to this phase of his activity. H. Koch proved that he knows of the direct intuition of God. The pioneer effort, however, at presenting a comprehensive summary of the teaching of 'the founder of mystic theology' is the contemporary J. Daniélou's important monograph on Gregory's relation to Platonism, in which the author contrasts him with Origen. On a broader basis, W. Völker investigates the connection between his mysticism and that of the Alexandrians, of Methodius, of Athanasius and of the other two Cappadocians, and stresses especially the ascetic and ethical orientation of Gregory's views on perfection.

There is no doubt that he played a very prominent part in founding and developing Christian mysticism. He is the link between Philo and the Alexandrians through Plotinus to Dionysius the Areopagite, Maximus Confessor and Byzantine mysticism. Although he was later wholly overshadowed by the authority of Pseudo-Dionysius and although western medieval writers such as Hugh and Richard of St. Victor, William of Paris, St. Bonaventure, Dionysius the Carthusian and John Gerson made commentaries on the *Theologia mystica* of 'the disciple of St. Paul' rather than on the treatises of St. Gregory, nevertheless they are all in a large degree indirectly indebted to the bishop of Nyssa.

Studies: F. DIEKAMP, op. cit. 91. — K. HOLL, op. cit. 205. — H. KOCH, Das mystische Schauen beim hl. Gregor von Nyssa: ThQ 80 (1898) 397-420. — E. v. IVANKA, Vom Platonismus zur Theorie der Mystik: Schol 11 (1936) 163-195. — J. MARÉCHAL, Études sur la psychologie des mystiques II. Paris, 1937, 101-111. — A. NYGREN, Eros und Agape. Gestaltwandlungen der christlichen Liebe II. Gütersloh, 1937, 232-251. — M. VILLER and K. RAHNER, Aszese und Mystik in der Väterzeit. Freiburg, 1939, 133-145. — H. U. v. BALTHASAR, op. cit. — A. LIESKE, Zur Theologie der Christus-mystik Gregors von Nyssa: Schol 14 (1939) 485-514; *idem*, Die Theologie der Christus-mystik Gregors von Nyssa (MBTh 22). Münster, 1943 (= ZkTh 70 (1948) 49-93, 129-168, 315-340). — J. TRINICK, St. Gregory of Nyssa and the Rise of Christian Mysticism. Shorne (Kent), 1950. — J. DANIÉLOU, Platonisme et théologie mystique. Essai sur la doctrine spirituelle de Saint Grégoire de Nysse. 2nd ed. Paris, 1954. — W. VÖLKER, Die Mystik Gregors von Nyssa in ihren geschichtlichen Zusammenhängen: ThZ 9 (1953) 338-354; *idem*, Gregor von Nyssa als Mystiker. Wiesbaden, 1955. — St. Gregory of Nyssa and St. Augustine on the Symbolism of the Cross: Late Classical and Medieval Studies in Honor of A. M. Friend, ed. by K. WEITZMANN. Princeton, 1955,

88-95. — H. LANGERBECK, Zur Interpretation Gregors von Nyssa: ThLZ 82 (1957) 82-90 (on Völker's book). — H. CROUZEL, Grégoire de Nysse est-il le fondateur de la théologie mystique?: RAM 33 (1957) 189-202. — R. LEYS, La théologie spirituelle de Grégoire de Nysse: PS II (TU 64). Berlin, 1957, 495-511.

1. *The Image of God in Man*

Gregory's teaching on the image of God in man is one of his basic ideas. It forms the foundation for his teaching not only on the intuition of God but also on the mystical ascent of man. As the crowning achievement of the work of creation, man, as a microcosm, displays the same order and harmony which we admire in the macrocosm, in the universe:

> If the orderly arrangement of the whole universe is a kind of musical harmony whose maker and artist is God,... and if man himself is a microcosm, then, he, too is an imitation of Him Who fashioned the universe. It is, therefore, reasonable to assume that the mind finds in the microcosm the same things that it discovered in the case of the macrocosm ...Thus all the harmony that is observed in the universe is rediscovered in the microcosm, i.e. in human nature, and it corresponds to the whole by virtue of its parts, as far, at least, as the whole can be obtained by the parts (*In Psalmos* I, c. 3, MG 44, 441 CD).

However, this ancient philosophical idea has been surpassed by the Christian doctrine. Man is much more than just a microcosm and an imitation of the material universe. His excellence and greatness rests 'not upon his likeness to the created universe, but upon the fact that he has been made in the image of the nature of the Creator' (*De hom. opif.* c. 16, MG 44, 180 A). Man is the faithful image of his Maker principally by reason of his soul, and more precisely because this soul possesses reason, freedom of the will, and supernatural grace. Gregory uses the term 'image' *(eikon)* as the comprehensive expression for man's entire endowment of divine gifts, his original state of perfection. Whereas for Clement and Origen the image of God in the human soul is the rational part of man, and for Irenaeus, the free will, for Gregory it consists not only in the νοῦς and αὐτεξούσιον, but also in his virtue, the ἀρετή. He does not adopt the Alexandrian distinction between εἴκων and ὁμοίωσις, which understands the latter as the ethical efforts of man on the basis of the εἴκων, but treats them as synonyms, in order to signify 'the purity, freedom from passion, blessedness, alienation from all evil, and all those attributes of the like kind which help to form in men the likeness of God' (*De opif. hom.* 5,1). By this likeness man 'is second to none of the wonders of the world, and easily the greatest of all things known to us, because none of the existing things has been made in the likeness of God except that creature which is man' (*De opif. hom.*, MG 44, 128A).

Studies: J. Gross, La divinisation du chrétien d'après les Pères grecs. Paris, 1938, 219-238. — J. T. Muckle, The Doctrine of Gregory of Nyssa on Man as the Image of God: MS 7 (1945) 55-84. — R. Leys, L'image de Dieu chez Saint Grégoire de Nysse. Paris, 1951. — H. Merki, 'Ομοίωσις θεῷ. Von der platonischen Angleichung an Gott zur Gottähnlichkeit bei Gregor von Nyssa (Paradosis 7). Fribourg, 1952; *idem*, Ebenbildlichkeit: RACh 4 (1958) 467-479. — G. B. Ladner, The Philosophical Anthropology of Saint Gregory of Nyssa: DOP 12 (1958) 58-94. For other studies on Gregory's anthropology, see above p. 264.

2. *Intuition of God*

By this image man becomes a relative of God and able to know God. Gregory adopts the famous axiom of the ancients 'like is known by like', when he emphasizes that the likeness of the soul to God is the *conditio sine qua non* of our knowledge of God's nature. This principle, which played an important role in the history of Greek philosophy, was first introduced by Pythagoras, received its definite formulation from Empedocles and had become a commonplace in Plato's time. It attained to special prominence in Neo-Platonic mysticism as a summary of the doctrine that Divine can be known only by Divine. Gregory repeats the Platonic formula, that the eye is able to behold rays of light because light is part of its nature. Similarly man can see God because there is a divine element in him:

> The eye enjoys the rays of light by virtue of the light which it has in itself by nature that it may apprehend the kindred... The same necessity requires, as regards the participation in God, that in the nature that is to enjoy God there be something kindred to Him Who is to be partaken of (*De infant.*, MG 46, 113 D, 176 A).

Thus the image of God in man enables him to attain the mystic vision of Him and compensates for the deficiencies of human reason and the limitation of our rational knowledge of God, as he explains in his sixth *Sermon on the Beatitudes:*

> The Divine Nature, whatever It may be in Itself, surpasses every mental concept. For It is altogether inaccessible to reasoning and conjecture, nor has there been found any human faculty capable of perceiving the incomprehensible; for we cannot devise a means of understanding inconceivable things. Therefore the great Apostle calls His ways unsearchable, meaning by this that the way that leads to the knowledge of the Divine Essence is inaccessible to thought. That is to say, none of those who have passed through life before us has made known to the intelligence so much as a trace by which might be known what is above knowledge. Since such is He Whose nature

is above every nature, the Invisible and Incomprehensible is seen and apprehended in another manner. Many are the modes of such perception. For it is possible to see Him Who has made all things in wisdom by way of inference through the wisdom that appears in the universe. It is the same as with human works of art, where, in a way, the mind can perceive the maker of the product that is before it, because he has left on his work the stamp of his art. In this, however, is seen not the nature of the artist, but only his artistic skill which he has left impressed on his handiwork. Thus also, when we look at the order of creation, we form in our mind an image not of the essence, but of the wisdom of Him Who has made all things wisely. And if we consider the cause of our life, that He came to create man not from necessity, but from the free decision of His Goodness, we say that we have contemplated God by this way, that we have apprehended His Goodness — though again not His Essence but His Goodness. It is the same with all other things that raise the mind to transcendent Goodness, all these we can term apprehensions of God, since each one of these sublime meditations places God within our sight. For power, purity, constancy, freedom from contrariety — all these engrave on the soul the impress of a Divine and transcendent Mind.

But the meaning of the Beatitude is not restricted to this alone that He Who operates can be known by analogy through His operations. For perhaps the wise of this world, too, might gain some knowledge of the transcendent Wisdom and Power from the harmony of the universe... No, I think this magnificent Beatitude proffers another counsel to those able to receive and contemplate what they desire.

If a man's heart has been purified from every creature and unruly affections, he will see the Image of the Divine Nature in his own beauty. I think that in this short saying the Word expresses some such counsel as this: There is in you, human beings, a desire to contemplate the true good. But when you hear that the Divine Majesty is exalted above the heavens, that Its glory is inexpressible, Its beauty ineffable, and Its Nature inaccessible, do not despair of ever beholding what you desire. It is indeed within your reach; you have within yourselves the standard by which to apprehend the Divine. For He Who made you did at the same time endow your nature with this wonderful quality. For God imprinted on it the likeness of the glories of His own Nature, as if molding the form of a carving into wax. But the evil that has been poured all around the nature beating the Divine Image has rendered useless to you this wonderful thing, that lies hidden under vile coverings. If, therefore, you wash off by a good life the filth that has been stuck on your heart like plaster, the Divine beauty will again shine forth in you.

For the Godhead is purity, freedom from passion, and separation from all evil. If therefore these things be in you, God is indeed in you. Hence, if your thought is without any alloy of evil, free from passion, and alien from stain, you are blessed because you are clear of sight. You are able to perceive what is invisible to those who are not purified, because you have been cleansed; the darkness caused by material entanglements has been removed from the eyes of your soul, and so you see the blessed vision radiant in the pure heaven of your heart (ACW).

This passage proves that Gregory sees, in the mystic vision of God that takes place within the soul, the greatest possible knowledge of the supreme Beauty, an anticipation of the Beatific Vision. He calls it on another occasion a 'divine and sober inebriation *(θεία τε καὶ νηφάλιος μέθη)* by which man steps out of himself' *(In Cant. cant. hom.* 10, MG 44, 992). Of course, such an extraordinary grace is given only to those who have prepared themselves for a return to the original Image of God in man by a *katharsis*, by a purification and a relentless battle against sin. They must continue to fight against the passions and the entanglements of the world until the state of *apatheia* has been reached.

Studies: G. HORN, L'amour divin. Note sur le mot 'Eros' dans S. Grégoire de Nysse: RAM 6 (1925) 378-389; *idem*, Le 'miroir', la 'nuée', deux manières de voir Dieu d'après S. Grégoire de Nysse: RAM 8 (1927) 113-131. — H. LEWY, Sobria ebrietas. Untersuchungen zur Geschichte der antiken Mystik (Beihefte zur ZNW 9). Giessen, 1929, 132-136. — A. A. WEISWURM, The Nature of Human Knowledge according to St. Gregory of Nyssa. Diss. Washington, 1952. — J. P. CAVARNOS, Gregory of Nyssa on the Nature of the Soul: The Greek Orthodox Theological Review 1 (1955) 135-150. — C. NICOSIA, Platonismo e pessimismo nel pensiero di Gregorio di Nisa: MSLC 6 (1956) 23-35 (purification of the soul).

3. *The Mystic Ascent*

It is only then that the mystic ascent can begin: 'Now the way which leads human nature back to heaven is none other than that of avoiding the evils of the world by flight; on the other hand, the purpose of fleeing from evils seems to me precisely to achieve likeness to God. To become like God means to become just, holy, and good and suchlike things. If anyone, as far as in him lies, clearly shows himself the characteristics of these virtues, he will pass automatically and without effort from this earthly life to the life of heaven. For the distance between the Divine and the human is not a local one so as to need some mechanical device by which this heavily weighted earthly flesh should migrate into the disembodied intelligible life. No, if virtue has really been separated from evil, it lies solely within the free choice of man to be there where his desire inclines him. Since, therefore, the choice of the good is not followed by any labor, — for possession of the things that are chosen follows the act of choice — you are entitled to be in heaven immediately, because you have seized God with your mind. Now, if according to Ecclesiastes (5,1), "God is in heaven" and you, according to the Prophet (Ps. 72, 28) "adhere to God", it follows necessarily that you should be where God is, because you are united to Him. Since then He has commanded in the prayer to call God Father, He tells you to do nothing less than to become like your heavenly Father by a life that is worthy of God, as He bids us do more clearly elsewhere when He says: "Be you therefore perfect, as also your heavenly Father is perfect" ' (Matth. 5, 48) (*De orat. dom.* 2 ACW).

Studies: H. RAHNER, Die Gottesgeburt. Die Lehre der Kirchenväter von der Geburt Christi im Herzen der Gläubigen: ZkTh 59 (1935) 373-376. — Gregory interprets the life of Moses in terms of the ascent of the soul to union with God. Cf. J. DANIÉLOU, Grégoire de Nysse. La vie de Moïse (SCH 1). Paris, 2nd ed. 1955, 9-46; *idem*, Mystique de la Ténèbre chez Grégoire de Nysse: DSp 2 (1953), 1872-1885; *idem*, Moïse exemple et figure chez Grégoire de Nysse: Cahiers Sion (1955) 386-400.

AMPHILOCHIUS OF ICONIUM

Amphilochius of Iconium is known to us best from the letters of the three Cappadocian Fathers. They were intimate friends; Basil dedicated *De Spiritu Sancto* to him, and Gregory of Nazianzus was very probably his cousin. Born at Diocaesarea in Cappadocia between 340 and 345 A.D., he attended the lectures of Libanius at Antioch and became a lawyer at Constantinople about 364. Six years later he withdrew from public life and returned to his native town. His desire to live as a hermit remained unfulfilled, because in 374 he was, at the request of Basil, consecrated bishop of Iconium and the first metropolitan of the new province of Lycaonia. It seems that Amphilochius accepted his new position only reluctantly, for in a letter addressed to him Basil says:

> Blessed is God, who selects those in each generation who are pleasing to Him and makes known the vessels of His election, and uses them for the ministry of the saints: He who even now has ensnared you with the inescapable nets of His grace, when, as you yourself admit, you are trying to escape, not us, but the expected call through us, and who has brought you into the midst of Pisidia, so that you may take men captive for the Lord and bring those who had already been taken captive by the devil from the depths into the light according to His will (*Ep.* 161 LCL).

Basil's choice proved an excellent one. Amphilochius governed his diocese very successfully, restoring order and discipline everywhere. A prominent figure in the controversies of his time, he defended the Christian doctrine in his speeches and in his writings against the Arians, Messalians and Encratites. He participated in the Ecumenical Council of Constantinople in 381 as one of its outstanding members, praised for his orthodoxy in the Law of the Emperor Theodosius of July 30, 381 (*Cod. Theod.* 16, 1, 3). He presided at a synod in Side on the gulf of Adalia in 390, which condemned the ascetic sect of the Messalians (cf. above, p. 164), Euchites or Adelphians as heretical (see the proceedings in Photius, *Bibl. cod.* 52). He is last mentioned in 394, when he attended the Synod of Constantinople which settled the episcopal succession in the diocese of Bostra. The year of his death remains unknown.

Studies: J. B. LIGHTFOOT, Amphilochius: DCB 1 (1877) 103-107. — G. BAREILLE, Amphilochius: DTC 1 (1902) 1121-1123. — A. TONNA-BARTHET, Amphiloque: DHG 2 (1914) 1346-1348. — G. BARDY, Amphiloque: DSp 1 (1937) 544. — K. HOLL, Amphilochius von Ikonium in seinem Verhältnis zu den grossen Kappadoziern. Tübingen, 1904, 5-42. — G. FICKER, Amphilochiana I. Leipzig, 1906. — For Amphilochius' relation to Gregory of Nazianzus, see K. BONES's study cited above p. 239 and H. M. WERHAHN, BZ 47 (1954) 414-418. The so-called *Vita S. Amphilochii* (MG 39, 13-26), and the *Vita* by Simeon Metaphrastes (MG 116, 955-970) have no historical value.

HIS WRITINGS

Although Amphilochius was recognized as a patristic authority as early as the fifth century, and the Ecumenical Councils since Ephesus quote him as such, his writings seem not to have been cherished like the works of his friends, the three great Cappadocians, and most of them are no longer extant. Some titles are known to us from citations in Conciliar Acts or in later writers.

Editions: MG 39, 9-130 (incomplete). For additions, see: K. HOLL, op. cit. 43ff., F. DIEKAMP, ThR 3 (1904) 332 and especially, G. FICKER, op. cit. 3ff.

1. *Synodical Letter*

Among the few things from his pen that have come down to us complete is the letter, which a synod held at Iconium in 376 commissioned him to write to the bishops of another diocese, apparently Lycia. It defends the true divinity and consubstantiality of the Holy Spirit against the *Pneumatomachoi* along the lines which St. Basil had developed the year before in his book *On the Holy Spirit* (cf. above, p. 210).

Editions: MG 39, 93-98. — MANSI, SS. Conc. Coll. 3, 505-508.

2. *Against the Apotactites and Gemellites*

This polemical treatise is extant in a Coptic version only. G. Ficker published it from a manuscript of the thirteenth century in the

Escorial (*Scorial.* T. 1. 17). The introduction and conclusion, as well as the title and the author's name, are lost. Ficker proved, however, by a critical analysis of its contents, that Amphilochius composed it, most probably between 373 and 381. He combats extremists, who for ascetical reasons repudiated marriage, wine, the partaking of the Blood of the Lord, and meat. The Gemellites disapproved even of the possession of domestic animals and of the wearing of woollen dress. The author traces the origin of these sects to Simon Magus, whom he calls an instrument of Satan. Their founder, Gemellus, was Simon's disciple at Rome, and it was he who spread this heresy in Asia Minor. The treatise was part of the great campaign which Amphilochius conducted against those puritanical and ecstatic cults of the East.

Edition: G. FICKER, op. cit. 1, 23-77.

Studies: J. SICKENBERGER, BZ 16 (1907) 303-312. — R. REITZENSTEIN, Historia monachorum und Historia Lausiaca. Göttingen, 1916, 205ff.

3. *Epistula iambica ad Seleucum*

Cosmas Indicopleustes refers (*Top. Christ.* 7, 265) to Amphilochius as the author of the *Iambics for Seleucus*, which consists of 333 trimeters, and has come down to us among the works of Gregory of Nazianzus, his relative. It belongs undoubtedly to Amphilochius and is, so far as we know, his only composition in verse. It instructs Seleucus in the life of study and virtue. The author admonishes him, to apply himself to the Scriptures more than to any other writing, and, apropos of this, adds a complete list of the books of the Bible in verses 251-319, which is very important for the history of the Canon (EP 1078).

Editions: MG 37, 1577-1600. New editions of the Canon: T. ZAHN, Geschichte des neutestamentlichen Kanons 2. Leipzig, 1890, 212ff. — M. J. LAGRANGE, Histoire ancienne du Canon du Nouveau Testament. Paris, 1933, 118-120.

Studies: K. BONES, Περὶ τῆς μητρὸς τῆς ἁγίας Ὀλυμπιάδος; Studi Biz. e Neoell. 8 (1953) 3-10 (*Iambics* not composed before 396).

4. *Homilies*

In his eight extant homilies on various texts from the Bible he discloses his rhetorical skill and fondness for puns. It is also a favorite device of his to represent the personages of Scripture engaged in a dialogue. One sermon, *In natalitia Christi*, was for the Christmas celebration on the 25th of December. Another, *In occursum Domini*, is among the oldest witnesses to the feast of the Purification on the 2nd of February. Three further titles are *In Lazarum quatriduanum*,

In mulierem peccatricem and *In diem sabbati sancti*. His *In mesopentecosten* published by Matthaei in 1776 (MG 39, 119-130), is one of the earliest references to the feast of Midpentecost, which evenly divided the Paschal period. A seventh discourse, first published by K. Holl, *In illud: Pater si possibile est, transeat calix iste* (Matth. 26, 39), was delivered on the feast of St. Stephen, December 26th, and was quoted by Theodoret of Cyrus, Pope Gelasius and Facundus of Hermiane. All three testify to Amphilochius' authorship. The sermon sees in the trembling and fear of the Lord a means of attracting Satan, who otherwise would not have dared to approach the Son of God. It is supposed to answer objections to the divinity of Christ which Arius and Eunomius based on this text. Ficker published in 1906 a long Coptic fragment of his homily on the sacrifice of Isaac, and C. Moss in 1930 the Syriac version of a homily on John 14, 28.

Editions: MG 39, 35-94, 119-130. — K. HOLL, op. cit. 91-102 (on Matth. 26, 39). — G. FICKER, op. cit. 1, 281-306 (German translation of the Coptic fragment by A. Jacoby). — C. Moss, S. Amphilochius of Iconium on John 14, 28 'The Father who sent me is greater than I': Mus 43 (1930) 317-364 (Syriac text, English translation, Greek, Latin and Syriac fragments). — New fragments are found in: J. LEBON, Severi Antiocheni liber contra impium Grammaticum. Orationis tertiae pars posterior (CSCO 102). Louvain, 1933, 143f. — K. V. ZETTERSTÉEN, Eine Homilie des Amphilochius von Iconium über Basilius von Caesarea: Festschrift E. Sachau, Berlin, 1915, 223-247, edited from Codex Sachau 321 of the Berlin Library and from Cod. add. 12174 of the British Museum the Syriac text of a homily on St. Basil the Great which seems to be spurious. For a German translation of this homily, see: K. V. ZETTERSTÉEN, Eine Homilie des Amphilochius von Iconium über Basilius von Caesarea: OC (1934) 67-98.

Studies: K. HOLL, op. cit. 58-83, was the first to prove that the five sermons (MG 39, 35-94) are authentic. — F. CAVALLERA, Amphilochiana: RSR 3 (1912) 68-74, reconstructed the homily *Pater me maior est* from Cod. Paris. Gr. 1234. — B. MARX, Procliana. Münster, 1940, 50, 60; *idem*, Der homiletische Nachlass des Basileios von Seleukeia: OCP 7 (1941) 355 n. 1 (thinks that the Good Friday sermon among the *Spuria Chrysostomi*, MG 50, 811ff., belongs to Amphilochius). — M. RICHARD, Le fragment XXII d'Amphiloque d'Iconium: Mélanges E. Podechard. Lyon, 1945, 199-210 (proves that this fragment dealing with the Incarnation is not authentic). — J. RIVIÈRE, Contribution au dossier des 'Cur Deus homo' populaires. Une homélie de saint Amphiloque d'Iconium: BLE (1945) 129-138.

LOST WRITINGS

St. Jerome states *De vir. ill.* 133: 'Amphilochius, bishop of Iconium, recently read to me a book *On the Holy Spirit*, arguing that He is God, and that He is to be worshipped, and that He is omnipotent'. This happened on the occasion of the Second Ecumenical Council at Constantinople in 381. Nothing remains of this treatise.

The titles and fragments of other works no longer extant are known to us from the quotations in Conciliar Acts and later writers. Almost all seem to have been sermons or orations and dealt with the Scriptural passages which the Arians used against the Niceans, for instance, Proverbs 8, 22; Mark 13, 32; John 5, 19; 14, 28; 16, 14 and 20, 17. One of them, *Oration on the Son (Λόγος περὶ υἱοῦ)*, was perhaps a treatise like that mentioned by Jerome *On the Holy Spirit*. Though little remains of Amphilochius' work, it is clear that he was deeply involved in the Arian controversy and deeply interested in the theology of the Trinity.

We get the same impression from extant excerpts of two of his letters. One of them was addressed to the Seleucus to whom he dedicated his iambic poem, the other to Pancharius, the deacon at Side. Both answer questions on the Trinity and the personality of Christ.

Studies: L. Saltet, La théologie d'Amphiloque: BLE (1905) 121-127, tried in vain to prove that the *Epistula ad Seleucum*, MG 39, 111-114, is a forgery which originated after the Council of Chalcedon. — F. Cavallera, Les fragments de St. Amphiloque dans l'Hodegos et le tome dogmatique d'Anastase le Sinaïte: RHE 8 (1907) 473-497, gave convincing reasons for its authenticity. — The *Florilegium Edessenum* contains a fragment *De recta fide* which represents perhaps an excerpt of the lost work *De Spiritu Sancto* mentioned by Jerome: I. Rucker, Florilegium Edessenum anonymum (SAM Phil.-hist. Abt., Jahrgang 1933, Heft 5). Munich, 1933, 87-92.

ASTERIUS OF AMASEA

Another Cappadocian Father is Asterius, metropolitan of Amasea in Pontus. He was a contemporary of Amphilochius and his three great countrymen. Little is known about his life. Like Amphilochius he had been lawyer before he became bishop between 380 and 390. The sixteen homilies and panegyrics on martyrs which are extant show his training in rhetoric and his familiarity with the classics. One, *Adversus kalendarum festum (Oratio 4)*, condemns the pagan customs and abuses of the feast and refutes everything which Libanius' oration had said in its favor. Asterius gave this sermon on the first of January 400 A.D. Oration 11, *On the Martyrdom of St. Euphemia*, is important for the history of art. Asterius describes a painting of the martyrdom of this Saint and compares it with the works of Euphranor and Timomachus. The Second Council of Nicaea in 787 quotes the entire text twice as a precious proof of the veneration of holy pictures.

Photius (*Bibl. cod.* 271) supplies quotations from ten other sermons no longer extant, except for the two found in manuscripts of Mount Athos by M. Bauer and first edited by A. Bretz. A number of homilies wrongly attributed to Asterius of Amasea have been proved to be the property of his namesake, Asterius the Sophist (cf. above, p. 194). In the sermons that Photius read he found evidence that Asterius attained a great age (*Quaest. Amphiloch.* 312, MG 101, 1161 or 40, 477).

Editions: MG 40, 155-480. Of these homilies only 14 are authentic: MG 40, 163-390. Two more were first edited by A. BRETZ, Studien und Texte zu Asterios von Amaseia (TU 40, 1). Leipzig, 1914, 107-121. The excerpts of Photius can be found: MG 104, 201-224. — For the quotation from the homily on St. Euphemia in the Acts of the Second Council of Nicaea (787), see: MANSI, SS. Conc. Coll. 13, 16-17 and 308-309.

Translations: English: H. ANDERSON and E. J. JOHNSON, Ancient sermons for modern times by Asterius, Bishop of Amasea. New York, 1904. — *German:* J.G.V. ENGELHARDT, Die Homilien des Asterius von Amasea (3 Progr.). Erlangen, 1830, 1832, 1833 (nine homilies). — L. KOCH, Asterius, Bischof von Amasea: Zeitschrift für histor. Theologie 41 (1871) 77-107 (translation of homily 5 on Matth. 19, 3). — J. STRZYGOWSKI, Orient oder Rom. Leipzig, 1901, 118ff. (translation of homily 11 *On the Martyrdom of St. Euphemia* by B. Keil).

Studies: M. BAUER, Asterios Bischof von Amaseia. Sein Leben und seine Werke. Diss. Würzburg, 1911. — M. SCHMID, Beiträge zur Lebensgeschichte des Asterios von Amasea und zur philologischen Würdigung seiner Schriften (Diss. Munich). Borna-Leipzig, 1911. — A. BRETZ, op. cit. — D. FECIORU, Asterius, Bishop of Amasea. His Life and his Works (in Rumanian): Biserica ort. rum. 55 (1937) 624-694.

CHAPTER IV

THE WRITERS OF ANTIOCH AND SYRIA

Arius received his theological training in the School of Antioch. The priest whose teaching led to the great trinitarian controversy belongs to the first generation of students which the founder of that school, Lucian, produced. Thus we cannot be surprised that he won many adherents among his former schoolmates. Antioch was the first episcopal see to be occupied by an Arian. After Eustathius had been deposed in 326, it remained in the hands of the Arians until 360. There cannot be any doubt that a great number of bishops of the patriarchate belonged to the different Arian parties. Yet it would be unjust to assume that the teaching of the School of Antioch inevitably had to end up in Arianism. The fact is that the most famous writers of this ecclesiastical province, Diodore of Tarsus, Theodore of Mopsuestia, John Chrysostom and Theodoret of Cyrus defended the Nicene faith with their pen against the Arians, though they must be regarded as the main representatives of the School of Antioch. The period under discussion sees this great center of learning reach its peak. Meanwhile Palestine gave birth to the Father of Church History in Eusebius of Caesarea and to a great pastor of souls in Cyril of Jerusalem.

EUSTATHIUS OF ANTIOCH

One of the most reputed representatives of the orthodox faith at the Council of Nicaea in 325 was Eustathius of Antioch. Born at Side in Pamphylia, he had been bishop of Beroea in Syria before he was appointed in 323 or 324 to the see of the Syrian capital. According to Theodoret (*Hist. eccl.* 1, 7), he was the first to speak at the Council and when the Emperor Constantine entered the assembly of the bishops, he had the honor to salute him with an address of welcome, in which 'he commended the diligent attention he had manifested in the regulation of ecclesiastical affairs' (cf. below, p. 342). It was the same emperor who in 330 drove him into exile to Trajanopolis in Thrace after an Arian synod at Antioch had deposed him in 326. There he must have died before the year 337, when Constantius recalled the banished bishops.

Studies: E. VENABLES, Eustathius: DCB 2 (1880) 382-383. — S. SALAVILLE, Eustathe d'Antioche: DTC 5 (1913) 1554-1565; *idem*, Eustathiens: DTC 5 (1913) 1574-1576. — E. PETERSON, EC 5 (1951) 862f. — F. CAVALLERA, Le schisme d'Antioche. Paris, 1905, 57ff. (deposition: time and reasons). — P. KRAUSE, Eustathius von Antiochien. Diss. Breslau, 1921 (typ.). — E. A. BURN, Saint Eustathius of Antioch. London, 1926. —

E. SCHWARTZ, Zur Kirchengeschichte des vierten Jahrhunderts: ZNW 34 (1935) 129-213 (schism of Antioch). — H. CHADWICK, The Fall of Eustathius of Antioch: JThSt 49 (1948) 27-35, regards 326 as the year of deposition. — W. SCHNEEMELCHER, Zur Chronologie des arianischen Streites: ThLZ 79 (1954) 398, shares this opinion. — M. RICHARD, MSR 8 (1951) 113, advocates 331 as the year of his fall. — For the question whether Eustathius delivered the address of welcome and was the president of the Council of Nicaea, see: V. C. DE CLERCQ, Ossius of Cordova. Washington, 1954, 235f.

I. HIS WRITINGS

St. Jerome (*De vir. ill.* 85) speaks of many treatises that Eustathius composed against the doctrine of the Arians. He mentions especially *De anima* and *De engastrimytho adversum Origenem* and countless letters which he could not list in detail (*Ep.* 70, 4; 73, 2). Sozomen (*Hist. eccl.* 2, 19) states that Eustathius 'was justly admired on account of his fine eloquence, as is evidenced by his transmitted works, which are highly approved for their choice of words, flavor of expression, temperateness of sentiments, elegance and grace of narration'. Nevertheless, most of his writings are lost. His tract *On the Witch of Endor against Origen* (1 Kings 28) is the only one completely extant. Eustathius rejects not only Origen's interpretation of this particular passage but his entire allegorical exegesis, because it deprives Scripture of its historical character. He most probably wrote it before the beginning of the Arian controversy.

Editions: MG 18, 613-674. New crit. ed.: E. KLOSTERMANN, Origenes, Eustathius und Gregor von Nyssa über die Hexe von Endor (KT 83). Bonn, 1912, 16-62.

Studies: A. BRINKMANN, Verbesserungsvorschläge zu Eustathius von Antiochien über die Hexe von Endor: RhM 74 (1925) 308-313 (emendations as to Klostermann's edition). — F. SCHEIDWEILER, Zu der Schrift des Eustathius von Antiochien über die Hexe von Endor: RhM 96 (1953) 319-329 (text. crit.).

Fragments

Of all other writings only excerpts have come down to us, chiefly in dogmatic florilegia. His most important work seems to have been *Adversus Arianos*, which counted at least eight books. Small fragments of it are found in Greek in Eulogius of Alexandria, the compiler of the anthology *Doctrina Patrum de incarnatione Verbi*, and in John of Damascus, in Latin in Facundus of Hermiane and Pope Gelasius.

His book *De anima* seems to have consisted of two parts. The first is a refutation of the philosophers, mostly Platonists, and their views regarding the relation existing between soul and body. The second attacks the Arians for their doctrine that the Logos assumed a human body without a human soul. The fragments which are extant defend the complete divinity and the complete humanity of Christ without the slightest indication that Eustathius favored a view which could have led to the Nestorian Christology of later Antiochenes, as has been asserted occasionally.

Of christological importance also are the remains of his exegetical treatises on the Psalms, especially Ps. 15 and 92, and on Proverbs 8, 22: 'The Lord created me in the beginning of His ways, before His works'. Of this last Theodoret has preserved a number of short passages in his *Ecclesiastical History*. It seems that Eustathius composed it about 329 after Eusebius of Nicomedia (cf. above, p. 190) had returned from exile.

Unfortunately, even his large correspondence is no longer extant except for a letter to bishop Alexander of Alexandria (cf. above, p. 13), which has been recently reconstructed from fragments in the *Catenae*. Eustathius apparently wrote it while still bishop of Beroea. It refutes the Melchisedechians, who were of the opinion that the Priest-King of Salem was greater than Christ, and others who identified him with the Holy Spirit. Eustathius declares that he was a man like ourselves and interprets Genesis 14, 18f in the light of St. Paul's Epistle to the Hebrews.

Some Syriac fragments of his homilies remain. The *Homilia christologica in Lazarum, Mariam et Martham* edited by F. Cavallera in 1905 is not authentic. The same is true of the *Commentarius in Hexaeméron* which Leo Allatius published in 1629, and the *Liturgia S. Eustathii*, a Syriac Anaphora extant in many manuscripts.

Editions: MG 18, 675-704. Useful collection of fragments: F. CAVALLERA, S. Eustathii ep. Antioch. in Lazarum, Mariam et Martham homilia christologica. Paris, 1905. — New crit. ed. of fragments by M. SPANNEUT, Recherches sur les écrits d'Eustathe d'Antioche avec une édition nouvelle des fragments dogmatiques et exégétiques. Lille, 1948. Cf. M. RICHARD, Note sur une édition récente des écrits d'Eustathe d'Antioche: MSR 7 (1950) 305-310. — F. SCHEIDWEILER, Die Fragmente des Eustathios von Antiocheia: BZ 48 (1955) 73-85 (text. crit. and exeget. stud.). — Fragments on Genesis: R. DEVREESSE, Anciens commentateurs grecs de l'Octateuque: Eustathe d'Antioche: RBibl (1935) 189-191. — New fragment: I. LEBON, Severi Antiocheni liber contra impium Grammaticum. Orationis tertiae pars posterior (CSCO 102). Louvain, 1933, 47. — Crit. reconstruction of the *Epistula* to Alexander of Alexandria: B. ALTANER, Die Schrift Περὶ τοῦ Μελχισεδέκ des Eustathios von Antiocheia: BZ 40 (1940) 30-47.

Studies: L. SALTET, Une prétendue homélie d'Eustathe: BLE (1906) 212-220 (*homilia christologica in Lazarum, Mariam et Martham* is spurious). — A. JÜLICHER, ThLZ 31 (1906) 683ff. and F. DIEKAMP, ThR 5 (1906) 405f. are of the same opinion. — N. P. KUDRJAVZEV, Eustathios von Antiocheia: Bogosl. Vjestm. 1 (1910) 453-465; 2 (1911) 59-77, 426-439; 3 (1912) 66-78. — F. E. ROBINS, The Hexaëmeral Literature. Diss. Chicago, 1912, 42ff. — L. RADERMACHER, Eustathius von Antiochien, Platon und Sophocles: RhM 73 (1924) 449-455. — E. SCHWARTZ, Der sogenannte Sermo maior de fide des Athanasius (SAM Phil.-hist. Kl. 1924, 6). Munich, 1925 (regards Eustathius as the author of the *Sermo maior* and the *Expositio fidei*). Cf. J. LEBON, Le Sermo maior de fide pseudo-athanasien: Mus 38 (1925) 243-260; *idem*, S. Athanase a-t-il employé l'expression 'Ο κυριακὸς ἄνθρωπος?: RHE 31 (1935) 309, 311, 317-318. Cf. above p. 30. — F. SCHEMMEL, Julian and Eustathius: PhW 46 (1926) 1262-1264 (thinks that *Ep.* 72

of the Emperor Julian is addressed by Eustathius to Julian, and *Ep.* 39 from Julian to Eustathius). — F. ZOEPFL, Der Kommentar des Pseudo-Eustathius zum Hexaëmeron. Münster, 1927. — W. BROCKMEIER, De S. Eustathii episcopi Antiocheni dicendi ratione. Accedit index vocabulorum libri contra Origenem scripti omnium (Diss. Münster). Borna-Leipzig, 1932. — M. SPANNEUT, Hippolyte ou Eustathe?: MSR 9 (1952) 215-220: the fragment on the Gospel of S. Luke attributed to Hippolytus of Rome (MG 10, 700D-701A) belongs in reality to Eustathius (cf. ed. Spanneut, p. 102, n. 23). — F. SCHEIDWEILER, Ein Glaubensbekenntnis des Eustathius von Antiochien?: ZNW 44 (1952/53) 237-249 (Eustathius is most probably the real author of the Pseudo-Athanasian Creed formula *Contra Theopaschitas* found in Codex Ambros. D. 51 (235) f. 221a-222b and published for the first time by H. G. OPITZ, Untersuchungen zur Überlieferung der Schriften des Athanasius, Berlin, 1935, 210-212).

II. HIS CHRISTOLOGY

Eustathius has been accused of being in his Christology a successor to Paul of Samosata (cf. vol. II, p. 140f) and a forerunner of Nestorius. Although the few fragments of his works make it very difficult to give a complete picture of his teaching, they certainly suffice to refute this accusation. In his letter on Melchisedech he clearly recognizes the *communicatio idiomatum*, when he says of St. John the Baptist: 'Johannes autem ipsum Verbum corpus factum, quod est principium imaginis et sigilli, manibus suis complexus deduxit in aquas' (frgm. 64). In his *Oratio coram ecclesia* he says of the Jews: 'Manifeste deprehensi sunt, qui Verbum occidissent et cruci affixissent' (frgm. 70). He uses without reservation the title *Theotokos* for the blessed Virgin (frgm. 68).

Eustathius is the first to attempt a Logos-Man Christology against the predominant Logos-Sarx doctrine. It is in his refutation of the latter theory that he wins a position of importance in the history of dogma. He perceived the danger inherent in this formula, namely, that the Arians could use it to show that Christ assumed a human body without a soul; they could then attribute all the changes to the Logos Himself and thus deprive Him of his divinity. For this reason he resorts to the Logos-Man formula and makes such a sharp distinction between the two natures in Christ that in some passages (frgm. 37, 48, 24) he appears to have retracted his statements in favor of the *communicatio idiomatum*. It is in his emphasis on the whole man in Christ against the Logos-Sarx Christology of the Arians that he coins formulas which could be misunderstood, like *homo deifer*, ἄνθρωπος θεοφόρος. However, it is only by an isolation of these words from his other affirmations that he can be made suspect of Adoptianism or Nestorianism.

Studies: H. BRUDERS, Die antiarianische Kampfesweise des Eustathius von Antiochien im Gegensatz zu der des hl. Athanasius: ZkTh 38 (1914) 631-633. — F. ZOEPFL, Die trinitarischen und christologischen Anschauungen des Bischofs Eustathius von

Antiochien: ThQ 104 (1923) 170-201. — R. V. SELLERS, Eustathius of Antioch and his Place in the Early History of Christian Doctrine. Cambridge, 1928. — A. GRILLMEIER, Die theologische und sprachliche Vorbereitung der christologischen Formel von Chalkedon: CGG I (1951) 124-130. — M. SPANNEUT, La position théologique d'Eustathe d'Antioche: JThSt N.S. 5 (1954) 220-224 (the Trinitarian and Christological ideas of Eustathius do not agree with Loofs's thesis that Eustathius is a typical representative of the School of Antioch); idem, La bible d'Eustathe d'Antioche. Thèse. Paris, 1956. Cf. MATHON, RSR 13 (1956) 97-102. — J. N. D. KELLY, Early Christian Doctrines. London, 1958, 281-284 (the Arians and Eustathius).

AËTIUS OF ANTIOCH

Antioch became a center of Arianism after Eustathius had been exiled. Among the literary defenders of the heresy was Aëtius, a native of the city. Socrates (*Hist. eccl.* 2, 35) says that he 'never had the advantage of an academic preceptor' and calls him 'a man of so superficial attainments, and so little acquainted with the Sacred Scriptures, and so extremely fond of caviling, a thing which any clown might do, that he had never carefully studied those ancient writers who have interpreted the Christian oracles'. He was ordained a deacon by Leontius, the Arian bishop of Antioch (344-358), and consecrated bishop in 362 (Philostorgius, *Hist. eccl.* 7, 6).

Of his works only one short treatise is entirely preserved by Epiphanius, *Haer.* 76, 11, the *Syntagmation* (Συνταγμάτιον περὶ ἀγεννήτου θεοῦ καὶ γεννητοῦ). It defends in 47 theses the watchword of the Arians, anomoios, against misrepresentations of his opponents and intends to show the essential difference between the ungenerated Father and the generated Son. Epiphanius adds that Aëtius composed 300 of such theses in all. Socrates *(l.c.)* knows of *epistles* he wrote 'to the Emperor Constantius and to some other persons, wherein he interwove tedious disputes for the purpose of displaying his sophisms'. The compiler of the *Doctrina Patrum de incarnatione Verbi* has preserved (311-312 ed. Diekamp) five passages of his letter to the tribune Mazon.

Studies: G. BARDY, L'héritage littéraire d'Aétius: RHE 24 (1928) 809-827. — V. GRUMEL, Les textes monothélites d'Aétius: EO 28 (1929) 159-166. — A. KREUZ, LThK² 1 (1957) 165.

EUNOMIUS OF CYZICUS

More important than Aëtius himself was his pupil Eunomius, who became the literary defender and leader of Neo-Arianism. We know nothing of his youth. Gregory of Nyssa (*Contra Eunom.* 1) says that his father was a farmer and 'an excellent man, except that he had such a son'. From the same source we get the information that he learned short-hand in order to earn a livelihood. Socrates (*Hist. eccl.* 4, 7) tells us that he became secretary to Aëtius and 'learned from him his sophistical mode of reasoning'. Eudoxius of Antioch ordained him a deacon and in 360, after he had become bishop of Constantinople, he promoted him to the see of Cyzicus. As a bishop he 'astonished his auditors by his extraordinary display of "dialectic" art, and thus produced a great sensation at Cyzicus. At length the people, unable to endure any longer his empty and arrogant parade of language, drove him out of their city. He therefore withdrew to Constantinople, and taking up his abode with Eudoxius, was regarded as a titular bishop' (Socrates, *l.c.*). After Aëtius' death he became the chief exponent of Anomoeanism and his adherents were called Eunomians. He retired to his estate in Chalcedon (Philostorgius, *Hist. eccl.* 9, 4). In 383 he attended a synod at Constantinople and was shortly afterwards exiled by the Emperor Theodosius. He lived until 394 in Halmyris in Moesia, Caesarea in Cappadocia and in near-by Dacora.

Studies: E. VENABLES, Eunomius: DCB 2 (1880) 286-290. — A. JÜLICHER, PWK 6 (1909) 1131-1132. — X. LE BACHELET, Eunomius: DTC 5 (1913) 1501-1514. — C. R. W. KLOSE, Geschichte und Lehre des Eunomius. Kiel, 1883. — M. ALBERTZ, Zur Geschichte der jung-arianischen Kirchengemeinschaft: ThStKr 82 (1909) 205-278. — L. PARMETIER, Eunomius tachygraphe: RPh (1909) 238-245 (Theodoret, *Hist. eccl.* 4, 18, 7).

HIS WRITINGS

His works were very numerous and provoked many refutations. Thus Didymus the Blind (cf. above, p. 88), Basil the Great (cf. above, p. 209), and Gregory of Nyssa (cf. above, p. 257), Sophronius, Apollinaris of Laodicea and Theodore of Mopsuestia wrote against him. Except for the treatises of the two Cappadocians, all these refutations have perished. Since successive imperial edicts from the time of Arcadius in 398, four years after the death of Eunomius, ordered his writings to be burnt and made the possession of them a capital crime, very little remains of his extensive literary activity.

Studies: M. ALBERTZ, Untersuchungen über die Schriften des Eunomius. (Diss. Halle.) Wittenberg, 1908. — F. DIEKAMP, Literargeschichtliches zur Eunomianischen Kontroverse: BZ 18 (1909) 1-13, 190-194. — W. WEINBERGER, Τὰ 'Εὐνομίου γράμματα: WSt (1912) 74-75.

1. *First Apology ('Ἀπολογία)*

The most important is his *Apology*, which is extant (MG 30, 835-868) and was published in 361. It is this short treatise that occasioned St. Basil the Great, Didymus the Blind and Apollinaris of Laodicea to write against Eunomius. The book found many readers and gives ample proof of the rhetorical skill of its author. Its philosophy is Neo-Platonic and Aristotelian with a leaning to rationalism and Nominalism. Theology is to Eunomius 'technology' (Theodoret, *Haer. fab.* 4, 3). The only true name for the divinity is 'Ungenerated', because not to be begotten is the very essence of God. The concept of 'Unbegotten' enables us to distinguish God from every other being. The Son is begotten and therefore of a different nature than God the Father (ἀνόμοιος). He is created from nothing. Eunomius, however, differs from Arius in so far as he concedes that Christ was adopted as Son of God from the beginning, not as a reward after a life of virtue.

Edition: MG 30, 835-868.

Translation: English: W. WHISTON, Eunomius's Apologetic against which Basil the Great wrote his Refutation: Primitive Christianity Revived I. London, 1711, 1-30.

Studies: F. DIEKAMP, Die Gotteslehre des hl. Gregor von Nyssa I. Münster, 1896, 122ff. — J. CHAPMAN, On the Date of the Clementines: ZNW (1908) 21-34 (*Apology* used as a source). — J. DE GHELLINCK, Quelques appréciations de la dialectique d'Aristote dans les conflits trinitaires du IVᵉ siècle: RHE 26 (1930) 5-42. — E. VANDENBUSSCHE, La part de la dialectique dans la théologie d'Eunomius 'le technologue': RHE 40 (1944/45) 47-72.

2. Second Apology (᾽Απολογία ὑπὲρ ἀπολογίας)

It took Eunomius at least twelve years to answer St. Basil's refutation of his first *Apology*. Unfortunately, this counter-reply, which he composed in 378, is not extant. But in Gregory of Nyssa's works against Eunomius (cf. above, p. 257) large excerpts are preserved. It consisted of at least three books, most probably of five. The first two refuted the first book of Basil's *Adv. Eunomium;* the third, the second. The last two, mentioned only by Philostorgius (*Hist. eccl.* 8, 12), seem to have been the rebuttal to Basil's third book. It is doubtful whether Eunomius published the entire work simultaneously. Photius (*Bibl. cod.* 138) speaks of three books only.

Editions: Partial collection of fragments: C. H. G. RETTBERG, Marcelliana. Göttingen, 1794, 125ff. — M. ALBERTZ, Untersuchungen, 15-36, tried to reconstruct the content and the order of the texts.

3. Confession of Faith (῎Εκθεσις πίστεως)

It has been mentioned above (p. 257) that Eunomius in 383 wrote a formal profession of faith which he sent to the Emperor Theodosius. Its entire text has survived the fate of his other writings. Gregory of Nyssa severely criticized it in a detailed refutation (cf. above, p. 257).

Editions: J. D. MANSI, SS. Conc. Coll. 3, 645-649. — New ed.: C. H. G. RETTBERG, op. cit. 147ff. — J. D. GOLDHORN, S. Basilii et S. Gregorii Theol. opp. dogm. sel. (Bibl. patr. Graec. dogm. cur. J. C. Thilo II). Leipzig, 1854, 618-629.

4. Commentary on the Epistle to the Romans

Nothing remains of his commentary *On the Apostle's Epistle to the Romans*, which consisted of seven books, according to Socrates, *Hist. eccl.* 4, 7.

5. Letters

Photius (*Bibl. cod.* 138) read 40 letters of Eunomius, addressed 'to different people'. None of them remains to enable us to form our own opinion. Philostorgius preferred them to any other of his writings (*Hist. eccl.* 10, 6 at the end), while Photius avers: 'In these he affects the same subtlety of form, since he is ignorant of the laws of epistolary style and has had no practice in them'.

Special Studies: A. SLOMKOWSKI, Doctrina Semiarianorum de circuminsessione personarum SS. Trinitatis: CTh 16 (1935) 95-103. — P. WORRALL, St. Thomas and Arianism: RTAM 23 (1956) 208-259. — J. DANIÉLOU, Eunome l'arien et l'exégèse néo-platonicienne du Cratyle: REG 69 (1956) 412-432.

EUSEBIUS OF CAESAREA

The golden age of patristic literature opens with the splendid productions of the 'Father of Ecclesiastical History', Eusebius Pamphili, bishop of Caesarea in Palestine. He combines with the greatest interest for the past a very active participation in the shaping of the present. He is at the same time an historian and a controversialist, a leading figure in the religious struggle of his times, one of the last Apologists and the first chronicler and archivist of the Church. He reflects the radical changes that were taking place at this turn in the world's history more faithfully than any other author. He remains the typical representative of the era which saw the first Christian Emperor.

It seems that Caesarea was not only the place of his intellectual training, of his literary activity and of his episcopal see, but also of his birth about 263. This city had developed into a center of learning from the time that the exiled Origen founded his famous school here; his literary bequest formed the basis of a library which the presbyter Pamphilus enlarged and made a seat of scholarship (cf. vol. II, p. 121, 144-146). The latter was in fact the one, to whom Eusebius owed his scientific education as well as his life-long admiration of the great Alexandrian Master. It was out of veneration and gratitude to his teacher and friend that he called himself Eusebius Pamphili, i.e. the spiritual son of Pamphilus, and that he honored his memory by a biography, after he had died as a martyr in the seventh year of the persecution of Diocletian, on February 6, 310. Eusebius himself escaped death only by his flight to Tyre, and thence into the Egyptian desert of the Thebais. Even there he was found, seized and imprisoned.

It seems that the same year that gave peace and freedom to the Church (313) saw his election to the see of Caesarea. As a bishop he was soon caught up in the Arian controversy, which he thought he could solve with suggestions of mutual concessions by the opposing parties, without realizing the importance of the doctrine at stake. He wrote several letters in favor of Arius and was very influential in a synod at Caesarea, which declared Arius' profession of faith to be orthodox, although it demanded his submission to his bishop. Soon afterwards a synod of Antioch in 325 excommunicated the bishop of Caesarea when he rejected a formula directed against the Arian teaching. At the Council of Nicaea in 325 he sought to continue his peace-making efforts as the main representative of the center party, which advocated a recognition of the true divinity of Christ in simply biblical terms and refused the Homoousian doctrine of Athanasius as leading logically to Sabellianism. He finally signed the Creed drawn up by the Council as a merely external conforming to the express wish of the Emperor but without any internal assent. Soon afterwards he openly sided with Eusebius of Nicomedia and took a prominent part in the synod of Antioch in 330, which deposed the local bishop Eustathius, and in the synod of Tyre in 335, that excommunicated Athanasius. He wrote in addition two treatises against Marcellus of Ancyra, who lost his episcopal see a year later.

His admiration for the Emperor, who established peace between Church and State after centuries of bloody persecutions, was unbounded and he himself enjoyed in a special degree the favor of Constantine. On the occasion of the twentieth and thirtieth anniversaries of the Emperor's assumption of the reins of government he delivered the panegyrics and when Constantine died on May 22, 337, he dedicated to his memory a lengthy eulogy. He may, in fact, have influenced the Emperor's measures against the orthodox bishops, because he appears to have been his chief theological adviser. He died a few years after Constantine, in 339 or 340.

Studies: J. B. LIGHTFOOT, DCB 2 (1880) 308-348. — E. SCHWARTZ, PWK 6 (1907) 1370-1439. — H. LECLERCQ, Eusèbe de Césarée: DAL 5 (1922) 747-775. — A. P. FRUTAZ and A. PENNA, EC 5 (1951) 841-854. — K. ALAND, RGG³ 2 (1958) 739-740. — M. WEIS, Die Stellung des Eusebius von Caesarea im arianischen Streit. Trier, 1920. —

F. J. F. JACKSON, Eusebius Pamphili. A Study of the Man and his Writings. Cambridge, 1933. — D. S. BALANOS, Ὁ χαρακτὴρ τοῦ ἐκκλησιαστικοῦ ἱστορικοῦ Εὐσεβίου: Studies in honor of S. Lampros. Athens, 1935, 515-522; idem, Zum Charakterbild des Kirchen-historikers Eusebius: ThQ 116 (1935) 309-322. — H. v. CAMPENHAUSEN, Griechische Kirchenväter. Stuttgart, 1955, 61-71. — E. SCHWARTZ, Griechische Geschichtsschreiber. Leipzig, 1957, 495-598.

HIS WRITINGS

Except for Origen, Eusebius outdistances all Greek Church Fathers in research and scholarship. He was an indefatigable worker and continued writing until a very advanced age. His treatises represent storehouses of excerpts which he collected from pagan and Christian works, many of them no longer extant. For this reason his literary productions have mostly survived, although his Arian tendency stood against them. They reveal a breadth of learning which is simply astonishing. He shows himself well versed in Scripture, pagan and Christian history, ancient literature, philosophy, geography, technical chronology, exegesis, philology and paleography. However, he lacks any feeling for form or composition. Photius remarks: 'His style is neither agreeable nor brilliant, but he is a man of great learning' (Bibl. cod. 13). Although he is a resourceful apologist, he does not belong to the outstanding theologians of Christian antiquity. If he has won eternal fame, it is by his great historical works.

Collections: MG 19-24. — New crit. ed.: GCS, 8 vols. so far (1902-1956), edited by I. A. HEIKEL, T. MOMMSEN, E. KLOSTERMANN, H. GRESSMANN, J. KARST, R. HELM, K. MRAS.

Translations: English: A. C. C. McGIFFERT and E. C. RICHARDSON, LNPF ser. 2, vol. 1 (1890). — German: J. M. PFÄTTISCH, BKV² 9 (1913) with an introduction by A. Bigelmair V-LXI. — P. HÄUSER, BKV³ 1 (1932). — French: G. BARDY, SCH 31 (1952), 41 (1955), 55 (1958).

Studies: E. FRITZE, Beiträge zur sprachlich-stilistischen Würdigung des Eusebios. Diss. Borna-Leipzig, 1910. — A. BIGELMAIR, Zur Theologie des Eusebius von Caesarea: Festschrift G. Hertling. Kempten, 1913, 65-85. — D. DE BRUYNE and A. WILMART, Membra disiecta: RB 36 (1924) 121-136 (list of manuscripts). — J. STEVENSON, Studies in Eusebius. Cambridge, 1929. — H. G. OPITZ, Euseb von Caesarea als Theologe: ZNW 34 (1935) 1-19. — H. BERKHOF, Die Theologie des Eusebius von Caesarea. Diss. Leiden. Amsterdam, 1939. — A. SIEGMUND, Die Überlieferung der griechischen christlichen Literatur in der lateinischen Kirche. Munich-Pasing, 1949, 73-80. — B. ALTANER, Augustinus und Eusebios von Kaisareia. Eine quellenkritische Unter-suchung: BZ 44 (1951) 1-6.

1. Historical Works

1. The Chronicle

Among his earliest compositions is one commonly called Chronicle but to which the author himself refers as the Χρονικοὶ κάνονες καὶ ἐπιτομὴ παντοδαπῆς ἱστορίας Ἑλλήνων τε καὶ βαρβάρων

(*Ecl. proph.* 1, 1; *Hist. eccl.* 1, 1, 6). It was written about 303 and consists of two parts. The first, which is actually the introduction, provided in short epitomes the history of the Chaldeans based on excerpts from Alexander Polyhistor, Abydenos and Josephus, of the Assyrians according to Abydenos, Castor, Diodorus and Cephalion, of the Hebrews based on the Old Testament, Josephus and Clement of Alexandria, of the Egyptians according to Diodorus, Manetho and Porphyry, of the Greeks according to Castor, Porphyry and Diodorus, and of the Romans according to Dionysius of Halicarnassus, Diodorus and Castor.

The second part was made up of synchronous tables arranged in parallel columns (χρονικοὶ κάνονες) and accompanied by notes marking the principal facts of universal, and especially sacred, history. For his point of departure Eusebius took the year of Abraham's birth (2016/15 B.C.) and made five divisions: from Abraham to the taking of Troy, from the taking of Troy to the first Olympiad, from the first Olympiad to the second year of the reign of Darius, from the second year of the reign of Darius to the death of Christ, from the death of Christ to 303 A.D. The object set himself by Eusebius was to prove that the Jewish religion, of which the Christian was the legitimate continuation, was older than any other. This idea was by no means a new one. As early as the second century the Christian Apologists had for the same reason tried to show the great antiquity of Moses. Moreover, at the beginning of the third century, Julius Africanus (cf. vol. II, p. 138) based his *Chronicles*, which represent the first synchronistic history of the world, on the same principle. There is no doubt that Eusebius found his model and a large part of his material in Africanus, even though he does not say so. Nevertheless, Eusebius' work is far superior, not only because he follows better and older authors almost everywhere, but also because he has a more critical approach. The most important advance over his predecessors is that he rid the Christian chronicle of millenarism. By his dating of scriptural events he wishes to prove that the system of Africanus was wrong and unscientific. He refuses to begin with Adam or the Fall, because nobody knows how long man was in Paradise, and also because the text of the numerals given in the Bible is sound and certain only from the time of Abraham on. Here we notice the judgment of an author skilled in textual criticism.

The Greek original has perished save for some fragments and excerpts. The entire text has survived only in an Armenian translation of the sixth century. The second part is in addition extant in a Latin version prepared by Jerome in 380 at Constantinople. Neither the Armenian nor the Latin edition is based on the original but on a revision which continues beyond 303 to the twentieth year of the reign of Constantine. Jerome, moreover, was not content to keep Eusebius' work just as it was, but expanded it, inserting a large number of entries on general, and especially Roman, history and bringing it up to date, i.e. from the year 325 down to the year 378, the death of Valens. It was in this form that the *Chronicle* reached the West and dominated the historiography of the Middle Ages. It is one of the fundamental books upon which all research on the past of mankind has been based.

Editions: MG 19, 99-598. — A. Schoene, 2 vols. Berlin, 1866-1875. Vol. I contains: Armeniam versionem Latine factam ad libros manuscriptos recensuit H. Petermann. Graeca fragmenta collegit et recognovit, appendices chronographicas sex adiecit A. Schoene. Vol. II: Armeniam versionem Latine factam e libris manuscriptis recensuit H. Petermann. Hieronymi versionem Latine factam e libris manuscr. rec. A. Schoene. Syriam epitomen Latine factam e libro Londinensi recensuit E. Roediger. — New crit. editions: J. K. Fotheringham, Eusebii Pamphili Chronici canones. Latine vertit, adauxit, ad sua tempora produxit Sanctus Eusebius Hieronymus. London, 1923. — R. Helm, GCS 24 (1913): Die Chronik des Hieronymus (Hieronymi Chronicon), I. Teil: Text; *idem*, GCS 34 (1926) II. Teil: Lesarten der Handschriften und quellenkritischer Apparat zur Chronik. GCS 47 (1956) combines GCS 24 and 34 in a new edition by R. Helm.

Translation: German: J. Karst, GCS 20 (1911), Eusebius' Werke V: Die Chronik aus dem Armenischen übersetzt. Mit textkritischem Apparat.

Studies: H. Gelzer, Sextus Julius Africanus und die byzantinische Chronographie 2, 1. Leipzig, 1885, 23-107 (the *Chronicle* of Eusebius). — A. Schoene, Die Weltchronik des Eusebius in ihrer Bearbeitung durch Hieronymus. Berlin, 1900. — H. Montzka, Die Quellen zu den assyrisch-babylonischen Nachrichten in Eusebius' Chronik: Klio (1902) 351-405. — J. K. Fotheringham, The Bodleian Manuscript of Jerome's Version of the Chronicle of Eusebius (reproduced in collotype). Oxford, 1905 (the best manuscript). — A. Rahlfs, Nachwirkungen der Chronik des Eusebius in Septuaginta-Handschriften: ZAW (1908) 60-62. — A. Bauer, Beiträge zu Eusebius und den byzantinischen Chronographen (SAW 162). Vienna, 1909. — D. Serruys, La notation ascendante des nombres dans la Chronique d'Eusèbe: RPh (1914) 215-218. — D. Dhorme, Les sources de la Chronique d'Eusèbe: RBibl (1910) 233-237 (Sennacherib). — P. Keseling, Die Chronik des Eusebius in syrischer Überlieferung. Diss. Bonn, 1917. Abstract: Duderstadt, 1921; OC 3rd ser., 1 (1926) 23-48, 223-241; 2 (1927) 33-56. — R. Helm, Eusebius' Chronik und ihre Tabellenform (AAB). Berlin, 1924; *idem*, De Eusebii in Chronicorum libro auctoribus: Eranos (1924) 1-40. — H. J. Lawlor, The Chronology of Eusebius: CQ (1925) 94-101. — R. Helm, Die Liste der Thalassokratien in der Chronik des Eusebius: Hermes (1926) 241-263; *idem*, Hieronymus' Zusätze in Eusebius' Chronik und ihr Wert für die Literaturgeschichte (Phil. Supplbd. 21, 2). Leipzig, 1929; *idem*, Die neuesten Hypothesen zu Eusebius' Chronik: SAB (1929) 371-408. — L. Santifaller, Über eine Unzialhandschrift der Chronik des hl. Hieronymus aus dem 5. Jahrhundert (Beiträge zur Paläographie II): HJG 59 (1939) 412-431. — J. Carcopino, Sur un passage de la Chronique de S. Jérôme: Mélanges F. Martroye. Paris, 1941, 73-79 (population of Rome). — H. Emonds, Zweite Auflage im Altertum. Leipzig, 1941, 45-55. — V. Grumel, Les premières ères mondiales: REB 10 (1952) 93-108. — G. d'Anna, Chronica di Cornelio Nepote fonte secondaria di S. Gerolamo: RIL 86 (1953) 211-232 (for the completion of the *Chronicon*). — J. R. Laurin, Orientations maîtresses des apologistes chrétiens de 270 à 361. Rome, 1954, 104-113. — H. Erbse, Vier Bemerkungen zu Herodot: RhM 98 (1955) 99-120. — M. Miller, Archaic Literary Chronography: JHS 75 (1955) 54-58. — D. S. Wallace-Hadrill, The

Eusebian Chronicle. The Extent and Date of Composition of its Early Editions: JThSt N.S. 6 (1955) 248-253. — R. SCHMID, Aetates mundi. Die Weltalter als Gliederungs-prinzip der Geschichte: ZKG 67 (1956) 288-317. — J. STEINMANN, Saint Jérôme. Paris, 1958, 102-106 (la Chronique d'Eusèbe).

2. The Ecclesiastical History

The work which made Eusebius immortal is his *Church History* (*'Εκκλησιαστικὴ ἱστορία*), which in its present form comprises ten books covering the period from the foundation of the Church to the defeat of Licinius (324) and the sole rulership of Constantine. The title should not be misunderstood, as if Eusebius intended to record the vicissitudes or even the development of the Church from its beginnings to his own day. He makes no effort at a complete or well-balanced account, much less does he attempt an orderly and reasoned exposition of the spread and growth of Christianity. His work represents an extremely rich collection of historical facts, documents and excerpts from a multitude of writings of the early Church. The introduction reveals the order in which the material is assembled:

> I have purposed to record in writing the succession of the sacred apostles, covering the period stretching from our Saviour to ourselves; the number and character of the transactions recorded in the history of the Church; the number of those who in each generation were the ambassadors of the word of God either by speech or pen; the names, the number and the age of those who, driven by the desire of innovations to an extremity of error, have heralded themselves as the introducers of knowledge, falsely so-called, ravaging the flock of Christ unsparingly, like wolves. To this I will add the fate which has beset the whole nation of the Jews from the moment of their plot against our Saviour; more-over, the number and nature and times of the wars waged by the heathen against the divine Word and the character of those who, for its sake, passed from time to time through the contest of blood and torture; furthermore the martyrdoms of our own time, and the gracious and favouring help of our Saviour in them all. My starting-point is therefore no other than the first dispensation of God touching our Saviour and Lord, Jesus Christ. Even at that point the project at once demands the lenience of the kindly, for confessedly it is beyond our power to fulfill the promise, complete and perfect, since we are the first to enter on the undertaking, as travellers on some desolate and untrodden way (LCL).

Thus it was the author's purpose to present (1) the lists of bishops in the most important communities, (2) the Christian teachers and authors, (3) the heretics, (4) the divine punishment of the Jewish people, (5) the Christian persecutions, (6) the martyrdoms and the final victory of the Christian religion. This arrangement betrays the apologetic aim of the entire work: to furnish the proof that the Church has been founded and guided by God to its final victory over the power of the pagan State.

Since Eusebius' own life was a period of fast-moving historical events of the greatest importance, he was forced to make additions several times to the original, in order to keep his principal work up to date. Thus his *Church History* passed through various stages, which have been called editions. E. Schwartz counted four such and advanced the theory that the first, consisting of books I-VIII, appeared in 312; the second, adding book IX, in 315; the third, adding book X, in 317; and the fourth, removing the passages inconsistent with the *damnatio memoriae* of Licinius and replacing them with an account of his downfall, in 325, at the time of the Council of Nicaea. A rival hypothesis has been propounded by H. J. Lawlor, who thinks that the work was published in its first form earlier than Schwartz suggested. Recent investigations favor the opinion that books I-VII appeared even before the outbreak of the persecution of Diocletian (303).

The *Church History* achieved world-wide success and was so often recopied that the present critical text can be based on seven Greek manuscripts from the 9th to the 11th century: three in the Bibliothèque Nationale at Paris (*Codex Parisinus* 1430, 1431, 1432), two in the Laurentian Library at Florence (*Codex Laurentianus* 70, 7 and 70, 20), one in St. Mark's Library at Venice (*Codex Marcianus* 338) and one in Moscow (*Codex Mosquensis* 50).

In addition, three translations have come down to us. The earliest is the ancient Syriac, most probably made in the fourth century, which served as the basis for a very literal old Armenian version. The Syriac is far better than Rufinus' Latin rendering of 403. He frequently paraphrases and misinterprets his original but he does bring the history down to the death of Theodosius the Great in 395, adding another 70 years. It is in this Latin translation that the *Church History* of Eusebius spread over the entire West.

Editions: MG 20, 45-906. — New crit. ed.: GCS 9 in 3 vols. Part I (1903) and II (1908) contain the text, Part III (1909) the introductions and indexes. Greek text edited by E. Schwartz. The Latin translation of Rufinus ed. by T. Mommsen. Separate edition: E. Schwartz, Eusebius' Kirchengeschichte. Kleine Ausgabe. 5th ed. Berlin, 1952. — K. Lake, Eusebius. The Ecclesiastical History. With an English Translation (LCL). 2 vols. London, 1926, 1932 (reprints the text of GCS). — E. Grapin, Eusèbe de Césarée. Histoire ecclésiastique. Texte grec et trad. française. 3 vols. Paris, 1905-1913. — G. Bardy, SCH 31 (1952), 41 (1955), 55 (1958). — A Syriac version was published by P. Bedjan, Leipzig, 1897 and in a much better edition by W. Wright and N. McLean, The Ecclesiastical History of Eusebius in Syriac, Cambridge, 1898. An Armenian translation of this Syriac version was edited by the Mechitarists, Venice, 1877. Remnants of a Coptic version were translated by W. E. Crum, Eusebius and Coptic Church Histories: Proceedings of the Society of Biblical Archaeology 24 (1902) 68-84.

Translations: English: A. C. McGiffert, LNPF ser. 2, vol. 1 (1890) 73-387. — K. Lake, op. cit. (volume 2 reprints Oulton's translation). — H. J. Lawlor and J. E. L. Oulton, Eusebius, The Ecclesiastical History and the Martyrs of Palestine, transl. with introd. and notes, 2 vols. (SPCK). London, 1927/1928. — R. J. Deferrari, FC 19 (1953), 29 (1955). — *French:* E. Grapin, op. cit. — G. Bardy, op. cit. — *German:* M. Stigloher, BKV (1870). — P. Häuser, BKV³ 1 (1932). — A German translation of the Syriac version was published by E. Nestle, TU 21, 2 (1901). The Armenian version of books VI and VII was translated into German by E. Preuschen, TU 22, 3 (1902). — *Italian:* G. del Ton, Eusebio, Storia ecclesiastica. Siena 1931, Florence 1943. — *Dutch:* H. Meyboom, Eusebius, Kerkgeschiedenis (Oudchristelijke geschriften in Nederlandsche vertaling, deel 2-4). Leiden, 1909. — D. Franses, Eusebius' Kerkelijke geschiedenis. Bussum, 1946. — *Swedish:* I. A. Heikel, Eusebius, Kyrkohistoria. Overs. fr. grekiskan med inledning och forklaringar. Stockholm, 1937.

Studies: A. Halmel, Die Entstehung der Kirchengeschichte des Eusebius von Caesarea. Essen, 1896. — H. J. Lawlor, Eusebiana. Essays on the Ecclesiastical History of Eusebius. New York, 1912 (Eusebius' sources, crit. of Schwartz's idea of four editions). — F. Jaskowski, Die Kirchengeschichte des Eusebius und der Primat: Kirchliche Zeitschrift (1909) 104-110. — E. Caspar, Die älteste römische Bischofsliste. Kritische Studien zum Formproblem des Eusebianischen Kanons sowie zur Genesis der ältesten Bischofslisten und ihrer Entstehung aus apostolischen Sukzessionsreihen. Berlin, 1926; *idem,* Paläographisches zum Kanon des Eusebius: Festgabe F. Degering. Leipzig, 1926, 42-56. — J. De Ghellinck, A propos d'un texte d'Eusèbe (l'histoire du symbole des apôtres): RSR 18 (1928) 118-125 (*H. E.* 5, 28, 3-6). — R. Laqueur, Eusebius als Historiker seiner Zeit. Berlin, 1929. — J. E. L. Oulton, Rufinus's Translation of the Church History of Eusebius: JThSt 30 (1929) 150-174. — J. Salaverri, La cronologia en la Historià eclesiàstica de Eusebio Cesariense: EE 11 (1932) 114-123; *idem,* La idea de tradición en la Historia eclesiástica de Eusebio Cesariense: Greg (1932) 211-240; *idem,* La sucesión apostólica en la Historia eclesiástica de Eusebio Cesariense: Greg (1933) 219-247. — N. H. Baynes, Eusebius and the Christian Empire: Mélanges Bidez. Brussels, 1934, 13-18 (*H. E.* 10, 4, 6off.). — J. Salaverri, El origen de la revelación y los garantes de su conservación en la Iglesia segun Eusebio de Cesarea: Greg (1935) 349-373. — M. Mueller, Die Überlieferung des Eusebius in seiner Kirchengeschichte über die Schriften des Neuen Testamentes und deren Verfasser: ThStKr 105 (1933) 425-455. — N. Zernov, Eusebius and the Paschal Controversy at the End of the Second Century: ChQ 116 (1933) 24-41. — F. J. F. Jackson, Eusebius Bishop of Caesarea and First Christian Historian. Cambridge, 1933; *idem,* A History of Church History. Cambridge, 1939, 56-70. — W. Nigg, Die Kirchengeschichtsschreibung. Grundzüge ihrer historischen Entwicklung. Munich, 1934. — W. Bauer, Rechtgläubigkeit und Ketzerei im ältesten Christentum. Tübingen, 1934, 13-16, 45f., 66f., 151-161, 193-195 (Eusebius unreliable). — H. Doergens, Eusebios von Caesarea, der Vater der Kirchengeschichte: ThGl 29 (1937) 446-448. — H. Grégoire, About Licinius' Fiscal and Religious Policy: Byz 13 (1938) 551-560 (*H. E.* 8, 14, 10). — H. Schöne, Ein Einbruch der antiken Logik und Textkritik in die altchristliche Theologie. Eusebios, Kirchengeschichte 5, 28, 13-19 in neuer Übertragung erläutert. Pisciculi. Festschrift F. J. Dölger. Münster, 1939, 252-265. — L. Allevi, Eusebio di Cesarea e la storiografia ecclesiastica: SC (1940) 550-564. — H. Emonds, op. cit. 25-45. — F. Tailliez, Notes conjointes sur un passage fameux d'Eusèbe: OCP 9 (1943) 431-449 (correction of *H. E.* 2, 25 dealing with the tomb of St. Peter). — C. C. Torrey, James the Just and his Name Oblias: JBL (1944) 93-98 (*H. E.* 2, 23). — F. X. Murphy, Rufinus of Aquileia. His Life and Works. Washington, 1945, 158-175. — M. Villain, Rufin d'Aquilée et l'histoire ecclésiastique d'Eusèbe: RSR 33 (1946) 164-210. — W. Seston, L'amnistie des vicennalia de Dioclétien d'après P. Oxy. 2187: Chronique d'Égypte (1947) 333-337. — F. M. Heichelheim - Schwarzenberger, An Edict of Constantine the Great. Study of

Interpolations: SO (1947) 1-19. — H. KATZENMAYER, Petrus und der Primat des römischen Bischofs in der Ἐκκλησιαστικὴ ἱστορία des Bischofs Eusebius von Caesarea: IKZ 38 (1948) 153-171. — R. H. CONNOLLY, Eusebius, H. E., V, 28: JThSt (1948) 73-79. — A. D'ACCINNI, La data della salita al trono di Diocleziano: RFIC (1948) 244-256. — W. KÜHNERT, Der antimontanistische Anonymus des Eusebius: ThZ 5 (1949) 436-446 (*H. E.* 5, 16-17). — O. PERLER, Das vierte Makkabäerbuch, Ignatius von Antiochien und die ältesten Martyrerberichte: RAC (1949) 47-72 (*H. E.* 5, 1-2). — J. ZEILLER, Légalité et arbitraire dans les persécutions contre les chrétiens: AB 67 (1949) 49-54 (*H. E.* 5, 1-4). — W. VÖLKER, Von welchen Tendenzen liess sich Eusebius bei der Abfassung seiner Kirchengeschichte leiten?: VC 4 (1950) 157-180. — H. GRÉGOIRE and P. ORGELS, La véritable date du martyre de S. Polycarpe (23 février 177) et le Corpus Polycarpianum: AB 69 (1951) 1-38 (chronology of Eusebius). — G. ZUNTZ, A Textual Note on Eusebius (Hist. Eccl. VI, 41, 15): VC 5 (1951) 50-54. — E. GRIFFE, A propos de la date du martyre de saint Polycarpe: BLE 52 (1951) 170-177 (retains 155 or 156 as the date of Polycarp's death against Grégoire's interpretation). — W. TELFER, The Date of the Martyrdom of Polycarp: JThSt (1952) 79-83 (against Grégoire). — G. G. SPAUDE, An Examination of Eusebius' Church History as a Source for N T Study. Diss. South. California Univ., 1952. — H. J. MARROU, La date du martyre de saint Polycarpe: AB 71 ('1953) 5-20 (against Grégoire). — E. GRIFFE, Un nouvel article sur la date du martyre de saint Polycarpe: BLE 54 (1953) 178-181. — J. CARCOPINO, Note sur deux textes controversés de la tradition apostolique romaine: Comptes Rendus de l'Académie des Inscriptions et Belles-Lettres (1952) 424-433 (*H. E.* 2, 27, 7). — H. GRÉGOIRE, Gélase ou Rufin? Un fait nouveau: NC 5 (1953) 472 (Gelasius wrote the continuation of *H.E.*). — J. MOREAU, Les 'Litterae Licinii': Annales Universitatis Saraviensis 2 (1953) 100-105 (*H. E.* 10, 5). — E. HONIGMANN, Gélase de Césarée et Rufin d'Aquilée: BAB 40 (1954) 122-161 (Gelasius could not have written the continuation). — M. ADRIANI, La storicità dell'editto di Milano: Studi Romani 2 (1954) 18-32. — G. S. P. FREEMAN - GRENVILLE, The Date of the Outbreak of Montanism: JEH 5 (1954) 7-15. — R. L. P. MILBURN, Early Christian Interpretations of History. London, 1954. — H. NESSELHAUF, Das Toleranzgesetz des Licinius: HJG 74 (1954) 44-61. — C. SAUMAGNE, Du mot αἵρεσις dans l'édit licinien de l'année 313: ThZ 10 (1954) 376-387. — W. SCHMID, Eusebianum. Adnotatio ad Epistulam Antonini Pii a Christianis fictam: RhM 97 (1954) 190f. (*H. E.* 4, 13, 5). — J. R. LAURIN, op. cit. 113-124. — G. BARDY, La théologie d'Eusèbe de Césarée d'après l'Histoire ecclésiastique: RHE 50 (1955) 5-20 (subordinatianism). — K. BALTZER and H. KOESTER, Die Bezeichnung des Jakobus als ὠβλίας: ZNW 46 (1955) 141-142 (*H. E.* 2, 23, 7). — J. ZEILLER, A propos d'un passage énigmatique de Méliton de Sardes relatif à la persécution contre les chrétiens: REAug 2 (1956) 257-263 (*H. E.* 4, 26, 5-6). — C. CECCHELLI, Un tentato riconoscimento imperiale del Cristo: Studi in onore di A. Calderini e R. Paribeni. Milan, 1956, I, 351-362 (*H. E.* 2, 2, 5). — M. SORDI, Un senatore cristiano dell'età di Commodo: Epigraphica 17 (1957) 104-112 (*H. E.* 5, 21, 2-5). — F. SCHEIDWEILER, Die Bedeutung der Vita Metrophanis et Alexandri für die Quellenkritik bei den griechischen Kirchenhistorikern: BZ 50 (1957) 74-98; idem, Zur Kirchengeschichte des Eusebios von Kaisareia: ZNW 49 (1958) 123-129 (*H. E.* 4, 13; 5, 11f. Edict of Antoninus Pius; Letter on the martyrs of Lugdunum).

3. *The Martyrs of Palestine*

Eusebius must have published a collection of ancient Acts of the Martyrs before he wrote his *Ecclesiastical History*, because in the fourth and fifth book of the latter he refers repeatedly to it. This valuable work has perished. Speaking of the martyrs of Palestine *Eccl. Hist.* 8, 13, 7, he adds:

It is not our part to commit to writing the conflicts of those who fought throughout the world on behalf of piety toward the Deity, and to record in detail each of their happenings; but that would be the special task of those who witnessed the events. Yet I shall make known to posterity in another work those with whom I was personally conversant (LCL).

Eusebius fulfilled this promise and gives us in his *Martyrs of Palestine* an eye-witness account of the martyrdoms of that province. The work has reached us in two recensions. The shorter alone is extant in Greek, preserved in four manuscripts of the *Church History* (*Codex Parisinus* 1430, *Codex Laurentianus* 70, 7 and 70, 20, *Codex Mosquensis* 50) as an appendix to the eighth book. Eusebius most probably wrote it soon after the first edition of his main work. The complete text of the longer recension is extant only in an ancient Syriac version. Of its Greek text, however, some fragments remain.

The arrangement is chronological and covers the entire duration of the persecution from 303 to 311. On the basis of this work we are better informed on the course of the persecution in Palestine and on the number of deaths there than in any other province of the East. It enables us to separate the victims of Diocletian from those of Galerius and Maximinus, an impossibility in other localities. During the reign of Diocletian a group of twelve Christians headed by the lector Procopius was sentenced to death in Caesarea. When Maximinus succeeded Diocletian, the persecution worsened. He gave the general order that all citizens should be forced to sacrifice and to eat of the sacrificial meat. The number of those who died as martyrs in this small corner of the Empire during the entire persecution from 303 to 311 is 83. The most famous among them is the presbyter Pamphilus, the teacher and friend of Eusebius. Far more numerous were the confessors: 'It is now no longer possible to tell the incalculable number of those who had their right eye first cut out with a sword and then cauterized with fire, and the left foot rendered useless by the further application of branding irons to the joints', and who after this were condemned to the provincial copper mines' (*Eccl. Hist.* 8, 12, 10 LCL). Eusebius does not hide the fact that in Palestine there were some who proved weak and apostatized at the first assault.

Editions: MG 20, 1457-1520. — New crit. ed.: E. SCHWARTZ, GCS 9, 2 (1908) 907-950. Schwartz has added (911ff.) the Greek fragments of the second and longer edition which were first published by H. DELEHAYE, De martyribus Palaestinae longioris libelli fragmenta: AB 16 (1897) 113-139. — G. BARDY, SCH 55 (1958) 121-174. The Syriac version of this longer edition was edited by W. CURETON, History of the Martyrs of Palestine by Eusebius. London, 1861 (with an English translation). — For the newly discovered Georgian version, see: G. GARITTE, Version géorgienne de la Passion de saint Procope par Eusèbe: Mus 66 (1953) 245-266.

Translations: English: W. CURETON, op. cit. — H. J. LAWLOR and J. E. L. OULTON, Eusebius, The Eccl. History and the Martyrs of Palestine (SPCK), vol. 2. London, 1928. — *German:* The Syriac version was translated into German by B. VIOLET, Die palaestinischen Märtyrer des Eusebius von Caesarea (TU 14, 4). Leipzig, 1896. — M. STIGLOHER, BKV 2 (1880) 614-654. — A. BIGELMAIR, BKV² 9 (1913) 273-313. — *French:* E. GRAPIN, Eusèbe de Césarée, Hist. ecclésiast., vol. 3. Paris, 1913. — G. BARDY, op. cit.

Studies: A. HALMEL, Die palaestinensischen Märtyrer des Eusebius von Caesarea in ihrer zweifachen Form. Essen, 1898. — H. J. LAWLOR, The Chronology of Eusebius' 'Martyrs of Palestine': Hermathena 25 (1908) 177-201. — A. EHRHARD, Überlieferung und Bestand der hagiographischen und homiletischen Literatur der griechischen Kirche I, 1 (TU 50). Leipzig, 1937, 1-18. — S. LIEBERMAN, The Martyrs of Caesarea: AIPh 7 (1939/44) 395-446. — G. RICCIOTTI, Le fonti storiche della persecuzione diocleziana: Orpheus 1 (1954) 59-67. — G. LAZZATI, Nota su Eusebio epitomatore di Atti dei martiri: Studi in onore di A. Calderini e R. Paribeni. Milan, 1956, I, 377-384.

2. *Panegyrics on Constantine*

In his writings on Constantine the Great Eusebius is less an historian than a panegyrist who placed himself and his pen unconditionally at the service of the Emperor both during his lifetime and even after his death, since he regarded his monarchy as the fulfilment of the highest Christian hopes. To Eusebius Constantine was God's chosen emissary to rescue the Church from persecution.

1. *Vita Constantini*

The so-called *Life of Constantine* in four books has perhaps provoked more criticism of Eusebius than any other work of his. Thus J. Burckhardt called him 'the first thoroughly dishonest and unfair historian of ancient times'. This condemnation is pointless because it does not do justice to the literary form of the *Vita*, which is by no means a historical biography but an *encomium* with all its eulogistic and exaggerated tone. Eusebius expressly states that he claims the right of all other imperial panegyrists to treat in the *Life* only what is good in the Emperor's career:

> It will contain a description of those royal and noble actions which are pleasing to God, the Sovereign of all. For would it not be disgraceful that the memory of Nero, and other impious and godless tyrants far worse than he, should meet with diligent writers to embellish the relation of their worthless deeds with elegant language, and record them in voluminous histories, and that I should be silent, to whom God himself has vouchsafed such an emperor as all history records not, and has permitted me to come into his presence, and enjoy his acquaintance and society? Wherefore, if it is the duty of any one, it certainly is mine, to make an ample proclamation of his virtues to

all in whom the example of noble actions is capable of inspiring the love of God. For some who have written the lives of worthless characters, and the history of actions but little tending to the improvement of morals, from private motives, either love or enmity, and possibly in some cases with no better object than the display of their own learning, have exaggerated unduly their description of actions intrinsically base, by a refinement and elegance of diction. And thus they have become to those who by the Divine favor had been kept apart from evil, teachers not of good, but of what should be silenced in oblivion and darkness. But my narrative, however unequal to the greatness of the deeds it has to describe, will yet derive luster even from the bare relation of noble actions. And surely, the record of conduct that has been pleasing to God will afford a far from unprofitable, indeed a most instructive study, to persons of well-disposed minds.

It is my intention, therefore, to pass over the greater part of the royal deeds of this thrice-blessed prince... the design of my present undertaking being to speak and write of those circumstances only which have reference to his religious character. And since these are themselves of almost infinite variety, I shall select from the facts which have come to my knowledge such as are most suitable, and worthy of lasting record, and endeavor to narrate them as briefly as possible. Henceforward, indeed, there is a full and free opportunity for celebrating in every way the praises of this truly blessed prince, which hitherto we have been unable to do, on the ground that we are forbidden to judge any one blessed before his death because of the uncertain vicissitudes of life (1, 10/11 LNPF).

This express acknowledgment of his purpose by the author has often not been taken into account by the critics, misled perhaps by the Latin title *Vita Constantini* under which the panegyric is commonly known. The Greek title is in fact: Εἰς τὸν βίον τοῦ μακαρίου Κωνσταντίνου βασιλέως, which is a better heading for the work. It does not profess to give a complete biographical record but limits itself to the Emperor's actions in so far as they advanced the Christian religion. Thus W. Telfer has recently suggested to render the Greek title in some such form as *Reflections on the Life of Constantine* (*Studia Patristica* I, p. 157).

The author paints a vivid picture of Constantine, 'who alone of all that ever wielded the Roman power was the friend of God, the Sovereign of all, and appeared to all mankind so clear an example of a godly life' (1, 3), whom God distinguished 'as at once a mighty luminary and most clear-voiced herald of genuine piety' (1, 4), who as the 'new Moses', delivered the new race of the chosen people from the tyrants and from the bondage of the enemies (1, 12). He gives (1, 27-32) a detailed description of Constantine's vision of the Cross and asserts that the Emperor on his oath assured him of the fact. The sixteen imperial orders and letters which Eusebius incorporated into the *encomium* and which amount to one fourth of the whole matter are extremely valuable. Their authenticity has been successfully defended by I. A. Heikel in his edition of the *Vita*, after A. Crivellucci and others had expressed their doubts.

The present form of the *Vita* raises some difficult questions. G. Pasquali has demonstrated that it is not the original work, the final revision of which was interrupted by Eusebius' death and published only posthumously. What has been handed down to us, has been considerably enlarged by inserted documents. J. Maurice thought that he found a tendency to justify the Arian policy of Constantius II in several passages, which, therefore, could not have been written by Eusebius. W. Seston contended that the whole account of the Vision of the Cross is an interpolation of the Theodosian period. H. Grégoire maintained that the *Life of Constantine* remained unknown during the whole of the fourth century and that it contains errors, falsifications and untruths which in such a form cannot be attributed to an historian like Eusebius; a Eusebian nucleus was possible, but the present form was of later date. P. Petit, P. Orgels and G. Downey have supported this thesis and pointed to other insertions and falsehoods. F. Scheidweiler went further, even questioning the existence of a Eusebian core, and put the entire work later than 430. In a more recent study he attributed most of the *Vita* to Eusebius, the rest to Gelasius. However, N. H. Baynes refuted most of the arguments of Pasquali and Maurice, and P. Franchi de' Cavalieri, F. Vittinghoff, J. Vogt and K. Aland those of the others. Nobody will reject the probability of a later revision. However, many of the reasons so far given for alterations of the original and for the date and purpose of such changes are such that they in many cases contradict and exclude one another. The difficulties created by the text in several passages have been too eagerly 'solved' by the theory of later interpolations. As a result new difficulties arise which make the posthumous Eusebius an even more complicated figure than the old and original one.

The *Vita Constantini* remains a genuine work of Eusebius though its plan and composition need further clarification. A fresh examination of the incorporated Constantinian documents and their authenticity has been undertaken by H. Kraft. A recently published papyrus has strikingly confirmed the genuineness of one of the edicts cited by Eusebius. The papyrus is *Papyrus London* 878 and was drawn up not long after 320. The text written on the back of the petition proved to be part of Constantine's letter to the provincials issued after the defeat of Licinius and it corresponds verbatim with Eusebius, *Vita Constantini* 2, 27 and 28, with the end of 26 and the opening of 29. Thus we have here in *Papyrus London*

878 a contemporary copy of the letter of A.D. 324, which had been called a falsification. A. H. M. Jones remarks: 'The papyrus proves beyond all reasonable doubt the authenticity of one of the Constantinian documents cited by Eusebius in the *Life*, and implies that of the rest. It does not of course prove that the *Life* in which they are quoted is a work of Eusebius, but I find it difficult to believe that a later forger would have troubled to search out the originals of old documents and copy them *in extenso*' (p. 200).

Editions: MG 20, 905-1440. — New crit. ed.: I. A. Heikel, GCS 7 (1902) 1-148.

Translations: English: E. C. Richardson, LNPF ser. 2, vol. 1 (1890) 481-540 (revision of the translation first published by S. Bagster, London, 1845). — *German:* J. Molzberger, Eusebius: BKV (1880) vol. 2, 11-225. — J. M. Pfättisch, BKV² 9 (1913) 1-190.

Studies: A. Crivellucci, Della fede storica di Eusebio nella Vita di Costantino. Livorno, 1888. — I. A. Heikel, op. cit. LXVI-LXXXII; *idem*, Kritische Beiträge zu den Konstantin-Schriften des Eusebius (TU 36, 4). Leipzig, 1911. — G. Pasquali, Die Komposition der Vita Constantini des Eusebius: Hermes 45 (1910) 369-386. — A. Casamassa, I documenti della 'Vita Constantini' di Eusebio Cesariense. Rome, 1914. — P. Batiffol, Les documents de la Vita Constantini: Bulletin d'ancienne littérature et d'archéologie chrétienne 4 (1914) 80-95 (regards 9 of the inserted letters as authentic and 6 as Semi-Arian forgeries). — F. J. Dölger, Die Taufe Konstantins und ihre Probleme: RQ Supplementheft 19 (1913) 377-447. — A. Baumstark, Die Modestianischen und die Konstantinischen Bauten am Heiligen Grabe zu Jerusalem. Paderborn, 1915, 65-74 (*Vita* 33-39). — H. Schrörs, Die Bekehrung Konstantins in der Überlieferung: ZkTh 40 (1916) 238-257; *idem*, Zur Kreuzeserscheinung Konstantins des Grossen: ZkTh 40 (1916) 485-523. — J. Maurice, La Vita Constantini: Bulletin de la Société nationale des Antiquaires de France (1919) 154-155. — P. Mickley, Die Konstantin-Kirchen im Heiligen Lande. Eusebius-Texte übersetzt und erläutert. Leipzig, 1923. — H. Baynes, Constantine the Great and the Christian Church (Raleigh Lecture on History. Proceedings of the British Academy 1929) 341-442; *idem*, Eusebius and the Christian Empire: Mélanges Bidez. Brussels, 1934, 13-18. — F. Staehelin, Constantin der Grosse und das Christentum: Zeitschrift für Schweizerische Geschichte 17 (1937) 385-417; *idem*, Nachlese zu Constantin: ibid. 19 (1939) 396-403. — G. Stuhlfaut, Konstantins Bauten am Heiligen Grabe in Jerusalem: ThBl 16 (1937) 177-188 (*Vita* 3, 33-39). — H. Lietzmann, Der Glaube Konstantins des Grossen: SAB Phil.-hist. Klasse (1937) 263ff. — I. Daniele, I documenti Costantiniani della 'Vita Constantini' di Eusebio di Cesarea (Analecta Gregoriana 13). Rome, 1938. — G. H. Evers, Zu den Konstantinsbauten am Heiligen Grabe in Jerusalem: Zeitschrift für ägyptische Sprache und Altertum 75 (1939) 53-60 (*Vita* 33-39). — H. Grégoire, Eusèbe n'est pas l'auteur de la 'Vita Constantini' dans sa forme actuelle, et Constantin ne s'est pas 'converti' en 312: Byz 13 (1938) 561-583; cf. N. H. Baynes, BZ 39 (1939) 466-469 (does not agree with Grégoire). — H. Grégoire, La vision de Constantin 'liquidée': Byz 14 (1939) 341-351; *idem*, Les pierres qui crient. Les chrétiens et l'oracle de Didyme: Byz 14 (1939) 318-321 (*Vita* 2, 50). — J. Zeiller, Quelques remarques sur la 'vision' de Constantin (et la Vita Constantini): Byz 14 (1939) 329-339. — A. Alfoeldi, Hoc signo victor eris. Beiträge zur Geschichte der Bekehrung Konstantins des Grossen: Pisciculi. Festschrift F. J. Dölger. Münster, 1939, 1-18. — H. Eger, Kaiser und Kirche in der Geschichtstheologie Eusebs von Caesarea: ZNW 38 (1939) 97-115. — J. Straub, Vom Herrscherideal in der Spätantike. Stuttgart, 1939, 113-129; *idem*, Konstantins christliches Sendungsbewusstsein: Das neue Bild der Antike 2 (1942) 374-394. — K. M. Setton, Christian Attitude towards the Emperor in the Fourth Century. New York, 1941, 40-56. — G. Stuhlfaut, Um die Kirchenbauten Konstantins des

Grossen auf Golgotha: ZKG (1941) 332-340. — E. Honigmann, The Original List of the Members of the Council of Nicaea (and the Vita Constantini): Byz 16 (1942/43) 20-80. — J. Vogt, Streitfragen um Konstantin den Grossen: MDAI (1943) 190-203 (for authenticity of the *Vita*). — W. Seston, Constantine as a Bishop: JRS 37 (1947) 127-131 (*Vita Constant.* 4, 24 and 1, 44). — H. Berkhof, Kirche und Kaiser. Eine Untersuchung der Entstehung der byzantinischen und theokratischen Staatsauffassung im 4. Jahrh. Zurich, 1947. — J. Vogt, Berichte über Kreuzeserscheinungen aus dem 4. Jahrhundert n. Chr.: AIPh 9 (1949) 593-606; *idem*, Constantin der Grosse und sein Jahrhundert. Munich, 1949. — A. Piganiol, L'état actuel de la question constantinienne: Historia 1 (1950) 82-96; *idem*, Sur quelques passages de la Vita Constantini: AIPh 10 (1950) 513-518 (against Grégoire). — H. Grégoire, Les persécutions dans l'empire romain, Brussels, 1951. Note complémentaire 12, 153-156; *idem*, L'authenticité de la Vita Constantini attribuée à Eusèbe de Césarée: BAB ser. 5, vol. 39 (1953) 462-479. — G. Downey, The Builder of the Original Church of the Apostles at Constantinople. A Contribution to the Criticism of the Vita Constantini Attributed to Eusebius: DOP 6 (1951) 53-80. — H. Karpp, Konstantin der Grosse und die Kirche: Theologische Rundschau N.F. 19 (1950) 1-21. — L. Petit, Libanius et la Vita Constantini: Historia 1 (1950) 562-582 (date of the *Vita*: 340); *idem*, Sur la date du Pro templis de Libanius: Byz 21 (1951) 285-310. — J. R. Palanque, Constantin, empereur chrétien d'après ses récents historiens: Études Mediévales offertes à M. le Doyen Fliche. Montpellier, 1952, 133-142. — E. Wistrand, Konstantins Kirche am Heiligen Grabe: Acta Univ. Gotoburg. 55, 1 (1952). — K. F. Stroheker, Das konstantinische Jahrhundert im Lichte der Neuerscheinungen 1940-1951: Saeculum 3 (1952) 654-680. — P. Orgels, A propos des erreurs historiques de la Vita Constantini: AIPh 12 (1952) 575-611. — F. E. Cranz, Kingdom and Polity in Eusebius of Caesarea: HThR 45 (1952) 47-66. — F. Vittinghoff, Eusebius als Verfasser der Vita Constantini: RhM 96 (1953) 330-373. — P. Franchi de' Cavalieri, Constantiniana (ST 171). Vatican City, 1953, 51-65. — E. Delaruelle, La conversion de Constantin, État de la question: BLE 54 (1953) 37-54, 84-100. — F. Scheidweiler, Die Kirchengeschichte des Gelasios von Kaisareia: BZ 46 (1953) 277-301. — J. Moreau, Sur la vision de Constantin: REAN 55 (1953) 307-333; *idem*, A propos de la persécution de Domitien: NC 5 (1953) 121-129. — L. Voelkl, Die konstantinischen Kirchenbauten nach Eusebius: RAC 29 (1953) 49-66, 187-206. — J. Vogt, Der Erbauer der Apostelkirche in Konstantinopel: Hermes 81 (1953) 111-117 (against Downey); *idem*, Die Vita Constantini des Eusebius über den Konflikt zwischen Konstantin und Licinius: Historia 2 (1954) 463-471 (against late redaction of *Vita Const.*); *idem*, Die Bekehrung Constantins: Relazioni X. Congresso int. Scienze storiche 6 (1955) 733-779. — K. Aland, Eine Wende in der Konstantin-Forschung: FF 28 (1954) 213-217 (discussion of recent studies). — A. H. M. Jones, Notes on the Genuineness of the Constantinian Documents in Eusebius's Life of Constantine: JEH 5 (1954) 196-200. — H. Dörries, Das Selbstzeugnis Kaiser Konstantins (AGWG Phil.-hist. Kl., 3. Folge, Nr. 34). Göttingen, 1954. — V. C. De Clercq, Ossius of Cordova (SCA 13). Washington, 1954, 153-158. — J. Moreau, Zum Problem der Vita Constantini: Historia 4 (1955) 234-245; *idem*, Vérité historique et propagande politique chez Lactance et dans la Vita Constantini: Annales Universitatis Saraviensis 4 (1955) 89-97. — H. Kraft, Kaiser Konstantins religiöse Entwicklung (BHTh 20). Tübingen, 1955. — A. Ehrhardt, Constantins des Grossen Religionspolitik und Gesetzgebung: ZSR 72 (1955) 127-190. — W. Seston, L'empire chrétien: Relazioni X. Congresso int. Scienze storiche 6 (1955) 792-796. — J. Vogt, Constantin der Grosse: RACh Fasc. 19 (1956) 362-364 — J. R. Palanque, Constantin le Grand: DHG 13 (1956) 593-608. — F. Scheidweiler, Nochmals die Vita Constantini: BZ 49 (1956) 1-32 (the greater part of the *Vita* must be attributed to Eusebius, the rest to Gelasius). — Petersen, Zur Religionspolitik der Tetrarchie, 303-313: Dansk Teol. Tidsskrift 19 (1956) 25-64 (against authenticity). — J. G. Davies, Eusebius' Description of the Martyrium at Jerusalem: AJA 61 (1957) 171-173 (*Vita Const.* 3, 38). —

L. H. VINCENT, L'Éléona, sanctuaire primitif de l'Ascension: RBibl 64 (1957) 48-71 (*Vita* 3, 41, 3). — K. ALAND, Kaiser und Kirche von Konstantin bis Byzanz: Berliner Byzantinistische Arbeiten 5 (1957) 188-212; *idem*, Die religiöse Haltung Kaiser Konstantins: SP I (TU 63). Berlin, 1957, 549-600. — H. KRAFT, Zur Taufe Konstantins: ibid. 642-648. — J. STRAUB, Kaiser Konstantin als ἐπίσκοπος τῶν ἐκτός: ibid. 678-695 (*Vita* 4, 24). — W. TELFER, The Author's Purpose in the Vita Constantini: ibid. 157-167; *idem*, Constantine's Holy Land Plan: ibid. 696-700 (*Vita* 3, 25-53). — L. VOELKL, Der Kaiser Konstantin. Annalen einer Zeitenwende. Munich, 1957. — C. HABICHT, Zur Geschichte des Kaisers Konstantin: Hermes 86 (1958) 360-378 (*Vita* 1, 48 - 2, 18). — H. DÖRRIES, Konstantin der Grosse. Stuttgart, 1958.

2. *Ad coetum sanctorum*

Eusebius reports in his *Life of Constantine* (4, 29) that the Emperor spent much of his time composing and delivering sermons, in which he exposed the error of polytheism and proved the superstition of the Gentiles to be mere fraud: 'He then would assert the sole sovereignty of God, passing thence to His Providence, both general and particular. Proceeding next to the dispensation of salvation, he would demonstrate its necessity, and adaptation to the nature of the case; entering next in order on the doctrine of Divine judgment... He reminded them that God Himself had given him the empire of the world, portions of which he himself, acting on the same Divine principle, had entrusted to their government; but that all would in due time be alike summoned to give account of their actions to the Supreme Sovereign of all' (LNPF). Eusebius adds:

> The Emperor was in the habit of composing his orations in the Latin tongue, from which they were translated into Greek by interpreters appointed for this special service. One of the discourses thus translated I intend to annex by way of specimen, to this present work, that one, I mean, which he inscribed *To the Assembly of the Saints*, and dedicated to the Church of God, that no one may have ground for deeming my testimony on this head mere empty praise (4, 32 LNPF).

The manuscripts of the *Vita Constantini* have indeed an appendix to the fourth book: *Oration of the Emperor Constantine which he addressed To The Assembly of the Saints*. The best manuscript calls it the fifth book of the *Vita*. Its text begins Κωνσταντῖνος Σεβαστὸς τῷ τῶν ἁγίων συλλόγῳ. It is an apology for the Christian religion. The introduction (1-2) contains the salutation and refers to the Day of the Passion, which has arrived as the prelude of the Resurrection. The first main part (3-10) deals with God, the Father of Christ, as the Creator and only Lord of the universe. It refutes the error of idolatry (4), the false concepts of the pagans, the superstitious belief in fate and chance (6) as well as the mistaken notions of the philosophers (9). In Plato's doctrines it is determined what can be accepted and what must be rejected. The mythological fictions of the poets are repudiated (10).

The second, more positive, part (11-15) treats of the Christian doctrine of Redemption through the crucified Christ who is God and God's Son. The author then (16-17) shows that the coming of Christ was foretold by the Prophets of the Old Testament. Even the pagan oracles are adduced as proof for the Divine nature of Christ (18). Thus the Erythraean Sibyl is cited: 'On one occasion, however, having rushed into the sanctuary of her vain superstition, she became really filled with inspiration from above, and declared in prophetic verses the future purposes of God; plainly indicating the advent of Jesus by the initial letters of these verses, forming an acrostic in these words: JESUS CHRIST, SON OF GOD, SAVIOUR, CROSS' (cf. vol. I, p. 169). The fourth eclogue of Vergil is given a detailed interpretation verse by verse as a prophecy predicting the Incarnation and Redemption (19-21).

In the third part (22-25) the Emperor attributes his victories to Christ, describes the miserable end of those rulers who persecuted the Church, and in the final chapter (26) stresses the duty of rendering thanks to the Saviour for all blessings bestowed on his government and his person.

Although all the manuscripts of the *Vita* contain this *Address to the Assembly of the Saints* and Eusebius explicitly declares his intention of appending it to the *Vita*, serious doubts have been voiced against its authenticity. Besides J. P. Rossignol and A. Mancini, it was especially I. A. Heikel who emphatically denied its genuineness after a careful examination of its sources and a detailed comparison with the true orations and letters of the Emperor. On the other hand, the number of scholars who unreservedly favor Constantine's authorship is by no means small. A. v. Harnack (*Chronol.* 2, 116) and E. Schwartz (PWK 6, 1427) are among its outstanding defenders. Moreover, J. M. Pfättisch came to the conclusion that the oration is a Good Friday Sermon composed between 313 and 325 and of great importance for the religious convictions of the first Christian emperor. He thought that it was in part a real translation from the Latin and in part a paraphrase in Greek by one of the imperial theological secretaries of an outline or draft prepared by Constantine. A. Kurfess maintained the authenticity in a series of articles which studied the Latin basis of the Greek text, its relation to the Sibylline Oracles and its date. He believed that the sermon was delivered on Good Friday 313, whereas A. Piganiol preferred April 7, 323. The latter regarded Constantine as its author but Lactantius as its reviser. More recently, H. Dörries after a renewed comparison of its ideas and style with those of the genuine imperial documents reached the conclusion that it would be easier to solve the difficulties than to suppose a forgery.

Editions: MG 20, 1253-1316. — New crit. ed.: I. A. HEIKEL, GCS 7 (1902) 149-192. *Translations: English:* E. C. RICHARDSON, LNPF ser. 2, vol. 1 (1890) 561-580. — *German:* J. MOLZBERGER, Eusebius: BKV (1880) vol. 2, 235-287. — J. M. PFÄTTISCH, BKV² 9 (1913) 191-272.

Studies: J. P. ROSSIGNOL, Virgile et Constantin le Grand. 1845. — A. MANCINI, La pretesa Oratio Constantini ad sanctorum coetum: Studi Storici 3 (1894) 92-117, 207-227. — I. A. HEIKEL, GCS 7 (1902) XCI-CII; *idem*, Kritische Beiträge zu den Constantin-Schriften des Eusebius (TU 36, 4). Leipzig, 1911, 2ff. — F. J. DÖLGER, IXΘYC. Das Fischsymbol in frühchristlicher Zeit. I. Band. Rome, 1910, 52-68. — J. M. PFÄTTISCH, Die Rede Konstantins des Grossen an die Versammlung der Heiligen auf ihre Echtheit untersucht. Freiburg i.B., 1908; *idem*, Platos Einfluss auf die Rede Konstantins an die Versammlung der Heiligen: ThQ 92 (1910) 399-417; *idem*, Die vierte Ekloge Vergils in der Rede Konstantins an die Versammlung der Heiligen (Progr.). Munich, 1913; *idem*, Die Rede Konstantins an die Versammlung der Heiligen (RQ Supplementheft 19: Konstantin der Grosse und seine Zeit, herausg. v. F. J. Dölger). Freiburg i.B., 1913, 96-121. — A. KURFESS, Observatiunculae ad P. Vergilii Maronis eclogae quartae interpretationem et versionem Graecam: Mnem (1912) 277-284; *idem*, Platos Timaeus in Kaiser Konstantins Rede an die heilige Versammlung: ZNW 19 (1919/20) 72-81; *idem*, Curae Constantinianae. Berlin, 1920; *idem*, Kaiser Konstantins Rede an die Versammlung der Heiligen, eine Karfreitagsrede vom Jahre 313: Verhandlungen der Versammlung Deutscher Philologen (1929) 130-131; *idem*, Zu Kaiser Konstantins Rede an die Versammlung der Heiligen: PhW 50 (1930) 366-368; *idem*, Kaiser Konstantins Karfreitagsrede im Jahre 313: Festschrift P. Meyer. Münstereifel, 1933, 26-30. — A. PIGANIOL, RHPR 12 (1932) 369-372. — A. KURFESS, Der griechische Übersetzer von Virgils vierter Ekloge in Kaiser Konstantins Rede an die Versammlung der Heiligen: ZNW 35 (1936) 97-100; *idem*, Latein-Griechisch: Glotta 25 (1936) 274-276 (Constantine composed the *Oratio* in Latin); *idem*, Kaiser Konstantin und die Sibylle: ThQ 117 (1936) 11-27; *idem*, Die griechische Übersetzung der vierten Ekloge Vergils: Mnem 3, 5 (1937) 282-288; *idem*, Zur Echtheitsfrage und Datierung der Rede Konstantins an die Versammlung der Heiligen: ZRG 1 (1948) 355-358; *idem*, ThGl (1949) 167-174; *idem*, ThQ (1950) 145-165; *idem*, Kaiser Konstantin und die Erythräische Sibylle: ZRG 4 (1952) 42-57. — A. BOLHUIS, Vergils 4. Ecloga in der Oratio Constantini ad sanctorum coetum. Diss. Amsterdam, 1950; *idem*, Die Rede Konstantins des Grossen an die Versammlung der Heiligen und Lactantius' Divinae Institutiones: VC 10 (1956) 25-32. — H. DÖRRIES Das Selbstzeugnis Kaiser Konstantins. Göttingen, 1954, 129-161. — J. VOGT, RACh Fasc. 19 (1956) 364-367.

3. Laudes Constantini

The *Oratio ad coetum sanctorum* is followed in the manuscripts of the *Vita* by the *Laus Constantini*. This misleading title combines in reality two different works.

a. Chapters 1-10 represent the panegyric which Eusebius delivered in the palace at Constantinople on July 25, 335, the thirtieth anniversary of Constantine's reign. Eusebius begins with the assurance that he intends to avoid any display of rhetoric. He believes that the Emperor is a human being set apart from other human beings in that he is 'perfect in wisdom, in goodness, in justice, in courage, in piety, in devotion to God: the Emperor truly and he alone is a philosopher, for he knows himself, and he is fully aware that an abundance of every blessing is showered on him from a source quite external to himself, even from heaven itself' (5). Eusebius compares him to the sun: 'Thus our Emperor, like the radiant sun, illuminates the most distant subjects of his empire through the presence of his Caesars, as with the far piercing rays of his own brightness' (3). His Empire is 'the imitation of the monarchical power in heaven' (5), because he has consciously modelled his government after that in heaven:

> Invested as he is with a semblance of heavenly sovereignty, he directs his gaze above, and frames his earthly government according to the pattern of that Divine original, feeling strength in its conformity to the monarchy of God. And this conformity is granted by the universal Sovereign to man alone of the creatures of this earth: for He alone is the author of the sovereign power, Who decreed that all should be subject to the rule of the one. And surely monarchy far transcends every other constitution and form of government: for that democratic equality of power, which is its opposite, may rather be described as anarchy and disorder (3 LNPF).

Throughout the rest of the oration Constantine is praised for his achievements, and for the blessings resulting from the freedom which he gave to the Church. In the last chapter Eusebius refers again to Constantine's own sermon: 'Discourses and precepts and exhortations to a virtuous and holy life, are proclaimed in the ears of all nations. Nay, the Emperor himself proclaims them: and it is indeed a marvel that this mighty prince, raising his voice in the hearing of all the world, like an interpreter of the Almighty Sovereign's will, invites his subjects in every country to the knowledge of the true God' (10 LNPF).

b. In chapters 11-18 of the *Laudes Constantini* we possess not an oration but the treatise which Eusebius presented to the Emperor at the dedication of the Church of the Holy Sepulchre (335). Although on the whole an apologetic tract, its first purpose is to justify the erection of the magnificent building: 'Those lofty and noble structures, imperial monuments of an imperial spirit, which thou hast erected in honor of the everlasting memory of the Saviour's tomb, the cause, I say, of these things is not equally obvious to all... The ignorant and spiritually blind regard these designs with open mockery and scorn, and deem it a strange and unworthy thing indeed that so mighty a prince should waste his zeal on the graves and monuments of the dead... In full persuasion, then, of thy approval, most mighty Emperor, I desire at this present time to proclaim to all the reasons and motives of thy pious works' (11, 2. 3. 7). However, with this special goal Eusebius combines a wider and more general one, since he sees in the Church of the Holy Sepulchre a symbol of the Emperor's God-given mission:

> I desire to stand as the interpreter of thy designs, to explain the counsels of a soul devoted to the love of God. I propose to teach all men, what all should know who care to understand the principles on which our Saviour God employs His power, the reasons for which He Who was the pre-existent Controller of all things at length descended to us from heaven: the reasons for which He assumed our nature, and submitted even to the power of death. I shall declare the causes of that immortal life which followed, and of His resurrection from the dead. Once more, I shall adduce convincing proofs and arguments, for the sake of those who yet need such testimony: and now let me commence my appointed task (11, 7).

Thus the author offers an introduction for pagan readers to the Christian faith, which consists mainly of a summary of the first three books of his *Theophany* (cf. below, p. 332) adapted to this special occasion.

Editions: MG 20, 1316-1440. — New crit. ed.: I. A. HEIKEL, GCS 7 (1902) 193-259.

Translation: English: E. C. RICHARDSON, LNPF ser. 2, vol. 1 (1890) 581-610.

Studies: N. H. BAYNES, Eusebius and the Christian Empire: Mélanges Bidez. Brussels, 1934, 13-18 (*Laus Constant.* 1-10; Eusebius appropriates the Hellenistic philosophy of kingship). — E. PETERSON, Der Monotheismus als politisches Problem. Ein Beitrag zur Geschichte der politischen Theologie im Imperium Romanum. Leipzig, 1935, 71-82. — K. M. SETTON, Christian Attitude towards the Emperor in the Fourth Century, Especially As Shown in Addresses to the Emperor. New York, 1941, 46-54.

3. Apologetic Works

In his apologetic treatises Eusebius sums up the entire literary efforts of the past for the defense of the Christian religion. He combines the ideas of the Greek Apologists with a new scholarly method, which overwhelms the reader by a plenitude of facts and arguments drawn from his amazing knowledge of ancient literature and history. Still he never loses himself in details but, following a well-conceived and clearly executed plan, he attempts to present in a grand historical vision the great religions of the past as a whole and as a preparation for the new. Unfortunately, some of his writings, which originally formed parts of this project, are no longer extant.

1. General Elementary Introduction

The oldest of his apologetic works is the *General Elementary Introduction* to the gospel, which he composed before he became a bishop.

It consisted originally of ten books, of which only books 6-9 and some few additional fragments are extant. This second part provides under the special title *Eclogae Propheticae* a collection and brief explanation of the Messianic prophecies of the Old Testament.

Editions: MG 22, 1021-1262. — New crit. ed.: T. GAISFORD, Eclogae propheticae. Oxford, 1842.

Studies: H. NOLTE, ThQ 43 (1861) 95-109 (textual crit.). — W. SELWYN, Journal of Philology 4 (1872) 275-280 (textual crit.). — G. MERCATI, La grande lacuna delle Ecloghe profetiche di Eusebio di Cesarea: Mémorial L. Petit. Bucarest, 1948, 1-3. — J. R. LAURIN, Orientations maîtresses des apologistes chrétiens de 270 à 361. Rome, 1954, 124-130.

2. *Praeparatio Evangelica*

The *General Elementary Introduction* served as preliminary studies for his great apologetic work in two parts: the *Preparation for the Gospel* and the *Proof for the Gospel*. The former is complete in fifteen books, all of which are extant in the original Greek. Its object is to refute pagan polytheism and show the superiority of the Jewish religion, which served as a 'preparation for the gospel'. Eusebius intended the *Praeparatio* to be 'a guide, by occupying the place of elementary instruction and introduction, and suiting itself to our recent converts from among the heathen' (3). At the beginning of the fifteenth book the author gives a summary of the *Praeparatio*. The first, second and third books expose the obscene and shocking myths of the pagans and attack the allegorical interpretation of them by Neo-Platonists. The fourth and fifth treat of the heathen oracles. The sixth answers those who believe in Fate. The seventh ushers in the second part, which comprises the next seven books and aims to show that the Christians were justified in giving up the religion and philosophy of the Greeks and in accepting the sacred books of the Hebrews. Here we meet again the familiar theme that Moses and the prophets lived long before the greatest Greek philosophers and that in fact the latter, especially Plato, borrowed from the former the best of their ideas. The fourteenth and fifteenth books reveal the contradictions among the Greek thinkers and the essential errors in their doctrines.

The *Praeparatio* opens with a remarkable claim to originality of method: 'the purpose, however, which we have in mind is to be worked out in a way of our own' (7a). In his refutation of idolatry he lets the pagans speak for themselves by the ample use of lengthy quotations from their own literature: 'I shall not set down my own words, but those of the very persons who have taken the deepest interest in the worship of them whom they call gods' (16d). Several passages (1, 4, 2f; 5, 1, 4f) indicate that the pressure of persecution

330 THE WRITERS OF ANTIOCH AND SYRIA

had ceased and peace was established when Eusebius wrote his *Praeparatio*. The allusion (135c) to the punishment of the Antiochene impostors (cf. *Hist. eccl.* 9, 11) by Licinius would place the date after A.D. 314.

Editions: MG 21. — Separate ed.: F. A. HEINICHEN, 2 vols. Leipzig, 1842/43. — T. GAISFORD, 4 vols. Oxford, 1843. — E. H. GIFFORD, Eusebii Pamphili Evangelicae Praeparationes, libri XV, ad codices manuscriptos denuo collatos recensuit, Anglice nunc primum reddidit. 4 vols. Oxford, 1903. — New crit. edition: K. MRAS, Praeparatio Evangelica. Part I: Einleitung, die Bücher I-X: GCS 43, 1 (1954); Part II: Die Bücher XI-XV: GCS 43, 2 (1956).

Translations: English: E. H. GIFFORD, op. cit. The translation was also issued separately in 2 vols. Oxford, 1903. — *Selections:* J. E. DE HIRSCH - DAVIES, Eusebius' Praeparatio Evangelica. Selections from Gaisford's text, translated with short explanatory notes. Lampeter, 1904. — *French:* SÉGUIER DE SAINT BRISSON, Préparation Évangélique d'Eusèbe de Césarée. Paris, 1846.

Studies: I. A. HEIKEL, De Praeparationis Evangelicae Eusebii edendae ratione quaestiones. Helsingfors, 1888. — M. FAULHABER, Die griechischen Apologeten der klassischen Väterzeit. I. Buch: Eusebius von Caesarea. Diss. Würzburg, 1895. — U. v. WILAMOWITZ - MOELLENDORFF, Ein Bruchstück aus der Schrift des Porphyrius gegen die Christen: ZNW 1 (1900) 101-165 (*Praep. Ev.* 1, 2, 1-4). — H. KUIPER, De Ezechiele poeta Judaeo: Mnem (1900) 237-280 (*Praep. Ev.* 9, 28ff., text and translation). — V. COSTANZI, L'imprecazione di Nabucodonosor in Abideno: Atene e Roma (1905) 143-150 (*Praep. Ev.* 9, 41). — H. DOERGENS, Eusebius von Caesarea als Darsteller der phoenizischen Religion (FLDG 12, 5). Paderborn, 1915; idem, Eusebius von Caesarea als Darsteller der griechischen Religion (FLDG 14, 3). Paderborn, 1922. — K. MRAS, Ein Fund bei Eusebius: WSt 47 (1929) 39-42 (*Praep. Ev.* 15, lacunae in the last ch.). — J. WIENEKE, Ezechielis Iudaei poetae Alexandrini fabulae quae inscribitur 'Εξαγωγή fragmenta rec. Münster, 1931 (*Praep. Ev.* 9, 28ff.). — P. HENRY, Recherches sur la 'Préparation Évangélique' d'Eusèbe et l'édition perdue des œuvres de Plotin publiée par Eustochius (Bibl. de l'École des Hautes Études. Sciences relig. T. 20). Paris, 1935; idem, Les états du texte de Plotin. Paris, 1938, 77-124 (*Praep. Ev.* 15, 10, 22). — J. BIDEZ, Le nom et les origines de nos almanachs: AIPh 5 (1937) 77-85. — O. EISSFELDT, Religionsdokument und Religionspoesie, Religionstheorie und Religionshistorie. Ras Schamra und Sanchunjaton. Philo Byblius und Eusebius von Caesarea: ThBl (1938) 185-197; idem, Zur Frage nach dem Alter der phoenizischen Geschichte des Sanchunjaton: FF (1938) 251-252. — K. MRAS, Zu den neu gefundenen Διηγήσεις des Kallimachos: WSt (1938) 45-54 (*Praep. Ev.* 3, 1). — C. PETERS, Zum Namen Abdalonymus: OLZ (1941) 265-268. — C. BONNER, An Unnoticed Fragment of Porphyry: HThR 35 (1942) 8-11 (*Praep. Ev.* 4, 22, 174d-175a). — K. MRAS, Ein Vorwort zur neuen Eusebius-Ausgabe mit Ausblicken auf die spätere Gräzität: RhM 22 (1944) 217-236 (new ed. of *Praep. Ev.*); idem, Meine Eusebius-Ausgabe: AAWW 84 (1947) 115-120 (language of the *Praep.*); idem, Eine neuentdeckte Handschrift des Eusebius: Die österreichische Nationalbibliothek. Festschrift J. Bick. Vienna, 1948, 485-487 (Cod. Athos Vatopedi 180 containing *Praep. Ev.*). — P. NAUTIN, Sanchuniaton chez Philon de Byblos et chez Porphyre: RBibl 56 (1949) 259-273 (*Praep. Ev.* 1, 9-10); idem, La valeur documentaire de l'Histoire phénicienne: RBibl 56 (1949) 573-578 (*Praep. Ev.* 1, 9-10); idem, Trois autres fragments du livre de Porphyre contre les chrétiens: RBibl 57 (1950) 409-416 (*Praep. Ev.* 1, 9-10). — E. DES PLACES, Les Lois de Platon et la Préparation Évangélique d'Eusèbe de Césarée: Aegyptus 32 (1952) 223-231. — O. EISSFELDT, Sanchunjaton von Berut und Ilumiku von Ugarit. Halle, 1952; idem, Taautos und Sanchunjaton. Berlin, 1952; idem, Adrammelek und Demarus: AIPh 13 (1953) 153-159 (Phœnician divinities described by Philo Byblius, quoted in *Praep. Ev.*). — R. FOLLET, Sanchuniaton, personnage mythique ou personne historique?: Bibl 34 (1953) 81-90. — K. MRAS, Zum Schluss der Praeparatio Evangelica des Eusebius: WSt 66 (1953) 92f. — J. R. LAURIN, op. cit. 344-367. — K. MRAS, Ariston von Keos in einem zweiten Bruchstück von Plutarchs Στρωματεῖς: WSt 68 (1955) 88-98 (*Praep. Ev.* 15, 62, 7-13); *idem*, Die Stellung der Praeparatio Evangelica des Eusebius im antiken Schrifttum: AAWW 93 (1956) 209-217 (*Praep. Ev.* contains Greek fragments of the lost works of Amelios, Severus, Numenius, Porphyry, Aristocles, Alexander of Aphrodisias and Abydenus). — E. DES PLACES, Le Platon de Théodoret. Les citations du Phédon, de la République et du Timée: Studi in onore di A. Calderini e R. Paribeni. Milan, 1956, I, 325-336 (Theodoret uses *Praep. Ev.*); *idem*, Eusèbe de Césarée juge de Platon dans la Préparation évangélique: Mélanges A. Diès. Paris, 1956, 69-77. — J. PÉPIN, La théologie tripartite de Varron: REAug 2 (1956) 282-285 (*Praep. Ev.* 3, 17, 1-2; 4, 1, 2-4). — E. DES PLACES, Deux témoins du texte des Lois de Platon: WSt 70 (1957) 254-259. — O. EISSFELDT, Textkritische Bemerkungen zu den in Eusebius' Praeparatio Evangelica enthaltenen Fragmenten des Philo Byblius: WSt 70 (1957) 94-99.

3. *Demonstratio Evangelica*

Whereas the *Praeparatio* defends the Christian religion against the pagans, the *Demonstratio*, as its sequel, answers the accusations of the Jews, that the Christians accepted Judaism only to claim the blessings promised to the chosen people for themselves without accepting the obligation of the Law. Eusebius answers this charge in twenty books, of which only the first ten and a considerable fragment of book 15 are extant. They suffice to show that the author in the *Proof of the Gospel* wrests the Old Testament from the Jews and proves its universal significance and the Christian religion as its fulfilment.

The first two books, which form the introduction, explain why the Christians accept the Jewish Scriptures but reject the legislation of Moses. Christianity is a continuation of the world-wide religion of the patriarchs, from which the Mosaic Law was only a temporary dispensation, serving as a transition between the age of the patriarchs and the coming of Christ. In the second book the author adduces abundant proof from the prophets that the downfall of the Jewish state, the coming of the Messias and the calling of the Gentiles were predicted. Books three to nine produce prophetic evidence for Christ's humanity (Book III), his divinity (Books IV and V), and the incarnation and earthly life of the Saviour (Books VI to IX). Book X treats of his passion and death. The other ten books no longer extant dealt most probably with his resurrection and ascension, the sending of the Holy Spirit and the foundation of the Church. The fragment of Book XV treats of the four kingdoms of the Book of Daniel.

Although nominally directed against pagans and Jews, the *Praeparatio* as well as the *Demonstratio* is really aimed at Porphyry's treatise *Against the Christians*. Eusebius refers to him again and again, and at times even takes from his work the wording of accusations against the Christian religion, e.g. *Praep. ev.* 1, 2, 1-4, thus refuting him out of his own mouth. This device reminds one of Origen's *Contra Celsum* (cf. vol. II, p. 52-57). However, Eusebius abstains from meeting the objections of Porphyry point by point, as Origen did with Celsus. He follows a different course, which does not permit the opponent to draw the author aside from his well-ordered and systematic program of Scriptural exposition into fruitless controversy on points of minor importance. This method proves far more effective and does much toward making his work not only a codification of the results achieved by his predecessors but probably the most important apologetic contribution of the early Church.

As for its date, the *Demonstratio* was most probably written immediately after the *Praeparatio*. Its theological language suggests that the Council of Nicaea was not imminent.

Editions: MG 22, 13-794. — Separatet ed.: T. GAISFORD, 2 vols. Oxford, 1852. New crit. ed.: I. A. HEIKEL, Die Demonstratio Evangelica, GCS 23 (1913).

Translation: English: W. J. FERRAR, The Proof of the Gospel being the Demonstratio Evangelica of Eusebius of Caesarea (SPCK). London, 1920, 2 vols.

Studies: K. LAKE, A Lost Manuscript of Eusebius's Demonstratio Evangelica Found: HThR 16 (1923) 396-397 (Cod. Maurocordati used by Fabricius is Codex Vatopedi 179 of Mt. Athos). — V. G. TASKER, The Text used by Eusebius in Demonstratio Evangelica in quoting from Matthew and Luke: HThR 28 (1935) 61-67. — D. S. WALLACE - HADRILL, An Analysis of Some Quotations from the First Gospel in Eusebius' Demonstratio Evangelica: JThSt N.S. 1 (1950) 168-175; *idem*, Eusebius and the Institution Narrative in the Eastern Liturgies: JThSt N.S. 4 (1953) 41-42 (*Demonstr. Ev.* 7, 1, 28). — J. R. LAURIN, op. cit. 369-380. — H. S. MURPHY, Eusebius' New Testament Text in the Demonstratio Evangelica: JBL 73 (1954) 162-168.

4. *Theophania*

The *Theophany* or *Divine Manifestation* is the last of Eusebius' apologetic works in date. Its subject is the manifestation of God in the Incarnation of the Logos. The author explains and defends this dogma against common objections in five books, which are written in a popular tone but with great rhetorical display. The first three deal with the manifestation of the Logos in the creation of the universe, in its maintenance and in the human mind, with the need of redemption and its final accomplishment by Christ. The fourth shows the fulfilment of the Old Testament prophecies, the fifth the foolishness of the hypothesis that Christ was a sorcerer and his disciples deceivers. The first three books are strongly dependant on the *Praeparatio* and *Demonstratio*. The fourth seems to be a new edition of a monograph on the prophecies fulfilled in Christ, which Eusebius mentions in his *Praeparatio* (1, 3, 12). The fifth reproduces the third book of the *Demonstratio* in its main section, as the author himself admits (4, 37). These literary connections together with the predominant concept of a victorious and flourishing Church, which permeates the entire work, prove that it was composed after 323 and Constantine's accession to sole rulership.

Except for numerous Greek fragments nothing remains of the original. But a very slavish Syriac translation has preserved the entire text. The latter must have been made at an early time, because the British Museum in London possesses a manuscript of it dated February 411 A.D.

Editions: Greek fragments: MG 24, 609-690. — New crit. ed.: H. GRESSMANN, Die Theophanie. Die griechischen Bruchstücke und Übersetzung der syrischen Überlieferungen, GCS 11, 2 (1904). — Syriac text: S. LEE, London, 1842.

Translations: English: S. LEE, Eusebius of Caesarea on the Theophania or Divine Manifestation of Our Lord and Saviour Jesus Christ, translated into English with notes, from an ancient Syriac version of the Greek original. Cambridge, 1843. — *German:* H. GRESSMANN, op. cit.

Studies: H. GRESSMANN, Studien zu Eusebs Theophanie (TU 23, 3). Leipzig, 1903. — F. J. DÖLGER, Zur antiken Embryotomie. Ihre moralische Bewertung durch Eusebius von Caesarea: AC 4 (1934) 280-281 (*Theoph.* 1, 71). — C. PETERS, Die Zitate aus dem Matthäus-Evangelium in der syrischen Übersetzung der Theophanie des Eusebius: OC 11 (1936) 1-25. — J. QUASTEN, Der Gute Hirte in hellenistischer und frühchristlicher Logostheologie: Heilige Überlieferung. Festschrift J. Herwegen. Münster, 1938, 51-58 (*Theoph.* 2, 83; 4, 24).

5. *Against Porphyry*

The powerful attack of Porphyry, the famous Neo-Platonist, in his fifteen books *Against the Christians* called forth a special refutation by Eusebius in twenty-five books which has entirely perished. Jerome (*De vir. ill.* 81, *Ep.* 70), Socrates (*Hist. eccl.* 3, 23) and Philostorgius (*Hist. eccl.* 8, 14) mention it and the first gives some hint of its contents (*Comm. in Dan.*, Prol.; *Comm. in Matth.*, ad 24, 16). The polemic apparently centered around the correct interpretation of some Gospel passages; Porphyry made much of the supposed contradictions in the Gospels about the genealogies of Jesus and about the accounts of the Resurrection.

Editions: Collected fragments ed. by E. PREUSCHEN in: A. HARNACK, Geschichte der altchristlichen Literatur 1, 2, 564f. — New fragment: E. v. D. GOLTZ, Eine textkritische Arbeit des 10. bzw. 6. Jahrhunderts (TU 17, 4). Leipzig, 1899, 41f.

6. *Against Hierocles*

The treatise against Porphyry was preceded by a refutation of Hierocles, the governor of Bithynia and author of a polemic alleging the superiority of Apollonius of Tyana to Jesus. The text of the small tract is preserved in the famous Codex of Arethas at Paris (cf. vol. I, p. 188). It is one of Eusebius' earliest works, composed most probably between 311 and 313, or even earlier.

Editions: MG 22, 795-868. — New crit. ed. by T. GAISFORD, Oxford, 1852 (together with *Contra Marcellum* and *De ecclesiastica theologia*). — The text is also found in the edition of the writings of Flavius Philostratus: C. L. KAYSER, Philostrati Opera. Leipzig, 1870, vol. 1, 369-413. Kayser's text was reprinted by F. C. CONYBEARE, Philostratus, The Life of Apollonius of Tyana and the Treatise of Eusebius Against Hierocles (LCL). London, 1912.

Translation: English: F. C. CONYBEARE, op. cit. 483-605.

Studies: M. FAULHABER, Die griechischen Apologeten der klassischen Väterzeit. I. Buch: Eusebius von Caesarea. Würzburg, 1895, 108-121. — H. DOERGENS, Apollonius von Tyana in Parallele zu Christus: ThGl 25 (1933) 292-304.

7. *Refutation and Defence*

Photius (*Bibl. cod.* 13) mentions that he read this work consisting of two books and that it was at his time extant in two slightly different editions. Both of them are lost. From his remarks it is evident that it was an apology answering pagan objections to the Christian religion. He thinks that Eusebius solved certain difficulties 'satisfactorily, though not entirely'.

4. *Biblical and Exegetical Works*

Eusebius deserves special credit for his efforts to provide a reliable edition of the Bible. With the assistance of his friend Pamphilus he reproduced Origen's Septuagint (the fifth column of the *Hexapla*) as a detached work with alternative readings from other versions on the margin. The history of the critical text of the Old and New Testaments is intimately connected with his and his friend's name and not a few of the extant manuscripts of the Bible go back to codices made by them. It was to Eusebius that Constantine turned when he needed fifty copies for the churches of Constantinople. In a letter the Emperor entrusted him with their preparation:

> It happens, through the favouring providence of God our Saviour, that great numbers have united themselves to the most holy Church in the city which is called by my name. It seems therefore highly requisite, since that city is rapidly advancing in prosperity in all other respects, that the number of churches should also be increased. Do you therefore receive with all readiness my determination on this behalf. I have thought it expedient to instruct your Prudence to order fifty copies of the Sacred Scriptures, the provision and use of which you know to be most needful for the instruction of the Church, to be written on prepared parchment in a legible manner, and in a convenient portable form, by professional transcribers thoroughly practised in their art. The Catholicus of the diocese has also received instructions

from our Clemency to be careful to furnish all things necessary for the preparation of such copies; and it will be for you to take special care that they be completed with as little delay as possible (*Vita Const.* 4, 36 LNPF).

Studies: J. SCHÄFER, Die fünfzig Bibelhandschriften des Eusebius für den Kaiser Konstantin: Der Katholik (1913) I, 90-104. — C. WENDEL, Der Bibel-Auftrag Kaiser Konstantins: ZBW 56 (1939) 165-175. — D. VOLTURNO, The Four Gospel Text of Eusebius. Diss. Boston, 1956 (microfilm). — D. S. WALLACE - HADRILL, Eusebius and the Gospel Text of Caesarea: HThR 49 (1956) 105-114. — M. J. SUGGS, The Eusebian Text of Matthew: Novum Testamentum I (1956) 233-245; *idem*, Eusebius and the Gospel Text: HThR 50 (1957) 307-310.

1. *The Evangelical Canons*

Eusebius introduced an important innovation into the Gospel manuscripts. It is a device for forming a sort of Harmony of the Gospels by showing which passages in each Gospel have parallel passages in any of the others. In his letter to Carpianus he explains the entire system and mentions that it was suggested to him by the *Gospel Harmony* or *Sections* of Ammonius of Alexandria (cf. vol. II, p. 101), which arrange the Gospels in four parallel columns. He developed the plan of Ammonius still further, wishing to remedy the disadvantage of his system, which permitted only the Gospel of Matthew to be read continuously.

He first divided the Gospels into small sections which were numbered in succession. He then prepared a table of ten canons, each containing a list of passages in the following order: Canon I. passages common to all four gospels; II. those common to the synoptics; III. those common to Matthew, Luke and John; IV. those common to Matthew, Mark and John; V. those common to Matthew and Luke; VI. those common to Matthew and Mark; VII. those common to Matthew and John; VIII. those common to Luke and Mark; IX. those common to Luke and John; X. those peculiar to each Gospel: first to Matthew, second to Mark, third to Luke, and fourth to John. These tables used in combination with the numbers of the sections in the text of the Gospels enable the reader to discover at a glance the parallel passages. The system passed over into Syriac and Latin manuscripts and became known as the *Eusebian Canons* or *Eusebian Sections*. St. Jerome adopted it for his Vulgate and gives an explanation of it in his letter to Pope Damasus.

Editions: MG 22, 1275-1292. — For editions of the letter to Carpianus, see below p. 345. *Studies:* G. H. GWILLIAM, The Ammonian Sections, Eusebian Canons, and Harmonizing Tables in the Syriac Tetra-evangelium: Studia Biblica et Ecclesiastica 2 (1890) 241-272. — E. NESTLE, Die Eusebianische Evangeliensynopse: NKZ 19 (1908) 40-51, 93-114, 219-232. — S. GRÉBAUT, Les dix canons d'Eusèbe et d'Ammonius: ROC (1913) 314-317.

336   THE WRITERS OF ANTIOCH AND SYRIA

— L. Canet, Sur le texte grec des Canons d'Eusèbe: Mélanges d'archéologie et d'histoire
de l'École Française de Rome (1913) 119-168. — C. Nordenfalk, Die spätantiken
Kanontafeln. Kunstgeschichtliche Studien über die Eusebianische Evangelien-
Konkordanz in den ersten vier Jahrhunderten ihrer Geschichte. Göteborg, 1938. —
M. Marcovic, De duobus codicibus novis: Živa Antika 3 (1953) 159-168. — A. Penna,
Il De consensu evangelistarum ed i Canoni Eusebiani: Bibl 36 (1955) 1-19. —
E. Elordury, Ammonio escriturista: EB 16 (1957) 187-217 (Eusebius' testimony). —
J. Leroy, Nouveaux témoins des Canons d'Eusèbe illustrés selon la tradition syriaque:
Cahiers Archéologiques 9 (1957) 117-140. — A. Vaccari, Le sezioni evangeliche di
Eusebio e il Diatessaron di Taziano nella letteratura siriaca: RSO 32 (1957) 433-452.

2. *Onomasticon*

The *Onomasticon* is a gazetteer of Biblical sites which provides
an alphabetical list of the place-names of the Bible together with
a geographical and historical description of each locality and its
designation in Eusebius' day. Highly esteemed by biblical scholars
in the Orient, it enjoyed no less repute in the West, to which it
became known in a Latin translation by Jerome, who furnished
some corrections and additions. Both the Greek original and the
Latin version are extant and present even today the most important
source for the topography of the Holy Land.

The *Onomasticon* is only the fourth part of a larger work on
biblical geography which Eusebius composed at the suggestion of
bishop Paulinus of Tyre. Since the latter died in 331, it must have
been written before that date. The first three sections are no longer
extant. They gave (1) an Interpretation of the Ethnological Terms
of the Hebrew Scriptures in Greek; (2) a Topography of Ancient
Judea with the Inheritances of the Twelve Tribes; (3) a Plan of
Jerusalem and of the Temple, accompanied with Memoirs relating
to the Various Localities. Eusebius refers to those three parts in the
preface to his *Onomasticon* and Jerome in the introduction to his
Latin version.

Editions: MG 23, 903-976 (incomplete). — P. de Lagarde, Onomastica sacra. Göttingen,
1870/1887, 2 vols. (Greek text and Latin version by Jerome). — New crit. ed.:
E. Klostermann, Das Onomastikon der biblischen Ortsnamen, GCS 11, 1 (1904)
(Greek text and Latin version of Jerome in parallel columns).

Studies: E. Klostermann, Eusebius' Schrift Περὶ τῶν τοπικῶν ὀνομάτων τῶν ἐν τῇ
θείᾳ γραφῇ (TU 23, 2b). Leipzig, 1902. — E. Lindl, Die Oktateuchkatene des Prokop
von Gaza und die Septuagintaforschung. Munich, 1902, 37ff. — P. Thomsen, Palaestina
nach dem Onomastikon des Eusebius: ZDP 26 (1903) 97-141, 145-188; *idem*, Untersuchungen zur älteren Palaestinaliteratur: ZDP 29 (1906) 101-132; *idem*, Textkritisches
zum Onomastikon: Berliner PhW (1905) 621-624; *idem*, Loca sancta I. Halle, 1907. —
E. Nestle, Zum Onomastikon des Eusebius: ZDP 28 (1905) 41-43. — W. Kubitschek,
Ein Strassennetz in Eusebius' Onomastikon: Jahreshefte des Österreichischen Archaeo-
logischen Instituts 1 (1905) 119-127; *idem*, Die Mosaikkarte Palaestinas: Mitteilungen
der k.k. Geographischen Gesellschaft in Wien (1900) 335-380. — A. Jacoby, Das
geographische Mosaik von Madaba, die älteste Karte des hl. Landes. Leipzig, 1905. —

J. ZIEGLER, Die Peregrinatio Aetheriae und das Onomastikon des Eusebius: Bibl (1931) 70-84. — G. BEYER, Die Stadtgebiete von Diospolis und Nikopolis im 4. Jahrhundert und ihre Grenznachbarn: ZDP 56 (1933) 218-253. — F. M. ABEL, La question gabaonite et l'Onomasticon: RBibl (1934) 347-373. — H. FISCHER, Geschichte der Kartographie von Palaestina: ZDP 62 (1939) 169-189. — M. NOTH, Die topographischen Angaben im Onomastikon des Eusebius: ZDP 66 (1943) 32-63. — J. STEINMANN, Saint Jérôme. Paris, 1958, 201-205 (the Hebrew names and the *Onomasticon* of Eusebius).

3. Gospel Questions and Solutions

This work consisted of two parts. The first, entitled *Gospel Questions and Solutions addressed to Stephanus* was in two books and discussed the discrepancies of the childhood narratives. The second, *Gospel Questions and Solutions addressed to Marinus*, had only one book; the author states, that having dealt with the difficulties presented by the beginning of the Gospels in the first part, he now proceeds to the discrepancies at the end, the resurrection narratives. Both parts have perished except for some Greek and Syriac fragments. However, an epitome, discovered and published by Mai (reprinted MG 22, 879-1006), provides valuable information about the original and its content. The entire work represents an important contribution to biblical criticism.

Editions: Greek fragments: MG 22, 879-1006. — Syriac texts: G. BEYER, Die evangelischen Fragen und Lösungen des Eusebius in jakobitischer Überlieferung und deren nestorianische Parallelen. Syrische Texte herausgegeben, übersetzt und untersucht: OC N.S. 12/14 (1922/24) 30-70; 3rd ser. 1 (1927) 80-97, 284-292; 3rd ser. 2 (1927) 57-69.

Translation: German: G. BEYER, art. cit.

Studies: A. BAUMSTARK, Syrische Fragmente von Eusebios' Περὶ διαφωνίας εὐαγγελίων: OC 1 (1901) 378-383. — G. BEYER, art. cit. — G. BARDY, La littérature patristique des Quaestiones et Responsiones sur l'Écriture Sainte: RBibl 41 (1932) 228-236.

In his exegesis Eusebius followed the School of Alexandria. He like Origen wrote voluminous commentaries on the books of the Old Testament. There is no indication that he did the same for the New Testament.

4. Commentary on the Psalms

The most important of his exegetical works seems to have been his large *Commentary on the Psalms*, which enjoyed a high reputation among the patristic writers for its learning and critical acumen. It was twice translated into Latin, by Hilary of Poitiers and Eusebius of Vercelli, the latter omitting the heretical passages (Jerome, *De vir. ill.* 81; *Ep.* 61, 2; 112, 20). While nothing remains of either version, such extensive excerpts of the original have been preserved that a complete reconstruction might be possible. Thus B. de

Montfaucon published a running commentary to Psalms 51-95 and *Catenae* fragments to Psalms 1-50 and 96-118 (MG 23, 65f). Cardinal Mai edited *Catenae* fragments to Psalms 119-150 (MG 24, 9f). What Pitra published as quotations from Eusebius is of very dubious authenticity. But G. Mercati discovered in a *catena* of the Ambrosian Library at Milan important portions of Psalms 96-100. It seems that the Commentary was one of Eusebius' very latest writings, though an exact date cannot be given in the present state of our information. The fragments indicate that the entire work must have been of gigantic proportions.

Editions: MG 23; 24, 9-76. — R. DEVREESSE, DB Suppl. 1 (1928) 1122-1124. — G. MERCATI, Osservazioni a proemi del Salterio di Origene Ippolito Eusebio Cirillo Alessandrino e altri, con frammenti inediti (ST 142). Vatican City, 1948.

Studies: G. MERCATI, L'ultima parte perduta del commentario d'Eusebio ai Salmi: RIL ser. 2, vol. 31 (1898) 1036-1045 (Cod. Ambros. F 126 sup.). — H. E. W. TURNER, A Psalm Prologue Contained in Ms. Bodl. Barocianus 15: JThSt 41 (1940) 280-287. — G. MERCATI, Note di letteratura biblica: Vivre et Penser 1 (1941) 5-15.

5. *Commentary on Isaias*

Jerome mentions (*De vir. ill.* 81) a *Commentary on Isaias* in ten books, but in the preface to his own *Comment. in Isaiam* he speaks of this Eusebian work as composed of fifteen, and when he refers to it again (*Comm. in Is.* lib. 5, praef.; lib. 5 ad Is., 18, 2) he adds that Eusebius promised in the title an historical exposition, but often forgets his promise and ends in the allegorism of Origen. For a long time it seemed as if the complete work was lost except for a large number of substantial *Catenae* fragments, which Montfaucon collected (MG 24, 89-526). R. Devreesse, after a careful comparison of this collection with the *catenae* manuscripts of the Vatican Library *Chig.* R VIII 54, *Ottob. gr.* 452, *Vat. gr.* 755 and *Vat. gr.* 1153 and with the editions of the commentaries on Isaias written by Basil the Great (cf. above, p. 218), Cyril of Alexandria (cf. above, p. 121) and Theodoret of Cyrus, was able to show that Montfaucon produces a number of fragments as Eusebian which in reality belong to the other commentators and omits many which these *catenae* manuscripts attribute to Eusebius. Moreover, A. Möhle found out that Eusebius' *Commentary on Isaias* is almost complete on the margin of a manuscript in Florence, *Bibl. Laur. Plut.* XI 4 and its volume doubles that of all the *Catenae* fragments together. This newly discovered text proves, (1) that Eusebius depended on Origen, whose *Commentary on Isaias* is cited seven times, and (2) that he based his exegesis on the Hexapla Septuagint, whereas Montfaucon's biblical text is that of the Sixtina.

Edition: A critical text will be edited by J. ZIEGLER in GCS.

Studies: R. Devreesse, L'édition du Commentaire d'Eusèbe de Césarée sur Isaïe. Interpolations et omissions: RBibl 42 (1933) 540-555. — A. Moehle, Der Jesaia-kommentar des Eusebios von Kaisareia fast vollständig wieder aufgefunden: ZNW 33 (1934) 87-89.

6. The Polygamy and Large Families of the Patriarchs

In his *Demonstratio Evangelica* (1, 9, 20) Eusebius remarks: 'If there is any question about the families of Abraham and Jacob, a longer discussion will be found in the book I wrote about the polygamy and large families of the ancient men of God'. He refers to the same work *Praeparatio* 7, 8, 29. Basil the Great, *De Spiritu Sancto* 29, 72 quotes a passage from it but calls it 'Difficulties respecting the Polygamy of the Ancients'. The contrast existing between the Christian concept of marriage and the life of the ancient patriarchs called for a statement accounting for the primitive freedom shown in Genesis, in order to answer the criticism of opponents. The treatise is lost.

7. On Easter (Περὶ τῆς τοῦ πάσχα ἑορτῆς)

Eusebius informs us in his *Vita Constantini* 4, 34 that the Emperor had written him personally a letter 'on the subject of the most holy feast of Easter'. The occasion for this communication was Eusebius' own treatise *On Easter* which he had dedicated to Constantine: 'For I had myself dedicated to him an exposition of the mystical import of that feast' *(ibid.)*. From these words it appears that Eusebius had given an explanation of the typical significance of the Jewish Passover and its fulfilment in the Christian Easter Festival. The letter of thanks which the Emperor sent to Eusebius indicates, however, that the Paschal controversy had been discussed, too. The Emperor writes:

> It is indeed an arduous task and beyond the power of language itself, worthily to treat of the mysteries of Christ and to explain in a fitting manner the controversy respecting the feast of Easter, its origin as well as its precious and toilsome accomplishments. For it is not in the power of even those who are able to apprehend them adequately to describe the things of God. I am, notwithstanding, filled with admiration of your learning and zeal, and have not only myself read your work with pleasure, but have given directions, according to your own desire, that it be communicated to many sincere followers of our holy religion (*Vita Const.* 4, 35 LNPF).

Unfortunately, the work is no longer extant in its entirety, but the *Catena* on Luke by Nicetas of Heraclea preserves a sizable fragment, which was first published by Mai and reprinted in Migne

(MG 24, 693-706). It contains twelve chapters devoted to a discussion of the nature of the Old Testament feast and its Christian counterpart, to the decision taken at the Council of Nicaea regarding the Paschal question and to the reasons for not celebrating Easter at the time of the Jewish Passover. We learn (*De solemnitate paschali* 8) that about one-fourth of the members of the Council of Nicaea followed the Antiochian custom and that Constantine addressed the assembly on the matter, obviously along the same lines as his letter to the Churches of the Orient, namely, that it was most unbecoming for Christians to keep the Easter feast according to the custom of the Jews, or even to celebrate it on different days in the various churches (*Vita Const.* 3, 19). The practice aimed at in the decision of the Council was not that of the Quartodecimans (cf. vol. I, p. 77, 243, 246), but the so-called Protopaschites. Many churches, namely in Syria, Mesopotamia and part of Cilicia, invariably celebrated Easter on the Sunday after the Jewish 14th of Nisan. The rest of the East followed the Alexandrian computation, just as the West accepted the Roman date; the two latter systems, while based on a different paschal cycle (cf. vol. II, p. 108, 177, 369), agreed on the principle — ignored by the Jews — that the paschal full moon could never occur before the vernal equinox. Thus whenever the Sunday after the Jewish Pasch occurred before the equinox, Antioch and Alexandria would celebrate Easter a month apart; hence Constantine's complaint: 'How grievous and scandalous is it that on the self-same days some should be engaged in fasting, others in festive enjoyment; and again that after the days of Easter some should be present at banquets and amusements, while others are fulfilling the appointed fast' (*Vita Const.* 3, 18). Eusebius reports (*De solemnitate paschali* 8) that as a result of the discussions at the Council 'the Syrians submitted' and agreed to follow the practise prevailing outside the patriarchate of Antioch. In ch. 7 the author gives a beautiful testimony to the holy sacrifice of the Mass as the Paschal meal of the New Dispensation. The time of composition of the Post-Nicene treatise is most probably before the Emperor's tricennalia (335).

5. *Dogmatic Works*

Of a dogmatic nature was the *Defence of Origen* which Eusebius completed after Pamphilus had died (cf. vol. II, p. 145/46). Photius (*Bibl. cod.* 118) tells us that it consisted of 'six books, five of which were written by Pamphilus when in prison in the company of Eusebius. The sixth is the work of Eusebius alone, after the martyr, having been deprived of life by the sword, was removed to God, for whom his soul longed'. Thus the first five books were composed with the assistance of Eusebius in the years 308 and 309. Only the first is extant in a Latin translation of Rufinus, which does not seem very reliable. Nothing remained of the sixth, the exclusive work of Eusebius. The loss is regrettable for several reasons. The work contained not only very important biographical evidence but a dogmatic refutation of the many accusations made by Methodius and others against the great Alexandrian with passages quoted from his works.

Edition: Rufinus' translation of the first book is found in MG 17, 542-615.

Study: F. X. MURPHY, Rufinus of Aquileia. His Life and Works. Washington, 1945, 83-84.

1. Contra Marcellum

In the last years of his life Eusebius wrote in defence of the Arian position two treatises against bishop Marcellus of Ancyra (cf. above, p. 198). After the latter had been deposed by the Arian Synod at Constantinople in 336, Eusebius published most probably within the same year his two books *Against Marcellus* in order to justify this condemnation. The first rejects the attacks of the bishop of Ancyra against the leaders of the Arian party, especially the sophist Asterius and Eusebius of Nicomedia. The second proves by citations from Marcellus' own work that his doctrines are those of the heretics Sabellius and Paul of Samosata. Both books are extant.

Editions: MG 24, 707-826. — T. GAISFORD, Eusebii Pamphili contra Hieroclem et Marcellum libri. Oxford, 1852. — New crit. ed.: E. KLOSTERMANN, GCS 14 (1906) 1-58.

Studies: F. C. CONYBEARE, The Authorship of the Contra Marcellum: ZNW 4 (1903) 330-334; 6 (1905) 250-270, denied the authorship of Eusebius of Caesarea for reasons of chronology, teaching and style and attributed the treatises *Contra Marcellum* and *De ecclesiastica theologia* to Eusebius of Emesa. He was refuted by F. H. CHASE and J. F. BETHUNE - BAKER, The Contra Marcellum and the De Ecclesiastica Theologia: JThSt 6 (1905) 512-521; by G. LOESCHKE, Contra Marcellum, eine Schrift des Eusebius von Caesarea: ZNW 7 (1906) 69-76; and by E. KLOSTERMANN, op. cit. IX-XVI. — M. J. SUGGS, Eusebius' Text of John in the Writings against Marcellus: JBL 75 (1956) 137-142.

2. De ecclesiastica theologia

The three books of his work *Ecclesiastical Theology* represent a more detailed refutation of Marcellus. Written about 337 they are dedicated to the Arian bishop Flaccillus of Antioch (334-342). While the *Contra Marcellum* is composed in a spirited tone, the present work enlarges in a tiresome manner upon the content of the former. Though there is good ground for the belief that Marcellus was Sabellianistic in tendency, the exposition of the doctrine of the

Logos which Eusebius offers here as 'the theology of the Church' is certainly not more than an advanced subordinationism: the Son of God is not of the essence of the Father but of His free will and the Holy Spirit is not more than a creation of the Son. He remains convinced (2, 7, 12) that to recognize the true divinity of the Son means to sacrifice the oneness of the Godhead. Despite its Origenistic leanings the work is extant in its entirety.

Editions: MG 24, 825-1046. — T. GAISFORD, op. cit. — New crit. ed.: E. KLOSTERMANN, GCS 14 (1906) 59-182.

6. *Orations and Sermons*

Eusebius mentions on several occasions (*Vita Const.* 1, 1; 3, 60. 61; 4, 33 and 45-46) the orations and sermons he was privileged to deliver in the presence of the Emperor. Only the panegyric discussed above (p. 326) is extant. The eleventh chapter of the third book in the *Vita* has the heading 'Silence of the Council after Some Words by the Bishop Eusebius', insinuating that at the opening of the Council of Nicaea Eusebius of Caesarea was the one who delivered the address of welcome to the Emperor, though Eusebius does not state this explicitly. After describing the majestic entry of the ruler, he continues:

> As soon as he [Constantine] had advanced to the upper end of the seats, at first he remained standing, and when a low chair of wrought gold had been set for him, he waited until the bishops had beckoned him, and then sat down, and after him the whole assembly did the same. The bishop who occupied the chief place in the right division of the assembly then rose and, addressing the Emperor, delivered a concise speech, in a strain of thanksgiving to Almighty God on his behalf. When he had resumed his seat, silence ensued, and all regarded the Emperor with fixed attention (*Vita Const.* 3, 11 LNPF).

Thus Eusebius fails to give the name of the bishop. This is not necessarily a sign of his modesty, but may mean that another orator was chosen. The chapter headings did not form part of the original text of the *Vita*. However, Sozomen in his *Ecclesiastical History* (1, 19) attributes the address of welcome to Eusebius: 'After they (the bishops) were seated, Eusebius Pamphili arose and delivered an oration in honor of the Emperor, returning thanks to God on his account'. Nevertheless, it remains very doubtful, since the bishop of Caesarea came to Nicaea under the cloud of a suspended condemnation and it is difficult to believe that the Fathers of Nicaea would have selected him for this honor. John of Antioch (*Ep. ad Proclum Constantin.*, MG 65, 878), Theodoret (*Hist. eccl.* 1, 6) and the African Facundus Hermianensis (*Pro defens. trium cap.* 11, 1) state that Eustathius of Antioch made the opening speech and was also the president of the Council (cf. above, p. 302). Nicetas Choniates (*Thesaurus* 1, 7), following Theodore of Mopsuestia and Philostorgius, asserts that Alexander of Alexandria delivered it. The attempt has been made to explain the discrepancy in all these reports by supposing that Eustathius and Alexander, the two great patriarchs, first directed a few words to the Emperor and that only then did Eusebius come forward. However, his excommunication speaks against this suggestion. E. Schwartz (PWK 6, 1413) is convinced that Eusebius of Nicomedia delivered the address but his opinion has not found any approval. As long as the question of the presidency at the Council has not been answered, there remains little hope for a satisfactory solution of the vexed problem.

There is very little information on any other sermons of Eusebius. In his *Ecclesiastical History* (10, 4, 12-72) he reproduces the full text of his address at the dedication of the basilica of Tyre about 316. The central theme is the resurrection. Christianity's recent triumph, the rebuilding of the cathedral and the erection of the baptistery are all associated as types of the resurrection and final glorification in heaven of Christ's bride, the Church.

In the London manuscript dated February 411 (*Brit. Mus. add. 12150*), which contains the Syriac version of the *Theophany* and of the second edition of his book *On the Martyrs of Palestine*, there follows a panegyric of the Martyrs of Antioch. The Syriac *Martyrologium* celebrated on the first of August the Maccabean heroes. It is probable that the sermon was delivered on that occasion because it includes an elaborate encomium on the mother and her seven sons who were tortured to death by Antiochus Epiphanes and were supposed to be buried at Antioch. The sermon was published by W. Wright.

Editions: W. WRIGHT, The Encomium of the Martyrs: Journal of Sacred Literature 4th ser. 5 (1864) 403-408; 6 (1864/65) 129-133 (Syriac text with an English translation by B. H. Cowper). — The Syriac treatise *On the Star of the Magi* attributed to Eusebius is not authentic. Syriac text and English translation by W. WRIGHT, Eusebius of Caesarea on the Star: Journal of Sacred Literature 4th ser. 9 (1866) 117-136; 10 (1867) 150-164.

7. *Epistles*

The number of his letters must have been great because of his large share in the disputes of his times. Nevertheless, almost all of them have perished. Strange as it may seem, no effort was ever made, apparently, to collect his correspondence.

Only three of his letters have come down to us complete: the dedicatory epistle to Flaccillus at the beginning of his *De ecclesiastica theologia*, that to Carpianus, a kind of introduction to his *Evangelical Canons*, and, lastly, that to his own people at Caesarea upon the conclusion of the Council of Nicaea.

The last is appended by Athanasius to his defence of the definition of Nicaea *De decretis Nicaenae Synodi*, written about A.D. 350 (cf. above, p. 61). Socrates (*Hist. eccl.* 1, 8, 35f), Theodoret (*Hist. eccl.* 1, 12, 1) and Gelasius (*Conc. Nic.* II 35, 1) evidently copied it from Athanasius. Eusebius informs his church of what happened at the Council and attempts to justify his own conduct, and especially his consent to the *homoousios*, lest they should get a misleading impression through gossip and hearsay. He then reproduces a lengthy paper which, he says, he read out at one of the sessions in the presence of the Emperor. It contains, after a short statement that he adheres unswervingly to the faith in which he had been baptized, a baptismal creed, which seems to be that of the church of Caesarea. There follows a brief theological explanation of its articles and the statement that such had been his belief and preaching in the past. Scholars formerly held that his motive for submitting the Caesarean Creed to the Council was to provide a basis for a new creed that might be drafted but it now seems certain that he did it in order to secure the rehabilitation of his own orthodoxy, which had been brought into question at the Council of Antioch held earlier in the same year.

After the document Eusebius continues with his letter:

> On this faith being publicly put forth by us, no room for contradiction appeared; but our most pious Emperor, before any one else, testified that it was entirely orthodox. He confessed moreover that such were his own sentiments and he advised all present to agree to it, and to subscribe its articles and to assent to them, with the insertion of the single word, *homoousios*, which moreover he interpreted as not in the sense of the affections of the body, nor as if the Son subsisted from the Father in the way of division, or any severance (4 LNPF).

The Council, however, 'on the pretext of adding *consubstantial* drew up the following formula' — and then Eusebius produces the text of the Creed of Nicaea with its anathemas. He ends his letter explaining how he 'resisted even to the last minute as long as we were offended at statements which differed from our own', but finally signed after a careful examination of the words of the new creed formula. In view of the fact that no official minutes of the Council exist, this letter forms one of our most important authorities for the proceedings at Nicaea and for the dubious position of Eusebius.

Of other letters concerning the Arian controversy, which Eusebius wrote before the Council, some quotations are extant. Eusebius of

Nicomedia (Theodoret, *Hist. eccl.* 1, 5) mentions in his communication to Paulinus of Tyre an epistle addressed to Alexander of Alexandria, in which Eusebius of Caesarea intervened for Arius (cf. above, p. 191). The Acts of the Second Council at Nicaea in 787 contain a lengthy quotation from an earlier missive to the same Alexander of Alexandria, in which Eusebius used the creed formula submitted by Arius at the synod of Nicomedia for the latter's defence (*Conc. Nic. II Act.* 6: Mansi, *SS. Conc. Coll.* 13, 316-317). According to these Acts Eusebius wrote to Alexander several times in favor of the teaching of Arius. Athanasius (*De syn.* 17) speaks of an epistle of Eusebius to bishop Euphrantion of Balaneae in Syria at the time of the Nicene Council in which 'he did not scruple to say that Christ was no true God' (Mansi, *l.c.* 317).

Finally, in a note to Constantia, sister of Constantine and wife of Licinius, Eusebius, in his later years, rebuked the Empress for wishing to procure a portrait of Christ. It has an iconoclastic tendency in so far as it opposes as a pagan custom not only the veneration of such pictures but even the making of them. Hence, it was cited by the heretics of the eighth century to justify their own condemnation of images. Nicephorus of Constantinople (d. 826) criticized it sharply and inserted the principal passages in his *Antirrhetica* (Pitra, *Spicil. Solesm.* 1, 383f); these are also found in the Acts of the Second Council of Nicaea (Mansi, *l.c.* 13, 313. 317) and it is this accident that has preserved it for us.

Editions: The text of the letter to Carpianus reprinted in: H. von Soden, Die Schriften des Neuen Testamentes I. Berlin, 1902, 388f. — For the Coptic version of this letter, see: A. Hebbelynck, Les κεφάλαια et les τίτλοι des Évangiles: Mus 41 (1928) 81-120. — For the Armenian version: A. Vardanian, Euthalius' Werke. Untersuchungen und Texte. Anhang: Brief des Eusebios von Kaisareia an Karpianos. Hergestellt und herausgegeben (Krit. Ausgabe der Altarmenischen Schriftsteller und Übersetzungen. T. 3, fasc. 1). Vienna, 1930. — New crit. ed. of the letter to the people of Caesarea: H. G. Opitz, Athanasius' Werke II, 1. Berlin, 1935, 28-31. For the numerous Latin versions of this letter, see: C. H. Turner, Ecclesiae Occidentalis Monumenta Iuris Antiquissima. Tom. I, fasc. 2. Oxford, 1913, 297. — The text of the letter to Constantia: MG 20, 1545-1549.

Studies: J. N. D. Kelly, Early Christian Creeds, London, 1950, 213-230, furnishes a thorough discussion of the letter to the people of Caesarea, its creed and its relation to the Nicene Creed. — For the letter to Constantia, cf. W. Elliger, Die Stellung der alten Christen zu den Bildern. Leipzig, 1930, 47-53. — G. Florovsky, Origen, Eusebius and the Iconoclastic Controversy: Church History 19 (1950) 3-22.

ACACIUS OF CAESAREA

Eusebius' successor in the see of Caesarea was his disciple Acacius, who was elected in 340 and died in 366. St. Jerome describes him as follows:

Acacius, whom, because he was blind in one eye, they nicknamed 'the one-eyed', bishop of the Church of Caesarea in Palestine, wrote seventeen volumes *On Ecclesiastes* and six of *Miscellaneous Questions* and many treatises besides on various subjects. He was so influential in the reign of the Emperor Constantius that he made Felix bishop of Rome in the place of Liberius (*De vir. ill.* 98 LNPF).

The last sentence may exaggerate somewhat, but the fact remains that Acacius played an important role in Church politics (Philostorgius, *Hist. eccl.* 5, 1). He was the principal representative of the Homoeans, the party of compromise intended to be the rallying point of all moderates with the watchword 'like in all respects'. Athanasius (*De synodis* 29), Epiphanius (*Haer.* 73, 25) and Socrates (*Hist. eccl.* 2, 40) have preserved the Creed which he proposed at the Council of Seleucia in 359. Philostorgius (*Hist. eccl.* 4, 12) mentions that Acacius drew up the acts of the Homoean Synod of Constantinople in 360. But nothing has survived of these elaborate documents. Though under Jovian he signed the Creed of Nicaea at Antioch in 363, he returned to Arianism under Valens and was therefore deposed by the Homoeousian Synod of Lampsacus in 365.

The two works *On Ecclesiastes* and *Miscellaneous Questions* which Jerome mentions, are no longer extant except for fragments. A passage of the second work is preserved by Jerome in his *Ep.* 119, 6. Since it deals with I Cor. 15, 51, the entire work seems to have concerned biblical questions. Fragments of a Commentary on Romans and on the Octateuch have been found in exegetical *Catenae*. Socrates (*Hist. eccl.* 2, 4) testifies that Acacius published among other books a biography of his master and predecessor Eusebius (*εἰς τὸν βίον τοῦ διδασκάλου αὐτοῦ*) which is lost. Epiphanius (*Haer.* 72, 5-10) preserves part of a polemical treatise against Marcellus of Ancyra (cf. above p. 199). The information supplied by all these sources is evidence of Acacius' interest in scholarship, which also accounts for his renovation of the famous library of Caesarea (Jerome, *Ep.* 34, 1).

Editions: Fragments of the Commentary on Romans: K. STAAB, Pauluskommentare aus der griechischen Kirche. Münster, 1933, 53-56. — Fragments of the Commentary on the Octateuch: R. DEVREESSE, Anciens commentateurs grecs de l'Octateuque: RBibl 44 (1935) 186-189.

Studies: J. GUMMERUS, Die homoeousianische Partei bis zum Tode des Konstantius. Leipzig, 1900, 63ff., 138ff. — J. LEBON, La position de saint Cyrille de Jérusalem dans les luttes provoquées par l'arianisme: RHE 20 (1924) 181-210, 357-386 (Acacius and Cyril). — G. BARDY, La littérature patristique des Quaestiones et Responsiones sur l'Écriture Sainte: RBibl 41 (1932) 341ff. (on *Miscellaneous Questions*). — J. N. D. KELLY, Early Christian Creeds. London, 1950, 290-292.

GELASIUS OF CAESAREA

The second successor to Eusebius as bishop of Caesarea was Gelasius, Cyril of Jerusalem's nephew. Theodoret (*Hist. eccl.* 5, 8) calls him 'a man distinguished by the purity of his doctrine, and the sanctity of his life'. A staunch defender of the faith of Nicaea, he was elected to the see of Caesarea in 367 but ousted during the reign of Valens. He returned, however, on the accession of Theodosius in 379. St. Jerome mentions (*De vir. ill.* 130) that he wrote in a more or less carefully polished style but did not publish his works. Some of them, however, must have been circulated, because quotations can be found in a number of authors, e.g. Theodoret, Leontius of Byzantium and the compiler of the *Doctrina Patrum*.

Edition: F. DIEKAMP, Analecta Patristica (Orientalia Christiana Analecta 117), Rome, 1938, 42-49, published 17 fragments of his dogmatic treatises, some of them hitherto unknown.

1. *Ecclesiastical History*

According to Photius (*Bibl. cod.* 89) Gelasius wrote a continuation of Eusebius' *Ecclesiastical History* (cf. above p. 314). A. Glas, P. Heseler and others hold that Gelasius' work formed the basis of the last two books of Rufinus' *Ecclesiastical History*, whereas P. van den Ven, P. Peeters and F. Diekamp think this section original. As Photius remarks Gelasius stated in his work that he had been encouraged to write it by his uncle Cyril, bishop of Jerusalem. He adds: 'I have read elsewhere that this Cyril and Gelasius translated the *History* of Rufinus the Roman into Greek, but did not compose any history of their own' *(l.c.)*. This seems to be impossible because, as E. Honigmann proves, Gelasius had died before Rufinus began after 401 on his translation of Eusebius. He supposes that the author of books 9 and 10 of Rufinus' *Ecclesiastical History* was not Rufinus the Roman, but some unknown Greek writer of that name. Scheidweiler rejects this new theory and thinks that Gelasius of Caesarea's *Ecclesiastical History* can be reconstructed for its greater part, since Rufinus, Gelasius of Cyzicus, the author of the *Vita Metrophanis*, Georgius Monachus and Socrates borrowed from it.

Studies: A. GLAS, Die Kirchengeschichte des Gelasios von Kaisareia, die Vorlage für die beiden letzten Bücher der Kirchengeschichte Rufins (Diss. Munich). Leipzig, 1914. — P. VAN DEN VEN, Fragments de la récension grecque de l'Histoire ecclésiastique de Rufin dans un texte hagiographique: Mus 2 (1915) 92-115 (against Glas). — P. HESELER, Hagiographica I/II. Beiträge zur Kirchengeschichte des Gelasios von Kaisareia (Phil. Diss. Bonn). Athens, 1934. Cf. F. DIEKAMP: ThR 34 (1935) 235-236. — J. BIDEZ, Fragments nouveaux de Philostorge sur la vie de Constantin: Byz 10 (1935) 438-442. — P. HESELER, Hagiographica: BNJ 9 (1932) 113-137, 320-337; 12 (1936) 347-351. — P. PEETERS, Les débuts du christianisme en Géorgie: AB 50 (1932) 5-58 (against Glas).

— F. Diekamp, Gelasius von Caesarea in Palaestina: Analecta Patristica. Rome, 1938, 16-32. — F. X. Murphy, Rufinus of Aquileia. His Life and His Works. Washington, 1945, 160-164. — P. van den Ven, Encore le Rufin grec: Mus 59 (1946) 281-294; *idem*, Gélase de Césarée et Rufin: AIPh 12 (1952) 648; *idem*, La légende de saint Spyridon. Louvain, 1953, 195-200. — H. Grégoire, Gélase ou Rufin? Un fait nouveau: NC 5 (1953) 472. — F. Scheidweiler, Die Kirchengeschichte des Gelasios von Kaisareia: BZ 46 (1953) 277-301. — E. Honigmann, Gélase de Césarée et Rufin d'Aquilée: BAB 40 (1954) 122-161. — F. Scheidweiler, BZ 48 (1955) 162-164 (against Honigmann); *idem*, Nochmals die Vita Constantini: BZ 49 (1956) 2-6; *idem*, Die Bedeutung der Vita Metrophanis et Alexandri für die Quellenkritik bei den griechischen Kirchenhistorikern: BZ 50 (1957) 74-98 (Gelasius is the basic source of the *Vita*).

2. *Expositio Symboli*

The *Doctrina Patrum* (31, 92 ed. Diekamp) attributes an *Explanation of the Symbol* to Gelasius. Only fragments survive, which suggest that it might have been a series of Catechetical instructions akin to his uncle Cyril's lectures, based on the articles of the Creed and dealing with the principal doctrines of the Church.

3. *Against the Anomoeans*

Photius (*Bibl. cod.* 88) remarks that he read a polemic *Against the Anomoeans* and that the title gave the name of the author as Gelasius, bishop of Caesarea in Palestine. The treatise is no longer extant.

EUZOIUS OF CAESAREA

When Gelasius was banished, the Arian Euzoius became bishop of Caesarea. Jerome (*De vir. ill.* 113) informs us that he, together with Gregory of Nazianzus, was educated at Caesarea by Thespius the rhetorician, and that when he later became bishop, he made every effort to restore the library of Origen and Pamphilus (cf. vol. II, p. 121; above p. 309), which had already suffered considerable damage. He was expelled when Theodosius became emperor. Although Jerome states, 'Many and various treatises of his are in circulation, and one may easily become acquainted with them', all have disappeared and even their titles are unknown.

EUSEBIUS OF EMESA

Eusebius of Emesa is a disciple of his namesake Eusebius of Caesarea. Born at Edessa about 300 A.D., he was early attracted to biblical studies. Since his mother-tongue was Syriac, he attended a local school to learn Greek. His first teacher in the Scriptures

was the Arian bishop Patrophilus of Scythopolis. He, but especially
Eusebius of Caesarea, had a decisive influence on his theological
views. He went to Antioch for further exegetical training and was
there when in 326 or 330 Patriarch Eustathius was deposed by the
Anti-Nicene community. Having completed his studies at Antioch,
he went to the other great educational center, Alexandria, to take
courses in philosophy. There he became the intimate friend of
George, later bishop of Laodicea, a native of Alexandria and
follower of Arius. Nevertheless, he wisely declined when the Arian
Synod of Antioch in 340, after his return to this city, elected him
to succeed Athanasius at Alexandria. Shortly afterwards he became
bishop of the small diocese of Emesa (now Homs), the capital of
Lebanese Phoenicia and ancient center of pagan sunworship.
Socrates reports (*Hist. eccl.* 2, 9) that the townspeople broke into
sedition at his appointment because they did not want a scholarly
bishop. He was forced to flee to George of Laodicea, who brought
him to Antioch. Through the intervention of the patriarch of this
city he was finally able to return to Emesa. According to St. Jerome
(*De vir. ill.* 91) he was buried at Antioch, which seems to indicate
that he died there, evidently before the Council of Seleucia in 359.
George of Laodicea wrote an encomium on him of which parts
survive in Socrates (*Hist. eccl.* 2, 9) and Sozomen (*Hist. eccl.* 3, 6).

   Though St. Jerome calls Eusebius of Emesa 'a standard-bearer
of the Arian faction' (*Chronicon*, GCS 7, 1, p. 236), there is no
justification for regarding him as an Arian. Unquestionably, he was
Anti-Nicene, but he strongly attacks pure Arianism in his writings.
Theodoret of Cyrus is more careful than Jerome. He states in his
Eranistes (MG 83, 312) that Eusebius' works were written under
the influence of the Arian doctrine since they intend to prove that
the Father is greater than the Son, but adds that he rightly defends
the total impassibility of Christ's divine nature. Thus he could be
called a Semi-Arian.

HIS WRITINGS

   We know from St. Jerome *(ibid.)* that Eusebius was a very
successful author. 'Eusebius of Emesa', he states, 'who had a fine
rhetorical talent, composed innumerable works suited to win popular
applause and his historical writing is most diligently read by those
who practise public speaking. Among these the chief are, *Against the
Jews, Gentiles and Novatians* and *Homilies on the Gospels*, brief but
numerous'. A commentary on Galatians in ten books is mentioned
by Jerome in the prologue to his own commentary on this Epistle.
Theodoret of Cyrus (*Haer. fab. comp.* 1, 25-26) speaks of his treatises
against Marcionites and Manicheans.

Fortunately, much more of his works is extant than was believed until recently. About 30 of his discourses are preserved complete and a number of others in fragments, Greek, Syriac and Armenian. One of the sermons, *De poenitentia*, found among the apocrypha of Basil the Great (MG 31, 1476-1488), has come down to us in the original Greek. Twenty-nine others, edited recently by E. M. Buytaert, survive in an old Latin version from the end of the fourth or the beginning of the fifth century. Of these, fourteen had already been published by J. Sirmond in 1643, though under the name of Eusebius of Caesarea, and portions of several exist in various other languages, of no. I in Greek in Theodoret's *Eranistes*, of no. II in Armenian and of no. XXVI in Syriac. The most important are the 17 homilies which A. Wilmart discovered in the Latin manuscript *Troyes* 523, formerly belonging to Clairvaux. Two of these, nos. 3 and 4 *adversus Sabellianos*, appear in Sirmond's older edition, but the rest were entirely unknown. Wilmart himself published only nos. 5 and 6, but Buytaert the whole collection. The authenticity of no. 12 is merely probable.

Excerpts from at least eight other sermons are extant in twenty-seven Syriac quotations in Philoxenus of Mabbug. Three discourses have reached us in Armenian fragments. There is good reason to hope that more of his sermons will be discovered in Armenian manuscripts.

Editions: MG 86, 1, 509-562: *Orationes sacrae et fragmenta.* — MG 24, 1047-1208 reprint of: Eusebii Pamphili Caesareae in Palaestina ep. opuscula XIIII nunc primum in lucem edita studio et opere J. Sirmondi. Paris, 1643. — A. WILMART, Le souvenir d'Eusèbe d'Émèse. Un discours en l'honneur des saintes d'Antioche Bernice, Prosdoce et Domnine: AB 38 (1920) 263-284 (discourse VI *De martyribus*); *idem*, Un discours théologique d'Eusèbe d'Émèse: Le Fils image du Père: ROC 22 (1921) 72-94 (discourse V *De imagine*). — New crit. ed.: E. M. BUYTAERT, Eusèbe d'Émèse. Discours conservés en latin. Textes en partie inédits. I. La collection de Troyes (Discours I à XVII). Louvain, 1953. II. La collection de Sirmond (Discours XVIII à XXIX). Louvain, 1957. — A new edition of the Greek text of the sermon *De poenitentia* is found in: E. M. BUYTAERT, L'héritage littéraire d'Eusèbe d'Émèse. Étude critique et historique. Textes (Bibl. du Mus. 24). Louvain, 1949, 16*-29*. Syriac and Armenian fragments of sermons: *ibid*, 31*-92* (with a Latin translation).

Studies: J. C. THILO, Über die Schriften des Eusebius von Alexandrien und des Eusebius von Emisa. Halle, 1832. — P. GODET, Eusèbe d'Émèse: DTC 5 (1913) 1537-1539. — M. ESPOSITO, Notes on Learning and Literature in Mediaeval Ireland: Hermathena 22 (1932) 253-271. According to Esposito, Eusebius of Emesa is perhaps the author of the *Liber de tribus habitaculis* (ML 40, 991-998) which some manuscripts ascribe to S. Patrick, others to Caesarius of Arles, some to Eusebius of Emesa and some to St. Augustine. However, W. DELIUS, Die Verfasserschaft der Schrift De tribus habitaculis: ThStKr 108 (1937) 28-39, is of the opinion that this treatise was composed in the 12th century. — E. M. BUYTAERT, L'authenticité des dix-sept opuscules contenus dans le ms. T. 523 sous le nom d'Eusèbe d'Émèse: RHE 43 (1948) 5-89; *idem*, L'héritage littéraire 3-192. — A. GRILLMEIER, Die theologische und sprachliche Vorbereitung der christologischen Formel von Chalkedon: CGG I (1951) 130-135. — E. M. BUYTAERT, On the

Trinitarian Doctrine of Eusebius of Emesa: FS 14 (1954) 34-48. — S. DERNERSESSIAN, An Armenian Version of the Homilies on the Harrowing of Hell: DOP 8 (1954) 201-224 (Armenian Version of the 5th or 6th century of homilies attributed to Eusebius of Alexandria or Eusebius of Emesa). — E. AMAND DE MENDIETA, La virginité chez Eusèbe d'Émèse et l'ascétisme familial dans la première moitié du IVe siècle: RHE 50 (1955) 777-820 (on homilies VI *De martyribus* and VII *De virginibus*). — O. PERLER, Pseudo-Ignatius und Eusebius von Emesa: HJG 77 (1958) 73-82. — J. MUYLDERMANS, Les homélies d'Eusèbe d'Émèse en version arménienne (Cod. Ven. Mech. 1706): Mus. 71 (1958) 51-56.

For the Pseudo-Eusebian collection of Gallican Sermons attributed to Eusebius of Emesa in the edition of J. GAIGNY, Divi Eusebii episcopi Emiseni homiliae ad populum et ad monachos, Paris, 1548, and A. SCHOTT, Maxima Bibliotheca Veterum Patrum 6 (Lyons, 1677) 618-686, see: G. MORIN, La collection gallicane dite d'Eusèbe d'Émèse et les problèmes qui s'y rattachent: ZNW 34 (1935) 92-116, who regards the corpus as the work of a sixth-century compiler. The homilies ns. 9, 10, 13, 26, 33, 34, 37, 42, 44, 51, 61 belong to Faustus of Riez, but he is not the author of the entire collection. *Sermo* 50 seems to be by St. Hilary of Arles. For the Latin and the Biblical text of the collection, see: A. SOUTER, Observations on the Pseudo-Eusebian Collection of Gallican Sermons: JThSt 41 (1940) 47-57. For additional editions, see: E. DEKKERS and A. GAAR, Clavis Patrum Latinorum (SE 3). Steenbrugge, 1951, 167-168 (n. 966). — E. M. BUYTAERT, L'héritage littéraire, 159-161, reached the conclusion that though the content of these sermons would not prevent them from being attributed to Eusebius of Emesa, there is no positive reason at all to ascribe them to him. None of the sermons contains anything of the authentic collections of Troyes and of Sirmond.

Biblical Commentaries

It seems that his commentary on the Epistle to the Galatians mentioned by St. Jerome perished except for a few fragments. His other exegetical works are partially preserved in an Armenian version. A great number of Greek fragments have been collected from *catenae*, especially of his commentaries on Genesis and Galatians. Eusebius' interpretation follows the rationalistic method of the Antiochene theologians.

Editions: R. DEVREESSE, Anciens commentateurs grecs de l'Octateuque: RBibl 45 (1936) 201-211. — K. STAAB, Pauluskommentare aus der griechischen Kirche. Münster, 1933, 46-52 (fragments of commentaries on Romans and Galatians). — E. M. BUYTAERT, L'héritage littéraire: 95*-122* (*In Genesim*), 123*-133* (*In Exodum*), 134*-135* (*In Leviticum*), 136*-139* (*In Numeros*), 140*-142* (*In Deuteronomium*), 143* (*In Josue, In Iudices*), 144* (*In Romanos*), 145*-152* (*In Galatas*).

Studies: A. ZANOLLI, Una interpretazione caratteristica di Eusebio Emeseno e la questione del 'Pseudo-Cirillo': Bazmavep 92 (1934) 186-192 (commentary of Genesis); *idem*, Nuove identificazioni nel commentario di Procopio per mezzo del 'Pseudo-Cirillo': Bazmavep 93 (1935) 413-418. — V. HOVHANNESSIAN, The Commentary of Eusebius of Emesa (*In Genesim*): Bazmavep 93 (1935) 345-352 (in Armenian). — K. STAAB, op. cit. XXI-XXIII. — E. M. BUYTAERT, op. cit. 169-188.

NEMESIUS OF EMESA

Nemesius was one of the successors of Eusebius in the see of Emesa. Beyond this fact nothing is known of his life. Nevertheless, he remains an interesting personality on account of the treatise *On the Nature of Man* which he wrote during the last decade of the fourth century. He emerges from this work as a man of liberal Greek education, widely read in philosophy and medicine, and with a good deal of knowledge of psychology and physiology. Valuable as a quarry to the classical philologist and historian of philosophy, it yields less to the theologian, though it is essentially a piece of Christian apologetic. The author attempts to construct on a mainly Platonic basis a doctrine of the soul and its union with the body which would be in agreement with revelation. Thus he deals in the introduction (ch. 1) with the nature of man, who consists of soul and body. He was created to be the link between two worlds, the phenomenal and the intelligible. The world was made for man and lower creatures exist for his sake. The first chapter ends with a panegyric on man:

> When we consider these facts about man, how can we exaggerate the dignity of his place in creation? In his own person, man joins mortal creatures with the immortal, and brings the rational beings into contact with the irrational. He bears about in his proper nature a reflex of the whole creation, and is therefore called 'the world in little'. He is the creature whom God thought worthy of such special providence that, for his sake, all creatures have their being, both those that now are, and those that are yet to be. He is the creature for whose sake God became man, so that this creature might attain incorruption and escape corruption, might reign on high, being made after the image and likeness of God, dwelling with Christ as a child of God, and might be throned above all rule and all authority.
>
> Knowing, then, the nobility of which we are partakers, and how we are 'a planting from heaven', let us do nothing that would put our nature to shame, or publish us as unfit to be the recipients of so great a bounty. Let us not cheat ourselves of all this power, glory, blessedness by bartering the enjoyment of all eternal things for a brief season of pleasure that cannot last. Let us, rather, safeguard our high standing by doing good and eschewing evil, and by keeping before us a good aim, whereby divine grace is especially wont to be invoked; and, of course, by prayer (LCC).

The chapters which follow study the soul (2), the union of soul with body (3), the body (4), the elements (5), the faculty of imagination (6), sight (7), feeling or the sense of touch (8), taste (9), hearing (10), smell (11), the faculty of intellect (12), memory (13), thought and expression (14). After this the author discusses a further way of dividing the soul (15), the irrational part of the soul, also called the passions (16), concupiscence (17), pleasures (18), grief (19), fear (20), anger (21), the irrational part of the soul over which reason has no control (22), the nutritive faculty (23), the pulses (24), the generative faculty (25), another way of dividing up the faculties that control the life of a living creature (26), impulsion depending upon the will (27), respiration (28), voluntary and involuntary acts (29-34). Chapters 35-38 form a polemic against fatalism. The treatise comes to an end with a defence of free-will (39-41) and the Christian doctrine of divine providence (42-44).

This table of contents indicates, that there is a lack of unity and logic in the arrangement of the material and that the book is unfinished. In fact the author promises on several occasions further discussion of details, but never mentions them later on. Presumably death overtook him, before he could revise his work.

In his method he prefers not to start at once from the faith as center, but to establish contact with non-Christian thought and to give an account of the views of the ancient philosophers. Only then does he proceed to select from the contradictory theories that idea which he prefers from his Christian point of view. Thus he discusses the concepts of Plato, Aristotle, Epicurus and Stoic philosophy, of the physician Galenus and the Peripatetic Aetius, of Ammonius, Plotinus, Porphyry, Jamblichus and many others. He believes with Plato in the pre-existence of souls, but rejects the Neo-Platonic trichotomy. He follows Aristotle in his notions of the faculties of the soul and the freedom of choice. His theology is basically that of the School of Antioch though in the Christological section of the third chapter he refutes the extreme view 'of certain men of note' that the union of the Godhead and manhood in Christ is moral and not hypostatic, is only by divine favor, but not grounded in nature. He seems here to be alluding to Theodore of Mopsuestia's youthful work *On the Incarnation* (cf. below, p. 410). Nemesius summarizes his own concept of this union in the following words:

> The Divine Word suffers no alteration from the fellowship which He has with the body and the soul. In sharing with them His own Godhead, He does not partake their infirmity. He is one with them, and yet He continues in that state in which He was, before His entry into that union. This manner of mingling or union is something quite new. The Word mingles with body and soul, and yet remains throughout unmixed, unconfused, uncorrupted, untransformed, not sharing their passivity but only their activity, not perishing with them, nor changing as they change; but, on the one hand, contributing to their growth, and, on the other, nowise degraded by contact with them, so that He continues immutable and unconfused, seeing that He is altogether without share in any kind of alteration (3 LCC).

He refers twice to Eunomius and on three occasions to Apollinaris of Laodicea as his contemporaries. Since Theodore became bishop of Mopsuestia in 392, and Eunomius died about 392 and Apollinaris at nearly the same time, the conclusion is safe that Nemesius wrote in the year 400 at the latest. There is not the slightest indication that Origen has been formally condemned nor is there any notice taken of Nestorius, Eutyches or Pelagius.

Nemesius' treatise was much read during the Middle Ages and was translated into several languages. St. John Damascene made ample use of it in the anthropological chapters (Book II, 12-29) of his *Exact Exposition of the Orthodox Faith*, but without mentioning explicitly his source. About a century later Meletius, a monk of the monastery of the Holy Trinity in the neighbourhood of Tiberiopolis in Phrygia, excerpted it verbatim to such an extent that his *Synopsis of the Views of the Church Fathers and Distinguished Philosophers on the Constitution of Man* amounts virtually to an additional manuscript of Nemesius. Neither, however, does he name our author. Probably through confusion with the similar title of Gregory of Nyssa's *De hominis opificio*, Nemesius' book was often quoted as Gregory's. Thus an Armenian bishop of the eighth century, who translated it into Armenian, attributes it to Gregory. Of the two oldest Latin versions, one was prepared by the physician and later archbishop Nicholaus Alfanus of Salerno (d. 1085), the other by Richard Burgundio, Professor of Law in the University of Pisa (d. 1194). The former gives no author and even changes the title to *Key to Nature (Premnon physicon)*, while the latter ascribes the original to Gregory of Nyssa. Alfanus's rendering is artistic and far superior to Burgundio's, which is closely literal. The latter was used by Peter Lombard and Thomas Aquinas, the former by Albert the Great. The Renaissance produced two more Latin versions: the first, by the Italian encyclopedist Georgio Valla (d. 1499), was printed in 1533 at Leyden by Sebastian Gryphius, the second, by the Dominican John Konow of Nuremberg, was published at Strasbourg in 1512 and reissued in the Basle edition of Gregory of Nyssa in 1562. The eighth-century Armenian version mentioned above was edited by the Mechitarist J. Tasean in 1889 from the San Lazzaro Press at Venice. Since it is slavishly literal, it is an important witness to the Greek manuscript tradition.

The oldest Greek text is preserved in a Patmos codex of the tenth century. The editions by J. Fell (Oxford, 1671) and C. F. Matthaei (Halle, 1802) are obsolete, since neither of them has made use of the Patmos manuscript. A new edition by F. Lammert will be published soon. Migne reprints that of Matthaei.

Editions: MG 40, 508-818. — The best edition of the Latin translation of Alfano: C. J. BURKHARD, Nemesii episcopi Premnon Physicon sive Περὶ φύσεως ἀνθρώπου liber ab Alfano in Latinum translatus (Bibliotheca Teubneriana). Leipzig, 1917. The Latin translation of Burgundio was edited by C. J. BURKHARD, Gregorii Nysseni (Nemesii

Emeseni) Περὶ φύσεως ἀνθρώπου liber a Burgundione in Latinum translatus (5 Progrs. of the Gymnasium Wien-Untermeidling). Vienna, 1891, 1892, 1896, 1901, 1902. — For manuscript tradition, see: C. J. BURKHARD, WSt 10 (1888) 93-135; 11 (1889) 143-152, 243-267. — For the Armenian version, see: E. TEZA, La 'Natura dell'uomo' di Nemesio e le vecchie traduzioni in italiano e in armeno: Reg. Istituto Veneto di scienze, lettere ed arti 3, ser. 7 (1892) 1239-1279; idem, Nemesiana. Sopra alcuni luoghi della 'Natura dell'uomo' in armeno: RAL vol. 2, fasc. 1 (1893) 1ff. — A. ZANOLLI, Osservazioni sulla traduzione armena del Περὶ φύσεως ἀνθρώπου di Nemesio: Giornale della Società Asiatica Italiana 19, 2 (1906) 213ff.; 21 (1908) 81ff.; 22 (1909) 155ff. — For Syriac fragments, see: J. DRÄSEKE, Zeitschrift für wissenschaftliche Theologie 46 (1903) 506ff. — For the Georgian version: A. ZANOLLI, Sulla versione georgiana del trattato di Nemesio: Atti dell'Istituto Veneto di scienze, lettere ed arti. Classe di scienze morali e lettere 107 (1948/49) 1-17.

Translations: English: G. WITHER, The Nature of Man. A Learned and Usefull Tract written in Greek by Nemesius, surnamed the Philosopher. Englished and divided into sections. London, 1636. — R. CROFT, The Character of Man, or his Nature exactly displayed, in a Philosophical Discourse by the Learned Nemesius, now made English. London, 1657. — W. TELFER, Cyril of Jerusalem and Nemesius of Emesa (LCC 4). London and Philadelphia, 1955, 224-453. — *German:* W. OSTERHAMMER, Nemesius, Über die Natur des Menschen. Salzburg, 1819. — E. ORTH, Nemesius von Emesa, Anthropologie. Maria-Martental bei Kaisersesch, 1925. — *French:* M. J. B. THIBAULT, Némésius, De la nature de l'homme. Traduit pour la première fois du grec en français. Paris, 1844. — *Italian:* D. PIZZIMENTI, Operetta d'un autore incerto, Della natura degli animati (s. a.).

Studies: General: E. AMANN, Némésius d'Émèse: DTC 11 (1931) 62-67. — E. SKARD, Nemesios: PWK Suppl.-Band 7 (1940) 562-566. — Special: M. EVANGELIDES, Zwei Kapitel aus einer Monographie über Nemesius und seine Quellen. Diss. Berlin, 1882. — D. BENDER, Untersuchungen zu Nemesius von Emesa. Diss. Leipzig, 1898. — B. DOMANSKI, Die Lehre des Nemesius über das Wesen der Seele. Diss. Münster, 1897; idem, Die Psychologie des Nemesius. Münster, 1900. — C. BURKHARD, Kritisches und Sprachliches zu Nemesius: WSt 30 (1908) 47-58; idem, Johannes von Damaskus' Auszüge aus Nemesius: Wiener Eranos. Vienna, 1909, 89-101; idem, Zur Kapitelfolge in Nemesius' Περὶ φύσεως ἀνθρώπου: Phil 69 (1910) 35-39. — W. JAEGER, Nemesios von Emesa. Quellenforschungen zum Neuplatonismus und seinen Anfängen bei Poseidonios. Berlin, 1914. — H. A. KOCH, Quellenuntersuchungen zu Nemesius von Emesa. Diss. Leipzig, 1921. — A. FERRO, La dottrina dell'anima di Nemesio di Emesa: RR 1 (1925) 227-238. — V. VALDENBERG, La philosophie byzantine aux IVe-Ve siècles: Byz 4 (1929) 237-268. — R. ARNOU, Nestorianisme et néoplatonisme: l'unité du Christ et l'union des Intelligibles: Greg 17 (1936) 116-131. — E. SKARD, Nemesiosstudien: SO 15/16 (1936) 23-43; 17 (1937) 9-25; 18 (1938) 31-45; 19 (1939) 46-56; 22 (1942) 40-48 (Nemesius depending on Origen and Galenus). — G. KLINGE, Die Bedeutung der syrischen Theologen als Vermittler der griechischen Philosophie an den Islam: ZKG 58 (1939) 363-373 (psychology of Nemesius in Mose bar Kepha). — F. LAMMERT, Hellenistische Medizin bei Ptolemaios und Nemesios. Ein Beitrag zur Geschichte der christlichen Anthropologie: Phil 94 (1940) 125-141 (Nemesius not depending on Galenus). — E. AMAND DE MENDIETA, Fatalisme et liberté dans l'antiquité grecque. Louvain, 1945, 549-569. — I. BRADY, Remigius and Nemesius: FS 8 (1948) 275-284. — F. LAMMERT, Zur Lehre von den Grundeigenschaften bei Nemesios, cap. 5: Hermes 81 (1953) 488-491. — W. TELFER, op. cit. 203-223. — E. DOBLER, Nemesius von Emesa und die Psychologie des menschlichen Aktes bei Thomas von Aquin. Fribourg, 1956.

CHRISTIANITY AND MANICHAEISM

The turn of the third and fourth century saw the beginning of the struggle between the Church and the strangest of all heresies, Manichaeism. A thorough-going syncretism akin to Gnosticism, it carries dualism to its logical extreme. Light is the power of good; all matter is evil; the works of creation originated from a commingling of light and darkness. The founder of this sect, Mani, 'the ambassador of light', set out in A.D. 240 at the age of twenty-four, to preach in Persia and Babylonia the new religion of which he was the prophet. He was crucified by the order of a Sassanian monarch in 273. But by the time of his death his religion had taken root all over the East, and in the succeeding century it had spread throughout the Roman Empire, where it lasted down into the Middle Ages.

Thanks to important discoveries in our times the knowledge of Manichaeism has greatly increased. Four scientific expeditions made in 1902/3 to Chinese Turkestan brought to light hundreds of written fragments of Manichaean manuscripts. Some are in a sort of Persian, more are in a Turkish dialect, and one in Chinese. Even more surprising was the discovery of a small Manichaean Library by C. Schmidt in 1931 in Egypt, near Lycopolis, consisting of six volumes in Coptic, containing hymns, letters, some historical accounts of the tragic deaths of Mani and his successor Sisinnius, and especially a lengthy work, called the *Chapters* or *First Principles* (κεφάλαια).

Additional information is supplied by a number of Christian refutations of the heresy. This literary opposition must have begun almost immediately. C. H. Roberts has published the second half of a pastoral that was issued against the Manichaeans as early as the third century.

Texts: A. ADAM, Texte zum Manichäismus (KT 175). Berlin, 1954. — F. C. ANDREAS and W. HENNING, Mitteliranische Manichaica aus Chinesisch-Turkestan I-III. SAB 1932/34. — H. J. POLOTSKY, Manichäische Homilien. Stuttgart, 1934. — C. SCHMIDT, H. J. POLOTSKY and A. BÖHLIG, Kephalaia. I. Hälfte. Stuttgart, 1940. — C. R. C. ALLBERRY, A Manichaean Psalm-Book. Part II. Stuttgart, 1938. See the list of sources: A. ADAM, op. cit. VI-IX. — C. H. ROBERTS, Catalogue of the Greek and Latin Papyri in the John Rylands Library 3 (1938) n. 469.

Studies: G. BARDY, Manichéisme: DTC 9 (1927) 1841-1895. Bardy gives a survey of the Anti-Manichaean writings of the Patristic authors: DTC 9 (1927) 1954-1957. — H. H. SCHAEDER, Manichäismus: RGG² 3 (1929) 1959-1973. — H. LECLERCQ, Manichéisme: DAL 10 (1931) 1390-1441. — H. J. POLOTSKY, Manichäismus: PWK Suppl.-Band 6 (1935) 240-271. — F. C. BAUR, Das manichäische Religionssystem nach den Quellen neu untersucht und entwickelt. Tübingen, 1831; reprint: Göttingen, 1928 (unsuperseded). — F. CUMONT, Recherches sur le manichéisme. I: La cosmogénie manichéenne. Brussels, 1908; II: Extrait de la CXXIIIᵉ homélie de Sévère d'Antioche;

III: L'inscription de Salone. Brussels, 1912. — P. ALFARIC, Les écritures manichéennes. Paris, I, 1918; II, 1919. — F. C. BURKITT, The Religion of the Manichees. Cambridge, 1925. — H. H. SCHAEDER, Urform und Fortbildungen des manichäischen Systems (Vorträge der Bibliothek Warburg 1924/25). Leipzig, 1927. — F. J. DÖLGER, Konstantin der Grosse und der Manichäismus. Sonne und Christus im Manichäismus: AC 2 (1930) 301-314. — A. V. W. JACKSON, Researches in Manichaeism. New York, 1932. — C. SCHMIDT, Neue Originalquellen des Manichäismus aus Ägypten: ZKG (1933) 1-28. — G. BARDY, Le manichéisme et les découvertes récentes: RAp 58 (1934) 541-559. — H. S. NYBERG, Forschungen über den Manichäismus: ZNW 34 (1935) 70-91. — H. H. SCHAEDER, Der Manichäismus nach neuen Funden und Forschungen: Orientalische Stimmen zum Erlösungsgedanken, hrsg. v. F. Taeschner (Morgenland 28). Leipzig, 1936, 80-109. — H. C. PUECH, Der Begriff der Erlösung im Manichäismus. Zurich, 1937. — C. R. C. ALLBERRY, Manichaean Studies: JThSt (1938) 337-349. — E. ROSE, Christologie des Manichäismus. Diss. Marburg, 1942. — G. WIDENGREN, Mesopotamian Elements in Manichaeism. Uppsala, 1946. — A. BÖHLIG, Die Bibel bei den Manichäern. Diss. Münster, 1947 (typ.). — G. MESSINA, Cristianesimo, buddhismo, manicheismo nell'Asia antica. Rome, 1947. — H. C. PUECH, Le manichéisme, son fondateur, sa doctrine. Paris, 1949. — T. SÄVE - SÖDERBERGH, Studies in the Coptic Manichaean Psalmbook. Uppsala, 1950. — R. H. STOCKS, Zum Canon Salemannius: ZKG 63 (1950/51) 333-337 (Manichaean Canon of Scriptures); idem, Manichäische Miszellen: ZRG 3 (1951) 148-151, 258-261, 358-363; 4 (1952) 77-78. — A. BÖHLIG, Probleme des manichäischen Lehrvortrags. Munich, 1953. — R. MANSELLI, Mani e il manicheismo alla luce di testi recentemente scoperti: Humanitas 12 (1954) 1212-1223. — M. CRAMER, Zur dualistischen Struktur der manichäischen Gnosis nach den koptischen Manichaica: OC 39 (1955) 93-101. — P. SIWEK, The Problem of Evil in the Theory of Dualism: Laval Théologique et Philosophique (1955) 67-80.

HEGEMONIUS

Among the many Christian refutations of this heresy special mention must be made of the so-called *Acta Archelai*, which represents the common source of all later Greek and Latin works on Manichaeism. It contains the narrative of a dispute between Archelaus, bishop of Charchar in Mesopotamia, and Mani (Manes), held in presence of learned arbiters who decided in favor of Archelaus. A second dispute likewise ended in a splendid victory for the prelate. With the single exception of Mani himself, there is no evidence for the historical reality of any of the participants in the debates. The form of the work is, therefore, simply a literary device for presenting effectively the arguments of the author against the Manichaean system.

This author was, according to Heraclian of Chalcedon (Photius, *Bibl. cod.* 85), a certain Hegemonius of whom we know nothing more. But Heraclian's statement has been confirmed by the new manuscript of the Latin version which ends with the signature: *Ego Egemonius scripsi disputationem istam exceptam ad describendum volentibus.*

The time of composition is the first half of the fourth century, most probably after the Council of Nicaea (325), because Archelaus uses the word *homoousios* (ch. 36, p. 52 Beeson) and declares (ch. 31,

p. 44) that if Mani were correct, Jesus sent the Paraclete only after three hundred or more years. It must have been written before 348, because Cyril of Jerusalem in his *Catechesis* 6, 20 ff. quotes from memory a part of the dialogue between Archelaus and Manes.

St. Jerome remarks (*De vir. ill.* 72): 'Archelaus, bishop of Mesopotamia, composed in the Syriac language a book of the discussion which he held with Manichaeus, when he came from Persia. This book which is translated into Greek, is possessed by many. He flourished under the Emperor Probus, who succeeded Aurelianus and Tacitus'. This information is entirely wrong. Jerome is of the false opinion that the disputes were an historical event and actually took place. Secondly, as a result of this mistaken belief he thinks that they were originally written in Syriac. The fact is that the work in its primitive form was composed in Greek. This can be proved from Epiphanius, who not only quotes a long passage of the Greek text verbatim in his *Panarium* (*Haer.* 66, 6-7. 25-31), but borrows most of his history of Manichaeism from the *Acta Archelai*. Unfortunately, the Greek original has been lost, except for the few quotations. But a Latin translation of the end of the fourth century has preserved the entire treatise. Though of rather poor quality, this version was made from a Greek, not a Syriac, original. First edited by L. A. Zacagni in 1698 at Rome, it was often reprinted, as e.g. in MG 10, 1405-1528. However, L. Traube discovered in 1903 a very valuable manuscript hitherto unknown, at the end of which is added a list of heretics drawn up in the second half of the fourth century. Thus this document provides a further proof for the early date of the Latin translation. It begins with the words: *Thesaurus verus sive disputatio habita in Carcharis civitate Mesopotamiae Archelai episcopi adversus Manen.* This seems to be the authentic title of the work, which was intended to be a refutation of a Manichaean treatise entitled *Thesaurus*, mentioned in ch. 62.

Editions: MG 10, 1405-1528. — M. J. ROUTH, Reliquiae Sacrae. 2nd ed. 5. Oxford, 1848, 1-206. — New crit. ed.: C. H. BEESON, Hegemonius, Acta Archelai, GCS 16 (1906).

Studies: H. v. ZITTWITZ, Acta disputationis Archelai et Manetis untersucht: Zeitschrift für historische Theologie 43 (1873) 467-528. — A. OBLASINSKI, Acta disputationis Archelai et Manetis. Diss. Leipzig, 1874. — K. KESSLER, Mani. Forschungen über die manichäische Religion I. Berlin, 1889, 87-171 (language and form of composition). Cf. T. NÖLDEKE, ZDMG 43 (1889) 535-549. — A. HARNACK, Die Acta Archelai und das Diatessaron Tatians (TU 1, 3). Leipzig, 1883; *idem*, Geschichte der altchrist. Literatur 1, 2, 540f.; 2, 2, 163ff. Harnack first thought of a Syriac original, but later changed his mind. — L. TRAUBE, Acta Archelai. Vorbemerkung zu einer neuen Ausgabe: SAM Phil.-hist. Klasse (1903) 533-549. — H. J. POLOTSKY, Koptische Zitate aus den Acta Archelai: Mus 45 (1932) 18-20. — A. L. KATZ, Manichaeism in the Roman Empire according to the Acta Archelai: Vestnik Drevnej Istorii (Moskva) 1 (1955) 3 n. 53, 168-179 (in Russian).

TITUS OF BOSTRA

The Emperor Julian the Apostate addressed on August 1, 362 a letter (*Ep.* 52) to the people of Bostra, the capital of the province Arabia (Hauran), in which he attacked their bishop Titus:

It is my pleasure to declare and publish to all the people, by this edict, that they must not abet the seditions of the clergy nor suffer themselves to be induced by them to throw stones, and disobey the magistrates. They may assemble together, if they please, and offer up such prayers as they have established for themselves. But if the clergy endeavour to persuade them to foment disturbances on their account, let them by no means concur, on pain of punishment.

I thought proper to make this declaration to the city of Bostra in particular, because the bishop, Titus, and the clergy, in a memorial which they have presented to me, have accused the people of being inclined to raise disturbances, if they had not been restrained by their admonitions. I transcribe the words which the bishop has dared to insert in that memorial: 'Though the Christians are as numerous as the Gentiles, they are restrained by our exhortations from being tumultuous'. These are the words of the bishop concerning you. Observe, he does not ascribe your regularity to your own inclination; unwillingly, he says, you refrain 'by his exhortations'. As your accuser, therefore, expel him from the city.

From these words of the emperor it appears that Bishop Titus had received a communication from the emperor, which blamed him for the unrest among the populace of Bostra. Titus thereupon presented an address to Julian and drew attention to the tense situation, which was only kept in hand by the bishop's exhortations. It was not skilful statesmanship but rather a deliberate effort to foment sedition among the Christians, when the emperor immediately responded by urging the citizens to throw the bishop out of the city for speaking ill of them. There is no indication whatsoever that Bostra followed this suggestion. On the contrary, Titus was still bishop there at the end of 363 when his signature appears on a declaration of a synod at Antioch acknowledging the *homoousion* and ratifying the Nicene Creed. Jerome (*De vir. ill.* 102) testifies that Titus died under Valens (363-378).

HIS WRITINGS

The same Jerome reports *(ibid.)* that the bishop of Bostra wrote 'vigorous works against the Manichaeans, and some other things'.

1. *Against the Manichaeans*

This treatise has made him famous. It consists of four books and must have been composed after Julian's death (June 26, 363), to which it alludes (2, 28). The first book vindicates the justice of God in permitting evil to exist and warns against subjective speculation about this problem. A solution cannot be found except in the Catholic doctrine that evil is not a cosmic and eternal principle but must be attributed to the free choice of man and his passions. The Manichaean myth of the incursion of the Dark on the Light and of the continuous battle between the two is successfully refuted with skilful logic and detailed reasoning. The second book is a defense of the Christian teaching on Divine Creation and Providence against the Manichaean idea of the eternal existence of matter and evil. The author then proceeds from speculative to biblical theology, and in the third book examines the Manichaean concept of revelation and inspiration. He proves the divine origin of the Old Testament and refutes the heretical opinion that the latter is a work of evil and the New Testament only partly inspired by the Holy Ghost. He demonstrates the non-Christian character of Mani's own writings and the falsity of his interpretation of a number of Old Testament passages. The fourth book turns to the New Testament and exposes the tendency of the opponents to revise its text to fit their own system. The doctrine of the Incarnation and Virginal Birth and the Scriptural texts dealing with the devil are carefully explained and contrasted with the dualism of the heretics.

The work won great repute and deservedly so. It was used again and again by later Anti-Manichaean writers as well as by compilers of dogmatic anthologies. It has a special historical value by reason of its numerous exact quotations and paraphrases of Manichaean works. There is, however, no clear distinction between the teachings of Mani himself and his disciples. This shortcoming, which Titus has in common with many other anti-heretical authors, explains perhaps the criticism of Heraclian of Chalcedon (Photius, *Bibl. cod.* 85) that Titus was supposed to be an opponent of the Manichaeans, whereas he rather attacked the writings of Addas.

At any rate, the four books prove the author's rhetorical skill and his excellent philosophic training as well as his sober exegetical judgment. He stresses the importance of authority in the teaching of the Church as a guide and a guardian of human reason. He refrains from using any controversial terminology in his Christology. Though clearly defending the pre-existence and eternal generation of Christ, he does not take any definite position on the relation between the Father and the Son. For this reason his above mentioned subscribing to the *homoousion* appears all the more interesting. Book II represents the most detailed treatise on theodicy in early Christian literature.

The entire work is extant in a Syriac translation made within five years of the author's death, and preserved in the manuscript *Brit. Mus. Add.* 12150, dated A.D. 411. Of the original Greek only the first two books and a small portion of the third (chapters 1-7) have survived in *Codex Genova, Biblioteca della Missione urbana gr.* 37 and several copies of it, e.g. *Athos Vatopedi* 236. The new critical edition projected by Brinkmann and Nix was never completed, but that by R. P. Casey for the GCS should appear soon.

Editions: MG 18, 1069-1264: Greek text. The Syriac text was edited by P. A. DE LAGARDE, Titi Bostreni contra Manichaeos libri quatuor Syriace. Berlin, 1859; reprint: Hannover, 1924; *idem*, Titi Bostreni quae ex opere contra Manichaeos edito in codice Hamburgensi servata sunt Graece. Berlin, 1859.

Studies: R. P. CASEY, The Text of the Anti-Manichaean Writings of Titus of Bostra and Serapion of Thmuis: HThR 21 (1928) 97-111; *idem*, Titus von Bostra: PWK II. Reihe 6 (1937) 1586-1591. — R. REITZENSTEIN, Eine wertlose und eine wertvolle Über-lieferung über den Manichäismus: NGWG (1931) 28-58 (Alexander of Lycopolis and Titus of Bostra). — A. BAUMSTARK, Der Text der Mani-Zitate in der syrischen Über-setzung des Titus von Bostra: OC (1931) 23-42; *idem*, Die syrische Übersetzung des Titus von Bostra und das Diatessaron: Bibl (1935) 257-299. — W. FRANKENBERG, Die Streitschrift des Titus von Bostra gegen die Manichäer: ZDMG (1938) 28-29.

2. *Commentary on St. Luke*

Only fragments have come down to us of his Commentary on Luke. They are found in *Catenae* of Nicetas of Heraclea (11th century) and others, in a commentary on Daniel by Johannes Drungarius (7/8th century) and in a *catena*-like compilation of quotations from Titus, Cyril of Alexandria and other Fathers, that cannot be earlier than the sixth century. These excerpts cover almost all the chapters of the Gospel of St. Luke and suggest that the commentary consisted of a series of homilies. The exegesis has much in common with the sober interpretation found in Titus' *Adversus Manichaeos*.

Editions: J. SICKENBERGER, Titus von Bostra. Studien zu dessen Lukashomilien (TU 21, 1). Leipzig, 1901. — P. BELLET, Excerpts of Titus of Bostra in the Coptic Catena on the Gospels: SP I (TU 63). Berlin, 1957, 10-14.

Study: J. SICKENBERGER, Über griechische Evangelienkommentare: BiZ 1 (1903) 182-193.

3. *Sermon on Epiphany*

The so-called *Florilegium Edessenum (Brit. Mus. Add.* 12156) of the sixth century contains several Syriac fragments of a sermon on Epiphany by Titus, which seems to be genuine.

The same cannot be said of an *Oratio in ramos palmarum*, which Combefis edited under the name of Titus in 1648 (reprinted in Migne, MG 18, 1263-78). First of all there is a definite predilection for the allegorical interpretation of Scripture, a trait that does not

fit the author of *Contra Manichaeos*. Secondly, the sermon betrays
a pronounced partiality for Monophysitism. Thirdly, it presupposes
the liturgical celebration of Palm Sunday and its connection with
a commemoration of the resurrection of Lazarus. The feast was by
no means universal at the time, though it existed in the liturgical
calendar of Jerusalem at least in the reign of Theodosius and is
mentioned in the so-called *Peregrinatio Aetheriae* (81/84 Geyer).

The *Explanation of the Parables of the Unjust Judge and of the
Pharisee and the Publican*, attributed to Titus, is nothing but a
borrowing from Pseudo-Titus' Commentary on the Gospel of
St. Luke, edited as a genuine work of Titus by Fronto Ducaeus in
1624, and not to be confused with the authentic commentary
mentioned above.

Edition: I. RUCKER, Florilegium Edessenum anonymum (SAM Phil.-hist. Abt., Heft 5).
Munich, 1933, 82-87 (Syriac fragments of Epiphany sermon).

CYRIL OF JERUSALEM

Among the bishops of Jerusalem of the fourth century, only one
has gained repute as an ecclesiastical writer, Cyril, the well-known
author of the famous series of catechetical lectures. The place and
date of his birth are unknown, though it has been generally supposed
that he was born at Jerusalem about 315. At any rate, he became
bishop of that city in 348. Since the metropolitan of Caesarea, the
Arian bishop Acacius, consecrated him, the suspicion arose early
that he obtained his appointment by concessions to Arianism.
Socrates (*Hist. eccl.* 2, 38) and Sozomen (*Hist. eccl.* 4, 20) even go
further and assert that Cyril's predecessor Maximus was banished
for his orthodoxy and Cyril intruded as an Arianizer. But this
statement is contradicted by Theodoret (*Hist. eccl.* 2, 22) and by
the Synodal Letter of the Council of Constantinople of 382 (*ibid.*
5, 9). The fact is that soon after his consecration a conflict arose
between Cyril and Acacius and the Arians began to attack the
bishop of Jerusalem as the confessor and defender of the Nicene
faith. He was expelled three times from his see. He was first deposed
at a Council in Jerusalem in 357 and took refuge in Tarsus. After
he was restored by the Council at Seleucia in the next year, Acacius
banished him again in 360, but he was allowed to return to his
see in 362 on Julian's accession. Though Acacius died in 366,
Cyril's longest exile was yet to come. In 367 the Emperor Valens
deprived him once more of his diocese, which he did not regain
until eleven years later (378) after the ruler's death. In 381 he
took part in the Second Ecumenical Council of Constantinople.

He most probably died on March 18, 386, the day which the liturgical Calendars of the East and West have kept as his feast.

Studies: J. MADER, Der hl. Cyrillus, Bischof von Jerusalem, in seinem Leben und seinen Schriften. Einsiedeln, 1891. — E. H. GIFFORD, Cyril of Jerusalem. London, 1893. — J. LEBON, La position de St. Cyrille de Jérusalem dans les luttes provoquées par l'arianisme: RHE 20 (1924) 181-210, 357-386. — J. PHOKYLIDES, 'Ο ἅγιος Κύριλλος ἐπίσκοπος 'Ιεροσολύμων : NS 25 (1933) 294-300. — X. LE BACHELET, DTC 3 (1908) 2527-2577. — G. BARDY, Cyrille de Jérusalem: DHG 13 (1956) 1181-1185; *idem*, DSp 2 (1953) 2683-2687. — M. JUGIE, Cirillo di Gerusalemme: EC 3 (1950) 1725-1729.

HIS WRITINGS

1. *The Catechetical Lectures*

The series of twenty-four catechetical lectures, most of which he delivered in the church of the Holy Sepulchre, is one of the most precious treasures of Christian antiquity. A note preserved in several of the manuscripts records that they were taken down in short-hand, which means that we have a transcript made by one of his listeners, and not the bishop's own copy. The lectures actually fall into two groups. The first comprises the *Procatechesis* or introductory discourse and eighteen *Catecheses* addressed to the candidates for baptism, the φωτιζόμενοι, who were to receive this sacrament at the coming Easter. They were delivered during Lent. The second consists of the last five instructions, called *Mystagogical Catecheses* and addressed to the neophytes *(νεοφώτιστοι)* during Easter week.

The *Procatechesis* opens with an enthusiastic welcome. 'Already the savour of bliss is upon you, who have come to be enlightened; you have begun to pluck spiritual flowers with which to weave your heavenly crowns. Already are you redolent of the fragrance of the Holy Spirit. You have reached the royal vestibule. O may the King himself conduct you within!' (LCC) The bishop then stresses the seriousness of the step to be taken by the candidates, the need for penance and prayer, for self-discipline and strengthening of the will, for the right intention and the purest motives in approaching the sacrament of initiation. There is a strong insistence on the rule of secrecy *(disciplina arcani)*. The candidates are solemnly warned not to disclose what they will be taught, not even to the ordinary catechumens:

> When the instruction is over, if any catechumen tries to get out of you what your teachers told you, tell nothing, for he is outside the mystery that we have delivered to you, with its hope of the age to come. Guard the mystery for his sake from whom you look for reward. Never let anyone persuade you, saying 'What harm is it that I should

know as well?'... Already you stand on the frontier of mystery. I adjure you to smuggle no word out (12 LCC).

This spirit of mystery pervades the entire corpus of lectures, especially the last five.

The first of the prebaptismal catecheses deals with the temper of mind requisite for baptism. It urges us to lay aside all mundane concern, forgive personal enemies and feed the soul by reading the Bible. The second treats of penitence and the remission of sins, of the devil and his temptations; the third of baptism and salvation, of the baptismal rite, its meaning and its effects. The fourth gives a summary of the Christian doctrine and the fifth discusses the nature and origin of faith. The following twelve catecheses (6-18) contain an exposition of the successive articles of the Jerusalem Creed, which shows great similarity with the so-called Symbol of the Council of Constantinople in 381.

The five *Mystagogical Catecheses* (19-23) are based on the liturgical ceremonies of the three sacraments which the neophytes had received in the course of the Easter Vigil. Thus the first two (19-20) deal with Baptism, the third (21) with Confirmation, the fourth (22) with Eucharistic doctrine and the fifth (23) with the liturgy of Mass.

There is disagreement among scholars as to the exact year when these lectures were delivered. Attempts have been made to determine the date by one or two casual references, especially the statement in *Cat.* 6, 20 that the heresy of Mani began seventy years before the date at which St. Cyril was speaking. This would give 347 or 348, and would imply that he preached these sermons while still a presbyter, because in Lent, 348, his predecessor Maximus was apparently still alive, since according to Jerome's *Chronicle*, he died between May 348 and May 349. However, nothing in the sermons implies that Cyril speaks as a priest entrusted by his bishop with the office of instructing the candidates. Thus other scholars have drawn the conclusion that he was a bishop himself when he delivered them and that the most probable date is 350.

More serious is the difference of opinion regarding the authenticity. Though there is today general agreement on the genuineness of the prebaptismal lectures, doubts have been cast in our times on that of the *Mystagogical Catecheses*. It is a fact that *Codex Monac. gr.* 394 expressly ascribes the latter to Cyril's successor in the see, Bishop John of Jerusalem (386-417). Three other manuscripts, *Ottobon.* 86 and 466, and *Monac. gr.* 278 attribute them to Cyril and John and yet others have the prebaptismal, but not the supplementary instructions. This manuscript evidence is the main reason why Th. Schermann, W. J. Swaans, M. Richard, W. Telfer and others think that the Mystagogic Catecheses must be attributed to John rather than to Cyril. Other arguments do not seem to be as cogent. Swaans regards the external attestation as relatively late, because Eustratius of Constantinople in the sixth or seventh century is the first who cites from the Mystagogic lectures as explicitly Cyril's. Schermann and Telfer are of the opinion that several characteristic features of the liturgy described in these five Catecheses are to be expected in a work of the 390's but would be surprising forty years earlier. Against all these considerations F. L. Cross and others have pointed to a number of allusions in either group to the other which suggest common authorship. Thus Cyril announces 18, 33 the *Mystagogical Catecheses*:

> After the holy and salvation-bringing feast of Easter, beginning on the Monday, you shall, God willing, hear further lectures, if you will come into the holy place of the resurrection each day of Easter week after the liturgy. In these you will be instructed again in the reasons for each of the things that took place. You will be given proofs from the Old and New Testaments, first, of course, for the things that were done immediately before your baptism, and next how you have been made clean from your sins by the Lord 'with the washing of water by the word', then how you have entered into the right to be called 'Christ' in virtue of your 'priesthood', then how you have been given the 'sealing' of fellowship with the Holy Spirit, then about the mysteries of the altar of the new covenant which had their origin here, what Holy Scripture tells us about them, with what virtue they are filled, then how these mysteries are to be approached and when and how received, and so, finally, how for the rest of your life you must walk worthily of the grace you have received both by deed and word, so as all to attain to the enjoyment of eternal life. If God will, then, these lectures will be given (LCC).

There cannot be any doubt that the contents of the five *Mystagogical Catecheses* correspond very closely with what Cyril here promises. However, the difficulty remains that he announces a mystagogic lecture for every day in Easter week and that there are only five in the manuscripts. This does not show that the five are not by Cyril but seems to indicate that if they are, they do not belong to the same year as the prebaptismal catecheses. Again, in 16, 26 he implies that in a later lecture he will tell his listeners how a laying on of hands will bring to them the gift of the Spirit:

> In Moses' time the Spirit was given by the laying on of hands. Peter likewise gave the Spirit by the laying on of hands. Now this grace is shortly to come upon you when you are baptized. I am not telling you just now, for I am not taking anything out of turn (LCC).

But he never fulfilled this promise because in the third mystagogical lecture on Chrism, he makes no reference to the laying
on of hands, though he refers to Moses anointing Aaron. On the
other hand, the *Mystagogical Catecheses* contain several (19, 9;
23, 1) clear allusions to an earlier series of prebaptismal lectures.

Under these circumstances it seems that neither the manuscript
tradition nor the allusions suffice to establish or to disprove Cyril's
authorship. The liturgy described by the author of the mystagogic
lectures is equally inconclusive as an argument. That it contains
an Epiclesis, a recitation of the Our Father and a prayer for the
Emperor in the plural does not demonstrate that these five lectures
were wrongly attributed to Cyril and must be ascribed to John of
Jerusalem. Nor does the fact that the author assigns the virtue of
Chrism to the Third Person of the Trinity and teaches a Eucharistic
presence of Christ by metabolism of the elements. Nevertheless,
Telfer is inclined to believe that Cyril's lectures were transcribed,
but only those which he gave before Easter; that by the 390's the
absence of mystagogic instructions was felt to be a defect in the
book in circulation, and so five such composed by John were added,
but without the attribution to John always being copied. However,
the manuscript evidence could be explained in a different way: The
fact that the mystagogic lectures were attributed to John in one of
the codices and to Cyril and John in three of them, could indicate
that Cyril prepared them and delivered them first, but that later
his successor John revised them.

Editions: A. A. TOUTTÉE and P. MARAN, Paris, 1720 (Maurists); reprinted: MG 33,
331-1180. — More recent ed.: W. K. REISCHL and J. RUPP, Munich, 1848/1860 (text.
improvements based on Cod. Monac. gr. 394). — J. QUASTEN, S. Cyrilli Catecheses
mystagogicae: FP 7 (1935) 69-111. — F. L. CROSS, St. Cyril of Jerusalem's Lectures
on the Christian Sacraments. The Procatechesis and the Five Mystagogical Catecheses
(SPCK). London, 1951. — An Armenian version of the *Catecheses* (without the
Mystagogical) was published by the Mechitarists, Vienna, 1832. — For another Armenian
version of chapters 8 and 9, see: R. P. CASEY, Armenian inedita: Mus 68 (1955) 55-59.
— Fragments of a Palestinian-Aramaic version were collected by H. DUENSING, Christlich
palästinisch-aramäische Texte und Fragmente. Göttingen, 1906, 41-62. — For Arabic
versions, see: G. GRAF, Geschichte der christlichen arabischen Literatur. I (ST 118).
Vatican City, 1944, 335. — A. VAILLANT, La traduction vieux-slave des Catéchèses de
Cyrille de Jérusalem, La dernière Catéchèse: Byzantinoslavica 4 (1932) 253-302, has in
addition to the Old Slavonic version a much improved Greek text of the second *Catechesis*.

Translations: English: R. W. CHURCH, LFC 2 (1838) with pref. by J. H. Newman; rev.
by E. H. GIFFORD, LNPF series 2, vol. 7 (1894) 1-157. — H. DE ROMESTIN, The Five
Lectures of St. Cyril on the Mysteries. Oxford, 1887 (with Greek text). — F. L. CROSS,
op. cit. (reproduces the transl. of R. W. Church). — R. M. WOOLLEY, Instructions on
the Mysteries of St. Cyril of Jerusalem. London, 1930. — W. TELFER, Cyril of Jerusalem
and Nemesius of Emesa (LCC 4). London and Philadelphia, 1955, 64-192 (selections
from the *Catechetical Lectures*). — *German:* J. NIRSCHL, BKV (1871). — P. HÄUSER,
BKV² 41 (1922). — L. A. WINTERSWYL, Des hl. Bischofs Cyrill von Jerusalem Reden

der Einweihung (*Mystagogical Catecheses*). Freiburg i.B., 1939; 2nd ed. 1954. — *French:* M. Véricel, Cyrille de Jérusalem (Collection Église d'hier et d'aujourd'hui). Paris, 1957 (selections). — *Italian:* G. Carraro, Cirillo di Gerusalemme, Le Catechesi, trad. e note. Vicenza, 1942. — *Dutch:* J. van Ruyven, Cyrillus van Jerusalem, Catechesen of toespraken tot de doopelingen I (Getuigen, 1e reeks, dl. 4). Amsterdam, 1941. — *Spanish:* A. Ubierna, San Cirilo de Jerusalén, Las Catequeses traducidas directamente del griego y precedidas de una introducción (Los grandes maestros de la dotrina cristiana 2). Madrid, 1926. — A. Ortega, Las Catequeses de San Cirilo de Jerusalén (Colección Excelsa 21/22). Madrid, 1946. — J. Solano, Textos Eucarísticos Primitivos I (BAC). Madrid, 1952, 322-337 (*Myst. Cat.* 4-5).

Studies: L. L. Rochat, Le catéchuménat au IVe siècle d'après les Catéchèses de St. Cyrille de Jérusalem. Geneva, 1875. — C. P. Caspari, Alte und neue Quellen zur Geschichte des Taufsymbols. Christiania, 1879, 146-160 (*Cat.* 4). — A. Heisenberg, Grabeskirche und Apostelkirche. Leipzig, 1908, I, 47-89. — J. P. Bock, Die Brotbitte des Vaterunsers. Ein Beitrag zum Verständnis des Universalgebetes und einschlägiger liturgisch-patristischer Fragen. Paderborn, 1911 (*Myst. Cat.* 5). Cf. T. Schermann, ThR 10 (1911) 575-579. — S. Salaville, Les 'Catéchèses mystagogiques' de S. Cyrille de Jérusalem. Une question critique littéraire: EO 17 (1915) 531-537 (against Schermann). — T. H. Bindley, On Some Points Doctrinal and Practical in the Catechetical Lectures of St. Cyril of Jerusalem: American Journal of Theology 21 (1917) 598-607. — A. Bludau, Der Katechumenat in Jerusalem im 4. Jahrhundert: ThGl 16 (1924) 225-242; *idem*, Die Pilgerreise der Aetheria. Paderborn, 1927, 41-190 (liturgy of Jerusalem). — L. Duchesne, Origines du culte chrétien. 5th ed. Paris, 1925, 57-65. — H. Leclercq, Jérusalem (La liturgie à): DAL 7 (1927) 2374-2392. — M. Bulacu, The Problem of the Christian Conscience according to the Catecheses of Cyril of Jerusalem: Studii Teol. 7 (1939) 141-178 (in Rumanian). — W. J. Swaans, A propos des 'Catéchèses mystagogiques' attribuées à S. Cyrille de Jérusalem: Mus 55 (1942) 1-43. Cf. M. Richard, MSR 6 (1948) 282; P. Peeters, AB (1943) 270f. (against Swaans). — G. Dix, The Shape of the Liturgy. London, 1945, 187-209, 349-354. — D. Moraitis, Cyril of Jerusalem as a Catechist and Educator: Greg. Palamas 30 (1948) 57-59, 122-130, 187-200, 238-246, 283-286 (in Greek). — J. C. M. Fruytier, Cyrillus' auteurschap van de Mystagogische Catechesen toch nog te redden?: StC 26 (1951) 282-288. — G. Touton, La méthode catéchétique de S. Cyrille de Jérusalem comparée à celles de St. Augustin et de Théodore de Mopsueste: Proche-Orient Chrétien 1 (1951) 265-285. — F. Cross, op. cit. IX-XLI. — W. Telfer, op. cit. 9-63. — J. H. Greenlee, The Gospel Text of Cyril of Jerusalem. Copenhagen, 1955. — A. A. Stephenson, St. Cyril of Jerusalem and the Alexandrian Heritage: TS 15 (1954) 573-593; *idem*, The Lenten Catechetical Syllabus in the Fourth-Century Jerusalem: TS 15 (1954) 103-116 (the Jerusalem Creed as subject matter of Cyril's teaching); *idem*, St. Cyril of Jerusalem and the Alexandrian Christian Gnosis: SP I (TU 63). Berlin, 1957, 147-156.

2. *Letter to the Emperor Constantius*

The Letter reports about the miraculous apparition of a great cross of light that was seen from Jerusalem on May 7, 351:

For in these very days of the holy feast of Pentecost, on the Nones of May, about the third hour a gigantic cross formed of light appeared in the sky above holy Golgotha stretching out as far as the holy Mount of Olives. It was not seen by just one or two, but was most clearly displayed before the whole population of the city. Nor did it, as one might have supposed, pass away quickly like something imagined, but was visible to sight above the earth for some hours, while it sparkled

with a light above the sun's rays. Of a surety, it would have been
overcome and hidden by them, had it not exhibited to those who saw
it a brilliance more powerful than the sun, so that the whole population
of the city made a sudden concerted rush into the Martyry, seized by
a fear that mingled with joy at the heavenly vision. They poured in,
young and old, men and women of every age... not only Christians
but pagans from elsewhere sojourning in Jerusalem, all of them as
with one mouth raised a hymn of praise to Christ Jesus our Lord, the
only-begotten Son of God, the worker of wonders (4 LCC).

The letter ends with the wish that God may grant the Emperor
health and a continuance of his wonted solicitude for the holy
Churches and the sovereignty of Rome through many cycles of
peaceful years, 'ever to glorify the holy and consubstantial Trinity,
our true God, to whom, as is due, be all glory, world without end,
Amen'. Since Cyril never uses the word *homoousios* in his catecheses,
its appearance in this passage has caused some scholars to question
the authenticity of the letter. There is no reason to do so. The
vocabulary and style are decidedly Cyril's and there are a number
of striking correspondances with the language of the lectures.
Sozomen (*Hist. Eccl.* 4, 5) mentions Cyril's letter to the Emperor
and says that pilgrims carried the news of the miracle of 351 all
over the world. The manuscripts attribute the Epistle unanimously
to Cyril. Two explanations for the *homoousios* are possible. It could
be that Cyril meanwhile had changed his attitude towards the term
or that a scribe added the doxology at the end of the letter to
vindicate Cyril's orthodoxy. The basis for the latter conjecture is
that the entire phrase beginning 'ever to glorify' is missing in the
Munich copy made in the sixteenth century by Andrew Damarius.

Another interesting feature of the letter (ch. 3) is its passing
reference to the discovery of the True Cross 'fraught with salvation'
in the days of Constantine the Great. This fact is also mentioned
in *Catecheses* 4, 10; 10, 19; and 13, 4. However, Cyril gives no hint
of the later legend of the miracles connected with the discovery.

Editions: MG 33, 1165-1176. — J. Rupp, op. cit. II, 434-440.

Translation: English: W. Telfer, op. cit. 193-199.

Studies: A. Heisenberg, op. cit. I, 85ff. — J. Straubinger, Die Kreuzauffindungslegende.
Paderborn, 1912, 104ff. — F. J. Dölger, Das Anhängekreuzchen der hl. Makrina und
ihr Ring mit der Kreuzpartikel: AC 3 (1932) 100-102 (*homoousios* inserted). — J. Vogt,
Berichte über Kreuzeserscheinungen aus dem 4. Jahrhundert n. Chr.: AIPh 9 (1949)
593-606.

3. *Homilies*

Of his homilies we possess only one in its entirely, that on the
paralytic: *In paralyticum iuxta piscinam iacentem* (John 5, 5). Cyril

must have delivered it while he was still a presbyter because he mentions (ch. 20) the exhortation of the bishop which was to follow his. There are striking parallels of expressions between this homily and the *Catecheses*.

Not more than four brief fragments remain of his other homilies. The homily on the feast of Hypapante and other writings are wrongly attributed to him.

Editions: Sermon *On the Paralytic:* MG 33, 1131-1154. — J. Rupp, op. cit. II, 406-426. — Homily on the feast of Hypapante: MG 33, 1187-1204. — Fragments: MG 33, 1181-1182; F. Diekamp, Doctrina Patrum de incarnatione Verbi. Münster, 1907, 20; 92-93. The fragment published by F. Diekamp, Analecta Patristica, Rome, 1938, 10-12, is spurious. — For other writings falsely ascribed to Cyril, see: A. Raes, Anaphora Cyrilli Hier. (Anaphorae Syriacae I, 3). Rome, 1944. — E. A. W. Budge, Miscellaneous Coptic Texts. London, 1915, 49-73, 183-230. — For Arabic spuria, see: P. Carali, L'exaltation de la Croix, homélie attribuée à S. Cyrille de Jérusalem: Al-Machriq (Beyrouth) 31 (1933) 575-589, 743-754, 839-852, 883-907; 32 (1934) 37-65, 212-234, 367-392, 510-539. Although Carali defends the authenticity, it seems to be not authentic; cf. G. Graf, OC 32 (1935) 274-276. — G. Graf, Geschichte der christlichen arabischen Literatur I, Rome, 1944, 335-337, gives a list of the other Arabic works attributed to Cyril. — For the 'Alexandrian' character of the sermon *On the Paralytic*, see: A. A. Stephenson, SP I (1957) 142-147.

THEOLOGICAL ASPECTS

Today it is generally agreed that there is no reason to assume that in his earlier life Cyril shared the Arian views of which he has been accused (cf. above, p. 362). It seems that for a long time he displayed an attitude of reserve towards the contemporary dogmatic controversies. Perhaps his mind was too practical to be really interested in such questions. In his *Catecheses* he never speaks of Arianism. Nevertheless, he frequently opposes its teaching and decidedly defends the complete unity of essence between the Father and the Son.

1. *Christology*

In his eleventh *Catechesis* he teaches clearly the divinity of Christ and parries the Arian argument that 'there was a time when He was not' and that He was the Son of God 'by adoption':

Being begotten of the Father, He is Son of God by nature, not by adoption... Now when you hear of God begetting, do not fall a-thinking in corporeal terms, or risk blaspheming by imagining corruptible generation. 'God is a Spirit' (John 4, 24). Divine generation is spiritual. Bodies are begotten from bodies, and there has to be an interval of time for it to be completed. But time does not come into the begetting of the Son from the Father. Bodies are begotten in an imperfect state, but the Son of God was begotten perfect. For what He is now, that has He been timelessly begotten from the beginning. We are begotten so as to develop from childishness to rationality. Being man, your first state is imperfect and your advance is by stages. But do not imagine anything of that sort in divine generation, or charge the Begetter with lack of power. For you might charge the Begetter with lack of power, if the Begotten was first imperfect and then reached perfection in time; that is if the Begetter did not fully grant from the beginning what was by supposition granted after the lapse of time.

Do not think, therefore, in terms of human generation, as when Abraham begat Isaac. For Abraham truly begat Isaac, but what he begat was not the product of his will, but what another rendered to him. But when God the Father begat, it was not as unknowing what should be, or only after some deliberation. It would be the extreme of blasphemy to say that God did not know whom He was begetting; nor would it be any less blasphemous to say that the Father became Father only after deliberating. For God was not at first childless, and then after lapse of time became Father, but He had his Son from all eternity, not begetting Him as men beget men, but as He alone knows Who begat Him, true God before all ages. The Father, being Himself true God begat a Son like to Himself, true God *(θεὸς ἀληθινός)*.

Here the Arian position is successfully refuted and Cyril's teaching is in complete accord with the Nicene faith. Christ is 'true God' in the same sense as the Father (11, 14) and he is one with the Father: 'One They are because of the dignity pertaining to the Godhead; one in respect of their kingdom; one because there is no discord nor division between Them; one because the creative works of Christ are no other than the Father's' (11, 16). He states explicitly: 'He Who for man's sake descended into hell is identical with man's Maker from the clay in the beginning' (11, 24).

Nevertheless, it remains a fact that Cyril never uses the Nicene ὁμοούσιος. This cannot be accidental. He must have avoided the term on purpose. There are two explanations for this strange attitude, so inconsistent with his general belief. Since he (*Cat.* 5, 12) insists on the necessity of scriptural language, it is possible that he disapproved of the introduction into the Creed of new words not to be found in the inspired writings of the evangelists and Apostles. Hitherto every Creed had been made up of expressions from the Bible. Thus Cyril describes that which the candidates for baptism should learn by heart: 'Now the one and only faith that you are to take and preserve in the way of learning and professing it is that which is now being committed to you by the Church as confirmed throughout the Scriptures. For seeing that not everyone can read the Scriptures, some because they lack the learning and others because for one reason or another, they find no opportunity to get to know them, we gain possession of the whole doctrine of the Christian faith in a few articles... These articles of our faith were not composed out of human opinion, but are the principal points collected out of the whole Scripture to complete a single doctrinal formulation of the faith' (*Cat.* 5, 12). The other reason for his objection to the term *homoousios* could be the Sabellian meaning which many saw in the word. He repeatedly (*Cat.* 4, 8; 11, 13. 16. 17; 15, 9; 16, 4) warns his listeners against this heresy. He shows that he is equally opposed to Arius as well as Sabellius, when he states:

> Believe also in the Son of God, Who is one and sole, our Lord Jesus Christ, God begotten from God, life begotten from life, light gendered from light, like in all things to Him that begat Him (ἐν πᾶσιν ὅμοιος τῷ γεγεννηκότι): Who did not receive His being in time but was begotten of the Father before all ages in a manner eternal and incomprehensible. He is God's wisdom and power and His righteousness existing hypostatically. He is enthroned at God's right hand from before all ages. For He was not, as some have supposed, crowned after His passion, as though God seated Him at His right hand for His endurance of the cross, but has royal dignity from that source whence He has His being, to wit, in being eternally begotten from the Father, and shares the Father's throne, being God, and, as we said, being the wisdom and the power of God. He reigns together with the Father, and through the Father is creator of all things. He falls in nothing short of the majesty of the Godhead and knows the Father that begat Him as He Himself is known of His Father. To state the matter in brief, I remind you of the gospel, 'None knoweth the Son, but the Father: neither knoweth any the Father, save the Son' (Matth. 11, 27).
>
> Nor must you make the Son alien from the Father [sc. as did Arius] nor, on the other hand, put your faith in a Father-who-is-His-own-Son (υἱοπατορίαν), by making the concepts coalesce [sc. as did Sabellius]; but you must believe that there is one only-begotten Son of one God, the Word Who is God before all ages (*Cat.* 4, 7/8 LCC).

Studies: J. MARQUARDT, S. Cyrilli Hieros. de contionibus et placitis Arianorum sententia. Braunsberg, 1881. — J. LEBON, cf. above, p. 363. — B. NIEDERBERGER, Die Logosidee des heiligen Cyrillus von Jerusalem (FLDG 14, 5). Paderborn, 1923. — V. ILIEV, The Orthodoxy of St. Cyril of Jerusalem: Duchovna Kultura (1930) 237-248; (1932) 136-151. Cf. RHE 28 (1932) 64* n. 1109 and 29 (1933) 73* n. 1209; BZ 34 (1934) 187. — H. A. WOLFSON, Philosophical Implications of the Theology of Cyril of Jerusalem: DOP 11 (1957) 1-19 (*homoousios*).

2. *Holy Spirit*

As the Son, so is the Holy Spirit sharer in the Father's divinity:

> Only the Holy Ghost, together with the Son, has a true vision of God, 'searcheth all things, and knoweth even the deep things of God'

(I Cor. 2, 10), as also the only-begotten Son has essential knowledge of the Father, together with the Holy Spirit: as He says 'neither knoweth anyone the Father save the Son, and he to whomsoever the Son will reveal Him' (Matth. 11, 27). For He has the essential vision, and reveals God through the Spirit according to each man's capacity. And this is because the only-begotten Son is, with the Holy Spirit, sharer in the Father's Godhead (*Cat.* 6, 6 LCC).

Cyril affirms repeatedly the distinct personality of the Spirit and draws attention to the directly personal action attributed to Him: 'He Who speaks and sends is living and subsisting [personal] and operating' (*Cat.* 17, 9. 28. 33. 34). Once he states:

> It is established that there are various appellations, but one and the same Spirit — the Holy Spirit, living and personally subsisting and always present together with the Father and the Son; not as being spoken or breathed forth from the mouth and lips of the Father and the Son, or diffused into the air; but as a personally existing being, Himself speaking and operating and exercising His dispensation and hallowing, since it is certain that the dispensation of salvation in regard to us which proceeds from Father and Son and Holy Spirit is indivisible and concordant and one (*Cat.* 17, 11).

He sums up his trinitarian belief: 'Undivided is our faith, inseparable our reverence. We neither separate the Holy Trinity, nor do we make confusion as Sabellius does' (*Cat.* 16, 4).

Studies: T. SCHERMANN, Die Gottheit des Heiligen Geistes nach den griechischen Vätern des vierten Jahrhunderts. Freiburg i.B., 1901, 17-47 (Cyril of Jerusalem). — P. GALTIER, Le Saint-Esprit en nous d'après les Pères grecs. Rome, 1946, 105-115.

The main theological interest of Cyril's *Catecheses* lies in their importance as an invaluable source of information for the history of the liturgy and the sacraments. Here we have for the first time a detailed description of the baptismal and eucharistic rites and the essentials of a theology of liturgy.

3. *Baptism*

Cyril expounds the sixth chapter of Romans in order to explain the early Christian liturgy of baptism: the sinner was submerged in the water just as Christ was buried in the grave, and following the example of the Lord, the baptized person came out of the water and rose to a new life:

> After that, you were led to the holy font of divine baptism, as Christ was brought from the cross to the Sepulchre which is before your eyes. And each of you was asked if he believed in the name of the Father and of the Son and of the Holy Ghost. And you made the saving

confession, and descended three times into the water and came up again, here also recalling by a symbol the three-days burial of Christ. For as our Saviour passed three days and three nights in the bosom of the earth, so you also in your first ascent out of the water imitated the first day of Christ in the earth, and by your descent, the night. For as he who is in the night no longer sees, but he who is in the day remains in the light, so in the descent, as in the night, you saw nothing, but in ascending again, you were as in the day (*Cat. myst.* 2, 4).

Combining the theology of St. Paul (Rom. 6, 3-5; Colossians 2, 10. 12) and St. John (1, 12-13; 3, 3-5) he presents baptism both as a grave and a mother:

> You died and were born at the same time. The saving water became for you both a tomb and a mother. And what Solomon spoke of others will suit you also; for he said, 'There is a time to bear and a time to die' (Eccl. 3, 2). But with you it is the opposite: The time to die is also the time to be born. One and the same season brings about both of these, and your birth went hand in hand with your death (*Cat. myst.* 2, 4).

Baptism is a sharing in the death and resurrection of Christ by way of imitation and image. It is more than remission of sins and adoption:

> O strange and inconceivable thing! we did not really *(ἀληθῶς)* die, we were not really buried, we were not really crucified and raised again, but our imitation was but in a figure *(ἐν εἰκόνι ἡ μίμησις)*, while our salvation is reality. Christ was actually crucified, and actually buried, and truly rose again; and all these things have been vouchsafed to us, that we, by imitation communicating in His sufferings, might gain salvation in reality. O surpassing loving-kindness! Christ received nails in His undefiled hands and feet, and endured anguish; while to me without suffering or toil, by the fellowship of His pain He vouchsafes salvation.
>
> Let no one then suppose that Baptism is merely the grace of remission of sins, or further, that of adoption; as John's baptism bestowed only the remission of sins. Nay we know full well, that as it purges our sins, and conveys to us the gift of the Holy Ghost, so also it is the counterpart of Christ's sufferings. For, for this cause Paul, just now read, cries aloud and says, 'Know ye not that as many of us as were baptized into Christ Jesus, were baptized into His death? Therefore we are buried with Him by baptism into death' (Rom. 6, 3). These words he spoke to them who had settled with themselves that Baptism ministers to us the remission of sins, and adoption, but not that further it has communion also in representation with Christ's true suffering.
>
> In order therefore that we may learn, that whatsoever things Christ endured, He suffered them for us and our salvation, and that, in reality and not in appearance, we also are made partakers of His

sufferings, Paul cried with all exactness of truth, 'For if we have been planted together in the likeness of His death, we shall be also in the likeness of His resurrection' (Rom. 6, 5). Well has he said, 'planted together'. For since the true Vine was planted in this place, we also by partaking in the Baptism of death, 'have been planted together with Him'. And fix thy mind with much attention on the words of the Apostle. He has not said, 'For if we have been planted together in His death', but, 'in the likeness of His death'. For upon Christ death came in reality, for His soul was truly separated from His body, and His burial was true, for His holy body was wrapt in pure linen; and every thing happened to Him truly; but in your case only the likeness of death and sufferings, whereas of salvation, not the likeness, but the reality (*Cat. myst.* 2, 5-7 Church).

In his *Procatechesis* (16) Cyril calls Baptism the 'Holy indelible seal' (σφραγὶς ἁγία ἀκατάλυτος) and mentions as its effects 'ransom for the captives, remission of offences, death of sin and regeneration of the soul'. He is firmly convinced that nobody can be saved except by baptism or martyrdom:

> Unless a man receive baptism, he has no salvation, excepting only martyrs, who receive the kingdom though they have not entered the font. For when the Saviour was redeeming the universe by means of His cross and His side was pierced, 'forthwith came there out blood and water' (John 19, 34), to show that in times of peace men should be baptized in water, and in times of persecution in their own blood. For the Saviour purposely spoke of martyrdom as baptism when He said 'Can you drink the cup that I drink of, and be baptized with the baptism that I am baptized with?' (Mark 10, 38) Moreover, martyrs make their profession of faith, 'Being made a spectacle to the world, and to angels, and to men' (I Cor. 4, 9).

Cyril is familiar with a blessing of the baptismal font in the form of an *epiclesis*. In order to explain the effectiveness and power of this invocation he refers to pagan parallels:

> Do not think of the font as filled with ordinary water, but think rather of the spiritual grace that is given with the water. For just as the sacrifices on pagan altars are in themselves indifferent matter and yet have become defiled by reason of the invocation (ἐπικλήσει) made over them to the idols, so, but in the opposite sense, the ordinary water in the font acquires sanctifying power when it receives the invocation of the Holy Spirit, of Christ and the Father (*Cat.* 3, 3 LCC).

He speaks of the baptismal font as of the 'Christ-bearing waters' (*Procat.* 15) and states that Christ 'imparted of the fragrance of His divinity to the waters when He was washed in the river Jordan' (*Cat. myst.* 3, 1).

Studies: J. MARQUARDT, S. Cyrillus Hieros. baptismi, chrismatis, eucharistiae mysteriorum interpres. Leipzig, 1882. — J. DANIÉLOU, Le symbolisme des rites baptismaux: Dieu vivant 1 (1945) 17-43. — J. QUASTEN, The Blessing of the Baptismal Font in the Syrian Rite of the Fourth Century: TS 7 (1946) 309-313.

4. *Eucharist*

It is in his Eucharistic doctrine that Cyril makes a more definite advance on his predecessors. He expresses himself more clearly regarding the Real Presence than all the earlier writers. After quoting I Cor. 11, 23-25, he adds:

> Since then He Himself has declared and said of the bread, 'This is My Body', who shall dare to doubt any longer? And since He has affirmed and said, 'This is My Blood', who shall ever hesitate, saying, that is not His blood? (*Cat. myst.* 4, 1 LNPF)
>
> Therefore with fullest assurance let us partake as of the Body and Blood of Christ: for in the figure of bread is given to thee His Body, and in the figure of wine His Blood; that thou by partaking of the Body and Blood of Christ, mayest become of one body and one blood with Him (σύσσωμος καὶ σύναιμος αὐτοῦ). For thus we shall become Christ-bearers (χριστοφόροι) because His Body and Blood are diffused through our members; thus it is that, according to St. Peter (2 Pet. 1, 4) 'we become partakers of divine nature' (*ibid.* 4, 3).
>
> That what seems bread is not bread, though bread by taste, but the Body of Christ; and that what seems wine is not wine, though the taste will have it so, but the Blood of Christ (*ibid.* 4, 9).
>
> Contemplate therefore the bread and wine not as bare elements, for they are, according to the Lord's declaration, the Body and Blood of Christ; for though sense suggests this to thee, let faith establish thee. Judge not the matter from taste, but from faith be fully assured without misgiving, that thou hast been vouchsafed the Body and Blood of Christ (*ibid.* 4, 6).

According to Cyril this Real Presence is brought about by a changing of the substances of the elements (μεταβάλλεσθαι) and thus he is the first theologian to interpret this transformation in the sense of a transsubstantiation. He illustrates it from the change of water into wine at Cana:

> He once turned water into wine (μεταβέβληκεν), at Cana in Galilee, at His own will, and shall not we believe Him when He changes (μεταβαλών) wine into blood? (*ibid.* 4, 2)

Cyril regards the calling down of the Holy Spirit upon the oblation by the epiclesis as that which effects the change of the bread and wine into the Body and Blood of Christ. He states clearly that 'The bread and wine of the Eucharist before the holy invocation (ἐπικλήσεως) of the Adorable Trinity was simply bread and wine, while after the invocation (ἐπικλήσεως) the bread becomes the Body of Christ, and the wine the Blood of Christ' (*Cat. myst.* 1, 7). He is the first to testify to the basic form of the epiclesis, which later became typical for the Oriental Liturgies:

> We call upon the merciful God to send forth His Holy Spirit upon the gifts lying before Him; that He may make the bread the Body of Christ, and the wine the Blood of Christ; for whatsoever the Holy Ghost has touched, is sanctified and changed (μεταβέβληται, *Cat. myst.* 5, 7 LNPF).

Most interesting is Cyril's highly developed concept of the Eucharist as a sacrifice. He calls it a spiritual sacrifice, a bloodless service, a propitiatory sacrifice, offered by the way of intercession for all who are in need of help, even for the departed (*Memento pro defunctis*). It is nothing less than Christ slain as a victim for our sins, that is offered in this oblation:

> After the spiritual sacrifice is perfected, the bloodless service upon that sacrifice of propitiation, we entreat God for the common peace of the Church, for the tranquillity of the world, for kings, for soldiers and allies, for the sick, for the afflicted, and, in a word, for all who stand in need of succour we all supplicate and offer this sacrifice.
>
> Then we commemorate also those who have fallen asleep before us, first, Patriarchs, Prophets, Apostles, Martyrs, that at their prayers and intervention God would receive our petition. Afterwards also on behalf of the holy Fathers and Bishops who have fallen asleep before us, and in a word of all who in past years have fallen asleep among us, believing that it will be a very great advantage to the souls, for whom the supplication is put up, while that holy and most awful sacrifice is presented... we offer up Christ slain for our sins in order to obtain pardon from our merciful God both for them [the departed] and for ourselves (*Cat. myst.* 5, 8-10).

Cyril is the first theologian to call this Eucharistic sacrifice 'awful' or 'awe-inspiring' (φρικωδέστατος) preparing the way for this particular religious sentiment found also in the other sources of the liturgy of Antioch, the Apostolic Constitutions (cf. vol. II, p. 184), St. John Chrysostom, Theodore of Mopsuestia and Narses.

Studies: BECKER, Der hl. Cyrillus von Jerusalem über die reale Gegenwart Christi in der heiligen Eucharistie: Der Katholik 1 (1872) 422-449, 539-554, 641-661. — V. SCHMITT, Die Verheissung der Eucharistie (Joh. 6) bei den Antiochenern Cyrillus von Jerusalem und Johannes Chrysostomus. Würzburg, 1903. — R. RIOS, St. Cyril of Jerusalem on the Holy Eucharist: Pax 25 (1935) 77-81. — J. C. M. FRUYTIER, Het woord 'mysterion' in de Catechesen van Cyrillus van Jerusalem (Diss. Nijmegen). Nijmegen, 1950. — J. QUASTEN, Mysterium tremendum. Eucharistische Frömmigkeitsauffassungen des vierten Jahrhunderts: Vom christlichen Mysterium (Festschrift

O. Casel). Düsseldorf, 1951, 66-75. — K. Baus, Die eucharistische Glaubensverkündigung der alten Kirche in ihren Grundzügen : Die Messe in der Glaubensverkündigung (Festschrift J. A. Jungmann), edit. by F. X. Arnold and B. Fischer. Freiburg i.B., 1953 55-70.

APOLLINARIS OF LAODICEA

Apollinaris is the author of the first great Christological heresy. Born about 310 at Laodicea in Syria as the son of a presbyter and grammarian, also named Apollinaris, he was a close friend of St. Athanasius and for this reason was excommunicated in 342 by George, the Arian bishop of his native city. Nevertheless he received Athanasius on his return from exile in 346 and about 361 became bishop of the Nicene community of Laodicea, a position which he occupied until he died. He was a very successful teacher who combined classical erudition with rhetorical ability, so that even St. Jerome was among his pupils at Antioch in 374 (cf. *Ep.* 84, 3). One of the most fertile and versatile ecclesiastical writers of his day, he fought side by side with Athanasius and Basil the Great against the Arians, only to be condemned in the end as a heretic himself. He was still alive when Gregory of Nyssa wrote his *Antirrheticus* in 385 against him (cf. above, p. 258), and must have died about 390.

Studies: R. Aigrain, DHG 3 (1924) 962-982. — G. L. Prestige, Fathers and Heretics. Oxford, 1940, 195-246. — G. Gentz, RACh 1 (1942) 520-522. — W. Schneemelcher, RGG³ 1 (1957) 474-475. — F. L. Cross, ODC (1957) 70-71. — H. de Riedmatten, LThK² 1 (1957) 714. — J. Steinmann, Saint Jérôme. Paris, 1958, 87-91.

HIS WRITINGS

1. *Exegetical Works*

According to St. Jerome (*De vir. ill.* 104) he composed 'innumerable volumes on the Holy Scriptures'.

Of these *Commentaries* on the books of the Old and New Testament only fragments remain scattered through a great number of *Catenae*, where they await collecting and critical editing. This is now being done by H. de Riedmatten. St. Jerome mentions explicitly works on Ecclesiastes (*Comm. in Eccl.* ad 4, 13f and ad 12, 5), Isaias (*Comm. in Is.*, prol.), Osee (*Comm. in Hos.*, prol.) and Malachy (*Comm. in Mal.*, prol.) but implies that he wrote such on other prophets, too (*Comm. in Hos.*, prol.). According to the same authority Apollinaris composed in addition commentaries on the Gospel of St. Matthew (*Comm. in Matth.*, prol.), First Corinthians (*Ep.* 49, 3; 119, 4), Galatians (*Comm. in Gal.*, prol.) and Ephesians (*Comm. in Eph.*, prol.). We know besides of a commentary on Romans, the fragments of which gathered by K. Staab from various *Catenae*, cast an interesting light on the writer's exegetical method. His interpretation stresses the dogmatic importance of the Epistle but shows no leaning to the philological approach of the School of Antioch or the allegorical of the Alexandrians. Jerome indicates that Apollinaris' explanations were far too brief and too few and sometimes consisted of little more than a table of contents (*Comm. in Is.*, prol.).

Fragments: R. Devreesse, Anciens commentateurs grecs de l'Octateuque: RBibl 45 (1936) 213-216. — K. Staab, Pauluskommentare aus der griechischen Kirche. Münster, 1933, 57-82. — J. Reuss, Matthäus-, Markus- und Johannes-Katenen. Münster, 1941; *idem*, Matthäus-Kommentare aus der griechischen Kirche (TU 61). Berlin, 1957, 1-54.

Study: H. de Riedmatten, Le texte des fragments exégétiques d'Apollinaire: RSR 44 (1956) 560-566.

2. *Apologetic Works*

Among his numerous apologetic works, his thirty books against the Neoplatonist Porphyry merited special praise from St. Jerome and Philostorgius. The former states (*De vir. ill.* 104) that they were 'generally considered as among the best of his works'; the latter does not hesitate to declare (*Hist. eccl.* 8, 14) that the earlier treatises against Porphyry by Methodius (cf. vol. II, p. 137) and Eusebius (cf. above p. 333) were eclipsed by Apollinaris' great refutation.

Another apologetic work, entitled *The Truth* ('Υπὲρ ἀληθείας) was directed against the Emperor Julian. It proved without any appeal to the authority of Scripture, but from reason, that the pagan philosophers, on which the Emperor relied, were far from having attained right opinions of God (Sozom., *Hist. eccl.* 5, 18).

Both writings are no longer extant except for a few fragments.

3. *Polemic Works*

We know only a few of his anti-heretical writings; one was against the Arian bishop Eunomius of Cyzicus (cf. above p. 307) and another against Marcellus of Ancyra (cf. above p. 197), whom he accused of Sabellianism (Jerome, *De vir. ill.* 86). Only the titles are preserved. Fragments remain of his treatises against Diodore of Tarsus and Flavian of Antioch, in which he defended the unity of Godhead and manhood in Christ. Nothing has survived of his works against Origen and Dionysius of Alexandria.

4. *Dogmatic Works*

It appears strange at first sight that some of his dogmatic works, in which his Christological errors can be found, survived complete. The reason is that they were preserved under the false names of orthodox writers, to whom they were intentionally attributed by his followers to camouflage the fact that the real author was a heretic. The *Adversus fraudes Apollinaristarum*, attributed to Leontius of Byzantium (485-543), asserts that Apollinarists and Monophysites had put in circulation certain writings of Apollinaris under the authoritative names of Gregory Thaumaturgus, Athanasius, and Pope Julius. The search of Caspari, Lietzmann and de Riedmatten has confirmed this assertion. Thus the following writings of Apollinaris survive:

a. A *Detailed Confession of Faith* (ἡ κατὰ μέρος πίστις) ascribed to Gregory Thaumaturgus.

b. Three works went under the name of St. Athanasius: (1) An Epiphany sermon, entitled *Quod unus sit Christus* (ὅτι εἷς ὁ Χριστός); (2) *De incarnatione Dei Verbi* (περὶ σαρκώσεως τοῦ θεοῦ λόγου); and (3) A *Profession of Faith* addressed to the Emperor Jovian.

c. Three works were detected under the name of Pope Julius I (337-352): (1) *De unione corporis et divinitatis in Christo*, (2) *De fide et incarnatione*, and (3) An extensive letter addressed to a presbyter Dionysius.

d. His main dogmatic work can be partially reconstructed from Gregory of Nyssa's attack on it in his above (p. 258) mentioned *Antirrheticus*. Its title was *Proof of the Incarnation of God according to the Image of Man* (Ἀποδείξις περὶ τῆς θείας σαρκώσεως). Composed between 376 and 380, it followed the threefold division of man, to which Plato gave currency, into body, soul and spirit. Gregory rejects this 'trichotomy' on the basis that Scripture recognized only a 'dichotomy' into body and soul, as can be seen in the account of the creation of man in Genesis and in the Gospel narrative of the death of the Lord (*Antirrhet*. 8, 35).

e. A small treatise *Recapitulatio* (Ἀνακεφαλαίωσις) can be culled from the fifth pseudo-Athanasian Dialogue *De sancta Trinitate*. It summarizes the main Christological doctrines and seems to be an epitome of a larger work no longer extant.

f. A great number of fragments of his Christological studies are preserved in florilegia and in quotations by other authors. Thus Theodoret's *Eranistes* contains several very substantial excerpts.

Texts: H. Lietzmann, Apollinaris von Laodicea und seine Schule (TU 1). Tübingen, 1904. — Syriac texts: J. Flemming and H. Lietzmann, Apollinaristische Schriften. Syrisch. Mit den griechischen Texten und einem syrisch-griechischen Wortregister (GAb N.F. 7, 4). Berlin, 1904; cf. H. Gressmann, ZDMG 59 (1905) 674-686. —

I. RUCKER, Florilegium Edessenum anonymum. Munich, 1933, 25f.; 47-50. — H. DE RIEDMATTEN, Les fragments d'Apollinaire à l' 'Éranistes': CGG I (1951) 203-212. — For fragments of Anti-Apollinaristic writings, see: A. SOUTER, An Unpublished Latin Fragment against the Apollinarists: Miscellanea F. Ehrle (ST 37). Rome, 1924, 39-49. — F. DIEKAMP, Analecta Patristica. Rome, 1938, 50-53 (Peter of Myra).

5. *Poetry*

When the Emperor Julian by a law in 362 stopped the children of Christians from frequenting the public schools and studying the Greek poets and authors, Apollinaris with his father rewrote much of the Bible in classical forms in order to compensate them for the loss. Thus he took Biblical material and made of it comedies, tragedies and epics:

> His [Julian's] sole motive for excluding the children of Christian parents from instruction in the learning of the Greeks, was because he considered such studies conducive to the acquisition of argumentative and persuasive power. Apollinaris, therefore, employed his great learning and ingenuity in the production of a heroic epic on the antiquities of the Hebrews to the reign of Saul, as a substitute for the poem of Homer. He divided this work into twenty-four parts, to each of which he appended the name of one of the letters of the Greek alphabet, according to their number and order. He also wrote comedies in imitation of Menander, tragedies resembling those of Euripides, and odes on the model of Pindar. In short, taking themes of the entire circle of knowledge from the Scriptures, he produced within a very brief space of time, a set of works which in manner, expression, character and arrangement are well approved as similar to the Greek literatures (Sozom., *Hist. eccl.* 5, 18; LNPF).

He even composed Platonic dialogues out of gospel material (Socrates, *Hist. eccl.* 3, 16). All of these works have been lost except for a *Paraphrase of the Psalms* in hexameters, richly interwoven with reminiscences of the old Hellenic poets. But even this is of doubtful authenticity. Golega believes that its author was perhaps the presbyter Marcianus, who died at Constantinople after 471. According to Sozomen (*Hist. eccl.* 6, 25, 4/5) Apollinaris wrote in addition liturgical hymns which by their sweetness induced many to cleave to him, and religious songs for private use: 'Men sang his strains at convivial meetings and at their daily labor, and women sang them while engaged at the loom. But, whether his tender poems were adapted for holidays, festivals, or other occasions, they were all alike to the praise and glory of God'. Nothing has survived of them.

Editions: MG 33, 1313-1538. — Crit. ed.: A. LUDWICH, Apollinaris Laodicensis, Metaphrasis psalmorum (Bibl. Teubneriana). Leipzig, 1912. — R. CANTARELLA, Poeti bizantini, Milan, 1948, 1-8, reprints the *Protheoria* of Ludwich's edition.

Studies: R. GANSZYNIEC, Zu Apollinarios von Laodicea: BNJ (1920) 375-376 (claims that the author of the *Paraphrase of the Psalms* was blind and cannot be Apollinaris). — R. KEYDELL, Über die Echtheit der Bibeldichtungen des Apollinaris und des Nonnos: BZ 33 (1933) 243-254. — P. S. MILLER, The Greek Psalter of Apollinarius: TP 65 (1934). — J. GITSCHEL, War der Verfasser der dem Apollinarios zugeschriebenen Psalmenmetaphrase wirklich körperlich blind?: Munera philologica I. Cwiklinski oblata. Poznań, 1936, 104-110 (against Ganszyniec). — J. GOLEGA, Verfasser und Zeit der Psalterparaphrase des Apollinarios: BZ 39 (1939) 1-22 (not authentic; composed perhaps at the request of a presbyter Marcianus who died at Constantinople after 471). — F. SCHEIDWEILER, Zur Protheoria der unter dem Namen des Apollinarios überlieferten Psalmenparaphrase: BZ 49 (1956) 336-344 (the *Paraphrase of the Psalms* is an authentic work of the young Apollinaris).

6. *Correspondence with Basil the Great*

His correspondence with Basil the Great, found among the letters of the latter (*Epp.* 361-364), and consisting of two letters of St. Basil and two answers of Apollinaris must probably be regarded as authentic according to the latest research by Prestige and de Riedmatten (cf. above, p. 224), though some doubts remain.

THEOLOGICAL ASPECTS

Though Apollinaris was an outstanding champion and vigorous advocate of the Nicene doctrine against the Arians, attempts have been made to derive his peculiar Christology from their teaching. Others are inclined to represent Apollinarianism as the scientific form of a naive Monophysitism based on Plato's anthropology. Both of these explanations fail to do justice to his ultimate motives. His works reveal him as a theologian of a keen and reflective mind. and exceptional dialectical skill. His philosophy is syncretistic, combining elements both peripatetic and stoic. It was in opposition to the Arians that he was led to devise his theory.

One of his foremost motives was his zeal for the absolute unity of Godhead and manhood in Christ and the divinity of the Redeemer. He saw a potential danger to these dogmas in the teaching of the Arians that there was a moral growth and development in Christ's life. The received doctrine of the School of Antioch did not satisfy him and he wanted by a better solution to exclude any mistaken tendency to interpret the close union of God and man in Christ as a double personality. The fear of a separation of the two natures and the endeavor to grasp the unity in the incarnate Logos as deeply as possible dominated his entire thought. For this reason he has recourse to the acts of the synod of 268 which condemned Paul of Samosata and his heresy.

Nevertheless, his own theory was no solution at all. His basic mistake was the mutilation of Christ's humanity. Following Plato he asserted that in man there coexist body, soul, and spirit (νοῦς). The second of these three elements is understood as the irrational (ψυχὴ ἄλογος) or animal soul and the principle of life; the third, the spirit or mind, as the rational soul (ψυχὴ λογική) and the controlling and determining principle. According to Apollinaris, in Christ were to be found the human body and irrational soul, the first two elements, but not the third, the human spirit or rational soul, the latter being replaced by the Divine Logos. Thus he possessed perfect Godhead but not complete manhood. This solution commended itself to Apollinaris as a way of escape from all the difficulties and as the correct interpretation of the passage in the prologue of St. John's Gospel 'The Word became flesh', which means that the Deity of the Logos united only with the corporeality of man and dwelt as soul in the body received from the Virgin Mary. Christ could not have a complete humanity for two reasons. The metaphysical reason is that two beings already perfect, God and man, cannot produce unity, but only a hybrid. Thus he regards the doctrine of the union of full Divinity and full humanity in one person as an absurdity, because two wholes cannot be in one whole. The psychological reason is that the rational soul constitutes the seat and centre of the power of self-determination for good or evil, which would attribute the possibility of sin to Christ. But the Saviour must be without sin, if redemption is to be accomplished. Apollinaris was convinced that there was only one nature in Christ, one incarnate nature of the God-Word (μία φύσις θεοῦ λόγου σεσαρκωμένη), since a complete 'nature' was to him the same thing as a 'person' (πρόσωπον, ὑπόστασις). It is extremely difficult to say how much of this conclusion resulted from the want of agreement as to the use of the terms φύσις, πρόσωπον and ὑπόστασις. But there cannot be any doubt that Apollinaris thought of one only real and biological unity in Christ, which links the Godhead directly with his body and forms one only nature (μία φύσις). He saw in this formula the sole genuine explanation for the *communicatio idiomatum*, for the Virginal conception, for the redemptive power of Christ's death and the salvific character of His flesh, that we receive in the Lord's Supper. He states in *De fide et incarn.* 6 (ed. Lietzmann 198/9): 'There is no separation between the Logos and His flesh mentioned in the Holy Scriptures, but the same (αὐτός) is one *physis*, one *hypostasis*, one power (ἐνέργεια), one *prosopon*, whole God and whole man'.

His solution satisfied superficial and rationalistic minds because it seemed to be an easy answer to a difficult question and the most telling proof of the sinlessness of Christ. Thus he gained adherents in the different provinces of the East, even among bishops. However, soon there arose doubts, because his daring theory was in direct contradiction with the ecclesiastical doctrine of the complete and perfect manhood in Christ. In denying to the person of Christ a human soul, the most important element in human nature, Apollinaris was depriving the Incarnation and Redemption of its meaning. Thus Athanasius, Basil the Great, Gregory of Nazianzus, Gregory of Nyssa, Diodore of Tarsus and Theodore of Mopsuestia wrote refutations. Teaching akin to that of Apollinaris was rejected at the synod of Alexandria in 362, which formulated the thesis that 'the Saviour did not possess a body without a soul, sense-perception, and understanding. Since the Lord became man for our sakes, it was impossible that His body should be without understanding (νοῦς). Moreover, not only the body but also the soul were redeemed by the Logos'. His errors had for a long time remained unnoticed on account of his friendship with Athanasius and his reputation as a theologian. Not until 377 and 382 was his teaching explicitly censured by synods at Rome under Pope Damasus. It was finally condemned at the General Council of Constantinople in 381.

Studies: G. Voisin, L'Apollinarisme. Louvain, 1901. — G. Furlani, Studi Apollinaristici I: La dottrina trinitaria di Apollinario di Laodicea: Studi filos. e relig. II (1921) fasc. 2-3. — C. E. Raven, Apollinarianism. Cambridge, 1923; cf. H. Lietzmann, ThLZ 50 (1925) 374-378; J. Lebon, RHE 26 (1925) 285-288; C. Gore, ChQ 98 (1924) 120-134. — G. Furlani, I presupposti psicologici della cristologia di Apollinare di Laodicea: RSFR 4 (1923) 129-146. — E. Weigl, Die Christologie vom Tode des Athanasius bis zum Ausbruch des nestorianischen Streites. Munich, 1925, 6-18. — A. d'Alès, Apollinaire. Les origines du monophysitisme: RAp 42 (1926) 131-149. — G. Bardy, Paul de Samosate. 2nd ed. Louvain, 1929, 139-144. — C. Papadopoulos, 'Ο ἅγιος Κύριλλος 'Αλεξανδρείας καὶ τὰ συγγράμματα τοῦ 'Απολλιναρίου: Θεολογία 10 (1932) 97-105. — M. Jugie, Quelques témoignages grecs nouveaux ou peu connus sur la doctrine catholique de la procession du Saint-Esprit: Apollinaire de Laodicée: EO (1936) 257-274. — G. Verbeke, L'évolution de la doctrine du pneuma du stoïcisme à S. Augustin. Louvain, 1945, 485-489. — M. Richard, L'introduction du mot hypostase dans la théologie de l'incarnation: MSR 2 (1945) 5-32, 243-270. — H. de Riedmatten, Some Neglected Aspects of Apollinarist Christology: Dominican Studies 1 (1948) 239-260. — A. Grillmeier, Die theologische und sprachliche Vorbereitung der christologischen Formel von Chalkedon: CGG I (1951) 102-117. — H. Ristow, Zwei Haeretiker der alten Kirche: Apollinaris von Laodicea und Nestorius. Diss. Berlin, 1954 (typ.). — P. Galtier, Saint Athanase et l'âme humaine du Christ: Greg 36 (1955) 553-589 (compared with Apollinaris' concept); *idem*, Saint Cyrille et Apollinaire: Greg 37 (1956) 584-609 (the influence of Apollinaris on Cyril of Alexandria's Christology). — H. A. Wolfson, The Philosophy of the Church Fathers I. Faith, Trinity and Incarnation. Cambridge, 1956, 433-444 (Christology). — H. de Riedmatten, La Christologie d'Apollinaire de Laodicée: SP II (TU 64). Berlin, 1957, 208-234. — H. J M. Diepen, Stratagèmes contre la théologie de l'Emmanuel. A propos d'une nouvelle comparaison entre saint Cyrille et Apollinaire: Divinitas 1 (1957) 444-478. — H. A. Wolfson, Philosophical Implications of Arianism and Apollinarianism: DOP 12 (1958) 3-28. — A. Gesché, L'âme de Jésus dans la christologie du IVe s.: RHE 54 (1959) 403-406.

EPIPHANIUS OF SALAMIS

The island of Cyprus produced only one important theological author, Epiphanius, bishop of Constantia, the ancient Salamis. Born about 315 in a hamlet near Eleutheropolis not far from Gaza in Palestine, he acquired at an early time the knowledge of Greek, Syriac, Hebrew, Coptic and some Latin, as Jerome informs us (*Adv. Rufin.*, 2, 22). An enthusiastic supporter of the monastic movement, he founded, after a visit with the most famous monks of Egypt c. 335, a monastery near his birthplace over which he presided for some thirty years. His reputation for learning and sanctity induced the bishops of Cyprus to choose him in 367 as their metropolitan. In this position he occupied the see of Constantia for an entire generation.

His life and his writings reflect his fiery zeal in defence of the purity of ecclesiastical doctrine, and at the same time his want of judgment and his lack of moderation and tact. He is the earliest representative of a school of thought that has been called realistic-traditionalistic. An ardent upholder of the faith of the Fathers, he was against all metaphysic speculation. This explains his complete inability to understand Origen, which grew into a real hatred of the great Alexandrian, whom he held responsible for Arianism and whose allegorical interpretation he regarded as the root of all heresies. Condemning Origenism as the most dangerous of them (*Haer.* 64), he was unyielding and relentless in its pursuit. Thus in 392 he went to Jerusalem, the home of Origen's most determined and influential admirers, and in the presence of John, the bishop of the city, and a great multitude assembled in the Church of the Holy Sepulchre, he delivered a vehement sermon against Origen. The result was a serious quarrel, during which Jerome, first an ardent defender of Origen, changed his views and attempted to obtain a condemnation of Origen from bishop John of Jerusalem. When the latter refused, Epiphanius broke off ecclesiastical communion with him. The controversy which followed reached its climax in the condemnation of Origen in 400 by a council at Alexandria, convoked by the local metropolitan Theophilus, who referred in his Festal Letter of 402 to Origen as the 'hydra of heresies'. Epiphanius did not hesitate to join forces with the artful and violent patriarch of Alexandria, in the expulsion from their monasteries in the Nitrian Desert of the famous 'Tall Brothers' and other Egyptian adherents of Origen. They took refuge with St. John Chrysostom, while Epiphanius in 400, at the instigation of Theophilus, went to Constantinople despite his advanced age, in order to wage war in person against Chrysostom, the bishop, and all Origenists of that city. When he finally realized that he had been used as a tool by Theophilus, he did not wait for the deposition of Chrysostom at the notorious 'Council of the Oak', but set out for Cyprus and died at sea, May 12, 403.

Epiphanius was one of the few bishops of his times to become the subject of a biography (MG 41). The work contains more legend than history, and, though purporting to be written by his disciples John and Polybius, was really composed much later.

Studies: B. EBERHARD, Die Beteiligung des Epiphanius an dem Streit über Origenes. Trier, 1859. — J. MARTIN, St. Épiphane: Annales de philosophie chrétienne 155 (1907/1908) 113-150, 606-618; 156 (1908/1909) 32-49. — K. HOLL, Die Zeitfolge des ersten origenistischen Streites: SAB (1916) 226-255; A. JÜLICHER, Bemerkungen: ibid. 256-275; both articles reprinted in: K. HOLL, Gesammelte Aufsätze zur Kirchengeschichte I. Tübingen, 1928, 310-350. — M. VILLAIN, Rufin d'Aquilée. La querelle autour Origène (rôle d'Épiphane de Salamine): RSR 37 (1937) 5-18. — F. X. MURPHY, Rufinus of Aquileia. Washington, 1945, 59-81 (the quarrel over Origen: first phase). — J. STEINMANN, Saint Jérôme. Paris, 1958, 243-246 (les gaffes de St. Épiphane).

HIS WRITINGS

According to Jerome (*De vir. ill.* 114) Epiphanius' works were 'eagerly read by the learned, on account of their subject matter, and also by the plain people, on account of their language'. We have to keep in mind that this is the judgment of a friend who held the *papa Epiphanius* πεντάγλωττος (*Adv. Rufin.* 3, 6) in great veneration, and has a reputation for being very partial. There cannot be any doubt that Epiphanius' writings remain precious because they preserve much invaluable material for the history of the Church and of theology. Moreover, they are highly important for the reconstruction of a great number of sources no longer extant, especially the Greek Irenaeus and the *Syntagma* of Hippolytus. Unfortunately, they reveal a total lack of critical acumen and depth and are far too one-sided. Most of his treatises are hasty, superficial and disorderly compilations of the fruits of his extensive reading. Their style is careless, verbose and according to Photius (*Bibl. cod.* 122) 'like that of one who is unfamiliar with Attic elegance'. This trait is no surprise because Epiphanius was an enemy of all classical education. He reckoned the Greek philosophical schools among the heresies and was suspicious of any Hellenistic learning. Thus he differs entirely from most of his Christian contemporaries who expressed vehement protests when the Emperor Julian by his edict on June 17, 362 A.D. excluded them from the study of the ancient authors.

According to K. Holl (GCS 25, p. VII), Epiphanius' language is a most interesting example of an 'elevated Koine'. This explains, why, on the one hand, even plain people liked to read his works, as Jerome reports, and why, on the other, several attempts have been made to revise his more important works in Attic. U. v. Wilamowitz-Moellendorff's judgment (SAB 1912, 759 f) is more severe. He is of the opinion that Epiphanius' language contains more vulgar elements than that of most of his contemporaries.

Formerly, his literary output was regarded as equal in volume to that of the great theologians of his age. However, modern criticism has proved a number of works attributed to him to be spurious. He owes his renown among the Fathers of the fourth century especially to two comprehensive writings, the *Ancoratus* and the *Panarion*. Both are devoted to the refutation of heresy.

Editions: MG 41-43. — W. DINDORF, Epiphanii episc. Constantiae opera. Leipzig, 1859-1862. 5 vols. — New crit. ed.: K. HOLL, GCS 25 (1915), 31 (1922), 37 (1933).

Translations: German: C. WOLFSGRUBER, BKV (1880). — J. HÖRMANN, BKV² 38 (1919). Other translations below with individual works.

Studies: K. HOLL, Die handschriftliche Überlieferung des Epiphanius (Ancoratus und Panarion) (TU 36, 2). Leipzig, 1910. — O. VIEDEBANTT, Quaestiones Epiphanianae metrologicae et criticae. Leipzig, 1911.

Theological Studies: T. SCHERMANN, Die Gottheit des Heiligen Geistes nach den griechischen Vätern des vierten Jahrhunderts. Freiburg i.B., 1901, 233-242 (Epiphanius' teaching on the Holy Spirit). — E. R. SMOTHERS, Saint Epiphanius and the Assumption: AER 125 (1951) 355-372. — T. GALLUS, Ad Epiphanii interpretationem mariologicam in Gen. III, 15: Verbum Domini 34 (1956) 272-279. — D. FERNANDEZ, De perpetua Mariae virginitate iuxta S. Epiphanium: Marianum 20 (1958) 129-154.

1. *Ancoratus (Ἀγκυρωτός)*

The earliest of them is the *Ancoratus* i.e. *The Firmly-Anchored Man*, written in 374 at the request of the Christian community of Syedra in Pamphylia, which felt disturbed by the Pneumatomachi. It provides its readers with the anchor of faith to secure them amidst the storms of heresy. Though it pays special attention to the doctrine of the Trinity and particularly the Holy Spirit, it amounts practically to a compendium of ecclesiastical dogma. Based on Scripture and tradition only, it could be compared with Gregory of Nyssa's *Great Catechism* (cf. above, p. 262), except for its polemic tendency and its frequent anti-heretical digressions. The author explains in chapters 2-75 the Church's teaching on the Trinity against the objections of the Arians and Pneumatomachi. He finds his proof for it in the baptismal formula (ch. 8), in the Trishagion of the angels (ch. 10-26) and in many passages of Scripture. The Spirit (ch. 5-7) as well as the Son (ch. 45-63) is true God. Chapters 65-71 describe the consubstantiality of the Son, and ch. 72-74 that of the Holy Spirit. Though the author dealt with the Incarnation in ch. 27-38, he returns to this dogma and defends it in ch. 75-82 against Apollinaris. Chapters 83-100 treat of the resurrection of the flesh with urgent appeals to pagans (83-86) and heretics i.e. Origenists (87-100) to believe in it. Epiphanius admonishes the faithful to cooperate with God for the conversion of the pagans (100-109). He refutes the opinions of the Manichaeans and Marcionites regarding the God of the Old Testament, decries the unbelief of the Jews and condemns the teaching of Sabellius. At the end he returns to a discussion of the errors of the Arians and Pneumatomachi and exhorts his readers to remain steadfast in their faith. There follow two Creeds which Epiphanius recommends to be used in baptism. The first and shorter one (119) is the baptismal creed of the metropolitan see of Constantia (Salamis), introduced as such not long before the election of St. Epiphanius. The Second Ecumenical Council of Constantinople in 381 accepted this profession of faith with a few modifications and made it thereby the baptismal creed of the whole East. The second and longer one (ch. 120) was composed by Epiphanius himself (EP 1081/9; ES 13 f.). The text of the *Ancoratus* is preceded in the manuscripts by two letters from Syedra requesting of Epiphanius an extensive explanation of the true and sound faith concerning the Holy Trinity and the Holy Spirit.

Editions: MG 43, 17-236. — F. OEHLER, Corpus haereseologicum T. 2. Berlin, 1859. — New crit. ed.: K. HOLL, GCS 25 (1915) 1-149. For the fragment of a very old Sahidic version comprising chapters 104-108, see: J. LEIPOLDT, Epiphanios' von Salamis 'Ancoratus' in saidischer Übersetzung: Berichte über die Verhandl. der K. Sächs. Gesellschaft der Wiss. zu Leipzig. Philol.-hist. Klasse (1902) 136-171.

Translations: German: C. WOLFSGRUBER, BKV (1880) 35-229. — J. HÖRMANN, BKV² 38 (1919) 6-182.

Studies: U. v. WILAMOWITZ - MOELLENDORFF, Ein Stück aus dem Ancoratus des Epiphanius: SAB (1911) 759-772 (chs. 103-106 containing a criticism of Greek legends of the gods). — H. RASCHKE, Der Römerbrief des Markion nach Epiphanios: Abhandlungen und Vorträge der Bremer wissenschaftlichen Gesellschaft 1 (1926) 128-201. — For the Creeds in chs. 118-119, see: J. N. D. KELLY, Early Christian Creeds, London, 1950, 318-322, 335-338.

2. *Panarion* (Πανάριον)

The most important of all his treatises is the *Panarion* or *Medicine Chest*, usually cited as *Haereses*. The Greek title finds its explanation in the author's intention to furnish an antidote to those who have been bitten by the serpent of heresy and to protect those who have remained sound in their faith. It deals with eighty heresies but the first twenty of them belong to the pre-Christian period; they are barbarism, Scythism, Hellenism with its different philosophical schools, and Judaism with its sects. The first of the Christian heresies is that of Simon Magus and the last, that of the Messalians (cf.

above, p. 163). The work culminates in a summary of the faith of the Catholic and Apostolic Church (*De fide*).

The *Panarion* is by far the most extensive ancient account of heresies. For the description of the earlier aberrations the author made wide use of S. Justin, St. Irenaeus' *Adversus haereses* and the lost *Syntagma* of Hippolytus (cf. vol. II, p. 169). The lengthy literal excerpts from these and many other scattered sources are priceless, though the whole is rather confused and uncritical. The work is divided into three books or seven volumes, the first book comprising three, each of the last two books two volumes. The number of 'eighty' heresies is probably borrowed from the 'four scores concubines' in the Canticle of Canticles (6, 7) and appears for the first time in *Ancoratus* 12-13, which indicates that the plan for the *Panarion* had been conceived by that time. When in 375 two readers of the *Ancoratus*, Acacius and Paulus, begged the author for a more detailed analysis and refutation of the eighty heresies, Epiphanius had already begun on the later treatise (*Pan.* 1, 2). He reports that he had reached the system of the Manichaeans in 376 or 377 (*Haer.* 66, 20) and he must have finished the entire work during 377. The preface consists of the answer to the letter of the two archimandrites Acacius and Paulus.

The manuscripts of Epiphanius' writings contain a small epitome of the *Panarion*, called *Anakephalaiosis* or *Recapitulatio*. Though it is attributed to Epiphanius himself, and St. Augustine, who made ample use of it in his *De haeresibus* in 428, is firmly convinced of its authenticity, it seems to be a rather clumsy compilation of a later author. It reproduces only the tables of contents preceding the volumes in the *Panarion* and a few poorly selected passages.

Editions: MG 41-42. — F. OEHLER, Corpus haereseologicum T. 2-3. Berlin, 1859-1861. — New crit. ed.: K. HOLL, GCS 25 (1915) 153-464 (*Panarion: Haer.* 1-33); GCS 31 (1922) *Panarion: Haer.* 34-64; GCS 37 (1933) *Panarion: Haer.* 65-80. — *Anakephalaiosis:* MG 42, 833-886. An Old Armenian version was published by J. DASHIAN, Vienna, 1895.

Translations: German: Anakephalaiosis: C. WOLFSGRUBER, BKV (1880) 236-286. — J. HÖRMANN, BKV² 38 (1919) 185-263.

Studies: For the manuscript tradition, see: K. HOLL, TU 36, 2 (1910), especially 95-98 (spuriousness of the *Anakephalaiosis*). — R. A. LIPSIUS, Zur Quellenkritik des Epiphanius. Vienna, 1865; *idem*, Die Quellen der ältesten Ketzergeschichte neu untersucht. Leipzig, 1875 (sources of *Haer.* 13-57). — A. CONDAMIN, St. Épiphane a-t-il admis la légitimité du divorce pour adultère?: BLE (1900) 16-21 (*Haer.* 59, 4ff.). — C. H. TURNER, Epiphanius' Chronology of the Ministry: JThSt 3 (1901) 115-120. — R. P. CASEY, Note on Epiphanius' Panarion 31, 5-6: JThSt 29 (1927) 34-40. — C. R. C. ALLBERRY, Das manichäische Bema-Fest: ZNW (1938) 2-10 (*Haer.* 66, 20). — W. SESTON, Le roi sassanide Narsès, les Arabes et le manichéisme (chez Épiphane): Mélanges Dussaud I. Paris, 1939, 227-234. — J. HERING, Dieu, Moïse et les anciens. Réflexions sur la critique du Pentateuque faite par le gnostique Ptolémée: RHPR (1941) 192-206 (*Haer.* 33, 3-7). — G. BLOND, L'hérésie encratite vers la fin du IVᵉ siècle (chez Épiphane): RSR (1944) 157-210. —

E. Amand de Mendieta, Fatalisme et liberté dans l'antiquité grecque. Louvain, 1945, 440-460. — E. Peterson, Ein Fragment des Hierakas: Mus (1947) 257-260 (*Haer.* 67). — J. Doresse, Nouveaux aperçus historiques sur les gnostiques coptes. Ophites et Séthiens: Bulletin de l'Institut d'Égypte 31 (1948/49) 409-419 (*Haer.* 40, 7). — J. Schoeps, Theologie und Geschichte des Judenchristentums. Tübingen, 1949, 457-479 (Epiphanius and the Pseudo-Clementines). — P. Nautin, Deux interpolations orthodoxes dans une lettre d'Arius: AB 67 (1949) 131-141 (*Haer.* 69, 6). — B. Altaner, Augustinus und Epiphanius von Salamis. Eine quellenkritische Studie: Mélanges J. De Ghellinck. Gembloux, 1951, 265-275 (Augustine used in *De haeresibus* the *Anakephalaiosis*, but not the *Ancoratus* and the *Panarion*). — M. Tetz, Zwei De fide-Fragmente des Epiphanius: ThZ 11 (1955) 466-467 (two fragments in Cod. Coislinianus 37 attributed to St. Athanasius belong in reality to St. Epiphanius; they are excerpts of ch. 22 of the final section of the *Panarion, De fide*).

3. *De mensuris et ponderibus (Περὶ μέτρων καὶ σταθμῶν)*

The title *On Weights and Measures* does not do justice to the contents of this work composed at Constantinople in 392 for a Persian priest. It is the preliminary form of a dictionary of the Bible, which deals in its first part with the Canon and the translations of the Old Testament, in the second with biblical measures and weights and in the third with the geography of Palestine. A Syriac version first edited by de Lagarde preserves the entire treatise, while of the original Greek only the first part and an excerpt of the second are extant. Fragments remain of Armenian and Sahidic versions.

Editions: Greek text: MG 43, 237-294 (incomplete). — P. de Lagarde, Symmikta 2. Göttingen, 1880, 149-216. — Syriac version: P. de Lagarde, Veteris Testamenti ab Origene recensiti fragmenta apud Syros servata quinque. Göttingen, 1880. — New crit. ed.: J. E. Dean, Epiphanius' Treatise on Weights and Measures. The Syriac Version (Studies in Ancient Oriental Civilization 11). Chicago, 1935.

Translation: English: J. E. Dean, op. cit.

Studies: G. Mercati, Note di letteratura biblica e cristiana antica (ST 5). Rome, 1901, 17-27: Sul canone biblico di S. Epifanio (*De mens. et pond.* 23); *idem*, Opere minori I (ST 76). Vatican City, 1937, 20-92 (thinks that *De mens. et pond.* was translated into Latin in the sixth century).

4. *De XII gemmis (Περὶ τῶν δώδεκα λίθων)*

The tract *On the Twelve Precious Stones* in the breastplate of the high priest of the Old Testament was written in 394 at the request of Diodore of Tarsus to whom it is dedicated. The author gives an allegorical interpretation of the stones, describes their medicinal use and assigns them to the twelve tribes of Israel. Of the Greek only fragments remain but an old Georgian version has preserved the entire text. More than half of it is extant in an Armenian and in a Latin translation. The latter forms an appendix to the Imperial and Papal Letters of the *Collectio Avellana*. There are in addition Coptic and Ethiopic fragments.

Editions: MG 43, 293-304: Greek fragments; MG 43, 321-366: old Latin version.
Crit. ed. of this Latin version in the *Collectio Avellana:* O. Guenther, CSEL 35 (Epistulae
imperatorum, pontificum, aliorum) 743-773. Facundus of Hermiane, *Pro defens. trium
capit.* 4, 2 (ML 67, 617ff.) indicates that there was another Latin version existing about
550 A.D. Cf. Guenther, op. cit. p. 743 A. — Georgian version: P. R. Blake and
H. De Vis, Epiphanius: De Gemmis (Studies and Documents 2). London, 1934, 1-96;
the five Armenian fragments: ibid. 197-235; the twelve Coptic fragments: ibid. 236-335.
Cf. I. Rucker, ThR 34 (1935) 329-335; G. Deeters, ZDMG 90 (1936) 209-220;
F. Drexl, BZ 37 (1937) 400-411.

Translations: English: P. R. Blake, op. cit. 97-193 (Georgian version); 197-235 (Armenian
fragments). — *German:* R. Blechsteiner, Jahrbuch der österreichischen Leogesellschaft,
Vienna, 1930, 232-270, translated the part of the Georgian version that was published
by Dschanaschwili, Tiflis, 1898, comprising only chapters 6-21.

5. *Letters*

Two of his letters are preserved in a Latin translation. One of
them is addressed to John of Jerusalem, the other to St. Jerome,
both documents pertain to Epiphanius' unrelenting fight against
Origenism. Jerome rendered the one addressed to the bishop of
Jerusalem into Latin. This version found as *Ep.* 51 among Jerome's
Letters soon became public and incurred severe criticism. Charged
with having falsified his original, Jerome defended his translation
in his Letter to Pammachius *On the Best Method of Translating*
(*Ep.* 57), in which he declared that he intended 'to give sense for
sense and not word for word' (*Ep.* 57, 5). The letter of Epiphanius
is a poor apology for having uncanonically conferred ordination on
Jerome's brother Paulinian, which John resented. The entire
communication, which he wrote in 393, casts an interesting light
on Epiphanius' personality. But one paragraph (9) especially is
very valuable as an early instance of the iconoclastic spirit.
Epiphanius narrates how he destroyed a church-curtain with a
likeness of Christ. The passage shows at the same time the bad
temper of the metropolitan of Cyprus:

> I came to a villa called Anablatha, and, as I was passing, saw a
> lamp burning there. Asking what place it was, and learning it to be
> a church, I went in to pray, and found there a curtain hanging on
> the doors of the said church, dyed and embroidered. It bore an image
> either of Christ or of one of the saints; I do not rightly remember
> whose the image was. Seeing this, and being loth that an image of a
> man should be hung up in Christ's church contrary to the teaching
> of the Scriptures, I tore it asunder and advised the custodians of the
> place to use it as a winding sheet for some poor person (LNPF).

We have remains of other letters recently brought to light: a
passage of great interest for the history of Holy Week published
by K. Holl; quotations in Severus of Antioch (III 41, csco 102,

1933, 235 f.); and eight fragments in two Monophysite florilegia to which Lebon first drew attention.

St. Jerome mentions in his preface to his *Life of Hilarion* a short epistle of Epiphanius on the virtues of this abbot who died on Cyprus in 371. Nothing survives of Epiphanius' letter to Pope Siricius, in which he denounced John of Jerusalem as a heretic, nor of those to Egyptian monks warning them against the latter (Jerome, *C. Joan. Hier.* 14, 39). Of a later missive to St. Jerome, we have only a Latin translation, namely *Ep.* 91 in the Hieronymian corpus. Composed about the end of 400 A.D., it exults over his victory against Origenism and the success of the council convened at the suggestion of Theophilus. It was accompanied by a copy of the synodical letter and it urged Jerome to continue his work of translating into Latin documents concerning the Origenistic controversy. A former letter to Jerome on this subject is mentioned, but this is lost.

Editions: MG 43, 379-392 (*Ep.* 51 and 91 in Jerome's collection). New crit. ed.: I. HILBERG, CSEL 54, 395-412 (*Ep.* 51), CSEL 55, 145-146 (*Ep.* 91). — K. HOLL, Ein Bruchstück aus einem bisher unbekannten Brief des Epiphanius: Festgabe A. Jülicher. Tübingen, 1927, 159-189; reprinted in: K. HOLL, Gesammelte Aufsätze zur Kirchengeschichte II. Tübingen, 1928, 204-224. — J. LEBON, Sur quelques fragments de lettres attribuées à saint Épiphane de Salamine: Miscellanea G. Mercati I (ST 121). Vatican City, 1946, 145-174. — Severus of Antioch III, 41: CSCO 102 (1933) 235ff. (fragments of three unknown letters).

Studies: S. VAILHÉ, Notes de littérature ecclésiastique: EO 9 (1906) 219-224, intended to prove that the letter to John of Jerusalem with the iconoclastic passage is a forgery of the eighth century. — P. MAAS, Die ikonoklastische Episode in dem Brief des Epiphanius an Johannes: BZ 30 (1930) 279-286, successfully refuted this idea.

6. *Three Treatises against Images*

The above quoted passage is by no means the only proof for Epiphanius' hostile attitude towards images. K. Holl has sufficiently demonstrated that Epiphanius wrote three treatises against making or venerating them. Fragments of these survive in the Acts of the Councils of 754 and 787, in the works of St. John of Damascus, Theodore Studita, but especially in a tract which Nicephorus composed in 815 against Epiphanius. The remains are sufficient for the reconstruction of the three works.

a. *The Pamphlet against the Images*

The earliest of them is a pamphlet which Epiphanius composed shortly after the letter to John of Jerusalem, perhaps in 394. The author calls it idolatry to manufacture images of Christ, the Mother of God, martyrs, angels and prophets. He rejects the excuse that they honor the saints. They are forgeries. First of all, the saints are with Christ and are spirits. How can anyone represent them as bodies? The angels and saints do not want veneration of their images, as can be proved from Scripture. It is even more reprehensible to paint Christ. How can anyone dare to depict the Inconceivable and the Ineffable after Moses was unable to look into his face? The fact that Christ became man does not justify the practice. Christ never sanctioned it while He was here on earth and if such a concession was ever granted in the Church, it came from the devil. The custom is forbidden in the Old as well as in the New Testament, because in both it is written: 'The Lord thy God shalt thou adore, and Him only shalt thou serve'.

b. Letter to the Emperor Theodosius I

The fore-going pamphlet did not have the desired result. For this reason Epiphanius found it necessary to write a letter to the Emperor Theodosius I, in which he complains of his futile attempts to stop the manufacture of images. People mocked him and even his fellow-bishops refused to listen. The author introduces himself as born of Christian parents and brought up in the Nicene faith. He has no doubt of being supported by the Ruler, who had won great admiration for the zeal with which he destroyed pagan idols. He explains, how Satan, after the dangers of heresies and paganism have been removed, intends to lead the Christians back to idolatry. The Emperor should reflect on, whether it is proper for Christians to have a painted God. This is a shocking innovation. Nobody among the Fathers or former bishops ever dishonored Christ by having an image of Him in the church or in a private house. The painters have never seen the subjects of their portraits. They represent them according to their own fancy. The saints are now young, and again old. Christ has long hair, most probably because He was called 'the Nazirite'. But Christ was no Nazirite; He drank wine, strictly forbidden for Nazirites. St. Peter appears as an old man with a short beard, St. Paul with a bald head and a long beard. All these images are forgeries. Epiphanius suggests that they should all be removed. The painted curtains should be taken out of the churches and used for the burial of the poor. The wall paintings should be covered with white paint. If the mosaics could not be destroyed, new ones at least should be forbidden. The letter was written c. 394, and is highly important for the history of Christian art.

c. The Testament

The letter apparently made little impression upon the Emperor. Thus Epiphanius seizes a last opportunity; he leaves a last will and

testament in which he adjures his own community to keep the
tradition as a priceless heritage and never to abandon it; never
should they place images of saints in churches or cemeteries, but
have the image of God in their hearts. 'If anyone should dare,
using the Incarnation as an excuse, to look at the divine image
of the God Logos painted with earthly colors, be he anathema'.

Editions: K. HOLL, Die Schriften des Epiphanius gegen die Bilderverehrung: SAB (1916)
828-868; reprinted in: K. HOLL, Gesammelte Aufsätze zur Kirchengeschichte II.
Tübingen, 1928, 351-398 (356-359: *The Pamphlet against the Images;* 360-362: *Letter to
the Emperor Theodosius;* 363: *The Testament).*

Studies: W. KOCH, Die altchristliche Bilderfrage nach den literarischen Quellen.
Göttingen, 1917, 58ff. — J. WILPERT, Die unbekannten bilderfeindlichen Schriften des
hl. Epiphanius: HJG (1917) 532-535, regards these treatises as authentic. —
G. OSTROGORSKY, Studien zur Geschichte des byzantinischen Bilderstreites, Breslau,
1929, 61ff., calls them forgeries of the eighth century. F. DÖLGER, in his review of
Ostrogorsky's book: GGA 191 (1929) 353-372, rejects this idea and regards them as
authentic; so does H. BARION in his review: RQ 28 (1930) 78ff. — E. J. MARTIN, A
History of the Iconoclastic Controversy, London, 1930, 134ff., believes that these
iconoclastic writings are forgeries since their teaching is too complicated for the times
of St. Epiphanius. — W. ELLIGER, Die Stellung der alten Christen zu den Bildern in den
ersten vier Jahrhunderten nach den Angaben der zeitgenössischen Schriftsteller, Leipzig,
1930, 53-60, regards them as genuine.

SPURIOUS WRITINGS

1. *Physiologus*

The most important among the spurious writings attributed to
Epiphanius is the Greek recension of the *Physiologus ('Επιφανίου ἐκ
τῶν 'Αριστοτέλους φυσιολόγου τῶν ζώων)*, the mediaeval lexicon or
manual of Christian nature symbolism. It consists of a collection
of marvellous stories and allegories in which religious truths are
symbolized by the manners and habits of animals. Thus Christ's
saving of mankind by His Crucifixion is represented by the pelican
who feeds its offspring by shedding its own blood. The name of
the work comes from the introductory words of each tale 'the
physiologus (naturalist) says'. Its basic form goes back to Alexandria,
as the Egyptian names for the months indicate, and to the first half
of the second century A.D. The Epistle of Barnabas, Clement of
Alexandria and Origen made use of the book. But some of its parts
must be much older. Though the Greek title mentions the name of
Aristotle, he had nothing to do with it. His name was used because
he wrote on animals *(Περὶ ζώων)* and was looked upon as the first
naturalist *(φυσιολόγος).* Various adaptations and revisions of the
original Greek text and translations into Latin, Syriac, Ethiopic,
English, German, French and many other languages have been

made in the Middle Ages. It was the principal source of the numerous *Bestiaries*. Its popularity was universal and it exerted a wide influence on mediaeval literature and ecclesiastical art, in which its symbolism persists to the present day.

Editions: Greek text: MG 43, 517-534. — Crit. ed.: F. LAUCHERT, Geschichte des Physiologus. Strasbourg, 1889, 229-279. — New crit. ed.: F. SBORDONE, Physiologus. Milan, 1936. Cf. B. E. PERRY, AJPh 58 (1937) 488-496. — Latin versions: F. WILHELM, Physiologus, Dicta Chrysostomi (Münchener Texte 8). Munich, 1916 (late revision). — F. J. CARMODY, Physiologus Latinus, Versio Y. Berkeley (Univ. of California Pr.), 1941. — Arabic version: J. P. N. LAND, Anecdota Syriaca IV. Leiden, 1875, 115-176. Cf. G. GRAF, Geschichte der christlichen arabischen Literatur I. Vatican City, 1944, 548-549. — For Syriac versions, see: A. BAUMSTARK, Geschichte der syrischen Literatur. Bonn, 1922, 170-171. — An Old Georgian version was edited by N. MARR, 1904. — Fragments of a Coptic version were edited by A. VAN LANTSCHOOT, A propos du Physiologus: The Bulletin of the Byzantine Institute 2 (1950) 339-363 (with a French translation).

Translations: English: J. CARLILL, Physiologus. The Epic of the Beast. London, 1924, 153-250. — B. THEOBALD and W. RENDALL, Physiologus, a Metrical Bestiary. London, 1928. — *German:* E. PETERS, Der griechische Physiologus und seine orientalischen Übersetzungen. Berlin, 1898. — G. GRAF, Caucasica. Leipzig, 1926,9 3-114 (translation of the Georgian version). — *French:* The Bestiary of Philippe de Thaon represents a French version of the Physiologus. For text and translation, see: T. WRIGHT, Le livre des créatures. London, 1841, 74-131. — *Icelandic:* H. HERMANNSSON, The Icelandic Physiologus. Ithaca (Cornell University Press), 1938 (facsimile edit.).

Studies: C. O. ZURETTI, Per la critica del Physiologus greco: SIF 5 (1897) 113-219 (Greek text from Cod. Ambros. C. 255); *idem*, Ancora per la critica del Physiologus greco: BZ (1900) 170-188. — J. STRZYGOWSKI, Der Bilderkreis des griechischen Physiologus. Leipzig, 1899; *idem*, Der illustrierte Physiologus in Smyrna: BZ (1901) 218-222. — M. GOLDSTAUB, Der Physiologus und seine Weiterbildung besonders in der lateinischen und byzantinischen Literatur: Philologus Suppl.-Band 8 (1901) 337-404. — J. SAUER, Der illustrierte griechische Physiologus der Ambrosiana: BNJ (1921) 428-441. — L. THORNDIKE, A History of Magic and Experimental Science I. New York, 1923, 497ff. — M. WELLMANN, Der Physiologus. Eine religionsgeschichtlich-naturwissenschaftliche Untersuchung (Philologus Suppl.-Band 22). Leipzig, 1930. — F. LAUCHERT, Zur Eingliederung des Physiologus in die altchristliche Literatur: ThR 30 (1931) 405-417. — F. J. CARMODY, De bestiis et aliis rebus and the Latin Physiologus: Speculum (1938) 153-159. — B. E. PERRY, Physiologus: PWK 20 (1940) 1074-1129. — F. J. CARMODY, Quotations in the Latin Physiologus from Latin Bibles earlier than the Vulgate. Berkeley and Los Angeles, 1944. — F. SBORDONE, La tradizione manoscritta del Physiologus latino: Athenaeum (1949) 246-280. — F. CORDASCO, The Old English Physiologus: Its Problems: Modern Language Quarterly 10 (1949) 351-355. — E. PETERSON, Die Spiritualität des griechischen Physiologus: BZ 47 (1954) 60-72. — A. GRILLMEIER, Der Logos am Kreuz. Zur christlichen Symbolik der älteren Kreuzigungsdarstellung. Munich, 1956, 84-86. — H. MENHARDT, Der Millstätter Physiologus und seine Verwandten. Klagenfurt, 1956.

2. *Commentary on the Canticle of Canticles*

A Latin version attributes to Epiphanius a Commentary on the Canticle of Canticles which really belongs to his contemporary

Bishop Philo of Carpasia in Cyprus, as the abbreviated Greek text of the work, edited by Giacomelli, proves.

Editions: Greek text: M. A. GIACOMELLI, Rome, 1772; reprinted: MG 40, 9-154. — Latin version: P. F. FOGGINI, Rome, 1750.

Studies: W. RIEDEL, Die Auslegung des Hohenliedes in der jüdischen Gemeinde und der griechischen Kirche. Leipzig, 1898, 76ff. — L. WELSERSHEIMB, Das Kirchenbild der griechischen Väterkommentare zum Hohen Lied: ZkTh 70 (1948) 436-440 (Philo of Carpasia).

3. Homilies

The five sermons *In festo palmarum, In sabbato magno, In die resurrectionis Christi, In assumptionem Christi, In laudes S. Mariae Deiparae,* and the two fragments which follow (the second only in Latin) are spurious (MG 43, 428-508). The same must be said of the Armenian excerpts on Genesis and Luke in a manuscript of 1750, of which Conybeare published an English translation; and also of the Coptic homily on St. Mary, edited by Budge, and of the Latin *Vita B.M.V.*

P. Nautin published recently the Greek text of a homily *On the Resurrection* which *Codex Vaticanus gr.* 1255 attributes to Epiphanius, while *Vatic. gr.* 455, 2013, 1636 ascribe it to St. John Chrysostom. Content and style prove that neither of the two composed it. Though the Greek original had not been known, a Latin translation is found at the end of the collection of Epiphanius' spurious works in Migne, MG 43, 505-508. The author of this version is Gerard Vossius, who published it at Rome in 1585. Petavius reproduced this in his *Opera omnia* of Epiphanius (Paris, 1622) vol. II, pp. 310-311, whence it passed into Migne's edition. Except for the opening and close the short sermon is taken from the second half of the homily *De anima et corpore deque passione Domini* of Alexander of Alexandria (cf. above, p. 17).

Editions: MG 43, 428-508. — F. C. CONYBEARE, The Gospel Commentary of Epiphanius: ZNW 7 (1906) 318-332; 8 (1907) 221-225. — E. A. W. BUDGE, Miscellaneous Coptic Texts. London, 1915, 120-146, 699-724 (homily on St. Mary). — P. NAUTIN, Le dossier d'Hippolyte et de Méliton. Paris, 1953, 151-159 (Greek text and French translation).

Studies: C. MARTIN, Fragments en onciale d'homélies grecques sur la Vierge attribuées à Épiphane de Chypre et à Hésychius de Jérusalem: RHE 31 (1935) 356-359. — E. FRANCESCHINI, Il Περὶ τοῦ βίου τῆς ὑπεραγίας Θεοτόκου di Epifanio nella versione latina medioevale di Pasquale Romano: Studi e note di filologia latina medioevale (1938) 107-128. — A. VAILLANT, L'homélie d'Épiphane sur l'ensevelissement du Christ: Radovi staroslavenskog instituta 3 (Zagreb, 1958) 5-100.

4. The Anaphora of St. Epiphanius

Among the extant anaphoras of the Ethiopic Liturgies there is one attributed to St. Epiphanius, edited by S. Euringer from two

Berlin manuscripts. It was used on the Day of Baptism (January 11 or 6) on which the Baptism of Christ is commemorated, in the Month of Rain (June), on the Feast of Epiphanius (May 17) and in the Prayer of the Fifth Day, that is most probably Maundy Thursday. The anaphora has some characteristic features. Thus the Eucharistic Prayer is not addressed to the Father but to the Son. The omission of the *Sanctus* is remarkable. The Lord's Supper is supposed to have taken place 'in the house of Lazarus His friend', a tradition which is mentioned by the Monophysite bishop Solomon of Bosra in Iraq in the 13th century. The epiclesis follows the words of the Institution and asks for the descent of the Holy Spirit.

Edition: Ethiopic text: S. EURINGER, Die äthiopische Anaphora des heiligen Epiphanius, Bischofs der Insel Cypern: OC 3rd ser. 1 (1926) 98-142.

Translations: English: J. M. HARDEN, The Anaphoras of the Ethiopic Liturgy (SPCK). London, 1928, 101-103. — *German:* S. EURINGER, loc. cit.

5. *Other Spuria*

The little work on the birth and burial places of all the prophets and the legends of the prophets, apostles and disciples ascribed to Epiphanius, Dorotheus and Hippolytus are certainly spurious. The legends of the prophets go back to a Jewish source with various additions by Christians of the third and fourth century. The legends and lists of the apostles and disciples do not antidate the eighth century. The treatise *De numerorum mysteriis* (MG 43, 507-518) is not by Epiphanius, nor is the register of the main churches, patriarchical and metropolitan sees (*Ἔκθεσις πρωτοκλησιῶν πατριαρχῶν τε καὶ μητροπολιτῶν*) which most probably belongs to the time of the Emperor Heraclius (610-641). The Greek text of the latter was edited by H. Gelzer and again by F. N. Finck, who published it together with an Armenian version. This catalogue is the earliest of the *Notitiae episcopatuum* extant.

The *Opusculum S. Epiphanii de divina inhumanatione* published by A. Morcelli in 1828 and not found in Migne, is a collection of Messianic prophecies of the Old Testament arranged in 102 chapters. The compiler is unknown.

Editions: MG 43, 393-413, 415-528. — New crit. ed.: T. SCHERMANN, Prophetarum vitae fabulosae, indices apostolorum discipulorumque Domini, Dorotheo, Epiphanio, Hippolyto aliisque vindicatae. Leipzig, 1907. — H. GELZER, AAM Philos.-philol. Klasse 21 (1901) 531-549. — F. N. FINCK, Des Epiphanios von Cypern *Ἔκθεσις πρωτοκλησιῶν πατριαρχῶν τε καὶ μητροπολιτῶν* armenisch und griechisch. Marburg, 1902. — A. MORCELLI, Memorie di Religione, di Morale e di Letteratura 13. Modena, 1828, 265ff.; cf. the edition of DINDORF IV 2, IIIff.

Study: T. SCHERMANN, Propheten- und Apostellegenden nebst Jüngerkatalogen(TU 31, 3). Leipzig, 1907.

DIODORE OF TARSUS

The Exegetical School of Antioch produced one of its greatest scholars and teachers in Diodore of Tarsus. Highly esteemed as a pillar of orthodoxy during his lifetime, he was accused of heresy and condemned as the originator of Nestorianism a century after his death. A native of Antioch, he received his theological training there as a student of Silvanus, the later bishop of Tarsus (Basil the Great, *Ep.* 244, 3), and Eusebius of Emesa (Jerome, *De vir. ill.* 119). He was no less successful in his classical studies at Athens because in a letter addressed to Photinus and preserved by Facundus of Hermiane (*Pro defens. trium capit.* 4, 2) Julian the Apostate states, that Diodore had equipped his malevolent tongue against the ancient gods with the wisdom of Athens herself. According to Socrates (*Hist. eccl.* 6, 3) and Sozomen (*Hist. eccl.* 8, 2) he later presided over a monastic community near Antioch. As a teacher at its famous school he defended the Nicene faith against pagans and heretics and counted among his pupils men like St. John Chrysostom and Theodore of Mopsuestia. He felt especially challenged when Julian the Apostate during his unfortunate Persian campaign had his quarters at Antioch from the end of June 362 to the fifth of March 363 and did all in his power to restore the worship of the ancient gods. While the Emperor was busy there composing his great work *Against the Galileans,* on which he labored 'many nights' (Libanius, *Or.* 18 n. 178), Diodore rose like 'a great rock in the ocean' (Theodoret, *Hist. eccl.* 4, 22) to defend the divinity of Christ. This but increased the imperial anger to such a degree that Julian calls him (in the above mentioned letter) a 'priest sorcerer of the Galileans' and 'a keen defender of a religion for farmers', whose gaunt figure and pale face, together with his wretched health were so many evidences of the anger of the gods. He terms Christ's divinity Diodore's invention and declares that the latter bases His eternity on a legend, while in reality Christ died a shameful death. Julian's successor Valens banished Diodore in 372 to Armenia where he entered into relations with Basil the Great (*Ep.* 135). He returned to Antioch after the Emperor's death and became bishop of Tarsus in Cilicia in 378. In this capacity he took part in the Second Ecumenical Council at Constantinople in 381. In the imperial edict of July 30, 381 which confirmed its decrees Theodosius I called him one of the reliable arbiters of orthodoxy (*Cod. Theodos.* XVI 1, 3). He must have died before 394.

As early as 438 Cyril of Alexandria accused Diodore in his work *Contra Diodorum et Theodorum* of being responsible for the teaching

of Nestorius. It was the same charge that led to his final condemnation by a synod at Constantinople in 499.

Studies: P. GODET, Diodore de Tarse: DTC 4 (1911) 1363-1366. — P. SHERWOOD,
EC 4 (1950) 1657-1660. — G. BARDY, DSp fasc. 20/21 (1955) 986-994. — P. N. FETISOV,
Diodore of Tarsus. His Life and his Works. Kiev, 1915 (in Russian); cf. ROC 20 (1915/17)
219-220; A. PALMIERI, Diodoro di Taro, sua vita e sue gesta: Bess 20 (1916) 188-197. —
R. ABRAMOWSKI, Untersuchungen zu Diodor von Tarsus: ZNW 30 (1931) 234-262
(ed. and translation of Syriac *Vita* of Diodore found in the *Ecclesiastical History* of
Barhadbesabba composed about 600 A.D.). — G. DOWNEY, Julian the Apostate at
Antioch: Church History 8 (1939) 303-315. — L. ABRAMOWSKI, Der Streit um Diodor
und Theodor von Mopsuestia zwischen den beiden ephesinischen Konzilien: ZKG 67
(1955/56) 252-287. — R. LECONTE, L'Asceterium de Diodore: Mélanges Bibliques
A. Robert. Paris, 1957, 531-536 (Diodore's monastic school).

HIS WRITINGS

Diodore's literary bequest was very large. It comprised a great
number of works on exegesis, apologetics, polemics, dogma,
cosmology, astronomy and chronology. The Syrian Ebedjesu
(d. 1318) speaks of sixty treatises. Unfortunately, only fragments
survive. Attempts have been made again and again to collect them.
The first effort goes back to the Jesuit Garnier (d. 1681) who in
his edition of Marius Mercator (reprinted by Migne, ML 48, 1146 ff.
III, 8) tried to assemble the remnants. His collection is neither
reliable nor complete. The same must be said of Migne's own
(MG 33, 1545 ff.), which endeavored to enlarge Garnier's. But
recently all of the theological fragments have been collected in a
new edition with German translation by R. Abramowski. Most
of them have been preserved in Syriac-Jacobitic florilegia and very
few in Nestorian texts. There are in addition some Armenian and
Latin excerpts and a small number in the original Greek. Brière
and Lebon have added French or Latin versions to those which
they edited. The paucity of these fragments is due to the thorough
destruction of his works by his enemies.

Fragments: MG 33, 1561-1628. — Syriac fragments: P. DE LAGARDE, Analecta Syriaca.
Leipzig and London, 1858, 91-100. — J. LEBON, Severi Antiocheni liber contra impium
Grammaticum, Orat. II, 7 (CSCO 112, 70), II, 21 (CSCO 112, 142), III, 15 (CSCO
94, 178), III, 23 (CSCO 102, 9), III, 24 (CSCO 102, 30), III, 25 (CSCO 102, 33-34),
III, 26 (CSCO 102, 45), III, 33 (CSCO 102, 111). — R. HESPEL, Sévère d'Antioche.
Le Philalèthe (CSCO 134 (1952) 125-126). — M. BRIÈRE, Fragments syriaques de
Diodore de Tarse réédités et traduits pour la première fois: ROC 10 (1946) 231-283
(with the Syriac text of P. de Lagarde). — R. ABRAMOWSKI, Der theologische Nachlass
des Diodor von Tarsus: ZNW 42 (1949) 19-69 (the German translation needs a revision). — E. SCHWARTZ, ACO I, 5, 177-179.

1. *Biblical Commentaries*

In his exegesis Diodore follows firmly the historical and grammatical method and strenuously opposes the allegorical interpretation

peculiar to the Alexandrian School. He does not look for a hidden meaning in the text, but for the sense intended by the inspired writer. Suidas (*Lex.* 1, 1, 1379) reports that Theodorus Lector was acquainted with commentaries by him to all the books of the Old Testament, to the four gospels, Acts and 1 John. Even this list does not seem exhaustive: Staab has discovered sizable fragments of a work on Romans in *Codd. Vat.* 762, *Monac.* 412 and *Pantokrat.* 28; St. Jerome mentions (*Ep.* 48, 3) a commentary on 1 Corinthians and (*Ep.* 119, 4) on 1 Thessalonians, of which he preserves a considerable quotation. He speaks (*De vir. ill.* 119) of Diodore's 'extant commentaries to the Apostle and many others'. Most of the excerpts of the commentary on Ps. 51-74 in Migne MG 33 belong really to Didymus of Alexandria as Mariès has proved. Mariès believed that Diodore was the author of the treatise *On the Psalms* preserved under the name of Anastasius III, bishop of Nicaea, and on the strength of this identification, declared him much more orthodox than the dogmatic fragments indicate. However, to this conclusion serious objections have been raised by Jugie, Devreesse and Richard. In any case, the commentary remains still unedited. A number of quotations from Diodore's commentaries have been discovered in an Octateuch *catena*.

Suidas mentions in his list of exegetical writings a treatise *On the Difference between Theory and Allegory*. The work is completely lost, but the title suggests that Diodore developed therein his hermeneutic principles.

Editions: J. DECONINCK, Essai sur la chaîne de l'Octateuque avec une édition des Commentaires de Diodore de Tarse qui s'y trouvent contenus. Paris, 1912. — K. STAAB, Pauluskommentare aus der griechischen Kirche. Münster, 1933, 83-112.

Studies: R. DEVREESSE, Anciens commentateurs grecs de l'Octateuque: RBibl 45 (1936) 217-220. — A. VACCARI, La 'teoria' esegetica antiochena: Bibl 1 (1920) 3-36, 15 (1934) 94-101. — E. SCHWEIZER, Diodor von Tarsus als Exeget: ZNW 40 (1941/42) 33-75. — L. MARIÈS, Aurions-nous le commentaire sur les psaumes de Diodore de Tarse?: RPh 35 (1911) 56-70; *idem*, Diodore ἀπὸ φωνῆς 'Αναστασίου: RPh 38 (1914) 169-173; *idem*, Le commentaire de Diodore de Tarse sur les psaumes. Examen sommaire et classement provisoire des éléments de la tradition manuscrite: ROC 24 (1924) 58-189; *idem*, Études préliminaires à l'édition de Diodore de Tarse 'Sur les psaumes'. La tradition manuscrite: RSR 22 (1932) 385-408, 513-540; *idem*, Études préliminaires à l'édition de Diodore de Tarse 'Sur les psaumes'. La tradition manuscrite. Deux mss. nouveaux. Le caractère diodorien du commentaire. Paris, 1933. — R. DEVREESSE, Bibl 34 (1925) 605ff. — M. JUGIE, A propos du commentaire des psaumes attribué à Diodore de Tarse: EO 7 (1934) 190-193. — M. RICHARD, Byz (1950) 219-222 (commentary *On the Psalms* not authentic).

2. *Dogmatic, Polemic and Apologetic Treatises*

His apologetic and polemic works comprise tracts against pagans, Jews and heretics. According to Heraclian, bishop of Chalcedon, quoted by Photius (*Bibl. Cod.* 85) he wrote twenty five books *Against the Manichaeans*, in the first seven of which he refuted the work of Mani's disciple Addas named *Modion* ('Bushel' referring to St. Mark 4, 19), while 'in the remaining books he explained and cleared up the meaning of certain passages in the Scriptures which the Manichaeans were in the habit of appropriating to support their own views'. A Syrian florilegium has preserved 33 excerpts of Diodore's work *Against the Synousiasts*, some of them falsified by Apollinarists. First published by P. de Lagarde in 1858, they have been brought out in a new edition by M. Brière. Theodoret (*Haer. fab. comp.* 2, 11) mentions treatises 'against Photinus, Malchion, Sabellius and Marcellus of Ancyra'. Suidas lists the following titles: *De eo, quod sit unus Deus in Trinitate; Contra Melchisedecitas; Contra Judaeos; De resurrectione mortuorum; De anima, contra diversas de ea haereticorum opiniones; Ad Gratianum capita; De providentia; Contra Platonem, de Deo et diis; De natura et materia, in quo opere tractatur de eo quod justum est; De Deo et falsa Graecorum materia; Naturas invisibiles non ex elementis, sed una cum elementis ex nihilo factas esse, ad Euphronium philosophum, per interrogationem et responsionem; De eo quomodo opifex quidem sempiternus sit, opera vero eius non semper exstent; Quomodo velle et nolle sit in Deo aeterno; Contra Porphyrium, de animalibus et sacrificiis.* Finally Photius (*Bibl. cod.* 102) calls attention to Diodore's work *Concerning the Holy Spirit*, 'in which he shows that he is already infected by the taint of the Nestorian heresy'. Nothing remains of all these works.

Fragments: MG 86, 1385-1388. See the editions of M. Brière and R. Abramowski above, p. 398. — M. Richard, Les traités de Cyrille d'Alexandrie contre Diodore et Théodore et les fragments dogmatiques de Diodore de Tarse: Mélanges F. Grat 1. Paris, 1946, 99-116. — G. Brandhuber, Diodor von Tarsus. Die Bruchstücke seines dogmatischen Schrifttums, gesammelt, übersetzt und untersucht. Gars/Inn, 1949 (manuscript).

Studies: V. Ermoni, Diodore de Tarse et son rôle doctrinal: Mus 2 (1901) 422-444. — M. Jugie, La doctrine christologique de Diodore de Tarse d'après les fragments de ses œuvres: Euntes Docete (1949) 171-191. — A. Grillmeier, Die theologische und sprachliche Vorbereitung der christologischen Formel von Chalkedon: CGG I (1951) 135-144. — F. A. Sullivan, The Christology of Theodore of Mopsuestia. Rome, 1956, 181-196 (Diodore's Christology).

Harnack and Fetisov attributed to Diodore the four Pseudo-Justinian treatises *Quaestiones et Responsiones ad orthodoxos, Quaestiones Christianorum ad gentiles, Quaestiones gentilium ad Christianos, Confutatio dogmatum Aristotelis.* This identification has not found approval with scholars. The *Quaestiones et responsiones ad orthodoxos* belong to Theodoret of Cyrus (see below p. 548).

Studies: A. Harnack, Diodor von Tarsus. Vier pseudojustinische Schriften als Eigentum Diodors nachgewiesen (TU 21, 4). Leipzig, 1901. — F. X. Funk, Le Ps.-Justin et Diodore de Tarse: RHE (1902) 947-971; *idem*, Kirchengeschichtliche Abhandlungen 3 (1907) 323-350 (Theodoret is the author of the *Quaestiones et Responsiones*). — N. FETISOV, op. cit. — G. BARDY, La littérature patristique des Quaestiones et Responsiones sur l'Écriture Sainte: RBib 42 (1933) 211-229.

3. *Astronomical and Chronological Works*

Diodore must have been quite an authority in astronomy. Suidas has preserved the following titles: *Contra astronomos et astrologos et fatum; De sphaera et septem zonis et contrario astrorum motu; De Hipparchi sphaera; Contra Aristotelem, de corpore coelesti; Quomodo sol sit calidus, contra eos qui coelum animal esse dicunt.* The first work, *Against Astronomers, Astrologers and Fate*, is the only one of which we know more owing to Photius' (*Bibl. cod.* 223) detailed report, in which he quotes long passages of this work. It consisted of eight books and defended the faith in God and Divine Providence against the belief in fate and the unlimited power of the stars. It discussed the origin of evil and refuted especially Bardesanes and his adherents.

Suidas mentions among his exegetical works a *Chronicon* which Diodore wrote against Eusebius of Caesarea. The fact that this title appears in the list of his Biblical commentaries seems to indicate that it dealt with chronological questions in Holy Scripture.

Studies: P. DOLL, De Diodori Tarsensis libro κατὰ εἰμαρμένης. Diss. Bonn, 1923. — E. AMAND DE MENDIETA, Fatalisme et liberté dans l'antiquité grecque. Louvain, 1945, 461-479.

THEODORE OF MOPSUESTIA

Diodore's pupil, Theodore, was like his teacher born at Antioch. He studied rhetoric and literature under the famous sophist Libanius (cf. above, p. 222), in whose school he began his lifelong friendship with St. John Chrysostom. The example and advice of the latter induced him to enter a monastery near Antioch before his twentieth year. Soon, however, his ardor cooled and he left the cloister in order to become a lawyer and marry. Two eloquent letters of St. Chrysostom *ad Theodorum lapsum* (MG 47, 277-316) succeeded in dissuading him from such a change and he returned to his monastic life. About 383 he was ordained a priest by Flavian, the bishop of Antioch, and in 392 he was consecrated bishop of Mopsuestia in Cilicia. He died in 428 after gaining a wide reputation for his learning and his orthodoxy. Highly esteemed by his contemporaries but condemned as a heretic 125 years after his death, he shared the fate of his master Diodore of Tarsus.

Studies: H. B. SWETE, DCB 4 (1887) 934-948. — F. LOOFS, RE 19 (1907) 598-605. — H. G. OPITZ, PWK II. Reihe 5 (1934) 1881-1890. — E. AMANN, DTC 15 (1946) 235-279.

— L. Patterson, Theodore of Mopsuestia and Modern Thought. London, 1926. — R. Devreesse, Essai sur Théodore de Mopsueste (ST 141). Vatican City, 1948; cf. J. L. McKenzie, A New Study of Theodore of Mopsuestia: TS 10 (1949) 394-408. — L. Abramowski, Der Streit um Diodor und Theodor von Mopsuestia zwischen den beiden ephesinischen Konzilien: ZKG 67 (1955/56) 252-287. — G. Jouassard, Ad Theodorum lapsum: HJG 77 (1958) 140-150 (against Theodore as recipient).

HIS WRITINGS

Theodore is the most typical representative of the Antiochene school of exegesis and by far its most famous author. The Nestorian Church venerates him as 'the great exponent of the Scriptures' second to none. He wrote commentaries to nearly all the books of the Bible which are remarkable for their free and critical investigations into questions of authorship and date and for their highly scientific, philological and historical approach. He was the first to apply literary criticism to the solution of textual problems. He composed in addition a large number of dogmatic and controversial treatises which prove his lively interest in all theological questions of his times and his independent judgment. His works, as those of a heretic, have mostly perished, but discoveries of Oriental versions in the past twenty-five years have made several of them available to modern scholarship; they cast an entirely new light on his theology. Migne's edition (MG 66) contains only the Greek and Latin fragments collected up to the middle of the 19th century, many of which are spurious. The best catalogue of the titles of Theodore's writings is that of the Nestorian Ebedjesu from the beginning of the 14th century (in J. S. Assemani, *Bibl. or. Clem.-Vat.* III, 1, 30 ff.) and that in the Chronicle of Seert (PO 5, 289 ff.) from the first half of the 13th century.

Editions: MG 66, 9-1020. — H. B. Swete, 2 vols. Cambridge, 1880/1882 (*Commentary on the Minor Epistles of St. Paul;* the second vol. contains in an appendix all the known fragments of Theodore's strictly dogmatic works). — F. Nau, PO 9 (1913) 637-667. — A. Mingana, Woodbrooke Studies 5 (1932), 6 (1933). — R. Devreesse, ST 93 (1939); R. Tonneau and R. Devreesse, ST 145 (1949). — J. M. Vosté, CSCO 115/116 (1940). — E. Schwartz, ACO I, 5, 173-177. — Collections of Syriac fragments: P. de Lagarde, Analecta Syriaca. Leipzig and London, 1858, 100-108. — E. Sachau, Theodori Mopsuesteni fragmenta Syriaca e codicibus Musei Britannici Nitriacis edidit atque in Latinum sermonem vertit. Leipzig, 1869. — A. Sanda, Severi Antiocheni Philalethes. Beyrouth, 1928, 28-29. — For other ed., see indiv. works.

Translations: English: A. Mingana, op. cit. — *French:* R. Tonneau, op. cit.

Studies: O. F. Fritzsche, De Theodori Mopsuesteni vita et scriptis commentatio historica. Halle, 1836; reprinted: MG 66, 9-78. — H. Kihn, Theodor von Mopsuestia und Junilius Africanus als Exegeten. Freiburg i.B., 1880. — L. Pirot, L'œuvre exégétique de Théodore de Mopsueste. Rome, 1913. — A. Baumstark, Geschichte der syrischen Literatur. Bonn, 1922, 102-104. — J. M. Vosté, La chronologie et l'activité littéraire de Théodore de Mopsueste: RBibl 34 (1925) 54-81; *idem*, L'œuvre exégétique de Théodore de Mopsueste au IIe concile de Constantinople: RBibl 38 (1929) 382-395, 542-554; *idem*, De versione Syriaca operum Theodori Mopsuesteni: OCP 8 (1942) 477-481. — D. TYING, Theodore of Mopsuestia as an Interpreter of the Old Testament: JBL 50 (1931) 298-303. — R. DEVREESSE, Par quelles voies nous sont parvenus les commentaires de Théodore de Mopsueste?: RBibl 39 (1930) 362-377; *idem*, La méthode exégétique de Théodore de Mopsueste: RBibl 53 (1946) 207-241. — W. LAISTNER, Antiochene Exegesis in Western Europe during the Middle Ages: HThR 40 (1947) 19-31 (influence of Theodore).

1. Biblical Commentaries on the Old Testament

a. On Genesis

Ebedjesu mentions that Theodore *Commentarium in librum Geneseos tribus edidit tomis ad magnum Alphaeum summa elaboratum methodo et speculatione*, while the Chronicle of Seert speaks of a commentary in three books on the Pentateuch. Photius (*Bibl. cod.* 38) seems acquainted only with an interpretation of Genesis. He states in his very biased report:

> Read the work of Theodore of Antioch entitled *Commentary on Genesis* (the history of Creation), the first book of which contains seven volumes. The style is neither brilliant nor very clear. The author avoids the use of allegory as much as possible, being only concerned with the interpretation of history. He frequently repeats himself, and produces a disagreeable impression upon the reader. Although he lived before Nestorius, he vomits up his doctrines by anticipation. This is that Theodore of Mopsuestia, from whom on several occasions John Philoponus (as the latter himself says) demanded a serious explanation of his method of interpretation in his own work on the Creation (SPCK).

Fortunately we are no longer limited to the fragments in the *Catena Nicephori* found in Migne. Additional parts of the text have been recovered from MS *catenae* published by Devreesse, citations of John Philoponus and Procopius of Gaza, and a Syriac fragment, which has preserved the end of the first chapter of the introduction with a general consideration of the Hexaemeron. Thus we are now in possession of Theodore's explanation of Genesis 1-3, covering the act of the creation, the organization of creatures, the invisible powers, day and night and the first day, plants and animals, the creation of man as an image of God, the rest on the seventh day, paradise and the tree of knowledge, the creation of Eve, the fall and the expulsion from paradise.

Though Ebedjesu does not mention a commentary on the other books of the Octateuch, the *catenae* preserve about half a dozen fragments which would indicate that the *Commentary on Genesis* was not the only one. Three excerpts explain Exodus 25, 8-20, 23-29 and 30-38. They are of special importance for the exegetic

principles and methods of Theodore. The rest concern the interpretation of Josue 7, 4-5 and Judges 13, 25 and 15, 17.

Fragments: MG 33, 633-646. — R. DEVREESSE, Chaînes exégétiques grecques: DB Suppl. I
(1928) 1102-1105. — Syriac fragments: E. SACHAU, Theodori Mopsuesteni fragmenta
Syriaca. Leipzig, 1879, 1-21. — R. M. TONNEAU, Théodore de Mopsueste, Interprétation
(du livre) de la Génèse: Mus 66 (1953) 45-64 (edition and French translation of additional
fragments found in Cod. Vat. Syr. 120, ff. I-V).

Studies: R. DEVREESSE, Anciens commentateurs grecs de l'Octateuque: RBibl 45 (1936)
364-384; *idem*, ST 141 (1948) 5-25 (on Genesis); 25-27 (on Exodus).

b. Commentary on the Psalms

The *Commentary on the Psalms* was Theodore's first work; he
wrote it when he was scarcely twenty years of age and regretted
its imperfections later in his treatise *Contra allegoricos*, of which only
this passage is extant (Facundus, *Pro defensione trium capit.* 3, 6;
ML 67, 602). According to Ebedjesu it comprised five volumes:
Davidem quinque tomis exposuit ad Cerdonem fratremque eius.
Of the fragments printed in MG 66, 648-696 Devreesse rejects
about one half as spurious. Nevertheless the greatest part of this
work is now available. While for Psalms 1-31 only small fragments
of the Greek original remain, Devreesse succeeded in recovering
the text almost complete to Psalms 32-80 from MS *catenae*. Moreover, an ancient Latin version in *Cod. Ambros. C* 301 *inf.* and in
Cod. Univers. Taurin. F IV 1, 5-6 (both of the eighth century) enabled
him to restore the entire commentary for Psalms 1 - 16,11, and
large sections for Psalms 16,12 - 40,13.

Theodore is the first interpreter to insist that the Psalms must
be read against a historical background. He recognizes the Davidic
authorship of all the Psalms but at the same time was convinced
that the context and setting of many of the Psalms are altogether
unsuitable to David. His solution to this problem is that those
Psalms which reflect another period were written by David, but
as a prophet revealing the future state of Israel. Thus he classifies
the Psalms chronologically from David to the Maccabees. He
maintains that the prophetic horizon of David did not reach further
than the Maccabees, and that there is consequently no directly
Messianic passage in the Psalms. He justifies the Messianic use in
the New Testament as an accommodation. But he recognizes four
exceptions: Pss. 2; 8; 44; 109. Though he does not regard even these as
properly Messianic in the sense of referring to the future prepared
for the chosen people, he explains them as describing the Incarnation
and the Church. He rejects the Messianic interpretations proposed
by the allegorical school of Alexandria which violate his sound
principle that each Psalm must be treated as a literary whole and

that a verse cannot be divorced from its context. He refuses to admit any change of person, time or situation in the same Psalm. Thus if a Psalm refers to the future, it refers entirely to the future. He declares the titles of the Psalms posterior additions. On the whole, his commentary corroborates the more moderate of the opinions which have been held about Theodore of Mopsuestia as an interpreter of Holy Scripture, that, without rejecting the mystical interpretation or denying the existence of typology in Scripture, he used it far less than the Alexandrian divines or even St. John Chrysostom.

Edition: R. DEVREESSE, Le commentaire de Théodore de Mopsueste sur les psaumes (1-80) (ST 93). Vatican City, 1939; cf. A. VACCARI, Bibl (1941) 209-210; H. LIETZMANN, DLZ (1940) 841-843; D. STONE, JThSt 42 (1941) 87-88; B. ALTANER, BZ 45 (1952) 64-66.

Studies: H. LIETZMANN, Der Psalmenkommentar Theodors von Mopsuestia: SAB (1902) 334-346. — G. MERCATI, I frammenti inediti dell'antica versione latina del commento di Teodoro Mopsuesteno ai salmi: Varia Sacra (ST 11). Rome, 1903, 93-105; *idem,* Opere minori II (ST 77). Vatican City, 1937, 66-72. — R. I. BEST, The Commentary on the Psalms with Glosses in Old-Irish Preserved in the Ambrosian Library (Ms. C 301 inf.). Collotype facsimile, with introduction, published by the Royal Irish Academy. Dublin, 1936 (description of the manuscript containing the old Latin version). — J. M. VOSTÉ, Théodore de Mopsueste sur les psaumes: Ang (1942) 179-198. — V. BULHART, Kritische Studien zum lateinischen Text des neuen Theodorus von Mopsuestia: WSt (1941) 134-145; cf. PhW (1943) 35-37. — A. VACCARI, Il testo dei salmi nel commento di Teodoro Mopsuesteno: Bibl (1942) 1-17; *idem,* In margine al commento di Teodoro Mopsuesteno ai salmi: Miscellanea G. Mercati I (ST 121). Vatican City, 1946, 175-198. — J. M. VOSTÉ, Sur les titres des psaumes dans la Pešittā: Bibl 25 (1944) 210-235; *idem,* Mar Išo'dad de Merw (vers 850) sur les titres des psaumes: Bibl 25 (1944) 261-296 (exégèse théodorienne). — R. DEVREESSE, ST 141 (1948) 28-33, 55-78.

c. Commentary on the Twelve Minor Prophets

This exegetical treatise is the only one of Theodore's many writings completely extant in its original Greek, no doubt because it offers almost nothing of Christological import. Composed very probably immediately after the *Commentary on the Psalms,* it is mentioned by Ebedjesu and by the Chronicle of Seert. The most important manuscript is *Cod. Vatic. Gr.* 2204 s. X, of which the others are merely copies, viz., *Cod. Vatic. Gr.* 618 s. XVI, *Cod. Vindob. suppl. Gr.* 10 s. XV, *Cod. Vindob. theol. Gr.* 55 s. XVI and *Cod. Vallic. Gr.* 29 s. XVI. Syriac fragments were published by Sachau. Though Theodore more readily admits directly Messianic passages in the prophets, he refers many texts generally regarded, even now, as Messianic, to the restoration of the Jewish state or to the victories of the Maccabees.

Nothing remains of his Commentary on Samuel which Elisa

of Nisibis completed. The Acts of the Fifth Council preserve a few fragments of his two books on Job which he composed after 412 and dedicated to Cyril of Alexandria. A Syriac version of his *Commentary on Ecclesiastes* had been discovered before the first World War at Damascus by H. v. Soden (SAB 1903, 825), but disappeared again. Two fragments remain of his Commentaries on the four major prophets, which Ebedjesu mentions: *Isaiam quoque et Ezechielem et Jeremiam et Danielem singulis tomis commentatus est.* These excerpts dealing with Isaias 10, 22-23, are preserved in the *Catena* of Nicolas Muzalon.

The Acts of the Fifth Council (553) quote a passage from one of Theodore's letters (Mansi, 9, 225-227) which indicates that he regards the Canticle of Canticles as Solomon's reply to the opponents of his marriage with the Egyptian princess and refuses to grant it any allegorical significance. However, the inference is not thereby warranted that he composed a commentary to the Canticle. Neither of the catalogues of his titles mention such a book nor are there any fragments extant.

Editions: Commentary on the Twelve Minor Prophets: MG 66, 124-632. — A. v. WEGNERN, Berlin, 1834 (based on Cod. Vindob. suppl. Gr. 10). Syriac fragments: E. SACHAU, Theodori Mops. fragmenta Syriaca. Leipzig, 1869, 22-27. — Fragments of the Commentary on Job: MG 66, 697ff.

Studies: H. KIHN, op. cit. 93-171. — L. PIROT, op. cit. 258-275, 282-286. — R. DEVREESSE, ST 141 (1948) 78-93 (Le commentaire des Petits Prophètes).

2. Commentaries on the New Testament

a. Commentary on the Gospel of St. John

Of Theodore's works on the New Testament the most notable discovery is that of his commentary on the Gospel of St. John. It has reached us in a complete Syriac version which Vosté published with a Latin translation in 1940. There were in addition the Greek fragments which Migne had collected from the *catenae* of Cordier, Cramer and Mai. However, Devreesse has shown that one third of these must be rejected as spurious. By comparison with the Syriac, he recovered from five families of MS *Catenae* the extant Greek fragments of Theodore's commentary that had been falsely attributed to other writers. They amount to 144 rather closely printed pages.

Editions: Greek fragments: MG 66, 728-785. — R. DEVREESSE, ST 141 (1948) 305-419. — Syriac version: J. B. CHABOT, Commentarius Theodori Mopsuesteni in evangelium D. Johannis in VII partitus. Versio Syriaca iuxta codicem Parisiensem CCCVIII edita. Tom. I. Textus Syriacus. Paris, 1897. Chabot promised a Latin translation but never published one. — New crit. ed. of the Syriac version with a Latin translation: J. M. VOSTÉ,

Theodori Mopsuesteni Commentarius in evangelium Johannis Apostoli. Textus: CSCO 115, versio: CSCO 116. Louvain, 1940.

Studies: J. M. Vosté, Le commentaire de Théodore de Mopsueste sur saint Jean d'après la version syriaque: RBibl 32 (1923) 522-551. — X. Ducros, La traduction syriaque du commentaire de Théodore de Mopsueste sur l'Évangile selon saint Jean: BLE 28 (1927) 145-159, 210-230. — J. Reuss, Matthäus-, Markus- und Johannes-Katenen nach den handschriftlichen Quellen untersucht. Münster, 1941, 148-220. — R. Devreesse, ST 141 (1948) 289-304. — X. Ducros, L'Eucharistie chez Théodore de Mopsueste d'après son commentaire sur l'Évangile selon Jean: Actes du 21e Congrès Internat. des Orientalistes. Paris, 1949, 366ff. — J. L. McKenzie, The Commentary of Theodore of Mopsuestia on John 1, 46-51: TS 14 (1953) 73-84.

According to Ebedjesu Theodore also wrote commentaries on St. Matthew and St. Luke; of the first we have numerous fragments. The same author mentions a work on Acts: *Actus apostolorum uno commentatus est tomo.* A brief quotation is given in the Acts of the Fifth Council, dealing with Acts 2, 38. Dobschütz claimed to have found the prologue to this commentary in *Cod. Neapol. bibl. nat.* II A a 7 s. XII, which he published with an English translation. Devreesse rejects on internal grounds its authenticity.

Fragments: Gospel of St. Matthew: MG 66, 703-714. — J. Reuss, Matthäus-Kommentare aus der griechischen Kirche (TU 61). Berlin, 1957, 96-150. — Syriac fragments: P. de Lagarde, Analecta Syriaca. Leipzig, 1858, 107, 12-29; 108, 19-24. — E. Sachau, Theodori Mops. fragmenta Syriaca. Leipzig, 1869, 69-70. — MG 66, 716 (fragments of the *Commentary on St. Luke*). — MG 66, 713-716 (fragments on St. Mark). — E. v. Dobschütz, A hitherto Unpublished Prologue to the Acts of the Apostles (probably by Theodore of Mopsuestia): The American Journal of Theology 2 (1898) 353-387. Cf. R. Devreesse, ST 141 (1948) 38-39.

b. Commentary on the Ten Minor Epistles of St. Paul

Theodore's commentary on Galatians, Ephesians, Philippians, Colossians, I and II Thessalonians, I and II Timothy, Titus and Philemon survives in a complete Latin translation of the fifth century under the name of Ambrose, which H. B. Swete discovered and published from two manuscripts of the ninth and tenth centuries, together with the Greek fragments found in *Cod. Coisl. 204.*

Editions: H. B. Swete, Theodori episcopi Mopsuesteni in epistolas B. Pauli commentarii. 2 vols. Cambridge, 1880/1882. — New fragments found in Cod. Paris. Bibl. Nat. 17177 saec. X were published by D. De Bruyne, Le commentaire de Théodore de Mopsueste aux Épîtres de Paul: RB 33 (1921) 53-54 (on I and II Timothy, Titus and Philemon).

Studies: W. L. Lorimer, Theodore of Mopsuestia, In Ep. I ad Tim. Swete II, p. 123, 11: JThSt 44 (1943) 58-59 (text. crit.). — E. Dekkers, Un nouveau manuscrit du commentaire de Théodore de Mopsueste aux Épîtres de saint Paul: SE 6 (1954) 429-433 (Codex 455 of the University of Gand which belonged originally to the abbey of Saint-Maximin at Treves and was written in the 9th century, contains the Commentary of Theodore on the Epistles of St. Paul from Galatians to Philemon).

c. Commentaries on the Four Major Epistles of St. Paul

Ebedjesu lists commentaries on all 14 Epistles of St. Paul. In fact, fragments of all exist, some of considerable length. K. Staab supplemented in 1933 Swete's work by collecting the excerpts in the Greek *catenae* on the major Epistles: Romans, I and II Corinthians, and Hebrews. He used as sources *Codd. Vat.* 762, *Monac.* 412, *Coisl.* 204, *Vindob. theol.* 166 with eleven fragments to Romans, and *Pantokrat.* 28 with exceptionally rich material for all four letters.

Editions: K. STAAB, Pauluskommentare aus der griechischen Kirche. Münster, 1933, 113-172 on Romans, 172-196 on I Corinthians, 196-200 on II Cor., 200-212 on Hebrews.

Study: U. WICKERT, Studien zu den Pauluskommentaren Theodors von Mopsuestia als Beitrag zu seiner Theologie. Diss. Tübingen, 1957. Cf. ThLZ 83 (1958) 728-730.

3. Works on Liturgy, Discipline and Theology

After the exegetical treatises Ebedjesu mentions the following writings: 'Exstat etiam eius liber de sacramentis et qui de fide inscribitur. Ac tomus unus de sacerdotio. Duo vero de Spiritu Sancto. Tomus unus de incarnatione. Duo adversus Eunomium. Ac duo alii contra asserentes peccatum in natura insitum esse. Duo adversus magiam. Unus ad monachos. Unus de obscura locutione. Et unus de perfectione operum. Quinque praeterea tomos composuit adversus allegoricos. Et unum pro Basilio. Unum de assumente et assumpto. Item librum margaritarum in quo epistolae eius collectae sunt. Demum sermonem de legislatione'.

a. Catechetical Homilies

The initial impulse for the marked revival of interest in the writings and doctrine of Theodore of Mopsuestia was given in 1932 by Mingana's discovery and publication with an English translation of a Syriac text of Theodore's *Catechetical Homilies*. These sermons are identical with the two works *De sacramentis* and *De fide*, which Ebedjesu names first among the non-exegetical tracts, while the Chronicle of Seert refers to them with the words: 'He has left us moreover an explanation of the Symbol of the 318 [Fathers] and of the Mass'. Hitherto they had been known only from isolated fragments. Now for the first time the full text was available of a work in which Theodore presented the faith of the Church to his catechumens. The sixteen Catecheses are divided into two parts; the first ten deal with the articles of faith as contained in the Nicene Creed, while the other six explain the Lord's Prayer (11), the liturgy of baptism (12-14) and the Eucharist (15-16). The former are addressed to the catechumens as their final preparation for the sacrament of initiation, the latter — mystagogical catecheses — to the neophytes in the course of the week following baptism. Thus the entire series of instructions forms an exact counterpart to Cyril of Jerusalem's pre-baptismal and post-baptismal lectures (see above, p. 363). Theodore delivered them most probably between 388 and 392 at Antioch while he was still a presbyter, though Lietzmann supposes that they come from the time when he occupied the episcopal see of Mopsuestia, therefore 392-428. It seems that they were translated into Syriac shortly after his death. The manuscript, however, *Cod. Mingana Syr.* 561, is only of the seventeenth century and is contained in the Mingana collection in Selly Oak Colleges' Library, Birmingham.

These *Catechetical Homilies* are of the greatest value for an understanding of Theodore's teaching in its threefold relation to dogma, ethics and cult. The first ten expound the creed, a variant of the Constantinopolitan formula, which, according to the author, was recited 'before our baptism'. The one on the Lord's Prayer (11) stresses the importance of good works: 'Prayer does not consist so much in words but in good works, love and zeal for duty... If you care for prayer, know that it is not performed by words but by the choice of a virtuous life and by the love of God and diligence in one's duty. If you are zealous in these things you will be praying all your life'. Theodore explains the 'daily bread' as the food that is necessary for the sustenance of the human body, thus differing from Origen (see vol. II, p. 68) and Cyril of Jerusalem. Sermons 12-14 give a very detailed description of the preparation for baptism e.g. the registration of the candidates and the different forms of exorcisms as well as of the blessing of the baptismal font and the liturgy of the sacrament of initiation. The two instructions on the Eucharist (15-16) provide an explanation of the Liturgy, that of fourth-century Antioch. They present us with an accurate and nearly complete picture of the services. The commentary on the ceremonies serves also as a framework for an exposition of the doctrine of the Eucharist and the Real Presence. As an introduction Theodore offers a brief treatment of the Eucharist considered first as a spiritual food and then as a sacrifice. After commenting on the Liturgy, he concludes with an instruction concerning the disposition of soul necessary for Holy Communion and to this adds a few words on auricular confession.

Editions: Syriac text: A. MINGANA, Commentary of Theodore of Mopsuestia on the Nicene Creed (Woodbrooke Studies 5). Cambridge, 1932; *idem*, Commentary of Theodore of Mopsuestia on the Lord's Prayer and on the Sacraments of Baptism and the Eucharist (Woodbrooke Studies 6). Cambridge, 1933. — R. TONNEAU (in collaboration with R. DEVREESSE), Les Homélies Catéchétiques de Théodore de Mopsueste (ST 145). Vatican City, 1949 (with a phototypic reproduction of the Syriac manuscript).

Translations: Latin: A. Rücker, Ritus baptismi et missae quem descripsit Theodorus episcopus Mopsuestenus in Sermonibus Catecheticis e versione Syriaca ab A. Mingana nuper reperta in linguam Latinam translatus (Opuscula et Textus, Series Liturgica II). Münster, 1933 (selections). — *English:* A. Mingana, op. cit. — *French:* R. Tonneau, op. cit. — *German:* H. Lietzmann, Die Liturgie des Theodor von Mopsuestia (SAB). Berlin, 1933 (selections).

Studies: H. Lietzmann, op. cit. — R. Devreesse, Les instructions catéchétiques de Théodore de Mopsueste: RSR 12 (1933) 425-436. — W. C. van Unnik, Een verloren dogmatisch geschrift van Theodorus van Mopsuestia teruggevonden: NTT 16 (1933) 152-161. — R. Abramowski, Neue Schriften Theodors von Mopsuestia: ZNW 34 (1934) 66-84. — J. Quasten, Der älteste Zeuge für die trinitarische Fassung der liturgischen εἰς ἅγιος. Akklamation: ZkTh 58 (1934) 253-254. — O. Casel, Neue Zeugnisse für das Kultmysterium: JL 13 (1933) 99-171. — F. J. Dölger, Theodor von Mopsuestia über zwei Zeremonien vor dem Genuss des eucharistischen Brotes: AC 4 (1934) 231; *idem*, Der Taufbürge nach Theodor von Mopsuestia: AC 4 (1934) 231-232; *idem*, Der Kaisername als Handtätowierung für die Rekruten nach einem Zeugnis des Theodor von Mopsuestia: AC 4 (1934) 230. — E. Amann, La doctrine christologique de Théodore de Mopsueste (à propos d'une publication récente): RSR 14 (1934) 161-190. — M. Jugie, Le 'Liber ad baptizandos' de Théodore de Mopsueste: EO 38 (1935) 257-271. — W. de Vries, Der 'Nestorianismus' Theodors von Mopsuestia in seiner Sakramentenlehre: OCP 7 (1941) 91-148. — F. J. Reine, The Eucharistic Doctrine and Liturgy of the Mystagogical Catecheses of Theodore of Mopsuestia (SCA 2). Washington, 1942. — J. Quasten, Theodore of Mopsuestia on the Exorcism of the Cilicium: HThR 35 (1942) 209-219. — J. M. Vosté, Theodori Mopsuesteni 'Liber ad baptizandos': OCP 9 (1943) 211-228; *idem*, Maroutha de Maipherqat et le 'Liber ad baptizandos' de Théodore de Mopsuestè: OCP 12 (1946) 201-205. — R. Tonneau, op. cit. — G. Touton, La méthode catéchétique de S. Cyrille de Jérusalem comparée à celles de St. Augustin et de Théodore de Mopsueste: Proche-Orient Chrét. 1 (1951) 265-285. — J. Quasten, The Liturgical Mysticism of Theodore of Mopsuestia: TS 15 (1954) 431-439.

b. De incarnatione

None of his works was quoted more often than *On the Incarnation*. It was not only the most important of his own but of all the treatises the School of Antioch ever produced. Addai Scher discovered in 1905 in Seert the entire text in a Syriac version. Unfortunately this manuscript perished during the first World War, before it could be published. Nothing remains but a number of Latin, Greek and Syriac fragments. Most of them are excerpts preserved by friends and enemies, among the latter especially Leontius of Byzantium, whose treatise *Contra Nestorianos et Eutychianos* has twenty-nine quotations. A critical study of the fragments in MG 66 remains to be done. M. Richard and R. Devreesse have made a beginning, and demonstrated the existence of extensive interpolations.

The treatise was composed before Theodore became bishop of Mopsuestia. It is directed against Arius, Eunomius and Apollinaris of Laodicea. Gennadius (*De vir. ill.* 12) gives the following information:

> Theodore, presbyter of the church at Antioch, a cautious investigator and clever of tongue, wrote against the Apollinarians and Anomoians

On the Incarnation of the Lord, fifteen books containing as many as fifteen thousand verses, in which he showed by the clearest reasoning and by the testimony of Scripture that just as the Lord Jesus had a plenitude of deity, so he had a plenitude of humanity. He taught also that man consists only of two substances, soul and body and that sense and spirit are not different substances, but inherent inborn faculties of the soul through which it is inspired and has rationality and through which it makes the body capable of feeling. Moreover, the fourteenth book of this work treats wholly of the uncreated and alone incorporeal and ruling nature of the holy Trinity and of the rationality of animals which he explains in a devotional spirit, on the authority of Holy Scriptures. In the fifteenth volume he confirms and fortifies the whole body of his work by citing the traditions of the fathers (LNPF).

Fragments: H. B. SWETE, Theodori ep. Mops. in epistolas B. Pauli commentarii II. Cambridge, 1882, 290-312. — Syriac fragments: P. DE LAGARDE, Analecta Syriaca. Leipzig, 1858, 100-108 (20 fragments found in Cod. Brit. Mus. add. 12156, ff. 83v-86). — E. SACHAU, Theodori Mopsuesteni fragmenta Syriaca. Leipzig, 1869, 28-57 (Syriac text and Latin translation of the fragments found in Cod. Brit. Mus. add. 14669), 63-68 (Latin translation of the fragments already published by de Lagarde). — A. SANDA, Severi Antiocheni Philalethes. Beyrouth, 1928, 19 (versio 28-29).

Studies: A. SCHER, Joseph Hazzaya, écrivain syriaque du VIIIe siècle: Rivista degli Studi Orientali 3 (1910) 62-63. — M. RICHARD, La tradition des fragments du traité Περὶ τῆς ἀνθρωπήσεως de Théodore de Mopsueste: Mus 46 (1943) 55-75. — R. DEVREESSE, ST 141 (1948) 44-48. — P. GALTIER, Théodore de Mopsueste. Sa vraie pensée sur l'Incarnation: RSR 45 (1957) 161-186, 338-360.

c. Disputatio cum Macedonianis

This treatise has reached us in a Syriac version preserved in *Cod. Mus. Brit. or.* 6714. It is evidently the minutes or a later summary of an actual disputation in which Theodore defended in 392 at Anazarbos the divinity of the Holy Spirit against the Macedonians, and is most probably identical with the tract *On the Holy Spirit* which Ebedjesu and the Chronicle of Seert mention. The former speaks of two books, the latter of one. The work is dedicated to Patrophilus, as Severus of Antioch (*Contra Grammaticum* 3, 26) informs us, who seems to be bishop of Aegae and a correspondent of St. Basil's (*Ep.* 280).

Edition: F. NAU, Théodore de Mopsueste, Controverse avec les Macédoniens: PO 9 (1913) 637-667.

d. Three Ascetic Works

The three tracts *De sacerdotio*, *Ad monachos* and *De perfectione regiminis* dealt with spiritual direction. Both Ebedjesu and the Chronicle of Seert list them, though the title for the third differs slightly. The former calls it *On the Perfection of Works*, the latter *On*

Perfect Direction. Mingana published some Syriac fragments of *De sacerdotio* and *De perfectione*, while *Ad monachos* seems totally lost.

Fragments: Dadisho at the end of the seventh century quotes in his work *On Solitude* a passage from *De sacerdotio* and summarizes the content of *De perfectione* which seems to have been an exhortation addressed to hermits. A. MINGANA, Early Christian Mystics (Woodbrooke Studies 7). Cambridge, 1934, 95-96 (*De sacerdotio*), 109-110 (*De perfectione*).

e. Contra Eunomium

Photius (*Bibl. Cod.* 4) refers to Theodore's refutation of Eunomius as follows: 'Read the twenty-five books of Theodore of Antioch against Eunomius in defense of Basil. His style is somewhat obscure, but the work is full of ideas and sound reasoning, and contains a wealth of evidence taken from the Scriptures. He refutes the arguments of Eunomius almost word for word, and amply proves that he is very ignorant of outside knowledge and still more so of our religion. I believe he is the Theodore who was bishop of Mopsuestia' (SPCK). From this passage the conclusion was drawn that the two titles which Ebedjesu mentions, *Duo adversus Eunomium* and *Unum pro Basilio*, are identical. According to Devreesse this seems not to be the case. The two books against Eunomius were most probably written about 380-381 and a counterpart to Gregory of Nyssa's refutation of the same heretic (cf. above, p. 257). Of these a small fragment in Facundus (754 C) dealing with the Jewish expectation of the Messias is all that remains. The defense of Basil against Eunomius was composed several years after Basil had died and is totally lost.

Fragment: H. B. SWETE II, 322-323 (Facundus). — For a new fragment, see: L. ABRAMOWSKI, Ein unbekanntes Zitat aus 'Contra Eunomium' des Theodor von Mopsuestia: Mus. 71 (1958) 97-104. — Theodore mentions this work in his *Commentary on the Gospel of St. John:* et quidem intendebam aliquid dicere ad defendenda Basilii verba adversus iniquum Eunomium (p. 1 ed. Vosté).

f. De assumente et assumpto

This title in Ebedjesu refers most probably to his work against Apollinaris which Facundus calls *De Apollinario et eius haeresi* and of which he translated the beginning. The Chronicle of Seert states explicitly that Theodore wrote a refutation of Apollinaris. It consisted of at least four books. Seventeen fragments survive of the third and fourth in a letter of Justinian, in Leontius, the *Constitutum* of Vigilius, the Acts of the Fifth Council (553) and Facundus. Theodore composed it between 415 and 418 as an answer to those who had interpolated his *De incarnatione*, Apollinarists and Synousiasts.

Fragments: H. B. SWETE II, 312-322. — E. SACHAU. Theodori M. fragmenta Syriaca. Leipzig, 1869, 60. — PO 13, 188.

g. *Adversus defensores peccati originalis*

Both Ebedjesu and the Chronicle of Seert testify that Theodore refuted 'those who maintained that sin is a part of our nature'. Photius (*Bibl. Cod.* 177) gives a detailed report about this work and speaks of five books whereas Ebedjesu mentions only two. The *Collectio Palatina* has preserved a number of extracts from a treatise which Theodore wrote against St. Augustine's defense of original sin in the Pelagian controversy.

Fragments: Collectio Palatina 51, 1-9: H. B. SWETE II, 332-337. — E. SCHWARTZ, ACO I, 5, 173-176.

Studies: E. AMANN, DTC 15 (1946) 270-276. — R. DEVREESSE, ST 141 (1948) 98-103. — J. GROSS, Theodor von Mopsuestia, ein Gegner der Erbsündenlehre: ZKG 65 (1953/54) 1-15.

h. *Adversus magiam*

The Chronicle of Seert knows of one, Ebedjesu of two and Photius of three, books against magic. The last-named supplies more information on its exact title and content, directed against Zoroastrianism: 'Read three short treatises by Theodore *On Persian Magic and wherein it differs from Christianity*, dedicated to Mastubius, an Armenian and suffragan bishop. In the first book the accursed doctrine of the Persians, introduced by Zarades [Zoroaster], concerning Zuruam [Zervan], whom he makes the beginning of all things and calls Fortune, is expounded; how that, having offered a libation to beget Horsmidas, he begot both him and Satan. Of the mixing of blood. Having set forth this impious and disgraceful doctrine in plain words he refutes it in the first book. In the other two books he discusses the Christian faith, beginning from the creation of the world and at the same time rapidly going down to the law of grace. This Theodore is believed to be Theodore of Mopsuestia, since he mentions with approval the heresy of Nestorius, especially in the third book. He also foolishly talks of the restoration of sinners to their former condition' (*Bibl. cod.* 81, SPCK). Nothing is extant of this work.

i. *Liber margaritarum*

This *Book of Pearls* according to the two catalogues, was simply his collected letters. A fragment of the second letter addressed to Artemius, a priest of Alexandria, is preserved by Facundus (599 BC), and three excerpts of a letter to Domnus are found in the *Doctrina Patrum* (Ed. Diekamp, p. 305-306). Nothing else survives.

k. Adversus allegoricos

The only fragment preserved by Facundus (*Pro def.* 3,6) indicates that the five volumes of his *Against the Allegorists* were directed against Origen. Nothing remains of his book *On Obscure Language* (*De obscura locutione*) which seems to have been an explanation of difficult Scriptural passages, nor of his treatise *On Legislation* (*De legislatione*).

The relatively extensive fragments of Theodore's literary remains recovered in recent years have given rise to a revival of interest in his teaching, and to a re-examination of the reasons which led to his condemnation by the Fifth General Council at Constantinople in 553. The same year (428) in which Theodore died in peace and communion with the Church, his pupil Nestorius ascended the episcopal chair at Constantinople and his fate is intimately connected with the downfall of the latter. The opposition to Theodore, whose orthodoxy was never in doubt during his lifetime, began shortly after the Council of Ephesus (431) and was initiated by Rabbula of Edessa, an attack that led to the first collection of extracts from Theodore's writings, the so-called *Capitula* presented to Proclus of Constantinople by Armenian monks. Cyril of Alexandria's letters 67. 69. 71. 73 and 74 contain very harsh condemnations of Theodore and charges of Nestorianism. Thus he states in *Ep.* 69 *Ad Acacium*: 'Pretending to detest the teachings of Nestorius, they applaud them in another way, by admiring the teachings of Theodore, although these are tainted with an equal, or rather much more grievous impiety. For Theodore was not the disciple of Nestorius, but rather the other way around, and both speak as from one mouth, emitting one and the same poison of heterodoxy from their hearts'. He mentions on that occasion that he had made some excerpts from Theodore and Diodore and had refuted them. He must be referring here to his *Contra Diodorum et Theodorum*, of which only fragments are extant, mostly in the Acts of the Fifth Council and in the writings of Severus of Antioch. M. Richard and R. Devreesse have demonstrated that the Fifth Council based its condemnation on extracts of Theodore's works taken from a hostile and falsified florilegium. Where the extracts can be tested and compared with the texts recently discovered, they betray omission, interpolation, truncation, alteration in almost every instance; and this is more than enough to cast doubt on the reliability of the other extracts. Thus Richard, Devreesse, Amann and others have come to the conclusion that one must renounce any attempt to use them in assessing Theodore's genuine thought. To arrive at a true estimate of his doctrinal position they should be completely rejected and recourse had only to 'friendly' sources, and in particular to authentic Syriac versions. Sullivan has recently challenged this sweeping verdict and concluded that absolute confidence in the literal accuracy of the Syriac versions does not seem warranted.

Studies: M. RICHARD, Les traités de Cyrille d'Alexandrie contre Diodore et Théodore: Mélanges Felix Grat I. Paris, 1946, 99-116; *idem,* Acace de Mélitène, Proclus de Constantinople et la Grande Arménie: Mémorial L. Petit. Bucarest, 1948, 393-412. — R. DEVREESSE, Essai sur Théodore de Mopsueste (ST 141). Vatican City, 1948, 125-161. — F. A. SULLIVAN, Some Reactions to Devreesse's new Study of Theodore of Mopsuestia: TS 12 (1951) 179-207. — P. PARENTE, Una riabilitazione di Teodoro di Mopsuestia: Doctor Communis 1 (1950) 3-15. — K. McNAMARA, Theodore of Mopsuestia and the Nestorian Heresy: ITQ 19 (1952) 254-278; 20 (1953) 172-191.

1. *Christology*

It is especially Theodore's Christology that still finds scholars divided and which has been responsible for the charge that he was the father of Nestorianism. This accusation is based principally on the lengthy excerpts from *De incarnatione* which were assembled by Leontius of Byzantium and presented to the Fifth Council, and the less extensive fragments of the *Contra Apollinarem* (Mansi 9,203-229; MG 66,969-1002). Thus Bardenhewer drew the following conclusion: 'We possess at present only isolated fragments of these works but enough, however, to make certain that Theodore was a Nestorius before Nestorius. Like Diodorus he taught that in Christ there were two persons. The divine nature is a person, and the human nature is a person. The unity of the two natures consists in the community of thought and will. The Christian adores one sole Lord because the man who was joined to the Logos in a moral union was raised, in reward of his perseverance, to a divine dignity' (*Patrology* p. 321). It seems that this judgment must be modified in the light of the recently discovered homilies. The eighth homily teaches beyond cavil the unity of two natures in one person:

> He is not God alone nor man alone, but He is truly both by nature that is to say God and man: God the Word who assumed, and man who was assumed. It is the one who was in the form of God that took upon Him the form of a servant, and it is not the form of a servant that took upon it the form of God. The one who is in the form of God is God by nature, who assumed the form of a servant, while the one who is in the form of a servant is the one who is man by nature and who was assumed for our salvation.
> The one who assumed is not the same as the one who was assumed

nor is the one who was assumed the same as the one who assumed, but the one who assumed is God while the one who was assumed is man. The one who assumed is by nature that which God the Father is by nature, as He is God with God, and He is that which the one with whom He was, is, while the one who was assumed is by nature that which David and Abraham, whose son and from whose seed He is, are by nature. This is the reason why He is both Lord and Son of David: Son of David because of His nature, and Lord because of the honour that came to Him. And He is high above David His father because of the nature that assumed Him (*Cat. Hom.* 8,1 Mingana).

But this clear distinction between the two natures does not result in two persons or *prosopa*:

In their profession of faith our blessed Fathers [at Nicaea] wrote... they followed the Sacred Books which speak differently of natures while referring [them] to one *prosopon* on account of the close union that took place between them, so that they might not be believed that they were separating the perfect union between the one who was assumed and the one who assumed. If this union were destroyed the one who was assumed would not be seen more than a mere man like ourselves (*Cat. Hom.* 6,3 Mingana).

This union is never broken up, as Theodore states in another passage of the eighth homily:

In this way the Sacred Books teach us the difference between the two natures, and so it is indispensable for us to ascertain who is the one who assumed and the one who was assumed. The one who assumed is the Divine nature that does everything for us, and the other is the human nature which was assumed on behalf of all of us by the One who is the cause of everything, and is united to it in an ineffable union which will never be separated... The Sacred Books also teach us this union, not only when they impart to us the knowledge of each nature but also when they affirm that what is due to the one is also due to the other, so that we would understand the wonderfulness and the sublimity of the union that took place (*Cat. Hom.* 8,10 Mingana).

We should also be mindful of that inseparable union through which that form of man can never and under no circumstances be separated from the Divine nature which put it on. The distinction between the natures does not annul the close union nor does the close union destroy the distinction between the natures, but the natures remain in their respective existence while separated, and the union remains intact, because the one who was assumed is united in honour and glory with the one who assumed according to the will of the one who assumed him.

From the fact that we say two natures we are not constrained to say two Lords nor two sons; this would be extremely folly. All things that in one respect are two and in another respect one, their union through which they are one does not annul the distinction between the natures, and the distinction between the natures impedes them from being one (*Cat. Hom.* 8,13 Mingana).

The clarity of these passages is extraordinary in a document which precedes the writings of Cyril of Alexandria and the definition of Ephesus, though they are not sufficient to prove Theodore's orthodoxy. There is no doubt that exaggerations and omissions are found in the system of Theodore, and his terminology, *homo assumptus*, as well as his antithesis *Filius Dei - Filius David* is sometimes objectionable. His understanding of the impeccability of Christ cannot be accepted because he thinks of *impeccantia* rather than impeccability. He lacked the true conception of the immutability of Christ and of the *communicatio idiomatum*. But all these shortcomings do not entitle us to impute to him errors of which he was not guilty, nor to refuse him his due in the development of theology. It has to be kept in mind that during Theodore's lifetime the doctrine of the Person of Christ, of the relation between *physis*, *hypostasis* and *prosopon* had not been formulated by any Ecumenical Council. It would be an anachronism to condemn him for failure to adhere to the Christological formula of the Council of Chalcedon. But Grillmeier after a careful examination of his authentic writings has come to the conclusion that nobody contributed more to the progress of Christology in the generation of theologians between 381 and 431 than Theodore of Mopsuestia. If his doctrine contained some dangerous tendencies, it is equally true that it had also positive elements which point in the direction of Chalcedon and prepared its formula (cf. fragmentum *De incarnatione* VIII 62: ed. Sachau 69).

His refutation of Apollinaris and the Logos-Sarx Christology deserves great credit. He succeeded where Athanasius failed, namely, in assigning to the soul of Christ the theological importance which is absolutely necessary. The fifth *Catechetical Homily* is very valuable for an appreciation of his contribution to the advancement of the Christological doctrine:

> The partisans of Arius and Eunomius, however, say that He assumed a body but not a soul, and that the nature of the Godhead took the place of the soul. They lowered the Divine nature of the Only Begotten to the extent that from the greatness of its nature it moved and performed the acts of the soul and imprisoned itself in the body and did everything for its sustenance. Lo, if the Godhead had replaced the soul He would not have been hungry or thirsty, nor would He have tired or been in need of food. All these things befall the body because of its weakness, as the soul is not able to satisfy its wants, but does for it only those things that belong to itself according to the nature given to it by God.
>
> If therefore, the Godhead was performing the acts of the soul, it

would also by necessity have performed the acts of the body. Only in this way could be right the opinion of the misleading heretics who deny that He assumed a body and was only seen in the same way as the angels and was a man in appearance only while He did not possess any qualities of human nature...

Therefore it was necessary that He should assume not only the body but also the immortal and rational soul; and not only the death of the body had to cease but also that of the soul, which is sin...

It was, therefore, necessary that sin should have first been abolished, as after its abolition there would be no entry for death. It is indeed clear that the strength of the sin has its origin in the will of the soul... It was therefore necessary that Christ should assume not only the body but also the soul. The enemy of the soul had to be removed first and then for the sake of it that of the body...

It is therefore, great madness not to believe that Christ assumed the soul; and he would even be madder who would say that He did not assume human mind, because such a one would imply that He either did not assume the soul or that He did assume the soul not of man but an irrational one akin to that of animals and beasts.

Because of all this our blessed Fathers warned us and said: 'He was incarnate and became a man', so that we should believe that the one who was assumed and in whom God the Word dwelt was a complete man, perfect in everything that belongs to human nature, and composed of a mortal body and a rational soul, because it is for man and for his salvation that He came down from heaven (*Cat. Hom.* 5 ed. Mingana 55-59).

Here we notice the progress made in realizing the two natures in Christ; He is no longer said to consist of Logos and Sarx but of Logos and Man.

Studies: H. KIHN, Theodor von Mopsuestia und Junilius Africanus. Freiburg i.B., 1880, 171-197, 393-409. — E. AMANN, La doctrine christologique de Théodore de Mopsueste: RSR 14 (1934) 160-190; *idem*, DTC 15 (1946) 235-279. — R. ARNOU, Nestorianisme et néoplatonisme. L'unité du Christ et l'union des 'Intelligibles': Greg (1936) 116-131. — M. JUGIE, Le 'Liber ad baptizandos' de Théodore de Mopsueste: EO 34 (1935) 259-271 (against Amann); *idem*, Theologia dogmatica Christianorum orientalium ab ecclesia catholica dissidentium T: V. Paris, 1935, 99-110. — M. RICHARD, L'introduction du mot hypostase dans la théologie de l'incarnation: MSR 2 (1945) 21-29. — R. DEVREESSE, op. cit. 109-118. — R. TONNEAU, Les Homélies Catéchétiques de Théodore de Mopsueste (ST 145). Vatican City, 1949, XV-XXXIX. — J. RIVIÈRE, Le dogme de la Rédemption dans la théologie contemporaine. Albi, 1948, 181-223. — M. V. ANASTOS, The Immutability of Christ and Justinian's Condemnation of Theodore of Mopsuestia: DOP 6 (1951) 125-160. — A. GRILLMEIER, Die theologische und sprachliche Vorbereitung der christologischen Formel von Chalkedon: CGG I (1951) 120-159. — F. A. SULLIVAN, The Christology of Theodore of Mopsuestia. Rome, 1956. — P. GALTIER, Théodore de Mopsueste. Sa vraie pensée sur l'Incarnation: RSR 45 (1957) 161-186, 338-360. — J. N. D. KELLY, Early Christian Doctrines. London, 1958, 303-309. — J. L. McKENZIE, Annotations on the Christology of Theodore of Mopsuestia: TS 19 (1958) 345-373. — F. A. SULLIVAN, Further Notes on Theodore of Mopsuestia: TS 20 (1959) 264-279.

2. Anthropology

Marius Mercator accused Theodore of being the Father of Pelagianism (*Comm. adv. haeresim Pelagii*, praef.; *Ref. symboli Theod. Mops.*, praef. n. 2). The excerpts of Theodore's writings which he presents as a proof for his charge, Photius' report about the latter's treatise *Adversus defensores peccati originalis* as well as the citations of the Fifth Council suggest that Theodore's teaching on original sin was as follows: Man was not created immortal, but mortal; Adam and Eve harmed only themselves by their sin; universal mortality is not a chastisement of Adam's sin; the effects of the sin of Adam — the present condition of man — are not penalties, but a test, an experiment instituted by God. The tortures of the damned will come to an end. Devreesse after a careful examination of the authentic works of Theodore now at our disposal came to the conclusion that absolutely nothing like this appears in them. He and Amann agree that from these works it is possible to gain a doctrinal synthesis on original sin which is in every detail orthodox. Devreesse is therefore convinced that the extracts of Marius Mercator and Photius were forgeries. Even if this were not the case, it is absolutely evident that today Theodore would not be called the Father of Pelagianism. Nevertheless, Gross thinks that he was opposed to the doctrine of original sin.

Studies: E. AMANN, DTC 15 (1946) 270-276. — R. DEVREESSE, ST 141 (1948) 98-103. — J. GROSS, Theodor von Mopsuestia, ein Gegner der Erbsündenlehre: ZKG 65 (1953/54) 1-15. — I. ONATIBIA, La vida cristiana tipo de las realidades celestes: Scriptorium Victoriense 1 (1954) 100-133 (concept of immortality). — W. DE VRIES, Das eschatologische Heil bei Theodor von Mopsuestia: OCP 24 (1958) 309-338.

3. The Baptismal Creed

In the first ten of his catechetical lectures Theodore expounds the baptismal creed to his catechumens. Since he cites its several clauses textually many times over, it is possible to piece the whole formula together:

> We believe in one God the Father almighty, maker of all things visible and invisible.
> And in one Lord Jesus Christ, the only-begotten Son of God, the first-begotten of all creation, who was begotten from His Father before all ages, not made, true God from true God, of one substance with His Father, through whom the ages were fashioned and all things came into being, who because of us men and because of our salvation came down from heaven and was incarnate and became man, being born from the Virgin Mary and was crucified under Pontius Pilate, was buried and rose again on the third day according to the Scriptures,

ascended to heaven, sits on the right hand of God and will come again to judge living and dead.

And in one Holy Spirit, who proceeds from the Father, a life-giving Spirit. (We confess) one baptism, one Holy Catholic Church, the remission of sins, the resurrection of the flesh, and life everlasting.

This Creed is definitely not identical with the *symbolum fidei* attributed to Theodore by Marius Mercator and condemned as Theodore's by Justinian, the Fifth Council, and Leontius. Thus the latter's authenticity appears very doubtful and it seems to be improper to associate it with Theodore in any way whatsoever. One cannot believe in the good faith of those who ascribe it to him.

Text: A. MINGANA, Commentary of Theodore of Mopsuestia on the Nicene Creed (Woodbrooke Studies 5). Cambridge, 1932 (Syriac text and English translation). — R. TONNEAU, op. cit. (Syriac text and French translation).

Study: R. DEVREESSE, ST 141 (1948) 103-120, 256-257.

4. *Eucharist*

The discovery of the *Catechetical Homilies* enables us to win an impression of Theodore's sacramental theology. He clearly teaches the Real Presence and the sacrificial character of the Eucharist. He explicitly denies a merely symbolic interpretation of the sacrament:

> It is with justice, therefore, that when He gave the bread He did not say: 'This is the symbol of My body', but: 'This is My body': likewise when He gave the cup He did not say: 'This is the symbol of My blood', but: 'This is My blood', because He wished us to look upon the [elements] after their reception of grace and the coming of the Spirit, not according to their nature but to receive them as they are the body and the blood of Our Lord. We ought... not to regard the elements merely as bread and cup, but as the body and blood of Christ (*Cat. Hom.* 5).

This passage has an exact counterpart in the text of the Greek fragment of his Commentary on the Gospel of St. Matthew:

> He [Christ] did not say: 'This is the symbol of My body and this of My blood', but: 'This is My body and My blood', teaching us not to consider the nature of the laid-out things, but through the accomplished thanksgiving they have been changed into the flesh and blood (MG 66,713).

The change of the bread and wine into the body and blood of Christ is effected by the Epiclesis, the calling down of the Holy Spirit upon the oblation. He states that the priest prays 'to God that the Holy Spirit may descend, and that grace may come therefrom upon the bread and wine that are laid [on the altar] so that they may be seen to be truly the body and the blood of our Lord. And we hold them to be henceforth immortal, incorruptible, impassible, and immutable by nature, as the body of our Lord was after the resurrection' (*Cat. Hom.* 6 Mingana). Having broken the 'holy bread', the priest 'with the bread makes the sign of the Cross over the blood, and with the blood over the bread... in order to reveal to all that... they are the remembrance of the death and the passion that affected the body of our Lord, when His blood was shed on the cross for us all' *(ibid.)*. Theodore explains explicitly that each communicant receives the entire Christ:

> Each one of us takes a small portion, but we believe that we receive all of Him in that small portion. It would, indeed, be very strange if the woman who had an issue of blood, received the Divine gift by touching the border of His garment, which was not even part of His body but only His garment, and we did not believe that we receive all of Him in a part of His body *(ibid.)*.

> All of us draw nigh unto Christ our Lord... who, firstly in the likeness of a carnal mother, strove to feed us from His body, and secondly placed before us the elements of bread and cup which are His body and His blood... Although He comes to us after having divided Himself, all of Him is nevertheless in every portion [of the bread], and is near to all of us, and He gives Himself to each one of us, in order that we may hold Him and embrace Him with all our might, and make manifest our love to Him *(ibid.)*.

As to the moment or form of the consecration, Theodore teaches that it is effected by the Epiclesis of the Holy Spirit:

> We ought not to regard the elements merely as bread and cup, but as the body and the blood of Christ, into which they were so transformed by the descent of the Holy Spirit (*Cat. Hom.* 5,76 Mingana).

> Those who have been chosen as the priests of the New Testament are believed to perform sacramentally, by the descent of the Holy Spirit... these things which we believe that Christ our Lord performed and will perform in reality *(ibid.* 86 Mingana).

> One is the bread and one is the body of Christ our Lord, into which the element of bread is changed; and it receives this great change from one descent of the Holy Spirit (*Cat. Hom.* 16,110 Mingana).

> It is indeed offered so that by the coming of the Holy Spirit it should become that which it is said to be: the body and blood of Christ *(ibid.* 111 Mingana).

> Picture in your mind the nature of this oblation, which, by the coming of the Holy Spirit, is the body of Christ *(ibid.* 113 M.).

> At first it is laid upon the altar as a mere bread and wine mixed with water; but by the coming of the Holy Spirit it is transformed into body and blood, and thus it is changed into the power of a spiritual and immortal nourishment *(ibid.* 118-119 M.).

Thus Theodore is of the same opinion as Cyril of Jerusalem, regarding the Epiclesis as that which effects the consecration.

Studies: M. JUGIE, Le 'Liber ad baptizandos' de Théodore de Mopsueste: EO 38 (1935) 263-266 (the Real Presence), 266-270 (the Epiclesis). — F. J. REINE, The Eucharistic Doctrine and Liturgy of the Mystagogical Catecheses of Theodore of Mopsuestia (SCA 2). Washington, 1942. — J. LÉCUYER, Le sacerdoce chrétien et le sacrifice eucharistique selon Théodore de Mopsueste: RSR 36 (1949) 481-516. — J. QUASTEN, Mysterium tremendum: Vom christlichen Mysterium. Düsseldorf, 1951, 66-75.

5. *Penance*

Theodore is a witness to the existence of the sacrament of penance and to its necessity as a preparation for Communion for all those who have fallen into grievous sin after baptism. Few of the early Christian writers give as much information on this subject as he does. He clearly distinguishes between 'involuntary' or venial and 'great' sins. He assures his neophytes that the former should not deter them from Communion, since they will obtain remission of them in the reception of the Eucharist, if they feel sorry for them:

> The body and blood of our Lord... will strengthen us... as long as we have committed them involuntarily, and they have come to us against our will, from the weakness of our nature, and we have fallen into them against our desire, and because of them we have sorrowed intensely and prayed God in great repentance for our trespasses... If we do good works with diligence and turn away from evil works and truly repent of the sins that come to us, we will undoubtedly obtain the gift of the remission of sins in our reception of the holy Sacrament (*ibid.* 117-118 M.).

On the other hand, grievous sins prohibit the guilty from partaking of the Eucharist, unless they make a sacramental confession to a priest and in secret:

> If a great sin contrary to the commandments, is committed by us... we must first induce our conscience with all our power to make haste and fittingly repent our sins, and not permit any other medicine to ourselves. Let us know that as God gave to our body, which He made passible, medicinal herbs of which the experts make use for our healing, so also He gave penitence, as a medicine for sins, to our soul, which is changeable. Regulations for this [penitence] were laid down from the beginning, and the priests and the experts, who heal and care for the sinners, bring medicine to the mind of the penitents who are in need, according to ecclesiastical ordinance and wisdom, which is regulated in accordance with the measure of the sins...
>
> This is the medicine for the sins, which was established by God and delivered to the priests of the Church, who in making use of it with diligence, will heal the afflictions of men.

Since you are aware of these things, and also of the fact that because God greatly cares for us gave us penitence and showed us the medicine of repentance, and established some men, who are the priests, as physicians of sins, so that, if we receive in this world through them, healing and forgiveness of sins, we shall be delivered from the judgment to come — it behooves us to draw nigh unto the priests with great confidence and to reveal our sins to them, and they with all diligence, pain, and love, and according to the rules laid down above, will give healing to sinners.

They [the priests] will not disclose the things that are not to be disclosed, but they will keep to themselves the things that have happened, as fits true and loving fathers, bound to safeguard the shame of their children while striving to heal their bodies (*ibid.* 120-123 M.).

Theodore adds that after the sinner has repented 'he should be reinstated in the same confidence as that he had before, because he had been rebuked and had amended his ways, and through true repentance, had received forgiveness of his sins' (*ibid.* 122 M.).

Studies: M. JUGIE, art. cit. 270-271. — F. J. REINE, op. cit. 50-54.

POLYCHRONIUS OF APAMEA

Polychronius, bishop of Apamea in Syria, was a brother of Theodore of Mopsuestia. Theodoret (*Hist. eccl.* 5,40,2) praises him as an excellent shepherd of the church of Apamea who 'ruled with wisdom and success and was distinguished for the charm of his discourse as well as for the sanctity of his life'. When Theodoret wrote these words (about 428) Polychronius was still alive, but he died before the bishops met at Ephesus in June 431. He composed commentaries on the books of the Old Testament and must be ranked among the great exegetes of the School of Antioch. For the scattered fragments so far known, concerned principally with Job, Daniel and Ezekiel, we have to depend on the *catenae*. Since some excerpts of his exegesis of the latter two prophets are found in that of John Drungarius, the anonymous *scholia* therein on Jeremias most probably belong also to our author. So, at least, Faulhaber concluded. Dieu's identification of Polychronius' work with a commentary on Jeremias preserved under the name of St. John Chrysostom in *Cod. Ott.* 7 s. XVI and other manuscripts and first published by M. Ghislerius at Lyons in 1623 (reprinted MG 64, 739-1038) remains doubtful. However few the fragments of Polychronius' works, they are enough to prove that he like his brother was strongly opposed to allegorical interpretation (on Ez. 28, 2), but well equipped with historical, chronological and archaeological knowledge to elucidate the literal sense of the Scriptures. His exposition betrays a rationalizing tendency in so far as he repeatedly tries to interpret Messianic prophecies as referring to events of the near future. If he has this in common with his brother, he definitely does not share his views regarding the canonicity of the Book of Job. Polychronius strongly defends the latter. None of the extant quotations shows any trace of Nestorianism. His interpretation of the Book of Daniel was found to have points of agreement with that of the Neo-Platonist philosopher Porphyry, which evoked later criticism.

Fragments: MG 93, 13-470.

Studies: O. BARDENHEWER, Polychronius, Bruder Theodors von Mopsuestia und Bischof von Apamea. Freiburg i.B., 1879. — M. FAULHABER, Die Propheten-Catenen nach römischen Handschriften. Freiburg i.B., 1899, 125-129, 149-153, 157ff., 181ff. — L. DIEU, Le commentaire sur Jérémie du Pseudo-Chrysostome serait-il l'œuvre de Polychronius d'Apamée?: RHE 14 (1913) 685-701. — L. DENNEFELD, Der alttestamentliche Kanon der antiochenischen Schule. Freiburg i.B., 1909, 61-67. — A. VACCARI, Un commento da Giobbe di Giuliano di Eclano. Rome, 1915 (main source Polychronius); cf. J. STIGLMAYR, ZkTh 43 (1919) 269ff. — C. WEIMANN, Der Hiobkommentar des Julianus von Aeclanum: ThR 15 (1916) 241-248. — U. BERTINI, La catena greca in Giobbe: Bibl 4 (1923) 129-142.

ST. JOHN CHRYSOSTOM

Among the four great Fathers of the East and the three great ecumenical teachers of the Greek Church only one is of the School of Antioch, St. John Chrysostom. None of the ancient Christian writers has had so many biographers and panegyrists as he, from the oldest and best writing before 415 by Bishop Palladius of Helenopolis (cf. above, p. 179) down to the last in late Byzantine times. Unfortunately none of them provide sufficient information to determine the exact date of his birth, which must have been between 344 and 354. Like his friend and fellow-disciple Theodore of Mopsuestia, he was born at Antioch of a noble and well-to-do Christian family. His early education was received from his pious mother Anthusa, who lost her husband when she was twenty years of age and John still an infant. He was taught philosophy by Andragathius and rhetoric by the famous sophist Libanius (cf. above, p. 222). 'At the age of eighteen', Palladius (5) reports, 'a boy in years, he revolted against the professors of verbosities; and a man in intellect, he delighted in divine learning. At that time the blessed Meletius the Confessor, an Armenian by race, was ruling the Church of Antioch; he noticed the bright lad, and was so much attracted by the beauty of his character, that he allowed him to be continually in his company. His prophetic eye foresaw the boy's future. He was admitted to the sacrament of the washing of regeneration, and after three years of attendance on the bishop, advanced to be reader' (SPCK). During this period he had as his master in theology Diodore of Tarsus. He led a life of strict mortification at home and would have withdrawn from the world but for his mother who begged him not to make her a widow again (*De sacerdotio* 1,4). Nevertheless, he finally turned to the neighboring mountains, and found there an old hermit, whose life he shared for four years. 'He then retired to a cave by himself, in his eagerness to hide himself from the world, and there spent twenty-four months, for the greater part of which he denied himself sleep, while he studied the covenants of Christ, the better to dispel ignorance. Two years spent without lying down by night or day deadened his gastric organs, and the functions of the kidneys were impaired by the cold. As he could not doctor himself, he returned to the haven of the Church' (Palladius 5 SPCK).

Back at Antioch he was ordained a deacon in 381 by Meletius and priest in 386 by Bishop Flavian. The latter appointed him to the special duty of preaching in the principal church of the city. For twelve years, from 386 to 397, he discharged this office with such zeal, ability and success that he established forever his title as the greatest of Christian pulpit orators. It was during this time that he delivered the most famous of his homilies.

This happy and blessed period of his life ended rather abruptly when Nectarius, the patriarch of Constantinople, died on the 27th of September 397 and John was chosen to succeed him. Since the latter did not show any willingness to accept, he was brought to the capital at the Emperor Arcadius' order by violence and cunning. Theophilus, patriarch of Alexandria, was compelled to consecrate him on February 26, 398. Chrysostom immediately set about the work of reforming the city and clergy, fallen into corruption under his predecessor. Soon, however, it became evident that his nomination to the see of the imperial residence was the greatest misfortune of his life. He did not fit this position. He never realized the essential difference between the poisoned atmosphere of the imperial residence and the purer climate of the provincial capital, Antioch. He had a soul too noble and unselfish to see through the intrigues of the court. His sense of personal dignity was too lofty to stoop to that subservient attitude toward the imperial majesties which would have secured him their lasting favor. On the contrary, his fiery temperament betrayed him only too often into inconsiderate, if not offensive, speech and action. His plan for reform of clergy and laity was unrealistic and his uncompromising adherence to his ideal resulted only in uniting all hostile forces against him; he was innocent of the adroit diplomacy that pits one enemy against another.

Though he himself gave an example of simplicity and devoted his large income to the erection of hospitals and the support of the poor, his zealous efforts to raise the moral tone of priests and people encountered strong opposition. This grew into hatred when in 401 at a synod of Ephesus he had six bishops guilty of simony deposed. His opponents at home and abroad now joined forces to destroy him. Though his relations with the imperial court had been friendly at the beginning, the situation changed rapidly after the downfall of the all-powerful and influential Eutropius (399), the favorite advisor and secretary of the weak-minded Emperor Arcadius. The imperial authority passed into the hands of the Empress Eudoxia, whose mind had been poisoned against John by the insidious suggestion that his strictures on luxury and depravity were directed against herself and her court. Moreover, Chrysostom's own episcopal colleagues, Severian of Gabala, Acacius of Beroea and Antiochus of Ptolemais did everything to foment the growing resentment of Eudoxia against the patriarch.

Their intrigue met with a large measure of success, especially after Chrysostom's blunt rebuke of the Empress over her seizure of a piece of property. His most dangerous enemy, however, was Theophilus of Alexandria, who resented the patriarch of Constantinople ever since he had been forced by the Emperor Arcadius to consecrate him. His dislike changed to rage when he was called in 402 to the capital to answer to the charges made against him by the monks of the Nitrian desert, before a synod presided over by Chrysostom. Theophilus regarded the latter as responsible for this summons and with the support of the Empress resolved to turn the tables upon Chrysostom. He called a meeting of 36 bishops, of whom all but seven were from Egypt and all were Chrysostom's enemies. This so-called Synod at the Oak, a suburb of Chalcedon, condemned the patriarch of the capital on 29 fabricated counts. (The Acts of this synod survive in Photius, *Bibl. cod.* 59.) After Chrysostom refused three times to appear before this 'episcopal court', he was declared deposed in August 403. The Emperor Arcadius accepted the synod's decision and exiled him to Bithynia. This first expulsion did not last long, because he was recalled the following day. Frightened by the riotous indignation of the people of Constantinople and by a tragic accident in the imperial palace the Empress herself had requested his return. Chrysostom re-entered the capital in a triumphal procession and delivered in the Church of the Apostles a jubilant address which is still preserved *(Hom. I post reditum)*. In a second sermon, perhaps on the following day, he spoke of the Empress in terms of the highest praise (Sozomen, *Hist. eccl.* 8,18,8). This peaceful condition came to an abrupt end two months later when Chrysostom complained about the noisy and indecent public amusements and dances that marked the dedication of Eudoxia's silver statue erected quite close to the cathedral. His enemies were not slow to represent this as a personal affront. Deeply wounded, the Empress did little to conceal her resentment, while Chrysostom, angered by the evidence of her renewed hostility and impelled by his fiery temperament, committed an act of imprudence that was fatal in its consequences. On the feast of St. John the Baptist he began his sermon with the words: 'Again Herodias raves; again she rages; again she dances; again she asks for the head of John upon a charger' (Socrates, *Hist. eccl.* 6,18; Sozomen, *Hist. eccl.* 8,20). His enemies regarded this sensational introduction as an allusion to Eudoxia and resolved to secure his banishment on a charge of unlawfully reassuming the duties of a see from which he had been canonically deposed. The Emperor ordered Chrysostom to cease performing ecclesiastical functions, which he refused to do. Thereupon he was forbidden the use of any church. When he and his loyal priests on the Eastervigil 404 gathered the catechumens in the baths of Constans in order to confer solemn baptism, the ceremonies were interrupted by armed intervention, the faithful driven from the place and the baptismal water stained with blood (Palladius 33. 34; Socrates, *Hist. eccl.* 6, 18,14). Five days after Pentecost, June 9, 404 Chrysostom was informed by an imperial notary that he had to leave the city at once, which he did. He was exiled to Cucusus in Lesser Armenia, where he remained for three years. Soon his former community of Antioch came in pilgrimages to see their beloved preacher. 'So when they [his enemies] saw the Church of Antioch migrating to the Church of Armenia, and the gracious wisdom of John chanted from there back again to the Church of Antioch, they longed to cut short his life' (Palladius 38). At their petition Arcadius banished him to Pityus, a wild spot on the eastern end of the Black Sea. Broken by the hardships of the way and by the enforced travelling on foot in severe weather, he died on September 14, 407 at Comana in Pontus before he reached his destination. His earthly remains were brought back in solemn procession to Constantinople on January 27, 438 and interred in the Church of the Apostles. The Emperor Theodosius II, a son of Eudoxia (who had died as early as 404), went out to meet the funeral train. 'He laid his face upon the coffin, and entreated that his parents might be forgiven for their ill-advised persecution of the bishop' (Theodoret, *Hist. eccl.* 5,36). Before Chrysostom had left the capital, he had appealed to Pope

Innocent I of Rome and to the bishops Venerius of Milan and Chromatius of Aquileia and had requested a trial. Palladius has preserved this communication (*Dialog.* 8-11). Theophilus of Alexandria had notified the Pope of John's deposition shortly afterwards. Innocent refused to accept the latter and demanded an inquiry by a synod consisting of Western and Eastern bishops. When this proposition was rejected, the Pope and the entire West broke off communion with Constantinople, Alexandria and Antioch until atonement had been made. Chrysostom's first successor Arsacius died November 11, 405. He was followed by Atticus. He and his friends were received into the communion of Rome only after they had agreed to restore the name of the meanwhile deceased John in the Diptychs.

Biographical Studies: For editions, translations and studies of the *Vita* by Palladius, see above p. 179. Further biogr. material in Socrates, *Hist. eccl.* 6, 2-23; 7, 25-45; Sozomen, *Hist. eccl.* 8, 2-28; Theodoret, *Hist. eccl.* 5, 27-36. — P. R. COLEMAN - NORTON, The Vita sancti Chrysostomi by Georgius Alexandrinus: CPh 20 (1925) 69-72 (its source is the *Vita* by Palladius). — C. BAUR, Georg Alexandrinus: BZ 27 (1927) 1-16. — K. I. DYOBUNIOTIS, EEBS (1925) 50-83 (edition of 5 encomia by Cosmas Vestitor on the translation of the relics from MS 231 of the Library of Athens); *idem*, EPh (1932) 80-91 (*encomium* on Chrysostom, Basil and Gregory of Naz.); *idem*, Θεολογία (1934) 51-68 (*encomium* of Nicetas Paphlagonius). — F. LUDWIG, Der heilige Johannes Chrysostomus in seinem Verhältnis zum byzantinischen Hof. Braunsberg, 1883. — P. UBALDI, La Sinodo ad Quercum dell'anno 403: Memorie della Reale Accademia delle Scienze di Torino. Ser. 2. Tom. 52 (1903) 33-97. — J. GOTTWALD, La statue de l'impératrice Eudoxie à Constantinople: EO 10 (1907) 274-276. — F. SCHEMMEL, Der Sophist Libanios als Schüler und Lehrer: Neue Jahrbücher für das klass. Altertum 20 (1907) 52-69. — H. KELLNER, Die Verehrung des hl. Johannes Chrysostomus im Morgen- und Abendland: Chrysostomika. Rome, 1908, 1007-1012. — A. NÄGELE, Chrysostomos und Libanios: *ibid.* 87-142. — A. ROCCHI, Lipsanologia o storia delle reliquie di S. Giovanni Crisostomo: *ibid.* 1039-1040. — E. WÜNSCHER - BECCHI, Saggio d'iconografia di S. Giovanni Crisostomo: *ibid.* 1113-1138. — P. MAAS, Libanios und Johannes Chrysostomos: SAB (1912) II, 1123-1126. — C. BAUR, Wann ist Chrysostomus geboren?: ZkTh 52 (1928) 401-406. — V. SCHULTZE, Altchristliche Städte und Landschaften. Leipzig, 1930, vol. 3 (Antiocheia). — P. COHAUSZ, Das Chrysostomusdrama: Theol.-Prakt. Quartalschrift 84 (1931) 1-20. — J. F. D'ALTON, Chrysostom in Exile: IER (1935) 225-238. — E. SCHWARTZ, Palladiana: ZNW 36 (1937) 168-192 (Theophilus and Chrysostom). — S. SCHIWIETZ, Das morgenländische Mönchtum 3. Mainz, 1938, 254-273, 290-293 (Chrysostom as a monk). — C. A. BALDUCCI, Il dissidio fra S. Giovanni Crisostomo e Eudossia: Atti IV. Congresso Nazionale di Studi Romani 1 (1938) 303-310. — K. M. SETTON, Christian Attitude towards the Emperor in the Fourth Century. New York, 1941, 163-195 (Chrysostom and the imperial court). — J. DUMORTIER, La valeur historique du Dialogue de Palladius et la chronologie de S. Jean Chrysostome: MSR 7 (1951) 51-56. — B. TZORTZATOS, John Chrysostom on the Basis of his Letters. Athens, 1952 (in Greek). — J. DUMORTIER, La culture profane de saint Jean Chrysostome: MSR 10 (1953) 53-62. — E. DEMOUGEOT, Quelques témoignages de sympathie d'Orientaux envers saint Jean Chrysostome exilé: Studi Bizantini e Neoellen. (1953) 44-54. — A. H. M. JONES, St. John Chrysostom's Parentage and Education: HThR 46 (1953) 171-173. — Q. CATAUDELLA, Giovanni Crisostomo nel romanzo di Achille Tazio: La Parola del Passato 9 (1954) 25-44. — E. DEMOUGEOT, A propos des interventions du pape Innocent Ier dans la politique séculière: RH 212 (1954) 23-38. — A. J. VISSER, Johannes Chrysostomus als anti-Joods polemicus: NAKG 40 (1954) 193-206. — J. H. GRUNINGER, Les dernières années de saint Jean Chrysostome 404-407. Son second exil et sa mort: Proche-Orient Chrét. 6 (1956) 3-10 (summary without documentation).

Monographs: E. VENABLES, DCB 1 (1877) 518-535. — E. PREUSCHEN, RE 4 (1898) 101-111. — G. BARDY, DTC 8 (1924) 660-690. — H. LIETZMANN, PWK 9 (1916) 1811-1828. — C. BAUR, LThK 2 (1931) 951-955. — Q. CATAUDELLA, EC 6 (1955) 534-543. — F. L. CROSS, ODC (1957) 282-283. — W. ELTESTER, RGG³ 2 (1957) 1818-1819. — J. A. NEANDER, Der hl. Johannes Chrysostomus und die Kirche. 2 vols, 5th ed. Berlin, 1858. English transl. of vol. I, 1838, all publd. — W. R. W. STEPHENS, Saint John Chrysostom. His Life and Times. London, 1880. — A. PUECH, S. Jean Chrysostome. 5th ed. Paris, 1905; English translat., 1902. — P. E. LEGRAND, Saint Chrysostome (Les moralistes chrétiens). Paris, 1924. — I. GIORDANI, S. Giovanni Crisostomo. Padova, 1929. — C. BAUR, Der hl. Johannes Chrysostomus und seine Zeit. 2 vols. Munich, 1929/1930 (vol. I Antioch, vol. II Constantinople). English translat. London, 1959. — A. CARILLO DE ALBORNOZ, San Juan Crisostomo y su influencia social en el imperio bizantino del s. IV. Madrid, 1934. — J. HADZEGA, The Life of St. John Chrysostom and an Analysis of his Works (in Russian). Uzhgorod, 1936. — B. H. VANDENBERGHE, Chrysostomus, de grote redenaar. Cultuurbeeld van het oude Antiochië. Utrecht, 1939. — D. ATTWATER, St. John Chrysostom. Milwaukee, 1939. — A. MOULARD, Saint Jean Chrysostome, sa vie, son œuvre. Paris, 1949. — M. COSTANZA, De Heil. Joh. Chrysostomus. Haarlem, 1952. — H. F. v. CAMPENHAUSEN, Griechische Kirchenväter. Stuttgart, 1955, 137-152. — C. V. GHEORGHIU, Saint Jean Bouche d'Or (trad. du roumain par L. Lamoure). Paris, 1957. — H. LIETZMANN, Kleine Schriften I (TU 67). Berlin, 1958, 1811-1828 (repr. of article in PWK).

HIS WRITINGS

Among the Greek Fathers none has left so extensive a literary legacy as Chrysostom. Moreover, he is the only one of the older Antiochenes whose writings are almost entirely preserved. They owe this preferred treatment to the personality of their author as well as to their own excellence. None of the Eastern writers has won the admiration and love of posterity to such a degree as he. The tragedy of his life caused by the extraordinary sincerity and integrity of his character served but to enhance his glory and fame. He remains the most charming of the Greek Fathers and one of the most congenial personalities of Christian antiquity. His rare gift of eloquence gained him the proud title of 'Chrysostom', 'Gold Mouth', which has almost taken the place of his real name ever since it was first bestowed on him in the sixth century. His remarkable purity of speech reflects his noble and natural thought and reminds one of classical times. The Attic qualities of his language were praised by Isidore of Pelusium (*Ep.* 5,2) and one of the greatest scholars of modern times, U. v. Wilamowitz-Moellendorff, declared that his style is 'the harmonious expression of an Attic soul'.

Studies: L. ACKERMANN, Die Beredsamkeit des heiligen Johannes Chrysostomus. Würzburg, 1889. — T. E. AMERINGER, The Stylistic Influence of the Second Sophistic on the Panegyrical Sermons of St. John Chrysostom. Washington, 1921. — H. DEGEN, Die Tropen der Vergleichung bei Johannes Chrysostomos. Diss. Freiburg (Switzerland), 1921. — U. v. WILAMOWITZ - MOELLENDORFF, Die griech. Literatur des Altertums. 4th ed. Berlin, 1924, 296ff. — H. M. HUBBEL, Chrysostom and Rhetoric: CPh 19 (1924) 261-276. — F. W. A. DICKINSON, The Use of the Optative Mood in the Works of St. John Chrysostom. Washington, 1926. — S. SKIMINA, De Joannis Chrysostomi rhythmo oratorio. Cracow, 1927. — E. PETERSON, Die Bedeutung der ὠκεανέ-Akklamation: RhM N.F. 78 (1929) 221-223. — M. A. BURNS, Saint John Chrysostom's Homilies on the Statues. A Study of their Rhetorical Qualities and Forms. Washington, 1930. — M. SOFFRAY, Recherches sur la syntaxe de saint Jean Chrysostome d'après les Homélies sur les statues. Paris, 1939. — P. KUKULES, Proverbs and Proverbial Phrases in Chrysostom (in Greek): Studies in Honor of Th. Borea. Athens, 1939, 355-368; cf. BZ 40 (1940) 264. — W. A. MAAT, A Rhetorical Study of St. John Chrysostom's De sacerdotio. Washington, 1944. — M. SIMONETTI, Sulla struttura dei Panegyrici di S. Giovanni Crisostomo: RIL 86 (1953) 159-180. — A. WENGER, Homélies patristiques et hymnes mélodiques. Jean Chrysostome et Romanos le Mélode: REB 13 (1955) 157-160.

Though Chrysostom wrote some treatises on practical subjects and a great number of letters, most of his works are in sermon form. They offer a colorful picture of the ecclesiastical and political, social and cultural conditions in the capitals of Syria and Byzantium and have remained a rich treasure-house for theologians, historians and archaeologists alike.

His great reputation as an orator, with whom in the West only Augustine can compare, caused many authors to seek immortality for their writings under the prestige of his name. The task of sifting the spurious from the genuine remains a fruitful field of research and must be finished before we can hope for a genuinely critical edition of his works, which is badly needed.

Fortunately we possess very abundant and excellent materials for the latter, because the host of Greek manuscripts is astonishing. The same holds for the countless fragments and excerpts of his works in exegetical *catenae* and ascetical florilegia. There are in addition a great number of translations for many of his writings. The oldest of them, the Latin, Syriac and Armenian, are especially valuable for the preparation of a critical text. But so far no satisfactory survey of the Greek manuscripts exists and the value of the different versions has yet to be established.

Collections: We owe complete editions to the Jesuit FRONTON DU DUC, 12 vols. Paris, 1609-1633, to the Anglican Henry SAVILE, 8 vols. Eton, 1612 (Greek text only), and to the Benedictine Bernhard DE MONTFAUCON, 13 vols. Paris, 1718-1738. This last was reprinted at Venice, 1734-1741 in 13 vols.; again in 1780 in 14 vols. It was reprinted also at Paris with revisions 1834-1840 in 13 vols. The same edition (increased by a rather doubtful *Supplementum*) is found in MG 47-64 except for the *Commentary on Matthew* reprinted from FIELD's edition (1839). J. BAREILLE republished Montfaucon's Greek text with a French translation in 19 vols. Paris, 1865-1873. Among all these Savile's edition is unsurpassed and offers the best text.

Fragments: Fragments have been collected from *catenae* and *florilegia* by S. HAIDACHER, Studien über Chrysostomus-Eklogen: SAW Phil.-hist. Kl. 144, 4. Vienna, 1902 (the collection of Theodore Daphnopates of the 10th cent.); *idem*, Chrysostomus-Fragmente zu den katholischen Briefen: ZkTh 26 (1902) 190-194; *idem*, Chrysostomus-Fragmente unter den Werken des hl. Ephräm Syrus: ZkTh 30 (1906) 178-183; *idem*, Chrysostomus-Fragmente im Maximos-Florilegium und in den Sacra Parallela: BZ 16 (1907) 168-201; *idem*, Chrysostomus-Fragmente: Chrysostomika. Rome, 1908, 217-234 (fragments on Job and from the correspondence of Nilus). — G. BARDY, Les citations de saint Jean Chrysostome dans le florilège du Cod. Vat. gr. 1142: ROC 23 (1923) 427-440, published 27 fragments. — C. MARTIN, Un florilège grec d'homélies christologiques des IVe et Ve siècles sur la nativité (Paris. Gr. 1491): Mus 54 (1941) 17-57.

Manuscript Tradition: J. PAULSON, Symbolae ad Chrysostomum Patrem. 1. De codice Lincopensi; 2. De libro Holmensi. Lund, 1889-1890 (represents the beginning of a systematic collation); *idem*, Notice sur un manuscrit de S. Jean Chrysostome utilisé par Érasme et conservé à la Bibliothèque Royale à Stockholm. Lund, 1890. — C. BAUR, S. Jean Chrysostome et ses œuvres dans l'histoire littéraire, Louvain, 1907, 29, counted 1917 manuscripts, among them 20 of the ninth century, 180 for the *Commentary on Genesis*, 174 for the *Commentary on Matthew*. — E. DIEHL, Eine neue Handschrift des Johannes Chrysostomus: Gno (1928) 57, describes a manuscript of the tenth century. — A. CARILLO DE ALBORNOZ, San Juan Crisostomo y su influencia social en el imperio bizantino del s. IV, Madrid, 1934, reports about 52 manuscripts. — J. E. POWELL, A Palimpsest of St. Chrysostom: JThSt 39 (1938) 132-140 (*Adv. Judaeos*). — G. ROCHEFORT, Une anthologie grecque du XIe siècle, le Parisinus Suppl. Gr. 690: Scriptorium 4 (1950) 3-17. — For a classification of manuscripts, see: J. DUMORTIER, De quelques principes d'ecdotique concernant les traités de saint Jean Chrysostome: MSR 9 (1952) 63-72. — P. HAMELIAN, Tome commémorative de la Bibliothèque Patriarchale d'Alexandrie. 1953, 225-230. — P. K. ENEPEKIDES, Le sommaire d'un manuscrit byzantin inconnu, égaré dans le fond français de la Bibliothèque Nationale à Paris: Studi Bizant. e Neoellen. 7 (1953) 66. — A. WENGER, La tradition des œuvres de saint Jean Chrysostome: REB 14 (1956) 5-47 (Cod. 6 of the monastery Stavronikita at Mount Athos).

Versions: Old Latin: For the Latin versions in general, see: C. BAUR, L'entrée littéraire de S. Chrysostome dans le monde latin: RHE 8 (1907) 249-265. — B. ALTANER, Beiträge zur Geschichte der altlateinischen Übersetzungen von Väterschriften: HJG 61 (1941) 208-226. — A. SIEGMUND, Die Überlieferung der griechischen christlichen Literatur in der lateinischen Kirche. Munich-Pasing, 1949, 91-101. — B. ALTANER, Augustinus und Johannes Chrysostomus. Quellenkritische Untersuchungen: ZNW 44 (1952/1953) 76-84. — E. HONIGMANN, Patristic Studies (ST 173), Vatican City, 1953, 54-58, deals with the Pelagian deacon Anianus of Celeda who between 415 and 419 translated the seven *Panegyrics on St. Paul* and the first 25 *Homilies on the Gospel of St. Matthew*; cf. below p. 456 and 438. — M. FLECHIA, La traduzione di Burgundio Pisano delle Omelie di S. Giovanni Crisostomo sopra Matteo: Aevum 26 (1952) 113-130. Anianus of Celeda's version in: MG 50, 471-514 and 58, 975-1058. — A. WILMART, La collection des 38 homélies latines de saint Jean Chrysostome: JThSt 19 (1917) 305-327. The version of this collection is known to Augustine, Leo the Great, Cassiodore and Bede. The author seems to be Anianus. At least 16 of these 38 homilies must be attributed to St. Chrysostom. — For *Syriac* versions, see: A. BAUMSTARK, Geschichte der syrischen Literatur. Bonn, 1922, 80-81. — For *Arabic* versions: C. BACHA, S. Jean Chrysostome dans la littérature arabe: Chrysostomika. Rome, 1908, 173-187 (comprehensive list of versions). — G. GRAF, Arabische Chrysostomos-Homilien, untersucht und zum Teil übersetzt: ThQ 92 (1910) 185-214; *idem*, Geschichte der christlichen arabischen Literatur I (ST 118). Vatican

City, 1944, 337-354. — E. MICHAELIDIS, Saint John Chrysostom in Arabic Literature (in Greek): EPh 47 (1948) 67-80, 161-167. — For *Armenian* versions, see: C. BAUR, op. cit. 196-197. — G. AUCHER, S. Giovanni Crisostomo nella letteratura armena: Chrysostomika (1908) 143-197. The Mechitarists published at Venice in 1826 two volumes comprising the *Homilies on Matthew* (see below p. 438), in 1861, and 1862 three volumes of *Homilies on the Epistles of St. Paul*. — For the *Armenian* versions of the *Commentary on Isaias*, see below p. 436. — For *Georgian* versions: M. TAMARATI, S. Jean Chrysostome dans la littérature géorgienne: Chrysostomika (1908) 213-216. — G. PERADZE, Die altchristliche Literatur in georgischer Überlieferung. Johannes Chrysostomus: OC ser. 3, 6 (1931) 97-107. — For *Coptic* versions, see: C. BAUR, op. cit. 198. Furthermore E. A. W. BUDGE, Coptic Homilies, London, 1910, 133-143 Coptic text, 275-285 English translation of the *Homilia in dimissionem Chananaeae* (MG 52, 449-460); 1-45 Coptic text and 147-191 English translation of the spurious *Sermo de poenitentia* (MG 88, 1937-1978); 46-57 Coptic text and 192-203 English translation of the spurious *Sermo de Susanna* (MG 56, 589-594). Another work attributed to Chrysostom, an *encomium* on Saint John the Baptist, will be found in E. A. W. BUDGE, Coptic apocrypha. London, 1913, 128ff. (Coptic text), 335ff. (English translat.). *Old Slavonic versions:* F. MIKLOSICH, Monumenta linguae Palaeoslovenicae, Vienna, 1851, published twenty homilies of Chrysostom. — For *Old Russian* version, see: A. PALMIERI, San Giovanni Crisostomo nella letteratura russa: Chrysostomika (1908) 189-212.

Modern Translations: English: LFC 16 vols. Oxford, 1839-1852 and LNPF ser. 1, vols. 9-14, New York, 1888-1893. — *German:* J. FLUCK, Die ascetischen Schriften des hl. Joh. Chrysostomus. Freiburg i.B., 1864. — BKV 10 vols. Kempten, 1869-1884; BKV² 23. 25-27. 39. 42; BKV³ 15. 16, Kempten, 1915-1937. — *French:* M. JEANNIN, 11 vols. Bar-le-Duc, 1863-1867; repr. Arras, 1887-1888. — J. BAREILLE, 19 vols. Paris, 1865-1873 (with the Greek text of Montfaucon). Separate translations and editions will be listed with the individual works below.

Selections: Greek: J. F. D'ALTON, Selections from St. John Chrysostom. The Greek Text edited with Introduction and Commentary. London, 1940. — *English:* A. C. PEGIS, The Wisdom of Catholicism. An Anthology. London, 1950. — *French:* P. E. LEGRAND, Saint Jean Chrysostome (Les moralistes chrétiens). Paris, 1924. — G. BARDY, Les plus belles pages de saint Jean Chrysostome. Paris, 1943. — *Italian:* G. MAMONE, S. Giovanni Crisostomo. Pagine scelte (Bibl. dei santi, T. 16). Milan, 1930.

Studies: Excellent bibliographies are found in: C. BAUR, S. Jean Chrysostome et ses œuvres dans l'histoire littéraire. Louvain, 1907; *idem*, Der heilige Johannes Chrysostomus und seine Zeit. Munich, 1929/1939, vol. 1, XXVIII-XL, vol. 2, 397-400. More up-to-date bibliographies in the English translation: C. BAUR, John Chrysostom and his Time. Transl. by Sr. M. Gonzaga. London, 1960, vol. 1, XIV-LXXIV, vol. 2, 476-480. — *Special:* A. NÄGELE, Johannes Chrysostomus und sein Verhältnis zum Hellenismus: BZ 13 (1904) 73-113; *idem*, Die Bedeutung des hl. Johannes Chrysostomus in der Literatur: Die Kultur 9 (1908) 135-160. — C. BAUR, S. Jérôme et S. Jean Chrysostome: RB 23 (1906) 430-436. — S. BEZDEKI, Joannes Chrysostomus et Plato: Ephemeris Dacoromana 1 (1923) 291-337. — P. R. COLEMAN - NORTON, Saint John Chrysostom and the Greek Philosophers: CPh 25 (1930) 305-317; *idem*, St. Chrysostom's Use of Josephus: CPh 26 (1931) 85-89; *idem*, St. Chrysostom's Use of the Greek Poets: CPh 28 (1932) 213-221. — M. SOFFRAY, Saint Jean Chrysostome et la littérature païenne: Phoenix 2 (1947/48) 82-85. — L. CASTIGLIONI, Decisa forficibus, XLIII-XLV: RIL 83 (1950) 41-62 (Greek philosophical tradition in Chrysostom, text. crit.). — J. DUMORTIER, Platon et saint Jean Chrysostome: Association G. Budé. Congrès de Tours et de Poitiers, 3-5 septembre 1953. Actes du Congrès. Paris, 1954, 262-265 (summary).

1. *Sermons*

In his sermons Chrysostom appears as the real physician of souls who diagnoses with unerring instinct their maladies and shows a sympathetic understanding of human frailty, but does not hesitate to castigate selfishness, luxury, arrogance and vice wherever he finds them. Though some of them are very long and lasted sometimes two hours, the applause which punctuated them shows that he reached the hearts of his hearers and kept their attention. His command of imagery is superb and his sincere concept of Christian life deserves our respect and admiration even today.

The written form in which we possess them today does not go back to a copy prepared for publication by the author but in most cases to notes of his stenographers. The manuscripts present not unfrequently two editions of the homilies, the one in a comparatively smooth style, the other in a rather rough state. The former is a deliberate later revision of the latter. Thus the superiority and greater antiquity of the rough text is too evident to be called in question. The smooth text is without authority.

Translations of Selected Sermons: Spanish: F. OGARA, Homilias selectas de San Juan Crisostomo. 3 vols. Madrid, 1905. — M. CALVO, Homilias de San Juan Crisostomo. Barcelona, 1916. — *Dutch:* B. H. VANDENBERGHE, Chrysostomus herleeft. Keur van preeken. Antwerpen, 1938. — *Polish:* T. SINKO, Dwadziescia homily i mow, przl. Cracow, 1947.

1. *Exegetical Homilies*

Most of Chrysostom's writings are exegetical homilies on the books of the Old and New Testament. Their manuscript tradition is even better and richer than that of the rest of his works, for the reason that the *Typica* or liturgical manuals, which indicate how the services are to be recited during the ecclesiastical year, prescribe the reading of these homilies for the countless monasteries of the Byzantine Church during Lent and the Paschal season.

Most of these sermons were delivered at Antioch between 386 and 397. They give evidence of his strict and intelligent training in the tenets of that School. Always anxious to ascertain the literal sense and opposed to allegory, he combines great facility in discerning the spiritual meaning of the Scriptural text with an equal ability for immediate, practical application to the guidance of those committed to his care. The depth of his thought and the soundness of his masterful exposition are unique and attract even modern readers. He is equally at home in the books of the Old and the New Testament and has the skill to use even the former for the conditions of the present and the problems of daily life.

The great difficulty in connection with the homilies is their chronology. Photius' criterion that the more finished works were composed at Antioch, would scarcely suffice for precise dating. Most of his voluminous Scriptural expositions do not provide enough clues to determine the time of composition or delivery or even their exact order. Some of them might have been published only in written form without having ever been preached.

Studies: F. H. CHASE, Chrysostom. A Study in the History of Biblical Interpretation. London, 1887. — S. HAIDACHER, Die Lehre des heiligen Johannes Chrysostomus über die Schriftinspiration. Salzburg, 1897. — O. RATHAI, Johannes Chrysostomus als Exeget: Pastor Bonus 30 (1918) 342-351. — M. VON BONSDORFF, Zur Predigttätigkeit des Johannes Chrysostomos. Helsingfors, 1922 (important for the chronology of the homilies on the New Testament). — C. BAUR, Der Kanon des Johannes Chrysostomus: ThQ 105 (1924) 258-271. — J. STIGLMAYR, Antike Grossstädte im Spiegel der Chrysostomus-Homilien: Stimmen der Zeit 58 (1927) 170-185. — J. A. SAWHILL, The Use of Athletic Metaphors in the Biblical Homilies of St. John Chrysostom. Diss. Princeton, 1928. — J. GOERLINGS, Chrysostom's Text of the Gospel of Mark: HThR 24 (1931) 121-142. — A. EHRHARD, Überlieferung und Bestand der hagiographischen und homiletischen Literatur der griechischen Kirche (TU 50). Leipzig, 1936, 130ff. (inedited homilies). — S. LYONNET, Témoignages de saint Jean Chrysostome et de saint Jérôme sur Jacques le frère du Seigneur: RSR 29 (1939) 335-351. — I. MOISESCU, Holy Scripture and its Interpretation in the Works of St. John Chrysostom (in Rumanian): Candela 50/51 (1939/1941) 116-238. — F. OGARA, De typica apud Chrysostomum prophetia: Greg 24 (1943) 62-77. — B. GIORGIATIS, Die Lehre des Johannes Chrysostomos über die hl. Schrift. Athens, 1947.

OLD TESTAMENT HOMILIES

a. Homilies on Genesis

There are two series of homilies on Genesis extant which seem to be the oldest of the exegetical. The first consists of *Homiliae 9 in Genesin* (MG 54, 581-630), delivered at Antioch during Lent 386. With the exception of the last all of them deal with the first three chapters of Genesis. The second series, *Homiliae 67 in Genesin*, presents a complete commentary on the Book of Genesis. The author explains the entire text from the beginning to the end, taking it up by sections. It seems that he preached these homilies in 388. Some of the homilies of the two series have passages completely and literally identical.

Edition: MG 53-54.

Translations: German: Max Herzog VON SACHSEN, 2 vols. Paderborn, 1913/1914. — French: DE BELLEGARDE. Paris, 1703.

Studies: C. BAUR, Chrysostomus in Genesim: ThQ 108 (1927) 221-232. — W. A. MARKOWICZ, The Text Tradition of St. John Chrysostom's Homilies on Genesis and Mss. Michiganensis 139, 78 and Holkhamicus 61. Diss. University of Michigan. Ann Arbor, 1953.

b. Homilies on the Psalms

By far the best of his homilies on the books of the Old Testament are those on 58 selected Psalms. Montfaucon and the elder scholars believed that these represent a choice made from a series on the whole Psalter. Such an opinion has no solid foundation, even though Chrysostom did preach on scattered passages of other Psalms, for instance, the beginning of Ps. 41 (MG 55, 155-167) given in 387, and Psalm 115, 1-3, the Greek text of which was published by S. Haidacher in 1907. In the series of homilies on 58 Psalms, dating most probably from the end of his Antiochene period, he interprets Psalms 4-12, 43-49, 108-117, 119-150 (MG 55). Quite a number of homilies on the Psalter attributed to Chrysostom are spurious.

It remains doubtful whether Chrysostom ever actually delivered these addresses on 58 Psalms. They have reached us under the title *Explanations ('Ερμηνεῖαι)* rather than 'homilies'. The content shows that here Chrysostom is at his best. We find his favorite ideas on vices and virtues (Ps. 100. 142. 146), on the right kind of prayer (Ps. 7. 9. 141), on the singing of Psalms and hymns in the Christian home (Ps. 41. 134. 150). He speaks of St. Peter's sojourn in Rome (Ps. 48), of pilgrimages to the Holy Land (Ps. 109), of sacerdotal dignity (Ps. 113. 116), of virginity (Ps. 44. 113) and of worthy reception of Holy Communion (Ps. 133). Here and there we find a polemic against the Arians, the Manichaeans and Paul of Samosata (Ps. 46. 109. 148).

It is interesting to note that his commentary on the Psalms differs from all his others on the Old Testament in that he does not limit himself to the text of the Septuagint but refers often to the translations of 'others' (cf. Ps. 4, 9; 55, 53 etc.). Thus he uses sometimes three or four readings side by side, even those of the 'Hebrew' and the 'Syrian'. The 'other' versions are those of Symmachus, Aquila and Theodotion.

Editions: MG 55. — S. HAIDACHER, Drei unedierte Chrysostomus-Texte einer Baseler Handschrift: ZkTh 31 (1907) 349-360.

Studies: C. BAUR, Der ursprüngliche Umfang des Kommentars des hl. Johannes Chrysostomus zu den Psalmen: Chrysostomika (1908) 235-242 (the commentary is complete; the original did not comprise the entire Psalter). — J. QUASTEN, The Conflict of Early Christianity with the Jewish Temple Worship: TS 2 (1941) 481-487 (MG 55, 494; 497). — G. MERCATI, Alla ricerca dei nomi degli 'altri' traduttori nelle omelie sui Salmi di S. Giovanni Crisostomo e variazioni su alcune catene del Salterio (ST 158). Vatican City, 1952.

c. Homilies on Isaias

Six homilies on Isaias 6 have survived in their Greek original (MG 56, 97-142). Some of them were delivered at Antioch, others at Constantinople. A complete commentary on Isaias is extant in an Armenian version and seems to be genuine. The one on Isaias 1, 1-8, 10, preserved in Greek, is probably nothing but an excerpt from homilies which the compiler stripped of their oratorical garb.

The *Homiliae 5 de Anna* (MG 54, 631-676) and the *Homiliae 3 de Davide et Saule* (54, 675-708) comment on some chapters of the Books of Kings and were delivered in 387. The two homilies *De prophetarum obscuritate* deal with the prophetic books in general and were composed at Antioch in 386.

A great number of *catenae* fragments which bear the name of Chrysostom are extant on Jeremias, Daniel, Proverbs and Job. Their authenticity remains to be established. But even if they are genuine, they are no proof for lost commentaries or homilies on these books, but should be considered as excerpts from other writings.

Editions: Commentary on Isaias 1,1 - 8,10: MG 56, 11-94. The Armenian version was published by the Mechitarists from a manuscript of the 12th century. Venice, 1880 (Armenian text); 1887 (Latin translation). The Prolegomena and Chapters I-II, 2 that are lacking in this edition have been published by J. AUETISEAN, The Newly Discovered Part of the Armenian Version of St. John Chrysostom's Commentary on Isaias (in Armenian): Sion 9 (1935) 21-24. Cf. OC 12 (1937) 160.

Translation: Spanish: Interpretación sobre Isaías profeta: Biblioteca Clásica del Catolicismo, por una Sociedad de Teólogos y Humanistas. Madrid, 1889, I, 137-283.

Studies: L. DIEU, Le commentaire arménien de S. Jean Chrysostome sur Isaïe (chs. 8-64) est-il authentique?: RHE 17 (1921) 7-30 (confirms authenticity). — P. N. AKINIAN, Des hl. Chrysostomos Kommentar zu Isaias in der armenischen Literatur (in Armenian with a German summary): HA 48 (1934) 43-55. — For fragments of a commentary on Job (MG 64, 503-506), see: S. HAIDACHER, Chrysostomus-Fragmente: Chrysostomika (1908) 217-234. — L. DIEU, Le commentaire de saint Jean Chrysostome sur Job: RHE 13 (1912) 640-658. — For the fragments on Jeremias (MG 64, 739-1038), see: L. DIEU, Le commentaire sur Jérémie du Pseudo-Chrysostome serait-il l'œuvre de Polychronius d'Apamée?: RHE 14 (1913) 685-701. — For *De prophetarum obscuritate* (MG 56, 163-192), cf. W. ELTESTER, Zum syrisch-makedonischen Kalender im IV. Jahrhundert: ZNW (1938) 286-288 (concerning MG 56, 172). — G. MERCATI, Postille del codice Q a Geremia tratte dal commento dello pseudo-Crisostomo: Miscellanea Biblica B. Ubach. Barcelona, 1953, 27-30.

NEW TESTAMENT HOMILIES

Suidas mentions in his *Lexicon* (s.v. *Joan. Antioch.*) that Chrysostom composed homiletic commentaries on all four Gospels. So far we possess a series on Matthew and John, but none on Mark and Luke. There are in fact a few manuscripts which contain explanations of Mark and Luke attributed to Chrysostom, but they amount to no more than florilegia. Nobody else ever speaks of works by Chrysostom on those two Gospels. Thus Suidas must be mistaken. Chrysostom expounded the first and last Gospel only.

a. Homilies on the Gospel of St. Matthew

The 90 homilies on Matthew represent the oldest complete commentary on the first Gospel that has survived from the patristic period. They were delivered at Antioch as is evident from a passage in the seventh homily (MG 57, 81) and most probably in 390. Chrysostom attacks the Manichaeans on many occasions and refutes their claim that the Old Testament differs widely from the New, in so far as the God of the Old Dispensation is a God of rigorism and justice, whereas the God of the New Testament is a God of Love. He demonstrates that both have the same lawgiver, but that the Old Covenant was only a preparation and forerunner of the New. The commandments of Christ complete the Law of the Jews and make up for its shortcomings. He calls the Gospels letters of the Divine King and explains slight apparent discrepancies disclosed by a comparison of the four Gospels, as a proof of their independence:

> Was not one Evangelist sufficient to tell all? One indeed was sufficient; but if there be four that write, not at the same times, nor in the same places, neither having met together, and conversed one with another, and then they speak all things as it were out of one mouth, this becomes a very great demonstration of the truth.
> But the contrary, it may be said, has come to pass, for in many places they are convicted of discordance. Nay, this very thing is a very great evidence of their truth. For if they had agreed in all things exactly even to time, and place, and to the very words, none of our enemies would have believed, but that they had met together, and had written what they wrote by some human compact; because such entire agreement as this does not come of simplicity. But now even that discordance which seems to exist in little matters delivers them from all suspicion and speaks clearly in the behalf of the character of the writers (*Hom.* 1, 5-6 LFC).

Throughout the entire series of homilies Chrysostom stresses against the Arians that the Son is equal to the Father and not below the Father, even if He speaks of Himself in a human way, when He refers to His human nature. The interpretation of the parables of Christ is masterly and the author's moral and ascetical exhortations reveal the customs and manners of the time. The theaters are the theme of his frequent reprobation, and the monks of his praise. Homilies 69 and 70 describe their mode of life, their dress, retreats, labors and contrast their singing with the stage. He pictures their victory over the vice and presents their devotion as an edifying example to all. Almsgiving is especially recommended and the poor are called Christ's brethren and ours.

The *Homilies on Matthew* have the distinction of being preserved, though incomplete, in the oldest manuscript of Chrysostom's writings that we possess, in Uncial-Codex 95 of the Dukal Library at Wolfenbüttel, dating from the sixth century. So far it has not been used by any editor. From the eleventh century on the number of manuscripts is relatively great. At least 175 from the ninth to the sixteenth century contain the complete text or parts of it. Even Field, who has prepared the best text so far (reprinted by Migne 57-58) did not consult more than 11 or 13 of them (cf. MG 57, V-VII).

The oldest Latin translation of the *Homilies on Matthew* is that prepared by the Pelagian deacon Anianus of Celeda. Unfortunately the persecution of the Pelagians which began about 420 prevented his finishing it, and as a result, none of the manuscripts offers more than the first 25 homilies. The earliest complete Latin version goes back to Burgundius Pisanus (d. 1194). It is preserved in *Codex Vat. Lat.* 383 saec. XII. The homilies were turned a third time into Latin by George of Trapezunt (d. 1486) at the request of Pope Nicholas V (1447-1455).

As early as the fifth century an Armenian version was made, of which the Mechitarists published the first 53 sections in 1826 at Venice. A Syriac version of the same period survives only in fragments in four sixth-century manuscripts of the British Museum. The deacon Theodul (Abdallah) translated the homilies into Arabic in the tenth century and Euthymius of Mount Athos (d. 1028) in the eleventh into Georgian. None of these has been printed so far.

Editions: MG 57-58 reprints the edition of F. FIELD, Cambridge, 1839, 3 vols. — MG 58, 975-1058: *Latin* version by Anianus of Celeda, but only the first part comprising Homilies 1-8. The complete text of Anianus' version of the first 25 homilies has never been printed. — For Anianus of Celeda: cf. E. HONIGMANN, Patristic Studies (ST 173), Vatican City, 1953, 54-58. — For the earliest complete Latin version by Burgundius Pisanus, see: M. FLECHIA, La traduzione di Burgundio Pisano delle Omelie di S. Giovanni Crisostomo sopra Matteo: Aevum 26 (1952) 113-130.

Translations: English: S. G. PREVOST, LFC 11 (1843), 15 (1843), 34 (1851); reprinted: LNPF 10 (1889) revised by M. B. Riddle. — *German:* Max Herzog VON SACHSEN, Des hl. Johannes Chrysostomus Homilien über das Evangelium des hl. Matthäus. 2 vols. Regensburg, 1910/12. — C. BAUR, BKV² 23 (1915), 25 (1915), 26 (1916), 27 (1916). — *Spanish:* D. RUIZ BUENO, Obras de S. Juan Crisostomo I. Homilias sobre S. Mateo (1-45), II. Homilias sobre Mateo (46-90) (BAC 141, 146). Madrid, 1955/1956.

Studies: P. A. VARDANIAN, Un fragment récemment découvert du commentaire de S. Jean Chrysostome sur l'évangile selon S. Matthieu: Monatsschrift für armenische Philologie 35 (1921) 353-364. — J. REUSS, Der Exeget Ammonius und die Fragmente seines Matthäus- und Johannes-Kommentars: Bibl (1941) 13-20 (belong to Chrysostom). — F. OGARA, De typica apud Chrysostomum prophetia: Greg 24 (1943) 62-77 (*Comment.*

on Matthew 2, 15). — A. WIKGREN, A Chrysostom Leaf in the Kurdian Collection: Byz 17 (1944/1945) 329 (part of ch. 53). — C. D. DICKS, The Matthean Text of Chrysostom in his Homilies on Matthew. Diss. Chicago, 1947; *idem*, JBL (1948) 365-376. — A. ULEYN, De zedeleer van Johannes Chrysostomus in zijn Matthëuskommentaar. Hellenistische en kristelijke faktoren. Diss. Louvain, 1956; *idem*, La doctrine morale de S. Jean Chrysostome dans le Commentaire sur S. Matthieu et ses affinités avec la diatribe: Revue Universit. Ottawa 27 (1957) 5*-25*, 99*-140*.

b. Homilies on the Gospel of St. John

The 88 homilies on John (MG 59) are far shorter than those on Matthew and were delivered later, probably about 391. Most of them could not have lasted more than ten to fifteen minutes. Homilies 31,5 and 18,2 indicate that they were given in the morning. The episode of the adulterous woman, John 7,53 - 8,11, is omitted. In fact, Chrysostom does not mention this pericope in any of his works. Undoubtedly he would have commented on it, if it had been in the copies of the Bible which he used at Antioch. The *Homilies on John* are far more controversial than those on Matthew. The reason is that he continually meets with texts which the Arians, especially the Anomoeans, perverted into evidence of their false teaching that the Son is not even of like substance with the Father. Chrysostom develops the doctrine of condescension against these misinterpretations of statements about the human weaknesses of Christ, His fear and His suffering. He introduces Christ saying: 'I am God and the really-begotten Son of God, and am of that simple and blessed essence; I need none to witness to Me; and even though none would do so, yet am not I by this anything diminished in My essence; but because I care for the salvation of the many, I have descended to such humility as to commit the witness of Me to a man' (*Hom.* 6 LFC). He returns to this theme on many occasions. Thus he states in the eleventh homily:

> For He became Son of man, who was God's own Son, in order that He might make the sons of men to be children of God. For the high when it associates with the low touches not at all its own honor, while it raises up the other from its excessive lowness; and even thus it was with the Lord. He in nothing diminished His own Nature by this condescension, but raised us, who had always sat in disgrace and darkness, to glory unspeakable (LFC).

Thus Chrysostom shows that the heretics have no right to use these texts for their own purpose, because they are perfectly consistent with the truth held by the Church. Owing to the special character of the Gospel of St. John, these homilies differ in form, arrangement and content from Chrysostom's other Scriptural expositions. However, there can be no doubt about their authenticity; as early as 451 the Ecumenical Council of Chalcedon quotes them as his work.

Editions: MG 59. — D. C. Tirone, S. Giovanni Crisostomo, Le omelie su S. Giovanni Evangelista (Corona Patrum Salesiana) 4 vols. Turin, 1944-1948 (reprints the text of Montfaucon's edition).

Translations: English: G. T. Stupart, LFC 28 (1848), 36 (1852); reprinted: LNPF 14 (1889) 1-334 with notes by P. Schaff. T. A. Goggin, F. C. 33 (1957). — *German:* F. Knors, Die Homilien des hl. Johannes Chrysostomus über das Evangelium des hl. Johannes. Paderborn, 1862. — *Italian:* D. C. Tirone, op. cit.

Studies: F. Fabbi, La 'condiscendenza' divina nell'ispirazione biblica: Bibl 14 (1933) 330-347. — P. W. Harkins, Text Tradition of Chrysostom's Commentary on John. Diss. Michigan Univ., Ann Arbor, 1948. — J. Förster, Die Exegese des vierten Evangeliums in den Johannes-Homilien des Chrysostomus. Diss. Berlin, 1951. — P. W. Harkins, The Text Tradition of Chrysostom's Commentary on John: TS 19 (1958) 404-412.

c. Homilies on the Acts of the Apostles

The sequence of fifty-five sermons is the only complete commentary on Acts that has survived from the first ten centuries. Chrysostom himself dates them to the third year of his residence at Constantinople, i.e. 400 A.D. Their literary form is less finished than we are accustomed to expect from him. It seems that the text was drawn up from notes taken by stenographers during the preaching and that Chrysostom never revised it, owing to his heavy responsibilities in that imperial city and the constant trouble and alarm, by which he was then harrassed. Nevertheless, the reader will perceive in them the same excellent qualities as mark his other exegetical works, especially the clear and full exposition of the historical sense. The first homily begins with the preacher's complaint that this portion of the New Testament was not so much read as it ought to be: 'To many persons this book is so little known, both it and its author, that they are not even aware that there is such a book in existence. For this reason especially I have taken this narrative for my subject, that I may draw to it such as do not know it, and not let such a treasure as this remain hidden out of sight. For indeed it may profit us no less than even the Gospels; so replete is it with Christian wisdom and sound doctrine, especially in what is said concerning the Holy Ghost. Then let us not hastily pass by it, but examine it closely' (LFC). Chrysostom follows indeed with close attention St. Luke's report and sometimes even counts up the days of the missionary journeys. Of religious and moral subjects he treats especially the delay of baptism (*Hom.* 1,23), which he condemns. He repeatedly deals with the nature and purpose of miracles, contrasts them with magic and points out that it is better to suffer for Christ and to cast out sin than to expel a demon. He stresses the need of prayer, of the study of the Scriptures, of gentleness and almsgiving and rejects oaths and swearing.

Unfortunately the text of the printed editions is very unsatisfactory. In the manuscripts it is found in two forms which differ so widely that there are two recensions. One of them is stylistically inferior to the other, and the latter must be a deliberate and late revision. Some of the manuscripts and all printed editions contain a mixture of both forms. H. Browne, the translator of the Homilies in LFC, was the first to present proof that the unpolished recension is the only one which can be called authentic and he based his English version on this. A new critical edition of the Greek text of the rough recension is being prepared by E. Smothers.

Cassiodorus (*Institutiones* 1,9,1) relates that his friends at his request translated 'the fifty-five Homilies on the Acts, by St. John, bishop of Constantinople' into Latin and that this version was deposited in the monastic library at Vivarium. Unfortunately this work is lost. The Canons of the Fifth and Sixth General Councils cite a long passage of the Greek text from the 14th homily containing St. Chrysostom's view of the seven deacons in the Acts.

The series of fifty-five homilies must not be confused with the group of four homilies on the beginning of the Acts of the Apostles (MG 51, 65-112) and the four on the change of names in the case of St. Paul and other biblical personages (MG 51, 113-156) all delivered at Antioch during the Paschal season of 388.

Edition: MG 60.

Translations: English: H. BROWNE, LFC 33 (1851), 35 (1852); reprinted: LNPF 11 (1889) 1-328, revised by G. B. Stevens.

Studies: E. R. SMOTHERS, Le texte des homélies de S. Jean Chrysostome sur les Actes des Apôtres: RSR 27 (1937) 513-548; *idem*, A Problem of Text in Saint John Chrysostom: RSR 39 (1951) 416-427 (Acts 20, 13-14 and Chrysostom's commentary); *idem*, Chrysostom and Symeon (Acts 15, 14): HThR 46 (1953) 203-215 (Chrysostom identifies the Symeon with the author of the *Nunc dimittis*); *idem*, Toward a Critical Text of the Homilies on Acts of St. John Chrysostom: SP I (TU 63). Berlin, 1957, 53-57.

Almost half of Chrysostom's extant homilies are devoted to an exposition of the Epistles of St. Paul. There is no subject which kindled his eloquence more than the personality and the achievements of the Apostle of the Gentiles. He saw in him the perfect model of the pastor of souls and a kindred spirit, fearless and unselfish and with much of his own fiery temperament.

Edition: A critical edition of all the homilies on the Epistles of St. Paul was published by F. FIELD, Interpretatio Omnium Epistularum Paulinarum. Oxford, 1845-1862, 7 vols.

Studies: S. K. GIFFORD, Pauli epistolas qua forma legerit Joannes Chrysostomus. Halle, 1902. — L. J. OHLEYER, The Pauline Formula 'Induere Christum' with Special

Reference to the Works of St. John Chrysostom. Diss. Washington, 1921. — A. MERZAGORA, Giovanni Crisostomo commentatore di S. Paolo: Studi P. Ubaldi. Milan, 1937, 205-246. — F. FROMM, Das Bild des verklärten Christus beim hl. Paulus. Nach den Kommentaren des hl. Johannes Chrysostomus. Rome, 1938. — E. HOFFMANN - ALEITH, Das Paulusverständnis des Johannes Chrysostomus: ZNW 38 (1939) 181-188. — F. OGARA, El Apóstol san Pablo visto a través de san Juan Crisóstomo. Rome, 1944.

d. Homilies on Romans

The 32 homilies on Romans are by far the most outstanding patristic commentary on this Epistle and the finest of all Chrysostom's works. Isidore of Pelusium said of them that 'the treasures of the wisdom of the learned John are especially abundant in his exposition of the Epistle to the Romans. I think (and it cannot be said that I write to flatter any one) that if the divine Paul wished to expound in the Attic tongue his own writings he would not have spoken otherwise than this famous master; so remarkable is the latter's exposition for its contents, its beauty of form, and propriety of expression' (*Ep.* 5, 32).

Allusions in the homilies point to Antioch as the place of origin. Thus in the eighth homily Chrysostom speaks of himself and his hearers as under one bishop, which proves that he himself was not a bishop yet but deacon or priest. The 33rd homily shows even better that it was delivered at Antioch because here the preacher refers to the place in which his listeners live as one in which St. Paul taught and was bound, which is true of Antioch but not of Constantinople. Thus the work on Romans must have been composed during his Antiochene period, i.e. between 381 and 398, most probably shortly after he finished with the Gospel of St. John.

The entire series of sermons bears the stamp of Chrysostom's authorship in style, language and exegetical method. In the Pelagian controversy in 422 St. Augustine quotes (*Adversus Julianum* 1, 27) eight passages of the tenth homily on Romans as a proof that Chrysostom did not hold any Pelagian view on original sin. He took those quotations most probably from a Latin translation already in existence at that time.

Though the Epistle to the Romans deals with great dogmatic problems, Chrysostom does not take the opportunity to discuss them. He has no leaning to theological speculation and feels more attracted by moral and ascetical questions. Thus from a theological point of view his sober Antiochene exegesis is sometimes disappointing. All the more does his impassioned enthusiasm for St. Paul catch the attention of the modern reader. The first homily begins with words of affection and admiration for the Apostle:

> As I keep hearing the Epistles of the blessed Paul read, and that twice every week, and often three or four times, whenever we are

celebrating the memorials of the holy martyrs, gladly do I enjoy the spiritual trumpet, and get roused and warmed with desire at recognizing the voice so dear to me, and seem to fancy him all but present to my sight, and to behold him conversing with me. But I grieve and am pained, that all people do not know this man, as much as they ought to know him; but some are so far ignorant of him, as not even to know for certainty the number of his Epistles. And this comes not of incapacity, but of their not having the will to be continually conversing with this blessed man. For it is not through any natural readiness and sharpness of wit that even I am acquainted with as much as I do know, if I do know anything, but owing to a continual cleaving to the man, and an earnest affection towards him (LFC).

As the entire commentary begins so it ends with a burst of enthusiasm for the beloved teacher of the Gentiles. There is hardly a passage in the whole range of patristic literature which praises Saint Paul with such fondness and devotion as this conclusion of the *Homilies on Romans*:

I love Rome even for this, although indeed one has other grounds for praising it, both for its greatness, and its antiquity, and its beauty, and its populousness, and for its power, and for its wealth, and for its successes in war. But I let all this pass, and esteem it blessed on this account, that both in his lifetime he [Paul] wrote to them, and loved them so, and talked with them while he was with us, and brought his life to a close there. Wherefore the city is more notable upon this ground, than upon all others together. And as a body great and strong, it has as two glistening eyes the bodies of these Saints. Not so bright is the heaven, when the sun sends forth its rays, as is the city of Rome, sending out these two lights into all parts of the world. From thence will Paul be caught up, from thence Peter. Just think and shudder at the thought of what a sight Rome will see, when Paul arises suddenly from the tomb together with Peter, and is lifted up to meet the Lord. What a rose will Rome send up to Christ! what two crowns will the city have about it! what golden chains will she be girded with! what fountains possess! Therefore I admire the city not for the much gold, not for the columns, not for the other display there, but for these pillars of the Church. Would that it were now given me to throw myself round the body of Paul, and be rivetted to the tomb, and see the dust of that body that filled up that which was lacking after Christ, that bore the marks, sowed the Gospel everywhere, yea, the dust of that body through which Christ spoke... Fain would I see the dust of those eyes which were blinded gloriously, which recovered their sight again for the salvation of the world; which even in the body were counted worthy to see Christ, which saw earthly things, yet saw them not, which saw the things which are not seen, which saw no sleep, which were watchful at midnight, which were not affected as eyes are. I would also see the dust of those feet, which ran through the world and were not weary; which were bound in the stocks when the prison shook, which went through parts habitable or uninhabited, which walked on so many journeys. And why need I speak of single parts? Fain would I see the tomb, where the armor of righteousness is laid up, the armor of light, the limbs which now live, but which in life were made dead; and in all whereof Christ lived, which were crucified to the world, which were Christ's members, which were clad in Christ. This body is a wall to that City, which is safer than all towers, and than thousands of battlements (*Hom.* 32 LFC).

Homily 23 is a compact and brilliant treatise on Christian political thought. Chrysostom here clearly distinguishes between the power, which is of divine, and the office, which is of human origin: 'To show that these regulations are for all, even priests, and monks, and not for men of secular occupations only, he has made this plain at the outset, by saying, as follows, "let every soul be subject to the higher powers", even if you be an Apostle, or an Evangelist, or a Prophet, insofar as this subjection is not subversive of religion. And he does not merely say *obey*, but *be subject;* and the first claim such an enactment has upon us, and the reasoning that suits the faithful, is that all this is of God's appointment. *For there is no power but from God...* It may be said, is then every ruler elected by God? I do not say that; he [St. Paul] answers. I am now not speaking about individual rulers, but about the thing in itself. For that there should be rulers, and some rule and others be ruled, and that all things should not be carried on in confusion, the people swaying like waves this way and that, this, I say, is the work of God's wisdom. Hence he does not say "there is no ruler but from God"; but it is the thing he speaks of, and says: "There is no power but from God. And the powers that are are ordained of God" ' (*Hom.* 23 LFC). Chrysostom is the first theological writer to find the origin of political authority in a pact among men: 'It was for this that from of old all men came to an agreement that rulers should be maintained by us, because of the neglect of their own affairs; they take charge of the public, and on this they spend their whole time and so our goods are safe' (*ibid.* LFC).

Some of the homilies on Romans are so long that it would take two hours to deliver them. Thus it remains doubtful whether they were actually preached in the present form.

Edition: MG 59, 13-384.

Translations: J. B. MORRIS, LFC 7 (1841); reprinted: LNPF 11 (1889) 329-564, revised by G. B. Stevens. — *German:* J. WIMMER, BKV 4 (1880) 15-662. — J. JATSCH, BKV² 39 (1922), 42 (1923). — *Spanish:* B. BEJARANO, S. Juan Crisóstomo, Homilias sobre la Carta de san Pablo a los Romanos (Colección Excelsa 16 y 30). Madrid, 1944/1947, 2 vols.

Studies: A. MEAN, Étude des homélies que Jean Chrysostome a prononcées sur le premier chapitre de l'Épître aux Romains. Neuchâtel, 1930. — H. KAUPEL, Die Wertung des

Alten Testamentes im Römerbrief-Kommentar des hl. Johannes Chrysostomus: ThGl 30 (1938) 17-25. — J. a Jesu MACIAS, La dotrina de la justificación en el comentario de S. Juan Crisóstomo a los Romanos. Diss. Greg. Rome, 1951. — B. ALTANER, Augustinus und Johannes Chrysostomus. Quellenkritische Untersuchungen: ZNW 44 (1952/1953) 76-84. — W. KEUK, Sünder und Gerechter. Römer 7, 14-25 in der Auslegung der griechischen Väter. Diss. Tübingen, 1955. — K. H. SCHELKLE, Paulus Lehrer der Väter. Die altkirchliche Auslegung von Römer 1-11. 2nd ed. Düsseldorf, 1959.

e. Homilies on the two Epistles to the Corinthians

Among the very best specimens of his thought and teaching are the 44 homilies on First and the 30 on Second Corinthians. In the 21st on First he mentions explicitly that he writes at Antioch (21, 6). Those on Second Corinthians were composed in the same place, as *Hom.* 26, 5 refers to Constantinople as 'there'. The exact date of composition cannot be determined. The author alludes in the series on First Corinthians *Homilia* 7, 2 to his commentary on Matthew and *Homilia* 27, 2 to that on the Gospel of St. John.

Homily 7, 1-2 on First Corinthians, a detailed discussion of the Pauline concept of the Christian Mystery, provides the best key to Chrysostom's own understanding of I Corinthians 2, 6-10. His profound exposition of this passage is directed against the rationalistic tendencies of the Anomoeans who denied the mystery aspect of the Christian religion. In Homily 40 on First Corinthians 15, 29 he quotes a fragment from what was apparently a declaratory Creed uttered before the candidates stepped into the baptismal font, during the Easter vigil. It is clear that this Antiochene symbol contained at any rate the clauses 'and in the remission of sins, and in the resurrection of the dead, and in life everlasting'. The entire homily is valuable for the history of the baptismal liturgy and the rule of secrecy *(disciplina arcani)*. Speaking about the latter Chrysostom remarks:

> But first I wish to remind you who are initiated of the response, which on that [Easter] Eve they who introduce you to the mysteries bid you to make; and then I will also explain the saying of Paul: so this likewise will be clearer to you; we after all other things ended, adding this, which Paul now says. And I desire indeed expressly to utter it, but I dare not, on account of the uninitiated; for these add a difficulty to our exposition, compelling us either not to speak clearly, or to declare unto them the ineffable mysteries. Nevertheless, as I may be able, I will speak as through a veil. As thus: after the enunciation of those mystical and fearful words, and the awful rules of the doctrines which have come down from heaven, this also we add at the end, when we are about to baptize, bidding them say, 'I believe in the resurrection of the dead', and upon this faith we are baptized. I say, after we have confessed this together with the rest, then at last are we let down into the fountain of those sacred streams. This therefore Paul

recalling to their minds, said, 'if there be no resurrection, why are you then baptized for the dead?', i.e. the dead bodies. For in fact, with a view of this are you baptized, affirming a resurrection of your dead body, that it no longer remains dead. And you indeed in the words make mention of a resurrection of the dead; but the priest, as in a kind of image, signifies to you by very deed, the things which you have believed and confessed in the appointed words. When without a sign you believe, then he gives you the sign also; when you have done your own part, then also does God fully assure you. How, and in what manner? By the water. For the being baptized and immersed, and then emerging, is a symbol of the descent into hell, and the return thence. Wherefore also Paul calls baptism a burial, saying, 'Therefore we are buried with Him by baptism into death' (*Hom.* 40, 2 LFC).

Chrysostom wrote in addition to the two series of homilies on First and Second Corinthians three sermons on I Cor. 7, 1 (MG 51, 207-242) and three on II Cor. 4, 13 (MG 51, 271-302), and one on I Cor. 15, 28. The Greek text of the latter was first published by Haidacher in 1907.

Edition: MG 61, 9-61. — S. HAIDACHER, Drei unedierte Chrysostomus-Texte einer Baseler Handschrift II: ZkTh 31 (1907) 150-171.

Translations: English: H. K. CORNISH and J. MEDLEY, LFC 4 (1839), 5 (1839): Homilies on I Corinthians; J. ASHWORTH, LFC 27 (1848): Homilies on II Corinthians; reprinted: LNPF 12 (1889) revised by T. W. Chambers. — *German:* J. C. MITTERRUTZNER, BKV 5 (1881) 9-782 Homilies on I Cor.; A. HARTL, BKV 6 (1882) 9-480 Homilies on II Cor.

Studies: H. USENER, Divus Alexander: RhM N.F. 57 (1902) 171-173. — G. H. WHITAKER, Chrysostom on I Cor. 1, 13: JThSt 15 (1914) 254-257. — K. PRÜMM, Der Abschnitt über die Doxa des Apostolats 2 Kor. III, 1-IV, 6 in der Deutung des hl. Johannes Chrysostomus. Eine Untersuchung zur Auslegung des paulinischen Pneuma: Bibl 30 (1949) 161-196, 377-400. — J. RUWET, Origène et l'Apocalypse d'Élie (à propos de 1 Cor. 2, 9): Bibl 30 (1949) 517-519 (Chrysostom's interpretation). — H. A. MUSURILLO, Fragment of a Homily on First Corinthians: Aegyptus (1953) 179-180.

f. Commentary on Galatians

The *Commentary on Galatians* is now in the same form as a modern work, i.e. a running elucidation of the text, verse by verse. Originally, however, like the exegesis of Isaias mentioned above, it must have consisted of a series of homilies, since Chrysostom occasionally addresses his hearers directly. Again we cannot assign an exact date, but it was most probably composed after the homilies on the Epistles to the Corinthians. At any rate Chrysostom was still at Antioch, since he refers to his homily *On the Change of Names* (cf. above, p. 441) as having been preached before the same audience: 'Moreover I partly discussed this subject when I discoursed before you on the change of his name from Saul to Paul;

which, if you have forgotten, you will fully gather from a perusal of that volume' (ch. 1, v. 16 LFC).

Edition: MG 61, 611-682.

Translations: English: Anonym, LFC 6 (1840) 1-98; reprinted: LNPF (1890) 13, 1-45, revised by G. Alexander. — *German:* J. SCHWERTSCHLAGER, BKV 7 (1882) 9-168. — W. STODERL, BKV³ 15 (1936).

g. Homilies on the Epistle to the Ephesians

The 24 homilies on Ephesians disclose their origin in Antioch by the familiar mentioning of St. Babylas in Homily 9 and of St. Julian in Homily 21, 3, both favorite Saints of that city, the latter of whom, according to Theodoret (*Hist. eccl.* 4, 27) visited Antioch on one occasion. In Homily 6 and 13 Chrysostom refers to monastic establishments in the neighboring mountains, and those near Antioch played an important role in his own life as a hermit. Moreover, Homily 11,5 contains an allusion to a schism as existing in the community of his listeners, which must be that of Meletius. Homily 20 is very important for Chrysostom's teaching on marriage. It reads like a moral code for husband and wife and testifies to his ideal concept of Christian matrimony.

Edition: MG 62, 9-176.

Translations: English: W. J. COPELAND, LFC 6 (1840) 99-381; reprinted: LNPF 13 (1890) 46-172, revised by G. Alexander. — *German:* N. LIEBERT, BKV 7 (1882) 169-558. — W. STODERL, BKV³ 15 (1936).

Studies: J. RIVIÈRE, Le sacrifice du Père dans la rédemption: RSR (1939) 1-23 (*Hom. in Eph.* 17, 1). — M. COSTANZA, Waar predikte Sint Chrysostomus zijn vier en twintig homilieën als commentaar op Sint Paulus' brief aan de Ephesiërs?: StC 27 (1952) 145-154 (Homilies 6, 10 and 11 were delivered at Constantinople between Advent of 403 and Easter of 404). — Q. CATAUDELLA, Aristophanes, Plut. 566: Antidoron U.E. Paoli oblatum. Genua, 1956, 73-76 (*Hom. 2 in Epist. ad Eph.* 1).

h. Homilies on Philippians

The 15 homilies on Philippians have been assigned to Antioch by Baur because, he thinks, only there could Chrysostom have had the leisure to compose them. However, there are several references to his responsibilities as a bishop, especially in Homily 9,5, which prove their later origin at Constantinople. Baur believes that the allusion to the reigning monarch in Homily 15 would fit Theodosius and the period at Antioch but not Arcadius and the time when Chrysostom was at Constantinople. 'And has not he', the preacher asks, 'who now rules, from the time he received the crown, been in toil, in danger, in grief, in dejection, in misfortune, exposed to conspiracies?' However, it seems that Chrysostom is thinking here of the weak-minded Arcadius rather than of the victorious Theodosius who overcame all difficulties. Homily 7 on Philippians 2,5-11 is a great defense of the doctrine of the Incarnation against heretics of old and new, Marcionites, Paul of Samosata and Arians. Chrysostom stresses the 'perfect' divinity and the 'perfect' humanity of Christ, the latter consisting of body and soul. 'Let us not then confound or divide the natures. There is one God, there is one Christ, the Son of God; when I say *One*, I mean a union, not a confusion, the one Nature did not degenerate into the other, but was united with it' (LFC).

Edition: MG 62, 177-298.

Translations: English: W. C. COTTON, LFC 14 (1843) 1-179; reprinted: LNPF 13 (1890) 173-255. — *German:* N. LIEBERT, BKV 8 (1883) 9-295. — W. STODERL, BKV² 45 (1924) 7-231.

i. Homilies on the Epistle to the Colossians

The 12 homilies on the Epistle to the Colossians were also written at Constantinople, since the end of the third clearly points to the preacher's episcopal office: 'You do not despise me, but the priesthood; when you see me stripped of this, then despise me; then no more will I endure to impose commands. But so long as we sit upon this throne, so long as we have the first place, we have both the dignity and the power, even though we are unworthy. If the throne of Moses was of such reverence, that for its sake they were to be heard, much more the throne of Christ. It, we have received by succession; from it we speak... Ambassadors, whatever be their sort, because of the dignity of an embassy, enjoy much honor... And we now have received a word of embassy, and we are come from God, for this is the dignity of the Episcopate... We are God's ambassadors to men; but, if this offend you, not we, but the Episcopate itself, not this man or that, but the Bishop' (*Hom.* 3,4 LFC).

Chrysostom must have delivered these homilies on Colossians in 399 because he alludes to the fall of Eutropius which took place in the summer of that year: 'He who was yesterday up high on his tribunal, who had his heralds shouting with thrilling voice, and many to run before, and haughtily clear the way for him through the forum, is to-day mean and low, and of all those things bereft and bare, like dust blast-driven, like a stream that has passed by'. There is no mention of Eutropius' violent death, which seems to indicate that the homily was given shortly after his downfall.

Though there are passages which show Chrysostom at his best, these homilies do not come up to the general level of excellence of the rest. In variety of content, however, they can vie with any. The first discusses the many kinds of friendship among men; the third deals with Col. 1,15-18 and is of Christological importance. The fourth answers the question why Christ did not come earlier into the world. Its close is most instructive with regard to the use of the historical books of the Old Testament. The fifth treats of human reason as unable to comprehend mysteries and insufficient for comprehending things above nature. Though Chrysostom does not by any means rigidly exclude the allegorical interpretation, he seldom gives it as free play as he does here. The sixth describes how Christ by his death blotted out the bond that was against man and then tore it in two. The seventh explains the destructive and regenerative effects of baptism. The eighth demonstrates thankfulness as a great philosophy of life and as equal to a martyrdom if given for injuries we receive from another. The ninth stresses the necessity of reading the Scriptures with earnestness and points out the great use of the Psalms for moral instruction. It urges parents to teach their children the singing of Psalms which will lead to hymns, 'the diviner thing': 'When he has been instructed out of the Psalms, he then will know hymns also, as a diviner thing. For the Powers above chant hymns, not psalms'. The twelfth, condemning the abuses of wedding-feasts, pictures Christ and His angels present at the Christian marriage.

Editions: MG 62, 299-392. — C. PIAZZINO, S. Giovanni Crisostomo, Omelie sulla lettera di S. Paolo ai Colossesi. Testo con versione introd. not. (Corona Patrum Sal., ser. Gr. 6). Turin, 1940.

Translations: English: J. ASHWORTH, LFC 14 (1843) 181-334; reprinted: LNPF 13 (1890) 257-321. — *German:* N. LIEBERT, BKV 8 (1883) 297-533. — W. STODERL, BKV² 45 (1924) 235-419. — *Italian:* C. PIAZZINO, op. cit.

k. Homilies on the two Epistles to the Thessalonians

Chrysostom delivered eleven homilies on the First Epistle to the Thessalonians and five on the Second. These two series belong to his episcopal period at Constantinople because he refers in both to the duties of his high office. Homily 8 on I Thess. he states (4) 'I shall have to answer for this office in which I preside over you' and Homily 4 (3) elaborates the same idea.

Edition: MG 62, 391-500.

Translations: English: J. TWEED, LFC 14 (1843) 385-514; reprinted: LNPF 13 (1890) 323-398. — *German:* B. SEPP, BKV 8 (1883) 573-813.

l. Homilies on the Epistles to Timothy, Titus and Philemon

The 18 homilies on the First Epistle to Timothy and the 10 on the Second seem to have been written at Antioch. He speaks of Timothy's office as bishop again and again without any hint that he was one himself. The large number of solitaries living in the neighborhood of the city, gives him occasion to praise their strict discipline and exemplary devotion as he does in other homilies delivered at Antioch. In Homily 8 on II Timothy 3 he evidently alludes to the burning of the temple of Apollo at Daphne, of which he gives a full account in his Homily on St. Babylas. All these features point to Antioch as the place of origin.

The six homilies on the Epistle to Titus must be placed at Antioch because Daphne and the cave of Matrona mentioned in the third sermon are located near the Syrian capital. The long essay on the burden of a bishop alludes to another, not himself.

The three homilies on the Epistle to Philemon are especially valuable for Chrysostom's ideas on the institution of slavery, which he regarded as an established fact and as a consequence of sin but refused to accept as a law of nature. He proclaims that the Church knows no distinction between bond and free (*Hom.* 1) and encourages in every way manumission by Christian masters (*Hom.* 3). He calls these menials brethren of Christ and demands that they be treated as such (*Hom.* 2). Most probably the homilies on Philemon belong to the same time as those on Timothy and Titus.

Edition: MG 62, 501-662 Timothy, 663-700 Titus, 701-720 Philemon.

Translations: English: J. TWEED, LFC 14 (1843) 1-270 Timothy, 271-331 Titus, 333-363 Philemon; reprinted: LNPF 13 (1890) 407-518 Timothy, 519-543 Titus, 545-557 Philemon. — *German:* J. WIMMER, BKV 9 (1883) 7-403 Timothy, 405-496 Titus, 497-541 Philemon. — A. NÄGELE, BKV³ 16 (1937). — *Polish:* T. SINKO, Homilie na listy pasterskie sw. Pawla i ̇na list do Filemona, prsel. i wstepem opatrzyl. Cracow, 1949.

Studies: A. NÄGELE, Des Johannes Chrysostomus Homilien zu den Timotheus-Briefen des hl. Paulus und die Zeit ihrer Abfassung: ThQ 116 (1935) 117-142.

m. Homilies on the Epistle to the Hebrews

The 34 homilies on Hebrews were composed in the last year of his episcopal office at Constantinople, i.e. in 403/404, because the title states that they were published after his death from stenographic notes by Constantine, a priest of Antioch.

Cassiodorus reports (*Inst.* 1, 8) that his friend Mutianus at his request translated these 34 homilies on Hebrews into Latin.

Though some *catenae* fragments to the Catholic Epistles have been edited under Chrysostom's name (MG 65, 1039-1062), he never wrote commentaries on them. Almost all of these scholia have been found to belong to other treatises of his.

Edition: MG 63, 9-236.

Translations: English: T. KEBLE, LFC 44 (1877); reprinted: LNPF 14 (1889) 335-524 revised by F. Gardiner. — *German:* J. C. MITTERRUTZNER, BKV 10 (1884) 7-510.

Study: S. HAIDACHER, Chrysostomus-Fragmente zu den katholischen Briefen: ZkTh 26 (1902) 190-194.

2. *Dogmatic and Polemical Homilies*

a. *On the Incomprehensible Nature of God*

Among the comparatively small number of dogmatic and polemical works there are 12 homilies in two series *On the Incomprehensible Nature of God*. The first consisting of five sermons, delivered at Antioch about 386-387, attacked the Anomoeans, the most radical of the Arian parties which pretended to know God, as God knows Himself (*Hom.* 2, 3), and maintained not merely the inequality but the dissimilarity of the Son's nature to that of the Father. Their founder was Aetius, but their chief teacher Eunomius, from whom they were also called Eunomians. Chrysostom castigates their blasphemous arrogance which dares to confine God to the limits of human reason and to empty out the mystery of divine essence. He defends the ineffable, inconceivable and incomprehensible nature of God against these rationalistic tendencies, which deny the transcendence of the Christian religion. At the same time he points out the co-equality of the Son with the Father. His sources, besides Scripture, are Philo, Basil the Great and Gregory of Nyssa. His terminology shows the influence of liturgical formulas. The second series of homilies was given at Constantinople in 397 but is not directed against the Anomoeans, although Montfaucon and Migne (48,701-812) list them under the title *Contra Anomoeos*.

Editions: MG 48, 701-812. — R. FLACIÈRE, F. CAVALLERA and J. DANIÉLOU, Jean Chrysostome, Sur l'incompréhensibilité de Dieu (SCH 28). Paris, 1951 (repr. the text of Montfaucon).

Translation: French: R. FLACIÈRE, ibid.

Studies: R. OTTO, Chrysostomus über das Unbegreifliche in Gott: Das ganz Andere. Aufsätze das Numinose betreffend. 4th ed. Gotha, 1929. — G. WUNDERLE, Zur religionsgeschichtlichen Würdigung der fünf Predigten des heiligen Johannes Chrysostomus über das Unbegreifliche in Gott: Festgabe J. Geyser. Regensburg, 1930, 69-82. — A. D'ALÈS, De incomprehensibili chez Jean Chrysostome: RSR (1933) 306-320. — J. DANIÉLOU, L'incompréhensibilité de Dieu d'après saint Jean Chrysostome: RSR 37 (1950) 176-194. — F. CAVALLERA and J. DANIÉLOU, SCH 28 (1951) 7-70. — J. DANIÉLOU, Der καιρός der Messe nach den Homilien des hl. Johannes Chrysostomus über die Unbegreiflichkeit Gottes: Die Messe in der Glaubensverkündigung. Herg. von F. X. Arnold und B. Fischer, 2nd ed. Freiburg i.B., 1953, 71-78.

b. *The Newly Discovered Baptismal Catecheses*

During the twelve years of his preaching at Antioch from 386 to 398 Chrysostom had the office of preparing the catechumens for the reception of the sacrament of Baptism. It was surprising that very little remained of these instructions. We had only two *Catecheses ad illuminandos* in Migne (49,223-240), delivered during Lent 388. In 1909 A. Papadopulos-Kerameus edited for the first time a series of four sermons addressed to candidates of baptism from *Codex Mosqu.* 216 saec. X and *Codex Petrop.* 76 saec. X. The first of these is identical with Migne's first. The liturgy described is that of Antioch. At the end of the third homily Chrysostom asks his listeners to pray for the bishop who will baptize them at Easter and for the priests among whom he numbers himself. Thus it is evident that all four were delivered at Antioch, most probably during Lent 388.

A. Wenger had the good fortune to discover in 1955 a series of eight baptismal catecheses in a manuscript (*Codex* 6) of the monastery of Stavronikita on Mount Athos. He edited them in 1957 and thus greatly enriched our knowledge of the baptismal liturgy of Antioch at the end of the fourth century. They were given shortly after 388, and one of them, the third, is identical with the fourth of Papadopulos-Kerameus, and with the Latin sermon *Ad neophytos* in the appendix of the second volume of Fronton's edition (Paris, 1609 f.), to which Savile, Montfaucon and Migne paid no attention. Since this Latin translation was used by St. Augustine, *Contra Julianum* (1,6,21) in 421, it was made at a very early time and most probably by the deacon Anianus of Celeda.

Editions: MG 49, 223-240. — A. PAPADOPULOS - KERAMEUS, Varia Graeca Sacra. Saint-Pétersbourg, 1909, XX-XXV and 154-183. — A. WENGER, Huit catéchèses baptismales inédites (SCH 50). Paris, 1957.

Translations: English: T. P. BRANDRAM, LNPF 9 (1889) 159-171 (the two found in MG 49, 223-240). — *German:* M. SCHMITZ, BKV 3 (1879) 90-131 (the two in MG 49, 223-240). — *French:* A. WENGER, op. cit. (the newly discovered).

Studies: S. HAIDACHER, Eine unbeachtete Rede des hl. Chrysostomus an Neugetaufte: ZkTh 28 (1904) 168-186. — A. WENGER, La tradition des œuvres de saint Jean Chrysostome. I. Catéchèses inconnues et homélies peu connues: REB 14 (1956) 5-48; *idem*, SCH 50 (1957) 7-107.

c. Homilies against the Jews

The eight homilies against the Jews delivered at Antioch from 386 to 387 were intended chiefly for Chrysostom's Christian listeners and only incidentally for Jews. We gather from them that his Christians were frequenting synagogues, attracted by the charms and amulets in which Jews of the lower class dealt freely. The first Homily warns his audience against the celebration of Trumpets (i.e. the New Year), Tabernacles, and Fasts. The third deals with those who held their Easter with the Jews on the 14th of Nisan, the so-called Protopaschites. All of these sermons try to show that the Jews have rejected the Messias, as the prophets foretold, and that they have been rightly and permanently punished for their treatment of Christ. They reveal, however, that the Jews at that time were still a great social, and even a religious, power in Antioch.

Edition: MG 48, 843-942.

Studies: L. CANET, Pour l'édition de S. Jean Chrysostome Adversus Judaeos: Mélanges d'archéologie et d'histoire de l'École Française de Rome 34 (1914) 97-200 (preparatory studies for a new edition). — M. SIMON, La polémique anti-juive de S. Jean Chrysostome et le mouvement judaïsant d'Antioche: AIPh 4 (1936) 403-421. — J. E. POWELL, A Palimpsest of St. John Chrysostom: JThSt 39 (1938) 132-140. — S. HAIDENTHALER, 'Nachweis der Gottheit Christi'. 'Acht Predigten über alttestamentliches Gesetz und Evangelium'. Linz, 1951. — A. J. VISSER, Johannes Chrysostomus als anti-Joods polemicus: NAKG 40 (1954) 193-206.

3. *Moral Discourses*

Although Chrysostom in all his sermons never forgets his main purpose, the moral betterment of his listeners, he confined himself in a number of discourses exclusively to attacks on superstition and vice. The most famous of such are those *In kalendas* (MG 48,953-962), in which he rebukes on the First of January the debaucheries and superstitious excesses with which the New Year was celebrated. Chrysostom gave this sermon at Antioch because in the introduction he regrets the absence of the bishop.

One of his most powerful denunciations is *Against the Circus Games and the Theatre, Contra circenses ludos et theatra* (56,263-270) with which he addressed his congregation at Constantinople on July 3, 399, when he found half of his church empty because many of his flock had gone to the circus. He voices his indignation that chariot races were being held even on Good Friday and a performance given in the theatre on Holy Saturday.

In his eyes the theatre is an 'assembly of Satan'; its temptations are described in the *Homiliae 3 de diabolo* (MG 49,241-276) which must be assigned to his Antiochene period. The *Homiliae 9 de poenitentia* (49,277-350) were preached at different times and only later combined into the present series, except for the seventh, which belongs to Severian of Gabala, as C. Martin has shown.

Translations: German: M. SCHMITZ, BKV 3 (1879) 8-28 (*In kalendas*). — J. C. MITTERRUTZNER, BKV 1 (1890) 347-490 (*Homiliae 9 de poenitentia*).

Studies: C. MARTIN, Une homélie De poenitentia de Sévérien de Gabala: RHE 26 (1930) 331-343. — G. J. THEOCHARIDES, Beiträge zur Geschichte des byzantinischen Profantheaters im 4. und 5. Jahrhundert hauptsächlich auf Grund der Predigten des Johannes Chrysostomos, Patriarchen von Konstantinopel. Diss. Munich, 1940. — P. M. STRIEDL, Antiker Volksglaube bei Johannes Chrysostomus. Diss. Würzburg, 1948 (typ.). — G. TRAVERSARI, Tetimimo e colimbètra. Ultime manifestazioni del teatro antico (in Chrysost.): Dioniso (1950) 18-35. — B. WYSS, Johannes Chrysostomos und der Aberglaube (Festschrift K. Meuli): Schweizer Archiv für Volkskunde 47 (1951) 262-274. — B. H. VANDENBERGHE, Saint Jean Chrysostome et les spectacles (with English summary): ZRG 7 (1955) 34-46.

Chrysostom's keen sense of social justice was shocked by the violent contrasts of wealth and poverty in both Antioch and Constantinople. He estimates (*In Act. Ap. Hom.* 11,3) the number of the poor in Constantinople at about 50,000 and the Christian population at 100,000. While he constantly upraids the rich for their selfish indifference to the fate of their less fortunate brethren, he never forgets to insist on the duty of almsgiving. This topic returns so often in his sermons that he has been called 'St. John the Almsgiver'. His discourse *De eleemosyna* (51,261-272) provides a detailed interpretation of the passage I Cor. 16,1-4, while *De futurorum deliciis et praesentium vilitate* (MG 51,347-354) is directed against the materialistic outlook of the people.

Translations: English: F. ALLEN, Four Discourses of Chrysostom chiefly on the Parable of the Rich Man and Lazarus. London, 1869. — M. M. SHERWOOD, Sermon on Alms by Saint John Chrysostom. New York, 1917. — *German:* M. SCHMITZ, BKV 3 (1879) 239-261 (*On Alms*), 3 (1879) 262-297 (*On the Rich Man and Lazarus*). — *Italian:* M. PELLEGRINO and G. CRIS, S. Giovanni Crisostomo, Ricchezza e povertà. Siena, 1938 (8 homilies).

Studies: A. CARILLO DE ALBORNOZ, Aspectos sociales del s. IV a través de las obras de Juan Crisóstomo: RF (1933) 204-217, 507-525. — E. F. BRUCK, Die Gesinnung des Schenkens bei Johannes Chrysostomus: Mnemosyna Pappoulia. Athens, 1934, 65-83; *idem*, Kirchlich-soziales Erbrecht in Byzanz. Johannes Chrysostomus und die Mazedonischen Kaiser: Studi Riccobono III. Palermo, 1933, 377-423. — A. CARILLO DE ALBORNOZ, Mas sobre el comunismo de San Juan Crisóstomo: RF 110 (1936) 80-98. — E. F. BRUCK, Ethics versus Law. St. Paul, The Fathers of the Church and the 'Cheerful Giver' in Roman Law: Traditio 2 (1944) 97-121. — S. GIET, La doctrine de l'appropriation des biens chez quelques-uns des Pères: RSR (1948) 55-91. — I. K. CONEVSKI, Social Ideas in the Church Fathers I. St. John Chrysostom. (in Greek) Sofia, 1948; cf. BZ 50 (1957) 232. — R. MEHRLEIN, De avaritia quid iudicaverit Johannes Chrysostomus. Diss. Bonn, 1951 (typ.). — A. SODANO, I beni terreni nella vita dei giusti secondo San Giovanni Crisostomo. Brescia, 1955. — E. F. BRUCK, Kirchenväter und soziales Erbrecht. Berlin, 1956, 21-29.

4. Sermons for Liturgical Feasts

Among the festal discourses none has been more discussed than the Christmas sermon *In diem natalem D.N. Jesu Christi* of December 25, 386 (MG 49,351-362). Its purpose is to demonstrate that the 25th of December is the real birthday of the Lord, the Sun of Justice. Chrysostom states that this feast had become known to the people of Antioch less than ten years previously — a very interesting sidelight on the history of Christmas in the East. The authenticity of a second Christmas sermon (MG 56,385-396) hitherto regarded doubtful, has been recently defended by C. Martin; the Epiphany address *De baptismo Christi et Epiphania* (MG 49,363-372), most probably given on January 6, 387, seems to be genuine. The two homilies for Maundy Thursday *De proditione Judae* (MG 49,373-392) are only different recensions of the same work; the third (MG 50,715-720) is perhaps spurious. Three Good Friday sermons survive; one *De coemeterio et cruce* and two *De cruce et latrone* (MG 49,393-418). The latter represent most probably the same homily in two different editions. Whereas Chrysostom in his Maundy Thursday instructions deals with the institution of the Lord's Supper and the treason of Judas, his Good Friday utterances expound the Holy Cross and the death of the Savior. The liturgy of Good Friday at Antioch took place in the Martyrium outside the city in the great cemetery since Christ was crucified outside Jerusalem, as Chrysostom explains. This custom was supposed also to be a reminder that those buried in the surrounding graves awaited the eternal resurrection. The services lasted all day and the greater part of the night. Of the two Easter sermons (MG 50,433-442, and 52,765-772) the first is entitled *Contra ebriosos et de resurrectione*, and the second of doubtful origin. Of the two Ascension discourses (MG 50,441-452, and 52,773-792), only the first seems to be genuine, whereas the two Pentecost sermons (MG 50,453-470) are both authentic.

Translations: German: M. SCHMITZ, BKV 3 (1879) 29-54 (Christmas sermon); 3, 55-72 (Epiphany sermon); 3, 132-155 (*De proditione Judae*); 3, 156-185 (Easter sermon); 3, 186-204 (Ascension sermon); 3, 205-227, 228-238 (2 Pentecost sermons).

Studies: A. BAUMSTARK, Die Zeit der Einführung des Weihnachtsfestes in Konstantinopel: OC 2 (1902) 441-446. — K. LÜBECK, Die Einführung des Weihnachtsfestes in Konstantinopel: HJG 28 (1907) 109-118. — H. USENER, Das Weihnachtsfest. 2nd ed. Bonn, 1911, 379-384. — C. ÉMÉREAU, Mélanges de philologie byzantine: EO (1921) 295-300 (Christmas sermon). — E. MAHLER, Zur Chronologie der Predigten wegen der Weihnachtsfeier: OLZ 24 (1921) 59-63 (Christmas sermon should be dated 387). — P. RADO, Die Ps.-Chrysostomische Homilie εἰς τὴν Χριστοῦ γέννησιν: ZkTh 56 (1932) 82-83. — C. MARTIN, Un discours prétendument inédit de S. Cyrille d'Alexandrie sur l'Ascension: RHE (1936) 345-350 (this Ascension sermon found among the *Spuria* should be attributed to Eusebius of Alexandria); *idem*, Un centon d'extraits de l'homélie in Salvatoris Nostri Jesu Christi Nativitatem de saint Jean Chrysostome: Mus 54 (1941) 30-33, 48-52 (The Christmas sermon MG 56, 385-394 is genuine; Greek text: 48-52). — R. V. SCHODER, St. Chrysostom and the Date of Christ's Nativity: ThSt 3 (1942) 140-144. — M. M. BEYENKA, Cemetery, a Word of Consolation: Classical Bulletin 28 (1951) 34 (*De coemeterio et cruce* 1). — For Easter sermons of Pseudo-Chrysostom, see: P. NAUTIN, Homélies Pascales I (SCH 27), II (SCH 36), III (SCH 48). Paris, 1950, 1953, 1957. — E. BICKERSTETH, John Chrysostom and the Early History of the Hypapante: Studi Biz. e Neoell. 8 (1953) 401-404, argues that the inedited homily on the Feast of the Purification is authentic. — A. WENGER, Notes inédites sur les empereurs Théodose I, Arcadius, Théodose II, Léon: REB 10 (1953) 47-59 (Cod. Sinait. Gr. 494 contains the concluding part of an Epiphany sermon attributed to Chrysostom and dated 402; first edition). — C. BAUR, Drei unedierte Festpredigten aus der Zeit der nestorianischen Streitigkeiten: Traditio 9 (1953) 101-126 (Codex Berolinensis

77 — Phillips 1481, saec. XII — contains an Easter sermon and two Ascension sermons falsely attributed to Chrysostom; they belong, if not to Nestorius himself, to a theologian of Antioch; first critical edition and commentary). — C. MOHRMANN, Note sur l'homélie pascale VI de la collection pseudo-chrysostomienne dite Des petites trompettes: Mélanges M. Andrieu. Strasbourg, 1957, 351-360. — J. BAUER, A propos d'un passage à corriger de l'homélie pascale VI de la collection pseudo-chrysostomienne: VC 13 (1959) 184-186.

5. *Panegyrics*

Chrysostom delivered a great number of panegyrics on the Saints of the Old Testament like Job, Eleazar, the Macchabees and their mother, on some martyrs like Romanus, Julian, Barlaam, Pelagia, Berenice, Prosdoce, and on martyrs in general. Of special interest are those on the holy bishops of Antioch Ignatius, Babylas, Philogonius, Eustathius and Meletius. That on his teacher Diodore of Tarsus was delivered in 392 in the latter's presence.

But none of his encomia has won a greater reputation than the *Homiliae 7 de laudibus S. Pauli*, in which he gives enthusiastic expression to his unbounded admiration of the Apostle of the Gentiles. Anianus of Celeda who translated them into Latin between 415 to 419, says that the great Apostle is not only portrayed but in a certain sense awakened from the dead, so that he becomes once more a living pattern of Christian perfection. In the opening panegyric Chrysostom praises him as the synthesis of all virtues and compares him to the great figures of the Old Testament from Abel to John the Baptist, only to conclude that he surpasses each in his peculiar excellence. In the second he demonstrates that St. Paul has shown by his example to what extraordinary heights frail human nature can rise. The third describes the obstacles which the Apostle overcame by his boundless courage and inexhaustible charity. The fourth deals with his conversion on the road to Damascus. Chrysostom compares Paul's reaction to God's calling with that of the Jews as a people, who have remained obdurate in their unbelief though they have witnessed many miracles. The fifth describes the Apostle's frailties over which he triumphed so gloriously and the sixth discusses his fear of death, in which, apparently, some had seen a defect. Chrysostom explains that symptoms of physical aversion do not dimm the lustre of true courage; the resolution of the soul is what counts. The last panegyric contrasts the standard-bearer of an ordinary army with Saint Paul, the standard-bearer of the crucified Lord and Heavenly King, who carried the Cross emblazoned on his banner through the whole world.

Editions: The panegyrics on the Saints are all found in MG 50; those on St. Paul: MG 50, 473-514.

Translations: English: T. P. Brandram, LNPF 9 (1889) 141-143 *On St. Babylas*, 135-140 *On St. Ignatius.* — *German:* M. Schmitz, BKV 3 (1879) 298-387 seven homilies on St. Paul; 3, 388-400 panegyric *On All Holy Martyrs..*

Studies: T. E. Ameringer, The Stylistic Influence of the Second Sophistic on the Panegyrical Sermons of St. John Chrysostom (PSt 5). Washington, 1921. — H. M. Hubbell, chrysostom and Rhetoric: CPh 19 (1924) 261-276. — A. Bartolozzi, Le due omelie Crisostomiane sul martire S. Romano: Studi P. Ubaldi. Milan, 1937, 125-132. — M. Simonetti, Sulla struttura dei Panegyrici di S. Giovanni Crisostomo: RIL 86 (1953) 159-180.

6. Occasional Discourses

a. The First Sermon

We still possess Chrysostom's first sermon that he delivered on the occasion of his elevation to the priesthood at the beginning of 386. He states in so many words that this is his first homily and he dedicates it to God who gave him tongue and speech. He thanks the then bishop of Antioch (Flavian) for having him ordained and praises him for his truly apostolic spirit. He asks the congregation to pray that he himself may be a good priest.

Edition: MG 48, 693-700.

Translation: German: M. Schmitz, BKV 3 (1879) 401-414.

b. Homilies on the Statues

The most famous among his occasional discourses are the *Homiliae 21 de statuis ad populum Antiochenum*. They rank among the finest achievements of his eloquence and challenge comparison with the noblest monuments of this art. The statues of the Emperor Theodosius and the Imperial family had been thrown down and mutilated by a mob at Antioch in 387 in a sedition occasioned by the imposition of an extraordinary tax. Theodosius felt so outraged as to consider destroying the city entirely. The aged bishop Flavian went to Constantinople to beg the Emperor's forgiveness. As the people were fluctuating between hope and fear, Chrysostom delivered these homilies *On the Statues*, which give us a vivid picture of those days of terror marked by numerous executions. He exerts all his powers to console and encourage the vast crowds that thronged the churches but seizes the opportunity to castigate at the same time the vices and offences that had brought down God's wrath upon them. In the final address given on Easter Sunday he was able to announce that Bishop Flavian's efforts were crowned with success and that the Emperor had granted a complete pardon to his people. Chrysostom proved himself a real guide and father of his fold in this crisis and his sense of responsibility is as admirable as his profound sympathy and passionate sincerity. Delivered at the beginning of his presbyterate these courageous homilies *On the Statues* made his name as an orator.

Editions: MG 49, 15-222. — *Separate ed.* of the 21st homily: L. DE SINNER, Paris, 1842. — E. SOMMER, Paris, 1856 (and later editions). — E. RAGON. Paris, 1887.

Translations: English: C. MARRIOTT, LFC 9 (1842); reprinted: LNPF 9 (1889) 317-489, revised by W. R. W. Stephens. — *German:* J. C. MITTERRUTZNER, BKV 2 (1874) 1-432. — J. OTEO, Las XXI Homilias sobre las Estatuas de San Juan Crisóstomo (Colección Excelsa, T. 19 y 20). Madrid, 1945/1946.

Studies: R. GOEBEL, De Ioannis Chrysostomi et Libanii orationibus quae sunt de seditione Antiochensium. Diss. Göttingen, 1910. — M. A. BURNS, St. John Chrysostom's Homilies on the Statues: A Study of their Rhetorical Qualities and Form (PSt 22). Washington, 1930. — M. SOFFRAY, Recherches sur la syntaxe de saint Jean Chrysostome d'après les Homélies sur les statues (Coll. G. Budé). Paris, 1939.

c. Two Homilies on Eutropius

Eutropius after his fall from power in the beginning of 399 escaped death only by a hasty flight to the church where he claimed the right of asylum, the very privilege that shortly before he had himself tried to curtail. On the following Sunday, January 17, 399, as he clung pitifully to the altar, Chrysostom, preaching on the text 'Vanity of vanities and all is vanity', delivered a touching address on the transitoriness of earthly glory as illustrated by the fall of Eutropius. A few days later, when the latter had left the church and had been banished to Cyprus, Chrysostom in a second homily denies the rumor that he had been betrayed by the ecclesiastical authorities.

Editions: MG 52, 391-414. — *Separate ed.* of the first homily: F. DÜBNER and E. LEFRANC. Paris, 1855 (and later editions). — E. SOMMER. Paris, 1858 (and later editions). — J. H. VÉRIN. Paris, 1875 (and later editions). — J. G. BEANE. Paris, 1893. — R. CASTELLI. Verona, 1899.

Translations: English: W. R. W. STEPHENS, LNPF 9 (1889) 245-265. — *German:* M. SCHMITZ, BKV 3 (1879) 427-438. — *Italian:* F. FANTIN, Discorso in favore di Eutropio. Livorno, 1928. — F. PINI, San Giovanni Crisostomo, Per Eutropio. Brescia, 1948. — *Spanish:* J. MUNDÓ, Defensa de Eutropio de San Juan Crisóstomo (Obras escogidas de Patrologia griega). Madrid, 1910. — *Dutch:* W. BILDERDIJK, Chrysostomus' Rede op Eutropius. Uitgeg. door J. Heyrmans. Louvain and Amsterdam, 1910.

Studies: T. BIRT, Zwei politische Satiren des alten Rom, 1888, 36ff., 55ff., 112ff. — R. CASTELLI, Il poema di Claudiano 'In Eutropium' e l'omelia di S. Giovanni Crisostomo Εἰς Εὐτρόπιον, Parallelo. Verona, 1899. — J. BERNARDI, La formule Ποῦ εἰσιν: saint Jean Chrysostome a-t-il imité saint Grégoire de Nazianze?: SP I (TU 63). Berlin 1957, 177-181 (*On Eutrop.* 1, 1 MG 52, 392).

d. Sermons before and after Exile

Intimately connected with his own tragedy are the two sermons which Chrysostom delivered on the eve of his first exile in 403 and on the day after his return from it. In the first (MG 52,427-430) he undertook to pacify the enraged populace by a splendid discourse on the invincibility of the Church and on the inseparable union of the head and members. In the second (MG 52,443-448) which is known to Sozomen (*Hist. eccl.* 8,18,8) he thanks the multitude for its loyalty and praises the chastity and love of his bride, the Church of Constantinople, who in his absence repulsed all seducers.

Translation: German: M. SCHMITZ, BKV 3 (1879) 415-421 (on the eve of his first exile); 422-426 (after his return).

2. *Treatises*

1. *De sacerdotio*

No work of Chrysostom is better known and none has been more frequently translated and printed more often than his six books *On the Priesthood*. Only a few years after his death Isidore of Pelusium declared 'No one has read this volume without feeling his heart inflamed with the love of God. It sets forth how venerable and how difficult is the office of the priesthood, and it shows how to fulfil it as it ought to be fulfilled. For John, bishop of Byzantium, that wise interpreter of the divine mysteries, the light of the whole Church, composed that work with so much skill and accuracy, that they who fulfil the priestly office as God desires, and they who fulfil it with negligence, find in it their virtues and faults portrayed' (*Ep.* 1, 156). To the mind of Suidas (*Lex.* 1,1023) it surpasses all the other writings of Chrysostom in sublimity of thought, purity of diction, smoothness and elegance of style. In fact, it has ever been regarded as a classic on the priesthood and one of the finest treasures of Patristic literature.

The work itself does not furnish any clue to its date. Socrates (*Hist. eccl.* 6,3) assigns it to the period of his deaconship (381-386). At any rate, in the year 392 Jerome read it (*De vir. ill.* 129). The treatise takes the form of a dialogue between Chrysostom and his friend Basil, in which the former tries to justify his conduct on the occasion of their election as bishops about 373. Basil had informed Chrysostom that he was ready to follow whatever course he should adopt, either in declining or submitting to such a dignity but requested that there should be concerted action. Leaving his companion under the impression that he agreed to this suggestion, Chrysostom fled from the burden without disclosing his resolution to him. Meanwhile Basil was told by others that Chrysostom had accepted and was thus induced to do the same. When he found out that he had been deceived by Chrysostom, he felt deeply hurt.

The closing chapters of the first book describe Basil's indignation and the beginnings of Chrysostom's defense which turns into a discussion of the priesthood in its highest grade, the episcopal office. In the second book he continues this defense proving that his policy was for the good of his friend and of his flock which obtained such a good shepherd in him. He himself had shrunk from the charge because such an office requires a great and noble soul and is full of difficulty and danger. It was not to insult the electors that he fled but because he was deeply conscious of his frailty. Basil's virtue and ardent charity make him eminently fit for this high dignity, though he will never admit it. In the third book Chrysostom refutes those who suspect that he declined from pride and from vainglory showing that they have no true conception of the priest. This leads him, in one of the finest passages, to discourse on the greatness of the priesthood:

> For the office of the priesthood is executed upon earth, yet it ranks amongst things that are heavenly, and with good reason. For it was neither an angel nor an archangel nor any other created power, but the Paraclete Himself that established that ministry, and commanded that men yet abiding in the flesh should imitate the functions of angels. Wherefore it behooves the priest to be as pure as if he stood in heaven itself amidst those Powers... Picture to yourself Elias, and the immense multitude standing around, and the victim laid on the altar, and all in stillness and deep silence, while the prophet alone prays; and the fire forthwith descends from heaven upon the altar. Then pass from thence to the sacrifice which is now offered, and you will behold what is not only wonderful, but what exceeds all admiration. For the priest stands bringing down not fire, but the Holy Ghost, and he prays long not that fire may descend from heaven and consume the oblation, but that grace may descend upon the victim, and through it inflame the souls of all and render them brighter than silver fire-tried...

> For if you consider what it is for a man yet clothed in flesh and blood to approach that pure and blessed nature, you will easily understand to what dignity the grace of the Holy Ghost has raised priests. For by them these things are accomplished, and others not inferior to these pertaining to our redemption and salvation. For they who have their abode and sojourn upon earth have been entrusted with a heavenly ministry and have received a power which God has not granted to angels or archangels. For it was not said to them, 'Whatsoever you shall bind on earth, shall be bound also in heaven, and whatsoever you shall loose, shall be loosed' (Matth. 18,18). They who rule on earth have the power of binding, but they can bind the body only. But this bond reaches to the soul itself, and transcends the heavens; and what priests do upon earth God ratifies above, and the master confirms the sentence of his servants...

> It is to priests that spiritual birth and regeneration by baptism is

entrusted. By them we put on Christ, and are united to the Son of God, and become members of that blessed head. Hence we should regard them as more august than princes and kings, and more venerable than parents. For the latter begot us of blood and the will of the flesh, but priests are the cause of our generation from God, of our spiritual regeneration, of our true freedom and sonship according to grace (3,4-6).

All this serves to prove that nobody should be blamed for fleeing such a high dignity. Even St. Paul trembled and was awe-struck when he considered the priesthood. The reason is that a priest has to be exceptionally virtuous and holy. Ambition especially should be banished from his mind. He should be most wise and prudent, cautious and clear-sighted, patient and enduring, even when he is blamed and insulted. If this holds for a simple priest, all the more for a bishop.

Book four deals with the terrible fate of those who enter the clerical state though conscious of their unworthiness and of those who against their will are forced to accept it though they lack the necessary qualifications especially that of preaching. In order to be a good preacher, the priest must be equipped with the knowledge required to meet the attacks of all Greeks, Jews and heretics, especially of the Manichaeans and the followers of Valentinus, Marcion, Sabellius and Arius. A shining example in this respect is St. Paul, who was remarkable not only for his miracles but also for his eloquence.

Book five could be called a manual for preachers because here the author discusses the great labor and diligence which they must devote to their office as well as the dangers involved in it. A good preacher must despise flattery, if he is successful, and should not yield to envy, if others gain greater applause than himself. His first aim should be to please God. Unfavorable criticism and lack of appreciation should not disturb him.

Book six contrasts the active and contemplative life. It is very interesting to note that Chrysostom who was always full of praise for the latter and lived several years as a solitary, here gives preference to the former, because it demands a far greater magnanimity of soul. The difficulties and dangers of the monastic life cannot be compared with those of the priestly apostolate. The life of a monk is not such a proof of virtue as that of a good prelate. It is far easier to save one's own soul than those of others. Priests are accountable even for the sins of others while monks have to answer only for their own. Thus the former require far greater perfection than the latter. For all these reasons Chrysostom feels unequal to the responsibilities and perils of the episcopal office.

The historical occasion of the dialogue as set forth in the first book and even the dialogue form itself seem to be more fiction than fact and serve only to provide a setting for the author's main theme — the greatness and responsibilities of the priesthood. All attempts to identify the Basil of the dialogue have so far remained unsuccessful. He is never mentioned in any of Chrysostom's works, not even in his letters. Basil the Great, Basil of Seleucia and Basil of Raphanea have been suggested and the last-named preferred, but it remains strange that there is not the slightest trace in any of Chrysostom's subsequent writings and correspondence of so intimate a friendship. Neither Palladius nor Socrates mentions the incident of Basil's election and consecration. It seems that in the introductory narrative and in the treatise Chrysostom took as his literary model Gregory of Nazianzus' *Or. II De fuga* (cf. above, p. 243) in which he defends his flight from the priesthood. There are many details even in the treatment of the subject in which Chrysostom seems to be indebted to Gregory though he surpasses him in depth of thought and sublimity of tone.

Editions: MG 47, 623-692. — *Separate ed.*: J. A. NAIRN, CPT 4. Cambridge, 1906 (remains the best of all existing editions). — S. COLOMBO, San Giovanni Crisostomo. Dialogo del sacerdozio, testo, versione, note (Corona Patr. Sal.). Turin, 1934.

Translations: English: W. R. W. STEPHENS, LNPF 9 (1889) 33-83. — H. HOLLIER. London, 1728. — S. RICHARDSON. London, 1759. — H. M. MASON. Philadelphia, 1826. — F. W. HOHLER. Cambridge, 1837. — E. G. MARSH. London, 1844. — B. H. COWPER, London, 1866. — T. A. MOXON, (SPCK). London, 1907. — P. BOYLE, 2nd ed. Dublin, 1910. — W. A. JURGENS, The Priesthood. A Translation of the Περὶ ἱερωσύνης of St. John Chrysostom. New York, 1955. — *German:* G. WOHLENBERG, Bibliothek theol. Klassiker 29. Gotha, 1890. — J. C. MITTERRUTZNER, BKV 1 (1890) 16-148. — A. NAEGLE, BKV² 27 (1916) 97-251. — *French:* F. MARTIN, S. Jean Chrysostome. Dialogue sur le sacerdoce. Trad. nouv. avec notes. Paris, 1932. — B. H. VANDENBERGHE, St. Jean Chrysostome, Dialogue sur le sacerdoce. Version nouvelle. Namur, 1958. — *Italian:* S. COLOMBO, op. cit. — E. NEGRIN, S. Giovanni Crisostomo. Del sacerdozio. Vicenza, 1931. — R. TONNI, S. Giov. Cr., Il dialogo del sacerdozio. Alba, 1942. — *Spanish:* D. RUIZ BUENO, San Juan Crisóstomo. Los seis libros sobre el Sacerdocio (Colección Excelsa 17). Madrid, 1945. — *Dutch:* F. VERMUYTEN, Johannes Chrysostomus. Over het priesterschap, 2nd ed. Tongerloo, 1941. — *Polish:* W. KANIA, Jana Chryzostoma, O kapłaństwie. Posnań, 1949.

Studies: J. VOLK, Die Schutzrede des Gregor von Nazianz und die Schrift über das Priestertum von Johannes Chrysostomus: Zeitschrift für praktische Theologie 17 (1895) 56-63 (historical situation fictitious). — A. COGNET, De Ioannis Chrys. dialogo qui inscribitur Περὶ ἱερωσύνης λόγοι ἕξ (thèse). Paris, 1900. — J. A. NAIRN, On the Text of the De sacerdotio of St. Chrysostom: JThSt 7 (1906) 575-590. — S. COLOMBO, Il prologo del Περὶ ἱερωσύνης di S. Giovanni Crisostomo: Didaskaleion 1 (1912) 39-47. — A. NÄGELE, Zeit und Veranlassung der Abfassung des Chrysostomus-Dialogs De sacerdotio: HJG 37 (1916) 1-48 (dialogue form fictitious and Basil no historical person). — J. STIGLMAYR, Die historische Unterlage der Schrift des heiligen Chrysostomus über das Priestertum: ZkTh 41 (1917) 413-449 (against Naegle). — A. KULEMANN, Das christliche Lebensideal des Chrysostomus auf Grund seiner Schrift Περὶ ἱερωσύνης.

Berlin, 1924. — C. BAUR, Chrysostomus De sacerdotio: ThGl 18 (1926) 569-576. — F. P. KARNTHALER, Die Einleitung zu Johannes Chrysostomus: Über das Priestertum: eine comparatio: BNJ 9 (1932/1933) 36-38. — W. A. MAAT, A Rhetorical Study of St. John Chrysostom's De sacerdotio (PSt 71). Washington, 1944. — F. OGARA, La homilia intitulada De sacerdotio liber septimus: Greg 27 (1946) 145-155. — W. KANIA, Ideal kaplana wedlug sw. Jana Chryzostoma: Ateneum Kaplanskie, 46 (1947) 105-130. — T. SINKO, De inventione, tempore, consilio librorum De sacerdotio S. Johannis Chrysostomi: AIPh 9 (1949) 531-545 (time of composition perhaps 404).

2. On Monastic Life

Several treatises are devoted to the defense of the ascetic life. The earliest are the *Paraeneses ad Theodorum lapsum* (MG 47,277-316), two exhortations to his friend Theodore, later bishop of Mopsuestia, who had yielded to the charms of a certain Hermione and grown weary of the monastic life (cf. above, p. 401). Only the first of these has the conventional form, the other that of an epistle. Both date from the time when Chrysostom himself was still an anchorite. To the same period belong the two books *De compunctione* (περὶ κατανύξεως) (47,393-422), book I addressed to the monk Demetrius, book II to the monk Stelechius. Chrysostom here shows the nature and need of genuine compunction.

The three books *Adversus oppugnatores vitae monasticae* attack the enemies of monasticism, refute their accusations and try to persuade the Christian fathers to send their sons to the monks for their higher education and moral training (MG 47,319-386). The entire work, composed between 378 and 385, is reminiscent of popular philosophy and rhetoric. The parallel drawn between a monk and a king which occurs in the second book (6) goes back to a Stoic commonplace and is more fully developed in the short essay *Comparatio regis et monachi* (MG 47,387-392) which forms a Christian counterpart to Plato's 'comparison between a philosopher and a tyrant' in the ninth book of his *Politeia*.

Translations: English: W. R. W. STEPHENS, LNPF 9 (1889) 87-116 (*Ad Theodorum lapsum*). — R. BLACKBURN, LNPF 9 (1889) 147-155 (*De compunctione*). — *German:* J. FLUCK, Die ascetischen Schriften des hl. Johannes Chrysostomus. Freiburg i.B., 1864, 7-103 (*Adversus oppugnatores vitae monasticae*); 107-114 (*Comparatio regis et monachi*). — J. C. MITTERRUTZNER, BKV 1 (1890) 283-345 (*Ad Theodorum lapsum*). — *French:* P. E. LEGRAND, S. Jean Chrysostome, Contre les détracteurs de la vie monastique. Exhortations à Théodore. Paris, 1933. — *Spanish:* L. DEL PARAMO, Tratados de San Juan Crisóstomo contra los perseguidores de los que inducen a otros a abrazarse con la vida monastica (Obras escogidas de Patrologia griega T. II). Barcelona, 1918. — D. RUIZ BUENO, Tratados asceticos. Texto griego, versión española y notas (Obras de San Juan Crisóstomo). Madrid, 1958.

Studies: S. HAIDACHER, Eine interpolierte Stelle in des hl. Chrysostomus Büchlein ad Demetrium monachum: ZkTh 18 (1894) 405-411 (*De compunctione*). — P. UBALDI, Di due citazioni di Platone in G. Crisostomo: RFIC 28 (1900) 69-75 (*Adversus oppugnatores*). — W. Heffing, Eine arabische Version der zweiten Paraenesis des Johannes Chrysostomus an den Mönch Theodorus: OC N.S. 12/14 (1925) 71-98. — C. Fabricius, Vier Libaniusstellen bei Johannes Chrysostomus: SO 33 (1957) 135-136 (*Comparatio regis et monachi* influenced by Libanius). — G. Jouassard, Ad Theodorum lapsum: HJG 77 (1958) 140-150 (Theod. of Mopsuestia is not the addressee).

3. *On Virginity and Widowhood*

The book *De virginitate* (MG 48,533-596) is mostly (ch. 24-84) a detailed interpretation of the words of the Apostle (I Cor. 7,38) that marriage is good but virginity better, so that Chrysostom refers to this work in his Homilies on First Corinthians (19,6) delivered later at Antioch.

Soon after he became patriarch of Constantinople (397) Chrysostom issued two pastoral letters which both deal with the problem of the *Syneisaktoi* or so-called *virgines subintroductae*, i.e. both men and women ascetics dwelling under one roof. The first *Adversus eos qui apud se habent virgines subintroductas* (MG 47,495-514) is addressed to the clerics and condemns the custom followed by some priests of having consecrated virgins in their homes to keep house for them, pretending to live with them as sisters in devotion. The second *Quod regulares feminae viris cohabitare non debeant* (MG 47, 513-532) insists that canonical women *(αἱ κανονικαί)* must not have men residing permanently with them under the same roof. Chrysostom admits that there has been no great amount of actual wrongdoing, but points out that scandal must inevitably arise. Though the two treatises breathe an apostolic zeal for a reform of the clergy, their language is often harsh and biting, comparing such houses even with brothels. Palladius mentions that 'this caused great indignation to those among the clergy who were without the love of God, and blazing with passion' (19).

The brief treatise *Ad viduam iuniorem* (MG 48,399-410), probably written about 380, seeks to console a young widow for the loss of her spouse Therasius, and the tract *De non iterando coniugio*, which advises widows in general to remain as they are (I Cor. 7,40), often printed as an appendix to the foregoing, is most probably of the same date.

Edition: New crit. ed.: J. Dumortier, S. Jean Chrysostome, Les cohabitations suspectes. Comment observer la virginité (Nouv. Coll. de Textes et Doc.). Paris, 1955.

Translations: English: W. R. W. Stephens, LNPF 9 (1889) 119-128 *(Letter to a young widow).* — *German:* J. Fluck, Die ascetischen Schriften des hl. Johannes Chrysostomus. Freiburg i.B., 1864, 117-145 *(Adversus eos qui apud se habent virgines subintroductas);* 149-174 *(Quod regulares feminae);* 177-277 *(De virginitate);* 283-298 *(Ad viduam iuniorem);* 299-312 *(De non iterando coniugio).* — J. C. Mitterrutzner, BKV 1 (1890) 149-282 *(De virginitate).* — *French:* F. Martin, S. Jean Chrysostome, Discours sur le mariage; Lettre à une jeune veuve. Paris, 1933 *(De non iterando coniugio; Ad viduam iuniorem).*

— *Spanish:* B. VIZMANOS, Las Virgenes cristianas de la primitiva Iglesia. Estudio historico y antologia patristica (BAC). Madrid, 1949, 1173-1272 (S. Juan Cris., Sobre la virginidad).

Studies: A. MOULARD, Saint Jean Chrysostome, le défenseur du mariage et l'apôtre de la virginité. Paris, 1923. — K. BÖCKENHOFF - R. STAPPER, Gedanken aes hl. Johannes Chrysostomus über Fragen der Sexualpädagogik: Vierteljahrsschrift für wissenschaftliche Pädagogik 2 (1926) 174-188. — J. STIGLMAYR, Zur Aszese des hl. Chrysostomus: ZAM 4 (1929) 29-49. — C. BAUR, Der Weg der christlichen Vollkommenheit nach der Lehre des hl. Johannes Chrysostomus: ThGl 20 (1928) 26-41. — L. MEYER, Perfection chrétienne et vie solitaire dans la pensée de St. Jean Chrysostome: RAM 14 (1933) 232-262; *idem*, Liberté et moralisme chrétien dans la doctrine spirituelle de St. Jean Chrysostome: RSR 23 (1933) 283-305; *idem*, St. Jean Chrysostome, maître de perfection chrétienne. Paris, 1933, 229-267. — J. Jean Chrysostome: Études Carmélitaines 21 (1936) 245-284. — G. BRUNNER, Die Zeit der Abfassung der Schrift Ad viduam iuniorem des hl. Johannes Chrysostomus: ZkTh 65 (1941) 32-35 (composed about the end of May, 392). — J. DUMORTIER, Le mariage dans les milieux d'Antioche et de Byzance d'après saint Jean Chrysostome: Lettres d'humanité 6 (Paris, 1946) 102-166. — J. DUMORTIER, La tradition manuscrite des traités de saint Jean Chrysostome adressés aux moines et aux vierges: Contra eos qui subintroductas habent, Quod regulares feminae viris cohabitare non debeant: Actes du Congrès de l'Association G. Budé, Grenoble 1948. Paris, 1949, 151-152 (summary); *idem*, La date des deux traités de saint Jean Chrysostome aux moines et aux vierges: Contra eos qui subintroductas habent, Quod regulares feminae viris cohabitare non debeant: MSR 6 (1949) 247-252 (the two treatises should be dated about 382); *idem*, De quelques principes d'ecdotique concernant les traités de saint Jean Chrysostome: MSR 9 (1952) 63-72 (study of the 18 manuscripts of the two treatises against the *Syneisaktoi*). — G. BRUNNER, Intorno ad un passo del Crisostomo: Aevum 29 (1955) 272-274 (text. crit. of the *Quod regulares feminae*, ch. 8). — J. DUMORTIER, Les idées morales de saint Jean Chrysostome: MSR 12 (1955) 27-36 (monastic virtues); *idem*, L'auteur présumé du Corpus asceticum de S. Jean Chrysostome: JThSt N.S. 6 (1955) 99-102 (Nicephorus of Constantinople); *idem*, Les citations scripturaires des Cohabitations (MG 47, 495-532) d'après leur tradition manuscrite: SP I (TU 63). Berlin, 1957, 291-296 (*Contra eos* and *Quod regulares*).

4. *Concerning the Education of Children*

None of Chrysostom's works gives such a condensed presentation of his educational ideas as the treatise entitled *De inani gloria et de educandis liberis*. It appears at first sight strange that he should combine these two topics in the same book. The first and much smaller section *On Vainglory* deals with the main vice of Antioch, luxury and debauchery, the second *On the Education of Children* intends to protect the youth from such serious vice by teaching the right way for parents to bring up their sons and daughters. The author explains the transition from the first subject to the second as natural, since the deepest root of all corruption is the lack of moral training of the future generation (15): 'The corruption of the world remains unchecked because nobody guards his children, nobody speaks to them of chastity, of despising riches and glory, of the commandments of God' (17). He urges parents to regard the education of their children as the highest and holiest of tasks and to provide them with the true riches of the soul rather than with worldly wealth. They must train their boys and girls not for time, but for eternity. The little book has a lasting interest as a document in the history of Christian pedagogy though Chrysostom gives little attention to the child's intellectual progress and does not lay claim to any profound psychological insight.

The number of manuscripts containing this treatise is very small. The editions of Fronton du Duc, Savile, Montfaucon and Migne do not include it. The Dominican F. Combefis printed it in 1656 for the first time and added a Latin translation. John Evelyn in 1659 brought out an English version, omitting however the first sixteen paragraphs on vainglory. Since Montfaucon and Migne rejected it as spurious, it was forgotten again until S. Haidacher aroused fresh interest with his publication of a German translation. In the introduction he proved that all doubts regarding its authenticity are completely unjustified. His early death in 1908 prevented him from publishing a new critical edition of the Greek text, which was brought out by F. Schulte in 1914. Both Haidacher and Schulte based their conclusions about the genuineness of the little book on its many resemblances to Chrysostom's confessedly authentic writings, especially the similarity in the choice of diction, the structure of clauses, the figurative language employed and the recurrence of favorite topics. A comparison of the opening of the treatise with the tenth Homily on the Epistle to the Ephesians was especially convincing for Haidacher, who assigns both to Antioch and the year 393.

Combefis and Schulte relied upon a single manuscript: *Codex Parisinus Gr.* 764 saec. X-XI, formerly in the library of Cardinal Mazarin. Though Schulte explained that he had searched in vain for other copies, there is a second, which A. Papadopulos-Kerameus had discovered in 1881 and described in a printed catalogue in 1885: *Codex Lesbiacus* 42 of the late tenth or early eleventh century, fol. 92v to fol. 118r. It seems that Kerameus' publication remained unnoticed because in 1929 C. Baur claimed credit for discovering this second manuscript.

Editions: F. SCHULTE, Johannes Chrysostomus, De inani gloria et de educandis liberis (Progr. 627 Collegium Augustinianum Gaesdonck). Diss. Münster, 1914. — New crit. ed.: B. K. EXARCHOS, Joh. Chrysostomus, Über Hoffart und Kindererziehung. Mit Einleitung und kritischem Apparat (Das Wort der Antike 4). Munich, 1955.

Translations: English: J. EVELYN, The Golden Book of St. John Chrysostom concerning the Education of Children. London, 1659. — M. L. W. LAISTNER, Christianity and Pagan Culture in the Later Roman Empire together with an English translation of John Chrysostom's Address on Vainglory and the Right Way for Parents to bring up their Children. Ithaca N.Y., 1951. — *German:* S. HAIDACHER, Des hl. Johannes Chrysostomus Büchlein über Hoffart und Kindererziehung samt einer Blumenlese über Jugenderziehung aus seinen Schriften übersetzt und herausgegeben. Freiburg i.B., 1907.

Studies: A. HÜLSTER, Die pädagogischen Grundsätze des hl. Johannes Chrysostomus: ThGl 3 (1911) 203-227. — S. SEIDLMAYER, Die Pädagogik des Johannes Chrysostomus. (Diss.) Munich, 1923, and Münster, 1926. — S. SKIMINA, De Johannis Chrysostomi De inani gloria et de educandis liberis libelli veritate: Eos (1929) 711-730. — J. DUMORTIER, L'éducation des enfants au IVe siècle: Revue des Sciences Humaines (1947) 222-238. — B. EXARCHOS, The Authenticity of John Chrysostom's Treatise De inani gloria et de educandis liberis (in Greek): Θεολογία 19 (1941/1948) 153-170, 340-355, 559-571. — D. MORAITIS, The Authenticity of the Treatise De inani gloria (in Greek): ibid. 718-733 (against authenticity). — In the introduction to his above-mentioned new edition (1955) B. Exarchos defends the authenticity against Moraitis; following Haidacher, he argues for inserting the treatise between the 10th and 11th homilies of the *Commentary on Ephesians* (against Schulte). — M. L. W. LAISTNER, The Lesbos Manuscript of Chrysostom's De inani gloria: VC 5 (1951) 179-185.

5. *On Suffering*

Chrysostom was only a deacon when he wrote the three books *Ad Stagirium a daemone vexatum*. Here he consoles his friend, the monk Stagirius, who was in great despair and spiritual desolation. Chrysostom discusses the purpose of adversity and advises Stagirius to recognize in his own trials the loving aim of divine Providence. The second and third books review the history of suffering from Adam to St. Paul in order to prove that precisely God's favorites have endured the greatest tribulations.

The other two tracts dealing with the problem of human misery date from the period of his second exile between 405 and 406 and are addressed to friends at home. In the first *Quod nemo laeditur nisi a se ipso* (MG 52,459-480) he endeavors to show that in reality no one can injure any man unless the latter cooperates. It remains always and everywhere in a man's own free will to avoid that which alone can harm him. In the second, *Ad eos qui scandalizati sunt ob adversitates* (MG 52,479-528) he consoles those who are scandalized at the sad conditions of the present and the gloomy outlook for the future. Even if God's intentions are not clear to us, the sorrows and adversities that fall to the lot of the just, should never induce us to question the divine order of the world.

Separate Edition: New crit. ed.: J. J. CANAVAN, Quod nemo laeditur nisi a se ipso. Diss. Cornell Univ. Ithaca N.Y., 1956 (microfilm).

Translation: English: W. R. W. STEPHENS, LNPF 9 (1889) 269-284 (*Quod nemo laeditur*).

6. *Against Pagans and Jews*

These two apologetic treatises seem, despite some lingering doubts, to be authentic. The first *De S. Babyla contra Julianum et Gentiles*, composed about 382, shows the victorious triumph of the Christian religion and the downfall of paganism in the history of the bishop and martyr Babylas of Antioch who died in the persecution of Decius. Julian the Apostate had ordered his remains to be taken away from the grove at Daphne near Antioch in 362 and restored there the ancient worship of Apollo. But on October 24, 362 the famous temple at Daphne burned down and nine months later Julian himself was struck down (June 26, 363). Chrysostom praises both events as a proof for the power of St. Babylas and quotes long passages from Libanius' oration (60) on the burning of the temple, whose lament he characterizes as drivelling nonsense.

The second treatise *Contra Judaeos et Gentiles quod Christus sit Deus* is 'a demonstration to Jews and Greeks that Christ is God, from the sayings concerning him everywhere in the prophets' as the complete title runs in Greek. The author establishes the divinity of Christ from the fulfilment of Christ's own prophecies and those of the Old Testament. Among the former he emphasizes especially those on the irresistible power of the Christian religion and the destruction of the temple of Jerusalem. He mentions that in the present generation that king who surpassed all others in iniquity, Julian, gave his sanction to the rebuilding of the Jewish temple but when a beginning was made fire sprang from the foundations and drove the Jews away. The Cross which was the symbol of a horrible death has become the subject of benediction. 'Kings put off their crowns, and take up the Cross, the symbol of Christ's death. The Cross is on their robes of state, and on their crowns. It is at their prayers, and on their weapons; and upon the Holy Table stands the Cross. Everywhere throughout the world the Cross shines out, beyond the brightness of the sun'. Christ's victory is complete: 'Kings and Generals and Rulers and Consuls, slaves and free, private persons, wise and foolish, barbarians, and all the varied races of mankind, and whatsoever land the sun overlooks — throughout this vast extent His name is spread, and His worship; that you may learn the meaning of that prophecy, 'And His rest shall be glorious' (Is. 11,10). The very tomb of His slain body, small and narrow though it be, is more revered than the countless palaces of kings, more honoured than the kings themselves'.

The treatise is most probably incomplete because it ends abruptly and Chrysostom does not fulfil his promise to speak later on more fully about the Jews. In content and in eloquence the treatise seems to be from his pen. There are a number of passages reminiscent of his other works. Opinions are divided regarding its exact date of composition. Bardenhewer (vol. 3, p. 348) places it about the year 387, while Williams thinks at the beginning of his diaconate (A.D. 381).

Editions: MG 50, 533-572 (*De S. Babyla*); 48, 813-838 (*Contra Judaeos*).

Studies: A. NÄGELE, Chrysostomos und Libanios: Chrysostomika. Rome, 1908, 111-142. — R. VAN LOY, Le 'Pro templis' de Libanius: Byz 8 (1933) 7-39. — A. L. WILLIAMS, Adversus Judaeos. A Bird's-Eye View of Christian Apologiae until the Renaissance. Cambridge, 1935, 135-138. — M. HEIDENTHALLER, Johannes Chrysostomus: 'Nachweis der Gottheit Christi'. Linz, 1951 (*Contra Judaeos* authentic). — Further studies above p. 453.

3. Letters

There are about 236 letters extant, all dating from his second exile. Though most of them are quite brief, they testify to the lively interest which Chrysostom took in the well-being of his friends in Syria and Constantinople despite the remoteness of his own abode. Addressed to more than one hundred different persons they answer correspondents anxious to know something about his condition, give touching evidence of his pastoral zeal, provide consolation for his friends and followers worried about the hopeless state of the Church at Constantinople and Chrysostom's own situation. The longest and most cordial are the 17 communications which he wrote to the widow and deaconess Olympias (MG 52,549-623) who never tired of taking steps for the improvement of Chrysostom's lot. Most important are the two letters he addressed to Pope Innocent. The first and longer one (52,529-536) written at Constantinople immediately after Easter 404 before his second exile, reports about the disturbances at the capital after the arrival of Theophilus of Alexandria, and his own deposition. The second dates from the end of 406, and was written at Cucusus.

Editions: MG 52. — *Separate ed.:* A. M. MALINGREY, S. Jean Chrysostome, Lettres à Olympias (SCH 13). Paris, 1947. — *Selected letters:* G. ZANDONELLA, S. Giovanni Crisostomo, Lettere scelte (Corona Patr. Sal.). Turin, 1933.

Translations: English: W. R. W. STEPHENS, LNPF 9 (1889) 287-303 (4 letters to Olympias); 307-314 (letters to Pope Innocent). — *German:* BKV 3 (1879) 461-610 (17 letters to Olympias); 445-460 '(letters to Pope Innocent). — *French:* P. E. LEGRAND, Lettres à Olympias. Paris, 1933. — A. M. MALINGREY, op. cit. — *Italian:* G. ZANDONELLA, op. cit. — *Spanish:* B. BEJARANO, Cartas a Santa Olimpiade (Colección Excelsa 12). Madrid, 1944.

Studies: F. BÖHRINGER, Johannes Chrysostomus und Olympias. 2nd ed. Stuttgart, 1876. — P. UBALDI, Gli epiteti esornativi nelle lettere di S. Giovanni Crisostomo: Bess 6, 2 (1902) 304-332. — J. BOUSQUET, Vie d'Olympias la Diaconesse: ROC 11 (1906) 225-250; *idem*, Récit de Sergia sur Olympias: ROC 12 (1907) 225-268. — H. DACIER, S. Jean Chrysostome et la femme chrétienne au IVe siècle de l'Église grecque. Paris, 1907, 119-264 (St. Jean Chr. et Olympiade). — S. HAIDACHER, Chrysostomus-Fragmente: Chrysostomika. Rome, 1908, 217-234 (fragments of correspondence with Nilus). — A. M. AMELLI, S. Giovanni Crisostomo anello provvidenziale tra Constantinopoli e Roma: Chrysostomika. Rome, 1908, 47-60 (letters to Pope Innocent). — G. ZANDONELLA, Epistolario Crisostomiano: Didaskaleion N.S. 7 (1929) 23-92. — P. R. COLEMAN -

NORTON, The Correspondence of St. John Chrysostom with Special Reference to his Epistles to Pope Innocent I: CPh 24 (1929) 279-284. — G. BARDY, La chronologie des lettres de saint Jean Chrysostome à Olympias: MSR 2 (1945) 271-284. — E. R. SMOTHERS, A Note on Luke 2, 49: HThR 45 (1952) 67-69 (*Ad Olympiadem, Ep.* 13, MG 52, 610ff.). — B. H. VANDENBERGHE, St. John Chrysostom and St. Olympias. London, 1959.

SPURIOUS WRITINGS

The prestige of Chrysostom's name has occasioned the false attribution to him of far more writings than to any other Greek Father: 300 spurious works printed, and 600 still in manuscripts. The true authors have been identified in some instances: Nestorius, Severian of Gabala, Flavian of Antioch, Amphilochius of Iconium, Eusebius of Alexandria, Hesychius of Jerusalem, Gregory of Antioch, Anastasius Sinaita, John Damascene and many others. Various *Spuria* belong materially but not formally to Chrysostom in so far as his authority led at a very early date to the habit of extracting his utterances on a certain subject from various homilies and combining such excerpts into a new homily on the same subject. Others are downright forgeries.

Studies: For liturgical homilies of Ps.-Chrysostom, see above p. 454. — P. VOGT, Zwei Homilien des hl. Chrysostomus, mit Unrecht unter die zweifelhaften verwiesen: BZ 14 (1905) 498-508, defended the authenticity of the two homilies *De precatione* (MG 50, 775-786). — J. WEYER, De homiliis quae Joanni Chrysostomo falso attribuuntur, Bonn, 1952 (Diss. typ.), proves their spuriousness. — K. HOLL, Amphilochius von Ikonium, Tübingen, 1904, 91-102, shows that the homilies *In mulierem peccatricem* (MG 61, 745-752) and *In paralyticum in die mediae Pentecostes* (MG 61, 777-782) belong to Amphilochius and that the homily *In illud: Pater si possibile est* (MG 61, 751-756) is a compilation from a homily of Amphilochius. An English translation of the homily *In paralyticum* was published by W. R. W. STEPHENS, LNPF 9 (1889) 211-220, and of the homily *In illud: Pater si possibile est, ibid.* 201-207. — The sermon *In dictum illud: In qua potestate haec facis?* (MG 56, 411-428) is by Severian of Gabala; cf. S. HAIDACHER, Pseudo-Chrysostomus. Die Homilie über Mt. 21, 23 von Severian von Gabala: ZkTh 32 (1908) 410-413. For other Severiana, see: C. MARTIN, Une homélie De poenitentia de Sévérien de Gabala: RHE (1930) 331-343. — B. MARX, Severiana unter den Spuria Chrysostomi bei Montfaucon-Migne: OCP (1939) 281-367. — For inedited sermons, see: E. BATAREIKH, Discours inédit sur les Chaînes de S. Pierre attribué à S. Jean Chrysostome: Chrysostomika. Rome, 1908, 937-1006 (Greek text). — I. SIMON, Homélie copte inédite sur S. Michel et le Bon Larron, attribuée à S. Jean Chrysostome: Orientalia 3 (1934) 227-242, 4 (1935) 222-234. — For other Coptic *Spuria*, see above p. 432. — For sermons belonging to Proclus of Constantinople, see: B. MARX, Procliana. Untersuchungen über den homiletischen Nachlass des Patriarchen von Konstantinopel. Münster, 1940; cf. below p. 522. — For those composed by Basil of Seleucia, see: B. MARX, Der homiletische Nachlass des Basileios von Seleukeia: OCP 7 (1941) 329-369. For the homily *Against Jews and Greeks and Heretics, and with Reference to the Words 'Jesus was called unto a marriage'* (MG 48, 1075-1080) and the sermon *Against Jews, with Reference to the Brazen Serpent* (MG 51, 793-802), see: A. L. WILLIAMS, Adversus Judaeos. Cambridge, 1935, 139-140. — For two homilies on Pelagia, see: P. FRANCHI DE' CAVALIERI, Note agiografiche (ST 65). Vatican City, 1935, 281-303. — For an Old Slavonic homily *In Annuntiationem*, see: M. VAN WIJK, Byzantinoslavica 7 (1937/38) 108-123. — The 'Prayer of St. Chrysostom' belongs more likely to St. Basil, as was shown by H. Holloway, The Prayer of St. Chrysostom: ExpT 46 (1935) 238. — Quite a number of spurious sermons seem to be by Hippolytus of Rome. R. H. Connolly, New Attributions to Hippolytus: JThSt (1945) 192-200, deals with MG 59, 723-746. H. de Lubac, L'arbre cosmique: Mélanges E. Podechard. Lyons, 1945, 191-198. P. Nautin, Homélies Paschales I (SCH 27), Paris, 1950, thinks that this homily is anti-Arian and not by Hippolytus; cf. Patrology vol. II, 178-179. — For the homily on Ps. 96, see: G. W. H. Lampe, The Exegesis of Some Biblical Texts by Marcellus of Ancyra and Pseudo-Chrysostom's Homily on Ps. XCVI: JThSt (1948) 169-175. — For excerpts of the spurious Commentary on Jeremias, see: G. Mercati, Postille del codice Q a Geremia tratte dal commento dello pseudo-Crisostomo: Miscellanea Biblica B. Ubach (Scripta et Monumenta I). Barcelona, 1953, 27-30.

1. Opus imperfectum in Matthaeum

Among the spurious treatises the so-called *Opus imperfectum in Matthaeum* deserves special mention since it enjoyed great reputation during the Middle Ages as a genuine work of Chrysostom (MG 56, 611-946). It presents an incomplete Latin commentary on Matthew consisting of 54 homilies whose real author is an Arian of the fifth century. For a long time the Latin was thought to be the original. J. Stiglmayr, however, adduced reasons to prove that the original must have been Greek and the Latin is a rather free revision. He drew the conclusion that perhaps the Arian presbyter Timotheus, who lived at Constantinople in the time of the Emperor Arcadius (395-408), composed the commentary, since Socrates (*Hist. eccl.* 7,6) praises his great knowledge of the Scriptures. But there is not the slightest evidence for any literary activity on the part of this Timotheus — a silence all the more surprising since the author of *Opus imperfectum* mentions that he had written in addition commentaries on Mark and Luke. Lastly, G. Morin came to the conclusion that the original was composed in Latin about 550 in Illyria.

Edition: MG 56, 611-946.

Studies: H. Boehmer - Romundt, Des Pseudo-Chrysostomus Opus imperfectum in Matthaeum: Zeitschrift f. wissenschaftl. Theologie 46 (1903) 361-407. — F. X. Funk, Zum Opus imperfectum in Matthaeum: ThQ 86 (1903) 424-428. — T. Paas, Das Opus imperfectum in Matthaeum. Diss. Tübingen, 1907. — F. Kaufmann, Zur Textgeschichte des Opus imperfectum des Matthaeum. Kiel, 1909. — J. Stiglmayr, Das Opus imperfectum in Matthaeum: ZkTh 34 (1910) 1-38, 473-499. — O. Schilling, Eigentum und Erwerb nach dem Opus imperfectum in Matthaeum: ThQ 92 (1910) 214-243. — F. Zehentbauer, Der Wucherbegriff in des Pseudo-Chrysostomus Opus imperfectum in Matthaeum: Festgabe A. Ehrhard. Bonn, 1922, 491-501. — G. Morin, Quelques aperçus nouveaux sur l'Opus imperfectum in Matthaeum: RB 37 (1925) 239-262; idem, Les homélies latines sur S. Matthieu attribuées à Origène: RB 54 (1942) 9-11; idem, Indices de provenance illyrienne du livre d'Évangiles q: Miscellanea G. Mercati I (ST 121). Vatican City, 1946, 99. Morin identifies the author of the *Opus imperfectum* with the anti-Arian translator of Origen's *Commentary on Matthew.* E. Klostermann, ThLZ 73 (1948) 49ff., does not agree with him.

2. *Synopsis Veteris et Novi Testamenti*

This is a kind of an introduction to Scripture with a detailed description of the contents of each book. The text of the Benedictine edition (reprinted MG 56,313-386) is incomplete. Additions amounting to several chapters have been published by Bryennios and Klostermann. But quite a number of chapters, especially on the books of the New Testament, are still lost. The oldest manuscripts go back to the eleventh century. Before the question of the authorship can be answered, a careful investigation of the relations of this synopsis towards the one falsely attributed to St. Athanasius (cf. above, p. 39) will be necessary, though there cannot be any doubt about its spurious character.

3. *The Liturgy of St. Chrysostom*

The so-called Liturgy of St. Chrysostom is in its present form very much later than the time of the Saint whose name it bears. Except for the few days of the liturgical year on which the Liturgy of St. Basil (cf. above, p. 226) is prescribed, it has remained until now in general use in the Churches of the East and was translated into several different languages. While there are strong reasons for connecting the Liturgy of St. Basil with the name of this Cappadocian Father, those for attributing the Liturgy of St. Chrysostom to the great Patriarch of Constantinople are all insecure. The oldest manuscript of the eighth or ninth century ascribes only two of the prayers to him, which means that it implicitly denies to him the authorship of the rest. Moreover, the Synod of Constantinople of 692 A.D., the so-called *Quinisexta*, speaks of a Liturgy of St. James and of a Liturgy of St. Basil, but not of a Liturgy of St. Chrysostom, though this would have been not only appropriate but inescapable in the context. It is only in later manuscripts that the entire Liturgy is called after Chrysostom. It probably owed its great influence to being the liturgy of the Imperial capital and superseded in the 13th century the older Liturgies of St. James and St. Mark. In its Greek form it spread to the Basilian monasteries of Italy and in its Slavonic Byzantine version to the most remote regions of the Russias. The oldest Latin translation, found in a manuscript written in the second half of the twelfth century, seems to go back to the times of the First Crusade (1096-1099) and to be of South Italian origin. A second was made at Constantinople about 1180 by the Pisan interpreter Leo Tuscus.

Editions: Greek text: F. E. BRIGHTMAN, Liturgies Eastern and Western I. Eastern Liturgies. Oxford, 1896, 309-344 (based on Cod. Barb. III, 55) and 353-390 (modern text). —

Separate ed.: P. DE MEESTER, The Divine Liturgy of our Father among the Saints John Chrysostom. Greek text with introduction and notes. English translation by the Benedictines of Stanbrook. 2nd ed. London, 1930; *idem,* Die göttliche Liturgie unseres heiligen Vaters Johannes Chrysostomus. Griechischer Text mit Einführung, Übersetzung und Anmerkungen. Munich, 1932.

Old Versions: Oldest *Latin* version ed. by A. STRITTMATTER, EL 55 (1941) 2-73; *idem,* Missa Grecorum. Missa Sancti Johannis Chrisostomi. The Oldest Latin Version Known of the Byzantine Liturgies of St. Basil and St. John Chrysostom: Traditio 1 (1943) 79-137. — *Georgian* version: M. TARCHNISVILI, Die georgische Übersetzung der Liturgie des hl. Johannes Chrysostomus nach einem Pergament-Rotulus aus dem X./XI. Jahrhundert: JL 14 (1938) 79-94 (German translation). — *Syriac* version: H. G. CODRINGTON, Anaphora S. Joannis Chrysostomi Syriace. Rome, 1940. — *Arabic* version: C. BACHA, Notions générales sur les versions arabes de la liturgie de S. Jean Chrysostome, suivies d'une ancienne version inédite: Chrysostomika. Rome, 1908, 405-472. — For the *Armenian* version, see: G. AUCHER, La versione armena della liturgia di S. Giovanni Crisostomo: *ibid.* 359-404. — *Old Slavonic* version: A. J. SHIPMAN, The Holy Mass according to the Greek Rite, being the Liturgy of St. John Chrysostom in Slavonic and English. New York, 1912.

Modern Translations: English: P. DE MEESTER, op. cit. — A. FORTESCUE, The Divine Liturgy of our Father among the Saints John Chrysostom, done into English. London, 1908. — F. E. BRIGHTMAN, The Divine Liturgy of Saint John Chrysostom. 2nd ed. London, 1931. — A. J. SHIPMAN, op. cit. — *German:* R. STORF, Griechische Liturgien: BKV² (1912) 205-262. — P. DE MEESTER. Munich, 1932 (cf. above). — M. TARCHNISVILI, art. cit. (*Georgian* version). — *French:* F. v. V. GHIGA, La divine liturgie de S. Jean Chrysostome. Paris, 1934. — *Dutch:* I. DOENS, De heilige liturgie van onzen Vader Johannes Chrysostomus. Amay (Belg.), 1937.

Studies: C. AUNER, Les versions romaines de la liturgie de saint Jean Chrysostome: Chrysostomika. Rome, 1908, 731-770. — J. BOCIAN, De modificationibus in textu slavico liturgiae S. Joannis Chrysostomi apud Ruthenos subintroductis: *ibid.* 929-972. — C. CHARON, Le rite byzantin et la liturgie chrysostomienne dans les patriarcats melkites (Alexandrie - Antioche - Jérusalem): *ibid.* 473-718. — H. W. CODRINGTON, Liturgia praesanctificatorum Syriaca S. Joannis Chrysostomi: *ibid.* 719-730. — P. DE MEESTER, Les origines et les développements du texte grec de la liturgie de S. Jean Chrysostome: *ibid.* 245-358. — A. PÉTROVSKI, Histoire de la rédaction slave de la liturgie de S. Jean Chrysostome: *ibid.* 859-928. — A. BAUMSTARK, Die Chrysostomosliturgie und die syrische Liturgie des Nestorios: *ibid.* 771-858; *idem,* Die konstantinopolitanische Messliturgie vor dem 9. Jahrhundert: KT 35 (1909) 1-16; *idem,* Zur Urgeschichte der Chrysostomosliturgie: ThGl 5 (1913) 299-313, 392-395. — L. PULLAN, A Guide to the Holy Liturgy of St. John Chrysostom. London, 1921. — P. DE MEESTER, Authenticité des liturgies de saint Basile et de saint Jean Chrysostome: DAL 6 (1925) 1596-1604. — J. MOREAU, Les anaphores des liturgies de S. Jean Chrysostome et de saint Basile comparées aux canons romain et gallican. Paris, 1927. — C. G. BENNIGSEN, The Byzantine Liturgy of St. John Chrysostom as Compared with the Roman Mass: Clergy Review 11 (1936) 363-371. — H. ENGBERDING, Die syrische Anaphora der Zwölf Apostel und ihre Paralleltexte: OC 34 (1937) 213-247. — A. GRABAR, Un rouleau liturgique constantinopolitain et ses peintures: DOP 8 (1954) 161-199 (containing the Liturgy of John Chrysostom). — H. ENGBERDING, Die westsyrische Anaphora des hl. Chrysostomus und ihre Probleme: OC 39 (1955) 33-47. — A. RAES, L'authenticité de la liturgie byzantine de S. Jean Chrysostome: OCP 24 (1958) 5-16 (the liturgy cannot be attributed to St. Chrysostom).

Among the great number of Chrysostom's writings there is none that could be properly called an investigation or study of a theological problem as such. He was not involved in any of the great dogmatic controversies of the fourth century. If he refutes heresies, he does it in order to provide the necessary information and instruction for his listeners. He was by nature and by predilection a pastor of souls and a born reformer of human society. Though no one has ever interpreted Holy Scripture as successfully as he, he had no speculative bent nor any interest in the abstract. However, this lack of inclination for systematic presentation does not exclude a deep understanding of difficult theological questions. Since this greatest pulpit orator of the Ancient Church bases his entire preaching on Scripture, the study of his literary bequest is of great importance for positive theology. His writings mirror the traditional faith with great fidelity and their doctrinal content must not be underestimated. Unfortunately, a comprehensive monograph on his theological thought has not been written so far, though it would be of unusual value and significance.

1. *Christology*

Though Chrysostom was a pupil of Diodore of Tarsus, he did not feel called upon to champion openly the Christology of the School of Antioch in the capital of the East. Perhaps he abstained through fear of further fomenting the rivalry between Alexandria and Constantinople. However, there cannot be any doubt that Chrysostom favored the teaching of Antioch in his exegesis as well as in his Christology. He distinguishes clearly between *ousia* or *physis* as terms for nature, and *hypostasis* or *prosopon* as terms for person. He teaches that the Son is of the same essence as the Father (MG 57,17; 59,290) and uses at least five times the Nicene formula *homoousios* to characterize the relation of the Son to the Father (*Hom.* 7,2 *contra Anomoeos* MG 48,758; *Hom.* 52,3 and 54,1 *in Joh.* MG 59,290 and 298; *Hom.* 54,2 *in Matth.* MG 58,534; *Hom.* 26,2 *in I Cor.* MG 61,214). He prefers however expressions like 'equal to the Father', 'equal in essence', 'equality in essence'. He states, 'You ought not, when you hear of *Father* and *Son* to seek anything else to the establishing of the relationship as to Essence, but if this is not sufficient to prove to you the Condignity and Consubstantiality, you may learn it even from the works' (*Hom.* 74 *in Joh.* 2). Proceeding from the Father, the Son must be eternal:

But if any one say, 'How can it be that He is a Son, and yet not younger than the Father? since that which proceeds from something else needs must be later than that from which it proceeds'; we will say that, properly speaking, these are human reasonings; that he who questions on this matter will question on others yet more improper; and that to such we ought not even to give ear. For our speech is now concerning God, not concerning the nature of men, which is subject to the sequence and necessary conclusions of these reasonings. Still, for the assurance of the weaker sort, we will speak even to these points.

Tell me, then, does the radiance of the sun proceed from the substance itself of the sun, or from some other source? Any one not deprived of his very senses needs must confess, that it proceeds from the substance itself. Yet, although the radiance proceeds from the sun itself, we cannot say that it is later in point of time than the substance of that body, since the sun has never appeared without its rays. Now if in the case of these visible and sensible bodies there has been shown to be something which proceeds from something else, and yet is not after that from whence it proceeds, why are you incredulous in the case of the invisible and ineffable Nature? This same thing there takes place, but in a manner suitable to that Substance. For it is for this reason that Paul too calls Him *Brightness* (Hebr. 1,3); setting forth thereby His being from Him and His co-eternity. Again, tell me, were not all the ages, and every interval created by Him? Any man not deprived of his senses must necessarily confess this. There is no interval therefore between the Son and the Father; and if there be none, then He is not after, but co-eternal with Him. For 'before' and 'after' are notions implying time, since, without age or time, no man could possibly imagine these words; but God is above times and ages (*Hom. 4 in Joh.* 1/2 LFC).

Like all Antiochenes he stresses the complete and perfect divinity of Christ against the Arians and the complete and perfect humanity against the Apollinarists. He insists on the reality and integrity of these two natures in Christ. Christ is of the same nature as the Father, τῆς αὐτῆς οὐσίας τῷ πατρί (*Hom.* 1 *in Matth.* n. 2 MG 57, 17; *Hom.* 4 *contra Anomoeos* n. 4 MG 48, 732). He had also a human body, not sinful like ours, but identical with ours in nature (*Hom.* 13 *in Rom.* n. 5). Despite the duality of natures, there is but one Christ: 'Remaining what He was, He assumed what He was not, and though He became man, remained God, in that He was the Word... He became the one [man], He took the one [man]. He was the other [God]. Thus there is no confusion, but also no separation. One God, one Christ, the Son of God. But when I say one [Christ], I mean thereby a union and not a commingling (ἕνωσιν λέγω, οὐ σύγχυσιν), not that one nature is transmuted into another, but is united to that other' (*Hom.* 7 *in Phil.* n. 2-3). 'By a union (ἑνώσει) and conjoining (συναφείᾳ) God the Word and the flesh are one, not by any confusion or obliteration of substances, but by a certain union ineffable and past understanding. Ask not how' (*Hom.* 11 *in Joh.* 2). This last sentence expresses his unvarying attitude towards the Christological problem and was already quoted in the collection of Patristic passages presented by the Antiochenes in 431 and by the Council of Chalcedon in 451. He does not want to investigate the nature of this union of the two natures in one person. If he occasionally makes the Logos dwell in the man Christ as in a temple (*In Ps.* 44, 3; *Hom.* 4 *in Matth.* 3), if he speaks of an 'assumption of the flesh' by God and of a 'taking flesh to Himself' (*Hom.* 11 *in Joh.* 2) no special stress can be laid on such rhetorical expressions common in the School of Antioch, though they became a dogmatic axiom with Nestorius.

Studies: E. MICHAUD, La christologie de S. Jean Chrysostome: Revue internat. de théologie 17 (1909) 275-291; *idem,* La sotériologie de S. Jean Chrysostome: ibid. 18 (1910) 35-49. — J. H. JUZEK, Die Christologie des hl. Johannes Chrysostomus. Zugleich ein Beitrag zur Dogmatik der Antiochener. Diss. Breslau, 1912. — E. MERSCH, Le Corps Mystique du Christ, 2nd ed. Brussels. 1936, 464-486. English translation: E. MERSCH, The Whole Christ. Transl. by J. R. Kelly, Milwaukee, 1938, 323-336. — F. FROMM, Das Bild des verklärten Christus beim hl. Paulus. Nach den Kommentaren des hl. Johannes Chrysostomus. Rome, 1938. — J. LECUYER, Le sacerdoce céleste du Christ selon Chrysostome: NRTh 72 (1950) 561-579.

2. *Mariology*

There is no doubt that his training in that School influenced his Mariology. He never in his many writings uses the title *Theotokos* for the Blessed Virgin to which the Antiochenes objected, but neither does he employ their expression *Christotokos* nor that of Diodore of Tarsus, *Anthropotokos,* — a proof that he deliberately exercised reserve and refused to take sides in the discussion that had begun as early as 380 (cf. Gregory of Nyssa, *Epist.* 3; above, p. 289). He clearly teaches (*Hom.* 4 *in Matth.* 3) the perpetual virginity of Mary: 'We are ignorant of many things, as for instance, how the Infinite is in a womb, how He that contains all things is carried, as unborn, by a woman; how the Virgin gives birth and continues a Virgin' (τίκτει ἡ παρθένος καὶ μένει παρθένος), but on other occasions he speaks of her in such a strange way that Thomas Aquinas remarks: *In verbis illis Chrysostomus excessit* (*S. Th.* 3, qu. 27, a. 4 ad 3). Thus he asks the question, why the angel announced the glad tidings to the Virgin before, but to St. Joseph after the conception:

> Why then, it may be asked, did he not do so in the Virgin's case also, and declare the good tidings to her after the conception? Lest she should be in agitation and great trouble. For the probability was,

that, had she not known the clear fact, she would have resolved something strange about herself, and had recourse to rope or sword, not bearing the disgrace (*Hom. 4 in Matth.* 4-5).

His comment on Matth. 12,47 is no less objectionable:

> Today we learn something else even further, viz., that not even to bear Christ in the womb, and to have that wonderful childbirth, has any merit without virtue. And this is especially true from this passage, 'As He was yet speaking to the multitude, behold His Mother and His brethren stood without, seeking to speak to Him' etc. This He said, not as ashamed of His Mother, nor as denying her who bore Him (for, had He been ashamed, He had not passed through that womb), but as showing that there was no profit to her thence, unless she did all that was necessary. For what she attempted, came of overmuch love of honor; for she wished to show to the people that she had power and authority over her Son, imagining not as yet anything great concerning Him. Therefore she came thus unseasonably. Observe then her and their rashness. Since when they ought to have gone in, and listened with the multitude; or if they were not so minded, to have waited for His bringing His discourse to an end, and then to have come near, they call Him out, and do this before all, evincing a superfluous vanity, and wishing to make it appear, that with much authority they enjoin Him. Had He wished to deny His Mother, He would have denied her then, when the Jews taunted Him with her. But no: He shows such care of her as to commit her as a legacy on the Cross itself to the disciple whom He loved best of all, and to take anxious oversight of her. But does He not do the same now, by caring for her and His brethren?... And consider, not only the words which convey the considerate rebuke, but also... who He is who utters it... and what He aims at in uttering it; not, that is, as wishing to cast her into perplexity, but to release her from a most tyrannical affection, and to bring her gradually to the fitting thought concerning Him, and to persuade her that He is not only her son, but also her Master (*Hom. 44 in Matth.* 1).

When the mother said to her Son at the marriage of Cana, 'They have no wine' (Joh. 2, 3), Chrysostom explains: 'For she desired both to do them a favor, and through her Son to render herself more conspicuous' (*Hom. 21 in Joh.* 2).

There cannot be any doubt that these passages are authentic. Those of his *Commentary on Matthew* are already found in the Armenian, Syriac and Latin versions of the fifth century.

Studies: S. VAILHÉ, Origines de la fête de l'Assomption: EO 9 (1916) 138-145. — M. JUGIE, La première fête mariale en Orient et en Occident: EO 22 (1923) 129-152. — C. BAUR, Der hl. Johannes Chrysostomus und seine Zeit. I. Munich, 1929, 297-300. — C. GIANELLI, Témoignages patristiques grecs en faveur d'une apparition du Christ ressuscité à la Vierge Marie: REB 11 (1953) 106-119 (Chrysostom identifies Maria Jacobi with the Blessed Virgin).

478 THE WRITERS OF ANTIOCH AND SYRIA

3. Original Sin

In his sermon *Ad neophytos* which Haidacher rediscovered (cf. above, p. 452) Chrysostom remarks in detailing the effects of baptism: 'Therefore do we baptize also little children although they have no sins' *(ἁμαρτήματα)*. From this passage the Pelagian Julian of Eclanum drew the conclusion that Chrysostom denied original sin. St. Augustine (*Contra Julianum* 1, 22) rightly replies that the plural 'sins' and the context prove that Chrysostom meant personal sins (*propria peccata*) and supports his argument with eight additional quotations from other works of Chrysostom to show that he openly taught the existence of original sin. In all these passages, nevertheless, Chrysostom's concept does not coincide exactly with the ideas and better terminology of Augustine. Though Chrysostom repeatedly avers that the consequences or penalties of Adam's sin affect not only our first parents, but also their descendants, he never states explicitly that the sin itself was inherited by their posterity and is inherent in their nature. Commenting on Rom. 5, 19, for instance he says:

> What is the question? It is the saying that through the offence of one many were made sinners. For the fact that when he had sinned and become mortal, those who were of him should be so also, is nothing unlikely. But how would it follow that from his disobedience another would become a sinner? For at this rate a man of this sort will not even deserve punishment, if, that is, it was not from his own self that he became a sinner. What then does the word 'sinners' mean here? To me it seems to mean liable to punishment and condemned to death (*Hom.* 10 *in Rom.* 1. 2. 4, LFC).

Studies: E. BOULARAND, La nécessité de la grâce pour arriver à la foi, d'après saint Jean Chrysostome (Analecta Gregoriana 18). Rome, 1939; *idem,* Greg 19 (1938) 515-542 (excerpt). — J. SOLANO, La παλιγγενεσία (Mt. 19, 28; Tit. 3, 5) según San Juan Crisóstomo: Miscelanea de la universidad de Comillas 2. Santander, 1944, 91-138. — B. ALTANER, Augustinus und Johannes Chrysostomus. Quellenkritische Untersuchungen: ZNW 44 (1952/53) 76-84.

4. Penance

Theologians like P. Martain and P. Galtier have appealed to St. Chrysostom, in order to prove that in his time, both in Antioch and in Constantinople, private confession to a priest was universally prevalent and obligatory in the case of all mortal sins. This appeal is in vain. He frequently speaks of the confession of sins, but he means either public confession in the presence of others, or the outpouring of the heart in the presence of God alone. This latter he insists on again and again, pointing out its necessity and advantages. He never insinuates that in the confession made before God he also includes the confession made to a priest acting as the representative of God; nay, in several passages he positively excludes this interpretation:

> Therefore I exhort and beg you again and again: Confess to God without ceasing! I do not lead you into the circle of your fellow servants, and I do not force you to reveal your sins to men. Unfold your conscience to God alone, show Him your wounds, and ask help from Him. Show yourself to Him who will not reproach you, but who will heal you. Even though you be silent, He knows all (*Hom. contra Anomoeos* 5).

> How shall we receive pardon, if our sins are never brought to mind? Were this the case, everything would be done. For just as he who enters within the gate is within, so he who ponders over his sins and meditates separately upon each one, attains a cure for them all. But if he says, 'I am a sinner', and does not weigh his sins and say, 'I have done this or that', he will never cease sinning, because, while he always confesses them, he takes no measures for his betterment (*Hom.* 9 *in Hebr.*).

There is no passage in the writings of Chrysostom that would prove him an unmistakable witness for the existence of private confession. It is typical that in his six books *De sacerdotio*, in which he elaborates upon the dignity and the duties of the priesthood, he mentions seventeen obligations of the priest, but never once the hearing of confessions. One very significant passage, however, occurs, in which Chrysostom declares that the priest is able to remit sins twice, once in baptism and a second time in extreme unction:

> And not only in our regeneration have they [the priests] the power to remit sin; but they have also the power to remit the sins committed after regeneration. For the Apostle says (Jac. 5, 14. 15): 'Is any man sick among you, let him bring in the priests of the Church, and let them pray over him, anointing him with oil in the name of the Lord. And the prayer of faith shall save the sick man, and the Lord shall raise him up, and if he be in his sins, they shall be forgiven him' (*De sacerdotio* 3, 6).

Studies: P. MARTAIN, St. Jean Chrysostome et la confession: Revue Augustinienne 6 (1907) 460-462. — J. TURMEL, St. Jean Chrysostome et la confession: Revue du Clergé français 49 (1907) 294-308 (against private confession). — P. GALTIER, St. Jean Chrysostome et la confession: RSR 1 (1910) 209-240, 313-350. — A. LAGARDE, St. Jean Chrysostome a-t-il connu la confession?: RHL (1914) 26-62. — H. KEANE, The Sacrament of Penance in St. John Chrysostom: ITQ 14 (1919) 305-317. — J. F. GILLIAM, Scylla and Sin: Philological Quarterly (Iowa) 29 (1950) 345-347.

5. *Eucharist*

In modern times St. John Chrysostom has been called *Doctor Eucharistiae*. Though this title has never found any official ecclesiastical sanction, there is no doubt that he is an eminent witness to the real presence of Christ in the Eucharist and its sacrificial character. His statements to that effect are numerous, clear, positive and detailed. He would have this sacrament approached with awe and devotion and calls the Eucharist 'a table of holy fear' (*Hom. de bapt. Christi* MG 49, 370), 'an awe-inspiring and divine table' (*Hom. in natal. Dom.* MG 49, 360), 'the frightful mysteries' (*Hom.* 25 *in Matth.* MG 57, 331; *Hom.* 46 *in Joh.* MG 49, 261; *Hom.* 24 *in I Cor.* MG 61, 919), 'the divine mysteries' (*Hom. in s. Pascha,* MG 52, 769), 'the ineffable mysteries' (*Hom.* 34 *in I Cor.* MG 49, 288), 'the mysteries which demand reverence and trembling' (*Hom. in nat. Dom.* MG 49, 392). The consecrated wine is 'the cup of holy awe' (*Cat.* 1 *ad illum.* MG 49, 223), 'the awe-inspiring blood' (*Hom.* 82 *in Matth.* MG 58, 746), and 'the precious blood' (*De sacerdotio* 3. 4. MG 48, 642; *Hom.* 16 *in Hebr.* MG 63, 124). Moreover, the Eucharist is an 'awe-inspiring and terrible sacrifice' (*Hom.* 24 *in I Cor.* MG 61, 203), 'a fearful and holy sacrifice' (*Hom.* 2 *de prod. Judae,* MG 49, 390), 'the most awe-inspiring sacrifice' (*De sacerdotio* 6, 3, MG 48, 681). Pointing to the altar, he says: 'Christ lies there slain' (*Hom.* 1 and 2 *De prod. Jud.,* MG 49, 381 and 390), 'His body lies before us now' (*Hom.* 50 *in Matth.* n. 2, MG 58, 507). 'That which is in the chalice is the same as what flowed from the side of Christ. What is the bread? The Body of Christ' (*Hom.* 24 *in I Cor.* n. 1, 2, MG 61, 200). 'Reflect, o man, what sacrificial flesh (θυσία) you take in your hand! to what table you will approach. Remember that you, though dust and ashes, do receive the Blood and the Body of Christ' (*Hom. in nat. Dom.* n. 7, MG 49, 361). Some of his expressions are still stronger. He does not hesitate to say: 'Not only ought we to see the Lord, but we ought to take Him in our hands, eat Him, set our teeth upon His Flesh and most intimately unite ourselves with Him' (*Hom.* 46 *in Joh.* n. 3, MG 59, 260). 'What the Lord did not tolerate on the Cross [i.e. the breaking of His legs], He tolerates now in the sacrifice through the love of you; He permits Himself to be broken in pieces that all may be filled to satiety' (*Hom.* 24 *in I Cor.* n. 2, MG 61, 200). Here he transfers to the substance of the Body and Blood of Christ what is strictly true of the accidents of bread and wine, in order to make the truth of the real presence and the identity of the Eucharistic Sacrifice with the Sacrifice on the Cross as clear as possible (EP 1180, 1195, 1222). It is a real sacrifice that is offered daily, but it is not one victim to-day and another to-morrow, but always the same; and therefore the sacrifice is one:

> There is one Christ everywhere, complete both in this world and in the other; one body. As then, though offered in many places, He is

but one body, so there is but one sacrifice... We offer that now which was offered then; which is indeed inconsumable... We do not then offer a different sacrifice as the high priest formerly did, but always the same; or rather, we celebrate a memorial of a Sacrifice (*Hom.* 17 *in Hebr.* 3).

The sacrificing priest is Christ Himself and the consecration takes place the moment that the words of the institution are pronounced:

Believe that there takes place now the same banquet as that in which Christ sat at table, and that this banquet is in no way different from that. For it is not true that this banquet is prepared by a man while that was prepared by Himself (*Hom.* 50 *in Matth.* n. 3, MG 58, 507). Today as then, it is the Lord who works and offers all (*Hom.* 27 *in I Cor.* n. 4, MG 61, 229). We assume the role of servants; it is He who blesses and transforms (ὁ δὲ ἁγιάζων αὐτὰ καὶ μετασκευάζων αὐτός, *Hom.* 82 *in Matth.* 5, MG 58, 744). It is not man who causes what is present to become the Body and Blood of Christ, but Christ Himself who was crucified for us. The priest is the representative when he pronounces those words, but the power and the grace are those of the Lord. 'This is my Body', he says. This word changes (μεταρρυθμίζει) the things that lie before us; and as that sentence 'increase and multiply', once spoken, extends through all time and gives to our nature the power to reproduce itself; even so that saying 'This is my Body', once uttered, does at every table in the Churches from that time to the present day, and even till Christ's coming, make the sacrifice complete (*Hom.* 1 and almost identical *Hom.* 2 *de prodit. Judae*, n. 6, MG 49, 380 and 389).

Studies: F. PROBST, Die antiochenische Messe nach den Schriften des heiligen Johannes Chrysostomus dargestellt: ZkTh 7 (1883) 250-303. — J. SORG, Die Lehre des hl. Chrysostomus über die reale Gegenwart Christi in der Eucharistie und die Transsubstantiation: ThQ 79 (1897) 259-297. — A. NÄGELE, Die Eucharistielehre des hl. Johannes Chrysostomus, des Doctor Eucharistiae. Freiburg i.B., 1900. — E. MICHAUD S. Jean Chrysostome et l'eucharistie: Revue internat. de théologie 11 (1903) 93-111. — S. SALAVILLE, L'épiclèse d'après St. Jean Chrysostome et la tradition occidentale: EO 11 (1908) 101-112. — A. D'ALÈS, Un texte eucharistique de saint Jean Chrysostome: RSR (1933) 451-462 (text, translation and commentary of De poenitentia 9, MG 49, 345). — W. LAMPEN, Doctrina S. Joannis Chrysostomi de Christo se offerente in missa: Ant 18 (1943) 3-16. — L. MORINS, Eucharistiae promissio secundum Joannem Chrysostomum in Hom. ad Joannem 6. Diss. Propag. Rome, 1949. — G. FITTKAU, Der Begriff des Mysteriums bei Johannes Chrysostomus. Bonn, 1953. — A. HOFFMANN, Der Mysterienbegriff bei Johannes Chrysostomus: Freiburger Zeitschrift für Philosophie und Theologie 3 (1956) 418-422. — G. TILEA, Eulavia eucharistica dupa Sfîntul Joan Gură de Aur: Studii Teologice 9 (1957) 631-648 (Eucharistic devotion). — G. STÖCKER, Eucharistische Gemeinschaft bei Chrysostomus: ST II (TU 64). Berlin, 1957, 309-316.

Other Studies: Ecclesiology: M. JUGIE, Saint Jean Chrysostome et la Primauté de St. Pierre: EO 11 (1908) 5-15; *idem*, Saint Jean Chrysostome et la Primauté du Pape: *ibid.* 193-202. — J. HADZSEGA, De discrimine inter sententiam theologorum orthodoxorum et S. Joannis Chrysostomi de Primatu S. Petri: Operum Academiae Velehradensis 4 (1912) 1-10. — N. MARINI, Il Primato di San Pietro e dei suoi successori in S. Giovanni Crisostomo.

2nd ed. Rome, 1922. — C. BAUR, Joh. Chrys. und seine Zeit. Munich, I (1929) 383-391, II (1930) 254-258 (against Marini). — J. LUDWIG, Die Primatworte Mt. 16, 18.19 in der altkirchlichen Exegese. Münster, 1952, 54-57. — E. MICHAUD, L'ecclésiologie de S. Jean Chrysostome: Revue internat. de théologie (1903) 491-620. — R. HEISS, Mönchtum, Seelsorge und Mission nach dem hl. Johannes Chrysostomus: Lumen Caecis. St. Ottilien, 1928, 1-23. — P. ANDRES, Der Missionsgedanke in den Schriften des hl. Johannes Chrysostomus. Huenfeld, 1935. — T. SPACIL, Fides catholica S. Joannis Chrysostomi: Greg (1936) 176-194, 355-376. — F. BAUER, Des heiligen Johannes Chrysostomus Lehre über den Staat und die Kirche und ihr gegenseitiges Verhältnis. Diss. Vienna, 1946.

Eschatology: E. MICHAUD, S. Jean Chrysostome et l'apocatastase: Revue internat. de théologie 18 (1910) 672-696. — S. SCHIWIETZ, Die Eschatologie des hl. Johannes Chrysostomus und ihr Verhältnis zu der origenistischen. Mainz, 1914. — S. BEZDECHI, La théorie des peines futures chez Platon et Jean Chrysostome (in Rumanian with a French summary): Anuarul Istitutului de Studii Clasice 2 (1933/35) 1-33.

For studies on *sociology,* see above, p. 454. — C. N. STRATIOTES, Ἡ ποιμαντικὴ τοῦ ἁγίου Ἰωάννου τοῦ Χρυσοστόμου. Saloniki, 1935. — M. S. WASYLYK, De servitute apud Joannem Chrysostomum. Diss. Propag. Rome, 1949. — For studies on *moral theology:* see above, p. 453. — For studies on Chrysostom's *asceticism,* cf. above, p. 465; on *education,* above p. 467; on *marriage* and *virginity,* above, p. 464. — S. GOSEVIC, Ἡ περὶ θείας χάριτος διδασκαλία Ἰωάννου τοῦ Χρυσοστόμου : Θεολογία 27 (1956) 367-389. — M. M. BRANISTE, Conceptia Sfîntului Joan Gurǎ de Aur despre prientenie si dragoşte: Studii Teologice 9 (1957) 649-672 (concept of friendship and charity). — S. CINDEA, Sfîntul Joan Gurǎ de Aur ca pastor de sufleote: Biserica Ortodoxa Romîna 75 (1957) 922-927 (Chrysostom as a pastor of souls).

ACACIUS OF BEROEA

Acacius was for a time a trusted friend of Chrysostom, but, offended by a supposed slight at the hands of the Patriarch, became one of his bitterest opponents (Palladius, *Hist. Laus.* 4, 18; 6, 21). Born about 322, he entered the monastic life at an early age and gained a reputation for sanctity and austere asceticism that was apparently well deserved. During this period he corresponded with Basil the Great and Epiphanius of Salamis. The latter composed the *Panarion* at his request (cf. above, p. 387). In 378 he was consecrated bishop of Beroea (i.e. Aleppo) in Syria by Meletius of Antioch. The latter sent him to Pope Damasus in order to settle the schism of Antioch. He participated in the Council of Constantinople in 381. At the Synod of the Oak he belonged with Antiochus of Ptolemais, Severianus of Gabala and Theophilus of Alexandria to the group of four bishops whom Chrysostom refused to accept as his judges. Old age prevented him from attending the Council of Ephesus. Nevertheless, he had a decisive influence in the negotiations which led to the union formula of 433. He must have died shortly afterwards. Sozomen (*Hist. eccl.* 7, 28) and Theodoret (*Hist. eccl.* 5, 23) extol his kindness and piety despite his bad judgment in the tragedy of Chrysostom. One of his *chorepiscopoi,* Balaeus, praises his virtues in five Syriac hymns.

Of his extensive correspondence only six letters remain. One is addressed to Cyril of Alexandria in favor of Nestorius and recommends peace. It is extant in the Greek original (MG 77, 99-102) and in a Latin translation (Mansi 5, 518-520). Two communications sent to the Nestorian Alexander of Hierapolis deal with the agreement to be reached between Cyril of Alexandria and the bishops of Antioch. They are preserved in a Latin version only (MG 84, 647-648; 660). The *Confessio fidei* attributed to him (MG 72, 1445-1448) seems to be spurious.

Editions: MG 77, 99-102; 84, 647-648, 658-660; 41, 156f. — E. SCHWARTZ, ACO I, 1, 1, 99f.; 7, 146f., 161f.; IV, 85; 92; 243. — Two fragments are found in Severus of Antioch, *Contra impium Grammaticum* III, 2, ed. J. LEBON, CSCO 93 (1929) 94. — A German translation of the five Syriac hymns of Balaeus by P. S. LANDERSDORFER, BKV² 6 (1912) 71-89.

Studies: E. VENABLES, DCB 1 (1877) 12-14. — V. ERMONI, Acace de Bérée: DHG 1 (1912) 241-242. — C. BAUR, Johannes Chrysostomus und seine Zeit 2. Munich, 1930, 137ff.; 161-163. — S. SCHIWIETZ, Das morgenländische Mönchtum 3. Mainz, 1938, 182-190. — G. BARDY, Acace de Bérée et son rôle dans la controverse nestorienne: RSRUS 18 (1938) 2-45.

ANTIOCHUS OF PTOLEMAIS

Antiochus, bishop of Ptolemais (the old Acco) in Phoenicia, was one of the leaders of the conspiracy against Chrysostom. He frequently preached at Constantinople and 'had so fine a voice and delivery that, by some persons, he was surnamed Chrysostom (Golden Mouth)', as Sozomen (*Hist. eccl.* 8, 10) and Socrates (*Hist. eccl.* 6, 11) inform us. He must have died shortly after the Synod of the Oak, at the latest 408 A.D. Gennadius (*De vir. ill.* 20) says that he 'wrote one great volume *Against Avarice* and composed a homily, full of godly penitence and humility *On the Healing of the Blind Man* whose sight was restored by the Saviour'. Both of these works have perished. The homily *On the Creation of the Soul of Adam and on the Passion of Christ* found among the sermons of Chrysostom (ed. H. Savile V, 648-653) which S. Haidacher attributed to Antiochus, does not belong to the latter but to Severianus of Gabala, as J. Zellinger has shown. Two Christmas sermons, quotations from which are preserved in Theodoret (*Dial.* 2, MG 83, 205), in the Acts of the Council of Chalcedon (Mansi 7, 469) in Leontius of Byzantium (*C. Nest. et Eut.* 1. 1, MG 86, 1316) and in Pope Gelasius (*De duabus naturis in Christo*, ed. Thiel 551. 552. 557) were discovered complete by Ch. Martin in a manuscript of the tenth century (*Paris. Gr.* 1491) and seem to be genuine.

Studies: R. AIGRAIN, DHG 3 (1924) 707-708. — S. HAIDACHER, Die Homilie des Antiochus von Ptolemais über die Erschaffung der Seele Adams und über das Leiden Christi: ZkTh 33 (1908) 408-410. — J. ZELLINGER, Die Genesishomilien des Bischofs Severian von Gabala. Münster, 1916, 44-47. — C. MARTIN, Un florilège grec d'homélies christologiques des IVe et Ve siècles sur la Nativité (Paris. Gr. 1491): Mus 44 (1941) 17-57. Quotations from three sermons can be found in Severus of Antioch, *Contra impium Grammaticum* III, 41, ed. J. LEBON, CSCO 101/102 (1933).

SEVERIAN OF GABALA

More important than Acacius and Antiochus was Severian bishop of Gabala in Syria (near Laodicea). He was of a rather passionate nature and took an almost overweening pride in his talents as an orator. He won a certain popularity by his occasional preaching in the capital and succeeded in consolidating his influence in Court circles, especially with the Empress Eudoxia. His originally friendly relations with Chrysostom soon turned to intense hostility. He played a leading part at Constantinople in the events leading up to the Synod of the Oak in 403 and he defended the deposition of Chrysostom from the pulpit (Socrates, *Hist. eccl.* 6, 16; Sozomen, *Hist. eccl.* 8, 18). Palladius (*Dial.* 11) is convinced that he was responsible for the transfer of the exiled Patriarch from Cucusus to Pityus. He died after 408 A.D.

He is chiefly important as an exegete of the strict Antiochene School. A fervent defender of the faith of Nicaea against heretics and Jews, he lacks originality and is full of hatred. His concept of the world is naive and unscientific since he does not hesitate to apply a literal interpretation even to the most daring imagery of Old Testament poetry and to use it as a sourcebook for natural science.

Studies: E. VENABLES, DCB 4 (1887) 625f. — H. LIETZMANN, PWK II. Reihe, 2 (1923) 1930-1932. — G. BARDY, DTC 14 (1941) 2000-2006. — E. PETERSON, EC 11 (1953) 463. — M. JUGIE, Sévérien de Gabala et le Symbole Athanasien: EO 14 (1911) 193-204; *idem*, Sévérien de Gabala et la causalité sacramentelle: Revue de Phil. et Théol. (1913) 467-471. — W. DÜRKS, De Severiano Gabalitano. Diss. Kiel, 1917. — J. ZELLINGER, Studien zu Severian von Gabala (MBTh 8) Münster, 1926. — C. BAUR, Johannes Chrysostomus und seine Zeit. 2. Munich, 1930, 134-145, 161-166. — H. D. ALTENDORF, Untersuchungen zu Severian von Gabala. Diss. Tübingen, 1957 (typ.); cf. ThLZ 83 (1958) 583-584.

HIS WRITINGS

Gennadius (*De vir. ill.* 21) gives the following description of Severian: 'Severian, bishop of the church of Gabala, was learned in the Holy Scriptures and a wonderful preacher of homilies. On this account he was frequently summoned by the Bishop John and the Emperor Arcadius to preach a sermon at Constantinople. I have read his *Exposition of the Epistle to the Galatians* and a most attractive little work *On Baptism and the Feast of Epiphany*. He died in the reign of Theodosius, his son by baptism' (LNPF).

The Commentary to Galatians has not survived but about thirty homilies are extant, mostly among the works of St. Chrysostom, the man whom he persecuted to the bitter end.

1. About 14 sermons are preserved in Greek, and among them the most important *Orationes sex in mundi creationem*, six homilies on the Hexaemeron (MG 56, 429-500). Though they have come down under Chrysostom's name, they actually belong to Severian, as Cosmas Indicopleustes (*Topogr. Christ.* 1, 10; MG 88, 417 ff) and numerous quotations in Biblical *catenae* testify. They were delivered during Lent according to the liturgical custom and remain valuable as a source for the Antiochene view of the universe. The exact date is unknown. Two other homilies akin to the series on the Hexaemeron are found in Savile's edition only. They deal with Adam and the tree of knowledge. Other sermons are: *Hom. in illud Abrahae dictum Genesis* 24, 2 (MG 56, 553-564), *Hom. de serpente quem Moyses in cruce suspendit* (MG 56, 499-516), *Hom. in dictum illud Matth.* 21, 23 (MG 56, 411-428), *Hom. de ficu arefacta* (MG 59, 585-590), *Hom. de sigillis librorum* (MG 63, 531-544).

The *Homilia de pace* which Severian delivered in 401 after Eudoxia had brought about a temporary reconciliation between him and Chrysostom, is found in Migne (52, 425-428), in Latin only and in a fragmentary condition. The original and complete Greek text was edited by A. Papadopulos-Kerameus in 1891.

The authenticity of two other addresses preserved in Greek remains doubtful, especially that of the *Sermo in dedicatione pretiosae et vivificae crucis*.

Recently B. Marx has ascribed 12 additional homilies among the works of Chrysostom to Severian, some of which are incomplete.

An old Armenian version of 15 homilies under the name of Severian was published by the Mechitarist J. B. Aucher with a Latin translation. Only the first nine of them belong to Severian.

Other sermons are extant in Syriac, Coptic and Arabic but their genuineness has not been established beyond doubt.

Editions: MG 56, 411-590. — A. PAPADOPULOS - KERAMEUS, ʼΑνάλεκτα ἱεροσολυμτικῆς σταχυολογίας I. St. Petersburg, 1891, 15-26 (Greek text of *Homilia de pace*). — J. B. AUCHER, Severiani Gabal. homiliae nunc primum editae ex antiqua versione Armena in Latinum sermonem translatae. Venice, 1827. Homilies 7 (Aucher 250-293) and 9 (Aucher 321-371) are also extant in the original Greek. Homily 7 can be found in MG 56, 553-564 and homily 9 in: J. ZELLINGER, Studien 9-21, and in: C. MARTIN, Note sur l'homélie de Sévérien de Gabala: Mus (1935) 311-321 (*In illud: Pater transeat*). Cf. T. TOROSSIAN, The Greek Text of the Ninth Homily of Severian of Gabala and the Armenian Version (in Armenian): Bazmavep 95 (1937) 4-11. — A fragment of a

Georgian version of this ninth homily was found in Codex 35 of Mount Sinai: G. GARITTE, Un fragment géorgien de l'homélie IX de Sévérien de Gabala: Mus 66 (1953) 97-102 (Georgian text with a French translation and collation with the Armenian version). — For Syriac, Coptic and Arabic homilies, see: J. ZELLINGER, Studien 101-116. Five quotations of five homilies hitherto unknown are preserved by Severus of Antioch, *Contra impium Grammaticum* III, 39, 41, ed. J. LEBON, CSCO 101/102 (1933). — For a newly discovered Syriac Christmas sermon, see: C. Moss, Homily on the Nativity of Our Lord by Severian, Bishop of Gabala: Bulletin of the School of Oriental and African Studies 12 (1948) 555-566 (Syriac text and English translation).

Studies: J. ZELLINGER, Die Genesishomilien des Bischofs Severian von Gabala. Münster, 1916. — W. DÜRKS, Eine fälschlich dem Irenaeus zugeschriebene Predigt des Bischofs Severian von Gabala: ZNW 21 (1922) 64-69. — C. MARTIN, Une homélie De Paenitentia de Sévérien de Gabala: RHE 26 (1930) 331-343 (the 7th of the *Homiliae 9 de paenitentia* attributed to John Chrysostom, MG 49, 241-276, belongs to Severian). — F. CAVALLERA, Une nouvelle homélie restituée à Sévérien de Gabala: BLE (1932) 141f. — B. MARX, Severiana unter den Spuria Chrysostomi bei Montfaucon-Migne: OCP 5 (1939) 281-367. An additional homily of Pseudo-Chrysostom was discovered to belong to Severian by A. WENGER, Notes inédites sur les empereurs Théodose I, Arcadius, Théodose II, Léon: REB 10 (1953) 47-59; *idem*, Le sermon LXXX de la collection augustinienne de Mai restitué à Sévérien de Gabala: Augustinus Magister I. Paris, 1954, 175-185. — For Marian sermons of Severian, see: R. LAURENTIN, Court traité de théologie mariale. Paris, 1953, 162f. — E. J. SOARES, Severianus of Gabala and the Protoevangelium: Marianum 15 (1953) 401-411.

2. Large fragments are extant of a *Commentary to all the Epistles of St. Paul* in Biblical *catenae*. They testify to the existence of two different recensions, one of which quotes St. Paul directly, the other in paraphrase. This great exegetical work proves him a pupil of Diodore of Tarsus. Severian does not limit himself to an interpretation of the text but brings in theological discussions, especially concerning the Trinity. Frequently he introduces polemics against heretics, like Sabellius, the Docetes, the Valentinians, Marcionites, Apollinarists. Most remarkable is his strong opposition to veneration of the angels which endangers the central position of Christ in the Church and in the universe. He blames especially the Christian converts from paganism for substituting the angels for the pagan gods which they adored before and for regarding them as mediators between God and creation. Against all such tendencies he stresses the fact that there is only one mediator, Christ.

Edition: K. STAAB, Pauluskommentare aus der griechischen Kirche aus Katenen-handschriften gesammelt. Münster, 1953, 213-351.

MACARIUS MAGNES

Photius (*Bibl. cod.* 59) informs us that at the Synod of the Oak (403) Macarius, bishop of Magnesia, stood forth as the accuser of Heraclides whom Chrysostom had ordained bishop of Ephesus. It seems that this Macarius is identical with Macarius Magnes, a

Christian apologist and author about the year 400 of a work in five books, which in appearance reports a dispute of five days duration between himself and a pagan philosopher. Commonly known under its abbreviated name, the *Apocriticus*, its full title Ἀποκριτικὸς ἢ Μονογενὴς πρὸς Ἕλληνας is obscure and puzzling. The meaning seems to be 'Answer-book or rather the Only-begotten Himself to the pagans'. As an apology for the faith, the *Apocriticus* does not merit serious attention, and, paradoxically its chief claim to our notice is its accurate presentation of the pagan viewpoint. It is generally conceded that the dialogue form is merely a literary device adopted in refuting some widely read publication against the Church. The objections raised by the unbelieving interlocutor are all quoted verbatim from this work, and its line of attack is thus, thanks to the *Apocriticus*, the best known of the various types of anti-Christian propaganda. Criticism is directed against selected verses of the Gospels, Acts and Pauline Epistles. One or two objections concern the Old Testament, while some in the latter part deal with purely doctrinal questions, like the Incarnation, the Monarchy of God and the Resurrection. In the Gospels the pagan questions particularly the miracles and words of Christ. He displays undoubted skill and learning. Duchesne was of the opinion that he was the Neoplatonist Hierocles, the governor of Bithynia, who wrote two books called *Philalethes* or 'Friend of Truth', and instigated the persecution of Diocletian (cf. above, p. 333). However, Wagenmann, Hauschildt and Harnack adduced good reasons for the theory that he must be identified with Porphyry and that his objections are taken from his lost treatise in fifteen books against the Christians (cf. above, p. 333), which would make the *Apocriticus* even more valuable. However, it seems that Macarius did not use Porphyry's own work but a shortened revision by a later anonymous writer.

About half of the text has survived but not one of its manuscripts. The editio princeps by C. Blondel (Paris 1876) is based on a 15th century manuscript discovered in 1867 at Athens that has since disappeared. It was mutilated, beginning in chapter VII of book II, and ending in the middle of chapter XXX of book IV. A Venice manuscript from which the Jesuit F. Torres (Turrianus) cited a great number of passages in his Eucharistic controversy with the Lutherans in the sixteenth century is no longer extant either. He not only quotes from all the books contained in the printed edition but from the lost fifth book also. In the ninth century the *Apocriticus* was used by the Iconoclasts in defense of their doctrine. Nicephorus, Patriarch of Constantinople, showing that his opponents had cited it wrongly, quotes in addition a

passage from the first book, which has not been preserved otherwise.

Edition: C. BLONDEL (and P. Foucart), Μακαρίου Μάγνητος Ἀποκριτικὸς ἢ Μονογενής.
Macarii Magnetis quae supersunt ex inedito codice ed. Paris, 1876.

Translation: English: T. W. CRAFER, The Apocriticus of Macarius Magnes (SPCK).
London, 1919.

Studies: G. SALMON, DCB 3 (1882) 766-771. — G. BARDY, DTC 9 (1927) 1456-1459. —
L. DUCHESNE, De Macario Magnete et scriptis eius. Paris, 1877. — T. ZAHN, Zu Makarius
von Magnesia: ZKG 2 (1878) 450-459. — J. A. WAGENMANN, Porphyrius und die
Fragmente eines Ungenannten in der athenischen Makariushandschrift: Jahrbücher f.
deutsche Theologie 23 (1878) 269-314. — C. J. NEUMANN, Scriptorum Graecorum qui
Christianam impugnaverunt religionem, quae supersunt, fasc. 3. Leipzig, 1880, 14-23;
245. — T. W. CRAFER, Macarius Magnesius, a Neglected Apologist: JThSt 8 (1906/7)
401-423. — H. HAUSCHILDT, De Porphyrio philosopho Macarii Magnetis apologetae
Christiani Ἀποκριτικῶν auctore. Bonn, 1907. — G. SCHALKHAUSER, Zu den Schriften
des Makarios von Magnesia (TU 31, 4). Leipzig, 1907 (manuscript tradition). —
J. GEFFCKEN, Zwei griechische Apologeten. Leipzig, 1907, 301-304; cf. DLZ 39 (1916)
1637ff. — A. HARNACK, Kritik des Neuen Testaments von einem griechischen Philo-
sophen des 3. Jahrhunderts (TU 37, 4). Leipzig, 1911; *idem*, Porphyrius, 'Gegen die
Christen', 15 Bücher, Zeugnisse, Fragmente und Referate (AAB, Phil.-hist. Kl.). Berlin,
1916. — G. BARDY, Les objections d'un philosophe païen d'après l'Apocriticus de
Macaire de Magnesie: Bulletin d'anc. litt. et d'archéol. chrét. 3 (1913) 95-111. —
T. W. CRAFER, The Work of Porphyry against the Christians and its Reconstruction:
JThSt 15 (1914) 360-395, 481-512. — R. BURN, Adversaria in Macarium Magnetem:
JThSt 23 (1921) 64-67 (text. crit.). — A. B. HULEN, Porphyry's Work against the
Christians (Yale Studies in Religion, fasc. 1). New Haven, 1933. — G. MERCATI, Nuove
note di letteratura biblica e cristiana antica (TS 95). Vatican City, 1941, 49-71 (on the
titles of books 1-3). — P. FRASSINETTI, Sull'autore delle Questioni pagane conservate
nell'Apocritico di Macario di Magnesia: Nuovo Didaskaleion 3 (1949) 41-56 (questions
remind one of Julian the Apostate). — F. CORSARO, L'Apocritico di Macario di Magnesia
e le Sacre Scritture: ibid. 7 (1957) 1-24 (no recording of a real dispute).

The ten short fragments of another work of Macarius, his *Homilies
on Genesis*, are spurious, except the longest one dealing with the coats
of skins (Genesis 3, 21) which God gave to the first parents after
the fall. Following Origen he interprets them as the human body
in its present form.

Editions: MG 10, 1375-1406 (excerpts only). — L. DUCHESNE, op. cit. 39-43. — C. PITRA,
Analecta sacra et classica. Paris, 1888, pars 1, 31-37. Additional fragments: A. SAUER,
Des Makarius Magnes Homiliae in Genesim (eine Ergänzung der Fragmente): Festschrift zum elfhundertjährigen Jubiläum des deutschen Campo Santo in Rom. Freiburg
i.B., 1897, 291-295.

Study: G. SCHALKHAUSER, op. cit. 113-201.

HESYCHIUS OF JERUSALEM

Little is known of the life of Hesychius except that he was a
monk and about 412 held in high repute as a priest and preacher
of the Church of Jerusalem according to Theophanes Confessor

(*Chronographia*, ed. de Boor I 83). Cyril of Scythopolis who praises him as 'teacher of the Church', as 'Theologian' and 'far famed luminary', reports that he accompanied in 428 or 429 Patriarch Juvenal of Jerusalem to the consecration of the church of the monastery of Euthymius (*Vita S. Euthymii*, MG 114, 629). He most probably died after 450. The Greek Church venerates him as a Saint and highly gifted interpreter of Holy Scripture (Feast day, March 28).

HIS WRITINGS

According to the Greek Menology (MG 117, 373) he commented on the whole Bible. Though this statement was first thought to be an exaggeration, manuscript research in recent times seems more and more to confirm it. The surviving treatises and fragments show that he generally follows the Alexandrian method of allegorical exegesis. With Origen he goes so far as even to deny a literal meaning for every passage of Scripture: *Inutilis vel fortassis etiam noxia est haec litera, si spolietur spirituali intelligentia* (MG 93,791 B). On another occasion he states: *Haec quodammodo ad literam videntur esse ridicula, unde nec ita ea custodiri a prophetis et spiritualibus invenimus* (MG 93,1030 A). He is a declared enemy of philosophy, which he calls a *sapientia exterior* because the heretics have used it to falsify the teaching of the Church, especially the Christological dogma. His theology is entirely biblical and his Christology unphilosophical. Words like Person, Hypostasis, Essence, Nature, Incarnation are purposely avoided and Scriptural expressions substituted. There is no proof for M. Faulhaber's opinion that the terminology of Ephesus (431) influenced him, much less that of Chalcedon (451). The basis of his Christological views is Alexandrian. He follows Cyril of Alexandria but without adopting his technical vocabulary. The point of departure for his Christology is the Logos who assumes flesh and makes it His own. The shortest Christological formula is the Λόγος σαρκωθείς, the *Verbum incarnatum*. There is no possibility of sin, of moral progress or of real ignorance in Christ. Hesychius defends orthodoxy against Arians, Apollinarians and the Antiochene doctrine of separation. Bishop John of Maiuma and the Roman deacon and later Pope Pelagius I counted Hesychius among the Monophysites. Jüssen denies any basis for such an accusation. However, there is no doubt that in some of his writings he shows a leaning to this heresy, though he avoids the gross expressions of Eutyches.

While a great number of his works have perished, some of his writings remain still unedited and await more thorough research.

Studies: M. FAULHABER, Hesychius of Jerusalem: CE 7 (1910) 303-304. — G. LOESCHKE, Hesychios: PWK 8 (1913) 1328-1330. — K. JÜSSEN, Die dogmatischen Anschauungen des Hesychius von Jerusalem (MBTh 17 and 20). Münster, 1931/1934, 2 vols (with a complete survey of his works vol. I, 10-47). — G. GRAF, Geschichte der christlichen arabischen Literatur I (TS 118). Vatican City, 1944, 367-369. — A. VACCARI, Esichio di Gerusalemme: EC 5 (1951) 581-582. — K. JÜSSEN, Die Mariologie des Hesychius von Jerusalem: Theologie in Geschichte und Gegenwart. Festschrift M. Schmaus, ed. by J. Auer and H. Volk. Munich, 1957, 651-670.

1. *Commentary on Leviticus*

The complete text of this extensive commentary is extant only in a Latin translation by a certain Jerome of the sixth century. The introduction attributes the work explicitly to Hesychius who dedicates it to a deacon Eutychianus: *Venerabili diacono Eutychiano peccator Christi servus Isychius presbyter in Christo salutem.* Its Palestinian origin is indicated in the preface where the author asks Eutychianus to pray, *ut fiat oblatio verbi mei acceptabilis, non solum in Jerusalem, sed in omni terra in qua Deo annuente defertur.* Nevertheless, the authenticity of this commentary has been denied again and again, because the Latin translation bases its explanation of Leviticus on the Vulgate. Thus M. Faulhaber wrote (CE 5,303): '(This) is extant only in Latin and is unauthentic, being based on the Vulgate text rather than on the Septuagint, and therefore the work of a later Latin (Isychius)'. G. Loeschke (PWK 8, 1329) drew the same conclusion. Vaccari deserves credit for having shown that the Latin is a rendition of a Greek work which can come from no one else than Hesychius of Jerusalem. This was based on the Septuagint, and the text of the Vulgate was substituted by the Latin translator or by a later hand. Vaccari's conclusion has been magnificently confirmed only recently by the discovery of a fragment of the original which was thought to have altogether perished. A. Wenger found in a manuscript of the Library of Strasbourg a florilegium which contains a portion of the Greek text. While this manuscript (*ms. Graec.* 12) is dated 1296, he came upon the same florilegium in the much older *Cod. Paris. Gr.* 924, of the tenth century. The fragment reproduces the commentary on Leviticus XIV, 4-7. A comparison with the Latin version proves that the translator has revised the text, especially the Christological parts, to bring them into agreement with the definition of Chalcedon (451).

Editions: MG 93, 787-1180. — A. WENGER, Hésychius de Jérusalem. Le fragment grec du commentaire 'In Leviticum': REAug 2 (1956) 464-470 (Greek text of the fragment in parallel columns with the Latin version from MG 93, 952, line 12).

Studies: A. VACCARI, Esichio di Gerusalemme ed il suo 'Commentarius in Leviticum': Bess 22 (1918) 8-46; reprinted: A. VACCARI, Scritti di erudizione e di filologia I. Filologia biblica e patristica. Rome, 1952, 165-206. — L. SANTIFALLER, Das Altenburger

Unzialfragment des Levitikuskommentars von Hesychius aus der ersten Hälfte des 8. Jahrhunderts: ZBW 60 (1943) 241-266 (fragment of the Latin version from the eighth century). — A. Siegmund, Die Überlieferung der griechischen christlichen Literatur in der lateinischen Kirche. Munich-Pasing, 1949, 87-88.

2. Commentary on Job

A Commentary consisting of 24 homilies on Job 1 to 20 has come down to us in an Armenian version which Tcherakian published (Venice, 1913) from *Codex* 339 of the 13th century in the Library of the Mechitarists on the island of San Lazzaro. It seems that the original work covered the entire Book of Job and that the Armenian translator in the sixth or seventh century stopped at ch. 20. Fragments of the rest have survived. Hesychius bases his interpretation on the Septuagint but makes use also of the Hebrew text and the other translations. He regards Job as an historical person and as a prophet, whose sufferings are a type of the sufferings of Christ. He explains the entire book as an allegorical foreshadowing of Christ and His Church.

Edition: C. Tcherakian, The Commentary on Job by Hesychius, Presbyter of Jerusalem (in Armenian). Venice, 1913. The fragments of the rest (beyond ch. 20) are found in Tcherakian's edition, Appendix I, p. 284-290, culled from the *Catena on Job* by John Vanakan Vardapet (13th century).

Study: C. Nahapetian, Il commentario a Giobbe di Esichio: Bess 19 (1913) 452-465.

3. Glosses on Isaias

Hesychius' commentary on Isaias was discovered by M. Faulhaber in 1900 in the anonymous marginal notes to the eleventh-century *Cod. Vatic.* 347. He published it with a facsimile in the same year. Since then the authenticity of the 2680 glosses of which it consists has been confirmed by a ninth-century Bodleian manuscript (*Miscell. Gr.* 5). Hesychius here imitates Origen in putting his exegesis into the form of the shortest possible marginal glosses. Thus his comment on Isaias 9, 1, 'the Lord will ascend upon a swift cloud, and will enter into Egypt', is 'Christ in the arms of the Virgin'.

Edition: M. Faulhaber, Hesychii Hierosolymitani interpretatio Isaiae prophetae. Freiburg i.B., 1900.

Study: M. Faulhaber, Eine wertvolle Oxforder Handschrift: ThQ 83 (1901) 218-232 (Codex Bodleianus Miscellaneus Graecus 5, saec. IX).

4. Glosses on the Minor Prophets

Scholia to the Twelve Minor Prophets are preserved in six manuscripts at Rome, Paris and Moscow and are still unedited except for the few on Abdias, Zacharias and Osee which Faulhaber published as samples.

Edition: M. FAULHABER, Die Prophetenkatenen nach römischen Handschriften. Freiburg i.B., 1899, 21-26 (on Abdias), 32f. (on Zacharias); *idem*, Hesychii H. interpretatio Isaiae proph. VIII-XII (on Osee I, 1-11). — The preface to the commentary on the Twelve Minor Prophets is found in MG 93, 1340-1344.

5. *Commentaries on the Psalms*

The most perplexing problem has been the connexion of Hesychius with commentaries on the Psalms attributed to him. If we compare the numerous citations ascribed to Hesychius in *catenae* with the commentaries handed down under his name, particularly in Oxford and Venice manuscripts, the variations are too radical to be laid to scribal errors and oversights in copying a single archetype. Recent investigations have shown that Hesychius was in fact the author of several works on the Psalms.

a. Glosses on the Psalms

Faulhaber and Mercati have satisfactorily proved that the bulk of the so-called Psalm-commentary published by Cardinal Antonelli in 1746 under the name of Athanasius and printed in Migne among his works (27, 649-1344) belongs to Hesychius. It represents not a set commentary but a series of glosses, usually little more than marginal notes, which purpose to edify by allegorical explanation. Thus the 'Lord' of verse one of Psalm 22 is described as the Good Shepherd who gave His life for us (MG 27, 729). 'In a place of pasture' means 'in the Church of God in which the saints flower'. 'He has brought me to the waters of refreshment' means 'to the grace of the Holy Ghost'. The author remarks on 'Thou hast prepared a table before me': 'The Psalmist calls the mystery of immortality the heavenly table'. Finally, as Hesychius interprets the oil as 'the grace of the Holy Spirit', it is evident that he conceives the Psalm as a hymn of thanksgiving for the sacramental initiation, the reception of Baptism, Confirmation and the Holy Eucharist.

Editions: N. ANTONELLI, S. Athanasii Alex. interpretatio psalmorum sive de titulis psalmorum. Rome, 1746; reprinted: MG 27, 649-1344.

Studies: M. FAULHABER, Eine wertvolle Oxforder Handschrift: ThQ 83 (1901) 218-232. — G. MERCATI, Note di letteratura biblica e cristiana antica (ST 5). Rome, 1901, 145-179: Il commentario di Esichio Gerosolimitano sui Salmi. — G. MERCATI, Sull'autore del De titulis Psalmorum stampato fra le opere di S. Atanasio: OCP 10 (1944) 7-22 (confirms his former opinion).

b. Great Commentary on the Psalms

Besides this glossing of the Psalms, Hesychius published an extensive and complete commentary. One part is printed in Migne

(93, 1179-1340) under his name, another (MG 55, 711-784) under that of St. Chrysostom, and a great section remains unedited in *Cod. Vatic. Gr.* 525 and *Cod. Paris. Gr.* 654, both of the eleventh century. A critical edition of the whole work would be of great value for the history of the Biblical text as well as for the Patristic theology of the fifth century.

Studies: R. DEVREESSE, La chaîne sur les psaumes de Daniele Barbaro II. Hésychius de Jérusalem: RBibl (1924) 498-521 (*Aurea in quinquaginta Psalmos doctorum Graecorum catena* interprete Daniele Barbaro, published at Venice, 1569, contains additional fragments for the first 50 Psalms). Devreesse regained most of the Commentary from manuscripts. — G. MERCATI, Un Salterio greco e una catena greca del Salterio posseduti dal Sadoleto: Miscellanea P. Paschini. Rome, 1949, 205-304 (the fragments of this *Catena* belong to Hesychius).

c. A second Commentary on the Psalms

Another commentary on the Psalms of medium size, edited by V. Jagič as a work *incerti auctoris,* was attributed to Hesychius by Devreesse on account of *Catenae* which ascribe it to him. There is, however, one great difficulty: the Christology of this commentary has definitely Antiochene color. However, Jüssen is of the opinion that Hesychius did not hesitate to employ expressions of the School of Antioch before the Nestorian controversy began. Later on he seems anxious to avoid them. Thus the commentary could be of that earlier period, though doubts remain.

Edition: V. JAGIČ, Supplementum Psalterii Bononiensis. Incerti auctoris explanatio psalmorum Graeca. Vienna, 1917.

Studies: V. JAGIČ, Ein unedierter griechischer Psalmenkommentar (Denkschriften der Kaiserl. Akademie der Wissenschaften. Phil.-hist. Kl. 52). Vienna, 1906. — R. DEVREESSE, art. cit. 501ff., 503.

6. Glosses on Biblical Canticles

Faulhaber found in a manuscript of the 9th century at Oxford (*Miscell.* 5) a *Catena* to the Biblical Canticles which contains 169 scholia of six or seven different authors, but 147 scholia on 13 Canticles of the Old and New Testament are by Hesychius. They have been edited by V. Jagič. There is so far no evidence that those on Exodus 15, Deuteronomy 32, 1 Kings 2 and Luke 1-2 have been culled from complete commentaries on these books, as Faulhaber thought.

Edition: V. JAGIČ, Supplementum 301-320.

Study: M. FAULHABER, Eine wertvolle Oxforder Handschrift: ThQ 83 (1901) 218-232.

7. Sermons

Only a few of the authentic sermons of Hesychius have been published so far. Among them are two discourses *De sancta Maria Deipara* (MG 93, 1453-1460 and 1460-1468) on the Annunciation, and another *In Hypapanten* (MG 93, 1467-1478) for the feast of the Purification *(καθάρσια)*. The latter represents the oldest extant address on the occasion of this feast which originated at Jerusalem. The Armenian homily on the Blessed Virgin, published by Tcherakian, is identical with the first on the Annunciation.

A. Wenger has recently given a list of eleven discourses not yet edited. *Cod. Vatic. Gr.* 1990, *Cod. Patmos S. Joh.* 181 and others have preserved a homily for the feast of the Hypapante which differs from that published in Migne and mentioned above. Its Mariology is highly interesting, especially its interpretation of Luke 2, 35 which follows the exegesis of Origen (*Hom.* 17 *on Luke*, MG 13, 1845) and St. Basil (*Ep. ad Optim.*, MG 32, 963).

Cod. Sinait. Gr. 491 of the eighth or ninth century contains a sermon on the advantages of fasting in the spirit of God. *Cod. Sinait. Gr.* 492 of the eighth or ninth century reproduces two Easter instructions, the first (ff. 64-69) an exhortation preached at the Vigil to the faithful in the Church of the Anastasis, and the second (ff. 70-73) highly important for its Christological formula.

Two homilies on the resurrection of Lazarus are extant in *Cod. Ottob. Gr.* 14 of the tenth and a number of manuscripts of the ninth and eleventh centuries. They are remarkable for their lofty eloquence rather than for their theology, though some of the ideas on the afterlife are noteworthy.

An encomium on St. Andrew is found in *Cod. Vatic. Gr.* 1641 of the 11th century. A Latin translation by Ch. Fabien was published in Magna Bibliotheca Patrum XII, pp. 188-190, at Lyons in 1677.

An encomium on St. Luke is preserved in *Cod. Athos Great Laura* D 50 of the year 1039 and in later manuscripts. Speaking about the Annunciation, Hesychius stresses the *virginitas in partu*.

An encomium on St. Peter and St. Paul survives in *Cod. Vatic. Gr.* 1667 of the tenth century. Though mostly devoted to St. Paul, it opens with a magnificent praise of St. Peter as the head of the Apostles, the trumpet of the mystery, the irreproachable shepherd, the ever vigilant pilot and unerring charioteer.

Cod. Sinait. Gr. 493 of the eighth century is the only manuscript which preserves an encomium on St. Stephen, whose feast was celebrated on December 27 at Jerusalem. It is by far Hesychius' most beautiful sermon. He praises the first martyr as the glory of Jerusalem and calls Jerusalem the altar of his sacrifice.

An encomium on St. Antony the hermit has come down to us in two manuscripts, *Cod. Ottob. Gr.* 411 of the 14th and in *Cod.* 30 of the Library Spyros Loberdos (Athens) of the 16th century.

An encomium on St. John the Baptist is found in a number of manuscripts and a portion of an encomium on the martyrs in *Cod. Vatic. Gr.* 1524 of the tenth century.

Finally two lost sermons deserve to be mentioned. The first was a Christmas homily contained in *Cod. Taurin. Gr.* 135 of the 14th century which perished in 1904. The second, a sermon on the Cross, is listed in the table of contents at the beginning of *Cod. Sinait. Gr.* 493 of the eighth century. Photius refers to two encomia no longer extant, the one on St. Thomas, the other on St. James, the brother of the Lord (MG 93, 1477-1480).

Editions: MG 93, 1453-1460 (on the Annunciation I); 1460-1468 (on the Annunciation II); 1468-1478 (for the feast of the Purification). — C. TCHERAKIAN, The Commentary on Job by Hesychius. Venice, 1913, 293-303.

Studies: A. BAUMSTARK, Rom oder Jerusalem? Eine Revision der Frage nach der Herkunft des Lichtmessfestes: ThGl 1 (1909) 89-105. — A. WENGER, Hésychius de Jérusalem. Les homélies grecques inédites d'Hésychius: REAug 2 (1956) 458-461. — For fragments (Cod. Paris. Bibl. Nat., Lat. 4403), see: C. MARTIN, Fragments en onciale d'homélies grecques sur la Vierge attribuées à Épiphane de Chypre et à Hésychius de Jérusalem: RHE 31 (1935) 356-359; *idem*, Mélanges d'homilétique byzantine I. Hésychius et Chrysippe de Jérusalem: RHE 35 (1939) 54-60 (Chrysippus depends on Hesychius).

8. *Church History*

Hesychius wrote a *Church History* also, an important chapter of which on Theodore of Mopsuestia, read at the Fifth Ecumenical Council in 553, survives in a Latin translation (Mansi 9, 248f.). It proves Hesychius a strong enemy of Nestorianism and charges Theodore with having called the Saviour *hominem per vitae provectionem et passionum perfectionem coniunctum Deo Verbo*. The end of the fragment indicates that this *Church History* was composed after 428, the date of Theodore's death.

9. *Collection of Objections and Solutions*

This συναγωγὴ ἀποριῶν καὶ ἐπιλύσεων is a kind of harmony illustrating by way of question and answer 61 Gospel problems. It most probably belongs to Hesychius (MG 93, 1391-1448) and seems to be an epitome of his lost Εὐαγγελικὴ συμφωνία.

Study: G. BARDY, La littérature patristique des Quaestiones et responsiones sur l'Écriture Sainte. Hésychius de Jérusalem: RBibl 42 (1933) 226-229.

The ascetical treatise *Ad Theodulum de temperantia et virtute* (MG 93, 1479-1544), a collection of spiritual maxims, consisting of 200 chapters on temperance and virtue, the *Kephalaia* on the Minor Prophets (MG 93, 1345-1386), the *Martyrium S. Longini* (MG 93, 1545-1560) and the *Laudatio S. Procopii Persae* (AB 24, 473-482) do not belong to Hesychius. The first work was composed by an abbot Hesychius of Mount Sinai who lived in the sixth or seventh century.

NILUS OF ANCYRA

According to recent investigations Nilus was the abbot or archimandrite of a monastery near Ancyra (i.e. Ankara) who lived around the turn of the fourth to the fifth century and died shortly before or after 430. Georgios Monachos in the ninth century mentions that he was a disciple of St. John Chrysostom and a contemporary of Proclus, Palladius, Mark the Hermit and Isidore of Pelusium. Nilus' own letters testify that he regarded Chrysostom as his teacher (cf. *Ep.* 2, 265. 294; 3, 279). When the Emperor Arcadius in 407 A.D. begged him to pray for the city of Constantinople, seriously afflicted by earthquakes and fires, Nilus answered in a letter (*Ep.* 2, 265) that he could not comply with his wish since these trials were caused by the crimes committed against the bishop of the capital (John Chrysostom).

The traditional biography differs considerably from these few and sober facts. Based on the *Narrationes* found among Nilus' works, it presents Nilus as a prefect of Constantinople at the time of Theodosius the Great (379-395), who resigned his high office and with his son, Theodulus, became a hermit on Mount Sinai. When the monks were attacked by hordes of barbarian robbers, Theodulus was captured, while Nilus himself was able to escape. But Theodulus finally succeeded in returning to his father and both were ordained priests by the bishop of Eleusa in Palestine, who sent them back to Mount Sinai. This legendary account of the *Narrationes* has influenced the liturgical books of the Greek Church, especially the Byzantine Synaxary of the tenth century, and has given rise to the erroneous name 'Nilus of Sinai' of modern times. However, K. Heussi has satisfactorily proved that the *Narrationes de caede monachorum in monte Sinai* has no autobiographical value whatever; it is a pure fiction of some unknown later writer. It is a literary product reminiscent of the Hellenistic novel and the adventures of Theodulus are obviously imaginary. Degenhart's and Schiwietz' defense of its historical character is not convincing, though all but one of the great number of manuscripts attribute it to Nilus. J. Henninger's ethnographic criticism has recently led to the same conclusion as Heussi.

Studies: Text of the *Narrationes de caede monachorum:* MG 79, 589-694. — S. SCHIWIETZ, Das morgenländische Mönchtum II. Mainz, 1913, 37-72. — F. DEGENHART, Der hl. Nilus Sinaita. Münster, 1915. — K. HEUSSI, Nilus der Asket und der Überfall der Mönche am Sinai: NJKA 37 (1916) 107-127; *idem*, Untersuchungen zu Nilus dem Asketen (TU 42, 2). Leipzig, 1917. — F. DEGENHART, Neue Beiträge zur Nilusforschung. Münster, 1918. — K. HEUSSI, Das Nilusproblem. Randglossen zu F. Degenharts Neuen Beiträgen zur Nilusforschung. Leipzig, 1921. — M. T. DISDIER, Nil l'ascète: DTC 11 (1931) 661-674. — K. HEUSSI, PWK 16 (1935) 2186-2187. — V. FRADINSKI, Nilus. His Life and his Literary Activity (in Serbian). Beograd, 1938. — C. ASTRUC, Miscellanea Graeca dans un recueil provenant de Charles de Montchal: Scriptorium 8 (1954) 293-296 (manuscript of the *Narrationes*). — J. HENNINGER, Ist der sogenannte Nilus-Bericht eine brauchbare religionsgeschichtliche Quelle?: Anthropos 50 (1955) 81-148.

HIS WRITINGS

His literary heritage confronts us with numerous problems the solution of which must wait upon a critical edition of his works. A considerable proportion of the ascetical corpus traditionally ascribed to Nilus must be the product of other writers. Many treatises by authors suspect of heresy, notably Evagrius Ponticus, have hidden behind his great reputation in the history of monasticism. The sifting of the spurious from the genuine is far from being completed though it has produced a number of interesting results in recent times.

Editions: MG 79. — For old Latin versions, see: A. SIEGMUND, Die Überlieferung der griechischen christlichen Literatur in der lateinischen Kirche. Munich-Pasing, 1949, 109-110. For Arabic versions: G. GRAF, Geschichte der christlichen arabischen Literatur I (ST 118). Vatican City, 1944, 399-400. For Syriac versions: W. WRIGHT, Catalogue of Syriac Manuscripts in the British Museum. London, 1870/1872, 3, 1311 s.v. 'Nilus'.

1. *Letters*

The second Council of Nicaea (788) and Photius (*Bibl. cod.* 201) refer to a collection of letters, which in the best and most complete edition by Leo Allatius (reprinted in MG 79, 81-582) comprises 1061 items divided into four parts. A critical examination discloses many of them have been arbitrarily broken up into several independent pieces. Others are so short — consisting at times of only one sentence — that they must have been mutilated. Moreover, there are a number of doublets, the same letters recurring in whole or in part. Several have proved to be merely excerpts from treatises by Nilus or others, especially Chrysostom, and epistolary only in form. Nevertheless, it would be a mistake to lower the corpus to the level of an anthology, as has been customary in modern times. It is homogeneous and basically genuine; it does actually go back to Nilus and began as his authentic correspondence. The first collector must have lived in his neighborhood and was perhaps a member of his monastic community at Ancyra. In the course of time repeated revisions added a number of letters and intruded spurious elements. The final product reminds one of the correspondence of Isidore of Pelusium, which suffered the same fate (cf. above, p. 102). Even in his personality Nilus has much in common with Isidore, his contemporary, a coarse frankness, a deep knowledge of Holy Writ, a rather quick temper, though his style does not attain to Isidore's perfection and elegance. His letters provide excellent guidance for all who turn to him for advice. He emerges from them as one of those early masters of spirituality who combined a deep insight into the human soul with considerable worldly wisdom. The recipients belong to all ranks of society, and, as a result, the content of his missives would be interesting for its variety alone.

Quite a number are devoted to the explanation of Scriptural passages. The author makes ample use of allegorical interpretation. Nevertheless, he remarks on several occasions that he does not wish to sacrifice the literal or historical sense (2, 223). Dogmatic discussion is rarer. Eight sent in response to Gainas, the leader of the Goths, contain a strong refutation of Arianism. The Christological teaching forms the subject of several others. Thus *Ep.* 3, 91 states, 'One is the Lord Jesus Christ, one *hypostasis*, one *prosopon*' (cf. *Ep.* 3, 92). He is God and Man in one person (*Ep.* 2, 292). His mother is therefore *theotokos* (*Ep.* 2, 180).

But the most important topic of his letters is the attainment of perfection by the imitation of Christ. Christ, the teacher of true philosophy, wishes us to be not only his pupils but his imitators by living a pure life and lifting our soul out of the passions of our body. He develops the concept of 'spiritual philosophy', φιλοσοφία πνευματική, and seems to have coined this term, since it is not found in any Patristic writings before. He calls monastic life 'spiritual philosophy', which is to him the only philosophy worthy of Christ. He speaks repeatedly of our obligation to 'philosophize after Christ', φιλοσοφεῖν κατὰ Χριστόν (*Ep.* 2, 257; 2, 305). He regards asceticism merely as a means to become free of passions, achieve *apatheia* and union with God (*Ep.* 2, 89; 2, 139; 2, 257). This goal can be reached here on earth but only by a lifelong contest. Even then it can be lost again because it is a gift and grace of God (*Ep.* 2, 139; 2, 46). On the other hand, it can be regained by penance (*Ep.* 2, 140).

Editions: MG 79, 81-581 (reprint of L. Allatius, Rome, 1668).

Studies: S. HAIDACHER, Chrysostomusfragmente in der Briefsammlung des hl. Nilus: Chrysostomika Rome, 1908, 226-234. — S. SCHIWIETZ, op. cit. 50-58. — J. STIGLMAYR, Der Asketiker Nilus Sinaita und die antiken Schriftsteller: ZkTh 39 (1915) 576-581. — K. HEUSSI, Untersuchungen 31-123. — V. WARNACH, Das Mönchtum als 'pneumatische Philosophie' in den Nilusbriefen: Vom christlichen Mysterium. Festschrift O. Casel. Düsseldorf, 1951, 135-151. — J. KIRCHMEYER, Écriture sainte et vie spirituelle: DSp 4 (1958) 166-167 (St. Nilus).

2. *Treatises*

His treatises deal mainly with ascetic and moral subjects, especially with the spiritual and monastic life.

a. *De monastica exercitatione* (λόγος ἀσκητικός)

Addressed to cenobites, this treatise composed before 425, consists of three parts. The first (ch. 1-20) explains the origin and idea of monasticism, the second (21-41) the duties of a religious superior and the third those of cenobites in general (42-66). The author describes monastic life as the true philosophy taught by Christ and as a life of poverty and toil (ch. 1; 4). He thinks that the monks of his day did not have the same zeal for poverty as their early predecessors (ch. 6-7). The responsibilities of the abbot are heavy; he has to lead the others to the life of the spirit and to perfection by example, by exhortations and corrections. The guidance of souls is the greatest of all arts (ch. 22) and demands in those who command wisdom and experience. Obedience consists in a complete renouncement of one's will and of all resistance to the superior (ch. 41). Those who have taken this vow have to be like clay in the hands of an artist. They are not permitted to examine or criticize orders but must forget themselves (ch. 42). Monastic life is like a wrestling match which we have to enter completely naked less we provide the demon with holds (ch. 64-66).

Twenty-one passages of this treatise can be found in the letters of Nilus. Heussi (p. 45) believes that these letters are older and that Nilus quotes from them in the present tract. But the converse remains possible that the letters copy the *De monastica exercitatione*.

Edition: MG 79, 720-809.

Study: K. HEUSSI, Untersuchungen 45-53.

b. *De voluntaria paupertate* (περὶ ἀκτημοσύνης)

On Voluntary Poverty is addressed to the deaconess Magna of Ancyra and refers to the author's former writing *De monastica exercitatione* in the introduction. Nilus distinguishes three kinds of poverty; the supreme, the medium and the lowest. The first dedicates itself exclusively to the service of God as our first parents did before the fall. The second cares in a limited way for the body and should characterize the true monk. The third is wholly devoted to longing for earthly possessions. Unfortunately the last is becoming more and more common in monastic circles and represents an apostasy from the ideal. The author does not hesitate to brand the extensive property and tremendous herds of cattle owned by the religious establishments as a worship of earthly goods (ch. 30). He urges a return to the 'medium poverty' (ch. 13), the poverty of those who live of the work of their hands and use the rest of their time for the care of the soul, for prayer, the reading of Scripture and the practice of virtue (ch. 29). This treatise also constitutes an implicit refutation of the Messalians who rejected poverty on the pretext that it made perpetual prayer impossible (ch. 21). Incidentally, Nilus mentions (ch. 21) the expulsion of the abbot Alexander, the founder of the *Akoimetai*, from Constantinople. Since this took place in 426 or 427, the present treatise seems to be the last of all his writings.

Edition: MG 79, 968-1060.

Study: F. DEGENHART, Der hl. Nilus Sinaita 100-102.

c. In Albianum oratio

The monk Albianus whose praise this panegyric sings, was born in Ancyra in Galatia and lived for a time in a near-by monastic community, made a pilgrimage to the Holy Land and died in the desert of Nitria where he went 'to devote himself entirely to the heavenly philosophy' (col. 705). The encomium was most probably composed at Ancyra.

Edition: MG 79, 696-712.

Study: C. ASTRUC, Scriptorium 8 (1954) 293-296 (new manuscript).

d. De monachorum praestantia

The treatise *On the Advantage to Monks of living far from the Cities in the Deserts* describes in detail the two great benefits of the eremitic life as compared with the ascetic life in the world. The former keeps distractions and temptations away (ch. 1-24) and avoids vainglory (ch. 24-26). It eliminates the occasions of sin and delivers from the praise of men, which ruins even the best works. The life in the desert leads to undivided union with God since it protects against the dangers of the world.

Edition: MG 79, 1061-1093.

Study: F. DEGENHART, op. cit. 93-95.

e. De magistris et discipulis

The small tract *On Teachers and Pupils* which P. van den Ven first published in 1908 in its original Greek text and in an old Latin version is a manual for superiors, novice-masters and novices, couched in sententious form or aphorisms.

Editions: P. VAN DEN VEN, Un opuscule inédit attribué à S. Nil: Mélanges G. Kurth. Liége, 1908, 2, 73-81. Textual corrections: J. MUYLDERMANS, Le De magistris et discipulis de S. Nil: Mus (1942) 93-96. — Armenian version: J. MUYLDERMANS, S. Nil en version arménienne: Mus (1943) 78-113.

f. De octo spiritibus malitiae

This work deals with the eight capital sins in the following order: gluttony, fornication, avarice, anger, sadness, sloth, vanity and pride. The theory of the eight capital sins was very popular in the monastic circles of the fourth century. Evagrius Ponticus (cf. above, p. 172) and John Cassian devoted special treatises to it. These sins are called capital, not because they are always grave sins, but because they give rise to other sins.

Editions: MG 79, 1145-1164. — New recension: J. MUYLDERMANS, Une nouvelle recension du De octo spiritibus malitiae: Mus 52 (1939) 235-274.

Translation: German: S. SCHIWIETZ, Das morgenländische Mönchtum II. Mainz, 1913, 58-84.

Study: E. PETERSON, Nilus' De octo spiritibus im Isaak-Florilegium: ZkTh 56 (1932) 596-599. Cf. above p. 172.

LOST WORKS

1. Commentary on the Song of Songs

Two *Catenae* testify that Nilus composed a commentary on the Canticle of Canticles no longer extant. The first is that of Procopius of Gaza of the sixth century, the second, that of Michael Psellus of the eleventh. Procopius quotes Nilus 61 times; the number and length of the excerpts show that he used a running commentary. Since Nilus interprets some verses of the Canticle in his letters (*Ep.* 1, 331; 2, 197; 2, 282) in exactly the same way as in Procopius' excerpts there is hardly any doubt of the authenticity of this commentary. Procopius and Michael Psellus both make it clear that Nilus explained the Canticle allegorically and identified the bride with the Church or with the human soul. Procopius' quotations also suggest that Nilus followed Origen rather closely.

Fragments: MG 87, 1545-1754 (Procopius); MG 122, 537-686 (Michael Psellus).

Studies: A. SOLIČ, De Nili monachi commentario in Canticum Canticorum reconstruendo: Bibl 2 (1921) 45-52; *idem,* BoS (1925) 1-22; *idem,* Nila monaha Pjesmi nad pjesmama.

Zagreb, 1932 (reports in these three publications about a Commentary on the Canticle of Canticles so far inedited). — L. WELSERSHEIMB, Das Kirchenbild der griechischen Väterkommentare zum Hohen Liede: ZkTh 70 (1948) 435-436.

2. *Sermons*

Photius (*Bibl. cod.* 276) quotes longer passages from five sermons of St. Nilus, two of them on Easter, three on Ascension. None has survived.

Fragments: MG 79, 1489-1502.

Studies: One of the homilies on the Ascension belongs to Proclus, see: C. MARTIN, Proclus de Constantinople, Nestorius et le 'bienheureux Nil', *Εἰς τὴν Ἀνάληψιν*: RHE 32 (1936) 929-932. — J. G. DAVIES, Proclus and Pseudo-Nilus: HThR 49 (1956) 179-181.

3. *Adversus gentiles*

Nicephorus Callistus (*Hist. eccl.* 14, 54) mentions a treatise *Against the Pagans* as worthy of being ranked among the best of Nilus' writings. Nothing is preserved of this work, and there is no other reference to it.

4. *Ad Eucarpium monachum*

Anastasius Sinaita (*Quaestio* 3) contains a fragment entitled *Nili ex iis quae scripsit ad Eucarpium monachum.* This is the only evidence for this lost letter or treatise.

Fragment: MG 89, 357.

SPURIOUS WORKS

1. *De oratione*

By far the most important work that has reached us under Nilus' name, is the treatise *On Prayer.* Though eight of its maxims occur in the *Apophthegmata Patrum* (cf. above, p. 174) under the name of Nilus (MG 65, 305), and in exactly the same sequence, and though Photius (*Bibl. cod.* 201) attributes *De oratione* to Nilus, it has been definitely proved that the work is not his but by Evagrius. It is under the latter's name that the Syrians quote it, and to the latter that the Syriac version ascribes it. Moreover, the tract *De malignis cogitationibus* certainly belongs to Evagrius (cf. above, p. 175), though it, too, was attributed to Nilus, and its author refers to *De oratione* (ch. 23) as a work of his own. Finally, in the latter, as shown by Hausherr, every detail of thought and style reflect the personality of Evagrius. Though small, the work has 153 chapters, all aphorisms.

Edition: MG 79, 1165-1200. For Arabic and Syriac versions, modern translations and studies, see above p. 174.

2. *De octo vitiosis cogitationibus*

Basically, this treatise is a compilation from Cassian; its eight chapters represent an abbreviation of the Pseudo-Athanasian second *Epistula ad Castorem* (MG 28, 872-905), itself nothing more than a Greek compendium of Cassian's doctrine of the eight capital sins. The gnomic part of each chapter adds passages from Nilus *(De octo spiritibus malitiae)* and Evagrius (cf. above p. 172).

Edition: MG 79, 1436-1464.

Studies: K. HEUSSI, Untersuchungen 163-166. — E. PETERSON, Zu griechischen Asketikern III: BNJ 9 (1932/33) 52. — S. MARSILI, Résumé de Cassien sous le nom de St. Nil: RAM 15 (1934) 241-245. For the doctrine of the eight capital sins, see above p. 172.

3. *Ad Eulogium monachum*

This exhortation addressed to the monk Eulogius is first mentioned in the fourteenth century by Nicephorus Callistus, who attributes it to Nilus. It belongs, apparently, to Evagrius, to whom several manuscripts and the Syrians and Armenians ascribe it. It deals with the watch over the heart against the temptations of the devil who attacks the monk everywhere.

Edition: MG 79, 1093-1140. Cf. above p. 175.

4. *Ad Agathium monachum Peristeria seu tractatus de virtutibus excolendis et vitiis fugiendis*

This tract owes its title to a famous Christian lady of Alexandria, Peristeria, who enjoyed a great reputation for her outstanding works of charity. Its three parts discuss first the duties and virtues of man that concern himself, then his obligations towards his neighbor and human society, which reach their perfection in alms-giving and care for the poor; finally the spiritual warfare which all must wage. It seems that the work was composed at Alexandria about the middle of the fifth century. Anastasius Sinaita (*Quaestio* 2, 11, 21) attributes it to a 'monk Nilus'. However, Nilus of Ancyra is for several reasons out of the question. His mentality and style are totally different.

Edition: MG 79, 812-968.

Study: K. HEUSSI, Untersuchungen 160-163.

5. *Gnomic or Sententious Collections*

Photius and Nicephorus Callistus explicitly testify that Nilus composed 'chapters' *(κεφάλαια)* or sayings. The former speaks of 'a hundred chapters' (*Bibl. cod.* 201). A number of gnomic collections have reached us under the name of Nilus. However, these are simply compilations from his writings, so that they are his property only in content not in form. Migne gives three series of maxims under Nilus: *Institutio ad monachos* (MG 79, 1235-1240); *Sententiae abducentes hominem a corruptibilibus et incorruptibilibus unientes* (79, 1239-1250) and *Capita paraenetica* (79, 1249-1264). Ns. 1-24 of the last form a gnomic alphabet and have been reedited by Elter under Evagrius' name, to whom all three series belong (cf. above p. 170).

Study: J. MUYLDERMANS, Evagriana: Mus (1938) 191-226 (Cod. Barber. Graec. 515 furnishes additional 24 maxims for the *Institutio ad monachos*).

6. *Epicteti enchiridion seu manuale*

A Christian paraphrase of the *Enchiridion* of Epictetus, the Stoic philosopher, is preserved in many manuscripts and attributed to Nilus. The real author has not been found yet but that it was some later writer and not Nilus is generally agreed. The work certainly does not ante-date the sixth century.

Edition: MG 79, 1285-1312.

Studies: C. WOTKE, Handschriftliche Beiträge zu Nilus' Paraphrase von Epiktets Handbüchlein: WSt 14 (1892) 69-74. — F. DEGENHART, Der hl. Nilus Sinaita 18-20. — O. SCHISSEL, Zur handschriftlichen Überlieferung des christlichen Epiktet: BNJ 7 (1930) 444-447. — F. LIGUORI, Il 'Manuale' di Epicteto tra i cristiani: SC 58 (1930) 297-303. — J. STELZENBERGER, Die Beziehungen der frühchristlichen Sittenlehre zur Ethik der Stoa. Munich, 1933, 478-488. — A. GRILLI, Seneca ed Epicuro: Paideia 12 (1957) 337-338 (MG 79, 1294ff.).

7. *Tractatus moralis et multifarius*

The origin of this sermon, which is extant also in an Arabic version, is unknown. There is nothing decisive in its content, but style and language rule out the authorship of Nilus.

Editions: MG 79, 1279-1286. — For Arabic version, see: G. GRAF, Geschichte der christlichen arabischen Literatur I. Vatican City, 1944, 400.

MARK THE HERMIT

Mark the Hermit was according to Nicephorus Callistus (*Hist. eccl.* 14, 30. 53. 54) a pupil of St. John Chrysostom and a contemporary of St. Nilus the Ascetic and St. Isidore of Pelusium. It seems that he was abbot of a monastery at Ancyra in Galatia in the first half of the fifth century, but in his old age lived as a hermit in the desert, most probably the desert of Juda. Since he took part in the controversy with the Nestorians, he must have died after 430.

Nicephorus mentions that Mark wrote at least forty ascetic treatises of which by sheer accident, he had eight at hand. Photius (*Bibl. cod.* 200) quotes and evaluates nine without mentioning any others and all of these nine have survived.

Edition: MG 65, 893-1140. — For Syriac versions in manuscripts of Vatican Library, see: J.S. ASSEMANI, Bibliotheca Orient. 3,1,45; for those of the British Museum: W. WRIGHT; Catalogue of Syriac Manuscripts in the B.M. 2. London, 1872, 1306 (s.v. 'Mark the monk') For a Berlin manuscript, see: F. BAETHGEN, ZKG 11 (1890) 443-445; E. SACHAU, Hand-schriftenverzeichnisse der Kgl. Bibliothek zu Berlin 23. Berlin, 1899, 102-109. Fo: Syriac commentaries on *De lege spirituali* and *De his qui putant se ex operibus iustificari*, see, Ebedjesu, in: ASSEMANI, op. cit. 3, 1, 96; 194. — For Arabic versions, see: G. GRAF. Geschichte der christlichen arabischen Literatur I (ST 118). Vatican City, 1944, 400-401, For Arabic versions of passages from *De lege spirituali*, *De his qui putant se ex operibus iustificari*, *De poenitentia*, *Disputatio cum quodam causidico* and *De baptismo* in a codex of the Bibliothèque Nationale at Paris and of the Library of the University of Strasbourg, see: I. A. KHALIFÉ, Les traductions arabes de Marc l'Ermite: Mélanges de l'Université de St. Joseph (Beyrouth) 28 (1949/1950) 117-224.

Studies: T. FICKER, Der Mönch Markus, eine reformatorische Stimme aus dem 5. Jahr-hundert: Zeitschrift für histor. Theologie 38 (1868) 402-430. — J. KUNZE, Markus Eremita. Leipzig, 1895, 31-54 (his life and his works). — J. KUNZE, RE 12 (1903) 280-287. — E. AMANN, DTC 9 (1927) 1964-1968. — H. DÖRRIES, PWK 14 (1930) 1867-1869. — H. G. OPITZ, PWK Supplement 6 (1935) 281-282. — M. VILLER and K. RAHNER, Aszese und Mystik in der Väterzeit. Freiburg i.B., 1939, 175-177.

1. *De lege spirituali* (Περὶ νόμου πνευματικοῦ)

The author interprets the 'law of the spirit' (Rom. 7, 14) as the life of perfection and gives in 201 sayings an analysis, which covers the entire code of monastic duties. The source of all sins is to forget God. The soul's supreme inspiration is the knowledge of God's presence and the perpetual remembrance of His benefits. 'Think of nothing and do nothing without a goal. Whoever travels without a goal becomes tired for no reason' (54). We notice in this treatise a polemic undertone which is directed against the Messalians (cf. 25. 66. 143. 192).

Edition: MG 65, 905-930. — For the Arabic version, see: I. A. KHALIFÉ, Les traductions arabes, 138-217 (text and Latin transl.).

2. *De his qui putant se ex operibus iustificari*

This tract *On Those who suppose Justification is from Works* seems originally to have formed part of the *De lege spirituali* of which its contents, 211 maxims, are merely a continuation, and to which its final chapter refers. As a matter of fact, the Syriac version puts both works together as one, though, it must be admitted, Photius cites them as distinct (*Bibl. cod.* 200). At all events, the author here comes into the open against the Messalians by energetically repudiating their basic principle, the identification of grace with mystical experience.

Edition: MG 65, 929-966.

3. De poenitentia

The 13 chapters of this writing regard penance as consisting principally in the war against sinful desires, in perpetual prayer and in patient suffering.

Edition: MG 65, 965-984.

4. De ieiunio

The short treatise *On Fasting* counts only four chapters which give the stock reasons for controlling our appetite. To take pride in feats of self-restraint, however, the author warns, would do more harm than good. 'The proud one does not know himself. If he knew himself and his own stupidity, he would not be conceited. How can a man who does not even know himself, attain to the knowledge of God?' (4)

Edition: MG 65, 1109-1118.

5. Ad Nicolaum praecepta animae salutaria

This treatise represents an answer to a letter which the ascetic Nicholas of Galatia addressed to Mark. The latter recommends the thought of God's benefits, especially of the grace of redemption through Christ, as the best means of overcoming all passions. He warns the young religious of the three main evils that endanger the soul: forgetfulness, negligence and ignorance. The first will be conquered by continuous remembrance of all the graces that we receive from God, the second by zeal and the third by spiritual knowledge. Mark mentions among the greatest of God's gifts to Nicholas the monastic habit or 'the angelic garment of the angelic order', as he calls it, and his entrance into the community. The treatise dates from the time when Mark lived as a hermit in the desert, as the introduction indicates.

Edition: MG 65, 1027-1050.

Study: P. Oppenheim, Symbolik und religiöse Wertung des Mönchskleides im christlichen Altertum. Münster, 1932, 110-119.

6. *De baptismo*

The tract *On Baptism* has a strong anti-Messalian tendency and in a series of questions and answers, deals with the effects of the sacrament of initiation. The exact title *Responsio ad eos qui de divino baptismate dubitant* refers to those who doubt that sin is actually taken away by baptism, since the Messalians maintained that even after its reception sin remains in the soul and must be destroyed by our own moral efforts. Mark declares against all such false doctrines that baptism not only takes away all sin but confers the Holy Spirit. The words 'I see another law in my members, fighting against the law of my mind' (Rom. 7, 23) are spoken by the unbaptized, not by the baptized. Nevertheless, life after baptism remains a continuous warfare because of the unending temptations from within and without. But every sin is the result of our own free will, not of our corrupted nature. The treatise has points of contact with the *Homilies* of Pseudo-Macarius (cf. above, p. 162).

Edition: MG 65, 985-1028.

Studies: E. PETERSON, Die Schrift des Eremiten Markus über die Taufe und die Messalianer: ZNW 31 (1932) 273-288. — K. RAHNER, Ein messalianisches Fragment über die Taufe: ZkTh 61 (1937) 266ff. — C. JÜSSEN, Dasein und Wesen der Erbsünde nach Marcus Eremita: ZkTh 62 (1938) 76-91.

7. *Consultatio intellectus cum sua ipsius anima*

This tract is akin to *De baptismo* in thought though not in form; it is not a dialogue but a soliloquy. The author here admonishes his own soul not to fall into self-deception, for sin cannot be ascribed to our origin from Adam, to the power of the devil or to the influence of others.

Edition: MG 65, 1103-1110.

8. *Disputatio cum quodam causidico*

The first part of this dialogue consists of a dispute between an advocate and an aged ascetic, most probably Mark himself. The lawyer is vexed at the monks because their preaching against lawsuits has curtailed his income. No agreement is reached and the advocate leaves. In the second part the old ascetic and 'his brethren' discuss the question whether a Christian should bring anyone into court. It is possible that the conclusion has been lost. Since the *Disputatio* evidently belongs to the period when Mark presided over a monastic community, it is most probably the earliest of his writings.

Edition: MG 65, 1071-1102.

9. *De Melchisedech*

This tract is a dogmatic polemic against those who believed that Melchisedech was an incarnation of the Logos, because in Hebr. (7, 3) he is described as 'without father, without mother, without genealogy' and 'a priest for ever' (7, 3). Here, Photius (*Bibl. cod.* 200) finds our author 'guilty of no small heresy', detecting in his teaching on the *communicatio idiomatum* the taint of Monophysitism. However, Mark bases his doctrine correctly on the unity of person in the two natures and does not betray any leaning towards error.

Edition: MG 65, 1117-1140.

10. *Adversus Nestorianos*

There is in addition to the nine treatises mentioned by Photius another which Papadopulos-Kerameus and Kunze edited from a Jerusalem manuscript (*Cod. Sab.* 366). Its title runs: *Against those who claim that the holy flesh of the Lord was not united with the Logos but surrounded Him like a garment and that therefore it is necessary to distinguish carefully between the one who carries and the one who is carried*. In agreement with the *Anathemas* of Cyril of Alexandria (cf. above, p. 127) the author refutes these heretics from Holy Scripture and from the Baptismal Creed, which both predicate divine and human properties of one and the same subject, but do not distribute them among two. Thus he puts special stress on the ἕνωσις καθ᾽ ὑπόστασιν (8; 10). Though the writer states on many occasions that the flesh of the Logos was united from the moment of the Incarnation or from the womb (ἐκ μήτρας), he does not use the term *Theotokos*. Several features of the work remind one of *De Melchisedech*. The *Adversus Nestorianos* seems to have been composed at the end of the year 430 or the beginning of 431.

Editions: A. PAPADOPULOS-KERAMEUS, Ἀνάλεκτα Ἱεροσολυμιτικῆς σταχυολογίας 1. St. Petersbourg, 1891, 89-113. — J. KUNZE, Markus Eremita, ein neuer Zeuge für das altkirchliche Taufbekenntnis. Leipzig, 1895, 6-30 (improved text). — The same treatise was edited from a manuscript at Grottaferrata (saec. X) with a Latin translation by J. COZZA-LUZI, Nova Patrum Bibliotheca, t. 10. Rome, 1905, 1, 195-252.

Studies: J. KUNZE, op. cit. — A. JURJEVSKIJ, Marcus Eremita and his Newly Discovered Treatise Against the Nestorians (in Russian). St. Petersbourg, 1900.

SPURIOUS WRITINGS

The *Capitula de temperantia* found in Migne (65, 1053-1070) under Mark's name represent a late compilation from the works of Maximus Confessor and Macarius the Egyptian and cannot be attributed to Mark. The Latin fragment *Ex S.P.N. Marci epistola* 2 (MG 65, 903f.) is not genuine either. Its text is a translation of the introduction to *De patientia et discretione*, a tract ascribed to Macarius the Egyptian (MG 34, 865-868).

Studies: J. Kunze, op. cit. 51ff. — I. A. Khalifé, L'inauthenticité du De temperantia de Marc l'Ermite: Mélanges de l'Université Saint-Joseph (Beyrouth) 28 (1949/1950) 59-66.

DIADOCHUS OF PHOTICE

Diadochus, bishop of Photice in Epirus, is one of the great ascetics of the fifth century. Almost nothing is known of his life. Photius (*Bibl. cod.* 231) mentions 'the bishop of Photice, Diadochus by name' among the opponents of the Monophysites at the time of the Council of Chalcedon (451). His signature appears in a letter addressed to the Emperor Leo by the bishops of Epirus after the murder of Bishop Proterius of Alexandria by the Monophysites, in 457. He most probably died about 468.

Studies: K. Popov, Blessed Diadochus, Bishop of Photice in Epirus and his Works (in Russian). Kiev, 1903. — F. Dörr, Diadochos von Photike und die Messalianer. Ein Kampf zwischen wahrer und falscher Mystik im 5. Jahrhundert. Freiburg i.B., 1937. — E. Oberhummer, Photike: PWK 20 (1941) 660-662. — H. I. Marrou, Diadoque de Photiké et Victor de Vita: REAN 45 (1943) 225-232. — E. des Places, Un Père grec du Ve siècle, Diadoque de Photicé: REAN 45 (1943) 61-80. — P. Christou, *ΔΙΑΔΟΧΟΣ 'Ο ΦΩΤΙΚΗΣ*. Thessalonike, 1952. — E. Honigmann, Patristic Studies (ST 173). Vatican City, 1953, 174-184 (Diadochus died about 468). — E. des Places, DSp 3 (1957) 817-834. — D. Stiernon, DHG 4 (1958) 374-378.

HIS WRITINGS

1. *Capita centum de perfectione spirituali*

His most outstanding work is *One Hundred Chapters on Spiritual Perfection*, a manual of asceticism, which remains of great importance for the history of Christian spirituality and mysticism. The author does not only show the true way to perfection but he endeavors also to distinguish between the right and the wrong means of striving for it, to clarify concepts and eliminate false ideas. Thus his work also constitutes a polemic against Messalianism, the pietistic movement condemned at the Council of Ephesus (431), which held that in consequence of Adam's sin everyone had a demon substantially united with his soul, and that this demon, which was not expelled by baptism, was completely exorcized only by ceaseless prayer. (For the history of this sect cf. above, p. 163.)

The author addresses himself to 'the brethren' *(ἀδελφοί)* and

mentions 'the ascetics' again and again, which suggests that he
speaks like a spiritual father to his monastic community. He distinguishes, however, between cenobites, hermits and solitaries (53).
The spiritual doctrine developed in the hundred short chapters or
maxims shows the influence of Evagrius Ponticus (cf. above, p. 169).
The first chapter bases all mystical contemplation on the three
theological virtues, especially on love, in terms which are at the
same time Pauline and Evagrian: '*Apatheia* leads to love and
charity to knowledge'. Chapters 2-5 contrast God and man, good
and evil, the natural image of God and the likeness of God. The
latter is the unfolding and enrichment of the life of grace given in
baptism, demands our cooperation through virtue and is con-
summated in perfect charity. Optimism pervades the entire work
and a deep confidence in the power of God's grace as well as in
the power of free will in man. Evil has no existence except by sin.
Here the anti-Messalian tendency is clearly evident. Chapters 6-11
deal with knowledge and wisdom, illumination and preaching, with
silence and prayer. Chapters 12-23 are devoted to the love of God
and the steps leading to it: humility (12-13), a burning desire (14),
the love of our neighbor (15), the fear of God (16-17), the detach-
ment from the world (18-19), faith and good works (20-21), purity
of conscience (22-23). Ch. 24-25 describe body and soul as the two
components of man and the influence of the spiritual element on
the senses. Ch. 26-35 present a theory of discernment of spirits;
ch. 36 and 40 treat of visions, ch. 37-39 of deceptions. Ch. 41-42
praise obedience because it creates humility. Ch. 43-47 recommend
abstinence from food which is necessary for two reasons: first,
because the body must be dominated by the soul, and secondly,
such abstinence enables us to give to the poor. No food is evil in
itself, as the Manichaeans maintain. Though the body has to be
chastised and kept in servitude, it must preserve enough strength
to endure the continuous battle. Fasting is only a means of attaining
a higher goal. Though it is useful, its importance should not be
exaggerated. Moderation is especially necessary in drinking (ch.
48-51). One should be abstemious in the use of wines mixed with
flavoring. Ch. 52 explains that nobody is obliged to abstain from
the refreshing effect of a bath. But for reasons of selfdiscipline the
author advises his readers to forgo this pleasure which softens the
body. Ch. 53-54 discuss illnesses. Whoever is sick, may call a
physician but should have confidence only in Christ, the true
physician. If one accepts sickness gratefully and endures it with
patience and courage, one approaches the ideal state of *apatheia*.
The following chapters (55-57) recommend indifference to the
comforts of life: It is better not to be involved in the things of the

world and not to look for honors and amusements but to live as a stranger here on earth expecting the eternal life to come. If we yield to one of the senses — it is irrelevant which one — it becomes an obstacle for the spiritual life. Ch. 58 teaches how to overcome the feeling of weariness, exhaustion and carelessness (ἀκήδεια) which many times befalls the soul after the passions of the body have been conquered, and how to return to new fervor. Ch. 59-61 outline the conditions for true joyfulness which consists in keeping God in mind and invoking the name of Jesus. Ch. 62 gives a positive evaluation of a choleric nature. Ch. 63-64 exhort the readers not to get involved in lawsuits and not to sue anyone even if he takes the clothes from our back. Far better would it be to sell all posses- sions at once and distribute the proceeds among the poor (ch. 65-66). Though this will make future almsgiving impossible, fervent prayer, patience and humility will make up for it. Voluntary poverty is the best preparation for those who intend to teach others the riches of the kingdom of God, i.e. for the 'theologian'. The chapters which follow (67-68) deal with the concept of 'theology', and its privileges. Since theology feeds on contemplation (68), ch. 69 describes its difficulties, ch. 70 silence and recollection. Ch. 71 treats of holy anger, ch. 72 distinguishes between the gifts of know- ledge and of wisdom, ch. 73 between vocal and mental prayer, ch. 74 between natural and spiritual fervor, ch. 75 between the purifying and vivifying breath of the Holy Spirit and the evil breath of the false spirit which seduces to sin. Ch. 76-89 present a theology of grace in which Diadochus refutes the Messalian heresy about the cohabitation of grace and sin in the soul. The presence of divine grace in the baptized and the deliverance from sin does not mean that there will be no further battle. Spiritual life is a continuous warfare and the true Christian is involved in a struggle which will last all his life. It is a contest against passions and against demons. *Apatheia* does not consist in freedom from assaults but in not being defeated by the demons. Virtue can be attained only by suffering and temptation, and perfection only by martyrdom. Since there is no opportunity for bloody martyrdom, the Christian must accept the unbloody and spiritual martyrdom of the ascetical life (ch. 90-100).

The *Capita centum* enjoyed great popularity in succeeding generations as proven by the number of manuscripts that have come down. Maximus Confessor, Sophronius of Jerusalem, the compiler of the *Doctrina Patrum*, Thalassius and Photius cite it and John Climacus and Simeon the New Theologian were inspired by it. It was printed in the Russian *Philocalia*, a Greek spiritual flori- legium of the 18th century and its influence extends to modern

Russian literature. Many of the principles contained in this little work show a remarkable resemblance with those of Ignatius of Loyola and Teresa of Avila. Diadochus is one of the spiritual authors that the Society of Jesus recommends to the masters of novices in the *Regulae magistri novitiorum*.

Of the editio princeps (Florence, 1578) no copy exist. A Latin translation by the Jesuit Fr. Turrianus (Torres) was published at Florence in 1570 and reprinted by Migne. The Greek text with the Latin translation of Torres was edited by J. E. Weis-Liebersdorf in 1911. A new critical edition by E. des Places appeared in 1955.

Editions: MG 65, 1167-1212 (Latin translation by J. Torres). — Greek text: K. Popov, op. cit. — J. E. Weis - Liebersdorf, Diadochi De perfectione spirituali capita centum (Bibliotheca Teubneriana). Leipzig, 1912 (with Torres' Latin translation). — New crit. ed.: E. des Places, Diadoque de Photicé. Œuvres spirituelles (SCH 5bis). Paris, 1955, 84-163.

Translations: French: E. des Places, Diadoque de Photicé. Cent Chapitres sur la Perfection Spirituelle (SCH 5). Paris, 1943; reprinted: SCH 5bis, Paris, 1955, 84-163. — *German:* J. E. Liebersdorf, Münchener Theologische Wochenschrift 1 (1904) 85-183 (Capita 1-33).

Studies: R. Reitzenstein, Historia monachorum und Historia Lausiaca, eine Studie zur Geschichte des Mönchtums und der frühchristlichen Begriffe Gnostiker und Pneumatiker. Göttingen, 1916, 123-142. — E. Peterson, Zu Diadochus von Photike: BNJ 5 (1926/1927) 412-418 (text. crit.). — G. Horn, Sens de l'esprit d'après Diadoqoe de Photicé: RAM 8 (1927) 402-419. — J. Hausherr, Les grands courants de la spiritualité orientale: OCP 1 (1935) 126-128. — F. Dörr, op. cit. — M. Rothenhäusler, La doctrine de la 'Theologia' chez Diadoque de Photiké: Irénikon 12 (1937) 536-553; *idem*, Zur asketischen Lehrschrift des Diadochos von Photike: Heilige Überlieferung (Festgabe I. Herwegen). Münster, 1938, 86-95. — M. Viller und K. Rahner, Aszese und Mystik in der Väterzeit. Freiburg i.B., 1939, 216-228. — N. Crainic, Das Jesusgebet: ZKG (1941) 341-353. — For studies on the Messalians, see above p. 165 f.

2. *Homily on the Ascension*

A homily on the Ascension from *Codex Vatic.* 455 was published by Cardinal Mai in 1840. In its periodic sentences and rhythmic style it has much in common with the *Capita centum* — a trait that confirms the authorship of Diadochus to whom it is assigned in the manuscript. The sermon defends with great eloquence the two natures in Christ. The Resurrection and Ascension of the Lord refute the views of the Jews and the 'sophists of evil'. The deification of man is a result of the Incarnation, in which the Son of God assumed a true human nature. The author ends with a Christological confession which contains a strong repudiation of Monophysitism.

Editions: MG 65, 1141-1148. — K. Popov, op. cit., 555-569. — New crit. ed.: E. des Places, SCH 5bis (1955) 164-168.

Translation: French: E. des Places, SCH 5bis (1955) 164-168.

3. The Vision ("Ορασις)

The *Vision* is in form a dialogue in which the author is engaged with St. John the Baptist in a dream. A series of questions and answers explains the nature of contemplation, of divine apparitions and of the beatific vision. There follows an angelology which reminds one of Pseudo-Dionysius the Areopagite.

The eleven manuscripts, none earlier than the thirteenth century, which contain this *Vision* attribute it unanimously to Diadochus of Photice.

Editions: V. N. Benešević, Mémoires de l'Académie Impériale des Sciences de Saint-Pétersbourg, VIIIᵉ série, cl. historico-philologique, vol. 8, n. 11, 1908 (based on Cod. Vaticanus Gr. 1167 saec. XIII). — I. Bithynos, NS 9 (1909) 247-254 (based on Cod. Jerusalem Bibl. Patriarch. 58 saec. XIII/XIV). — New crit. ed.: E. des Places, SCH 5bis (1955) 169-179.

Translation: French: E. des Places, *ibid.* 169-179.

4. The Catechesis

The *Catechesis* known only since 1952 in the Greek original, is a small work consisting of a series of questions and answers dealing with the relations of God to the world, especially His omnipresence which should not lead to a confusion of God with the universe. Others concern the angels and their knowledge of God, man and the beatific vision. God appears in a halo of light and on a throne of glory. There are some features which this Catechesis has in common with the *Vision*. E. des Places is of the opinion that the author is the same as that of the *Vision*, and in fact, some of the manuscripts attribute it to Diadochus. Most of them, however, ascribe it to Simeon the New Theologian (d. March 12, 1022 A.D.). The possibility exists that Simeon composed it but published it under the name of Diadochus, his spiritual father.

Editions: Greek text: E. des Places, Une catéchèse inédite de Diadoque de Photicé?: RSR 40 (1952) 129-138; *idem*, SCH 5bis (1955) 180-183.

Translations: Latin translation by the Jesuit Pontanus (among the works of Simeon): ML 120, 709-712. — *French:* E. des Places, RSR 40 (1952) 129-138; *idem*, SCH 5bis (1955) 180-183.

Studies: E. des Places, RSR 40 (1952) 129-130; *idem*, SCH 5bis, 80-81. — B. Krivocheine, The Writings of St. Symeon the New Theologian: OCP 20 (1954) 301, note 2, and 315-327 (attributes the *Catechesis* to Simeon). — J. Darouzès, Notes d'histoire des textes: REB 15 (1957) 169-175 (the manuscript tradition reveals that the *Catechesis* was attributed to Diadochus only by a mistake of the copyists; it belongs to Simeon).

NESTORIUS

Nestorius who has been mentioned above (p. 116) as the opponent of Cyril of Alexandria and father of the heresy condemned at Ephesus in 431, was born (after 381) of Persian parents at Germanicia in Syria Euphratensis. He received his theological training at the School of Antioch and probably studied under Theodore of Mopsuestia. He entered the monastery of St. Euprepius near Antioch and as a presbyter of the Church of Antioch became a renowned preacher (Gennadius, *De vir. ill.* 53). His great reputation induced Theodosius II, overriding the claims of the local candidates, to elevate him in 428 to the see of Constantinople, vacant since Sisinnius' death on December 24, 427. Thus he was the second Antiochene to attain this eminence occupied a generation earlier by St. John Chrysostom. He at once resolved to reform the city by strong measures against heretics, schismatics and Jews. He attacked Arians and Macedonians, Novatians and Quartodecimans, sparing only the Pelagians, who had been forced to withdraw from the West. But soon he himself became suspect of heresy owing to his disputatious and impetuous nature. Whereas Chrysostom abstained from proclaiming the theology of Antioch from the pulpit, Nestorius on the contrary made its Christology a favored subject of his sermons; he is supposed to have preached that there are two separate Persons in the Incarnate Christ and that the Blessed Virgin could not be called *Theotokos*. The violent controversy that ensued and his deposition on June 22, 431 by the Council of Ephesus, called by the Emperor Theodosius at his instigation, has been described above (p. 118). At the beginning of September 431 Nestorius was sent back by imperial order to his monastery at Antioch. He lived there for four years in peace until the emperor in 435 banished him to Oasis in Upper Egypt. He outlived Theodosius, i.e. July 28, 450, but how long is unknown.

Studies: F. Loofs, Nestorius: RE 13 (1903) 736-749. — J. Chapman, Cath. Encyclopedia 10 (1911) 755-759. — A. J. Maclean, Encyclopaedia of Religion and Ethics ed. by J. Hastings 9 (1917) 323-332. — E. Amann, Nestorius: DTC 11 (1931) 76-157. — I. Rucker, Nestorios: PWK 17 (1937) 126-137. — M. Jugie and G. de Vries, Nestorio e nestorianesimo: EC 8 (1952) 1780-1787. — F. L. Cross, Nestorianism: ODC (1957) 946-947. — J. F. Bethune - Baker, The Date of the Death of Nestorius: JThSt 9 (1908) 601-605; *idem*, Nestorius and his Teaching. A fresh examination of the existence, with special reference to the newly recovered Apology of Nestorius (the *Bazaar of Heraclides*). Cambridge, 1908. — F. Nau, La naissance de Nestorius: ROC 14 (1909) 424-426 (of Persian origin). — L. Fendt, Die Christologie des Nestorius. Kempten, 1910. — L. Duchesne, Histoire ancienne de l'Église 3. Paris, 1910, 313-388. — F. Nau, Nestorius d'après les sources orientales. Paris, 1911. — M. Jugie, L'épiscopat de Nestorius: EO 14 (1911) 257-268; *idem*, Nestorius et la controverse nestorienne. Paris, 1912. — J. Junglas, Die Irrlehre des Nestorius. Trier, 1912. — F. Loofs, Nestorius and his Place in the

History of Christian Doctrine. Cambridge, 1914. — C. PESCH, Zur neueren Literatur über Nestorius. Freiburg, 1914. — L. HODGSON, The Metaphysic of Nestorius: JThSt 19 (1918) 46-55. — C. PESCH, Nestorius als Irrlehrer. Paderborn, 1921. — F. S. MUELLER, Fuitne Nestorius revera Nestorianus?: Greg 2 (1921) 266-284; 352-386. — L. LOHN, Doctrina Nestorii de mysterio incarnationis: CTh (1933) 1-37. — R. ARNOU, Nestorianisme et néoplatonisme. L'unité du Christ et l'union des 'Intelligibles': Greg (1936) 116-131. — I. RUCKER, Studien zum Concilium Ephesinum zur 1500-Jahrfeier des dritten ökumenischen Konzils, 5 Hefte, privately published (Oxenbronn über Günzburg a. D., 1930-1935). — A. DENEFFE, Schol (1935) 548-560; (1938) 522ff. (against Rucker). — M. JUGIE, Theologia dogmatica christianorum orientalium ab Ecclesia Catholica dissidentium, t. V: De theologia dogmat. Nestorianorum. Paris, 1935; idem, L'ecclésiologie des nestoriens: EO 34 (1935) 5-25. — R. V. SELLERS, Two Ancient Christologies (SPCK). London, 1940, 107-201. — W. DE VRIES, Sakramententheologie bei den Nestorianern (Orient. Christ. Analecta 130). Rome, 1947. — E. v. IVANKA, Hellenisches und Christliches im frühbyzantinischen Geistesleben. Vienna, 1948, 73-94. — E. AMANN, L'affaire Nestorius vue de Rome: RSR 23 (1949) 5-37, 207-244; 24 (1950) 28-52, 235-265. — M. LAIGNEL - LAVASTINE, Le rôle de l'hérésie de Nestorius dans les relations médicales entre l'Orient et l'Occident: Actes du VIe Congrès Internat. des Sciences. Amsterdam, 1950, 334-343. — H. CHADWICK, Eucharist and Christology in the Nestorian Controversy: JThSt N.S. 2 (1951) 145-164. — T. CAMELOT, De Nestorius à Eutyches. L'opposition de deux christologies: CGG 1 (1951) 213-242. — A. GRILL-MEIER, Die theologische und sprachliche Vorbereitung der christologischen Formel von Chalkedon: CGG 1 (1951) 159-164. — W. DE VRIES, Die syrisch-nestorianische Haltung zu Chalkedon: CGG 1 (1951) 603-635. — I. ORTIZ DE URBINA, Il dogma di Efeso: REB 11 (1953) 233-240. — P. GALTIER, Nestorius mal compris, mal traduit: Greg 34 (1953) 427-433. — H. RISTOW, Zwei Häretiker der alten Kirche: Apollinaris von Laodicea und Nestorius. Diss. Berlin, 1954 (typ.). — L. ABRAMOWSKI, Der Streit um Diodor und Theodor zwischen den beiden ephesinischen Konzilien: ZKG 57 (1956) 252-287 (important for the chronology of the Nestorian controversy). — H. A. WOLFSON, The Philosophy of the Church Fathers. I: Faith, Trinity, Incarnation. Cambridge (Mass.), 1956, 451-463 (Christology). — E. DELEBECQUE, Sur une lettre du Concile d'Éphèse (431): Bulletin de l'Association G. Budé (1956) 2, 74-78 (announcing the condemnation of Nestorius, ACO I, 1, 2, 70, n. 69). — J. N. D. KELLY, Early Christian Doctrines. London, 1958, 310-317. For further studies, see above p. 140.

HIS WRITINGS

Gennadius reports that Nestorius 'composed a great many treatises on various questions' (*De vir. ill.* 53) and the *Catalogue* of Ebedjesu (20) confirms this statement. Nevertheless, very little remains, since Theodosius II in 435 ordered all his writings condemned and burned. Some of them found their way to the Syriac Nestorians as Ebedjesu indicates, but even these have in greater part perished. The fragments of his sermons, letters and treatises were collected and edited by F. Loofs in 1905. Since then a number of new Syriac fragments have been made available by Lebon's and Sanda's first edition of the works of Severus of Antioch.

Editions: F. LOOFS, Nestoriana. Die Fragmente des Nestorius, gesammelt, untersucht und herausgegeben, mit Beiträgen von S. A. Cook und G. Kampffmeyer. Halle, 1905. Additions: G. MERCATI, Nestoriana: ThR (1907) 63-64. — W. LÜDTKE, Armenische Nestoriana: ZKG 29 (1908) 385-387. — J. LEBON, Fragments syriaques de Nestorius dans le 'Contra Grammaticum' de Sévère d'Antioche: Mus 36 (1923) 47-65. — J. LEBON, Severi Antiocheni liber contra impium Grammaticum: CSCO 93/94 (1929), 101/102 (1933), 111/112 (1938). — A. SANDA, Severi Philalethes. Beyrouth, 1928. — R. HESPEL, Sévère d'Antioche. Le Philalèthe: CSCO 133/134 (1952). — C. MARTIN, Proclus de Constantinople, Nestorius et le 'bienheureux Nil', Εἰς τὴν ’Ανάληψιν: RHE 32 (1936) 929-932. — A. E. GOODMAN, An Examination of Some Nestorian Kephalaia (Or. 1319, University Library, Cambridge): Essays and Studies Presented to S. A. Cook. London, 1950 (translation of fragments of theological treatises attributed to Nestorius). — E. SCHWARTZ, ACO I, vol. 1, pars 1-6. Editions of the *Bazaar*, see below.

Studies: L. ABRAMOWSKI, Untersuchungen zum literarischen Nachlass des Nestorius. Diss. Bonn, 1956.

1. *Treatises*

1. *Bazaar of Heraclides of Damascus*

The only treatise extant in its entirety is the *Bazaar of Heraclides*, a rather extensive work composed in his last years. It was discovered in 1895 in a Syriac translation and first published in 1910, from the unique manuscript in the Patriarchal Library at Kotchanes. Nestorius gives here in the form of a dialogue with the Egyptian Sophronius a defense of his teaching and at the same time a history of his life. He severely criticizes the decisions of Ephesus and the teaching of Cyril of Alexandria and Dioscurus, claiming that his own belief was identical with that of Pope Leo I and Patriarch Flavian of Constantinople, so that it would be hard to charge him, on the basis of this treatise, with wilful heresy. 'Heraclides of Damascus' is a pseudonym which the exiled and condemned author uses as the only way of getting his book published. The concluding lines contain a moving plea for forgiveness and charity. The *Bazaar* proves that Nestorius survived the death of Theodosius on July 28, 450. Its literary form testifies to his eloquence and to his high reputation as a pulpit orator. It was this work which led a number of scholars, like Harnack, Loofs, Fendt, Ficker, Bethune-Baker, Duchesne and Rucker to a revision of the traditional opinion regarding Nestorius, though his person and doctrine still present a problem. His teaching has been discussed above, p. 117.

Edition: P. BEDJAN, Nestorius, Le livre d'Héraclide de Damas. Paris, 1910.

Translations: English: G. R. DRIVER and L. HODGSON, Nestorius, The Bazaar of Heracleides. Newly translated from the Syriac. Oxford, 1925. Cf. R. H. CONNOLLY, JThSt 27 (1926) 191-200. — *French:* F. NAU, Nestorius, Le livre d'Héraclide de Damas. Paris, 1910.

Studies: J. F. BETHUNE - BAKER, op. cit. (with extracts from the *Bazaar*). — L. FENDT, op. cit. — L. DUCHESNE, op. cit. — E. W. BROOKS, Some Historical References in the Πραγματεία ‘Ηρακλείδου: BZ 21 (1912) 94-96. — F. LOOFS, Nestorius and his Place in the History of Christian Doctrine. Cambridge, 1914. — F. C. BURKITT, Two Notes on the 'Bazaar of Heracleides': JThSt 27 (1926) 177-179. — I. RUCKER, Rundum das Recht der zwanzig ephesinischen Anklagezitate aus Nestorius wider Nestorius im Lichte des Liber Heraclidis. Oxenbronn/Günzburg, 1930; *idem*, Das Dogma von der Persönlichkeit Christi und das Problem der Häresie. Die Quintessenz der syrischen Nestorius-Apologie genannt Liber Heraclidis (Damasceni). Oxenbronn/Günzburg, 1934. — A. R. VINE, An Approach to Christology. The Bazaar of Heracleides. London, 1948. — L. I. SCIPIONI, Ricerche sulla Cristologia del 'Libro di Eraclide' di Nestorio. La formulazione teologica e il suo contesto filosofico (Paradosis 11). Fribourg, 1956.

2. *The Twelve Counter-Anathemas*

These 'Counter-Anathemas', by which Nestorius is supposed to have answered the twelve Anathemas of Cyril (cf. above, p. 127) are preserved in a Latin translation. Though they have been ascribed for some time to the unfortunate patriarch of Constantinople, in reality they were not written by him but long after his death, as E. Schwartz proved in 1922; nor can the Latin version be attributed to Marius Mercator, since there is sufficient evidence to show that it originated much later.

Edition: F. LOOFS, Nestoriana. Halle, 1905, 203-224.

Study: E. SCHWARTZ, Die sogenannten Gegenanathematismen des Nestorius (SAM Phil.-hist. Kl.). Munich, 1922, 1-29.

3. *Tragedy*

Among the fragments collected by Loofs there are some portions of a work called *Tragedy (Τραγῳδία)* in which Nestorius seems to have given a thorough presentation of his case. Loofs thinks that he composed it during the four years (431-435) spent at the monastery near Antioch after the Council of Ephesus and before his exile to Egypt. The little that remains is in Greek, Latin and Syriac.

Fragments: F. LOOFS, Nestoriana 203-208.

Study: R. ABRAMOWSKI, Zur 'Tragödie' des Nestorius: ZKG 47 (1928) 305-324.

4. *Theopaschites*

A few Syriac fragments are extant of his *Theopaschites*, a refutation of Cyril of Alexandria in the form of a dialogue. The title refers to Cyril since Nestorius accuses him of making God suffer in Christ.

Fragments: F. LOOFS, Nestoriana 208-211. — H. G. OPITZ, Untersuchungen zur Überlieferung der Schriften des Athanasius, Berlin, 1935, 210-212, first published from Cod. Ambros. D 51 (235) f. 221a-222b the Pseudo-Athanasian Creed formula *Contra Theopaschitas*. He thinks that Nestorius himself or Eutherius of Tyana could be the author. — F. SCHEIDWEILER, Ein Glaubensbekenntnis des Eustathius von Antiochien: ZNW 44 (1952) 237-249, believes that Eustathius composed it.

2. Sermons

Since Nestorius preached with great success for about twenty-three years at Antioch and Constantinople, there must have been a considerable number of sermons extant before they were committed to the flames in 435. Nestorius himself sent some of them to Pope Celestine as did Cyril of Alexandria. The Nestorians spread his homilies in the fifth and sixth centuries. That four sermons under Chrysostom's name belong rightfully to Nestorius has been proven for one, on Hebr. 3, 1, by Loofs and Haidacher, and for three, on the temptation of Christ (from *Codex Paris. Gr.* 797), by their editor F. Nau. C. Baur edited recently from *Codex Berolinensis* 77 (*Phillips* 1481, saec. XII) three homilies, one on Easter, two on the Ascension, attributed to Chrysostom, the language, style and thought of which assign them definitely to the time of the Nestorian controversy. There are reasons to believe that Nestorius is the author of the second. The possibility remains that more of his works may be hidden amongst the writings of others. Loofs's collection comprises 30 items, ten more or less complete, and nine preserved in a Latin translation by Marius Mercator, five Christological, and four anti-Pelagian.

Editions: F. Loofs, Nestoriana 225-361. The Greek text of the homily on Hebr. 3, 1: MG 64, 479-492. New ed.: F. Loofs, Nestoriana 230-242. The three sermons on the temptation of Christ: MG 61, 683-688. New ed.: F. Nau, Le texte grec de trois homélies de Nestorius: ROC 15 (1910) 113-124; reprinted: F. Nau, Le livre d'Héraclide de Damas, suivi du texte grec des trois homélies de Nestorius sur les tentations de Notre Seigneur. Paris, 1910, 333-358. — C. Baur, Drei unedierte Festpredigten aus der Zeit der nestorianischen Streitigkeiten: Traditio 9 (1953) 101-126; cf. above, p. 455 f.

Studies: P. Batiffol, Sermons de Nestorius: RBibl 9 (1900) 329-353 (regards Nestorius as the author of 52 sermons hitherto attributed to Athanasius, Amphilochius, Basil of Seleucia and John Chrysostom); cf. F. Loofs, Nestoriana 150f. — S. Haidacher, Rede des Nestorius über Hebr. 3, 1 überliefert unter dem Namen des hl. Chrysostomus: ZkTh 29 (1905) 192-195. — J. B. Chabot, A propos du nestorianisme: CRI (1947) 152-155. — For the numerous quotations from Nestorius' homilies in Cyril of Alexandria's *Adversus Nestorii blasphemias contradictionum libri quinque,* see: I. Rucker, Rundum das Recht der 20 Anklagezitate aus Nestorius. Oxenbronn/Günzburg, 1930.

3. Letters

Of the fifteen letters listed by Loofs, ten are complete or virtually so. Of the ten, three survive in Greek in *Acta Ephesina Graeca,* two to Cyril of Alexandria (cf. above, p. 117) and one to Theodosius II. The rest have come down only in Latin or Syriac. Those in Latin are: two to Pope Celestine I in *Acta Ephesina Latina;* two others to him also and a third to the Pelagian Caelestius in a version by Marius Mercator; one to Theodoret of Cyrus in *Collectio Cassinensis*

209 (Acta Concil. ed. E. Schwartz, tom. I, vol. 4, 150f.) of which Loofs publishes only the Syriac fragments. The Syriac translation of an interesting epistle to the people of Constantinople penned in Nestorius' last years has been edited by E. W. Brooks and F. Nau.

Editions: F. LOOFS, Nestoriana 165-202. New crit. ed.: E. SCHWARTZ, ACO I. — E. W. BROOKS and F. NAU, La lettre de Nestorius aux habitants de Constantinople: ROC 15 (1910) 275-281. The discovery of the *Bazaar* has eliminated Loofs's (Nestoriana 70) objections against the authenticity of this letter.

Translations: French: E. W. BROOKS and F. NAU, art. cit. — F. NAU, Nestorius, Le livre d'Héraclide de Damas. Paris, 1910, 370-376 (to the people of Constantinople). — F. NAU, Traduction française des lettres de Nestorius à S. Cyrille et à S. Célestin et des douze Anathématismes de Cyrille: ROC 16 (1911) 176-199. — *German* (Letters of Nestorius to Pope Celestine): S. WENZLOWSKY, Die Briefe der Päpste und die an sie gerichteten Schreiben III (BKV). Kempten, 1877, 399-404, 404-407, 452-454, 532.

Studies: I. RUCKER, Ephesinische Konzilsakten in armenisch-georgischer Überlieferung (SAM Philos. Kl.). Munich, 1930; *idem*, Ephesinische Konzilsakten in lateinischer Überlieferung. Oxenbronn/Günzburg, 1930/1931.

EUTHERIUS OF TYANA

Eutherius, archbishop of Tyana in Cappadocia was one of the first to side with Nestorius. The Council of Ephesus (431) excommunicated him without being able to silence him. He warned John of Antioch against negotiations for a union between Cyril and the Oriental bishops (cf. above, p. 118), and called him a Judas when he made peace with the patriarch of Alexandria. He was deposed in 434 and exiled to Scythopolis in Palestine, finally to Tyre in Phoenicia. The date of his death is unknown.

1. Confutationes quarundam propositionum

His *Refutations of Various Propositions* survives among the works of St. Athanasius (MG 28, 1337-1394) and those of Theodoret of Cyrus (ed. Schulze V, 1113-1174), and more complete in a manuscript of the Escorial of the 14th century, also under the name of Athanasius, from which Ficker made his additions. Apparently, it consisted originally of 21 or 22 chapters and was written in the last months of the year 431. Photius who thought it came from Theodoret's pen speaks of 27 chapters (*Bibl. cod.* 46) but the first five chapters he mentions are identical with the *Pentalogus* of Theodoret (cf. below, p. 546) and the sixth with the same author's anonymous writing *That there is One Son Our Lord Jesus Christ* (cf. below, p. 549). So only ns. 7-27 describe the *Confutations* of Eutherius. Photius reports:

Read twenty-seven books by Theodoret, bishop of Cyrus, against various heretical propositions. The first book is directed against those who assert that the God-Word was one nature and that It took Its beginning from the seed of David, and also against those who attribute passions to the Godhead. In the second, he supports his contentions more by arguments from Scripture. The third deals with the same subject. The fourth contains the teaching of the holy Fathers concerning the glorious Dispensation of our Lord Jesus Christ the Son of God. The fifth contains a collection of the opinions of the heretics, which are compared with the opinion of those who do not admit two natures in Christ and shown to be nearly akin. The sixth distinctly states that there is one Son, our Lord Jesus Christ. The seventh [i.e. *Confutations* book I] is in the form of a letter completing the first book. The eighth is written against those who judge the truth only by the opinion of the multitude. The ninth is against those who assert that we should neither seek arguments nor quote from Scripture but that we must be satisfied with our faith. The tenth is against those who malevolently bring forward the argument that *the Word was made flesh*. The eleventh is against those who forbid us to assume two natures in the Incarnation. The twelfth is against those who assert that he who says the Word is one thing and the flesh another, assumes there are two Sons. The thirteenth is against those who say that to regard Christ as a man is to put one's hopes in a man. The fourteenth is against those who say, *He suffered without suffering*. The fifteenth is against those who say, *He suffered as He willed*. The sixteenth is against those who say that we ought to accept the words without regard to what is signified by them, which is beyond all men's understanding. The seventeenth is against those who say, *The Word suffered in the flesh*. The eighteenth is against those who ask what punishment the Jews would have suffered, if they had not crucified God. The nineteenth is against those who declare that he who does not believe that God was crucified, is a Jew. The twentieth is against those who assert that the angels who ate with Abraham did not entirely put on the nature of flesh. The twenty-first is against those who depreciate each of the miracles, by denying the flesh. The twenty-second is against those who injure our race, by denying that the Saviour began with our nature. The twenty-third is against those who bid us simply believe what is said, without considering what is seemly or what is unseemly. The twenty-fourth is against those who do away with the difference of the two natures, after the Passion and the Ascension. The twenty-fifth is a summary of all that has already been stated in detail. The twenty-sixth deals with the subsequently manifested composition or consubstantiation; the twenty-seventh with the example from the ordinary man, applied to Christ. The subject alone in each case is sufficient to indicate which of the above confirm the orthodox faith, and which are at variance with it (SPCK).

The table of contents which Photius gives for the chapters 7–27 corresponds closely to the text of the Codex of the Escorial.

This analysis of the chapters indicates that Eutherius criticized especially the propositions concerned with the one Person in Christ and the *communicatio idiomatum*. The rationalistic tendency which characterizes Nestorianism, appears unmistakably in these *Confutations*.

Editions: MG 28, 1337-1394. — J. L. SCHULZE and J. A. NOESSELT, Theodoretus, Opera omnia V. Halle, 1774, 1113-1174. — E. SCHWARTZ, ACO I, 5, 179-181.

Studies: T. W. DAVIDS, DCB 2 (1880) 397-398. — G. FICKER, Eutherius von Tyana. Ein Beitrag zur Geschichte des ephesinischen Konzils vom Jahre 431. Leipzig, 1908, 18ff. (additions to the text).

2. *Letters*

Five letters are preserved in a poor Latin translation in the so-called *Synodicon adversus tragoediam Irenaei*, addressed to John of Antioch (ch. 73), Helladius of Tarsus (ch. 74), Alexander of Hierapolis and Theodoret of Cyrus (ch. 116), Pope Sixtus III (ch. 117), and Alexander of Hierapolis (ch. 201). In the first Eutherius refers to a greater work of his, in which he had refuted the views of Cyril and his friends: *De quibus convincere quidem latius facile est, sicut factum in contradictionibus, quae a multis et quae a nobis ipsis factae sunt* (MG 84, 683). This is the *Confutationes*.

Editions: E. SCHWARTZ, ACO I, 4, 109-112, 144-148, 213-231. — H. G. Opitz attributed the Pseudo-Athanasian Creed *Contra Theopaschitas* to Eutherius. F. Scheidweiler thinks that Eustathius of Antioch is the real author; cf. above p. 305. — A new fragment can be found in Severus of Antioch, *Contra impium Grammaticum* III, 17, ed. J. LEBON, CSCO 94 (1929) 207.

PROCLUS OF CONSTANTINOPLE

Proclus was the second successor to Nestorius and became patriarch of Constantinople in 434. It was he who in 438 had St. John Chrysostom's body transferred to the capital and carried in solemn procession to the Church of the Apostles amidst the homage of the entire population. He had been consecrated archbishop of Cyzicus in the Propontis in 426 without being able to take possession of his see. Forced thus to remain at Constantinople he gained great renown as a preacher, and in 428 or 429 delivered a famous sermon in the presence of Nestorius in which he praised the Blessed Virgin as *Theotokos*. Nestorius answered in a homily in which he warned against this title. Proclus did not take active part in the subsequent controversy nor in the Council of Ephesus, but contributed to a large degree to the reception of its definition in the capital. He was instrumental in strengthening the union achieved in 434 among the Orientals and Cyril of Alexandria. He gained the confidence of the party of the Johannites and brought about their reconciliation. He settled the dangerous quarrel about Theodore of Mopsuestia which threatened the Church of Armenia, before it could spread further. His introduction of the *Trisagion* into the Liturgy of Constantinople shows that he was equally interested in the promotion of worship. He died in 446.

Studies: E. Schwartz, Konzilsstudien (Schriften der wissenschaftl. Gesellschaft in Strassburg, Heft 20, 1914) 18-53. — F. X. Bauer, Proklos von Konstantinopel. Ein Beitrag zur Kirchen- und Dogmengeschichte des 5. Jahrhunderts. Munich, 1919. — G. Fritz, DTC 13 (1936) 662-670. — M. Richard, Acace de Mélitène, Proclus de Constantinople et la Grande Arménie: Mémorial L. Petit. Bucarest, 1948, 393-412. — W. Ensslin, Proklos, Bischof von Konstantinopel: PWK 23 (1957) 183-186.

WRITINGS

1. *Sermons*

Socrates (*Hist. eccl.* 7, 28. 41. 43) mentions on several occasions that Proclus had studied rhetoric and was an outstanding pulpit orator. There is no doubt that he ranks among the best preachers of the Greek Church in the fifth century and was a worthy successor to Chrysostom in the see of Constantinople. About 27 homilies are attributed to him, some of them of doubtful authenticity, and three surviving only in a Syriac translation. Most were delivered on liturgical feasts of the Lord, as *De nativitate* (*Hom.* 4), *De circumcisione octavo post nativitatem die* (2), *In s. theophaniam* (7), *In transfigurationem* (8), *In ramos palmarum* (9), *In s. quintam feriam* (10), *In s. parasceven* (11), *In resurrectionem* (12).

Or. 1, 5 and 6 are devoted to the Blessed Virgin. The first, *Laudatio in sanctissimam Dei genitricem Mariam* (MG 65, 679 ff) is the one mentioned above as delivered in the presence of Nestorius. Its Greek text is found also in the Acts of the Council of Ephesus (Mansi 4, 577-588). We have in addition Syriac, Armenian and Ethiopic translations.

Or. 6 *Laudatio S. Dei genitricis Mariae* is spurious. It gives an imaginative description of the Annunciation with long dialogues between Joseph and Mary (9), and Mary and Gabriel (11). Its metrical form seems to have been influenced by the *contakia* of Romanos and other poets. It must have been composed at a much later date.

Or. 18 is a panegyric on St. Paul, 19 on St. Andrew, 20 on St. Chrysostom, 25 on St. Clement of Ancyra, a martyr of the fourth century. B. Marx has recently ascribed more than 80 of the sermons preserved in the *spuria* of Chrysostom to Proclus, two still unedited. Some of these attributions are not too convincing.

Most of Proclus' sermons deal with dogmatic questions, especially the dogma of the Incarnation. In *Hom.* 3 *De dogmate incarnationis* he states: 'There is only one Son because the two natures are not torn asunder into two persons but the adorable plan of salvation (economy) unites the two natures to one Person'. This dictum was often quoted by Greek patristic authors (cf. *Doctrina Patrum de incarnatione Verbi*, ed. Diekamp 48). The interesting homily has survived not only in the Greek original, but also in a Syriac and a Coptic version. Only the latter two preserve the complete text. Lebon believes that Proclus must be given part of the credit for a sermon on Our Lady by Atticus of Constantinople (MG 65, 716-721; MG 59, 707-710) of which he edited a Syriac version with a Latin and M. Brière with a French translation. Here the Blessed Virgin is called *Theotokos*, wherefore Cyril of Alexandria (*De recta fide ad reginas* MG 76, 1213; *Ep.* 14, MG 77, 97) and the Council of Ephesus (Mansi 4, 1193-1196) quote it as a testimony of the orthodox faith against Nestorianism. C. Martin has shown that the Ascension sermon attributed to Nilus by Photius (*Bibl. cod.* 200) belongs in reality to Proclus.

Amand de Mendieta published a Pseudo-Basilian Christmas sermon which perhaps belongs to Proclus. There is every reason to think that more homilies will turn up in manuscripts or among the *spuria* of other authors.

Editions: MG 65, 679-850. — New crit. ed. of the famous Marian sermon (*Or.* 1): E. Schwartz, ACO I, 1, 1 (1927) 103-107. — A Coptic version of *Hom.* 3 *De dogmate incarnationis* was published by E. A. W. Budge, Coptic Homilies in the Dialect of Upper Egypt. London, 1910, 97-104 (Coptic text), 241-247 (English translation), 381-386 (English translation of the Syriac version). The Syriac text was edited by J. B. Chabot, RAL ser. 5, vol. 5 (1896) 178-197 (*Hom.* 3-5). — C. Moss, Proclus of Constantinople's Homily on the Nativity: Mus 42 (1929) 61-73, filled the gap in the Syriac version of one of the homilies on the Nativity published by Chabot. — C. Martin, Un florilège grec d'homélies christologiques du IVe et Ve siècles sur la Nativité (Paris. Gr. 1491): Mus 54 (1941) 20-30 and 40-48, was the first to publish the Greek text (hitherto regarded to be lost) of the two Christmas sermons of which MG 65, 841-846 gives a Latin and Chabot, loc. cit. the Syriac version. — For the sermon attributed to Atticus (MG 59, 707-710), see: J. Lebon, Discours d'Atticus de Constantinople 'sur la sainte Mère de Dieu': Mus 46 (1933) 167-202 (Syriac text and Latin translation); M. Brière, Une homélie inédite d'Atticus, patriarche de Constantinople: ROC 29 (1933/1934) 160-180 (Syriac text and French translation). — For an Armenian version of the Epiphany sermon, see: G. Sarkissian, Proclus of Constantinople's Homily on the Epiphany (in Armenian): Bazmavep 92 (1934) 5-8. — For Syriac, Armenian and Ethiopic versions of the *Oratio* 1, see: F. X. Bauer, op. cit. 24. — E. Amand de Mendieta, Une homélie grecque inédite antinestorienne du Ve siècle sur l'Incarnation du Seigneur: RB 58 (1948) 223-263 (Greek text and French translation). Cf. *idem*, A propos d'une édition princeps: RB 62 (1952) 300-301 (notes on the *theotokos*). — S. Y. Rudberg, Le texte de l'homélie pseudo-basilienne sur l'Incarnation du Seigneur: RB 62 (1952) 189-200 (text. crit.).

Studies: For manuscripts, see: A. Ehrhard, Überlieferung und Bestand der hagigraphischen und homiletischen Literatur der griechischen Kirche I, 1 (TU 50). Leipzig, 1937, 132ff. — A. KIRPITSCHNIKOW, Reimprosa im 5. Jahrhundert: BZ 1 (1892) 527-530 (on the spurious *Or.* 6). Cf. P. MAAS, Das Kontakion: BZ 19 (1910) 285-306. — G. LA PIANA, Le rappresentazioni sacre e la poesia ritmica dramatica nella letteratura bizantina dalle origini al sec. IX: Roma e l'Oriente 2 (1911); 3 (1911/1912); 4 (1912) 47ff.: Testo dell'omelia attribuita a S. Proclo; 167ff.: Ricostruzione metrica dei frammenti dramatici conservati nell'omelia attribuita a S. Proclo. — C. MARTIN, Proclus de Constantinople, Nestorius et le 'bienheureux Nil', Εἰς τὴν 'Ανάληψιν: RHE 32 (1936) 929-932 (this Ascension sermon belongs to Proclus); *idem*, Hippolyte de Rome et Proclus de Constantinople, Εἰς τὸ ἅγιον Πάσχα. A propos de l'originalité d'une homélie attribuée à Proclus de Constantinople: RHE 33 (1937) 255-276 (shows that the Easter sermon MG 65, 796-800 uses Hippolytus of Rome as a source). — B. MARX, Procliana. Untersuchungen über den homiletischen Nachlass des Patriarchen Proklos von Konstantinopel. Münster, 1940. — F. OGARA, La homilia intitulada De sacerdotio liber septimus: Greg 27 (1946) 145-155 (the homily MG 48, 1067ff. belongs to Proclus). — For the authenticity of the Marian sermons, see: R. LAURENTIN, Court traité de théologie mariale. Paris, 1953, 161, 163, 164f. — J. G. DAVIES, Proclus and Pseudo-Nilus: HThR 49 (1956) 179-181 (the Ascension sermon mentioned by Photius as belonging to Nilus, must be attributed to Proclus).

2. *Letters*

The seven letters of his that have reached us deal with the Nestorian controversy. The most famous among them is *Ep*. 2 addressed to the Armenians and commonly called *Tomus ad Armenios*. This exposition of the doctrine of the one Christ in two Natures directed against Theodore of Mopsuestia is also extant in a Latin translation by Dionysius Exiguus. Though Theodore is not mentioned by name, the inquiry of the Armenian bishops preserved in Syriac, to which Proclus is replying, shows that he is meant.

The other six communications exist in Latin translation only, most of them mutilated. *Ep*. 4 contains the famous sentence 'One of the Trinity was crucified according to the flesh', destined to play an important part in the Theopaschite Controversy of the sixth century, though Proclus can hardly be charged with having coined this formula. The six letters are addressed to John and Domnus of Antioch and to the deacon Maximus. Of the seventeen items in Migne (65, 851-886) the rest are not by Proclus, but written to him or to others. Of the entire collection only nos. 2, 3, 4, 10, 11, 13, 17 belong to Proclus.

Another epistle of Proclus that resembles a profession of faith and is addressed *Ad singulos occidentis episcopos* was first edited by A. Amelli, Spicilegium Cassinense I (1888) 144 ff. and again by E. Schwartz (Acta concil. oec. IV 2, 65 ff). It discusses the doctrine of the Trinity and the Incarnation and defends the freedom of the human will against astrological superstition. Schwartz regards it as spurious, but A. Ehrhard (BZ 23, 1914/9, 485) and F. Diekamp (ThR 16, 1917, 357f.) are convinced of its authenticity.

The fragment *De traditione divinae missae* (MG 65, 849-852) is not by Proclus but by a later author.

Editions: MG 65, 851-886. — *Tomus ad Armenios:* MG 65, 856-875. New crit. ed.: E. SCHWARTZ, ACO IV, 2 (1914) 187-195 (Greek text); 196-205 (Latin translation by Dionysius Exiguus, who adds at the end the date: 435 A.D.). — Syriac version: J. P. N. LAND, Anecdota Syriaca 3, 2. Leiden, 1870, 103-115. — Armenian version: A. VARDANIAN, Kleine klassische Texte, vol. 2. Vienna, 1923. Cf. A. VARDANIAN, Ein Briefwechsel zwischen Proklos und Sahak: Wiener Zeitschrift für die Kunde des Morgenlandes 27 (1913) 415-441. — *Epistola uniformis ad singulos occidentis episcopos:* E. SCHWARTZ, ACO IV, 2 (1914) 65-68.

Translation: German: K. AHRENS and G. KRÜGER, Die sogenannte Kirchengeschichte des Zacharias Rhetor. Leipzig, 1899, 27-41 (*Tomus ad Armenios*).

Studies: For the *Tomus ad Armenios*, see: R. DEVREESSE, Le début de la querelle des Trois Chapitres: la lettre d'Ibas et le tome de Proclus: RSR 11 (1931) 543-565; *idem*, Essai sur Théodore de Mopsueste (ST 141). Vatican City, 1948, 125-152, 180-183, 186-189. — For *Ep.* 4, see: M. RICHARD, Proclus de Constantinople et le théopaschisme: RHE 38 (1942) 303-331 (Proclus not the author of the phrase: *Unus de Trinitate passus est carne*). — W. ELERT, Die theopaschitische Formel: ThLZ 75 (1950) 195-206 (history of this formula). — For the six letters to John and Domnus of Antioch and the deacon Maximus, see: R. DEVREESSE, Essai de Théodore de Mops. 151-152, 167-168.

GENNADIUS OF CONSTANTINOPLE

Gennadius was patriarch of Constantinople from 458 to 471. His namesake Gennadius of Marseilles informs us (*De vir. ill.* 89): 'Gennadius patriarch of the Church of Constantinople, a man brilliant in speech and of strong genius, was so richly equipped by his reading of the ancients that he was able to expound the prophet Daniel entire commenting on every word. He composed also many homilies. He died while the elder Leo was Emperor' (LNPF). Not one of these writings has survived and they were by no means the only ones. In addition to his commentary on Daniel, he expounded Genesis, Exodus, the Psalter and all the Epistles of St. Paul. Considerable fragments of these have survived, mainly in *Catenae*. Those of Genesis and Romans deserve special mention. Devreesse published seven of his commentary on Genesis and one of that on Exodus. K. Staab succeeded in reconstituting about three quarters of the commentary on Romans. Thus *Cod. Vindob. theol.* 166 furnished a complete exegesis of Romans 1, 5-2, 5, and *Cod. Vatic.* 762 of Romans 5, 12-15, 52. These remains show clearly that he followed the School of Antioch.

His dogmatic writings are no better preserved than his exegetical. Facundus of Hermiane mentions a treatise against the *Twelve Anathemas* of Cyril of Alexandria (*Pro def. trium capit.* 2, 4 ML 67,

571) of exceptional sharpness and bitterness. Facundus quotes several passages of this polemic, most probably written about 431.

St. John Damascene cites in his *Sacra Parallela* (MG 86, 2, 2044) a passage from his treatise *Ad Parthenium*, a follower of Nestorius. The excerpt deals with the origin of the human soul. From other fragments of the same treatise which Diekamp published it is evident that the work consisted of at least two books.

Gennadius also composed an encomium on the Tome of Pope Leo the Great *Ad Flavianum* which the Pontiff had directed especially against the heresy of Eutyches and which was given formal recognition by the Council of Chalcedon (451) as the classical authoritative statement of the Catholic doctrine of the Incarnation. The extant fragment of the encomium shows the author's full agreement with Chalcedon and proves his point of view orthodox.

The only work which has come down to us completely is his *Epistola encyclica* against simony from a synod held at Constantinople in 458 or 459. This encyclical has reached us in two recensions.

Gennadius died in 471 and was succeeded by Acacius the instigator of the so-called Acacian schism, which broke off all relations between Rome and Constantinople, and persisted until the accession of Justin in 518. The Eastern Church venerates Gennadius as a Saint and celebrates his feast on August 25 and November 17.

Editions: MG 85, 1613-1734. *Epistola encyclica:* MG 85, 1613-1622. — K. STAAB, Paulus-kommentare aus der griechischen Kirche. Münster, 1933, 352-418. — F. DIEKAMP, Analecta Patristica (Orientalia Christiana Analecta 117). Rome, 1938, 73-108 (fragments of the treatise against the *Twelve Anathemas* of Cyril, of the treatise *Ad Parthenium*, of the encomium on the Tome of Pope Leo, of the *Epistola encyclica*, of several letters). — R. DEVREESSE, Anciens commentateurs grecs de l'Octateuque: RBibl 45 (1936) 384.

Study: F. DIEKAMP, op. cit. 54-72 (his life and his works).

BASIL OF SELEUCIA

Basil, archbishop of Seleucia in Isauria from about 440, played a strange part in the events leading up to the Council of Chalcedon in 451. He first voted against Monophysitism at the Synod of Constantinople in 448, at the Robber-Synod of Ephesus in 449 he declared in favor of Eutyches, but at Chalcedon he subscribed to the Tome of Pope Leo the Great *Ad Flavianum* which condemned Eutyches and Dioscurus. In 458 together with the rest of the Isaurian bishops he wrote a letter to the emperor Leo I to the effect that the decisions of the Council of Chalcedon must be sustained and the intruded patriarch of Alexandria, Timothy Aelurus, a Monophysite, be deposed. This letter with his signature is extant in a

Latin translation (Mansi 7, 559-563; Schwartz, Act. conc. II 5, 46-49). He died about 468.

Studies: A. JÜLICHER, PWK 3 (1899) 55. — P. GODET, DTC 2 (1905) 459-460. — T. CAMELOT, De Nestorius à Eutyches: CGG 1 (1951) 233-234. — E. HONIGMANN, Patristic Studies (ST 173). Vatican City, 1953, 174-184 (time of his death: 468).

HIS WRITINGS

His extant treatises show that he was well read in classical literature and well trained in rhetoric. Photius (*Bibl. cod.* 168) blames his lack of simplicity and naturalness and his excessive use of tropes and figures. He remarks on his exegesis the influence of Basil the Great and Chrysostom.

1. *Sermons*

Photius is familiar with 15 homilies but speaks in addition of 'other works' which might also have been sermons. Migne (85, 27-474) has a series of 41 addresses by Basil on the Scriptures and biblical characters. However, B. Marx has proved that n. 38 *Contra Judaeos de Salvatoris adventu demonstratio* on Daniel 9, 20f. and n. 39 on the Annunciation cannot be authentic. The latter belongs most probably to Proclus of Constantinople (cf. above, p. 523). The rest of the series consists of discourses on passages of the Old and New Testament and events of biblical history. Basil is inclined to dramatize these events and to introduce Scriptural personages speaking in monologues and dialogues. Some of the latter provided the great Greek hymn-writer Romanos Melodos in the sixth century with inspiration for his *contakia*. N. 27, *In Olympia*, castigates those Christians who attend the immoral Olympic games. The last, n. 41 is entitled *Laudatio S. Christi protomartyris Stephani deque eius pretiosi corporis inventione*. Its authenticity has been questioned.

In addition six Pseudo-Athanasian sermons (MG 28, 1047-1061; 1073-1108) must be attributed to Basil, as some of the manuscripts do. Camelot published a homily *In Lazarum* from *Cod. Vat. Ottob. Gr.* 14, and there are two more still unedited (cf. MG 85, 17f.).

Editions: MG 85, 27-474. — T. P. CAMELOT, Une homélie inédite de Basile de Séleucie: Mélanges A. M. Desrousseaux. Paris, 1937, 35-48.

Studies: P. MAAS, Das Kontakion: BZ 19 (1910) 285-306 (Romanos and Basil of Sel.); cf. A. BAUMSTARK, Zwei syrische Weihnachtslieder: OC N.S. 1 (1911) 193-203. — F. FENNER, De Basilio Seleuciensi quaestiones selectae. Diss. Marburg, 1912. — B. MARX, Procliana. Münster, 1940, 84-89 (*Hom.* 39); idem, Der homiletische Nachlass des Basilius von Seleukia: OCP 7 (1941) 329-369. — F. HALKIN, Hagiographie grecque et patrologie: SP II (TU 64). Berlin, 1957, 465-467 (*Hom. In Lazarum*).

THE WRITERS OF ANTIOCH AND SYRIA

2. De vita et miraculis S. Theclae libri II

The first of these two books contains a prolix narrative of the life of the so-called protomartyr Thecla, the second of the 31 miracles that took place at her sepulchre in Seleucia. The first mainly paraphrases, interpolates and revises the apocryphal *Acta Pauli et Theclae* (cf. vol. I, p. 131). The second, mutilated at the end, is highly interesting for the history of pilgrimages and Christian substitutes for pagan miracle-workers. The work has no historical value except for the kernel of truth that the apocryphal Acts might contain.

Since it is prose, it cannot be identified with a 'poem' by Basil on the protomartyr Thecla described by Photius as 'the deeds, contest and victories' of the great Saint.

Edition: MG 85, 477-618.

Studies: See the bibliography vol. I, 132-133. — E. Lucius, Die Anfänge des Heiligenkultes in der christlichen Kirche. Tübingen, 1904, 205-214. — L. Radermacher, Hippolytus und Thekla. Studien zur Geschichte von Legende und Kultus: SAW 182, 3 (1916) 121-126. — H. Delehaye, Les recueils antiques de miracles des saints: AB 53 (1925) 49-57 (Les miracles de sainte Thècle). — B. Kötting, Peregrinatio religiosa. Münster, 1950, 141-144, 151-155. — H. Leclercq, DAL 15 (1953) 2225-2236.

CHURCH HISTORIANS OF CONSTANTINOPLE

Four Church Historians chose Constantinople as the place to compose their voluminous works. Three of them, laymen, wrote continuations of Eusebius of Caesarea's *Ecclesiastical History*, among them an Arian, Philostorgius. The priest, Philip, went further and published a *Christian History* beginning with the creation of the world.

PHILIP SIDETES

Philip was, as his surname indicates, a native of Side in Pamphylia. He was ordained deacon at Constantinople by St. John Chrysostom one of whose letters (MG 52, 729) testifies, that they became great friends. As a priest he was three times an unsuccessful candidate for the patriarchate, 426, when Sisinnius, 428, when Nestorius, and 431, when Maximianus was elected.

Between 434 and 439 he published a voluminous work under the title *Christian History* (Χριστιανικὴ ἱστορία) in 36 books comprising almost 1000 *tomoi*, extending from the creation of the world to about 426. Only small fragments remain but Socrates and Photius provide some valuable information on the character of this work. The former says (*Hist. eccl.* 7, 27):

This composition he has entitled not an *Ecclesiastical*, but a *Christian History*, and grouped in it abundance of very heterogeneous materials, wishing to show that he is not ignorant of philosophical and scientific learning: for it contains a medley of geometrical theorems, astronomical speculations, arithmetical calculations, and musical principles, with geographical delineations of islands, mountains, forests, and various other matters of little moment. By forcing such irrelevant details into connection with his subject, he has rendered his work a very loose production useless alike, in my opinion, to the ignorant and the learned; for the illiterate are incapable of appreciating the loftiness of his diction, and such as are really competent to form a just estimate, condemn his wearisome tautology. But let everyone exercise his own judgment concerning these books according to his taste. All I have to add is, that he has confounded the chronological order of the transactions he describes: for after having related what took place in the reign of the Emperor Theodosius, he immediately goes back to the times of the bishop Athanasius; and this sort of things he does frequently (LNPF).

Photius in whose day one could still read twenty-four books of the originally thirty-six books, as he himself tells us, describes the language and style (*Bibl. cod.* 35) as follows:

Read the work of Philip of Side, entitled a *Christian History*, beginning with the words 'In the beginning God created the heavens and the earth'. He gives an account of the Mosaic history, sometimes brief, sometimes full, although wordy throughout. The first book contains twenty-four volumes, like the twenty-three other books, which we have seen up to the present. His language is diffuse, without urbanity or elegance, and soon palls, or positively disgusts; his aim is rather to display his knowledge than to benefit the reader. Most of the matter has nothing to do with history, and the work might be called a treatise on all kinds of subjects rather than a history, tasteless effusion. Philip was a contemporary of Sisinnius and Proclus, patriarchs of Constantinople. He frequently attacks the former in his history, because, while both filled the same office and Philip was considered the more eloquent, Sisinnius was elected to the patriarchate (SPCK).

Perhaps the immense size of this work also contributed to its disappearance. Despite Socrates' and Photius' criticisms it is to be regretted that it did not come down to us because it must have contained much information lacking in Eusebius' Church History. What little survives is found in the collection of excerpts of *Codex Baroccianus* 142 of the 14th or 15th century at Oxford. One of them contains the much-discussed assertion that Papias had stated that the Apostles John and his brother James were martyred by the Jews. The fragment runs as follows:

Papias, bishop of Hierapolis, a disciple of John the Theologian and friend of Polycarp, wrote *The Lord's Gospel* in five books. There he gave a list of Apostles and, after enumerating Peter and John, Philip and Thomas and Matthew, recorded as 'disciples of the Lord' Aristion and another John, whom he also called 'presbyter'. As a result, some believe that (this) John is the author of the two short Catholic Epistles, which circulate under the name of John, their reason being that the men of the primitive age accepted the First Epistle only. Some have also erroneously believed the Apocalypse to be this man's work. Papias, too, is in error about the Millennium, and so is, in consequence Irenaeus. Papias says in the second book that John the Evangelist and his brother James were slain by the Jews. The aforesaid Papias related, alleging as his source of information the daughters of Philip, that Barsabas, the same Justus that passed the scrutiny, was forced by the unbelievers to drink snake poison, but was in the name of Christ preserved unharmed. He relates still other marvellous events, in particular the rising of Manaemus's mother from the dead. Regarding those who were raised from the dead by Christ, he says that they survived till Hadrian's time (ACW 6).

Another fragment found in the same Codex was published by Dodwell in 1689. It deals with the Alexandrian Catechetical School and contains a list of its heads.

The *Christian History* was not the only work of Philip of Side. Socrates mentions that he composed several others: 'Affecting the Asiatic style, he became the author of many treatises, attempting among others a refutation of the Emperor Julian's treatises against the Christians' (*Hist. eccl.* 7, 27 LNPF). Nothing is known of the last-named work.

Fragments: H. DODWELL, Dissertationes in Irenaeum. Accedit fragmentum Philippi Sidetae hactenus inediti de catechistarum Alexandrinorum successione. Oxford, 1689, 488. — C. DE BOOR, Neue Fragmente des Papias, Hegesippus und Pierus in bisher unbekannten Exzerpten aus der Kirchengeschichte des Philippus Sidetes (TU 5, 2). Leipzig, 1888, 165-184. — A. WIRTH, Aus orientalischen Chroniken. Frankfurt a.M., 1894, 208-210 (on Adam and Eve). — E. BRATKE, Das sogenannte Religionsgespräch am Hof der Sassaniden (TU 19, 3). Leipzig, 1899, 153-164.

Studies: E. BRATKE, *ibid.* — D. SERRUYS, Autour d'un fragment de Philippe de Side: Mélanges d'archéol. et d'histoire 26 (1906) 335-349 (on Adam and Eve). — F. J. DÖLGER, *IXΘYΣ* II. Münster, 1922, 252-262 (Der Kult von Hierapolis und das Religionsgespräch am Hof der Sassaniden). — P. HESELER, Neues zur 'Vita Constantini' des Codex Angelicus 22: Byz 10 (1935) 400. — H. G. OPITZ, PWK 19 (1938) 2350-2351. — E. HONIGMANN, Patristic Studies (ST 173). Vatican City, 1953, 82-91.

PHILOSTORGIUS

Philostorgius was born about 368 at Borissus in Cappadocia Secunda but went at the age of twenty to Constantinople where he spent most of his life. Though a layman he became a follower and warm admirer of Eunomius (cf. above, p. 306).

While at Constantinople he published between 425 and 433 a *Church History* in twelve books covering the period 300-425 ostensibly a continuation of Eusebius but in reality a late apology for the extreme Arianism of Eunomius. Photius describes (*Bibl. cod.* 40) its size, content, style and tendency as follows:

Read the so-called *Ecclesiastical History* by Philostorgius the Arian, the spirit of which is different from that of nearly all other ecclesiastical historians. He extols all Arians, but abuses and insults all the orthodox, so that this work is not so much a history as a panegyric of the heretics, and nothing but a barefaced attack upon the orthodox. His style is elegant, his diction often poetical, though not to such an extent as to be tedious or disagreeable. His figurative use of words is very expressive and makes the work both pleasant and agreeable to read; sometimes, however, these figures are overbold and far-fetched, and create an impression of being frigid and ill-timed. The language is variously embellished even to excess, so that the reader imperceptibly finds himself involved in a disagreeable obscurity. In many instances the author introduces appropriate moral reflections of his own. He starts from the devotion of Arius to the heresy and its first beginnings, and ends with the recall of the impious Aëtius. This Aëtius was removed from his office by his brother heretics, since he outdid them in wickedness, as Philostorgius himself unwillingly confesses. He was recalled and welcomed by the impious Julian. The history, in one volume and six books, goes down to this period. The author is a liar and the narrative often fictitious. He chiefly extols Aëtius and Eunomius for their learning, as having alone cleansed the doctrines of faith overlaid by time, therein showing himself a monstrous liar. He also praises Eusebius of Nicomedia (whom he calls the Great), Theophilus the Indian, and several others, for their lives and wonderful works. He severely attacks Acacius, bishop of Caesarea in Palestine, for his extreme severity and invincible craftiness, in which, he declares, Acacius surpassed all his fellow-heretics, however filled they were with hatred of one another, as well as those who held different religious opinions. This was the extent of our reading. Soon afterwards six other books were found in another volume, so that the whole appears to have filled twelve books. The initial letters of each book are so arranged that they form the name of the author. The work goes down to the time of Theodosius the Younger, when, after the death of Honorius, Theodosius handed over the throne of the West to his cousin Valentinian the Younger, the son of Constantius and Placidia.

Notwithstanding his rage against the orthodox, Philostorgius does not venture to attack Gregory the Theologian [i.e. of Nazianzus], but unwillingly accepts his doctrines. His attempt to slander Basil the Great only had the effect of increasing his reputation. He was forced to admit the vigour and beauty of his sermons from actual knowledge,

although he timidly calls Basil overbold and inexperienced in controversy, because he ventured to attack the writings of Eunomius (SPCK).

Apart from this interesting report Photius published separately
an *Epitome*, a series of excerpts culled from the twelve books. Since
Philostorgius' work has perished, this *Epitome* serves as a skeleton
for its reconstruction. It survives in a number of manuscripts whose
archetype is *Cod. Barocc.* 142 s. XIV. Scattered fragments are also
extant in the *Passio Artemii* composed by John of Rhodos in the
ninth century, in Suidas and in a *Vita Constantini* found in *Cod.
Angelicus* 22 and edited by Opitz; still others in the *Thesaurus
orthodoxae fidei* by Nicetas Acominatus, and in two epigrams of the
Anthologia Palatina. These remains show that Philostorgius used
excellent sources no longer extant, especially documents of Arian
origin, which furnish very valuable information for the history of
this controversy and its chief personalities. For this reason the loss
of the complete text is deplorable despite its bias and inaccuracy.

One of the fragments reveals that Philostorgius wrote earlier a
Refutation of Porphyry and an *Encomium on Eunomius* of which we
know nothing.

Editions: MG 65, 459-624. — Crit. ed.: J. BIDEZ, Philostorgius Kirchengeschichte:
GCS 21 (1913) 1-150; Anfang der Artemii Passio mit Philostorgius Angaben über
Artemius, ibid. 151-157. — H. G. OPITZ, Die Vita Constantini des Cod. Ang. Gr. 22:
Byz 9 (1934) 535-593 (contains the complete text of the *Vita* with the fragments of
Philostorgius). — New fragments: P. HESELER, Neues zur 'Vita Constantini' dès Codex
Angelicus 22: Byz 10 (1935) 399-402. — J. BIDEZ, Fragments nouveaux de Philostorge
sur la vie de Constantin: Byz 10 (1935) 403-442.

Translation: English: E. WALFORD, The Ecclesiastical History of Sozomen... also the
Ecclesiastical History of Philostorgius as Epitomized by Photius. London, 1855.

Studies: P. BATIFFOL, Fragmente der Kirchengeschichte des Philostorgius: RQ 3 (1889)
252-289; *idem*, Die Textüberlieferung der Kirchengeschichte des Philostorgius: RQ 4
(1890) 134-143; *idem*, Quaestiones Philostorgianae (thesis). Paris, 1891; *idem*, Un
historiographe anonyme arien du IVe siècle: RQ 9 (1895) 57-97 (a source of Philostorgius). — L. JEEP, Zur Überlieferung des Philostorgius (TU 17, 3b, 2). Leipzig,
1899. — J. R. ASMUS, Ein Beitrag zur Rekonstruktion der Kirchengeschichte des Philostorgios: BZ 4 (1895) 30-44. — J. BIDEZ, GCS 21 (1913) IX-CLXIII (important
introductions on manuscripts, sources, life, education and purpose of Philostorgius). —
J. MARQUART, Die schwarzen Syrer des Philostorgios: ThLZ 38 (1913) 705-709. —
G. FRITZ, DTC 12 (1935) 1495-1498.

SOCRATES

The Church Historian Socrates was born about 380 at Constantinople where he was educated by the pagan grammarians Helladius
and Ammonius and later became a lawyer.

At the instance of a certain Theodore he wrote a *Church History* in seven books designed to be a continuation of Eusebius' treatise, as he formally announces in the introduction. It extends from the abdication of Diocletian in 305 to 439 A.D., each book covering the reign of one of the emperors to his death. It represents by far the best continuation of Eusebius whom he even surpasses in objectivity and sincerity though his treatment suffers from a certain lack of color and theological interest. His main attention is focused on the vicissitudes of the Church, but secular history is by no means forgotten. Events connected with Constantinople attract his special interest and the Novationists arouse a certain sympathy. He examines his sources carefully and mentions them in most cases. He draws on Rufinus, Eusebius, the historical and polemical treatises and letters of Athanasius, on Gelasius of Caesarea, Eutropius, episcopal lists, and especially on a collection of Conciliar Acts issued about 375 by the Macedonian Sabinus of Heraclea, letters of emperors and bishops. Since he reproduces a great number of these sources verbally, his work which is completely extant remains an invaluable storehouse of information for the historian.

The existing text represents a second edition. After publishing the first Socrates found out that some of the sources he used (especially Rufinus) were unreliable. Thus he felt obliged to make a drastic revision. The reasons with which he justifies this second edition at the beginning of book II testify to his conscientiousness as a historian:

> Rufinus who wrote an Ecclesiastical History in Latin, has erred in respect to chronology. For he supposes that what was done against Athanasius occurred after the death of the Emperor Constantine: he was also ignorant of his exile to the Gauls and of various other circumstances. Now we in the first place wrote the first two books of our history following him; but in writing our history from the third to the seventh, some facts were collected from Rufinus, others from different authors, and some from the narration of individuals still living. Afterwards, however, we perused the writings of Athanasius, wherein he depicts his own sufferings and how through the calumnies of the Eusebian faction he was banished, and judged that more credit was due to him who had suffered, and to those who were witnesses of the things they describe, than to such as have been dependent on conjecture, and had therefore erred. Moreover, having obtained several letters of persons eminent at that period, we have availed ourselves of their assistance also in tracing out the truth as far as possible. On this account we were compelled to revise the first and second books of this history, using, however, the testimony of Rufinus where it is evident that he could not be mistaken. It should also be observed, that in our former edition, neither the sentence of deposition which was passed upon Arius, nor the Emperor's letters were inserted, but simply the

narration of facts in order that the history might not become bulky and weary the readers with tedious matters of detail. But in the present edition, such alterations and additions have been made for your sake, o sacred man of God, Theodore, in order that you might not be ignorant what the princes wrote in their own words, as well as the decisions of the bishops in their various Synods, wherein they continually altered the confession of faith. Wherefore, whatever we have deemed necessary we have inserted in this later edition. Having adopted this course in the first book, we shall endeavor to do the same in the consecutive portion of our history, I mean the second (LNPF).

The Theodore, to whom he dedicated his work, seems to have been a member of the clergy or a religious order, whereas Socrates himself was a layman.

The best manuscripts are two *Codd. Florentini* of the 10th and 11th centuries. A new critical text is badly needed and in preparation for GCS. An Armenian translation of the seventh century was published in 1897.

Editions: MG 67, 29-872. — *Separate ed.*: R. Hussey, Socrates Scholast.: Historia Ecclesiastica. 3 vols. Oxford, 1853. — W. Bright, Oxford, 1878 and 1893 (reprint of Hussey's text). — An Armenian version: by Ter Mosesean, Edschmiadzin, 1897; cf. E. Preuschen, ThLZ (1902) 210; P. Peeters, A propos de la version arménienne de l'historien Socrate: Mélanges J. Bidez 2. Brussels, 1934, 647-675.

Translations: English: A. C. Zenos, LNPF series 2, vol. 2 (1890) 1-178; reprinted: Grand Rapids, 1952. — *French:* L. Cousin, Paris, 1675, and Amsterdam, 1686.

Studies: L. Jeep, Quellenuntersuchungen zu den griechischen Kirchenhistorikern: Jahrbuch f. klass. Philologie, Supplementband 14. Leipzig, 1885, 105-137 (Socrates' sources). — S. P. Lambros, Eine neue Fassung des 11. Kapitels des 6. Buches von Sokrates' Kirchengeschichte: BZ 4 (1895) 481-486. — F. Geppert, Die Quellen des Kirchenhistorikers Sokrates Scholastikus. Leipzig, 1898. — G. Loeschke, Sokrates: RE 18 (1906) 481-486. — W. Eltester, PWK II. Reihe, 3 (1927) 893-901. — H. G. Opitz, Untersuchungen zur Überlieferung der Schriften des Athanasius. Berlin, 1935, 155-157 (text. crit.). — P. Heseler: Byz 10 (1935) 438ff. (Socrates draws on Gelasius of Caesarea). — F. J. F. Jackson, A History of Church History. Studies of Some Historians of the Christian Church. Cambridge, 1939, 73-82. — E. Peterson, EC 11 (1953) 883. — B. C. Stephanides, Ἱστορικαὶ διορθώσεις εἰς τὴν Ἐκκλησιαστικὴν Ἱστορίαν τοῦ Σωκράτους: EEBS 26 (1956) 57-129.

SOZOMEN

Sozomen, a contemporary of Socrates, likewise practiced law at Constantinople. He was, however, not a native of the capital but of Bethelia near Gaza in Palestine. After travelling as far as Italy (2, 24; 7, 16) he settled at Constantinople. It was here that he wrote between 439 and 450 his *Church History* covering the period from 324 to 425 and intended to be a continuation of Eusebius' work.

His full name was Salaminius Hermias Sozomen. From the first chapter of his *Church History* we learn that this was not his first work but that previously he had composed a compendium of ecclesiastical history from the Ascension to 323, the year of the overthrow of Licinius, that has not come down to us:

> I at first felt strongly inclined to trace the course of events from the very beginning; but on reflecting that similar records of the past up to their own time had been compiled by those wisest of men, Clemens and Hegesippus, successors of the Apostles, by Africanus the historian, and by Eusebius, surnamed Pamphilus, a man intimately acquainted with the Sacred Scriptures and the writings of the Greek poets and historians, I merely draw up an epitome in two books of all that is recorded to have happened to the Churches, from the Ascension of Christ to the deposition of Licinius. Now, however, by the help of God, I will endeavor to relate the subsequent events as well (LNPF).

His *Church History* consists of nine books and is preceded by an address to the Emperor Theodosius II to whom he dedicates the treatise with the following words: 'Receive from me this writing, and marshal its facts and purify it by thy labors, out of thy accurate knowledge, whether by addition or elimination. For whatever course may seem pleasing to thee, that will be wholly advantageous and brilliant for the readers, nor shall anyone put a hand to it after thine approval'. He then gives a table of contents which proves that the end of the last book covering the events of the years 425-439 is lost:

> My history begins with the third consulate of the Caesars, Crispus and Constantine, and stretches to thy seventeenth consulship (i.e. 439). It seemed proper to divide the whole work into nine parts: the first and second books will embrace the ecclesiastical affairs under Constantine; the third and fourth, those under his sons; the fifth and sixth, those under Julian, the cousin of the sons of the great Constantine, and Jovian, and further, of Valentinian and Valens; the seventh and eighth books, o most powerful Emperor, will open the affairs under the brothers Gratian and Valentinian, until the proclamation of Theodosius, thy divine grandfather, as far as thy celebrated father Arcadius, together with thy uncle, the most pious and godly Honorius, received the paternal government and shared in the regulation of the Roman world. The ninth book I have devoted to thy Christ-loving and most innocent majesty (LNPF).

Since Theodosius died 450, it is evident that the work must have been written between 439, the end of the period covered, and the year of the Emperor's death, and since his contemporary Socrates describes the events from 305-439, and he himself those from 324 to 439, a frequent parallelism of narrative can be expected. However, there are long passages in both works which are literally identical or differ only in a few words. Thus there is a strong dependence of one upon the other and it has been ascertained that Sozomen frequently copies the text of Socrates, although he never mentions him. Nevertheless he has consulted a number of sources himself and there are many passages for which no parallel can be found in Socrates, as for instance the long report about the persecutions of the Christians in Persia under Sapor II (2, 9-14), which he evidently based on the Acts of Persian martyrs. Perhaps he intended to correct and to enlarge Socrates' work. He certainly has used more Western sources than the latter. 'His style is better than that of Socrates' according to Photius (*Bibl. cod.* 30), though his historical sense and critical judgment seem to be weaker and many legends find their way into his narrative.

Editions: MG 67, 844-1630. — *Separate ed.*: R. HUSSEY, Sozomenus Salam.: Historia Ecclesiastica. Oxford, 1860, 3 vols.

Translations: English: C. D. HARTRANFT, LNPF series 2, vol. 2. New York, 1890, 236-427; reprinted: Grand Rapids, 1952. — *French:* L. COUSIN, Histoire de l'Église écrite par Sozomène (Hist. de l'Église III). Paris, 1676; reprinted: Amsterdam, 1686. — *German:* C. HEDIO, Eusebii Pamphili, Sozomeni, Socratis und Theodorets Kirchen-Historie. Strasbourg, 1545.

Studies: J. V. SARRAZIN, De Sozomeni historia num integra sit: Commentationes philologae Ienenses 1. Leipzig, 1881, 165-168. — L. JEEP, Quellenuntersuchungen zu den griechischen Kirchenhistorikern: Jahrbuch f. klass. Philologie. Supplementband 14. Leipzig, 1885, 137-154 (Socrates and Sozomen). — P. BATIFFOL, Sozomène et Sabinos: BZ 7 (1898) 265-284. — G. LOESCHKE, Sozomenos: RE 18 (1906) 541-547. — J. BIDEZ, La tradition manuscrite de Sozomène et la Tripartite de Théodore le Lecteur (TU 32, 2b). Leipzig, 1908. — G. SCHOO, Die Quellen des Kirchenhistorikers Sozomenos. Berlin, 1911. — W. ELTESTER, PWK II. Reihe, 3 (1927) 1240-1248. — J. BIDEZ, Le texte du prologue de Sozomène et des chapitres (VI, 28-34) sur les moines d'Égypte et de Palestine: SAB 18 (1935) n. 18. — F. J. F. JACKSON, op. cit. 82-84. — G. BARDY, DTC 14 (1941) 2469-2471. — N. H. BAYNES, Sozomen, Ecclesiastica Historia I, 15: JThSt 49 (1948) 165-168. — W. TELFER, Sozomen I, 15. A Reply: JThSt 50 (1949) 187-191 (against Baynes).

THEODORET OF CYRUS

The last great theologian of Antioch was Theodoret of Cyrus. Born at Antioch about 393, and educated in its monasteries he was in 423 elected bishop of Cyrus, a small town near Antioch, and governed this diocese with great wisdom and zeal for 35 years. Very active in promoting the spiritual and temporal welfare of his flock, he indefatigably fought pagans, Jews and heretics, but at the same time he generously beautified the city, built an aqueduct and a canal to provide a water supply previously lacking, repaired baths and erected public galleries and bridges. Though it cannot be proved that Theodore of Mopsuestia was his master and Nestorius and John of Antioch were his fellow-students, he soon became involved in the controversy between Cyril of Alexandria and Nestorius, whose cause he espoused. Deeply imbued with the theological ideas of the Antiochene School, he was convinced that the heresy of Apollinaris lurked in the teaching of Cyril and at the beginning of 431 gave expression to his fear in a polemical work no longer extant *Refutation of the Twelve Anathematisms of Cyril of Alexandria*. At Ephesus he sided with John of Antioch and maintained his views even after Nestorius had been condemned. Moreover, he now published a comprehensive work of five books, in which he attacked Cyril and the decisions of the Council. He refused to give his adhesion to the terms of reconciliation between Cyril and the bishops of the East though the declaration of faith, the so-called Union-Creed that Cyril accepted, in 433, had probably been composed by Theodoret himself (cf. above, p. 118). He finally joined the 'Union' only after the demand for a formal recognition of the condemnation of Nestorius had been dropped.

Soon, however, he became involved in another controversy over the heresy of Eutyches, which was the directly contrary error and the opposite extreme to Nestorianism. For while the latter denied that the divine nature was truly united to the human nature in Christ in one Person, the former denied that the two natures in Christ remained distinct. Thus at the Robber-Synod of Ephesus (449) Theodoret was deposed by Dioscurus, the successor of Cyril of Alexandria, and forced into exile. He appealed to Pope Leo I, who declared the decision of the *Latrocinium* null and void. Thanks to the new Emperor Marcian he could return to Cyrus in the following year. At the Council of Chalcedon (451) his appearance met at first with great opposition. A special session dealt with his case, and insisted upon his pronouncing anathema against Nestorius. After great reluctance he finally complied with this demand and exclaimed, 'Anathema to Nestorius, and to all who do not confess that the Blessed Virgin Mary is the Mother of God and divide into two the only Son, the only-Begotten'. Thereupon he was formally reinstated in his episcopal dignity and recognized by all the Fathers as 'an orthodox teacher' (Mansi 7, 189). He ruled the Church of Cyrus for seven more years and died about 466. There is every reason to believe that his declaration at Chalcedon was honest and that he cannot be accused of having abandoned his own convictions under pressure, which would not tally with what we know of his character and personal integrity. The years between his joining of the Union in 434 and the Council in 451 most probably enabled him to harmonize the correct elements of the two different

Christologies, that of Antioch and that of Alexandria, as did the authoritative decision of Chalcedon. In the third of the famous 'Three Chapters' the Fifth Ecumenical Council at Constantinople in 553 condemned his writings against Cyril and the Council of Ephesus together with some of his sermons and letters.

Studies: E. VENABLES, DCB 4 (1887) 904-919. — H. G. OPITZ, PWK II. Reihe, 5 (1934) 1791-1801. — G. BARDY, DTC 15 (1946) 299-325. — L. S. N. TILLEMONT, Mémoires pour servir à l'histoire ecclésiastique 15. Paris, 1711, 207-340; 868-878. — N. N. GLUBO-KOWSKIJ, The Blessed Theodoret. His Life and his Works (in Russian). Moscow, 1890, 2 vols. — J. SCHULTE, Theodoret von Cyrus als Apologet. Vienna, 1904. — K. GÜNTHER, Theodoret von Cyrus und die Kämpfe in der orientalischen Kirche vom Tode Cyrills bis zur Einberufung des sogenannten Räuberkonzils (Progr.). Aschaffenburg, 1913. — A. SEIDER, BKV² 51 (1926) IX-IC. — M. RICHARD, Notes sur l'évolution doctrinale de Théodoret: RSPT 25 (1936) 459-481. — T. CAMELOT, De Nestorius à Eutyches: CGG I (1951) 232-242. — I. ORTIZ DE URBINA, Das Symbol von Chalkedon. Sein Text, sein Werden, seine dogmatische Bedeutung: CGG I (1951) 400-409. — Y. AZÉMA, Théodoret de Cyr d'après sa correspondance. Étude sur la personnalité morale, religieuse et intellectuelle de l'évêque de Cyr. Diss. Paris, 1952. — E. HONIGMANN, Theodorct of Cyrrhus and Basil of Seleucia. The Time of their Death: Patristic Studies (ST 173), Vatican City, 1953, 174-184. — H. M. DIEPEN and J. DANIÉLOU, Théodoret et le dogme d'Éphèse: RSR 44 (1956) 243-248.

HIS WRITINGS

Theodoret is one of the most successful writers of the Eastern Church and his literary bequest has greater variety than that of the other theologians of Antioch. He composed works in almost all the different fields of sacred science. In 450 he himself estimates the number of his books at 35 (*Ep.* 145; cf. *Ep.* 116). Only a comparatively small number of these has survived, but enough to give evidence of his learning. Conversant with classical literature, he seems to have read Homer and Plato, Isocrates and Demosthenes, Herodotus and Thucydides, Hesiod, Aristotle, Apollodorus and Plotinus, Plutarch and Porphyry. He was acquainted with several languages besides his own, which was the Syriac. The Greek, in which he wrote, is perfect, and his style clear and simple, so that Photius (*Bibl. cod.* 203) praises the purity of his Attic.

Collections: J. L. SCHULZE and J. A. NOESSELT, Theodoretus, Opera omnia. Halle, 1769/1774, 5 vols.; reprinted: MG 80-84. Separate editions and translations will be found below with the individual works.

Translations: English: B. JACKSON, LNPF series 2, vol. 3. New York, 1893. — *German:* G. M. SCHULER and L. KÜPPER, BKV (1878). — K. GUTBERLET, BKV² 50 (1926). — A. SEIDER, BKV² 51 (1926). — *French:* Y. AZÉMA, SCH 40 (1955). — R. P. CANIVET, SCH 57 (1958).

Studies: E. SCHWARTZ, Zur Schriftstellerei Theodorets: SAM (1922) 1, 30-40. — J. LEBON, Restitutions à Théodoret de Cyr: RHE 26 (1930) 523-550. — M. RICHARD, L'activité littéraire de Théodoret avant le concile d'Éphèse: RSPT 24 (1935) 83-106.

— D. C. Fives, The Use of the Optative Mood in the Works of Theodoret, Bishop of Cyrus. Washington, 1937. — E. des Places, Le Platon de Théodoret. Les citations des Lois et de l'Épinomis: REG 68 (1955) 171-184; *idem*, Les citations de Platon chez les Pères: SP II (TU 64). Berlin, 1957, 340-341.

Theological Studies: A. Bertram, Theodoreti episcopi Cyrensis doctrina christologica. Hildesheim, 1883. — K. Jüssen, (below p. 542). — P. C. da Mazzarino, La dottrina di Teodoreto di Ciro sull'unione ipostatica delle due nature in Cristo. Rome, 1941. — J. Montalverne, Theodoreti Cyrensis doctrina antiquior de Verbo 'inhumanato' (Studia Antoniana 1). Rome, 1948. — F. Rossiter, Messianic Prophecy according to Theodoret of Cyrus. Diss. Greg. Rome, 1950. — A. Grillmeier, Die theologische und sprachliche Vorbereitung der christologischen Formel von Chalkedon: CGG I (1951) 183-191. — K. McNamara, Theodoret of Cyrus and the Unity of Person in Christ: ITQ 22 (1955) 313-328.

1. *Exegetical Writings*

Though Theodoret does not pretend to originality, his exegetical writings are among the finest specimens of the Antiochene School and remarkable for their combination of terseness and lucidity. In his interpretation of Holy Scripture he adopts a middle course, avoiding the radicalism of Theodore of Mopsuestia and his excessive literalness and allowing an allegorical and typological explanation, whenever this appears preferable. He composed both complete commentaries on a number of biblical books and treatises arranged in the form of question and answer on selected difficult passages.

1. *Quaestiones in Octateuchum*

One of the latter class is his series of questions on the Pentateuch with an appendix on the books of Josue, Judges and Ruth. Composed after 453 at the request of 'the dearest of his sons' Hypatius, the work was amply used by Anastasius Sinaita in the seventh and Photius in the ninth century.

Editions: MG 80, 75-528. — R. Devreesse, Anciens commentateurs grecs de l'Octateuque: RBibl 44 (1935) 167-170.

Studies: E. Montmasson, L'homme créé à l'image de Dieu d'après Théodoret de Cyr et Procope de Gaza: EO 14 (1911) 334-339; 15 (1912) 154-162 (*Quaest. in Gen.* 19-20). — G. Bardy, La littérature patristique des Quaestiones et responsiones sur l'Écriture Sainte: RBibl 42 (1933) 219-225 (manuscript tradition); 343 (Anastasius Sinaita). — J. Gross, La divinisation du chrétien d'après les Pères grecs. Paris, 1938, 273ff. (*Quaest. in Gen.* 1, 20). — W. J. Burghardt, The Image of God in Man according to Cyril of Alexandria (SCA 14). Washington, 1957, 62-63 (*Quaest. in Gen.* 20).

2. *Quaestiones in libros Regnorum et Paralipomenon*

This series represents a continuation of the above. While the author sticks to the question-and-answer form for the Books of

Kings, he abandons it for the Chronicles of which he gives a running explanation.

Edition: MG 80, 527-858.

Study: A. RAHLFS, Septuaginta-Studien, Heft 1. Studien zu den Königsbüchern. Göttingen, 1904, 16-46 (Theodorets Zitate aus den Königsbüchern und dem 2. Buch der Chronik).

3. *Interpretatio in Psalmos*

This *Interpretation of* all *the Psalms* is a continuous exposition of the entire Psalter. The author states in the preface that he read a number of commentaries on the Psalms, some extremely allegorical, others explaining Messianic prophecies as referring to events of the past, — the latter an interpretation which would fit Jews better than the children of the faith. 'I have regarded it as my duty', he continues, 'to avoid the one extreme as well as the other. Whatever refers to history, I shall explain historically but the prophecies about Christ the Lord, about the Church from the gentiles, about the Gospel and the preaching of the Apostles shall not be explained as referring to certain other things, as is customary with the Jews'. The commentary does not furnish a clue for an exact date. M. Brok concluded that it was written between 441 and 449. An Old Slavonic version is extant in manuscript.

Editions: MG 80, 857-1998; additions: MG 84, 19-32. — For the Old Slavonic version, see: V. JAGIČ, Ein unedierter griechischer Psalmenkommentar. Vienna, 1904, 5.

Studies: E. GROSSE - BRAUCKMANN, Der Psaltertext bei Theodoret: NGWG Phil.-hist. Klasse (1911) 336-365 (Biblical text and manuscript tradition). — M. BROK, Touchant la date du commentaire sur le psautier de Théodoret de Cyr: RHE 44 (1949) 552-556.

4. *Interpretatio in Canticum Canticorum*

This continuous explanation of the Canticle of Canticles represents his earliest exegetical work, composed at the request of bishop John of Germanicia. Rejecting the view that the subject treated in the Song of Songs is the mutual love of man and woman, the author reminds the reader in the preface of the spiritual character of this book. His ecclesiological interpretation makes ample use of Origen who in his commentary and in his homilies regards the Church as the bride and Christ as the spouse. Theodore of Mopsuestia's explanation of the Canticle as Solomon's reply to the opponents of his marriage with the Egyptian princess is repudiated as 'a story not even fitting in the mouth of crazy women'.

Edition: MG 81, 27-214.

Studies: W. RIEDEL, Die Auslegung des Hohenliedes in der jüdischen Gemeinde und der griechischen Kirche. Leipzig, 1898, 86-95 (Theodoret). — L. WELSERSHEIMB, Das Kirchenbild der griechischen Väterkommentare zum Hohen Liede: ZkTh 70 (1948) 440-441 (Theodoret depends on Origen).

5. Interpretatio in Danielem

This continuous commentary betrays a strong anti-Jewish tendency. The preface castigates the shamelessness of the Jews in excluding Daniel from the choir of the prophets. The story of Susanna and the narrative of Bel and the dragon are not mentioned. In his preface to the Psalms, Theodoret indicates that his *Interpretatio in Danielem* was his first commentary on the prophets. It must have followed immediately after that on the Canticle of Canticles.

Edition: MG 81, 1255-1546.

Study: L. CANET, Pour l'édition de S. Jean Chrysostome Λόγοι κατὰ 'Ιουδαίων et de Théodoret 'Υπόμνημα εἰς τὸν Δανιὴλ: Mélanges d'archéologie et d'histoire 34 (1914) 97-200 (Prolegomena for a new edition).

6. Interpretatio in Ezechielem was written after the commentary on Daniel as stated in the preface to the Psalms.

Edition: MG 81, 807-1256.

7. Interpretatio in duodecim Prophetas Minores followed that on Ezechiel according to the same preface.

Edition: MG 81, 1545-1988.

Studies: F. A. SPECHT, Der exegetische Standpunkt des Theodor von Mopsuestia und Theodoret von Kyros in der Auslegung messianischer Weissagungen aus ihren Kommentaren zu den kleinen Propheten dargestellt. Munich, 1871. — A. MERX, Die Prophetie des Joel und ihre Ausleger. Halle, 1879, 147-152 (Theodoret's commentary on Joel). — F. ROSSITER, op. cit. (above, p. 539).

8. Interpretatio in Isaiam

This commentary was until recently known only from fragments in *Catenae*. Papadopulos-Kerameus discovered a manuscript of the entire text and notified the world of scholars of this very valuable finding in 1899 in the fourth volume of his 'Ιεροσολυμιτικὴ Βιβλιοθήκη. But nobody paid any attention to his remark until A. Möhle's eyes fell on it in 1929 and he proceeded to edit the work in 1932 from Codex no. 17 of the Metochion of the Holy Sepulchre at Constantinople. It consists of twenty *tomoi* in two books of ten. The prologue states explicitly that it was the last but one of his commentaries on all the prophets and written just before that on Jeremias. The same excellent qualities which we admire in his other exegetical works, the transparent lucidity and compactness of diction, make this rediscovered work a model of Scriptural exposition. As a rule the author elucidates the literal sense with sober and critical judgment. This does not prevent him from adopting the allegorical and typological interpretation when occasion demands it. In many instances he reports the opinions of others in order to confront them with his own for which he gives a scientific proof. Several times he assails that exegesis which refers the Messianic prophecies to events of later Jewish history and which refuses, as Theodore of Mopsuestia did, to recognize the Christian sense of these passages. He uses such opportunities to attack the Jews for their unsatisfactory and false expositions of Scripture. His excellent philological training is wary of consulting only one recension and seeks out the variants in Lucian's and others' editions, especially those of Aquila, Symmachus and Theodotion and even a Syriac translation, in order to do full justice to the meaning of the inspired word. He also pays attention to the *Hexapla* recension of the Septuagint. The commentary is very valuable for Theodoret's Christological views.

Edition: A. MÖHLE, Theodoret von Kyros, Kommentar zu Jesaia (Mitteilungen des Septuaginta-Unternehmens der Gesellschaft der Wissenschaften zu Göttingen. T.: V). Berlin, 1932.

Study: K. JÜSSEN, Die Christologie des Theodoret von Cyrus nach seinem neuveröffentlichten Isaias-Kommentar: ThGl 27 (1935) 438-452.

9. *Interpretatio in Jeremiam*

This commentary deals not only with Jeremias but also with the Book of Baruch and the Lamentations. It is the last of his expositions on the prophets as he remarks at the end.

Edition: MG 81, 495-806.

10. *Interpretatio in quatuordecim epistolas S. Pauli*

The commentary on the 14 Epistles of St. Paul is most probably of a later date than those on the books of the Old Testament and is his only surviving work on the New Testament.

Edition: MG 82, 35-878.

Study: O. CULLMANN, Le caractère eschatologique du devoir missionnaire et de la conscience apostolique de S. Paul. Étude sur le κατέχον(ων) de 2 Thess. 2, 6-7: RHPR 16 (1936) 210-245 (MG 82, 664-665).

2. *Apologetical Works*

1. *Graecarum affectionum curatio*

The most important of Theodoret's apologetical writings is *The Cure of Pagan Maladies or The Truth of the Gospels Proved from Greek*

Philosophy, as the complete title runs. This last of the Christian apologies is completely preserved and considered as perhaps the best refutation of paganism which has come down to us. It consists of twelve discourses in which the author places side by side the pagan and the Christian answers to fundamental questions of philosophy or religion so that, as the subtitle indicates, the superiority of the Gospel over the philosophy of the Greeks can be immediately recognized. The foreword gives full information about purpose, content and form of the work:

> I have often encountered certain people still attached to the fables of pagan mythology who ridicule our belief and assert that faith is all we require of those whom we give religious instruction. They also point with scorn at the Apostles' lack of education and stigmatize these men as uncouth and ignorant of the niceties of cultivated speech. They further say that the veneration shown to the martyrs is absurd. And as for the living seeking to obtain the intercession of the dead, this, they declare, is the utmost folly.
>
> Sundry other charges such as these have been made which this work will expose. In refuting their accusations, I have given full treatment to the topics that required it. If I had ignored these men and the deceit they practice on the unsophisticated, I would have been lacking, it seemed to me, in piety and devotion to religion. Hence, I have written this work as a complete refutation of their empty charges.
>
> I have divided the work into twelve discourses, and, in composing it, I have adopted a discursive style, considering this style suitable to a didactic work. Besides, in view of the fact that I make use of Plato and the other philosophers as my authorities, I found it expedient to present my arguments in a form not entirely out of keeping with theirs and even somewhat resembling it.

The first of the discourses is devoted to faith, its justification and necessity as a source of religious knowledge. The second answers the question of the origin of all things and of the essence of God. The third compares the Christian angelology with the pagan fables of inferior gods; the fourth Christian with pagan cosmogony. The fifth deals with the nature of man; the sixth with Divine Providence. The seventh denounces pagan and Jewish sacrifices and sets forth the true concept of this supreme act of worship. The eighth defends the veneration of martyrs; the ninth reveals the superiority of Christian ethics by comparison with the laws of the Greeks, Romans and other nations. The tenth discusses pagan oracles and their nature. The eleventh describes what pagans and Christians teach concerning the end of the world and final judgment. The twelfth contrasts the lives of the Apostles and those who follow in their footsteps with the lives of pagan philosophers.

The *Curatio* displays more than any other of his works his classical erudition. The author quotes more than one hundred pagan philosophers, poets and historians in about 340 passages. However, the great majority of these quotations have not been taken directly from the originals but from secondary sources, among them especially the *Stromata* of Clement of Alexandria and the *Praeparatio evangelica* of Eusebius of Caesarea, though he mentions the latter only once, the former never. Since he refers to the *Curatio* in his *Ep.* 113, it must have been composed before 449. Most scholars place its publication about the year 437, but on insufficient grounds. According to M. Richard the terminology points to a period when the doctrine of Christ had not yet divided the theologians. R. P. Canivet thinks that Theodoret composed it before he became bishop of Cyrus in 423.

Editions: MG 83, 783-1152 (reprint of T. Gaisford's ed. Oxford, 1839). — Crit. ed.: J. RAEDER, Theodoreti Graecarum affectionum curatio (Bibliotheca Teubneriana). Leipzig, 1904. — N. FESTA, Teodoreto, Terapia dei morbi pagani. Vol. I. Libri 1-6. Florence, 1930. — New ed.: R. P. CANIVET, Théodoret de Cyr, Thérapeutique des maladies helléniques. 2 vols. (SCH 57). Paris, 1958.

Translations: French: R. P. CANIVET, op. cit. — *Italian:* N. FESTA, op. cit.

Studies: C. ROOS, De Theodoreto Clementis et Eusebii compilatore. Diss. Halle, 1883. — J. R. ASMUS, Theodorets Therapeutik und ihr Verhältnis zu Julian: BZ 3 (1894) 116-145 (intends to prove that Theodoret has Julian's books *Against the Galilaeans* in mind). — J. RAEDER, De Theodoreti Graecarum affectionum curatione quaestiones criticae. Copenhagen, 1900 (manuscript tradition); *idem*, Analecta Theodoretiana: RhM N.F. 57 (1902) 449-459 (Cod. Vatic. 2249, saec., ut videtur, X, the oldest and most reliable of the 28 manuscripts). — J. SCHULTE, Theodoret von Cyrus als Apologet. Vienna, 1904, 28-41, 46-105, 110-165; *idem*, Das Verhältnis von Theodorets Therapeutik zu den Schriften Kaiser Julians: ThQ 88 (1906) 349-356 (against Asmus). — L. KÖSTERS, Zur Datierung von Theodorets Ἑλληνικῶν θεραπευτικὴ παθημάτων: ZkTh 30 (1906) 349-356 (composed in 437). — N. FESTA, Lo stilo di Teodoreto nella Terapia: RAL 6th ser. 4 (1928) 584-588. — O. SCHISSEL, Die προθεωρία des Theodoretos von Kyrrhos zur Ἑλληνικῶν θεραπευτικὴ παθημάτων: BZ 30 (1930) 18-22. — M. RICHARD, L'activité littéraire de Théodoret avant le concile d'Éphèse: RSPT 24 (1935) 89ff. — P. HENRY, Études Plotiniennes I. Les états du texte de Plotin. Paris, 1938, 141-154 (quotations from Plotinus). — L. FRÜCHTEL, PhW (1939) 765-766 (quotations from Clement of Al.). — P. CANIVET, Précisions sur la date de la 'Curatio' de Théodoret de Cyr: RSR 36 (1949) 585-593. — M. F. A. BROK, De waarde van de 'Graecarum affectionum curatio' van Theodoretus van Cyrus als apologetisch werk: StC 27 (1952) 201-212 (against G. Bardy, who calls the *Curatio* 'a rather poor summary of arguments used in the past'). — E. DES PLACES, Le Platon de Théodoret. Les citations des Lois et de l'Épinomis: REG 63 (1955) 172-184 (quotations in the *Curatio*). — P. CANIVET, Histoire d'une entreprise apologétique au Vᵉ siècle. Paris, 1957.

2. *De providentia orationes decem*

The series of *Ten Discourses on Providence* is one of the best specimens of Theodoret's eloquence and style. Addressed to an educated audience at Antioch, the first five sermons prove Divine Providence from the natural, the other five from the moral and social order, to climax with the Incarnation of the Saviour as the best and most striking evidence of God's loving care for all mankind. Opinions are very much divided regarding the date of delivery. Garnier (MG 84, 433), Schulte (p. 24), Bardenhewer (4, p. 232) and Opitz (PWK II, 5, 1798) argue for before the Council of Ephesus (431), whereas Bertram (p. 106), Richard (RSPT 24, p. 105) and Brok (RHE 44, p. 553) will not put the series before 435 on account of the doctrinal development of the author.

Edition: MG 83, 555-774.

Translations: German: G. M. Schuler, BKV (1878) 25-199. — *French:* Y. Azéma, Discours sur la Providence. Trad., introd. et notes. Paris, 1954.

Study: J. Schulte op. cit. 23-28, 42-46, 107-110.

3. *Ad quaesita magorum*

The treatise has not survived except in the author's own occasional quotations (*Hist. eccl.* 5, 39; *Ep.* 82 and 113; *Quaestiones in Levit.* 1). Theodoret answers and refutes the objections of the Persian magi against the Christian faith, attacks their deification of the elements and blames them for the severe and long persecutions of the Christians during the reign of the Persian kings Bahram V and Jezdegerd II. It remains doubtful whether the interesting fragment in the *Catena* on the Books of the Kings in *Codex Coislin Graec.* 8 belongs to this work, as Opitz thinks (p. 1798).

Studies: J. Schulte, op. cit. 2-6. — M. Brok, Le livre contre les mages de Théodoret de Cyr: MSR 10 (1953) 181-194.

4. *Contra Judaeos*

The treatise *Against the Jews* which is also lost, intended to show 'that the prophets foretold Christ', as *Ep.* 145 indicates. Opinions differ regarding the fragment in *Codex Laur.* 6, I saec. XIV. Glubokowskij (II, p. 200), Schulte (p. 8), Bardenhewer (4, p. 231) and Opitz (p. 1798) are convinced of Theodoret's authorship, whereas M. Brok and others have grave doubts. About the date we are completely in the dark. The passages in the letters 113, 116 and 145 where Theodoret sums up his works, furnish only a *terminus ante quem* (449). M. Richard lists it among those works which Theodoret composed before the Council of Ephesus (431).

Fragment: A. M. Bandinius, Catalogus codicum manuscriptorum bibliothecae Medicae Laurentianae I. Florence, 1764, 110-112; reprinted: J. Schulte, op. cit. 6-22. — New crit. ed.: M. Brok, Un soi-disant fragment du traité Contre les Juifs de Théodoret de Cyr: RHE 45 (1950) 490-494 (based on four manuscripts).

Translation: German: J. Schulte, loc. cit.

Studies: J. Schulte, op. cit. — M. Brok, art. cit. 487-507.

3. Dogmatic and Controversial Treatises

1. Reprehensio duodecim capitum seu anathematismorum Cyrilli

At the request of John of Antioch Theodoret wrote at the beginning of 431 a sharp *Refutation of the Twelve Anathemas of Cyril of Alexandria against Nestorius,* from November 430. Therein he explains the Antiochene point of view, defends the orthodoxy of Nestorius and accuses Cyril of Monophysitism. Since the Fifth Ecumenical Council (553) condemned it, the original was lost, but the entire text seems to be preserved in Cyril's answer *Epistola ad Euoptium adversus impugnationem duodecim capitum a Theodoreto editam* (cf. above p. 127). Theodoret's work was according to the Nestorians translated into Syriac.

Editions: MG 76, 385-452. — New crit. ed.: E. Schwartz, ACO I, 1, 6, 107-146; also I, 1, 7, 33ff. For the Syriac version, see: A. Baumstark, Geschichte der syrischen Literatur. Bonn, 1922, 106.

2. Pentalogium

The five books written also in 431 against Cyril and the Council of Ephesus have perished for the same reason as the *Refutation of the Anathemas:* they were condemned by the Fifth Ecumenical Council (553). A considerable number of Latin excerpts survives in the *Collectio Palatina.* Greek quotations are preserved in the *Catena on Luke* by Nicetas of Heraclea. Here the title of the work is *Pentalogos,* a pseudonym given to it after it had been condemned. Schwartz has brought out a new edition of these fragments and Richard several additions. Photius describes the treatise (*Bibl. cod.* 46) without mentioning its title.

Editions: Greek fragments: E. Schwartz, Zur Schriftstellerei Theodorets: SAM Phil.-hist. Klasse (1922) 1, 32ff. — M. Richard, Les citations de Théodoret conservées dans la chaîne de Nicétas sur l'Évangile selon Luc: RBibl 43 (1934) 88-96. — Latin fragments: E. Schwartz, ACO I, 5, 165-169.

3. De sancta et vivifica Trinitate and De incarnatione Domini

The two books *On the Holy and Vivifying Trinity* and *On the Incarnation of the Lord* which have come down to us under the name of Cyril have been successfully restored to Theodoret by A. Ehrhard. *De incarnatione* shares the same views as the *Refutation of the*

THEODORET OF CYRUS 547

Anathemas. Moreover, a number of Greek and Latin extracts have survived under the name of the real author, Theodoret, and two of his letters testify that he composed a work *On Theology and Divine Incarnation* (*Ep.* 133) or *On the Trinity and Divine Dispensation* (Latin letter: ACO I, 4, p. 85, 7 Schwartz). New fragments have been added by E. Schwartz and especially by Lebon, who found a number of passages in Severus of Antioch. The latter mentions even the exact title *De theologia sanctae Trinitatis et de oeconomia.* The two books formed one work, which, as Schwartz has proved, was composed before 430. The author explicitly denies any polemical purpose and pretends only to be defending the orthodox faith against the Apollinarists. But the 'Apollinarists' turn out to be, of all people, Cyril and the Fathers of Ephesus! At the end the term *anthropotokos* is defended as being at least as exact as *theotokos.* The work was first published by Cardinal Mai from a Vatican Codex under the name of Cyril of Alexandria and reprinted thus by Migne.

Editions: A. Mai, Script. vet. nova collect. 8, 27-1073 and Nova patr. bibl. 2, 1-74; reprinted: MG 75, 1147-1190, 1419-1478 (based on Codex Vatic. Gr. 801, f. 176-203). — New fragments: E. Schwartz, Zur Schriftstellerei Theodorets: SAM (1922) 1, 32-40. — J. Lebon, Restitutions à Théodoret de Cyr: RHE 26 (1930) 524ff. — Latin fragments: E. Schwartz, ACO I, 5, 169-170 (from the *Collectio Palatina* n. 41).

Study: A. Ehrhard, Die Cyrill von Alexandrien zugeschriebene Schrift Περὶ τῆς τοῦ Κυρίου ἐνανθρωπήσεως, ein Werk des Theodoret von Cyrus. Tübingen, 1888.

4. *Eranistes seu Polymorphus*

Theodoret's main dogmatic or Christological work is the *Eranistes* or *Beggar,* a treatise against the Monophysites. Since their heresy is no more than a miscellany of ancient absurdities collected, beggarwise, from Simon Magus, Cerdo, Marcion, Valentinus, Bardesanes, Apollinaris, Arius and Eunomius, the author feels justified, as he states in the preface, in using the strange title. Composed about 447, the work consists of four books, all extant. The first three have the form of dialogues between an orthodox believer and a beggar (Monophysite), and deal with the unchangeable character of the divinity of Christ, the non-mixture of the divinity and humanity, and the impassibility of the divinity. The fourth summarizes the three dialogues in 40 syllogisms. The treatise is invaluable for its quotation of 238 passages from 88 different patristic sources. However, Saltet was able to prove that the arrangement of the entire work, the threefold division of the argument and the great number of quotations from the Fathers were borrowed from a comprehensive dogmatic florilegium which the bishops of Antioch intended to use against Cyril and his Christology at the Council of Ephesus (431).

The treatise is extant not in the first but in the second enlarged edition issued after the Council of Chalcedon (451) and incorporating at the end of the second dialogue the twenty patristic passages appended by Pope Leo I in 450 to his *Epistola dogmatica* of the previous year.

Editions: MG 83, 27-336. — A new critical text of the dogmatic fragments of Apollinaris of Laodicea preserved in the *Eranistes* was published by H. DE RIEDMATTEN, Les fragments d'Apollinaire à l'Éranistes: CGG I (1951) 203-212.

Studies: L. SALTET, Les sources de l'"Ἐρανιστής de Théodoret: RHE 6 (1905) 289-303, 513-536, 741-754. — R. DEVREESSE, Essai sur Théodore de Mopsueste (ST 141). Vatican City, 1948, 166-168. — M. RICHARD, Notes sur les florilèges dogmatiques du Ve et du VIe siècle: Actes du Congrès d'Études Byzantines. Paris, 1948, 307-318; cf. P. NAUTIN, La valeur des lemmes dans l'Éranistes de Théodoret: RHE 46 (1951) 681-683.

5. *Expositio rectae fidei*

This *Expositio* has come down to us under the name of St. Justin the Martyr, to whom it does not belong. The long dispute over its real authorship was ended by Lebon who showed that Severus of Antioch quotes it in his *Contra impium Grammaticum* (3, 1, 5) as a work of Theodoret. It must have been published before the controversy between Cyril and Nestorius started, as most scholars agree and as Richard and Brok have shown again. The argumentation as a whole proves that the author is not an exponent of Nestorianism, but the ambiguity in both his reasoning and his terminology caused Severus and others to reproach him with this error. There is no allusion to Eutychianism, a sign that Theodoret was not yet involved in the struggle against this heresy. The work opens with the words: 'Now that sufficient attention has been paid to the refutation of the Jews and Greeks'. Richard is convinced that Theodoret refers here to his work against the Jews (now lost) and his *Curatio*. The treatise is intended for the initiated in the mysteries of the Faith whom the author addresses as 'Sons of the Church'.

Edition: J. C. T. OTTO, Corpus apol. Christ. 4.

Studies: J. LEBON, Restitutions à Théodoret de Cyr: RHE 26 (1930) 536ff. — M. RICHARD, L'activité littéraire de Théodoret avant le concile d'Éphèse: RSPT 24 (1935) 83-106; *idem*, Notes sur l'évolution doctrinale de Théodoret: RSPT 25 (1936) 489-481. — R. V. SELLERS, Pseudo-Justin's Expositio rectae fidei, a Work of Theodoret: JThSt 46 (1945) 145-160. — F. L. CROSS, Pseudo-Justin's Expositio rectae fidei. A Further Note on the Ascription: JThSt 47 (1946) 57-58. — M. F. A. BROK, The Date of Theodoret's Expositio rectae fidei: JThSt N.S. 2 (1951) 178-183.

6. *Quaestiones et responsiones ad orthodoxos*

Since the *Expositio rectae fidei* and another Pseudo-Justinian work, the *Quaestiones et responsiones ad orthodoxos*, seem to come from the same pen, the latter must also be ascribed to Theodoret. This inference finds support in the fact that the *Catena* on Luke by Nicetas of Heraclea quotes a passage of *quaestio* 58 as belonging to Theodoret and that the manuscript of the Metochion of the Holy Sepulchre at Constantinople n. 452 saec. X, from which Papadopulos-Kerameus published the *Quaestiones*, itself attributes the treatise to Theodoret. It provides answers to 61 questions altogether on historical, dogmatic, moral and exegetical subjects.

Editions: J. C. T. OTTO, Corpus apol. Christ., vol. 5. — A. PAPADOPULOS - KERAMEUS, Sapiski istor.-fil. fakultete imper. S. Petersburg Universitet 36 (1895).

Translation: German: A. HARNACK, Diodor von Tarsus. Vier pseudo-justinische Schriften als Eigentum Diodors nachgewiesen (TU 21, 4). Leipzig, 1901, 69-160.

Studies: F. X. FUNK, Le Ps.-Justin et Diodore de Tarse: RHE (1902) 947-971; *idem*, Pseudo-Justin und Diodor von Tarsus: Kirchengeschichtliche Abhandlungen und Unter-suchungen 3. Paderborn, 1907, 323-350. Funk refuted Harnack (who attributed the *Quaestiones* to Diodore) and proved that they belong to Theodoret; cf. above, p. 400. — G. BARDY, La littérature patristique des Quaestiones et responsiones sur l'Écriture Sainte: RBibl 42 (1933) 211-229. — M. RICHARD, Les citations de Théodoret conservées dans la chaîne de Nicétas sur l'Évangile selon S. Luc: RBibl 43 (1934) 92.

7. *That there is One Son, Our Lord Jesus Christ*

Photius mentions (*Bibl. cod.* 46) in his description of the Theodoret Codex twenty-seven books by Theodoret, 'against various heretical propositions'. The first five books are identical with Theodoret's *Adversus beatum Cyrillum sanctumque concilium Ephesenum libri quinque* (cf. above, p. 537), ns. 7-27 with Eutherius of Tyana's *Confutationes* (cf. above, p. 519), but the sixth 'That there is One Son, Our Lord Jesus Christ' is the anonymous treatise *That there is even after the Incarnation only One Son, Our Lord Jesus Christ*, which has come down to us in *Codex Basiliensis* A III4. Schwartz and Richard have sufficiently proved that Theodoret refers to this treatise in *Ep.* 16, *Ep.* 109 and *Ep.* 130.

Edition: MG 83, 1433-1441.

Studies: E. SCHWARTZ, ACO I, 1, 6, p. III. — M. RICHARD, Un écrit de Théodoret sur l'unité après l'incarnation: RSR 14 (1934) 34-61.

Other controversial works against Arians and Eunomians, against Macedonians, Apollinarists, Marcionites, against Origen, a *Liber mysticus* in twelve books and *Libri de virginitate* are no longer extant. Of his *Defense of Diodore of Tarsus and Theodore of Mopsuestia* against Cyril of Alexandria composed after 438 only excerpts survived which were used against Theodoret at the Robber Synod of Ephesus in 449. Theodoret refers to this work in *Ep.* 16.

Fragments: J. FLEMMING, Akten der ephesinischen Synode vom Jahre 449 syrisch (with a German translation by G. Hoffmann): AAWG Phil.-hist. Kl. N.F. 15, 1 (1917) 104ff. — Mansi 9, 252D-254. — L. ABRAMOWSKI, Reste von Theodorets Apologie für Diodor und Theodor bei Facundus: SP I (TU 63). Berlin, 1957, 61-69 (52 excerpts from Facundus).

Studies: E. SCHWARTZ, Konzilsstudien. Schriften der wissenschaft. Gesellschaft in Strassburg. Heft 20 (1914) 27ff. — L. ABRAMOWSKI, Der Streit um Diodor und Theodor zwischen den beiden ephesinischen Konzilien: ZKG 67 (1955/56) 252-287.

4. Historical Writings

1. Historia religiosa seu ascetica vivendi ratio

Theodoret's earliest historical work is his *History of the Monks* which describes in 30 chapters the lives of 28 men and 3 women ascetics (Mara, Cyrina and Domnina). Most of them lived near Antioch and were personally known to Theodoret. The first twenty chapters deal with 'athletes of Christ' who have gone to their eternal reward, the last ten with such who are still engaged in the contest, among them Simeon Stylites (ch. 26). Chapters 14-25 are devoted to the hermits of the diocese of Cyrus. The work could be compared with Palladius' *Historia Lausiaca* except that the scope of the latter is much broader, covering the whole Roman Empire. Theodoret has added as an appendix an *Oratio de divina et sancta caritate*, in order to prove that the love of God alone enabled these heroes to gain the victory over all the temptations of the devil and of the world. The date of composition is about 444. A considerable number of these 'lives' have been also preserved in a Syriac version.

Editions: MG 82, 1283-1496. — New crit. ed. of ch. 26: H. LIETZMANN, Das Leben des hl. Symeon Stylites (TU 32, 4). Leipzig, 1908, 1-18. — For the Syriac version, see: A. BAUMSTARK, Geschichte der syrischen Literatur. Bonn, 1922, 106.

Translation: German: K. GUTBERLET, BKV² 50 (1926).

Studies: S. SCHIWIETZ, Das morgenländische Mönchtum 3. Mödling/Vienna, 1938, 238-253. — P. PEETERS, Syméon Stylite et ses premiers biographes: AB 61 (1943) 29-71; reprinted in his posthumous book: Le tréfonds oriental de l'hagiographie byzantine. Brussels, 1950, 93-136. — M. RICHARD, Théodoret, Jean d'Antioche et les moines d'Orient: MSR 3 (1946) 147-156. — E. HONIGMANN, Patristic Studies (ST 173). Vatican City, 1953, 92-100 (the monks Symeon, Jacobus and Baradatus).

2. Historia ecclesiastica

Theodoret's *Ecclesiastical History* takes up the narrative where Eusebius (cf. above, p. 314) left off, but extends only from 323 to 428, beginning with the Arian controversy and ending with the death of Theodore of Mopsuestia. Nestorius who became patriarch of Constantinople in 428 is not mentioned. The Nestorian controversy in which the author was himself involved, is totally excluded, perhaps as a matter of objectivity and propriety. Nevertheless, the five books have a strong anti-heretical and apologetic tendency and their purpose is to show the victory of the Church over the Arians. They present all heretics as black sheep and glorify all orthodox rulers without mentioning their faults. There is no doubt that this Church History has a lasting value for the many documents which it preserves, some of them not found in any other author. But there has been a long discussion of its sources. The earlier impression was that the author did not hesitate to plagiarize his predecessors, especially Socrates, Sozomen and Rufinus, and we have enough evidence that he knew their works. But L. Parmentier, the editor of the best and most recent edition, is convinced that in most cases the striking similarities must be explained from the use of the same collections of materials. Their selection and evaluation appear in many instances to be hasty and uncritical. The chronology is unreliable. Theodoret finished off the entire work in 449-450 during his exile in Apamea.

Editions: MG 82, 882-1280. — *Separate ed.:* T. GAISFORD. Oxford, 1854. — New crit. ed.: L. PARMENTIER, Theodoret, Kirchengeschichte: GCS 19 (1911); 2nd ed. revised by F. Scheidweiler (1954).

Translations: English: B. JACKSON, LNPF series 2, vol. 3 (1893) 1-348. — *German:* L. KÜPPER, BKV (1878). — A. SEIDER, BKV² 51 (1926). — *French:* L. COUSIN, Paris, 1675; reprinted: Amsterdam, 1686.

Studies: A. GÜLDENPENNING, Die Kirchengeschichte des Theodoret von Kyrrhos. Eine Untersuchung ihrer Quellen. Halle, 1889. — G. RAUSCHEN, Jahrbücher der christlichen Kirche unter dem Kaiser Theodosius d. Grossen. Freiburg i.B., 1897, 559-563 (on Theodoret's sources). — L. PARMENTIER, GCS 19 (1911) IX-CX (manuscript tradition, sources, earlier editions). — W. GÖBER, Quaestiones rhythmicae imprimis ad Theodoreti Historiam Ecclesiasticam pertinentes. Diss. Halle, 1926; cf. A. W. DE GROOT, Gno 5 (1929) 577-580. — F. J. F. JACKSON, A History of Church History. Cambridge, 1939, 84-86. — C. H. ROBERTS, Early Christianity in Egypt: Journal of Egyptian Archaeology 40 (1954) 92-96 (*Hist. eccl.* 4, 18).

3. *Haereticarum fabularum compendium* (αἱρετικῆς κακομυθίας ἐπιτομή)

The last of Theodoret's historical treatises is his *History of Heresies* in five books. The first four describe all heresies from Simon Magus to Nestorius and Eutyches. The fifth confronts these 'variations of error' with a systematic presentation of the Church's teaching in 29 chapters which is unique in Greek patristic literature and very valuable for the history of dogma. Theodoret mentions among his sources Justin Martyr, Irenaeus, Clement of Alexandria, Origen, Eusebius of Caesarea, Eusebius of Emesa and others. He relies mainly on the first book of Irenaeus' *Adversus haereses*, the tenth book of the *Philosophumena* — which, however, is assigned not to Hippolytus but to Origen — and the *Church History* of Eusebius. It seems strange that he is unacquainted with the *Panarion* of Epiphanius. The author refers on several occasions to his *Ecclesiastical History*, especially when he speaks of Arius and Eudoxius of Germanicia (4, 1-2). The authenticity of the chapter on Nestorius, at the end of the fourth book, has been questioned, but without sufficient reason. Spurious, on the other hand, is the so-called *Libellus contra Nestorium ad Sporacium* (MG 83, 1153-1164) which repeats this chapter word by word and adds a new polemic against Nestorius. Theodoret composed the *Compendium* about 453.

Edition: MG 83, 335-556.

4. *On the Council of Chalcedon*

Zacharias Rhetor reports (*Hist. eccl.* 7, 6-7) that Theodoret wrote a book about the Council of Chalcedon which was used by bishop Macedonius of Constantinople about 510 for a florilegium of Antiochene theologians. The work has not come down to us.

5. *Sermons*

Little more than fragments remain of his many sermons except those on Divine Providence (cf. above, p. 544) and that on the love of God at the end of his *History of the Monks* (cf. above, p. 550). In the Acts of the Fourth and Fifth Ecumenical Councils, we have the addresses which Theodoret delivered at Chalcedon in 451 as representative of the Antiochene party at the Council of Ephesus, as also his discourse at Antioch after the death of Cyril of Alexandria. Photius (*Bibl. cod.* 273) gives a detailed report of five panegyrics on St. John Chrysostom, from which he quotes a number of passages. The encomium on the Nativity of St. John the Baptist (MG 84, 33-48) is spurious.

Fragments: Latin: MG 84, 53-64. — *Greek:* E. Schwartz, Neue Aktenstücke zum ephesinischen Konzil von 431. Munich, 1920, 25-27 (Greek text of the fragment MG 84, 56-58). — E. Schwartz, ACO I, 1, 7, 82-83; more fragments will be found in the other volumes of ACO.

6. *Letters*

In the 14th century Nicephorus Callistus still possessed more than 500 of Theodoret's letters. Though less than half of them have reached us, they are a mine of information for the history of the fifth century, of Theodoret's life and of the history of dogma in general. There are 232 letters extant: 147 of them were published for the first time by the Jesuit J. Sirmond in 1642 and reprinted in MG 83, 1173-1409; 47 were first made known in 1885 by Sakkelion from *Codex Patmensis* 706, saec. XI/XII; 36 letters, dated between 431-437, are preserved in Conciliar Acts (four of them in Greek and 32 in a Latin version of the *Collectio Cassinensis*); there are in addition the letter to Abundius (MG 83, 1492-1494) and the letter to John of Aegea, of which some Syriac fragments remain. The communications discovered by Sakkelion are mostly addressed to imperial magistrates at Constantinople and from about 449. This large correspondence is distinguished for its unpretentious learning, felicitous diction and perfect grace of style. *Ep.* 113 is his letter of appeal to Pope Leo of the year 449, in which he states: 'With the aid of divine grace I have cleansed more than a thousand souls from the virus of Marcion, and from the party of Arius and Eunomius. I have led back many others to Christ the Lord'.

Scattered here and there in Sakkelion and Migne the reader will find 14 specimens of a new and interesting literary genre, the Festal Letters, as Theodoret himself calls them. They have nothing in common with the Festal Letters of the patriarchs of Alexandria (cf. above, p. 130). Apparently, it was the etiquette at Antioch and Cyrus to exchange good wishes with friends, both clergy and lay, on the occasion of the great liturgical feasts. What seems a little strange to us is that most of Theodoret's were sent out, not before, but after the holiday, which he speaks of as already passed (cf. *Ep.* 4-6, 25, 26, 38, 39, 40, 41, 54-56, 63, 64, 74).

Most important, of course, are the epistles that take part in the theological controversies of the time. They are very valuable sources for the history of the Eastern Church. In twelve of them, addressed to influential personages at Constantinople, Theodoret asks for protection against the calumny that he divided the One Son of God into two Sons (*Ep.* 92-96, 99-101, 103, 104, 106, 109).

Editions: MG 83, 1173-1409. — J. SAKKELION, Τοῦ μακαριωτάτου Θεοδωρήτου ἐπιστολαί, Athens, 1885. The Patmos manuscript contains 52 letters. Five of them, letters 16, 21. 24, 25 and 26, are identical with letters 58, 23, 19, 20 and 22 of the collection in MG. Sakkelion missed the double 16 and thus thought he had found 48 new letters. — New crit. edition of the letters of this Patmos collection: Y. AZÉMA, Théodoret de Cyr, Correspondance I (SCH 40). Paris, 1955. A further volume will print the letters of the *Collectio Sirmondiana* found in MG. — The letters preserved in Conciliar Acts were published by E. SCHWARTZ, ACO I, 1, 7 and *idem*, Neue Aktenstücke zum ephesinischen Konzil von 431, Munich, 1920, 23-24 (*Ep.* 169: *Ad Alexandrum Hierapolitanum*). — *Latin:* E. SCHWARTZ, ACO I, 1, 4. Excerpta ex epistolis: ACO I, 5, 170-172. — *Syriac:* fragments of the letter to John of Aegea: F. NAU, PO 13, 190-191: Réponse à Jean d'Égée; new fragments: Severus of Antioch, *Contra impium Grammaticum* III, 18 (ed. J. LEBON, CSCO 94, Louvain, 1929; reprinted: 1952, 218)); 29 (ed. J. LEBON, CSCO 102, Louvain, 1933; repr. 1952, 174-175).

Translations: French: Y. Azéma, *op. cit.* — *German:* S. Wenzlowsky, Die Briefe der Päpste und die an sie gerichteten Schreiben, vol. 4: BKV (1878) 280-287 (*Ep.* 113 to Pope Leo).

Studies: P. N. Papageorgiu, Zu Theodoretos und Georgios Burtzes: BZ 2 (1893) 585-590 (text. crit.). — A. d'Alès, La lettre de Théodoret aux moines d'Orient: ETL 8 (1931) 413-421. — M. Richard, Notes sur l'évolution doctrinale de Théodoret: RSPT 25 (1936) 473-474 (*Ep. ad Abundium*); *idem*, La lettre de Théodoret à Jean d'Égée: RSPT 2 (1941/42) 415-423 (for authenticity of the Syriac fragments). — M. M. Wagner, A Chapter in Byzantine Epistolography. The Letters of Theodoret of Cyrus: DOP 4 (1948) 119-181 (form and style). — M. F. A. Brok, A propos des Lettres Festales: VC 5 (1951) 103-110. — Y. Azéma, Théodoret de Cyr d'après sa correspondance. Diss. Paris, 1952. — Y. Azéma, Sur la chronologie de trois lettres de Théodoret de Cyr: REG 67 (1954) 82-94 (the letters 66 and 67 of the Sirmond collection and letter 32 of the Patmos manuscript dealing with the dedication of a church belong to the earliest pieces of the entire corpus). — A. H. M. Jones, Military Chaplains in the Roman Army: HThR 46 (1953) 239-240 (*Ep.* 2). — Y. Azéma, SCH 40 (1955) 9-71 (the historical and religious setting of the letters, the correspondents). — J. Darrouzès, Un recueil épistolaire byzantin, le manuscrit de Patmos 706: REB 14 (1956) 87-121 (description of the manuscript containing the letters first edited by Sakkelion).

INDEXES

1. REFERENCES

1. OLD AND NEW TESTAMENT

2. ANCIENT CHRISTIAN WRITERS

(Brackets enclosing the name or the passage = Pseudo-)

3. MODERN AUTHORS

Bonsdorff, M. von, 434
Bonwetsch, G. N., 224, 225
Boon, A., 155, 157, 158, 161
Boor, C. de, 530
Boos, R., 85
Bornhäuser, K., 72
Boularand, E., 478
Boulenger, F., 215, 243
Bourget, P. du, 186
Bousquet, J., 469
Bousset, W., 116, 147, 155, 159, 171, 176, 178, 188, 224
Bouvy, E., 185
Bouyer, L., 44, 76
Boyd, H. S., 245
Boyle, P., 462
Bradshaw, H., 33
Brady, I., 355
Brandhuber, G., 400
Brandram, T. P., 452, 457
Braniste, M. M., 482
Bratke, E., 530
Braun, F., 115
Braune, J., 115
Brémond, A., 147
Brémond, J., 147
Bretz, A., 300, 301
Brewer, H., 32, 33
Brière, M., 104, 398, 400, 523
Bright, W., 23, 28, 55, 56, 93, 101, 534
Brightman, F. E., 84, 143, 144, 227, 472, 473
Brinkmann, A., 81, 82, 303, 361
Brockmeier, W., 305
Brok, M. F. A., 248, 540, 544, 545, 546, 548, 554
Brooke, D., 149
Brooks, E. W., 197, 516, 519
Brou, L., 241
Browne, C. G., 239, 240, 242, 247
Browne, H., 441
Bruck, E. F., 220, 235, 454
Bruckmayr, P. A., 241
Bruders, H., 305
Brunner, G., 465
Bruyne, D. de, 10, 194, 311, 407
Bryennios, Ph., 472
Buckle, D. P., 186
Budge, E. A. W., 17, 44, 48, 50, 52, 104, 105, 106, 157, 188, 369, 395, 432, 523
Budilovic, A., 241
Buehring, G., 113
Bugnini, A., 144
Bulacu, M., 367
Bulhart, V., 405
Buonaiuti, E., 45, 147, 149, 171, 221
Burch, V., 45
Burckhardt, J., 319
Burdach, K., 265
Burgess, H., 23, 54, 55

Burghardt, W. J., 121, 141, 280, 539
Burkhard, C. J., 352, 353
Burkitt, F. C., 357, 517
Burmester, O. H. E., 52, 186
Burn, A. E., 33
Burn, E. A., 302
Burn, R., 488
Burns, M. A., 430, 458
Busch, L., 209
Busquets, A. M., 220
Butler, C., 156, 178, 179, 180, 188
Büttner, G., 215, 235
Buytaert, E. M., 350, 351

Cabrol, F., 144
Caillau, A. B., 239
Calasanctius, P., 209
Callahan, J. F., 204, 236, 265, 285
Callahan, V. W., 256, 269
Calvi, G. B., 178
Calvo, M., 433
Camelot, Th., 22, 24, 25, 148, 515, 527, 538
Campbell, J. M., 216
Campenhausen, H. F. v., 22, 108, 118, 147, 207, 255, 311, 429
Canavan, J. J., 467
Canet, L., 336, 453, 541
Canisius, Petr., 81
Canivet, R. P., 538, 544
Cantarella, R., 246, 380
Capelle, B., 52, 84, 143, 144, 145
Capmany, J., 141
Capo, N., 185
Cappuyns, M., 33
Carali, P., 369
Carcopino, J., 313, 317
Carillo de Albornoz, A., 429, 431, 454
Carlill, J., 394
Carmody, F. J., 394
Carraro, G., 367
Cary, G., 180
Casamassa, A., 322
Casel, O., 254, 410
Casey, R. P., 23, 25, 26, 30, 31, 45, 46, 47, 50, 51, 52, 60, 61, 81, 82, 361, 366, 388
Casoli, V., 243
Caspar, E., 235, 316
Caspari, C. P., 31, 200, 367, 379
Casseder, N., 165
Casson, L., 112
Castelli, R., 458
Castiglioni, L., 115, 432
Cataudella, Q., 116, 238, 240, 246, 428, 429, 447
Cattaneo, E., 33
Cauwenbergh, P. van, 147
Cava, F. la, 185
Cavallera, F., 188, 203, 299, 300, 302, 304, 451, 486

Giamberardini, G., 150
Gianelli, C., 477
Gibbon, F., 100
Giet, S., 207, 209, 214, 217, 218, 220, 239, 264, 280, 434
Gifford, E. H., 330, 363, 366
Gifford, S. K., 441
Gigli, G., 7
Gilliam, J. F., 479
Gillmann, F., 223
Giordani, I., 429
Giorgiatis, B., 434
Gismondi, H., 245
Gitschel, J., 381
Giudici, G., 124, 141
Glas, A., 347
Glubokowskij, N. N., 538, 545
Glueck, P. B., 185
Gnolfo, P., 157
Göber, W., 551
Gobillot, P., 147
Godet, P., 255, 350, 398, 527
Goebel, R., 458
Goemans, M., 215
Goerlings, J., 434
Goggin, T. A., 258, 283
Goldhorn, J. D., 309
Goldstaub, M., 394
Golega, J., 116, 380, 381
Goltz, E. v. d., 45, 333
Gomes de Castro, M., 287
Gonzales, S., 285, 287
Goodman, A. E., 516
Gorce, D., 147, 189, 465
Gore, C., 383
Gosevic, S., 482
Gottwald, J., 428
Gottwald, R., 239
Gouillard, J., 171
Grabar, A., 473
Graef, H., 256, 268
Graf, G., 23, 105, 120, 152, 159, 162, 170, 186, 188, 241, 257, 366, 369, 394, 431, 490, 497, 504, 505
Grande, C. del, 144
Grandsire, A., 230
Grapin, E., 315, 316, 319
Grébaut, S., 174, 335
Greenlee, J. H., 367
Grégoire, H., 185, 222, 316, 317, 321, 322, 323, 348
Gressmann, H., 173, 311, 333, 379
Gretser, J., 176, 282
Gribomont, J., 207, 208, 209, 211, 212, 213, 222, 235
Griffe, E., 317
Grilli, A., 504
Grillmeier, A., 9, 19, 55, 73, 74, 75, 134, 141, 253, 306, 350, 383, 394, 400, 417, 418, 515, 539

Gröhl, R., 185
Grohmann, A., 186
Gronau, K. (C.), 204, 209, 217, 220, 235, 265, 285
Gröne, V., 209, 211, 214
Groot, A. W. de, 551
Groot, J. F. de, 141
Gross, J., 72, 293, 413, 419, 539
Grosse-Brauckmann, E., 540
Grotz, J., 235
Grumel, V., 207, 235, 306, 313
Gruninger, J. H., 429
Grützmacher, G., 108, 109, 155
Guchteneere, P. de, 214
Guenther, O., 390
Guérand, O., 90
Guerrier, H., 33
Guétet, F. M., 211, 214
Guidi, J., 121
Guidi, M., 105
Guignet, M., 241, 248
Guillaumont, A., 174
Guillaumont-Boussace, C., 171, 174
Güldenpenning, A., 551
Gummerus, J., 9, 63, 202, 346
Günther, K., 538
Günthör, A., 31, 89, 90
Gutberlet, K., 538, 550
Guy, J. C., 189
Gwatkin, H., 6, 7, 19
Gwilliam, G. H., 335

Habicht, C., 324
Hadzsega, J., 429, 481
Haeringen, J. H. van, 217
Hagel, K. F., 22, 36
Hahn, A., 31
Haidacher, S., 115, 431, 434, 435, 436, 446, 451, 453, 463, 466, 467, 469, 470, 483, 484, 499, 518
Haidenthaler, S., 453
Halcomb, T. R., 108
Halkin, F., 149, 152, 158, 178, 278, 527
Halmel, A., 316, 319
Hamelian, P., 431
Hannay, J. O., 147
Hansmann, K., 280
Harden, J. M., 396
Hardy, E. R., 7, 10, 11, 242, 247
Haring, N. M., 136
Harkins, P. W., 440
Harnack, A. v., 19, 147, 200, 230, 231, 325, 333, 358, 400, 487, 488, 516, 549
Hartel, G., 64, 65
Hartl, A., 446
Hartranft, C. D., 536
Hauck, A., 108
Hauret, C., 70
Hauschildt, H., 487, 488

Johnston, C. F. H., 210
Jones, A. H. M., 36, 322, 323, 428, 554
Jonge, L. F. M. de, 246
Joosen, J., 209
Jordachescu, P. C., 262
Jouassard, G., 118, 120, 123, 125, 128, 134, 141, 402, 464
Jugie, M., 33, 52, 118, 140, 189, 228, 363, 383, 399, 400, 410, 418, 422, 423, 477, 481, 484, 514
Jülicher, A., 163, 165, 218, 219, 258, 304, 307, 385, 527
Junglas, J., 514
Jungmann, J. A., 144
Jurgens, W. A., 462
Jurjevskij, A., 508
Jüssen, K., 490, 493, 507, 539, 542
Juzek, J. H., 476

Kampffmeyer, G., 515
Kania, W., 462, 463
Karlsson, G., 112
Karnthaler, F. P., 463
Karpp, H., 323
Karst, J., 311, 313
Kattenbusch, F., 31
Katz, A. L., 358
Katzenmayer, H., 317
Kaufmann, F., 471
Kaupel, H., 444
Kayser, C. L., 334
Kayser, H., 131
Keane, H., 479
Keble, T., 450
Keenan, M. E., 44, 239, 257, 273, 283
Keil, B., 283
Kellner, H., 428
Kelly, F. J., 9
Kelly, J. N. D., 9, 10, 13, 62, 63, 70, 76, 141, 143, 145, 200, 231, 233, 250, 306, 345, 346, 387, 418, 515
Kelly, J. R., 140
Kemmer, A., 166, 275
Kerrigan, A., 120, 121, 122, 123
Keseling, P., 148, 313
Kessler, K., 358
Keuk, W., 445
Keydell, R., 114, 115, 116, 245, 246, 381
Khalifé, I. A., 505, 509
Kidd, J., 133, 134, 135
Kihn, H., 402, 406, 418
King, C. W., 243
Kinkel, G., 116
Kipling, R. C., 111
Kirchmeyer, J., 499
Kirpitschnikow, A., 524
Kleffner, A. J., 108
Klejna, F., 150, 152, 154
Klinge, G., 355
Klose, C. R. W., 307

Klostermann, E., 92, 166, 199, 200, 267, 303, 311, 336, 341, 342, 471, 472
Klostermann, R. A., 166
Kmosko, M., 154, 166
Knackstedt, H. O., 272
Knors, F., 440
Koch, H., 108, 147, 291, 355
Koch, L., 301
Koch, W., 393
Koester, H., 317
Koetting, B., see Kötting, B.
Kolbe, B., 111, 114
König, E., 157
Kopallik, J., 118
Koperski, V., 288
Kösters, L., 544
Kostits, B., 235
Kötting, B., 132, 283, 528
Kotynski, L., 111
Koukoules, P., 215, 430
Kozman, F., 148
Krabinger, J. G., 108, 109, 110, 114, 256, 261, 262, 268, 279
Kraft, H., 321, 323, 324
Krampf, A., 264
Kraus, 152
Krause, P., 302
Krestan, L., 243
Kreuz, A., 306
Krivocheine, B., 513
Krottenthaler, S., 178
Krüger, G., 17, 30, 45, 525
Krumbacher, K., 246
Krusch, B., 102, 131
Kubitschek, W., 336
Kudrjavzev, N. P., 304
Kugener, M. A., 277
Kuhn, A., 116
Kuhn, K. H., 50, 187
Kühnert, W., 317
Kuiper, H., 330
Kuiper, W., 116
Kukules, P., see Koukoules, P.
Kulemann, A., 462
Künstle, K., 33
Kunze, J., 505, 508, 509.
Küpper, L., 538, 551
Kurfess, A., 114, 177, 325, 326

Labriolle, P. de, 148, 188
Lacombrade, C., 108, 109, 110, 111, 113, 114
Ladeuze, P., 155, 159, 161
Ladner, G. B., 264, 293
Lagarde, P. A. de, 235, 336, 361, 389, 398, 400, 402, 407, 411, 479
Lagrange, M. J., 298
Laico, A. de, 220
Laignel-Lavastine, M., 515
Laistner, M. L. W., 403, 466, 467

Maclean, A. J., 514
McLean, N., 315
McNamara, K., 415, 539
Mader, J., 363
Madoz, J., 33
Maffei, S., 22, 65
Mahé, J., 118, 134, 141
Mahler, E., 455
Mai, A., 17, 53, 84, 85, 91, 120, 259, 268, 337, 338, 339, 512, 547
Maier, J., 204, 254
Malden, R. H., 33
Malevez, L., 141, 288
Malin, A. N., 243
Malingrey, A. M., 469
Malone, E. E., 44, 148
Mamone, G., 432
Mancini, A., 325
Manoir, H. du, 118, 130, 132, 134, 136, 140, 141. 142
Manselli, R., 357
Mansi, J. D., 32, 59, 297, 301, 309, 550
Maran, P., 208, 366
Marcellus, C. 'de, 116
Marcovic, M., 336
Maréchal, J., 171, 291
Marić, I., 123, 140
Mariès, L., 91, 122, 399
Marini, N., 481
Mariotti, S., 114
Markowicz, W. A., 434
Markowski, H., 223
Marquardt, J., 371, 375
Marquart, J., 532
Marr, N., 394
Marriott, C., 458
Marriott, G. L., 162, 163, 165, 166, 167, 275
Marrou, H.-I., 108, 317, 509
Marsh, E. G., 462
Marsili, S., 171, 503
Martain, P., 478, 479
Martin, C., 132, 147, 395, 431, 453, 454, 455, 470, 483, 484, 485, 486, 495, 502, 516, 523, 524
Martin, E. J., 393
Martin, F., 462, 464
Martin, J., 385
Martin, V., 148
Martroye, F., 238
Marx, B., 299, 470, 485, 486, 522, 524, 527
Marx, M., 44, 148
Mason, A. J., 165, 242
Mason, H. M., 462
Maspéro, J., 118
Mathon, 306
Matthaei, C. F., 354
Maunoury, A. F., 43
Maurice, J., 321, 322
Max Herzog zu Sachsen, 434, 438

Mayer, A., 148
Mazzarino, P. C. da, 539
Mean, A., 444
Medlay, J., 446
Meehan, D., 239
Meester, P. de, 148, 228
Mehler, J., 115
Mehrlein, R., 454
Meinhold, P., 31, 259
Melcher, R., 176, 224
Meloni, P., 131
Menhardt, H., 394
Menn, 244
Mensbrugghe, A. van der, 148
Mercati, G., 38, 55, 122, 131, 176, 185, 200, 208, 225, 247, 260, 281, 283, 329, 338, 389, 405, 435, 436, 471, 488, 492, 493, 515
Méridier, L., 257, 263
Merki, H., 218, 268, 293
Mersch, E., 76, 140, 252, 288, 476
Mertel, H., 24, 44, 159
Merx, A., 122, 541
Merzagora, A., 442
Messenger, E. C., 148
Messina, G., 357
Meunier, M., 113, 115
Meyboom, H., 316
Meyer, L., 465
Meyer, R. T., 44, 179
Meyer, W., 285
Meyier, K. A. de, 241
Michaelidis, E., 432
Michaud, E., 141, 290, 476, 481, 482
Michels, T., 113, 240, 243
Mickley, P., 322
Miklosich, F., 432
Milburn, R. L. P., 317
Miller, M., 313
Miller, P. S., 381
Milne, J. G., 7
Mingana, A., 85, 105, 106, 125, 402, 408, 409, 410, 412, 420
Mioni, E., 189
Misch, G., 110, 246
Mitterrutzner, J. C., 446, 450, 453, 458, 462, 463, 464
Moeller, C., 134
Moesinger, 268
Möhle, A., 338, 339, 541, 542
Möhler, J. A., 22
Mohrmann, C., 43, 456
Moisescu, I., 434
Möller, E. W., 264
Molzberger, J., 322, 326
Momigliano, A., 246
Mommsen, T., 311, 315
Monachino, V., 155
Monceaux, P., 149
Mönnich, C. W., 9

Pack, R., 109
Padelford, F. M., 215
Palanque, J. R., 33, 323
Palmer, P. F., 144, 145
Palmieri, A., 398, 432
Pando, J. C., 108
Papadopoulos-Kerameus, A., 452, 466, 485, 508, 541, 549
Papadopulos, C., 118, 119, 131, 132, 383
Papageorgiu, P. N., 554
Papakonstantinu, T., 235
Paramo, L. del, 220, 240, 463
Paranikas, M., 113, 245
Parente, P., 415
Pargoire, J., 207
Parmentier, L., 56, 307, 551
Parpal, M., 88
Pasquali, G., 111, 221, 223, 256, 280, 282, 283, 321, 322
Passow, F., 116
Pasté, C. R., 33
Paton, W. R., 245
Patterson, L., 402
Paulson, J., 431
Payne Smith, R., 124
Pease, A. S., 218
Peeters, P., 22, 54, 159, 178, 347, 367, 534, 550
Pegis, A. C., 432
Pellegrino, M., 93, 245, 246, 261, 285, 454
Penna, A., 310, 336
Pépin, J., 331
Pera, C., 231
Peradze, G., 432
Pericoldi-Ridolfini, F., 119
Perler, O., 202, 317, 351
Perry, B. E., 394
Pesch, C., 515
Pesenti, G., 207
Petavius, D., 108, 395
Petermann, H., 313
Peters, A., 82
Peters, C., 330, 333
Peters, E., 394
Petersen, 323
Peterson, E., 154, 162, 165, 170, 175, 302, 328, 389, 394, 430, 484, 501, 503, 507, 512, 534
Petit, P., 321, 323
Pétré, H., 266
Petrides, S., 241
Petrovski, A., 473
Pezopulos, E. A., 109, 113
Pfättisch, J. M., 311, 322, 325, 326
Pfeilschifter, G., 226
Pfister, F., 180
Phokylides, J., 363
Phytrakes, A. J., 148, 185
Piana, G. La, 524
Piazzino, C., 449

Pichler, T., 211
Picus, J., 162
Pieper, M., 53
Piganiol, A., 323, 325, 326
Pinault, H., 239
Pini, F., 458
Pirot, L., 402
Pitra, J. B., 38, 63, 81, 84, 85, 223, 238, 338, 488
Pizzimenti, D., 355
Places, E. des, 330, 331, 509, 512, 513, 539, 544
Plagnieux, J., 249
Polakes, P., 141
Pollard, T. E., 7, 9, 16, 70, 76
Polotsky, H. J., 105, 356, 358
Pontanus, Jac., 513
Popov, K., 509, 512
Portmann, F. X., 249
Powell, J. E., 431, 453
Praechter, K., 119
Preger, F., 285
Prestige, G. L., 9, 70, 141, 224, 225, 377, 381
Preuschen, E., 55, 178, 316, 333, 429, 534
Prevost, S. G., 438
Priessnig, A., 44
Probst, F., 481
Pruche, B., 209, 210, 211
Prümm, K., 72, 446
Przychocki, G., 247, 248
Puech, A., 257, 429
Puech, H. C., 90, 91, 357
Puig de la Bellacasa, J., 134
Pullan, L., 473
Pullig, E. A., 246
Puniet, P. de, 143, 144
Pusey, P. E., 120, 122, 123, 125, 126, 127, 128, 129, 132, 133, 134, 135

Quasten, J., 37, 84, 144, 145, 148, 333, 366, 375, 376, 410, 422, 435
Quattrone, A., 88, 97
Queffébe, H., 149
Quentier, V., 243

Radermacher, L., 304, 528
Rado, P., 455
Raeder, J., 544
Raes, A., 228, 369, 473
Ragon, E., 458
Rahlfs, A., 313, 540
Rahner, H., 90, 207
Rahner, K., 31, 44, 148, 165, 171, 189, 211, 291, 296, 505, 507, 512
Ramsay, W. M., 226
Randell, T., 120, 123
Rapisarda, E., 239
Raschke, H., 387
Rasneur, J., 230

Schelkle, K. H., 445
Schemmel, F., 207, 304, 428
Schepens, P., 33
Scher, A., 410, 411
Scherer, J., 90
Schermann, T., 29, 77, 84, 87, 88, 97, 143, 144, 210, 251, 365, 367, 372, 386, 396
Scheve, B., 235
Schiller, F., 115
Schilling, O., 471
Schiltz, E., 33
Schissel, O., 504, 544
Schiwietz, S., 147, 149, 155, 162, 171, 172, 178, 428, 482, 483, 496, 497, 499, 501, 550
Schladebach, J., 202
Schmid, A., 185
Schmid, M., 301
Schmid, R., 314
Schmid, W., 317
Schmidt, C., 55, 356, 357
Schmitt, V., 376
Schmitz, A. L., 147
Schmitz, M., 452, 453, 454, 455, 457, 458, 459
Schneemelcher, W., 6, 7, 10, 17, 22, 23, 303, 377
Schodde, G. H., 157
Schoder, R. V., 455
Schoemann, J. B., 72, 264
Schoeps, J., 389
Scholl, E., 235
Schöne, A., 313
Schöne, H., 316
Schoo, G., 7, 536
Schott, A., 351
Schrörs, H., 322
Schubach, M., 246
Schuett, M., 44
Schuler, G. M., 538, 545
Schulte, F., 466
Schulte, J., 538, 544, 545, 546
Schultze, V., 428
Schulze, J. L., 521, 538
Schwartz, E., 6, 7, 11, 22, 23, 25, 26, 30, 31, 52, 54, 60, 65, 102, 103, 119, 120, 126, 127, 128, 131, 132, 133, 134, 135, 177, 182, 184, 193, 202, 207, 223, 303, 304, 310, 311, 315, 316, 318, 325, 343, 398, 402, 413, 428, 483, 516, 517, 519, 521, 522, 523, 524, 525, 527, 538, 546, 547, 549, 550, 552, 553
Schweizer, E., 399
Schwertschlager, J., 447
Scipioni, L. I., 517
Seeck, O., 6, 7, 15, 110, 112, 193, 223, 243
Seel, O., 22
Segovie, A., 31, 90
Séguier de Saint Brisson, 330
Seider, A., 11, 15, 538, 551

Seidlmayer, S., 467
Seiler, R., 36
Sellers, R. V., 7, 76, 140, 306, 515, 548
Selwyn, W., 329
Sepp, B., 449
Septickij, A., 211
Serra, M., 249
Serruys, D., 121, 313, 530
Seston, W., 316, 321, 323, 388
Setton, K. M., 22, 36, 109, 322, 328, 428
Shapland, C. R. B., 58, 77
Sharpe, N. W., 22
Shean, T. L., 209
Sherwood, M. M., 454
Sherwood, P., 398
Shipman, A. J., 473
Sickenberger, J., 124, 298, 361
Sicking, J. L., 185
Siegmund, A., 23, 56, 60, 120, 209, 311, 431, 491, 497
Simenschy, T., 262
Simeon, X. H., 112
Simon, I., 278, 470
Simon, M., 453
Simonetti, M., 29, 34, 220, 430, 457
Sinko, T., 115, 241, 243, 246, 433, 450, 463
Sinner, L. de, 458
Sinthern, P., 132
Sirmond, J., 350, 553, 554
Siwek, P., 357
Skard, E., 196, 197, 355
Skimina, S., 241, 430, 467
Slomkowski, A., 309
Smith, M., 185
Smothers, E. R., 25, 386, 441, 470
Smulders, P., 31
Smythe, H. R., 58, 87
Snellmann, P., 6, 7, 11
Soares, E. J., 486
Sodano, A., 454
Soden, H. v., 345, 406
Soell, G., 204, 253, 277, 289
Soffray, M., 430, 432, 458
Solano, J., 367, 478
Solič, A., 501
Sollert, R., 108
Sommer, E., 215, 458
Sordi, M., 317
Sorg, J., 481
Sostin, A. P., 24
Soury, G., 215
Souter, A., 45, 109, 351, 380
Souvay, C. L., 134
Spacil, T., 482
Spanneut, M., 304, 305, 306
Spaude, G. G., 317
Specht, F. A., 541
Spies, O., 172
Srawley, J. H., 262, 263, 288

Turner, H. E. W., 338
Turrado, L., 123
Turrianus, F., 81, 487, 512
Tweed, J., 449, 450
Tyciak, J., 248
Tying, D., 403
Tzortzatos, B., 428

Ubaldi, P., 179, 428, 463, 469
Ubierna, A., 367
Ueding, L., 10, 159
Uleyn, A., 439
Ullmann, C., 238
Unger, D., 72
Unnik, W. C. v., 263, 410
Unterstein, K., 204
Urtiz de Urbina, I., 135
Usener, H., 243, 277, 279, 446, 455

Vacandard, E., 33
Vaccari, A., 120, 336, 399, 405, 424, 490
Vailhé, S., 391, 477
Vaillant, A., 28, 203, 366, 395
Valdenberg, V., 355
Vandenberghe, B. H., 429, 433, 454, 462, 470
Vandenbussche, E., 210, 258, 308
Vardanian, A., 345, 438, 525
Vellay, C., 113
Ven, P. v. d., 347, 348, 501
Venables, E., 207, 302, 307, 429, 483, 484, 538
Verbeke, G., 383
Vergote, J., 44
Véricel, M., 367
Vérin, J. H., 458
Vermuyten, F., 462
Viedebantt, O., 386
Villain, M., 316, 385
Villecourt, L., 163, 165, 167, 168, 188, 275
Viller, M., 44, 148, 165, 171, 175, 189, 211, 291, 505, 512
Vincent, L. H., 324
Vine, A. R., 517
Violet, B., 319
Vis, H. de, 105, 219, 390
Vischer, L., 209
Vismara, S., 101
Visser, A. J., 108, 429, 453
Vittinghoff, F., 321, 323
Vizmanos, F. de B., 45, 272, 465
Voelkl, L., 323, 324
Vogel, C. J. de, 28
Vogt, J., 241, 321, 323, 326, 368
Vogt, P., 470
Vögtle, A., 172
Voisin, G., 73, 76, 383
Volk, J., 244, 462
Völker, W., 166, 222, 285, 291, 292, 317
Vollert, W., 290

Völter, D., 147
Volturno, D., 335
Vööbus, A., 220
Vossius, Ger., 395
Vosté, J. M., 402, 403, 405, 406, 407, 410, 412
Vries, G. J. de, 112
Vries, W. de, 410, 419, 514, 515

Waddell, H., 147, 188
Wagenmann, J., 48
Wagenmann, J. A., 487, 488
Wagner, M. M., 211, 219, 244, 283, 554
Walford. E. 532
Wallace-Hadrill, D. S., 313, 332, 335
Wallis, F., 23
Walther, G., 268
Warnach, V., 499
Warren, H. B. de, 148
Wasylyk, M. S., 482
Watson, E. W., 178
Way, A. C., 221, 222, 225
Wegern, A. v., 406
Weigl, E., 76, 101, 140, 141, 252, 383
Weimann, C., 424
Weinberger, W., 307
Weingarten, H., 147
Weis, M., 310
Weis-Liebersdorf, J. E., 512
Weismann, H., 187
Weiss, H., 204
Weiss, K., 256, 261, 263, 268
Weiss, R., 111
Weiswurm, A. A., 295
Weitzmann, K., 291
Wellmann, M., 394
Welsersheimb, L., 122, 266, 395, 502, 541
Wendel, C., 335
Wenger, A., 166, 170, 275, 430, 431, 452, 455, 486, 490, 494, 495
Wenger, L., 197
Wenzlowsky, S., 519, 554
Werhahn, H. M., 239, 245, 297
Wesley, John, 163, 165
Wessely, C., 144
Weyenborg, R., 225
Weyer, J., 470
Weyh, W., 13
Weyman, C., 113, 215
Whiston, W., 308
Whitaker, G. H., 446
Whitall, J., 149
White, H. G., 147, 162
Wickert, U., 408
Widengren, G., 357
Wieneke, J., 330
Wiesmann, H., 186
Wifstrand, A., 109
Wijk, M. v., 470
Wikgren, A., 439

4. GREEK WORDS

II. GENERAL INDEX

Codex Theodosianus, 397

coenobium, 154

Collectio Avellana, 389

Collectio Cassinensis, 518, 553

Collectio Palatina, 413, 546, 547

Colluthus, 14

colonies, monastic, 151

Colossians, commentaries on St. Paul's Epistle to the, 407, 448f.

Coma, in Egypt, 148

Comana, in Pontus, 427

comedies, biblical, 380

Commentaries, biblical, 3,175; see: Old Testament, New Testament; see: the titles of the individual biblical books

communicatio idiomatum, 75, 139, 288, 305, 382, 417, 508

Communion, Holy, 235, 421; ritual of, 234; prayer of, 143, 144; preparation for, 422; disposition of soul for, 409; worthy reception of, 435; taken in hands, 480; daily, 225, 233f.; at home, 234; see: Eucharist

Compline, origin of, 226

compunctio, 463

concupiscence, 352

condescension, doctrine of, 439

confession of sins, public, 478; auricular, 234f., 409, 422-423, 478, 479; monastic, 234

confessor, concept of, 80; confessors in Palestine, 318

confirmation, 82, 364, 492

Hesychius of Jerusalem, 2, 3, 38, 169, 470, 488-496
Hexaemeron, 216-218, 263, 264, 304, 403, 485
hexameters, 116, 380
Hexapla, 91, 334, 338
Hierocles, Neoplatonist, governor of Bithynia, 333f., 487
Hilarion, abbot, 391
Hilary of Poitiers, 11, 32, 337
Himerius of Athens, 240
Hippolytus of Rome, 175, 385, 388, 396, 551
Historia acephala, 20
Historia Lausiaca, 177-179
Historia monachorum, 147, 178
historiography, 313
history, 328; a Christian, 529; first attempt of Church h., 3, 314-317; of heresies, 314, 388, 551f.; synchronous tables of world h., 312
Holy Ghost, see: Spirit
Holy Land, topography of, 336; see: Palestine
Holy Week, at Alexandria, 160; history of, 390f.; Lectionary of, 51
Homer, 182, 538; Christian attitude toward, 214; substituted by biblical poetry, 380
homilies, 3, 114, 216-220, 298f., 425; dogmatic, 451-453; spiritual, 162; reading of, in liturgy, 433; see: sermons
Homoeans, 62, 82, 230, 346
Homoeousians, 62, 201, 202, 230; theology of the, 202; Synod of the, at Lampsacus (365), 346
homoousios, 18, 61, 62, 69, 70, 82, 84, 93, 96, 177, 183, 201, 230, 310, 344, 357, 359, 360, 368, 370, 371, 474; rejected by many bishops, 20; see: consubstantiality
Honorius, Emperor, 531, 535
Hormisdas, 413
Horsiesi, abbot, 101, 102, 159-160
Hosius of Cordova, see: Ossius
hospitals, established by Basil, 205; by Chrysostom, 426
humanism, Christian, 1, 2
humilitas, 183, 215, 510
hymns, Christian, 4, 113, 240; liturgical, 380; of thanksgiving, 290, 492; at home, 435; children sing, 449; of praise to Christ, 196, 368
Hypapante, 369, 455; origin of, 494; see: Purification
Hypatia, philosopher, 106, 111, 117
hypostasis, 28, 29, 55, 139, 202, 228, 229, 249, 252, 260, 281, 382, 417, 474, 489, 498
hypostatic union, 46, 128, 138, 139-140, 184, 353, 448, 475f., 508

Iconium, synod at (376), 297
iconoclasm, 280, 345, 390-393, 487
idolatry, 24, 41, 324, 329, 391, 392
idols, 374, 392
Ignatius of Antioch, panegyric on, 456
Ignatius of Loyola, 512
image, of God in man, 292, 379, 510; treatises against images of Christ and the saints, 345, 390-393; see: iconoclasm
imagery, 433
imitation, of Christ, 273, 498
immortality of the soul, 24, 419
Incarnation, 24, 26, 28, 29, 95, 130, 131, 132, 136, 137, 199, 244, 258, 328, 353, 360, 379, 382, 383, 386f., 393, 448, 487, 489, 508, 512, 520, 523, 524, 545, 546f.; classical doctrine of the, 526; purpose of, 439; necessity of, 71; benefits of, 290; restored primitive order, 262; in the Psalms, 404; foretold by Vergil, 325; reasons for, 24; Virginal Birth in the, 253, 360, treatise on the, 410f.
India, 180
inebriation, divine and sober, 295
initiation, sacrament of, 78, 178, 363, 409, 492; see: baptism
Innocent I, Pope, 103, 226, 428, 469
inspiration, 360; see: Scripture
Institution, of the Eucharist, 83, 143, 455, 481
intellect, faculty of the, 352
intercession, in Mass, 376
intermediaries, 8
intuition, of God, 292-295
invocation, 83, 374, 375; see: epiclesis
Irenaeus, 289, 385, 388, 530, 551
Iris in Pontus, 237, 261, 276
Isaac, 370; sermon on the sacrifice of, 299
Isaac of Ninive, 169
Isaias, commentaries on, 90, 91, 121-122, 218, 338, 377, 406, 435f., 491, 541
Isidore of Pelusium, 117, 180-185, 429, 442, 459, 496, 498, 504
Isocrates, 538
Israel, 284, 389; see: Jews, Hebrews

Jacob, patriarch, 49, 339
Jamblichus, 113, 353
James, martyrdom of the Apostle, 529f.; Liturgy of St., 226, 472; encomium on, 495
jealousy, sermon on, 219
Jeremias, 436; commentaries on, 122, 423, 541
Jerome, 40, 82, 85, 87, 91, 102, 103, 155, 257, 312, 313, 336, 338, 364, 377, 378, 384, 390, 391
Jerusalem, 169, 176, 362, 367, 384; synods at, 9, 37, 362; plan of, 336; liturgy of, 365, 366; pilgrimage to, 47,

spirituality, Christian, doctrine of, 146, 269, 509f.; see: asceticism
Stagirius, monk, 467
State, and Church, 1, 3, 132, 315
Statues, Chrysostom's homilies on the, 457f.
Stelechius, monk, 463
stenographers, 3, 363, 433, 440
Stephen, Feast of St., 299; sermons on, 278, 494, 527
Stoa, Stoics, 245, 274, 280, 284, 353, 381, 463
Strasbourg, University Library, 145, 490
subintroductae, 47
subordinationism, 8, 17, 69, 87, 342
subsistentia, 31, 55
substantia, substance, 228; unity of divine, 94, 230
Suidas, 112, 116, 399, 459, 532
sun, in theology of the Logos, 68, 69, 196, 475; image of the Emperor, 327; pagan worship of the, 349
sundays, liturgy of, 226; rest on, 403
superstition, 43, 324, 401, 453
Susanna, story of, 541
swearing, rejected, 441
Syedra in Pamphylia, 386, 387
symbol, see: Creed, faith
symbolism, 393, 394
Symeon, the Messalian, 164, 167
Symmachus, version of, 435
synagogues, 452
synaxary, Byzantine, 496; of Constantinople, 181; of the Monastery of the Archangel Michael at Hamouli, 51
syncretism, 112, 356
syneisaktoi, 47, 464
Synesius of Cyrene, 3, 4, 106-114
Synopsis Scripturae Sacrae, 39
Synopsis Veteris et Novi Testamenti, 472
synousiasts, 400, 412
Syntagmation, 195f.
Syria, writers of, 302-554; Church of, 101; anaphora, 304; poetry, 4; monastic movement of, 177
Syriac translations, 17, 20, 23, 37, 40, 43, 46, 48, 50, 53, 60, 85, 104, 105, 119, 124, 125, 127, 128, 129, 133, 151, 152, 153, 154, 158, 163, 170, 171, 174, 175, 176, 186, 187, 212, 240, 299, 304, 315, 318, 333, 335, 337, 340, 350, 360, 361, 389, 393, 402, 403, 405, 406, 409, 415, 430, 431, 438, 473, 477, 485, 502, 505, 506, 516, 519, 522, 523, 524, 538, 546
Syrus, abbot, 158

Tabennisi, 154
Tabernacles, Feast of, 452
table, divine, 480; see: altar
tachygraphs, 212; see: stenographers

Tall Brothers, 101, 384
Tarsus, 362
teachers, Christian, 314; ecumenical, 208
temperance, 496
temples, of idols in Egypt, 105
temptations, 364, 453, 507
Teresa of Avila, 512
Thalassius, 511
Thalia, 11-13, 26, 62
theater, 453; condemned, 437; assembly of Satan, 453
Thebaid, 20, 154, 310
Thebes, 185
Thecla, protomartyr, narrative, 528
theodicy, treatise on, 360
Theodore, the martyr, panegyric on, 278
Theodore, Pachomian abbot, 152, 159, 160-161
Theodore Studites, 213, 280, 391
Theodore, Roman deacon, 179
Theodore of Mopsuestia, 3, 118, 128, 226, 302, 307, 343, 376, 383, 397, 401-423, 424, 463, 495, 514, 522, 524, 537, 539, 540, 542, 549
Theodoret of Cyrus, 3, 10, 14, 29, 90, 118, 124, 127, 299, 302, 304, 338, 347, 379, 400, 518, 519, 521, 536-554
Theodorus Lector, 399
Theodosius I, Emperor, 1, 100, 102, 105, 118, 184, 207, 238, 257, 267, 278, 297, 307, 308, 315, 347, 348, 362, 392, 397, 447, 457, 496, 529
Theodosius II, Emperor, 126, 127, 131, 177, 182, 427, 514, 515, 518, 531, 535
Theodotion, 435
Theodul, deacon, 438
Theognis, poet, 214
Theognis of Nicaea, 192, 193-194
Theognostus, 61
theology, concept of, 242, 511; object of, 248; sources of, 248; centers of, 117; method of, 195f., 248; beginnings of research in, 6, 217; development of, 1, 66; terminology, 123, 137, 140; biblical, 360, 373, 489; Patristic, 135; reason in, 136, 285; of grace, 511; sacramental, 420; mystical, 291-296; in monasteries, 2; of the liturgy, 372; feeds on contemplation, 511; rationalism in, 8; "technology", 308; see: faith, reason, revelation
Theopaschites, 517, 524
Theophaneia, 332
Theophanes Confessor, 489
Theophilus of Alexandria, 90, 100-106, 107, 112, 160, 169, 179, 258, 384, 385, 391, 425, 426, 428, 469, 482, 531
theotokos, 19, 52, 116, 117, 118, 123, 126, 128, 253, 289, 305, 476, 498, 508, 514, 521, 523, 547
Thesaurus, Manichaean treatise, 358

IMPRIMATUR

Gerh. A. M. Abbink S. Th. drs.
Censor a. h. d.
Driebergen, d. 11 m. febr. A. D. 1959